AUG    2006

# EUROPEAN NATIONS

# FRANCE

## A REFERENCE GUIDE
### FROM THE RENAISSANCE TO THE PRESENT

William J. Roberts

☑®

Facts On File, Inc.

**France: A Reference Guide from the Renaissance to the Present**

Facts On File, Inc.
132 West 31st Street
New York NY 10001

**Library of Congress Cataloging-in-Publication Data**
Roberts, William J.
  France : a reference guide from the Renaissance to the present /
  by William J. Roberts.
    p. cm. — (European nations series)
  Includes bibliographical references and index.
  ISBN 0-8160-4473-2
  1. France—History—Dictionaries. I. Title. II. Series.
  DC35.R64 2004
  944'.003—dc22                                                          2003061581

Facts On File books are available at special discounts when purchased in bulk quantities for businesses, associations, institutions or sales promotions. Please call our Special Sales Department in New York at (212) 967-8800 or (800) 322-8755.

You can find Facts On File on the World Wide Web at http://www.factsonfile.com

Text design by David Strelecky
Cover design by Semadar Megged
Maps by Jeremy Eagle

Printed in the United States of America

VB FOF 10 9 8 7 6 5 4 3 2 1

This book is printed on acid-free paper.

# CONTENTS

# FOREWORD

This series was inspired by the need of high school and college students to have a concise and readily available history series focusing on the evolution of the major European powers and other influential European states in the modern age—from the Renaissance to the present. Written in accessible language, the projected volumes include all of the major European countries: France, Germany, Great Britain, Italy, and Russia, as well as other states such as Spain, Portugal, Austria, and Hungary that have made important intellectual, political, cultural, and religious contributions to Europe and the world. The format has been designed to facilitate usage and includes a short introduction by the author of each volume, a specialist in its history, providing an overview of the importance of the particular country in the modern period. This is followed by a narrative history of each nation from the time of the Renaissance to the present. The core of the volume consists of an A–Z dictionary of people, events, and places, providing coverage of intellectual, political, diplomatic, cultural, social, religious, and economic developments. Next, a chronology details key events in each nation's development over the past several centuries. Finally, the end matter includes a selected bibliography of readily available works, maps, and an index to the material within the volume.

—Frank J. Coppa, General Editor
St. John's University

# INTRODUCTION

France has been, since its national beginnings, a center of Western political, economic, social, scientific, and cultural history. At times almost synonymous with the achievements of Western civilization, France has often led the way to the developments of the early modern and modern European eras. While today the preeminence of French culture and civilization might seem less evident, France nonetheless remains a locus of the vital developments of the modern era. Nature and geography have favored France and its role in history, and it is the second-largest European state in area. Nearly all of France's boundaries and borders are natural ones, being formed in part by the Alps, the Jura, the Pyrenees, the Rhine, and the sea. It is a fertile and varied land, still agricultural, and embraces within its borders the cultures of both northern and southern Europe. In many ways, the history of France is a story of forming a nation and national identity out of diversity, beginning with Charlemagne, continuing through the dynasties, and into the modern era. By the 16th and 17th centuries, French culture and language were becoming the standards by which other nations often measured themselves, and with the beginnings of a global empire, that culture was spread beyond Europe. The center and in many ways the source of the Enlightenment during the 18th century, France epitomized the critical thinking that ushered in the modern era. The French Revolution of 1789 brought the concepts of human freedom and equality to the world and set the pattern for future political and social struggles. Already recognized for leadership in mathematics and other disciplines, France in the 19th century, while continuing to be a world cultural center, became a scientific one as well. By 1900 Paris was the world's recognized artistic and literary capital and was second only to London as a financial one. But the vagaries of nationalism that produced World War I would challenge and change that role and also presage the eventual breakup of the French global empire in the 20th century. France experienced, too, the ideological turmoil of the modern era and in a sense was often at the focal point of the conflicts that were the products of this age of upheaval. Now, in the 21st century, France plays a most vital and leading role in the creation of a newly defined Europe—politically, culturally, socially, and economically—and plays a significant part in developing an independent and definitive role on the global stage for that entity.

—William J. Roberts

# HISTORY OF FRANCE

# ORIGINS

The oldest identifiable culture in what is now France was the Paleolithic (50,000–8,000 B.C.E.). It left a rich culture of cave paintings, most notably those of Lascaux in the Dordogne region, done between 15,000 and 14,000 B.C.E. From 8,000 to 4,000 B.C.E., a Mesolithic culture existed in what is present-day France. The peoples, like their ancestors, were food gatherers, but relatively little evidence of their culture remains. The following Neolithic culture (4000–2000 B.C.E.), however, left several thousand remarkable stone monuments as evidence of its existence. These include the menhirs in Brittany, statuelike menhirs in the southern part of France, and the dolmens, or chamber tombs, in the Loire valley, the Parisian basin, and Champagne. France continued to be inhabited during the Bronze Age (2000–800 B.C.E.) and, toward the end of that era, the Hallstatt people, a part of the Celtic culture, appeared, coming from the Alpine region into France and producing and working with iron. They also produced pottery with rigid geometric patterns. In the Iron Age (800–200 B.C.E.), Celtic culture, with its Druidian beliefs, spread to many parts of what is today France. At the same time (seventh century B.C.E.), the Greeks established a colony, Massilía, at what is present-day Marseille and carried on trade up into the Rhône valley. During the eighth to the seventh century, Celts, known as Gauls, dominated many areas of modern-day France, known also as Gaul. A particular Celtic culture, known as La Téne culture, emerged in eastern Gaul. During the late Iron Age, they produced fine jewelry and pottery. In 121 B.C.E., the Romans took control of the Greek colony of Massalía and established one at Narbonne. Roman conquest continued, and in 58 B.C.E., Julius Caesar initiated the Gallic Wars to further Roman domination. In his *De Bello Gallico*, he describes all Gaul as being "divided into three parts," known as Gallia Belgica, Gallia Lugdunensis, and Aquitania. A center of administration was established at Lugdunum (present-day Lyon). In 52 B.C.E., Vercingétorix, the chief of the Arverni, a Gallic tribe, led a revolt that included various other Gallic tribes against the Romans. He was, however, defeated and captured at Alésia (near present-day Dijon) by Julius Caesar. Roman administration created two main divisions of Gaul, Gallia Cisalpina and Gallia Transalpina, and in 49 B.C.E., Roman citizenship was extended to their inhabitants and the Gauls began often to identify their gods with those of the Romans. In 27 B.C.E., Augustus divided Gaul into four administrative regions, and the area enjoyed the general peace of the early Roman Empire. Christianity was introduced into Gaul in the first century (Christians were martyred at Lyon in 177), and by the third century, the apostles to the Gauls (Denis, Gatien, Matial, Hilaire) helped to introduce the faith to the region, so that by the fifth century, it was rather widespread. The emperor Diocletian, in the third century, divided Gaul into two administrative areas, each containing several provinces. Subsequently, Gaul suffered from the decline that affected the rest of the Roman Empire. Beginning in 406, Germanic tribes started to settle peacefully in Gaul and served as military allies to the Romans. But they were soon followed by violent tribal invasions of the Vandals, Suevi, and Alans, and especially the Visigoths, who settled in the south, and the Burgundians, who settled in the east, each respectively creating separate kingdoms. In the northwest, the Celtic culture continued in Brittany, and in 451 the Huns invaded Gaul. But the Franks, one of the Germanic tribes who had settled in the north, would conquer much of Gaul under the leadership of Clovis, and the Gauls themselves would adopt the name of the Franks.

# THE FRANKISH KINGDOM

In a certain sense, one can consider the history of France as beginning with the Franks. Their power rested in part in the personality of their chiefs, including Clovis. By the end of the fifth century, they had made themselves masters of nearly all France and conquered adjacent territory east of the Rhine. In 481 Clovis, leader of the Salian Franks, established the first dynasty, called the Merovingian, with his capital at Paris, and reigned until his death in 511, when his kingdom was divided among his four sons. The country was subsequently divided among other rulers under a general law of inheritance, by which numerous principalities arose. There was a brief period of unity, beginning in 613 under Clotaire II and Dagobert I, then a decline until Pepin, the mayor of the royal palace, took power. His son, Charles Martel, in 732 repelled a Muslim army from Spain at Poitiers, and in 751 Martel's son, Pepin the Short, deposed the last Merovingian ruler and had himself crowned king of the Franks. He began a new dynasty that would later be called the Carolingian. In 754, Pope Stephen journeyed to France to anoint Pepin and his sons, and in 756 Pepin was succeeded by his son Charles (Charlemagne). Charlemagne was the sole ruler of the Franks until his death in 814. His early years were spent, like those of his father, in military campaigns. In 800 in Rome, he was crowned emperor of the Romans (Holy Roman Emperor), the first emperor in the West since the late fifth century. His main residence was at Aix-la-Chapelle (now Aachen, Germany). Under Charlemagne, there was a cultural revival (called often the Carolingian renaissance), with artisans producing in metallurgy, the goldsmith's art, and jewelry, and a scholarly and clerical revival occurring with schools in Reims and Tours. Charlemagne was succeeded by his son Louis the Pious, who decreed in 817 (Ordinatio Imperii) that his sons would each inherit parts of the empire. In 843, under the terms of the Treaty of Verdun, his son Charles received the area that is the forerunner of modern France (Francia Occidentalis), another, Louis, received Francia Orientalis (the East Frankish kingdom, corresponding to Germany), and the third, Lothair, inherited the territory in between that would be fought over in modern times by France and Germany. The disunity of the Franks facilitated successful Viking raids, with especially many northern towns and monasteries being attacked. The Vikings soon made permanent settlements, however, and in 911 a group (Normans) under Rollo accepted from the West Frankish king, Charles III, territory in the

Hugh Capet
*(Hulton/Archive)*

lower Seine valley to become known as Normandy. In 888, the West Frankish crown was offered to Eudes, count of Paris, and after his death, it reverted to the Carolingians. But when their power declined after the death of Louis V, the great magnates offered the crown, in 987, to Hugh Capet, a descendant of Eudes.

# THE CAPETIANS

The true founder of the French monarchy was Hugh Capet, who established the Capetian dynasty and added the fiefs of Orléans and Paris to the monarchy. Until the 12th century, however, the Capetian dynasty remained too weak to take part in the great political events of the era: The king of France did not intervene in either the conquest of England or the conflict between the Empire and the papacy. Meanwhile, power passed into the hands of the clergy and the nobles (with the bourgeoisie, the three "orders" that persisted until the French Revolution of 1789 would henceforth be established), and royalty seemed to fulfill mainly a spiritual and inefficacious role. Nonetheless, the Capetian dynasty did try to recover its prerogatives from vassals (Louis VI, who ruled from 1108 to 1137, consolidated royal power in the Île-de-France and arranged for the marriage of his son, the future Louis VII, to Eleanor of Aquitaine) and sought to resist English pretensions to the crown of France (Eleanor's remarriage to Henry, duke of Normandy, and later king of England, gave the English a claim on French territory). And Capetian monarchs established the principle of royal inheritance, having their sons crowned during their lifetimes, an advantage not enjoyed, for example, by the emperors. The church at this time played a preeminent role, with the first crusade being preached by a French pope, Urban II, and with monasticism in France experiencing a great expansion and reform (Cluny, Citeaux, Clairvaux). Romanesque art was abundantly represented in places such as Reims (Saint-Remi), Poitiers (Notre-Dame-la-Grande), Toulouse (Saint-Sernin), Jumièges, Moissac, Vézalay, Autun, and Mont-Saint-Michel. Philosophy flourished at schools in Paris and elsewhere, and theologically, Catharism, or ALBIGENSIANISM, a Christian sect, rose in the south. Courtly literature also developed, in both the *langue d'oïl* in the north and in the *langue d'oc* in the south among the troubadours. Royal authority increased under King Philip II Augustus (1180–1223), who acquired territory for the Crown, especially by leading the crusade against Catharism in the south, which he saw as an opportunity for intervention. The conquest of the south continued under his son, Louis VIII, so that royal authority eventually would extend to the Mediterranean. The cost of the brutal suppression of Catharism, however, would be, besides the political integration of the south into the kingdom of France, the destruction of the independent Occitan culture of Provence and Languedoc. Paris meanwhile became not only a political center but also one of the most important cities of Europe. Its university influenced the intellectual life of the entire West and attracted many important foreign scholars (Albert the Great, Thomas Aquinas, Duns Scotus, Eckhart, William of Occam). The reign of Louis IX, or Saint Louis (1226–70), was marked by an expansion in royal government and by that king's participation in the Crusades. He was succeeded by Philip III the Bold (1270–85). Under Philip IV the Fair (1285–1314), governmental administration increased and a class of legalists developed who, being familiar with Roman law, developed a new concept of the state, in which the king was not only a ruler but the living representation of the law. The new administration provoked the conflict that put Philip at odds with the church and also caused the first ESTATES GENERAL to be called in 1302. The Estates, consisting of the three orders—nobles, clerics, and bourgeois—were convened to support the king and the "freedoms of the kingdom" against the pope. The Estates were again convened in 1308 and 1314, without playing a true political role. But Philip, seeking increased revenues needed because of his intervention in Flanders and other regions (he annexed Franche-Comté, Lyon, and parts of Lorraine), was also willing to begin a persecution of the Jews in France and the persecution and suppression of the Templars, a rich and powerful military order. This period was also marked by the assault on the pope at Agagni (1303), which led to the 60-year-long Avignon papacy (1309–76). Yet as resources were squandered, the prestige of the monarchy declined and its prerogatives were challenged. Between 1314 and 1328, Philip's three sons—Louis X, Philip V, and Charles IV—held the crown in succession. As each died without a legitimate male heir, the throne passed to PHILIP VI OF VALOIS. This brought an end to Capetian rule.

# THE HUNDRED YEARS' WAR AND AFTER

The crisis over succession that developed upon the death of Philip the Fair and the accession of Philip IV of Valois would reawaken the old conflict between France and England, already exacerbated by their rivalry in Flanders. The HUNDRED YEARS' WAR would be a particularly somber period for France, which already was involved in the general crisis in western Europe, the economic aspect of which can be attributed to a halt in agricultural expansion during the 14th century (there were numerous famines, in particular those of 1316–17, which were followed by epidemics and a reduction of the population). The Hundred Years' War (a period of intermittent warfare between England and France between 1337 and 1453), in its first phase, produced great defeats for the French, at Sluys (1340), Crécy (1346), and especially at Poitiers (1356). A French resurgence began in 1370, and then a period of peace. War then resumed, and the French were defeated at Agincourt (1415) and had to sign the Treaty of Troyes, which recognized King Henry V of England as heir to the French throne. A French revival, however, began with the relieving of the siege of Orléans by JOAN OF ARC in 1429 (and her subsequent bringing of the king to Reims for his coronation). And between 1450 and 1453, the English were finally driven from Normandy and Gascony; thus almost all their control on the continent was ended (Calais was held until 1558). The Treaty of Étaples, signed in 1492, effectively settled the outstanding differences between France and England. Nonetheless, the victory was not complete for France, especially regarding subsequent economic developments. French domination in the Near East, a result of the Crusades of the 13th century, had clearly begun to diminish. The development of Venetian and Genoese maritime trade caused the end of the fairs at Champagne. Currency became quite unstable. These socioeconomic problems, aggravated by the war, put the nation in a position of weakness regarding its adversary; thus, the anarchy and the uprisings, brought about, too, by a threatened feudal system (feudal league, *grandes compagnies,* etc.), as well as by a constrained bourgeoisie and a suppressed peasant population (the *grand Jacquerie* of the Île-de-France in 1358, the Parisian uprising of ÉTIENNE MARCEL, the revolts of 1382 and 1413). The coming of the bubonic plague in 1348 (it would reappear, in slightly less virulent forms, over the course of the century), had also devastated the nation for a period of about two years, as it did the rest of Europe, decimating a large percentage of the population. For these reasons and others, this period did at least produce large social changes; at the end of the Hundred Years' War, the freeing of the serfs occurred generally, while the nobility began to give up some land, because of financial difficulties, to the advantage of the bourgeoisie. This gave rise to a wealthy class that became politically active (Étienne Marcel, JACQUES CŒUR) and a class of well-to-do peasants. Finally, the economic crisis began to subside.

Both Kings CHARLES VII and LOUIS XI (1461–83) sought to encourage strong economic measures (regulation of urban corporations and guilds, development of the textile industry and of the trade fairs at Lyon, strengthening of the currency, and measures favorable to cooperation between the nobility and the bourgeoisie). Their centralizing policies corresponded to the reinforcement of royal power, which would often be tested, and a sense of national unity developed, centered on the monarch (a phenomenon already enhanced earlier by the actions of JOAN OF ARC). Louis XI's principal adversary was CHARLES THE BOLD, but after his defeat and death (1477), Louis acquired a part of the Burgundian domains, as well as Roussillon, and the succession of Anjou (Anjou, Maine, and Provence, 1481). France also now had a permanent army (*compagnies d'ordonnance*). And despite the dangerous policies pursued by the noble houses that ruled during the 14th and 15th centuries (House of Burgundy, Orléans, Bourbon, Armagnac, Albret), the kingdom of France was further enlarged with the acquisition not only of Burgundy and Artois but, at the end of the 15th century, Brittany as well. While hardly propitious for the development of the arts, the Hundred Years' War brought a certain number of large construction projects. Soon the minor arts did flourish greatly, with manuscript illuminating (JEAN PUCELLE, the LIMBOURG brothers, JEAN FOUQUET), enamel work (particularly at Limoges), and tapestries (*Apocalypse d'Angers*). Sculpture (Claus Sluter) and painting (ENGUERRAND QUARTON, the Master of Moulins) also had a revival. Influenced by all events, literature became more realistic (CHRISTINE DE PISAN, CHARLES D'ORLÉANS, ALAIN CHARTIER, EUSTACHE DESCHAMPS, FRANÇOIS VILLON).

# THE RENAISSANCE AND THE RISE OF THE MONARCHY

France, during its decline, had left cultural preeminence to Italy, but the prestige France enjoyed explains why there was still an attraction to French culture. The wars in Italy would, however, bring the diffusion of the Italian Renaissance. The coming to France of several Italian artists, such as il Vignola, il Primaticcio, il Rosso Fiorentino, and Niccolò d'Abate, influenced French art (PIERRE LESCOT, JEAN GOUJON, the Fontainebleau school). On the other hand, humanism brought the flowering of philosophical studies (GUILLAUME BUDÉ, JACQUES AMYOT, ÉTIENNE DOLET, HENRI ESTIENNE) that exposed the literate French public not only to classical authors but also to translations of biblical texts (JACQUES LEFEVRE D'ETAPLES, OLIVÉTAN, CLÉMENT MAROT). A determinant element in the development of the pre-Reformation, humanism also permitted the establishment and enrichment of the French language (Pléiade group, FRANÇOIS RABELAIS, GEOFFROY TORY), sometime the influence of those who were inspired by Petrarch (MARGUERITE DE NAVARRE, MAURICE SCÈVE, PHILIPPE DESPORTES, AGRIPPA D'AUBIGNÉ), and would encourage a complete renewal in philosophy (MICHEL DE MONTAIGNE, JEAN BODIN, RAMUS). The great artists of the French Renaissance were above all architects and sculptors. The architects built vast palaces for court ceremonials. The most celebrated are the châteaux of the Loire, where the earlier French traditions combined with the new style: Amboise, Blois, Chambord, the châteaux of Francis I, the work of Pierre Nepveu, and the like. In Paris the Louvre, the work of PIERRE LESCOT, represents the Renaissance where the classical style prevails. Of the great architect PHILIBERT DELORME, there remains only part of the château of Anet near Dreux. Like the architects, the French sculptors remained at first faithful to the French realist tradition, as seen in the works of the Breton MICHEL COLOMBE and LIGIER RICHIER from Lorrain. But JEAN GOUJON is a pure classicist, as is obvious in his sculpture *Diane* at Anet or the *Nymphes de la fontaine des Innocents*. GERMAIN PILON, a classicist when he produced the tomb of Henry II, returned at times to the French tradition, for example, when he sculpted the funerary statue of Birague in a vigorously realistic style. In the minor arts, BERNARD PALISSY, from Périgord, a scholar and artist, rediscovered the secret of applying enamel to terracotta and produced the most original works, ornamented with figures of animals, fish, shells, and other aspects of nature.

The claims of the French monarchs over the kingdom of Naples served as a pretext for the campaigns of CHARLES VIII (during whose minority the regent, Anne de Beaujeu, led the country from 1483 to 1492) and LOUIS XII, the latter setting his aims on Milan also. The idea of a vast crusade, too, against the Ottomans was a part of their plans. But Charles VIII first conquered and then lost Naples, and Louis XII did the same at Milan. If these plans of conquest had succeeded, they would have actually cost the nation little and would have had the advantage of channeling the restlessness of the nobility. Instead, the result was to create a European coalition against France that degenerated into a struggle between the French and Austrian dynasties, under King FRANCIS I (1515–47), of the House of Valois-Orléans-Angoulême, and the Habsburg emperor Charles V, over the Burgundian inheritance. Francis I was defeated at Marignan (1515) and later at Pavia (1525), where he was captured, then forced to sign the disastrous Treaty of Madrid (1526). Later, at the Peace of Cateau-Cambrésis (signed after the defeat of Emperor Charles at Metz), King HENRY II (1547–59) renounced entirely his predecessors' claims in Italy to gain advantages in the north and the east of the country, particularly, the Trois-Évêchés, the three bishoprics of Metz, Toul, and Verdun. Contemporary opinion, however, considered the terms of that treaty as quite unfavorable. The peace was a compromise between two financially depleted adversaries. They had each tried to channel to themselves as much capital as possible to impoverish the other, and it was this game that France lost, when Emperor Charles V, financed by the Fuggers, a German family of financiers from Augsburg, was elected. One can also consider that in economic matters, the 16th century marks a break in the rapport among the medieval orders; these came apart and made room for a type of "capitalism," which was less a large economic structure than a preponderant commercial function (contemporaries spoke of mercantilism). The major global explorations and the influx of precious metals that followed gave a new impulse to the economy of the 15th century that was already expanding. Credit developed, as well as letters of exchange, accompanied by the growth of a truly industrial, not just an artisan, economy.

This evolution was accompanied by social changes. The rise in prices had as a consequence the triumph of a capital economy over the landed feudal one; the wealthy bourgeoisie, now in a position to purchase the possessions of the nobility, who were forced to sell, moved closer socially to that class (they thus formed a new aristocracy, from which would arise, for example, the Villeroi or the Gondi), while distancing themselves from the masses. The financial system that supported and favored the bourgeoisie, and its weakening of the nobility, reinforced royal power in the short term. Francis I, who never called the Estates General, in effect made triumphant a concept of an absolute monarchy that presaged LOUIS XIV, during whose reign that idea became a divine right. The king held all power, he became temporal head of the church (CONCORDAT OF BOLOGNA negotiated with Pope Leo X), with the right to fill all bishoprics and benefices, but he had, nonetheless, to respect certain contracts and customs. Brittany, already tied to the Crown under Louis XII, was definitively integrated into the kingdom. The last great fiefs disappeared, while the idea of the inalienability of the kingdom was born, in virtue of which the Parlement had to abrogate the Treaty of Madrid, which had given Burgundy to the emperor Charles V. Royal authority, emanating from the role of the king as sole lawmaker, was reinforced by the development of officers of the court. In 1539, Francis I banned the use of Latin in judicial proceedings and required instead the exclusive use of French. Also a generous and discerning patron of the arts, he helped to bring about the flowering of the French Renaissance. Edifices built during his era still attest to the power, influence, and wealth of the monarchy at this time.

# THE WARS OF RELIGION

The later decades of the 16th century were a period of great difficulty and unrest in France. The population had increased, as did inflation, causing poverty and discontent. The Reformation, especially in the 1540s and 1550s, through the influence of the ideas of JOHN CALVIN, spread through France, attracting many followers known as Huguenots, among the nobility and the lower ranks. King HENRY II saw a threat and tried to suppress Protestantism and, under the brief reigns of his three sons, the Wars of Religion broke out, with an inextricable combination of religious, political, and dynastic factors involved. Fanaticism and extreme brutality characterized much of the events of this violent period. In 1559, FRANCIS II became king but ruled for only two years, succeeded by his brother, CHARLES IX. Their mother, CATHERINE DE' MEDICI, had exercised regency during their reigns, and her influence continued during that of her third son, HENRY III (1574–89). She always sought a religious compromise so as to secure a peaceful reign, but she was powerless against religious fanaticism. Protestant leaders from the upper nobility included ANTOINE DE BOURBON, king of Navarre, and his brother Louis I, the PRINCE DE CONDÉ, and great lords, such as GASPARD DE COLIGNY. Catholic nobles, who were in the majority, were led by Francis of Guise and his brother, the cardinal of Lorraine (under Charles IX, there had been an attempt at reconciliation, but the Massacre at Vassy in 1562 of a hundred Calvinist leaders unleashed civil strife that involved foreign intervention). In time, Catherine became involved in the events leading to the SAINT BARTHOLOMEW'S DAY MASSACRE (August 24, 1572) in Paris in which thousands of Protestants were killed, and which was organized by Henry of GUISE, who sought to eliminate the Huguenot leadership. The horrible slaughter reached the provinces and there were many more victims.

The Wars of Religion would set the power of the great feudal lords against that of the Crown; they took advantage of the minority of Francis II and Charles IX, presaging the events that would occur later under LOUIS XIII, where the FRONDE, led by the great provincial nobles, would exploit the troubles that had originated during the Reformation and the religious wars. The creation of the HOLY LEAGUE (Sainte Ligue) (1576), a large league of the Catholic nobility led by Henry of Guise that was secretly antiroyalist, put the monarchy in peril. In the long term, these events would arrest the development of the economy and the rise of the bourgeoisie, and would favor the development of absolutism (in contrast to what was occurring in England at the same time). During the reign

This engraving depicts the St. Bartholomew's Day Massacre, August 25, 1572. *(Hulton/Archive)*

of Henry III (1574–89), anarchy spread, and the dynasty itself was threatened by the ambitions of Henry of Guise, who entered Paris in 1588, provoking an uprising, the "DAY OF THE BARRICADES," that forced the king to flee, and in response to whose assassination that same year, HENRY III himself would be assassinated (1589).

In the immediate sense, the monarchy was saved in this period by government officials, such as MICHEL DE L'HOSPITAL, who through legislative activity upheld the principle of monarchic continuity. The civil and religious war had degenerated into a foreign one; Philip II of Spain, for example, considered placing his daughter on the French throne (leaders of the League in 1585 had concluded a secret treaty with that monarch, which forced Henry III to outlaw Protestantism). But the eventual coming together of various political factions, which had been slowly developing in the face of foreign intervention, allowed HENRY IV (1589–1610) finally to reestablish peace in 1594. In 1572, Henry of Navarre (Henry IV) had married the sister of King CHARLES IX (the occasion of the marriage, attended by many Huguenot leaders, facilitated the Saint Bartholomew's Day Massacre), and thus upon the death of Charles in 1589, the crown passed to Henry, the first of the Bourbon kings. The leader of the Protestants, he seemed at first unable to achieve reconciliation with the Catholics. After four years of continued warfare, in which he defeated the League at Arques and then Ivry (1589–90), he was unable to take Paris, which was under the League's control. The denouement took place in 1593, when the League convened the Estates General to elect a king. Philip of Spain at this point put forth his daughter as a candidate for queen and, in the face of this foreign threat there was a sudden revival of national sentiment. The Leaguers hesitated and, on July 25, 1593, Henry IV, in the church of Saint-Denis, solemnly abjured Protestantism. The great nobles and the cities made their submission, and in 1594 the king entered Paris. There remained the religious question. After long negotiations, Henry IV prevailed on both parties to accept the EDICT OF NANTES (1598), by which Protestants obtained freedom of worship, equal access with Catholics to all positions, and the creation of councils, or *parlements,* consisting of both Protestants and Catholics, and political and military privileges (the right to convene synods, the right to garrison and keep secure certain towns). The edict was a great and wise political achievement, as it gave France peace and religious freedom at a time when other nations suffered from intolerance and conflict.

# THE AGE OF ABSOLUTISM

After 30 years of civil wars, not only was the nation devastated, the state was disorganized, with royal authority nearly dissipated. Provincial governors and former League leaders had formed a new feudal class, the *parlements* were accustomed to opposing the Crown, and there were many peasant uprisings. During the reign of Henry IV, this would change. He did not convene the ESTATES GENERAL and began to restrain the political power of provincial leaders, reducing their role to a purely military one. To appease both sides, he surrounded himself with individuals from all factions. Huguenots such as SULLY and Leaguers like Villeroy, meanwhile, continued to extend royal control throughout the realm (the governor of Burgundy, Marshal Biron, who had conspired with the Spanish, was executed in 1602). But the fervor of the League had not been completely extinguished. In 1610, as Henry IV, allied with the German Protestants, was preparing for a war against Spain and Austria, he was assassinated by a fanatic. His son, LOUIS XIII, was not even nine years old. The Parlement proclaimed the queen mother, MARIE DE' MEDICI (Marie de Médicis), as regent with full powers. Of limited ability, she put all her confidence in two Italian adventurers, LÉONORA GALIGAÏ and her husband, CONCINO CONCINI. Soon, all the achievements of Henry IV were lost, with the great nobles revolting when a depleted treasury could not longer pay their pensions. The Estates General was convened in 1614, but nothing was accomplished. In 1617, the young king had both Concini and his wife killed and gave power to one of his hunting companions, de Luynes, who died in 1621 as disorder and revolts continued.

After two years of intrigues, Marie de' Medici, who had regained influence, had her confidant, Cardinal RICHELIEU, named to the Royal Council. Three months later, he became head of the council, that is, leading minister. He remained until his death the true head of the government (1624–42). Despite various cabals, Louis XIII placed all his confidence in him. Between the factious nobles and Richelieu, there was a fight to the death. From 1624 to 1632, the plots and uprisings against the cardinal were incessant, with the king's brother GASTON D'ORLÉANS instigating almost all of them. Their conspiracies foiled or suppressed, the great nobles (les Grands) remained meanwhile strong in the provinces, where, as governors, they remained often semi-independent of the Crown's authority. Richelieu then either replaced them or placed an administrator (*intendant*) with them. Armed with dictatorial powers in matters of security, justice, and finance, the *intendants* little by little became the leaders of the provincial administration. More than any other governmental institution, they helped to strengthen absolutism in France. Richelieu also instituted, in 1634, the ACADÉMIE FRANÇAISE, the oldest of the five academies that constitute the INSTITUT DE FRANCE. He also encouraged the further extension of the French empire in North America.

Richelieu died at the end of 1642 and the king died shortly after, leaving as a successor a five-year-old child, LOUIS XIV (1643). Following the example of Marie de' Medici, the Parlement granted the regency with full powers to the queen mother, ANNE OF AUSTRIA. The princes and the Grands were waiting to regain their control. To everyone's surprise, Anne of Austria gave power to the protégé of Richelieu, Cardinal MAZARIN, and protected him against all the cabals of the nobility. The wars in which France had been engaged since 1635 had depleted the treasury. To deal with the deficit, Mazarin increased expediency measures, sold offices, and imposed duties and various taxes that weighed most heavily on the Parisians and exasperated them also. Finally, discontent was so great that a revolt broke out (1648).

Emboldened by the minister's unpopularity and by the example of the revolution in England, the Parlement of Paris, with popular support, decided that the time had come for a strong move. By the Decree of Union (Arrêt d'Union), the Parlement invited the other sovereign courts (*cours des comptes, cour des aides,* and *grands conseils*) to deliberate on the "reform of the kingdom" and then, with the Declaration of 27 Articles, an actual constitution, they claimed to limit royal power. In the declaration, in particular, they called for the suppression of intendancies and forbade the raising of new taxes without the consent of Parlement. The regent tried to deal with the matter with force; she arrested several of the opposition leaders, among them the popular adviser PIERRE BROUSSEL.

Immediately, a strong uprising broke out: the DAY OF THE BARRICADES (August 26, 1648). Lacking a sufficient number of troops, Anne of Austria had to concede and released Broussel. Shortly after, she fled to Saint-Germain with the young king and Mazarin, and the civil war began. It was called the FRONDE, after a children's game that had been forbidden by the police. The first revolt, called the Fronde parlementaire, ended after three months. The royal army blockaded Paris, and, refusing the help offered by the king of Spain, the Parlement concluded with the royal court the Peace of Rueil (March 1649). A second revolt in the provinces, the Fronde des Princes (1650–52), was more threatening for the Crown. Following the Parisian revolt came the revolt in the provinces— Normandy, Guyenne, Burgundy, Poitou—which the great nobles (les Grands) successfully launched. The scheming Paul de Gondi, famous later under the name of cardinal de RETZ, brought the Parlement again into the revolt. But the rebels fought among themselves; LOUIS II DE BOURBON, PRINCE DE CONDÉ, chief leader of the revolt, had to flee and seek refuge with the Spanish. The state of anarchy was such that at the request of the Parlement itself, the royal court reentered the capital and was enthusiastically received. After that, and until his death (1661), Mazarin governed without resistance or limitations.

The Fronde revolt, along with the foreign war, left France in ruins. There was some relief: Saint VINCENT DE PAUL, especially, with the help of the Sisters of Charity, worked with admirable devotion to alleviate suffering, but charity was insufficient against such misery. The Fronde had another unexpected consequence; it assured the triumph of absolutism. France, because of all the problems that the revolts caused, had come to detest instigators of unrest. All thought of opposition to the king was abandoned, and, wishing much for internal peace, the nation awaited someone who could bring it about.

Upon the death of Mazarin (1661), King Louis XIV announced his determination to govern by himself, and he carried out that intention for the rest of his reign (1661–1715). Louis XIV never had a prime minister and instead most diligently and conscientiously fulfilled the duties of that office himself. Louis XIV brought to everything he did, even his gestures, an air of nobility and majesty. If he did not have great personal qualities, he had a good sense of politics and, having self-confidence, acted with determination. But his driving sentiment was his passionate love of glory, and he sought because of that to be a great monarch. He was filled with the idea that he was the representative, or lieutenant, of God. This coincided also with the theory, already widely accepted in France, of the divine right of princes.

With a belief in a divine foundation for his authority, Louis XIV consequently became the master of the wealth, freedom, and lives of his subjects. The idea that he was God's representative filled him with prodigious conceit. His life was regulated by a ceremonial that became more and more rigid (etiquette) and a true cult of royal majesty. Each of the activities of his daily routine became an aspect of this cult, a ceremony in which nothing was left to chance. Following the example of King Francis I, Louis XIV made the royal court the center of his government and gave it extraordinary power. His bad memory of the Fronde persisted, so to occupy the idle and restless nobility so they would not return to conspiracies and revolts, he resolved to control them and keep them at the court by a foolproof strategy, the distribution of favors. Thus, by the thousands, the nobles came to the court at Versailles, with even the greatest lords disputing among themselves the honor of holding the candle or the shirt of the king at his daily *levée* (rising) or *coucher* (going to bed). Jealous of his authority, Louis XIV systematically excluded from power the great lords and the prelates. He appointed only nobles to positions at court or in the army. For his government and administration, he preferred the service of lesser individuals who, powerless themselves, owed him everything. The king governed assisted by three or four persons who had his trust and bore the title of ministers of state. Only the ministers of state attended the High Council, where all important matters were discussed. In truth, the ministers were merely the executors of the king's wishes. They were generally chosen from among the leaders of the public services: the chancellor; head of justice; the comptroller general of finances; the four secretaries of state (war, foreign affairs, royal household, navy). Certain ministers, such as JEAN-BAPTISTE COLBERT (1661–83) and FRANÇOIS DE LOUVOIS (1672–91), played a large role in the government, but the king, at least in appearance, made the final decisions.

Outside the High Council, which was the principal government council, the king also presided over four other grand councils that dealt with finances, interior administration (the intendancies), justice, and matters of the Chancellery. In the provinces, the intendants carried out the royal will and authority. Under this regime, order and security were well assured, but they were purchased at the cost of the servitude of the entire nation. Royal power was limitless and Louis's government was unchecked. The king never convened the Estates General, and the Parlement effectively lost the right of remonstrance (1673). The nation found itself submitting to the most arbitrary royal policies, and absolutism turned into despotism. Control was maintained by a system of policing, especially in Paris, where there was a lieutenant general of police (1667), and the king had spies everywhere, at the court and in the cities. With the use of lettres de cachet, anyone could be imprisoned indefinitely and without charges. By the time of the king's death, France had grown tired of absolute monarchy and the abuses of personal power. Following the end of the reign, there were incessant conflicts, countless acts of violence and injustice, and financial disorganization, with a great part of the nation reduced to misery. As a consequence, a critical spirit reawoke, with some proposing reforms, including a fair and equal system of taxation and the participation of the people in their government.

# FRANCE DURING THE SEVENTEENTH CENTURY

In the 17th century, France was the most populous nation in western Europe, with about 19 million inhabitants. Between the classes was great inequality. Officially, there were two privileged orders, or estates—the clergy and the nobility—beneath which were the masses, or the Third Estate. The clergy were the first order, or estate, and had their own assemblies and tribunals. Exempt from taxation, they gave instead to the king an annual subsidy (the *"don gratuit"*) and possessed immense properties that made the church the wealthiest landowner in the kingdom. But only the upper clergy—bishops and abbots—held this authority and riches, while the lower clergy lived on a small income or stipend. Since the Concordat of 1516, the upper clergy depended on the king, who dispensed all titles and benefices of the church. These were given to members of the noble families and sometimes to the bourgeoisie (BOSSUET, who was bishop of Meaux, was the son of an attorney). Most often, the high aristocratic clergy was a court clergy, for whom the duty to reside in their diocese was a punishment. The nobility who held on their estates honorific privileges and ancient feudal rights, were divided into the nobility of the court (*noblesse de cour*), entitled and pensioned by the king, and the provincial nobility (*noblesse de province*), themselves very diverse and often poor and idle. Between them, there was often hatred and jealousy; the only common sentiment was their aristocratic pride and disdain for those who were not of the nobility. On penalty of derogation, or loss of title, the nobility was forbidden to engage in labor or trade. Instead, they were expected to "live nobly," without making commercial profits. Because of this, they became something of a parasitic class, dependent on royal favors and positions at court.

The Third Estate comprised about 18.5 million people, all of them nonprivileged. But this class was not homogeneous. It included, in particular, bourgeoisie, artisans, and peasants, in effect, three separate classes. The bourgeoisie formed an educated and increasingly influential class. The "men of letters," those who would today be called "professionals"—doctors, attorneys, writers, and the like; businessmen—financiers, shipowners, and wealthy merchants; the innumerable groups of secondary royal officials—judges, notaries, court clerks, and tax collectors—all were part of this class that sought to increase its privileges and to rise in the social hierarchy. The artisans filled the manual positions and for the most part were organized into guilds as in the Middle Ages. Correspondingly, among them existed the ranks of apprentice, journeyman, and master. The lives of such workers, especially if they were not masters, was hard, and they often worked for many hours each day on fixed wages. In the countryside could be found the landowning peasants who lived in some comfort. The great majority, however, were sharecroppers who lived in poverty, weighed down by taxes, feudal dues, tithes, and corvées, or local and royal duties, and were expected also to give quarter to soldiers. Their misery often provoked revolts that were usually brutally suppressed.

In terms of religious affairs, the 17th century was a period of true Catholic revival, marked by many works of charity and piety. As noted, Vincent de Paul founded the Lazarist order to evangelize the countryside and the Daughters of Charity to help the poor and the orphaned (1638). Others were involved in founding Catholic schools, such as the Oratorian colleges, which competed with the Jesuits for the education of the young nobility and bourgeoisie. The religious fervor of the period was also manifested in the first part of the century by the growth of JANSENISM. Based on the doctrines of a Belgian bishop, Cornelis Jansen, Jansenism approached Calvinism in its emphasis on divine grace. Violently attacked by Jesuit theologians and condemned by the pope, Jansenism, with its emphasis on morality, nonetheless attracted many, including the abbot of Saint-Cyran; the Grand ARNAULD, a Jansenist spiritual leader; Pierre Nicole; BLAISE PASCAL; and others. They lived in a community at the convent of Port-Royal des Champs, near Paris, dedicated to meditation, prayer, and work.

The Jansenists came under the suspicion of royal authority and in particular that of Louis XIV for their independent spirit and their contempt for worldly things. In 1660, the *Provinciales,* written by Pascal to defend Jansenism against the Jesuits, were condemned. At the end of the reign, the persecution of the Jansenists was renewed but more rigorously. The convent of Port-Royal was razed and the religious expelled (1709). In 1715, more than 2,000 persons were imprisoned because of their Jansenist sentiments. But the doctrine survived, admired for its high sense of morality and independence, and in the 18th century it constituted a force against absolutism. Thanks to the concessions that Henry IV granted in the Edict of Nantes, Protestants not only enjoyed freedom of worship and equality before the law, they also were able to keep their political and military organizations. But such organizations also presented a permanent threat of civil war.

This became apparent after Henry IV's death. Fearing a Catholic reaction, the Protestants, or Huguenots, went on the defensive. Their principal fortified places included Montauban, Montpellier, and especially La Rochelle. LOUIS XIII and Charles d'Albert, duke de LUYNES, besieged these without success (1620–22). So long as they were a force, Richelieu attacked the Protestants, not because of intolerance but for reasons of state, because they constituted the most dangerous political faction in the kingdom. The decisive struggle took place between 1627 and 1629. The center of the Huguenot resistance was the port of La Rochelle. Richelieu besieged it and blockaded the port with an enormous dike that stopped the English relief fleets. After more than a year of siege, the town, suffering from starvation, surrendered (1628). The war continued in the Cévennes until the Protestants, discouraged, asked for peace. Then the king proclaimed the Edict of Alès (1629), which allowed the Protestants to return to common law. They lost their secure sites and their political privileges; in return, they retained their religious freedoms and equal status with Catholics as stipulated in the Edict of Nantes. After that, the Protestants remained loyal subjects, but the religious peace lasted only until the personal reign of Louis XIV.

Convinced that he was the "lieutenant of God" on Earth, and persuaded also that religious unity was a condition for political unity, Louis was resolved to extirpate what he saw as a heresy from his kingdom. At first, the Edict of Nantes was applied in the most rigorous way and one that was most favorable to the Protestants. The regime, however, then began a persecution that kept increasing in intensity. Everything that the edict did not explicitly stipulate was forbidden. Little by little, all public functions were closed to Protestants. Protestant marriages and burials were subjected to vexatious regulations, and churches constructed after the edict were demolished. All methods were used to achieve conversions: A fund for converts was established to reward those who abjured, and an edict of 1681 authorized that children over the age of seven could convert and leave their families. Finally, to constrain the most recalcitrant, it was ordered that the Protestants had to lodge the king's dragoons, who, in turn, were permitted to commit all manner of excesses and abuses. The king's minister Louvois generalized this practice into a system known as the dragonnades. The king recommended that only bankers and leading manufacturers be spared, but the terror inspired by the soldiers was such that Protestants abjured in the thousands. As the lists of conversions grew, Louis XIV believed that only a few "obstinate" Huguenots remained in France. He decided to sign the revocation of the Edict of Nantes (1685). The Protestant cult was now forbidden; all its churches had to be demolished; its pastors were forced to leave the kingdom or be sent to the galleys.

The revocation was welcomed with enthusiasm not only by the clergy, who had long demanded it, but also by the great majority of the people, the elite included. The revocation, however, had disastrous consequences for the country. The Protestants were still very numerous, and although there were penalties for emigration, they emigrated en masse. Certain provinces were for the moment ruined and several industries gravely affected. By contrast, the refugees became a source of strength and prosperity for the countries that gave them asylum, especially England, Holland, and Brandenburg. On the other hand, Calvinist peasants remained numerous in the Cévennes, and during the War of the Spanish Succession, they revolted. It took an army led by the duc de Villars to suppress the CAMISARD revolt (1702–04), as it is known. Finally, the revocation of the edict aroused the hatred of the Protestant states against France and produced coalitions that in the end Louis XIV was unable to defeat.

The economic life of France changed during the 17th century. The Wars of Religion had devastated the nation. Some years of peace and the good government of HENRY IV were sufficient, however, to encourage productivity. The principal collaborator of Henry IV was a Protestant noble, the duke of SULLY, a comrade in arms of the king who was made superintendent of finances and grand overseer of France. Sully severely cut royal and administrative expenses, reducing state debts, economizing, and demanding exact accountability. As grand overseer, he restored roads and bridges, and dug the canal at Briare. But above all, he energetically protected and encouraged agriculture and the peasantry. Cultivation and pasturage, he said, fed France. He reduced agricultural taxes and the *taille,* a personal tax, forbade fiscal agents to seize farm animals and tools, and tried at the same time to introduce the new agrarian methods outlined by OLIVIER DE SERRES in his treatise *Théâtre d'agriculture et ménage des champs.*

In matters of trade and commerce, Henry IV put forth the boldest initiatives, on the advice of BARTHÉLEMY DE LAFFÉMAS, comptroller general of commerce. He encouraged production of luxury goods, introduced into France the planting of mulberry trees and at Tours and LYON the production of silks and velvets, and subsidized tapestry and glass factories. He concluded trade agreements with England and the Ottoman Sublime Porte and encouraged colonial enterprises; the first French colony was Canada, where SAMUEL CHAMPLAIN founded Quebec (1608).

The rapid economic resurgence was not permanent. Its results were partially wiped out by the 50 years of troubles and war that preceded the personal government of Louis XIV. Also during the course of the 17th century, the economic revival constantly faced obstacles, such as the relative insufficiency of monetary circulation in Europe and the low prices that resulted, especially in the second half of the century. And until 1660, it was often undermined by royal policies. Soon after the death of Henry IV, the economies of Sully were squandered. During the ministries of Richelieu and Mazarin, internal conflicts and foreign wars impoverished the country. Richelieu sought to develop the wealth of the public sector. He supported the trading companies and colonial enterprises. Bank branches were founded in Senegal (1626), the Antilles, and Madagascar, and commercial agreements were signed with Russia, Denmark, and the sultan of Morocco. Prospective missions were sent as far away as Persia. The work of economic revival outlined by Henry IV and Richelieu received a decisive impetus with the arrival of JEAN-BAPTISTE COLBERT to power. Colbert was the most industrious of the ministers of Louis XIV (1661–83). Comptroller general of finances, then secretary of state of the royal household and of the navy, he served effectively as minister of national works and wanted to make France the wealthiest nation in Europe.

To achieve that, he believed it was necessary to prevent French gold from leaving the country and to attract foreign gold, in that way developing industries and trade in export. He planned thus to develop France as the greatest financial, manufacturing, and merchant power. Colbert developed existing industries; Elbeuf, Sedan, and Carcassonne became great centers for the production of drapery cloth; the GOBELIN works in Paris manufactured admirable tapestries; Lyon produced silk cloth. Moreover, Colbert created industries that France lacked: at Saint-Gobain, glassmaking; at Alençon and Chantilly, lace; at Sèvres, porcelains; at Saint-Étienne, steel and armaments. To produce large quantities, the small workshop no longer sufficed. Colbert sponsored large factories that could employ many workers. Large government-financed enterprises also developed, the royal factories that employed hundreds of workers.

This, then, was the beginning of large, or capitalist, industry that began in France. To gain foreign customers, French products had to be of high quality. Also, Colbert believed it essential to regulate and supervise production. His decrees described to the smallest detail the method of production. Factory inspectors exercised rigorous surveillance and defective products were seized and destroyed. In the long run, this excessive regulation would be an impediment to industrial progress. To discourage foreign imports and close French markets to foreign competition, Colbert imposed a protective system of high duties on foreign ships and products entering France. Certain products, like Venetian glass and lace, were completely prohibited. Meanwhile, Colbert continued war with Holland to ruin that nation's trade. To extend French commerce throughout the world, he also employed other policies. Inside the kingdom, Colbert was unable to create a system of uniform weights and measures, or to suppress the agreements or customs duties between the provinces. But he did repair the roads and developed canals, such as the Canal d'Orléans and the Canal des Deux-Mers, conceived by the engineer PIERRE RIQUET to connect the Mediterranean and the Atlantic.

Maritime trade was the most fruitful, having assured the fortunes of Venice and Holland. Colbert therefore demanded the development of a merchant marine. He paid well shipbuilders and buyers of foreign vessels. To create a trade in exotic goods, he created trading companies, such as the East Indies Company. It was organized as a stock company. But the results he hoped for did not materialize, and few of these companies prospered. Trade became more active and the merchant fleet doubled between 1670 and 1680. Colbert could not establish the vast colonial empire that he had wished, but he did much achieve the settlement of Canada and lay the foundation for the French territory of Louisiana. He sent around 4,000 Breton and Norman peasants to Canada, while at the same time, the French domains were enlarged by bold explorations. In 1673, a merchant from Quebec, LOUIS JOLIET, and a Jesuit, Père Marquette, sighted the Mississippi River. In 1682, RENÉ-ROBERT CAVELIER, SIEUR DE LA SALLE, reached the delta of that river and the Gulf of Mexico, naming the region Louisiana in honor of the king. In India, the East Indies company acquired the territories of Chandarnagar and Pondicherry (1676) and founded settlements on the island of Réunion. Finally, to protect the merchant fleet and the colonies, Colbert created a powerful navy. He worked not only for the enrichment of the nation, but also for a better administering of royal finances, and he fought against financial waste. He demanded exact and daily accounts from the Treasury and reduced official benefices and percentages from taxation. But beginning in 1672, wars, building projects, festivals and spectacles, and pensions paid to courtiers increased, raising expenses for the state. As in the past, Colbert had to increase taxes, sell positions, and put the nation in debt.

What stopped Colbert in the end was the financial disorder that remained the incurable problem of absolute monarchy. After his death, the economic and financial situation did not improve. It was not enough to increase existing taxes (*taille, aide, gabelle*), but new direct taxes now had to be created, such as a head tax (capitation), in 1695 and the *dixième* (or "tenth"), imposed on revenues

*Ifrael ex. Cum Priul. Reg.*

fin ces Voleurs infames et perdus ,   Monfrent bien que le crime (horrible et noire engeance)   Et que ceft le Deftin des hommes vicieux
me fruits malheureux a cet arbre pendus   Eft luy mefme inftrument de honte et de vengeance ,   Defprouver toft ou tard la iuftice des Cieux . 1

Prisoners of war and entire communities were massacred during the Thirty Years' War by both sides, as depicted in this drawing. *(Hulton/Archive)*

(1710), taxes that weighed most heavily on the nonprivileged. Among the mass of people, burdened by taxes, misery increased. The population fell from 19 million to 17 million. A large part of the kingdom remained fallow. Louis XIV became extremely unpopular and, at his death (September 1715), the people, said the memorialist LOUIS DE ROUVROY, DUKE DE SAINT-SIMON, gave "thanks to God for a deliverance so ardently desired."

In the 17th century, French political preponderance increased in Europe. Initially, at the beginning of the century, the House of Habsburg (Austria) seemed to many to be the most powerful on the continent. Since the abdication of the Emperor Charles V (1556), there were two branches of the Habsburgs, one in Spain and one in Austria. But the two families remained quite united. Masters of Artois and Flanders, of Luxembourg, Alsace, Franche-Comté, and Roussillon, the Habsburgs blocked France on all its borders. The struggle against the House of Habsburg, therefore, was a necessary condition for French security and expansion. Careful in reorganizing his kingdom, Henry IV at first practiced prudent policies, while still concerned about checking the Habsburgs. The duke of Savoy meanwhile took the side of Spain. A short war forced him to cede to France Bresse and Bugey (1601). The United Provinces (Netherlands) had revolted against Spanish rule and Henry IV supported them. Only in 1610 did he decide to make war directly on the Habsburgs. He was preparing to intervene in Germany on the side of the Protestant princes when he was assassinated (1610). The struggle planned by Henry IV had to wait.

The inabilities of his successors favored the ambitions of Austria. These ambitions were at the source of a war that ravaged first Germany, then reached a large part of Europe, the THIRTY YEARS' WAR (1618–48). Emperor Ferdinand II, who was devoutly Catholic, wanted to restore that faith in all his states and in all Germany. As Emperor, he wanted to transform the constitution of Germany and bring it effectively under his authority. His power was also formidable and, thus, his plans put not only Protestant Germany at peril but the European balance, too, hence, the intervention of the other European powers in German affairs.

At first the Emperor was successful. He defeated the rebellious Czechs in Bohemia (1618–20), the German Protestants led by the Palatine elector (1620–23), and the king of Denmark, who had come to their aid (1625–29). With the help of Spain and a powerful army recruited and commanded by General Wallenstein, he seemed the master of Germany.

Coming to power in 1624, Richelieu resolved to halt the progress of Austria. At first, France intervened only indirectly through diplomacy in the struggle. Richelieu supported a new adversary of the Emperor, the king of Sweden, Gustavus-Adolphus (1630), who was a great military leader, but he was killed at the battle of Lützen in Saxony. The Imperial forces having taken the advantage after the death of Gustavus-Adolphus, Richelieu decided to intervene militarily in 1635. Skillful at invoking the European balance menaced by the Habsburgs, he gathered around France a great number of allies, without distinction of religion: Sweden, the United Provinces, the Protestant states of Germany, and the Swiss. France had to fight at the same time against the Imperial forces and the Spanish.

The war did not go well at first. Imperial troops invaded Burgundy and the Spanish took Corbie on the Somme and threatened Paris (1636). But beginning in 1637, the French armies took the offensive. By the time of Richelieu's death (1642), they occupied Artois, Alsace, and Roussillon.

Mazarin skillfully continued Richelieu's work. Led by the great commanders Admiral Condé and HENRI DE TURENNE, the French armies would demonstrate a growing superiority. In 1643, Condé defeated the Spanish army at Rocroi and, with Turenne, defeated the Imperial forces in Germany at Fribourg (1644) and Nordlingen (1645). In 1648, at Lens, he again defeated the Spanish, while Turenne, working in concert with the Swedes, invaded Bavaria, forcing the Emperor to negotiate. Since 1645, the belligerents had been negotiating at Münster and Osnabrück in Westphalia.

The treaties of Westphalia gave France control in Alsace, without Strasbourg, and the complete sovereignty of all the member states of the Holy Roman Empire. Imperial pretensions were ruined and Germany remained disunited. With Spain, the war continued for 10 more years. To end it, Mazarin allied with the English dictator Cromwell (1657). With English reinforcements, Turenne won the battle of the Dunes (1658), near Dunkerque. Spain decided to sign the Treaty of the Pyrénées (1659), by which France received Roussillon, a part of the Cerdagne, Artois, and some fortified places in the north. Louis XIV married the Spanish king's eldest daughter, MARIE-THÉRÈSE.

Enlarged by three provinces, having defeated Austria, France became the preponderant power in Europe. Ambitious for military glory and conquests, Louis XIV wanted to have the strongest army in Europe. The army was reorganized by MICHEL LE TELLIER and his son Louvois, who served as secretary of state for war from 1662 to 1691. Louvois, who was brutal and imperious, was a brilliant administrator, and he made the French army the most powerful implement of war. The manpower was augmented considerably, with 125,000 infantrymen and 12,000 cavalry. An artillery corps was specially created for the cannons. The army became a regular one, with the same discipline, rules, and marches. Each regiment had its own distinctive uniform. No one could be an officer without spending two years in the cadet corps. Louvois also built barracks and hospitals, creating an engineering corps under the direction of SÉBASTIEN LE PRESTRE DE VAUBAN, the leading military engineer of the time. The navy, which had fallen into neglect under Mazarin, was rebuilt by Colbert. After 1677, France had 116 ships of the line, to become a naval power capable of holding its own with Holland and England. The crews were recruited by a system of maritime conscription that imposed obligatory military service on seamen. During times of war, corsairs reinforced the royal navy.

Louis XIV intended to use this powerful military to continue the work of Richelieu and Mazarin: to aggrandize France at the expense of the Habsburgs. But the two great ministers had succeeded in rallying nearly all of Europe to their cause and carried on the fight against the Habsburgs in the name of maintaining the European balance of power. Louis XIV, on the contrary, followed from the beginning a policy of glory and supremacy that alarmed all the powers, and it was henceforth against France that coalitions were formed.

When Louis XIV came to power, the Turks were menacing Austria, and Spain was in decline. The king wanted to profit therefore from this favorable situation and first attacked Spain. King Philip IV of Spain had died in 1664, leaving as his successor Charles II, a son born from a second marriage. Louis had married Philip IV's oldest daughter and, invoking a tradition of Brabant, claimed for his part all the Spanish Low Countries. The Spanish were not in a position to wage war. In two months, Turenne conquered a part of Flanders; then Condé, in 15 days, conquered Franche-Comté. Meanwhile, the advance of France into Flanders had worried the Dutch and the English. Together with Sweden, they offered their mediation, which Louis judged was prudent to accept. By the Peace of Aix-la-Chapelle (1668), France gave up Franche-Comté but kept the territory conquered in Flanders, with Lille and Douai. Because Holland had been an obstacle to his plans for conquest, Louis XIV resolved to break that nation. In 1672, he suddenly attacked. Holland, isolated and invaded by 120,000 troops, seemed lost. Then the Dutch made a heroic decision. They opened the floodgates and broke the dikes that protected their lowlands from the sea. The French offensive had to stop. Meanwhile, a revolution brought to power, with the title of stathouder, the young prince William of Orange.

Louis XIV never had such a bitter adversary. Skillful and tenacious, William succeeded in forming against France a first coalition that comprised Austria, Spain, and Brandenburg (1673). Nonetheless, France kept the advantage. Holland was abandoned, but Franche-Comté and Flanders were conquered again. In the east, Alsace, invaded by the Germans, was taken by a skillful campaign led by Turenne (1674), who was killed shortly after at Salsbach. On the sea, ABRAHAM DUQUESNE defeated the illustrious Dutch admiral Michiel Andriaanszoon De Ruyter off the coast of Syracuse, Sicily. The powerless coalition had to sign the Peace of Nijmegen (1678). Spain paid the cost of the war by ceding Franche-Comté and another part of Flanders, with Valenciennes, Maubeuge, and Cambrai, to Louis XIV.

The Peace of Nijmegen marked the apogee of Louis XIV's power, and pride inspired him to more audacious acts. Tribunals, or *chambres de réunion,* were established to identify the dependencies of the territories ceded in the earlier treaties; thus Montbéliard, the towns of the Sarre, and Luxembourg were annexed during peacetime. Strasbourg, a city of the empire, was also occupied (1681). To the anger of Europe was added the hatred of all the Protestant countries after the revocation of the Edict of Nantes (1685). The Emperor formed a defensive league, the League of Augsburg (1686), which included the German princes, Spain, and Sweden. Louis XIV responded by occupying the Palatinate, and war broke out.

Meanwhile, a revolution made William of Orange king of England. The league was strengthened therefore by two maritime powers, England and Holland. Without allies, Louis XIV had to fight much of Europe. Nearly everywhere France remained victorious over the coalition. In Italy, General Nicholas Catinat forced the duke of Savoy to negotiate (1693). In the Low Countries, Marshal FRANÇOIS-HENRI DE LUXEMBOURG won three brilliant victories, at Fleuris (1690), Steinkerque (1692), and Nerwinden (1693). The French fleet suffered a grave defeat at La Hougue, but the war subsequently saw great English and Dutch losses. Exhausted, the opponents signed the Peace of Ryswick, near La Haye (1697). Except for Strasbourg, Louis gave up most of the territories occupied since Nijmegen. In fact, Ryswick marked a halt to French power. Charles II of Spain had died, and it was to control the partition of his succession that Louis XIV had signed the peace. Louis XIV negotiated first with England and Holland a secret treaty of partition in 1700. But Charles II had not wanted partition; he willed all of his states to the duc d'Anjou, grandson of Louis XIV. While the partition treaty was more profitable for France, Louis decided to accept the will. The duc d'Anjou became the king of Spain, Philip V. But Louis XIV behaved from then on as if he had been king of Spain himself. William of Orange profited from this by forming against France the Great Alliance of The Hague, which included England, Holland, the Emperor, and most of Germany (1701).

The subsequent War of the Spanish Succession lasted 13 years (1701–14). For the first time, the French armies suffered grave reversals. In 1704 began a series of disasters: the defeat at Hochstädt in Bavaria, the taking of Gibraltar by the English (1704), the defeat at Ramillies and the loss of Belgium (1705), the defeat at Turin and the loss of Italy (1706), defeat at Oudenarde in Flanders and the loss of Lille (1708), the brutal battle of Malplaquet and the retreat of the French in the north (1709). The terrible winter of 1709 added to the misery. The kingdom seemed to be depleted of resources and talks for peace were failing. Finally, in 1712, through a supreme military effort, the victory of Marshal CLAUDE-LOUIS-HECTOR VILLARS at Denain allowed the signing of an honorable peace. The Treaties of Utrecht (1713) and Rastatt (1714) ended the war and thus determined the Spanish succession. Philip V kept Spain and its colonies but renounced all his rights to the French throne. The Emperor received the Low Countries, Milan, the kingdom of Naples, and Sardinia; the duke of Savoy obtained Sicily. England forced France to cede Newfoundland, Acadia, and Hudson Bay, and, near Spain, Minorca and Gibraltar, key to the Mediterranean. Thus, the Spanish Crown remained in the House of Bourbon. The kingdom of France was intact but drained of blood and money; its colonial domains were reduced and its preponderance was lost. The actual victors of the Treaty of Utrecht were the English, who achieved both maritime and colonial supremacy.

# FRENCH CULTURE IN THE SEVENTEENTH CENTURY

The 17th century was an important period for French arts and sciences. In mathematics, BLAISE PASCAL and his associate, PIERRE DE FERMAT, set down the bases for calculus, paralleling the discoveries made by Isaac Newton in England in the same period and those made earlier by such figures as Galileo Galilei, Johannes Kepler, Gottfred Leibnitz, and Christiaan Huygens. In France, RENÉ DESCARTES defined the scientific method, and botany was studied by the abbé Mariotte. French letters are illustrated in an early period by the names of PIERRE CORNEILLE, René Descartes, and Blaise Pascal. There were efforts also, especially by the poet FRANÇOIS DE MALHERBE, to purify the French language, which was seen to be encumbered by Greek, Latin, and other foreign words or provincial locutions. To this end, Richelieu founded the ACADÉMIE FRANÇAISE (1635), which began work on a *Dictionnaire*. Unity and purity in language were achieved in the writings of various eminent authors, and, under Louis XIV, a classical era emerged. France ranked intellectual prestige as important as political and military paramountcy and established various other academies, of sciences, architecture, and fine arts. The achievements of this classical age continued in letters with the masterpieces of MOLIÈRE, RACINE, LA FONTAINE, BOILEAU, BOSSUET, LA BRUYÈRE, FÉNELON, BAYLE, and FONTENELLE and, in the fine arts with the works of such artists as POUSSIN, LE LORRAIN, Champaigne, LA TOUR, LE BRUN, PUGET, Girardon, and COYSEVOX. Architectural achievement culminated in the building and renovation of the Palace of Versailles, the work especially of the architects MANSART and LE VAU.

# The French Monarchy during the Eighteenth Century

The French monarchy in the 18th century was first marked by the long reign of LOUIS XV (1715–74). The great-grandson of Louis XIV, Louis XV was only five years old when he became king. In his will, Louis XIV had entrusted the regency to his nephew, PHILIP, DUC D'ORLÉANS, but with powers limited by a Regency Council. Solicitous, the Parlement canceled the will and declared that the regent had full authority. The regent was intelligent but indifferent and corrupt. As a reaction to the austerity of the later period of the previous reign, the regency was a period of loose morals, with the regent and his friends, the "roués," setting the example for libertinage. The reaction in morals was accompanied by one in politics, with an attempt by the nobility and the Parlement to regain part of their power. Each secretary of state was replaced by a council composed mostly of nobles, who lacked experience, however. The Parlement, as in the days of the Fronde, opposed royal edicts. The financial situation, an inheritance of Louis XIV, seemed without solution.

As an expediency, the regent decided to try a system that had been proposed to him by a Scottish banker, JOHN LAW. His plan was to make the state a banker and a merchant and to create a state bank that would issue paper money and raise capital by means of privileged trading companies. Alongside the national bank, Law formed the Mississippi Company, which was given the monopoly on the development of Louisiana, and individuals could purchase shares in the company, with titles being held by the state, thus reducing the national debt. Greatly impressed, the regent named Law comptroller general of finances, and his bank became the Royal Bank (1718). Emboldened by success, Law quickly expanded his field of operations. His company absorbed all other companies, becoming the Indies Company (1719). Everyone wanted to purchase his shares and a great speculation ensued. Quickly everything fell apart. The first dividends seemed insufficient and speculators sought to sell their shares and exchange their currency for gold and silver.

Despite the efforts of the government, the system went bankrupt. Law fled the country (1720), leaving all France greatly affected by the crisis, the first speculative crisis in the nation's history. Nonetheless, the public debt was reduced and maritime trade was given impetus, but the state would be wary of the use of paper currency and credit institutions.

In 1723, the regent died. Louis XV confided the power in another royal prince, the duke de Bourbon, who arranged for his marriage to MARIE LESZCZYN-SKA, the daughter of Stanislaus, the dethroned king of Poland (1725). But Louis XV trusted only his old tutor, Cardinal ANDRÉ-HERCULE DE FLEURY, and in 1726, Fleury was brought to power; his ministry lasted 17 years until his death in 1743. Prudent and peace-loving, Fleury was careful to maintain peace and order, and to be economical. Assisted by a good administrator, PHILIBERT ORRY, the comptroller of finances (1730–45), he improved the country's financial situation and, for a time, balanced the budget. This wise administration favored economic development; trade prospered and rivaled that of England. This was a lucrative period for the ports, with Océan, Le Havre, Nantes, and Bordeaux becoming the great centers of sugar importation from the Antilles.

Fleury also sought to settle the recurring religious quarrels. The pope had definitively condemned Jansenism in 1713 in his papal bull *Unigenitus;* opposed to controversy, Fleury made every effort to have the Parlement accept this judgment. But in midcentury, unrest and then violence erupted again. After Fleury's death began the period known as the personal reign of Louis XV. This period was marked by the monarch's indifference and the weakness and disorganization of his government. In 1743, at age 33, Louis XV, wanting to follow the example of Louis XIV, personally assumed all power. Handsome, affable, and intelligent, he was at first popular, hence his sobriquet Bien-Aimé ("Beloved"). In 1745, for instance, when the king fell ill at Metz, all over France people went to the churches to pray for his recovery. But his good reputation did not last. Weak, secretive, and sometimes moody, the king was given to extreme indolence and carelessness and was incapable of sustained activity.

Without the king actively taking part, the government became directionless, and for many years, France was ruled by the king's favorites and lovers, among these Jeanne Poisson, whom Louis made MARQUISE DE POMPADOUR. For the rest of her life she exerted such an influence that she could appoint and remove ministers and military commanders. The great patronage that she gave to artists and writers brought her a certain popularity, especially among the philosophes, but the people held her responsible for draining the nation's finances and for the incompetence of French political policies.

Some of the various ministers in power from 1743 to 1774 were capable, but the king's inertia in general offset their efforts JEAN-BAPTISTE DE MACHAULT D'ARNOUVILLE, comptroller of finances from 1745 to 1754, attacked aristocratic and other privileges. To reduce the debt, he instituted a 5 percent tax on all the king's subjects (1745), but because of the opposition of the privileged classes, upheld by the Parlement of Paris, the tax fell more and more only on the Third Estate. Machault was himself dismissed for having displeased Mme de Pompadour. From 1758 to 1770, the principal minister was her protégé, ÉTIENNE-FRANÇOIS, DUKE DE CHOISEUL, successively minister of state for foreign affairs, war, and the navy. An adroit courtier, Choiseul was also an active minister and a capable diplomat. He was, however, unable to stop the reversals in the SEVEN YEARS' WAR; but he worked energetically for France's revenge by rebuilding the army and the navy. He annexed two important territories, Lorraine and Corsica, in 1766 and 1768, respectively, but his enemies, supported by a new favorite of the king, Mme DU BARRY, had him dismissed (1770). Choiseul was succeeded by what is known as the "triumvirate," consisting of the abbé TERRAY for finances, the incapable duke D'AIGUILLON for foreign affairs, and the chancellor RENÉ-NICOLAS DE MAUPEOU.

Conscious of the danger posed to royal authority by the claims of the Parlement, Maupeou in 1771 undertook a complete reform of the judicial structure. In this period, the problems that Fleury had tried to solve intensified. Religious strife broke out with new violence. From 1752 to 1757, for example, the issue of the "billets de confession" caused much popular resentment. The archbishop of Paris had ordered that the sacraments be refused to anyone who could not present a statement attesting to his or her submission to the bull *Unigenitus* (1752). This, however, required the approval of the Parlement, and hence a long and sometimes tumultuous conflict ensued, with finally a compromise in 1757 bringing some appeasement. But supported by public opinion, the Parlement then ended by triumphing over the Jesuits whose great influence was of concern. In 1762, apropos of a trial in which the Jesuits were involved, the Parlement of Paris declared that that religious order's constitution was contrary to the laws of the kingdom and ordered the suppression of the order in France. Louis XV ratified the Parlement's decision (1764), and the abolition of the Jesuits seemed to many to be a victory of a revolutionary spirit.

Not content to overrule the government by its constant interventions in religious affairs, the Parlement revived its old political claims, including the right to control the royal power. This was brought about particularly by the financial problems of the time. The Parlement energetically resisted the creation of new taxes, refusing to register financial edicts. In 1771, Chancellor Maupeou resolved to end this resistance by radical measures. The Parlement of Paris was suppressed and replaced by six superior councils whose members, nominated and appointed by the king, were only to be his agents. In this way, an old and official practice of selling government offices was also abolished. The reform was good, but after the death of Louis XV it was abandoned and the Parlement of Paris, as well as provincial ones, were reestablished. The reign ended amid public protest and unrest, and so great was the discontent that when Louis XV died in 1774, the royal cortege had to bypass Paris to convey him to the royal tomb at Saint-Denis.

Louis XV left to his grandson, LOUIS XVI, aged 20, a heavy legacy, with ruined finances, unhappy subjects, and a faulty and incompetent government. The people, meanwhile, still had confidence in royalty, and the accession of Louis XVI was welcomed with enthusiasm. The confidence of the people was hardly justified. Louis XVI was a mediocre prince and lacked authority. Honest and good-hearted, he desired to do well but was at the mercy of many influences. One of these was his wife, MARIE ANTOINETTE, daughter of the empress Maria Theresa of Austria. Lively and gracious but naive and somewhat capricious, she often opposed economic and other indispensable reforms. Advised by an old courtier, JEAN, COUNT DE MAUREPAS, the king appointed to foreign affairs an excellent diplomat, CHARLES GRANIER DE VERGENNES; a liberal magistrate, CHRÉTIÉN DE

MALESHERBES, became secretary of state of the royal household. The most important post, that of comptroller general of finances, was entrusted to a man of great ability, ANNE-ROBERT TURGOT, already famous as an economist and for having instituted reforms in his intendancy at Limousin (1761–74).

The financial situation was critical and bankruptcy seemed imminent. Turgot had an ambitious plan with which he hoped to lead the kingdom out of its financial difficulties: first, by economizing, and second, by increasing the general wealth through tax reforms. The reforms in economic matters involved freeing up the economy. Turgot began by abolishing all the regulations that limited the trade in wheat and allowed it to circulate freely from province to province. His first edict established free trade in grain within the kingdom (1774), and a second established the freedom to work in various industries by abolishing the guilds (1776). A third edict abolished the royal corvée (1776), the obligation of peasants to work for free on the repair and construction of roads. The corvée was replaced by a tax, leveled on all properties, privileged or not. But Turgot came up against growing opposition. His economizing irritated the queen and the court. The edict on grain exasperated the speculators, who organized uprisings, and the edict was soon revoked. The edicts of 1776 brought against Turgot all the privileged groups, courtiers, factory owners, and financiers. The Parlement led this opposition and addressed solemn appeals to the king, who resisted at first, then gave in, and asked Turgot for his resignation (1776). A few days before he left, Turgot wrote prophetically to the king: "Never forget, Sire, that it was weakness that put the head of Charles I on the block."

To address the still critical financial situation, the king called a noted banker from Geneva, JACQUES NECKER. The latter soon had to deal with new difficulties because of French involvement in the war in America and so resorted to loans. But he also wanted, like Turgot, to pursue an economic and reformist policy. He abolished serfdom in the royal domains, then instituted in two provinces, Berry and Guyenne, provincial assemblies to assist the intendants with regional administration. After being violently criticized, Necker justified his actions and sought to gain public confidence by publishing a complete accounting of royal and governmental finances. The publication caused a scandal, because it revealed the expenses of the court, which until then were kept secret. The queen had Necker recalled (1781). His fall made a profound impression as it effectively signified the failure of reformist policy. The Old Regime had demonstrated that it was incapable of reforming itself and revolution became inevitable.

After the departure of Necker, the financial crisis became worse. With CHARLES-ALEXANDRE DE CALONNE (1783–87), a capable individual but prodigal and without character, after three years the treasury was depleted and state credit was ruined. The government faced insoluble problems. Widespread unrest then followed, a prelude to more grave events. First came the conflict with the nobles, followed by that with the Parlement. Calonne had to present a plan for reform and new taxes inspired by Necker and Turgot (1786). Fearing the opposition of the Parlement, he thought to win their approval by creating an Assembly of Notables, to be chosen by the king. The assembly, far from being complacent, demanded Calonne's accounts (1787), which he refused to hand over. To end this, the queen had Calonne replaced by the archbishop of Toulouse, ETIENNE-CHARLES DE LOMÉNIE DE BRIENNE, who dismissed the notables and modified Calonne's plan. But when Brienne wanted to register with the Parlement the edicts creating new taxes, that body refused, denying the king's right to create new taxes on his own. While thus engaged, a great conflict broke out between the royal government and the Parlement which had the support of public opinion. Brienne arrested or exiled the principal instigators, the Parlement resisted stubbornly, and, taking a revolutionary view, proclaimed solemnly by the decree of May 3, 1788, the fundamental laws of the nation including the right of the Estates General to grant financial subsidies freely. The government responded by rescinding the right of appeal from the Parlement. But the opposition organized everywhere and uprisings broke out. In Dauphiné, the deputies of the three orders, meeting at Vizille, encouraged all the provinces to refuse to pay taxes while the Estates General had not been convened (July 1788).

The crisis had reached its peak. The government gave in because it had neither funds nor means to restore order. The Estates General was to be convened on May 1, 1789. To procure immediate resources and avoid bankruptcy, the king dismissed Brienne and recalled Necker, who was immensely popular (August 1788). Imbued with revolutionary principles, public opinion expected from the meeting of the Estates a change in government. Those who led this movement, the "nationaux" or "patriotes," wanted the Estates General to become a true national assembly. To achieve this, it was necessary for the three orders to unite, with voting by membership and not by order, as the Third Estate, being the majority of the nation, had a number of delegates at least equal to those of the two privileged orders together. Despite the opposition of the Parlement, which defended privilege more than freedom, Necker convinced the king to accept a doubling of the Third Estate. In each bailiwick, the nobles and the clergy directly elected their deputies; for the Third Estate, the scrutiny was general and in two stages. The elections were a great success for the Patriote faction, and out of nearly 300 deputies for the Clergy, around 200 curés were ready to join with the Third, thus assuring its majority in the Estates, on the condition that the orders were united into one single assembly.

# French Foreign Policy in the Eighteenth Century

European foreign policy in the 18th century had unique characteristics. Not only was there no longer a preponderant power, but to the old rivalries were added new ones, such as that between Prussia and Austria, the question of Poland, and above all the colonial rivalry between France and England. French policy never succeeded in adapting to these new conditions. While content until 1740, it was to be unlucky in later dealings. The ruling on the Spanish succession again was left open: Neither the king of Spain, Philip V, nor the Emperor had accepted the decision on the succession in Spain. All of France's efforts were at first to maintain the terms of the Treaty of Utrecht. The adviser to the regent Philip of Orléans, the abbé GUILLAUME DUBOIS, concluded in 1716 a treaty of alliance between France and England to uphold the threatened peace. After a short war (1717–20), the Treaty of Vienne (1725), by which Italian territories were reshuffled, ruled definitively on the Spanish succession.

Wanting peace, Cardinal Fleury sought also to maintain peace through the English alliance. Meanwhile, he could not prevent the war that broke out in 1733 over the succession in Poland. Two claimants disputed the elective Polish crown, Augustus III, elector of Saxony and nephew of the Emperor, and Stanislaus Leczinski, father-in-law of Louis XV. Stanislaus was elected but was driven from his throne by Austro-Russian forces. To avenge his father-in-law, Louis declared war on Russia and Austria. Fleury sought to end the conflict as quickly as possible. After some successes in Italy and on the Rhine, negotiations began and resulted in the Treaty of Vienna (1738). Stanislaus renounced Poland and accepted the duchy of Lorraine, which, upon his death, would revert to France. Don Carlos, the son of the king of Spain, received Naples and Sicily.

Fleury, his authority declining, could not prevent a war that subsequently broke out over the succession in Austria. By a ruling known as the Pragmatic Sanction, the emperor Charles VI, drawing on previous agreements, had assured the succession to his daughter Maria Theresa. Once on the throne, Maria Theresa faced a large coalition that included the elector of Bavaria, Charles-Albert, the Bourbons of Spain and Italy; France; and the new king of Prussia, the ambitious Frederick II, who also wanted Silesia. All seemed lost for Maria Theresa. With great energy and commitment, she faced the coalition, soon broke it up, and succeeded in making an alliance with England and Holland. She disarmed Frederick II by ceding to him Silesia (1742) and negotiated also with Bavaria (1745). Isolated France had to bear all the weight of the war. Fortunately, the French armies were led by a skilled commander, Marshal MAURICE DE SAXE. The Austrian Netherlands—Belgium—was conquered by the victories at Fontenoy (1745), Raucoux (1746), and Lawfeld (1747). In 1748, the Peace of Aix-la-Chapelle was signed. Frederick II kept Silesia, but France had to give up all its conquests; its efforts had been for the king of Prussia.

The Peace of Aix-la-Chapelle was merely a truce; two powers wanted war—Austria, to retake Silesia from Prussia, and England to destroy French commerce. Rather than engaging fully in a colonial war, France became involved in a continental war where it was at a disadvantage. The war was preceded by a complete change in the system of alliances. For two centuries, Austria had been France's enemy; France now was allied with that power against a former ally, Frederick II, who, for his part, had allied with the king of England, George II, who was at the same time elector of Hanover (1756). The war that broke out in 1756 is called the Seven Years' War (1756–63) because of its duration. Prussia and England would fight a coalition comprised of Austria, France, Russia, and most of the German principalities. England was committed above all to a maritime struggle. Frederick II therefore had to bear nearly all the fighting on the continent. The small kingdom of Prussia was saved by his genius, the superiority of the Prussian army, and the mediocrity of his adversaries. France, neglecting the colonies, sent large armies into Germany, where they fought in Westphalia. Encircled by his enemies, Frederick II found himself in great danger but disengaged by skillful maneuvers. In 1757 at Rossbach in Saxony, he defeated the French and Swabian armies, and at Leuthen in Silesia, the Austrian. Meanwhile, in 1762, he was almost exhausted when an unexpected event saved him. The new Russian czar, Peter III, left the war. With the defection of Russia, Maria Theresa decided to negotiate, and the peace was signed at Hubertsburg in 1763. Frederick kept Silesia. At the same time, England, victorious on the seas and in the colonies, imposed the disastrous Treaty of Paris on France.

After the war, Choiseul had at least the sense to recognize what mistakes had been made. He reorganized the army and the navy, and tried to replace by new acquisitions the losses suffered as a result of the war. Lorraine and Corsica were annexed to France. But Choiseul was dismissed in 1770; placed in inexperienced hands, it would not be long before France's fortunes again faltered. Taking advantage of the French lack of power and anarchy in Poland, Frederick II and the Russian empress Catherine II reached an understanding with Maria Theresa in 1772 to divide Poland by the Treaty of Partition. In France, because of the ties of friendship that united that nation with Poland, the partition was considered another French defeat.

Succeeding Spain and Portugal, France and England became the major colonial powers. But nearly all their colonies bordered each other or were rivals. Franco-English colonial rivalry occurred principally in North America, in the Antilles, and in the Indian Ocean. France and England had already fought in the colonies during the two last wars of Louis XIV and, by the Treaty of Utrecht,

France had ceded Newfoundland and Acadia to the British. From 1715 to 1740, during a period of peace, French colonial trade increased tremendously. Anxious because they were being outdistanced, English merchants and colonists pushed for a conflict, which occurred in the War of the Austrian Succession. This first colonial war (1744–48) ended without a result; in the Peace of Aix-la-Chapelle, France and England both retained their conquests (1748).

At this time, French colonization of India began. The empire of the Great Mogul, which in the 17th century included all of India, had been disintegrating. In this situation, JOSEPH-FRANÇOIS DUPLEIX, governor of the French Indies Company in 1741, played an important part; in a few years, he established a large French empire in India. But Dupleix's policies met with English resistance, and he was obliged to ask for reinforcements. In France both the government and the company preferred peace. Dupleix, who was misunderstood and considered to be an adventurer, was abruptly recalled (1754). By the terms of the treaty negotiated by French Indies Company director Godeheu, concluded with the English East India Company, the French company willingly renounced all rights in all indigenous territory, and thus France lost its Indian empire. These great sacrifices made during peacetime were useless to the French. The war that the English desired, the Seven Years' War, broke out the following year. In Canada, the conflict was carried on by General LOUIS JOSEPH, MARQUIS DE MONTCALM, a military leader who succeeded in holding off the English for two years. But lacking resources, he was thrown on the defensive. In 1759, a decisive battle took place before Quebec in which Montcalm and his adversary, General Wolfe, were both killed. The English took Quebec and, in 1760, Montreal. Canada was lost. In India, the French, commanded by LALLY-TOLLENDAL, at first won important victories. But left without reinforcements, Lally ended by being blocked in Pondicherry, where, after a heroic defense, he was forced to surrender (1761). That ended French domination in India. France had then to sign the humiliating Treaty of Paris (1763), as mentioned above, by which Louis XV ceded to the English Canada and the left bank of the Mississippi, a part of the French Antilles, and posts in Senegal, and renounced French claims in India. Only five towns—Pondicherry, Chandarnagar, Yanaon, Karikal, and Mahé—remained to the French Indies Company. France also lost Louisiana west of the Mississippi, which it gave to Spain in compensation for Florida, which had been taken by the English.

After the Treaty of Paris, with peace being reestablished on all the high seas, there was again an opportunity for maritime exploration. These voyages, which were scientific in nature, took place especially in the Pacific Ocean, the largest and least known of the world's seas. The principal explorers were French and English, and their encounters this time were peaceful. The most remarkable of the French navigators was LOUIS-ANTOINE, COUNT DE BOUGAINVILLE. From 1766 to 1769, he made a voyage around the world during which he visited Tahiti and rediscovered the Samoan Islands, the New Hebrides, and the Solomon Islands. Another French officer, JEAN-FRANÇOIS DE GALAUP, COUNT DE LA PÉROUSE, in 1785 explored the coasts of Korea and Siberia. Sailing into the Southern Hemisphere, his expedition lost men and equipment in the Hebrides. Among the English, the

American ambassador
Benjamin Franklin is
given an audience
with King Louis XVI
of France, 1778.
*(Hulton/Archive)*

most illustrious was Captain James Cook, who, in three voyages, also explored the Pacific. After a short lull, Franco-English rivalry was soon renewed on the occasion of the revolt of the English colonies in America. In 1774, the thirteen English colonies in America revolted against England and, after two years of struggle, the Declaration of Independence of the United States of America was issued.

The rebels soon had a powerful ally in France, where the American cause was immediately popular. Beginning in 1777, noble French officers, young and enthusiastic, like the MARQUIS DE LA FAYETTE, enlisted as volunteers in George Washington's American army.

The foreign minister, CHARLES GRAVIER DE VERGENNES, wanted to seize this opportunity to reduce English power, and the American Benjamin Franklin came to France to work for a Franco-American alliance. An English army commanded by General Burgoyne surrendered at Saratoga (1777), and France entered the War of American Independence, which Spain soon joined as an ally. This was the start of the fourth war between France and England since the beginning of the century. The French held the English in check in both the Atlantic and the Indian Oceans. In America, the struggle was indecisive for a long period; finally, after the arrival of French reinforcements led by JEAN-BAPTISTE, COUNT DE ROCHAMBEAU, General Washington stopped the main English forces at Yorktown, forcing them to surrender (1781). But the allies did not succeed in taking Gibraltar, and a French fleet was defeated at Saintes in the Antilles (1782). England meanwhile sued for peace and signed the Treaty of Versailles (1783), by which it recognized the United States and returned Florida to Spain, and Senegal and some of the Antilles to France.

# French Civilization and Its Influence in the Eighteenth Century

Louis XIV imposed monarchical authority on both society and culture, including arts and letters and, by the end of his long reign, many of the French were weary of this yoke. The inevitable reaction occurred in intellectual life as well as in politics. There had been created outside of the court new centers of intellectual life, the Parisian salons. There, on a set day, one could meet great lords, churchmen, writers, artists, and financiers. Following the spirit of the age, the conversations generally took on a free and irreverent tone, as was the case at such salons as those of Mme MARIE-THÉRÈSE RODET GEOFFRIN and Mlle JULIE DE LESPINASSE. The tastes and mores of the era were faithfully reflected in the arts. Under the influence of Louis XIV, the art of the 17th century had produced works that were majestic and somewhat cold. Free of official interference, the art of the 18th century sought new paths where grace, freedom, and ease prevailed. The architecture of the period remained faithful to the classical tradition, and the main architects, JACQUES GABRIEL and GERMAIN SOUFFLOT, continued the style of CLAUDE PERRAULT and FRANÇOIS MANSART. But the châteaux of the age, like the Petit Trianon at Versailles, and country houses reflected the new taste for intimacy and comfort. In painting, in place of nobility and grandeur, there was a sense of fantasy, grace, and elegance, often associated with the natural and the realistic. The masters of genre during the regency were ANTOINE WATTEAU (whose main disciples were FRANÇOIS BOUCHER and JEAN-HONORÉ FRAGONARD), JEAN-BAPTISTE CHARDIN, JEAN-BAPTISTE GREUZE, and Quentin de la Tour. Sculpture, characterized by a sense of realism often exemplified in marble busts and portraits, was represented by EDME BOUCHARDON, JEAN-BAPTISTE PIGALLE, ÉTIENNE FALCONET, and above all JEAN-ANTOINE HOUDON.

The desire for scientific knowledge in this period was also very strong. The general public, instructed through popularized works, sought more such information. The physical sciences saw achievements by ANTOINE-LAURENT LAVOISIER and, in natural science, GEORGES-LOUIS LECLERC, COUNT OF BUFFON, who described all of nature in his *Histoire naturelle* and made the Royal Gardens (today the Botanical Gardens) one of the principal scientific sites in the world. Science also achieved practical applications, such as the steam engines of Cugnot (1769) and Jouffroy (1776) and the hot-air balloon flights of the MONTGOLFIER BROTHERS (1783).

The 18th century was above all one of great and universal criticism. Writers questioned the traditional structures and propagated new political and social ideas. It was the beginning of the ENLIGHTENMENT, or Age of Reason. The organization of the kingdom rested on a certain number of principles held to be indisputable until the 18th century: in politics the concept of divine right absolutism; in society the inequity of rights and responsibilities; in religious matters the rule of intolerance; in economics that of regulation and protectionism. Already, SÉBASTIEN DE VAUBAN and FRANÇOIS FÉNELON had spoken out against such an organization and for fiscal justice, and a "kingdom governed by laws." In the same period, Pierre Bayle, a French Protestant who had fled to Rotterdam and strongly proclaimed the unlimited primacy of reason in all matters, was an indefatigable defender of freedom of thought and tolerance in the face of organized religion. But it was especially in England where such ideas were first accepted, with their principal spokesperson being the philosopher John Locke, who formulated the doctrine of the natural rights of man, of religious tolerance, and of the sovereignty of the people.

In France, two groups of thinkers and writers were the continuers of Vauban, Bayle, and Locke: the philosophes, who were concerned especially with political, social, and religious and moral questions, and the economists, who sought a means of developing national wealth. The main French philosophes were MONTESQUIEU, VOLTAIRE, ROUSSEAU, and DIDEROT. Montesquieu, in the guise of his quaint *Lettres persanes,* in 1721 wrote a lively satire on social mores and institutions. In 1748, he published his great work, *L'Esprit des lois,* dedicated to the study of diverse types of government. There, he praised the English constitutional monarchy and recommended the separation of the executive, legislative, and judicial branches as the only guarantee of liberty. Voltaire was at once the most prolific, brilliant, and caustic of the writers of the 18th century. After a stay in England, he published his *Lettres philosophiques,* or *Lettres sur les Anglais* (1734). He, too, praised the English political freedoms and attacked absolutism and intolerance. After 20 years of an errant life, he settled at Ferney in Gex (1755). Thence recognized as the leader of the philosophes, he exercised a kind of intellectual sovereignty. From Ferney came a multitude of satirical works, usually signed with a fictitious name, which were a series of barbs against despotism or the church. Until his death, Voltaire carried on a determined campaign against injustice and intolerance. His writings, ironic and destructive to the established order, contributed more than any others to causing questioning and doubt.

Rousseau, in contrast to Montesquieu and Voltaire, who upheld liberal monarchy, was democratic and revolutionary. He presented his ideas in an educational treatise, *Émile* (1762), and above all in *Le Contrat social,* his main work (1762). In eloquent language and with passionate conviction, he held that all humans are by right free and equal, and that sovereignty rests in the people alone. His writings led to the establishment of the republic and would become the gospel of ROBESPIERRE and the JACOBINS.

These new ideas were condemned by the French government and so their diffusion often had to take place in roundabout or secret ways: in salon discussions, the theater, and particularly through anonymous books and pamphlets clandestinely published outside the country. But the principal means of propagation was the *Encyclopédie*, "a broad tableau of the achievements of the human spirit." The work was published by the philosopher Diderot, who was assisted by D'ALEMBERT, a mathematician. As contributors they enlisted the majority of writers and scholars of the time. The *Encyclopédie*, which gathered together all the new ideas and all the criticisms of the regime, was twice banned by the government (1751 and 1772).

While the philosophes attacked the political and religious policies of the Old Regime, other theorists, the economists, questioned its traditional economic policies. The economic structure then in place was one of complete regulation. The economists, like the philosophes, however, believed in the benevolence of the natural order. They maintained, contrary to the doctrines of Jean-Baptiste Colbert, that natural laws should be allowed to act freely. They were known as physiocrats, because they posited that all power derives from nature, or the natural. This concept was first developed by FRANÇOIS QUESNAY, who was the king's physician, and VINCENT DE GOURNAY, the intendant for trade. They both stated that duties, tariffs, and regulations hindered agricultural and industrial activity, and both recommend a free economic system expressed in the formula "laissez-faire, laissez-passer." The most outstanding disciples of Quesnay and Gournay were, in England, Adam Smith, and in France Turgot. Smith, in his treatise *The Wealth of Nations* (1776), made labor the true source of wealth. Turgot, the son of a Parisian trade supervisor, was, besides an original theorist, a careful administrator. Intendant of Limousin (1761–64), he sought to put these new ideas into practice and, one by one, to the poorest provinces, he brought 13 years of prosperity. At the beginning of the reign of Louis XVI, he sought to apply the principles of liberal economics. It was only under the revolution, however, that free labor was established following the complete suppression of the guilds.

# THE FRENCH REVOLUTION OF 1789

The Estates General, which was so eagerly awaited, finally met at Versailles on May 5, 1789. Following tradition, the deputies brought the *cahiers*—lists of the grievances and wishes of their electors. Collected in each parish, town, and bailiwick, these cahiers were the most valuable testimony of the aspirations of the French people on the eve of the Revolution. They attributed all the problems of the nation to the "arbitrary power" of the king and asked for a "constitution" that would define the "rights of the king and of the nation" in a way that would put an end to the abuses of absolutism. This constitution had to guarantee individual freedom; there were to be, for example, no more "lettres de cachet," or the practice of arbitrary arrest and imprisonment. They demanded the end of censorship and the right of freedom of thought and expression. Justice and finances would be reorganized to end odious abuses. Equality in taxation would be established, with the clergy and the nobility renouncing all their exemptions, although they could keep their other privileges. All the cahiers were put together and edited in a spirit of confidence in the monarchy. Reforms were desired, but they were to be achieved through the goodwill of the king.

The conflict between the Third Estate and the privileged classes became an issue of power among the elected delegates. The Third Estate proposed that the three orders meet and approve all decisions in common. The nobility refused. The question was of prime importance: If the three orders deliberated separately, and if voting was done by order and not by delegate, what advantage would that be to the Third Estate? After more than a month of waiting, the Third Estate took a revolutionary initiative, and on June 17, 1789, understanding that it represented "at least ninety-six percent of the nation," proclaimed itself the National Assembly and set about the work of reforming the state.

Louis XVI, urged on by the royal court, took a position against the Third Estate and sought to act authoritatively. On June 20, under the pretext of preparing for a royal meeting, he closed the hall where the assembly met. The deputies quickly reassembled in an indoor tennis court. There, under the presidency of JEAN-SYLVAIN BAILLY, they swore never to leave before establishing a constitution for the kingdom. This was called the TENNIS COURT OATH. On June 23, the royal meeting took place. The king declared the assembly's decisions null and void and ordered the deputies to leave and meet again divided into three distinct chambers. The privileged orders obeyed. The Third Estate resisted and stayed in the tennis court.

This was the decisive moment, in which the opposing wills of the king and the nation confronted each other. To the grand master of ceremonies, HENRI ÉVRARD, MARQUIS DE DREUX-BREZÉ, HONORÉ-GABRIEL RIQUETI, COUNT OF MIRABEAU, a noble who had been elected as a deputy to the Third Estate, replied in a thunderous voice: "Go tell your master that we are here by the will of the people, and that we can be removed only with the force of bayonets." A shocked Louis XVI did not dare use force and so gave in. Four days later, he rescinded his orders and instructed all the delegates to join the Third Estate. On July 9, the assembly took the name of Constituent Assembly. The political revolution had been achieved: It was the end of absolutism.

The king, however, who only seemed to be resigned to these circumstances, was preparing a strong move against the assembly. With troops having been ordered to concentrate around Versailles, on July 11 the crisis broke. Necker, the only popular minister, was dismissed. But the intervention of the people of Paris saved the assembly and assured the triumph of the revolution. The news of Necker's dismissal caused great unrest. At the Palais-Royal, spontaneous speakers appeared, among them a young writer, CAMILLE DESMOULINS, who appealed to the people to take up arms in defense of freedom. The resistance was organized. The mob looted any places where they could find weapons. At the Hôtel-de-Ville, or City Hall, a standing committee was formed creating a revolutionary municipality.

On July 14, all the rage of the populace was directed against the Bastille, a state prison and symbol of arbitrary power. After a brutal siege, the fortress, defended by Swiss troops and retired soldiers, surrendered. The victory of the people had decisive consequences. For the second time, the king admitted defeat; he recalled Necker and sent the troops away. On July 17, he came to the Hôtel-de-Ville and accepted the tricolored cockade—blue, white, red—joining the colors of Paris with those of the king, a symbol of a renewed France. These events made a profound impression on many. Everywhere in the kingdom, following the example of Paris, people organized and armed themselves. They formed militias, the national guards, and in the municipalities elected individuals took over government functions.

In the countryside, a kind of panic, the Great Fear (la Grande Peur) took place. The peasants angrily attacked the châteaux seeking to destroy the seigneurial archives—it was a true JACQUERIE revolt. To stop the disorders, the worried assembly decided to ratify the popular will. On August 4 the noble deputies were the first to propose the abolition of privileges. At two in the morning, in an enthusiastic delirium, the deputies voted equal rights for all, free employment for all, equal justice, abolition of the privileges of the guilds, the provinces, the towns, and of individuals, and the abolition of feudal dues and services, such as the corvée and other remnants of feudalism. It was now necessary to rebuild. The National Assembly voted the famous Declaration of the Rights of Man and the Citizen and the main articles of the constitution. But the king hesitated to ratify them. On the other hand, the provisioning of Paris was breaking down and anger and hunger brought a new revolutionary situation, the October Days.

In the beginning of October, the rumor reached Paris that at a banquet given at Versailles for the Royal Guards, the tricolored cockade had been trampled on. This unleashed the popular fury. On October 5, thousands of women, soon followed by thousands of men, marched on Versailles to demand bread from the king. The palace was blockaded and then on October 6 it was entered. To appease the rioters, Louis XVI and the royal family had to leave Versailles and go to live in the Tuileries. The assembly also left Versailles for Paris. The October Days made the people of Paris the masters of the situation. In the midst of this armed populace, the king and the assembly soon found themselves dependent on them. Meanwhile, in village after village, and in province after province, with the enthusiasm of a newly won freedom, people came together; the supporters of the Revolution, or *patriotes,* swore to remain united as *fédérés* in defense of liberty, hence the name "federation" given to this movement, that, beginning in Dauphiné, spread throughout France and culminated in a great national festival, celebrated in Paris on July 14, 1790. That day, at the Champ-de-Mars, in the name of 14,000 delegates of the national guards of France, the MARQUIS DE LA FAYETTE swore, on the Altar of the Homeland, loyalty to the nation, the law, and the king. And the king himself swore to uphold the constitution. The festival of the Fédération was a major event. By this solemn ceremony, national unity was established on a solid foundation, the freely expressed will of the people.

But, if the revolutionary masses dreamed only of unity, the deputies in the National Assembly became more and more divided. In the beginning, all the *patriotes,* or supporters of the new order, had stood together against those of the Old Regime, the so-called aristocrats. But more and more, the moderates among the *patriotes,* the "monarchists," concerned about violent revolutionary activities, made overtures to the aristocrats. In contrast, some deputies, like MAXIMILIEN DE ROBESPIERRE, were more democratic—supporters of popular power—than the majority of *patriote* deputies. The majority had as its main leader La Fayette, who was also very popular. But the assembly listened most willingly to the great orators, Mirabeau and ANTOINE BARNAVE.

Outside the assembly, politically interested individuals had adopted the English fashion of meeting in "clubs." Since 1789, the revolutionary bourgeois elite had been meeting at the Jacobin Club, its name derived from the former convent in Paris that served as its headquarters. Soon, a large number of provincial branches were affiliated with it. The CORDELIERS CLUB had a more populist and violent tone. There, demonstrations and, at times, uprisings were organized, and one could find not only attorneys, like GEORGES-JACQUES DANTON, and journalists like JEAN-PAUL MARAT, but also tradesmen, like the butcher LOUIS LEGENDRE and the brewer ANTOINE-JOSEPH SANTERRE. Thanks to freedom of the press, the number of journalists greatly increased and some, like Camille Desmoulins, Jean-Paul Marat, and JACQUES HÉBERT, became very popular. Marat, in his newspaper, *l'Ami du Peuple,* violently attacked the royal court, the assembly, Mirabeau, and La Fayette. Hébert, beginning in 1790, published *Le Père Duchêne,* and other newspapers, such as *Le Petit Gauthier,* spoke of renewing France through a "bloodbath."

The accord between the king and the nation that seemed to have been established by the Festival of the Federation soon came apart. The principal cause of this rupture was the religious policy of the Constituent Assembly. In July 1790, the assembly voted on the CIVIL CONSTITUTION OF THE CLERGY, by which the number of bishops was reduced from 134 to 83, one for each department, and bishops and parish priests were henceforth to be elected. The pope, in turn, would not give spiritual investiture to these bishops, and thus, his spiritual authority over the church in France was considerably reduced. Such a reform naturally met with strong resistance. To break it, the assembly demanded from the clergy an oath of loyalty to the constitution (1790); thousands of priests refused the oath. The church in France thus found itself divided in two: On one side the juring, or constitutional, clergy; on the other the nonjuring, or refractory, clergy. The events had grave consequences. The schism increased counterrevolutionary activity, supported henceforth by the refractory clergy.

Another result of the schism was to end the king's hesitation and make him determined to flee. During the night of June 20–21, 1791, Louis XVI, disguised as a valet, left the Tuileries with the royal family. He had already been secretly negotiating with foreign rulers, asking them to mass troops at the borders to intimidate the revolutionaries. Louis himself was going to meet the French army of the marquis de Bouillé in Lorraine, with troops stationed along the route to Metz assuring his safe passage. But the troop movements aroused curiosity and suspicions. The king was recognized at Varennes and arrested and, under the surveillance of commissioners from the assembly was brought back to Paris with the royal family and then was provisionally suspended from his office.

The attempted flight of the king had the most serious consequences. Not only did it destroy the confidence of the people in the king but it began to shake faith in the monarchy and gave credence to previously rare republican ideas. The Cordeliers Club took the lead in the republican movement. Large demonstrations were organized to demand the deposition and trial of the king. But the assembly, remaining monarchist, on July 17, 1791, sent the National Guard to stop these demonstrations that were taking place on the Champ-de-Mars. The demonstrators were dispersed with a deadly fusillade. Masters of the situation, the moderate deputies decided to restore Louis XVI to his powers as a constitutional monarch. Louis accepted the constitution and swore to uphold it. The Constituent Assembly stepped down and was replaced by the Legislative Assembly (September 30, 1791).

The Constituent Assembly had had as its basic task the development of a constitution and decided, first of all, to put forth the philosophic principles on which the new order would be founded, to be derived from the Declaration of the Rights of Man and the Citizen, which had been proclaimed in August 1789. The Declaration, inspired by the new philosophic doctrines, in particular proclaimed: "That men are born free and equal in their rights: that the principle of all sovereignty resides in the nation; that all citizens, equal before the law, are equally admissible to all public positions without any distinctions except their abilities and talents; that no one can be accused, arrested, nor detained except in cases determined by law; that no one can be silenced for their opinions or beliefs; that all citizens can speak, write, and publish freely; and that property is an inviolable and sacred right." Meanwhile, the constitution only applied these principles prudently. Thus, they did not dare to establish universal suffrage. Contrary to the principle of equality, they distinguished between "passive citizens," who did not have the right to vote, and "active citizens"—those who paid a tax equal to three days' salary—who alone had the right to vote.

The constitution when completed and promulgated was known as the Constitution of 1791. It included the principle taken from Montesquieu of the separation of powers and established a new government, a constitutional monarchy, in which the nation delegated executive power to the king, now called the "king of the French," legislative power to an elected assembly, and judicial power to elected judges. The constituents wanted to organize a simplified and uniform administration for all France. The old structures were suppressed and France was divided into 83 departments. Each of these was further divided into districts, each district into cantons, and each canton into communes. In these new units, administration was confided not only to the king's agents, but to delegates elected by the inhabitants—thus producing a decentralized administration. The old duties, hated by all, were replaced by three direct taxes upon individuals, residences, and businesses. The new taxes were borne equally by all citizens, without exemption. Nearly all the indirect taxes were suppressed and duties and customs were collected only at the nation's borders.

But it was necessary to resolve the financial crisis, the main cause of the Revolution. To avoid bankruptcy, the assembly decided to confiscate the properties of the clergy and sell them at a profit to the state (November 1789). In compensation, the state would provide for each religion's expenses and for the upkeep of its clergy. Becoming national properties, the properties of the clergy served to back a paper currency, the assignats. The sale of these properties had a great political and social significance. There was a vast transfer of rebel estates, with an enormous increase in the number of landowners, both among the bourgeoisie and the peasantry. The assembly also undertook a great number of reforms that profoundly changed French society. Not only was the organization of the Catholic Church modified, but also political rights were now accorded to non-Catholics, Protestant and Jewish. Within the family, equality was established among siblings by the abolition of the right by which only the eldest son inherited from his parents. In economic matters, in conforming to the doctrines of the physiocrats, the constitution established the right of freedoms of work and trade, or commerce. The guilds and the interior duties were suppressed. But the assembly did nothing to ameliorate the condition of workers. Professional trade unions were forbidden and it continued to be a crime to strike. Finally, concerned about popular education, the framers of the constitution decreed that public instruction available to all citizens would be established. But for want of time, they did not create necessary institutions for this and left that task to the assemblies that followed.

The Constitution of 1791 stipulated that there would be a Legislative Assembly, elected for two-year terms. This assembly met on October 1, 1791, and included members of the former assembly. The majority of deputies, who came without preconceived views, gathered in the center under the name *indépendants* and wavered between the right, made up of deputies from the FEUILLANTS CLUB, and the left, comprised of members adhering to the Jacobin Club. The Feuillants, originally revolutionary, had become moderates like La Fayette, agreeing to defend Louis XVI and constitutional royalty against the popular unrest. The Jacobins also declared themselves as constitutionalists, but they were hostile to the king and encouraged popular demonstrations against him; many of them had republican tendencies. The Right was more numerous than the Left, but the Left included more better-known individuals, including the philosopher the MARQUIS DE CONDORCET and the journalist JACQUES-PIERRE BRISSOT, and the Left had the best orators: the deputies from the Gironde, like PIERRE V. VERGNIAUD, and ARMAND GENSONNÉ. The name Girondins, or Brissotins, was given to this group of political figures who would play a principal role in the legislature. An agreement between the king and the Feuillants seemed natural and necessary. But Louis XVI and especially Marie Antoinette hated the constitutionalists as much as the Jacobins. They would favor the Jacobins, however, hoping that the worse matters became, the better would be the chance to restore absolutism.

At the end of 1791, thanks to the intrigues of the royal court, the Jacobin JÉROME PETION became mayor of Paris, and the popular Cordelier orator Danton, became the commune's prosecutor. The new regime needed peace and order to function normally. To domestic problems, however, was added that of the threat of war. The king's intrigues precipitated the crisis. The main cause of the trouble was the religious question. In Anjou and in the Vendée, bands of peasants, encouraged by refractory priests, drove out the constitutional clergy. The Legislative Assembly declared that all the priests had to swear the civil oath within eight days, under penalty of being interned as suspects (November 29, 1791). Louis XVI vetoed this decree. The threat of war had already been apparent to the Constituent Assembly, despite a solemn declaration of peace voted by that body in 1790. As soon as it occurred, it was apparent to the sovereigns of Europe that the French Revolution posed a danger to their thrones. Immediately after Varennes, the Emperor and the king of Prussia published the Declaration of Pilnitz, threatening revolutionary France (August 1791). On the other hand, in two other cases France found itself in conflict with foreign rulers, first, in Alsace, where certain German princes held territories, the abolition of feudal rights provoked their protests, in the name of the Treaty of Westphalia; second, in the territory of Avignon, which belonged to the pope, the people rose up and voted for annexation to France (1790). After a plebiscite, the assembly approved the annexation (1791). In these two cases, the Revolution broke with treaty agreements and in their place posed the right of peoples to rule themselves.

Thereafter the threat of war only intensified. The main cause would be the machinations of the émigrés, the princes and nobles who had fled France to escape the Revolution. They were grouped around the king's brother, the count of Provence, at Koblenz, in the domains of the elector of Treves, prince of the Empire, and they encouraged the sovereigns to go to war to crush the Revolution. In response to the émigrés' counterrevolutionary intrigues, the Legislative

Assembly issued a decree in November 1791, summoning the émigrés, under penalty of death, to return before January 1, 1792. The king vetoed this decree but agreed to send a demand to the elector to disperse the émigré army. Louis secretly hoped that a war would restore him to power. For their part, the Girondins saw in a war the way to test the loyalty of the monarchy. War was avoided at this moment only by the prudence of Emperor Leopold. In March 1792, two events occurred that ruined the last chances for peace. In Austria, Leopold died suddenly; his successor was his son Francis II, militant and absolutist. In France, the Girondins obliged the king to form a new ministry whose principal members were CHARLES DUMOURIEZ and JEAN-MARIE ROLAND. Dumouriez, minister of foreign affairs, was talented, ambitious, and unscrupulous; offering his services to the king as well as the Jacobins, he sought power above all else. Roland, minister of the interior, was honest but lacked great abilities; the true interior minister was his wife, Mme Roland, who, by her intelligence, grace, and passionate convictions greatly influenced the Girondins. From then on, war was inevitable. In April, the assembly voted for war against the king of Hungary and Bohemia (Francis II).

The declaration of war marked a turning point in the history of the Revolution. Henceforth each military event had repercussions in Paris. The war began badly. Prussia allied with Austria. The French army had been disorganized by the emigration. A tentative French offensive in Belgium failed. France's frontiers were open to invasion. The situation became all the more critical as religious troubles worsened. To reduce the danger, the assembly voted two decrees: the first deported the refractory priests; the second formed, under the command of Paris, a force of 20,000 *fédérés,* or volunteer national guards. The king vetoed these decrees and, in a new about-face, dismissed the Girondin ministers (June). In response, the Girondin clubs decided to hold a large popular demonstration to intimidate the king. On June 20, 1792, an armed mob entered the Tuileries. The king had to submit to the popular threat but, despite the danger, did not rescind his veto or recall the Girondin ministers. Mayor Pétion evacuated the Tuilieries. The demonstration failed.

Meanwhile, as the danger of invasion increased and the attitude of the king appeared more and more suspicious, the Jacobins had patriotic sentiment on their side. In the beginning of July, it was learned that the Prussian army, reinforced by émigrés, was preparing to invade France. On July 11, the assembly declared *"la patrie en danger"*—the nation is in danger. The decree produced the deepest emotion, and from many quarters came the demand for the king to abdicate. The Parisian revolutionaries were reinforced by the arrival of volunteers from the provinces who set out despite the king's veto. The most ardent were the Marseillais, who entered Paris singing a war song that henceforth would be called "La Marseillaise."

On August 1 news reached Paris of the manifesto sent by the Prussian general, the duke of Brunswick, the leader of the armies preparing to invade France. The manifesto was a declaration of support for Louis XVI and a threat to the assembly and the National Guard. Nothing could better demonstrate the accord between the enemies of France and the king. The people of Paris and the volunteers responded to the Prussian manifesto with an uprising. On the night of August 9–10, an insurrectional commune was installed in the Hôtel-de-Ville. In the morning, the insurgents marched on the Tuileries. A bloody struggle ended with the people victorious. The popular victory of August 10 had consequences of major importance. Under popular pressure, the assembly voted for the suspension of the king, who was interned in the Temple Prison.

To strengthen its position, it decreed that a Convention would be elected by universal suffrage and confided the government to a provisionary Executive Council that included Roland and Danton. Elected by universal suffrage, the Convention had more republican and democratic tendencies than the assembly. Its first act was to abolish royalty (September 21, 1792) and decree that public acts would be dated from Year 1 of the republic (September 22). The Convention consisted of 750 delegates. In the center the majority of deputies formed the Plain, or the Marais. They wavered between two groups, the Girondins on the right, and the MONTAGNARDS on the left, separated often by great personal hatred. The Girondins, who included Brissot, Vergniaud, Roland, and Pétion, and nearly all the provincial deputies, were opposed to the dictatorship of the Paris Commune, where their adversaries were dominant. The Montagnards, wanting to be the party of the people, accepted the Parisian dictatorship. Among them were Maximilien Robespierre, Danton, and Marat, who were joined by Camille Desmoulins, LOUIS-ANTOINE SAINT-JUST, and the attorney GEORGES COUTHON.

The struggle between the two factions opened with the issue of the fate of the king. At the Tuileries, documents were found revealing the secret intrigues of Louis XVI. The Convention decided to try him itself. After passionate debating, the assembly declared the king guilty and condemned him to death; he was executed on January 21, 1793. This only served to widen the gap between the Girondins and the Montagnards, who accused their adversaries of having wanted to save the king and create a federal republic. They demanded the arrest of the Girondins, who, in turn, accused Marat and Robespierre of wanting a dictatorship; they had Marat tried before the Revolutionary Tribunal, but he was acquitted (April). They also tried to break up the commune. This was forcefully resisted, and on June 2, the Convention decreed the arrest of 29 Girondins.

Never had the revolution been in such peril. After the events of June 2, Girondin uprisings broke out in Bordeaux, Normandy, and the Midi. Including the royalist Vendée, 60 departments, three-quarters of France, was in arms against Paris, where a young woman, CHARLOTTE CORDAY, had stabbed Marat to avenge the Girondins. At the same time, all the borders were crossed by the armies of the Coalition and the royalists delivered to the English the port and the fleet at Toulon (August). In response, the Convention formed a strong government armed with dictatorial powers that, in turn, created a Committee of General Safety to search for suspects; a Revolutionary Tribunal to judge them without appeal; and a Committee of Public Safely composed of nine members elected by the Convention that was armed with the most extensive civil and military powers. To the nation's departments were sent representatives with full powers to control the actions of civilian and military authorities. And in each commune, a Surveillance Committee was charged with enumerating and arresting suspects.

In July, the most intransigent of the Montagnards, Robespierre and his friends Couthon and Saint-Just, replaced Danton and his associates on the Committee of Public Safety. The revolutionary government had to continue the civil and foreign wars and also deal with the economic crisis. National defense was assured by the decree of a *levée en masse*, and to halt the economic crisis, the Convention voted a law that punished with death anyone who tried to monopolize necessary goods, established a maximum price, or set up a committee to control production. Montagnard policy became more and more egalitarian and hostile to wealth and to Catholicism, and appeals were made to the SANS-CULOTTES ("without breeches")—the masses. A revolutionary calendar was adopted and churches were converted into temples of Reason (November 1793). All these measures were met with innumerable acts of resistance that, in turn, were met with the Terror. Already, émigrés and refractory priests had been outlawed. The Law of Suspects declared traitors all "the enemies of liberty," and each day the Revolutionary Tribune sent many to the guillotine. In the insurgent departments, there were mass executions. Horrendous excesses were committed. Between March 1, 1793, and July 27, 1794 (9 Thermidor), 2,627 persons were guillotined in Paris. Among the victims were Marie Antoinette, MME ROLAND, the early revolutionaries who were now declared traitors, Bailly, Barnave, the Girondins, weak or suspect generals, such as ADAM PHILIPPE CUSTINE, Jean Houchard, and ALEXANDRE DE BEAUHARNAIS, first husband of the empress Joséphine. Mass executions were carried out in Lyon, and in Nantes, mass drownings of the guilty and suspected.

In this merciless war, the republic at least survived. At the end of 1793, the military situation had improved. Only the economic one remained unresolved. Doubtlessly, famine had been avoided in the cities, but at the price of strict rationing. Rationing, and the taxing of commodities and salaries, increased greatly the number of discontented, especially in Paris, within all classes of society. Since the middle of 1793, Robespierre had been, without the title, the recognized leader of the government. But he soon had to fight against new opponents. Two of these threatened the Committee of Public Safety. On the left, the Hébertists, led by JACQUES-RENÉ HÉBERT, were extremely anti-Catholic and sought a new social structure. On the right, the Indulgents, who stood behind Danton and Desmoulins and protested against the excesses of the Terror. Robespierre hated the atheism of the Hébertists, and the dishonesty of certain Dantonists. Successively, he had one after the other arrested and guillotined (March–April 1794). Robespierre decided that this was the time to establish the Republic of Virtue, which he ceaselessly spoke of. Drawing on the writings of Jean-Jacques Rousseau, he had conceived the idea of a democratic republic, founded on equality and virtue. To apply these doctrines, the Convention issued two decrees (February–March 1794): confiscating the property of suspects and distributing it to poor patriots. For almost five months, Robespierre exercised a veritable dictatorship to achieve his program. He wanted first of all to give the regime a moral and religious basis, and he instituted the Cult of the

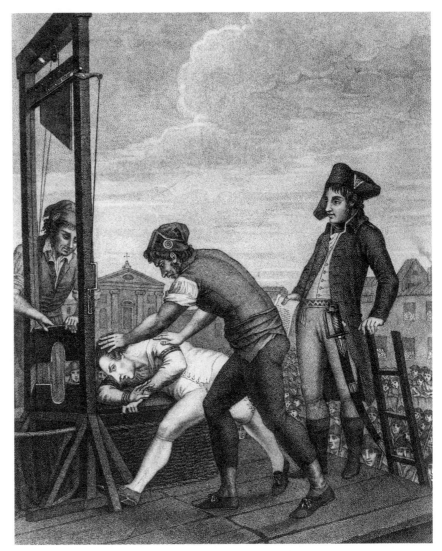

Robespierre being
put to the guillotine
after the French
Revolution, 1794
(Hulton/Archive)

Supreme Being. Then was instituted the Law of Prairial, which allowed the
Revolutionary Tribunal to impose the death sentence without defense or witnesses. This brought the Great TERROR that had many illustrious victims, such
as the scientist ANTOINE-LAURENT DE LAVOISIER and the poet ANDRÉ CHENIER. Suddenly, Robespierre was overthrown by a conspiracy of all his enemies, terrorist and moderate. At its 9 Thermidor (July 27, 1794) meeting, to cries of "Down
with the tyrant," the Convention voted his arrest along with Saint-Just and
Couthon. The Paris Commune tried to save him; but, condemned, he was guillotined along with 21 of his supporters (10 Thermidor).

Power soon reverted to moderates like FRANÇOIS COUNT DE BOISSY D'ANGLAS and to "reformed" terrorists like PAUL DE BARRAS and JEAN-LAMBERT TALLIEN. This is called the Thermidorian Reaction. The Terror regime was progressively abolished. The Revolutionary Tribunal was disbanded, its laws were rescinded, and the COMMUNE OF PARIS was suppressed. The Jacobin Club was closed and the policy of de-Christianization was ended. A new constitution was approved. There was also a sudden change in customs and tastes; the salons were reopened, luxuries reappeared, and the youth led the way with a deliberate attempt to enjoy life and its pleasures. The Jacobins responded with uprisings in the faubourgs (districts or neighborhoods). But these were put down and their leaders arrested. The defeat of Jacobinism, however, emboldened the royalists. In many regions, a WHITE TERROR developed. Jacobins were massacred in the Midi, and in the Vendée, people again took up arms. The English fleet landed an émigré army at Quiberon, Brittany (July 1795). The Convention had to revert to a defensive policy. The émigrés at Quiberon were defeated, and to avoid a royalist electoral victory, the Convention decreed that the two ranks of future deputies must be chosen from among its members.

The royalists organized the insurrection of 13 Vendémiaire (October 1795) against the Convention, but they were suppressed by the young general Napoléon Bonaparte (see NAPOLÉON I). The financial, moral, and political situation of the country at the end of 1795, however, was profoundly troubled. The war, which went on against England and Austria, emptied the treasury. To deal with the debts, the printing of paper money continued and monetary disorder led to speculation. The luxury of a class of nouveaux riches contrasted with the misery of the poor. The political situation was no better and became the legacy of the Directory government (1795–99).

The extremes of wealth would bring a return of Jacobinism. The Jacobins had formed the Panthéon Club, where some members adhered to the communist doctrines of FRANÇOIS-NOËL BABEUF. Democrats and communists conspired against the Directory, but the principal leaders, among them Babeuf, were arrested and executed. The royalist party was more frightening. Owing to the recall of the refractory clergy and an active propaganda supported by English subsidies, the royalists won a majority among the Counsels in the 1797 elections. This brought them into conflict with the Directors, of whom three were former members of the Convention. Since the constitution had not provided for this, the conflict was resolved by force. The Directors, with the help of one of Bonaparte's lieutenants, took control in the coup d'état of 18 Fructidor.

Once fully in power, the Directory undertook in all areas, particularly the financial, an important work of reorganization, including monetary reforms. But the population was tired of war and the strife among the political parties. At the same time, the enemy was menacing France on all its borders, and there was the CHOUANNERIE peasant uprising in the West. Within the Directory a group wanted to revise the constitution, but to achieve this end another coup d'état was necessary, under a popular leader. This would be General Napoléon Bonaparte, who, having just returned from a campaign in Egypt, was welcomed as a hero. Bonaparte resolved to make the coup d'état, but to his own advantage.

Along with EMMANUEL-JOSEPH SIEYÈS and Bonaparte, the principal architects of the conspiracy were the Director ROGER DUCOS, the Minister of Justice JEAN-JACQUES DE CAMBACÉRÈS, Bonaparte's brother LUCIEN BONAPARTE, president of the Council of Five Hundred, and the master intriguer TALLEYRAND. The coup was achieved when, with the help of the military, the deputies were chased from their meeting place at Saint-Cloud on 18 Brumaire (November 9, 1799).

In reality, the coup d'état of 18 Brumaire marked the end not only of the Directory but also of the republic. Bonaparte had first come to the attention of the nation by his stunning military victories, beginning at Toulon in 1793 and continuing with his brilliant campaign in Italy, with victories at Lodi, Arcoli, and Rivoli (1796). After conquering northern Italy, he forced the Austrians to sign the Treaty of Campo-Formio (1797), by which France gained Belgium and other territories and a dominant influence in Italy (Cispalpine Republic). In 1798, in a move against England and its interests in India, Bonaparte conquered Egypt (battle of the Pyramids). The French fleet, however, was annihilated by the British at Aboukir.

# The Era of Napoléon Bonaparte

Despite all its efforts, the Directory had left France in anarchy and impoverished. The most urgent need, therefore, was for internal peace. To achieve this, Bonaparte practiced a policy of reconciliation. The Vendée and Brittany were pacified and roads were improved, thereby reducing brigandage. To replace the Constitution of the Year III, Bonaparte put in place the Constitution of the Year VIII, which, under a republican appearance, established a monarchical regime. The constitution was founded on national sovereignty with the right to vote extended to all male citizens aged 21 and living for at least a year in a commune. But the voting was only for a list of candidates already chosen by the government; there were no representative elections. Legislative power, too, was weak, with the four assemblies—Council of State, Tribunate, Legislative Corps, and Senate—dependent on Bonaparte as first consul and deprived of any real authority. Executive power was in the hands of the three consuls—Bonaparte, Cambacérès, and CHARLES LEBRUN—but in fact, the first consul held all power, proposing laws and nominating ministers, officials, functionaries, and most judges. The constitution was accepted by a plebiscite.

At the same time that he proceeded with the reorganization of the country, the first consul continued the struggle against the Second Coalition. Austria was disarmed first in the campaign of 1800 (battle of Marengo, June), and by the Treaty of Lunéville (1801), Austria had to recognize French annexation of the left bank of the Rhine and the new republics created in Italy. England remained victorious at sea but no longer had allies. By the terms of the Peace of Amiens (1802), after 10 years of war, a general peace was established in Europe.

Just as he had done in war, Bonaparte proceeded with extraordinary activity to reorganize the state, society, and church. State reorganization included centralization of the government and the creation of the Bank of France. Education was reformed with the creation of lycées (high schools) that granted scholarships (1802). The LEGION OF HONOR was created to recognize both military and civilian achievements (1802). Assisted by the Council of State, Bonaparte undertook what was his masterwork, the reform of legislation. He decided to unite in one unique code the various laws dealing with family, property, and contracts. The Civil Code was completed in 1804. Inspired by Roman law, royal ordinances, and Revolutionary rights, the code addressed the needs of the society that emerged from the revolution. It has since been used in France and has been imitated or adopted by a large number of other countries.

Bonaparte saw religion as one of the most important elements in maintaining order. Since the end of the Terror, a strong Catholic revival had taken place in France. The first consul wanted to take advantage of this to reconcile the clergy and separate them from royalism. Beginning in 1800, despite his supporters, he held negotiations with Pope Pius VII. Long and difficult, these resulted in the signing of the Concordat of 1801. In exchange for the pope's recognition of the sale of church property during the Revolution and the reorganization of its dioceses, the French government assured free exercise of religion but maintained the right to appoint bishops and pastors. Following Gallican tradition, Bonaparte reinforced the prerogatives of the state with the Organic Articles. With this Concordat, church and state in France would be connected until 1905. Bonaparte felt that the powers of the first consul, as outlined in the constitution, were limiting, so after the Peace of Amiens, he had himself named consul for life (1802). The constitution was modified and became the Constitution of the Year X. The first consul also was granted the right to designate his successor, in effect creating a hereditary monarchy. Meanwhile, Bonaparte's dictatorship had discontented many, both republicans and royalists. The latter at first thought that he could work for a restoration of the Bourbons; but their offers were rejected with disdain. Exasperated, they resorted to plots and assassination attempts. The epilogue of one such plot was the abduction and execution of the DUKE D'ENGHIEN (1804).

The political evolution that had begun in 1799 ended in 1804 with the reestablishment of an imperial monarchy. Since 1803, France's war had recommenced with England. Taking advantage of his popularity during this time of national peril, Bonaparte granted himself the title of Napoléon I, hereditary emperor. The constitution was modified a second time, taking the name Constitution of the Year XII (1804). A plebiscite approved these amendments by a vote of 4 million to fewer than 3,000. The constitution also created an imperial family, with each of the emperor's brothers and sisters receiving the title of French princes and princesses, and a hierarchy of notables. The emperor Napoléon was one of the most powerful figures of modern times and one of the most astonishing leaders in history. In 1804, at the time of his accession to the throne, his genius and character had reached their full development, but his passion for glory and power would also be his downfall. His regime became despotic, with a large surveillance police force throughout the nation, internments without trial, and censorship and strong limitations on freedom of the press. Under the First Empire, domestic reforms begun under the Consulate continued in all areas—education, religion, agriculture, and industry—but general discontent also was present because of conscription and the economic hardships caused by import duties and the policy of the Continental System, designed to blockade British trade to the continent.

In foreign policy, France between 1804 and 1815 had to deal constantly with hostile military coalitions. These incessant wars had their origins both in the fears of the major powers regarding France and in Napoléon's insatiable need for conquests. In 1803, England took the initiative in a new war against France, and while Bonaparte continued his conquests on the continent, the main

French fleet was defeated at Trafalgar by the British (1805). At the same time, England, with Austria and Russia, formed the Third Coalition. The campaign of 1805 was marked by an astonishing French rapidity and precision, with French victories at Ulm (October 20) and at Austerlitz (December 2). The subsequent Treaty of Pressburg (December 1805) brought France more territory. Napoléon completely reorganized Germany, creating the Confederation of the Rhine with himself as its protector. In 1806, he defeated Prussia and the following year signed the Peace of Tilsit with Russia.

Only England remained unsubdued, and against it Napoléon ordered a continental blockade (1806). But for the blockade to be effective, it had to extend to all of Europe; thus Napoléon was caught in a policy of perpetual wars and annexations. In 1808, he intervened in Spain, exploiting a division between the royal family and the government. This led to the war in Spain, which would be fatal for the French, who, for the first time, faced national resistance in the form of guerrilla warfare, supported by the English. Austria sought to take advantage of the situation by forming a new coalition (1809) but, defeated at Wagram, had to submit again to territorial losses to France by the terms of the Treaty of Vienna.

In 1811, French hegemony extended over the greater part of Europe. The Peace of Vienna marked the apogee of Napoléon's power. Vassal states were given to members of his family or were controlled directly by Napoléon himself. To establish a dynasty, he divorced JOSEPHINE and married the daughter of the emperor of Austria, MARIE-LOUISE OF HABSBURG-LORRAINE (1810). In 1811, a son, to be known as the king of Rome, was born. To maintain his European empire, Napoléon had to insure that his power rested in the imperial army. But the bloody series of wars had taken a enormous human toll, and by this time, there was great discontent among the French people because of these losses. The hatred of French domination, too, had awakened national sentiment among the many conquered peoples of Europe, and this would be an important legacy of the Bonaparte era.

In 1812, England succeeded in detaching Russia from the French alliance and in forming a sixth coalition. Czar Alexander I was alarmed by France's creation of a new Polish state on Russia's border, and his nobility encouraged him to oppose the French. War broke out in June 1812. Napoléon took the offensive with 400,000 troops—the Grande Armée. He believed it would be a quick campaign. The French took Moscow in September, but the Russians set fire to the city and the czar refused to negotiate. Napoléon decided, too late, to retreat (October 1812). The retreat turned into a disaster as his army was decimated by the Russian winter and the attacks of Russian forces. On December 16, only 18,000 retreating soldiers crossed the Neman River into Poland. A new coalition was formed against the French, and by 1814 Napoléon had been defeated. The victorious allies recalled the Bourbons to power, beginning what is known as the First RESTORATION. Napoléon, having abdicated and been exiled to the island of Elba in the Mediterranean did return (March 1815), only to be defeated a second time, after the HUNDRED DAYS in power, at the Battle of Waterloo. With Bonaparte now permanently exiled, the Bourbons were again recalled and the Second Restoration began (1815).

# The Restoration

LOUIS XVIII, who returned from exile in England in 1814 to France behind the invaders, had to negotiate a new peace, the second Treaty of Paris. In contrast to the concessions achieved by Talleyrand in the first treaty (Congress of Vienna), France lost Savoy as well as places at its northern and eastern borders. It paid an indemnity and had to submit to five years of foreign occupation. France was now smaller than at the beginning of the Revolution and for a long time remained weakened, diminished, and suspected by all of Europe. By the declaration of Saint-Ouen (May 2, 1814), Louis XVIII was urged to accord a new constitution, the Constitutional Charter. The Charter guaranteed to the French people the essential gains of the Revolution: equality before the law, access to all employment, individual liberty, and freedom of religion and of the press. It maintained the Civil Code and the Legion of Honor and declared irrevocable the sale of national properties. It kept the departments, the prefectures, and the judicial and financial administration of the Empire, thus maintaining the administrative structure inherited from Napoléon. Moreover, the Charter established representative government modeled on the English system. Executive power rested with the king alone, assisted by his ministers. But the king shared legislative power with two chambers, the Chamber of Peers (upper house) and the Chamber of Deputies (lower house). The peers were named by the king, with hereditary titles and without limitation to their number. The deputies were elected for terms of five years by those citizens who paid at least 300 francs in direct taxes.

The new regime, more liberal than the Empire, granted to the representatives a certain part in administering public affairs. The general policy thus depended on the king and political parties, of which there were three principal ones: the Ultra-royalists, or Ultras, the Independents, and the Constitutionals. The Ultras only grudgingly accepted the Charter and hoped for a return to the Old Regime. For the most part former émigrés, they wanted their confiscated properties returned and the Catholic clergy given a prominent place in the government. The Independents, in contrast, included all the enemies of the Bourbons and the regime, republicans, Bonapartists, or liberal and democratic monarchists who upheld the principle of the sovereignty of the people. Between these two extremes, the Constitutionals, or moderates, wanted to remain loyal to the Charter. Among them was a faction known as the Doctrinaires. Within the ranks of the Constitutionals was the émigré ARMAND-EMMANUEL DU PLESSIS DE CHINON, DUKE OF RICHELIEU, revolutionaries like PIERRE-

PAUL ROYER-COLLARD, and important functionaries from the Empire like DECAZES. But the majority within this party were from the upper bourgeoisie.

There were also secret societies established in France, such as the Charbonnnerie, modeled on the Neapolitan Carbonari. Louis XVIII during an exile of 23 years had gained much experience and wisdom, but also indolence and egoism. So as not to loose a throne regained in such an unexpected way, he was desirous of respecting the laws established under the constitutional government and of reconciling the new France with the old. He did not want, he said, "to be the king of two peoples."

The new regime was inaugurated by the vengeful acts of the White Terror. In the Midi, at Marseille, Nîmes, and Avignon, the royalist population committed massacres. In Paris, Marshal MICHEL NEY and several generals were put on trial and executed for renewing their loyalty to Bonaparte. All regicides, that is, those who voted for the death of Louis XVI, were banished. The chamber elected during this period was composed almost completely of Ultras. Louis XVIII, at first satisfied, declared that another such chamber could not be found (*"introuvable"*), hence the name *la Chambre introuvable*. This chamber voted for extremely reactionary laws such as that which imposed a penalty for flying the tricolor. Freedom of the press and assembly were curtailed. The following elections (1816) gave the majority to the Constitutionals, who remained in power until 1820.

This was a good period for the regime. Under the leadership of Decazes especially, a policy of moderation and reconstruction prevailed and important laws were passed. In 1818, Marshal GOUVION-SAINT-CYR reorganized the military so that France could again take its place among the major powers. Laws of conscription were thus modified. Decazes passed the Law of 1819, very liberal for the time, which suppressed censorship and allowed much more press freedom. Finances, too, were reorganized, with annual budgets being submitted for approval to the chambers. Meanwhile, Decazes's situation became precarious. Pursued by the hatred of the Ultras, he was also abandoned by his party compatriots who feared the progress of the Independents, and was supported only by the king. A catastrophe led to his fall. On February 13, 1820, a worker stabbed the son of the count of Artois (the future CHARLES X), the DUKE OF BERRY. This act was soon used against Decazes by the Ultras. Giving in to the appeals of the count of Artois, his brother Louis XVIII abandoned his minister.

This was the end of the policy of moderation and conciliation pursued since 1816. Decazes was replaced by Richelieu (1820–21); then, the latter seemed also too moderate to one of the Ultra leaders, the count DE VILLÈLE (1821–27). To stop the progress of the Independents in the chamber, Richelieu pushed through a law of double voting (June 1820) by which the wealthiest electors voted twice, thus giving the majority to the great property owners. Another law also set the legislative terms at seven years, helping the Ultras to perpetuate their power. Freedom of the press was suspended and censorship reestablished.

Louis XVIII died in 1824, and his brother, the count of Artois, succeeded him as Charles X (1824–30). With Charles, the Ultras and the counterrevolution came to power. Supported by Charles X, Villèle undertook to realize the entire Ultra program. In 1825, the chamber voted a huge indemnity to the émigrés

French rebels taking a Royalist canon in the Rue Saint Honoré in Paris during the July Revolution of 1830 (Hulton/Archive)

whose lands had been confiscated during the Revolution. The same year, the Law of Sacrilege was passed. It made punishable by death the profanation of sacred objects. The nation saw in this law a revival of religious fanaticism. Discontent increased throughout the country. A dozen military plots aimed at overthrowing the Bourbons took place in 1821 and 1822. All failed and ended with executions. Even in the chamber itself, a certain number of royalist deputies were concerned about this extreme reactionary policy. To break their opposition, Villèle dissolved the Chamber. But his adversaries returned in a stunning election victory and he resigned (January 1828).

The triumph of the liberal opposition at first made Charles X back down. He agreed to replace Villèle with a moderate, the count de MARTIGNAC (1828), who after a year and a half had to step down. Charles then formed a ministry that shared his own views, under JULES DE POLIGNAC (August 1829). Comprised of the most intransigent Ultras, this was a provocative and confrontational ministry. The expected conflict occurred at the opening parliamentary session in 1830. The king gave a speech to which the chamber replied with the "Address of 221," the number of deputies who voted for it. In respectful terms, the Address reiterated the rights of the nation and of its representatives. Charles X immediately prorogued the chamber, then declared it dissolved. In the new elections held between June 23 and July 19, the opposition increased from 221 to 270. The king did not for an instant, however, dream of acceding to the will of the country. On July 25, Charles signed the Four Ordinances, which expressed the royal will to legislate without resorting to the chambers and also to suspend freedom of the press.

The publication of the ordinances on July 26 immediately unleashed a revolution in Paris. All the opposition came together to fight against the king's attempted coup. The journalists, affected by the ordinance on the press, protested with a great demonstration. The republicans also joined the armed resistance. After three days of fighting—"The Three Glorious Days" of July 27, 28, 29—they became the masters of Paris.

The triumph of the insurrection appearing assured, royalist liberals ADOLPHE THIERS, and JACQUES LAFFITTE, advised by Talleyrand, offered the crown to Louis-Philippe, duke of Orléans, known for his liberal views. The republicans, who knew that public opinion was not yet ready, did not dare to proclaim a republic. La Fayette, who had been named commander of the National Guard, rallied to Louis-Philippe, and the new king received him acting as the lieutenant general of the kingdom, while Charles X left for England.

The departure of Charles X facilitated the establishment of a new regime. The deputies came over to Louis-Philippe, trying to maintain the charter that they had revised. On August 9, having sworn to uphold the revised charter, the lieutenant general became LOUIS-PHILIPPE I, "king of the French." The dynastic change had been achieved, but it was the result of a skillful political maneuver, not a large national consensus.

In foreign affairs, France, after 1815, was considered the center of Revolutionary ideas and was closely watched by the allies, whose armies occupied France until 1818. The occupation ended by the terms of the Treaty of Aix-la-Chapelle. In fact, Louis XVIII was invited to join the League of Sovereigns and make the Quadruple a Quintuple Alliance. France soon was engaged in a reactionary foreign policy for which Prince Klemens Metternich of Austria had set the example. At the Congress of Verona (1822), France was given the mission to intervene in Spain to restore the reactionary king Ferdinand VII to the throne as an absolute monarch. Encouraged by the success of this expedition, the government of the Restoration practiced an independent policy, under Charles X, with the Greek revolt providing an occasion to act. France joined England and Russia in the mediation that resulted in Ottoman recognition of Greek independence (1829). But the Greek expedition brought no material advantage to France. To satisfy public opinion, Charles X and his minister Polignac sought bolder initiatives, and, in exchange for freedom, the French people were given the glory of restored territories. Also, Charles and Polignac initiated a colonial policy that resulted in the French occupation of Algiers in 1830.

# THE JULY MONARCHY

The new king, Louis-Philippe, was known and admired by the Parisian bourgeoisie for his simple and familiar habits; but he also had an obstinate, authoritarian nature and wanted to impose his will on the government. He desired peace and order. This conservative policy quickly produced a break with the liberals (1831). The individuals who had brought Louis-Philippe to power did not agree on which policy to pursue. Some, like the banker Laffitte and La Fayette, wanted to open the way for democratic reforms and also work toward annulling the treaties of 1815. They formed the party of *mouvement*. The others, peace loving and conservative, believed it was necessary to resist popular demands and, by a policy of prudence, reassure the European rulers who were ill disposed toward the "king of the barricades." They formed the party of *résistance*, of whom the leaders were CASIMIR PERIER, LOUIS-ADOLPHE THIERS, and FRANÇOIS GUIZOT, the party that the king preferred.

Louis-Philippe nonetheless at first believed that he could govern with the party of *mouvement,* which was the more popular grouping. Jacques Laffitte took power (November 1830–March 1831), but his ministry was marked by a period of continual uprisings. The revolution had increased unemployment. Remaining armed, the people took every opportunity to demonstrate, while the government was powerless. Moreover, the Revolution of 1830 had provoked by repercussion uprisings elsewhere in Europe. Laffitte wanted to intervene in support of the insurgents, at the risk of bringing back the coalition of 1814 against France. Louis-Philippe believed that the moment had come to break with the liberals. Openly supporting the résistance faction, he called to power Casimir Perier, a banker and authoritative figure who wanted to impose respect for the new regime on the nation (March 1831). Perier died of cholera in 1832, but in a year he had reestablished order, organized the conservative party, stabilized the monarchy, and strengthened its position in Europe. After Périer's death, his policies were continued by the leaders of the conservative party, Achille, duke DE BROGLIE, Thiers, and Guizot.

Meanwhile, the Orléanist monarchy had to defend itself against three adversaries: the legitimists, the Bonapartists, and above all the republicans. Remaining faithful to the Bourbon claimant, the legitimists came from the old nobility and the great landowners. A clerical party, they were not, however, dangerous to the regime. After the death of Napoléon's son, the duke of Reichstadt (1832), the Bonapartists recognized the emperor's nephew, Louis-Napoléon Bonaparte (eventually NAPOLEON III), who, taking his role as pretender quite seriously, twice attempted armed uprisings, one at Strasbourg (1836), the other at Boulogne (1840). Both were suppressed. Only the republican opposition, which most recently had embraced socialist ideas, could imperil the monarchy.

Accustomed to revolutionary action and organized into secret societies the most important of which was the Droits de l'Homme, the republicans increased the number of uprisings and actions against the state: the insurrection of the workers of Lyon in 1831, more social than political, provoked above all by extreme poverty; the insurrection of June 1832 in Paris on the occasion of the funeral of the republican general MAXIMILIEN LAMARQUE; and the insurrections of April 1834, in Lyon, Marseille, and Paris. The government's response to the revolutionaries was to pass the Laws of September 1835. The most important of these was the Law of the Press. It forbade any attack on the king, the government, and the principle of property, threatened by socialist doctrines. Censorship and prior authorization were reestablished for plays, drawings, and caricatures. Ruined by the costs of trials and fines, the republican newspapers quickly disappeared. But republican propaganda nonetheless continued in satirical journals, almanacs, novels, such as those by EUGÈNE SUE and GEORGE SAND, and in historical works.

Having disarmed the revolutionary opposition, the regime, after 1836, seemed assured of its future. The king took advantage of the parliamentary struggles (1836–40) to pursue a more personal policy. After having imposed, between 1836 and 1839, the Molé ministry, which he controlled but which was overthrown by a coalition of all the parties, he appointed Thiers to lead the government. But the king took advantage of the Egyptian Question, the crisis in the East involving the Ottoman Empire, to replace Thiers with Guizot (October 1840). Guizot's ministry lasted for eight years because he was in complete agreement with the king's views and because the government was able to maintain a majority in the chamber. His political and social policies were completely conservative: order at home, peace abroad; no reforms, no chance ventures.

This policy was strongly fought by the parties on the Left. Their attack was based on two main points, the English alliance and reform. A supporter of an entente with England, Guizot, to uphold that aim, made concessions that were often seen as humiliating. The opposition also denounced the corrupt practices of the government and demanded electoral and parliamentary reform. An extreme leftist group, led by ALEXANDRE LEDRU-ROLLIN, demanded universal suffrage. The regime served the interests of the upper bourgeoisie. But it neither appealed to the intellectual elite and the idealist youth nor to the working classes, whose conditions were very poor. Also, outside the parliamentary parties, two new ones emerged, the Catholic and the Socialist Parties.

Under the Restoration, the clergy, allied with reaction, had become unpopular, and there had been a violent anticlerical reaction after the Revolution of 1830. Some ardent Catholics, the abbés FÉLICITÉ DE LAMENNAIS and HENRI LACORDAIRE and CHARLES, COUNT DE MONTALEMBERT, resolved to demonstrate that the Catholic faith could accommodate liberty. They demanded the separation of church and state, freedom of association, and above all freedom in education. Grouped under the name of socialists were all those who wanted to change not only the political regime, but also social organization, the regime of property and labor. Numerous especially among the republicans, some, like LOUIS-AUGUSTE BLANQUI, had adopted the communist doctrines of Babeuf. Others were the disciples of two more recent theorists, CLAUDE HENRI, COUNT DE SAINT-SIMON and CHARLES FOURIER. In 1839, a young journalist, LOUIS BLANC, published a very successful book, *L'Organisation du travail.* In it, he proclaimed the right to work and demanded the intervention of the state in establishing social workshops and the distribution of benefits.

Unbeknownst to the government, the nation each day distanced itself further from the regime, thus explaining the suddenness and easy success of the Revolution of February 1848. Powerless within the Chamber, the opposition resolved, in 1847, to appeal to public opinion. Throughout the country, meetings were organized, at which speakers stressed the need for reform. The campaign was to culminate in a large banquet in Paris, but Guizot prohibited it. In protest, a demonstration was quickly improvised that he also prohibited. At this point, an uprising broke out and for two days, February 23 and 24, there was fighting. On February 23, the uprising seemed to be directed only against Guizot and it generally was believed that it could be stopped by his dismissal. Paris celebrated. But in the evening, on the Boulevard des Capucines, demonstrators were killed by a fusillade and the fighting began again. On the 24th, the uprising turned against the monarchy. The National Guard, themselves supporters of reform, refused to march against the insurgents. Worried and discouraged in the Tuileries, Louis-Philippe abdicated in favor of his grandson, the count of Paris, and like Charles X, fled to England.

This time, the republicans were resolved not to lose the prizes of victory, as in 1830. Although politically conservative, the July monarchy did achieve certain administrative, educational, and economic reforms. In foreign affairs, because the Revolution of 1830 had everywhere awakened national and liberal aspirations, especially in Belgium, Poland, and Italy, France became more involved in European matters. Louis-Philippe, extremely peace loving, had to deal with the issue of various peoples of Europe seeking liberty and try to guarantee order over anarchy. The Belgian revolution provided France with an opportunity to tear up the treaties of 1815 and, at the London Conference (1830–31), stood with the other major powers in recognizing Belgian independence. So as not to be isolated again in Europe, Louis-Philippe drew closer to Britain. The policy of a Franco-Russian entente was followed by a Franco-English one, seen as the best guarantee of peace in Europe. But the accord was fragile and, tested by the intransigent policy of British prime minister Palmerston, was broken twice, over the Eastern Question and the crisis of 1840 involving Egypt, and the war in 1844 between France and Morocco. France then, under Guizot, turned to Austria (1847) and agreed to cooperate in Metternich's struggle against the nationalist and liberal agitation that was spreading in Europe.

Between 1815 and 1848, there was also a resurgence of French colonialism. Algeria had been occupied by the French under Charles X, but the July Monarchy hesitated at first to maintain interests in Africa and adopted a policy of restraint (1830–35). When this policy was reversed, France undertook the colonization of Algeria and an extension of interests in North Africa and elsewhere. Outposts were established on the Ivory Coast and Gabon (1842–43). In the Indian Ocean, Mayotte and Nossi-Bé, near Madagascar, were occupied, as were archipelagos and islands in the Pacific (Marquises, Wallis and Futuna, and Tahiti, 1842–47). The July Monarchy thus inaugurated a policy of expansion that would be more aggressively pursued by subsequent French governments.

# SCIENTIFIC, ECONOMIC, AND CULTURAL DEVELOPMENTS

During the first half of the 19th century, a great number of revolutionary scientific discoveries were made. The French governments after 1789 had encouraged scientific research and practical applications, and these were manifest in a wide area of achievements. During the Revolution and the First Empire, France had a number of illustrious mathematicians, produced in large part by the new educational system. They included JOSEPH-LOUIS, COUNT DE LAGRANGE, GASPARD MONGE, and PIERRE-SIMON, MARQUIS DE LAPLACE, to be followed by BARON AUGUSTIN CAUCHY and ÉVARISTE GALOIS. In astronomy, URBAIN LE VERRIER stands out. In the study of physics, the most important French scientists were AUGUSTIN FRESNEL, NICHOLAS-LÉONARD-SADI CARNOT, and ANDRÉ-MARIE AMPÈRE. In chemistry, Lavoisier was followed by LOUIS-JOSEPH GAY-LUSSAC and EUGÈNE CHEVREUL. In France, the main center of the study of natural sciences was the Natural History Museum, where such naturalists as JEAN LAMARCK, GEORGES BARON CUVIER, and ÉTIENNE GEOFFROY SAINT-HILAIRE taught.

Various scientific discoveries led to important practical applications. PHILIPPE LEBON, through a distillery process of wood, produced a gas that led to the public illumination of cities and of private residences. The utilization of light processes led to the experiments of JOSEPH NIÉPCE and JACQUES DAGUERRE that formed the first type of photography. The considerable work also of PHILIPPE PINEL, CLAUDE, COUNT DE BERTHOLLET, and ANTOINE, COUNT DE FOURCROY mark the scientific achievements of the age. In economic theory, the ideas of Saint-Simon, Auguste Comte, Fourier, and Blanc led to the development of socialist alternatives to the unbridled capitalism of the era.

The first decades of the century were a period, too, of great artistic development. Such painters as DAVID, GROS, PRUD'HON, and Anne-Louis Girodet set the tone of the imperial age, to be followed by DELACROIX, COURBET, GÉRICAULT, and others who reflect the romantic style. In literature, the work of pre-romantics and romantics formed a significant contribution to French culture. In fact, in France the romantic movement was also a literary revolution that was followed by the political one, with CHATEAUBRIAND and MME DE STAËL setting the tone, followed by LAMARTINE, HUGO, VIGNY, MÉRIMÉE, BALZAC, STENDHAL (who coined the term "romanticism"), SAINTE-BEUVE, MICHELET, MUSSET, George Sand, ALEXANDRE-DAVY DUMAS, and NERVAL.

# THE SECOND REPUBLIC

After the Revolution of 1848 and the fall of the July Monarchy, the provisional government was installed in Paris and, with the new republic proclaimed, decreed the convocation of a Constituent Assembly to be elected by universal manhood suffrage. To make political participation accessible to the poor as well as to the rich, the government instituted salaries for parliamentary deputies. The provisional government decreed total liberty of the press and assembly; political clubs were opened everywhere. It freed those detained for debt and abolished the death penalty in political matters and slavery in the colonies.

The aspirations of the new government quickly dissipated. The republicans were divided on the social question, made more pressing by the poverty of the working classes. The socialists wanted to apply immediately their doctrine of social transformation; the majority, the moderate or bourgeois republicans, wanted only political reforms. In reality, a class struggle had developed between the workers and the bourgeoisie, and the first month of the republic came to be dominated by the antagonism between these two groups. The socialists acted first. Socialist leaders LOUIS BLANQUI, ARMAND BARBÉS, and FRANÇOIS-VINCENT RAS-PAIL founded several political clubs. By organizing popular demonstrations, they achieved the recognition of the right to work, the establishment of national workshops, and the creation of a commission for workers, charged with initiating social reforms. The worried bourgeoisie prepared to resist. The National Guard was reinforced by the creation of an auxiliary force comprised of young volunteers. A new socialist demonstration, on April 16, was met with the cry "down with the communists!" The elections (April 14–23) were a decisive victory for the moderates; they took 750 out of 900 seats in the Constituent Assembly. The socialist clubs then organized a demonstration on May 15. But the demonstrators were dispersed and the clubs closed.

This success inspired in the bourgeoisie the will to break definitively with the worker agitation. The closing of the national workshops offered them the occasion. The national workshops (*ateliers nationaux*) had been organized to occupy the mass of the unemployed. Instead of being production workshops, they became charitable ones, where workers were employed randomly at various tasks. More and more numerous and restless, they became an organized army of discontents. To put an end to the workshops and to disperse the socialist army, the assembly, on June 21, closed the national workshops. The workers responded with an insurrection (June 22–26). The assembly gave General CAVAIGNAC dictatorial powers. The worst street battle that had ever been seen in Paris lasted four days. It ended on June 26, with the crushing of the insurgents at their last retrenchment in the Place de la Bastille. Many were shot after the battle; 4,000 were deported by a simple decree.

The June Insurrection saved the bourgeoisie, but it proved fatal to the republic, whose main defenders, the workers, became irrevocably hostile because of the struggle and subsequent repression. On the other hand, the frightened bourgeoisie and peasants wanted a strong government, capable of protecting them against the revenge of the "reds." Out of this spirit, the Second Empire was born. The faction that had so much supported the republicans in February would, in less than a year, be lost and the application of the constitution would bring about the republican defeat.

The Constitution of 1848 was founded on the dual principles of the sovereignty of the people and the separation of powers. The legislative power was granted to a unique assembly, elected for three years by direct universal manhood suffrage; it passed laws, imposed taxes, and dealt with the budget; its members were inviolable. The executive power was delegated to a president, also elected by universal suffrage for four years. He could not be immediately reelected and was responsible to the assembly. For the presidency there were four candidates: Cavaignac, the candidate of the moderate republicans; Ledru-Rollin, the progressive republicans' candidate; Raspail, the socialists' candidate; and Louis-Napoléon Bonaparte. Louis-Napoléon had the only name in France that was known and popular. He also had behind him the parti de l'Ordre, a coalition of Orléanists, legitimists, and Catholics. He was elected by 5.5 million votes, far more than the other candidates. The president chose his ministers also from the parti de l'Ordre, thus taking executive power from the republicans.

In May 1849, the Legislative Assembly replaced the Constituent Assembly. The elections had been a disaster for the republicans. Henceforth, all power was in the hands of the enemies of the republic. At first, the president and the assembly worked together to destroy the government and the republican party. The party was attacked first. The military expedition sent to protect the Roman Republic against the Austrians was transformed into an enterprise against that republic. Having protested in vain, the democratic republicans, or Montagnards, on June 13 organized a demonstration that was put down by force. The leaders were arrested and the republican faction found itself in disarray. The victorious majority then attacked the government itself. It passed several laws designed to weaken it and strengthen the social order; the most durable was the Falloux Law, named for its initiator. It established freedom of instruction by suppressing the control of the university. The work principally of the Catholic faction, the law was especially advantageous to the clergy, who now gained the upper hand in education. The assembly then attacked universal suffrage. It passed the Law of 31 May: to qualify as a voter, it was necessary to have resided for at least three years within a community. The right to vote was thus taken away from 3 million citizens. The president and the assembly had united against the republicans, but the goal that each envisioned was not the same. In the minds of the majority leaders, the reactionary laws were only the preface to a monarchic restoration.

For his part, Louis-Napoléon had only one ambition: to keep power. The constitution forbade his reelection after his mandated term. In July 1851, he requested a revision of that article from the assembly, and then the "Prince-President" resolved to use force. The date of his coup d'état was set for December 2, 1851, the anniversary of the Battle of Austerlitz. The plot was boldly organized under the direction of MORNY, minister of the interior. During the night, while the police arrested the main opposition leaders, the president decreed the dissolution of the assembly and, to win over the workers, the reinstitution of universal suffrage.

An attempt at resistance was tried by some of the majority deputies. They voted for the dismissal of the president for perjury, but they were arrested en masse. Some republican deputies, including Victor Hugo and JULES FAVRE, tried to organize an armed resistance in the faubourgs. But the workers, hostile to the republic since the June Days and unarmed besides, remained indifferent. In the provinces, however, rigorous resistance was organized by secret republican societies, with uprisings in 15 departments. These attempts at resistance would assure the success of the coup d'état. To frighten the bourgeoisie, they were denounced by Bonaparte's supporters as socialist uprisings, or "jacqueries," dangerous to the social order. The repression for a long time disabled the republican party. Just as after the 18 Brumaire, the coup d'état was ratified by a plebiscite: officially there were 7,349,000 yes, 646,000 no. The mass of the population had approved, out of fear of the "reds." Again, the revolution led to despotism.

# The Second Empire

After the coup d'état of December 2, 1851, Louis-Napoléon, using the powers that were conferred on him by the plebiscite of December 20, promulgated a new constitution (January 1852). Inspired by the Constitution of the Year VIII, it was conceived to give the head of state dictatorial powers. Elected for 10 years, the president of the republic exercised at the same time executive power and most legislative power. He declared war, signed treaties, appointed all posts, alone initiated laws, and chose members of the Senate and the ministers, who only reported to him. He was responsible only to the people. To conceal the dictatorship of the head of state, the constitution kept the appearance of a representative and democratic regime: an assembly, the Legislative Corps, elected for six years by universal suffrage, deliberated and voted on taxes and legal projects presented by the president of the republic. A more important role was assigned to the Senate, composed of high dignitaries or members appointed for life by the Prince-President. "Guardian of the Constitution," he regulated, through "Senate decree," all legislation that it reviewed and examined before promulgation. Under the name of the republic, the constitution had, in fact, created a monarchy in disguise.

The reestablishment of the Empire was only a question of time. It took place before the end of 1852. After a second plebiscite, Louis-Napoléon was proclaimed "Hereditary Emperor of the French" and took the name Napoléon III (December 2, 1852). Public opinion had been prepared by a visit of the president to the principal provincial cities. In well-orchestrated demonstrations, he was acclaimed everywhere with cries of "Vive l'Empereur!" After a triumphal return to Paris, the plebiscite of November 20 decided on the "reestablishment of the Imperial dignity in the person of Louis-Napoléon" by a vote of 7,839,000 yes against 253,000 no. But nearly all those whom France considered eminent individuals were opposed.

The dictatorial nature of the regime was reinforced by a series of measures designed to subdue all opposition. A decree of 1852 reestablished preliminary authorization for all publications and warning and judicial proceeding for all offenses of the press. It instituted a new system of administrative repression: newspapers could be warned, suspended, or suppressed simply by the decision of the prefect. The constitution maintained universal suffrage, but the government controlled elections under the guise of circumspections, the banning of electoral meetings, and through official candidatures. Police surveillance extended to all matters, even conversations. Each citizen ran the risk of arbitrary arrest. The University of Paris was suspected of liberalism, and courses considered dangerous were suppressed, such as philosophy and contemporary history.

The government took advantage of every occasion to strike at all whom it deemed hostile, especially the republicans. In this way the Orsini assassination attempt (January 1853) by FELICE ORSINI served as a pretext for more restrictions. The government responded with a draconian law of general security that allowed the expulsion or internment without trial of hundreds of suspects, not connected to Orsini's crime. But the repression was relaxed progressively beginning in 1860. The causes for this development were found above all in the domestic problems caused by the war of unification in Italy and by the government's new commercial policy. The war (1859) undertaken to liberate northern Italy from Austrian control had as a consequence the almost complete loss of the pope's temporal power (1860); this profoundly displeased French Catholics. In another area, Napoléon III, a supporter of free trade, concluded a commercial treaty with England (1860) that considerably reduced the customs tariffs between the two countries; this treaty upset the industrial bourgeoisie who were attached to protectionism. A decree of 1860 inaugurated the new policy. The chambers would have the right to put forth an "Address" in response to the statement from the throne, so as to debate the government's general policy. A summary of their debates would be published in a *Journal officiel* that the newspapers could reprint; ministers without portfolio would represent the government before the Legislative Corps.

This was the first return to the practices of a parliamentary regime. But the emperor did not know how to follow through. Tired and irresolute, he never ceased wavering between the old authoritarian and liberal politics. France was subjected to an incoherent regime. The majority of the government's opponents remained irreconcilable. Some had meanwhile seemed ready to accept the empire on the condition that it would quickly become a liberal parliamentary regime. They would bring with them a certain number of Bonapartist supporters of such a transition. Thus, around 1866, the Third Party was born. Its leader was a republican who had come over to the empire, ÉMILE OLLIVIER, who was able to gain the emperor's confidence. Abroad, the empire found itself involved with increasing difficulties: the Mexican affair, the duchies, the Roman Question, and the resurgence of Prussian power at Sadowa.

To consolidate the regime, Napoléon III decided to grant further concessions to the nation. In 1867, the right of interpellation, or the right to question the government's acts, was granted to the deputies. In 1868, a law of the press abolished preliminary authorization for the establishing of newspapers, as well as administrative repression. Freedom of assembly was partially restored also.

Still, the regime was not a free parliamentary government. But the criticisms and success of an opposition emboldened by the same concessions would in time bring about a radical transformation of the regime. The clerical opposition did not end, but the republicans, for the most part irreconcilable, would use the new concessions to establish new newspapers and undertake an angry campaign of the press and of public meetings against the government. The strongest attacks were made by a young attorney, LÉON GAMBETTA, who, before the imperial judges, dared to disparage the coup d'état, and especially by an outspoken pamphleteer, HENRI ROCHEFORT, in his newspaper *La Lanterne,* which had great success. Each week Rochefort wrote epigrams about the regime and the imperial family.

The elections of 1869 would attest to the progress of the opposition. The partisans of the authoritarian regime—the "mameluks"—were put in the minority. The Third Party controlled the situation with 116 deputies.

To save his dynasty, the emperor undertook a complete transformation of the regime, in three stages between 1869 and 1870. A Senate decree of September 6, 1869, gave to the Legislative Corps legislative initiative and the full right of interpellation and amendment. The ministers would be responsible now not only to the emperor. A parliamentary ministry was formed (January 2, 1870), and a Senate decree of April 20, 1870, transformed the Senate into a second legislative chamber, but confirmed with the emperor most of its prerogatives. The emperor however, remained only "responsible to the French people to whom he always had the right of appeal." He retained the right to nominate and remove ministers who therefore were not strictly responsible to the chambers, a necessary condition of all parliamentary governments. The Senate decree established a strange combination of Caesarism by plebiscite and a parliamentary form.

The republicans had not been appeased. But the murder in Paris of a republican journalist, Victor Noir, by a Bonaparte prince failed to unleash a revolution. Worried, the emperor had recourse to a plebiscite. By a decree of April 23, 1870, voters were asked to approve the liberal reforms that had been operating under the constitution since 1860. In fact, they were being asked to vote for or against the Empire. Despite a strong republican campaign in favor of rejection, the plebiscite (May 8, 1870) was in the emperor's favor, with strong support from the peasantry, while Paris and the large cities voted no. With this plebiscite, the Empire seemed to be consolidated and established for a second time. But it would collapse three months later in the great disaster of September 4, 1870.

# SOCIAL, ECONOMIC, AND FOREIGN POLICY DEVELOPMENT DURING THE SECOND EMPIRE

The Second Empire was a period of intense economic activity. The development of business had various causes: the progress of science and technology, the growth of mechanization and large industry, construction of railways and telegraphs, and an influx of money from the discovery of gold mines overseas. To these factors, which were not limited to France, can be added the personal and systematic efforts of Napoléon III to stimulate economic activity. The emperor, as well as several of his advisers, had come under the influence of Saint-Simonism, for which economic progress was the condition for social progress. Seen from the point of view of economic achievements, the Second Empire seemed like a vast Saint-Simonian experiment. To stimulate economic life, increase the regime's prestige, maintain social peace, and give employment to the mass of workers, the Empire began a vast program of public works. Until this time, the role of the railway and the telegraph had been secondary. Their development had been suspended by the Revolution of 1848; the majority of industries were stagnant. To activate the construction of railways, a monopoly was granted to six large development companies for 99 years. Technological progress allowed the realization of two gigantic enterprises, the crowning glories of the Second Empire: the Mont Cenis Tunnel, the first great Alpine breakthrough, and the Suez Canal, the latest feature of a link between the West and the Far East. Important improvement works were also undertaken in such large cities as Lyon, Marseille, Bordeaux, Lille, and especially Paris. The work in Paris was done under the direction of the prefect of the Seine, BARON GEORGES-EUGÉNE HAUSSMANN, and involved the creation of great avenues and boulevards, squares and parks, and important public buildings. Thus transformed, Paris was, more than in the past, the European capital of luxury and elegance, and the later years of the Empire semed somewhat like an unending celebration.

All these enterprises required enormous capital investments. To this effect, the government encouraged the creation or the development of numerous credit establishments, including Crédit Lyonnais and the Société Générale. The

Paris stock market became, for a few years at least, the financial center of the world. This was the golden age of the Paris Exchange and of speculation. With these stimuli, economic activity increased. Though agricultural progress would remain slower, large industry made decisive advances. In place of the traditional protectionist system, the emperor encouraged free trade. In 1860, the treaty already mentioned was concluded with England, and similar agreements were reached with other European states. It was an economic revolution. To put in full light the progress realized by French industry, to gain foreign customers, and to encourage all initiatives, the government organized the Universal Expositions of 1855 and 1867. Both were very successful, particularly the second one.

With the rapid development of large industry, the question of the worker's place took on a new importance and a new acuity. During this period, workers were again subject to a discriminatory regime. They had to have a *livret,* or passbook, detailing their activities, their gathering places were under police surveillance, and they had no right to strike or assemble. They were powerless in relation to their employers, with insufficient wages, excessive work, and no unemployment, accident, or illness benefits. But Napoléon III wanted to ameliorate working conditions and bring workers over to the regime. He helped workers through charitable measures and encouraged mutual aid societies, assistance works, and credit institutions. The imperial government was resolved to accord the workers some of the freedoms that they demanded. In 1864, strikes ceased to be illegal, and in 1867, cooperatives were legalized. These measures were accompanied by an official tolerance toward workers associations. In the same period (1863–69), public instruction was instituted.

Despite these reformist measures, the workers moved toward internationalism as a form of organization and action. The idea of an international workers union was born of the meetings that took place in London, on the initiative of Napoléon III, in 1862, 1863, and 1864, between English and French workers. There then were elaborated the statutes of the International Association of Workers, the First International (1864). In the French section of the International, moderates were soon replaced by extremists, determined supporters of the republic. The bloody strikes that broke out near Saint-Étienne (1869) confirmed the break of the proletariat with the regime. The Empire ended with a rebirth of revolutionary socialism.

In foreign as in domestic policy, Napoléon III had ambitious plans. These were inspired, at least in Europe, by two powerful ideas that were at the same time contradictory, the new principle of nationalities, and the principle of natural boundaries. In the new Europe that Napoléon III dreamed of, the states would be founded on the free consent of the governed. The people of the same nationality, while they might be divided into distinct political groups or controlled by a foreign power, would be enfranchised or united in a unique state. Under the guise of the territorial reshufflings that would be brought about by the policy of nationalities, Napoléon III hoped to erase the humiliating treaties of 1815, and return France, at least partially, to its natural boundaries, the Rhine and the Alps. In this way, he obtained Savoy during the development of Italian unification, and he tried to take Belgium and the left bank of the Rhine during the process of German unification.

French foreign policy tended to disrupt the existing European political framework. Many of the emperor's advisers would disapprove. To have his ideas prevail, Napoléon III worked through secret negotiations, unknown to his ministers. French policy also was often one of disconcerting incoherence.

Before assuming the throne, in 1852, Louis-Napoléon declared: "L'Empire, c'est la paix." But the Second Empire, supported by the army and growing out of the Napoleonic tradition, could not bypass military glory.

France also was engaged, during this period, in wars inside and outside of Europe. In Europe, France participated in the Crimean War (1854–56), against Russia; the war in Italy (1859) against Austria; and the Franco-Prussian War of 1870–71. Outside of Europe, Napoléon III intervened in Africa, Asia, Oceania, and America. French troops were in Algeria (1857), Senegal, China and Indochina (1858–60), Syria (1860), and Mexico (1861–67).

Among these expeditions, the first were profitable and enlarged the colonial empire of France; in contrast, the war in Mexico was a costly and useless adventure that demonstrated the weaknesses and defects of imperial policy. Napoléon III intervened in Mexico under the pretext of financial claims; then allying with the Mexican clericals, he resolved to establish there an empire to the benefit of the archduke Maximilian, brother of the emperor of Austria. After taking Puebla and Mexico City (1863), Maximilian was crowned emperor (1864), but the Mexicans offered strong resistance aided by the mountainous countryside. Finally, with threats of intervention from the United States, French troops were recalled and Maximilian was abandoned (1867). This denouement dealt a rude blow to the prestige of the Empire.

In Europe, Prussian victories during the 1860s would engender a latent conflict between France and Prussia that led to a disastrous war for France. Imperial France exercised in Europe a sort of supremacy based on military prestige. This prestige was eclipsed by the Prussian victories. To this blow to national honor were added concerns for national security: the unification of Germany under the leadership of Prussia threatened French borders. But after the Prussian defeat of Austria at Sadowa (1866), Napoléon III had asked for nothing, although he was in a position to do so. He then decided too late to ask for compensations. Successively and in secret he asked for the Bavarian territory on the left bank of the Rhine (August 5, 1866), then with the objections raised by German premier Bismarck, he tried to assert the right of France to annex Luxembourg and Belgium, in return for which Napoléon III would not oppose the union of northern and southern Germany (August 20). With such a request, he renounced all his former protestations regarding the right of nationalities. The plan for annexation aroused German public opinion. For a moment, war seemed imminent. A transaction intervened: a conference in London made Luxembourg a neutral state. It was a setback for Napoléon and his policies. Bismarck skillfully took advantage of these mistakes, and France was presented as the only obstacle to German reunification. In both Germany and France there were factions that wanted war. On the French side, many, faithful to the classic tradition, considered German unification under Prussia as a mortal peril for France. Others, to restore the Empire's prestige, also wanted war, never doubting a victorious outcome. On the German side, Bismarck was inclined to believe that a war against France was the surest way to achieve unification.

The two sides made military and diplomatic preparations. In France, Napoléon III tried in vain to negotiate a treaty with Austria and Italy. At the same time, a plan for military reform was only in its preliminary states. Bismarck, suspecting France of seeking to form a coalition against Prussia, put forth a Hohenzollern candidate for the Spanish throne in 1870. To the French, the plan seemed a dangerous machination and, after categorical declarations by the imperial government, the candidate was withdrawn. Under pressure from his entourage and notably the empress, Napoléon III then ordered his ambassador to demand from the Prussian king a guarantee against any such candidate in the future. The king refused the request and, from Ems, telegraphed his statement to Bismarck. The latter soon published this Ems dispatch, editing it in a manner that seemed to insult France. Napoléon III fell into the trap. Despite the objections of Thiers and the Legislative Corps, France declared war (July 19, 1870).

The Franco-Prussian War lasted six months (August 2, 1870–February 1, 1871) and fell in two periods; the imperial war, marked by the destruction of the regular armies and the fall of the Second Empire, and the period of national defense, led by the republican government. In less than a month, the imperial armies were successively destroyed, blocked, or captured. Alsace was lost after the defeat of General PATRICE DE MAC-MAHON at Froeschwiller (August 6). The same day, Lorraine was invaded and the French were defeated at Forbach. The decisive operations took place at the fortified site at Metz, where the French army, commanded by General FRANÇOIS BAZAINE, was held up. The third shock was even more disastrous. Napoléon and Mac-Mahon formed a large army at Châlons, but, stopped at Beaumont on the Meuse, the French army was forced back to Sedan, where it was obliged to surrender (September 2). The emperor was taken prisoner with 100,000 troops.

The chief cause of France's defeat was the inferiority of its military command. The imperial regime had never suffered such a debacle. Upon the news of Sedan, on Sunday, September 4, Paris rose up in anger and overthrew the imperial government. The deputies in Paris proclaimed a republic and formed a government of National Defense. In the face of the exigencies of Bismarck, they would decide to continue the struggle, but the situation was desperate. Except for the army at Metz, there remained no regular army in France. Strasbourg capitulated on September 28 and Paris was in danger of falling. For five months, all efforts were made to protect the capital. The government had resolved to stay in the besieged capital while the deputy Léon Gambetta escaped by balloon to organize resistance at Tours. At that same time, Metz capitulated (October 27), allowing German forces to regroup and block the route to Paris of Gambetta's armies. To break the city's resistance, the Germans bombarded Paris with long-range cannons. After a brutal siege that took place during one of the coldest winters of the century, the government ended the futile resistance and signed an armistice at Versailles (January 28, 1871).

Among the direct consequences of the war, the two main ones were the achievement of German unification and the loss of French territory. On January 18, 1871, in the Hall of Mirrors at Versailles, William I was proclaimed emperor of Germany by the princes of the Confederation. During the armistice, elections took place in France for the National Assembly, which decided then to negotiate. It ratified the preliminary terms agreed to by Thiers after bitter discussions. France lost Alsace, except for Belfort, and the north of Lorraine, including Metz. It had to pay 5 billion francs over a period of three years and submit to German occupation for that period. These harsh conditions became definitive with the Treaty of Frankfort (May 10, 1871). The inhabitants of Alsace and Lorraine had the right individually to choose French nationality, on condition that they emigrate from France.

# THE THIRD REPUBLIC

The Government of National Defense was only provisional in nature. The question remained what type of government the country would have after peace was restored. In February 1871, during the armistice, France elected a National Assembly. But the issue that the electors had to decide was war or peace. The majority, including royalists and moderate republicans, voted for peace. The assembly, meeting at Bordeaux, named Thiers, the most visible political figure, as "head of the executive power of the French Republic," pending his constitutional approval.

Thiers soon faced an insurrection in Paris. This uprising is explained by the extraordinary circumstances that existed in that city. The Parisian population had come out of the hardships of the siege in a state of physical and moral fatigue. The misery was aggravated by the measures taken by the assembly. Workers had only their small salaries (1 franc 50 per day) as members of the National Guard on which to live. The assembly ordered the suppression of this salary, then decreed that the payment of debts, loans, and bills, suspended during the siege, had to resume. Parisians also suffered a blow to their pride, their republican convictions, and their patriotism. The election of a royalist majority to the National Assembly concerned them; the entrance of the Prussians into Paris—accepted by Thiers in exchange for Belfort—was an indignity and an affront, and the decision of the assembly to meet at Versailles instead of Paris drove them to exasperation.

The insurrection began with the uprising of May 18, 1871. Thiers wanted to remove the cannons placed at Montmartre, but the people attacked the troops that were sent, and seized and shot two generals. Thiers left for Versailles with the government and troops. Paris, left to itself, formed a new government, the COMMUNE, made up of extreme republicans and socialists. The Commune adopted the red flag and claimed to legislate for all France but soon found itself involved in a merciless struggle against the government of Versailles. The Prussians saw this as a second siege of Paris. After two months of fighting, the troops from Versailles succeeded in taking the city by surprise (May 20). Then began the Bloody Week (May 20–28), a bloody urban war in the midst of fires that the insurgents, in their desperation, had started. The Tuileries, part of the Louvre, the Assize Court, and the Hôtel de Ville were burned. The battle degenerated into a massacre and the Communards were killed without mercy. An estimated 20,000 perished. "I profoundly believe," said a mayor of Paris, "that more people were shot than were behind the barricades."

The repression lasted until 1875. Just as after June 1848, the extreme parties were for a long time left out of political life. Although victorious, the assembly did not dare immediately to reestablish a royal government. It let Thiers govern with the title president of the republic. He devoted himself above all to reconstruction. To the 5-billion-franc indemnity was added the crushing cost of supporting the occupying army, but after 1873, the reparations were paid and France was evacuated. To pay for the war, new funds were obtained by increasing indirect taxes, customs duties, transcriptions, monopolies on match sales, and the like. No less rapid was the military reorganization, put in place despite the occupation of territory by the Law of 1872, which intended to give France an army equal to that of Germany. The law established the concept of personal obligatory service.

The forces of the country strengthened, Thiers asked the assembly to rule on the form of government and proposed definitively to organize the republic. But the majority in the assembly wanted the restoration of a monarchy. On May 24, 1873, they forced Thiers to resign. He was soon replaced by Mac-Mahon, a soldier without political experience, destined to be only a figurehead. To prepare the way for a restoration of the monarchy, power was conferred on an aggressive ministry led by the duke de BROGLIE. The coronation of HENRY V was planned, but the pretender declared that, faithful to the white Bourbon flag, he could not

A barricade at the Porte Maillot during the revolt by supporters of the Paris Commune, May 1871 *(Hulton/Archive)*

accept the tricolor, symbol of popular sovereignty. This intransigence brought an end to the restoration. The paradoxical condition, as in 1850, remained in which the republicans were treated as enemies under the republic. Waiting for more favorable circumstances, the royalists wanted to keep power. Mac-Mahon was given the presidency for seven years (November 1873).

The Septennat regime was also that of moral order. Under the pretext of reestablishing "the moral order," the de Broglie ministry facilitated the clergy and, with new ardor, pursued the antirepublican campaign. Meanwhile, unrest was growing in the rest of the country. The Catholic faction caused serious problems in foreign affairs for the government with Italy by demanding the reestablishment of the temporal power of the pope, with Germany in attacking Bismarck's religious policy. The republican faction, despite the government's efforts, increased its influence day by day. Its progress was due principally to the efforts of Gambetta. In the assembly itself, the royalist coalition slowly came apart. Fearing the loss of power, the majority decided finally to begin debate on the constitutional laws.

The question of the government was resolved first. The word *republic,* introduced apropos of the form of election for the president, was accepted. The republic would have a majority voice. Legislative power was conferred on a parliament comprised of two chambers, the Chamber of Deputies and the Senate. The Senate, destined to play a moderating role, would comprise 75 permanent senators elected for life by the assembly, then confirmed by the Senate, and 225 senators elected for nine years. The Chamber of Deputies was elected by direct universal suffrage for four years. Being the only political power chosen directly by universal suffrage assured it an incontestable preponderance. Theoretically, the executive power rested in the president of the republic, elected for a seven-year renewable term by the chambers. The Constitution of 1875 established a parliamentary government. The actual head of government was the prime minister. But the ministry had to have the confidence of the parliament, to which it was accountable for all its actions; if it received a vote of no confidence from either of the chambers, it had to resign.

The elections of February 1876 sent a republican majority to the chamber. But the royalists would not accept defeat. Mac-Mahon broke with the republican ministry and formed a royalist one (May 16, 1877). The chamber voted an order of the day in defiance. Instead of resigning, the ministry obtained the dissolution of the chamber and began a struggle against the republicans, with their eyes on new elections. But in spite of the pressure from the government and the clergy, the republicans prevailed. Mac-Mahon accepted a republican ministry. The republican victory was won in 1879. Thanks to partial elections, the Senate also became republican. Mac-Mahon resigned and was replaced by a committed republican (January 1879). The republicans also controlled all public power and, until 1940, held power uninterruptedly. But they were also profoundly divided.

The struggles soon intensified between the radicals, whose leader was GEORGES CLEMENCEAU, and the moderates, led by Gambetta, and then after 1882 by JULES FERRY. Nearly always in power between 1879 and 1885, Ferry passed important educational laws, dissolved the Jesuit order, and developed the policy of colonial expansion. Attacked from the Right and the Left, and having become very unpopular, he was overturned in 1885.

Taking advantage of these parliamentary divisions, the adversaries of the government attempted a new assault against the republic: this was the crisis of Boulangerism (1886–89). The attempted overthrow, however, only helped to consolidate republican institutions. Political passions broke out violently again on the occasion of a grave judicial error, the Dreyfus affair (1897–99). A victim of anti-Semitism, a Jewish officer, Captain ALFRED DREYFUS, had been found guilty of high treason. Influential powers prevented for a long time a review of his trial. The affair divided France, some fighting "for justice," others for "the honor of the army." The adversaries of the government formed a nationalist faction.

The Dreyfus affair thus degenerated into a grave political crisis. The nationalists would try to march on the ÉLYSÉE (February 1899), but their attempted coup was stopped. The affair ended with Dreyfus being exonerated. Among the outstanding figures who rose to Dreyfus's defense were writers ÉMILE ZOLA and JEAN JAURÈS. Since then and until 1940, the republic was never seriously threatened and the electors never ceased to send a strong republican majority to parliament.

From 1899 to 1914, political evolution was made to the advantage of the parties of the Left, most often Radicals, Radical-Socialists, and Republican Socialists. On the extreme Left a socialist group formed a united Socialist Party (1905–20), then divided into rival factions. The division of parties and the parliamentary rivalries engendered ministerial instability, corrected somewhat by the frequent presence of the same ministers in diverse combinations. No party being strong enough alone to constitute a majority, all the ministries had to depend on majority coalitions that often fell apart soon after they were formed.

Under the conservative governments of the National Assembly and of May 16 (Seize Mai) in 1877, all forms of restrictions limited public liberties. After the definitive triumph of the republicans (1879), they were progressively reestablished and increased. In 1881, freedom of the press was established by law. Censorship and prior authorization were suppressed. The right of response, that is, the right to a rebuttal, was assured to the accused. In 1881, freedom of assembly was guaranteed by a law that authorized all meetings, including political ones, that made a simple declaration. That was superseded by a law of 1907 that removed all restrictions on public assemblies. A law of 1884 authorized the formation of labor unions and professional and student associations. Thus, workers associations, which had been more or less proscribed since the Revolution of 1789, were legalized. With the right to strike, union freedom would become one of the more effective means of action for the working classes. Freedom of conscience was fully established by a series of laws abolishing all previous restrictions. Religious freedom would be enlarged when churches became completely independent of the state by the Law of Separation of 1905.

The republicans undertook to complete the work of public education, begun by Guizot and continued by subsequent governments. Illiteracy in France was not uncommon, especially among women. Jules Ferry, minister of public instruction, first gained free primary education by a law of 1881. The following year, a law made primary instruction obligatory for all children aged six to 13, and strictly neutral from the religious viewpoint in public schools. The recruitment of teachers was assured by the creation of normal primary schools in all the departments of the country. Superior normal schools were created also for the formation of professors in the primary normal schools. Considerable attention was paid also to the education of adolescents leaving the primary schools. Adult education courses were offered and schools were established for technical, industrial, commercial, and artistic educations under the Astier Law of 1919. In secondary education, the principal reform was the creation of lycées and collèges for young women (1880). Secondary education for boys was also greatly modified in both curricula and methodology. A law of 1896 reconstituted the universities, now grouped regionally into faculties of sciences, letters, law, and medicine. Further reforms continued, with coordination of technical and secondary schools in 1946.

The reorganization of the military advanced as well. The Law of 1872 created the national army and decreed obligatory military service. Successive laws sought more equality in military status. Later modifications allowed exemptions but with the requirement of administrative or economic service in its place. A great plan of development in communications—railways, navigation routes, ports—was undertaken by the Third Republic, beginning in 1878. The policy of free trade, practiced since the treaties of 1860, was abandoned for protectionism. The large industries, which had always fought free trade, attacked it more vigorously after 1871. A law of 1892 established a double customs tariff, based on the advantages obtained from the foreign trading partner.

More and more numerous in the industrial regions, workers organized and fought to obtain improvement in their working conditions and in their lives. Under the Second Empire, workers had gained some union rights. These increased during the Third Republic (Waldeck-Rousseau Law, 1884). In 1895 the CONFÉDÉRATION GÉNÉRALE DU TRAVAIL (CGT) was formed and in 1902 was enlarged. The trade unionists were divided according to tactics: the revolutionaries sought continued confrontation; the reformists wanted to continue with gradual reforms. The influence of the revolutionaries was demonstrated by the violent strikes of 1908–09 and 1948. A cabinet post, the Ministry of Labor, was established in 1906. In terms of reforms, the workday was progressively reduced: in 1900, by the Millerand Law, workers gained a 10-hour day; in 1906, a weekly day of rest; in 1919, the eight-hour day; in 1936, the 40-hour week and a paid vacation of at least 15 days per year. In these matters, France was ahead of the other industrial nations, including the United States. A law of 1936 provided for collective bargaining and arbitration.

The most important social laws dealt with matters relevant to work assurances. The law of 1898 on work accidents made the factory owner responsible and liable. In 1910, compensation paid with contributions by the worker, the owner, and the state was instituted. This law was expanded (1928–32), with insurance for various risks, such as illness, injury, old age, and unemployment. In 1947, under the title of Social Security, these benefits were extended to the majority of the population. During the Third Republic, too, advances in French feminism and the French feminist movement were made. Building to an extent on the work of the Positivists (PROSPER ENFANTIN), Charles Fourier and, earlier, that of such writers as OLYMPE DE GOUGES, and moving in stages through the early 19th century and the Second Empire, the efforts of such feminists as FLORA TRISTAN, JEANNE DEROIN, LÉON RICHER, MARIE DERAISMES, HUBERTINE AUCLERT, EUGÉNIE POTONIE-PIERRE, and others sought to translate the vision of equal social and political rights into a reality. Strengthened by the extension of education to girls and women and by laws liberating the press from such restrictions as prior approval, feminist newspapers and journals flourished. One result was a further connecting of the French feminist movement with the international one. While various rights for women, including suffrage (not granted until 1946), would be achieved only later, the work of the 19th-century feminists formed an important basis for the achievements of the later era.

# CULTURAL AND SCIENTIFIC DEVELOPMENTS, 1850 TO 1914

The Second Empire (1852–70) for France was also a period of prodigious artistic development. A pivotal time, it bridged the traditional age with that of modernity. Leading architects (Charles Garnier, Henri Labrouste, Jacques Hittorf, Louis Baltard) embellished the new Paris created by Baron Haussmann, and in painting, while JEAN-AUGUSTE-DOMINIQUE INGRES, ALEXANDRE CABANEL, and WILLIAM BOUGUEREAU reigned with their classical and official style, GUSTAVE COURBET, with realism, led the way to the later impressionists (MONET, RENOIR, SISLEY, BAZILLE, DEGAS). The same contrasts were found in literature (THÉOPHILE GAUTIER, Théodore de Banville, Charles Marie Leconte de Lisle, CHARLES BAUDELAIRE, GUSTAVE FLAUBERT, EDMOND HUOT DE GONCOURT), historiography (JULES MICHELET), and music (JACQUES OFFENBACH, CHARLES GOUNOD). The first decades of the Third Republic were a fecund time for the arts in France. During the exhilarating Belle Époque, Paris became the world's artistic center, with all the arts involved. In painting, the ideas of PAUL CÉZANNE marked a fundamental break with the past. He was the precursor of fauvism and cubism, and an inspiration for expressionism. In architecture, LE CORBUSIER and others had already set down the precepts of the modern style. Musicians (CAMILLE SAINT-SAËNS, Jules Massenet, VINCENT D'INDY, HENRI DUPARC, Ernest Chausson, Emmanuel Chabrier) moved progressively from the Wagnerian form, culminating in the works of GABRIEL FAURÉ, DEBUSSY, RAVEL, and SATIE. Correspondingly, through the influence of Diaghilev's Ballets Russes in Paris, a current developed that led to experimental musical expressions (Stravinsky, the Groupe des Six). Philosophy moved from Comte's Positivism to the ideas of HENRI BERGSON, then those of ALAIN (Emile Chartier) and GASTON BACHELARD, while a strong religious current was expressed in the writings of JACQUES MARITAIN and GABRIEL MARCEL.

Literature found with the naturalism of ÉMILE ZOLA a way to attempt the systematization of reality. But the experience contrasted with symbolism (APOLLINAIRE, MALLARMÉ, RIMBAUD, VERLAINE), and then with the decadent writers (HUYSMANS, BLOY). The literary field was quite brilliant and, if writers such as PROUST, GIDE, MAURIAC, MONTHERLANT, Roger Martin du Gard, MALRAUX, and VALÉRY brought a classic conception to writing, others (Mallarmé, Rimbaud, LAUTRÉAMONT, Apollinaire) would write skeptically of humanist and bourgeois values.

Equally prodigious were the scientific achievements of this period. The work of LOUIS PASTEUR, MARIE and PIERRE CURIE, Louis-Antoine de Broglie, and Henri Poincaré made France a world scientific center and contributed to the formation of the modern era, which would already see such inventions as the cinema and the automobile. With the optimism expressed conceptually in the EIFFEL TOWER (1889), the Belle Époque, which evoked the joyful life of the Parisian cabarets and music halls (as represented in the art of HENRI DE TOULOUSE-LAUTREC), also signified France on the eve of the coming world conflict.

# FRENCH EXPANSION OVERSEAS SINCE 1850

The colonial expansionist movement begun by the July Monarchy developed broadly during the second half of the 19th century. As noted, Napoléon III increased the number of French involvements outside of Europe. The causes were generally the desire to extend French trade and to protect Catholic missions that were very active. It resulted in a notable growth in the colonial domain. In Africa, after Algeria was conquered, the colony of Senegal was established (1854–65) and Obok was acquired on the Somali coast (1862). A new colonial empire in Asia was founded with the conquest of Cochin China and the occupation of Cambodia (1858–67). In the Pacific Ocean, France took possession of New Caledonia (1853). Under the Third Republic, Jules Ferry was the premier who broke with the policy of *recueillement* (meditation) that had been observed since 1870. He succeeded in putting forth a methodical policy of colonial expansion the aim of which was to give France new commercial outlets, new refueling ports for its fleet, and the future grandeur of the nation.

North Africa all together formed a single natural region, the Maghreb; thus, French expansion in the area is explained. Diverse methods of colonization were successively applied in Algeria, which had already been occupied under the Second Empire (1857). A policy of assimilation (1870) was followed by one of autonomy (1896). Suffrage was extended in 1937 and was broadened after 1946, during the Fourth Republic. Tunisia, once a Roman province, was governed by a Turkish bey who was the vassal, or regent, of the Ottoman sultan. The area was coveted by the Italians. To cut short their attempts, Ferry quickly sent in French troops under the pretext of controlling the pillaging tribes. The bey, by the Treaty of Bardo (1881), had to recognize the French protectorate. Morocco, protected by its massifs, constituted, in the 19th century, a separate region. France and England disputed the preponderant influence, then, in 1904, in exchange for concessions in Egypt, England abandoned Morocco to French influence, except for the northern area reserved for Spain. German opposition arose, which it was necessary to appease by the cession of territories in the Congo (1911). At the Fez Convention (1912), the French protectorate of North Africa was officially recognized.

With the pacification of Morocco, all the important regions of the Maghreb were under French influence. Also, a great part of sub-Saharan Africa was explored and conquered by the French. In less than half a century (1855–1901), in the region of Niger, Sahara, Congo, and Lake Chad, France built an empire of 8 million square kilometers. In this area, French expansion took the form of exploitation as well as conquest. After the conquest and occupation of Senegal, the Niger River area was explored, and by 1893, the French had reached Timbuktu. French North and West Africa were connected by the occupation of oases in the Sahara. Between 1879 and 1885, by winning the confidence of the indigenous people, a French officer, PIERRE DE BRAZZA, established the French Congo in equatorial Africa. From bases on the Niger and the Congo, French expansion reached Lake Chad. The area was controlled by Muslim rulers whose power was overcome in 1901 by the French. Thus French domination extended over most of West Africa. In the Indian Ocean, France, which already held the island of Réunion, by 1895 had taken all the large island of Madagascar, which was declared a French colony. In Asia, in the second half of the 19th century, France occupied Indochina. After French missionaries were massacred there in 1858, Napoléon III sent an expedition that conquered Cochin China (1858–63). At the same time, the king of Cambodia, worried about threats from his neighbor, Siam (Thailand), placed his nation under a French protectorate (1863). The conquest of Tonkin and Annam was the consequence of French explorations (1866–68) toward China. When hostilities broke out (1882), Ferry acted decisively. A large fleet sent to the area obliged Annam to accept a French protectorate (1883). Then, after a brief conflict with China (1885), Tonkin was taken. In 1929, the area was designated as French Indochina, with some participation by the indigenous peoples in local governments. French culture, as in other colonial areas, was adopted by much of the population, and there was great exploitation of agricultural and mineral resources.

# INTERNATIONAL RELATIONS FROM 1871 TO 1914 AND WORLD WAR I

From 1871 to 1914, Europe was more often than not in a state of alert. The last 10 years especially were like an armed vigil. France could not resign itself to a defeat that also had cost it some of its territory. The Treaty of Frankfort thus had as a direct effect the perpetuation of Franco-German enmity. To this rivalry could be added another no less disturbing Austro-Russian rivalry, aggravated by incessant crises in the Balkans. At another level, the rapid development of large industry engendered or strengthened imperialism, the policy of economic or territorial conquests. Competition increased among the colonial powers England, France, and Russia, to which was joined Italy, then Germany. Such competition would create, initially, a double antagonism, Anglo-French and Anglo-Russian—which lasted until 1904–07—then an Anglo-German antagonism that became, at the beginning of the 20th century, one of the main issues of European politics.

These rivalries engendered a state of armed peace. Following the example of Germany, which sought to maintain its preponderance, all countries would strive to increase their armaments. Military budgets became more crushing by the day. The route to armaments could only increase the risk of war. Yet there were tentative attempts to preserve peace. Two international conferences took place at The Hague—in 1898 and in 1907—to study the possibility of limiting armaments and substituting arbitration for armed conflicts. But none of the powers unconditionally accepted arms limitations, and Germany opposed obligatory arbitration. The major powers continued on the course of arming and colonial expansion. At the same time as they built up their armaments, the rival powers sought allies. Germany set the example. In 1875, the Three Emperors' League was created as an alliance with Austria and Russia, designed in large part to contain France. After the Congress of Berlin (1878), however, this agreement broke down and in 1882 was replaced by the Triple Alliance. Italy, annoyed by the French occupation of Tunisia, moved closer to Germany and Italy's traditional enemy Austria. The result was the Triple Alliance, in which Germany was the strongest power.

France and Russia remained isolated and, as a result, in 1893, after advances made by France, the Franco-Russian Alliance was formed. A rapprochement between France and Italy was also achieved by 1896 and, in 1904, the Entente Cordiale was signed between France and England. This, in 1907, developed into the Triple Entente among France, England, and Russia. But France's treaties seemed threatening to Germany, and German policy henceforth would be to try to weaken them. To demonstrate that the accord of 1904 with England was inoperable, Germany abruptly vetoed France's actions in Morocco. While a French delegation at Fez negotiated an accord with the sultan, William II of Germany arrived at Tangiers and, in a menacing speech, took a clear stand against France (1905). This was accompanied by strong diplomatic pressure. Germany forced the resignation of THÉOPHILE DELCASSÉ, who for seven years had directed French foreign policy, and called for an international conference at Algeciras (1906) to rule on the Moroccan question. But the Algeciras Conference recognized French influence in Morocco. New incidents occurred. In 1911, French troops entered Fez to deal with a rebellion. Germany in turn sent a warship to Agadir, in southern Morocco, to constrain France. Seeking a peaceful solution, France, after initially difficult negotiations, reached an accord. In exchange for a free hand in Morocco, France ceded a part of the French Congo to Germany (1911). Far from achieving appeasement, however, this accord only increased Franco-German antagonism. Both sides increased production of armaments and the size of their armies and, in 1912, the Poincaré ministry sought new accords with Russia and England.

After the assassination at Sarajevo in Bosnia (June 28, 1914), the major powers moved toward war. In secret meetings (July 5–7), the risk of a major European war was weighed and accepted. The brusque Austrian ultimatum to Serbia (July 23) and subsequent declaration of war (July 28) was followed by Russian general mobilization (July 30), the German declaration of war on Russia (August 1), then on France (August 3). Soon, all the major French political parties, including the Socialists, united behind RAYMOND POINCARÉ's government in a *"Union sacrée."* But the union would be severely strained during the course of the war. Germany was sure of victory, and the German plan was to remove France quickly from the fighting, then turn against Russia. At first, it seemed that this would happen. The adversaries had all taken the offensive, and the first large battle, the battle of the borders, took place between August 20 and 30. The French offensive ventured into difficult terrain and was broken at Morhange in Lorraine and in the Ardennes. The left Franco-English wing, attacked at Charleroi and threatened with encirclement, succeeded in falling back but was defeated in its retreat (August 23). The result of the German victory was the loss of Belgium and the invasion of France. Through a rapid advance, the Germans hoped to surround their adversaries. But the French armies responded methodically, until the time when GENERAL JOSEPH JOFFRE halted the retreat and attacked at the Battle of the Marne (September 6–13). After six days of fighting, the Germans were forced to retreat to the Aisne. Meanwhile GENERAL JOSEPH GALLIENI defended Paris, which was never reached by German forces.

The two adversaries extended their battle lines to the seacoast. The Germans tried to take Calais, but their assaults were repelled at Ypres and at the Yser

(October-November). Thus, the campaign of 1914 ended without a decisive result on the western front. On the eastern front, the Russians were badly defeated by the Germans at Tannenberg but held out against the Austrians in Galicia. Masters of the sea, the Allies would take most of the German colonies. But through the Dardanelles straits of their Turkish ally, the Germans threatened to take Egypt.

The year 1915 was above all one of reversals for the Allies, underscored by the defeat at Gallipoli and setbacks on the western front. The war in 1916 was marked particularly by Verdun, the largest battle of the entire conflict. The furious German assaults on this French fortress lasted for five months but were finally broken by the French resistance led by General PHILIPPE PÉTAIN. The Allies went on the offensive in France at the Somme and in Italy on the Isonzo, while in the North Sea, the Battle of Jutland, the only major sea battle, took place between the German and English fleets. In 1917, the most difficult year of the war, submarine warfare and the Russian Revolution imperiled the Allies. But political and economic events would overshadow the military ones, with uprisings among the French and other Allied troops against the futility of the conflict. On the home front, around 100,000 French strikers protested the rise in the cost of living. These occurrences led to the fall of two cabinets and ceased only when Clemenceau came to power in November. On the western front, Germany had fallen back on powerfully fortified positions, the Hindenburg Line. From there, the Allied offensives at the Aisne and in Flanders could be broken. In the east, Austrian forces broke through the Italian front at Caporetto and invaded the Veneto. With Russia out of the war immediately after its revolution, German forces were freed up in the east. The entrance of the United States in April would not yet prove decisive for the Allies.

The last phase of the war in the west was entirely taken up by the great battle of France (March–November 1918). Germany concentrated all its strongest forces on the western front in the hope of striking a decisive blow at the Allies before the Americans arrived at the front. The German offensive lasted from March 21 to July 18. At three points, in Picardy, in Flanders, and on the Aisne, the English and French fronts were broken. The Germans would approach Amiens, Calais, and Paris itself, which they bombarded by air and with long-range cannons during the most critical period for the Allies. The battle was reversed between July 15 and 18 at the Second Battle of the Marne, the decisive event of the war at this point. Stopped completely by a new offensive in Champagne, the Germans retreated in the face of a large Allied advance. While the Allied forces increased their pressure, a new attack was prepared in Lorraine, just as the Central powers were suffering more defeats on the eastern front (September-October). To avoid a total disaster, Germany, now in revolution, accepted all the terms set by the armistice of November 11.

The peace terms were decided by the interallied Paris Peace Conference (1919). Twenty-seven nations were represented, but important decisions were made in conference by Clemenceau (France), Lloyd George (Britain), Orlando (Italy), and Wilson (United States). Clemenceau dominated the conference, and the defeated nations were admitted only to learn the terms that had been imposed. The Allies finally reached agreement in imposing the Treaty of Versailles on Germany and in forming the League of Nations to guarantee peace. By the terms of the Treaty of Versailles, Alsace-Lorraine was restored to France, and reparations were paid by Germany for the destruction of the war, which devastated especially France's northeast industrial area. Germany was also forced to accept the infamous war-guilt clause (article 231), the loss of territory in the east, and a drastic reduction in its armed forces. The war, which took millions of lives, cost the French 1,350,000 casualties, thus greatly affecting the national population of the next generation.

# THE INTERWAR YEARS

France emerged from World War I as a victor but economically and demographically weakened. The most pressing issue immediately after the war was the stabilization of the franc, which, by 1926, was set at one-fifth of its prewar value. This issue especially affected the bourgeoisie. Politically, moderates and conservatives came together in the BLOC NATIONAL (1919), while at the Congress of Tours (1920), a schism occurred between socialists and the communists. The war had encouraged a rallying to nationalist values, and the 1919 elections brought overwhelming conservative success. A new electoral system benefited parties that formed coalitions. This caused great difficulty for the Left. The Socialist Party, isolated by its break with the Union Sacrée in 1917 and internally divided over support for the revolution in Russia, did not want to compromise with the bourgeois parties. The Radicals were forced to negotiate with the conservatives, thus forming the Bloc National, whose leaders, ALEXANDRE MILLERAND and Georges Clemenceau, stressed the continuation of wartime unity. A government was formed led by Millerand and, after 1922, by Raymond Poincaré.

It pursued an aggressive foreign policy, especially regarding Germany and reparations, and culminating in 1923 with the occupation of the Ruhr. Public concern over these policies led to an electoral victory of the center-left alliance, the CARTEL DES GAUCHES. By 1924, however, the various parties, which differed on social policies, agreed to work together for peace through collective security, especially through the League of Nations. This led in 1925 to the signing of the Locarno Pact, by which Germany recognized France's eastern borders, with a British and Italian guarantee. France also signed defensive treaties with Poland and Czechoslovakia.

After the interlude of the Cartel des Gauches (1924–26), and in the face of the great economic crisis, the Union Nationale government was formed under the leadership of Poincaré. Meanwhile, as stated, the Left had split at the Congress of Tours, with the majority of delegates voting to adhere to the Communist International, thus greatly reducing the membership of the Section Français de l'Internationale Ouvrière (SFIO). While the Socialist Party was now established as the major proponent of social reform, it would remain internally much divided on tactics. This division increased when, after the failure of the general strike in 1920, the major trade union, the CONFÉDÉRATION GÉNÉRALE DU TRAVAIL, also split, with a communist minority forming the CGT Unitaire (1922).

Another new force in politics was Christian Democracy. In 1924, some former members of the prewar Sillon movement, which had been dedicated to reconciling Catholic doctrine with the principles of the Revolution of 1789, founded the Popular Democratic Party. Although the Catholic Church had condemned the Sillon movement, it now accepted the Popular Democrats, whose numbers, however, remained small.

The most threatening problems to the nation, inflation and a series of unbalanced budgets, seemed resolvable only when the Poincaré government achieved financial stabilization. But this ended after the October 1929 stock market crash and resultant worldwide depression. The crisis affected France later than other industrialized nations, and so 1930 was still a prosperous year. But while the crisis was less severe in France than elsewhere, it was more prolonged and the decade would be one of continual crises. In May 1932 the electorate turned toward the Left for a solution and the result was its greatest success since before the war. But change, while attempted, was made more difficult by political instability. The international situation, too, was a cause for alarm. In July 1932, at Lausanne, Switzerland, the major powers had recognized both Germany's inability to pay war reparations and its right to rearm.

In January 1933, Adolf Hitler became German chancellor and in October withdrew Germany from the Geneva disarmament conference. By June 1934, with French military expenditure at its lowest, the government considered increasing arms production. Within the middle class these domestic and foreign factors resulted in a loss of confidence in the government and in democracy. The Right sought to unite nationalism, clericalism, economic liberalism and anticommunism. German Nazism was reflected to an extent in France in the growing influence of extreme right-wing leagues in the 1930s. Beginning with the Jeunesses patriotes, formed in 1924, followed by the Croix-de-feu (1927), their popularity reflected the lack of public confidence in the official parties, tainted by a series of political scandals, the most notorious being the STAVISKY affair (1934), in which the fraudulent financial activity of a naturalized Ukrainian Jew, apparently involving leading political figures, provided an excuse for a campaign by the extreme Right that combined its usual themes of xenophobia, anti-Semitism, and antiparliamentarianism. An outlet was found in the ACTION FRANÇAISE, a monarchist and anti-Semitic movement and newspaper founded by CHARLES MAURRAS at the time of the Dreyfus affair. The movement was influential in organizing a massive right-wing demonstration in Paris (February 6, 1934). After a night of violent fighting between the Right and Left, 15 people were killed and approximately 2,000 injured. For a time the republic seemed in some danger as Prime Minister ÉDOUARD DALADIER resigned, but the rioting was contained and the Action Française went into decline. The insurrection, which could have divided France, led decisively to the Front populaire, a coalition of left-wing parties that won the general elections of 1936. For the first time, France had a socialist prime minister, LÉON BLUM. Although his regime was not of long duration (he resigned in 1938), it was marked by particularly important developments, including the reduction of the workweek to 40 hours, the introduction of paid vacations, and the inclusion of women in the cabinet. However, the political tensions of the period caused open hostility in certain areas to Blum and his government, mixed with anti-Semitism from certain factions.

In foreign affairs, despite little initial fear of Hitler and German aggression, construction on the Maginot Line (1929–40), fortified defenses designed by ANDRÉ MAGINOT, continued. However, the threat did grow greater, as Germany's militarization of the Rhineland (1936), in violation of the Treaty of Versailles and the Locarno Pact, which stipulated permanent demilitarization, was followed in 1938 by the German invasion of Czechoslovakia and the *Anschluss* with (annexation of) Austria. After that, there was a major shift in French public opinion. In 1933, Foreign Minister LOUIS BARTHOU had reaffirmed France's ties with the smaller eastern European states and sought to bring Italy and the Soviet Union into the system. His assassination, however, in 1934, undermined that policy, and the events of 1935–36, including Italy's invasion of Ethiopia, aroused tensions. France came more to depend on British support in areas of foreign policy, and it was partly due to this that the Blum government followed British advice and adopted a policy of nonintervention in the Spanish civil war (1936).

Then on September 1, 1939, Germany invaded Poland. On September 3, France and Great Britain declared war, and the new world conflict erupted. World War II began rather uneventfully in France, with eight months of "phony war," lasting until May 10, 1940. Up to that point, the French, with their British allies, remained solidly entrenched along the fortifications of the Maginot Line. This apparent absence of danger also encouraged internal political dissent, in contrast to the Union Sacrée of 1914. Then, the German blitzkrieg of Belgium and the advance on Paris began. Over 1,850,000 Allied prisoners were taken and some 92,000 servicemen were killed, a figure that testifies to the intensity of the fighting in some sectors. By June 12, the French command was demanding an armistice. Marshal MAXIME WEYGAND in particular seems to have been concerned with preserving the army intact to secure social order and prevent a communist takeover after hostilities. He vigorously opposed Premier PAUL REYNAUD's proposal to capitulate to avoid further useless sacrifice and to allow the option of later continuing the war from the overseas empire.

On June 16, Reynaud was pressured to resign in favor of Marshal Philippe Pétain, the hero of Verdun, and the next day, Pétain announced his intention to seek an armistice. The terms were harsh, with France being divided into four zones, the most important being the Free Zone, with its capital at Vichy, and the Occupied Zone, which covered Paris and the north. Pétain set up headquarters at Vichy, while General CHARLES DE GAULLE, then relatively unknown, fled to London, where he made his appeal on the BBC on June 11 to the French people to continue the struggle. On July 10, the National Assembly voted full powers to Pétain. The Third Republic came to an end, being replaced by the État français, the most autocratic regime in modern French history. Its slogan "Travail, Famille, Patrie" replaced the familiar republican "Liberté, Egalité, Fraternité" as the Vichy regime sought to remold the nation's political and social structures.

Meanwhile, in such areas as Alsace, the Nazis pursued a policy of Germanization. At Vichy, Pétain's right-hand aide was PIERRE LAVAL, who, although removed from office in 1941, was returned to power in 1942. Deportations, especially of French Jews, soon became a policy of the regime. As war continued, the

RESISTANCE movement increased because of patriotism and such factors as the instituting of obligatory work service, or Service de Travail Obligatoire (STO), which occurred in February 1943. Under that policy, 650,000 French workers were sent to Germany to serve the German war effort. In France, civil war almost broke out between the Resistance and the Milice, the Nazi-led Vichy police, even after the Normandy invasion (June 6, 1944). The fighting between the often Communist-led Resistance, which began essentially in the urban areas, and the Milice of the Vichy regime continued throughout the country.

During this time, a guerrilla army, known as the *maquis*, had been formed in the mountains of central and southeastern France. Beginning in 1942, a closer relationship developed between the underground and the Free French in London. The paramilitary units of the Resistance were also combined under a single command and came to be called the French Forces of the Interior (FFI). Reprisals were often taken against collaborators (although active collaboration involved only a small minority), and when de Gaulle arrived in France in 1944, he quickly moved to restore centralized authority. The Resistance, persuaded by leaders like JEAN MOULIN, had declared their support of General de Gaulle and worked with the Free French forces under his command. On August 25,

French crowds cheer American troops as they enter Paris, 1944. *(Hulton/Archive)*

Paris was liberated (to a great extent, the city, rising up on August 19, had liberated itself) and on August 15 American troops landed in the south and advanced up the Rhône valley. By the end of the year, most of the country was free of German troops. In the face of the onslaught, the Vichy regime collapsed. De Gaulle's French Committee of National Liberation was recognized by the Allies as the de facto provisional government of France.

# THE FOURTH
# AND FIFTH REPUBLICS

For a little over a year after the liberation of Paris, President de Gaulle governed France almost without restrictions. He was assisted only by an advisory Consultative Assembly, representing the various political parties, Resistance groups, and labor unions. On October 21, 1945, French voters, including women for the first time, elected a Constituent Assembly and in a concurrent referendum rejected a return to the Third Republic. By November, however, it became clear that the Communists favored a unicameral legislature for the new government, with almost complete powers, while the MOUVEMENT RÉPUBLICAIN POPULAIRE (MRP), the successor to the Christian Democrats, sought a strong executive branch. When the Socialist Party gave its support to the Communist position, de Gaulle abruptly resigned from the presidency (January 20, 1946) and announced his withdrawal from politics, hoping that the politicians would call him back to power. This did not happen and the left-wing parties proceeded to draft a constitution. This first draft was rejected in a referendum (May 5, 1946), and a second Constituent Assembly was elected on June 2. A referendum of October 13, 1946, produced a positive result with a bicameral legislature being established, resembling that of the Third Republic.

The new Constitution of the Fourth Republic guaranteed equal gender rights, the right to work, and the right to education, health care, and social benefits.

The effects of the war, however, combined with the lack of a broad national consensus, presented the new government with many difficulties. The earlier coalitions had broken down by 1947, and changes in Soviet foreign policy made it difficult for cooperation to occur between the Communists and other parties. The cabinets of 1947 to 1951, therefore, lacked the full support of the French Communist Party, on the one hand, and that of the newly organized Gaullist movement, the RASSEMBLEMENT DU PEUPLE FRANÇAIS (RPF), on the other. The center coalition of Socialists, Popular Republicans, and Radicals, which adopted the label Third Force, maintained a small majority in parliament but dealt successfully with two challenges, in 1947 and 1948. The Communist-led CONFÉDÉRATION GÉNÉRALE DU TRAVAIL (CGT), the main labor organization, twice started a series of strikes, but police measures in each case averted a larger conflict, and the Communists backed off rather than start a civil war. The Third Force also put in place a plan for the democratic structuring of the nation's economy, developed by a group of experts led by JEAN MONNET.

The postwar reconstruction plan, guided by Keynesian economics, depended on state intervention and assistance. The general elections of June 1951 posed a serious threat to the unstable Third Force coalition, and from 1951 to 1956, France was governed by a right-of-center coalition of Radicals, Popular Republicans, and Independent-Peasants. A large segment of de Gaulle's followers supported the government, and in response he repudiated the RPF and again withdrew from politics. This coalition, too, was hindered by "immobilism," or lack of solidarity and broad national support. But this was a period of the greatest commercial expansion since the Second Empire, with industrial production rising 10 percent annually and the rate of productivity increasing more rapidly than that of any other nation. The era of prosperity that it inaugurated came to be known as the "Trente glorieuses," or "Thirty glorious" years of economic increase (an analogy with the "three glorious" days of the July 1930 Revolution).

A continuing problem for the Fourth Republic was colonial conflict. The new government had given new freedoms to the colonial populations and had reorganized the French Empire as the French Union. Colonial territories were allotted seats in the French parliament, and government investment in these areas increased. Nevertheless, those same areas experienced a rise in nationalism. In December 1946, a full-scale rebellion occurred in Indochina led by the Communist HO CHI MINH. The unpopular and costly war continued to drain the French treasury and morale until 1954, when, after the French military defeat at DIEN BIEN PHU, the National Assembly accepted the plan of the new PIERRE MENDÈS-FRANCE government to end the conflict. The Geneva agreements of July 21, 1954, left North Vietnam under Communist control, while the South remained under nationalists. French influence there and in Laos and Cambodia greatly diminished. Since 1945, a strong independence movement had also been developing in Tunisia and Morocco. Mendès-France averted conflict in those regions by negotiating independence for both protectorates (1956).

Next, violence broke out in ALGERIA, where rebels began a campaign of guerrilla warfare and terrorism (November 1954). But the Mendès-France government fell before it could deal with this issue. On December 2, 1955, Premier EDGAR FAURE dissolved the National Assembly before the end of its five-year term, a procedure that had not been implemented since 1877. The subsequent elections of 1956 failed to lead to a coalition, while the Communists made significant gains and the new Union de Défense des Commerçants et Artisans de France (UDCA, known also as the Poujadist movement), of PIERRE POUJADE, representing shopkeepers and artisans, emerged with almost 2 million votes and 52 seats. A majority was achieved only by bringing together the Socialists, MRP, Radicals, and Independent-Peasants with the Socialist GUY MOLLET as premier. Mollet's cabinet lasted 16 months and dealt with the Algerian rebellion by concentrating 400,000 French troops in the region without, however, halting the rebellion. The war caused financial problems that, coupled with, inflation, forced the Mollet government to resign. It was replaced by new coalitions (1956–57) that also collapsed, bringing the government system to a crisis.

On May 13, 1958, when the new premier, PIERRE PFLIMLIN, was due to seek confirmation of his cabinet, demonstrators gathered in Algiers to protest his alleged intention to seek a negotiated peace in Algeria. The demonstration turned into a riot; the mass of demonstrators went to the government head-

quarters and proclaimed a self-appointed Committee of Public Safety as the
new governing authority in Algiers. The uprising was the product of conspiracies planned by right-wing factions representing the colons, or French settlers
in Algeria who feared that Paris would abandon them as they struggled to keep
Algeria, French. They were supported by sympathetic elements in certain army
circles. Antiparliamentary groups, too, had been plotting actions in Algiers and
Paris, hoping to subvert the republic and put an authoritarian system in its
place. Some of these activists looked to a return of de Gaulle to power, even
though he had refused to encourage them. After the initial coup d'état of May
13, Gaullist agents infiltrated the Committee of Public Safety in Algiers and
gained the support of General RAOUL SALAN, the military commander in Algeria. For two weeks, Paris negotiated with the committee. The Pflimlin cabinet
and the National Assembly at first were determined to uphold the regime, but
many politicians soon turned to de Gaulle as the only person with the stature
to save the republic from the various hostile forces. On May 15, General de
Gaulle announced that he would assume power if called by the nation and, on
June 1, the National Assembly voted by a margin of 329 to 224 to approve him
as premier, with a grant of almost unlimited powers for six months.

De Gaulle quickly used his emergency powers to create the Fifth Republic.
To achieve national unity, he appointed to his cabinet members of all the important political parties except the Communists. MICHEL DEBRÉ led the committee
that drafted a new constitution that was approved overwhelmingly in a referendum of September 28, 1958. Combining features of a presidential and a parliamentary system, the Fifth Republic vested much more authority in the
executive than had the Third and Fourth Republics. The premier was named
by the president, although he could be overthrown by a formal vote of censure
in the National Assembly. The president, in turn, could dissolve the assembly
and call for new elections and could even assume emergency powers in times
of crisis, thus making the Élysée the locus of power.

The constitutional referendum offered the French overseas territories (but
not Algeria, which was technically considered a part of France) an opportunity
to vote for independence or for autonomous status in a newly organized French
Community. In subsequent years, a number of the members received sovereign
status, while voluntarily retaining loose ties with France in the French Community. The elections of November 1958 resulted in a strong move to the right.
A new Gaullist Party, the Union pour la défense de la République, won a near
majority in the assembly, while the Communists lost heavily. Using his transitional powers, de Gaulle issued decrees that devalued the franc (December
1958) and issued a new one, and the government instituted reforms (1959) to
encourage housing and improvement of the nation's administrative, judicial,
and educational systems.

The situation in Algeria, however, remained unresolved. The Right, which
included military leaders, the colons, and their sympathizers in France, believed
that de Gaulle would not permit French withdrawal and would favor keeping
Algeria an integral part of France. But de Gaulle seemed convinced that Algerian nationalism, like anticolonial movements elsewhere, was irrepressible and

would have to be accepted. In September 1959, he spoke for the first time of Algerian self-determination. To nationalists and some Gaullists, like JACQUES SOUSTELLE and General Jacques Massu, this was seen as a betrayal, and on January 24, 1960, European settlers in Algeria, with the backing of certain army officers, openly revolted. The revolt was soon suppressed and de Gaulle then announced plans (November) to offer Algeria a choice between independence and autonomy. More than 75 percent of French voters in a referendum of January 1961 approved this proposal. In April there was another revolt in Algiers led by the army, which was suppressed. Two generals, Salan and Jouhaud, then set up an anti-Gaullist underground, the OAS (ORGANISATION DE L'ARMÉE SECRÈTE), and launched a terrorist campaign in Algeria and France with the intention of preventing a cease-fire. In France, various groups, including the left-wing parties and committees of intellectuals and artists who had long supported French withdrawal, organized huge protests against OAS terrorism. On March 18, 1962, negotiations with the Algerian nationalist leaders culminated in an agreement signed at Évian-les-Bains, which ended more than seven years of warfare and conceded full independence to Algeria.

It was a victory for the Algerian National Liberation Front, while granting concessions protecting French oil interests and air bases in the region. On July 3, after referenda in France and Algeria, Algerian independence was formally recognized. By the end of the year, more than 750,000 European settlers had fled Algeria for southern France. At the end of the conflict, Premier Debré resigned and was succeeded by GEORGES POMPIDOU, a close associate of de Gaulle. In September 1962, Pompidou proposed a referendum providing for direct election of the president by universal suffrage. Almost all political parties disapproved, then the National Assembly censured the government and brought about Pompidou's resignation. De Gaulle responded by dissolving the assembly and proceeding with the referendum, which passed (October).

In the November elections for the National Assembly, the UNR won a majority of the seats. Economically, the Fifth Republic continued to prosper and progress, benefiting from membership in the Common Market (European Economic Community), although de Gaulle blocked the development of supranational institutions that would limit national independence. His attitude toward Great Britain remained antagonistic, and he strongly opposed that nation's entrance into the EEC, owing to concern with the economic strength of the British Commonwealth (1963). While supporting the Atlantic Alliance, de Gaulle insisted on French equality with Britain and the United States in leadership, rejecting any hint of French "vassalage." He refused to place a part of the French Mediterranean fleet under NATO command and demanded that NATO headquarters be removed from French soil. He decided also that France must develop its own nuclear force and proceeded to build a nuclear striking force (*force de frappe*). In 1960, France conducted its first atomic explosion in the Sahara and continued testing, refusing to sign the international atomic Test Ban Treaty of 1963.

Believing that international tensions were due to power relationships and not ideology, he rejected the American cold war policies against communism and sought closer diplomatic and economic relations with the USSR and the countries of Eastern Europe, and in 1964, France recognized mainland China. He sought, too, a rapprochement in Europe, particularly with West Germany, and maintained close relations with West German chancellor Konrad Adenauer. At the same time, he denounced U.S. policy and involvement in Vietnam.

In the elections of 1965, certain dissatisfaction with de Gaulle's policies became apparent. While trained professional bureaucrats governed the nation, de Gaulle presided like a republican monarch. But the public became skeptical and restless with this arrangement. The two leading opposition candidates, FRANÇOIS MITTERRAND, representing the Left, and JEAN LECANUET, representing the center, were supported by much of the electorate. In December, de Gaulle received only 55.2 percent of the vote. In the parliamentary elections of March 1967, the opposition, led by Mitterrand and PIERRE MENDÈS-FRANCE, formed a coalition of the noncommunist Left and the election results were a setback for the Gaullists. After the election, Pompidou, who was given authority to govern by decree for six months, sought to stimulate the economy and appeal to both workers and farmers, but without great success. In 1967, de Gaulle appeared to intensify his nationalistic foreign policies, especially in terms of NATO and the Common Market. He also involved France more in the Middle East and made his celebrated visit to Canada, during which he stated *Vive le Québec libre* ("Long live free Quebec"), causing widespread resentment.

The Gaullist party, now renamed the UDR, had a small majority in parliament and there seemed to be a sense of stability at home. The great upheaval of 1968, therefore, came as a surprise for which no one was prepared and proved to be the regime's strongest challenge. It began with the student demonstrations in March on the Nanterre campus of the University of Paris; by May, it had spread to the SORBONNE. Eventually hundreds of thousands of students from universities and secondary schools around the country became involved. In Paris's Latin Quarter, student activists built barricades and fought with riot troops and the police, whose violence initially caused great sympathy for the students. On May 13, 800,000 students marched in Paris, parading black and red flags but maintaining no single political allegiance. Antiquated and overcrowded conditions in French schools and highly centralized educational policies and structures were the initial causes, but the Gaullist regime and bourgeois society itself came under violent criticism from the demonstrators. The Communists were caught off guard and dismissed the participants as political adventurers and extremists, while de Gaulle went on a previously scheduled trip to Romania and Pompidou promised educational reforms.

By mid-May, a new element emerged as thousand of workers throughout France engaged in sit-down strikes and demanded reduction in hours, increases in wages and benefits, and a role in management. Eventually, nearly 10 million workers paralyzed the economy. But a worker-student alliance was not achieved and was rejected by the labor unions and political parties. De Gaulle, on May 18, promised reforms and a referendum, but on the 28th, was advised by Pompidou that he must either call for new elections or resign. De Gaulle disappeared the next day, and while the press speculated as to his whereabouts,

French students protest in the Latin Quarter of Paris, May 1968. *(Hulton/Archive)*

he flew to Baden-Baden, West Germany, to seek the support of General Massu, commander of the French army in Germany. On May 30, he told the French people that he would not resign, and his speech was followed by a massive demonstration by right-wing and conservative groups and the middle classes. An agreement was reached with labor, and by mid-June production was resumed in most factories. The June elections resulted in a large Gaullist victory, and many French rallied to the general who, resentful of Pompidou's independence during the crisis, dismissed the premier and appointed MAURICE COUVE DE MURVILLE in his place.

While these events ended in a triumph for de Gaulle, in the following year he would face defeat. Having proposed a plan to restructure the Senate and to decentralize the country's general administration he asked for a vote of confidence from the nation in April 1969, through a referendum, in both the plan and in himself. He stated unequivocally that he would resign if a substantial majority did not approve the adoption of his proposal. When only 47.6 percent of the voters gave their support in the referendum of April 27, he resigned.

Although there had been speculation about France's political stability after de Gaulle, the transition proved to be orderly and uneventful. Pompidou won the election and assumed office in June. He chose as premier the Gaullist JACQUES CHABAN-DELMAS, who was replaced in 1972 by PIERRE MESSMER. That same year, Pompidou reversed de Gaulle's policy and began negotiations with Great Britain regarding the latter's entrance into the Common Market, which was achieved on January 1, 1973. In March 1973, the general election for the National Assembly produced a union of the Socialists, led by Mitterrand, the Communists, led by GEORGES MARCHAIS, and a faction of the Radical Party of the Left. The government's strength in the assembly was thus reduced to the benefit of the Union of the Left. The Socialist Party's strength increased when the PSU (Parti Socialiste Unifié) joined its ranks (1974).

On April 2, 1974, Pompidou died. In the May elections, the Left had an advantage and in the first round of voting Mitterrand won, but in the face-off in the second round with VALÉRY GISCARD D'ESTAING, the leader of the Independent Republicans, Mitterrand was defeated by an extremely narrow margin. Giscard's first choice as premier was the Gaullist JACQUES CHIRAC, but after great differences, the latter resigned in August 1976 and was replaced by RAYMOND BARRE, whose program of economic austerity caused a great drop in Giscard's popularity by early 1977, and, in the 1978 elections, the Right won by only a small margin over the Left, which was divided by a split between the Socialists and the Communists. Barre continued as premier until 1980, although it had become clear that his austerity measures failed and had caused inflation.

Several important developments took place during Giscard's tenure, including the endorsement of France's nuclear deterrent policy by the Communists in 1977 (they had also abandoned the doctrine of the dictatorship of the proletariat in 1976), and by the Socialists in 1978, the founding of the Republican party (May 1977) and of the UDF (February 1978), and the president's meeting with Leonid Brezhnev in Warsaw, Poland, in May 1980.

In the next presidential election (May 10, 1981) Mitterrand was elected at a time when inflation was at 14 percent and unemployment at 8 percent. His platform included the nationalization of major industries and most of the banking system, the decentralization of government, and an increase in public expenditures. The Socialists won at the expense of the Communists, and their victory was repeated in the National Assembly in June. Nonetheless, the new cabinet, led by PIERRE MAUROY, a Socialist, included four Communist ministers. Mitterrand, with a Socialist majority in the National Assembly, implemented several policies: raising the minimum wage and increasing benefits, nationalization, and abolishing capital sentencing. Caught by inflation, however, especially after 1986, and with right-wing control of the assembly, he appointed Jacques Chirac as prime minister (they were sharply divided over the question of privatization), the first example of what the French called "cohabitation." In 1979, under Giscard, France had joined the European Monetary System, in which the écu (European Currency Unit) was established, but beginning in 1981, Mitterrand gave even more emphasis to moving France toward a federalist position on Europe. This policy was strengthened when Finance Minister JACQUES DELORS became president of the European Commission. In 1986, the Single Europe Act was signed with the projected creation of a single market by 1993. The Maastricht Treaty (February 1992) on the European Union extended the EU parliament's powers and sought common foreign and defense policies and a single currency. It was approved in France by referendum in September of that year.

Mitterrand also left a great architectural legacy in Paris that includes the Pyramide du Louvre, the Arche de la Défense, the Opéra de la Bastille, and the new Bibliothèque Nationale. In foreign affairs, in his first term he made an important official visit to Israel (March 1982), addressed the German Bundestag (January 20, 1983), and held the first summit of francophone countries (February 17–19, 1986). There was, however, also the regrettable incident of the sinking of the Greenpeace organization's vessel, *Rainbow Warrior* (July 10, 1985), which had been sent to the South Pacific to protest French nuclear testing in the region. The incident, while minimized by Premier LAURENT FABIUS and other French officials, caused great outrage in New Zealand (which arrested two French agents) and other countries. Later, in January 1984, the Greens were constituted as a united party and began to show electoral strength in several French regions (in 1988 Premier Michel Rocard appointed the ecologist Brice Lalonde as secretary of state for the environment). A later event of Mitterrand's first term was the trial of Klaus Barbie (May–June 1987), the wartime Gestapo leader in Lyon, awakening bitter memories and recriminations of that period.

In May 1988, Mitterrand was elected to his second term as president of the republic. He appointed MICHEL ROCARD as premier, while within the Socialist ranks, Pierre Mauroy defeated Fabius for the position of party first secretary. The Socialists returned to the National Assembly with a reduced majority (June). In November, a referendum was held on New Caledonia, one of France's last colonies, in the South Pacific. It recognized the Matignon agreement, which had provided for eventual independence of the region.

The entire issue brought into direct conflict the demands of France's liberating and civilizing mission with those of French greatness and honor. France has always sought to play a determining role in world affairs, including preserving peace. In fact, this is reinforced by France's presence in other former colonial regions, especially in Africa. Even after independence had been granted to the 13 African states (Cameroon, Togo, Senegal, Sudan, Ivory Coast, Dahomey, Upper Volta, Niger, Mauritania, Central African Republic, French Congo, Gabon, and Chad, along with the island of Madagascar), the influence of France in Africa did not wane but simply took other forms. Under military agreements, armies and gendarmeries in each state were built up and trained by the French. France was allowed to keep bases at strategic points, and an intervention force, stationed in France, was held at the disposal of the new governments. To perpetuate the French language and a francophone and Francophile elite, French citizens who wished to perform civilian instead of national military service were sent out, usually as teachers, while African students were encouraged to study in France. Immigration from the African states to France also continued. The diversity of the population within France and the issue of the growing Muslim population was underscored by the controversy of Muslim females' wearing headscarves in school (October 1989). (In March 2004 the French government banned the display of religious symbols in state schools, which includes wearing of headscarves by Muslim females.) The increasing presence of Islam heightened the multicultural aspect of French society and the debate over whether assimilation should be a criterion for French citizenship and the full exercise of political rights. In January 1991, France joined the coalition of powers in the Gulf War against Iraq, causing the resignation of Defense Minister Jean-Pierre Chevènement over protest of the American "big stick" policy and what he viewed as U.S. manipulation of the U.N. Security Council. Traditionally, too, France's sympathies had usually been with the Arab states of the Middle East, and the French government favored an embargo rather than a war, together with an international conference on the region, including the Palestinian question.

Mitterrand, in May 1991, appointed ÉDITH CRESSON as France's first woman prime minister. She had earlier served as agricultural minister (1982), and her appointment to the premiership coincided with a growing awareness of the great underrepresentation of women in French political life. Only 33 women had been elected to the National Assembly in 1988 and 35 in 1993. As the 50th anniversary of women's securing the right to vote approached, attention was focused on the organization Réseau Femmes pour la Parité, which demanded "liberty, equality, and parity." The Réseau also campaigned for the transfer to the Panthéon of the remains of OLYMPE DE GOUGES, author of the *Declaration of the Rights of Women* in 1791 (those of MARIE CURIE were eventually transferred).

The elections of March 1993 produced a landslide for the Right and constrained Mitterrand to recognize cohabitation as a fact of life in French politics as he appointed a banker, ÉDOUARD BALLADUR, as premier. In May, the French law on nationality was revised, reflecting the growing debate on cultural assimilation; likewise, changes were made in those laws dealing with the right of asylum. In December 1993, through pressure from the Right, a revision of the Falloux Law of 1850 on private education was pushed through parliament. It provoked a strike by public-sector teachers and was criticized by both Mitterrand and the cardinal-archbishop of Lyon, who feared that it would reopen the "school law." On January 13, 1994, however, the reform was censured by the Conseil Constitutionnel for violating the principle of equality between citizens, and a mass demonstration of 900,000 in Paris on January 16 endorsed their ruling. The same month, Georges Marchais resigned as secretary-general of the French Communist Party (PCF), and the party also abandoned its doctrine of democratic centralism.

The end of Mitterrand's term (1994) saw the resignation of Rocard as first secretary of the Socialist Party (June), the foundation of the Independent Ecologist Movement (September), and the passage of a law against political corruption (December). In the May election of 1995, JACQUES CHIRAC defeated the Socialist candidate, LIONEL JOSPIN, for the presidency of the republic in the second round of balloting, thus ending the second period of cohabitation. He chose as premier ALAIN JUPPÉ, a graduate of the ENA and former foreign minister under Mitterrand. Several reforms were then undertaken, notably that of Social Security, which was strongly contested (November–December 1995) and the military (emphasizing professionalism and suppressing national service). In April 1997, Chirac dissolved the National Assembly to move the general elections forward, even though he had a conservative majority. The move was counterproductive, however, as the Socialists won more seats than any other party on the Left. Chirac had to name the Socialist Jospin as premier. An "Achilles' heel," as it has been described, of the Constitution of the Fifth Republic is its provision that while the president of the republic is elected for a seven-year term, that of the National Assembly is only five years; hence, an incumbent president might have to deal with an assembly controlled by opponents but might not want to risk dissolving it and calling for new elections. This could result in cohabitation.

During this period, the growth of the extreme right-wing National Front, which had erupted onto the political scene after 1981, became an issue and, its gains in the presidential election of 2002 also produced national concern. In that election, Chirac was given a second mandate, defeating Jospin (who subsequently retired from political life) for the presidency. Chirac continued the foreign policy of previous governments, asserting both European unity (France, along with most of western Europe, adopted the euro as its sole currency in January 2002) and France's independence. France, for instance, did not support the U.S. invasion of Iraq (2003), and instead sought the path of peaceful negotiations and a more rigorous inspection process. Antiglobalization demonstrations by many French and other Europeans show the growing concern not only with the political and cultural, but also the environmental consequences of that phenomenon.

# MODERN FRENCH CULTURE

From the later years of the 19th century until the present, France continues to be a determining force in Western cultural developments. In architecture, the short-lived Art Nouveau style ended the eclectic forms of the 19th century, and 20th century architects sought to use new materials and concepts for the new era, such as the cantilever and ferroconcrete. Although iron and concrete had been used, for example, at the Paris Exhibition of 1867, and were fairly familiar by 1890, it was not until AUGUSTE PERRET in 1903 perfected the techniques of modern building that they became typical. French architects advocated a simplified style that eliminated all extraneous ornamentation and stressed clean lines and function. Important in the use of ferroconcrete were Tony Garnier and Le Corbusier. The Centre National d'Art et de Culture Georges Pompidou (known as the Pompidou Centre, or the Centre Beaubourg) is not only a locus of contemporary artistic theory and practice (with library, cinema, facilities for musical and acoustical research) but, in its revolutionary design and conception, is a signature building of the high-tech, postmodern era. Modern French painting, especially of the 20th century, has origins going back to the last impressionist exhibition (1886) and the beginnings of the postimpressionist style. The works exhibited at the Paris International Exhibition of 1900 emphasized the break with the past and presented the aspects of modern art. In 1905, the Fauvist exhibition was held in Paris during a period that saw the exhibition there of such seminal artists as HENRI MATISSE, GEORGES ROUAULT, Pablo Picasso, MAURICE UTRILLO, MAURICE DE VLAMINCK, and RAOUL DUFY. Cubism, like fauvism, also represented the advent of the modern era. Expressionism, as represented by the works of JEAN DUBUFFET, PIERRE SOULANGES, Georges Mathieu, and others is a direct product as well of the conceptual changes developed in French painting. By midcentury, France also was a center of performing arts, and Pop and op art. Modern French sculpture can be seen to begin with the work of AUGUSTE RODIN, who suggested that the modern era must evolve a completely new concept of that art form. When Constantin Brancusi arrived in Paris from Romania in 1903, he formulated what would become that dominant concept for the new century. Also, art from Africa and Micronesia, in which the material dictates form, opened a new vision for 20th-century sculptors, many of whom were based in Paris. Cubism contributed to this vision with mobile sculptures and Dadaism, founded by MARCEL DUCHAMP and others and emanating from France and a product clearly of the challenges and issues of the modern era, contributed to the variety and broadness of 20th-century French art.

It is difficult to classify modern French literature by a dominant outlook, style, or philosophical movement. Unlike the literature of previous eras, it defies classification and, instead, is often a response to such modern phenomena as world war and the development of such sciences as psychology and sociology. The center of interest, for example, of such 20th-century French authors as ANDRÉ GIDE, MARCEL PROUST, JEAN GIRAUDOUX, and ALAIN FOURNIER was the human mind itself. While neglected by the symbolists of the late 19th century, the novel was embraced by such early 20th-century French writers as ANATOLE FRANCE, ROMAIN ROLLAND, MAURICE BARRÈS, and PAUL BOURGET. EDMOND ROSTAND and Maurice Maeterlinck revived romantic drama, but it was in French poetry most of all that a new modern spirit especially emerged. Guillaume Apollinaire is the most outstanding example, with his sense of both sentimentality and irony. There was also, for the first time in centuries, a revival of Catholic writing, as represented by the poems of CHARLES PÉGUY and particularly by the poetry, dramas, and essays of PAUL CLAUDEL. André Gide, too, found inspiration in Christianity, and the influence of his Protestant background is quite evident in his works. The most important French writers of the first half of the 20th century include the novelists Marcel Proust and Colette and the critic and poet Paul Valéry. A later generation, including François Mauriac, Jules Romains, the poet St.-John Perse, the playwright Jean Giraudoux, and the poet, playwright, and essayist Jean Cocteau, all contributed to France's leading reputation in modern literature. The postwar period, dominated at first by the surrealists, was an era of significant change and growth. Led by ANDRÉ BRETON, writers such as LOUIS ARAGON, Benjamin Péret, PAUL ÉLUARD, Robert Desnos, and RENÉ CHAR fill the ranks of the finest poets of the period. The French stage at this time was dominated by the enormous talents of JEAN ANOUILH, EUGÈNE IONESCO, Samuel Beckett, and JEAN GENET. The latter, especially by his concepts, themes, and style, led the way to the literary forms of the post–World War II era. After the war, existentialism, a successor to surrealism, was chiefly identified with its French proponents. JEAN-PAUL SARTRE, SIMONE DE BEAUVOIR, and ALBERT CAMUS rank not only as its greatest and most original thinkers, but are among the finest of 20th-century French writers. De Beauvoir's writings, too, are considered landmarks in the development of modern feminism. Clearly, France's determining and premier cultural role in the modern era is demonstrated by the cultural achievements of the past century, and the role that France has historically played will continue to be expressed in a broad spectrum of ideas and creativity consistent with the centuries-old reputation of the nation and its people.

# HISTORICAL
# DICTIONARY
# A–Z

# A

## About, Edmond (1828–1885)
*writer and journalist*
Born in Dieuze, Edmond About wrote essays about the theater before he became recognized for a collection of short stories (*Les Mariages de Paris*, 1856; *Les Mariages de province*, 1868); inspired by depictions of contemporary mores described by HONORÉ DE BALZAC in his works. Evoking imaginary situations, often suggested by scientific progress (*Le Roi des montaignes*, 1857; *L'Homme à l'oreille cassé*, 1862), About's writings are lively and bright accounts. A political journalist, known for his clear and incisive style, he was outspoken in his anticlerical views. Edmond About was elected to the ACADÉMIE FRANÇAISE in 1884.

## Académie française (French Academy)
The oldest of the five academies that form the INSTITUT DE FRANCE (French Institute), which was founded by Cardinal RICHELIEU in 1634, the Académie française was at first composed of a group of literary figures who were joined, little by little, by statesmen, lawyers, and doctors. Officially authorized in 1635 by LOUIS XIII, the Académie française held its first meetings at the homes of its members, then at the Chancellery, and finally at the LOUVRE up to the REVOLUTION of 1789. It was dissolved in 1793, then reestablished in 1803 when NAPOLÉON I installed the Académie française in the Collège de Quatre-Nations, today the site of the French Institute. The Academie française includes, at its full meetings, 40 members who have the tasks of editing and updating the *Dictionnaire de la langue française* (the present ninth edition of which includes words done since 1986) and to award the prizes for literature, history, and achievement. In 1980, the Academie française elected MARGUERITE YOURCENAR as its first female member.

## Action française
A political movement of the extreme Right, founded during the Dreyfus Affair by CHARLES MAURRAS, JACQUES BAINVILLE, and LÉON DAUDET. The movement published a newspaper, *L'Action française*, which was at first a bimonthly. The founders of this journal created a Committee of French Action, which was nationalistic and anti-Dreyfusard (see ALFRED DREYFUS) and soon transformed it into the League of French Action (Ligue d'action française). Under the influence of Maurras, the movement sought "integral nationalism," the reestablishment of a monarchy that was "hereditary, antiparliamentary, and decentralized," and the establishment of the Catholic Church as the guarantor of order. The vendors of the newspaper *l'Action française* (which became a daily in 1908) quickly evolved into a royalist street force known as the *"camelots du roi."* Pope Pius XII lifted the 1926 condemnation of the Action française movement by the church in 1939. Having given support to the VICHY regime during WORLD WAR II, the newspaper itself was banned after the Liberation. Later, its supporters regrouped and rallied to the *Aspects de la France* of Pierre Boutang.

## Adélaïde, Eugénie-Louise, princess d'Orléans (Madame) (1777–1847)
*sister of Louis-Philippe*
Born in PARIS, the daughter of the LOUIS-PHILIPPE DUC D'ORLÉANS (Philippe Égalité) and Louise-Marie de Bourbon-Penthièvre, Princess Adélaïde was the sister of King LOUIS-PHILIPPE I. She emigrated in 1792, accompanied by her governess, Mme de Genlis, and returned to France in 1817. She played a role in placing her brother on the throne in 1830 and continued to serve as his adviser during his reign (see REVOLUTION OF 1830).

## Ader, Clement (1841–1925)
*engineer and inventor*

Called the "Father of Aviation," Clement Ader was born in Muret. In 1870, he manufactured a balloon that was launched successfully and then, in 1890, a heavier-than-air apparatus (*Éole*) powered by steam; it flew for a distance of 50 miles on October 9 of that year at Armainvilliers. The flight was not sustained, however, as he continuously brushed the ground from a height of about 20 centimeters, Ader's later attempts, supported by the War Ministry, were also unsuccessful. Greatly discouraged, he destroyed his plans and his inventions. Clement Ader coined the word *avion* to describe his various models: Avion I, Avion II, and so forth.

## Adjani, Isabelle (1955–  )
*actor*

Known for her sensitive character portrayals, Isabelle Adjani was born in PARIS and had her stage debut at the COMÉDIE FRANÇAISE (*L'École des Femmes, Ondine*). She very soon had a film success with *La Gifle* (1974) and above all *L'Histoire d'Adèle H.* (1975), directed by FRANÇOIS TRUFFAUT, for which she received an Academy Award nomination. In that film, she demonstrated her extraordinary skill at portraying complex, intelligent heroines, especially in period pieces. Since then, her star has not dimmed, as she played the main role in *Les Soeurs Brontë* (1979), *Possession* (1981), and *Quartet* (1981), winning the best actress award at the Cannes Film Festival for the last two. Other films include *L'Été meutrier* (1983), for which she won the Cesar Award, *Le Métro* (1985), and *Camille Claude* (1988), a film based on the story of the sculptor whose life was overshadowed by that of her lover, AUGUSTE RODIN, and for which Isabelle Adjani again received an Academy Award nomination for best actress. Her later films include *La Reine Margot* (1994).

## Africa, French in

The French colonial presence in Africa (aside from ALGERIA) consisted in two large administrative areas: French West Africa and French Equatorial Africa.

French West Africa, once one of the largest colonial zones in Africa, presently consists of seven independent nations: Benin, Ivory Coast, Senegal (formerly French Guinea), Mali and Mauritania (formerly French Sudan), Burkina Faso (formerly Upper Volta), and Niger.

The Europeans first explored the west coast of Africa in the 15th century with the arrival of the Portuguese. French influence began in the 17th century with the establishment of trading posts on the Senegal River. Between 1854 and 1865, the French explored the area around the river and entered present-day Senegal and Mauritania.

Territory was taken from the local Wolof and Serer peoples and from the Tukulor Empire, which controlled an area along the Niger River in what is today Mali. In the 1860s the French established outposts on the coasts of Guinea and the Ivory Coast. In 1883 they established a protectorate over the area around Dahomey.

After 1876 the French pushed further into the interior toward the Nile. But prevented from extending further by the British, they concentrated on establishing a colonial empire in West Africa. By the 1890s, they had control of an area extending from Algeria in the north to the Gulf of Guinea in the south. In 1895, these areas were organized into the administrative unit of French West Africa, which officially would consist of several colonial areas defined in the early 20th century.

During WORLD WAR II, French Africa was initially loyal to the VICHY regime, but in 1942, after the Allied invasion of North Africa, French West Africa became Free French territory under CHARLES DE GAULLE.

French Equatorial Africa, the former French colonial possession in central Africa, consisted of the present-day nations of Chad, Gabon, Central African Republic, and Republic of the Congo. The French presence in this area dates back to 1839, when a settlement was built on the coast of what is now Gabon. Colonial development occurred rapidly, and by 1862, the French had consolidated their power in this coastal region. Later in the century, several explorers, notably PIERRE-PAUL SAVORGNAN DE BRAZZA, charted and explored the interior of central Africa. At the BERLIN WEST AFRICA CONFERENCE of 1884–85, the major European powers decided upon a mutual division of Africa. France, by 1891, had control of most of Gabon and an area north of the Congo River. Between 1894 and 1916, despite strong resistance from the African inhabitants, the French conquered most of what is now the Central African Republic and Chad. In 1910, all these areas were organized into an administrative unit known as French Equatorial Africa. A capital was established at Brazzaville.

During World War II, French Equatorial Africa was the first French overseas possession to break with Vichy and rally to the Free French. In 1946, the four former colonies of this area were made overseas territories within the French Union and their inhabitants were given French citizenship. By 1956, the right to vote was extended to all inhabitants. In 1958, the four territories voted to become autonomous republics within the newly created French Community.

## Aguesseau, Henri-François d' (1668–1751)
*magistrate*

Born in Limoges, Henri-François d'Aguesseau was appointed advocate general of the parlement of PARIS in 1691 and in 1700 was named procurator general. Becoming chancellor in 1717, he was exiled to Fresnes from 1718 to 1720 for having opposed the economic system of JOHN LAW, and again from 1722 to 1737 for his hostility to the influential Cardinal GUILLAUME DUBOIS. By his important ordinances regarding donations (1731), testaments (1736), and substitutions (1747), Aguesseau contributed greatly to the codifying and unifying of the parlement's legislation.

## Aiguillon, Emmanuel-Armand de Vignerot, duke d' (1720–1788)
*statesman and minister*

A great-nephew of Marie-Madeleine, duchess d'Aiguillon, a niece of Cardinal RICHELIEU (who also had encouraged the development of charities and missions in Canada), Emmanuel-Armand de Vigernot served as governor of BRITTANY in 1753. There, he brought about the opposition of the parlement and the nobility when he attempted a fiscal reform in the central government. This caused his recall in 1769. After the fall of the duke of CHOISEUL, Aiguillon was put in charge of foreign affairs, forming a triumvirate with MAUPEOU and TERRAY. He could not, however, preserve the accomplishments of

CHOISEUL or prevent the partition of Poland; he fell from power early in the reign of LOUIS XVI. His son, Armand de Vignerot du Plessis de Richelieu (1761–1800), also duke of Aiguillon, was a delegate to the Estates General in 1789 who, after having opposed the measures of the Legislative Assembly, left for exile in Germany.

## Aix-la-Chapelle, Congress of

The Congress of Aix-la-Chapelle, meeting between September 29 and November 21, 1818, brought together the powers of the Quadruple Alliance, who, at the request of the French Restoration government, decided to end the occupation of France by that alliance's allied troops (see PARIS, TREATY of). After the beginning of the evacuation of these forces (October 9, 1818), the French plenipotentiary, ARMAND-EMMANUEL DU PLESSIS DE CHINON, duke de Richelieu, was invited to participate in the congress and France also joined the Quadruple Alliance.

## Alain (1868–1951)
### (Émile-Auguste Chartier)
*philosopher and essayist*

A student of JULES LAGNEAU, Émile-Auguste Chartier, or Alain, as he is known, was born in Mortagne-au-Perche, Orne. He taught philosophy in the provinces and in Paris, his ideas appearing in his *Propos* (1908–19), the *Dépêche de Rouen*, and the *Nouvelle Revue française*. Alain wanted to reintroduce ethics into philosophy, that is, reflect on our conduct so as to use our wisdom, passion, and senses, and guide our imagination and heart by the spiritual. He believed that liberal-democratic radicalism would save humankind from all tyrannies. His spiritualism was anti-intellectual but optimistic. Following the example of Socrates, Alain wished to be a master of thought and an educator, and in this regard he viewed existence through a quasi-phenomenological approach. His principal works include *Système des beaux-arts*, 1920; *Mars, ou la guerre jugée*, 1921; *Éléments d'une doctrine radicale*, 1925; *Souvenirs concernant Jules Lagneau*, 1925; *Les idées et les âges*, 1927; *Propos sur le bonheur*, 1928; *Idées*, 1932; *Vigiles de l'esprit*, 1942; *Les Dieux*, 1947.

## Alain-Fournier (1886–1914)
### (Henri Alban Fournier)
*novelist*

Born in La Chapelle-d'Angillon, Cher, Henri Alban Fournier, or Alain-Fournier as he is known, left Berry and Sologne, where he had spent his early years, to come to Paris to prepare for the entrance exam to the École normale supérieure. There, with his classmate JACQUES RIVIÈRE (who would marry his sister Isabelle), he began an important *Correspondance* (1905–14, published 1926–28) in which he discussed his literary tastes. His only novel, *Le Grand Meaulnes* (1913), became a success when the author was lost in combat in September 1914 during WORLD WAR I. His remains, discovered and identified in 1991, were interred in 1992 in the national cemetery at Saint-Rémy-la-Calonne (Meuse).

## Albigensians

Albigensians (Albigeois) was the name given to the Cathari (Cathars), or followers of Catharism, in the region of Albi and extended to all such believers in the Midi region of France during the 13th century. Catharism, a Manachaean belief that spread throughout many parts of Europe (the Balkans, Lombardy and central Italy, the Rhineland, Catalonia, and Champagne), was particularly strong in the Midi (Albi, Toulouse, Carcassonne) and was considered a heresy by the Catholic Church. As such, its followers, known for their austerity, charity, and high sense of morality, were the objects of a crusade launched by the Catholic Church (1209) and of the Catholic Inquisition (1229). The principal leaders of the Albigensians included many nobles of the LANGUEDOC. The crusade called by Pope Innocent III and led by Simon de Montfort, a French military figure, led to brutal massacres and the appropriation of Cathari properties. But, the last Albigensian stronghold, at Montségur, only fell, however, in 1244, and the Cathar Church survived in Languedoc until the 14th century. The involvement of king Louis VIII of France (1226) in the attacks on the Albigensians, and the subsequent Treaty of Paris (1229), gave to the Crown the territories conquered by de Montfort. The crusade against the Albigensians therefore marks the entrance of royal French authority into the regions of southern France.

## Alembert, Jean Le Rond d' (1717–1783)
*philosopher, writer, physicist, and mathematician*

A major figure of the Enlightenment, Jean Le Rond d'Alembert was born in Paris, the natural son of the writer CLAUDINE GUERIN DE TENCIN. With DIDEROT, he was one of the authors of the *Encyclopédia*, in which he edited the *Discours préliminaire* (1751), as well as numerous scientific and philosophical articles, all marked by the spirit of the Age of Reason. Using the three principles of Newton, d'Alembert also wrote his most important work, a treatise on physics and the science of mechanics, *Traité de dynamique* (1743), in which he describes movement and equilibrium between two bodies, and presents the principle that bears his name (the resultant of the forces impressed upon a system is equivalent to the effective force of the entire system). In the following works (*Traité de l'équilibre et du mouvement des fluides*, 1744; *Théorié générale des vents*, 1745), his studies led to the first conception of the calculus of partial differential equations. In *Précession des équinoxes* (1749), he proposed the first analytical solution to the precession of the equinoxes. He also discovered the theorem that bears his name, in which all algebraic equations have at least a real or an imaginary root. His other writings include *Éléments de musique* (1752), *Mélanges de littérature et de philosophie* (1753), and *Éloges académiques*. A rationalist, he opposed religious absolutism and spoke out for tolerance and for the access to scientific knowledge for all. His correspondence with VOLTAIRE was published by CONDORCET. D'Alembert was elected to the Academy of Sciences in 1741 and to the ACADÉMIE FRANÇAISE in 1754.

## Algeria, French in

The French presence in Algeria dates to the early 19th century, when, in 1830, King CHARLES X sent an expedition against Algiers. This action had been inspired by earlier naval blockades of the Algerian ports by the French and other European powers in response to Turkish corsairs that had been attacking merchant vessels. French occupation and annexation of the region (1834) soon followed. The objective of the annexation was to colonize the territory. But this immediately provoked fierce resistance from the local tribes, who had been accustomed to the earlier indirect rule of the

Ottomans. The tribal leader, Abd al-Qatar, fought an effective campaign against the French until he was defeated in 1847. At that point, France began the colonization of Algeria in earnest, and consequently there was a huge influx of European settlers. The French encouraged this by confiscating or purchasing at low prices Algerian-owned properties. Algeria became an overseas department of France, controlled effectively by the European minority (colons), who formed a privileged elite. The colons soon developed a modern economy similar to that in France. Agriculture too was geared to the French economy, with large estates producing wine and citrus fruit intended for export to Europe. Additionally, all colons, whatever their economic status, shared a strong belief in an *"Algérie française."* The Muslim population, however, although benefiting from economic development and social services, remained a disadvantaged majority without political rights and with many restrictions. Their population continued to grow and reached 5 million by 1930. That of the Europeans had grown from 36,000 in 1840 to nearly a million.

Algerian nationalism developed after WORLD WAR I (1914–18) among groups who sought parity with the Europeans. In the 1920s and 1930s, Ferhat Abbas and Ahmed Messali Hadj were among the more prominent nationalist leaders. In 1936, the French government presented a plan (Blum-Violette Proposal) that would have granted full equality to Muslim Algerian war veterans and professionals, but it was vetoed by colon deputies in the French National Assembly. In response, the Algerian nationalists organized militant anti-French movements during WORLD WAR II (1939–45). By 1946 the two most important of these were the Union démocratique du manifeste algérien (UDMA) of Ferhat Abbas and the Mouvement pour le triomphe des libertés démocratiques (MTLD) of Messali Hadj. In 1947, the French government approved the Algerian Organic Statute, which established Algeria's first parliamentary assembly, with an equal number of European and Algerian Muslim delegates. But this satisfied neither group and proved ineffective. By the early 1950s, militant nationalists were preparing for an armed revolt. In March 1954, AHMED BEN BELLA, an ex-sergeant in the French army, formed with others in exile the Front de Libération Nationale (FLN). By November, the group had begun attacks on military and government installations. Guerrilla actions intensified and, by 1956, 400,000 French troops were stationed in Algeria. Terrorism and guerrilla tactics on the part of the nationalists brought counterterrorist actions from the French military and the colons. By 1956, the conflict had spread to the cities, producing harsh reprisals from the military and government authorities. International criticism of France increased because of this policy, and there was a wide division of public opinion in France. In May 1958, the colons and French army officers joined to overthrow the French government in Algiers, charging it with vacillation. A Committee of Public Safety demanded the return to office of General CHARLES DE GAULLE. Once in power, however, de Gaulle realized that the war could not be won and, in 1959, announced his intention of allowing Algerians to choose between independence or continued association with France. The colons and their supporters revolted in early 1960 and, in 1961, a group of army officers tried to overthrow de Gaulle. Both times, however, the majority of the military remained loyal to the government. Associated with the general's plot was the Organisation de l'armée secrète (OAS), a group of colon and military extremists who simultaneously launched a counterattack on both the FLN and the French authorities. In March 1962, a cease-fire was finally arranged at Évian, France, between government and FLN representatives. In a referendum of July 1963, Algerians voted overwhelmingly for independence, and the colons began a mass evacuation with nearly all leaving by the end of the year. Those who remained could choose, after three years, either Algerian or French citizenship. France also ceded the Sahara oil and gas deposits to the Algerians and provided special aid for postwar recovery. French casualties from the conflict were about 100,000, the Algerian more than 1 million, and 1.1 million inhabitants became refugees.

## Alkan (1813–1888)
### (Charles-Valentine Morhange)
*pianist*

A virtuoso who is sometimes called the "Berlioz of the piano" Alkan (the pseudonym of Charles-Valentine Morhange) was born in Paris. Beginning in 1828, he had great success as a pianist-composer, but his career was soon eclipsed. Alkan has left three pieces of chamber music (*Grand duo concertant* for piano and violin, 1840; Trio for piano, violin, and violincello, 1841; *Sonate de concert* for piano and violincello, 1856), some diverse works and especially texts for piano, which are often as difficult as those of Liszt (25 *préludes dans tous les tons majeurs et mineurs*, 1847; *Grand sonate "Les Quatre Âges,"* 1847; 12 *Études dans tous les tons majeurs*, 1848; 12 *Études dans tous les tons mineurs*, 1857). Because of the formidable difficulty of these works, they were neglected until the 1970s.

## Allais, Maurice (1911–   )

*economist*

A neoliberal economist, Maurice Allais was born in PARIS, where he studied at the École polytechnique and at the École nationale supérieure des Mines. He joined the state mine administration in 1937 and became a professor at the École nationale des mines in 1944. Later appointed director of research at the National French Research Council, he was named an officer of the LEGION OF HONOR in 1977. In 1988 he was awarded the Nobel Prize in economic science for his contribution to the study of markets and the effective use of resources. He was the first French citizen to receive the prize in that category. His work is considered to have helped improve the economic and social efficiency of state-run monopolies, which largely developed in Western Europe after WORLD WAR II. Allais demonstrated that, even with a monopoly, optimum prices could be found that would be socially efficient. His principle that price, rather than state regulation, should guide the planning of state monopolies became essential to the running of such institutions. Even after the 1980s trend towards privatization, his work continued to be applied to such private and monopolistic public-service enterprises as the English Channel tunnel project. Allais's work has now gained wide international recognition.

## Allégret, Marc (1900–1973)

*film director*

Born in Basel, Switzerland, Marc Allégret entered the film industry in his youth. Because of the fine craftsmanship and interpretation of a number of young actors (Jean-Pierre Aumont, Danièle Delorme, Simone Simon, Michèle Morgan, Gérard Philipe) whose debut roles he directed, Marc Allégret's films had a great success: *Lac aux dames* (1934), *Gribouille* (1937), *Entrée des artistes* (1938). Also, two documentaries by Allegret bear witness to his friendship with ANDRÉ GIDE: *Voyage au Congo* (1927) and *Avec André Gide* (1951).

## Allégret, Yves (1907–1987)

*film director*

Born in Asnières, Yves Allégret, in contrast to his brother, MARC ALLÉGRET, became a specialist in the French cinematic film noir genre: *Dédée d'Anvers* (1948), *Une si jolie petite plage* (1949), *Manèges* (1950), and *La Meilleure Part* (1956). Yves Allegret, however, introduced a sense of optimism into this typically pessimistic film style.

## Alps, French

Forming an arc of 1,200 kilometers from the Gulf of Genoa to the Danube River at Vienna, the Alps are the highest and most densely settled mountain chain of Europe. Structurally, the alpine mountain system is divided into the Western and Eastern Alps. The Western Alps, where the French Alps are located, average about 1,000 meters higher and are more rugged and narrower than the Eastern Alps. Among the principal ranges are the Alps Grees in France, with the Jura Mountains as a northeastern outlier of this French chain. The Rhône River also passes through the French Alps.

The highest peak of the Alps, Mont Blanc (15,771 feet [4,807 m]) is on the French-Italian border, largely situated in the Haute-Savoie Department of France. Geologically, it is known as a massif. Chambéry, an important tourist and winter sport center, is located at the base. There are large glaciers nearby, the most notable being the Mer de Glace on the northern slope.

Part of the alpine region in France is formed also by the Cottian Alps, along the French-Italian border, located primarily in southeastern France, but partly in northwestern Italy. Among its highest peaks is Aiguille de Chambeyron (12,602 feet [3,841 m]) in France. Prior to WORLD WAR II, the

French side of the Cottian Alps was heavily fortified. After the war, the Mont Cenis plateau and the Mont Tabor-Charberton area of this range was ceded by Italy to France.

In the south of France is the Alps maritime area, with Nice as the largest city. This range extends to the Mediterranean Sea and is lower than the French alpine region to the north.

In the Dauphiné region, Les Écrins (13,462 feet [4,103 m]) and Mont Pelvoux (12,970 feet [3,953 m]) are the two highest peaks of the French Alps in this area.

Winter sports, especially skiing, are important activities in the French Alps, and it is there that the first Winter Olympics were held at Chamonix/Mont Blanc in 1924. They also were held in the region, at Grenoble, in 1968, and at Albertville, in 1992.

The Alps receive high precipitation at the north side (about 3,000 mm/120 inches) annually, sustaining the forests and the rivers of the region. Elevation and exposure to maritime air masses and to the sun's rays are the prime variables influencing vegetation. Oak, hornbeam, pine, beech, fir, spruce, mountain maple, and larch are the most prevalent arbors. Other flora are rhododendron, edelweiss, rock flora, sedges, rowan, creeping pine, and dwarf shrubs. Fauna includes ibex, chamois, woodchuck, snow grouse, snow mouse, and alpine daw.

## Alsace-Lorraine

The area of Alsace-Lorraine (German, Elsass-Lothringen) makes up the historic frontier area of northeastern France, separated from Germany in the east by the Rhine River and drained by the Moselle River. The Vosges Mountains are in the east. Alsace-Lorraine consists of three departments: Bas-Rhin and Haut Rhin in the administrative region of Alsace, and Moselle, part of the region of Lorraine. The main cities are STRASBOURG, Mulhouse, and Metz.

Historically, the region has been the object of disputes between French and Germanic rulers since the breakup of Charlemagne's empire in the ninth century. The term "Alsace-Lorraine" was first used in 1871 when, under the terms of the Peace Treaty of Frankfurt, concluding the FRANCO-PRUSSIAN WAR, the former provinces of Alsace and Lorraine, French since the mid-17th century, were annexed by Germany. Returned to France in 1919, they were again annexed and occupied by Germany from 1940 to 1945.

French is now the dominant language in both areas, but Alsatian, a German dialect, is also spoken. The whole region has a culture that reflects both French and German elements. The area produces textiles and chemicals and, in agriculture, important crops including grain, grapes, and tobacco.

## Althusser, Louis  (1918–1990)
*philosopher*

Best known for his views concerning the origin and developments of the theories of Karl Marx, Louis Althusser was born in Birmandreis, Algeria. A professor at the École Normale Supérieure, Althusser, in his many writings, proposed a traditional scientific reading of Marx, particularly of *Capital*, in place of the "ideologic" reading of the evolution and influence of that philosopher's theories. He viewed Marx's writings as consisting of two distinct stages—the early works of the humanistic and ideological young Marx, and a later, scientific phase, characterized by the revolutionary *Capital*. Between the two stages Althusser postulated an epistemological break, creating a more complex Marxian model. His most significant innovation regarding Marxism was his rejection of a strict economic determinism. He also posited that Marxism was not so much a moral philosophy as a humanistic science and, therefore, a purely theoretical doctrine. Althusser also defined the idea of an "ideological state apparatus." His principal writings include *Pour Marx* (1965), *Lire le Capital* (1965–68), *Lénine et la philosophie* (1969), and *L'avenir dure longtemps, Journal de captivité* (posthumous, 1994).

## Ampère, André-Marie  (1775–1836)
*scientist, mathematician*

Born near LYON, the son of a city official, André-Marie Ampère became interested in mathematics at an early age. He is best known for his important contributions to the study of electrodynamics, the "ampere"—the unit of electrical current—being named after him. His electrodynamic theory and his views on the relationship between electricity and magnetism were published in his *Recueil d'observa-*

*tions électrodynamiques* (1822) and in his *Mémoire sur la théorie des phénomènes électrodynamiques, uniquement déduits de l'expérience* (1827). Ampère also invented the astatic needle, which made possible the modern astatic galvanometer, and the electric telegraph, and he was the first to show that parallel conductors carrying currents that travel in the same direction will attract each other, while, traveling in opposite directions, they will repel each other. André-Marie Ampère was named to the Academy of Sciences in 1814.

## Ampère, Jean-Jacques (1800–1864)
### writer, historian

The son of ANDRÉ-MARIE AMPÈRE, Jean-Jacques Ampère was an enthusiastic and creative scholar, interested above all in the literature of northern Europe (eddas, sagas, nibelungen). Born in LYON and educated in PARIS, in 1827 he made the first of many visits to the Scandinavian countries, where he studied lore and poetry and folksongs, comparing them to Norse mythology. Professor at the COLLÈGE DE FRANCE (1833–64), he published the *Histoire littéraire de la France avant le XIIe siècle* (1830) and the *Introduction à l'histoire de la littérature française au Moyen-Age* (1841). After several lengthy trips abroad, he dedicated himself to his *Histoire romaine à Rome* (1858), followed by *L'Empire romain à Rome* (posthumous, 1867). Jean-Jacques Ampère also left an interesting correspondence with Mme JEANNE RÉCAMIER. He was elected to the ACADÉMIE FRANÇAISE in 1848.

## Amyot, Jacques (1513–1593)
### humanist

Born in Melun, Jacques Amyot is known for his translation from the ancient Greek of *Theagenes and Charicles* (*Théagene et Chariclée*)(by Helidorus), completed in 1547, which gained him the favor of the royal court. He became the tutor to the children of King HENRY II, the grand almoner of France and bishop of Auxerre, and, in 1559, published a translation of *Daphnis and Chloe* by Longus. He also translated Plutarch's *Lives* (*Vies des hommes illustres*, also known as *Vies parallèles*; 1559) and his *Moralia* (*Oeuvres morales*; 1572).

## Andrault, Michel (1926–   )
### architect

Born in Montrouge, Michel Andrault is a leading modernist architect who perfected the techniques of building comfortable dwellings for the public. In his apartment houses at Sainte-Geneviève-des-Bois (1968–70), he overcame the banality and bulk of large buildings and created "intermediary" dwellings. This is evidenced also in his buildings at Evry (1971–72), which feature graduated terraces. In 1973, he built the Havas social center at Neuilly-sur-Seine, an impressive structure marked by great horizontal beams and a cylindrical hall, done in a lyrical style. The University of Paris–Tolbiac (1972–73), the Totem tower at quai de Grenelle in PARIS (1970), and the Palais omnisport at Bercy (1984) all bear witness to this architect's ability to combine the concepts of modern architecture, especially the massive use of concrete, with an esthetic articulation of volume.

## André, Louis (1838–1913)
### general, political figure

Born in Nuit-Saint-Georges, Louis André was named minister of war and replaced the marquis de GALLIFET in the WALDECK-ROUSSEAU cabinet (1901). He also held that portfolio in the COMBES government. His name remains tied to the affaire des FICHES, which brought about a scandal, the resignation of André, and the fall of the ministry of EMILE COMBES (1904).

## André, Maurice (1933–   )
### musician

Born in Ales, Maurice André, who is known for his virtuosity, broad musical interests, and flamboyant personality, was one of the first modern trumpet players to have a career as an individual performer rather than as a member of an orchestra. André took up trumpet playing as a youth while he worked in a coal mine. He was taught by his father, an amateur musician, and, in 1951, studied musicology and trumpet at the Paris Conservatory. There, he twice (1952, 1953) won the prestigious Prix d'Honneur for his performance on the cornet and trumpet. He played with such major ensembles as the Paris Radio Orchestra (1953–62), the Lamoureux Orchestra (1953–60), and the orchestra of the Opéra-Comique (1966–67). Playing also in jazz groups, he won the international music competition in Geneva (1953) and the German Radio Competition in 1963. He then began a famed international career as a trumpet soloist, touring with an orchestra from Stuttgart, Germany. André, who is a specialist in the ornate and difficult repertoire of 18th-century music, has been recognized also for his modern works. A number of these were written for him by such noted composers as A. JOLIVET, H. TOMASI, and B. Blacher. André has made nearly 300 recordings, including over 30 various trumpet concertos.

## Angoulême, Louis-Antoine de Bourbon, duke of  (1775–1844)
*last dauphin of France*

Born at VERSAILLES, Louis-Antoine de Bourbon, the last dauphin of France, was the son of the count d'Artois (the future CHARLES X) and Marie-Thérèse of Savoy. He left France with his family at the beginning of the REVOLUTION (1789) and married his cousin, MARIE-THÉRÈSE CHARLOTTE, DUCHESS OF ANGOULÊME in exile (1799). As part of General Wellington's forces, he entered BORDEAUX in March 1814, then attempted in vain to initiate uprisings in the Midi against NAPOLÉON I, during the HUNDRED DAYS. A member of the military expedition to Spain sent in 1823 to help King Ferdinand VIII, he took part in the capture of Trocadero. Louis-Antoine de Bourbon became dauphin on the succession of his father to the throne in 1824, but he renounced his own claim to the throne after the REVOLUTION of July 1830.

## Angoulême, Marie-Thérèse Charlotte, duchess of  (1778–1851)
*royal figure*

Born at VERSAILLES, the daughter of king LOUIS XVI and MARIE ANTOINETTE of Austria, princess Marie-Thérèse was known as "Madame Royale." In 1792, during the REVOLUTION OF 1789, she was held prisoner with her family in the Temple Prison, then later (1795) was sent to Austria. In 1799, she mar-

ried her cousin, LOUIS-ANTOINE DE BOURBON, DUKE OF ANGOULÊME. She returned to France in 1814, but because of her support of the clerical reactionism there remained unpopular.

See also QUINETTE, NICOLAS-MARIE.

## Anguier, François  (1604–1669)
*sculptor*

Born in Eu, François Anguier studied with the leading sculptor, SIMON GUILLAIN, then traveled to Rome (1641–43), where he observed the works of the Italian baroque masters. Returning to France, he worked at decorating the LOUVRE then, with his brother, MICHEL ANGUIER, sculpted the mausoleum of Henry II de Montmorency (1653–58). The kneeling statue with reserved decoration of *Gaspard de Montmorency* is considered François Anguier's masterpiece.

## Anguier, Michel  (1612–1686)
*sculptor*

Born in Eu, Michel Anguier was the brother of the sculptor FRANÇOIS ANGUIER and, like him, studied with the noted sculptor SIMON GUILLAIN. He then spent 10 years in Rome, where he studied in particular with D'Algardi. Michel Anguier was commissioned by NICOLAS FOUQUET to work at Saint-Mandé and at Vaux, and later adorned the stuccos in the LOUVRE for ANNE OF AUSTRIA (1654–55). He also did most of the decorated sculpture in the Val-de-Grâce (group of *La Nativité, 1662–67).* He then executed the reliefs for the portal of Saint-Denis (1671–77) after a design by LEBRUN. Michel Anguier worked in marble, ivory, bronze, and silver, producing numerous groupings and religious statues that bear the mark of Italian baroque models.

## Anjou, François, duke of  (1554–1584)
*royal figure*

Born in Saint-Germain-en-Laye, François, duke of Anjou, was the fourth son of HENRY II and CATHERINE DE' MEDICI. At first called the duke of Alençon, he was very ambitious and intrigued with the Protestants, rejoining the prince de CONDÉ and putting himself forth as a leader of the rebels. After the

Peace of Monsieur (1576), he intrigued with William of Orange and went to the Netherlands. But he quickly became unpopular. His death left the succession to the throne to Henry of Navarre, the future HENRY IV.

## Anne of Austria (1601–1666)
*queen of France*

The queen of France, Anne of Austria was born in Valladolid, the daughter of Philip III, king of Spain, and Marguerite of Austria. In 1615, she married LOUIS XIII of France and they had two sons (LOUIS XIV and PHILIPPE D'ORLÉANS) after 23 years of an unhappy marriage. Compromised by her love for the duke of Buckingham, she joined in conspiracies against RICHELIEU, who accused her of treason for having corresponded with her brother, the king of Spain. Upon the death of Louis XIII, she became regent (1643–61) for the young Louis XIV and governed with MAZARIN, whom she perhaps married. As regent, Anne upheld the authority of the Crown during the Fronde uprisings and, in 1661, retired to Val-de-Grâce when her son assumed power.

## Anne of Brittany (1477–1514)
*duchess of Brittany, queen of France*

Born in Nantes, Anne of Brittany was duchess of Brittany (1488–1514) and queen of France. The daughter of Francis II, the last duke of Brittany, whom she succeeded in 1488, she was engaged (1490) to the future Holy Roman Emperor Maximilian I, but finally married the king of France, CHARLES VIII (1491). Being widowed in 1498, she remarried in 1499 with LOUIS XII, who had ended his marriage to JEANNE OF FRANCE. Anne had two daughters by this second marriage: CLAUDE OF FRANCE, the future wife of FRANCIS I, and RENÉE OF FRANCE, the future duchess of Ferrara.

## Anne of France (1461–1522)
*duchess of Bourbon, regent*

Born in Genappe, Brabant, Anne of France was known as the "dame de Beaujeu." The daughter of LOUIS XI and Charlotte of Savoy, she married Pierre II of Beaujeu (1438–1503), duke of Bourbon (1448). Regent during the minority of her brother

CHARLES VIII, she ruled with competence, convoking the Estates General (1484) and fighting against the "Grands." During the Guerre folle, his troops fought the duke of Orléans (future LOUIS XII) and Francois II, duke of Brittany, at Saint-Aubin-du-Cormier in 1488. She arranged the marriage of CHARLES VIII with ANNE OF BRITTANY (1491).

## Anouilh, Jean (1910–1987)
*playwright, director, and producer*

One of the best-known French playwrights, at home and abroad, Jean Anouilh, noted for his provocative dramas, was born near BORDEAUX and spent most of his life immersed in the theater world of PARIS. After studying law and working briefly at an advertising agency, Anouilh, during the 1930s, began to write his first plays. His work reflects his sustained search for an explanation of the failure of idealism in the real world. Such plays (*Le Voyageur sans bagages*, 1937; *Le Sauvage*, 1938) seek their explanation in the nature of society. Anouilh termed them "Pieces noirs," describing their pessimistic tone. Other works, termed "Pieces roses" (*Le Bal de voleurs*, 1938; *Le Rendez-Vous de Senlis*, 1939; *Léocadia*, 1939) are more optimistic. He also wrote what he called "Pieces brillantes" (*L'Invitation au château*, 1947; *Le Répétition ou l'Amour puni*, 1950), or "Pieces grinçantes" (*Pauvre Bitos*, 1956), "Pieces costumes" (*L'Alouette, 1953; Becket ou l'Honneur de Dieu*, 1959; *La Foire d'empoigne*, 1962; *Léonora*, 1977), "Pieces secrètes" (*L'Arrestation*, 1975), and "Pieces farceuses" (*Le Nombril*, 1981). With *Cher Antoine* (1969) and *Les Poissons rouges* (1970), Anouilh seemed to have turned to a more autobiographical style. In other works (*Medea*, 1937; *Eurydice*, 1942; *Antigone*, 1942), he sought explanation for human failures in Greek mythology. *Antigone* is considered one of his masterpieces. Anouilh is known as a consummate master of the well-made play.

## Antoine, André (1858–1943)
*stage director, actor, theorist*

Born in Limoges, André Antoine was the founder of the Théâtre-Libre (1887) and was at first, as an artist, attracted to the works of ÉMILE ZOLA and to naturalism. Antoine staged the plays of contemporary writers (Strindberg, Ibsen, Tolstoy) and set the initial parameters of theatrical realism. He directed the Théâtre-Antoine, then the Odéon, where he produced elaborate stagings of Shakespeare and MOLIÉRE. Coming late to film, he brought an element of realism and sobriety, although these were not so appreciated at the time: *La Terre* (1921), *L'Hirondelle et la mésange* (1924, revived in 1983).

## Antoine, Jacques-Denis (1733–1801)
*architect*

Born in PARIS, where he studied architecture, Jacques-Denis Antoine, following a contest in which he competed with ÉTIENNE-LOUIS BOULLÉE, was commissioned to build the hotel de la Monnaie in that city (1771–77). This building constitutes one of the first examples of the Louis XVI style in civil Parisian architecture. Beginning in 1776, Antoine produced a number of buildings in Paris, notably the hôtel de Fleury and the École des ponts et chaussées. He also built the château of Herces (Yvelines) and Mussy-l'Évêque (Haute-Marne), the hôtel des Monnaies in Berne (1790), and the hôtel de Berwick in Madrid.

## Antoine de Bourbon (1518–1562)
*king of Navarre*

Born the duke de Vendôme in Les Andelys, Antoine de Bourbon became king of Navarre (1555–62) by his marriage to JEANNE III D'ALBRET (1548). With her, he had a son, the future king HENRY IV of France. Converting to Catholicism, Antoine de Bourbon took part in the religious wars, fighting against the Protestants commanded by his brother, LOUIS I DE CONDÉ, but was fatally wounded during the siege of Rouen.

## Apollinaire, Guillaume (1880–1918)
**(Wilhelm Apollinaris de Kostrowitzy)**
*poet*

A poet, novelist, dramatist, and art and literary critic who is believed to have coined the term "surrealist," Guillaume Apollinaire, as he is known, was a leader of the avant-garde in PARIS in the early 20th century. Born Wilhelm Apollinaris de Kostrowitzy, in Rome, the natural son of an Italian officer and Angelica de Kostrowitzy, the daughter of a Polish noble in the papal court, Apollinaire studied for a time in schools in Cannes and Nice before settling in Paris (1902). After some minor jobs there, he took a post as a tutor in the Rhineland, which allowed him to travel throughout Germany and Austria-Hungary. Upon returning to Paris, he submitted his writings to various literary revues (*La Revue blanche, La Plume*) and became a friend of several symbolist writers. In 1909, his first book, *L'Enchanteur pourrissant,* was published. In the symbolist spirit, it reflects the idea that the imagination is the source of all ideas. Apollinaire also championed cubism and the cubists, and was a friend of many artists, including Picasso, and wrote of their works (*Les Peintres cubistes, méditations esthétiques,* 1913). He was fascinated by the relationship among the arts, especially poetry and painting, and his own poems are themselves very pictorial (*Calligrames: poèmes de la paix et de la guerre,* 1918). Apollinaire's writings also reflect his fascination with the modern world. The Eiffel Tower, airplanes, and cosmopolitanism are among the motifs in his great collection, *Alcools, poèmes* (1913). In his novel, *Le Poète assassiné* (1913), he rejected 19th-century realism and wrote a work of fantasy and satire. His play *Les Mamelles de Tirésias* (1917) anticipates both surrealism and the theater of the absurd. It had a significant influence on such dramatists as Artaud and Ionesco. Apollinare, who was wildly inconsistent in all but one thing—his intellectual commitment to the avant-garde—lived a life of controversy (it was typical of him that he spent a few days in jail on suspicion of having stolen the *Mona Lisa*). And it was characteristic also of him that he should have died two days before the armistice of World War I—of influenza in the 1918 pandemic. Apollinaire's other works include the novels *L'Hérésiarque et Cie* (1910), *La Bestiare ou Cortège d'Orphée* (1911) and *La Femme assise* (1920), a collection of poems (*Vitam impendere amore,* 1917) and *Le Flâneur des deux rives* (1917). His *Oeuvres complètes* was published in 1966.

## April 1834, Days of

The Days of April 1834 were an insurrection against the JULY MONARCHY, organized by workers' mutual corporations and the Society of the Rights of Man (Société des droits de l'homme). This uprising took place first in Lyon (April 9–12) and then in Paris (April 13). ADOLPHE LOUIS THIERS, minister of the interior, called upon the army to suppress the revolutionary movement. Under the command of General THOMAS BUGEAUD, the soldiers massacred many on the rue Transnonain in Paris (April 14).

## April 1848, Day of

The Day of April 1848 (April 16) was that of a workers' demonstration in Paris incited by socialist clubs after the REVOLUTION OF 1848. Poorly organized, however, it was quickly suppressed by the provisional government, which called out the National and Civil Guards.

## Arago, François (1786–1853)
*astronomer, physicist, political figure*

Born in Estagel, Pyrénées-Orientales, François Arago, through the influence of PIERRE-SIMON LAPLACE, was appointed secretary of the Bureau of Longitudes. In 1806, with JEAN-BAPTISTE BIOT, he measured the arc of the terrestrial meridian in Spain, which, in turn, led to the discovery of the phenomenon of the production of magnetism by rotation and proof of the relationship between the Aurora and variations in terrestrial magnetism. Professor at the École polytechnique, director of the Observatory, then of the Bureau of Longitudes, he served as a leftist deputy from 1830 to 1848. A member of the provisional government after the Revolution of February 1848, as minister of war and the navy, he helped to pass the laws abolishing slavery in the colonies. Elected to the Constituent Assembly, member of the executive commission, and deputy to the Legislative Assembly (May 1849), he left political life after the coup d'état of December 2, 1851. Arago's other scientific work covered various fields. A supporter of the undulatory theory of light, he measured, with Biot, the index of reflection of several gases, discovering the rotary and chromatic polarization of light, especially by observing the Aurora. With ANDRÉ-MARIE AMPÈRE, he studied electromagnetic phenomena and measured the terrestrial magnetic field to determine planetary diameters. In 1839, he helped in the invention of photography by presenting the work done by

JACQUES DAGUERRE before the Academy of Sciences. François Arago was himself named to the Academy of Sciences in 1809.

## Aragon, Louis (1897–1982)
*writer*

A novelist, poet, and essayist, Louis Aragon, who was also a leader in the dadaist and surrealist literary movements in France, was born in PARIS. During his early years he wrote a number of experimental works, including the collection of poems *Feu de joie* (1920) and a long essay, *Traité du style* (1928), as well as *Anicet ou le Panorama* (1921) and *Le Paysan de Paris* (1926). Aragon also founded, with other surrealist writers, the revue *Littérature* (1919). Along with ANDRÉ BRETON, he joined the COMMUNIST PARTY in 1927 and adhered to the related aesthetic doctrine of socialist realism. He would become one of the most active French Communist propagandists. Aragon praised the Soviet Union in his *Persécuté persécuteur* (1930–31) and *Hourras l'Oural* (1934), and presented his theme of socialist realism in a vast work, *Le Monde réel*, completed between 1934 and 1951. During WORLD WAR II, he was a leading figure in the RESISTANCE. In his other works, including *Le Crève-Coeur* (1941), *Cantique à Elsa* (1942), *Les Yeux d'Elsa* (1942), *Brocéliande* (1942), *Le Musée Grevin* (1943), and *La Diane française* (1946), he exalts subjects dear to the French, such as love and hope. Among Aragon's other works are *Le Nouveau Crève-Coeur* (1948), *Élégie a Pablo Neruda* (1966), *La Mise à mort* (1965), *Le Fou d'Elsa* (1963), *Blanche ou l'Oubli* (1967), *Je n'ai jamais appris à écrire ou les Incipit* (1969), and *Henri Matisse, roman* (1971). Until 1972, he directed the journal *Les Lettres françaises*. Aragon became a member of the French Communist Party's Central Committee in 1954 and, in 1957, was awarded the Lenin Peace Prize.

## Arc de Triomphe

In 1806, Emperor NAPOLÉON 1 commissioned the construction of the Arc de Triomphe in PARIS as a monument to his troops. It was completed and dedicated in 1836, and was constructed according to the plans of JEAN-FRANÇOIS CHALGRIN and com-

L'Arc de Triomphe, ca. 1900  *(Library of Congress)*

pleted after his death by J. A. Raymond in the neoclassical style. It was inspired by the ancient Roman arch of Constantine but is twice its size. With its colossal proportions (50 m high by 45 m wide), the monument dominates Paris. Twelve avenues radiate from its center (Place Charles de Gaulle, formerly Place de l'Étoile), and is situated at the western end of the Champs-Élysées. The inner walls of the arch bear the names of Napoléon's military victories and of many of his generals. Sculptures in high relief by F. RUDE, J. Pradier, J. P. Cortot, and A. Elex depict such themes as "Victory" and "la Marseillaise." Since 1920, the tomb of the unknown soldier has lain beneath the arch where an eternal flame is also kept burning. The arch has been the scene of important historical events, including the return of Napoléon's remains from St. Helena in 1840, and CHARLES DE GAULLE's victory parade through Paris in 1944 after the liberation of the city.

## Argonne, Battle of

The battle of the Argonne was a major battle of WORLD WAR I, fought in fall 1918 between the U.S. First Army, including units of the XVII French Corps, and German forces. Part of an Allied assault in the Meuse-Argonne offensive, as it is also known, it was part of an effort to weaken the highly fortified German Hindenburg Line of western Europe. The American general John J. Pershing commanded the Allied forces. Lasting for two months, the Argonne offensive involved 1,200,000 U.S. troops, of whom 60,000 took an active part in the battle. The conflict extended over 500 square miles [1,295 sq km] and took 117,000 Allied casualties, killed or wounded. German losses were 94,000 killed or wounded, with 30,000 captured by the French and 26,000 taken prisoner by the Americans. The Battle of the Argonne was a major factor in the final breakdown of the German line of resistance and helped to bring about the German initiative for an armistice, which was finally achieved on November 11, 1918.

## Argonne Forest

The Argonne Forest is a wooded plateau region of northeastern France, bounded by the Aisne and Meuse Rivers. The area covers parts of the departments of Ardennes, Meuse, and Maine, and extends to the Belgian border. The forest, which also contains steep cliffs and wide river valleys, is a natural area of defense for France. During the FRENCH REVOLUTION in 1792, the French general DUMOURIEZ led a successful campaign there against the Prussians, culminating in the victory of Valmy. During the FRANCO-PRUSSIAN WAR, in 1870, the Argonne was the scene of the French army's retreat under Marshal MAC-MAHON, culminating in the battle of Sedan. In 1918, during WORLD WAR I, the Argonne was again the site of a major battle (see ARGONNE, BATTLE OF).

## Arnauld, Antoine  (1612–1694)
## (the Grand Arnauld)
*theologian*

The most famous French exponent of JANSENISM, Arnauld was born in PARIS and studied theology at the SORBONNE. There, he came under the influence of the leaders of the Jansenist movement. In 1641, he was ordained a priest and, in 1643, the same year that he was made a member of the Society of the

Sorbonne, he published *De la fréquente Communion*—a basic exposition of Jansenist principles. The work would provoke the Jesuits with whom he would be engaged in controversy and debate for the rest of his life. For a time, Arnauld was a member of the Jansenist community of Port-Royal, near Paris. In 1665, the Jesuits had him expelled from the Sorbonne and, despite the protection of LOUIS XIV, forced him into exile in Belgium in 1679. He did research for BLAISE PASCAL's *Provinciales* and continued to publish his polemics against his many other adversaries, including Calvinists and freethinkers. Arnauld's other major works are *Apologie pour les Saints-Pères* (1651, *Lettre d'un docteur de Sorbonne à une personne de condition* and *Seconde Lettre à un duc et pair* (1655). Other works include *Grammaire générale et raisonnée* or *Grammaire de Port-Royal* (1660), *Logique de Port-Royal* (1662), and *La Perpétuité de la foi* (1669–79). Besides his eminent place in the history of Christianity, Antoine Arnauld is a major figure in logic and the philosophy of language.

## Arnauld family

A family of French Jansenists who brought Jansenism to the Abbey of Port-Royal in Paris. Antoine Arnauld (1560–1619), born in Paris, was a member of that city's parlement, advocate-general, then a state comptroller. He supported the SORBONNE against the Jesuits (1594) and restored the Abbey of Port-Royal, with which his family never ceased to be connected. Among his eight children was his eldest son, Robert Arnauld D'Andilly (1589–1674), also born in Paris, who returned to Port-Royal in 1646. He has left his *Mémoires*, a *Journal*, and a translation, *Vie des Pères des déserts*. Jacqueline Marie Angélique Arnauld (religious name Merè Angélique) (1591–1661), the daughter of Antoine, born in Paris, was after 1602 abbess of Port-Royal. She reformed that monastery (1609), founded the institut du Saint-Sacrement with SÉBASTIAN ZAMET, bishop of Langres, and in that she placed JEAN DUVERGIER DE HAURANNE, the abbé of Saint-Cyran, in charge of the spiritual direction of her nuns (1636), and introduced JANSENISM to Port-Royal. Jeanne Catherine Agnès Arnauld (religious name Mère Agnès) (1593–1671) was the daughter of Antoine. Born in Paris, she was the abbess of

Port-Royal from 1636 to 1642 and from 1658 to 1661. She refused to sign the formulation of 1661 regarding Jansenism and was subsequently confined to the convent of the Visitation (1663–65). ANTOINE ARNAULD (1612–94), known as "le Grand Arnauld," was born in Paris, the son of Antoine. A theologian under the influence of the abbot of Saint-Cyran, he willingly accepted the most extreme Augustinian theories and became leader of the Jansenist faction. Expelled from the Sorbonne in 1656, he lived clandestinely for a time, doing research for BLAISE PASCAL for the latter's *Provenciales*, then returned to Port-Royal. Upon the renewal of anti-Jansenist restrictions (1679), he went into self-imposed exile in Flanders, then in the Netherlands. His principal writings include *De la fréquente Communion* (1643), *Apologie pour les Saints-Pères* (1651), *Lettre d'un docteur de Sorbonne à une personne de condition* (1655), *Second Lettre a un duc et pair* (1655), in which he presented his views on the five propositions attributed to Jansenism, *Grammaire généralé et raisonnée*, or *Grammaire de Port-Royal* (1660), *Logique de Port-Royal* (1662), *La Perpétuité de la foi* (1669, with Nicole), and various other writings against Protestantism. Besides his eminent place in the history of Christianity, le Grand Arnauld is considered a major figure in the study of logic and philosophy of language. According to his theory, which is essentially Cartesian, the syntax of natural languages is the product of a rational and universal analysis by the thinking subject. Angélique Arnauld d'Andilly (religious name, Mère Angélique de Saint-Jean) (1624–84), the daughter of Robert, was born in Paris. She was the prioress, then abbess (1678–84), of Port-Royal des Champs.

## Aron, Raymond (1905–1983)
*philosopher and sociologist*

Born and educated in Paris, Raymond Aron was a prominent political thinker who served as editor in chief of *La France libre* in London during World War II (1941–44) and, with JEAN-PAUL SARTRE, was one of the founders of *Temps modernes*. Later, he was editorial writer for LE FIGARO (1947–77). Aron taught sociology at the SORBONNE and also the COLLÈGE DE FRANCE. Author of a study on contemporary German sociology (*La Sociologie allemande contemporaine*, 1935), his philosophy was critical of relativist and pluralistic historiography. He questioned the monistic theories (idealistic and materialistic), and also the deterministic viewpoint (*Introduction à la philosophie d'histoire*, 1938 and 1950; *Dimensions de la conscience historique*, 1962). Aron's moderate conservatism and skepticism regarding ideologies isolated him from the mainly left-wing French intelligentsia for much of his career. He is considered, through his later works (*La Grande Schisme*, 1948; *L'Opium des intellectuels*, 1957; *La Société industrielle et la guerre*, 1959; *Dix-huit Leçons sur la société industrielle*, 1963) one of the main theoreticians of technologic ideology and, in his economic, social, and political analyses, a principal critic of Marxism. Aron's ideas gained popularity in recent years, and his *Mémoires*, published in 1983, drew much favorable notice.

## Arp, Jean (1887–1966)
*sculptor*

An avant-garde sculptor, painter, and poet, Jean Arp was born in Strasbourg and studied art in Paris and Weimar, then later painted in Switzerland for a number of years. By 1912, he had become associated with the Blue Rider (Der Blaue Reiter) group of experimental artists in Munich. During World War I, he found refuge in Zurich, Switzerland, where he helped launch the revolutionary dadaist movement with such artists as Ball, Janco, Huelsenbeck, and Tzara. By 1917, Arp's own style of art had evolved to the abstract and curvilinear forms that characterized his later work. In 1924, in Paris, he became associated with the surrealists and their style and began producing painted wooden basreliefs and cut-cardboard constructions. By the 1930s, he was working in freestanding carved and molded sculpture in various substances. An example is his biomorphic form *Human Construction* (1935). He has also worked in collage and gouache, as well as lithography and engraving. A poet and essayist, Arp, recalling his bilingual Alsatian background, referred to himself as both "Jean" and "Hans." In 1921, he married Sophie Taeuber, a Swiss artist and one of the earliest painters of geometric abstraction.

## Artaud, Antoine-Marie-Joseph (1896–1948) (Antonine)
*writer*

Born in MARSEILLE, Antoine-Marie-Joseph Artaud, or Antonine Artaud, as he was known, whose work influenced the development of experimental theater, was for a time part of a surrealist group of artists (*L'Ombilic des limbes*, 1925; *Le Pèse-Nerfs*, 1925), but soon left and turned toward theatrical writings. A founder, with ROGER VITRAC, of the Theatre Alfred Jarry, Artaud wrote, between 1931 and 1935, a collection of essays, *Le Théâtre et son double* (1938), which is the basis for the concepts of modern theater direction (theater of the absurd, ensemble theater, environmental and virtual theater). Meanwhile, his early play, *Les Cenci* (1935), was not a success. His most significant works remain his *Lettres de Rode* (published 1946), written in a psychiatric hospital, where his friends had committed him because of his mental illness, and his correspondences (*Artaud le Mômo*, 1947; *Van Gogh ou le suicidé de la société*, 1947; and *Les Tarahumaras*, posthumous, 1955), at once poems and firsthand accounts. Artaud developed the concept of "the theater of cruelty"—a term he used to define a new theater that minimized the spoken word, relying instead on a combination of physicality, gestures, nonspecific sound, and elimination of spatiality, forcing the audience to confront instead their inner primal self. Because of lifelong mental and physical illness, Artaud was unable to implement his theories. He was equally known as a film actor, notably in *Faits divers* (1923); ABEL GANCE's *Napoléon* (1927), and *Passion de Jeanne d'Arc* by DREYER (1928). His other writings include *Correspondence avec Jacques Rivière* (published 1927) and the text of a controversial radio broadcast, *Pour en finir avec le judgement de dieu* (1948).

## Arthur III (1393–1458)
*duke of Brittany*

Born near Vannes, Arthur III, duke of Brittany, was the son of Jean IV, duke of Brittany (ca. 1340–99). As count of Richemont, Arthur succeeded his nephew, Pierre II, as duke. A prisoner of the English after the Battle of Agincourt, he became constable of France in 1425 and was a friend and comrade-in-arms of JOAN OF ARC. He was also one of the most faithful supporters of King CHARLES VII.

## Atget, Eugène (1857–1921)
*photographer*

Now recognized as one of the major figures in the history of photography, Eugène Atget, who was born in BORDEAUX, went to sea at an early age, then became a painter and actor. In the late 1890s, he began his photographic career and soon began producing an impressive documentary series on Parisian life: cafés, parks, shop windows, markets, streets, architecture, and portraits of tradespeople. He sold very little of his work and, in 1921, received his only commission—to document the bordellos of Versailles and PARIS. Atget's photography was discovered by the American artist Man Ray in the 1920s. Man's student, the American photographer Berenice Abbott, recognizing Atget's genius, brought the bulk of his work to the United States in 1927. It now forms the Abbott-Levy Collection in the New York City Museum of Modern Art. As a photographer of what is now a bygone era, Atget had an influence on the surrealist movement.

## Attiret, Jean-Denis (1702–1768)
*Jesuit priest, painter*

Born in Dole, Jean-Denis Attiret arrived in China in 1738 as a Jesuit missionary and worked as a painter for the court of the Qing dynasty under the Chinese name of Wang Zhicheng. He produced numerous works celebrating the glories of the conquests of Qianlong and is the author of the famous letter describing the "houses of pleasure" of the emperor of China (the "Yuanminguan"), which was widely circulated in Europe and contributed to the development of a taste for the "Anglo-Chinese" gardens of the 18th century.

## Aubanel, Théodore (1829–1886)
*poet of the Languedoc*

Born in Avignon, Théodore Aubanel was, along with FRÉDÉRIC MISTRAL and JOSEPH ROUMANILLE, one of the founders of the Félibrige (1854), a society dedicated to the revival of the Provençal language. Théodore Aubanel collaborated on the *Armana Prouvencau,* a colorful and homey almanac that would help to propagate an interest in and attachment to Provence and a knowledge of its language. A beloved poet, he expressed his passionate nature in his collection of lyrical poetry, *La Grenade entrouverte (La Mióugrano entreduberto,* 1860). In 1878, he wrote a Shakespearian drama, *Le Pain du peche (Lou pen dou pecat),* followed by *Le Pâtre (Lou Pastre,* posthumous, 1928), and *Le Rapt (Lou Raubatòri,* posthumous, 1944). His second collection of poetry, in which a fervid sensuality is linked to the theme of death, *Les Filles d'Avignon (L'Fihho d'Avignoun,* 1885), was condemned by the religious authorities of the time.

## Auber, Daniel-François-Esprit (1782–1871)
*composer*

A leading operatic composer, Daniel-François-Esprit Auber was born in Caen and was a pupil of the Italian composer Luigi Cherubini. Auber chose EUGÈNE SCRIBE as his librettist and composed nearly 50 operas (*Le Maçon,* 1825; *Fra Diavolo,* 1830; *Le Domino noir,* 1837; *Manon Lescault,* 1856), which were quite successful because of their melodic content. His masterpiece remains *La Muette de Portici* (1828), an opera seria composed in a naturalist spirit. Its production in Brussels, in 1830, was the signal for the Belgian uprising against the Netherlands. Auber served as the director of the Paris Conservatory (1842).

## Aubert, Jacques (1689–1753)
*violinist and composer*

Born in Paris, Jacques Aubert was first violinist at the Paris Opéra (1728), played at the Concert spirituel, and published more than 30 books of sonatas, trios, and concertos (of which the 10 sonatas for four violins and base were the first to be written by a Frenchman [1735]).

## Aubert, Jean (unknown–1741)
*architect, designer, ornamentalist*

A student of JULES HARDOUIN-MANSART, Jean Aubert built the great stables at Chantilly (1719–35), which were commissioned by the duke of Bourbon. A major work in the Regency style, they are characterized by their ample conception and space, the use of a refined design and décor, the adoption of separate roofs, and a large original circular riding school. Jean Aubert also built the abbatial buildings at Chaalis, in PARIS (1736), as well as several private mansions, and was one of the architects of the Palais-Bourbon.

## Aubert, Louis (1871–1968)
*composer*

Born in Paramé, Louis Aubert became well known for his compositions, which are characterized by a delicate sensibility, colored by impressionism, and having diverse dimensionality. Author of a comic opera (*La Forêt bleue*), instrumental works (*Fantaisie pour piano et orchestra*), symphonic poems (*Habañera, Offrandes, Le Tombeau du Chateaubriand*), he has also composed a number of melodies (*Six poèmes arabes*), and ballets (*La Nuit esorcelée, Cinéma*).

## Aubignac, François Hédelin, abbé d' (1604–1676)
*theatrical theorist, dramatist, critic*

François Hédelin, abbé d'Aubignac, whose studies of dramatic technique and presentation were based on the classics and had a great influence on the the 17th century and subsequently influenced 17th-century French theater, was born in Paris. A self-educated lawyer, he was ordained a priest and became the tutor to the nephew of Cardinal RICHE-LIEU. Aubignac's most noted work is his *Pratique du théâtre* (1657), which, while being based to an extent on Aristotle, defines verisimilitude as the essence of tragedy, and tragedy itself as a meditation on the human condition, in which the script must prevail over the action. Through the importance that he placed on the "rule of three unities," he represented the bases of classical drama. Aubignac also wrote a number of tragedies, including *Cyminde* (1642), *La Pucelle d'Orléans* (1642), and *Zenobiel* (1647). His *Conjectures académiques sur l'Iliade* (posthumous, 1715) speculates on the existence of the Greek poet Homer. This theory anticipated the work of the scholar Friederich Wolf, who argued

that the *Iliad* and the *Odyssey* had more than one author. After Aubignac was not invited to join the ACADÉMIE FRANÇAISE, he founded his own society, the so-called Little Academy (1654).

## Aubigné, Agrippa d' (1552–1630)
*writer*

Born in Pons, Saintonge, Agrippa d'Aubigné served as a military attaché to the future king HENRY IV, and was a staunch Calvinist who bore the memory of the Amboise conspiracy (1563) and the SAINT BARTHOLOMEW'S DAY MASSACRE (1572), which he survived. He was an erudite humanist as well as a valiant soldier, and wrote an ardent and diverse literary work describing his impassioned life, *Histoire universelle depuis 1550 jusqu'en 1601* (1616–18), which is also a vivid and lively personal account of the HUGUENOT community during the latter part of the 16th century. He was at first, however, a lyric poet, celebrating his love, Diane Saliviati (whom he could not marry because of the difference in religion) in the Petrarchan verses of *Printemps du sieur d'Aubigné* (composed between 1568 and 1575). He then demonstrated his religious zeal and his satirical nature in *Les Tragiques* (begun in 1577, published in 1656), in which he praises Divine Providence and Protestantism, speaks against the cruelty of war, and notes the sciences and the occult, and the political and military issues of the day. It is a long (seven cantos) work. After the abjuration of Henry IV, he retired to a political post in Maillerzais Vendée, where he continued to write. But his defense of Calvinism caused him to be exiled to Geneva, where he finished his colorful biography, *Sa Vie à ses enfants* (posthumous, 1729). Previously, his caustic style was apparent in his prose and in realistic and humorous pamphlets in which he criticized self-interested religious abjurations (*Confession du très catholique sieurs de Sancy*, posthumous, 1660) and ridiculed the court of MARIE DE' MEDICI (*Les Aventures du baron de Faeneste*, published 1617–20). In the later years of his life, Aubigné was saddened by the setbacks to the Protestant party in France and by the abjuration of his son Constant (the father of FRANÇOISE D'AUBIGNÉ, MARQUISE DE MAINTENON). "One of the most expressive figures of the 16th century" (SAINTE-BEUVE), Agrippa d'Aubigné is equally by his art, in which a daring realism is combined with an elaborate and rich metaphysical style, one of the greatest representatives of baroque literature in France.

## Auclert, Hubertine (1848–1914)
*feminist*

Born in Allier, Auvergne, to a wealthy provincial family, Hubertine Auclert was the leading figure in the struggle for women's suffrage in France. Educated in a convent, she became a republican and in 1876 founded a feminist group, Le Droit des femmes (later, 1883, Le Suffrage des femmes). In 1880 she tried to register as a voter and, in 1881, led a women's tax strike, arguing that taxation without representation was unfair. In 1878 Hubertine Auclert attended the International Women's Conference in Liverpool, England, and met with many leading suffragists. She admired the methods of the British women's suffrage movement and, in 1908, smashed a ballot box in emulation of British feminist tactics, but the action did not cause the expected scandal, and so only a fine was imposed on her. Inspired by MARIE DERAISMES and LÉON RICHER, she joined them in PARIS, where she fought not only for women's right to vote, but also for equal access to professions, equal pay, civil rights, and divorce reform. From 1888 to 1892, she lived in Algeria, where she concerned herself also with women's rights issues. Her writings include *Les Femmes arabes en Algérie* (1900), *La Vote des femmes* (1908), and *Les Femmes au gouvernail* (1921). Hubertine Auclert was the first to use and popularized the terms "feminism" and "feminist."

## Audiberti, Jacques (1899–1965)
*writer*

Born in Antibes, Jacques Audiberti, through the combined influence of STÉPHANE MALLARMÉ and surrealism, developed an exalted lyrical style and expressiveness, and his passion for language is evident in all his works. As a poet, Audiberti published *L'Empire et la trappe* (1930), *Des tones de semence* (1941), *Toujours* (1943), and *Rempart* (1953). As a novelist, he was still poetic in his works, which are filled with creativity, vicissitudes, and adventure (*Abraxas*, 1938; *Des jardins et des fleuves*, 1954; *La Poupée*, 1956), as are his more classically styled writings (*Le Maître de Milan*, (1950); *Marie Dubois*, 1952). He also wrote essays (*La nouvelle Origine*, 1942; *L'Abhumanisme*, 1955) and recollections (*Dimanche m'attend*, 1965). Finally, Audiberti is, for the theater, the creator of a world in which the word, more than even the logic of the characters and the ingeniousness of the plots, fascinates the audience. As a writer for the theater of the absurd, in which he mixes the allegorical with the absurd, Audiberti evokes the great romantic dramas of VICTOR HUGO (*L'Ampélour*, 1928; *Quoat-Quoat*, 1946; *Le mal court*, 1947; *La Haberaute*, 1957; *L'Effet Glapion*, 1959; *La Logeuse*, 1960).

## Audran, Claude (1657–1734)
*painter, designer, ornamentalist*

Born in LYON, Claude Audran was the nephew of GÉRARD AUDRAN and thus, too, a member of the artistically prolific Audran family. He specialized in ornamental painting and produced decorative works for the châteaux of Sceaux, Marly, la Muette, and Meudon, and for the menagerie at VERSAILLES. Employing a verve and an imagination filled with the most fanciful concepts, he used in his arabesques, grotesques, and other pieces Chinese motifs, anthropomorphized animals, and scenes from the circus and theater, in which, like the works of JEAN BERAIN, there is a continuous lively narrative, always however, in a systematic and regular framework and setting. Intendant of the Luxembourg Palace, he employed ANTOINE WATTEAU as his collaborator, and produced for the GOBELIN works the cartoons from the eight panels known as "des Dieux" (1708). Because of the contoured grace of his motifs, as well as his sense of freedom and fantasy, Claude Audran is considered one of the creators of the rococo style that later fully developed during the reign of LOUIS XV.

## Audran, Gérard (1640–1703)
*engraver*

Born in LYON, Gérard Audran came from a productive family of French engravers, ornamentalists, painters, and sculptors of the 17th and 18th centuries. He studied in Rome with Carlo Maratta. A member of the Academy, in 1674 he was an engraver for CHARLES LE BRUN, for whom he reproduced *Les Batailles d'Alexandre* (1672–78), in which his technical mastery is most evident. He also engraved works of the Bolognese painters, as well as the tableaux of NICOLAS POUSSIN and EUSTACHE LE SUEUR, and published *Les Proportions du corps humain d'après les plus belles statues d'Antiquité* (1693). Gérard Audran was the uncle of the painter and ornamentalist CLAUDE AUDRAN.

## Augereau, Pierre-François-Charles (1757–1816)
*field marshal*

Born in PARIS, Pierre-François-Charles Augereau enlisted as a volunteer at age 17, then deserted and served with the Neapolitan and Prussian forces. He returned to France in 1792 to support the Revolution and was made a division commander in December 1793. During the Italian campaign, under Napoléon Bonaparte (see NAPOLÉON I), he won the victory at Millesimo (April 14, 1796), distinguished himself at Lodi and at Castiglione, and played a decisive role in the victory at Arcole (November, 16–17). Upon returning to France, he carried out the coup d'état of 18 Fructidor (September 4, 1797). Named marshal (1804), he fought in all the campaigns of the Empire (Jena, Eylau, Spain, Leipzig) but, in 1814, went over to the side of LOUIS XVIII, who made him a peer of France. Augereau refused to sit in judgment at the trial of Marshal MICHEL NEY.

## Aulnoy, Marie-Catherine Le Jumel de Barneville, countess d' (ca. 1650–1705)
*writer*

Born at Barneville, Marie-Catherine Le Jumel de Barneville, countess d'Aulnoy, was forced, because she tried to escape her husband, to sojourn in Spain, then in England (from 1669 to 1685), where in 1690, she produced her *Mémoires de la cour d'Espagne*, followed by *Relation du voyage en Espagne* (1691), and *Mémoires de la cour d'Angleterre* (1695), inexact but lively chronicles. Upon her return to France (1685), she opened a literary salon fre-

quented by worldly society and published a romantic account that enjoyed a great success, *Histoire d'Hippolyte, comte de Douglas* (1690). Her *Contes de fées* (or *Les Fées à la mode*, 1697) are charming fairy tales meant especially for children (*L'Oiseau bleu; Gracieuse et Percinet; La Chatte blanche*), while *Les Illustres Fées* (1698) evokes an elegant society more than a world of fantasy.

## Aumale, Charles of Lorraine, duke d' (1556–1631)
*Catholic leader in Wars of Religion*

Charles of Lorraine, duke d'Aumale, was one of the leaders of the HOLY LEAGUE. Governor of PARIS (1589), he forced King HENRY IV to give up the siege of the capital. Condemned to death for contempt (1595) because of his alliance with the Spanish, he took refuge in the Low Countries and died in Brussels.

## Aumale, Henri-Eugène-Philippe-Louis d'Orléans, duke d' (1822–1897)
*soldier, writer, royal figure*

Born in PARIS, the fourth son of LOUIS-PHILIPPE and Marie-Amélie, Henri the duke d'Aumale joined the military and took part in the Algerian campaign of 1843. He was named governor of ALGERIA in 1847, but after the REVOLUTION OF 1848, resigned his post and went to England. There, he dedicated himself to historical research and writing (*Histoire des princes de Condé*, 1869) and publishing pamphlets against the SECOND EMPIRE and NAPOLÉON III. After the beginning of the FRANCO-PRUSSIAN WAR in 1870, he offered his services to France but was rejected. He returned nonetheless in 1871 and was elected to the National Assembly. Rejoining the army, he presided over the tribunal that condemned Marshal FRANÇOIS BAZAINE. The duke d'Aumale later was part of the monarchist faction that forced the resignation of LOUIS ADOLPHE THIERS in 1873. In 1883, he served as inspector general of the army but was proscribed by the decree of 1886. Author of a work, *Instructions militaires de la France* (1868), he left much of his property to the Institut and the Museum of Chantilly. The duke d'Aumale was elected to the ACADÉMIE FRANÇAISE in 1871.

## Auriol, Vincent (1884–1966)
*political figure*

Born in Revel, Vincent Auriol, an attorney, worked within the ranks of the Socialist Party and became the financial expert of the Section Francaise de l'Internationale Ouvrière (SFIO). He served as minister of finances in the Popular Front government of LÉON BLUM (1936), then as minister of justice (1937). Having refused to support the Vichy regime of PHILIPPE PÉTAIN, he fled to London in 1943. After the Liberation, he served as president of the two Constituent Assemblies. Elected president of the FOURTH REPUBLIC, he exercised during the whole period of his term (1947–54) a real influence on the government by favoring a middle course of policy. Vincent Auriol is the author of *Journal du septennat 1947–1954.*

## Aymé, Marcel (1902–1967)
*writer*

Marcel Aymé was born in Joingy and, after a childhood spent in the countryside, came to Paris (1925), where he held various jobs. Later, he became a journalist. The success of his account *La Jument verte* (1933), in which sexuality is the source of satirical comedy, allowed him to dedicate himself to writing. The novels of Aymé often explore rural life and are descriptions, too, of the mediocrity and hypocrisy that he observed. This pessimism is apparent in *Travelingue* (1941), and especially in *Le Chemin des écoliers* (1946), *Le Vin de Paris* (1947), and *Uranus* (1948). All bear ironic witness to the period of the Occupation and the Liberation of World War II. To mitigate the boredom of modern life, Marcel Aymé resorted to imaginative, picturesque, and hilarious characters (*La Table-aux-crevés*, (1929); *Le Boeuf clandestine*, 1939) in familiar tales of the real and the imaginary (*La Vouivre*, 1943). His taste for the lively vernacular, both rural and Parisian, is represented skillfully in brief and incisive narration, and his sense of parody is original and remarkable. An imaginative realism colors his accounts in *Passe-muraille* (1943) and in the *Contes du chat perché* (1934, augmented in 1950 and 1958)—"simple stories without love or money," which combine, with a knowing naïveté, the marvels and the daily routine of rustic life. Interested in film, which often transposed his work, Aymé also wrote for the theater: *Lucienne et le Boucher* (1932) and *Clérambard* (1950) are truculent comedies, while *La Tête des autres* (1952) is a bitter satire on bourgeois justice. Aymé has done two adaptations of works by Arthur Miller: *Les Socières de Salem* (1954) and *Vu du Pont* (1958).

## Aznavour, Charles (1924–  )
*writer-composer, singer, and actor*

Of Armenian origin, Charles Aznavour was born Varenagh Aznavourian in PARIS. He wrote for ÉDITH PIAF, JULIETTE GRÉCO, and GILBERT BÉCAUD before beginning his own career as a singer. His direct and descriptive style, his distinct, rough, but velvetlike voice, as well as the quality of his tunes, gained for him during the 1960s a large international audience (*"La Mamma," "Les Comédiens," "J'me vouais déjà"*). He also acted in a number of films including *Tirez sur le pianiste* (1960), *Un taxi pour Tobrouk* (1961), and *Le Tambour* (1979), among others.

# B

## Babeuf, François-Noël (1760–1797)
### ("Gracchus")
*revolutionary*

Born in Saint-Quentin, and spending his early years in the service of the landed aristocracy, François-Noël, or Gracchus, Babeuf as he is known, wrote initially on the problems of agrarian law and land distribution. Arriving in PARIS during the REVOLUTION of 1789, he was briefly imprisoned at the time of the TERROR. Upon his release, he attacked the Revolution because it had not developed along the lines of socialism. Writing under the pen name "Gracchus Babeuf," he published a journal, *Tribun du peuple,* in which he strongly condemned the enemies of the Revolution. As a supporter of common ownership of land and property, and of the absolute equality of all citizens, he advocated the abolition of all private ownership of property and of inheritance. He was also one of the earliest advocates of nationalization. His principles became known as Babouvism. Along with PHILIPPE BUONARROTI and others, he organized the Conspiracy of the Equals to overthrow the Directory government (1796) and establish a communistic state. Babeuf's part in this conspiracy resulted in his execution.

## Bachelard, Gaston (1884–1962)
*philosopher*

Born in Bar-sur-Aube, Gaston Bachelard worked for the Ministry of Communications and studied both the sciences and philosophy, then taught in the Faculty of Letters at Dijon (1930–40) and later at the SORBONNE. Analyzing the parameters of scientific knowledge, he maintained that progress could be attained only by overcoming epistemological obstacles (immediate perception, opinion, results considered to be definitive) as he sought to "establish the rudiments of a rational psychoanalysis." An open philosopher (dialectic), Bachelard integrated aspects of philosophy and psychoanalysis. His philosophy of science can be described as an applied rationalism (*Le Nouveau Esprit scientifique,* 1934; *La Formation de l'esprit scientifique,* 1938; *Le Rationalisme appliqué,* 1948; *Le Matérialisme rationnel,* 1953). To the world of rationality, he juxtaposed a complimentary universe of the poetic imagination and its symbols, which draw inspiration from the natural elements (earth, air, fire, water) and which Bachelard attempted to apply to a method of psychoanalysis (*La Psychoanalyse du feu,* 1937; *L'Eau et les rêves,* 1941; *L'Air et les songes,* 1943; *La Terre et les rêveries de la volonté,* 1948; *La Terre et les rêveries du repos,* 1948; *La Poétique de la rêverie,* 1960).

## Baïf, Jean de (1532–1589)
*writer*

The natural son of LAZARDE DE BAÏF, Jean de Baïf was born in Venice. As a student of the humanist JEAN DORET, his classmates included JOACHIM DU BELLAY and PIERRE DE RONSARD. Together, they formed the "Brigade" (which was to become the PLÉIADE group of poets and writers). Baïf demonstrated his admiration for ancient classical culture by adopting the style of the Latin and Greek playwrights (*Le Brave,* 1567, after Plautius; *Antigone,* 1573, after Sophocles). A learned poet, Baïf wrote love poetry in the style of Petrarch (*Amours de Méline,* 1552) and more spontaneous works (*Amours de Francine,* 1555), and finally *Mimes, enseignements et proverbes* (1576, 1581, and posthumous, 1597), which were a varied collection of moral and satirical reflections. A reformer and bold thinker, Baïf conceived the idea of adopting a phonetic orthography and the intimate prosody of antiquity, and maintained that through its vocal quality, poetry should be measured by the same melodic rules as music (this led him to establish, with the endorsement of King CHARLES IX, an academy for poetry and music). Baïf failed, however, in his attempt to introduce foreign phonetic rules into French.

## Baïf, Lazare de  (1496–1547)
*diplomat, humanist*

Born in Les Pins, near La Fléche, Lazare de Baïf was an aid to the cardinal de Lorraine and became an adviser to King FRANCIS I and ambassador to Venice (1529). He later served in Germany. A student of the Greek humanist John Lascaris, Baïf became one of the greatest Hellenists of his times (a translation of the four *Lives* of Plutarch and, in French verse, Sophocles' *Electra*). He also published works on archaeology that for a long period were considered among the most authoritative in that field (*De re vestiaria*, 1526; *De re navali*, 1536).

## Bailly, Jean-Sylvain  (1736–1793)
*astronomer, historian, revolutionary*

Born in PARIS, Jean-Sylvain Bailly was early recognized as a brilliant astronomer and mathematician. At age 26, he was nominated to the Academy of Sciences, with his main work as an astronomer being *Essai sur la théorie des satellites de Jupiter* (1766). In this work he applied Newtonian physics to the theory of Jupiter's moons. Bailly's five-volume history of astronomy is his best-known tome. Combining scientific writing with scholarly wisdom and journalistic clarity, it includes *Histoire de l'astronomie ancienne* (1775), *Histoire de l'astronomie moderne* (3 volumes, 1779–82), and *Traité de l'astronomie indienne et orientale* (1787). Bailly was appointed to a royal commission to investigate the work of the Austrian physician Franz Frederich Anton Mesmer and his practice of mesmerism, which claimed to induce trancelike states. Bailly's report would discredit Mesmer's hypothesis of magnetism and pave the way for the foundation of modern psychotherapy. Elected to the ACADÉMIE FRANÇAISE in 1784 and to the Académie des inscriptions et belles-lettres in 1785, he was one of only two people appointed to all three of France's royal academies. Politically,

Bailly served as secretary of the General Assembly of Electors in Paris at the beginning of the REVOLUTION (1789). He was named deputy from Paris to the ESTATES GENERAL and became third president of the Third Estate. He would be the first to swear the Oath of the Tennis Court (see REVOLUTION OF 1789), then became president of the National Assembly. Bailly's defiance of the king made him a popular hero, and he was named mayor of Paris by acclamation after the taking of the BASTILLE. His proclamation of martial law, however, after the riot of the Champ-de-Mars in July 1791, in which he ordered troops to fire on the crowds, led to his downfall. In 1793, he was arrested and falsely accused of plotting with the king and queen. Shortly after, Bailly was executed. His three-volume *Mémoire d'un témoin de la Révolution*, published in 1804, describes many of the events of the times.

## Bainville, Jacques  (1879–1930)
*historian*

Born in Vincennes, Jacques Bainville was a disciple of CHARLES MAURRAS, with whom he collaborated on the latter's right-wing newspaper *L'Action française*. Bainville expressed his own thoughts on the relation between France and Germany and his support of monarchy in two works, *Histoire de France* (1924) and *Napoléon* (1931). In another history, *La Troisième République*, he demonstrated his preoccupation concerning the future of France in which democratic policies seem to be, at best, merely weak safeguards against a rising pan-Germanism (*Histoire de trois générations*, 1934). This pessimism recurs in his chronicles in *Revue universelle*, which he edited beginning in 1920 with HENRI MASSIS and JACQUES MARITAIN. Jacques Bainville was elected to the ACADÉMIE FRANÇAISE in 1935.

## Baker, Josephine  (1906–1975)
*singer, dancer, actor, philanthropist*

Born in St. Louis, Missouri, Josephine Baker first gained notice as a dancer in New York City. During the 1920s, she appeared regularly there at the Cotton Club and other New York night spots. In 1925, she went to Paris and won enormous fame in the production *Le Revue nègre* and in other revues at the

Folies-Bergère and the Casino de Paris. The style of her dance and her songs ("La petite tonkinoise," "J'ai deux amours") enhanced her international reputation as she introduced her black American art style to European audiences. Settling permanently in Paris, Josephine Baker became a French citizen in 1937. She played an active role in the RESISTANCE (1939–45) and, later, in the spirit of inclusiveness, adopted and supported several children of diverse racial backgrounds.

## Balandier, Georges (1920–  )
*anthropologist and sociologist*
Born in Aillevillers, Haute-Saône, Georges Balandier, shortly after World War II (1946), went with a group from the Musée de l'homme to do anthropologic and sociologic studies in Senegal, Guinea, Mauritania, and Congo. His subsequent work has had a profound effect upon the study of contemporary African societies (*Sociologie actuelle de l'Afrique noire, dynamique sociale en Afrique centrale,* 1955), notably through the study of urban phenomena (*Sociologie des Brazzavilles noires,* 1955). His work is based on a dynamic sociology that studies the mechanisms of stability and instability, especially in phenomena that are not readily apparent (*Sens et puissance, les dynamiques sociales,* 1971; *Le Désordre: éloge du mouvement,* 1988). He also was interested in the way in which symbolic configuration can express social channels (*Anthropo-logiques,* 1974) and in the mechanism of power (*Anthropologie politique,* 1967; *Le Pouvoir sur scenes,* 1980). Georges Balandier, who taught at the École normale superieure and at the SORBONNE, served as director of the Institut français d'Afrique noire (IFAN) in Guinea and later at Brazzaville.

## Balladur, Édouard (1929–  )
*political figure*
Born in Smyrna (Izmir), Turkey, Édouard Balladur served as an envoy (1964), then as a technical adviser to GEORGES POMPIDOU (1966–68) and, after the latter's election as head of state, became adjunct secretary-general (1969), then secretary-general to the presidency of the republic (1973–74). During the first cohabitation between the govern-

ment of JACQUES CHIRAC and President FRANÇOIS MITTERRAND, Édouard Balladur was minister of the economy, finances, and privatization (1968–88) and, as a supporter of a liberal economy, led in the privatization of several large public enterprises. After the massive victory of the Union pour la France (UPF) (Rassemblement pour la République [RPR] and Union pour la democratie française [UDF]) in the legislative elections of March 1993, he became prime minister, while a new period of cohabitation began (1993–95). Édouard Balladur followed a policy of restraint but found himself confronted with an economic depression and unemployment. He was a candidate in the presidential election of 1995.

## Balthus (1908–2001)
### (Balthasar Klossowski de Rola)
*painter*
Born in PARIS, Balthasar Klossowski de Rola, or Balthus, as he is known, was the brother of PIERRE KLOSSOWSKI. He learned to paint in the LOUVRE and in Italy, and his technique is similar to fresco, with a tempera base. His treatment of space is influenced by the Italian primitives. He caused a sensation and became widely known in the 1930s for interior scenes depicting disturbing eroticism (*Alice: la leçon de guitare*). Inspired by Emily Brontë's *Wuthering Heights,* he brought to his own work the atmosphere of the Gothic novel in his enigmatic portraits of young women shown in bleak surroundings. Always on the edge of artistic trends, Balthus painted landscapes in the same vein. His work, which later became more academic, is still based on the dual theme of a provocative and suggestive eroticism and monumentalism (*La Rue,* 1933; *Le Passage du Commerce-Saint-André,* 1952–53). Balthus served as the curator of the Villa Medici in Rome from 1961 to 1976.

## Balzac, Honoré de (1799–1850)
*writer*
Considered one of the world's great novelists, Honoré de Balzac wrote, along with many short stories, essays, and plays, *La Comédie humaine* (1842–48), a cycle of about 90 novels describing French society

in detail. Balzac was born in Tours and, at age 20, with his family's consent, gave up the study of law to devote his life to writing. He was influenced early by his mother's interest in mysticism and began his literary career writing works that reflected a romantic sentimentality and his youthful intoxication with abstract theory. Discouraged by an initial lack of success, he turned to publishing for financial security but soon fell into debt. It was the first of several financial disasters in his life. Balzac then wrote, often for magazines, on a per-word basis to get out of debt, which he never fully accomplished. Balzac's first important novel was *Les Chouans* (1829), based on the civil war in the VENDÉE during the REVOLUTION OF 1789. Although clearly influenced by romanticism, the historical accuracy and factual descriptions that characterize this work became hallmarks of Balzac's fictional style. The relative success of *Les Chouans* was followed by the triumph of his two philosophical novels, *La Peau de chagrin* (1831) and *Louis Lambert* (1832). At this time, he also met Eveline Hanska, a Polish countess with whom he remained for the rest of his life. Balzac reached his full creative maturity between 1833 and 1835, when he wrote and published his masterpieces *Le Médecin de campagne* (1833), *Eugènie Grandet* (1833), *Père Goriot* (1834), and *Le Lys dans la vallée* (1835). At this time he conceived the idea of connecting his novels with a larger work, depicting a detailed study of French life and society, from the Revolution to the ascendance of LOUIS-PHILIPPE I in 1830. After 1834, he wrote his novels with this in mind, as parts of *La Comédie humaine*, and a 17-volume edition appeared under that title between 1842 and 1848. In his introduction to this edition, Balzac reflects the influence of the groundbreaking theories of LAMARCK and GEOFFROY SAINT-HILLAIRE concerning the evolution of animal species. Balzac used the word *studies* to describe the three groupings of his work in which he extends the ideas of those two scientists on environment and heredity to his own description of human behavior and character. The goal of *La Comédie humaine* was to describe the human species in France from 1789 to 1830. In doing so, Balzac presages, by his significant degree of historical realism, the later movement of literary realism. At the same time, however, he writes in the genre of literary romanticism. Balzac's use of heightened realism, through which he

attempted objectively to describe French society, as well as the development of the panoramic historical novel, had an enormous influence on other authors, including MARCEL PROUST and ÉMILE ZOLA, both of whom wrote lengthy novel cycles.

## Balzac, Jean-Louis-Guez, sieur de (1595–1654)
*writer*

Considered in his lifetime the "most eloquent" man of his era, Jean-Louis Guez de Balzac was born in Angoulême, where he was first educated. He later studied law at Poitier, Paris, and Leiden, the Netherlands. Balzac began writing letters in 1618 and then, visiting Italy (1620–22), there found further inspiration and material for his prose. The first edition of his *Lettres,* full of enthusiasm for the ancient world, was published in 1624. They were all well received because of their fine writing style. His attempts to write longer works, however, were not as successful, and his first lengthy publication, *Le Prince* (1631), a veiled description of King LOUIS XIII, was coldly received. Balzac continued a steady correspondence with his friends in Paris and elsewhere and, in 1634, was elected to the ACADÉMIE FRANÇAISE. His first book of letters was republished many times during the 17th century. Seven other collections of letters were later published, but none had the success of the first. Other books by Balzac include *Le Baron* (1648), a satire on pedagogues, and *Le Socrates chrétien* (1652), and a series of religious essays. Other works, including his favorite, *Aristippe ou de la cour*, with his reflections on Machiavellianism in politics, and *Entretiens* (1657), a work of literary criticism, were published posthumously in 1658 and 1659, respectively, and the only nearly complete edition of his works, in two folio volumes, appeared in 1658.

## Barante, Prosper-Brugière, baron de (1782–1866)
*historian and political figure*

Born in Riom, Prosper-Brugière, baron de Barante was an intimate friend of both Mme DE STAËL and Mme RÉCAMIER. He had a brilliant administrative career, and while maintaining liberal views, held high posts under the FIRST EMPIRE and during the

RESTORATION. Named a peer of France in 1819, he was appointed ambassador to Russia in 1835 (*Souvenirs de Russie,* 1859). He left the diplomatic service in 1848. Already known for his *Tableau de la littérature française au XIIIe siècle* (1808), Barante acquired more literary notoriety with his dozen volumes of *Histoire des ducs de Bourgogne de la maison de Valois* (1824–26). In these texts, relying on accurate sources, he wrote a colorful chronicle, free of any political doctrine or rhetoric. His other works include *Études historiques et biographiques* (1857), *Études littéraires et historiques* (1858), and eight volumes of *Souvenirs* (posthumous, 1889–1901). He was elected to the ACADÉMIE FRANÇAISE in 1828.

## Barbaroux, Charles-Jean-Marie (1767–1794)

*political figure*

Born in MARSEILLES, Charles-Jean-Marie Barbaroux, an attorney, embraced the ideas of the REVOLUTION OF 1789 and, on August 10, 1792, led the Federalist section from Marseille during the taking of the Tuileries in Paris. Elected deputy for Bouche-du-Rhône to the Convention, he joined the GIRONDINS and, while they were being eliminated from power by the MONTAGNARDS, tried to organize a resistance in Normandy during the FEDERALIST INSURRECTION with FRANÇOIS BUZOT and JÉROME PÉTION DE VILLENEUVE (Caen, 1793). He failed and, after fleeing to Bordeaux, Barbaroux was captured, condemned, and executed.

## Barbès, Armand (1809–1870)

*revolutionary*

Born in Point-à-Pitre, Armand Barbès arrived in Paris in 1830 and immediately joined the republican opposition to the JULY MONARCHY. He was imprisoned after the April Days of 1834 (see APRIL 1834, DAYS OF), and again in 1835 after an assassination attempt on the king, in which, however, he had no part. Upon his release, Barbès organized and led, with LOUIS AUGUSTE BLANQUI, the May 12, 1839, uprising. He was sentenced to death, but the sentence was commuted to life in prison, in part owing to the intervention of VICTOR HUGO. Released after the February 1848 REVOLUTION, Barbès took a seat in the National Assembly as a deputy of the extreme Left. But having been one of the principal instigators of the May 15 demonstrations, he was again sentenced to prison. Held at Doullens and later at Belle-Île-en-Mer, he refused the pardon granted by NAPOLÉON III in 1854 and, freed against his will, went into voluntary exile in Holland.

## Barbey d'Aurevilly, Jules-Amédée (1808–1889)

*novelist, critic*

Born in Saint-Sauveur-le-Vicomte, Jules-Amédée Barbey d'Aurevilly was descended from Norman nobility and was a staunch Roman Catholic and royalist. His novels, which are tragic stories of violent emotions, deal with the typical characters and types of the Cotentin region of his native NORMANDY. Among his major works of fiction are *Une Vieille Maîtresse* (1851), *L'Ensorcelée* (1854), and *Les Diaboliques* (1874). Most of his critical work is found in *Les Œuvres et les hommes* (26 volumes, 1860–1909). Barbey wrote against the romantic dandyism of the age (*Du dandysme et de George Brummel*) and was a supporter of the ultramontanist position within the Catholic Church. Barbey d'Aurevilly influenced such writers as GEORGES BERNANOS.

## Barbizon School

Situated near the Fontainebleau forest, outside of Paris, Barbizon was a favorite gathering place of landscape painters during the mid-19th century. The style of these painters of the Barbizon School was derived especially from that of CAMILLE COROT and GUSTAVE COURBET and played an important role in the development of IMPRESSIONISM.

See also MILLET, JEAN-FRANÇOIS; ROUSSEAU, THÉODORE.

## Bardot, Brigitte (1934–   )

*actor, animal rights advocate*

Born Camille Javal in Paris, Brigitte Bardot, as a film actress, became an international sex symbol before retiring from show business to devote herself to the cause of animal rights. She began her career modeling in fashion magazines and, at the age of 15, made her film debut in the comedy *Le trou normand*

(1952). In 1956, she was featured in *Et Dieu créa la femme*, directed by ROGER VADIM, which was a showcase for her physical beauty and sensual personality. The film was an international success, especially in the United States, where it represented different and controversial film standards. Bardot's image was further advanced in a series of minor French and Italian comedies, but she gained respect in her field as an actress, in *La Vérité* (1960), directed by JEAN-LUC GODARD, and *Le mépris* (1963) and *Viva Maria* (1965), directed by LOUIS MALLE. After this, she made other films and maintained her worldwide celebrity. Following her retirement from acting in 1973, Brigitte Bardot mostly withdrew from public life but continued to keep her notoriety through her tireless efforts and selfless advocacy for animal rights. She established a foundation under her name for the protection of animals (1970) and was awarded the LEGION OF HONOR in 1985.

## Barnave, Antoine (1761–1793)
*revolutionary*

Born in Grenoble, Barnave was a lawyer and member of the estates for the Dauphiné region. In 1789, he was elected to the Third Estate of the Estates General and, at the beginning of the REVOLUTION, became spokesman for the liberal bourgeois position. As one of the most brilliant speakers in the National Assembly, he spoke against MIRABEAU and his defense of royal prerogatives. After the king's failed attempt at escape in 1791, Barnave was charged with returning the monarch to Paris. He then rallied to the constitutional monarchist side and joined the CLUB DES FEUILLANTS. One of the authors of the Constitution of 1791, Barnave favored a "free and limited" monarchy. Denounced by the Jacobins, he was guillotined during the Terror. As author of an *Introduction à la Révolution française* (1792, published 1843), Barnave described both the political and the social implications of that event.

## Barras, Paul, viscount de (1755–1829)
*political figure*

Born in Fox-Amphoux, Provence, to a noble family of the region, Paul, viscount de Barras, served as an officer in the Indies campaigns before being elected deputy in 1792 to the Convention. There, he took his place with the Montagnards, the radical group that abolished the monarchy during the Revolution. Barras was soon sent as an envoy to the French army in Italy and then to southeastern France, where he organized and directed the suppression of the counterrevolutionaries after the siege of Toulon (December 19, 1793). With JEAN-LAMBERT TALLIEN and JOSEPH FOUCHÉ, he was one of the principal figures responsible for the overthrow of MAXIMILIEN ROBESPIERRE (9 Thermidor, Year II—July 27, 1794) and, as commander in chief of the Army of the Interior under the Thermidorian Convention, suppressed the royalist insurrection against the government (13 Vendémiaire, Year IV—October 5, 1795). As a director in 1795, Barras was one of the organizers of the coup d'etat of 18 Fructidor, Year V (September 4, 1797), and served as head of state until the coup d'etat of 18 Brumaire, Year VIII (November 9, 1799), that brought Napóléon Bonaparte to power (see NAPOLÉON I). Bonaparte subsequently forced Barras to retire. Exiled in 1810, then interned at Montpellier, he reemerged after the Restoration. Barras's *Mémoires* give an interesting account and description of political and social life under the Directory.

## Barrault, Jean-Louis (1910–1994)
*actor, director, and producer*

Born in Le Vinsinet, Jean-Louis Barrault was a student of CHARLES DULLEN and was initially influenced by the ideas of Antonine Autaud, who saw the art of theater as a ritual. Barrault also studied mime with ETIENNE DECROUX. His meeting with PAUL CLAUDEL, for whom he would later direct (*Numance*, 1937; *Le Soulier de satin*, 1943; *Le Partage de midi*, 1948), and his joining the Comédie-Française mark the beginning of his career. With his wife, the actress MADELEINE RENAUD, he founded the troop that would be attached to the Marigny Theater. He served, too, as the director of the Odéon Theater from 1958 to 1968. A director of the avant-garde, he also produced many of the great classical works (*Hamlet*, 1946; *L'Orestie*, 1955), contemporary pieces (Claudel's *Tête d'or*, 1959; Ionesco's *Rhinoceros*, 1960; Beckett's *Happy Days*, 1963). After completing several tours, Barrault directed *Rabelais* (1970) and served as director of the Renaud-Barrault Theater (1974–80), where he staged *Zarathustra* (1975). He then served as director of the theater of Rond-Point (1981–91). In cinema, Barrault appeared in well-known films, notably *Drôle de drame* (1937), *Les Enfants du paradis* (1945), *Le Rond* (1950), and JEAN RENOIR's *Le Testament du docteur Cordelier* (1961).

## Barre, Raymond (1924–  )
*economist and political figure*

Born in Saint-Denis, La Réunion, and educated in Paris (Institut d'études politiques), Raymond Barre is a distinguished professor of laws and economic sciences and has served as vice president of the Commission for the European Community (1967–72), president of the Commission for Financial Reform and Reconstruction (1975), minister of foreign trade (1976), and premier (1976), after the resignation of JACQUES CHIRAC. Raymond Barre undertook a rigorous policy of financial reform to redress the nation's economic situation (plans Barre). As an economist without party affiliation he was charged with overcoming industrial stagnation, the deficit in foreign trade, and inflation. He sought to move France toward a free-market economy by removing price controls and limiting government aid to failing companies. High technology and competition were encouraged and, to deal with energy prices, the building of nuclear power plants was accelerated. Closer ties with Arab nations were developed to safeguard important sources of petroleum for France. Barre, however, had to resign after the defeat of VALÉRY GISCARD-D'ESTAING in the presidential election of 1981. In the presidential election of 1988, Barre himself ran and gained 16.55 percent in the first round of voting. He has served since 1978 as deputy for Rhône and, after 1995, as mayor of LYON.

## Barrès, Maurice (1862–1923)
*writer, political figure*

Born in Charmes, Vosges, Maurice Barrè's began his literary career shortly after he entered political life. The first of two volumes of his trilogy *Le Culte du moi* (*Sous l'œil des barbares,* 1888; *Un Homme libre,* 1889) are affirmations of his moral and social individual-ism, appearing when he was elected a Boulangist deputy for Nancy (1889). *Le Jardin de Bérénice* (1891) completed the cycle. An anti-Dreyfusard (see DREYFUS, ALFRED), defender of the military, and preoccupied with the German threat, Barrè's presented his nationalistic ideas in a new trilogy, *Le Roman de l'énergie nationale* (1897–1902); (*Les Déracinés, L'Appel au soldat, Leurs figures*). Conscious henceforth of the need for action, he never ceased to exalt revanchist patriotism (*Colette Baudoche,* 1909; *La Colline inspirée,* 1913), until World War I made him a supporter of the Union sacrée. A deputy for Paris since 1906, he was, in the same year, named to the ACADÉMIE FRANÇAISE. *Mes Cahiers,* his journal, contains his intellectual memoirs, in which he also expresses "the melodies that are inside him" and explains his many personal complexities—"a blood that demands action, a spirit that wishes to remain free" (HENRI DE MONTHERLANT).

## Barricades, Days of

The term "Days of the Barricades" is given to several Parisian insurrections throughout French history. The Day of May 12, 1588, the duke of GUISE took PARIS. King HENRY III wanted to recapture the city with his troops, but the population rose up, blocking the streets with large barrels and casks (*barriques*) filled with earth. The king had to flee, leaving the city to the duke de Guise. The Day of August 26, 1648, the city rose up following the arrest of popular figures by the regent ANNE OF AUSTRIA, who was then forced to free them. This day marks the beginning of the FRONDE. The Days of July 1830 mark the beginning of the REVOLUTION OF 1830; those of February and June 1848 signal the beginnings of the REVOLUTION OF 1848 and of the subsequent popular uprising. The Day of December 3, 1851, was a day of revolutionary protest against the coup d'état of LOUIS-NAPOLÉON BONAPARTE (December 2, 1851), and like many Days of the Barricades, was centered in the faubourg Saint-Antoine. The Days of the COMMUNE OF Paris of 1871 mark the resistance of the Commune of Paris against the national troops sent from Versailles. The Days of August 1944 occurred during the Liberation of Paris. The Week of the Barricades (January 24,–February 1, 1960) was an insurrection against the policies of General CHARLES DE GAULLE and the conflict in ALGERIA. The Days of May 1968 mark the student uprisings in Paris that helped to bring about the end of the de Gaulle government.

See also NAPOLÉON III.

### Barrot, Odilon  (1791–1873)
*political figure*

Born in Villefort, Lozère, Odilon Barrot, who became an attorney in 1811, soon took a position against the regime of the RESTORATION, which he had initially supported. A liberal constitutional monarchist, he upheld, during the REVOLUTION OF JULY 1830, the idea of a "kingdom surrounded by republican institutions." Under the July Monarchy, he became the leader of the dynastic opposition (constitutional monarchists of the Left: parti du Mouvement). Organizer of the "Banquets campaign" (1847) for electoral reform, he was overtaken by the democratic forces during the REVOLUTION OF 1848 and unwittingly became one of the initiators of the fall of the monarchy. For a time a supporter of NAPOLÉON III, who named him minister of justice and head of his first ministry (1848–49), he soon went over to the Orléanist opposition and was arrested (December 2, 1851). In 1872, LOUIS-ADOLPHE THIERS named him president of the Council of State. Odilon Barrot's *Mémoires* were published in 1875–76.

### Barry, Jeanne Beçu, countess du  (1743–1793)
*nobility*

Born in Vaucouleurs, Jeanne Beçu, countess, or Madame, du Barry, as she is known, was the natural daughter of a seamstress and a tax collector. After a brief convent education and a somewhat restless youth, she became the mistress of the chevalier Jean du Barry and, shortly after, to LOUIS XV. As his favorite, she had great influence over the king until his death in 1777, when she then retired to her chateau at Louvciennes, near VERSAILLES. Much celebrated for her beauty and wit, she often found herself at the center of court intrigues. She also was a generous patron to many artists and literary figures. In 1792, during the REVOLUTION, she

made at least one visit to England and then, upon her return to France, was arrested and executed at the beginning of the TERROR.

### Bart, Jean  (1650–1702)
*naval officer*

Born in Dunkerque, Jean Bart enlisted in the naval service of Holland, then joined that of King LOUIS XIV at the time of the Dutch War (1672). In that capacity, as a corsair, he was quite successful. Notably, he broke the English blockade of Dunkerque (1694) and took or burned more than 80 Dutch merchant vessels (1696). For his exploits, Bart was ennobled by Louis XIV and made commander of a fleet (1697). There are many anecdotes of his courage and bluntness as a sailor, naval commander, and popular hero of the period.

### Bartas, Guillaume de Salluste, seigneur de  (1544–1590)
*poet, military figure*

Born in Montfort, near Auch, Guillaume de Salluste, lord of Bartas, a Huguenot, had a reputation as a renowned soldier when he entered the service of Henri de Navarre (HENRY IV). For that king, he also carried out various diplomatic missions to England and Denmark. As a writer, his abundant literary works include especially religious poetry, in which he emerges as an austere moralist: *Uranie, Le Triomfe de la foi* (1583), *Judith* (1583). Bartas's principal work, which had a prodigious success, is *La Sepmaine ou la Création du monde* (1578–84), a poem in seven cantos, inspired by the Old Testament. It was followed by *La Seconde Sepmaine* (unfinished, 1585) and evokes the history of humanity. More than a religious work, however, it is a scientific poem that can be considered part of the baroque aesthetic.

### Barthes, Roland  (1915–1980)
*literary critic, semiologist*

A leader in structuralist and semiotic movements, Roland Barthes was born in Cherbourg. After receiving degrees in classical studies and having experience in the theater (Groupe de Théâtre antique de la Sorbonne, 1936), he was, beginning in 1945, influenced by the works of Karl Marx and JEAN-PAUL SARTRE. A reading of ALBERT CAMUS's *L'Étranger* gave Barthes the idea for a new form of literature, a neutral, or "blanche," style of writing, employing the written text alone. *Le Degré zéro de l'écriture* (1953), a reflection on literary language and on the historical condition, was a collection of his thoughts on structuralism. This essay can be considered the manifesto of a "new criticism." His works on *Michelet* (1954), *Racine* (1963), and on others illustrate this critical approach in which Freudian psychoanalysis plays a large role. Social criticism dominates in *Mythologies* (1957), a reflection on the myths of daily life through which society accepts as natural the historical results of ideology. These concepts brought Barthes to structural linguistics. *Élements de semiologie* (1964) and *Système de la mode* (1967) analyze statements concerning the feminine mode and the "code" that it represents, contributing with a rigorous method borrowed from the Danish linguist Louis Hjelmslev to the understanding of the laws of signification. Barthes published a detailed exegesis on a story by HONORÉ DE BALZAC, which puts forth particularly the theme of sexual ambiguity and castration (*S/Z*, 1970). Other essays on *Sade, Fourier, Loyola* (1971), show a growing interest in the significance of the unconscious. Barthes has also written on the group *Tel Quel* and on Japanese society (*L'Empire des signes*, 1970). A precursor of critical formalism, Barthes, with five volumes of *Essais critiques* (1964–84), *Le Plaisir du texte* (1973), then *Roland Barthes par lui-même* (1975), avoids being "scientific" so as to give the reader a more humanistic approach (*Fragments d'un discours amoureux*, 1977). He has also written a meditation on photography (*La Chambre claire*, 1980), a statement on the rapport between an image and its times. In 1976, Barthes was named to the chair of Literary Semiology at the COLLÈGE DE FRANCE.

## Bartholdi, Frédéric-Auguste (1834–1904)
*sculptor*

Best known for his creation the *Statue of Liberty*, standing in the harbor of New York City, Frédéric-Auguste Bartholdi was born in Colmar and was trained there and in Paris as an architect. He also studied painting and, in 1855, traveled to the Middle East to continue his studies. He soon devoted himself to sculpture, however, with his first major achievement being a statue of General JEAN RAPP (1853). Then, at official request, he was commissioned to express patriotic sentiments in a work done in the academic style, and produced *La Liberté eclairant le monde* (*Statue of Liberty*), a monument 33 meters high (dedicated in 1886) as a gift from France to the United States (a reproduction stands in Paris at the pont de Grenelle). The statue was done in bronze set on a steel armature made by GUSTAVE EIFFEL. Bartholdi's architectural training enabled him to handle successfully extreme problems of material and structure. Another of his monuments, and perhaps his greatest tour de force, is *Le Lion de Belfort,* completed in 1880 (a reproduction is in Paris, at place Denfert-Rochereau). Carved out of red sandstone on a hill over that city, it honors the French during the FRANCO-PRUSSIAN WAR.

## Barthou, Louis (1862–1934)
*political figure*

Born in Oloron-Sainte-Marie, Louis Barthou served as a center-right deputy and was several times minister during the THIRD REPUBLIC. President of the Council (March–December 1913), he put through the law providing for three years of military service, thus drawing the hostility of the Radicals and the Socialists. Senator (1922), then foreign minister (1934), he worked for the realization of a policy of alliance with eastern Europe (in particular the USSR), but was killed during the assassination attempt against King Alexander I of Yugoslavia that took place in MARSEILLE. Barthou is the author of several historical works and was elected into the ACADÉMIE FRANÇAIS in 1918.

## Barye, Antoine-Louis (1796–1875)
*sculptor, watercolorist*

Born in Paris, Antoine-Louis Barye was the son of a goldsmith and studied with the Monegasque sculptor F. Bosio, then with the painter ANTOINE GROS. He became well known as a painter of animals with his *Tigre dévorant un gavial* (1831) and then a *Lion écrasant un serpent* (1833). The nonconformity of his works was violently criticized, however, but he continued to receive official commissions (*Lion en marche*, for the July Column, 1840) and also produced works in a more classical spirit (*Le Lapithe et le Centaure*, 1850; *Thésée combattant le Minotaure*, 1855). Barye had a great sense of movement and an understanding of large animated forms, and he could exalt the epic and dramatic character of his subjects with a marked predeliction for the romantic theme of the struggles of wild beasts. A keen observer, he often went to paint at Barbizion, and his watercolors and drawings done there have great expressive power.

## Basque français, Pays

The Pays Basque français is a region of southwest France that extends in the west from the pic (peak) d'Anie, on the approach to the Pyrenees in the department of Pyrénées-Atlantiques. It comprises the former lands of la Soule, Labourd (Bayonne and Ustaritz), and the lower Navarre. The mountainous area is generally not very elevated (900 m at la Rhune) but reaches 2,017 m at pic d'Orhy. There are numerous streams and rivers and a hilly, wooded countryside. The Basque population is essentially agrarian.

## Bastiat, Frédéric (1810–1850)
*economist, philosopher, statesman*

Born near Bayonne, the son of a merchant in the Spanish trade, Frédéric Bastiat had limited success working in trade and farming on the family estate at Mugron. He became a strong proponent of free trade, following the principles of the British economist Richard Cobden. Bastiat founded a society for that purpose and also edited the society's journal. After the REVOLUTION OF 1848, he spent a number of years combating the growth of socialism, especially that of PIERRE PROUDHON. In August 1848, he was elected to the Constituent Assembly and in May 1949, to the Legislative Assembly. His works include *Harmonies économiques* (1848), *Propriété et loi* (1849), and *Protectionisme et communisme* (1850). As an economist and thinker, Bastiat is considered a partisan of "optimistic liberalism," in contrast to the views of Thomas Malthus and David Ricardo.

## Bastille, la

A former French prison fortress in PARIS, the Bastille, at the time of the REVOLUTION OF 1789, was regarded as a symbol of royal tyranny. Built around 1370, it was originally part of the fortifications of the east wall of the city. Beginning with Cardinal RICHELIEU and throughout the 17th and 18th centuries, the Bastille was used primarily for housing political prisoners. Citizens of any class and profession, who for whatever reason were deemed a liability to the royal establishment, were arrested by "lettres de cachet"—secret warrants that would imprison them indefinitely in the Bastille without accusation or trial. Among the more illustrious of the fortress's prisoners were VOLTAIRE and the marquis DE SADE. At the beginning of the Revolution (July 14, 1789), the Bastille was attacked and captured by a mob assisted by royal troops. Two days later, the demolition of the fortress was begun amid great public rejoicing. The event marked the transition of the Revolution from the parliamentary to the popular stage. The site is now an open square, known as the place de la Bastille. In its center is the large bronze July Column surmounted by a figure of the spirit of Liberty, erected in 1833. Bastille Day is celebrated annually as the national holiday of France on July 14.

La Bastille *(Library of Congress)*

## Bataille, Gabriel (ca. 1575–1630)
*composer, lutist*
Music master to QUEEN ANNE (1617–30), Gabriel Bataille composed tunes for the court ballets and published six books on *Airs de différents auteurs mis en tablature de luth* (1608–15). He is also the author of 10 psalms, based on the poems of PHILIPPE DESPORTES.

## Bataille, Georges (1897–1962)
*writer*
Born in Billom, Puy-de-Dôme, Georges Bataille, persuaded that "authentic literature must be Promethean," sought to put that principle into all his work. A convert to Catholicism, then to Marxism, he was drawn to sociology and psychology and, borrowing their aesthetic techniques, combined them with Oriental mysticism. His idea of society and history, based on the concept of transgression (*La Part maudite*, 1949; *Lascaux ou la Naissance de l'art*, 1955), his mystical experience, and his conception of literature (*La Littérature et la Mal*, 1957) are all apparent in his writings. Bataille proposed that, considering sexuality and death as disorder, society tries to remove them, but then turns to religion and contradiction (*L'Érotisme*, 1957). Bataille also wrote a trilogy: *Somme athéologique* (*L'Éxperience intérieure*, 1943; *La Coupable*, 1944, *Sur Nietzsche*, 1945). His other works include *L'Abbé C* (1950), *Histoire de l'œil* (1928), *Anus solaire* (1931), *Alleluiah* (1947), *Le Bleu de ciel* (written in 1935, published in 1957), *Madame Edwarda* (1941), and *L'Impossible* (1962).

## Bataille, Henry (1872–1922)
*dramatist, poet*
Considered the foremost French dramatist of the pre–World War I period (1900–14), Henry Bataille was born in Nîmes. In his work, he sought to present a complaisant picture of decadent morals in a style that came to be called "sentimental realism." He gives psychological studies of passion as a motivating force in human behavior. Bataille's principal writings include *Maman Colibri* (1904), *La Marche nuptiale* (1905), *La Femme nue* (1908), and *La Vierge folle* (1910). His verse includes a book of war poems, *La Divine Tragédie* (1917).

## Bauchant, André (1873–1958)
*painter*
Born in Château-Renault, André Bauchant was the son of a vintner and was himself a horticulturist. He began painting during World War I and exhibited at the Salon d'automne in 1921. Influenced by LE CORBUSIER, JACQUES LIPSHITZ, and ANDRÉ LURÇAT, Bauchant received recognition at his own show in 1927, and soon after, the impresario Sergey Diaghilev commissioned him to do the ballet sets for Stravinski's *Apollon musagète* (1927). A representative of art naïf and considered a painter of popular realism, Bauchant devoted himself to "grand genre," portraying with ingenuity and imagination biblical, mythological, and historical subjects, often done in a range of bright colors. He also painted bouquets, landscapes, rustic scenes, and portraits in deep and warm tones.

## Baudeau, Nicolas (1730–1792)
*economist, abbot*
Born in Amboise, Abbé Nicolas Baudeau was the founder of a periodic compilation, *Ephemeúdes du citoyen* (1796). He was initially hostile to the Physiocrats but eventually adopted their ideas and developed and explained the system of FRANÇOIS QUESNAY in *Première Introduction à la philosophie économique ou Analyse des États polices* and, in doing so, also supported the theories of ANNE-ROBERT TURGOT.

## Baudelaire, Charles (1821–1867)
*writer*
A poet and critic, Charles Baudelaire, who was to become a leader of the symbolist school of literature, was born in Paris and educated at the Collège Louis-le-Grand. His childhood and adolescence were unhappy, as his father died when he was six, and he resented his mother's marriage to his stepfather, whom he disliked. Even then, as he later wrote, he felt that he was "destined to be always alone." Scandalized by the bohemian life that he adopted in his youth, his family sent him on a sea voyage to India. He soon returned to Paris, however, determined to devote himself to writing. To support himself, he began to write critical journal-

ism. He also continued a life of dandyism and exploration of the demimonde and the use of stimulants and drugs. Much of his writing expresses his desire to escape from the bonds of life, age, and death. Baudelaire's first important publications were two booklets of art criticism, *Les Salons* (1845–46), dealing with the work of such contemporaries as EUGÈNE DELACROIX and HONORÉ DAUMIER. Baudelaire then achieved literary acclaim with his translations of the works of Edgar Allan Poe, with whom he felt a strong affinity. Baudelaire's major work, a volume of poetry entitled *Les Fleurs du mal*, appeared in 1857. Immediately after its publication, the government prosecuted him on charges of offending public morals. Although the elite of French literature came to his support, he was fined, and six poems were removed from later editions. His next work, *Les Paradis artificiels* (1860), a self-analytic book, was inspired by Thomas De Quincey's *Confessions of an English Opium-Eater*. Baudelaire was also inspired by Richard Wagner (*L'Art romantique*, 1868) and other artists with whom he identified. Baudelaire possessed great skill for choosing perfectly appropriate phrases, and his gift for language has produced some of the finest verse in the French language. His originality, too, set him apart from the dominant literary schools of his time. His poetry has been praised as a final brilliant summation of romanticism and as a precursor of symbolism. His work deals with the eternal conflict between the ideal and the sensual and depicts all human experiences, from the most sublime to the most sordid. Among Baudelaire's other writings are a collection of prose poems, *Petits Poëmes en prose* (or *Le Spleen de Paris*) and his intimate journals, *Fusées* and *Mon Coeur mis a nu*, all published posthumously in 1869. Like JORIS-KARL HUYSMANS, Baudelaire is a leading exponent of decadence, a literary style designed to shock, that cultivates artifice and the abnormal and seeks inspiration in aestheticism.

## Baudot, Anatole de (1834–1915)
*architect, theorist*

Born in Saarebourg, Anatole de Baudot was the student of E. VIOLLET-LE-DUC and worked on the restoration of old monuments (château de Blois, cathedrals of Clermont and Puy) and supported rationalist architectural concepts and the use of

modern techniques. He employed reinforced concrete and, at Saint-Jean-de Montmartre, the first religious structure built entirely in this way, he created forms that, as well as being inspired by Gothic architecture, are in part determined by their materials (supports lighting, unified surfaces, hollowed out walls). In 1999, at Tulle, he built the first theater in reinforced concrete. Baudot published *L'Architecture: le passé, le present* and *L'Architecture et le béton armé*.

## Baudrier, Yves (1906–1988)
*composer*

Born in Paris, Yves Baudrier was the cofounder, along with O. MESSIAEN, A. JOLIVET, and DANIEL-LESUR, of the group Jeune France (1936), which advocated a "return to the human" in music. Baudrier is the author of works of great freshness, often inspired by the region of Brittany: symphonic poems (*Raz de Sein*, 1935; *Le Grand Vollier* 1939; *Le Musicien dans la cité*, 1946), a symphonie (1945), and melodies and musical scores for films (*La Bataille du rail*, 1946).

## Baumé, Antoine (1728–1804)
*chemist, pharmacist, botanist*

Born in Senlis, Antoine Baumé, who studied at the College of Pharmacy in Paris, experimented with quite diverse materials: preparations of mercury, sulfur, platinum, fat bodies, boric acid; crystallization of salts; and fermentation. He put in place the procedures for the tinting of fabrics, was interested in the production of porcelain, and invented the aerometer, which bears his name, as does a scale to measure density (degré Baumé). Combining his botanical interests with the scientific techniques of his age led to developments in the pharmaceutical and therapeutic use of oils, extracts, syrups, and distilled water. Antoine Baumé was named to the Academy of Sciences in 1772.

## Bayard, Pierre Terrail, seigneur de (1474–1524)
*nobleman, military leader*

Known in legend and tradition as "chevalier sans peur et sans reproche" (fearless and blameless knight), Pierre Terrail, seigneur de Bayard, considered a model of chivalry, was born in Dauphiné, near GRENOBLE. As a young soldier, he came to the attention of CHARLES VIII, and was knighted for his bravery after the battle of Fornovo in Italy (1495). He was cited for contributing to LOUIS XII's conquest of Milanais (1499–1500) and distinguished himself in the defense of the bridge at Garigliano (1503) against a Spanish force, and in the battle against the Venetians at Agnadel (1509). Such was Bayard's reputation for valor that several incredible stories were told of him, including one in which he single-handedly defended a bridge against 200 of the enemy. He was captured twice, but his chivalrous character and reputation secured his release without a ransom payment. During the war between FRANCIS I of France and Holy Roman Emperor Charles V, Bayard held the fortress town of Mezières with only 1,000 men for six weeks, against a force of 35,000. He also played a part in the decisive victory of Marignan (1515). Bayard was mortally wounded while covering the retreat at the Sesia River in Italy.

## Bayle, Pierre (1647–1706)
*writer, philosopher*

Born a Calvinist at Carla-Bayle and educated at the Jesuit College in Toulouse, Pierre Bayle converted to Roman Catholicism in 1669, but a year later again adopted Protestantism. In 1675, he became professor of philosophy at the Protestant Academy of Sedan and, in 1681, was appointed independent professor of philosophy and history at the Protestant Academy of Rotterdam. His first popular work was *Pensées diverses sur la Comète de 1680* (1682), a rationalistic statement on the widespread fear caused by the appearance at the time of the great comet. In 1693, he was dismissed from his post at Rotterdam because of the suspicion that he had written a tract expressing religious skepticism. He soon compiled his *Dictionnaire historique et critique* (4 volumes, 1695–97), in which he forcefully advocated freedom of thought and conscience, questioned authority, and adopted a rationalist view of religion. This work in particular would have a great influence on the French Encyclopedists and philosophes of the 18th century and make Bayle a precursor of modern historical criticism. His other

Pierre Bayle *(Library of Congress)*

writings include *Critique de l'histoire du calvinisme du P. Mainbourg* (1682); *Nouvelles de la république des lettres* (a literary publication appearing monthly from 1684 to 1687), and *La France toute catholique sous le règne de Louis le Grand* (1685), a pamphlet defending civil liberties.

## Bazaine, François Achille (1811–1888)
*military figure, marshal of France*

François Achille Bazaine was born in Versailles and received his military education in Paris. After having fought in Algeria and in Spain against the Carlists, he was made a general and distinguished himself during the Crimean War (the capture of Sevastopol) and again during the campaign in Italy (victory of Solferino). In 1862, he was sent to Mexico, where he was named commander in chief and made a marshal of France (1864). Having married a Mexican woman, he intrigued, in part because of her influence, to oust the emperor Maximilian. In disgrace for a time upon his return to France, he was nonetheless named commander of the Imperial Guard by NAPOLÉON III (1869). Commander in chief of the French army in Lorraine during the FRANCO-PRUSSIAN WAR (1870), he fell back upon Metz without trying to establish a connection with the army at Châlons, commanded by General MAC-MAHON. Wishing to exploit the abdication of Napoléon III and the fall of the SECOND EMPIRE (September 4, 1870), he tried to negotiate with German prince Bismarck and the empress Eugènie, but was finally forced to surrender (October 27, 1870). In 1873, he was condemned to death for treason by a military tribunal. His sentence was commuted to 20 years in prison, but having escaped from the fortress of Sainte-Marguerite, he eventually reached Spain, where he died.

### Bazaine, Jean  (1904–2001)
*painter*
Born in Paris, Jean Bazaine had his first personal exhibition in 1932, and in 1945, he organized the show "Vingt Jeunes peintres de tradition française" in reaction to the political and cultural climate of the Occupation regime. The effects of this show were significant. Bazaine himself began to reject all the "abstract" rules (*Notes sur la peinture d'aujourd'hui,* 1948, 1953, and 1955). Concerned about painting reality, he affirmed that his paintings reflected his feelings toward nature. His paintings are characterized by the use of line and color and irregular patterns, with dense tones, fragmentation, and juxtaposed or mixed forms (*La Clairière,* 1951). Interested also in monumental art, Bazaine worked in stained glass (church of Assy, 1944–46, church of Saint-Séverin in Paris, 1965–69), and in mosaics.

### Bazille, Frédéric Jean  (1841–1870)
*painter*
Born in Montpellier, Frédéric Jean Bazille abandoned his medical studies in Paris to dedicate himself to painting. At the studio of CHARLES GLEYRE, he met CLAUDE MONET, PIERRE RENOIR, and ALFRED SISLEY and went with them to paint at Fontainebleau. Bazaine supported his friends financially and was part of the beginnings of IMPRESSIONISM. His art owes much to ÉDOUARD MANET. In his portraits and family scenes, the use of clear colors, clean forms, and a sense of volume are evident. He shows, too, a certain naïveté in his somewhat dry drawings and in the character of his expressions, but because of his very subtle sense of light, Bazaine is considered one of the founders of the impressionist movement (*Réunion de famille,* 1867).

### Bazin, Hervé  (1911–1996)
*writer*
Born Jean-Pierre Hervé-Bazin in Angers, Hervé Bazin, as he is known, was the great-nephew of the writer RENÉ BAZIN. Author of a number of collections of poetry (*Jour,* 1947; *Torchères,* 1991), Bazin gained his notoriety through his novels, which are indictments of bourgeois society. Rebelling against all coercive societal forces (*La Tête contre les murs,* 1949), fiercely opposed to authority (*Vipère au poing, La Mort du petit cheval,* 1950; *Cri de la chouette,* 1972), including conjugal (*Madame Ex,* 1975), bold in his portrayal of incest (*Qui j'ose aimer,* 1956) and childhood relations (*Au nom du fils,* 1961), he succeeded also in appealing to the modern world, but not without a certain sense of irony (*L'Église verte,* 1981; *Le Démon de minuit,* 1988; *L'École des pères,* 1991). Bazin was elected to the Académie Goncourt in 1958 and served as its president in 1973.

### Bazin, René  (1853–1932)
*writer*
Born in Angers, René Bazin was a professor of law and gained great notoriety among the French Catholic bourgeoisie because of his novels, through which he demonstrated his attachment to traditional values. In his works, Bazin represents the antithesis of the naturalism that characterizes the writings of, for example, ÉMILE ZOLA. Instead of presenting characters in an objective manner, Bazin sought to reveal the positive aspects of human nature, and to stress such virtues as humility, faith, and sacrifice. *Le blé qui lève* (1907) and *Davidée Birot* (1912) had real success, as did even more those of his works that evoked a sense of the lives of the peasantry and the bonds that tied them to their land (*La Terre qui meurt,* 1899), or to the religious and patriotic traditions of their soil (*Les Oberlé,* 1901; *Les Nouveaux Oberlé,* 1919; *Magnificat,* 1931).

He also wrote biographies, including *Charles de Foucault* (1921) and *Pie X* (1928). Bazin was elected to the ACADÉMIE FRANÇAISE in 1928.

## Beaudin, André  (1895–1979)
*painter, engraver, sculptor*
Born in Mennecy, André Beaudin was influenced by cubism after meeting the Spanish artist Juan Gris. Beaudin would then, in his art, deal with a variety of themes in still lives, sleeping figures, horses, birds, plants, rivers, and the bridges of Paris, but in these works, the subject and the human form tend to disappear or are reduced to a group of strong lines, decorative contours, and finely colored areas. He decorated the ceiling of the church of Saint-Jean-Marie-Vianney at Rueil-Malmaison and illustrated the works of various authors (FRANCIS PONGE, PAUL ÉLUARD).

## Beaudouin, Eugène  (1898–1983)
*architect, urban planner*
Born in Paris, Eugène Beaudouin built, in collaboration with MARCEL LODS, the city area of Champs-des-Oiseaux (Bagneux, 1931–32) and the open-air school Suresnes (1935). There, he systematically utilized prefabricated materials. He also constructed numerous collective administrative buildings (university residences at Antony, 1954), as well as large housing units. He conceived various urban, regional, and rural development models, and is one of the authors of the concept for the renewal of the Maine-Montparnasse district in Paris. Beaudouin was named to the Academy of Fine Arts in 1961.

## Beaufort, François de Bourbon-Vendôme, duke de  (1616–1669)
*admiral*
The grandson of GABRIELLE D'ESTRÉES, duchess de Beaufort, and youngest son of CÉSAR DE VENDÔME, François de Bourbon-Vendôme was one of the leaders of the FRONDE. His popularity earned him the sobriquet "roi des Halles." Returning to the side of the Crown, he was given the command of a fleet against the Barbary pirates, whom he twice fought (1665). Continuing to fight for France, he was lost during the siege of Candie in the Mediterranean.

## Beauharnais, Alexandre, viscount de  (1760–1794)
*military figure*
Born in Fort-Royal, Martinique, Alexandre, viscount de Beauharnais, in 1779 married JOSÉPHINE Tascher de la Pagerie, the future empress of France. The couple had two children: EUGÈNE DE BEAUHARNAIS, a future general, prince, and viceroy of Italy, and HORTENSE, who became the queen of Holland. Alexandre de Beauharnais fought in the American War of Independence and then, after serving as a deputy for the nobility to the ESTATES GENERAL, during the REVOLUTION OF 1789, served as president of the Constituent Assembly. Promoted to the rank of general in 1792, he declined being named minister of war. Accused of having poorly defended Mainz from attacking anti-Revolutionary Coalition forces (1793), he was guillotined.

## Beauharnais, Eugène de  (1781–1834)
*prince, general*
The son of ALEXANDRE BEAUHARNAIS and JOSÉPHINE Tacher de la Pagerie, and brother of HORTENSE DE BEAUHARNAIS, Eugène de Beauharnais was born in Paris and was later adopted by Napoléon Bonaparte (see NAPOLÉON I) who married his widowed mother in 1796. Eugène accompanied Napoléon on his campaigns in Italy (1797) and in Egypt (1798), and he became a general in 1804. The next year, Napoléon made him a prince of the Empire and viceroy of Italy. Eugène de Beauharnais distinguished himself in Russia in 1812 and at the battle of Lutzen, Germany (1813). Then, after having courageously defended Italy against the Allies, he sought refuge in Munich with Maximilian I of Bavaria, whose daughter, Augusta, he had married in 1809. In 1817, Eugène's father-in-law made him duke of Leuchtenberg and prince of Eichstätt.

## Beauharnais, Hortense de  (1783–1817)
*queen of Holland*
Queen of Holland, Hortense de Beauharnais was born in Paris, the daughter of ALEXANDRE DE BEAUHARNAIS and JOSÉPHINE Tacher de la Pagerie. Hortense was married against her will by her stepfather, Napoléon Bonaparte (see NAPOLÉON I), to his brother LOUIS BONAPARTE. She became queen of

Holland in 1806 and, after the abdication of her husband in 1810, separated from him and kept a brilliant salon in Paris. During the first Restoration, LOUIS XVIII made her duchess of Saint-Leu. Exiled during the second RESTORATION, she went to Switzerland (1817) and resided in the château of Arenenberg. From her marriage to Louis Bonaparte were born Napoléon-Charles (1802), Napoléon-Louis (1804), and Charles-Louis-Napoléon (1808), who later became NAPOLÉON III. From a liaison with the count de FLAHAUT, she had a son, the future duke de MORNY. Hortense Beauharnais has left her *Mémoires.*

## Beaujoyeux, Balthazar de (ca. early 16th century–1587)
*dancer, ballet master, choreographer*
Born Badassarino di Belgioioso in Piedmont, Italy, Balthazar de Beaujoyeux, as he was known in France, was at first a violinist-composer and organizer of festivals for the courts of Mary Stuart, CHARLES IX, HENRY III, then CATHERINE DE' MEDICI. For the latter, he composed *La Défense du paradis,* a work of political allusions representing the four days preceding the Saint Bartholomew's Day Massacre. Balthazar de Beaujoyeux is also the author of the celebrated *Ballet comique de la reine* (1581), considered to be the first court ballet of genuine dramatic nature.

## Beaumarchais, Pierre-Augustin-Caron de (1732–1799)
*playwright*
Born in Paris, the son of a watchmaker, Pierre-Augustin-Caron de Beaumarchais began his career as a music teacher to the daughter of King LOUIS XV. In 1756, he married and took the name of the widow of a court official and was subsequently ennobled himself. He then served as an official under Kings LOUIS XV and LOUIS XVI and was sent on a trade mission in 1764 to Madrid by Joseph PÂRIS. Beaumarchais's literary fame comes from his two comedies, *Le Barbier de Seville* (1775) and *Le Mariage de Figaro* (1784). In both, he satirized the French aristocracy and expressed dissatisfaction with the ruling classes in the years before the REV-

OLUTION. The plays would be made into popular operas, *Le nozze di Figaro* (1786) by Mozart, and *Il barbiere di Siviglia* (1816) by Rossini. Beaumarchais's earlier works include *Eugénie ou la Vertu de désespoir* (1767) and *Les deux Amis ou le Négotiant de Lyon* (1770).

## Beauneveu, André (ca. 1330–1413)
*sculptor, painter, miniaturist*
Born in Valenciennes, André Beauneveu was one of the most celebrated artists of his time. After working in Flanders (ca. 1360), then Valencienne, he was commissioned by King CHARLES V to carve the tombs of PHILIPPE VI and JEAN LE BON in Saint-Denis; he sculpted them from images taken from their death masks. Beauneveu also worked in England (1366), at Courtai for the count of Flanders (1374–76) and, settling in Bourges, worked for JEAN DE BERRY (decoration of the château de Mehun-sur-Yèvre and the *Psaultier de Jean de Berry,* ca. 1384). The latter is a masterpiece composed of 24 finely modeled figures.

## Beauvoir, Simone de (1908–1986)
*writer*
One of the most important writers of her generation, Simone de Beauvoir was born in Paris, where she was to spend most of her life. She was educated at the École Normale Supérieure and at the SORBONNE, where she received a degree in philosophy (1929). She taught philosophy for a time but left that profession in 1943, when her first novel, *L'Invitée,* was published. De Beauvoir then dedicated herself to the writing of essays (*Pyrrhus et Cinéas,* 1944; *Pour une morale de l'ambiguïté,* 1947) and novels (*Le Sang des autres,* 1945; *Tous les hommes sont mortels,* 1946). Her life and her thought were linked to those of JEAN-PAUL SARTRE, whom she met while at the Sorbonne. They resided in Paris during World War II (1939–45) and were active in the RESISTANCE. At that time, they refined the principles of existentialism. They also collaborated on the political and literary journal *Les temps modernes* and traveled through Europe and the United States. In 1949, *Le Deuxième Sexe,* de Beauvoir's existential analysis of women's status and situation

in modern society, was published. Drawn from her personal experience, it was extremely influential in the formation of feminist theory. A following work, the novel *Les Mandarins,* received the prestigious Prix Goncourt. De Beauvoir continued in the autobiographical genre with *Mémoires d'une jeune fille rangée* (1958); *Tout compte fait* (1972); and *La Cérémonie des adieux* (1981), her farewell to Sartre. In her later years, she also wrote essays on age, including *Une Mort tres douce* (1954), which she dedicated to her mother, and *La vieillesse* (1970), a critique of the poor treatment given to older people in Western societies. After de Beauvoir's death, her autobiographic *Journal de guerre* (1990) and *Lettres à Sartre* (1990) were published. In her philosophic writings, de Beauvoir sought above all to create "significant" works, to elucidate the relationship between men and women, and, through an exploration of her own experiences, achieve a definition of authentic morality applicable to the modern world and society.

## Becquerel family

The Becquerel were a family of noted French physicists. Antoine Becquerel (1788–1878), born in Châtillon-sur-Loing (today Châtillon-Coligny), studied the phenomenon of diamagnetism, but he is particularly known for his work in the field of electrochemisty, notably for his invention of a polarized dual liquid battery (1829). He was named to the French Academy of Sciences in 1829. Edmond Becquerel (1820–1891), born in Paris, was the son of Antoine Becquerel. He conducted a photographic study of the Sun, proving the existence of Fraunhofer rays in its untraviolet areas (1842). With others, he developed thermodynamic coupling and studied the magnetic properties of minerals and the phenomena of phosphorescence. He was named to the Academy of Sciences in 1863. Henri Becquerel (1852–1908), the son of Edmond Becquerel, was born in Paris. He studied effects of X-rays and fluorescence on uranium salts and discovered the phenomenon of radioactivity (1896) as well as the ionizing properties of new radiations. He was named to the French Academy of Sciences in 1889 and, in 1903, with PIERRE and MARIE CURIE, was awarded the Nobel Prize in physics.

## Bédier, Joseph (1863–1938)
*medievalist*

Born in Paris, Joseph Bédier, who would contribute valuable research to the study of medieval literature, taught from 1880 to 1903 at the University of Freiburg, Switzerland, and in France at the University of Caen and the École normale supérieure. From 1903 to 1936 he was professor at the COLLÈGE DE FRANCE and, in 1920, was elected to the ACADÉMIE FRANÇAISE. Bédier's first major scholarly work was *Les Fabliaux, études de littérature populaire et d'histoire littéraire du moyen âge* (1893). In this work he described the origins of the *fabliau* (short comic stories) in 13th-century French society. This study also established his reputation as a leading medievalist. His next book, *Le Roman de Tristan et Iseult* (1900), made him a world-famous writer. It was considered to be a masterpiece of French prose. In 1902, Bédier published *Le Roman de Tristan par Thomas* (2 volumes, 1902–05), considered one of the most important contributions to the field of medieval literary studies. In it, the author demonstrated the single original source for the many Tristan legends. Bédier also wrote a groundbreaking four-volume study of Old French medieval epics, *Les Légendes épiques* (1908–13), which became the definitive work in that field. His scholarship culminated in his critical study *Le Chanson de Roland* (1922), in which he produced a modern French translation of the 12th-century version of the legend of the medieval hero Roland. Additionally, Bédier published *Histoire illustrée de la littérature française* (1923–24).

## Béjart, Maurice (1927–   )
*dancer, choreographer*

Born Maurice Berger in MARSEILLE, Maurice Béjart, as he is known, made his debut at the Opéra de Marseille (1945) and, with Jean Laurent, founded the Ballets de l'Étoile (1954), which later became the Ballet-Théâtre de Paris (1957). He was named ballet director of the Théâtre royal de la Monnaie in Brussels (1960–87) and led the Ballet du xxe siècle (1960–80), which became the Béjart Ballet Lausanne in 1987. Dissatisfied with the traditional and academic ballet forms that he considered to be outdated, Béjart, as a director as well as a dancer, encouraged a renewal of dance based on the great stories of Western civilization (*Faust, Tristan, Don Juan*) and of Eastern sources, too. He produced works that were original or based on his research into mythology, with the goal of combining song and the spoken word with dance, to produce, in his words, "ceremony for the greatest number" (*Symphonie pour un homme seul,* music by PIERRE HENRY and PIERRE SCHAEFFER, 1955; *Le Sacre du printemps,* 1955; *La Damnation de Faust,* 1964; *Messe pour temps présent,* 1967; *À la recherche de . . .,* 1968; *Le Marteau sans maître,* music by PIERRE BOULEZ 1973; *Gaîté parisienne,* 1978; *Éros Thanatos,* 1980). Béjart was named to the Academy of Fine Arts in 1995.

## Bellange, Jacques de (ca. 1575–1616)
*painter, engraver*

Born probably near Nancy, Jacques de Bellange was a popular artist, many of whose paintings, notably portraits and decorative works that he produced for the ducal palace at Nancy while he was in the service of Charles III of Lorraine (1602–16), have disappeared. But his engravings and sometimes lightly retouched drawings reveal a personal talent of mystical and strange inspiration, which is often sensual. The elongated forms, studied poses, and tension and elegance of his drawing are related to Florentine mannerism and the Fontainebleau School, which he seems to have continued.

## Belleau, Remi (1528–1577)
*poet, scholar*

Born in Nogent-le-Rotrou, Remi Belleau, a noted humanist, was a protégé of the powerful House of Lorraine. He could, therefore, pursue his poetic vocation and is counted, after 1554, among the seven members of the Pléiade, the group of Renaissance poets named after the ancient poets of Alexandria. The group's goal was the elevation of French to the level of the classical languages and Italian. After having gained the admiration of PIERRE DE RONSARD for his translation of *Anacreon* (1556), Belleau began the composition of a sensitive interpretation of nature in *La Bergerie* (1556; augmented in 1572), a mixed work of verse and prose in which he praises the beauties of rustic scenes and the pleasures of love. Belleau also evokes with equal grace the myths of antiquity in his *Amours et Nouveaux Échanges de pierres précieuses* (1576).

## Bellay, Joachim du (1522–1560)
*poet, scholar*

An influential figure of the French Renaissance, Joachim du Bellay was born in Liré. Abandoning a military career and under the influence of Peletier du Mans, he took up poetry. Inspired by the humanistic spirit of PIERRE DE RONSARD (whom he met in 1547), he studied under the Hellenist JEAN DORAT (1547–49), then joined the Pléiade, the group of Renaissance poets named for the seven poets of ancient Alexandria. The group had as its goal the elevation of the French language and literature to the illustrious level of ancient Greek and Latin and of Italian. In 1549, Bellay wrote the Pléiade manifesto, *La Défense et illustration de la langue française,* and *L'Olive,* 115 sonnets inspired by the writings of Petrarch. Falling ill and almost deaf, Bellay went to Rome in 1553, where he studied for four years. Upon his return to France, he wrote two more sonnet collections, *Les Regrets* (1558) and *Les Antiquités du Rome* (1558). In 1558 also appeared *Divers Jeux rustiques,* one of his most notable works. This was followed a year later by *Discours du Roi* and the satire *La Poète courtisan.*

## Belley, Jean-Baptiste (ca. 1765–1830)
*political figure*

Born in Guadeloupe, Jean-Baptiste Belley, a black descendant of slaves, was sent during the REVOLUTION OF 1789 to the National Convention (1792) in Paris to ask for recognition of Saint-Domingue (Haiti) and Guadeloupe as free departments of France. There, he made such a rousing and moving appeal to the assembly for the abolition of slavery that he drowned out all opposition. The Convention, taken by his eloquence, voted at once to abolish all slavery in Guadeloupe, Saint-Domingue, and all other French territories. Belley was later made an adjutant general by NAPOLÉON I and took part in the defense of Guadeloupe against the British.

## Belmondo, Jean-Paul (1933–   )
*actor*

A leading actor of the New Wave (Nouvelle Vague) genre, Jean-Paul Belmondo was born near Paris in Neuilly-sur-Seine. He made his debut in the first feature film of JEAN-LUC GODARD, *À bout de soufflé* (1960), and later *Pierrot le Fou* (1965). A versatile actor, Belmondo easily shifted his character from humor to despair, and his portrayals as a coolly detached gangster or an unpredictable lover assured his popularity. In the late 1980s, he had a great stage success playing a bold Cyrano de Bergerac. Some of Belmondo's other films are *La Ciociara* (1960), *L'Homme de Rio* (1963), *Paris brûle-t-'il* (1965), *Casino Royale* (1967), *Borsalino* (1970), *Stavisky* (1973), *L'animal* (1977), *Le guignolo* (1980), and *Les misérables* (1995).

## Ben Bella, Ahmed (1916–   )
*Algerian political figure*

Born in Marnia, ALGERIA, Ahmed Ben Bella was a former officer in the French army who became one of the leaders of the Algerian uprising against French rule. He was interned in France from 1956 to 1962. Freed after the ÉVIAN ACCORDS, he served as president of the Council of Ministers and then as president of the Algerian Republic (1963). Overthrown in 1965, he was imprisoned. Released in 1980 and exiled to Europe, Ben Bella returned in 1990 to Algeria where he founded the Mouvement pour la démocratie en Algérie (MDA).

## Benda, Julien (1867–1956)
*writer, philosopher*

Born in Paris, Benda first published his writings in 1898 in *La Revue blanche,* in which he proclaimed himself a "Dreyfusard by reason." In his writings, and especially in his essays, *Le Bergsonisme, ou une philosophie de la mobilité* (1912) and *La France byzantine* (1945), Benda, who was connected for a time with CHARLES PÉGUY and contributed to *Cahiers de la quinzaine,* condemned the philosophers who based their thinking on intuition and emotion, in particular, HENRI BERGSON. In 1927, he published his major work, *La Trahison des clercs,* a manifesto on the necessity of devotion to the absolute truth, which he felt his contemporaries had betrayed. He called upon fellow intellectuals to be "administrators of abstract justice" and defenders of democratic rationalism, and not submit to temporal or even spiritual authorities. Benda later reiterated these themes in other works, including an autobiographical trilogy, *La Jeunesse d'un clerc* (1936), *Un régulier dans le siècle* (1938), and *Exercise d'un enterré vif* (1946).

## Benoist, Marie-Guillemine (1768–1826)
*painter*

Born in Paris, Marie-Guillemine Benoist was the daughter of a government official. She studied under ÉLISABETH VIGÉE-LEBRUN, whose influence is apparent in Benoist's earlier works. Benoist also studied with JACQUES-LOUIS DAVID, and her later paintings reflect the neoclassical tradition and style. She painted in a variety of genres, including portraiture and historical themes. Napoléon Bonaparte (see NAPOLÉON I) commissioned her to paint his portrait as well as those of his family. Benoist dealt with contemporary subjects, too; her *Negresse* (1800), for instance, was inspired by the decrees abolishing slavery.

## Benoist, Michel (1715–1774)
*Jesuit, mathematician, astronomer, geographer*

Born in Dijon, Michel Benoist, after joining the Jesuit order, arrived in China in 1744 as a missionary. He served at the Qing court under the Chinese name Jiang Youren. Benoist took part in the creation of a general map of the Chinese Empire engraved on copper (1764) and, with the Italian Jesuit Giuseppe Castiglione (who had arrived in China earlier), collaborated on the hydraulic works that supplied the fountains and water displays at the European Palace (formerly the Summer Palace) of the emperor Qianlong at Yuanmingyuan.

## Benveniste, Émile (1902–1976)
*linguist*

Born in Aleppo, Émile Benveniste is known for his influential theories and writings in comparative Indo-European grammar (*Essai de grammaire sogdiane,* 1929; *Les Infinitifs avestiques,* 1935). He proposed a theory of language roots ("consonant-vowel-consonant"—from which full sounds develop). In lexicography, he developed a structuralist viewpoint (*Noms d'agent et Noms d'action en indo-européen*, 1948; *Vocabulaire des institutions*, a series of lectures at the Collège de France). Benveniste's principal theoretical works were collected together in *Problèmes de linguistiques générales* (1966; 1974), writings in which he studied in particular the problems of case, verbal pronouns, verb tense, and the relationship between function (or semantics) and forms. Benveniste debated the theory of the arbitrariness of signs and enriched syntax of the possibilities of the relationships between the speaker and his or her discourse. Finally, Benveniste put forth important theoretical hypotheses in semiology. He was named to the Académie d'inscription et belles lettres in 1960.

## Berain, Jean (1639–1711)
*decorative designer, engraver, and ornamentalist*
Born in Saint-Mihiel into a noted family of 17th-century French designers and engravers (of which Jean, or Jean le Vieux as he is known, was the most brilliant), Jean Berain was commissioned to decorate the king's chamber in 1674, and he continued to design the sets and costumes for the carnivals, ballets, operas, spectacles, and ceremonies during the reign of LOUIS XIV. The creator of interior decorations and tapestry cartoons (*Tentures à grotesques, Triomphes marins*) for the tapestry works of Beauvais, he had a notable influence also in Holland, England, and Germany (Berain style). Through his finesse, the elegance of his drawings, and his imaginative motifs, Berain augured the rococo style prevalent during the reign of LOUIS XV.

## Beranger, Jean-Pierre (1780–1857)
*poet and songwriter*
Known for his political songs, Jean-Pierre Beranger was born in Paris. He became a topographer working in the bank that his father founded (1796), then as a clerk in the offices of the University of Paris (1809). He wrote his first verses early on, a satirical comedy and an epic poem, and became a member of the societé du Caveau, a well-known

group of songwriters. He had already come to the notice of LUCIEN BONAPARTE, and Napoléon Bonaparte (see NAPOLÉON I) would actually later support the songwriter for a number of years. With the Restoration (1814–15), Beranger found his true style: "the liberal republican and patriotic song that was and would remain his greatest achievement" (SAINTE-BEUVE). Evoking the spirit of earlier times (notably the Napoleonic era), Beranger's anticlerical satires and political pamphlets in single verse and prose were quite popular (*Le Roi d'Yvetot, Le Vieux Sergent, Le Dieu des bonnes gens, Le Sacre de Charles le Simple, La Sainte-Alliance des peoples*), but also caused him twice to be imprisoned (1815, 1828) for his sentiments. Beranger's songs were published in four collections (1815, 1821, 1828, and 1830), and his *Biographie* appeared in 1857 and his *Correspondance* in 1860.

## Bérégovoy, Pierre (1925–1993)
*political figure*
Born in Déville-les-Rouen, Pierre Bérégovoy, the son of an immigrant, was a former RESISTANCE fighter and worker. A socialist and staunch supporter of FRANÇOIS MITTERRAND, he became, after the arrival of the Left in power in 1981, secretary-general of the presidency of the republic, minister of social affairs and national solidarity, then minister of the economy, finances, and the budget (1984–86; 1988–92), and, finally, prime minister from April 1992 to March 1993. A supporter of a rigorous economic policy, his program was based on the stabilizing of the franc and reducing inflation and government expenses. But faced with the subsequent rising unemployment that in turn became one of the principal reasons for the Left's defeat in the legislative elections of March 1993, he took responsibility for the situation and committed suicide.

## Bergson, Henri (1859–1941)
*philosopher*
Born in Paris, Bergson was professor at the COLLÈGE DE FRANCE from 1900 to 1914. As a thinker, he left an abundance of philosophical writings, including *Essai sur les données immédiates de la con-*

science (1889), *Matière et mémoire* (1896), *Le Rire* (1900), *L'Évolution créatrice* (1907), *L'Énergie spirituelle* (1919), *Durée et simultanéité* (1922), *Les Deux Sources de la moral et de la religion* (1932), and *La Pensée et le mouvant* (1934). Hostile to formalistic intellectualism, and in particular to Kant and neo-Kantianism, as well as to scientific and materialistic positivism, Bergson developed his thought through a critical analysis of the scientific method. He presented, in contrast, theories on the freedom of the mind and on duration, which he regarded as the succession of unconscious states, intermingling and unmeasured. Bergson defined the mind as pure energy—the *élan vital*—responsible for all organic evolution. Although often associated with the intuitionalist school of philosophy, Bergsonism is too original and eclectic to be so categorized. Nonetheless, Bergson did emphasize the importance of intuition over intellect and the idea of two opposing currents: inert matter in conflict with organic life as the vital urge strives toward free creative activity. The influence of Bergson's lectures and writings on 20th-century philosophers, writers, and artists is extensive and includes CHARLES PÉGUY, MARCEL PROUST, and others. Bergson was elected to the ACADÉMIE FRANÇAISE in 1914 and was awarded the Nobel Prize in literature in 1927.

## Berlin West Africa Conference

Also called the Berlin Conference, this meeting of the major European powers was convened in 1884–85 to deal with questions of rivalry and trade and to address territorial claims in Africa made by these same powers. Attended by representatives of 14 European states and the United States, the conference reached agreement on possession of the territory surrounding the Congo River. Various colonial powers had claims in that area, with France, on the basis of treaties negotiated in 1880 by the explorer PIERRE SAVORGNAN DE BRAZZA, claiming most of the territory. At the conference, the French claims were recognized, while Germany received large areas and Portugal was granted access to the Congo River. Belgian control in the region was also recognized. The representatives at the conference did not actually divide up African territory, as is commonly believed. In fact, they recognized territorial claims that had been in existence for some time.

## Bernadette Soubirous, Saint (1844–1879)
*religious figure*

Born to a peasant family in Lourdes, Bernadette Soubirous had, at age 14, visions of the Virgin that are themselves the origin for the celebrated pilgrimages to Lourdes. She entered the convent of the Sisters of Charity at Nevers in 1866 and was canonized in 1933. The Catholic Church celebrates her feast on February 18.

## Bernanos, Georges (1888–1948)
*writer*

Born in Neuilly-sur-Seine, Georges Bernanos began his career in journalism as a militant supporter of the ACTION FRANÇAISE and soon undertook a strong critique of politics, vehemently denouncing the moral bankruptcy of the French bourgeoisie (*La Grande Peur des bien-pensants*, 1930). At first supportive of the Falangist uprisings in Spain, he eventually spoke against the collusion of the church with Francisco Franco and with CHARLES MAURRAS (*Les Grandes Cimetières sous la lune*, 1938; *Nous autres Français*, 1939), then against the VICHY regime (*Lettre aux Anglais*, 1941, written during his stay in Brazil, 1940–45), which made Bernanos one of the moving spirits of the RESISTANCE. He later spent time in Tunisia (1946–48) and there wrote the play *Dialogues des carmélites* (posthumous, 1949), a forceful statement of the theme of anguish and the loss of virtue. Coming late to literature (1926), Bernanos, over a period of 10 years, composed the essential parts of his important works of fiction (especially during his stay in Palma, Majorca, 1934–37). A realist and visionary, he advocated the pursuit of spiritual rather than material goals. His devotion to Roman Catholicism and his mysticism are also clearly evident in his other writings, which include *Sous le soleil de Satan*, 1926; *L'Imposture*, 1928; *Le Joré*, 1929; *Le Journal d'un curé de campagne*, 1936, one of his best-known works; *Monsieur Ouine*, 1933–46; and *La Nouvelle Histoire de Mouchette*, 1937. His motion picture scenario for *Dialogues des carmélites* was the basis for the successful opera of the same name by FRANCIS POULENC (1957).

## Bernard, Claude (1813–1878)
*physiologist*

Regarded as a founder of experimental medicine, Claude Bernard was born in Saint-Julien, Rhône. He received his early education in the humanities and only after 1834 enrolled in medical school. Bernard obtained a position at the COLLÈGE DE FRANCE, where he began his work in physiology. By the late 1840s, he had made several important discoveries in that field, including that of the role of the pancreas in digestion and of the liver in glucose transformation. He also explored the functions of the nervous system, discovering the purpose of the vasometer nerves that regulate the blood supply. He made other contributions to experimental physiology and was the first to propose the concept that came to be known as homeostasis. In 1854, he was given the newly created chair of physiology at the SORBONNE and that same year was named to the Academy of Sciences. Considered a prominent scientist during his lifetime, Bernard, upon his death, was the first scientist in France to be given a public funeral. His writings include *Introduction à l'étude de la médecine expérimentale* (1865) and *La Science expérimentale* (1876). He was named to the ACADÉMIE FRANÇAISE in 1868. Although considered important in his era, Bernard's methodology in particular is now considered dated.

## Bernard, Émile (1868–1941)
*painter*

A postimpressionist, Émile Bernard, who was born in Lille, studied art (1884) in Paris, where he met HENRI DE TOULOUSE-LAUTREC. He soon became friends with Vincent Van Gogh, PAUL CÉZANNE, and ODILON REDON, with whom he conducted a continuous correspondence. Often inspired by folk art and by Japanese prints, Bernard went to paint at Pont-Avers, in Brittany, where he met PAUL GAUGUIN. Bernard had already painted *Le Christ jaune* and *Le Pouldu*. Along with other painters who joined them, he and Gauguin developed (1888) what is known as the School of Pont-Avers, which became an important part of the symbolist movement in painting. Often compared to cloisonné, it uses color decoratively and symbolically to express emotion over reality (*Madeleine au Bois d'Amour; La Gardeuse d'oies.*) In 1892, Bernard exhibited with the NABIS group, who shared his colorful style. In 1893, he traveled to Italy and then to Egypt, where he remained for six years. At that time, he developed a more conventional style, inspired by Byzantine and early European religious art. His theoretical writings on art and art history (published between 1905 and 1910) still had a decisive influence on modern painting.

## Bernard, Tristan (1866–1947)
*novelist, playwright*

Born Paul Bernard in Besançon, Tristan Bernard, as he is known, was educated in Paris and studied law, although he never practiced it. After a brief business career, he began to contribute humorous pieces and other articles to the periodical *La Revue Blanche*. He would eventually become equally successful as a moralist, essayist, and playwright. His first play, *Les Pieds nickelés*, was produced in 1895, followed in 1899 by *L'Anglais tel qu'on le parle*, a popular one-act farce that has been repeatedly revived, and by a novel, *Les Mémoires d'un jeune homme rangé*. Other works include *Triplepatte* (1905) and *Le Petit Café* (1911). Known for its fine sense of irony and comedic phrasing, Tristan Bernard's stage writings have been compared to those of MOLIÈRE, while the humor of his novel is considered reminiscent of that of Charles Dickens.

## Bernhardt, Sarah (1844–1923)
*actor*

Born Rosine Bernard in Paris, Sarah Bernhardt, one of the most celebrated actors of her time, made her debut at the COMÉDIE-FRANÇAISE. After acting there, she founded her own company and toured in many countries. At home, she appeared at the Odéon and other Parisian theaters. Her portrayals in *Phèdre* (1874), *Hernani* (1880), *La Dame aux camélias* and *L'Aiglon* (1900) have become famous.

She also appeared in several motion pictures (*La Tosca*, 1906; *Adrienne Lecouvreur*, 1913; *La Voyante*, 1923). Known as "La Divine Sarah," Bernhardt was world renowned not only for her acting, voice, beauty, celebrated lifestyle, and many eccentricities but also for her charitable works.

## Bernis, François-Joachim de Pierre de (1715–1794)

*prelate, statesman*

Born in Saint-Michel-d'Ardèche, François-Joachim de Pierre de Bernis began his career by gaining the favor of Mme de POMPADOUR because of his literary and political talent, charm, and wit. Ambassador to Venice, then minister of foreign affairs, he was the author of the system of alliances that led to the Seven Years' War (1756–1763). Falling out of favor for having advised peace after the Battles of Rossbach and Leuthen (1758), he became archbishop of Albi (1764), then ambassador to Rome (1768), where he lived during the REVOLUTION OF 1789. Bernis is the author of a *Correspondance* with VOLTAIRE and *Mémoires*, where one can see in him the libertine spirit of the period.

See also LOUIS XV.

## Berque, Jacques (1910–1995)

*sociologist, orientalist*

Born in Molière, Algeria, Jacques Berque was a colonial administrator and director of studies at the École pratique des hautes etudes and professor at the COLLÈGE DE FRANCE. There, he dedicated himself to important studies of the Arab world from a sociological and historical perspective (*Structures sociales du Haut-Atlas*, 1955; *Le Maghreb entre deux guerres*, 1962; *Égypte, Impérialisme et révolution*, 1967; *L'Intérieur du Maghreb, XVe–XIXe siècles*, 1978). In his political writings, Berque advocated progressive decolonization (*Les Arabes d'hier à demain*, 1960), and in his later years, his interest turned toward the sacred writings of Islam (*Le Coran*, 1991). Through his style of writing and his erudition, Berque sought to represent the symbolic and actual dimensions of the Arab world, and hence had a great influence on contemporary studies in that field.

## Berry, Charles Ferdinand, duke of (1778–1820)

*ultraroyalist political figure*

Born at Versailles, the second son of the count of Artois (the future CHARLES X) and Marie-Thérèse of Savoy, the duke of Berry left France at the beginning of the REVOLUTION OF 1789 and served with Condé's royalist army (1792). He then went to England, where he married Ann Brown, with whom he had two daughters. Upon the RESTORATION, he returned to France with his uncle King LOUIS XIII. But because his family did not recognize his marriage, he was married again, to princess Marie Caroline de Bourbon-Sicilie, with whom he had a daughter and a son, Count Henri de Chambord. An ultraroyalist, Berry was assassinated in 1820, and his death brought about the fall of the DECAZES government.

## Berry, Jean de France, duke of (1340–1416)

*art patron, royal personage*

A Capetian prince, Jean de France, duke of Berry, was born in Vincennes, the third son of JEAN II LE BON and Bonne de Luxembourg, and the brother of CHARLES V. He was one of the guardians of his nephew, CHARLES VI, and served as governor of Languedoc (1388). Removed from office because of the "Marmousets"—the grotesque church sculptures carved in derision of the king's advisers (1388)—he regained his authority when Charles VI went mad. An ostentatious patron of the arts, Jean de France commissioned from ANDRÉ BEAUNEVEU the *Psaulter de Jean de Berry*, then from JACQUEMART DE HESDIN the *Très Belles Heures* and the *Grands Heures*, and from the LIMBOURG BROTHERS the *Très Riches Heures du duc de Berry*, one of the most beautiful illuminated manuscripts of its time.

## Berryer, Pierre-Antoine (1790–1868)

*advocate, political figure*

Born in Paris, Pierre Antoine-Berryer was the son of an eminent advocate and adviser to the parlement. He was educated at the Collège de Juilly and, like his father, was an ardent legitimist. After the Restoration, he was an outspoken advocate of moderation in the treatment of various military figures, and is famous for his eloquent defenses during the trials of MICHEL NEY, PIERRE CAMBRONNE, FÉLICITÉ LAMENNAIS, FRANÇOIS CHATEAUBRIAND, and Louis-Napoléon (later NAPOLÉON III) (after the attempted uprising in Boulogne). Berryer was elected a deputy in 1830 and became involved in the legitimist intrigues of the duchess of Berry to restore her family to the throne. He was tried but acquitted, and was later (1841) elected to the National Assembly. He was also later a member of the imperial legislature (1868), although he had opposed both the coup d'état of December 2 and the SECOND EMPIRE. His writings include *Discours parlementaires* (1872–74) and *Plaidoyers* (1875–78). Berryer was elected to the ACADÉMIE FRANÇAISE in 1854.

## Bert, Paul (1833–1886)
*physiologist, political figure*
Born in Auxerre, Paul Bert was a student of CLAUDE BERNARD and did his initial research on grafts and transplants, the physiology of respiration, the variations in functionary atmospheric pressure, and anesthetics. In 1878, he did the first comprehensive studies of the health effects of altered air pressure and composition, published under the title *La Pression barometrique*. Then leaving science for politics, he served as minister of public instruction in the GAMBETTA cabinet (1881–82) and contributed to reforms in education, in particular, the adoption of free schooling and obligatory primary instruction. In 1886, he was named governor-general of Annam and Tonkin in Indochina. Bert was elected to the Academy of Sciences in 1882.

## Berthelot, Marcelin (1827–1907)
*chemist, political figure*
Born in Paris and educated at the COLLÈGE DE FRANCE, Marcelin Berthelot received a doctorate in 1854 with a thesis on the nature of fats, glycerin, and polyhydric alcohols. In 1856, he synthesized methane. With his success in the area of sythesization, he helped to discredit the prevailing notion that only living organisms can create organic compounds. In fact, Berthelot contributed to the knowledge of almost every class of organic chemical compounds, especially dyestuffs and explosives, and on the energy in chemical reaction. He was a professor at the École Supérieure de Pharmacie (1859) and at the COLLÈGE DE FRANCE (1865). A member of the French Academy of Sciences (1873), he succeeded LOUIS PASTEUR as perpetual secretary of that academy in 1889. As a member of the French government, he served as inspector general of education (1876) and was elected senator for life in 1881. He was minister of public instruction from 1886 to 1887, and minister of foreign affairs from 1895 to 1896. Berthelot's writings include *Les origines de l'alchimie* (1885), *Traité practique de calorimetrie chimique* (1893), and *Recherches expérimentales* (1901).

## Berthier, Louis-Alexandre (1753–1815)
*marshal of France*
Born in Versailles, Louis-Alexandre Berthier, after an early military career, in 1789 was made major general of the National Guard and was charged with protecting the royal family. Later, as a division commander and chief of staff to the French Army in Italy (1796), he was sent to Rome and, on orders of the Directory (1798), arrested the pope, Pius VI, and brought him to France. Serving as minister of war (1800–1807), Berthier was also made a marshal of France and then major general of the Grande Armée (1805–14). A close adviser and aide to Napoléon Bonaparte (see NAPOLÉON I), he was given the principality of Neuchâtel (1806) and later the title prince of Wagram (1809) for his part in the battle of the same name. In 1814, after Bonaparte began to suffer defeat, Berthier rallied to King LOUIS XVIII, who named him a peer of France. Taking refuge in Bamberg, Germany, during the HUNDRED DAYS, Berthier was killed in an accident.

## Berthier de Sauvigny, Louis-Bénigne (ca. 1742–1789)
*administrator*
Born in Paris, where he served as an assistant in the Intendancy, Louis-Bénigne Berthier de Sauvigny was named intendant in 1776. He soon under-

took a series of administrative reforms. Charged with supplying army headquarters at the beginning of the REVOLUTION OF 1789, he introduced measures that made him unpopular. Accused of speculating on the grain supply, he was killed, shortly after the execution of his father-in-law, the intendant-general, JOSEPH FRANÇOIS FOULLON, by revolutionary rioters on July 22, 1789.

## Berthollet, Claude-Louis, count (1748–1822)

*chemist*

Born in Talloires, Claude-Louis, count Berthollet was a chemist who made notable contributions to several areas of that discipline. He was educated at the University of Turin and, in 1785, proposed the use of chlorine as a bleaching agent. A noted scientist, Bertholett would later, after some period of doubt, become one of the first to support the theories of ANTOINE DE LAVOISIER, although he opposed his erroneous ideas that oxygen is the fundamental acidifying agent. With Lavoisier and others, Berthollet developed a new system of chemical nomenclature (1787) that is the basis for the present system. He also made significant contributions to the chemistry of explosives and to the field of metallurgy. His important work, *Essai de statique chimique* (2 volumes, 1803), presented his theories on chemical affinity and the reversibility of reactions. In 1780, Berthollet was named to the Academy of Sciences, and in 1794, he became a professor at the École Normale in Paris. He was one of the scholars who accompanied Napoléon Bonaparte to Egypt in 1798, and in 1804, NAPOLÉON I, now emperor of the French, made him a senator and later a grand officer in the LEGION OF HONOR and, under the Empire, a count. Berthollet was, with PIERRE DE LAPLACE, a cofounder of the Société d'Arcueil, a group of noted scientists and scholars who met regularly. He was named to the Academy of Sciences in 1780.

## Berthoud, Ferdinand (1727–1807)

*French-Swiss watchmaker*

Known as a marine clockmaker and writer on horological matters, Ferdinand Berthoud was born in Neuchâtel, Switzerland, and settled in Paris in 1745. His extensive skill and technical training led to his invention of the marine clock, used to determine longitude at sea. He also developed various other types of watches, including one in which the hour and minute hands were mounted and traveled separately. For his achievements, especially inventing the mechanisms of marine clocks, Berthoud was made a member of the French Academy of Sciences and of the Royal Society, London. His writings on horology include *Traité des horloges marines* (1773), *Essai sur l'horlogerie* (1786), and *Histoire de la mesure du temps par les horloges* (2 volumes, 1802).

## Bertillon, Alphonse (1853–1914)

*criminologist*

Born in Paris, Alphonse Bertillon was a chief of the judicial identification bureau of the Paris police prefecture. In 1882, he created the field of anthropometry (known also as the Bertillon System), as a method for identifying criminals. The system records anthropometric measurements and personal characteristics, such as eye color and distinctive markings. Because the Bertillon measurements are difficult to assess with uniform exactness, his system has largely been superseded by the use of fingerprinting and other methods as the principal means of identification in modern police procedures.

## Berton, Jean-Baptiste (1769–1822)

*military figure*

Born near Sedan, Jean-Baptiste Breton, or Berton, as he is known, graduated from the military schools of Brienne and Châlons, and fought in various campaigns of the empire, distinguishing himself particularly at Austerlitz, Friedland, and in Spain (capture of Málaga). After the defeat at Waterloo in 1814 (*Précis historique de la bataille de Waterloo*), he joined, during the RESTORATION, the Charbonnerie (Carbonari) and was instructed to lead the insurrection at Saumur (February 1822). This having failed, General Berton was arrested and executed.

## Bertrand, Aloysius  (1807–1841)
*writer*

Born in Ceva, Italy, Aloysius Bertrand was an ardent follower of VICTOR HUGO. He came to Paris to pursue a career in writing but initially had little success. Then, his "poems in prose" (*Gaspard de la nuit, Fantaisies à la manière de Rembrandt et de Callot*, posthumous, 1842) were praised by CHARLES BAUDELAIRE in the introduction to his *Spleen de Paris*. These same writings of Bertrand would also inspire three piano pieces by MAURICE RAVEL. Considered evocative of former times and "strangely picturesque," his poems in prose show a romantic taste for an imaginative and picturesque vision of the Middle Ages. In fact, his studies of strange imagery and the secret resonance of certain of his writings make Bertrand a precursor of surrealism.

## Bérulle, Pierre de  (1575–1629)
*cardinal*

Born in the château de Sérilly, near Troyes, Pierre Cardinal de Bérulle, with the help of Mme Acarie (religious name, MARIE DE L'INCARNATION) established (1604) the Carmelite order in France. He also founded the secular congregation of the Oratory (1611), which was a body of priests living in community but without monastic vows and subject to its own superior general. A contemplative and mystic, Bérulle was also an adviser to LOUIS XIII and was often in opposition to CARDINAL RICHELIEU. Made a cardinal in 1627, Bérulle profoundly influenced the 17th-century French school of spirituality (JEAN DUVERGIER DU HAURANNE, ST. VINCENT DE PAUL, Charles de Condren). Cardinal de Bérulle's major writing, *Discours de l'estat et des grandeurs de Jésus* (1622), is itself inspired by the Augustinian heritage and Ignacian spirituality.

## Besnard, Albert  (1849–1934)
*painter, etcher*

Born in Paris, Albert Besnard was a student of ALEXANDRE CABANEL and, in 1874, won the prix de Rome. From 1880 to 1884, he was a much sought-after portraitist of the socially prominent in the tradition of Joshua Reynolds, Thomas Gainsborough, and Thomas Lawrence. Besnard's career was filled with official commissions, and he was rewarded with many important projects to decorate with murals the interior of several large and significant buildings (École de pharmacie, 1884; Hôtel de Ville de Paris; Sorbonne, 1896; Petit Palais, 1909; Théâtre-Français, 1910–13; palais de la Paix de la Haye). Greatly influenced by the academic tradition, he was nonetheless open to certain modernist trends (art nouveau, pre-Raphaelites–style symbolism). Besnard was elected to the ACADÉMIE FRANÇAISE in 1924.

## Beuve-Méry, Hubert  (1902–1989)
*journalist*

Born in Paris, Hubert Beuve-Méry was a correspondent in Prague for *Le Temps* (1934). However, because of his disagreement with that newspaper's position regarding the Munich Pact, he resigned his post. After having fought in the RESISTANCE (1943–44), he founded, in December 1944, the daily *Le Monde*, which he directed until 1969. His integrity and prestige allowed him to produce a highly respected newspaper, which became one of the most important in France. Beuve-Méry is the author of works on politics (*Réflexions politiques*, 1951; *Onze ans de règne, 1958–1969*, 1974).

## Bidault, Georges  (1899–1983)
*political figure, Resistance leader*

Born in Moulins, Georges Bidault was educated at the SORBONNE. Before WORLD WAR II, he was editor of the Roman Catholic newspaper *L'Aube* and leader of the Popular Democratic Party, a left-wing Catholic organization. He also was an outspoken critic of the prewar policy of appeasement that led to the Munich Pact. In 1939, he joined the French army and was taken prisoner. After his release, he joined the RESISTANCE and, in 1943, succeeded JEAN MOULIN as its leader. One of the founders of the Popular Republican Movement (see MOUVEMENT RÉBULICAN POPULAIRE), a liberal Catholic party, Bidault joined the postwar government in 1946. Serving in a number of government positions during the 1940s and 1950s, including defense minister, foreign minister, and premier of a coalition government in 1949 and 1950, Bidault was one of the promoters of the idea of European unity under the FOURTH REPUBLIC. Also, during his career in the

National Assembly, from 1945 to 1962, he opposed the policy of Algerian independence (see ALGERIA) of CHARLES DE GAULLE. Instead, he supported the Organisation de l'armée secrète (OAS), of which he became a leader. Advocating terrorism, he was charged with conspiracy and went into exile in 1963. He lived in Belgium and Brazil until his return to France in 1968, when he was granted amnesty. Bidault is the author of *Résistance* (1965), an autobiographical work.

## Billaud-Varenne, Jean-Nicolas (1756–1819)
*political figure*

Born in La Rochelle, Jean-Nicolas Billaud-Varenne studied law in Paris and Poitiers. An attorney for the Paris Parlement, when the REVOLUTION OF 1789 began, he joined the JACOBIN CLUB and, in 1789, published a violent critique of the government, *Despotisme des ministres de France*, and later a pamphlet, "Acéphalocratie" (1792), in which he affirmed his republican convictions. A Montagnard deputy to the National Convention and later to the Insurrectionary COMMUNE OF PARIS (after August 10, 1794), he advocated the establishment of a federal republic and the execution of LOUIS XVI. In September 1793, he became a member of the Committee of Public Safety, joining MAXIMILIEN ROBESPIERRE in his struggle against the GIRONDIN moderates, Hebertists, and Dantonist factions. Although he became one of the instigators of the 9 Thermidor (July 27, 1794) attack on Robespierre, Billaud-Varenne was nonetheless himself arrested, prosecuted as a terrorist, and deported to Guyana (1795). He later refused NAPOLÉON I's amnesty and went to Haiti after the return of the Bourbons, where he remained.

## Binet, Alfred (1857–1911)
*physiologist, psychologist*

Born in Nice, Alfred Binet, who studied with noted psychologists, was a founder of *L'Année psychologique* and contributed to the progress of experimental psychology (*Introduction à la psychologie expérimentale*, 1894). He is above all known for his work (with THÉODORE SIMON) on the measuring of the development of intelligence in young children. His metric scale (Binet Scale) of intelligence, established in 1905, was later modified.

## Biot, Jean-Baptiste (1774–1862)
*physicist, mathematician, astronomer*

Born in Paris, Jean-Baptiste Biot became professor of physics at the COLLÈGE DE FRANCE in 1800 and was elected to membership in the Academy of Sciences in 1803. In that year he discovered the celestial origin of meteorites, and began his studies of the density of gases. Biot is best known for his optical law on polarized light, and was the first to use the saccharimeter in determining the nature and amount of sugars in solutions. He also formulated, with the French physicist Félix Savart in 1820, the Briot-Savart Law concerning the effect of an electric current on a magnetic field. Biot was made a member of the ACADÉMIE FRANÇAISE in 1856.

## Bissière, Roger (1888–1964)
*painter, engraver*

Born in Villeréal, Lot-et-Garonne, Roger Bissière, after studies at the École des beaux-arts in BORDEAUX, settled in Paris, where he frequently saw ANDRÉ LHOTE and the Spanish artist Juan Gris and, beginning in 1922, became friends with GEORGES BRAQUE. Bissière collaborated, too, on LE CORBUSIER and AMÉDÉE OZENFANT's revue, *L'Esprit nouveau*, and was professor at the Académie Ranson from 1925 to 1938. Settling in the Lot region in 1939 with vision problems, he abandoned painting until 1945. Meanwhile, he produced fabric wallpapers. After his recovery, he painted nonfigurative works, abandoning cubism and painting subtle nuances, creating more or less compact canvases that gave the entire work an original tonal unity. These works, in which color tends to become the primary vehicle for emotion, often reveal a sustained contemplation of nature (*Le Jardin cette nuit*, 1962). Bissière also produced numerous engravings, as well as stained-glass windows for the cathedral of Metz.

## Bizet, Georges (1838–1875)
*composer*

Best known for his operas, Georges Bizet was born in Paris, where he entered the Paris Conservatory

Georges Bizet *(Library of Congress)*

work of his youth, *Jeux d'enfants,* 12 pieces for piano duet (1871); and the celebrated incidental music for the play *l'Arlésienne* (1872).

## Blanc, Charles (1813–1882)
*art critic*

Born in Castres, Charles Blanc was the brother of the revolutionary LOUIS BLANC. Author of a *Histoire des peintres français du XIXe siècle* (1845), he was named an administrative director of fine arts (1848–50), then dedicated himself to the editing of his *Histoire des peintres de toutes les écoles* (14 volumes, 1876). Blanc was elected the ACADÉMIE FRANÇAISE in 1876.

## Blanc, Louis (1811–1882)
*socialist and historian*

Born in Madrid, Spain, the son of the inspector general of finances for the king, JOSEPH BONAPARTE, Louis Blanc was educated in Paris, where he soon became an advocate of socialism and socialist reform. A contributor to various political journals, he established, in 1839, *Revue du Progrès,* which served as an organ for his socialist doctrines. Blanc's concept of the social order anticipated a number of later thinkers in that it declared that revolutionary action was the only feasible path for the working classes. He also formulated, in *L'Organisation du travail* (1839), the social principle, "from each according to his abilities, to each according to his needs," which was later adopted by Marx. Blanc believed that this could be achieved through the creation of "social workshops"—the "ateliers" that were associations of workers financed by the state. In 1841, he published a violent pamphlet, "Histoire de dix ans," against the July Monarchy and, during the REVOLUTION OF 1848, became a leader of the provisional republican government that came to power after the abdication of LOUIS-PHILIPPE I. But after the brutal suppression of the worker's uprising in Paris in June 1848, he was forced to flee and lived in exile in England for 22 years. There, he wrote his 12-volume *Histoire de la Revolution française* (1847–62). After the fall of the Second Empire in 1870, he returned to France and was elected to the National Assembly (February 1871), but he opposed the extremism of the COMMUNE, which was then in

at age 10. After a brilliant career as a student, he went on to win first place in the Grand prix de Rome (1857). Among the numerous works that he composed for the theater, certain of his opéras comiques and operas stand out: *Les Pêcheurs de perles* (1863), *La Jolie Fille de Perth* (1866), *Djamileh* (1871), and, above all, *Carmen* (1875), a masterpiece of French lyrical drama in which the music conveys the most eloquent interpretation of the characterization. Although not an immediate success, *Carmen* soon became one of the most popular works in operatic history. Bizet was an outstanding dramatist, and his style would have a strong influence on the verismo school of opera of the late 19th century. Bizet's other works include the Symphonie in C (1855); a power. He served as a member of the Chamber of Deputies from 1876 until his death.

## Blanchard, Jean-Pierre  (1753–1809)
*aeronaut*
In 1784, just after the French physicist JEAN ROZIER made the first manned balloon ascent, Jean Blanchard, who was born in Les Andeleys, made a successful ascent in his own balloon. In 1785, accompanied by John Jeffries, an American physician, he made the first aerial crossing of the English Channel from Dover to Calais by balloon. In the same year, he gave the first successful demonstration of a parachute, using a basket containing an animal. In 1793, at Philadelphia in the United States, Blanchard made the first balloon ascent in North America. He was often accompanied in his trial ascents by his wife, Sophie Armant, who was killed when a balloon exploded.

## Blanchot, Maurice  (1907–2003)
*essayist and novelist*
Born in Saône-et-Loire, Maurice Blanchot, through his writings, was initially brought into the ranks of the extreme right. He contributed to, in particular, *La Revue française* and to *Réaction,* and took part in the VICHY regime's cultural movement, Jeune France. His encounter with GEORGES BATAILLE in 1941, however, was decisive. In 1942, Blanchot joined the RESISTANCE and, in July 1944, was captured, but escaped from the Germans. Much later (1960), as an activist, he played an important part in editing the "Manifeste des 121" and was a member of the Committee of Students and Writers (1968). With *Thomas l'Obscur* (1941 and 1951), *Aminadab* (1942), *Le Trés Haut* (1948), *L'Arrêt du mort* (1948), *Ce-lui qui ne m'accompagnait pas* (1953), *Le Dernier Homme* (1957), and *L'Instant de ma mort* (1994), and dedications to *Lautreament et Sade* (1949), to MALLARMÉ (*Faux Pas,* 1943), to Kafka, Rilke, and Hölderin (*La Part de feu,* 1949; *Le Livre à venir,* 1959; *De Kafka à Kafka,* 1982; *La Communauté inavouable,* 1983), the essays of Blanchot represent the same literary quest as his novels. The narratives *L'attente, L'oubli* (1962), then *L'Entretien infini* (1969), *L'Amitié* (1971), and *Le Pas au delà* (1973), three

"theoretical" works, are fictional dialogues that poignantly illustrate Blanchot's developments. His internal conflict in reconciling with modernity is expressed also in *La Réssassement éternal* (1983) and in *L'Écriture du désastre* (1980).

## Blanqui, Louis-Auguste  (1805–1881)
*revolutionary, socialist*
Born in Puget-Théniers, Alpes-Maritimes, Louis-Auguste Blanqui studied law and medicine in Paris. Shortly afterward, he became a republican and joined the French Carbonari, participating in the antimonarchist uprisings of 1827. By then, he had become familiar with the ideas of HENRI DE SAINT-SIMON, CHARLES FOURIER, and above all, GRACCHUS BABEUF. He took part in the JULY REVOLUTION OF 1830, and was a supporter of King LOUIS-PHILIPPE I during his early reign. But after 1831, Blanqui was involved in organizing several secret republican and socialist societies, as well as numerous conspiracies against the government. He was arrested and, in his defense statement, gave a strong denunciation of bourgeois capitalist society. Arrested again in 1839 for conspiracy, he was sentenced to life in prison. Pardoned in 1847, he participated in the overthrow of Louis-Philippe's regime the next year, but was again imprisoned for 10 years for his part in the failed leftist uprising of May 1848. During his years in prison, he developed several theories within socialism, among them the concept of the "dictatorship of the proletariat." While believing in the necessity of revolution, he also favored gradual economic evolution from capitalism to communism. Upon returning from exile in Belgium in 1870, he attempted another uprising, but the fall of the SECOND EMPIRE of NAPOLÉON III occurred shortly after (September 1870). By this time, Blanqui had founded the journal *La Patrie en danger.* He briefly led a provisional government (October 1870), and his followers formed the majority of the members of the COMMUNE of Paris, which would end with the slaughter of more than 20,000 communards in May 1871. Blanqui was then again imprisoned but released in 1879. He subsequently published the journal *Ni Dieu ni Maïtre,* in which he criticized the utopian socialist movement. Blanqui's own doctrine, "blanquisme," is considered the necessary link between French

socialism and Marxism. His most important work, *Critique sociale,* was published posthumously in 1885.

## Blin, Roger (1907–1984)
*actor, stage director*

Born in Neuilly-sur-Seine, Roger Blin was the friend of ANTONIN ARTAUD, and acted in his play *Les Cenci* (1935); he also worked with JACQUES PRÉVERT in the groupe Octobre (a revolutionary theater company of the years 1934–35) and with JEAN-LOUIS BAR-RAULT (*Numance,* 1937; *La Faim,* 1939). Recognized at the time of his first stage direction (*La Sonate des spectres* by Strindberg, 1949), Blin helped to develop the idea that the stage director was the creative source of theatrical entertainment through interpretation and presentation of scripts and aspects of staging. As his reputation grew, the most serious and demanding of contemporary authors entrusted him with their works: Arthur Adamov (*La Grande et la petite Manœuvre,* 1950; *La Parodie,* 1952), Samuel Beckett (*En attendant Godot,* 1953; *Fin de partie,* 1957; *La Dernière bande,* 1960, *Oh les beux jours,* 1963), JEAN GENET (*Les Nègres,* 1959; *Les Paravents,* which caused a scandal when it was produced in 1966).

## Bloch, Marc (1886–1944)
*historian*

Born in LYON, the son of Gustave Bloch, the noted professor of Roman history at the SORBONNE, Marc Bloch, along with LUCIEN FEBVRE, compiled the *Annales d'histoire économique et sociale* (1929). Appointed professor of history at the Sorbonne in 1936, Bloch joined the RESISTANCE in 1942 and was soon captured and killed by the Germans. His writings (*Les Rois thaumaturges,* 1924; *Les Caractères originaux de l'histoire rurale française,* 1931; *La Société féodale,* 1939–40) revitalized medieval historiography and considerably enlarged the general field of historical research. His posthumous work, *Apologie pour l'histoire* (1952), in which he defined his idea of history, led to his becoming one of the most important historians of his generation.

## Bloc national

The Bloc national was a political alliance formed in France immediately after the FIRST WORLD WAR (1919) grouping moderates and conservatives to meet the challenge of the Radical-Socialists and the Socialists. Winning in the legislative elections of November 16, 1919, the Bloc national governed France for four years (see ALEXANDRE MILLERAND, ARISTIDE BRIAND, RAYMOND POINCARÉ), then was defeated by the CARTEL DES GAUCHES in May 1924.

## Blondel, François (1618–1686)
*mathematician, military engineer, diplomat, architect, theorist*

Born in Ribemont, near Saint-Quentin, François Blondel, who had a solid scientific and literary background and had traveled throughout Europe, was entrusted by the French government with important diplomatic missions, notably to Egypt, Constantinople, and the Antilles. There, he built fortifications, developed the urbanization plans for Rochefort, and restored the ancient bridge at Saintes. He entered the Academy of Sciences, as the protégé of JEAN-BAPTISTE COLBERT and helped to establish the Royal Academy of Architecture (1671). Drawing freely from Roman models, he built the triumphal arch at the porte Saint-Denis in PARIS (1671–72), and was one of the principal theorists of the classical dogma, extolling the imitation of the "Ancients" and the architecture of the Italian Renaissance, while condemning the "fantasies and excesses" of the Italian baroque. His conception of a single, universal, and rational beauty (*Cours d'architecture,* 1675) was opposed within the academy by CLAUDE PERRAULT.

## Blondel, Jacques-François (1705–1774)
*architect, urbanist, theorist*

Jacques-François Blondel, the nephew of FRANÇOIS BLONDEL, was born in Rouen. He played an important role in the development of the LOUIS XVI style by opening a private school of architecture (1734) and by publishing several theoretical and practical works (*De la distribution des maisons de plaisance et de la décoration en général,* 1737; *L'Architecture française,* 1752–56; *Cours d'architecture civile,* 1771–77). Condemning the use of rococo decoration, Blondel extolled ornamental simplicity, the perfection of proportions, and respect for rules, and expressed his admiration for the French masters of the 17th century (FRANÇOIS MANSART) and for the ancient classical styles. He conceived the plan for the renovation of the city of Metz, and built there the Parlement, the Archepiscopal Palace, and, notably, the City Hall (begun in 1765).

## Blondel, Maurice (1861–1949)
*philosopher*

Born in Dijon and educated at the École normale supérieure, Maurice Blondel taught at the universities of Mautaubon, Lille, and Aix-Marseille. Trying to formulate a theory in which no true division would exist between thought and experiential reality, Blondel, in his doctoral thesis, *L'Action: essai d'une critique de la vie et d'une science de la pratique* (1893), sought to resolve the problem of the relationship between the speculative and the practical. A religious thinker, he wanted to reconcile reason and faith, the immanent and the supernatural. His work holds an important place in the intellectual history of the Catholic Church. At first discussed among philosophers and then theologians, Blondel has strongly influenced the development of Catholic thought (*Vers un réalisme intégral*, 1898; *La Philosophie et l'Esprit chrétien*, 1944–47).

## Bloy, Léon (1846–1917)
*writer*

Born in Périgueux, Léon Bloy was a critical journalist (in literature he attacked the whole naturalist school, especially ÉMILE ZOLA in *Je m'accuse*, 1900). An ardent Catholic who castigated the Vatican (*Brelan d'excommuniés*) and denounced materialism, democracy, and positivism in violent invectives. Bloy is the author of a number of novels, sometimes semiautobiographic (*Le Désespéré*, 1886; *La Femme pauvre*, 1897) and other polemical works (*Le Salut par les Juifs*, 1892; *Celle qui pleure*, 1908).

## Blum, Léon (1872–1950)
*statesman, writer*

Born in Paris and educated at the École Normale Supérieure and at the SORBONNE, Léon Blum, after leaving the university, practiced law and also gained a reputation as a literary and drama critic. Brought into politics by the Dreyfus affair (see ALFRED DREYFUS), he joined the Socialist Party in 1899. As a Socialist, he collaborated, after 1904, with JEAN JAURÈS on *L'HUMANITÉ*. In 1920, after the Congress of Tours, at which the Communist and Socialist Parties split, Blum was responsible for rebuilding the French Socialist Party. From 1919 to 1928, and from 1929 to 1940, he was a member of the Chamber of Deputies. In the 1930s, he helped to organize the Popular Front, a coalition of leftists and centrists that gained a majority in the Chamber in 1936. It was the first time that the Socialists controlled the government in France. Blum became premier (the first Socialist and also the first Jew to do so), and immediately encountered conservative opposition through his program of extensive social reform. The 40-hour workweek was introduced, along with paid vacations. Labor disputes were brought to arbitration, and the Bank of France and the munitions industry were nationalized. As there was a strong concentration on domestic issues, Blum's government was criticized for failing to give precedence to rearmament (especially after the German remilitarization of the Rhineland in 1936). Blum was criticized by the Communists for his policy of nonintervention in the Spanish civil war. In March 1938, Blum's Socialist Party broke with the Popular Front government of ÉDOUARD DALADIER over the Munich Pact signed with Germany, Italy, and Great Britain. After the French surrender in 1940, Blum was arrested by the VICHY government and charged with treason. At his trial, however, his remarkable and eloquent defense so embarrassed the Vichy regime that the proceedings were stopped and he was sent to a concentration camp. Freed by the Allies in 1945, Blum subsequently served as French ambassador extraordinary to several countries and also would lead an interim government from December 1946 to January 1947. In that capacity, he helped to put in place the foundations of the Fourth Republic. As a writer, Blum's works include *Nouvelles Conversations de Goethe avec Eckermann* (1901); *Du mariage* (1907), *Stendhal et la beylisme* (1914), and *À l'échelle humaine* (1945), in which he wrote of the RESISTANCE and also presented his views on the differences between socialism and communism.

## Bodin, Jean (ca. 1530–1596)

*economist, philosopher*

An early defender of the political theory of absolutism, Jean Bodin was born in Angers and was an attorney for the Parlement of PARIS before becoming lieutenant-general, then royal procurator, for the district of Laon. In his treatise *Methodus ad facilem historiarum cognitionem* (1556), he demonstrated the importance of historical knowledge in the development of law and politics. An economist, he analyzed the phenomenon of rising prices in the 16th century and their relationship to the importation of precious metals from the Americas (*Réponse aux paradoxes de Malestroit*), finally, as author of *La République*, he became in politics the theorist of absolute monarchy. One of the first thinkers to defend absolutism without relying on religious arguments, Bodin asserted the right of monarchs to partake of the power of the Holy Roman Emperor and, at the same time, to exert their right to rule over all their own subjects, constrained, however, by social customs and natural law. This theory became a central tenet of absolutism in the 17th century.

## Boileau, Nicolas (1636–1711)

*poet, critic*

Of bourgeois background, Nicholas Boileau, or Boileau-Despréaux, as he is known, was born in Paris and educated at the SORBONNE. Considered to have had an important influence on French literature, as both a poet and a critic, he established the principles for French classical writing and, in this regard, was known as the "lawgiver of Princes." His earliest significant works include his 12 *Satires* (begun in 1660) in rhymed couplets, in which he gives witty and sharp critiques of contemporary writers. Other important works include the several volumes of his *Épîtres* (1669–90); *Art poétique* (1674), which was inspired by Horace's *Ars Poetica* and in which Boileau analyzed various forms of poetry and set down the guidelines for their composition; and *Le Latin* (1674), a mock heroic poem that would later be used by the English poet Alexander Pope as a model for his *Rape of the Lock*. In 1670, Boileau-Despréaux was granted a pension by LOUIS XIV, was made royal historiographer in 1677, and, in 1684, was elected into the ACADÉMIE FRANÇAISE.

## Boissy d'Anglas, François-Antoine, count de (1756–1826)

*political figure*

Born in Saint-Jean-Chambre, Ardèche, François-Antoine, count de Boissy d'Anglas was a deputy for the third estate to the ESTATES GENERAL (1789), and as such, he usually voted with the constitutional faction. Reelected, during the REVOLUTION OF 1789, to the Convention, he served as its president after 9 Thermidor Year II (July 27, 1794), when MAXIMILIEN ROBESPIERRE was overthrown. A member of the Council of Five Hundred, after having taken part in the drafting of the Constitution of the Year III, he was proscribed during the coup d'état of 18 Fructidor (September 4, 1797), in which the more extreme republican faction of the Directory removed the more moderate and royalist (absolutist and constitutional) members of the government. Boissy d'Anglas, however, escaped deportation and, after the coup d'état of 18 Brumaire (November 9, 1799) that brought Napoléon Bonaparte (see NAPOLÉON I) to power, became a member of the Tribunal, a senator, and eventually a count of the Empire. He was named a peer during the RESTORATION.

## Bombois, Camille (1883–1970)

*painter*

Born in Venarey-les-Laumes, Camille Bombois, who had worked as a farmhand, dockworker typographer, and itinerant entertainer, was one of that generation of painters, like HENRI ROUSSEAU ("le Douanier"), who had raised painting from the usual criterion of simple reproduction to another view of reality. In 1922 in Paris, when he exhibited his paintings at the Foire aux croûtes de Montmartre, his talent was recognized by the critic Wilhelm Uhde, who bought an important part of his work. Beginning in 1925, Bombois supported himself by painting landscapes, nudes, and circus characters (on luminous colored surfaces) that were also comments on various aspects of daily life (*Le Pont du Chablis*, 1923; *Nature morte au homard*, 1932). In his paintings, the stiffness of the personages, in frontal positions, in which the simplified shapes are often cut short by a dark bottom, at times evoke the surrealist style and indicate a certain detachment of the artist from his subject.

## Bonaparte, Carlo Maria (1746–1785)
*father of Napoléon I*

The husband of MARIA LETIZIA RAMOLINO, and father of NAPOLÉON I, as well as of CAROLINE, ÉLISA, JÉRÔME, JOSEPH, LOUIS, LUCIEN, and PAULINE BONAPARTE, Carlo Bonaparte was born in Ajaccio, Corsica, where he was a lawyer. He fought along with PASQUALE PAOLI for Corsican independence (1768–69), then, after 1770, went over to the side of the French. He died before his son came to power in France.

## Bonaparte, Caroline (1782–1839)
*princess, sister of Napoléon I*

Born in Ajaccio, Corsica, the daughter of MARIA LETIZIA RAMOLINO and CARLO MARIA BONAPARTE and sister of NAPOLÉON I, Caroline Bonaparte, as she was called, married JOACHIM MURAT in 1800. Quite ambitious, she had a strong influence on her husband. As queen of Naples (1808), she patronized the arts and cultured life in her kingdom. After her husband's death, she took the title of countess of Lipona.

## Bonaparte, Élisa (1777–1820)
*princess, sister of Napoléon I*

Born Maria-Anna Bonaparte in Ajaccio, Corsica, the daughter of MARIA LETIZIA RAMOLINO and CARLO MARIA BONAPARTE and sister of NAPOLÉON I, Elisa Bonaparte, as she was called, married and became princess of Lucca and Piombino and grand duchess of Tuscany. In 1797, she married Félix Bacciochi, from whom she separated in 1801. An intelligent and active woman, in many ways resembling her brother Napoléon, Élisa Bonaparte proved to be a capable administrator of her principalities and duchies. After the fall of the empire, she settled in Bologna and then in Germany.

## Bonaparte, Eugène-Louis-Jean-Joseph-Napoléon (1856-1879)
*imperial prince*

Born in Paris, Prince Eugène-Louis-Napoléon was the only son of NAPOLÉON III and Empress EUGÉNIE. After the fall of the SECOND EMPIRE, he went into exile with his mother in England. There, he was allowed to join the military as an observer in South Africa, where he was killed in the Zulu War. Prince Eugène-Louis had been proclaimed Napoléon IV by his father's adherents.

## Bonaparte, Jérôme (1784–1860)
*king of Westphalia, brother of Napoléon I*

Born in Ajaccio, Corsica, the son of MARIA LETIZIA RAMOLINO and CARLO MARIA BONAPARTE, and the brother of NAPOLÉON I, Jérôme Bonaparte served in the French navy, and in 1803, while in the United States, married Elizabeth Patterson. Napoléon, however, arranged for a second marriage in 1807 to princess Catherine of Würtemburg. Jérôme Bonaparte became king of Westphalia that same year. In 1813, he went into exile but returned in 1815 to command a French division at Waterloo. After Napoléon's defeat and abdication, he went into exile again, returning to Paris in 1848, when his nephew, Louis-Napoléon (the future NAPOLÉON III), came to power. Jérôme then, in 1849, was made governor of the Invalides and, subsequently, a marshal of France (1850), and president of the Senate (1852). The present Bonaparte line and claimants are descended from him.

## Bonaparte, Joseph (1768–1844)
*king of Spain, brother of Napoléon I*

Born in Corte, Corsica, the son of MARIA LETIZIA RAMOLINO and CARLO MARIA BONAPARTE, and the older brother of NAPOLÉON I, Joseph Bonaparte served as deputy for Corsica to the Council of Five Hundred (1796). He also participated in the planning of the coup d'état of 18 Brumaire (1799), which brought his brother to power (see NAPOLÉON I). In charge of various diplomatic missions during the Consulate, Joseph Bonaparte, in 1801, signed the Treaty of Lunéville, the Peace of Amiens, and the Concordat. His brother then made him king of Naples (1806–08), and subsequently king of Spain (1808–13). He went to the United States after Waterloo, then to England, and finally to Florence, Italy. He married Julie Clary in 1794.

## Bonaparte, Louis (1778–1846)
*king of Holland, brother of Napoléon I*

Born in Ajaccio, Corsica, the son of CARLO MARIA BONAPARTE and MARIA LETIZIA RAMOLINO, and younger brother of NAPOLÉON I, Louis Bonaparte served as aide-de-camp to Napoléon during that commander's campaigns in Italy and in Egypt. He was married against his will to HORTENSE DE BEAUHARNAIS, the daughter of JOSÉPHINE BEAUHARNAIS, in 1802. Napoléon made Louis king of Holland in 1806. There, out of concern for the welfare of his subjects, Louis refused to continue the Continental Blockade imposed by Napoléon. Because of his conflicts with the emperor, Louis was forced to abdicate in 1810. He had three children, one of whom, Louis-Napoléon, became NAPOLÉON III.

## Bonaparte, Lucien  (1775–1840)
*brother of Napoléon I*

Born in Ajaccio, Corsica, the son of CARLO MARIA BONAPARTE and MARIA LETIZIA RAMOLINO, and brother of NAPOLÉON I, Lucien Bonaparte was extremely intelligent and always possessed an independent spirit. He was a member (1797), and then president, of the Council of Five Hundred and was chiefly responsible for the coup d'état of 18 Brumaire (1799), which brought his brother to power. Minister of the interior (1799) and ambassador to Spain (1800), he became a member of the Tribunate after his return to France. Breaking with Napoléon over the issue of the latter's authoritative exercise of power, Lucien went into exile in Rome (1804), then to Canino, where a principality was created for him by Pope Pius VII. He reconciled with the emperor during the Hundred Days. Lucien had two daughters from his marriage to Christine Boyer (1795). Against the wishes of Napoléon, he married a second time to Alexandrine de Bleschamps, widow of a stockbroker. From that marriage, he had nine children.

## Bonaparte, Maria Letizia Ramolino (1750–1836)
*mother of Napoléon I*

The wife of CARLO MARIA BONAPARTE, and the mother of JOSEPH, NAPOLÉON, LUCIEN, ÉLISA, LOUIS, PAULINE, CAROLINE, and JÉRÔME BONAPARTE, Maria Letizia Ramolino was born in Ajaccio, Corsica. She was supportive of Napoléon and her other children as her family came to power in France and, under the Empire, was given the title of "Madame Mère."

Extremely intelligent and possessing an energetic character, she lived a modest life away from the imperial court, while serving as patroness to a number of charitable and educational institutions. She advised and maintained an influence on her children, including the emperor. After the fall of the Empire, Letizia Bonaparte retired to Rome.

## Bonaparte, Marie  (1882–1962)
*psychoanalyst*

Born in Saint-Cloud, Marie Bonaparte was the granddaughter of Pierre Napoléon Bonaparte. She helped to popularize the work of Sigmund Freud and was one of the founders of the Psychoanalytic Society of Paris (1926). Like Karen Horney, she emphasized the role of sociocultural factors in nervous disorders.

## Bonaparte, Mathilde Letizia Wilhelmine  (1820–1914)
*niece of Napoléon I, salon hostess*

Born in Trieste, Mathilde Letizia Wilhelmine Bonaparte, who was known as princess Mathilde, was the daughter of JÉRÔME BONAPARTE and Catherine of Würtemburg, and was the niece of NAPOLÉON I. She was at first engaged to marry the future NAPOLÉON III, but the engagement was broken following his imprisonment at Ham. After an unhappy marriage, princess Mathilde settled in Paris, where, before and after the FRANCO-PRUSSIAN WAR (1870), which forced her to leave the country, her salon was the meeting place for some of the most brilliant personages of the artistic and literary world (HIPPOLYTE TAINE, ERNEST RENAN, the GONCOURTS, GUSTAVE FLAUBERT).

## Bonaparte, Napoléon  See NAPOLÉON I.

## Bonaparte, Napoléon-Joseph-Charles-Paul  (1822–1891)
*nephew of Napoléon, senator, diplomat, imperial pretender*

Born in Trieste, Napoléon-Joseph-Charles-Paul Bonaparte, who was known as prince Jérôme, was the son of JÉRÔME BONAPARTE and Catherine of Würtemburg and was the nephew of Napoléon

Bonaparte (NAPOLÉON I). A senator during the SEC-OND EMPIRE, then minister of colonies (1858), in 1859 he married Clotilde, daughter of King Victor Emmanuel II of Italy. From this union was born Napoléon-Victor Bonaparte, known as prince Victor (1862–1926). Imperial pretender (1879), prince Jérome was expelled from France (1886) and settled in Brussels, Belgium. His son, Louis-Napoléon-Jérome Bonaparte, became the claimant. Their descendant Charles-Napoléon Bonaparte (1950–  ) is the present claimant.

## Bonaparte, Pauline (1780–1825)
*princess, sister of Napoleon Bonaparte*
Born Marie-Paulette Bonaparte in Ajaccio, Corsica, the daughter of MARIA LETIZIA RAMOLINO and CARLO MARIA BONAPARTE, and the younger sister of Napoléon Bonaparte, Pauline Bonaparte married General LECLERC but was widowed in 1802, when her husband died of yellow fever in the course of trying to suppress the rebellion that led to the establishment of independent Haiti (the former French colony of St-Domingue). In 1803 she married prince Camille Borghese and became princess Pauline Borghese. She was soon separated from him, however, and lived independently, much celebrated for her beauty. In 1806, Napoléon made her duchess of Guastalla. Banished from the French imperial court in 1810 because of a dispute with the empress Marie-Louise, Pauline Bonaparte always remained loyal to her brother. She joined him in exile on Elba (1814) and wanted to follow him to Saint Helena. The sculptor Canova produced a famous statue of her as Venus victrix.

## Bonnat, Léon (1833–1922)
*painter, portraitist*
Born in Bayonne, Léon Bonnat, after having worked on religious subjects, during the THIRD REPUBLIC became the preferred portraitist of the leading political figures of the period (*Thiers; Jules Ferry*). Influenced by the realism of GUSTAVE COURBET, he gave a quasi-photographic tone to his portraits and is considered one of the best representatives of the French academic style. At his Parisian workshop, Bonnat's own students included HENRI DE TOULOUSE-LAUTREC and GUSTAVE CAILLEBOTTE. Bonnat left to the

French nation a remarkable collection of paintings and portraits, now exhibited at the LOUVRE and the Musée Bonnat in Bayonne.

## Bonnefoy, Yves (1923–  )
*poet*
Born in Tours, Yves Bonnefoy is a critic, translator of Shakespeare and Yeats, and professor at the Collège de France. He developed an intense poetic meditation on the inertia of all matter. Recognizing that words have a living effect on objects, he has confided in them the hope of a return to the innocence of the world, to be achieved by poetry. His thought, expressed in a language that suggests more than is being described, transmits also a sense of anguish. Bonnefoy's poetry, which includes *Du monument et de l'immobilité de Douve* (1975), *Dans le Leurre du seuil* (1975), *Ce qui fut sans lumière* (1987), and *Début et fin de la neige* (1991), is inseparable from his narratives (*L'Arrière-pays*, 1972; *Rue Traversière*, 1977) and his text-meditations on art (*L'Improbable*, 1959; *Entretiens sur la poésie*, 1990; *Alberto Giacometti*, 1991). With *Vie errante* (1933), Bonnefoy seemed to want to meld all genres into a simple and discreet poetic word.

## Bordeaux
A city of southwestern France, Bordeaux, capital of the Gironde Department, is on the Garonne River, which flows into the Bay of Biscay. Canals also link the city with the Mediterranean, and it is the chief trade and shipping center for the region's wines. Manufactures include ships, motor vehicles, refined petroleum, chemicals, and processed food. Bordeaux is crescent-shaped (lying along a broad bend in the Garonne), and the north section is well planned with wide streets and spacious squares, notably the Place des Quinconces, and many imposing buildings. The south section, constructed during the 18th century, is older, with narrow streets and many wooden structures, some dating to an earlier period. Points of interest include the Porte de Bourgogne and the Porte d'Aquitaine; the Cathedral of Saint-André from the 11th century; the church of Saint Croix, a Romanesque basilica of the 12th and 13th centuries; and the church of Saint Seurin, from the 11th to the 15th centuries.

Other important and historic buildings are the Hôtel de Ville; the Bordeaux Library, with many significant manuscripts; the Grand-Théâtre, from the 18th century, and several art museums. Bordeaux and nearby Talence are the sites of the universities of Bordeaux I, II, and III, established in the early 1970s to supplement the University of Bordeaux (1441). Before the Roman conquest of Gaul, the city of Bordeaux, then known as Burdigala, was the capital of the Bituriges Vivisques, a Celtic tribe. The Romans took the city in the first century and developed a commercial center. In the fourth century it became the capital of the province of Aquitania Seconda and also the seat of an archbishopric. From the fifth to the 12th centuries, it was held for varying periods by the Goths and the Normans. In 1154, through the marriage of Eleanor of Aquitaine to Henry II of England, Bordeaux became an English possession. During the HUNDRED YEARS' WAR, the English withdrew and the city, accustomed to regional autonomy, until the late 17th century, often rebelled against subsequent French rule. During the REVOLUTION OF 1789, Bordeaux was a stronghold of the moderate republican faction, the GIRONDINS. Because of this, the city suffered greatly during the TERROR. Bordeaux was one of the first to rally to the Bourbon cause in 1814, at which time King LOUIS XVIII granted the title duke of Bordeaux to his nephew and later heir, the count of CHAMBORD. The city served as the seat of the French government in the final stages of the FRANCO-PRUSSIAN WAR and, during WORLD WAR I, the government again for a time was also located there. Bordeaux was the seat of a government, too, in 1940, but was then occupied by German forces until 1945.

## Bosse, Abraham (1602–1676)
*painter, engraver, theorist*

Abraham Bosse began his artistic career in his birthplace, Tours, making etchings. He eventually settled in Paris, where he met JACQUES CALLOT, who introduced him to the process of making etchings (aqua fortis) on hardened varnish. Using this process in a different way, Bosse sought to create the effect of an engraving. He was named professor of perspective when the Academy of Painting & Sculpture was established (1648), but stubborn and polemic, he

was excluded from that body following a dispute with CHARLES LE BRUN on the subject of perspective in art. He then founded a free school (which the king ordered closed) and wrote numerous statements in its defense. A great part of his work (more than 1,500 plates) constitutes a document on the mores of the first half of 17th-century France; they are exceptionally varied and rich in details. His meticulous depictions reveal a rigorous and temperate mind and comfortable workmanship (*La Galerie du palais; La Saignée; Les Cris de Paris*). His writings, *Traité des manières de graveur en taille-douce* (1645) and *Leçon de géométrie et de perspective pratique* (1648), were popular and influential on other artists and engravers.

## Bossuet, Jacques-Bénigne (1627–1704)
*prelate, theologian, and writer*

One of the greatest French preachers and religious writers, Jacques-Bénigne Bossuet was born in Dijon and educated in Jesuit schools in Paris. In 1652, he was ordained a priest and, after being initially guided by Saint VINCENT DE PAUL, soon earned a reputation for his erudition and ability as a preacher. From 1670 to 1681, he was tutor to the son of LOUIS XIV and MARIE THÉRÈSE, the grand dauphin for whom he wrote his great *Discours sur l'histoire universelle* (1681), one of the first philosophical interpretations of history. In it, Bossuet argued that all history is impelled by Divine Providence. In 1681, he became bishop of Meaux. A peerless orator, Bossuet is best known for his *Oraisons funèbres*, which he gave between 1656 and 1687 and which are his panegyrics on major national figures. The virtual head of the French Catholic Church, he participated in the quarrel between Louis XIV and Pope Innocent XI over the respective rights of the king and the pope in France and edited the *Déclaration du clergé de France* (1682), in which he presented his theses. Supporting the monarch, Bossuet's ideas became the basis for subsequent claims of both king and church in France for independence from the papacy (see GALLICANISM). He also took part in a famous dispute with the French prelate FRANÇOIS FÉNELON over the mystical teachings of quietism. While Fénelon supported quietism, Bossuet considered it a heresy. His opinion influenced the pope, who soon condemned Fénelon's writings. An intense and dramatic preacher, as well as a prolific scholar, Bossuet was elected to the ACADÉMIE FRANÇAISE in 1671. His other works include *Histoire des variations des Églises protestantes* (1688), *Défense de l'histoire des variations* (1691), and *Relation sur le quiétisme* (1698).

## Bouchardon, Edme (1698–1762)
*sculptor*
Born in Chaumont-en-Bassigny, Edme Bouchardon studied first in France, then spent time in Rome (1722 to 1732), where he produced several busts. In Paris, he first designed medals and engravings for the royal furnishings and then worked in the gardens of VERSAILLES, where his work adorned several fountains. An admirer of ancient sculpture, he was opposed to the rococo style then in vogue, and worked in the neoclassical mode (a copy for king LOUIS XV of the *Barberini faun*, 1726–1730; *L'Amour taillant son arc*, 1739–50). Bouchardon sculpted and finished the fountain of Quatre-Saisons, rue de Grenelle in Paris (1739–50) and the equestrian statue of Louis XV dressed in ancient Roman costume (1748–62).

## Boucher, François (1703–1770)
*painter, designer, decorator, engraver*
Known for his pastoral and mythological scenes embodying the sensuousness and frivolity of the rococo, François Boucher was born in Paris, the son of a lace designer. There, he studied with various artists but was most influenced by the delicate style of ANTOINE WATTEAU. In 1725, Boucher won the prix de Rome, then studied in Italy from 1727 to 1731, where he was especially inspired by the works of Correggio and Tiepolo. Through his many decorative works (the Queen's Chamber, VERSAILLES, 1734; the first floor of the hôtel de Rohan-Soubire, Paris), his drawings and designs for the Gobelins works (*Fêtes chinoises*, 1734), his cast models for Sèvres and his mythological scenes (*Le Triomphe de Venus*, 1740), his pastorals, and his libertine scenes and nudes (*Odalisque*, 1745), Boucher became the master of rococo and of sensuous painting, by which he created an amorous

and gracious world. In 1755, he became director of the Gobelins tapestry works and, in 1765, was made first painter to King LOUIS XV and became director of the Royal Academy. The protégé of MME DE POMPADOUR, he painted her portrait many times. Boucher's delicate, lighthearted depiction of classical deities and French shepherdesses delighted the public, and he became the most fashionable painter of his day. His sentimental and facile style, however, became too widely imitated, and would be less preferred during the rise of neoclassicism.

## Boucher de Perthes (1788–1868)
*archaeologist, paleontologist*
Born in Rethel, Jacques Boucher de Crévecoeur de Perthes, or Boucher de Perthes, as he is better known, was a customs official by profession. He made his first discoveries in the gravel deposits of the Somme valley near Abbeville in 1844. There, he found flint implements that he believed to be from the Pleistocene era. In subsequent research done from 1846 to 1864, he proved that humans had lived during the Pleistocene Epoch, 1 million to 12 million years ago. This was proof of the antediluvian existence of humans, a theory in contrast to the established beliefs of the time. His ideas were upheld by the British Royal Society, and Boucher de Perthes is now recognized as one of the founders of prehistoric studies.

## Bouchotte, Jean-Baptiste-Noël (1754–1840)
*political figure*
Jean-Baptiste-Noël Bouchotte, who was born in Metz, was a cavalry officer at the beginning of the REVOLUTION OF 1789. After serving at Cambrai, he was named by the Convention to be minister of war, a post he retained until 1794. During the rule of the Committee of Public Safety, he promoted such military officers as JEAN-BAPTISTE KLÉBER, JEAN VICTOR MOREAU, ANDRÉ MASSÉNA, and Napoléon Bonaparte (NAPOLÉON I). He organized the program of wartime defense but, because he was connected with the Hébertists, was arrested and dismissed in 1794. Amnestied, Bouchotte left politics and lived quietly in retirement.

## Boudin, Eugène (1824–1898)
*painter, watercolorist, chalk artist*

Eugène Boudin, who is noted for his seascapes and coastal scenes, was born in Honfleur. Discovered by CONSTANT TROYON and JEAN-FRANÇOIS MILLET, he went to study in Paris and later traveled in Belgium, the Netherlands, and the north of France. He worked especially on the Norman coast and, around 1856, with GUSTAVE COURBET and the Dutch artist Johan Barthold Jongkind, founded the Saint-Siméon school at Honfleur. Boudin, one of the first artists to paint in the open air, painted marine themes, views of harbors, beach scenes, and studies of the sky, all with a clear palette, bright shifting sunlight, iridescent sand and water, and vibrant and shimmering tones. Boudin was the teacher of CLAUDE MONET, and he was strong influence and the direct precursor of the impressionist painters with whom he exhibited in the first impressionist show in 1874 (*La Plage de Trouville,* 1863; *La Jetée à Deauville,* 1869).

## Boudon, Raymond (1934–   )
*sociologist*

An internationally renowned, and one of the most influential of contemporary sociologists, Raymond Boudon was born in Paris and educated at the École Normale Superieure. He is a leading proponent of the tradition of methodological individualism (*L'Analyse mathématique des faits sociaux,* 1967). This sociological tradition rejects holistic concepts and is founded on theories of individual interaction (*La Logique du social,* 1973). After having studied scholastic inequality (*L'Inégalité des chances,* 1973), Boudon demonstrated, in *Effets pervers et Ordre social* (1977), how a series of actions can end in a contrary result to that which was desired; thus, the multiplication of the number of diplomas diminished the value of the diplomas. His other writings include an epistemological reflection, *La Place du désordre; Critique des théories du changement social* (1983); *Dictionnaire critique de la Sociologie* (1982); *L'idéologie ou l'origine des idées reçues* (1986); *L'art de se persuader* (1990); *Le juste et le vrai: études sur l'objectivité des valeurs et de connaisance* (1995), and *Le sens des valeurs* (1999). Raymond Boudon, a professor at the SORBONNE, has taught at more than 16 universities worldwide, is a member of the French

Institute (1990), and was elected to the Academy of Sciences in 1995.

## Bouguer, Pierre (1698–1758)
*astronomer and mathematician*

Born in Le Croisic, Pierre Bouguer was a member of an expedition sent to Peru (1735) to measure the arc of the meridian on the equator (see LA CONDAMINE). His works on the factors of transmission and reflection make him one of the creators of photometry. In 1748, Bouguer invented the photometer and the heliometer. He was named to the Academy of Sciences in 1735.

## Bougainville, Louis-Antoine, count de (1729–1811)
*navigator*

Born in Paris, Louis-Antoine, count de Bougainville studied law and mathematics, then (1754) began a military career. The author of a work on calculus (*Traité de calcul intégral,* 1749–56), he was made a member of the Royal Society in London in recognition of his scholarship. He served as an officer in CANADA (1756) and later (1763) joined the navy. In 1764, he established a colony in the Falkland Islands, then crossing the Pacific, became the first Frenchman to sail around the world. During that voyage, Bougainville visited Tahiti, Samoa, the Solomon Islands, and the New Hebrides. Accompanied by astronomers and naturalists, he made many geographic and scientific discoveries—the flowering tropical vine, Bougainvillea, for example, being named for him. Bougainville published his experiences in his *Voyage autour du monde* (1771). He was made a founding member (1796) of the Institut de France, and NAPOLÉON I made him a senator and count of the empire and also a member of the LEGION OF HONOR. The largest of the Solomon Islands and a strait there are named for him, as is a channel in Vanuatu.

## Bouguereau, Adolphe-William (1825–1905)
*painter*

Born in La Rochelle, William Bouguereau, who won the Prix de Rome in 1830, was an admirer of

Raphael and, thus like ALEXANDRE CABANEL, sought to maintain strict academic principles for the Salon, the official venue for the exhibition of works of art. He painted meticulous portraits and received commissions to decorate the Grand-Théâtre of BORDEAUX and the churches of Saint-Augustin and Sainte-Clotilde in PARIS. There, the influence of the pre-Raphaelites on his work is apparent (*Vierge consolatrice,* 1877). Bouguereau, above all, painted allegorical and mythological compositions, with subdued tones and smooth surfaces portraying, for example, in an "archeologic" style, pale female nudes (*Les Oréades; Bacchante sur une panthère*). Both Bouguereau's critics and supporters saw him as a leading exponent of academism and, in his time, he was highly respected; for the impressionists, however, he represented insipid bourgeois taste.

## Bouillé, François-Claude-Amour, marquis de (1739–1800)
*general*

Born in Cluzel-Saint-Eble, Auvergne, François-Claude-Amour, marquis de Bouillé became a colonel in 1761, then served as a governor in the colonies (Guadeloupe, 1768; îles du Vent, 1777). He fought in the American War of Independence and, in 1782, was made a lieutenant general. He was the military commander of Trois-Évêchés, and of Alsace, Lorraine, and Franche-Comté (1789). General in chief of the Army of the Meuse and the Moselle, he suppressed the garrison revolt against the officers in Nancy (1790), then helped to organize the flight on June 20, 1791, of LOUIS XVI (Varennes-en-Argonne), himself crossing the border on June 22. After two visits to the Antilles, Bouillé ended his days in England. He is the author of *Mémoires sur la révolution française.*

## Bouillon, Emmanuel Théodore de la Tour d'Auvergne, Cardinal de (1643–1715)
*prelate, diplomat*

Born in Turenne, Emmanuel Théodore de la Tour d'Auvergne was the son of Frederick Maurice, prince of Sedan, and Elénore-Catherine-Febronie de Bergh. A nephew of Marshal TURENNE, in 1658

he was named a canon at Liège, in 1667 received a doctorate from the SORBONNE, and in 1669 was made a cardinal and named chief almoner to King LOUIS XIV. But he fell from royal favor due to the intrigues of François-Michel Le Tellier, marquis de LOUVOIS, who was an enemy of the House of Turenne. Bouillon then (1697), against the king's wishes, championed FRANÇOIS FÉNELON against JACQUES BOSSUET in the Gallican controversy. As a consequence, he had his properties confiscated and was forced to retire to the abbey of Tournus. He later (1710), during the War of the Spanish Succession, corresponded with the English duke of Marlborough and other enemies of Louis XIV. Bouillon eventually fled to the Netherlands and then to Rome, where he died.

## Bouillon, Henri de la Tour d'Auvergne, viscount of Turenne, duke de (1555–1623)
*military figure, marshal of France*

Born in Joze, Henri de la Tour d'Auvergne, viscount de Turenne and duke of Bouillon, served under King HENRY IV and was one of the leaders of the Protestant party. He was the father of Marshal TURENNE and Frédéric Maurice de la Tour d'Auvergne, duke de Bouillon (1604–52), who was constantly conspiring during the ministry of Cardinal RICHELIEU (allied with the Spanish, he defeated the French at Marfée) and during the FRONDE.

## Boulanger, Georges (1837–1891)
*general, politician*

Born in Rennes and educated at Saint-Cyr, Georges Boulanger began his military career serving in Kabylie, in Italy, and in Cochin-China, and fought in the FRANCO-PRUSSIAN WAR (1870–71). He was made director of infantry for the Ministry of War, then division commander of troops in Tunisia (1884). Supported by GEORGES CLEMENCEAU and also by the duke d'AUMALE, in 1886 he was named minister of war. The army reforms that he undertook (the law of exile for princes, which affected, among others, the duke d'Aumale, his patron; suppression of draft lottery) and his hostile attitude toward Germany in the Schnaebelé affair (April 1887), however, caused him to be removed from the ministry. Already, there had crystallized around Boulanger a large number of the opposition, with nationalists bent on revenge (Boulanger was given the name "General La Revanche" or General Revenge), Bonapartists, and even monarchists. His departure for Clermond-Ferrand, where he had been named commander of the 13th army corps, was the scene of an important popular demonstration (gare de Lyon). Forced to back down by the government, Boulanger, nonetheless, stood for election. Encouraged by his supporters (DÉROULÈDE and others) who were members of the Ligue des patriots, he was elected in four departments and then in Paris (January 1889), and was encouraged to attempt a coup d'état. But, in part owing to the influence of his mistress, Mme de Bonnemain, he hesitated, leaving the government time to take measures against him. Accusing him of conspiracy, the minister of the interior threatened him with arrest and ordered the dissolution of the Ligue. Boulanger, who had fled abroad, was condemned in absentia to life in prison. He reached Belgium (April 1889) and spent some time in England before returning to Belgium and committing suicide at the tomb of his mistress, who had died shortly before.

Nadia Boulanger *(Library of Congress)*

### Boulanger, Louis-Candide (1806–1867)
*painter, lithographer*

Born in Vercelli, Piedmont, Louis-Candide Boulanger achieved notoriety through his work in the revue *Le Supplice de Mazeppa,* which also brought him the admiration of VICTOR HUGO. He did paintings of historical and literary subjects in a classical yet moving style. He illustrated, too, the works of Victor Hugo and produced portraits of numerous writers, including HONORÉ BALZAC.

### Boulanger, Nadia (1887–1979)
*composer, professor of music*

Born in Paris, Nadia Boulanger was a remarkable musician (she was the first woman to win the grand prix de Rome, 1913) and, during a quite brief public career, dedicated her life to teaching music. Among her students were Igor Markevitch, Aaron Copland, and PIERRE HENRY.

### Boulez, Pierre (1925–  )
*composer, conductor*

Pierre Boulez, who was to gain an international reputation for his profound effect on postwar avant-garde music, was born in Montbrison and educated at the Paris Conservatoire (1945). His principal teacher was the composer OLIVIER MESSIAEN. In 1948, Boulez became music director of the Renauld-Barrault Company at the Théâtre-Marigny in Paris. During the late 1940s and 1950s, he composed many critically acclaimed, highly experimental works, including some for electronic instruments, based on the 12-tone system. He also began to propose going beyond traditional harmony and melody to include other elements such as rhythm, pitch, tone color, and dynamics.

In 1967, he became guest conductor of the Cleveland (Ohio) Orchestra and, in 1971, was appointed both chief conductor of the British Broadcasting Company (BBC) Symphony Orchestra in London and music director of the New York Philharmonic Orchestra. While Boulez always focused on his own compositions and those of his contemporaries, he also became known for his interpretations of the works of such composers as CLAUDE DEBUSSY and Igor Stravinsky. In 1976, he conducted the centenary production of Richard Wagner's Ring cycle at the Wagner Festival in Bayreuth. In 1977, Boulez left his position at the New York Philharmonic to direct the Institut de Recherche et de Coordination Scientifique/Musique, which he had founded in 1974 at the Centre National d'Art et de Culture Georges Pompidou in Paris. He subsequently returned to New York to perform his own works with the Ensemble InterContemporain. Boulez's compositions include *Le Visage nuptial,* for chorus and orchestra (1946–50); *Le Soleil des eaux,* for solo, chorus, and orchestra (1948); *Polyphonie X,* for 18 instruments (1951); *Le Marteau san maître,* for alto voice and six instruments (1955); *Pli selon pli,* for soprano and orchestra (1960); *Cummings ist der Dichter* (1970); *Rituel "in memoriam Maderna"* (1975); and *Repons* (3 versions: 1981, 1982, and 1984). He is also the author of a number of books (*Points de repère,* 1981; *Jalons pour une décennie,* 1989).

## Boulle, André-Charles  (1642–1732)
*cabinetmaker*

André Boulle, who was born in Paris, developed as a furniture maker what would come to be known as the Buhl style of furniture inlay. In his early career, he worked for CHARLES LE BRUN and gained the patronage of JEAN-BAPTISTE COLBERT. After 1672, he was one of the most important furniture makers to the king and members of the royal court. He developed an ornate baroque style, influenced by JEAN BERAIN (the Mazarin cabinet), in a monumental and geometric form. While he did not invent, nor was he the sole producer of furniture in ebony and other precious woods encrusted with highly colored inlay shaped to depict landscapes, flowing draperies, and geometric arabesques, richly overlaid with designs in pewter, copper, and brass, Boulle has given his name to this type of furnishings (cabinets, chests, desks, clocks, and parquet floors). His four sons imitated and continued his

work. The vogue for Buhlwork, as it is called, during the SECOND EMPIRE is the result of a large number of reproductions that were made. In 1891, the name École Boulle was given to a municipal school in Paris, which would become an institute dedicated to producing technicians and artists.

## Boullée, Étienne-Louis  (1728–1799)
*architect, artist*

Born in Paris, Étienne-Louis Boullée was a neoclassical architect, best known for his visionary but unrealized designs for ideal buildings. At first trained as a painter, after 1740 he built private mansions (hôtel de Brunoy, 1774) and châteaux (Chaville, 1764), in which, going against the prevailing rococo style, he employed many ancient Greek and Roman architectural elements, recalling the classicism of the 17th century now considered characteristic of the LOUIS XV style. Influenced by the drawings of Piranesi and documents on early Hellenic, Oriental, and Egyptian architecture published as a result of numerous archaeological expeditions done at the time, he conceived projects of colossal monuments (the cenotaph for Isaac Newton, 1788–Boullée's best-known design—with an immense exterior sphere of light). Developing a symbolism in accord with the secular spirit of the Revolution of 1789 and its ideals, he put forth an esthetic founded on an imitation of ancient architecture and, above all, inspired by geometric forms found in nature (*Essai sur l'art,* 1783–93). A gifted teacher, Boullée influenced a generation of French architects. And certain of his revolutionary and monumental conceptions would prefigure those of the Russian avant-garde movement of the 1920s.

## Bourbon, Charles III, duke of (1490–1527)
*constable of France*

Born in Montpensier, Charles III, duke of Bourbon, the constable of France (or le connétable de Bourbon, as he was known), count of Montpensier (1501), and duke of Auvergne (1503) became heir to the county of Montpensier in 1503. He married his cousin, a daughter of Pierre II de Beaugeu, and unified the immense domains of the two lines of the

HOUSE OF BOURBON. Charles III, duke of Bourbon fought brilliantly at the Battle of Agnadel (1509), received the title of constable (1514), played a decisive role at the Battle of Marignan (1515), then served as governor of Milan. After the death of his wife (1521), he refused the hand of Louise of Savoy, mother of FRANCIS I, who claimed the Bourbon inheritance. Charles then offered his services to the Holy Roman Emperor Charles V and took part in the defeat of the French at Pavia (1525). He was later killed at the siege of Rome in 1527. The sculptor Benvenuto Cellini, who was among the city's defenders, claimed to have fired the fatal shot. With the death of Charles III, the elder branch of the Bourbons became extinct, and Francis I confiscated his domains.

## Bourbon, House of

A leading dynasty of French history, the House of Bourbon (Bourbon-l'Archambaut) dates from the 10th century. The seigneurie of Bourbon passed by marriage to the House of Dampierre, then to the first Capetian line of Burgundy, and finally to Robert de Clermont, the sixth son of Saint Louis through his marriage to Béatrice of Burgundy-Bourbon. The son of Robert, Louis I le Grand was made duke de Bourbon in 1327; nine dukes of Bourbon succeeded him up to CHARLES III, the constable, who died in 1527. From a Bourbon cadet branch, that of de la Marche, issued the branch of the Vendôme, who inherited the throne of Navarre with Antoine (1555) and the throne of France with HENRY IV (1589), whose son, LOUIS XIII, had two sons. From the elder line, the issue of LOUIS XIV, the eldest son of Louis XIII, came the French branch, ending with the count of CHAMBORD in 1883.

## Bourdaloue, Louis (1632–1704)

*preacher*

Born in Bourges, Louis Bourdaloue, after becoming a Jesuit, began his career as a preacher in 1666. He came to Paris in 1669 and gained notoriety at the royal court, where he often preached during Lent and Advent (from 1670 to 1693). After the revocation of the Edict of NANTES (1685), he was sent by King LOUIS XIV to teach new converts in Languedoc; after 1696, he devoted himself essentially to works of charity. The most popular French preacher of the 17th century, Bourdaloue struck his audiences with his exacting moral tone and the austere style of his sermons. Taking a rigorous stance and using meticulous psychological analyses, he did not hesitate to critique sins or faults in the "personal" portraits of his subjects (*Sermon sur la médisance*, in which he evokes BLAISE PASCAL; the allusion to the Grand ARNAULD in *Sermon sur la sévérité chrétienne*, to JEAN-BAPTISTE MOLIÈRE and *Tartuffe* in his *Sermon sur l'hypocrisie*). His *Sermons et oeuvres diverses* (posthumous, 1707–34) were reprinted in an edition of 1822–26.

## Bourdelle, Antoine (1861–1928)

*sculptor, painter*

One of the forerunners of 20th-century monumental sculpture, Antoine Bourdelle, the son of a cabinetmaker, was born in Montauban, where he was also educated. He went to Paris in 1855 and studied in the studio of ALEXANDRE FALGUIÈRE. Later (1893–1903), he worked as an assistant to AUGUSTE RODIN and, from that point, his career began to rise. In an heroic and moving style, he produced the monument to the fallen heroes of Montauban (1893 to 1902), in which he used naturalism to create rough and simplified forms with expressive distortion. He developed also a personal style, as he referred to Roman, Gothic, and archaic Greek sculpture (*Tête d'Apollon*, 1900; *Héracles archer*, 1900, inspired by the Egine pediment). In defining his basic structures (relief of the théâtre du Champs-Élysées, 1912), Bourdelle sought powerful rhythms, the effect of mass, and monumental character, but without abandoning dynamic expression. Of a lyrical temperament, he aimed for epic expression (monument to Alvear, in Buenos Aires, 1914–19; monument to Mickiewicz in Paris, 1928), but sometimes fell into pomposity. Bourdelle has, nonetheless, contributed to the freeing of modern sculpture from a strict naturalist style.

## Bourdichon, Jean (ca. 1457–1521)

*painter, miniaturist*

Born probably in Tours, Jean Bourdichon found favor as an artist with LOUIS XI and then with CHARLES VIII, for whom he became court painter

(1484). Later, he was commissioned by FRANCIS I to do the decoration for the Field of Cloth of Gold. Bourdichon directed an important workshop of illustrators and produced a large number of works himself. He is the creator of the *Grandes Heures d'Anne de Bretagne* (ca. 1503–08), which features margins decorated with flowers, fruits, and insects and which reveals his fine talent. He sought above all to reproduce gracefully gestures and faces. For a long time the *Heures de Ferdinand d'Aragon, Heures de Charles VIII,* and *Heures de François de Vendôme* (ca. 1480) were attributed to Bourdichon, but they are instead most likely the work of a disciple of JEAN FOUQUET.

## Bourdieu, Pierre (1930–2002)
*sociologist*

A leading champion of the antiglobalization movement, Pierre Bourdieu was born in Deguin, Pyrénées-Atlantique, and educated in Paris at the École normale supérieure. After teaching at the University of Algiers, he became professor at the Collège de France and began his writings. His works are based on a triple translation of Karl Marx, Max Weber, and ÉMILE DURKHEIM. He sought to analyze such issues as force, legitimacy, and belief in groups. Bourdieu also considered the work of CLAUDE LÉVI-STRAUSS and borrowed ideas from Sigmund Freud (for example, that of "denial"). Beginning with *Les Héritiers* (1966), up to *La Distinction critique sociale du jugement* (1979), Bourdieu was interested particularly in the sociology of culture and the link between domination and symbolic violence. The dominated internalize the condition under the form of a disposition to act, or "habitus" (*Le Sens pratique,* 1980). His notion of space, considered as a series of rooms, allows an analysis of the constraints that weigh on individuals; this is essentially reproduced in the school system (*La Reproduction: éléments d'une théorie du système d'enseignement,* 1970). The difference of capital culture between students, which the school treats in an egalitarian fashion, gives children of different social categories unequal chances for success. Bourdieu and his students were critical of the concept of public opinion and the use of opinion polls, as well as the mechanisms that claim to represent the views of dominant groups. *Règles de l'art: genèse et structure du champ littéraire* (1992), a study of the work of GUSTAVE FLAUBERT, is also an important contribution to the socialization of art. One of France's leading sociologists, Bourdieu has been described as the "intellectual reference" for any opposition to free-market orthodoxy and globalization.

## Bourdon, Sébastien (1616–1670)
*painter*

Known for his paintings of historical events and landscapes, Sébastien Bourdon was born in Montpellier, the son of a stained-glass maker. He developed his talent in Paris, then around 1634, he was employed in Rome, where he painted landscape pastiches after such contemporaries as CLAUDE LORRAIN and NICOLAS POUSSIN. Returning to painting in 1637, he produced decorative works and painted numerous genre scenes, inspired by the work of LOUIS LE NAIN. Bourdon was one of the founders of the Royal Academy of Painting and Sculpture (1648) and later (1653) became chief painter to Queen Christina of Sweden (*Portraits de la reine, du prince héritier*). In France (1654), he accepted large commissions, notably for the hôtel des Bretonvilliers (1663, now destroyed). An eclectic painter, Bourdon is the creator of mythological composition done in a classical spirit that shows the influence of Poussin (*Moïse sauvé des eaux*), genre scenes with realistic and picturesque details, and portraits in which the ease of his technique is clearly apparent (*L'Homme aux rubans noirs*).

## Bourgeois, Léon (1851–1925)
*political figure*

Born in the château d'Oger, Marne, Léon Bourgeois was a radical deputy (1888), several times minister and premier (1890–96), president of the Senate (1920–29), and the author of *Essai d'une philosophie de la solidarité* (1902). In this essay, he developed the doctrine of solidarity ("the third way"), between collectivism and liberalism. This reformism resulted in several social measures, such as the law on workers' restraints, or the democratization of secondary education, and contributed in the international arena to the creation of the Societé des Nations, of which Bourgeois was one of the promoters. He was awarded the Nobel Peace Prize in 1920.

## Bourget, Paul (1852–1935)
*writer*

Known at first for his poetry, Paul Bourget, who was born in Amiens, with his *Essais de psychologie contemporaine* (1883–85), proposed to analyze, according to the scientific and naturalistic process, the "moral ills" of his age. A traditionalist and didactic novelist, opposed to the naturalism of ÉMILE ZOLA, Bourget extolled a return to spiritualism (*Le Disciple,* 1889) and to Catholicism (*Un divorce,* 1904; *Le Sens de la mort,* 1915), and wanted to bring his readers to study the dilemmas of society (*André Cornélis,* 1887; *Mensonges,* 1887). He then turned to social studies (*Cosmopolis,* 1892; *L'Étape,* 1902) and major works, notably *Némésis* (1918) and *Nos actes nous suivent* (1927). Gifted with a sensitive imagination, he brought to his art a rigorous moral analysis, which evokes HENRI STENDHAL or BENJAMIN CONSTANT, to whom he dedicated some of his essays. His works offer a documentary of the age, but he has also been criticized for painting a positive and flattering image of the wealthy society of the period. Bouret was elected to the ACADÉMIE FRANÇAISE in 1894.

## Bourrienne, Louis-Antoine-Fauvelet de (1769–1834)
*political figure*

Born in Sens, Louis-Antoine-Fauvelet de Bourrienne was a schoolmate friend of Napoléon Bonaparte (NAPOLÉON I) and, after a diplomatic career in the pre-Revolutionary period, became his secretary in 1797. He was made chargé d'affaires in Hamburg in 1804, where he had been sent to enforce the Continental System. In 1814, he rallied to LOUIS XVIII and was made prefect of police and minister of state. Bourrienne left his *Mémoires* (1829–31), which are considered an important source for personal information on Bonaparte and on the Napoleonic era.

## Bousquet, Joë (1897–1950)
*writer*

Born in Carcassonne, Joë Bousquet was paralyzed for most of his life because of a severe wound that he suffered in World War I. He led a reclusive existence as a poet and as a thinker enamoured of shadow and silence. At the limits of the physical and supernatural world, nourished by solitude and contemplation, his thought is expressed in a language of transparent purity. He was an associate of such writers as ANDRÉ GIDE and of surrealists and the Carcassone group (PAUL ELUARD, FRANÇOIS-PAUL ALIBERT, MAX ERNST, and others). Bousquet has left collections of poetry that are detached fragments of an intimate journal: *Traduit du silence* (1936), *Le Meneur de lune* (1946), and *La Connaissance du soir* (1947), as well as an important *Correspondance.*

## Braque, Georges (1882–1963)
*painter, designer, engraver, pioneer of cubism*

One of the leading artists of the 20th century, Georges Braque was born in Argenteuil, near Paris. In 1899, following his father's occupation, he apprenticed himself as a house painter. By 1902, however, he settled in Paris to study art. There, he was greatly influenced by a fauvist exhibit that featured the works of HENRI MATISSE and ANDRÉ DERAIN. Braque soon adopted the fauvist style as his own work (*Le Pont de l'Estaque,* 1906). In 1908, inspired by the works of PAUL CÉZANNE, he began to develop a style of distorted forms and unconventional perspective that came to be known as cubism. From that period, Braque began more to question artistic conventions, calling attention to the very nature of visual illusion and artistic representation. After seeing Pablo Picasso's *Demoiselles d'Avignon* in 1909, Braque began to work closely with that artist, both producing a style called analytic cubism, of which Braque's *Violon et Cruchel* (1910) is a prime example. Braque also began to introduce elements of trompe l'oeil (faux wood and marble) into his works. And both he and Picasso began to experiment with collages, especially in the period 1911 to 1914. Their collaboration continued until World War I, when Braque, who had enlisted, was severely wounded. After the war, he resumed his artistic career alone. He began to develop a more personal style, characterized by brilliant color and textured surfaces and, after his move to the Norman coast, the reappearance of the human figure. He also painted many still lifes at this time, as well as a large number of other paintings, graphics, and sculptures. Works from this period include *La Musicienne* (1917); a series of Guéridons, Canélphores, and Natures mortes (1922–30), also Plages, Falaises, and Baigneuses (1928–31); Billiards (1944); Ateliers (1950–56); and Oiseaux (1955–63).

## Braudel, Fernand (1902–1985)
*historian*

A leading proponent of the Annales school of historiography, Fernand Braudel was born in Lunéville-en-Ornois, Meuse. Educated at the SORBONNE, he was a student of LUCIEN FEBVRE and was a professor at the COLLÈGE DE FRANCE (1949). In 1929, with MARC BLOCH, he established the journal *Annales d'histoire économique et sociale,* and in 1935, accepted a post at the University of Brazil, São Paulo. He also taught in Algeria (1923–33). Later, as a prisoner of war, he developed and wrote many of his theses in prison camps, with limited resources. In *La Méditerranée et le Monde méditerranée à l'époque de Philippe II* (1949), Braudel, greatly impressed by Febvre's new approach to history, sought to present the concept of a profound unity between the natural and social sciences, and to integrate into his historical research the ideas of geography and economics. The essence of Braudel's works, in accord with the theories of the Annales school, are marked by the importance he gives to the different periods of history, especially those of the longest duration (*Écrits sur l'histoire,* 1969). He give in them an incisive view of the profound evolution of European economic infrastructures (*Civilisation matérielle, économie et capitalisme, xve-xviiie siecle,* 1967–79; *Histoire économique et social,* 1979). In *L'Identité de la France,* t. I "Espace et Histoire," t. II [2 vols.] "Les Hommes et les Choses," 1986), he connected with the vast synthesis of French history. Braudel was elected to the ACADÉMIE FRANÇAISE in 1984.

## Brazza, Pierre Savorgnan de (1852–1905)
*explorer*

Born in Castel Gandolfo, near Rome, Pierre Savorgnan de Brazza was of Italian origin. He studied at the French naval academy (1868–70) and was later (1874) granted French citizenship. Begin-

ning in 1875, he undertook several expeditions in Africa, during which he explored the estuaries of the Gabon and Ogooue Rivers. This brought him to the region north and west of the Congo, which he claimed for France (1879–82). He then founded a settlement that became the city of Brazzaville (see AFRICA, FRENCH IN; BERLIN CONFERENCE). From 1887 to 1897, Brazza served as commissioner general of the region (French Congo), which was declared a French protectorate. Among the native population, he gained a reputation for his sense of fairness and equality. His explorations, however, also helped to stimulate the rush by major European powers to claim African territory during the last decades of the 19th century.

## Bréal, Michel (1832–1915)
*philologist, linguist*

Born in Landau, Bavaria, Breal studied first in Germany under noted linguists, including Franz Bopp. Bréal became an instructor of comparative grammar at the COLLÈGE DE FRANCE (1864) and also served as secretary to the Linguistic Society of Paris (1868). In his major work, *Essai de sémantique* (1897), he developed a new branch of linguistics studies—semantics—"a science of signification," or the study of the evolution of words and their meaning. As the translator of Franz Bopp's major work (*Grammaire comparée,* 1866–74), Bréal attempted to synthesize the formal functionalism of German linguistics with the French rationalist tradition. Bréal was also an ardent student of mythology.

## Bremond, Henri (1865–1933)
*literary critic, historian, priest*

Born in Aix-en-Provence, Henri Bremond, in his monumental *Histoire littéraire du sentiment religieux en France* (unfinished, 11 volumes, 1916–32), made a significant study of modes of expression of religious spirituality and, earlier, expressed his opposition to JACQUES BOSSUET and issues related to JANSENISM, in *Apologie pour Fénelon* (1910). There, he affirmed also his tendencies toward mysticism. Suspected by orthodox Catholics, Bremond also drew criticism when he defended the romantic spirit and individualistic literature in *Pour le romanticisme* (1923).

Assimilating the poetic art with mystical experience (*Prière et Poésie*, 1927), he began a passionate debate (notably with PAUL VALÉRY) on the essence of poetry; Bremond was a defender of pure poetry (*La poésie pure*, 1926) based on "intuition," which he considered universal. He also strongly opposed intellectualism and neoclassicism. Bremond was elected to the ACADÉMIE FRANÇAISE in 1923.

## Bretecher, Claire (1940–  )
*illustrator, narrator*

Born in Nantes, Claire Bretecher began her career as a comic-strip artist and narrator in 1964. One of her main characters, Cellulite, a romantic and silly medieval princess with an ungainly physique, appeared for the first time in the newspaper *Pilote* in 1969. Beginning in 1973, Bretecher published in *Le Nouvel Observateur* the stories of *Frustrés*, followed by *Mères*, then *Agripinne*. A strong satirist, she has poked fun at her contemporaries, caricaturing their language and conversation, ridiculing fashions and fads, and creating the most pertinent of social criticism through her drawings and dialogues.

## Breton, André (1896–1966)
*writer*

A poet, critic, and leader of the surrealist movement, known for his "automatic" style, André Breton was born in Tinchebray, Orne. At first he studied medicine (1913), but soon took up writing, especially poetry. He corresponded with many notable figures, including GUILLAUME APOLLINAIRE. His first work of poetry was *Le Mont de Piété* (1919). In 1924, along with other surrealist writers such a PAUL ELUARD and LOUIS ARAGON, he published the *Manifeste du surréalisme* (1924) and with PHILIPPE SOUPAULT the first surrealist text, *Les Champs magnétiques*. In 1927, Breton, along with Aragon, joined the Communist Party and from that point on took an active part in political life (*Position politique du surréalisme*, 1935). He broke with Stalinism (1938) after a meeting with Leon Trotsky. Breton's views of surrealism reflect his study of the works of Freud. Breton was also influenced by the poets PAUL VALÉRY and ARTHUR RIMBAUD. In his writings, Breton sought to celebrate love in all its forms. His best creative work is considered to be the novel *Nadja* (1928), based partly on his own experiences. He organized two international surrealist exhibitions (1947, 1965) and had a great interest also in pre-Columbian cultures of the New World (Breton left France and stayed in North America for a period after the banning of his work *Anthologie de l'humour noir* in 1940). Breton's other writings include *Union libre* (1931), *L'Amour fou* (1937), *Arcane 17* (1947), *Ode à Charles Fourier* (1947), *Poèmes* (a collective edition, 1948), and two essays on art (*Le Surréalisme et la Peinture*, 1946; *L'Art magique*, 1957).

## Breuil, Henri (1877–1961)
*paleontologist, historian, priest*

Born in Mortain, Henri Breuil was a professor of prehistoric ethnography at the COLLÉGE DE FRANCE. He specialized in the study of Paleolithic art and participated in the discovery and authentication of the most important prehistoric cave sites (Combarelles, Font-de-Gaume, Altamira, Lascaux, Marsoulas) and is the author of *Quatre Cents Siècles d'art pariétal* (1952).

André Breton *(Library of Congress)*

## Briand, Aristide (1862–1932)
*statesman, Nobel laureate*

The editor of *L'HUMANITÉ* and a Nobel laureate, Aristide Briand was born in Nantes and educated in law at Paris. Secretary-general of the French Socialist Party, he was elected to the Chamber of Deputies in 1902 and was one of the legislators responsible for the Law of Separation of Church and State, passed in 1905. By 1906, Briand had left the Socialist Party (after the Amsterdam Conference) and became minister of education and religion, the first of 26 ministries, including 11 premierships, that he would eventually hold. As premier in 1909, he was responsible for the controversial use of force in the suppression of a railway strike. From 1915 to 1917, he headed a wartime coalition government and also directed the Foreign Ministry, organizing the campaigns in Salonika and the Balkans. In 1929, Briand formed a new government and represented France at the Washington Conference. He also urged a postwar policy of conciliation with Germany. Briand resigned a year later, but in 1925, again as foreign minister, he was instrumental in achieving the Locarno security treaty. In 1926, he shared the Nobel Peace Prize with Gustave Stresemann, the foreign minister of Germany. Briand, who enjoyed one of the longest ministerial careers of the THIRD REPUBLIC, served as premier again in 1925 and 1926, and as foreign minister from 1926 to 1932. In that capacity, he drafted and sponsored the Kellogg-Briand Pact, aimed at outlawing war. Briand was defeated for the presidency in 1931.

## Briconnet, Guillaume (1445–1514)
*cardinal*

A trusted adviser to CHARLES VII and later LOUIS XI, Guillaume Briconnet, after the death of his wife, became bishop of Saint-Malo, archbishop of Reims, and later of Narbonne, and cardinal. It was said that Charles VII would undertake nothing without his advice. His most important role was as a negotiator between the French Crown and the papacy, in particular with Pope Alexander VI. He also encouraged Charles to invade Italy, and later, entered into a great dispute with Pope Julius II, who excommunicated Briconnet after he called a council at Pisa in opposition to that pope's practices

and policies. Briconnet was later restored to his position as cardinal by Pope Leo X, and, as archbishop of Reims crowned LOUIS XII in 1498. He then retired to Narbonne.

## Brissot, Jacques-Pierre (1754–1793)
*journalist, political figure*

Known also as Brissot de Warville, Jacques-Pierre Brissot, a leading figure of the French REVOLUTION OF 1789, was born in Chartres. After having served in the procurator's offices in Paris, he threw himself into political writing, affirming himself as a partisan of the new revolutionary ideas of the time. He traveled to England, where he collaborated on the editing of the *Courrier de l'Europe*, to Holland, and to the United States, where he became interested in the problems of race and racism. Upon his return to France, he founded the newspaper *Le Patriote français* and an antislavery group, the Societé des amis des Noirs. A member of the Jacobin Club (see JACOBINS) at the beginning of the Revolution, he called for the proclamation of a republic after the flight of the king to Varennes (June 20–21, 1791). He also helped to write the petition that was brought to the Champ-de-Mars (July 17, 1791). Elected deputy to the Legislative Assembly, he sat with the Left and, being one of the leaders of the GIRONDINS (sometimes identified as "Brissotin"), took a firm stand in favor of a declaration of war against Austria. Reelected to the Convention, he vehemently opposed the MONTAGNARDS and, most particularly, MAXIMILIEN ROBESPIERRE. Proscribed along with the other Girondin leaders (June 2, 1793), he succeeded in fleeing but was arrested at Moulins, tried by the Revolutionary Tribunal, and guillotined. Besides his *Mémoires* (published 1830), Brissot left a work on criminology (*Théorie des lois criminelles*, 1781) and a political study entitled *De la France et des États-Unis* (1787).

## Brittany

Brittany as a French duchy was united with the crown under King CHARLES VIII (1491) through his marriage to ANNE OF BRITTANY and was annexed by King FRANCIS I in 1532. The capital of Brittany is Rennes, and the province comprises the departments of Finistère, Côtes-du-Nord, Morhiban, Ille-et-Vilaine, and Loire-Atlantique. Bordered by NOR-MANDY, Anjou, and Maine, Brittany is the western-most province of France and for a long time remained relatively isolated. Agriculture and tourism are main industries. The inhabitants are known as Bretons.

## Broglie family

A French family descended from a 17th century Piedmontese noble FRANCESCO MARIA BROGLIA, who entered the service of France and, in 1643, received the title of count de Broglie. The most important of his descendants, many of whom served France as soldiers, statesmen, or scientists, include his son, Victor Maurice, count de Broglie (1646–1727), who was named marshal of France in 1724. François-Marie Broglie (1671–1745), third son of Victor Maurice, was made a marshal of France in 1734 and won military victories in Italy (Parma, Guastalla), and was made duke of Broglie in 1742. Victor François, duke de Broglie (1718–1804), the son of François Marie, was born in Münster and distinguished himself during the SEVEN YEARS' WAR. He was named marshal of France and prince of the Holy Roman Empire in 1759. He emigrated at the time of the REVOLUTION OF 1789, and led the princes' army (1792) before entering the service of the Russian czar. Charles Louis Victor de Broglie (1756–94), son of Victor François, was a deputy for the nobility to the ESTATES GENERAL in 1789. He was executed during the Terror. Achille Léon Charles Victor, duke de Broglie (1785–1870) was born in Paris, a descendant of the third duke de Broglie. He entered the diplomatic service under Napoléon Bonaparte and was charged with several diplomatic missions during the Empire. He was later a member of the Chamber of Peers under the Restoration. A constitutional moderate and a liberal, desirous of reconciling the gains of the Revolution with the political regime of the Restoration, he supported LOUIS-PHILIPPE after the JULY REVOLUTION OF 1830. He then served as premier (1835–36) and as a minister. Elected a representative to the Legislative Assembly after the REVOLUTION OF 1848, he took a position against the democratic movement and retired from political life after December 2, 1851. His *Souvenirs* (4 volumes, posthumous, 1885–88) are a useful reference for the Napoleonic and RESTORATION periods. Achille, duke de Broglie was elected to the ACADÉMIE FRANÇAISE in 1855. Albert, duke de Broglie (1821–1901), the son of Achille, was born in Paris and, under the Third Republic, was an Orléanist deputy to the National Assembly (1871). He also served as ambassador to London (1871–72). He played a role in the downfall of LOUIS-ADOLPHE THIERS (May 24, 1873) and his government, and became deputy premier but had to resign after the second attempt to restore monarchy failed (see CHAMBORD, COUNT OF) in May 1874. Recalled by Marshal EDME MAC-MAHON to lead the government after the dismissal of JULES SIMON (May 16–17, 1877) for trying to bring the Ordre moral to power, he dissolved the chamber, which had a republican majority, but was forced to resign himself after a new republican victory in the election of November 19, 1877. Albert de Broglie is also the author of a number of works on European history—*L'Église et l'Empire romain au IVe siècle* (1856–66), *Frédéric II et Marie-Thérèse* (1882), *Mémoires de Talleyrand* (1891)—and was elected to the ACADÉMIE FRANÇAISE in 1862. Maurice, duke de Broglie (1875–1960), the grandson of Albert, was born in Neuilly-sur-Seine. A physicist, he studied the spectrums of X-rays, and invented a method of determining crystalline structures by diffraction (the revolving crystal method) and discovered the photoelectrical nuclear effect (1921). He was elected to the Academy of Sciences in 1924 and to the ACADÉMIE FRANÇAISE in 1934. Louis, (later duke) de Broglie (1892–1987), the brother of Maurice, was born in Dieppe and was also a physicist. A Nobel laureate, he made important contributions to the theory of quantum mechanics. The founder of ondulatory mechanics, he demonstrated that all corpuscles can be considered as a wave (and vice versa), and established the formula that allowed the calculation of a wave as it is associated with a particle ("De Broglie's formula"). In his work, he attempted to rationalize the dual nature of matter and energy, and his studies of electromagnetic radiation form the basis for the modern quantum theory. He also published popular works on science (*La Physique nouvelle et les Quanta* 1937). Louis de Broglie, a professor of theoretical physics at the University of Paris, was awarded the Nobel Prize in physics in 1929, was elected to the Academy of Sciences in 1933 and the ACADÉMIE FRANÇAISE in 1944, and in 1945 became adviser to the French Atomic Energy Commission.

## Brongniart, Alexandre  (1770–1847)
*mineralogist, geologist*
Born in Paris, Alexandre Brongniart was one of the principal founders of stratigraphic paleontology (*Sur les caractères zoologiques de formations,* 1821). He defined the Secondary Jurassic system and introduced systematically the idea of structure and texture in the description of boulders. Brongniart studied under ANTOINE LAURENT DE LAVOISIER and later graduated from the École de Medicine in Paris. In 1797, he was appointed professor at the École de Quatres Nations, and in 1822 became professor of mineralogy at the Museum of Natural History. His interest in geology and paleontology led to a long and successful collaboration with GEORGES CUVIER (*Essai sur la géographie minéralogique des environs de Paris* (1811). In 1800, he was appointed director of the Sèvres porcelain factory (1800–47), where with his assistants he laid the foundation for the modern knowledge of ceramic chemistry and revived the forgotten art of painting on glass. He also established there a museum of ceramics (1824) and is the author of *Traité des arts céramiques* (1842). Brongniart was named to the Academy of Sciences in 1815.

## Brosses, Charles de  (1709–1777)
*magistrate, writer*
Born in Dijon, where he served as first president of the parlement, Charles de Brosse was, because of his independent and irreverent nature, twice exiled to his estates. A bon vivant, spirited, and learned, de Brosses was interested in Roman history, art, and archaeology (*Lettres sur Herculanum,* 1750), geography (*Histoire des navigations aux terres australes,* 1756), and the origin of languages. A passionate reader of the works of Salluste, of which he attempted to write a critical edition, he was led by his research to make a visit to Italy (1739–40), later described in *Lettres familières écrites d'Italie à quelques amis* (posthumous, 1799) in which he clearly portrayed the monuments and cities, as well as giving perspicacious observations on the mores of society and the church. Of an appealing vivacity of tone and freedom of thought that often approached cynicism, these *Lettres* were greatly valued by STENDHAL.

## Brousse, Paul  (1844–1912)
*political figure*
Born in Montpellier, Paul Brousse was a physician and an anarchist disciple of Mikhail Bakunin. He was a member of the First International, took part in the COMMUNE of Paris, and with Peter Kropotkin founded a secret society at La Chaux-de-Fonds. Brousse became a reformist socialist (1880) and formed the Possibilist (or Broussist) Party, which extolled social change without revolution.

## Broussel, Pierre  (1575–1654)
*counselor to parlement*
Born in Paris, where he served as adviser to the Parlement, Pierre Broussel took a stand against the measures of the royal government and was consequently arrested on the orders of ANNE OF AUSTRIA (1648). This arrest unleashed the uprising of the populace (DAY OF THE BARRICADES) and the FRONDE.

## Bruant, Aristide  (1851–1925)
*songwriter*
Born in Courtenay, Aristide Bruant began, around 1875, to perform his own songs in the music halls of Montmartre. He became popular at the well-known Chat noir, which was his main locale. His songs, which have remained famous, evoke the daily life of the Parisian districts (*À la Villette, À ménilmontant*), reflecting the anarchy and the particular social reality of the fin de siècle period (*À la Roquette, Nini Peau d'chien*), or expressing the sentimentalism of his era (*Rose blanche*). Colorful and sad ballads, written in the popular language, making free use of Parisian argot, were assembled in collections (*Dans la rue. . .,* 3 volumes, 1889–1909; *Chansons et monologues,* 1896–97; and *Sur la route,* 1897). The author of a number of serialized stories, Bruant also composed a *Dictionnaire de l'argot au XXe siècle* (1901).

## Brunschvicg, Léon (1869–1944)
*philosopher*

Born in Paris, Léon Brunschvicg, as a philosopher, rejected positivistic empiricism and spiritualism, and adopted a critical idealist position in his studies on the conditions and evolution of the scientific spirit. Considering reason as a legislative activity that puts forth and perfects its principles and demonstrable rules, Brunschvicg saw in mathematics his most perfect expression (*Les Étapes de la philosophie mathématique*, 1912; *Les Âges de l'intelligence*, 1922; *L'Expérience humaine et de causalité physique*, 1922; *Le Progrès de la conscience dans la philosophie occidentale*, 1927).

## Buchez, Philippe-Joseph-Benjamin (1796–1865)
*philosopher, political figure*

Born in Matagne-la-Petite in the Belgian Ardennnes, Philippe-Joseph-Benjamin Buchez was at first a supporter of the theories of HENRI DE SAINT-SIMON and contributed to *Producteur* (the Saint-Simonian revue) before becoming one of the founders of Christian Socialism. The director of the Catholic newspaper *L'Européen* (1831–32; 1835–38) and a moving spirit behind *L'Atelier*, in 1848 he served for a time as president of the Constituent Assembly. In his *Histoire parlementaire de la Révolution française* (40 volumes, 1833–38), he sought to demonstrate that the REVOLUTION OF 1789, in establishing popular sovereignty and equality, was in line with the message of the Gospel. Buchez's other writings include *Introduction à la science de l'histoire* (1833) and *Traité complet de philosophie* (1839–40).

## Budé, Guillaume (1467–1540)
*humanist*

Born in Paris, Guillaume Budé is also known by his Latin name, Budaeus. He acquired a vast erudition at an early age and became a well-known Hellenist. One of the most learned men of the Renaissance, he held several important posts, including those of royal librarian and provost of Paris. At his suggestion, King FRANCIS I in 1530 founded the institute that later became the COLLÈGE DE FRANCE, and also the famed library at Fontainebleau, which later

became the basis for the Bibliothèque Nationale. As a scholar, Budé carried on a correspondence with the most illustrious figures of his age, including Erasmus and FRANÇOIS RABELAIS. His own writings on philosophy, philology, and jurisprudence (*Annotations aux Pandectes*, 1508), include translations of treatises by Plutarch. Budé also wrote on Roman civil law, on numismatics (*De asse*, 1514), and on mathematics. He was also an author on works on language and literature, especially Greek, by which he essentially established the science of philology and greatly advanced the study of Greek literature in France and elsewhere. His major study in this area is *Commentaires sur la langue grec* (1529).

## Bueil, Jean V de, count of Sancerre (ca. 1405–1480)
*military figure*

Surnamed the "scourge of the English," Jean V de Bueil, count of Sancerre, was a companion in arms to JOAN OF ARC and became an admiral of France (1450). He helped in the retaking of Normandy (1450) and Guyenne (1453) and is the author of an autobiographical work, *Le Jouvencel*.

See also XANTRAILLES.

## Buffon, Georges Louis Leclerc, count de (1707–1788)
*naturalist, writer*

Born in Montbard into an aristocratic family, Georges Louis Leclerc, count de Buffon, studied medicine, botany, and mathematics in Paris. His early scientific pursuits gained him admittance to the Royal Academy of Sciences (1733), and, in 1740, he was made intendent (keeper) of the Royal Gardens (now the National Museum of Natural History in Paris). Buffon's major work, *Histoire naturelle* (36 volumes, published 1749–89), provided the first naturalistic account of the history of the Earth, including a complete description of its botanical, zoological, and mineralogical, aspects. In it, he employed an empirical causation to explain natural phenomena. This caused him, however, to criticize the classification system of the Swedish naturalist Linnaeus and to support the theory of spontaneous generation upholding the idea of 38 original species as the basis of all living matter. Nonetheless, Buffon's writings, including his *Épilogue de la nature* (1751) and *Discours sur la style* (1753), are considered some of the best literary achievements of the Enlightenment. His position within the French intellectual community was recognized by King LOUIS XV, who made him a count in 1773. Buffon earlier had been named to the Academy of Sciences (1733) and the ACADÉMIE FRANÇAISE (1753).

## Bugeaud, Thomas-Robert, marquis de la Piconnerie, duke d'Isly  (1784–1849)
*military figure*

Thomas-Robert Bugeaud, who was born in Limoges, after distinguishing himself as a young officer in the wars of the Empire, notably in Spain, went over to the Bourbons (1814), then to NAPOLEON I during the HUNDRED DAYS, during the course of which he repelled the Austrians in Savoy. Named field marshal at the beginning of the July Monarchy and elected deputy in 1831, he was charged with guarding the duchess of Berry in 1832, and with suppressing the uprising of April 1834, which made him very unpopular. Sent for the first time to Algeria in 1836, where he won the victory at Sikkah (July), he at first opposed this occupation, which he deemed too costly for France. In 1837, he signed with the Emir Abd el-Kader the Treaty of Tafna. This having been broken, Bugeaud, named governor-general of Algeria (1840), then declared a fierce war, employing scorched-earth tactics, and organized the conquest of the country. Promoted to marshal in 1843, and made duke d'Isly after his victory over the Moroccans on the banks of the Isly (1844), he tried to establish an indirect form of government there (indigenous leaders would take orders from the French through the Office for Arab Affairs). But lacking support from the French government, he resigned and was replaced by the duke d'AUMALE. Bugeaud returned to France, where he died of cholera.

## Buisson, Ferdinand  (1841–1932)
*educator, political figure*

Born in Paris, Ferdinand Buisson served as inspector-general of public instruction (1878) and is the author of a large *Dictionnaire de pédagogie* (1882–87). Beginning in 1880, he worked unceasingly in the ministry of JULES FERRY, and then as a Radical-Socialist deputy (1902–14; 1919–24), for the secularization of public education, free education, obligatory professional training, as well as women's suffrage. President of the Ligue des droits de l'homme (1913–26), Buisson was awarded the Nobel Peace Prize in 1927.

## Bullant, Jean  (1520–1571)
*architect, artist, theorist*

An important architect of the French Renaissance, Jean Bullant was born in Amiens and traveled to Italy around 1577. Upon returning to France, he worked for the duchess of Montmorency, probably on the château of Fère-en-Tardenois, and especially on the château of Ecouen; he built the chapel, as well as the porticos. He often built on a large scale, demonstrating his penchant for the monumental. He succeeded PHILIBERT DELORME as architect of the Tuileries (1570) and built there two pavilions. He also built, for CATHERINE DE' MEDICI in Paris, the mansion of Soissons (1570), of which only the astronomical column remains. Bullant published a collection, *Horlogiographie*, and *Règle générale d'architecture* (1564). Beyond the influence of the Italian Renaissance, Bullant sought inspiration in antiquity; and above all, influenced by Philibert Delorme, he became a mannerist, especially in the importance that he gave to decoration.

## Buonarroti, Philippe  (1761–1837)
*revolutionary*

Of Italian origin, Philippe Buonarroti was born in Pisa and received an education in law and music in Florence. He became a journalist and bookseller and, with the advent of the FRENCH REVOLUTION OF 1789, moved to CORSICA, where he would later denounce the Corsican nationalists to the National Convention. He was appointed by MAXIMILIEN ROBESPIERRE to oversee the occupied Ligurian territories. With FRANÇOIS-NOËL BABEUF, Buonarroti was also one of the leaders of the Conspiracy of Equals (1796). He was imprisoned until 1806, after which he settled in Geneva and Brussels. He had a brief association with the Italian nationalist and revolutionary Giuseppe Mazzini, but they broke over ideological and methodological differences. Concerned with the social problems of a growing industrialized society in France, Buonarroti organized such new groups as the Société des Familles to address these issues. In 1828, he published *La Conspiration pour l'Égalité* that would later influence LOUIS-AUGUSTE BLANQUI.

## Bureau, Jean (unknown–1463)
*military figure*

Jean Bureau, lord of Montglat, was grand commander of artillery under CHARLES VII along with his brother Gaspard Bureau (died ca. 1469). Bureau fought in the Battle of Castillon (1453) and was named mayor of BORDEAUX, where he built several defensive battlements. For the rest of his career, he continued to serve as an important and trusted military adviser to Charles VII.

## Bussy-d'Amboise, Louis, seigneur de (ca. 1459–1579)
### (Louis de Clermont d'Amboise, seigneur de Bussy)
*military figure*

Louis de Clermont d'Amboise, lord of Bussy, or Bussy-d'Amboise as he is known, was a favorite of the duke of Alençon (duke of ANJOU) who made him governor of Anjou (1576), a region that Bussy-d'Amboise quickly exploited for his own benefit. Famous for his bravery and his duels, he was killed by the count of MONSOREAU, whose wife he had seduced. ALEXANDRE DUMAS made Bussy-d'Amboise the hero of his *Dame de Monsoreau.*

## Bussy-Rabutin (1618–1693)
### (Roger de Rabutin, count de Bussy)
*writer*

Born in Épiry, Nivernais, Roger de Rabutin, count de Bussy, or Bussy-Rabutin as he is known, took part in the FRONDE and won the respect of the prince de CONDÉ, before fighting under the viscount de TURENNE. After 1659, Bussy-Rabutin fell into disgrace because of his reputation as a libertine and his remarks concerning the love affairs of LOUIS XIV. The king's hostility increased when there anonymously appeared at Liège (1665) a *Histoire amoureuse de Gaules*, a satirical novel, inspired by the *Satyricon* of Petronius, in which Bussy-Rabutin described the vices of the court and the amorous intrigues of the young king. After imprisonment in the BASTILLE and banishment henceforth to his estates, he wrote his *Mémoires* (posthumous, 1856), while continuing an important *Correspondance* (posthumous, 1697 and 1858) with the literary figures of his time, notably with his cousin, Mme de SÉVIGNÉ. An intelligent writer but one with a biting and often cruel wit, Bussy-Rabutin left incisive portraits of a number of his famous contemporaries.

## Buzot, François (1760–1794)
*political figure*

Born in Évreux, François Buzot was elected a deputy for the Third Estate to the ESTATES GENERAL (1789) and, at the beginning of the REVOLUTION OF 1789, was elected to the Convention, taking his place with the GIRONDINS. He took part in the FEDERALIST INSURRECTION and when that uprising failed, committed suicide to escape the guillotine. Buzot has left his *Mémoires sur la Révolution française.*

# C

## Cabanel, Alexandre (1823–1889)
*painter*

Born in Montpellier, Alexandre Cabanel was a representative of the academic school of painting and, under NAPOLÉON III, was given many honors and important official commissions. He produced works on great historical themes, portraits, and softly figured female nudes (*Naissance de Vénus*, Museum of Orsay). Cabanel also taught leading artists of the period at his studio in Paris.

## Cabanis, Pierre-Jean-Georges (1757–1808)
*physician, philosopher, political figure*

Born in Cosnac, Limousin, Pierre-Jean-Georges Cabanis, who was a professor of hygiene and clinical medicine, after Thermidor took an active role in French political life. He helped NAPOLÉON I take power, and he also later dared to disavow him. A member of the Idéologues group, he broke with CONDILLAC when he affirmed in his treatise, *Rapports du physique et du moral* (1802), the need to connect psychological facts to physiology, seeing in instincts the link between the organic and the intellectual world. He also developed a naturalistic monism. His other works include *Observations sur les hôpitaux* (1789) and *Coup d'œil sur les révolutions et la réforme de la médecine* (1804). Cabanis was elected to the ACADÉMIE FRANÇAISE in 1803.

## Cabet, Étienne (1788–1856)
*socialist*

Born in Dijon and educated as an attorney, Étienne Cabet was an active Carbonarist (la Charbonnerie) and in 1830 took part in the insurrection against the monarchy. After the JULY REVOLUTION of that year, he was elected to the Chamber of Deputies. A founder of the newspaper *Le Populaire*, in 1832 he published his first work, *Histoire de la révolution de 1830*. Being forced to emigrate in 1834 for his attacks on the government, Cabet went to England, where he soon was influenced by the theories of the British Socialist Robert Owen. On his return to France, he published *L'Histoire populaire de la Révolution française de 1789* (1839) and his philosophical novel, *Le Voyage en Icarie* (1840 and 1842), in which he put forth the concept of a utopian and pacifistic communism. A supporter of the idea of community property, he accorded to the state a primordial role, charged with setting up the system in which, thanks to technological developments, the principle of "to each according to his needs" could be applied. In 1848, Cabet, with a large number of his followers, known as "Icarians," immigrated to the United States to found communities based on his theories.

## Cadoudal, Georges (1771–1804)
*conspirator*

Born in Kerléano, near Auray, Georges Cadoudal fought in the WAR OF THE VENDÉE and was one of the leaders of the CHOUANNERIE. He took refuge in London in 1800 and was named lieutenant general by the count of ARTOIS. Cadoudal organized two plots against Napoléon Bonaparte: on December 24, 1800, a bomb exploded on the rue Saint-Nicaise near Bonaparte, who was on his way to the Opéra. Bonaparte escaped injury, but 22 others were killed. The second plot (1803), in complicity with General CHARLES PICHEGRU, was foiled, and Cadoudal was arrested and then executed on June 25, 1804.

## Caillaux, Joseph (1863–1944)
*political leader*

A controversial figure in French politics, Joseph Caillaux was born in Le Mans. He was elected to the Chamber of Deputies in 1898 and, as a member of the Radical Socialist Party, served three times as minister of finance between 1899 and 1911. Later, as prime minister (1911–12), he won Germany's agreement to a French protectorate over Morocco. As finance minister again (1913–14), he sponsored passage of France's first income tax law. In 1914 his wife, in a famous incident, shot and killed the editor of LE FIGARO, GASTON CALMETTE, for having published personal letters written by Caillaux. Caillaux resigned from the government to defend her at her trial, and won an acquittal. During WORLD WAR I, Caillaux favored a negotiated peace with Germany and, for that reason, was accused by the premier, GEORGES CLEMENCEAU, of treasonable correspondence with the enemy. Found guilty by a high court, he was imprisoned from 1918 to 1920. Later amnestied, Caillaux subsequently returned to the government as a senator (1925) and again as finance minister (1925, 1926, and 1935). He is the author of his *Mémoires*.

## Caillebotte, Gustave (1848–1894)
*painter, collector*

Born in Paris, Gustave Caillebotte is known for his scenes of contemporary French urban life, especially of the Parisian upper middle class. He was a patron also of the impressionists, with whom he exhibited. His own work is characterized by its lack of sentimentality and use of the extraordinary perspectives of Paris, and especially of its boulevards. He also employed stylized and unconventional viewpoints, as in *Les Raboteurs de parquet* (1875). As a core member of the Impressionist group, Caillebotte participated in the exhibitions of 1876, 1877, 1879, 1880, and 1882. Caillebotte began to study painting in 1872 at the studio of LÉON BONNAT and at the École des beaux-arts. In particular, he was influenced by EDGAR DEGAS, especially in technique and perspective. In 1894, he donated his own collection of 67 impressionist masterpieces to the French government, whereupon he provoked a scandal—conservatives having condemned his gift as an affront to French art. Today this great legacy forms the central part of the collection at the Musée d'Orsay.

## Calas, Jean (1698–1762)
*merchant*

Born in Lacabarède, near Castres, Jean Calas was a Calvinist merchant. Following the suicide of his eldest son, Calas tried to hide the fact but was accused of killing him to prevent his conversion to Catholicism. Jean Calas was subsequently condemned and executed. His family, with the help of VOLTAIRE, who wrote *Traité sur la tolerance* (1763) about the circumstances, succeeded in proving Calas's innocence and having him rehabilitated (1765). The Calas affair became an example of Catholic intolerance and persecution of Protestants.

## Callot, Jacques (1592–1635)
*engraver, etcher*

Born in Nancy, Jacques Callot is considered an important and influential innovator in both the technique and the subject matter of printmaking. He first studied in Italy, where later, as a court printmaker to the Medicis (1612–21), he developed a new etching medium (a linseed oil and mastic varnish), the texture of which would make possible greater detail and fineness. This innovation later facilitated the work of other great etchers of the period, including Rembrandt. In such works as his *Foire de l'Impruneta* (1620), Callot became one of the first artists to depict a complete cross section of the society of the time. He returned to France in 1621, where he produced works for LOUIS XIII (*Siège de la Rochelle*; *Siège de Saint-Martin-de-Ré*). After this period, Callot adopted a more realistic and less courtly style. His masterpieces are the two series, each entitled *Les Misères et Malheurs de la guerre* (both 1633), in which he removed any glory or romance from the acts of warfare by showing it as a merciless distress for the common people. An artist with a wide repertoire, however, Callot has among his lighter subjects the figures *Razullo et Cucurucu* and *Scaramuche et Fricasso*. Callot's prints were especially admired in the 19th century by the romantics.

## Calmette, Gaston  (1858–1914)
*journalist*

Born in Montpellier, Gaston Calmette studied law in Paris and, in 1883, joined the staff of *Le Figaro*. His reporting caused a sensation in December 1892, at the height of the PANAMA AFFAIR, when one of his interviews led to the resignation of the minister of finance. In 1894, he was named an editor, and soon (1896–97) wrote articles on the Dreyfus affair that were widely read. Made director of *Le Figaro* in 1903, he increased the paper's circulation over the next decade. In 1914, he began an intense campaign against JOSEPH CAILLAUX, minister of finance, accusing him and others of improper political activity. Consequently, on March 16 of that year, he was assassinated in his office by Caillaux's wife, and Caillaux subsequently resigned. Her trial caused a sensation in France.

## Calonne, Charles-Alexandre de (1734–1802)
*political figure*

Born in Douai, where he served (1759) as procurator general of the parlement, Charles-Alexandre de Calonne became intendant general of Metz (1766), then of Lille (1778), where he proved his administrative qualities by building roads and canals, and developing the maritime commerce at Dunkerque. Called to the Finance Ministry in 1783, shortly after the resignation of JACQUES NECKER, he at first practiced a policy of expediency (loans, major works), then faced with the economic and financial crisis of 1785, he proposed a more radical plan of reforms (August 20, 1786) to unify the provincial administration and, above all, establish fiscal equity. The Assembly of Notables, which he convened in 1787, rose up strongly against his proposals. Calonne was forced to resign (April 1787) and was replaced by LOMÉNIE DE BRIENNE.

## Calvin, Jean  (1509–1564)
### (John Calvin, Jean Cauvin)
*religious reformer*

A major figure of the Protestant Reformation, Jean Calvin (or Cauvin) was born in Noyens and studied for the priesthood at the University of Paris. Encour-aged by his father, however, to study law and theology, he also attended the universities at Orléans and Bourges. Calvin studied Hebrew and Greek, too, and this humanistic formation is apparent in his early writing *Commentaire du "De Clementia" de Seneca* (1532). In 1533, he embraced the Reformation, and it was his association with Nicholas Cop, the newly elected rector of the University of Paris, which forced him to flee the city when Cop announced his own support of the teachings of the reformer Martin Luther in 1535. Calvin moved about frequently in the next two years as a preacher (Saintonge, Angoumois) and was finally forced to leave France altogether for Basel. There, he published the first edition (in Latin) of his *L'Institution de la religion chrétienne* (1536), which he later translated into French (1541). He soon went to Geneva, where he was asked by Guillaume Farel to assist in that city's reform movement. In 1538, however, both were asked to leave and Calvin journeyed to Strasbourg, where he taught theology, took part in the French reform movement, met the reformer Melancthon, and married Idette de Buse, a widow. Recalled to Geneva in 1541, he led the reform movement there again and helped to draft the *Ordonnances ecclésiastiques*, which became the basis for the reformed church of the city. Calvin also took charge of and reorganized the educational life of Geneva and supervised its citizens' religious formation. Calvin's role and his extremely strict teachings were not without opposition, however. In response, he condemned his political and religious critics to exile or death, as in the case of Michael Servetus, whom Calvin had burned in 1553.

## Cambacérès, Jean-Jacques-Régis de (1753–1824)
### (duke of Parma)
*jurist, political figure*

Born in Montpellier, where he served in the financial office (1771), Jean-Jacques-Régis de Cambacérès, who was educated as an attorney, in 1789 became president of the criminal court of Hérault. Elected to the National Convention during the REVOLUTION OF 1789 (1792), he voted for the death of King LOUIS XVI and called for the arrest of the Girondin leaders after the treason of CHARLES

DUMOURIEZ. Later, avoiding party politics, he edited a first draft of the Civil Code, which was presented to the Convention in August 1793 and rejected (it later would be a basis for the Code Napoléon). A member of the Council of Five Hundred and Minister of Justice (June 18, 1799), Cambacérès was named second consul at the request of Napoléon Bonaparte (see NAPOLÉON I). President of the Senate and of the Council of State, he specialized in issues of judicial administration and contributed to the formulation of the Civil Code. Named archchancellor of the Empire (1804) and duke of Parma (1808), he went over to the Bourbons in 1814 but, during the Hundred Days, again served Napoléon as minister of justice and as president of the House of Peers. After the Restoration of the Bourbons, he was proscribed as a regicide and went into exile (1815), but three years later his legal and political rights were restored and he returned to France. Cambacérès was elected to the ACADÉMIE FRANÇAISE in 1803 but expelled in 1816.

## Cambon, Joseph  (1756–1820)

*political figure*

Born in Montpellier, Joseph Cambon was, during the REVOLUTION OF 1789, a deputy to the Legislative Assembly, then to the Convention, where he left the neutral Plains group to join the radical Montagnards. He was a member of the first Committee of Public Safety (April–July 1793), then president of the Finance Committee (until 1795). He tried without much success to halt inflation and institute a policy (August 24, 1793) by which the new regime would assume the debts of the old. Opposed to MAXIMILIEN ROBESPIERRE, he voted against him on 8 Thermidor, thus contributing to his fall the next day. Nonetheless, Cambon was himself suspected by the Thermidorian Convention and had to stay in hiding until the amnesty of the Year IV. A proscribed regicide, he went into exile in Belgium during the RESTORATION (1815).

## Cambon, Jules  (1845–1935)

*administrator, diplomat*

Born in Paris, Jules Cambon was the brother of the diplomat PAUL CAMBON. After an administrative career, in particular in government in Algeria

(1891), he was named (1897) ambassador to Washington, where, in part, he later helped to negotiate the peace treaty ending the Spanish-American War. He then served as ambassador to Madrid and to Berlin (1907–14) and, in that capacity, helped to settle the diplomatic question relating to Morocco (the Agadir incident). He then was the secretary-general to the minister of foreign affairs (1915–19) and was one of the signers of the Treaty of Versailles. Cambon published *La Diplomate* (1925), and was elected to the ACADÉMIE FRANÇAISE in 1918.

## Cambon, Paul  (1843–1924)

*diplomat, administrator*

Born in Paris, Paul Cambon was the brother of the diplomat JULES CAMBON. Head of the cabinet of JULES FERRY after September 4, 1870, he had an administrative career in France and then was named resident general in Tunisia (1882), before entering diplomacy. Named ambassador to Madrid (1886), Constantinople (1891), and London (1898), where he remained until 1920, he worked to achieve cooperation between France and Great Britain (Entente Cordiale). Paul Cambon published his *Correspondence*.

## Cambronne, Pierre-Jacques-Étienne, viscount  (1770–1842)

*military figure*

Born in Nantes, Pierre-Jacques-Étienne, viscount Cambronne, joined the army as a volunteer in 1792 and took part in the military campaigns of the Revolution and the Empire, being named brigadier, then major general in the Imperial Guard. Having accompanied Napoléon Bonaparte (see NAPOLÉON I) to Elba (1814), he returned with him in 1815, during the HUNDRED DAYS and was made a count and a peer of France. During the Battle of Waterloo (June 1815), he was part of the "last division" of the Old Guard and, summoned to surrender, according to tradition famously replied, "the Guard dies, it does not surrender" (a phrase that would later be used by VICTOR HUGO in his *Les Misérables*). At the Battle of Waterloo, Cambronne was wounded and was taken prisoner to England. Upon his return to France, he was tried before a military tribunal. Defended by PIERRE BERRYER, he was acquitted and shortly after was given the command of a post at Lille.

## Camisards

Derived from the Languedoc word *camiso,* meaning "shirt," *Camisards* was the name given to the Calvinists of the Cévennes because they wore a white shirt under their garments as a sign of recognition among themselves during their night raids against government troops. After the revocation of the EDICT OF NANTES (1685) and the religious persecution that followed, they rose up in 1702, and one of their leaders, JEAN CAVALIER, defied royal troops sent to put down the rebellion. Although Cavalier made peace with the royal commander, Marshal VILLARS (1704), the Camisards continued their rebellion until 1710.

## Camus, Albert (1913–1960)
*writer, philosopher*

One of the most important and influential writers of the 20th century, Albert Camus was born in Mondovi, Algeria, into modest circumstances and raised by his widowed mother and his grandmother. He began his studies in philosophy but did not obtain a degree because he suffered from a tubercular condition. Becoming interested in politics, he was briefly a member of the Communist Party (1934–37) and, in the 1930s, began a career in journalism. During this time, Camus also formed the Théâtre du Travail and published his first collection of essays, *L'Envers et Endroit* (1937). Unable to serve during World War II, he went to Paris to work for *Paris-Soir* as an editor. He joined the RESISTANCE and, after the Liberation, resumed his editorial work. The publication in 1942 of his novel *L'Étranger* (*The Stranger*), and an essay, *Le Mythe de Sisyphe* (1944), brought him a renown that continued with the publication of his other works, *Le Malentendu* (1944) and *Caligula* (1945). At the time of the Setif uprising in Algeria (1945), Camus tried in vain to mobilize the public conscience there regarding the plight of the Muslims. In 1951, the publication of Camus's *L'Homme révolté* initiated a strong polemic and then a definite break with the leading existentialist thinker and writer, JEAN-PAUL SARTRE. The latter criticized Camus for attacking Stalinism along with Nazism. Camus, for his part, was seeking a collective morality that would elevate human solidarity in the face of evil. This is best expressed in his novel *La Peste* (*The Plague*, 1947),

and in his chronicles, collected together under the title *Actuelles* (1950, 1953, 1958). During the Algerian war for independence (1954–57) (see ALGERIA), Camus was deeply troubled by the moral implications of the conflict and the role of the French, the French military, and French public opinion. In 1956, his novel *La Chute* (*The Fall*), appeared in which he backed further away from Sartre's existentialism. In 1957, he published *L'Exil et la Royaume* and *Réflections sur la guillotine*, and received the Nobel Prize in literature "for having brought to light the problems of our day that trouble the human conscience." Camus died in an automobile accident. He left a novel, *Le Premier Homme,* that was published posthumously (1994). While classified, in a sense, as an existentialist, Camus actually went through an evolution that made him more of a skeptical humanist. Many readers have come to consider him just that—a most profound, effective, and honest spokesman of our age for liberal humanism.

## Canada, French in

The first European presence in Canada occurred during the ninth and 10th centuries (Vinland, Leif Eriksson), followed by initial exploration in the 15th (John Cabot). In the 16th century, King FRANCIS I of France sent Giovanni de Verrazano (1524) then JACQUES CARTIER (1534–36), who reached the Indian village of Hochelaga. The colonization of Canada, then named Nouvelle-France, began, however, only under King HENRI IV with SAMUEL DE CHAMPLAIN, the founder of Quebec (1608), who encouraged the coming of French settlers. In Acadia, the settlements reached to the St. Lawrence River. Then in 1627, under the impetus of Cardinal RICHELIEU, the Compagnie de la Nouvelle-France, or the Cent-Associés, was created. Paul de Chomedey, sieur de Maisonville founded Ville-Marie (Montreal) in 1642, and the first public and religious institutions were established. The conquest of various indigenous peoples (Algonquin, Assiniboine, Huron, Micmac, Montagnai, Outaouai, Sioux, and above all the Iroquois of the Five Nations) was undertaken simultaneously with their proselytization. The initial colonizations encouraged COLBERT in 1663 to establish in Nouvelle-France the royal administration that governed the region like a French province. At the same time, the exploration of the interior was undertaken by various French missionaries.

Meanwhile, the English, through the Hudson's Bay Company, claimed the Canadian territories that became objects of continuous contention between the two countries (the city of Quebec was occupied from 1629 to 1632, then Acadia from 1654 to 1667). Under king LOUIS XIV, by the terms of the Treaty of Utrecht (1713), Acadia (Nova Scotia), Newfoundland, and the Hudson Bay were ceded to the English. There then followed a period of peace during which the French pursued the development of their remaining possessions and the exploration of the hinterland. But the SEVEN YEARS' WAR would renew the armed conflict between France and Great Britain, and after the French defeat on the Plains of Abraham followed the British taking of Quebec (1759) and Montreal (1760) and the brutal displacement and exile of thousands of Acadians to places as far away as Louisiana. By the terms of the subsequent Treaty of Paris (1763), all of Nouvelle-France (New France) was ceded to Great Britain, ending French domination in Canada. French language and culture, however, still dominate in the province of Quebec and other areas, especially in Lower Canada, and the French political presence still exists on the small islands of St. Pierre and Miquelon, off the coast of Newfoundland, which form a department of the Republic of France.

## Canguilhem, Georges (1904–1995)
*philosopher*

Born in Castelnaudary, Georges Canguilhem was educated both in philosophy and in medicine. He proposed, over the course of a series of works, a philosophy of living without opposing analytical knowledge. Thus, vitalism (see HENRI BERGSON) could not be radically condemned according to Canguilhem. The clinic and pathology are "the basis of physiology," and are part of a questioning of "normalcy." More largely, Canguilhem proposed a theory of science as the production of problematics and concepts, which is closer to the history of science than to formal logic. He had a strong influence on MICHEL FOUCAULT in particular.

## Cannes

Cannes is a city on the Côte d'Azur, facing the Lérin Islands. It features the Old City, and seaside (la Croisette) buildings, casinos, the palais des Festivals and des Congrès. There is a museum of archaeology and ethnography, the Musée de la Castre. A famous sea resort and tourist and vacation center, Cannes is the site of the celebrated Cannes Film Festival, held annually since 1946. It was during the SECOND EMPIRE that British (notably Lord Brougham) and Russian tourists came to the small port of Cannes for their winter holidays.

## Canrobert, François-Certain (1809–1895)
*military figure*

Born in Saint-Céré, Lot, François-Certain Canrobert, after graduating from SAINT-CYR, took part in the conquest of ALGERIA. General and aide-de-camp to Louis-Napoléon Bonaparte (see NAPOLÉON III), to whom he gave support during the coup d'état of December 2, 1851, Canrobert became commander of the French forces in the Crimea (1854–55), and was promoted to the rank of marshal upon his return to France. During the FRANCO-PRUSSIAN WAR (1870), he helped to defend Saint-Privat-la-Montagne, but had to fall back to Metz, where he was taken prisoner. During the THIRD REPUBLIC, Marshal Canrobert was one of the leaders of the Bonapartist Party.

## Carco, Francis (1886–1958)
*writer*

Born in Nouméa, NEW CALEDONIA, François Carcopino-Tusoli, or Francis Carco, as he is known, was associated with such poets as PAUL-JEAN TOULET and became known for his intimate poems ("La Bohème et mon coeur," 1912; "Chansons aigres-douces," 1913), evocations that were followed by his chronicles *De Montmartre au Quartier latin* (1927) and *Mémoires d'une autre vie* (1934). Known for his novels that portray a milieu of troublesome youths (*Jésus la Caille*, 1914; *L'Équipe*, 1918), Carco is equally known for his deep psychological studies (*L'Homme traqué*, 1922), evoking two mediocre personages linked by the knowledge of a crime, and *Rien qu'une femme* (1924), an analysis of a morbid jealousy. He also published *Le Roman de François Villon* (1926), *La Légende et la Vie d'Utrillo* (1927), *Verlaine* (1939), and *Gerard de Nerval* (1953).

See also FARGUE, LÉON-PAUL.

## Carcopino, Jérome (1881–1970)
*historian, political figure*

Born in Verneuil-sur-Avre, Jérome Carcopino was a professor of history at the SORBONNE (1920–27), director of the École française of Rome (1937–40), and for a time served as minister of education and youth in the VICHY government (1940–41). Pursued after the Liberation, he benefited from a pardon because of his services to the RESISTANCE. A Hellenist and Latinist, he is known for his works on the last century of the Roman Republic (*Sylla ou la Monarchie manqué*, 1931; *César*, 1936), Roman imperialism and religion (*Aspects mystiques de la Rome païnne*, 1941), early Christianity (*De Pythagore aux apôtres*, 1956; *Les Fouilles de Saint-Pierre et la tradition*, 1963). Carcopino has also written a study on *Les Secrets de la correspondance de Cicéron* (1948). He was elected to the ACADÉMIE FRANÇAISE in 1955.

## Carême, Marie-Antoine (1784–1833)
*chef, gastronome*

Born in Paris, Marie-Antoine Carême, in his youth, rose from tavern apprentice to pastry chef in an elegant Parisian patisserie. In 1805, he became cook to the statesman TALLEYRAND, and subsequently served as head chef in the households of the English prince regent (later George IV), the Russian and Austrian emperors, and the financier Baron JAMES DE ROTHSCHILD. He also achieved great notoriety by preparing the cuisine for the Congresses of Aix-la-Chapelle, Vienna, and Laibach. He wrote numerous works on gastronomy and cuisine, including *Les Déjeuners de l'empereur Napoléon* (1815), *Le Pâtissier pittoresque* (1815), *Le maître d'hôtel français ou Parallele de la cuisine ancien et moderne* (1822), and his five-volume *L'Art de la cuisine française au xixe siècle* (1833–37), which was completed by an assistant after his death and which set the standard for classical French cuisine and solidified the French culinary tradition.

## Carné, Marcel (1906–1996)
*film director*

Born in Paris, Marcel Carné was an assistant to the director RENÉ CLAIR and then, from 1936 to 1946, worked with the writer JACQUES PRÉVERT, who wrote his screenplays. Carné's principal works include: *Le Quai des brumes* (1938), *Hôtel du Nord* (1938), *Le jour se lève* (*Daybreak*, 1939), *Les Portes de la nuit* (1946). At the same time, Carné and Prévert collaborated on three works that can be considered masterpieces: *Drôle de drame* (*Bizarre, Bizarre*, 1937), *Les Visiteurs du soir* (1942), and *Les Enfants du paradis* (*The Children of Paradise*, 1945). Carné was named to the Academy of Fine Arts in 1979.

## Carnot, Lazare Hippolyte (1801–1881)
*political figure*

Born in Saint-Omer, Lazare Hippolyte Carnot was the son of General LAZARE-NICOLAS-MARGUERITE CARNOT, with whom he went into exile in 1816, when the latter was condemned as a regicide. Returning to France (1823), Hippolyte for a time was a follower of Saint-Simon, but then broke with the movement. After having taken part in the Revolution of July 1830, he was elected deputy for PARIS (1839–49) and supported the republic after the Revolution of February 1848. At that time, he was named minister of public instruction (1848). Elected again in 1850 and 1857, he refused to take the oath and thus could not sit in the legislature. A member of the Legislative Body in 1864, republican deputy in the National Assembly (1871), Carnot became a senator in 1875.

## Carnot, Lazare-Nicolas-Marguerite (general) (1753–1825)
*military figure*

Known as "le Grand Carnot" and "Organisateur de la victoire," Lazare-Nicolas-Marguerite Carnot was born in Nolay, Burgundy. A military engineer before the Revolution, which he supported, Carnot was elected to the Legislative Assembly, then to the Convention, where he sat with the deputies for the Plain, before joining the MONTAGNARDS. A member of the Committee of Public Safety (July 1793), where he dealt with military matters, he established the 14 armies of the republic, was sent on a mission with the Army of the North, and helped to achieve the victory of Wattignies (October 16, 1793). Associated with the dictatorial policies of the Terror stood against MAXIMILIEN ROBESPIERRE, GEORGES COUTHON, and LOUIS SAINT-JUST during the events of 8 and 9 Thermidor (July 26–27, 1794). A member of the Directory in 1795, he was removed after the coup d'état of 18 Fructidor, Year V (September 4, 1794). Recalled after 18 Brumaire, Year VIII (November 9, 1799) coup d'état, he was named minister of war by NAPOLÉON I but, dismissed in 1800. Opposed to the Consulate and the Empire, he retired from public life and dedicated himself to his scientific projects and research until 1814. He then took part, as governor, in the defense of Antwerp (1814). Minister of the interior during the HUNDRED DAYS, he was banished in 1816 as a regicide. Considered the principal strategist of French victories in the crucial years from 1792 to 1795, Carnot is also the author of important scientific works in which he specified the laws of force, enunciated the law of the conservation of labor, and is considered one of the founders of analytical geometry. Carnot was named to the Academy of Sciences in 1796.

## Carnot, Marie-François-Sadi (1837–1894)
*statesman*

The son of LAZARE-HIPPOLYTE CARNOT, Marie-François-Sadi Carnot was born in Limoges and educated in Paris at the École polytechnique. He served as engineer in charge of bridges and roads and, after the fall of the SECOND EMPIRE (September 14, 1870), was made prefect of what is now the department of Seine-Maritime, and was elected to the National Assembly (1871). Twice a minister (public works, 1879–80; finance, 1885–86), he then became president of the republic (1887). The beginning of his tenure was marked by the Boulangist agitation, then by the rallying of various Catholics to the republican government (1890), and finally by the PANAMA AFFAIR (1892). Because of legislation passed during his term against anarchism and syndicalism,

he was assassinated by an Italian anarchist while visiting an exposition at LYON.

## Carnot, Nicolas-Léonard-Sadi (1796–1832)
*physicist, military engineer*

The son of LAZARE NICOLAS MARGUERITE CARNOT, Nicolas-Léonard-Sadi Carnot was born in Paris, where he was educated at the École polytechnique. Nicolas Carnot was responsible for first discovering the relationship between heat and energy and, studying engines and machines, he put forth the principle, known as Carnot's Theorom (Carnot Cycle), which later became the second law of thermodynamics. It states that heat cannot pass from a colder to a warmer body. In 1824, he described his concept of the perfect engine, the so-called Carnot Engine, in which all available energy is utilized. Nicolas Carnot is chiefly responsible for establishing the field of thermodynamics.

## Carpeaux, Jean-Baptiste (1827–1875)
*sculptor, designer, painter*

Born in Valenciennes, Jean-Baptiste Carpeaux studied at the studio of the sculptor FRANÇOIS RUDE. He then traveled to Italy, where he was inspired by the works of the Renaissance masters, especially Donatello and Michelangelo, as well as by 18th-century rococo sculpture. A leading exponent of romanticism, Carpeaux produced works outstanding for their lifelike grace and animation. The best example is his masterpiece, *La Danse* (1867–69), done for the Paris Opera. It expresses joyful abandon with graceful intertwined figures, strong facial expressions, and flowing draperies, and has a clear affinity with rococo art. Carpeaux gained the favor of NAPOLÉON III, who commissioned a series of portraits of members of the imperial family and of other prominent individuals. In 1874, Carpeaux finished *Les Quatres Parties du monde* for the fountain of the Observatory of Paris.

## Carrel, Alexis (1873–1944)
*surgeon, physiologist, Nobel laureate*

Born in Foy-lès-Lyon and educated at the university of LYON, Alexis Carrel, who did his research both in France and in the United States, was awarded the Nobel Prize in physiology in 1912 for his earlier (1902) development of a technique for suturing blood vessels. When he returned to France in 1939, he worked for the VICHY regime as head of the Fondation française, which studied human physiological problems (1941). Because of this, and his theories on eugenics, he was much criticized. Carrel, who had also done some of his work in the United States in collaboration with Charles Lindbergh, wrote *L'Homme, cet inconnu* (1936), in which he put forth his elitist and racist philosophy.

## Carrel, Armand (1800–1836)
*journalist, political figure*
Born in Rouen, Armand Carrel, shortly after graduating from the military academy of Saint-Cyr, took a strong stand against the regime of the Restoration. During France's Spanish campaign (1823), he arrived in Barcelona and joined the forces fighting against King Ferdinand VII and the troops of LOUIS XVIII. Arrested and tried, then sentenced to death, he was eventually acquitted. A collaborator for some time with the historian AUGUSTIN THIERRY, he was a political pamphlet against the Restoration regime. The founder of a liberal constitutional opposition newspaper, *Le National* (1830), with AUGUSTE MIGNET and LOUIS

ADOLPHE THIERS, from whom he later politically separated, Carrel joined the republican opposition at the time of the July Monarchy (1830). Following a public dispute that was being carried on in his newspaper, he was killed in a duel with ÉMILE DE GIRARDIN.

## Cartel des gauches
The Cartel des gauches was formed in 1924 to meet the challenge of the moderates and conservatives of the BLOC NATIONAL. It brought together the radical Left (Radicals and Radical-Socialists), Republican Socialists, and the Socialists (SFIO). Its victory in the elections of May 24, 1924, brought about the resignation of the president of the republic, ALEXANDRE MILLERAND, who was succeeded by GASTON DOUMERGUE, and the formation of a Radical-Socialist government (ÉDOUARD HERRIOT, who would succeed PAUL PAINLEVÉ and ARISTIDE BRIAND). This government itself, after the failure of its financial policies, was replaced by one of national unity, led by RAYMOND POINCARÉ (1926).

## Cartier, Jacques (1491–ca. 1557)
*navigator*
Born in Saint-Malo, Jacques Cartier, while seeking a northwest passage to Asia through the New

Jacques Cartier *(Library of Congress)*

World, reached Newfoundland and the coast of Labrador, which had already been discovered by John and Sebastian Cabot (1497). Cartier discovered the estuary of the St. Lawrence and, at Gaspé, took possession of CANADA in the name of King FRANCIS I of France. He undertook two other voyages (1535, 1541) during the course of which he proved the insularity of Newfoundland, sailed up the St. Lawrence (which he believed to be the Northwest passage to "Cathay") until he reached the site of Quebec, and went on to found a settlement at Hochelaga, the site of the future Montreal. Jacques Cartier was called the "discoverer of Canada."

### Cartier-Bresson, Henri (1908– )
*photographer*
Born in Chanteloup, Henri Cartier-Bresson was educated at the Lycée Condorcet in Paris. Known for his reportage work, he was originally interested in painting and took up photography later, in 1930. Beginning in 1931, he traveled worldwide, and his photographs were published in books, magazines, and newspapers and also frequently exhibited. He had a unique ability to capture the fleeting moment in which his subject's significance is revealed. This Cartier-Bresson terms the "decisive moment." During WORLD WAR II, he spent over two years in German prison camps. After his escape, he joined the RESISTANCE as a member of a photographic unit that recorded the Occupation and the German retreat. In 1945, he directed the documentary film *Le Retour* and two years later had a major one-person exhibit at the Museum of Modern Art in New York City. In 1955, he became the first photographer to exhibit at the LOUVRE. Cartier-Bresson highlighted through photography the spirit and events of contemporary life.

### Casimir-Perier (1811–1876)
**(Auguste Casimir Perier)**
*political figure*
Born in Paris, Auguste Casimer Perier, or Casimer-Perier, as he is known, was the son of CASIMIR PERIER, a minister in the government of King LOUIS-PHILIPPE. A diplomat, he was elected to the Chamber of Deputies (1846–48), then to the Legislative Assembly (SECOND REPUBLIC, May 1849). Retiring from political life during the Second Empire, he was elected as a deputy to the National Assembly and named minister of the interior in the government of LOUIS ADOLPHE THIERS, whose policies he supported (1871–73).

### Casimir-Perier, Jean (1847–1907)
*statesman*
Born in Paris, Jean Casimer-Perier was the son of CASIMIR-PERIER. He began his political career after the fall of the SECOND EMPIRE, and was elected deputy in 1876 and named undersecretary of state for war in 1883, but resigned following the decree that deprived the princes of Orléans of their military ranks (1886). Premier in 1893, he helped in the repression of workers' movements and anarchist agitation, and put through the "lois scélérates" (five years' imprisonment for inciting manslaughter, theft, and arson, and the banning of all anarchist propaganda). Named president after the assassination of SADI CARNOT (June 1894), Casimir-Perier, socially and politically a conservative, was strongly criticized by the Socialists, particularly JEAN JAURÈS, and resigned in January 1895.

### Cassagnac, Bernard Granier de (1806–1880)
*political figure, journalist*
Born in Avéron-Bergelle, Bernard Granier de Cassagnac, as editor of the *Globe* and of *L'Époque*, supported the policies of FRANÇOIS GUIZOT, then opposed to the republican regime, rallied to the cause of Louis-Napoléon Bonaparte. He then served as a deputy from 1852 to the end of the SECOND EMPIRE, all the while remaining a journalist. A deputy also under the Third Republic (1876–77), Cassagnac was one of the leaders of the Bonapartist Party. A writer, his works include *Histoire de la Révolution française* (1850), and *Souvenirs du Second Empire* (1879–82).

### Cassagnac, Paul Granier de (1843–1904)
*political figure, journalist*
The son of BERNARD GRANIER DE CASSAGNAC, Paul Granier de Cassagnac was born in la Guadeloupe.

He served as the literary and political editor of various newspapers (*La Nation, Diogène, Le Pays*) and was the founder of *L'Autorité*. He served as a representative of the Bonapartist Party in the Chamber of Deputies (1876, 1898) and took part in the Boulangist agitations (see BOULANGER, GEORGES).

## Cassin, René (1887–1976)
*jurist, Nobel laureate*

Born in Bayonne, René Cassin, after having served in various capacities under General CHARLES DE GAULLE in London during WORLD WAR II, became a member of the Consultative Assembly at Algers in 1944. Vice president of the Council of State (1944–60), then a member of the Constitutional Council (1960–71), he participated in numerous international conferences, helped to put through the Universal Declaration of Human Rights, and served as president of the European Court on Human Rights from 1965 to 1968. Cassin was awarded the Nobel Peace Prize in 1968.

## Cassini family

A family of French astronomers and geodesists who served as directors of the Paris Observatory for four generations. Jean-Dominique Cassini (1625–1712), known as Cassini I, was born in Perinaldo, near Nice. He is the author of numerous works on the planets Jupiter, Mars, and Venus, and discovered two satellites of Saturn. He was named to the Academy of Sciences in 1669. Jacques Cassini, or Cassini II (1677–1756), the son of Jean-Dominique Cassini, was born in Paris and is considered to be the founder of topographic cartography. He produced works on the representation of the surface of Earth, and was named to the Academy of Sciences in 1699. César Cassini, or Cassini III (1714–84), born in Thury, created an unfinished map of France on the scale of 1:86,400, which served as the model for such works until the middle of the 19th century, when it was replaced by more advanced charts. César Cassini was named to the Academy of Sciences in 1735. Dominique, count de Cassini (1748–1845), the son of César Cassini, was born in Paris and completed the map begun by his father. He was named to the Academy of Sciences in 1770.

## Castellion, Sébastien (1515–1563)
### (Sébastien Castalion, Sébastièn Chateillon)
*humanist*

Born in Saint-Martin-du-Fresne in le Bugey, Sébastien Castellion, a Protestant, met the reformer JOHN CALVIN in Strasbourg (1540) and, with his encouragement, accepted the post of regent of the College of Geneva (1541). In 1544, following a dispute he had regarding the canonical status of the Song of Songs, and also the belief in Christ's descent into Hell, Castellion left Geneva for Basel, where he taught Greek. He subsequently did Latin (1551) and French (1553) translations of the Bible and is considered to be the author of a manifesto on tolerance (*De haereticus*, 1554), which appeared after the execution of the Spanish theologian Miguel Servetus for heresy by the Calvinist regime in Geneva. Sébastien Castellion published this work under the pseudonym of Martinus Bellius.

## Catherine de' Medici (1519–1589)
### (Catherine de Médicis)
*queen of France*

One of the most influential queens of France and mother of the last three Valois kings, Catherine de' Medici was born in Florence, Italy, the great-granddaughter of Lorenzo de' Medici (the Magnificent) and daughter of Lorenzo, duke of Urbino. In 1537, she married the duke of Orléans, the future HENRY II. She had little effect during the reigns of her husband and of her eldest son, FRANCIS II, but as regent for her second son, CHARLES IX, she began to exercise great political control. To preserve royal power, Catherine played the Catholics, led by the House of Guise, against the Protestant Bourbons. Free from fanaticism herself, and acting always in the interests of political expediency, she appointed the tolerant MICHEL DE L'HOSPITAL as minister and adopted, initially, a policy of conciliation toward the Protestants (Edict of Tolerance, 1561; Edict of Amboise, 1563; Peace of Saint-Germain, 1570). In 1560, Catherine arranged for her daughter, ÉLISABETH OF FRANCE, to marry Philip II of Spain and, in 1572, for another daughter, MARGUERITE DE VALOIS, to marry the Protestant king Henri de Navarre, later HENRY IV. In that same year, alarmed by growing HUGUENOT influence, particularly that of Admiral GASPARD DE COLIGNY, over her son, CHARLES IX, she instigated the

plot that led to the ST. BARTHOLOMEW'S DAY MAS-
SACRE. In 1574, her third son, HENRY III, ascended
the throne. Apart from her political role, Catherine
was also a patron of the arts. She added a new wing
to the royal residence at the LOUVRE and rebuilt
parts of the Tuileries gardens and the château of
Monceau. Her personal library, with many rare
manuscripts, was renowned in Renaissance France.

## Cauchy, Augustin, Baron (1789–1857)
*mathematician*

Born in Paris, Baron Augustin Cauchy worked in
mathematics (differential equations) and physics
and developed the theory of functions with a variable complex that would play a great role in the
evolution of the study of mathematics. He also did
studies on the mechanics of elasticity, on the propagation of light, and on astronomical mathematics.
Cauchy was named to the Academy of Sciences in
1816.

## Cavaignac family

A family of French political and military figures
who served in the 18th and 19th centuries. Jean-
Baptiste Cavaignac, baron of Lalande (1763–1829),
born in Gourdon, was elected during the REVOLU-
TION OF 1789 to the Convention (1792), and was
known for his extreme revolutionary views.
Named prefect during the HUNDRED DAYS, he was
banished as a regicide at the time of the Restoration
(1815). Godefroy Cavaignac (1801–45), the son of
Jean-Baptiste Cavaignac, was born in Paris and,
after participating in the JULY REVOLUTION OF 1830,
joined the republican opposition. Imprisoned after
the troubles of June 1834, he escaped and reached
England; returning to France (1841), he served as
president of the Society of the Rights of Man,
which he had helped to found. Louis-Eugène
Cavaignac (1802–57), the brother of Godefroy
Cavaignac, was born in Paris. A military officer
with republican convictions, he was sent to Algeria
(1832), where he was named governor-general in
1848. Shortly after, he was then recalled to France
to become minister of war. In that capacity, he suppressed the workers' uprising of June 1848 and,
invested by the National Assembly with quasi-dic-
tatorial powers, undertook a policy of severe

repression. Defeated in the elections of December
1848 by Louis-Napoléon Bonaparte (see NAPOLÉON
III), he joined the opposition. Elected to the legislature in 1852, he refused to take his place because
he would have had to swear the oath.

## Cavalier, Jean (1679–1740)
*Camisard leader*

Born in Ribaute, Gard, Jean Cavalier was the leader
of the CAMISARDS, the Protestants who formed a
resistance to the French government's policy of religious persecution implemented after the revocation
of the EDICT OF NANTES (1685). Cavalier held out
against royal troops led by various commanders,
including Marshal CLAUDE VILLARS, but laid down his
arms when the latter offered him a pension in 1704.
Cavalier then served in Savoy and England and as
the governor of the Isle of Jersey, where he died.

## Cellemare Plot

A plot named for Antonio de Giudice, duke of Gio-
venazzo, prince of Cellemare, who was the Spanish
ambassador to France (1715). The plot, carried out
on the orders of the Spanish minister, Cardinal Giulio
Alberoni (1664–1752), involved LOUIS-AUGUSTE DE
BOURBON, duke of MAINE, and his wife, the duchess
Anne-Louise-Bénédicte de Bourbon Condé (1676–
1753). The participants in the plot sought to replace
PHILLIPE D'ORLÉANS as regent of France with Philip V
of Spain. The conspiracy failed, and the duke of
Maine was briefly imprisoned (1719). Upon his
release (1720), he retired from political life.

## Cénacle, le

The Cénacle was the name given to a group of
writers who met at first at the home of CHARLES
NODIER and then at that of VICTOR HUGO to define
and delineate the ideas of emerging romanticism
and to oppose the strictures classical formalism
(1823 to 1828).

## Cendrars, Blaise (1887–1961)
*writer*

Best known for his use of literary forms, Blaise
Cendrars (nom de plume of Frédéric Sauser) was

born in La Chaud-de-Fonds, Switzerland. His feverish poetic conquest "of the whole world" superimposes an unusual image of possible adventures. Via innumerable journeys through all parts of the world (by 17, he had visited Moscow), he gained the various experiences and memories that would be the basis for his half-mythic autobiographies, *L'Homme foudroyé* (1945) and *La Main coupée,* 1946. While serving in the FOREIGN LEGION, Cendrars lost an arm during World War I (influencing *Bourlinguer,* 1948, and *Le Lotissement du ciel,* 1949). Cendrars's works are part travel journal and part reflection. He created a style using a succession of photographic impressions, feelings, and ideas, which combine nostalgia and disillusionment with an endless world vision.

## Cerdan, Marcel (1916–1949)
*sports figure, boxing champion*
Born in Sidi Bel-Abbès, Algeria, Marcel Cerdan won the French light middleweight championship boxing title in 1938 and the world middleweight championship title in 1948. A celebrated and internationally popular French sports figure, he was killed in an airplane crash in the Azores the following year. Cerdan was married to the singer ÉDITH PIAF.

## Césaire, Aimé (b. 1913–   )
*poet, political figure*
Born in Basse-Pointe, Martinique, and educated in Paris at the École normale supérieure, Aimé Césaire, who was a descendent of slaves, was a professor and then a Communist deputy in the National Assembly for Martinique, where, upon his return, he served as mayor of Fort-de-France. In his writings, he uses elements of surrealism to express the great desire of his people for emancipation. His fiery words and epic images translate as a rejection of the colonial system and as an assertion for *negritude* (a term he coined) and for the colonized. These concepts he would develop further with his associates Léopold Senghor and LÉON-GONTRAN DAMAS. His writings, however, also demonstrate a powerful faith in life and a universal aspiration for justice and happiness. They include his poetry (*Cahier d'un retour au pays natal,* 1938–39, published

1947; *Soleil cou coupe,* 1948; *Cadastre,* 1961), as well as politically inspired plays such as *La Tragédie du roi Christophe* (1963), *Une saison au Congo* (1966) and *Une Tempête,* a free adaptation of Shakespeare (1969), in which one hears the same message of revolt: "I will give with such force, the great Black cry, that the very foundations of the world will be shaken!"

## Cézanne, Paul (1839–1906)
*painter*
Born in Aix-en-Provence, Paul Cézanne, who is considered a father of modern art and who had a profound effect upon the art of the 20th century, was the son of a banker. In his youth he was a friend of ÉMILE ZOLA. After studying classics and the law and against the wishes of his family, Cézanne dedicated himself to painting. In 1863, he arrived in Paris, where he became influenced by the works of EUGÈNE DELACROIX and other artists such as Tintoretto and Rubens. In his early works, Cézanne adopted the color theories of Delacroix and the idea of "simultaneous contrasts" formulated by EUGÈNE CHEVREUL. Cézanne's early paintings reveal a romantic sensibility in their dramatic and sometimes violent themes (*Les Assassins, L'Orgie, L'Enlèvement*), as well as lyrical ones (*Jugement de Pâris, Déjeuner sur l'herbe*), and he also painted at this stage a series of portraits (*L'Homme au bonnet de coton, Paul Alexis lisant à Zola*). These early works show the influence of GUSTAVE COURBET, but those dated from the period 1872–73 demonstrate an assimilation of the impressionist style, acquired at Auvers-sur-Oise from CAMILLE PISSARRO (*Maison de pendu à Auvers*). Cézanne soon separated himself from the usual impressionist style to develop his own vigorous technique, characterized by large and accentuated compositions (*Mer à l'Estaque*). His ambition, as he stated, was to go beyond impressionism. Having a great respect for the old masters (Veronese, CHARDIN), he attempted to combine their techniques with those of the impressionists to create a new form. As he developed these theories and techniques, Cézanne, especially in his later works (*Les Joueurs de cartes*), achieved a form in which color and design are closely combined in the development of the composition. In the 1880s and 1890s, he discovered a means of rendering both the

*The Bathers*, by Paul Cézanne *(Library of Congress)*

light and the form of nature with a single application of color. He sought to use color to solve the technical problems of impressionism through what he called "color modulation." Volumetric forms were also juxtaposed with strokes of pure color. Abstraction prevails and spaces are very flat, while images are defined by geometric patches of color. Exterior and interior scenes that demonstrate this style and technique include *La Montagne Sainte-Victoire, Tables de cuisine, Portrait de Gustave Geffroy, Les Grandes Baigneuses (The Bathers),* and *Le Grand Pin.* Cézanne's work, little appreciated for the greater part of his life, had an enormous influence on modern artists. He was the greatest single influence on HENRI MATISSE, who drew upon Cézanne's use of color, and a major influence on Pablo Picasso, who developed Cézanne's planar compositional struc-

ture into the cubist style. Known initially to only a few of his impressionist colleagues, Cézanne was finally featured in major exhibitions in 1896 and 1904, and, by his death in 1906, he was recognized as a master of the modern era. He is considered to have contributed to the greatest change in Western art since the Quattrocentro and as a beginning point for the art of the 20th century.

## Chaban-Delmas, Jacques (1915– )
*political figure*

Born in Paris, Jacques Chaban-Delmas served as inspector of finances and played an active role in the Resistance, being promoted to the rank of brigadier general in 1944. A Radical deputy (1946), and mayor of BORDEAUX (1947–95), he joined the RASSEMBLEMENT DU PEUPLE FRANÇAIS (RPF) of CHARLES DE GAULLE and presided, after the dissolving of that party, over the group of social republicans in the National Assembly. Several times a minister, notably in the cabinets of PIERRE MENDÈS-FRANCE (1954–55) and of GUY MOLLET (1956–57), he actively participated in the return of De Gaulle in 1958. A member of the Union pour la nouvelle République (UNR) then of the UNIONS DES DÉMOCRATES POUR LA RÉPUBLIQUE (UDR) and president of the National Assembly (1958–69), he was prime minister (1969–72) during the presidency of GEORGES POMPIDOU. But his "new society" (nouvelle societé) project raised much opposition from conservatives. He won only 14.5 percent of the vote during the presidential election of 1974. Joining the RPR formed by JACQUES CHIRAC in 1976, Chaban-Delmas again served as president of the National Assembly from 1978 to 1981, then again from 1986 to 1988.

## Chabannes, Antoine de  (1408–1488)
*military figure*
Born in Saint-Exupéry, Limousin, Antoine de Chabannes was a former comrade in arms of JEANNE D'ARC, then became a leader of a band of *écorcheurs* (armed nobles who ravaged France during the reign of CHARLES VII, then were integrated into the French army; they disappeared after the end of the Hundred Years' War). Antoine de Chabannes himself entered the service of CHARLES VII (1430) and, after 1468, served LOUIS XI and then his son CHARLES VIII, who named him governor of PARIS.

## Chabot, Philippe de  (ca. 1480–1543)
**(seigneur de Brion)**
*admiral*
Seigneur de Brion and childhood companion to FRANCIS I, Philippe de Cabot was named admiral and governor of Burgundy (1526) after having negotiated the ransom for the king following the defeat at Pavia (1525). He conquered Piedmont (1536) but fell into disgrace as a result of court intrigues. His properties were confiscated and he was banished (1540), but was restored to favor in 1541.

## Chabot, François  (1759–1794)
*political figure*
Born in Aveyron, François Chabot was a defrocked Capuchin who was made the constitutional (juring) bishop of Blois and was elected also as a deputy to the Legislative Assembly, then the Convention (1792). A member of the JACOBIN and the CORDELIERS CLUBS, whose extreme views he shared, Chabot wrote a *Catéchisme des sans-culottes* and promoted the cult of the Goddess of Reason. He then married a banker's daughter and went into business. Implicated in the scandal involving the liquidation of the Indies Company (1793), he was denounced before the Committee of Public Safety. Accused of embezzlement, he was condemned to death and guillotined along with GEORGES JACQUES DANTON and the Indulgents.

See also REVOLUTION OF 1789.

## Chagall, Marc  (1887–1985)
*Russian-born painter, sculptor, designer*
A leading artist of the 20th century, Marc Chagall was born in Vitebsk, Russia (now Belarus), studied art in St. Petersburg, and, between 1910 and 1913, in PARIS. He returned to Russia and, after the Russian Revolution of 1917, was director of the Art Academy in Vitebsk (1918–19) and art director of the Moscow Jewish State Theater (1919–22). In 1923, Chagall returned to France, where he spent the rest of his life, except for a period in the United States (1941–48). Known for his distinctive style, Chagall used color and form in a way that was derived partly from Russian expressionism and was strongly influenced by French cubism. This was already apparent in his early work (*Moi et le village,* 1910; *La Violoniste,* 1912; and *Vue de Paris par une fenêtre,* 1913). He also produced the print series *Mein Leben* (1922) in the same vivid motif. In addition to Jewish secular and biblical themes, Chagall's work combines recollections with fantasy and folklore (*Le Songe d'une nuit d'été,* 1950), and there are many prints illustrating other literary classics. Religious themes, however, prevail in many works, including a series of etchings done between 1925 and 1939 illustrating the Old Testament, and 12 stained-glass windows done for the Hebrew University Medical Center in Jerusalem (1962). In

1973, the Musée National Marc Chagall opened in Nice, to house hundreds of his works. Among Chagall's pieces with secular themes are his *Écuyères aux colombes* (1960), depicting themes used frequently by the artist in both painting and ceramics—figures with flowers, birds, and other animals. Chagall also completed in 1964 a huge canvas to cover the ceiling of the Paris Opera, and two large murals for the lobby of the Metropolitan Opera House in New York City. Chagall died in Saint-Paul-de-Vence.

## Chalgrin, Jean-François (1739–1811)
*architect*

A leading French architect of the 18th century, Jean-François Chalgrin was born in Paris and, in 1758, won the prix de Rome. He subsequently went to Italy to study ancient buildings and monuments and, returning to France, became architect to the king and to the count of Provence. He produced structures that, because of their simplicity and elegance, were especially characteristic of the LOUIS XVI style. He also added to, or enlarged, buildings for the COLLÈGE DE FRANCE, the Luxembourg Palace, and various Parisian churches (e.g., Saint-Sulpice). A representative of the "Greek," or Doric, phase of neoclassicism, he adapted to the church of Saint-Philippe-du-Roule a colonnaded style reminiscent of early Christian basilicas (1769–84). During the Directory and Consulate periods, Chalgrin developed a more grandiose style and drew up a plan for a triumphal arch in Paris.

## Chalier, Joseph (1747–1793)
*political figure*

Born in Beaulard, Piedmont, Joseph Chalier, after adopting the various ideals of the REVOLUTION OF 1789, became one of the principal representatives of the MONTAGNARD Party of LYON and a member of that city's governing Commune. There, he was condemned to death and decapitated after the city's successful royalist and FEDERALIST INSURRECTION (July 17, 1793). Consequently, like LE PELETIER DE SAINT-FARGEAU and JEAN-PAUL MARAT, Chalier became one of the "divinities" of the French revolutionary pantheon.

## Challe, Maurice (1905–1979)
*military figure*

Born in Le Pontet, Vaucluse, Maurice Challe, after having served as an aviator in various operations during WORLD WAR II (1944–45), was named a major general of the armed forces. Commander in chief in ALGERIA (1959), then of the Central European division of NATO, he was one of the authors of the attempted coup d'état of Algiers (1961). Condemned to 15 years in detention, he was pardoned by General CHARLES DE GAULLE in 1966.

## Challemel-Lacour, Paul-Armand (1827–1896)
*political figure*

Born in Avranches, Paul-Armand Challemel-Lacour, after an early political career, was exiled until 1859 because of his opposition to the coup d'état of December 2, 1851, which brought NAPOLÉON III to power. After the fall of the SECOND EMPIRE (September 4, 1870), he was named a prefect and elected a deputy to the National Assembly, where, with LÉON GAMBETTA, he took a position against the monarchist coalition. Challemel-Lacour was named minister of foreign affairs in the cabinet of JULES FERRY (1883) and served as president of the Senate (1893). He was elected to the ACADÉMIE FRANÇAISE in 1893.

## Chambord, Henri d'Artois, duke of Bordeaux, count of (1820–1883)
*royalty*

The last representative of the senior branch of the Bourbons, Henri d'Artois, duke of Bordeaux and count of Chambord, was born in Paris, the posthumous son of the duke of BERRY and the princess Marie-Caroline of Bourbon-Sicily. He went into exile after the REVOLUTION OF JULY 1830, was raised by his aunt, the duchess of ANGOULÊME, and married a princess of Modena (1846). The last Legitimist pretender to the throne (under the name Henri V) after the abdication of CHARLES X, he renounced his claims only in 1871. Following discussions between the Legitimists and the Orléanists, his accession to the throne seemed for a moment certain; but his intransigence in refusing to renounce, among other things, the white Bourbon flag ended the negotiations. Having died without issue, Henri, count of Chambord left the House of Orléans as the sole heir to the throne.

### Champion de Cicé, Jérôme  (1735–1810)
*prelate, political figure*

Born in Rennes, Jérôme Champion de Cicé was made archbishop of BORDEAUX in 1781 and, in 1789, was elected to represent the clergy at the ESTATES GENERAL. He was one of the first to rally to the Third Estate. Named keeper of the seals (August 3, 1789), he gained a certain popularity because he convinced LOUIS XVI to ratify the CIVIL CONSTITUTION OF THE CLERGY (July–August 1790). However, the ministry to which he belonged was accused, on several occasions, of favoring counter-revolution, and in November 1790, Champion de Cicé resigned and emigrated. On his return to France, he was named archbishop of Aix shortly after the signing of the Concordat (1802); see REVOLUTION OF 1789.

### Championnet, Jean-Étienne  (1762–1800)
*military figure*

Born in Valence, Jean-Étienne Championnet fought in various campaigns of the REVOLUTION OF 1789 and, as a brigadier general, distinguished himself in 1794 at Fleurus against the Anglo-Dutch forces. In Italy, he fought the troops of Ferdinand IV and in 1799, in Naples, created the Parthenopean Republic. He was arrested on the orders of the Directory, then freed. General Championnet, at the command of the Army of the Alps, was defeated at Genola and died shortly after.

### Champlain, Samuel de  (ca. 1567–1635)
*explorer*

Called the father of New France, Samuel de Champlain was born in Brouage, but little is known of his early years before 1603. After probably studying cartography, he became a naval captain and, in 1603, made his first visit to North America. He

Samuel de Champlain *(Library of Congress)*

explored the area of the St. Lawrence River in CANADA during his first visit. Upon returning to France, he published his account (*Des Sauvages*) of that journey and then, in 1604, made his second exploratory expedition to the area. At that time, he explored a region south of Canada (Acadia) and established a French colony. Champlain left, but in 1607, made his third visit and at that time established a trading post that was to become Quebec. In 1612, he was made lieutenant of the viceroy of

New France. In 1613, he explored the area of the Ottawa River. Champlain had already (1608) allied himself and his men with the Algonquian and Huron Indians in their conflict with the Iroquois. Much of the time, Champlain, when not exploring in North America or organizing the French colony there, was in France, raising funds for that enterprise. In 1629, when British privateers took Quebec, Champlain was taken prisoner to England, where he was held until 1632. In 1633, he returned to New France, after the Treaty of Saint-Germain-en-Laye restored Quebec to France. Champlain accomplished much during his career. He produced the first accurate chart of the Atlantic coast from Newfoundland to Cape Cod, and made maps of the St. Lawrence River valley and the Great Lakes basin. He also published accounts of the indigenous peoples and helped to establish the basis for the French Empire in North America.

### Champollion, Jean-François  (1790–1832)
*Egyptologist*

One of the founders of the science of Egyptology, Jean-François Champollion was born in Figeac, in the Midi, and came to Paris in 1807 to study Oriental languages at the COLLÈGE DE FRANCE. He had already begun the study of Egyptian, and especially Coptic, texts convinced that the Coptic language was a later form of ancient Egyptian. Champollion obtained a facsimile of the Rosetta Stone, which previous scholars had already analyzed and which seemed to offer solutions to the problem of deciphering the hieroglyphics. It was this stone, along with the text taken from an obelisk found at Philae, Egypt, in 1821, that allowed Champollion to discover the relationship among hieratic, demotic, and hieroglyphic symbols in Egyptian script. In 1822, he reported his findings in his *Lettre à M. Dacier relative à l'alphabet des hiéroglyphes phonétiques,* followed in 1824 by his *Traité sur l'écriture démotique* and his noted *Précis du système hiéroglyphique.* His discovery of the complex system (part phonogram, part ideogram) of ancient Egyptian script was indispensable in the eventual deciphering of the entire hieroglyphic code and the building of a complete vocabulary and grammar. In 1826, Champollion was named curator of the Department of Egyptology at the LOUVRE. From 1828 to 1830, he led a scientific expedition in Egypt, followed by his publication of *Monuments de l'Égypte et de la Nubie* (1830). In 1831, a chair of Egyptology was created for him at the Collège de France. At the time of his death, Champollion left an unfinished *Grammaire égyptienne* and *Dictionnaire égyptien,* which were later published by his brother in 1835 and 1843, respectively.

### Chanel, Coco  (1883–1971)
**(Gabrielle Chasnel)**
*fashion designer*

One of the modern leaders of haute couture, whose name is synonymous with elegance and chic, Gabrielle Chasnel, or Coco Chanel, as she is known, was born in Saumur, Maine-et-Loire. In 1916, she opened a shop in Paris where she designed simple and elegant clothing. Her style soon became part of the liberating movement in women's fashion, which her classic Chanel look would dominate during the 1920s and 1930s. It consisted of a casual but extremely well-cut wool jersey suit with a straight, collarless cardigan jacket and short, full-cut skirt, worn with art deco costume jewelry and often a sailor hat over short hair. Chanel was also the first couturière to launch a brand of perfume—Chanel No. 5 (1921)—which itself became world famous. It was one of several that she created. Coco Chanel designed little during WORLD WAR II and in the immediate postwar years, but in 1954, she successfully revived the understated Chanel look, which soon became universally popular. The American musical *Coco* (1969), by Alan Jay Lerner and André Previn, is based on her life.

### Changarier, Nicolas-Anne-Théodule  (1793–1877)
*military and political figure*

Born in Autun, Nicolas-Anne-Théodule Changarier joined the personal guard of LOUIS XVIII and served in the Spanish Campaign (1823), and then again with distinction over the course of the conquest of ALGERIA (1830–48), where he was named governor after General CAVAIGNAC. Elected to the Constituant Assembly (1848) and named commander of the troops in Paris, he was relieved of his duties by

NAPOLÉON III because he was an Orléanist, and was proscribed after the coup d'état of December 2, 1851. Returning to France in 1859, he fought in the FRANCO-PRUSSIAN WAR (1870–71) with the French army in Metz. Elected to the National Assembly in 1871, he formed a group of royalist deputies who helped to organize the fall of LOUIS ADOLPHE THIERS (May 24, 1873). In 1875, Changarier voted against the constitutional laws recognizing the republic.

## Chanoine, Charles-Paul-Jules (1870–1899)

*officer, explorer*

Born in Paris, Charles-Paul-Jules Chanoine, with PAUL VOULET, went to Africa and explored the Mossi and Gourounsi regions of the Sudan and contributed to their annexation (1896–97). In 1898, he participated in explorations in Chad, but having committed violent reprisals against the indigenous populations, was dismissed along with Voulet. They then assassinated the officer in charge of the expedition, JEAN-FRANÇOIS-ARSÈNE KLOBB, but, in turn, were killed by their own soldiers who had accompanied them. (See also AFRICA, FRENCH IN.)

## Chanzy, Antoine-Alfred-Eugène (1823–1883)

*military and political figure*

Born in Nouart, Ardennes, Antoine-Alfred-Eugène Chanzy served with the Zouaves in ALGERIA and fought in the campaigns in Italy (1859) and in Syria (1860–61). Given the command of the 2nd Army of the Loire during the FRANCO-PRUSSIAN WAR (1870–71), he surrendered to Prince Frederick-Karl after a battle at Vendôme. A deputy to the National Assembly (1871), he opposed the Treaty of Frankfort that ended the war. Named governor of Algeria (1873), he then served as ambassador to Russia (1879).

## Char, René (1907–1988)

*poet*

Born in L'Isle-sur-la-Sorgue, in PROVENCE, René Char came to poetry early, especially after reading the poems of the French surrealist PAUL ELUARD. By the 1930s, as a poet himself, Char befriended other French surrealist poets, notably LOUIS ARAGON and ANDRÉ BRETON, and collaborated with them in collective writing. Char's first independently written collection of surrealist poems, *Le Marteau sans maître* (1934), was later put to music by PIERRE BOULEZ. During WORLD WAR II, Char became a leader in the RESISTANCE and, as chief of a sabotage sector, made many parachute drops behind enemy lines. He joined General CHARLES DE GAULLE in ALGERIA in 1944 and participated in the liberation of PARIS in that same year. After the war and until his death, he devoted himself to poetry, spending much of his time in his native Provence, writing and conferring with friends, including ALBERT CAMUS and the German philosopher Martin Heidegger. He worked regularly, too, with various artists, such as HENRI MATISSE, Pablo Picasso, MARIA VIEIRA DA SILVA, and Joan Miró. Char also wrote tributes to those who influenced him, including ARTHUR RIMBAUD, as well as surrealistic works. Two collections of poetry reflect his experience in the Resistance, *Seuls demeurent* (1945) and *Feuillets d'Hypnos* (1946). Many of his other works evoke the rustic atmosphere and beauty of his beloved Provence. Considered one of the most important French poets of the postwar era, Char, who translated the works of such poets as Petrarch, William Shakespeare, Emily Dickinson, and Ossip Mandelstam, believed poetry could provide a nonrational and intuitive understanding of a constantly changing and mysterious world.

## Charcot, Jean (1867–1936)

*scholar, explorer*

Born in Neuilly-sur-Seine, Jean Charcot was the son of the noted physician JEAN-MARTIN CHARCOT. After having studied medicine, he turned to oceanography and, in the course of two expeditions to the Antarctic on board the *Français* and then the *Pourquoi-Pas?* (1903–05, 1908–10), he charted the austral region of the Palmer archipelago to the island that now bears his name. From 1912 to 1936, he made a number of expeditions in the Atlantic, the English Channel, and the North Sea (the Hebrides, 1921; Greenland, 1925–26), pursuing his work in oceanography and hydrography. During his final expedition, Charcot died at sea.

## Charcot, Jean-Martin (1825–1893)
*physician, neurologist*

Jean-Martin Charcot was born and educated in Paris, where he later taught as a professor of anatomical pathology at the Salpetrière. There, where his most famous pupil would be Sigmund Freud, he opened what would become the most highly regarded neurological clinic of the time, where he specialized in the study of hypnosis, hysteria, ataxia, and aphasia. The condition of cerebrospinal sclerosis is named after him. In 1881, Charcot was made an honorary member of the American Neurological Association, and he was elected to the Academy of Sciences in 1883.

## Chardin, Jean (1643–1713)
*traveler, writer*

Born in Paris, Jean Chardin visited the Indies and Persia, where he stayed for several years at Esfahãn. Returning to Europe, he published *Le Récit du couronnement du roi de Perse Soliman III* (1670) and, after a second journey in that country, *Voyages en Perse et aux Indes orientales* (1686). Both books were widely read at the time in Europe. Settling in England, Chardin served as an agent for the English East Indies Company in Holland.

## Chardin, Jean-Baptiste-Simeon (1699–1779)
*painter*

Born in Paris the son of a cabinetmaker, Chardin, although he studied under a student of LEBRUN, was largely self-taught. One of the great artists of the 18th century, he documented the life of the Parisian bourgeoisie in his genre paintings and still lifes. Chardin was originally influenced by 17th-century Dutch masters and, like them, devoted himself to simple subjects and common themes. His lifelong work in this style contrasted greatly with the heroic and historic subjects and rococo scenery that were the main themes of mid–18th-century art. After being admitted to the Royal Academy of Painting and Sculpture in 1728, on the basis of two early still lifes (*La Raie* and *Le Dressoir*), Chardin began producing such scenes of everyday bourgeois life. About 1755, he returned to the still life genre with *Le Gobelet d'argent*. All Chardin's works are characterized by subdued color tones, lighting, and celebration of the beauty of the commonplace. There is always an air of intimacy, domesticity, and honesty in each. Also, his technique was to achieve a realistic texture in his paintings. Known as the "grand magicien" by his critics, Chardin achieved an unequaled mastery in these areas. Later works (after 1770) included three self-portraits in the same style.

## Charette de la Contrie, François-Athanase de (1763–1796)
*counterrevolutionary leader*

Born in Couffé, in the Nantais region, François-Athanase de Charette de la Contrie was a naval officer before the REVOLUTION OF 1789. He then became a leader of the counterrevolutionary movement in the Vendée, leading the uprising at Machecoul (March 1793), participating in the siege of Nantes, then fighting in the Poiteven Marais. On February 17, 1795, he signed the peace treaty of La Jaunaye with the Thermidorian Convention, but took up arms again in June of that year to help the émigrés who had tried to land at Quiberon. After the failure of this attempt, he was arrested by General LAZARE HOCHE, condemned to death, and executed at Nantes.

See also VENDÉE, WAR OF THE.

## Charivari, Le

*Le Charivari* was a French satirical daily that was published in Paris from 1832 to 1937. Hostile to the regime of King LOUIS-PHILIPPE, it moved, in the face of rising socialism, towards a certain conservatism during the SECOND EMPIRE and then, during the THIRD REPUBLIC, abandoned political satire for moral critique. But, thanks to the spirit of its illustrators, including HONORÉ DAUMIER, and the use of new technologies, such as lithography, *Le Charivari* played a primordial role in the history of caricature.

See also DAUMIER, HONORÉ.

## Charles, Jacques-Alexandre-César (1746–1823)

*physicist*

Born in Beaugency, Jacques-Alexandre-César Charles conceived the idea of using hydrogen to inflate the aerostats invented by the MONTGOLFIER brothers to achieve the first ascent in a balloon of this type, reaching an altitude of 3,000 meters (December 1, 1783). Charles established the law that bears his name, according to which the relationship between the temperature and the constant volume pressure of a gas is constant. Charles was named to the Academy of Sciences in 1795.

## Charles II the Bad (1332–1387)
### (Charles II le Mauvais)

*king of Navarre*

Charles II the Bad, king of Navarre (1349–87), was the son of JEANNE II of Navarre and the grandson of LOUIS X, king of France. Through his grandfather, he was a pretender to the French throne. He supported the revolt of ÉTIENNE MARCEL during the reign of JEAN II THE GOOD and allied himself with England (1358). Charles II of Navarre helped to repress the JACQUERIE and was defeated by BERTRAND DU GUESCLIN at Cocherel, near Evreux (1364), but then would no longer be involved in French affairs.

## Charles III the Noble (1361–1425)

*king of Navarre*

The son of CHARLES II THE BAD, Charles III the Noble succeeded his father as king of Navarre. He reconciled with the House of Valois and was thus able to obtain the duchy of Nemours and the title of peer. He spread French culture throughout Navarre.

## Charles V the Wise (1338–1380)
### (Charles V le Sage)

*king of France*

Born in Vincennes, the son of King JEAN II and Bonne de Luxembourg, Charles V was king of France from 1364 to 1380. In 1350, he married Jeanne of Bourbon and, during his father's captivity, he served as regent, suppressed the JACQUERIE uprising and the revolt of ÉTIENNE MARCEL, and

signed the Treaty of Brétigny with England (1356–64). Upon becoming king, he surrounded himself with capable military leaders (JEAN BOUCICAUT, ROBERT FIENNES) and, thanks to BERTRAND DU GUESCLIN, was able to end the struggle with CHARLES II THE BAD, king of Navarre. CHARLES V also rid the kingdom of the GRANDES COMPAGNIÉS and renewed the war against the English (1368), seizing most of their possessions in France. At the time of his death, the English then held only some maritime cities (notably BORDEAUX and Calais) and some strongholds. During his reign, Charles V ended the War of Succession in Brittany. He surrounded himself, too, with good chancellors and advisers, such as NICOLAS ORESME (finances). A patron of the arts and letters, Charles V established the royal library, rebuilt the LOUVRE, and built the Saint-Pol residence and the BASTILLE in PARIS, and the château de Beauté. He instituted a new system of taxation, reestablishing a solid currency. During the Great Schism, he took the side of Pope Clement VII. The life of Charles V, who was the father of CHARLES VI, is known especially through the writings of CHRISTINE DE PISAN.

## Charles VI (1368–1422)

*king of France*

Born in Paris, Charles VI was the son of King CHARLES V and Jeanne de Bourbon. He governed at first as king of France under the tutelage of his uncles, the dukes of Anjou, Burgundy, Berry, and Bourbon, who, during their guardianship, suppressed various uprisings in Paris, Rouen, Languedoc, and that of Philip van Artevelde in Flanders. After a period of good government by his ministers (*les marmousets*—so called because of the images carved of them on public buildings), Charles VI was struck with dementia (1392), and France was thrown into a civil war between the Armagnacs (House of Orléans) and the Burgundians. The king of England, Henry V, took advantage of this internal strife and invaded France, allying with the Burgundians and winning the Battle of Agincourt (1415). He also conquered Normandy (1417) and captured Rouen (1419) and Paris (1420). The English then imposed on Charles VI the disastrous Treaty of Troyes (1420), which, with the compliance of the queen, ISABEAU OF BAVARIA, disinherited the dauphin (the future CHARLES VII), recognized Henry V of England as heir to the kingdom of France, and conferred on him the regency. Abandoned by his family, the demented Charles VI spent his remaining days being cared for by his mistress, Odette de Champdivers.

## Charles VII (1403–1461)
*king of France*

Born in Mehun-sur-Yèvre, near Bourges, Charles VII, king of France (1422–61), was the oldest surviving son of King CHARLES VI and ISABEAU OF BAVARIA. During the civil war between the Armagnacs and the Burgundians, he left Paris and took refuge in Bourges. His mother had signed the Treaty of Troyes (1420), which disinherited him to the benefit of the king of England, Henry V, who was his nephew. Upon the death of Henry V, Henry VI of England succeeded him under the regency of the duke of Bedford. Charles VII was recognized as king of France only in the southwest and in the Midi. Despite the support of ARTHUR III, count of Richemont, he did not have confidence in himself until he was recognized as the true king of France by JEANNE D'ARC, who liberated Orléans and had him crowned at Reims (1429). After a part of northern France was retaken (Orléanais, Vendômois, Champagne, Brie, Valois, Beauvaisis), Charles VII reconciled with PHILIPPE III LE BON, duke of Burgundy, who had been allied with the English (by the Treaty of Arras [1435]). Paris being retaken (1436), and the truce of Tours signed with the English (1444), Charles VII reorganized his kingdom, limiting the power of the papacy in France through the Pragmatic Sanction of Bourges, and created a new army by the ordinances of 1445–48 (companies of skilled archers were formed). He reestablished a sound currency and raised regular taxes. With his financial adviser JACQUES COEUR, France experienced a full economic uplift. Charles VII rid the kingdom of swindlers and forgers and put down the PRAGUERIE revolt. Thanks to capable military leaders (JEAN DUNOIS, PHILIPPE DE LA HIRE, JEAN BUREAU, JEAN XAINTRAILLES), the reconquest of France continued. The victory at Formigny (1450) allowed the retaking of Normandy and Castillon (1453), the surrender of BORDEAUX (1453), and the recapture of La Guyenne,

with only Calais remaining in the hands of the English. Charles VII's mistress, AGNES SOREL, who was the first officially recognized favorite in French history, had an important influence on the king and his policies. Charles had earlier married MARIE D'ANJOU, who was the mother of LOUIS XI.

## Charles VIII (1470–1498)
*king of France*

The king of France (1483–98), Charles VIII was the son of LOUIS XI and Charlotte of Savoy. His sister, ANNE DE FRANCE, who served as regent (1483–91), was the wife of Pierre de Beaujeu, who himself was able to gain subsides from the Estates General of Tours (1484) and fought against the rebellious nobles in the Guerre folle (1485–88). This conflict ended with the victory at Saint-Aubin-du-Cormier over the duke of Orléans and François II, duke of Brittany. Anne then married her brother to Anne of Brittany (1491), thus adding that duchy to the Crown. Charles VIII subsequently signed the Treaties of Étaples with Henry VII of England and of Senlis with Maximilian of Austria, which restored to him Artois and Franche-Comté. On the advice of GUILLAUME BRIÇONNET, Charles VIII undertook to have recognized the claims that LOUIS XI, his father, had inherited, through the House of Anjou, on the kingdom of Naples, thus beginning the wars in Italy. He easily conquered the kingdom of Naples, but Milan, Venice, Maximilian of Austria, Ferdinand of Aragon, and Pope Alexander VI all being allied against him, he was forced to retreat and return to France after the Battle of Fornoue, thus losing the territory that he had taken. Charles VIII was succeeded by his cousin, the duke of Orléans, who became LOUIS XII.

## Charles IX (1550–1574)
*king of France*

Born in Saint-Germain-en-Laye, the son of HENRY II and CATHERINE DE' MEDICI, Charles became king upon the death of his older brother, FRANCIS II. During Charles's minority, and even after 1563, when he assumed active power, he remained under the strong influence of his mother. The religious conflicts and war between Roman Catholics and Pro-

Charles IX *(Library of Congress)*

testants in France (see HUGUENOTS) characterized his entire reign. In 1572, Catherine, alarmed by the influence of the Protestant Admiral COLIGNY over the young king, persuaded Charles to give his con-

sent to the SAINT BARTHOLOMEW'S DAY MASSACRE. Charles was succeeded by his brother, HENRY III.

## Charles X (1757–1836)
*king of France*

The grandson of LOUIS XV and the younger brother of LOUIS XVI and LOUIS XVIII, Charles, known as the count of Artois until he became king, was born at VERSAILLES. In 1773, he married Marie-Thérèse of Savoy, with whom he had two sons (the dukes of ANGOULÊME and of BERRY). Greatly attached to the ideas of the ancien regime and to the principle of royal absolutism, he was generally disliked and, at the beginning of the REVOLUTION OF 1789, became one of the leaders of the émigrés. At first, Charles was active with the counterrevolutionary forces, but then, in 1795, he went to England, where he remained until 1814. After the RESTORATION, he returned to France to serve as lieutenant-general of the kingdom and became a leader of the ultras. Upon the death of his brother King Louis XVIII in 1824, he became king and began his reign by being crowned at Reims, the historic site of royal coronations, in the tradition of the ancien régime. Charles's rule was characterized by reactionary and autocratic policies. Favoritism was shown to the Roman Catholic Church and to the aristocracy, and conservative ministers were put in charge of the government (see JEAN-BAPTISTE DE VILLÈLE, JEAN-BAPTISTE DE MARTIGNAC, JULES DE POLIGNAC). Subsequently, liberal opposition to the regime intensified. After the suppression of freedom of the press and other liberties by Charles's government, particularly as stipulated in the Ordonnances de Saint-Cloud, the people, on July 29, 1830, rose up. The resultant REVOLUTION OF JULY 1830 forced Charles to abdicate. His overthrow marked the end of Bourbon rule, with that dynasty being succeeded by the house of Orléans. Charles spent his remaining years in exile in Britain and later on the Continent.

## Charles XIV (1763–1844)
### (Charles-Jean-Baptiste Bernadotte)
*marshal of France, king of Sweden*

Born in Pau, Charles-Jean-Baptiste Bernadotte served as a soldier in the REVOLUTION OF 1789 and became a brigadier general in 1794. In 1797, he served under Napoléon Bonaparte (see NAPOLÉON I) in Italy, then as ambassador to Vienna in 1798. The same year, he became, by marrying Desirée Clary, the brother-in-law of JOSEPH BONAPARTE. As minister of war, Bernadotte refused to participate in the coup d'état of 18 Brumaire (1799). He was made a marshal by Napoléon in 1804, and governor of Hanover that same year. Bernadotte distinguished himself at the Battle of Austerlitz (1805), for which he was created prince of Pontecorvo. He also took part in the victories of Halle and Lubeck over the Prussians (1806), and those of Mohrungen and Spander, where he was wounded, over the Russians. As governor of the Hanseatic cities, he led the campaign against the Swedish forces of Gustave IV (1808). After Wagram, however, Bernadotte broke with Napoléon. The Swedes, who appreciated his policies toward them, offered Bernadotte the throne (1810). Chosen crown prince by the Swedish Riksdag (parliament), he was adopted by Charles XIII, who had no heirs, and installed in Sweden with Bonaparte's approval. When the danger of the continental blockade, imposed by Napoléon, began to affect Sweden, Bernadotte, as crown prince, turned against him and, in 1812, allied Sweden with Russia. As a member of the coalition against Bonaparte and France, Bernadotte fought against the French forces at Grossbeeren and at Dennewitz, and against those commanded by Napoléon at Leipzig, where he contributed to the French defeat (1813). After a campaign in Holstein, Bernadotte signed the Peace of Kiel (1814) with Denmark, by which Norway was returned to Sweden. Bernadotte with enthusiasm became king of Sweden, succeeding Charles XIII in 1818, and dedicated himself to his role as monarch. He founded the present royal house of Bernadotte and was succeeded by his son Oscar I.

## Charles of Blois (ca. 1319–1364)
### (Charles de Châtillon)
*pretender to French throne*
Pretender to the duchy of Brittany, Charles de Blois married the duchy's heiress, JEANNE OF PENTHIÈVE, in 1337. His rights were then recognized by France (1341), but he had to negotiate with Jean de Mon-

fort, who disputed his claims to the duchy. The war, called the War of the Succession of Brittany, ensued and Charles of Blois was defeated and killed at Auray by JEAN II OF BRITTANY.

## Charles of Orléans (1394–1465)
*poet, duke of Orléans*
The duke of Orléans, Charles of Orléans was born in Paris, the grandson of King CHARLES V, the nephew of King CHARLES VI, and the brother of King LOUIS XII. The leader of the Armagnacs, he was taken prisoner at Agincourt (1415) and held for 25 years as a captive in England. Upon his return to France, he made his court at Blois a center of poetry. There, he composed and sang allegorical songs, in the form of ballads and rondos, about his exile (*En regardant vers le Pays de France*), of time passed and solitude (*En la Forêt d'ennuyeuse tristesse*), or about nature (*En regardant ces belles Fleurs*). Charles of Orléans is, with FRANÇOIS VILLON, the principal French poet of the 15th century.

## Charles the Bold (1433–1467)
### (Charles le Téméraire)
*duke of Burgundy*
Born in Dijon, Charles the Bold, duke of Burgundy, was the son of PHILIPPE III THE GOOD, duke of Burgundy, and Isabelle of Portugal. He took part in the LIGUE DU BIEN PUBLIC (League of public welfare) against the king of France, LOUIS XI and, after the indecisive battle of Montlhéry, obtained the restoration of the towns of the Somme through the Treaty of Conflans (1465). All his policy was an attempt to unify his estates through a strong administrative structure and to assume a connection between the two parts of the Burgundian territory (Flanders and Burgundy). This constituted a grave menace to the French monarchy and its neighbors (Lorraine, Switzerland). The inhabitants of Liège, supported by LOUIS XI, had revolted against their bishop, who was Charles's ally. Charles, in turn, obliged the king to help him repress the revolt and to sign the Treaty of Peronne (1468). Charles then invaded PICARDY but was stopped at Beauvais (see JEANNE HACHETTE), then again at Rouen (1472). He conquered Lorraine but was defeated at Grandson and at Morat by the

Swiss supplied by Louis XI (1476). He died at the siege of Nancy.

## Charpentier, Marc-Antoine (1643–1704)
*composer*

Marc-Antoine Charpentier, whose masses, operas, and songs are admired for their elegant structure and style, was born in Paris and studied in Italy, where he was a student of the noted composer Giacomo Carissimi. Returning to France, Charpentier worked for several years with PIERRE CORNEILLE and MOLIÈRE, composing musical pieces for their theatrical productions (*Malade imaginaire*, 1673). An intense rivalry also developed between Charpentier and JEAN-BAPTISTE LULLY, who dominated French court music as the official composer of LOUIS XIV. From 1679, Charpentier composed music for the private masses of the dauphin and, in the 1680s, was also composer and music director for the prince of Guise. In 1698, he became music director of the royal chapel—Saint-Chapelle—in Paris, where he served, too, in that capacity at the church of St. Louis. Among Charpentier's major compositions are *Leçons et Répons de ténèbres* (for Port-Royal) and a *Te Deum* for soloists, choir, organ, and orchestra, featuring festive trumpets. His secular works include three tragedies set to music (*Celse martyr*, 1687; *David et Jonathas*, 1688; and *Médée*, 1691). Charpentier's full collection of compositions is vast, with more than 500 pieces. Seen as a precursor to Handel, he is considered one of the greatest French composers of the 17th century.

## Charrat, Janine (1924–   )
*dancer, teacher, ballet director*

Born in Grenoble, Jeanne Charrat danced as the partner to ROLAND PETIT (1941) and produced her first choreography for the Ballets des Champs-Élysées, *Jeu de cartes* (music by Igor Stravinsky, 1945). After having danced the ballets of SERGE LIFAR, she performed the *Concerto no. 3* by Serges Prokofiev at the Opéra-Comique (1947), then, with the Ballets de Paris, *La Femme et son ombre* and *Adame Miroir* (music by DARIUS MILHAUD, story by JEAN GENET, 1948). Charrat founded her own company, Les Ballets Janine Charrat, in 1952, for which

she choreographed and produced *Le Massacre des Amazons* 1952), *Les Algues* (1953), and *La Valse* (music by MAURICE RAVEL, 1955). In 1957, this ballet troupe became the Ballets de France, where Charrat has in particular performed *Électre* (1960) and *Les Sept Péchés capitaux* (1961).

## Châtelet, Émilie le Tonnelier de Breteuil, marquise de (1706–1749)
*writer*

Born in Paris, Émilie le Tonnelier de Breteuil, marquise of Châtelet, was brilliant and well-educated, especially in mathematics (her tutor was the noted mathematician PIERRE DE MAUPERTUIS) and the sciences. She wrote various treatises (*Institutions de physique*, 1740; a translation of Isaac Newton's *Principia*, 1742) and was highly regarded as a unique woman and scholar. Émilie du Châtelet had a long sentimental and intellectual liaison with VOLTAIRE, whom she welcomed to her château at Cirey. She also inspired the poet JEAN-FRANÇOIS DE SAINT-LAMBERT.

## Chartier, Alain (ca. 1385–ca. 1433)
*diplomat, writer*

Born in Bayeux and educated at the University of Paris, Alain Chartier, who served both CHARLES VI and the dauphin (later CHARLES VII) as secretary during the 14th century, enjoyed a great literary renown (court pages, at the time, for example, were required to memorize some of his verses). The author of courtly (*La belle Dame sans mercy*, 1424) and patriotic poems, he was above all the first French political orator, with his *Quadrilogue invectif* (1422), a debate in prose among four allegorical characters representing the French social classes in an appeal for unity and in support of the king. Chartier wrote this after the great French defeat at Agincourt.

## Chartres

An important site in French history, Chartres (the ancient *Carnutes* of the Gauls) is located in the north central area of the country and is the capital of the department of Eure-et-Loir. It is also an agricultural and manufacturing center, producing machinery, electrical equipment, and fertilizer. The town consists of upper and lower sections connected by steep streets. The high point of Chartres is its world-famous Cathedral of Notre-Dame (12th–13th centuries), noted for its beautiful spires and stained-glass windows and its Renaissance choir screen. Its north tower, known as the "Clocher neuf," was erected in 1513. An ancient settlement (it was the capital of the Gauls and a sacred center of Druidism), Chartres was burned by the Normans in 858 and became a possession of the French kings in 1286. Besieged by HUGUENOT forces during the religious wars of the 16th century, it was the site of HENRY IV's coronation in 1594. The House of Orléans was given the title dukes of Chartres by King LOUIS XIV. The city was occupied by German forces in 1870 and 1871, and again during WORLD WAR II from 1940 to 1944. The population is presently about 28,000.

## Chasseloup-Laubat, François, marquis de (1754–1833)
*military engineer*
Born in Saint-Sornin, Saintonge, François, marquis de of Chasseloup-Laubat, joined the REVOLUTION OF 1789 as a military officer and was promoted to the rank of general in 1797. He took part in the campaigns of the FIRST EMPIRE and built numerous fortification works, in particular in Piedmont. Rallying to LOUIS XVIII, he was made a peer of France.

## Chasseloup-Laubat, Justin (1805–1873)
*political figure*
Born in Alessandria, Piedmont, Justin Chasseloup-Laubat was the son of FRANÇOIS DE CHASSELOUP-LAUBAT. Elected as a deputy in 1837, he was named minister of the navy, then held the portfolio of the navy and the colonies under the SECOND EMPIRE (1860–67). He helped to reorganize the French war fleet and supported the annexation of Cochin-China and the establishment of a French protectorate in Cambodia (1863). Minister-president of the Council of State in 1869, he was elected deputy to the National Assembly (1871) after the fall of NAPOLÉON III.

## Chateaubriand, François-René, viscount de (1768–1848)
*writer*
Born in Saint-Malo, in Brittany, where he also spent his youth, Chateaubriand entered the army in 1786, but soon saw his military career interrupted by the REVOLUTION OF 1789. He left France and traveled to the United States (1791), then returned to fight on the side of the royalist forces. Later (1793), he escaped to England. After publishing his *Essai sur les révolutions* (1797), he returned to France (1800) and dedicated himself to writing. He also found favor with NAPOLÉON I, who gave him a diplomatic post. He resigned and turned against Napoléon, however, after the execution of the duke of Enghien (1804). After the RESTORATION, Chateaubriand was made a peer of France (1815) and ambassador to Britain (1822). He represented France at the Congress of Verona and served as foreign minister (1823–24). As one of the most important French writers of the early 19th century, Chateaubriand introduced the European audience to the new and exotic life of North America, especially its rustic scenery and the Native American culture. His other writings emphasized introspection and are often pessimistic, as exemplified by his novels *Atala* (1801) and *René* (1802). In his famous *Génie du christianisme* (1802), he presented his view that Christianity was the moral and aesthetic superior to other religions. This thesis had a strong effect on the religious and literary culture of the period. Chateaubriand's other writings, often further defenses of Christianity or descriptions of his travels in America, include *Les Martyrs* (1809). Hostile to Orléanism, Chateaubriand wrote works that are also political in outlook, as in his *Études historiques* (1831). He left an account of his life, *Mémoires d'outre-tombe*, published posthumously in 1849. Chateaubriand was elected to the ACADÉMIE FRANÇAISE in 1811.

## Chatelain, Eugène-Pierre-Amabile (1829–1902)
*political figure, writer*
Born in Paris, Eugène-Pierre-Amabile Chatelain, who worked as a chaser, took part in the REVOLUTION OF 1848 and was deported in 1851 because of

his opposition to NAPOLÉON III. Affiliated with the First International, he was a member of the Central Republican Committee of the arrondissements (zones) of Paris after September 4, 1870 (see COMMUNE) and took part in the fighting of the Bloody Week of May 22–28, 1871. Taking refuge in Jersey and then London, he was condemned to deportation for contempt of court (1874). After the amnesty of 1880 Chatelain became the editor of the revue *Le Coup de feu*. He is also the author of several collections of poems.

## Chassériau, Théodore  (1819–1856)
*painter, engraver*

Born in Sainte-Barbe-de-Samana, Santo Domingo, Théodore Chassériau studied between the ages of 11 and 15 in Paris with JEAN INGRES. In works like *Vénus marine* (1838) and *Suzanne au bain* (1840), he expressed a languorous sensuality and created an original female type. If the lines of his figures are in the style of Ingres, the treatment of color is inspired by that of EUGÈNE DELACROIX. But the "classical" austerity of *Portrait de Lacordaire* (1840) and that of his two sisters (1843) gives witness to another aspect of Chassériau's temperament. After 1840, he broke with his master, Ingres. His painting then evolved; the choice of subjects (Shakespeare, the East, especially after a visit to ALGERIA in 1846) and his taste for bright hues reveal a romantic spirit. Chassériau also contributed to the revival of mural painting in France (church of Saint-Meni, 1841–45; Assizes Court, 1844–48). The artists GUSTAVE MOREAU and PUVIS DE CHAVANNES were influenced by Chassériau.

## Chaumette, Pierre-Gaspard (1763–1794)
*revolutionary*

Born in Nevers, Pierre-Gaspard Chaumette, during the REVOLUTION OF 1789, became a member of the CORDELIER'S CLUB and legal adviser for the insurrectionist Commune of Paris (1792). He took part in the SEPTEMBER MASSACRES (1792) and the movement for de-Christianization and the installation of the cult and the Festival of Reason (late 1793). He proposed democratic policies for the nation and the teaching of public health. Chaumette was arrested and guillotined with the Hébertist extremists.

See also HÉBERT, JACQUES-RENÉ.

## Chautemps, Camille  (1885–1963)
*political figure*

Born in Paris, Camille Chautemps, who as a deputy had represented the Radical-Socialist Party (1919), served several times as minister (1924 to 1926), and was premier in February 1930 and again from November 1933 to January 1934, when he had to resign after the STAVISKY affair. He succeeded LÉON BLUM as head of the government (June 1937–January 1938, and January–March 1938), and tried to modify the policies of the POPULAR FRONT. For this reason, he disappointed the Socialists and the Communists. Recalled to the government shortly after the Anschluss between Nazi Germany and Austria (April 1938) he became a member of the cabinet of PAUL REYNAUD (1940) but left when Marshal PHILIPPE PÉTAIN formed a government in July of that year.

## Chauvelin, François-Bernard, marquis de  (1766–1832)
*political figure*

Born in Paris, François-Bernard, marquis de Chauvelin, although being of the nobility and serving as master of the wardrobe of king LOUIS XVI, came to support the REVOLUTION OF 1789. Named ambassador to London (1792), he tried to gain the neutrality of Great Britain but was asked to leave his post after the occupation of Belgium and Holland by the revolutionary French armies and the execution of Louis XVI. On his return to France, he was imprisoned during the TERROR until 9 Thermidor (July 27, 1794). A member of the Tribunal of 18 Brumaire (November 9, 1799), and a prefect in 1804, he was elected a deputy during the Restoration and took his place with the liberal opposition.

## Chénier, André  (1762–1794)
*poet*

Regarded as one of the most important French classical poets and as a forerunner of the romantics, André Chénier was born in Constantinople, where his father was serving as French consul general. In the salon of his mother, who was of Greek origin, he became absorbed with Hellenic culture and also was inspired by the works of the Enlightenment philosophers. At first a poet of the liberal REVOLUTION OF 1789, he became outraged by the excesses of the TERROR and, as his writings antagonized MAXIMILIEN ROBESPIERRE, he was guillotined. His work (posthumous, 1819) caused a sensation among the romantic youths of the period who saw in it "a new poety, about to be born" (VICTOR HUGO). In *L'Invention*, Chénier defends his poetic art, while in *Idylles ou Bucoliques*, he seeks to rediscover the physical beauty and musicality of the works of antiquity. In two long poems, "L'Hermès" and "L'Amérique," epics of science and progress, he turns to more modern inspirations. A lyrical poet, in *Élegées* and *Pièces à Fanny*, he sang of love and themes dear to the poets of the 18th century. Finally, in *Iambes*, Chénier expresses, in strong and incisive satire, his distain and hatred of the political excesses of the day.

## Chénier, Marie-Joseph (1764–1811)
*political figure and writer*

The brother of ANDRÉ CHÉNIER, Marie-Joseph Chénier, like his brother, was born in Constantinople, where their father was French consul general. Leaving a military career to dedicate himself to literature, Chénier composed lyrical poems (*Poésies*, posthumous, 1844) and the words to a number of patriotic songs (notably "Le Chant du depart"). Animated by an ardent revolutionary spirit, his tragic plays had, at the time, considerable success: *Charles IX ou l'École des rois* (1788, performed by TALMA in 1789), *Henri VIII* (1791), and *Caius Gracchus* (1792). A member of the JACOBIN CLUB, then the Convention, the Council of Five Hundred, and, finally, the Tribunate, and the author of numerous epigrams and moral and political satires, he was the object of attack from his literary rivals and his political enemies. Accused of having betrayed his brother, he was forced to pen a vigorous defense: *Épitre sur la calonnie* (1797). A supporter of Napoléon Bonaparte (see NAPOLÉON I), and named during the FIRST EMPIRE inspector-general of the university, after 1806 he fell somewhat into disfavor; his *Tibère*, for example, could not be performed until after his death. Meanwhile, Chénier devoted himself to his major work, *Tableau de la littérature française de 1789 à 1808* (posthumous, 1816), in which he defends the neoclassical school of literature.

## Chéret, Jules (1836–1932)
*poster artist*

Born in Paris, Jules Chéret, as a designer, revolutionized the look of poster art. He began in 1855 by producing posters in black and white, then in three colors (*Orphée aux Enfers*, 1888). In London from 1859 to 1866, he studied the industrial processes of producing lithographs in several colors. His posters (more than a thousand) became part of the art of the late 19th and early 20th centuries, and are characterized by their vivacity, lightness, and effervescence (*La Saxoléine*, 1891). Whereas formerly, posters were literal and unimaginative, with the illustrations subordinate to the text, in Chéret's works, the illustrations are dominant and he departs from literal depiction. Specializing in theatrical posters, he portrayed can-can dancers and stage personalities with minimal use of text. Chéret's influence spread quickly and inspired such artist as HENRI DE TOULOUSE-LAUTREC and PIERRE BONNARD.

## Chevalier, Maurice (1888–1972)
*singer, entertainer, actor*

Born in Paris, Maurice Chevalier began his career at the age of 13, singing in cafés. There, he quickly developed the style and characteristics (smoking a cigarette and wearing a straw hat with an air of insouciance) that would become his famous and widely imitated trademark. At age 21, Chevalier was a featured performer at the Folies-Bergère and, after serving in WORLD WAR I, returned to the operetta and music hall stages of Paris and London. Since 1914, he had also appeared in some minor films of the director Max Linder, but his cinematographic career reached its apogee when, between 1928 and 1935, he made 12 films for Hollywood. These included *The Love Parade* (1929), *The Smiling Lieutenant* (1931), *Love Me Tonight* (1932), *The Merry Widow* (1934), and *Folies Bergère* (1935). Among later films were *Gigi* (1958), *Can-Can* (1960), and *Fanny* (1961). Chevalier returned to France in 1935 and remained in seclusion during WORLD WAR II. Later, he toured various parts of the world with his one-man shows, the last of these being in Paris in 1968. Chevalier's charm and style are also evident in a number of brief memoirs that he wrote in his later years.

## Chevalier, Michel (1806–1879)
*economist*

Born in Limoges, Michel Chevalier was initially an enthusiastic convert to Saint-Simonism (see SAINT-SIMON, HENRI DE). He then became a proponent of free trade and contributed, with the English economist Richard Cobden, to the signing of a free-trade agreement between France and Great Britain (1860).

## Chevreul, Eugène (1786–1889)
*chemist*

Born in Paris, Eugène Chevreul was one of the first to become interested in organic chemistry. He discovered the role of fatty acids and was the author of the theory of saponification (1823), in which, through a thorough investigation of their chemical nature, he concluded that simple fats do not combine with alkali to form soap, but are first decomposed to form fatty acids or glycerol. His studies led to changes in the composition of soaps and candles during their manufacture. Director of dyes at the GOBELIN factories, he was interested in colored substances and developed a theory of colors and a chromatic schema that inspired impressionist painters. Chevreul was named to the Academy of Sciences in 1826.

## Chevreuse, Marie de Rohan-Montbazon, duchess de (1600–1679)
*nobility*

The wife of the duke de Luynes, then of Claude de Lorraine, duke de Chevreuse, Marie de Rohan-Montbazon, duchess de Chevreuse, who was an intimate of Queen ANNE OF AUSTRIA, led a life filled with intrigues and amorous adventures. The discovery of a plot against Cardinal RICHELIEU, for example, cut short the life of her young lover Chalais (an ancestor of TALLEYRAND). And she attempted, during one of her exiles, to bring Charles IV, duke of Lorraine, to whom she was mistress, into a conspiracy against court figures. Returning to France after the death of LOUIS XIII, she took part in the "Importants" plot (1643), comprised mainly of those of Richelieu's victims who, hoping to gain revenge after the death of Louis XIII, planned to eliminate Cardinal MAZARIN. Just before marrying the marquis de Laigues, she also was involved in the FRONDE. The duchess de Chevreuse had an influence on François, duke de La Rochefoucauld, with whom she had an intimate friendship.

## Chiappe, Jean (1878–1940)
*administrator, political figure*

Born in Ajaccio, Corsica, Jean Chiappe, as prefect of police, was known for his sympathies regarding the right-wing leagues. He was transferred to Morocco by Premier ÉDOUARD DALADIER (February 3, 1934), an assignment that he refused and that led to the riot of February 6 of that year. In 1940, the VICHY government named him high commissioner in Syria. But the plane that he was taking to go there was shot down in the eastern Mediterranean by the Royal Air Force of Great Britain, and he was killed.

## Chirac, Jacques (b. 1932–   )
*statesman, president*

Born in Paris, Jacques Chirac studied at the Institut d'études politiques (1956) and, after military service, at the École nationale d'administration (1959). In 1962, he joined the staff of GEORGES POMPIDOU and, in 1972, became minister of agriculture and rural development. In 1974, when VALÉRY GISCARD D'ESTAING became president, Chirac was appointed prime minister. He also became secretary-general of the conservative UDR (Union des Démocrates pour la République), but after continuing differences with Giscard, he resigned as premier in 1976. He then became president of the UDR, which he reorganized into the neo-Gaullist party, RPR (Rassemblement pour la République). In 1977, he was elected mayor of Paris, a position he held until 1995. Chirac lost his first run for president of France to FRANÇOIS MITTERRAND in 1981, but in 1986 he

Jacques Chirac *(Embassy of France)*

the influence of Mme DE POMPADOUR. He served as ambassador to Rome (1754) and secretary of state for foreign affairs (1758). In that capacity, combined with his authority over the naval and war ministries (his reform and buildup of the army and navy contributed later to French success in the American War of Independence), Choiseul controlled France's foreign policy for several years. His power increased during the Seven Years' War (1756–63). Although it was a disastrous conflict for France, he softened the defeats by negotiating the "Family Compact" alliance with Spain (1761) and directing the peace talks (1763). After the war, he restored France's power through an ambitious reform of the army and navy. In 1768, he acquired CORSICA for France and strengthened ties with Austria in 1770 by arranging the marriage of the dauphin (later LOUIS XVI) and Princess MARIE ANTOINETTE. But Choiseul's foreign policy did have some weaknesses, as in his failure to prevent Russian expansion into Poland. After 1764, with the death of Mme de Pompadour and the rise of Mme DU BARRY, whose enmity he incurred, Choiseul's position was weakened. In 1770, when his policies threatened to provoke another war with England, LOUIS XV dismissed him. He did not play an active political role after this.

was appointed prime minister under the policy of agreement known as "cohabitation." In 1998, he lost again to Mitterrand in the presidential election, but would win that office in the 1995 vote by 53 percent. As president, Chirac focused on domestic issues, such as unemployment, taxes, reform of the educational system, and development of a volunteer army. In foreign policy, he continued Mitterrand's move toward European integration and a single currency, and stood for an independent and leading role for France and Europe in international affairs.

## Choiseul, Étienne-François, duke de (1719–1785)
*statesman*
Born in Lorraine, Étienne-François, duke of Choiseul rose to power during the reign of LOUIS XV through

## Chopin, Frédéric (1810–1849)
*Polish-French composer*
Born in Zelazowa-Wola, near Warsaw, to a Polish mother and a French father, Frédéric Chopin, who some consider the greatest composer of music for piano, was a prodigy who published his first composition in 1817 and gave his first concert as a piano virtuoso in 1829. Chopin, who greatly influenced Franz Liszt, Richard Wagner, and CLAUDE DEBUSSY, has among his many compositions 55 mazurkas, 27 études, 25 préludes, 19 nocturnes, 13 polonaises, four waltzes, three piano sonatas, as well as piano concertos in E minor and F minor, and 17 songs. (Sources differ as to the number of each type of musical composition and may include works on which Chopin collaborated with other composers.)

Settling in PARIS, Chopin had a liaison with the writer GEORGE SAND and enjoyed a long friendship with EUGÈNE DELACROIX. Through his works, Chopin

Frédéric Chopin *(Library of Congress)*

is admired for his originality, and no one else was so exclusively dedicated to the piano.

## Chouannerie, La

A guerrilla movement of the 18th century in which French peasants fought against the REVOLUTION OF 1789. It developed especially after 1793 in the northern area of the Loire, in Brittany principally, Normandy, Maine, and Anjou. The movement was born at the same time as the Vendean War (see VENDÉE, WAR OF THE )and for the same reasons: economic difficulties, antireligious revolutionary policies, and the decree conscripting 300,000 men issued by the Convention (February 24, 1793). Led usually by individuals from the region—count of BOURMONT, LOUIS DE FROTTÉ, the marquis de LA ROUËRIE, the COTTEREAU brothers, PIERRE CORMATINE—the Chouans (the term is derived from an old Breton word for

"owl") spread imperceptibly throughout the countryside aided by a network of agents and sympathizers. Their principal objective was to destroy civil authority, intercept convoys, and assassinate revolutionary leaders in their regions. La Chouannerie was combated rigorously by General HOCHE, who pacified areas in the west by 1795, but it remained, nonetheless, until the beginning of the FIRST EMPIRE.

## Chrétien, Jean-Loup  (1938–   )
*astronaut*
Born in La Rochelle, Jean-Loup Chrétien, a military officer, was the first Frenchman to travel in space. He spent a week on board the Soviet space station *Saliout* 7 in 1962. In 1988, Chrétien spent a month in the orbital station *Mir.*

## Christine of France  (1606–1663)
*royalty*
Born in Paris, Christine of France was the daughter of King HENRY IV and Queen MARIE DE' MEDICI. She married Victor-Amadeus I (1619) and became duchess of Savoy. Upon the death of her husband, she assumed the regency for her son, Charles-Emmanuel II, and vigorously resisted French ambitions toward her duchy.

## Christine de Pisan  (ca. 1363–ca. 1430)
*writer, humanist*
Born in Venice, Italy, Christine de Pisan spent her childhood at the court of King CHARLES V of France and later wrote his biography (*Le Livre des faits et bonnes moeurs du roi Charles,* 1405). Widowed at age 25, she began writing to support her family. Using poetic, historical, and moral genres, she wrote in defense of women, especially against the satires of JEAN DE MEUNG (*Épître au dieu d'amour,* 1399). She wrote especially in that sense to counter the attitudes of courtly love of the period. De Pisan's abundant writings include *Seulette m'a mon douz ami laissiée* (ca. 1389); *La Mutacion de Fortune* (1403); *Le Livre de la cité des Dames* (1405), an account of women's heroic deeds; *La vision de Christine* (1405), her autobiography; and *Le Dictié en l'honneur de la Pucelle* (1429), in honor of JOAN OF ARC.

## Christophe, Henry (1767–1820)
*king of northern Haiti*

Born a slave on the island of Grenada, Henry Christophe at first served in the French army and then became one of the principal insurgent generals during the Haitian war of liberation. After the death of JEAN-JACQUES DESSALINES, he became his successor (1807) and established a dictatorship, proclaiming himself king (1811). His kingdom, which constituted the north of the country, tried to control the Republic led by ALEXANDRE in the south, without success. Christophe died in his magnificent palace of Sans-Souci which he built not far from Cap-Haïtien. His kingdom did not survive him. His life inspired *La Tragédie du roi Christophe* (1963) by AIMÉ CÉSAIRE.

## Civil Constitition of the Clergy

Decreed at the time of the REVOLUTION OF 1789 (July 12, 1790) by a vote of the National Constituent Assembly and sanctioned by the king (August 24), this constitution, of liberal and Gallican inspiration (see GALLICANISM), sought to organize the Catholic Church in France along the lines of the local civil administration (dioceses to correspond to each of the 83 departments; election of bishops and pastors). While waiting for canonical sanctioning of this constitution, the Constituent Assembly imposed on all priests an oath of fidelity to the Constitution of the kingdom (November 1790). From then on, Catholic priests would be divided into juring (constitutional) and non-juring (refractory) clerics. The formal condemnation of the Civil Constitution of the Clergy by Pope Pius VI (April 1790) began a schism within the French Church. This religious crisis was also a political one, as the majority of the refractory priests supported the counter-revolution; some emigrated, many were massacred during the TERROR.

See also GRÉGOIRE, HENRI.

## Citroën, André (1878–1935)
*engineer, industrialist*

Born in Paris, André Citroën built his first factory in 1915 at quai de Javel, where he produced 55,000 artillery shells per day. After World War I (1919), he undertook there the mass production of automobiles, becoming the first in France to do so. He built new factories at Saint-Ouen, Clichy, and Levallois—suburbs of Paris—and began using the assembly line process. Always interested in transportation (taxis, automobiles), he introduced the first cruising Citroën models (Croisière noire, 1924–25; Croisière jaune, 1931–32). In 1934, Citroën introduced his famous automobile with forward traction.

## Cixous, Hélène (1937– )
*writer, feminist*

Born in Oran, Algeria, Hélène Cixous is a graduate of the University of Paris and, as a specialist on James Joyce and English literature, directs the Center for Women's Studies (Centre d'études féminines), which she founded. She is also a professor at the Collège international de philosophie. Her abundant writings include novels and works of fiction: *Dedans* (1969), *Souffles* (1975), *Le Livre de Prométhéa* (1983), *L'Ange au secret* (1991); essays: *Un K. incompréhensible: Pierre Goldman* (1975), *Entre l'écriture* (1986); plays: *L'Indiade* (produced in 1987 by ARIANE MNOUCHKINE), works for the Théâtre du Soleil troupe with whom she has regularly collaborated; and histories: *L'Histoire (qu'on ne connaîtra jamais)*, 1944. A leading French feminist, Cixous has developed a complex concept of human sexuality, affirming that each human expresses masculinity and femininity, and based her work as a writer in a critical relationship with society. One gets a sense of these ideas in the Groupe information-prison, created with MICHEL FOUCAULT (1971), or in her play *La Ville parjure* (1994), where, in the tradition of ancient Greek tragedies, she treats blood contaminated with the AIDS virus as a metaphor for a defect in the system of justice, and as a metaphor for societal ills.

## Clair, René (1898–1981)
*film director*

Born René Chomette in Paris, René Clair, as he is known, demonstrated even in his early films a sense of inventive rhythm and insolent humor that became his trademark (*Paris qui dort*, 1924; *Entr'acte*, 1924; *Un chapeau de paille d'Italie*, 1928;

*Les Deux Timides,* 1929). After a very good debut in talking films (*Sous les toits de Paris,* 1930; *Le Million,* 1931; *Quatorze Juillet,* 1933), his reputation was enhanced. He worked in the United States (*I Married a Witch,* 1942) and, returning to France, continued with successful films (*Le silence est d'or,* 1947; *Les Grands Manoeuvres,* 1955). Clair also penned a collection of short stories, *Jeux du hazard* (1976). He was elected to the ACADÉMIE FRANÇAISE in 1960.

## Claudel, Camille (1864–1943)
*sculptor*

The sister of the writer PAUL CLAUDEL and an artistic collaborator with AUGUSTE RODIN, Camille Claudel was born in Fère-en-Tardenois, Aisne. In 1884, she was apprenticed to Rodin and soon became his assistant and his companion. Her early works (*L'Abandon,* 1888; *La Valse,* 1893; *Les Bavardes,* 1897; and *L'Âge mûr,* 1899) show both his influence and her sensitivity and lyricism. Her portrait of *Rodin* is probably her best-known work; her later sculptures are more classical in conception. She concentrated mainly on portraits of tableaux of nude figures, often with allegorical subject matter. Claudel received an important government commission in 1893 and continued to exhibit regularly until 1913, when she was institutionalized for an emotional disorder.

## Claudel, Paul (1868–1955)
*writer, poet, diplomat*

Born in Villeneuve-sur-Fère, Aisne, Paul Claudel was of a provincial bourgeois background. Early influences on him were the scientific, naturalistic, and materialistic ideas of the late 19th century. It was at Notre-Dame Cathedral in Paris (December 25, 1886) that he said he had a revelation of the Catholic faith. Certainly, his volumes of poetry, plays, religious prose, travel writing, and literary criticism often expressed his ardent Roman Catholicism. His early works are influenced also by STÉPHANE MALLARMÉ (*Tête d'or,* 1890; *La Ville,* 1893). Claudel studied for a diplomatic career that began in 1893 with an assignment to the United States, where he wrote *L'Échange* (1895). From 1895 to 1909, he was posted in the Far East, which also enriched his literary experiences. Returning to Europe, he served successively as French consul in Prague, Frankfurt, and Hamburg, until he left Germany in 1914. He subsequently was a minister plenipotentiary in Rio de Janeiro, then in Copenhagen, then was named French ambassador to Japan (1921), the United States (1927), and Belgium (1933–36). During these periods he wrote *L'Otage* (1911), *L'Annonce faite à Marie* (1912), *Le Pain dur* (1914), *Le Père humilié* (1916), and *Le Soulier de satin* (1929). Claudel frequently used themes relating to spiritual conflict and the salvation of the soul, and he was, in many ways, influenced, as noted, by the symbolists, Richard Wagner, and Friedrich Nietzsche, as well as the philosophies of the Far East. These multiple influences would convince him also to equate poetry with action. Other of Claudel's works include *Présence et Prophétie* (1942), *L'Apocalypse* (1952), and a translation of Aeschylus's *Oresteia* (1916). His correspondence with ANDRÉ GIDE (1899–1926) was published in 1952. Claudel was elected to the ACADÉMIE FRANÇAISE in 1946.

## Clemenceau, Georges (1841–1929)
*political figure*

Born in the Vendée at Mouilleron-en-Pareds, Georges Clemenceau was trained as a physician but took up a political career in 1870, just after the fall of the SECOND EMPIRE. He became mayor of the 18th arrondissement (Montmartre) of PARIS and also a Radical deputy to the National Assembly in 1871. By 1876, he was the leader of the Left in the assembly, where, after his opposition to the rightist policies of EDME MAC-MAHON, he contributed also to the fall of a number of ministers (LÉON GAMBETTA, 1882; JULES FERRY, 1885), earning him the title of "tombeur de ministeries" ("feller of ministries") and later, "Tigre" (Tiger). After having supported the candidacy of GEORGES BOULANGER for minister of war, Clemenceau soon denounced his attempts at a monarchist revival. But being compromised himself in the PANAMA AFFAIR, and accused of being an agent of Great Britain, Clemenceau was defeated in the election of 1893. His support of Captain ALFRED DREYFUS (ÉMILE ZOLA's *J'Accuse* was published in Clemenceau's newspaper *L'Aurore* [1898]) brought him back to politics. A senator in 1902, he was named president of the Council and minister of the interior in 1906. Clemenceau pursued a policy of separation of church and state but was hostile to some social movements, and he used military force to break up a miner's strike in Pas-de-Calais (1909), earning him the enmity of the Socialists. Chosen premier in that year, his ministry soon fell and he again became a senator. Returning to the opposition, he founded the newspaper *L'Homme libre* (1913), in which he denounced the German threat and the inefficiency of the French military. Suppressed at the beginning of WORLD WAR I, it soon reappeared under the name *L'Homme enchaîné*. In 1917 during WORLD WAR I, Clemenceau was called by RAYMOND POINCARÉ to lead the government and restore the national confidence with a struggle against defeatism. Despite opposition, he made General FERDINAND FOCH a marshal of France and rallied the country for an all-out victory effort. After the war, Clemenceau presided over the Paris Peace Conference and negotiated the TREATY OF VERSAILLES (1919). Known as "le Père la Victoire," Clemenceau was defeated in the presidential election of 1920 because of his hostility to factions on both sides of parliament. He spent much of the remainder of his life traveling (in particular in the United States) and writing. Clemenceau was elected to the ACADÉMIE FRANÇAISE in 1918.

## Cloots, Jean-Baptiste du Val-de-Grâce, baron de (1755–1794)

*revolutionary*

Of Prussian origin, Jean-Baptiste du Val-de-Grâce, baron de Cloots, who would later be known as Anacharis, was born in Gnadenthal, near Clives. He came to Paris in 1776, where he contributed to the *Encyclopédie* of DENIS DIDEROT and, in 1789, became a supporter of the REVOLUTION OF 1789. He styled himself "orator of the human race" and a "citizen of humanity," and was a member of the Jacobin Club, where he stood out because of his extreme revolutionary views. A deputy to the Convention (1792), he joined the Hébertists and played an active role in the de-Christianization movement (late 1793) and in the establishment of the cult of Reason. Shortly after the denunciation

of a foreign conspiracy by FABRE D'EGLANTINE (October 1793), Cloots was arrested and guillotined with the Hébertists (March 24, 1794).

## Clouet, François (ca. 1515–1572)

*painter*

Born in Tours around 1515, François Clouet, a painter of the French Renaissance, was the son of JEAN CLOUET and is also known by that name. He developed his talent in his father's workshop, became painter to the king in 1541, and perhaps traveled to Italy around 1549–50. Like his father, whose style he imitated, he produced many drawings. The model's faces there are portrayed with gentleness yet serenity and a sense of animation (*La Reine Marguerite enfant; Catherine de Médicis*). Few of his paintings, however, have survived, except some portraits (*Pierre Quthe*, 1562; *La Duchesse de Bouillon; Jeanne d'Albret; Portrait équestré de François I*). Attributed to Clouet is *Le Bain de Diane*. The theme, the form and shapes, and the elegant character of his poses reflect his ties with the mannerism of the Fontainebleau school. He also painted a *Dame au bain,* which seems to be the prototype of a series that doubtlessly was produced in his studio up to the beginning of the 17th century.

## Clouet, Jean (ca. 1485–1541)

*painter, miniaturist*

Renowned for his royal portraits, Jean Clouet (or Janet Clouet as he is also known), an important French Renaissance artist, was of Flemish origin. He settled in Tours in 1515 and became painter to the king, FRANCIS I. He painted religious subjects (these painting have disappeared) and produced cartoons for tapestries. Attributed to him are also a series of eight miniatures, the *Preux de Marignon*, and several painted portraits: *François I en costume d'apparat* (ca. 1520–30), *Le Dauphin François, Guillaume Budé*, and *L'Inconnu avec un livre de Petrarque*. His style, characterized by minute attention to detail and delicacy of line, is not without comparison to that of Hans Holbein, but it is also a tribute to the art of the miniaturist. There is his series of a hundred drawings, portraits done according to nature with black and red chalk and heightened color, distinguished by an extreme sharpness of features, which are a testimony to the success of this style at the Valois court. Janet Clouet was widely imitated and his genre continued into the 17th century, thanks to several artists of that period.

## Cocteau, Jean (1889–1963)
*writer*

A leading and influential French writer, poet, novelist, dramatist, designer, painter, and filmmaker, Jean Cocteau was born in Maisons-Laffitte, near Paris. He was a poor student who early dropped out of school, but at age 16, he met the actor Édouard de Max, who launched his career as a poet. Cocteau gave a reading of his work in 1908 and his first volume of verse, *La lampe d'Aladin,* which appeared the next year, quickly established him as an important writer. Eventually, Cocteau's versatility, unconventionality, and enormous output in virtually all artistic and literary fields brought him international acclaim. Despite this, he insisted that he was essentially a poet and that all of his work was poetry. As a leading member of the surrealist movement, he would also have great influence on the work of many others. Cultivating the friendship of many diverse individuals, Cocteau soon broadened his views and areas of productivity. In 1909, he met the impresario Sergey Diaghilev, who encouraged him to create ballet scenarios. During WORLD WAR I, Cocteau served as an ambulance driver and, during that period, met GUILLAUME APPOLINAIRE, Pablo Picasso, Amedeo Modigliani, and many other writers and artists with whom he later collaborated or who influenced his work. He was also inspired by the writings of STÉPHANE MALLARMÉ and ARTHUR RIMBAUD. His first novels were *Le Potomak* (1913), *Thomas l'Imposteur* (1922), and *Le Grand Écart* (1923). In 1923, he became addicted to opium after the tragic death of his companion, Raymond Radiquet. He described his recovery in *Opium: journal d'un désintoxication* (1930). During his recovery he produced other major works, including the dramas *Orphée* (1926), based on his favorite Greek myth, and *La machine infernale* (1934), and a novel, *Les enfants terribles* (1929), and his first film, *Le sang d'un poète* (1930). His films, most of which he wrote and directed, were instrumental in bringing surrealism

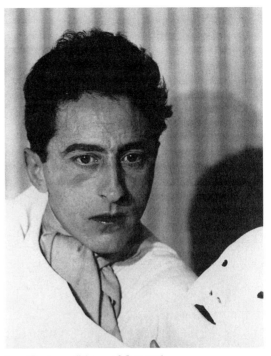

Jean Cocteau *(Library of Congress)*

to French cinema. A number of them, in particular *La belle et la bête* (1945), *Orphée* (1950), *Les enfants terribles* (1950), and *Le testiment d'Orphée* (1959), are regarded as modern classics. He was elected to the ADADÉMIE FRANÇAISE in 1955.

## Coeur, Jacques (ca. 1395–1456)
*merchant, banker*

Born in Bourges around 1395, Jacques Coeur was a merchant who worked to develop French commercial relations with Spain, Italy, and the Levant, and established bank branches at Avignon, LYON, Limoges, Rouen, PARIS, and Bourges. He engaged in a variety of business and trading activities (banking, exchange, mining, precious metals, spices, and cloth). A creditor and banker to King CHARLES VII, he held other official posts and contributed to the reform and strengthening of the nation's currency and the development and stabilization of its economy. He was sent on various diplomatic missions and subsidized the reconquest of Normandy (1449). Much envied because of his immense wealth, he was arrested for embezzlement but escaped from prison after three years. One of the most successful businessmen of his age, Coeur built a sumptuous palace at Bouges. He died while commanding a papal fleet against the Turks in the eastern Mediterranean.

## Cohn-Bendit, Daniel (1945–   )
*student leader, anarchist*

Born in Montauban, Daniel Cohn-Bendit, whose parents had emigrated from Germany, where he later received part of his education, spent his youth in Paris. In May 1968, he led the student uprisings there, culminating in the takeover of the university at Nanterre. These events, reflecting the political, economic, and cultural malaise of the period, were followed by labor union strikes and, finally, the electoral circumstances that culminated in President CHARLES DE GAULLE's leaving power. Cohn-Bendit later lived and taught in Frankfurt, Germany, where he joined the German Green Party (1984) and served as a deputy mayor (1989). In 1994, he helped to form the European Green Party (GUPE).

## Colbert, Jean-Baptiste (1619–1683)
*statesman*

Known for his efforts to reorganize France's economic structure so as to increase revenue and reach self-sufficiency, Jean-Baptiste Colbert was born in Reims, the son of a drapery merchant. He obtained employment at age 19 in the Ministry of War and, in 1651, was hired by King LOUIS XIV's chief minister, CARDINAL MAZARIN, to handle his personal finances. Before he died, Mazarin recommended Colbert to the king for preferment. As adviser to the monarch, Colbert prosecuted the superintendent of finance for embezzlement and, in doing so, gained the king's confidence. After serving as intendant of finances, superintendent of royal buildings, arts and manufactures, and secretary of state to the royal household and the navy, in 1665 Colbert was made comptroller general of finance. Proceeding to reconstruct industry and

commerce along the lines of mercantilism, he began a large-scale overhaul of state finances while continuing to prosecute officials for graft and corruption. With government control of industry and protective tariffs and navigation laws, Colbert organized state colonization and trading companies, established model factories, including Gobelins, Beauvais, and La Savonnerie, and extended French trade and industry. The name "Colbertism" is given to his mercantile fiscal and economic system, and he created the East and West India Companies based on the Dutch model. As secretary of state for naval affairs, Colbert directed the building of a network of roads and canals, the fortification of seaports, strengthening of the navy, and the writing of marine and colonial legal codes. His policies can be considered, however, to have inhibited agriculture and the free development of industry in France. Colbert gave positions to his own family, made brilliant marriages for his daughters, and was the head of a clan that continuously opposed that of the marquis de LOUVOIS, the LE TELLIER family. As a patron of the arts and culture (with CHARLES LE BRUN), he also founded several learned academies (Inscriptions, 1663; Sciences, 1666) and societies (now part of the Institut de France), established the Paris Observatory (1667), and sponsored many public works. Colbert was named to the ACADÉMIE FRANÇAISE in 1667.

## Colet, Louise Revoil (1810–1876)
*writer*

Born in Aix-en-Provence, Louise Revoil Colet, or Mme Colet as she is known, had initial success with her literary career with a collection of poems (*Fleurs du Midi*, 1836), then composed numerous works in verse, of which *Le Poème de la femme* (*La Paysanne*, 1883; *La Servante*, 1854; *La Religieuse*, 1856), along with various prose works, assured her a sometimes scandalous notoriety (*Les Coeurs brisés*, 1843; *Lui*, 1860—which evokes the liaison of GEORGE SAND and ALFRED DE MUSSET, 1860). Between 1842 and 1859, Mme Colet's salon was frequented by the leading personalities of the literary and political world, with some of whom she had numerous and often stormy relations (VICTOR COUSIN, ABEL VILLEMAIN, ALFRED DE MUSSET, ALFRED DE VIGNY, and GUS-

TAVE FLAUBERT). These relationships are discussed in her voluminous correspondence.

## Colette, Sidonie-Gabrielle (1873–1954)
*novelist*

Known by her pen name of Colette, Sidonie-Gabrielle Colette, whose novels probed deeply into the life of the senses and into human relationships, was born in Saint-Sauveur-en-Puisaye, Burgundy. She spent her early years there (described in *Claudine à l'école*, 1906), then, in 1893, married the first of her three husbands, the writer Henri Gauthier-Villars, and moved with him to Paris. Although they collaborated on four novels (the *Claudine* series, 1900–03), using his pen name (Willy), these frank semiautobiographical works were largely written by Colette. Divorced in 1906, she spent a few years satisfying her theatrical ambitions by appearing on the music-hall stage. Then, writing under the name Colette, she began to establish her reputation as the leading female novelist in France. This reputation was firmly established with the

Colette *(Library of Congress)*

publication of *Chéri* (1920), a bittersweet story of an older woman's love affair with a selfish youth. Colette had also married again, to Henri de Jouvenel, and with him collaborated on the *Matin* series (*Les Heures longues*, 1917; *Dans la foule*, 1918; *Aventures quotidiennes*, 1924). Among Colette's other highly praised novels are *Retraite sentimentale* (1907), *Les Vrilles de la vigne* (1908), *L'Ingénue libertine* (1909), *Mitsou* (1919), *Le Blé en herbe* (1923), and *Sido* (1924), about her mother. She also explores her love of nature and domestic animals. Her later important works include *Julie de Carneilhan* (1941), *L'Étoile Vesper* (1947), and *Le Fanal bleu* (1949). Colette was also a journalist, playwright, and critic, and her own works, strong in characterization and drama, have frequently been adapted for the stage and screen. In 1945, she became the first woman elected to the Académie Goncourt.

## Coligny, Gaspard de Châtillon, seigneur de (1519–1572)
*admiral, Protestant leader*

Born in Châtillon-sur-Loing, Gaspard de Châtillon, seigneur de Coligny was born into the French aristocracy and was raised in the Catholic faith. Early in his career, he found favor with the royal court, being named admiral and governor of PICARDY. He was responsible for a number of military victories (Renty), until he was captured by the Spanish at Saint-Quentin (1557). Shortly after, he converted to Protestantism and, with the prince of CONDÉ, became the principal leader of the HUGUENOTS. In 1560, CATHERINE DE' MEDICI conspired with Coligny against the Catholic GUISE family. The plot failed, but Coligny, in the Treaty of Amboise (1563), gained some degree of religious freedom for the Protestants. He played a major role in the subsequent religious wars (Battles of Jarnac and Moncontour, devastation of GUYENNE and LANGUEDOC), which finally ended in 1570 with the Treaty of Saint Germain. Catherine, however, alarmed by Coligny's influence over her young son, CHARLES IX and over Henri de Navarre (later HENRY IV), plotted with the Guises and prompted her son to agree to the massacre of August 24, 1572 (see SAINT BARTHOLOMEW'S DAY MASSACRE), in which Coligny and thousands of other Protestants were slain.

## Coligny, Odet de (1517–1571)
*religious figure*

The brother of Admiral de COLIGNY, Odet de Coligny, known as the cardinal de Coligny, was born at Châtillon-sur-Loing. He converted to Protestantism and helped to bring his brother with him into the Reformed religion. He died in exile in England, poisoned.

## Coligny d'Andelot, François de (1521–1569)
*military figure*

The brother of the admiral and cardinal de COLIGNY, François de Coligny d'Andelot, like them, converted to Protestantism. A soldier, he distinguished himself at the Battles of Dreux (1562) and Jarnac (1569).

See also RELIGION, WARS OF.

## Collège de France

An establishment of higher education, located in Paris, near the SORBONNE, the Collège de France was founded by FRANCIS I in 1530 at the request of GUILLAUME BUDÉ as the Collège des trois langues (Latin, Greek, Hebrew). It then became the Collège royal de France, and then the Collège de France during the Restoration. In 1852, it was placed under the Ministry of Public Instruction (today, National Education), while remaining administratively independent of the university of Paris. Endowed presently with 52 chairs (including a European chair created in 1989), the Collège de France offers free teaching that is considered universal and does not grant diplomas. The professors, who are appointed by the government, plan the curriculum. Research laboratories are attached to the teaching units. The buildings that house the college were built under LOUIS XIV (1610) by JEAN-FRANÇOIS CHALGRIN and were notably enlarged after 1930.

## Colleyre, Roger de (ca. 1470–ca. 1540)
*poet, actor*

Born around 1470 in either Paris or Auxerre, Roger de Colleyre was a member of the Confrérie des Enfants-sans-Soucy, for which he wrote farces and comedies. His *Œuvres, contenant diverses matières pleines et passé temps* were put together in 1536. De Colleyre is the creator of the carefree and free-spirited character Roger Bontemps.

## Collot d'Herbois, Jean-Marie (1750–1796)
*political figure, writer*

Born in Paris, Jean-Marie Collot d'Herbois was an actor and writer of comedies, as well as the author of the *Almanach du père Gérard* (1791), considered, at the time of the REVOLUTION OF 1789, to be the best patriotic almanac of the JACOBIN CLUB. He joined the insurrectionist Commune of Paris after August 10, 1792, and took part in the September Massacres (1792). A MONTAGNARD deputy to the Convention and a collaborator with the Committee of Public Safety in September 1793, he was concerned mostly with domestic issues. An organizer and supporter of the TERROR, with JOSEPH FOUCHÉ he directed the suppression of the royalist federalist uprising in LYON (November 1793). Opposed, however, to MAXIMILIEN ROBESPIERRE, he contributed, as president of the Convention, to his downfall. Nonetheless, Collot d'Herbois was deported in April 1795 (after the Days of 12 and 13 Germinal Year III), with several other Montagnard deputies to Guyana, where he eventually died.

## Colombe, Michel (ca. 1430–ca. 1512)
*sculptor*

Born in Tours around 1430, Michel Colombe was one of the most famous French Renaissance sculptors of the late 15th century, although, his work has now in part disappeared. He worked for LOUIS XI (ca. 1462) and the duke of Bourbon (1484–88), then, in Tours in 1501, he entered the service of ANNE OF BRITTANY and sculpted the tomb of duke François II and Marguerite de Foix (1502–07), after a model by JEAN PERREAL. On the corners of this work, the statues of the four Virtues are noted for their fullness and suppleness of design, elegance of line, and serenity of expression. Colombe's art, one of restrained realism, makes the transition between the phase of Gothic "détente" and that of the French Renaissance. It is characterized especially by the adoption of decorative Italian motifs (*Relief de saint Georges,* carved for the château at Gaillon).

## Combes, Émile (1835–1921)

*political figure*

Born in Rocquecourbe, Tarn, Émile Combes earned a doctorate in theology, then left his studies for the priesthood to study medicine, which he also quit to enter politics. Joining the Radical Party, he served successively as president of the Senate (1894–95), minister of public instruction (1895–96), and president of the Council after PIERRE WALDECK-ROUSSEAU (1902–05). Combes's anticlerical policies and legislation (including the law of 1904 ending teaching and instruction by religious orders and congregations) culminated in the Law of Separation (1905), which effectively ended the CONCORDAT OF 1801 and achieved the separation of church and state in France. Combes himself resigned in January 1905 after the affaire des FICHES scandal.

## Comédie-Française

The Comédie-Française, the national theater of France, is a cooperative theater company, organized in two groups, the "pensionnaires," probationary salaried members, and the "sociétaires," full members with governing powers. The Comédie-Française was founded in 1680 in PARIS by a decree of LOUIS XIV that joined together the Hôtel Guénégaud (formerly the troupe de Molière) and the Hôtel de Bourgogne acting companies. The Comédie-Française was dissolved in 1792 but reorganized in 1812 by a decree of NAPOLÉON I and relocated to the Théâtre-Français (the present Théâtre-Richelieu). The reopening of the Théâtre du Vieux-Colombier in 1993, then the inauguration in 1996 of the Studio-Théâtre, gave the Comédie-Française two additional locations. Throughout its history, the Comédie-Française, the home of many of France's most outstanding stage artists, has always been respected for its high-quality repertoire, production, and dramatic training.

## Communauté, La

La Communauté was an association created by the Constitution of the FIFTH REPUBLIC (1958) that brought together the French Republic, the overseas departments and territories, and various African states, which heretofore had been under French administration. La Communauté had a brief existence, lasting only until 1960, the date on which nearly all the African states became completely independent. Nevertheless, they remained linked to France through various military and economic accords.

## Commune, La

La Commune, or the Paris Commune as it is also known, is the name applied to the revolutionary government installed by the people of PARIS during the FRANCO-PRUSSIAN WAR (1870–71). After the surrender of the emperor NAPOLÉON III at Sedan in September 1870, the republicans of Paris staged a bloodless revolution and proclaimed the THIRD REPUBLIC. In January 1871, the city capitulated to the Germans and, in February, a National Assembly, which was to meet at VERSAILLES, was elected by the rest of the country. The monarchist majority in the assembly favored the peace terms dictated by Bismarck, but the radical Republicans and the Socialists in Paris supported the continuation of the war. On March 18, the Parisians led an uprising against the national government. A proletarian dictatorship was established in Paris and, on March 28, the Commune of 1871 was proclaimed. A majority of its members, the Communards, were followers of the revolutionary LOUIS BLANQUI, who was then being held prisoner at Versailles by LOUIS THIERS, who was leading the government there. The other Communards supported the socialist model of PIERRE PROUDHON or were members of the International Workingmen's Association and were close to a form of Marxism. The Commune proposed or adopted several measures favorable to the workers, but before these could be implemented, the National Assembly sent troops from Versailles to suppress the revolt. After occupying strategic points in the city's outlying areas, the assembly's troops bombarded Paris and civil war began. These troops entered the city on May 21 and a week of carnage and savagery (May 21–28), known as "Bloody Week," ensued. More than 20,000 Communards were slaughtered and, in turn, the Communards burned a number of public buildings and shot a number of hostages. The Commune fell on May 28. Considered to be the first proletarian revolution, the Commune of 1871 was disavowed at the time by the bourgeoisie, even the most liberal, while it was viewed favorably by members of the Left and the extreme Left.

## Commune of Paris

The Commune of Paris (to be distinguished from LA COMMUNE, or the PARIS COMMUNE OF 1871), was the radical government of Paris during the REVOLUTION OF 1789. Set up in the Hôtel de Ville after the fall of the BASTILLE, the Commune was in power from 1789 to 1795 and had successively as its mayors JEAN-SYLVAIN BAILLY and PÉTION DE VILLENEUVE. In August 1792, an insurrectional Commune replaced the legal one and, superceded by the Committee of Public Safety during the TERROR, the commune of Paris was finally replaced by two commissions set up under the DIRECTORY government in 1795.

See also SANS-CULOTTES; SEPTEMBER MASSACRES; FEDERALIST INSURRECTIONS.

## Communist Party, French (Parti communiste français [PCF])

The Parti communiste français (PCF), or French Communist Party, was founded in 1920 under the name Section française de l'Internationale communiste (SFIC), becoming officially the Parti communiste—section française de l'Internationale communiste in 1922. The rallying of the socialists during WORLD WAR I to the policies of the Union sacrée of RAYMOND POINCARÉ (cabinet of RENÉ VIVIANI, August–September 1914), the failure of the Second International, the consequences of the long and imprudent war (especially in 1917 when mutinies and strikes occurred), and finally the victory of the Russian Revolution and the coming to power of the Bolsheviks led to a severe crisis within the socialist movement (see SOCIALIST PARTY). After the founding by Lenin of the Third International (1919), the SFIO at first decided to leave the Second International (Congress of Strasbourg, February 1920); then the majority of its representatives favored joining the Communist International and formed the SFIC. Accepting the Marxist-Leninist theory of the proletarian revolution and supporting the Bolsheviks, the Communists would develop a tightly structured party (local cells, departmen-

tal sections and federations, central committee in which the political bureau formed the executive body, general secretariat), whose official organ was *L'HUMANITÉ*. After initial success in the 1924 elections (26 seats), the French Communist Party lost in later electoral contests (1928, 1932), abandoning its relative isolation to fight against the efforts of the extreme right and rising fascism. The PCF (and its secretary-general MAURICE THOREZ) allied with the SFIO (1934), leading to the formation of the Front populaire, and, after the elections of 1936, supported the government of LÉON BLUM and worked for the reunification of the CONFÉDÉRATION GÉNÉRALE DU TRAVAIL (CGT). On the eve of WORLD WAR II, the refusal of the party to disavow the German-Soviet non-aggression pact (August 1939) provoked a strong reaction (dissolution of communist organizations by the cabinet of ÉDOUARD DALADIER). During the Occupation, the communists played a determining role in the RESISTANCE (Francs-Tireurs et Partisans français [FTPF], clandestine press). During the unifying of the resistance network, the Communists were represented on the Conseil national de la Résistance and in the provisional government in Algiers. With Liberation, the PCF became one of the leading French political groups and had great success in the 1945 elections. Entering the government along with representatives of the Mouvement républicain populaire (MRP) and the socialists (tripartism, 1945–47), the Communist ministers, who had fought for nationalization of the major businesses and industries, the creation of Social Security, and an increase in the public sector, were excluded from the cabinet formed in May 1947 by PAUL RAMADIER because of the cold war between East and West and France's pro-American foreign policy (which supported the Marshall Plan and NATO). Becoming the opposition party, the PCF benefited from a relatively stable electoral base (a little more than 20 percent of the vote), in spite of anticommunist campaigns and the defection of a part of the French Left after the Soviet interventions in Hungary and Czechoslovakia (1968). The PCF then tried after 1965 to end its isolation and in 1972 signed with the Socialist Party a common governmental agreement. After the breakup of this leftist coalition (Union de la gauche) in 1978, and the election of FRANÇOIS MITTERRAND (1981), the PCF had approximately 700,000 members (secretary-generals: WALDECK-ROCHET, then GEORGES MARCHAIS) and four ministers in the government (1981–84). Since 1981, there has been a continuous and serious electoral decline. Besides internal dissent, the PCF had to confront the additional problem of the collapse of communism in eastern Europe and its own identity crisis, which led it to abandon in 1994 (national secretary: ROBERT HUE) the organizational principle of democratic centrism.

## Concini, Concino  (1575–1617)
### (Marshal d'Ancre)
*Italian adventurer, political figure*
Born in Florence, Italy, Concino Concini, who was known also as Marshal d'Ancre, took advantage of the favoritism shown to his wife, LEONORA GALIGAÏ, by Queen MARIE DE' MEDICI to rapidly advance his political career, especially after the death of King HENRY IV. Named marquis of Ancre and marshal of France, he tyrannically and greedily exercised his political powers. The young king, LOUIS XIII, who despised Concini, aided by CHARLES D'ALBERT DE LUYNES, had him arrested and then killed.

## Concordat of 1801
The Concordat (a treaty between the Holy See and a state) of 1801 was concluded between Napoléon Bonaparte (see NAPOLÉON I) and Pope Pius VII. It forced the resignation of émigré bishops and reorganized Catholicism in France. Napoléon, however, unilaterally imposed an addendum to the treaty, known as the Organic Articles, which for all practical purposes restored the control of the state over the church (see GALLICANISM), and were never accepted by the Holy See.

## Concordat of Bologna
The Concordat (a treaty between the Holy See and a state) of Bologna (1516) was an important negotiation between King FRANCIS I and Pope Leo X that superceded the Pragmatic Sanction of Bourges and recognized the supremacy of the pope's authority over the church in France but left ecclesiastical nominations, and thereby the real power, in the hands of the king.

See also GALLICANISM.

## Condé, Louis I, prince de  (1530–1569)
*nobility*
The founder of the House of Condé and a HUGUENOT leader, Louis I, prince de Condé, the youngest son of CHARLES III DE BOURBON, duke de Vendôme, and brother of Antoine de Bourbon, the father of HENRY IV, was born in Vendôme. Raised as a Protestant, he fought in the French War (1551–57) against Charles V, the Holy Roman Emperor. In 1560, Condé led the Protestant conspiracy against FRANCIS II of France and was condemned to death. A change in policy, however, at the accession of CHARLES IX, saved his life, and the following year he was appointed governor of PICARDY. Shortly after, the religious wars between French Catholics and Protestants began, and Condé took command of the Huguenot army. He was defeated at the Battle of Dreux (1562), however, and later at Jarnac (1569), after which he was assassinated at the instigation of the duke of Anjou, the future HENRY III.

## Condé, Louis II de Bourbon, prince de (1621–1686)
### (the Grand Condé)
*leader of anti-royalist revolt known as the Fronde*
The French general who led the nobles against the Crown in the last revolt of the FRONDE, Louis II de Bourbon, prince de Condé (known for his military achievements as "le Grand Condé"), was born in Paris, the great-grandson of LOUIS I, PRINCE DE CONDÉ. Until the death of his father, he was known as the duke of Enghien. In 1641, he married a niece of Cardinal RICHELIEU. Trained from youth for a military career, Condé was given command of the French armies in the north at age 22 and, in 1643, during the THIRTY YEARS' WAR, won a great victory over the Spanish at Rocroi. In 1645, he defeated an army of the Holy Roman Empire at Nordlingen, Germany. He later (1646) defeated the Spanish at

Dunkerque and again (1648) at Lens. In 1646, he succeeded his father as prince de Condé. His military fame and growing power, as lord of Burgundy, Berry, and sections of Lorraine, however, was of concern to Cardinal MAZARIN, the king's minister. In 1648, during the Fronde, Condé led the royal forces, but his brother, Armand de Bourbon, prince de Conti, and his brother-in-law, the duke de Longueville, supported the Frondeurs. Condé himself soon wavered between the two opposing forces and, after the truce of 1649, joined the Fronde. In 1656, these three nobles were arrested but were freed the following year after a new uprising by the Frondeurs. Condé, thereafter, fought on the side of Spain against the French Crown until he was defeated (1658) by Henri de la Tour d'Auvergne, viscount de Turenne, near Dunkerque. A year later, Condé was pardoned by King LOUIS XIV, then he retired. He later reentered the service of the king and, in 1668, conquered Franche-Comté and subsequently fought in the Dutch wars. He was made commander of the French army in 1675, the year of his last battle, fought against the army of the Holy Roman Empire on the Rhine. Retiring finally to Chantilly, Condé in his later years surrounded himself with writers and poets, including JEAN RACINE. His funeral oration was given by JACQUES BÉNIGNE BOSSUET.

## Condillac, Étienne Bonnot de (1715–1780)
*philosopher*

Born in Grenoble, Étienne Bonnot de Condillac left the priesthood in 1740 and traveled to Paris, where he became an acquaintance of the philosophes (DENIS DIDEROT, JEAN-JACQUES ROUSSEAU) and at this time wrote his *Essai sur l'origine des connaissances humaines* (1749) and the *Traité des sensations* (1755), this latter being regarded as a decisive contribution to the science of psychology. From 1758 to 1767, Condillac was the tutor to the son of the duke of Parma. He then returned to the Abbey of Flux, where he wrote *Le Commerce et le Gouvernement considérés relativement l'un à l'autre* (1776), a treatise on political economy. The leading French advocate of the ideas of the English philosopher John Locke, Condillac argued that all human knowledge and conscious experience are derived from sensory perception. He also tried to clarify and support Locke's theory of knowledge, asserting with Locke the impossibility of innate ideas. Some of Condillac's theories were anticipated by the 16th-century thinker PIERRE GASSENDI. Condillac, whose writings also were precursors of modern linguistic theories, was elected to the ACADÉMIE FRANÇAISE in 1768.

## Condorcet, Marie-Jean-Antoine-Nicolas de Caritat, marquis de (1743–1794)
*philosopher, mathematician, political figure*

Born in Ribemont, Marie-Jean-Antoine-Nicolas de Caritat, marquis de Condorcet was educated at the Collège de Navarre in Paris. His first work was *Essai sur le calcul intégral* (1765), followed by a study, *Problème des trois corps* (1767). He became a mem-

Marquis de Condorcet *(Library of Congress)*

ber of the Academy of Sciences (1769) and was chosen its permanent secretary. In 1782, he was elected to the ACADÉMIE FRANÇAISE. Condorcet's literary reputation was later assured by his *Vie de Turgot* (1786) and his *Vie de Voltaire* (1789). A disciple of FRANÇOIS QUESNAY and the physiocrats, and of ANNE ROBERT TURGOT, VOLTAIRE, and JEAN D'ALEMBERT, Condorcet edited articles on political economy for DENIS DIDEROT's *Encyclopédie* and himself wrote against the death penalty and slavery, and in support of equal rights. As a deputy to the Legislative Assembly and the Convention during the REVOLUTION OF 1789, he proposed a law for public education (1792). Arrested as a Girondin during the Terror, he wrote in prison his principal work, *Esquisse d'un tableau historique des progrès de l'esprit humain* (1794), in which he outlined the progress of humanity through nine stages, beginning with the primitive. Convinced of the indefinite development of the sciences, Condorcet also proposed a 10th stage in which, he affirmed, that through education, human perfection might be attained. Condemned to death during the terror for his moderate views, he poisoned himself in prison.

## Confédération française de l'encadrement–Confédération générale des cadres (CFE-CGC)

The Confédération française de l'encadrement –Confédération générale des cadres (CFE-CGC) is a French labor union formed in 1944 under the name Confédération générale des cadres. After 1981, it took the name Confédération française de l'encadrement. Opposed to the leveling of salaries, it seeks a greater role for workers in management as well as an improvement in wages.

## Confédération française des travailleurs chrétiens (CFTC)

The Confédération française des travailleurs chrétiens (CFTC) is a French labor union that, when formed in 1919, sought to apply Christian principles to the labor struggle. It is a member of the Confédération internationale des syndicates chrétiens (CISC, founded in 1920). In 1964, the majority of members of the CFTC renounced the sectarian orientation of the union and formed the CONFÉDÉRATION FRANÇAISE DÉMOCRATIQUE DU TRAVAIL (CFDT), while the minority (between 80,000 and 100,000 members) voted to maintain the religious aspect of the union.

## Confédération française démocratique du travail (CFDT)

The Confédération française démocratique du travail (CFDT) is a French labor union founded in 1964 by the majority of members of the CONFÉDÉRATION FRANÇAISE DES TRAVAILLEURS CHRÉTIENS (CFTC) who wished to abandon the sectarian aspect of their labor movement. Long supportive of self-management, the CFDT, which counts nearly 500,000 members and belongs to the Confédération mondiale du travail, since 1980 has given up a policy of confrontation for one of negotiation, and has evolved toward a more pragmatic and contractual policy.

## Confédération générale du travail (CGT)

The Confédération générale du travail (CGT) is a French labor union that was formed at Limoges in 1895. In 1902, it brought together various other French labor movements. Despite its Charter of Amiens (1905), affirming the independence of the labor union movement from party politics, the CGT was divided into factions with different tendencies and, until WORLD WAR I, was dominated by revolutionaries and anarchosyndicalists. In 1920, the failure of the general strike considerably reduced its membership. The anarchosyndicalist and the Socialist majority (who had joined the Communists at the Congress of Tours, 1920), separated from the CGT after their setback at the Congress of Lille (1921) and formed the CGTU (Confédération générale du travail unitaire, 1922), which adhered to the policies of the Internationale syndicale rouge (1932). Reunited at the Congress of Toulouse (1936), CGT and CGTU supported the program of the Front populaire and with the Confédération générale du patronat français signed the Matignon Accords (June 1936), which granted the 40-hour workweek and paid vacations. Dissolved by the VICHY government (1940), the CGT has been controlled, since the end of WORLD WAR II, by members with communist views. The CGT joined the Fédération syndicate mondiale, which provoked new dissensions within the labor union movement resulting in the formation of the anarcho-syndicalist Confédération nationale du travail (CNT, 1946) and the CONFÉDÉRATION GÉNÉRALE DU TRAVAIL–FORCE OUVRIÈRE (1948), a reformist union. The CGT, which is the most important main French labor union, has approximately 700,000 members (see LÉON JOUHAUX).

## Confédération générale du travail–Force ouvrière (CGT-FO)

The Confédération générale du travail–Force ouvrière (CGT-FO) was formed in 1948 by the schism within the CONFÉDÉRATION GÉNÉRALE DU TRAVAIL (CGT) caused when members opposed to the preponderant communist influence in that union left under the direction of LÉON JOUHAUX. Toward reformist tendencies, the CGT-FO has, since 1989, developed a more confrontational policy. It has a membership of approximately 700,000.

## Constant de Rebecque, Benjamin (1767–1830)
*writer, political figure*

Of Swiss origin, Benjamin Constant de Rebecque was born in Lausanne and educated at British and German universities. Hostile to Napoléon Bonaparte (see NAPOLÉON I), he spent most of the period of the Napoléon regime in exile in Germany and Switzerland, during which time he maintained an intense relationship with Mme GERMAINE DE STAËL. She would influence his famous semiautobiographical novels *Adolphe* (1816) and his unfinished *Cécile*, which was discovered only in the 20th century. As an important contributor to the development of romanticism and the psychological novel, Benjamin Constant, as he is known, in these early works reflected the romantic spirit and probed the psyche of his protagonists. He also wrote the tragic poem *Wallenstein* (1809), several journals, and a treatise on religion. After the restoration of the monarchy, he lived in Paris, where he served in the Chamber of Deputies (1819–22, 1824–30) and founded two liberal periodicals.

## Consulate

The Consulate (Consulat) was the government of France that derived from Napoléon Bonaparte's coup d'état of 18 Brumaire Year VIII (November 9, 1799) and replaced the DIRECTORY (see NAPOLÉON I). It lasted from November 10, 1799, to May 18, 1804. The Constitution of the Year VIII outlined the organization of the government and named the three consuls: Bonaparte, JEAN-JACQUES CAMBACÉRÈS, and CHARLES LEBRUN. In fact, Bonaparte, as First Consul, held all the power. During this period, Bonaparte decided to exploit the coup d'état to achieve his ambitions and, while pursuing a brilliant foreign policy, reorganized France, along semi-dictatorial lines. The Civil Code was promulgated in 1804, and the LEGION OF HONOR created in 1802. Slavery was reestablished in the colonies (1802), strikes were forbidden (1803), and the *livret*, or identity book, was required to be carried by all workers. On August 4, 1802, the First Consul was named Consul for Life, the constitution was then revised strengthening his powers at the expense of the legislative. A new state of peace abroad favored the development of trade and industry. The suppression of the opposition was matched by some measures at appeasement, especially toward the old émigrés. The general policies of the Consulate opened the way for the FIRST EMPIRE.

## Copeau, Jacques (1879–1949)
*writer, theater figure*

Born in Paris, Jacques Copeau was the founder with ANDRÉ GIDE and JEAN SCHLUMBERGER of the *Nouvelle Revue française* (1909), and soon denounced the commercialism and vulgarism of the theater. With a troop of young actors, including LOUIS JOUVET, he formed the Compagnie du Vieux-Colombier (1913). Inspired by the ideas of Gordon Craig and Stanislavski, he tried to rediscover the "laws" of true theater. The Vieux-Colombier produced, besides new interpretations of the classics, interesting works of contemporary authors, such as André Gide, and had a considerable influence on European theater. Copeau left the company in 1924 and, in the years that followed, he gained popular acclaim with a traveling acting troop. Creator of a school and an actor, Copeau was also an author and adapter. One of his last writings was his spiritual testament: *Le Théâtre populaire* (1942).

## Coquille, Guy  (1523–1603)
*jurisconsul, writer*

Born in Decize, Guy Coquille was actively involved in the political life of the period. Being a duputy to the Third Estate of the Estates General of Orléans (1560), and then to that of Blois (1576 and 1588), he was one of the editors of that body's official records. He also wrote polemical works against the Leaguers and the Ultramontanists, such as his *Dialogue sur les causes de la misère de la France* (1590). Eager, like CHARLES DUMOULIN, to unify the common law in France, he wrote in particular *Les Coutumes du pays et duché de Nivernais* (1590), dealing with public rights. His other writings, especially his two *Traités des libertés de l'Église de France* (1594), inspired the works of PIERRE PITHOU.

## Corbière, Tristan  (1845–1875)
*poet*

Born near Morlaix, Édouard-Joachim, or Tristan, Corbière, as he is known, in his youth suffered from fragile health and had to leave his studies and move to BRITTANY. He made several visits to Paris and a trip to Italy. The collection of his verses went unappreciated until PAUL VERLAINE brought them to notice, citing their author in *Poètes maudits* (1883) along with ARTHUR RIMBAUD and STÉPHANE MALLARMÉ. The poets LÉON BLOY, JORIS-KARL HUYSMANS, and JULES LAFORGUE celebrated the freedom of Corbière's imagery and his baroque tendencies, as when he evoked Brittany and its sailors ("Armor," "Gens de mer"), the sun of Naples, or his sad passion for "Marcelle."

## Corday d'Armont, Charlotte de  (1768–1793)
## (Charlotte Corday)
*revolutionary figure*

Born in Saint-Saturnin-des-Ligneries, Orne, Charlotte de Corday d'Armont was educated in a convent and was an ardent reader of classical writers such as Plutarch and Tacitus and Enlightenment thinkers like JEAN-JACQUES ROUSSEAU. Adopting the ideas of her age, she became a supporter of the REV-OLUTION OF 1789. After the proscription of the GIR-ONDINS (June 2, 1793), she joined a number of leaders of the federalist insurrection in NORMANDY in a plot to assassinate JEAN-PAUL MARAT, the member of the revolutionary government who, in her eyes, was responsible for the Reign of TERROR. Arriving in Paris in early July 1793, she gained admittance to Marat's house on the pretext of offering to disclose to him the names of several Girondins of Caen. Instead, taking a knife from the kitchen of his residence, she stabbed him in his bath, declaring "For Liberty." Captured by Marat's friends before she could escape, Charlotte Corday, as she is known, was tried by a revolutionary tribunal and executed on July 17. Despite the horror that her act evoked, she is regarded by many as a heroine of the Revolution. Her act is portrayed in a famous painting by JACQUES-LOUIS DAVID.

## Cordeliers Club  (Cordeliers, Club des)

The Club des Cordeliers, or Cordeliers Club, known also as the Société des amis des droits de l'homme, was a revolutionary club founded in April 1790, during the REVOLUTION OF 1789 by GEORGES DANTON. It counted among its members CAMILLE DESMOUS-LINS, FABRE D'EGLANTINE, LOUIS LEGENDRE, ANTOINE SANTERRE, and JEAN-PAUL MARAT and held its first meetings at the Cordelier convent (rue de l'École-de-Médicine, today the Dupuytren Museum) in Paris. It was in a great part due to the influence of the Cordeliers Club that the petition brought to the Champ-de-Mars (July 17, 1791) was made, leading to the overthrow of King LOUIS XVI. During the Convention, the club was led by the extreme revolutionaries JACQUES-RENÉ HÉBERT and his followers, the Hébertists, and became the mouthpiece for the SANS-CULOTTES, the working-class population of the *faubourgs* (Saint-Antoine and Saint-Marceau). After the elimination of the Hébertists (April 1794), the Cordelier's Club was suppressed and its remaining members joined the JACOBINS.

## Cormatin, Pierre Dezoteux, baron de  (ca. 1750–1812)
*counterrevolutionary*

Born in Paris, Pierre Dezoteux, baron de Cormatin served as a military aide-de-camp during the course of the American War of Independence, and then as a member of the Constitutional Guard of King LOUIS XVI (1791). He emigrated in 1792, and, as one of the leaders of LA CHOUANNERIE, took part in several émigré military expeditions in western France. Named major general in the Royal Catholic Army, he signed the peace treaty of Mabilais (1795) with the Thermidorian Convention. Accused of having violated this treaty, Cormatin was tried before a military tribunal and imprisoned.

## Corneille, Pierre (1606–1684)
*dramatist*

Born in Rouen, the son of a government official, Pierre Corneille, one of the leading French dramatic writers of the 17th century, served as a government official but soon turned to drama and poetry as a career. His first dramatic work was a comedy, *Mélite* (1629), soon followed by a tragic comedy, *Clitandre* (1630), then by four other comedies, *La Veuve, La Galerie du palais, La Suivante,* and *La Place royale* (1631–34). Recognized by Cardinal RICHELIEU, Corneille became one of five writers who enjoyed his patronage, eventually receiving a government pension. Corneille soon published his first tragedy, *Médée* (1635), then *L'Illusion comique* (1636), a fantasylike work in which he gave a marvelous description of the world of the theater. This was soon followed by *Le Cid* (1636), which provoked a controversy over the form of classic drama, finally settled only by the intervention of the ACADÉMIE FRANÇAISE at the orders of Richelieu. Quite prolific as a playwright in the following years, Corneille published *Horace* (1640), *Cinna* (1641), and *Polyeucte* (1642), all set in ancient Rome. These important plays, along with *Le Cid,* created the standards for French tragedy, to be further developed by his younger contemporary JEAN RACINE. Also a master of comedy, Corneille's *Le Menteur* (1643) is considered the best of that genre before those of MOLIÈRE. Like the earlier *Mélite,* it is a comedy of manners, a form Corneille himself originated. In 1647, Corneille became a member of the Académie française and, with his large family, including his brother, Thomas Corneille, who was also a successful playwright, moved to Paris. Established as a major dramatist, Corneille saw his next productions—*Don*

Pierre Corneille *(Library of Congress)*

*Sanche d'Aragon* (1649), *Andromède* (1650), and *Nicomède* (1651)—well received. After his next work, *Pertharite* (1651), failed, he stopped writing for the stage for seven years. Later, with the government's encouragement, he returned to playwriting and produced a number of works, mainly tragedies (*Tite et Bérénice,* 1670, *Psyché,* with Molière, 1670; *Suréna,* 1674). Corneille also wrote several discourses on the art of drama.

## Corneille, Thomas (1625–1709)
*writer, dramatic poet*

Born in Rouen, Thomas Corneille was the younger brother of the dramatist PIERRE CORNEILLE. His abundant works are very diverse: tragedies (*Timocrate,* 1656, which was the greatest success of the 17th century), tragicomedies (*Circé,* 1675), comedies (*La Devineresse,* 1679), and operas (*Bellérphon,* 1679). A contributor to *Mercure galant* (1677), Corneille wrote *Dictionnaire des terms d'arts et de sciences* (1694) and *Dictionnaire géographique et historique* (1708).

## Corneille de Lyon (ca. 1500–ca. 1574)
*portraitist*

Of Dutch origin, Corneille de Lyon, as he was known, was born in The Hague between 1500 and 1510. He came to France sometime before 1534, settled in LYON, probably around 1540, and became a naturalized French citizen in 1547. In 1551, he was commissioned to paint the portrait of King HENRY II. Corneille de Lyon preferred to do portraits in small dimensions on wood, and showing a bust of the subject in full face with a green or blue background. His works, characterized by their finesse and precise treatment and subtlety of subject, precocity of tone, and meticulous rendering of details, are in the Franco-Flemish portrait tradition and show the influence of the miniaturists. A large number of his portraits were engraved on medallions and were reproduced in the *Promptuarium iconum* (1553). Corneille de Lyon had numerous assistants and was widely imitated by other artists.

## Corot, Camille (1796–1875)
*painter, designer*

Renowned for his romantic, realistic, and proto-impressionist style of landscapes, Camille Corot was born in Paris, the son of a draper. He studied painting at the studio of Victor Bertin, then went to Italy, where he produced some of his early works (*Forum*, 1826; *Le Pont de Narni*, 1827). For the rest of his life, Corot lived in Paris, traveling throughout Europe during spring and summer. Many of his associates were from the Barbizon School of artists who, like Corot, painted landscapes while out of doors instead of in studios, as was the classical tradition. Corot's work is characterized by filmy romantic atmosphere, achieved by silvery tones and soft brushstrokes. Examples of this proto-impressionist style are versions of *Ville-d'Avray* and *Mortefontaine* (1864). He also did *La Cathédral de Chartres* (1830) and *Le Beffroi de Douai* (1871), both in a more classical style. In addition, Corot, considered the greatest French landscapist of the 19th century, produced a number of figure studies and portraits. His compositions done for the Salon, are of religious or mythological themes set in the French or Italian countryside, filled with such figures as nymphs, shepherds, and fauns. Generous to his students and friends with both his time and his money, he earned the title "Père Corot."

## Corsica (Corse)

Located in the Mediterranean Sea, Corsica is considered a territorial collectivity, or region, of France. Separated from Sardinia by the Strait of Bonifacio, the island's principal towns are Ajaccio, Bastia, Sartene, Corte, Calvi, L'Île-Rousse, Porto-Vecchio, and Bonifacio. Corsica is divided into two departments (Haute-Corse and Corse-du-Sud) and covers an area of 8,780 square kilometers. The interior is mountainous, with the highest peak at Mont Cinto (2,710 m). The west coast is indented and rocky, and the east is filled with swamps and lagoons. The largest rivers are the Golo and the Tavignano. Farming and manufacturing are the main economic activities, with grapes, olives, vegetables, citrus fruit, and wheat being cultivated. Goats and sheep are raised, and the forests, which have been depleted, produce chestnuts and cork. The island is known for its heavy undergrowth, the *maquis,* which provides natural hiding places. Other industries of the island are quarrying of marble and granite, winemaking, mining, and tourism. Corsica has an ancient history, with settlements going back to the Neolithic period. In antiquity, the Phoenicians, Greeks, and Etruscans successively occupied the island, and in 259 B.C. Corsica was conquered by the Romans. After the fifth century A.D., Corsica was ruled by the Vandals, Byzantines, Lombards, and the Moors. In the late 11th century, it became subject to the papacy, which divided it between Pisa and Genoa. Corsica remained under Genoese rule until the 18th century, when it was ceded to France (1768). The following year, NAPOLÉON I was born at the island's capital, Ajaccio. During the Napoleonic Wars, Corsica was held by the British. During WORLD WAR II, it was occupied by the Germans and Italians, but the Allies liberated it in 1943. In 1958, Corsica was controlled by elements of the rebellious OAS (see ALGERIA). In the 1970s, a movement developed to achieve greater autonomy for the island, with radical groups resorting to terrorism in an effort to gain independence. In 1982, as part of a decentralizing program, the French government created the Corsican Regional Assembly. Comprising 50 members, it controls local financial, educational, and cultural affairs. These powers were increased in 1992. Corsica has a dry and sunny climate, similar to PROVENCE. The population is around 250,000.

## *corvée*

The *corvée* in pre-Revolutionary France was a service of compulsory labor required of every villager under the age of 60 on several days during the year. It usually consisted of road making, repairs, bridge building, and, generally speaking, maintenance of communications. It was not uniformly imposed, however, and in certain areas, known as the *pays d'état*, it did not exist. In other areas, although compulsory, the *corvée* was paid labor. The *corvée* was abolished during the REVOLUTION OF 1789.

## Cottereau brothers

The Cottereau brothers were leaders of the counterrevolutionary CHOUANNERIE movement that developed first in the lower Maine region at the time of the FRENCH REVOLUTION OF 1789. They were given the name Chouans because it was customary for them to call their followers at night by hooting like an owl ("chat-huant"), and the name was then applied to all the supporters of the uprising. Pierre Cottereau (1756–94) was arrested and guillotined. Jean Cottereau (1757–94) died while fighting, as did his brother François Cottereau (1760–94). Only the last, René Cottereau (1764–1846), survived the insurrection.

## Coty, René (1882–1962)

*statesman*

Born in Le Havre and educated at the University of Caen, René Coty practiced law in his native city, where he also held a number of administrative posts. He served with distinction in WORLD WAR I, after which (1923) he was elected to his first term in the Chamber of Deputies. There, he became interested in constitutional reform. From 1935 to 1940, he served in the Senate, but after that he was not active until 1944, when General CHARLES DE GAULLE asked him to join a provisional government. As a member of the Constitutional Assembly, Coty was asked to help draft a new constitution. In 1946, after the establishment of the FOURTH REPUBLIC, he served in the National Assembly and, in 1948, in the Council of the Republic. He was elected president of France in 1953, serving until 1959. Coty supported De Gaulle's return to power and afterward served as a member of the Constitutional Council.

## Coubertin, Pierre Frédy, baron de (1863–1937)

*educator, founder of modern Olympic Games*

Born in Paris, Baron Pierre de Coubertin, the founder of the modern Olympic Games, was originally encouraged to follow a military career, but, convinced of the necessity to give an important place to physical education in the formation of the individual, he oriented himself toward the encouragement of sports. A product himself of the École libre des sciences politiques in Paris, Coubertin started to promote his ideas by publishing several articles and founding numerous sporting societies. In 1894, at a conference that brought together representatives from 14 nations, he proposed reviving the Olympic Games. Two years later, Pierre de Coubertin created the International Olympic Committee, on which he served as president until 1925. The committee organized the first Olympics (1896), which, symbolically, were held in Athens.

## Coulomb, Charles-Augustin de (1736–1806)

*physicist*

Born in Angoulême, Charles-Augustin de Coulomb served as a military engineer in the French West Indies before retiring to Blois at the time of the REVOLUTION OF 1789. A pioneer in electrical theory, he continued his research on electricity, magnetism, and friction. He invented the torsion balance (1777) to measure the force of electrical attraction and magnetism, then formulated the principle known as Coulomb's Law, governing the interaction between electrical charges. He published his treatise, *Théorie des machines simples,* in 1779, and later, during the Revolution, assisted the French government in developing a metric system of weights and measures. The unit of quantity used to measure electrical charges, the coulomb, is named for him. De Coulomb was named to the Academy of Sciences in 1781.

## Couperin, François  (1668–1733)
*composer, organist, harpsichordist*
Called "Le Grand" Couperin, François Couperin is celebrated for his musical compositions that stand at the apex of French baroque music. Born in Paris, the son and nephew of the organists there at the church of Saint-Gervais, Couperin was trained early to follow in their profession (the Couperin family would hold that position until 1826). In 1693, he became organist of the royal chapel and director of music at court. He was soon known throughout Europe. The epitome of the French baroque tradition, Couperin was also influenced by Italian works and artists such as Arcangelo Corelli. In his mature period he achieved a fusion of the French and Italian musical styles. His four volumes of harpsichord music (1713–30) are a monument of French keyboard music that influenced other great composers, such as J. S. Bach. They are groupings of short, lilting pieces, cast in dance rhythms varying from elegant to satirical to profound. His treatise, *L'Art de toucher le clavecin* (1716–17), is a major statement of 18th-century performance practices. Couperin also introduced the sonata to France, adding to this Italian genre a typically French form of ornamentation and melody. Of particular importance, too, are his collections of *Les Nations* (1726) and the 12 concerts for harpsichord and other instruments (1714, 1724). In church music are the three *Leçons de ténèbres* (1714–15) for solo voices, organ, and other instruments. Couperin's organ masses are considered among the finest examples of French baroque organ music.

## Courbet, Gustave  (1819–1877)
*painter, lithographer*
Born in Ornans, the son of farmers, Gustave Courbet in 1840 went to Paris to study art. A most

Gustave Courbet *(Library of Congress)*

influential and prolific painter, he spent much of his time copying masterpieces in the LOUVRE and was strongly influenced by THÉODORE GÉRICAULT and EUGÈNE DELACROIX. A founder, along with HONORÉ DAUMIER and JEAN-FRANÇOIS MILLET, of the school of realism, Courbet reflected the romantic influence in his early works. These include an *Odalisque* (1840), *Walpurgis Night* (1841), and self-portraits (*Self-portrait with a Black Dog,* 1842; *The Lovers in the Country,* 1844; *The Wounded Man,* 1844), in which he often presented himself in the style of a Byronic hero. He journeyed to Holland and England and, under the influence of socialist ideas, developed a popular and democratic conception of art. After the REVOLUTION OF 1848, he became a friend of PIERRE-

JOSEPH PROUDHON and CHARLES BAUDELAIRE, and an ardent champion of realism, trying in his work to reflect social realities. In this genre, he painted *After Dinner at Ornans* (1849); *The Stonebreakers* (1849); and the enormous *A Burial at Ornans* (1850). These are polemical works, evoking the daily realities of the people. Courbet also defied convention in another huge painting, *The Artist's Studio* (1855), which, he explained, was a true allegory of his life. He painted other controversial works, including *The Bathers* (1853), that was criticized because Courbet tried to liberate the nude form from the idealistic conventions of the age. From 1869 to 1870, he traveled and painted in Normandy with the American painter James Mc Neill Whistler (*The Wave*, 1869; *The Cliff at Étretat after the Storm*, 1870) then returned to Paris to give his support to the COMMUNE. Placed in charge of the city's art museums by the revolutionary government, Courbet was responsible for saving the city's treasures from looting by the mob. After the fall of the Commune, however, he was accused of allowing the destruction of the triumphal column dedicated to NAPOLÉON I in the place Vendôme and, as a result, was imprisoned and ordered to pay for its reconstruction. He fled to Vevey, Switzerland, where he continued to paint until his death.

## Courier, Paul-Louis (1772–1825)
*pamphleteer, writer*

Born in Paris, Paul-Louis Courier, who embraced humanist culture and was a translator of the ancient Greek authors (Herodotus, Longus, Lucius of Patras, and Xenophon) whose clear and elegant style he wished to imitate, resigned his officer's position to retire to his estate, Véretz, in Touraine. There, he published his PAMPHLETS against the political and religious order that had been established by the Restoration. Notable among them are *Pétition aux deux Chambres* (1816), *Lettres au rédacteur du "Censeur"* (1820), and *Simple discours* (1821). Using specific examples, he expressed, with incisiveness and irony, his support for the liberal and anticlerical bourgeoisie. He was the spokesperson especially for that class in his *Pamphlet des pamphlets* (1824). Courier was assassinated, but the accused were never punished, and the crime remained unsolved.

## Cournot, Antoine-Augustin (1801–1877)
*mathematician, economist, philosopher*

Born in Gray, Antoine-Augustin Cournot, who was not well known in his lifetime, wrote works on economics (*Recherches sur les principes mathématiques de la théorie des richesses*, 1838) that made him a precursor of the mathematical school of economic theory, later developed by such thinkers as LEON WALRAS. A specialist in probabilities (*Exposition de la théorie des chances et des probabilitiés*, 1843), Cournot formulated a probabilistic and relativistic theory of knowledge; without denying the concept of order in nature and in history, this theory gives an important place to chance, defined as the intersection of a series of independent circumstances, and proposed a classification of the sciences that recognized their irreducible nature (*Traité de l'enchaînement des idées fondamentales dans les sciences et dans l'histoire*, 1861; *Matérialisme, Vitalisme, Rationalisme*, 1875).

## Cousin, Jean (ca. 1490–ca. 1561)
*painter, sculptor, engraver*

Born in Soucy, near Sens, around 1490, Jean Cousin, who was called Le Père, was a leading artist of the Fontainebleau school. He probably produced the cartoons for the stained glass windows of the cathedral of Sens (*Les Sibylles*), as well as the cartoons for important tapestries (*Histoire de saint Mammès*). He wrote a treatise on painting, *Traité de perspective* (1560), and did illustrations for books (*Orus Apollo*, 1543). Cousin was a representative of the mannerist style of the Fontainebleau school, but few of his paintings have survived except *Charité* and *Eva prima Pandora*, which is one of the first important French paintings of a nude.

## Cousin, Victor (1792–1867)
*philosopher*

Born in Paris, Victor Cousin was professor at the École normale supérieure and at the SORBONNE, and served as minister of public instruction (1840) in the cabinet of LOUIS-ADOLPHE THIERS. In that capacity, he reorganized the system of primary education and encouraged philosophical studies at the higher levels. Influenced by other thinkers of the period, Cousin can perhaps be considered the founder of the modern philosophical school of eclecticism and of the history of philosophy. Stating that no single philosophical system is entirely correct, he combined aspects of mysticism, skepticism, idealism, and materialism into his own eclectic system of thought. He was the first to introduce into France the philosophy of G. F. W. Hegel (*Fragments de philosophie*, 1826; *Cours d'histoire de la philosophie*, 1828). Cousin was elected to the ACADÉMIE FRANÇAISE in 1830.

## Cousteau, Jacques-Yves (1910–1997)
*naval officer, oceanographer, filmmaker*
A leading figure in the field of modern oceanography, Jacques Cousteau, as he is known, was born in Saint-André-de-Cubzac and was educated at the Naval School in Brest. While serving as a naval gunnery officer, he began his underwater explorations. In 1943, with Émile Gagnan, a French engineer, Cousteau perfected the aqualung, enabling divers to stay underwater for several hours at a time. From his base on his ship, *Calypso*, he made his award-winning underwater films, including *Le Monde du silence* (1950) and *Le Monde sans soleil* (1965). He also produced several acclaimed television documentaries and film shorts. Cousteau served as director of the Oceanographic Museum in Monaco (1957–88) and was active in environmental programs, in particular those that protected the ecology of the seas and oceans of the world. He was elected to the ACADÉMIE FRANÇAISE in 1988.

## Couthon, Georges (1755–1794)
*revolutionary, political figure*
Born in Orcet, Auvergne, Georges Couthon was an attorney in Clermont-Ferrand, where he served as president of the city tribunal (1789) and gained a reputation for fairness and prudence. At the beginning of the REVOLUTION OF 1789, he was elected to the Legislative Assembly and sat with the democratic Left. Reelected to the Convention as a MONTAGNARD, he became a member of the Committee of Public Safety (July 10, 1793) and, forming a triumvirate with MAXIMILIEN ROBESPIERRE and LOUIS SAINT-JUST, took control of the government. He showed a certain moderation in the repression of

Jacques-Yves Cousteau *(Library of Congress)*

the federalist and royalist insurrection at LYON (late August–early September 1793), and could not bring himself to destroy that city completely, as was ordered by the Convention. Meanwhile, returning to Paris, he was elected president of the Legislative Assembly (December 12, 1793) and fought strongly against the Hébertists as well as the Dantonists, or Indulgents. He was also largely responsible for the Convention's adopting the Law of 22 Prairial (June 10, 1794), which reorganized the Revolutionary Tribunal by eliminating defense attorneys, witnesses, and preliminary instruction in the trials of suspects. On 9 Thermidor (July 27, 1794), Couthon was ordered arrested along with Robespierre, and was guillotined the next day.

## Couve de Murville, Maurice  (1907–1999)
*diplomat, political figure*

Born in Reims, Maurice Couve de Murville served as inspector of finance during World War II and, in that capacity, helped to rally ALGERIA to the Allies after their landing in North Africa. He was made commissioner of finances of the National Committee for French Liberation at Algiers (1943–44), then served as the provisional government's ambassador to Rome (1945), director general of political affairs in the Foreign Ministry (1944–50), ambassador to Egypt (1950–54), to Washington (1955–56), and to Bonn (1956–58), foreign minister from 1958 to 1960 (in which capacity he pursued a policy of keeping France out of NATO's military operations and Great Britain out of the European Economic Community), then minister of the economy and finance (May–July 1968). Couve de Murville, a loyal Gaullist, became premier in July 1968. He resigned in June 1969, after the departure of President CHARLES DE GAULLE. His writings include *Une Politique étrangère 1598–1969* (1971) and *Le Monde en face* (1989).

## Coypel family

This was a family of four French painters, all born in Paris. Noël Coypel (1628–1707) decorated the LOUVRE and became director of the French Academy in Rome (1622). He also decorated the Tuileries and the chapel of Les Invalides, and designated tapestries. He was elected to the ACADÉMIE FRANÇAISE in 1659. Antoine Coypel (1661–1722), the son of Noël Coypel, with whom he studied in Rome, was greatly influenced by the baroque style and was instructed by Gian Lorenzo Bernini. Antoine Coypel decorated the ceilings of the Palais Royal and the chapel at VERSAILLES, and already a favorite of the regent, in 1716 became principal painter to the king. He, too, designed tapestries for the GOBELINS factory. Influenced also by Peter Paul

Rubens and Anthony Van Dyck, his mythological paintings herald the rococo style (*Persée et Andromède*) and his works are known for their ease of technique and sense of verve (*Démocrite*, 1692; *Jeune Noir tenant une corbeille de fruits et jeune fille caressant un chien*, c. 1682). Noël-Nicolas Coypel (1690–1734), also a son of Noël Coypel, painted minor subjects in the rococo style. Charles-Antoine Coypel (1694–1752), the son of Antoine Coypel, was a painter to the king, director of the Academy of Fine Arts, and produced the illustrations for a number of works of JEAN-BAPTISTE MOLIÈRE and for Miguel Cervantes's *Don Quixote*.

## Coysevox, Antoine  (1640–1720)
*sculptor, decorator*

The principal baroque sculptor of the French court during the reign of LOUIS XIV, Antoine Coysevox was born in LYON, the son of a wood sculptor. In 1676, he became a member of the Academy of Fine Arts and was soon one of the king's preferred sculptors. The variety and abundance of his work is evident at VERSAILLES, where he worked at first under the direction of CHARLES LE BRUN. Coysevox played a large role in the decoration of the Versailles Marble Court, the Greek Gallery, and the salon de la Guerre relief, *Louis XIV terassant ses ennemis* (1688), and the Great Staircase (destroyed). For the gardens, he produced statues and groups of allegorical and mythological subjects (*La Garonne; La Dordogne; Le Vase de la guerre*). He also sculpted classic works based on themes from antiquity (*Vénus accroupie*, 1688; *La Renommée*, and *Mercure*, 1700–1702, presently at the Tuileries). His baroque style is most clearly evident in his theatrical funerary monuments for JEAN-BAPTISTE COLBERT (1685–1712), Cardinal MAZARIN (1689–93), and Le Brun. In some works (*Marie-Adélaïde de Savoie en Diane*), he heralds the rococo style. Coysevox's masterpieces are most likely his portrait busts, including 10 of Louis XIV and of Le Grand CONDÉ (1686).

## Crémieux, Gaston  (1836–1871)
*jurist, political figure*

Born in Nîmes, Gaston Crémieux was an attorney in Aix-en-Provence and, during the SECOND EMPIRE, served in the republican opposition, for which he was sentenced several times to prison. In March 1871, he tried to play a conciliatory role as president of the Departmental Commission of the Commune of MARSEILLE, but after that movement was crushed (April 4, 1871), he was condemned to death and shot.

## Crémieux, Isaac Moïse  (1796–1880)
*political figure*

Born in Nîmes, Isaac Moïse Crémieux, or Adolphe Crémieux as he is known, was an attorney, deputy for the opposition (1842), and minister of justice in the provisional government after the REVOLUTION OF 1848. Elected to the Constituent Assembly (April 1848), he sat with the Left while supporting Louis-Napoléon Bonaparte (see NAPOLÉON III) for the presidency. Reelected to the Legislative Assembly (May 1849), he took a position against the policies of the prince-president and was imprisoned after the coup d'état of December 2, 1851. A deputy for the extreme Left in 1869, he was named minister of justice in the government of National Defense after the fall of the SECOND EMPIRE and, in that capacity, helped to put forth the decree (Crémieux Decree) granting French citizenship to the Jews of ALGERIA (1870). He was also one of the founders of the Alliance israélite universelle.

## Cresson, Édith  (1934–   )
*political figure, prime minister*

The first woman to become prime minister of France, Édith Cresson was born in Boulogne-sur-Seine and educated in Paris. She served as a Socialist deputy in the National Assembly from 1981 to 1993, during which time she also served as minister of agriculture (1981–83), minister of foreign trade and tourism (1983–84), of industrial redevelopment and trade (1984–86), and of European affairs (1988–90). Chosen as the first woman prime minister of France in 1991 by FRANÇOIS MITTERRAND, whom she had staunchly supported, Cresson was known for her energy and candor. Always an outspoken and controversial figure, Édith Cresson was replaced in April 1992 by PIERRE BÉRÉGOVOY after the Socialists lost in regional elections.

## Crèvecoeur, J. Hector St. John de  (1735–1813)
## (Crèvecoeur, Michel-Guillame-Jean de)
*writer*

Born in Caen, Michel-Jean de Crèvecoeur left France to join General MONTCALM in Canada during the SEVEN YEARS' WAR (1754–63), then settled as a farmer in the colony of New York, becoming a citizen (1765). He lived in the United States until 1790, when he returned to France, remaining there until his death. Under the name Hector St. John de Crèvecoeur (Saint Johnsbury, Vermont, was named in his honor), he published, first in London, then in Paris, in translation the *Lettres d'un fermier américain* (1784), which were popular among French writers of the day. In them, he describes in detail life in the New World. He was named French consul to New York, and was acquainted with Benjamin Franklin, Thomas Jefferson, and George Washington.

## Crimean War

The Crimean War (1854–55) was a conflict between Russia and a coalition consisting of Turkey, Great Britain, France, and Sardinia that ended with the defeat of Russia and the signing of the Treaty of Paris (1856). The rival ambitions of Russia and Great Britain in the east and the pretext of the quarrel between NAPOLÉON III and Czar Nicholas I regarding the religious sites in the Holy Land, mixed with the Eastern Question, were the causes of this war. In response to the refusal of the Turkish sultan to recognize the czar's protectorate over Orthodox Christians in the Ottoman Empire, Russia occupied the Moldavian principalities and destroyed a Turkish fleet at Sinope (1853), thus provoking the Franco-British alliance with Turkey and the intervention in the Crimea. The allied powers landed at Eupatoria (September 14, 1854); led by Marshal SAINT-ARNAUD and Lord Raglan, they defeated the Russians at Alma (September 20) and besieged Sevastopol for a year. Meanwhile, the Franco-British fleet destroyed the fortress of Bomarsund in the Baltic (1854), while Odessa, on the Black Sea, was bombarded. The campaign, marked by the battles of Balaklava, Inkerman, and Tchernaia, continued with the victorious assault on

Malakoff (September 1855), which led to the fall of Sevastopol. The Crimean War, in which a number of French military figures, including Generals MAC-MAHON and CANROBERT, served with distinction, helped to consolidate the SECOND EMPIRE and brought a number of social reforms to Russia under Czar Alexander II, who began his reign in 1855.

## Cros, Charles  (1842–1888)
*poet and inventor*

Charles Cros, who independently invented sound recording, was born in Fabrezan, Aude. Self-taught, he became interested in Oriental languages (Sanskrit and Hebrew), then in mechanical sciences and physics, and carried on his own scientific studies while pursuing a literary career. Cros discovered, independently of LOUIS DUCOS DU HAURON, the trichromium process of color photography (1869), as well as an apparatus that he called a paleophone, which preceded Thomas Edison's invention of the phonograph (the Académie Charles Cros annually honors his memory with an award for that year's best recordings). Cros also frequented the bohemian literary world (with PAUL VERLAINE, VILLIERS DE L'ISLE-ADAM, and others), and composed a lyric work that for a long time remained unappreciated. Behind the mask of a whimsical writer, expert in humourous monologues (*Le Hareng saur; Le Bilboquet; L'Obsession*), he was also a poet of the absurd and of solitude, as in *Le Coffret de santal* (1873), much praised by Verlaine, and of a long poem, *Le Fleuve* (1874). *Le Collier de griffes* was published by his son in 1908.

## Cujas, Jacques  (1520–1590)
*jurist*

Born in Toulouse, Jacques Cujas dedicated himself to the study of law and taught at Toulouse (1547), Bourges (1555), and Valence (1567), inspiring his students, including PIERRE PITHOU. Favored by CHARLES IX and HENRY III, he remained neutral during the WARS OF RELIGION, dedicating himself to his writings (*Tractatus ad Africanum, Recitationes sollemnes, Observationum et emendationum libri XXVII*, from 1556 on: the last eight volumes being published by Pithou). Considered the most illustrious represen-

tative of the historic school, founded by A. Alciat, he worked on the exegesis of Latin legal texts (restoration of the Justinian Code).

## Curie, Marie Sklowdowska  (1867–1934)
*physicist and Nobel laureate*

Of Polish origin (born in Warsaw), Marie Sklowdowska continued her studies in Paris at the SORBONNE, where she graduated at the top of her class in physics and mathematics. In 1894, she met the French chemist PIERRE CURIE, whom she married the following year. Beginning in 1896, they worked together on radioactivity (to which she gave the name), building on the work of HENRI BECQUEREL and the German physicist Wilhelm Roentgen. In 1898, after searching for the source of radioactivity, the Curies announced the discovery of the elements polonium and radium. In 1906, after the death of Pierre Curie in a road accident, Marie Curie took over his post at the Sorbonne, becoming also the first woman to teach there. In 1910, she collaborated with the French chemist André Debierne to isolate pure radium metal. Later (1914), the University of Paris built the Institut du radium (now the Institut Curie) to facilitate their further research. During WORLD WAR I, Curie helped to equip ambulances with X-ray equipment and drove them to the front lines. The International Red Cross made her chief of the Radiological Service, and she and her colleagues at the Institut du radium held courses instructing medics and doctors in the use of this new technique. Continued exposure to radium would, however, eventually cause her health to deteriorate and, after some years of illness, she died of its effects. Her remains were transferred to the Panthéon in 1995. Marie Curie received the Nobel Prize in physics along with her husband and Henri Becquerel in 1903, and the Nobel Prize in chemistry in 1911.

## Curie, Pierre  (1859–1906)
*physicist and Nobel laureate*

Born in Paris, Pierre Curie studied physics at the university there and, with his brother Paul, worked on crystallography and magnetism. Their research led to discoveries that would be of great use in the later studies of radioactivity. Other discoveries included the Curie Point—the temperature at which various metals lose their magnetic properties. In 1894, he met and soon married MARIE SKLOWDOW-SKA (CURIE) and together they worked on radioactivity. In 1898, they isolated the element radium from pitchblende—a radioactive material that also contains uranium. They later (1903) shared the Nobel Prize in physics with HENRI BECQUEREL for their work on radioactivity. In 1904, Pierre Curie was appointed professor of physics at the University of Paris and, a year later, was named to the Academy of Sciences. He was killed in 1906, when he was struck by a horse-drawn carriage. His remains were transferred to the Panthéon in 1995.

## Custine, Adam-Philippe, count de (1740–1793)
*general, deputy*

Born in Metz, Adam-Philippe, count de Custine was named field marshal after serving in the American War of Independence. In 1789, he was elected a deputy for the nobility to the Estates General and supported the REVOLUTION OF 1789. He did, however, vote with the Right on certain issues, notably on the question of the king's right to declare war and peace. Commanding the Army of the Rhine, he captured, in turn, Speyer (September 25, 1792), Worms (October 5), Mainz (October 21), and Frankfurt (October 23). After the defeat and treason of General CHARLES DUMOURIEZ (March 1793), Custine's forces were pushed back in the south by the duke of Brunswick, who retook Worms and Speyer and besieged Mainz. On his return to Paris, Custine was named general in chief of the Army of the North (May 13, 1793). But after the surrender of Condé and the loss of Mainz, he was accused of treason, condemned to death by the Revolutionary Tribunal, and guillotined.

## Custine, Astolphe, marquis de (1790–1857)
*writer*

The grandson of ADAM-PHILIPPE, COUNT OF CUSTINE, Astolphe marquis of Custine was born in Niederwiller, Meurthe. He was an associate of FRANÇOIS

RENÉ CHÂTEAUBRIAND, HONORÉ DE BALZAC, VICTOR HUGO, and HENRI STENDHAL; CHARLES BAUDELAIRE wrote of his great talent. But being gay, he was excluded by the bourgeois society of the 19th century. His novels *Aloys* (1829), *Le Monde comme il est* (1835), and *Ethel* (1839) make him one of the most renowned representatives of literary dandyism. Custine also wrote a drama, *Béatrix Cenci* (1830), as well as travel accounts (*La Russie en 1839,* 1843), and after his death were published the *Lettres à Rahel* (1870) and the *Lettres au marquis de la Grange* (1925).

## Cuvier, Georges (1769–1832)
## (Baron Cuvier)
*zoologist and paleontologist*

Born in Montbéliard, Georges, baron Cuvier, who is considered the founder of comparative anatomy, served as an instructor in France. Invited to Paris in 1795 to work at the newly reorganized Museum of Natural History, he was soon appointed professor of zoology. Cuvier formulated two anatomic principles: that of the subordination of organs, and that of the correlation of forms. He also attempted to establish a zoological classification (Vertebrata, Articulata, Radiata, and Mollusca). Regarding fossils, he proved the existence of extinct species, thereby laying the foundations for the study of paleontology. His work served too as the basis for the transformist theory of existence, while at the same time he was a supporter of the theory of catastrophism and other ideas of his associates ÉTIENNE GEOFFREY SAINT-HILAIRE and JEAN-BAPTISTE LAMARCK, with whose theories he later broke. In contrast to their evolutionary ideas, Cuvier argued that species are immutable. Cuvier's system of classification dominated natural history until the publication of Darwin's *On the Origin of the Species* in 1859. Among Cuvier's principal works are *Leçons d'anatomie comparée* (1800–1805); *Recherches sur les ossements fossiles* (1812–13); *La Règne animal distribué selon son organisation* (1816–17); *Description géologique des environs de Paris* (1822); *Discours sur les révolutions de la surface de la globe* (1825); and *Histoire naturelle de poissons* (1828). Cuvier was named to the Academy of Sciences in 1795 and to the ACADÉMIE FRANÇAISE in 1818.

## Cyrano de Bergerac, Savinien (1619–1655)
*writer*

Born in Paris, Cyrano de Bergerac as he is known, whose many duels and other escapades gained him a reputation as a romantic hero, became a soldier but had to give up that career because of a battle wound. He was perhaps the friend of MOLIÈRE and was introduced to the libertine teachings of PIERRE GASSENDI (1641), which he no doubt adopted. His attitude during the FRONDE is not well understood. If, as is believed, he had published (1649) a series of pamphlets against Cardinal MAZARIN, he did an about-face with his *Lettre contre les Frondeurs* (1652). He continued to write and produce several tragedies (*La Mort d'Agrippine,* 1653) and later a number of satirical comedies featuring prominent individuals of his day. His most famous works are two prose fantasies, *L'autre Monde ou les États et Empires de la lune* (posthumous, 1657) and *Des États et Empires du soleil* (posthumous, 1662). Both works by Cyrano de Bergerac are considered precursors to modern science fiction.

# D

## Dacier, André (1651–1722)
*scholar*

Born in Castres, André Dacier was the husband of the scholar ANNE LEFEBVRE DACIER. A convert to Catholicism (1685), he translated numerous Greek and Latin works. Dacier was elected to the ACADÉMIE FRANÇAISE in 1695 and became the king's librarian in 1708.

## Dacier, Anne Lefebvre (1647–1720)
*scholar*

Born in Preuilly-sur-Claise, Anne Lefebvre Dacier, or Mme Dacier as she is known, like her husband, ANDRÉ DACIER, was a scholar who translated the ancient Greek and Latin authors. She took part in the second debate between the Ancients and the Moderns and, as a translator of Homer's *Iliad* (1699) and *Odyssey* (1708), opposed the liberal adaptations of those works. She took a strong position in support of the Ancients in her treatise *Causes de la corruption de goût* (1714).

## Daguerre, Jacques (1789–1851)
*painter, inventor*

Jacques Daguerre, the inventor of the daguerreotype, was born in Cormeilles-en-Parisis, first worked as a scene painter for the Paris opera. After initial success in the art, he began to paint extensive panoramas, developing finally (in 1822) the diorama, which attracted much attention. In 1829 he began a collaboration with the physicist JOSEPH NIÉPCE, who was the inventor of photography. After Niépce's death, Daguerre refined the process they had been working on and eventually discovered the methods for developing (1835) and making (1837) images. In 1838 he perfected the daguerreotype. This method of photography, using metal plates, was the earliest widely practiced form of photography and led to important developments in the arts and sciences.

## Daladier, Édouard (1884–1970)
*statesman*

Born in Carpentras and educated in Paris at the École normale supérieure, Édouard Daladier taught history until 1919, when he was elected as a Radical-Socialist deputy (1919–40). Beginning in 1924, he also served several times as minister and, as premier (January–October 1933), tried to deal with the financial crisis. Returned to power in January 1934 to fight against the development of the extreme right-wing leagues after the STAVISKY affair, he demanded the resignation of the prefect of police, JEAN CHIAPPE (February 3, 1934), but had to resign himself after the demonstrations of February 6 of that year. One of the leaders of the Popular Front, Daladier was named minister of national defense (1936–37) and was called, after the fall of the second LÉON BLUM cabinet, to form a government (April 1938–March 1940). He signed the Munich Pact (September 1938), tried to halt the financial crisis and organize national defense, and took vigorous measures against the Communists after the signing of the German-Soviet Pact (1939). When Germany invaded Poland on September 1, 1939, his government declared war on Germany on September 3, 1939. Minister of war, then of foreign affairs in the cabinet of PAUL REYNAUD, Daladier was arrested by the VICHY government (after June 1940) and brought to trial at Riom (1942). Deported to Germany (1943–45), Daladier was reelected as a Radical deputy after the Liberation (1946–58). He took a position against the continuation of the war in Indochina, the constitution of the European Defense Community, and the Constitution of 1958.

## Danton, Georges-Jacques (1753–1794)
*political figure, revolutionary*

Born in Arcis-sur-Aube, Georges-Jacques Danton was a radical but pragmatic leader of the FRENCH REVOLUTION OF 1789. He began his career as a lawyer in Paris and, when the revolution began, quickly became a leader of the CORDELIERS CLUB, which he helped found, and earned a reputation as a radical orator. He was also suspected (1791) at the same time of taking bribes from royalists. Elected to a minor post in Paris, Danton achieved prominence with the fall of the monarchy in August 1792. Elected to the national Convention, he served as minister of justice (August 1792) and bore a great responsibility for the September massacres. He was soon attacked, along with JEAN-PAUL MARAT and MAXIMILIEN ROBESPIERRE, by the GIRONDINS, the moderate deputies who considered him to be a dangerous radical. Danton's efforts at reconciliation with the moderate faction failed, but the issue was ended when the Girondins fell from power in June 1793. Danton, who served too as envoy to Belgium (late 1792–early 1793) had at this point become a member of the Committee of Public Safety, but as such was unsuccessful in securing an end to the war. At the same time, Robespierre was rising as the committee's central figure. Danton was caught in the factional conflicts of 1794 and was accused of treason and corruption. Seeking to end or modify the TERROR, he sympathized along with CAMILLE DESMOULINS and others with the "Indulgents." Danton's position was further undermined by the intrigue and corruption of several of his associates, including FABRE D'ÉGLANTIN, especially in the scandal over the issue of the liquidation of the Compagnie des Indes at a loss. Danton's position in the policy of de-Christianization led Robespierre to conclude reluctantly that the government's integrity could be maintained only by removing both the extreme radicals and the Indulgents. Danton was found guilty by the Revolutionary Tribunal and executed along with most of his supporters in April 1794. He is judged both as a realist who never fully accepted the revolutionary fervor and/or an opportunist who threatened the Revolution's security.

## Darlan, François (1881–1942)
*naval officer, political figure*

Born in Nérac, François Darlan was chief of staff of the navy (1936), which he helped to modernize, and for that he requested and was given the rank of admiral of the fleet, to be on a par with the British first lord of the sea. Minister of the navy and the merchant marine in the VICHY government (June 16, 1940), he became vice president of the Council of Ministers with the portfolio of interior and foreign affairs; he was also the designated successor to Marshal PHILIPPE PÉTAIN after the dismissal of PIERRE LAVAL (December 1940). He then engaged in a policy of collaboration (meetings with Adolf Hitler, concessions to the Germans over rights to the French ports in Africa and Syria, the Darlan-Warlimont Accord, which was repudiated by the Vichy government). The Germans having demanded the recall of Laval, Darlan resigned his government posts, while remaining commander in chief of the armed forces. He was in Algiers during the Allied landing (November 8, 1942) and ordered a cease-fire. He joined the Allied side and regrouped French forces in the fight against the Axis, being recognized as commander by French military leaders in North Africa, Alexandria, the Antilles, and Dakar. His leadership, however, was repudiated by General CHARLES DE GAULLE and divisions of the metropolitan forces. In December 1942, Darlan was assassinated and replaced by General HENRI GIRAUD.

See also WORLD WAR II.

## Daudet, Alphonse (1840–1897)
*writer*

Known for his accounts of his native Provence, Alphonse Daudet, a naturalistic, semiautobiographical short story writer, was born in Nîmes. After a happy and carefree childhood, he was forced, because of his family's financial problems, to become a school supervisor at Alès (a period recalled in *La Petite Chose,* 1868), then went to Paris to try his fortune. With his first work, a verse collection, *Les Amoureuses* (1858), he gained notoriety and began to write for various newspapers. Famous for his stories (*Les Lettres de mon moulin*, 1866), he sang again of Provence in the heroic and comic trilogy of *Tartarin* (*Aventures prodigieuses de Tartarin de Tarascon* 1872; *Tartarin sur les Alpes*, 1885; and *Port-Tarascon*, 1890). Drawn to the theater, Daudet made from *Lettres de mon moulin* a drama, *L'Arlésienne* (1872), which would be immortalized by the music of GEORGES BIZET. Involved also in the writing of realistic novels, he describe contemporary mores (*Fromont jeune et Risler aîné*, 1874; *Jack*, 1876; *Le Nabab*, 1878; *Numa Roumestan*, 1881; *Sapho*, 1884), or evokes with poignancy and humor the fall of the SECOND EMPIRE (*Contes du lundi*, 1873).

## Daudet, Léon  (1868–1942)
*journalist, writer*

The son of ALPHONSE DAUDET, Léon Daudet was born in Paris and, after abandoning medical studies, went into journalism, contributing articles to *La Libre Parole* and working especially on *L'Action française* with CHARLES MAURRAS (1907). He served as a deputy from 1919 to 1924 and, affected by his son's mysterious death, held the government responsible and in turn was convicted of defamation. Imprisoned (1927), he escaped to Belgium. Pardoned, he returned to France in 1929 and published virulent editorials in *L'Action française*. Daudet left several works, including *Les Morticoles* (1894, against doctors and medical schools), *Le Monde des images* (1919, a psychopathologic study against Sigmund Freud), and others describing the intellectual and political life during the Third Republic (*Fantômes et Vivants*, 1914; *L'Entre-deux-guerres*, 1915; *Charles Maurras et son temps*, 1928). He was named to the Académie Goncourt in 1897.

## Daumier, Honoré  (1808–1879)
*painter, lithographer, caricaturist, sculptor, designer*

Born in MARSEILLE, Honoré Daumier, as a youth, moved to Paris with his family. He studied art at the Académie Suisse and, on his own, frequently visited and sketched at the LOUVRE. He began a career by drawing for advertisements and joined the staff of the comic journal *La Caricature*, where he earned a reputation for his bold and satirical political prints. One such irreverent caricature published in 1832 portrayed King LOUIS-PHILIPPE I as "Gargantua" and resulted in Daumier's imprisonment for six months. He continued, however, to defend his liberal views and ideals, and zealously continued to caricature and satirize both political figures and bourgeois society in a successful journal, LE CHARIVARI. These satirical lithographs (*Le Ventre législative*, 1834) were also supplemented by a number of statuettes that he produced on the same subjects. After the REVOLUTION OF 1848, his political caricatures and satires increased. He also produced a number of prints of scenes of daily life that also have a political and social message (*Les Juges; Le Wagon de troisième classe; Les Immigrants; Le Fardeau*). Forced by infirmities to retire to a home offered to him by CAMILLE COROT, Daumier was recognized and praised as the greatest caricaturist of his age by HONORÉ DE BALZAC, CHARLES BAUDELAIRE, and many others. His prints and lithographs, as well as his sculptures in plaster and bronze, used as models for his drawings, are highly sought after today by galleries and collectors.

## Daunou, Pierre-Claude-François  (1761–1840)
*political figure, historian*

Born in Boulogne-sur-Mer, Pierre-Claude-François Daunou, an Oratorian priest, joined the REVOLUTION OF 1789 and was elected to the Convention (1792). Of moderate political views, he opposed the execution of LOUIS XVI and the proscription of the GIRONDINS, and subsequently was imprisoned until 9 Thermidor Year II (July 17, 1794). A member of the Council of Five Hundred, then the Tribunate, he left politics because of his independent views and was named conservator of the National Archives (1807–15) and, after 1830, professor of history at the COLLÈGE DE FRANCE. He published the *Journal des savants;* a collection, *Historiens de France;* and *Histoire littéraire de la France*. His *Cours d'études historiques* appeared after his death (1842–49). Daunou was named to the Academy of Moral and Political Sciences in 1832.

## Dautry, Raoul (1880–1951)
*engineer, political figure*

Born in Montluçon, Raoul Dautry joined the administration of the French Northern Railroads and was named to the general directorship of the West-State system (1928). There, he became known for his management methods and contributed to the formation of the French national railway system (SNCF) in 1938. Minister of armaments (1939–40), he held the portfolio of reconstruction and urbanization at the end of World War II (1944–45), then was named general administrator of the Atomic Energy Commission (1946).

## David, Jacques-Louis (1748–1825)
*painter*

Known for introducing the neoclassical style in France, as well as being its leading proponent, Jacques-Louis David was born in Paris and studied at the Académie Royale under the rococo painter J. M. Vien. He won the Prix de Rome (1774) and, during a visit to Italy, was strongly influenced by the classical work of NICOLAS POUSSIN. David soon developed his own style of neoclassicism, inspired also by themes from ancient sources and using the gestures and forms of Roman sculpture. Returning to Paris, he produced a number of portraits on this motif—*Belisarius* (1780), *Andromache Mourning Hector* (1782)—and achieved a full statement of this new neoclassical style with *The Oath of the Horatii* (1784). In it his characteristic uses of ideal forms, gesture, clarity, and dramatic lighting are emphasized. With its highly moralistic and patriotic theme, this work became the principal mode for such paintings for the next two decades. He would return to this style in the allegorical *Rape of the Sabines* (1799), which he considered his greatest work. For some years after 1789, however, David, an ardent revolutionary, adapted a more realistic tone to record the contemporary scenes of the REVOLUTION OF 1789, as seen in his *Death of Marat* (1795). From 1799 to 1815, he was the official painter for NAPOLÉON I, whose reign he chronicled in such works as the huge *Consecration of Napoléon I* (1805–07, LOUVRE) and *The Distribution of the Eagles* (1810). Also throughout his career, David was a prolific portraitist. His portraits such as *Mme Récamier* (1800, Louvre) and *Pius VII* (1805) show great understanding of character as

well as technical mastery. With his career bridging the transition from 18th-century rococo to 19th-century realism, David would strongly influence such pupils as ANTOINE, BARON GROS and JEAN-AUGUSTE INGRES. His heroic and patriotic themes also paved the way for the romantics. Exiled during the RESTORATION, David died in Brussels.

## Déat, Marcel (1894–1955)
*political figure*

Born in Guérigny, Marcel Déat was elected a Socialist (SFIO) deputy in 1932 but left the party shortly afterward to found the reformist Socialist Party of France. Air minister in 1936, he was reelected deputy in 1939, and supported a policy of compromise with Germany ("Should we die for Danzig?" was an article that appeared in *L'Œuvre*, the newspaper that Déat directed after 1940). The founder, in February 1941, of the Rassemblement national populaire, a fascist and collaborationist party, Déat joined the VICHY government as secretary of state in 1944, but took refuge in Italy, where he died, after the Liberation.

## Debray, Régis (1940– )
*political writer*

Born in Paris, Régis Debray is the author of a work on the revolutionary struggle (*La Révolution dans la revolution*, 1967) and, as a comrade in arms to Che Guevara, took part in the guerrilla struggles in Latin America. Arrested in 1967 in Bolivia, he was sentenced to 30 years' imprisonment but was freed in 1970. Named an assistant to President FRANÇOIS MITTERRAND (1981–85, 1987–88), he is the author of numerous essays: *Le Pouvoir intellectual en France* (1979), *Que vive la République* (1989), *À demain de Gaulle* (1990), *L'État séducteur* (1993), as well as a text *Cours de médiologie générale* (1991).

## Debré, Michel (1912–1996)
*political figure*

The first prime minister of the FIFTH REPUBLIC, Michel Debré, the son of a noted physician, was born in Montlouis-sur-Loire. In his early career, he played an active role in the Resistance, was cofounder of the École nationale d'administration, and was a member of the Council of the Republic (1948–58). In that capacity, he was noted for his many stands against the successive governments of the FOURTH REPUBLIC and for his ardent defense of a French Algeria. During the events of May 1968, he helped in the recalling to public service of General CHARLES DE GAULLE. Named minister of justice (June 1958), he assisted in the drafting of the constitution of the Fifth Republic. Appointed prime minister (June 1959), he put through the law linking private and state education (Debré Law, 1959). Replaced by GEORGES POMPIDOU (April 1962), he served as a deputy (1963–66, 1967–68, 1973–88), was minister of the economy and finances (1966–68), foreign affairs (1968–69), then defense (1969–73). His unwavering support of Gaullism led him to oppose the policies of VALÉRY GISCARD D'ESTAING, particularly in European affairs, as well as distancing him from the Rassemblement pour la République, and to run for president in 1981 (1.66 percent of the vote) against JACQUES CHIRAC. Among his writings are *Refaire la France* (1944), *La Mort de l'état républican* (1947), *Ces princes qui nous gouvernent* (1957), *Lettre ouverte aux Français sur la reconquête de la France* (1980), and three volumes of *Mémoires* (1948–88). Debré was elected to the ACADÉMIE FRANÇAISE in 1988.

## Debussy, Achille-Claude (1862–1918)
*composer*

Born in Saint-Germain-en-Laye, Claude Debussy as he is known, entered the Paris Conservatoire at the age of 10, then at 16 became the private musician to Nadezdha van Meck, Pyotr Tchaikovsky's patroness. In that capacity he traveled to Venice, Florence, Vienna, and Moscow. While in Russia he became acquainted with the works of a number of Russian composers and with Russian and Romanian folk music. In 1884 Debussy won the Grand Prix de Rome for his cantata *L'enfant prodigue*. Studying in Rome, he then composed such works as the symphony suite *Printemps* and the cantata *La demoiselle élue*. During the 1890s his works were performed with increasing frequency, and despite their controversial (because of their innovations) nature, he gained a recognition. *Prélude à l'après-midi d'un faune* (1894) based on the poem by STÉPHANE MALLARMÉ, and Debussy's opera *Pelleas et Mélisande* were produced in 1902. Regarded by some critics as a perfect

union of music and drama, *Pelleas* earned him widespread fame. From 1902 to 1910, Debussy composed mostly for the piano, but in nontraditional modes. (*Estampes*, 1903; *L'Île joyeuse*, 1904; *Images*, 1905–07; *Children's Corner*, 1908). He also composed 24 *Préludes* in homage to FRÉDÉRIC CHOPIN (1910–13). Most of Debussy's other works include chamber music, with sonatas for violin, cello, flute, and harp. Other works are the orchestral poem *La Mer* (1905) and songs for *Cinque poèmes de Baudelaire* (1889). For Sergey Diaghilev, who had asked Vaslav Nijinsky to do the choreography for *Prèlude à l'après-midi d'un faune*, Debussy composed another ballet, *Jeux* (1913). Debussy's harmonic innovations helped pave the way for the great musical change of the 20th century, and he was the first composer to exploit the whole-tone scale. The dreamlike quality of Debussy's music made some critics refer to it as musical impressionism, a term still used to describe his contemporaries.

## Decazes and of Glücksberg, Élie, duke (1780–1860)
*political figure*

Born in Saint-Martin-de-Laye, Élie, duke Decazes and of Glücksberg, was an attorney in Libourne, judge for the tribunal of the Seine (1806), then adviser in the cabinet of LOUIS BONAPARTE, king of Holland (1807). In 1814, he went over to the Bourbons, was named prefect and minister of police, replacing JOSEPH FOUCHÉ. Of liberal constitutionalist tendencies, he quickly became adviser to LOUIS XVIII and, after the fall of the duke of RICHELIEU cabinet, served as the effective head of government (1818–20). Seeking the support of the moderates, who favored a more equitable social order, Decazes reversed the majority in the upper chamber by naming 60 new peers (1819), removed Ultra prefects from office, and tried to gain support for liberal policies (in particular in the area of freedom of the press in March 1819). After the partial reconstituting of the Chamber of Deputies in favor of the Independents, he tried to work from behind the scenes but could not bring the Ultras over to his side. He was forced to resign after the assassination of the duke of BERRY (February 1820), and was replaced by the duke of Richelieu. Made a duke and peer of France, Decazes in 1830 supported

LOUIS-PHILIPPE, but after that, he concerned himself mainly with farming and industry, establishing the Decazes forges in Aveyron.

## Deffand, Marie-Anne de Vichy-Chamrond, marquise du (1697–1780)
### (Madame du Deffand)
*writer, salon hostess*

Born in the chateau of Chamrond, BURGUNDY, Marie, marquise du Deffand was a hostess who received in her celebrated literary salon such writers and thinkers as BERNARD LE BOVIER DE FONTANELLE, the count de MONTESQUIEU, PIERRE DE MARIVAUX, and the Encyclopedists, whom she introduced to various political and social figures of the age. In her vast correspondence (to VOLTAIRE, JEAN D'ALEMBERT, and the British political figure Horace Walpole), Mme du Deffand describes in a picturesque manner the aristocratic and literary world of 18th-century France.

See also LESPINASSE, JULIE DE.

## Defferre, Gaston (1910–1986)
*political figure*

Born in Marsillargues, Gaston Defferre was, since 1933, a militant Socialist (SFIO) and, during World War II, a member of the Resistance. He was mayor of MARSEILLE (1944–45 and from 1953 until his death), served as a deputy (1946–58, 1962–86), and senator (1959–62). Named minister for France overseas in the GUY MOLLET cabinet (1956–57), he contributed to the passing of the law modifying the status of the countries of the French Union (July 23, 1956). Minister of the interior of decentralization (1981–84), then of the Plan for Territorial Development (LAURENT FABIUS cabinet, 1984–86), Defferre was the author of the law on decentralization (1982).

## Degas, Edgar (1834–1917)
### (Hilaire-Germain-Edgar de Gas)
*painter, pastelist, sketcher, and engraver*

Born in Paris to a family of bankers, Edgar Degas, as he is known, studied law before he took up painting. In 1859, he traveled to Italy, where he copied the works of the Quatrocentrists. Degas's first works were on historical themes (*Semiramis*

*Building Babylon,* 1861) and portraits that show Ingres's influence but also Degas's personal style (*The Belleli Family,* 1858–67). Abandoning academic conventions, Degas came under the influence of naturalism and photography, and was inspired by Japanese prints. About 1868 he became part of the group that met at the Café Guerbois and included ÉDOUARD MANET, (*Portrait of Manet,* 1864) AUGUSTE RENOIR, and CLAUDE MONET. With them, in 1874 Degas took part in the first impressionist exhibit. Like Monet, who influenced him, he had an acute sense of modernist style, represented in his scenes of everyday life, street scenes, and the world of horse racing (*Before the Start,* 1862) and the stage (*Mlle Fiocre in the Ballet "La Source,"* 1868). Following a visit to the United States (1872–73), he painted *Cotton Merchants in New Orleans* (1873), which showed his naturalistic style. He had a passion for the world of dance (*Dancer Taking a Bow,* 1878; *Dancer at the Bar,* 1880) and produced works showing the effect of artificial light devoid of all idealism. He had an exceptional ability to capture the rapid gestures and the particular characteristics of his subjects. In portraying dressmakers and women ironing, (1882–83), he approached stylistically certain works of HONORÉ DAUMIER, while works such as *Women at Their Toilette* (1885–98) evoke instead the lifestyle of HENRI DE TOULOUSE-LAUTREC. Suffering from vision problems, Degas had a preference for pastels, working with crayon and gouache as well as with paints. Painted from memory, his works show a free and audacious style and are more suggestive than descriptive, often having the quality of rough sketches. Influenced by Japanese art, Degas sought unusual modes of presentation for his subjects, decentralized, with planes oblique and sloped, or straight scenes, and in doing so helped to end traditional perspective in painting (*The Tub,* 1866; *After the Bath,* 1898). PAUL VALÉRY would dedicate an essay on painting (*Degas, danse, dessin,* 1936) to the works of Degas.

## Delacroix, Eugène (1798–1863)
*painter, naturalist, designer, lithographer*

Eugène Delacroix, whose work exemplified 19th-century romanticism and whose influences extended to the impressionists, was born at Saint-Maurice near Paris. He studied first under the French

Eugène Delacroix *(Library of Congress)*

painter PIERRE GUÉRIN. Although trained in the formal neoclassical style of JACQUES-LOUIS DAVID, Delacroix was strongly influenced by the more colorful, opulent style of such earlier masters as Rubens and Veronese. He also absorbed the spirit of his contemporary, THÉODORE GÉRICAULT, whose works exemplified the active, romantic themes of the turbulent post-Napoleonic era. Delacroix's career began in 1822 when his first painting, *Dante and Virgil in Hell,* was accepted by the Paris, Salon. He achieved popular success soon after with *The Massacre at Chios* (1824, LOUVRE), itself considered a manifesto of the romantic school. In 1825 Delacroix traveled to England, and the influence of the English artist R. P. Bonington is evident in a subsequent work *The Death of Sardanapalus* (1828), a lavish, colorful, and dramatic painting. Delacroix also excelled in other dramatic allegorical paintings such as *Greece Expiring at Missolonghi* (1827), his famous *Liberty Leading the People,* and historic themes such as *Murder of the Bishop of Liège* (1831) and *The Decapitation of Doge Mario Falerio* (1827). His *Liberty Leading the People,* a semiallegorical glorification of the idea of liberty,

confirmed a clear division between the romantic and the neoclassical styles of painting. Delacroix himself remained the dominant romantic painter throughout his life. In 1852, a visit to North Africa provided him subjects for a large number of canvases, including *The Sultan of Morocco* (1845), *Jewish Wedding in Morocco* (1839), and *Algerian Women* (1834). Such works also helped to popularize the exotic Oriental style among other romantic painters. Additionally, Delacroix received many government and church commissions for murals and ceiling paintings. Many of his later, smaller paintings, especially animal pictures and marine subjects, are superb, and he also illustrated various works of William Shakespeare, Sir Walter Scott, and J. W. von Goethe. The recognized master of the romantic style, Delacroix would have an important influence on the impressionists. In his writings (*Journals; Correspondence;* and *Notes*), which are well known, he displays considerable literary talent as he expresses his views in life, art, and politics. "What is most real to me," he wrote, "are the illusions that I create with my paintings."

## Delambre, Jean-Baptiste-Joseph, chevalier (1749–1822)
*astronomer*

Born in Amiens, Jean-Baptiste-Joseph, chevalier Delambre was commissioned during the REVOLUTION OF 1789 by the Constituent Assembly (1791) to collaborate with PIERRE MÉCHAIN on the measuring of the arc of the meridian between Dunkerque and Barcelona. This was done to form the basis for the determination of a meter, thus helping to develop the metric system. Delambre was named to the Academy of Sciences in 1795.

## Delaunay, Robert (1885–1941)
*painter*

A pioneer of abstract art, Robert Delaunay was born in Montpellier. After an apprenticeship in the workshop of a theater set designer, he was influenced by PAUL GAUGUIN and the Pont-Avers school, became interested in the neoimpressionism of GEORGES SEURAT, then moved away for cubism and to the style of Orphism (the name was given by GUILLAUME APOLLINAIRE), which emphasized circular forms and light colors. His early series—*Saint-*

*Severin* (1909), *La Tour Eiffel* (1910), *Les Tours de Laon* (1910–12), *La Ville de Paris* (1910–12)—caught the attention of Wassily Kandinsky, Paul Klee, and others, and his series done in 1912 and entitled *Fenêtres et Disques circulaire* was described by Apollinaire as the "first manifestation [of] totally abstract art." His love of rhythm and movement led to other series and works (Hélices, 1923; *Portraits, Coureurs,* 1924–26; *Joie de vivre,* 1930; *Rythmes sans fin,* 1933–34).

## Delaunay, Sonia (1885–1979)
*painter*

Born in Odessa, Ukraine, Sonia Terk (in 1910 she married ROBERT DELAUNAY) studied first in St. Petersburg and in Germany before coming to Paris in 1906. Her first exhibition (paintings, fabrics, bookbindings) showed the influence of PAUL GAUGUIN and Vincent van Gogh. Having assimilated the ideas of PAUL CÉZANNE and the cubists (*Bal Bullier,* 1913), she became interested especially in the possibilities of pure color. A pioneer in geometric abstraction, she developed a style of "simultaneous contrast" of bright prismatic colorations and illustrated the first "simultaneous" book, *La Prose du Transsibérien et de la petite Jehanne de France* by BLAISE CENDRARS. Following a trip to Portugal and Spain, she produced large geometric compositions with strong colors (*Marché à Minho*). Beginning in 1911, Delaunay was involved in decorative arts and also created theatrical costumes. In the 1920s, she became a fashion designer, with her brilliant hand-painted fabrics revolutionizing textile design. Later, in the 1940s, her style evoked a more delicate and restrained level.

## Delcassé, Théophile (1852–1923)
*political figure*

Born in Pamiers, Théophile Delcassé served as a Radical deputy (1889) and minister for colonies (1894–95) and then was given the portfolio of foreign affairs, which he held from 1898 to 1905. As minister of foreign affairs, he contributed, with the help of PAUL CAMBON, to development of the rapprochement between France and Italy (1898), as well as to strengthening France's alliance with Russia (1900). After the FASHODA incident, he was, with Cambon, the initiator of the ENTENTE CORDIALE with Great Britain. This alliance, which would cause concern for Germany, took into account French rights in Morocco (the French-English Convention of 1904) in exchange for the renouncing of French rights of Egypt. This convention, which was made to the detriment of Germany, brought a strong reaction from Berlin (Emperor Wilhelm II's Tangier statement, 1905). To avert a conflict, the prime minister asked Delcassé to resign, probably without stating the reason, and accepted the terms of the Algeciras Conference. Named minister of the navy (1911–13), then ambassador to Russia (1913–14), Delcassé was recalled as foreign minister at the beginning of World War I to serve in the cabinet of RENÉ VIVIANI. Delcassé supported Italy's entrance into the war, but as he was criticized for not having gained the neutrality of Bulgaria, which had joined the Central Powers, he resigned from the government.

See also MARCHARD, JEAN-BAPTISTE.

## Delorme or De L'Orme, Philibert (ca. 1510 or 1515–ca. 1570)
*architect and architectural theorist*

The leading French architect of the 16th century, whose works and theories influenced the creation of French classical design, Philibert Delorme was born in LYON, the son of a master mason. He developed his talents in Italy, where he probably met Baldassare Peruzzi, Antonio Sangallo, and Sebastiano Serlio and where he developed his love for the buildings of antiquity, of which he made many reliefs. Returning to France, he gained the favor of King HENRY II and conceived the model for the tomb of FRANCIS I at Saint-Denis. Inspired by the models of the Italian Renaissance, he produced numerous works at the châteaux of Fontainebleau, Chenonceau, Villers-Cotterêts, and Surtout, and for DIANE DE POITIERS, the chapel at the château d'Anet which was the first domed church built in France (1548–52). On the death of Henry II, Delorme edited *Nouvelles inventions pour bien bâtir à petits frais* (1561) and the first volume of *Architecture.* Commissioned then by CATHERINE DE' MEDICI to build the great palace of the Tuilieries (1564–67), he developed a grandiose plan, only the central body of which was erected. Delorme, who influenced many of the major French architects of the period, brought the ideals of the Renaissance to France, played an important role as an architectural theorist, and helped to change the function and social status of the architect.

## Delors, Jacques (1925– )
*political figure*

Born in Paris, Jacques Delors, after a career at the Bank of France (1945–62), joined the cabinet of Premier JACQUES CHABAN-DELMAS (1965–72) as minister of social and cultural affairs. A member of the Socialist Party (1974), European deputy (1979), minister of the economy and finances from 1981 to 1984, he proposed in 1982 a pause in social reforms and an austere plan to freeze prices and wages. President of the European Commission in Brussels (1985–95), Delors was a proponent of a political, economic, and monetary union of Europe, and he contributed to the drawing up of the Maastricht Treaty.

See also EUROPEAN UNION.

## Demy, Jacques (1931–1990)
*director, screenwriter*

Born in Pontchâteau, Jacques Demy produced his first full-length film, *Lola,* in 1961. It was praised for its subtle surrealism, which is evident also in his other works, *Les Parapluies de Cherbourg;* 1964), *Les Demoiselles de Rochefort; 1967, Peau-d'Âne; 1970 , Une chambre en ville;* 1982), and *Trois Places pour les 26; 1988).* In 1982 he was awarded the Grand Prix des Arts et Lettres for lifetime achievement. Demy's wife, the cinematographer AGNÈS VARDA, paid him a moving tribute in her film *Jacquot de Nantes; 1991.*

## Deneuve, Catherine (1943– )
*actor*

Born Catherine Dorléac in Paris to French actors Renée Deneuve and Maurice Dorléac, Catherine Deneuve first attracted attention when ROGER VADIM starred her in *La Vice et la vertu* (1962). She then achieved much renown with her role in *Les Parapluies de Cherbourg* (1964) by Jacques Demy. She also appeared in *Les Demoiselles de Rochefort* (1967) with her sister Françoise Dorléac. Deneuve's

later roles were often based on characters whose dark personalities were hidden behind beautiful facades (*Repulsion,* 1965; *Belle de Jour,* 1967). Her subsequent roles include performances in *Tristana* (1970), *Le dernier Métro* (1980), *Le Lieu du crime* (1986), and *Indochine* (1992), for which she received an Academy Award nomination for Best Actress. Deneuve's mysterious screen persona and beauty have made her an icon of European film.

## Denon, Dominique Vivant, baron (1747–1825)
*writer, engraver, administrator*

Born in Givry, Dominique Vivant, Baron Denon, who initially dedicated himself to literature, was commissioned to restore the cabinet de Médailles of King LOUIS XVI. Under that monarch, he was also charged with various diplomatic missions (to Russia, Switzerland, and Naples). During the REVOLUTION OF 1789 he was protected by the painter JACQUES LOUIS DAVID, then gained the favor of NAPOLÉON I. During the Egyptian campaign, he restored a number of monuments (*Voyage dans la haute et basse Égypte,* 1802). He became director general of museums and organized the LOUVRE museum and, at the time of the Napoleonic campaigns, cataloged works of pillaged art. He worked in engraving and lithography, producing copies of the great Italian masters and portraits (*Voltaire à Ferney*) and designed for the *Voyage historique et pittoresque* of the abbot of Saint-Non and engraved the *Serment de jeu de paume.*

## Denis, Maurice (1870–1943)
*painter, engraver, writer*

Born in Granville, Maurice Denis in 1888, at the Académie Julian in Paris met PAUL SÉRUSIER, who introduced him to the synthesized style of PAUL GAUGUIN. Denis joined the symbolist movement and with Sérusier founded the NABIS group, becoming its main theorist. His works (above all, family and intimate scenes) reflect the esthetic of Art Nouveau and the Japanese-inspired style that was then in fashion. After two visits to Italy, in 1895 and 1897, where he was influenced by Nazarenes, a group who wanted to revive medieval Christian artistic values, and the fresco-artists of the 14th and 15th centuries, Denis turned completely to religious painting, to which he tried to introduce modern techniques, and a return to the style of the "primitives." In 1919, he founded the Ateliers d'art sacré. Denis also did large decorative murals (Théâtre des Champs-Élysée, Paris 1912–13), but could not find the proper mode for his modernist theories (*Théories*, 1912; *Nouvelles Théories sur l'art moderne et sur l'art sacré*, 1922).

## Depardieu, Gérard (1948–  )
*actor*

The incarnation of a certain type of spirited, virile, and spontaneous modern French screen hero, Gérard Depardieu, who was born in Châteauroux, soon rose to the ranks of an international film star. Depardieu's successes are numerous and include *Les Valseuses* (1974), *Le dernier Métro* (1980), *Danton* (1983), *Sous le soleil de Satan* (1987), and *Cyrano de Bergerac* (1990).

## Derain, André (1880–1954)
*painter, sculptor*

Born in Chatou, André Derain studied at the Julian and Carrière academies in Paris, where he met HENRI MATISSE. He also worked with his friend Maurice de Vlaminck in a studio in Chatou. The influence of GEORGES SEURAT and especially of VINCENT VAN GOGH encouraged Derain to give a primary importance to color, which he applied in his painting with large fragmented strokes (*Le Bal des soldats*, 1903). He later (1905) worked with Matisse and then made several visits to London (*London Bridge*). He was interested, too, in popular imagery, Byzantine mosaics, and Roman art, and under the influence of PAUL CÉZANNE moved toward cubism (*Baigneuse*, 1908). Derain produced portraits, still-lives, fantasy forms, stage decorations, numerous book illustrations, and, especially after 1939, sculptures, which constitute an ensemble of stylistically quite disparate works.

## Deraismes, Marie (1828–1894)
*feminist*

Born in Paris to a bourgeois republican family, Marie Deraismes was quite well educated. Financially independent, she became a well-known writer, lecturer, and anticlericalist during the 1860s. In 1866, she cofounded the Societé pour la revendication de droits de la femme with PAULE MINK and LOUISE MICHEL. In 1870, she founded the Association pour les droits des femmes, a leading moderate French feminist organization. She collaborated with LÉON RICHER, with whom she organized several international congresses and founded the newspaper *Le Républican de Seine et Oise*. Deraismes, who sought also to gain membership for women in Masonic lodges, has among her writings *Le Théâtre chez soi* (1863), *Aux femmes riches* (1865), *Nos Principes et nos moeurs* (1867), *Les Droits des enfants* (1886), and *Eve dans l'humanité* (1891).

## Deroin, Jeanne (1805–1894)
*feminist*

Born in Paris into a working-class family, Jeanne Deroin spent her youth as an embroiderer. Around 1831, she was drawn, through articles in the *Globe*, to the Saint-Simonians, attracted particularly by their views on the emancipation of women. Under the name Jeanne Victoire, she eventually contributed articles to the Saint-Simonian working women's journal, *Femme libre*. She married a fellow Saint-Simonian and, especially after the REVOLUTION OF 1848, wrote and petitioned for broad social reform and even attempted herself to campaign for public office. With Desirée Gay, she founded the Societé d'éducation mutuelle des femmes. In support of women's rights, she rebutted the view of PIERRE-JOSEPH PROUDHON that women should be relegated to household activities, and proposed self-governing women's associations. After the coup d'état of December 2, 1851, Deroin went into exile in Great Britain, where she continued to write, publishing two women's almanacs, and to campaign for female emancipation. LÉON RICHER published her letter on the problems of children born out of wedlock in his *Le Droit des femmes*.

## Déroulede, Paul (1846–1914)
*writer, political figure*

Born in Paris, Paul Déroulede served as a volunteer in the FRANCO-PRUSSIAN WAR (1870–71) and, after the French defeat, published his *Chants du soldat* (1872–75), a drama in verse, *L'Hetmann,* and a play, *La Moabite,* which was banned. Founder and president of the Ligue des patriotes (1882) and a supporter of General BOULANGER, he was elected deputy (1889). Forced to resign in 1892, he was reelected in 1898. Déroulede attempted, two days after the funeral of the president of the republic, FÉLIX FAURE, to raise the army against the parliamentary republic (February 1899) and was subsequently sentenced to 10 years in exile. He settled in Spain and then was pardoned in 1905. Déroulede's writings (*Marches et Sonneries,* 1881; *Chants patriotiques; Livre de la Ligue des patriotes*) express his strong nationalistic and revanchist patriotic views.

## Derrida, Jacques  (1930–    )
*philosopher*

Jacques Derrida, a leading contemporary French philosopher whose writings form the basis for the deconstructionist school, was born in El Biar, ALGERIA, and educated in Paris at the École normale supérieure, where he later taught. He was also a professor at the SORBONNE and began his writings with essays on the Greeks, Hegelian phenomenology, and antimetaphysics. He questioned the primacy of the word, or "logo-centrism," as the common foundation of religion and metaphysics, and centered his work on a critique of "signs." Derrida first put forth this philosophy in *L'Écriture et la différence* (1967), in *La Voix et le phénomène* (1967), and in *De la Grammatologie* (1967). His writings are also concerned with the human sciences (notably the fundamentals of linguistics and textology) and, after *La Dissémination* (1972), *Marges de la philosophie* (1972), and *Glas* (1974), which illustrate his theories on the author and the graphical juxtaposition of critical and literary texts apropos of G. W. F. Hegel and JEAN GENET, he continued to write prolifically and to break with the classical modes of philosophic exposition (*La Carte postale: De Socrate à Freud et au-delà,* 1980; *Droit de regard,* a work of photographs with the Belgian photographer Marie-Françoise Plissart, 1985). His detractors have accused Derrida of seeking to destroy reason, but his critical interpretation at all times seeks to achieve a synthesis among psychoanalysis (*Résistances,* 1996),

Marxism (*Spectres de Marx,* 1993), and the ideas of Martin Heidegger (*Heidegger et la question,* 1990; *Apories,* 1996). Derrida's other writings include *Schibboleth* (1986), *Antonin Artaud* (1986), *Parages* (1986), and *Signéponge* (1988).

## Desaix de Veygoux  (1768–1800)
## (Louis-Charles-Antoine de Aix)
*military figure*

Born Louis-Charles-Antoine de Aix in Saint-Hilaire d'Ayat, near Riom, Desaix de Veygoux, as he is known, joined the REVOLUTION OF 1789 and distinguished himself serving with the Army of the Rhine. He accompanied Napoléon Bonaparte (NAPOLÉON I) to Egypt and was put in charge of the organization of Fayoum. His fair governing earned him the name "the just Sultan." Returning to France in 1800, General Desaix de Veygoux went to fight at Marengo, where he was killed.

## Desargues, Gérard  (1593–1662)
*engineer, mathematician*

Born in LYON, Gérard (or Gespard) Desargues was dedicated to research in pure geometry and was the first to understand the fundamental role of perspective. He gave, after Apollonios, the basis for the projective geometry of conic sections (*Brouillon project d'une atteinte aux événements des rencontres du cône avec un plan,* 1639). Among his most important conclusions, he was able to prove the idea that all conic forms can be considered as the projection of a circle, the concept of an infinite point in a right angle, the subsequent identification of a cluster of parallel right angles, and a cluster of concurrent right angles, as well as that of a cone and a cylinder, the theory of the involution on a right angle and the Desargues Theorem on homologic triangles.

## Des Autels, Guillaume  (1529–1581)
*poet*

Born in Vernoble, Burgundy, Guillaume Des Autels, with MAURICE SCÈVE, PIERRE DE RONSARD, and others, became a member of the PLÉIADE group (1555) and composed sonnets similar to those of Petrarch

(*Amoureux repos,* 1553). A supporter of the house of GUISE after 1559, he was, in his writings, an ardent defender of Catholicism (*Remontrance au peuple français* and *Éloge de la paix*). He is also the author of *Mitistoire barragouyne de Fanfreluche et Gaudichon* (1574), which is similar to the works of FRANÇOIS RABELAIS.

## Descartes, René (1596–1650)

*philosopher, scholar*

Born in La Haye, Touraine, the son of a minor nobleman, René Descartes began his education at the Jesuit school of La Flèche in Anjou. He studied law at the University of Poitiers, and in 1618 entered the service of the prince of Nassau with the intention of beginning a military career. His attention, however, was soon drawn to philosophy and mathematics. After a period in Italy (1623–24) and in France (1624–28), Descartes settled in the Netherlands, where he spent the rest of his life devoted to the study of philosophy and science. His first major work was *Essais, philosophies* (1637). In certain essays on geometry, optics, and meteors, and his *Discours de la méthode*, he presents his philosophical views. This latter work was followed by *Méditations métaphysiques* (1641) and *Principes de philosophie* (1644). The latter was dedicated to Princess Elisabeth Stuart of Bohemia, with whom he had a deep friendship. In 1649 Descartes was invited to instruct at the court of Queen Christina of Sweden, and it is there that the rigors of a northern climate caused his death. Descartes's philosophy is based on his attempt to apply the rational inductive methods of mathematics to philosophy. He began his investigation with what was to him the single sure fact expressed in his words "Cogito ergo sum" (I think, therefore I am). His philosophy, sometimes called Cartesianism, led him, however, to a number of erroneous conclusions. He rejected the heliocentric view of the solar system, for instance, and in physiology, misinterpreted the nature of blood in its circulation. In the area of optics, however, his study led him to independent discovery of the law of reflection. Descartes's most important contribution to the study of mathematics was his systematization of analytic geometry. He was the first mathematician to attempt to classify curves according to their types of equation. He also formulated the rule, known as Descartes's rule of signs, for finding the number of positive and negative roots in algebraic equations.

## Deschamps, Eustache (ca. 1344–ca. 1406) (Eustache Morel)

*poet*

Born in Vertus, Eustache Deschamps, known also as Eustache Morel, was one of the great personages of the courts of Kings CHARLES V and CHARLES VI. A student of GUILLAUME DE MACHAUT, Deschamps was a theorist of the poetic art (*Art de dictier et de fere chançons,* 1392) and the author of historical poems, ballads, and rondos. His work deals realistically with all subjects, amorous, satirical, and anecdotal.

## Deshoulières, Antoinette de Ligier de la Garde, Mme (1637–1694)

*poet*

Born in Paris, Antoinette de Ligier de la Garde, or Mme Deshoulières as she is known, was married in her youth to a nobleman who was a supporter of the Grand CONDÉ. She was an admirer of PIERRE CORNEILLE and joined in the cabal against JEAN RACINE by writing a famous epigram about his play *Phèdre* (1677). Having followed the ideas of PIERRE GASSENDI, she held a salon in which she had the originality to "mingle the precious and the audacious with beautiful strong minds" (SAINTE-BEUVE). There, she received the Corneille brothers and many of the other leading artistic and intellectual personages of the time. Beginning her own literary career in 1672, Mme Deshoulières wrote in various genres (tragedy, comedy, opera), but above all she was known for her poetry (*Poésie,* 2 volumes, collected in 1688 and 1695), in which she shows, in both idyll and elegy, a grace and style that can already be considered romantic.

## Desmoulins, Camille (1760–1794)

*political figure, writer*

Born in Guise, Camille Desmoulins was a fellow student with MAXIMILIEN ROBESPIERRE at the lycée Louis-le-Grand in Paris. He was admitted to the bar in 1785 and joined the REVOLUTION OF 1789, taking part in the Parisian uprisings of July 12–14 of that year. He published violent pamphlets against the ancien régime (*La France libre; Le Discours de "la Lanterne" aux Parisiens*) and founded the journal *Les Révolutions de France et de Brabant* (1789–91). A member of the CORDELIERS CLUB, where he allied himself with GEORGES JACQUES DANTON, a Montagnard deputy to the Convention, he expressed his hostility to JACQUES BRISSOT and the Girondins in a pamphlet, *Brissot démasqué*, then in his *Fragment de l'histoire secrete de la Révolution* (1793). After the elimination of the Girondin leaders, Desmoulins tried to fight against establishing the TERROR and gain acceptance with the moderates with his newspaper *Le Vieux Cordelier* (1793–94). He was then arrested, condemned to death, and guillotined with Danton and the Indulgents (April 1794). His wife, Lucile Desmoulins (1771–94), met the same fate for sending Robespierre a letter protesting her husband's arrest.

## Des Périers, Bonaventure (ca. 1510–ca. 1543)

*humanist, poet, storyteller*

Born in Arnay-le-Duc, Bonaventure Des Périers was a member of the entourage of MARGUERITE DE NAVARRE and was the student and friend of CLÉMENT MAROT. His life is not well known, but he worked with OLIVÉTAN in translating the Bible (1535), helped ÉTIENNE DOLET to correct the *commentarii linguae latinae* (1536–38), and translated and annotated Plato, Horace, and Terence. The enigmatic *Cymbalum mundi* (1537) and his *Nouvelles récréations et joyeux devis* (1558) show a freedom of expression and a mastery of the art of storytelling that place the author alongside FRANÇOIS RABELAIS. The attribution of these two works to Des Périers, however, is still a matter of contention.

## Despiau, Charles (1874–1946)

*sculptor*

Born in Mont-de-Marsan, Charles Despiau, after studying at the Beaux-Arts academy in Paris, became an assistant to AUGUSTE RODIN (1907). His statues and bas-reliefs, representing mythological themes (*Bacchante*, 1909; *Faune*, 1912; *Léda*, 1917; *Apollon*, 1936–46), nudes (*Assia*, 1938) and less traditional subjects (*Petite fille des Landes*, 1909), reveal, despite the influence of naturalism, a classicist tendency that translates into quiet expression, calm composition, and harmonious and supple form. He produced some commemorative works (monument at Mont-de-Marsan, 1920–22), but above all he emerges as a portraitist in his numerous busts. His concern for precision in the rendering of features and psychological truth go together with his fine modeling and seem to reconcile with a tendency toward idealization, translated into a formal harmony and serene expressive character (*Mme Faure*, 1927; *Mme Agnes Meyer*, 1929). Despiau's work, with its technical mastery, can be seen as a continuation of the classical tradition.

## Desportes, Philippe (1546–1606)

*poet*

Born in CHARTRES, Philippe Desportes was the court priest and official poet to King HENRY III. He is the author of *Élégies* and profane poems ("Les Amours de Diane," "Les Amours d'Hippolyte," 1573) that have a certain precocity. His translation of psalms (published in 1603) is, in contrast, in spirit close to that of CLÉMENT MAROT.

## Dessalines, Jean-Jacques (ca. 1758–1806) (Jacques I)

*Haitian emperor*

Born in Grand-Rivière-du-Nord, in what was then the French colony of Saint-Domingue, Jean-Jacques Dessalines, a slave, soon joined the revolt against the colonial rule. Successively a battalion leader, colonel, and brigadier general (1797), he helped, under orders from TOUSSAINT LOUVERTURE, to expel the British, who had landed in Saint-Domingue during the Napoleonic Wars, from parts of Hispaniola. After Toussaint Louverture was taken captive by the French, Dessalines became leader of the insurgent armies, winning the Battle of Vertières against General DONATIEN DE ROCHAMBEAU (November 18, 1803) and proclaiming the independence of the Republic of Haiti (January 1, 1804). He named himself emperor under the title Jacques I, but his authoritarian policies alienated the other Haitian leaders, who killed him near Port-au-Prince (October 1806).

See also PÉTION, ALEXANDRE; CHRISTOPHE, HENRY.

## DeStutt de Tracy, Antoine-Louis-Claude, count (1754–1836)

*philosopher*

Born in Paris, Antoine-Louis-Claude, count DeStutt de Tracy was the leader of the Ideologues (a group of philosophers who adhered to the theories of CONDILLAC) and, under the DIRECTORY, was a member of the Committee of Public Instruction. Author of the five-part *Éléments d'idéologie* (*Idéologie,* 1801; *Grammaire générale,* 1803; *Logique,* 1805; *Traité sur la volonté,* 1815), he affirmed in that work his psychological materialism. He believed that sensibility (of which the fundamental forms are to feel, to remember, to judge, to desire) defines our own existence as well as that of the external world. It is the source of our judgments and ideas in general. For this reason, DeStutt de Tracy was especially interested in language (in the power of words themselves and in the value of discourse). DeStutt de Tracy, who would have a great influence on STENDHAL, was elected to the ACADÉMIE FRANÇAISE in 1808.

## Dézamy, Théodore (1808–1850)

*Socialist*

Born in Luçon, Théodore Dézamy was the editor of a Socialist newspaper, *L'Égalitaire* (1840). He was critical of the Christian Socialism of FÉLICITÉ LAMENNAIS, as well as the utopian communism of ÉTIENNE CABET, with whom he had first worked (*Code de la communauté,* 1842). A member of a Neobabouvist group (see FRANÇOIS BABEUF, RICHARD LAHAUTIÈRE, ALBERT LAPONNERAYE), Dézamy can be considered one of the first representatives of materialist socialism in France.

## Diagne, Blaise (1872–1934)

*statesman*

The first black African deputy to the French National Assembly (1914–34), Blaise Diagne was born on the island of Gorce, off the coast of Dakar, Senegal. Educated in France and Senegal, he served with the French customs service from 1892 to 1914, being frequently transferred throughout the French Empire in Africa and South America because of his outspoken criticism of racial privilege. Returning to Senegal in 1903, he ran for and won a seat in the French Chamber of Deputies, becoming the first black African to do so. During WORLD WAR I, he served as governor-general for military recruitment in FRENCH WEST AFRICA, and in exchange for assurances of expanded citizenship, veterans' benefits and imperial social services, he was able to enlist 100,000 Africans. In 1919 he founded the Republican Socialist Party, the first such political party in sub-Saharan Africa. He soon came to dominate Senegalese politics. In 1923 Diagnes's policies, however, alienated many of his African supporters. In 1930 he was appointed French undersecretary for the colonies, and during the Great Depression negotiated France's first subsidies for African farmers.

## Diane de Poitiers, duchess de Valentinois (1499–1566)

*nobility*

The daughter of Jean de Poitiers, sieur de Saint-Vallier, Diane de Poitiers, duchess de Valentinois, married Louis de Brézé, a grandson of King CHARLES VIII, who left her a widow at age 32. She soon became the mistress of the future king HENRY II, who was 19 years younger than she. At first her influence over him was shared with the duchess d'Étampes, mistress of FRANCIS I, until the latter's death. Henceforth having great power, Diane de Poitiers supported the suppression of Protestantism. She encouraged the arts, and Henry II built a château for her at Anet.

## Diane de Valois (1538–1619)
## (Diane de France)

*nobility*

The natural daughter of HENRY II and a Piedmontese woman, Filippa Duci, or, as some said, DIANE DE POITIERS, Diane de Valois, or Diane de France, as she is also known, was legitimized and married Orazio Farnese (1553). Her second husband was FRANÇOIS DE MONTMORENCY (1557), whom she saved from the Saint Bartholomew's Day Massacre of French Protestants in Paris. Intelligent and cultivated, she exerted an important influence at court and reconciled King HENRY III with the future HENRY IV.

## Diderot, Denis (1713–1784)

*writer, philosopher*

Born in Langres to a well-to-do bourgeois family, Denis Diderot, a major figure of the ENLIGHTEN-

Denis Diderot *(Library of Congress)*

MENT, studied theology, philosophy, and law at the SORBONNE, while living a bohemian existence. There he spent several years pursuing a variety of professions. His first serious work, published anonymously, was *"Pensées philosophiques"* (1746), in which he presented his deistic philosophy, followed by *Les Bijoux indiscrets* (1748). In 1747 he was invited to edit a French translation of the English *Encyclopaedia*. Instead, collaborating with JEAN LE ROND D'ALEMBERT, Diderot converted the project into a vast, controversial, and new work, the 35-volume *Encyclopédie ou dictionnaire raisonné des sciences, des arts et des métiers*, usually known as the *Encyclopédie*. He worked on this project from 1747 to 1766 with the assistance of the most celebrated writers and thinkers of the age, including MONTESQUIEU, VOLTAIRE, and others. Diderot, ever the skeptic and rationalist, used the *Encyclopédie* to attack the conservatism, superstitions, religious authority and semifeudal social norms of the period. Consequently, the Conseil du roi suppressed

the early volumes (published after 1751) and the remainder Diderot had printed secretly. Diderot's other voluminous writings include *La religieuse* (1760), an attack on convent life; *Le fils naturel* (1757); *Le Père de famille* (1758); a social satire, *Le Neveu de Rameau* (1761–74), published by J. W. von Goethe in 1805; *Est-il bon? Est-il méchant* (1781); and *Jacques le Fataliste et son maître* (published 1796), which explored the psychology of determination and free will. Diderots's materialist theories are found in his *Lettre sur les aveugles à l'usage de ceux qui voient* (1749) on learning among the blind, and dramatic philosophical dialogues, *Le rêve d'Alembert* (1769) and *Supplement au voyage de Bougainville* (published 1796). In his *Correspondance* with SOPHIE VOLLAND, he exalts nature as a "divine" force. As a leader in aesthetic criticism, Diderot, in 1759, founded *Les Salons,* a journal in which he critiqued the annual Paris art exhibition. In an age of famous letter writing, he was unexcelled in his correspondence. He won the patronage of Catherine the Great of Russia, whom he visited in 1773, and was a major influence on other thinkers of the Enlightenment.

## Dien Bien Phu (Dienbienphu)

Dien Bien Phu, which is located on a plain in northern Vietnam, was the site of a decisive battle (May 7, 1954) between the French forces and the Front de libération du Viêtnam (Viet Minh). Encircled and bombarded by artillery, the French troops had to end their resistance after 57 days of fighting. The subsequent Geneva Accords would declare the end of hostilities and of French hegemony in INDOCHINA.

## Dior, Christian (1905–1957)
*couturier*

Born in Granville, Christian Dior came late to fashion, founding his own couture house in 1946. He was an immediate success with his "new look" collection (shirtwaist dresses, long and ample skirts). Encouraged by his success, he built a commercial empire founded on an international network of trademark licensing that flourished even after his death. Dior was succeeded by his protégé YVES SAINT LAURENT and other designers.

## Directory (Directoire)

The Directory (Directoire) was the government that functioned during the REVOLUTION OF 1789 from 5 Brumaire Year IV (October 27, 1795) to 18 Brumaire Year VIII (November 9, 1799), when it was overthrown by Napoléon Bonaparte (see NAPOLÉON I). The Directory governed with the help of two chambers: the Council of Elders (Conseil des Anciens), and the Council of Five Hundred (Conseil des Cinq-Cents). The Directory, a regime instituted by the Constitution of the Year III, was a bourgeois republic. In foreign affairs, it practiced a policy of conquering territories and establishing sister republics, made war on the Holy Roman Empire (campaign in Italy) and on Britain (campaign in Egypt), and provoked the formation of the Second Coalition against France. In terms of domestic policy, the Directory regime, quite dissolute, was marked by attempted coup d'états and a terrible financial crisis. Leading members of the Directory government included PAUL BARRAS, Abbé EMMANUEL SIEYÈS, and LAZARE CARNOT.

## Dolet, Étienne (1509–1546)

*humanist, printer*

Born in Orléans, Étienne Dolet was a leading French humanist. He produced commentaries on the ancient authors and the Latin language (*Commentarii linguae latinae,* 1536–38), as well as editions of CLÉMENT MAROT and FRANÇOIS RABELAIS, and was an ardent defender of religious toleration and of the French language. Dolet also worked with other humanists, such as BONAVENTURE DES PÉRIERS. Because of his free spirit and his activities, Doret was condemned to the stake for heresy and atheism.

## Dorat (1508–1588)

## (Jean Dinemandi)

*humanist*

Born in Limoges, Jean Dinemandi, who is known as Dorat, was a renowned author of Latin and Hellenistic poems who held the chair of Greek at the Collège royal (1566). Having communicated his enthusiasm for Greco-Latin culture, notably to PIERRE DE RONSARD, JOACHIM DU BELLAY, and JEAN-ANTOINE DE BAÏF, he formed the Brigade, which would later become the PLÉIADE.

## Doriot, Jacques (1898–1945)

*political figure*

Born in Bresles, Oise, Jacques Doriot was a metallurgist and secretary-general of the Jeunesses communistes, and served as deputy (1924) and as mayor of Saint-Denis. He was excluded from the Communist Party (1934) and moved toward fascism, founding the Parti populaire française (PPF, 1936) and the newspaper *La Liberté,* and he took a position against the Front populaire. A supporter of collaboration with Germany (1940), Doriot helped to form the Légion des volontaires français (LVF), an anti-Bolshevik group, and fought alongside the Germans on the Russian front.

## Doré, Gustave (1832–1883)

*illustrator, engraver, and painter*

Gustave Doré, whose highly imaginative engravings accompanied many important 19th-century literary works, was born in Strasbourg. At age 15, he drew caricatures for the Parisian *Journal pour rire,* for *Caricature,* and for CHARIVARI. He produced nearly 10,000 illustrations for newspapers, and was above all known as a book illustrator. In that area especially, he showed his inexhaustible imagination. His energetic graphics reveal a sometimes vivid fantasy (*Pantagruel,* 1854; *Les contes drolatiques,* 1856), as well as a romantic and visionary lyricism (*L'Enfer de Dante,* 1861; *La Bible,* 1866). He practiced lithography and engraving with a great mastery, and excelled in conveying great dramatic action and mysterious and even gloomy settings.

## Doumergue, Gaston (1863–1937)

*statesman*

Born in Aigues-Vives, Gard, to an old HUGUENOT family, Gaston Doumergue studied law in Paris and, in 1885, became an attorney in Nîmes, then served as a judge in INDOCHINA and in ALGERIA. Known for his impartiality and fairness, he was elected as a Radical deputy in 1893, and was several times named a minister between 1902 and 1917 (in particular for colonies and for foreign affairs) and was also premier (1913–14). Elected president of the republic after the Cartel des gauches victory and the resignation of ALEXANDRE MILLERAND (1924), Doumergue retired from politics at the end of his term

(1931), but was recalled after the political unrest of February 1934 and formed a government of national union. This drew the opposition of the Left because of his support for constitutional reform (strengthening the executive power) and he had to resign in November of that year.

## Dreux-Brezé, Henri Évrard, marquis de (1766–1829)
*courtier*

Born in Paris, Henri Évrard, marquis de Dreux-Brezé was, beginning in 1781, the grand master of ceremonies to King LOUIS XVI. As such, he was charged in June 1789 with conveying to the deputies of the Third Estate the king's order to leave the meeting hall, where he was then met with the famous apostrophe of MIRABEAU: "Go and tell those who have sent you that we are here by the will of the nation and that we shall not leave save at the point of bayonets." An émigré from the REVOLUTION OF 1789 (after August 10, 1792 when the monarchy fell), Dreux-Brezé resumed his functions under king LOUIS XVIII.

## Dreyfus, Alfred (1859–1935)
*military officer*

Alfred Dreyfus is best known for being the center of the major controversy known as the Dreyfus affair. Born in Mulhouse to a Jewish-Alsatian family, Dreyfus pursued a military career and, in 1893, as an artillery captain, was assigned to the general staff in Paris. Accused on the basis of handwriting of passing secrets to the Germans, he was found guilty (1894) of treason by a court-martial, reduced in rank, and sent to Devil's Island for imprisonment for life. in 1896, Lieutenant GEORGES PICQUART, chief of French military intelligence, uncovered evidence that another officer, Major CHARLES ESTERHAZY, was actually the guilty party. Picquart was, however, silenced by his superior and dismissed from the service. In January 1898, ÉMILE ZOLA wrote his impassioned letter "J'accuse," which was published in the Paris newspaper *L'Aurore* and in which Zola denounced both the civil and the military authorities for their part in the case. In August of the same year, Lieutenant Colonel HUBERT HENRY confessed that as Picquart's successor as the head of intelli-

gence, he had forged documents implicating Dreyfus. He was arrested and committed suicide. In 1899 the Dreyfus case was brought before the Cour de cassation (Supreme Court of Appeal), which ordered a new trial. A second court-martial again pronounced Dreyfus guilty, but 10 days later the government of Premier PIERRE WALDECK-ROUSSEAU and President ÉMILE LOUBET nullified the verdict and pardoned Dreyfus. In 1906 Dreyfus was finally fully rehabilitated by the Cour de cassation, returned to the army with the rank of major, and awarded the LEGION OF HONOR. He served in WORLD WAR I with the rank of lieutenant colonel. The Dreyfus case was the spark for an inevitable major political and social controversy in the France of the THIRD REPUBLIC. Extremists of the Right and Left used the affair to illustrate their disillusionment with the prevailing order. The case also unleashed a strong anti-Semitism in various factions in France, including the military. The nation was divided sharply between "Dreyfusards"—intellectuals, including ANATOLE FRANCE and CHARLES PÉGUY, Socialists, Radicals, Republicans, moderates, and antimilitarists— and "anti-Dreyfusards"—the anti-Semites and clericals, and the nationalist Right. As a result of the Dreyfus affair, a liberal government was voted into power, the military was reformed, and legislation was introduced that led to the 1905 separation of church and state.

## Drouet, Jean-Baptiste (1763–1824)
*political figure*

Born in Sainte-Ménehould, where his father was postmaster, Jean-Baptiste Drouet recognized King LOUIS XVI when he attempted to flee France (June 21, 1791) and, proceeding to Varennes, raised the alarm, resulting in the king and the royal family's arrest. Deputy for the Maine in the Convention, Drouet fought in the war and was captured at Maubeuge by the Austrians (1793), who exchanged him for the king's daughter (December 1796). A member of the Council of Five Hundred during the Directory, he took part in the BABEUF Conspiracy (1796). Imprisoned in the Abbaye, he escaped and emigrated. During the FIRST EMPIRE he returned to France and was named prefect of Sainte-Ménehould. Proscribed as a regicide during the Restoration, he remained in hiding under the name Merger.

## Drouet d'Erlon, Jean-Baptiste, count (1765–1744)

*military figure*

Born in Reims, Jean-Baptiste, count Drouet-d'Erlon was an army volunteer in 1792 and took part in the campaigns of the REVOLUTION OF 1789 and the FIRST EMPIRE. Imprisoned during the First RESTORATION, he joined NAPOLÉON I during the HUNDRED DAYS, was made a peer of France, and fought in the Battle of Waterloo (1815). Exiled to Prussia during the Second Restoration, then condemned to death for contempt, he returned to France after the REVOLUTION OF 1830 and was named governor of ALGERIA (1834–35). There he helped in the creation of departments to deal with Arab affairs and in the establishment of a central government.

## Drouyn de Lhuys, Édouard (1805–1881)

*political figure*

Born in Paris, Édouard Drouyn de Lhuys was elected deputy (1842) under the July Monarchy, joined the opposition and, after the REVOLUTION OF 1848, was elected to the Constituant Assembly. Named minister of foreign affairs under the SECOND EMPIRE (1852), he favored an Austrian alliance but had to resign after having meetings in Vienna (1855). Recalled to his post in 1862, he was disavowed by NAPOLÉON III for having wanted to obtain from Prussia territorial compensations on the left bank of the Rhine in exchange for French mediation during the Austro-Prussian War of 1866.

## Drumont, Édouard (1844–1917)

*publisher, journalist, political figure*

Édouard Drumont, who was born in Paris, was a Catholic journalist and contributor to *L'Univers*, published by LOUIS VEUILLOT. Drumont attacked the powerful figures of high finance and, in particular, Jewish financiers, especially in an essay entitled *France juive, essai d'histoire contemporaine* (1886), which is generally considered to be the most systematic of anti-Semitic manifestos. He also founded a nationalist and anti-Semitic newspaper, *La libre Parole* (1892), in which he denounced, among other issues, the PANAMA AFFAIR. This is also the theme of his work *De l'or, de la boue et du sang* (1896). A lead-

ing anti-Dreyfusard, Drumont served as a rightist deputy (1898–1902).

## Dubois, Guillaume (1656–1723)

*cardinal, political figure*

Born in Brive-la-Gaillarde, the son of an apothecary, Guillaume Dubois served as tutor to PHILIPPE D'ORLÉANS, who, upon becoming regent, brought him to power. Venal, libertine, hypocritical, scheming, but intelligent, Dubois was a skillful diplomat. Reconciling the interests of the regent with those of Hanover, which thus made them acceptable to England, he concluded with that nation and Holland the Triple—then the Quadruple—Alliance against Spain (1717). After having held in check the CELLAMARE PLOT (1718), he conducted a short war against Spain (1719–20) to obtain the dismissal of Cardinal Alberoni and stop the rebuilding of Spanish military power. Extremely ambitious, Dubois was not content to be foreign minister and obtained for himself, after the archbishopric of Cambrai and the cardinal's hat, the title of first minister (1722). He had himself elected to the ACADÉMIE FRANÇAISE and named president of the Assembly of the Clergy.

## Dubuffet, Jean (1901–1985)

*painter, sculptor, writer*

Born in Le Havre, Jean Dubuffet pursued his work as wine merchant while being interested in the fine arts (*Masques et Marionettes*, 1933). After 1942, he devoted himself entirely to painting, while placing himself on the margins of traditional cultural expression (*Notes pour les fins lettres*, 1946; *Positions anti-culturelles*, 1951; *Asphyxiante Culture*, 1968). Admiring ingenuity and spontaneity (he was interested in the art of children and the insane), he developed the concept of "art brut" (*L'Art brut préféré aux arts culturels*, 1949), or basic primitive art. Many of his pieces are assemblages as well as paintings. Dubuffet's works include series (*Marionettes de la ville et de la campagne*, 1943–45; *Mirobolus, Macadam et Cie*, 1945; *Portraits Plus beaux qu'ils croient*, 1947; *Corps des dames*, 1951; and later, *Paris-Circus*, 1962), and other pieces (*Sols et Terrains*, 1952; *Pâtes battues; Phénomènes*, or *Empreintes; Assemblages,*

1953–57; *Topographies, Texturologies, Matériologies;* and *L'Hourloupe,* 1962; and *Closerie Falbala,* 1970–73).

## Duchamp, Marcel  (1887–1968)
*painter*

Marcel Duchamp, who has had a major influence on modern art, was born in Blainville-Crevon, the brother of the artists RAYMOND DUCHAMP-VILLON, SUZANNE DUCHAMP, and JACQUES VILLON. His early works, which he began at age 15, were in the impressionist style. Later, he moved to fauvism (*À propos de jeune Soeur,* 1911; *Yvonne et Magdeleine déchiquetées,* 1911; *Jeune homme triste dans un train,* 1911; *Le Roi et la Reine entourés de nus vites,* 1912), and works of this period show the influence of PAUL CÉZANNE. Duchamp then moved to cubism, and his famous *Nu descendant un escalier* (*Nude Descending a Staircase;* 1912) caused an uproar when shown in Paris and later in New York City at the Armory show, the first major exhibition of modern art in the United States. His nonconformism is also evident in his *Moulin à café* (1911) and *Broyeuse de chocolat* (1913), and he continued to court controversy with his "readymades," assemblages from ordinary materials, in particular his bicycle wheel mounted on a kitchen stool (1913), and a reversed urinal, entitled *Fontaine* (1917), and signed R. Mutt, and a Mona Lisa with a mustache, entitled *L.H.O.O.Q.* (1917), an acronym with a risqué sexual connotation. He also in this period produced his mysterious masterpiece, *La Mariée mise à nu par ses célibataires, même* (1915–23), a complex work made of foil, oil paint, and wire forms set between large panes of glass. Duchamp also produced a short motion picture, *Anémic cinéma,* with Man Ray (1926), and one of his last works is a monumental and also controversial piece assembled out of various materials and entitled *Étant donnés: 1 la chute d'eau, 2 le gaz d'éclairage* (1946–66).

## Duchamp, Suzanne  (1889–1963)
*painter*

Born in Blainville-Crevon, Normandy, Suzanne Duchamp was the sister of the artists JACQUES VILLON, RAYMOND DUCHAMP-VILLON, and MARCEL DUCHAMP. She began her art studies at Rouen and her early work reflects the influence of impressionists and cubists. Settling in Paris in 1896, she soon exhibited at the Salon des Indépendants. By 1916, Duchamp, who was also a poet, was painting in the dadist style (*Multiplication*).

## Duchamp-Villon, Pierre-Maurice-Raymond  (1876–1918)
*sculptor*

Pierre-Maurice-Raymond Duchamp-Villon, or Raymond Duchamp-Villon as he is known, was born in Damville, Eure, the brother of the artists JACQUES VILLON, SUZANNE DUCHAMP, and MARCEL DUCHAMP. Considered one of the masters of the early 20th-century modernist style, he was first influenced by AUGUSTE RODIN, then the cubists, seeking to simplify forms and achieve a more geometric abstract style. He did busts of individuals (*Tête de Baudelaire,* 1911), and animals, notably horses (*Petit-Cheval, Cheval-Majeur*). Progressively he abandoned all representational aspects in his art to achieve angular volume and spherical or cylindrical forms, evoking action (*L'Athlète*). Despite the brevity of his career, Duchamp made a significant contribution to the development of modern sculpture and the movement toward cubism.

## Ducis, Jean-François  (1733–1816)
*poet*

Born at Versailles, Jean-François Ducis was a translator into French of William Shakespeare's works, which he tried to adapt to the theater with the rules of classical tragedy (*Hamlet,* 1769; *Romeo and Juliette,* 1772; *King Lear,* 1783; *Macbeth,* 1784; *Othello,* 1792). In his academic adaptations, he is the first to introduce the works of the great English dramatist to the French public. Ducis was elected to the ACADÉMIE FRANÇAISE in 1778.

## Duclaux, Émile  (1840–1904)
*biochemist*

Born in Aurillac, Émile Duclaux succeeded LOUIS PASTEUR as the director of the Pasteur Institute (1895) in Paris and, in particular, did research on microbic fermentation and illnesses. He also developed the theory of capillaric phenomena. Duclaux was one of the founders of the Ligue des droits de l'homme, and in 1888 was named to the Academy of Sciences. He was succeeded as director of the Pasteur Institute by ÉMILE ROUX.

## Duclos, Charles Pinot  (1704–1772)
*novelist, moralist*

Born in Dinan, Charles Pinot Duclos is the author of the libertine-inspired *Confessions du comte de \*\*\** (1714). A friend of the philosophes and the libertines, he wrote *Considérations sur les mœurs de ce siècle* (dedicated to King LOUIS XV, 1751), a series of tableaux and caricatures of the era whose historical and psychological interest is undeniable. His *Commentaire sur la grammaire générale et raisonnée de Port-Royal* (1754) served as the basis for the *Essai sur l'origine des langues* by JEAN-JACQUES ROUSSEAU. Duclos was elected to the ACADÉMIE FRANÇAISE in 1747 and in 1755 was named its permanent secretary.

## Duclos, Jacques  (1896–1975)
*political figure*

An influential leader of the FRENCH COMMUNIST PARTY (SFIC), Jacques Duclos was born in Louey, Hautes-Pyrénées. As a youth, he worked in the pastry trade until entering the French army in WORLD WAR I. After the war, in which he was wounded, he founded with others the Association républicaine des anciens combatants (ARAC). Already a member of the Communist Party, he joined its Central Committee (1926), then its Political Bureau (1931), and finally rose to the Executive Committee of the Communist Third International (1935). A deputy in the National Assembly from 1926 to 1932, and from 1936 to 1939, he was then a member of the clandestine secretariat that directed the actions of the French Communist Party during the German Occupation (1941–44). With the approval of General CHARLES DE GAULLE, he planned an uprising in PARIS in August 1944. Reelected and serving as a deputy after the Liberation (1945–58), he went to Poland in 1947 to help establish the Cominform, the central information office of the Communist Party. Duclos's influence in world Communist circles increased greatly, and he served as president of the Communists in the National Assembly (1946–48), vice president of the National Assembly (1946–48), senator (1959), and was a candidate for the presidency of the Fifth Republic (1969).

## Ducos, Roger  (1747–1816)
*political figure*

Born in Dax, Roger Ducos, during the REVOLUTION OF 1789, was a MONTAGNARD deputy to the Convention, a member of the Council of Ancients (from which he was excluded after 22 Floréal Year VI), a member of the Directory 30 Prairial Year VII (June 18, 1799), and supporting the coup d'état of 18 Brumaire, was named third consul, being replaced shortly after by CHARLES FRANÇOIS LEBRUN. Vice president of the Senate, having been made a count of the Empire, he voted for the abdication of NAPOLÉON I (1814). He was, nonetheless, a peer during the Hundred Days. Proscribed as a regicide under the Restoration, Ducos died in exile near Ulm, Germany.

## Ducos, Théodore  (1801–1855)
*political figure*

Born in BORDEAUX, Théodore Ducos, whose family had been GIRONDINS during the REVOLUTION OF 1789, was named minister of the navy by NAPOLÉON III (1851). In that capacity, he was ordered to carry out the deportation to Cayenne, in French Guiana, of the opponents of the coup d'état of December 2, 1851. He then supported a policy of French entrance into Senegambia and New Caledonia, and helped in the preparation for the Crimean War.

## Ducos du Hauron, Louis  (1837–1920)
*physicist*

Born in Langon, Louis Ducos du Hauron, like CHARLES CROS, but independently of him, helped to invent color photography. He established the principles of subtractive synthesis and described the methods of obtaining trichromatic photographs (1869). He also conceived the idea of anaglyphic stereoscopy (superimposition of negatives in complementary colors, 1891).

## Ducrot, Auguste-Alexandre (1817–1882)
*military figure*

Born in Nevers, Auguste-Alexandre Ducrot served in ALGERIA and in the Italian campaign (1859). During the FRANCO-PRUSSIAN WAR (1870), he fought at the battle of Woerth (or Reichshoffen, August 6, 1870). A prisoner after the defeat at Sedan, he escaped and was placed in command of the Second Army of Paris during the capital's siege by Prussians. A monarchist deputy to the National Assembly (1817–72), then commander of the 8th Corps of Bourges (1872–78), General Ducrot attempted a monarchist coup d'état but was forced to retreat after the republican suppression of the attempted overthrow.

## Dufaure, Jules-Armand-Stanislas (1798–1881)
*attorney, political figure*

Born in Saujon, Charente-Maritime, Jules-Armand-Stanislas Dufaure was a liberal deputy (1834), then minister of public works (1839–40). He became a member of the Constituent Assembly immediately after the REVOLUTION OF 1848 and was named minister of the interior by Premier JEAN-BAPTISTE CAVAIGNAC (October–December 1848). Reelected to the Legislative Assembly (May 1849), he left political life after the coup d'état of December 2, 1851. After the fall of the SECOND EMPIRE, he served in the National Assembly as a moderate deputy and was called a number of times to serve as minister of justice, or premier (May 1873, 1876) under the Third Republic. Dufaure was elected to the ACADÉMIE FRANÇAISE in 1863.

## Dufy, Raoul (1877–1953)
*painter, engraver*

Known for his lively outdoor scenes, Raoul Dufy was born in Le Havre and studied at the workshop of LÉON BONNAT in Paris. His first scenes show the influence of HENRI DE TOULOUSE-LAUTREC, while his landscapes and seascapes show that of CLAUDE MONET (*14 Juillet,* 1906). He moved toward fauvism (1906) and spent time with GEORGES BRAQUE at l'Estaque (1908), as evidenced by his use of a more somber palette (*Maison dans les arbres*). He took up engraving (wood engravings for GUILLAUME APOL-LONAIRE's *Bestiaire*), then, after 1919, developed a more personal style, making frequent trips to the Midi as well as to Italy (1922–23) and Morocco (1925). He produced works with diverse themes: boaters on the Marne, nudes (1918–30), racing scenes, circuses, regattas, flowers, outdoor amusements, portraits, and landscapes (1944) in a lighter and more luminous style, dominated by line. His elegant engravings, as well as his lively vision of the world, show his genius. Dufy also produced a large mural for the Palais de Chaillot in Paris and for other venues, including an immense work (60 m × 10 m), *La Fée Électricité* (1937). He worked, too, in ceramics, textiles, and tapestries, and created sets for the theater and the ballet.

## Dugommier, Jacques (1738–1794)
*military figure*

Born Jacques François Coquille, in La Basse-Terre, Guadeloupe, General Dugommier as he is known, enthusiastically embraced the REVOLUTION OF 1789 and was named commander of the National Guards of Martinique (1790). A deputy to the Convention (1792) and brigadier general, he served in Italy (1793) and played an active role at the siege of Toulon (1793–94). While commanding the Army of the Pyrenees, Dugommier was killed fighting the Spanish forces in Catalonia.

## Duguay-Trouin, René (1673–1736)
*naval officer*

Born in Saint-Malo, René Duguay-Trouin, a naval officer, distinguished himself in the wars of LOUIS XIV against the Dutch and the English, but his principal exploit was the taking of Rio de Janeiro (1711) from the Portuguese. During the reign of LOUIS XV, he fought against the Barbary pirates.

## Du Guesclin, Bertrand (ca. 1320–1380)
*military figure*

Known as the "Eagle of Brittany," Bertrand du Guesclin was born in La Motte-Broons, near Dinon. He joined the service of the king of France around 1350 and defeated King CHARLES II THE BAD of Navarre at Cocherel (1364). Du Guesclin fought alongside CHARLES OF BLOIS at the Battle of Auray (1364), where he was taken prisoner. King CHARLES V of France payed his ransom and gave him a large company of mercenaries, the Grandes Compagnes (1366), which he led out of France to fight in Castile. There, they aided King Henry of Trastamara (the future Henry II of Castile and Léon) in his war against his half brother, Peter the Cruel. Du Guesclin was defeated there by Edward, prince of Wales, at Najera in 1367, but eventually recovered the throne of Castile for Henry. Upon returning to France, he was made constable and fought a war of harassment against the English (the HUNDRED YEARS' WAR) and other enemies of France, chasing them out of Poitou, Normandy, Guyenne, and Saintonge. Du Guesclin would crystallize the French hatred for the English, signaling one of the first patriotic manifestations of the French kingdom.

## Dullin, Charles (1885–1949)
*actor, stage director*

Born in Yenne, Savoy, Charles Dullin dedicated his career to renewing the staging and interpretation of both classical and modern French drama. His stagings of Aristophanes (*Les Oiseaux*), Pirandello (*Chacun sa vérité*), Ben Jonson (*Volpone*), Salacrou (*La Terre est ronde*), MOLIÈRE (*L'Avare*), Achard (*Voulez-vous jouer avec môa?*), Shakespeare (*Richard III*), and BALZAC (*Le Faiseur*) are among the most remarkable of the period. An incomparable teacher, he greatly influenced several other actors and directors, including JEAN-LOUIS BARRAULT and JEAN VILAR.

## Dumas, Alexandre (1802–1870)
## (Alexandre Dumas Davy de la Pailleterie)
*novelist, playwright*

Born in Villers-Cotterêts, Aisne, the son of a general born in Jérémie, Saint-Domingue (now Haiti), and grandson of the marquis Davy de la Pailleterie, Alexandre Dumas, or Dumas père, as he is also known, had little formal education but, while working as a clerk in Paris, achieved notoriety with his play *Henri III et sa cour* (1825), which was produced by the COMÉDIE-FRANÇAISE along with a later work, *Christine* (1830). Both were resounding successes. Dumas became a prolific writer, with about 1,200 volumes eventually published under his

Alexandre Dumas *(Library of Congress)*

name. Many, however, were the products of collaboration or the work of hired writers, but all bear the mark of his personal inventiveness and genius. Dumas is best remembered for his historical novels, *Les Trois Mousquetaires* (*The Three Musketeers;* 1844) and *Le Comte de Monte-Cristo* (*The Count of Monte Cristo;* 1844). More of a writer than a historian, however, Dumas described history as "merely a peg to which he could hook his works on." Dumas spent much of his enormous earnings from his writings on an extravagant lifestyle (one of his numerous mistresses was the mother of his son ALEXANDRE DUMAS FILS). He died nearly bankrupt. Besides his historical novels, Dumas's works include the plays *Antony* (1831), *La Tour de Nesle* (1832), *Catherine Howard* (1834), and *L'Alchimiste* (1839). His own life as well as a vivid account of his times are found in his *Mémoires* (1852–54) and *Impressions de Voyage* (1835–58).

## Dumas fils, Alexandre  (1824–1895)
*novelist, playwright*

Born in Paris, the natural son of ALEXANDRE DUMAS, Alexandre Dumas fils, as a child, was often taunted about his illegitimacy. His first literary work was a volume of poetry, *Péchés de jeunesse* (Sins of Youth; 1847). This was followed by his first novel, *Camille* (1848), and his subsequent dramatization of that work (*La Dame aux camélias*) in 1852, establishing his name as a playwright. The story, which has served as a vehicle for many actors on stage and in film, was immortalized by Giuseppe Verdi in his opera *La Traviata* and by Greta Garbo in the film *Camille* (1936). Although Dumas continued to write novels, he was much more successful as a dramatist. His plays include *Le Demi-Monde* (1855), *La Question d'argent* (1857), *Le Fils naturel* (1858), *Monsieur Alphonse* (1874), *Denise* (1885), and *Francillon* (1887). He was elected to the ACADÉMIE FRANÇAISE in 1874.

## Dumont d'Urville, Jules-Sébastien-César  (1790–1842)
*navigator, explorer*

Born in Condé-sur-Noireau, Jules-Sébastien-César Dumont d'Urville, after having taken part in hydrographic expeditions in the Aegean Sea (where he recognized the recently unearthed Venus de Milo and secured its acquisition by the French government), and the Black Sea (1819–20), participated in an expedition that circumnavigated the globe (1822–25). He then was given command of the *Astrolabe*, on which he began an expedition to survey Oceania, during the course of which he studied the hydrography of a number of islands (New Zealand, Viti, Loyalty, New Guinea, NEW CALEDONIA, and others) and was sent to the island of Vanikoro, where he found evidence of the earlier explorer JEAN-FRANÇOIS LA PÉROUSE, who had been shipwrecked and killed. From 1837 to 1840, Dumont d'Urville explored the Antarctic regions, discovering Louis-Philippe Land, Joinville Island (1839), and Adelie Land (Terre Adélie) (1840). He has left accounts of his voyage: *Voyages et découvertes autour du monde et à la recherche de La Pérouse* (1822–34), *Voyages au pôle Sud et en Océanie* (1842–46). Various regions, including D'Urville Sea, off Adélie Coast, and Cape d'Urville, Indonesia, and D'Urville Island, off New Zealand, bear his name.

## Dumoulin, Charles  (1500–1566)
*jurist*

Born in Paris, where he served as an adviser to the parlement (1522), Charles Dumoulin passed from Calvinism to Lutheranism and, having to leave France due to his religion, taught law in Germany. Returning to France in 1557, he questioned the authority of the pope in his *Conseil sur le fait du concile de Trente*, which caused him to be imprisoned until 1564. He returned to Catholicism before dying. Called the "prince of jurisconsuls" because of his important works on the origins and history of French law, he expressed in his writings, and especially in *Révision de la coutume de Paris* (1539), his hostility to the old feudal legal system and his wish to codify civil law.

## Dumouriez, General  (1739–1823)
### (Charles-François du Périer)
*military figure*

One of the most important and controversial generals of the REVOLUTION OF 1789, Charles-François du Périer, or General Dumouriez, as he is known, became an officer in 1758 and fought in the Seven Years' War. In 1763, he joined the diplomatic espionage service and was sent by the duke of CHOISEUL on several missions. Head of the National Guard, Dumouriez, having embraced the principles of the revolution, as well as having ties to the count of MIRABEAU, the MARQUIS DE LA FAYETTE, and the duke of ORLÉANS, and, being a member of the JACOBIN Club (1790), would be named foreign minister during the Girondin government (1792) and helped to encourage King LOUIS XVI to declare war against the coalition of forces invading France. After the recall of the GIRONDIN ministers (June 13), he resigned (June 15). Commander in chief of the Armies of the North, with General FRANÇOIS KELLERMANN he won the celebrated Battle of Valmy against the Prussians, then that of Jemmappes against the Austrians, then occupied Belgium. After the formation of the First Coalition (February 1793), Dumouriez proposed an offensive plan that was adopted, entering into Holland (February 16), and seizing Breda (February 25), but he was defeated at Neerwinden (March 18), then again at Louvain (March 21) by the duke of Saxe-Coburg, with whom he had entered into negotiations. Accused of treason, Dumouriez handed over to the Austrians the commissioners sent by the Convention to inquire into his conduct, before he himself went over to the enemy's side. His defeats and the consequences (the loss of Belgium and Holland, then the left bank of the Rhine) contributed to the fall of the Girondins. Dumouriez died in exile in England.

## Dunois, Jean, count de Longueville (1402/3–1468)
### (Jean d'Orléans, le Bâtard d'Orléans)
*military figure*

Known as "le Bâtard d'Orléans," Jean Dunois, count of Longueville, was born in the château de l'Hay, the natural son of Louis, duke of Orléans. In 1418, he joined the Armagnacs in the civil war and was captured by the Burgundians. A companion in arms to JOAN OF ARC, he fought during the defense of Orléans and assisted in the victory at Patay (1429), contributing to the reconquest of Normandy and Guyenne (1448–53). He took part in the coronation of King CHARLES VII, his half brother, whom, as part of the Praguerie, he later opposed. In 1465, Dunois joined the LIGUE DE BIEN PUBLIC against King LOUIS XI (1465).

## Dupanloup, Félix (1802–1978)
*prelate, political figure*

Born in Saint-Félix, Savoy, Félix Dupanloup was the bishop of Orléans when, in 1849, as a leader of the liberal Catholics, he took a stand against LOUIS VEUILLOT's ultramontanist newspaper, *L'Univers*, and, for personal reasons, opposed the definition of papal infallibility (although when that doctrine was proclaimed in 1870, he accepted it). Dupanloup was a member of the commission that developed the law (Falloux Law, 1855) on education and later, as a deputy, helped to pass the law of 1875 on upper-level teaching. At odds with the writers ERNEST RENAN, HIPPOLYTE TAINE, and MAXIMILIEN LITTRÉ, he tried to overturn the latter's election to the ACADÉMIE FRANÇAISE, from which he resigned when Littré was elected in 1871. Dupanloup, who became a senator in 1876, is the author of various pedagogic works and catechisms, and of a famous pamphlet in which he supports the papal encyclical *Quanta cura* and the *Syllabus* of Pope Pius IX.

## Duparc, Henri (1848–1933)
### (Henri Fouques-Duparc)
*composer*

Born in Paris, Henri Fouques-Duparc, or Henri Duparc, as he is known, was the student of CÉSAR FRANCK and was one of the founders of the Société nationale de musique (1871). Neurasthenia and rheumatism, however, brought an end to his career (1885). Author of works for piano (*Laendler*, 1874) and orchestra (*Lénore*, 1875), he destroyed the majority of his compositions, leaving only a collection of 13 melodies (1868–83), which passed into the canon of traditional lieder and are considered among the major works of vocal art (*Soupir*, the famous *Invitation au voyage*, *Extase*, *Phydilé*, *La Vie antérieure*).

## Du Perron, Jacques-Davy (1556–1618)
*prelate, statesman, writer*

Born in Val-de-Joux, Switzerland, Jacques-Davy Du Perron, a convert from Calvinism, became the bishop of Évreux and, as an emissary of King HENRY IV to Pope Clement VIII, obtained from Rome a reconciliation (1595) with that monarch. Jacques Du Perron, who upheld the Catholic theses at the meeting in Fontainebleau (see PHILIPPE DUPLESSIS-MORNAY), became, in turn, a cardinal (1604), archbishop of Sens (1606), and, in 1610, a member of the Regency Council. His writings comprise works of religious polemics, sermons, and poetry.

## Dupin, André-Marie-Jean-Jacques (1783–1865)
*magistrate, political figure*

Born in Varzy, Nivernais, André-Marie-Jean-Jacques Dupin, or Dupin Aîné as he is known, was a highly respected attorney who, in particular, defended Marshal MICHEL NEY and the singer and satirist PIERRE BÉRANGER. Elected a deputy in 1827, he sat with the liberal opposition and played an active role in the revolutionary days of July 1830. President of the Chamber of Deputies (1832–37), he supported the republic (1848) and was named president of the Legislative Assembly. He then, however, became close with Louis-Napoléon (see NAPOLÉON III) and, under the SECOND EMPIRE, became a senator (1857). Dupin Aîné was elected to the ACADÉMIE FRANÇAISE in 1832.

## Dupin, Charles, baron (1784–1873)
*mathematician, political figure*

The brother of ANDRÉ DUPIN, Charles, baron Dupin was born in Varzy, Nivernais. Serving in turn as councilor of state (1831) and as minister of the navy (1833), he was a member of the Constituant, then the Legislative Assembly and became a senator in 1852. In mathematics, he determined the surface in which all lines on a curve are circular (*cyclide de Dupin,* 1801), studied the triple orthogonal systems, and introduced the idea of conjugant directions and asymptotic lines. He applied his discoveries to the construction of roads, to the study of stability in ships, and to optics. Dupin was elected to the Academy of Sciences in 1818.

## Dupleix, Joseph-François (1697–1763)
*colonial administrator*

Born in Landrecies, Joseph-François Dupleix served as the director of the French Indies Company (1720), then as the director general of all French bank branches in India. He had a military, as well as a commercial, career, and taking advantage of the divisions among the indigenous principalities, conquered additional territory in India for France. Great Britain opposed this expansion, and a conflict developed, with Dupleix taking Madras from the British but losing it later by the terms of the Treaty of Aix-la-Chapelle (1748). Dupleix continued to try to extend French hegemony over southern India by intervening in the quarrels that divided its various states, especially in the Dekkan. But he was successfully opposed by the British under Robert Clive (1754). He was then recalled to France. His policies were disavowed and his conquests were lost in the SEVEN YEARS' WAR.

## Duplessis-Mornay (1549–1623)
*Protestant leader*

Born in Bugy, Philippe de Mornay, lord of Plessis-Marly, or Duplessis Mornay as he is known, was a supporter of Henri de Navarre (HENRY IV), to whom he became principal adviser and ambassador (1576). After that monarch's abjuration (1593), he retired to Saumur, where he founded the first Protestant academy (1599). Author of *Traité de l'eucharistie,* which opened a debate with JACQUES

DU PERRON (Fontainebleau, 1600), he also left his *Mémoires* (4 volumes, posthumous.)

## Dupont de l'Eure (1767–1855)
*political figure*

Born in Le Neubourg, Eure, Jacques-Charles Dupont, or Dupont de l'Eure as he is known, was an advocate for the Parlement of Normandy, a member of the Council of Five Hundred under the DIRECTORY (1797), a member of the Legislative Corps in 1813, and of the Chamber of Representatives during the HUNDRED DAYS. He sat as an opposition deputy during the RESTORATION and, after having taken part in the REVOLUTION OF JULY 1830, was for some time minister of justice before rejoining anew the ranks of the opposition under the July Monarchy. Dupont de l'Eure was named president of the provisional government in 1848.

## Dupont de Nemours, Pierre-Samuel (1739–1817)
*economist, political figure*

Born in Paris, Pierre-Samuel Dupont de Nemours was a disciple of FRANÇOIS QUESNAY and author of several works on political economy (*Physiocratie,* 1767; *Origines de progrès d'une science nouvelle,* 1768; *Table raisonnée des principes de l'économie politique,* 1773). He was a collaborator with ROBERT TURGOT and a deputy to the Third Estate (1789) at the time of the REVOLUTION OF 1789. A royalist, he went into exile in the United States after 18 Fructidor. His son, Éleuthère Irénée Du Pont (1771–1834), was a chemist who worked in France with ANTOINE LAVOISIER and founded a gunpowder mill in the United States that was the origin of the Du Pont de Nemours company.

## Duport (or Du Port), Adrien-Jean-François (1759–1798)
*political figure*

Born in Paris, Adrien-Jean-François Duport was a deputy for the nobility of that city to the ESTATES GENERAL (1789), and was one of the first to join the Third Estate at the beginning of the REVOLUTION OF 1789. Within the National Assembly, he formed with ANTOINE BARNAVE and ALEXANDRE DE LAMETH a triumvirate that tried to reconcile the revolution's principles and the monarchy. He stood out for his influence on the reorganization of the judicial system, which in turn contributed to the adoption of the institution of juries. After August 10, 1792, Duport succeeded in escaping to England. He returned to France after 9 Thermidor Year II (July 1794), then was forced to emigrate to Switzerland in 1797 to escape his Directory enemies.

## Duprat, Antoine (1463–1535)
*prelate, political figure*

Born in Issoire, Antoine Duprat, an attorney and the first president of the parlement of PARIS (1507), became tutor to the future FRANCIS I, who made him chancellor (1515). Taking holy orders in 1516, he was the chief negotiator of the Concordat of Bologna. He became archbishop of Sens, then cardinal (1527). Duprat was the instigator of the policy to repress Protestantism.

## Duquesne, Abraham, marquis (1610–1688)
*naval officer*

Born in Dieppe, Abraham, marquis Duquesne, after having served in Sweden, returned to France and distinguished himself as a naval officer, notably against the Dutch in the Mediterranean, gaining a number of victories over Dutch admiral Michiel Adriaanszoon de Ruyter (Stromboli, 1675; Augusta, 1676) and against the Barbary pirates (Tripoli, 1681; Algiers, 1682). He was one of the few Protestants spared by the revocation of the EDICT OF NANTES, which had upheld religious toleration.

## Duras, Marguerite (1914–1996)
*novelist, playwright, screenwriter, film writer*

Born Marguerite Dennadieu in French Indochina, Marguerite Duras as she is known, was left in poverty by the death of her father when she was four, leaving her mother struggling to support her and her siblings. In 1930, Duras moved to Paris to study law and government, and soon began publishing. Her memoirs (*Une banage contre le Pacifique*, 1950) recall the difficult period of her youth and also brought her critical acclaim. Several other works, *Petits chevaux de Tarquina* (1953), *Dix heures et demie du soir en été* (1960), *Le Ravisissement de Lol V. Stein* (1964), *Le Vice-Consul* (1966), and *L'Amour* (1971) followed, but it was in *Moderato Contabile* (1958) where her distinctive style that dispensed with traditional narrative structures and plots and focused instead on silences and ambiguity first appeared. In 1959, Duras's career took a new turn when ALAIN RESNAIS asked her to write the screenplay for his film *Hiroshima mon amour*. It was similar in style to *Moderato Contabile*. This screenplay won her worldwide critical acclaim and was followed by others, including *Une aussi longue absence* (1961). Duras also wrote for and directed other films, *Jaune le Soleil* (1971), *Nathalie Granger* (1973), *India Song* (1974), and *Le Camien* (1977). Duras's later works include the autobiographical novel *L'Amant* (prix Goncourt 1984), *L'Amant de la Chine du Nord* (1991), *La pluie d'été* (1990), and *Yann Andrea Steiner* (1992). Her plays include *Les Viaducs de Seine-et-Oise* (1960), *Le Square* (1962), *Les Eaux et Forêts*, *La Musica* (1965), and *Savannah Bay* (1982).

## Durkheim, Émile (1858–1917)
*social theorist*

One of the founders of modern sociology, Émile Durkheim was born in Épinal and graduated from the École normale supérieure in Paris. He began his career teaching social sciences, first at the University of Bordeaux and later at the University of Paris. In the line of AUGUSTE COMTE's positivism, Durkheim believed that the scientific method should be applied to the study of society. He proposed that groups had characteristics that varied from those of individuals and was also concerned with the basis of social stability, mores, and religion. Values, he believed, were the bonds that held the social order together. Their breakdown leads to the loss of one's individual stability and to feelings of anxiety and dissatisfaction. In this light, he explained suicide as a result of the lack of integration into society. In his work, Durkheim often applied anthropological themes and approaches, especially of aboriginal societies, to support his theories. His principal works include *De la division du travail social* (1893), *Regles de la méthode sociologique* (1895), *Le Suicide* (1897), *Les Formes élémentaires de la vie religieuse: le système totémique en Australie* (1912).

## Duruy, Victor (1811–1894)
*historian, political figure*

Born in Paris, Victor Duruy was inspector general of secondary schools (1861–62), was named minister of public instruction by NAPOLÉON III (1863–69), and helped to put through important reforms liberalizing education, reestablishing exams in philosophy, introducing contemporary history in the curricula, and developing new primary and secondary curricula (e.g., creation of courses for girls). Author of a number of historical works, including an important *Histoire des Romains* (1876–85), Duruy was elected to the ACADÉMIE FRANÇAISE in 1884.

## Duvergier, Maurice (1917– )
*jurist, political theorist*

Born in Angoulême, Maurice Duvergier is the author of numerous texts and scholarly manuals (*Droit constitutionnel et institutions politiques*, 1951; *Le Système politique français*, 20th edition in 1990; *La Nostalgie de l'impuissance*, 1988; *Le Lièvre libéral et la Tortue européenne*, 1990), and was for a long time one of the principal writers for the newspaper *Le Monde*. His study, *Les Partis politiques* (1951), has become a classic of political sociology. In it, he proposes a typology of parties, distinguishing the membership parties (partis de notables) from mass parties (partis des militants). He has shown that the portional party type (the Italian or French FOURTH REPUBLIC model) tends toward a multiplication of parties and that that of majority scrutiny (the British model) tends toward a biparty structure. In 1989, Duvergier was elected to the European Parliament (see EUROPEAN UNION) on a list presented by the Italian Communist Party.

## Duvergier de Hauranne, Jean (1581–1643)
*theologian*

One of the founders of JANSENISM, Jean Duvergier de Hauranne, abbot of Saint-Cyran, was born near Bayonne and studied at Louvain and Paris where he became a close friend of the Dutch theologian Cornelius Jansen. Together they developed a theory of predestination based on Augustinian lines. After 1630, Duvergier became the spiritual counselor at the Jansenist convent of Port-Royal and was closely associated with other leading Jansenist theologians. His insistence on strict doctrines and theology, hostility to the Jesuits, and political ties to the parlements, as well as his opposition to the foreign and religious policies of Cardinal RICHELIEU, caused him to be put into prison (1638). He remained there until Richelieu's death in 1642, but his health was ruined, and he died shortly after. An erudite thinker, Duvergier, through his writings, mirrored Jansenist theology. The strength of the Jansenist movement, lasting into the 18th century, was largely due to his influence.

See also ARNAULD, ANTOINE; ARNAULD FAMILY.

## Duvergier de Hauranne, Prosper (1798–1881)
*political figure*

Born in Rouen, Prosper Duvergier de Hauranne was elected a deputy in 1831 and, while at first doctrinaire, became one of the principal reformist proponents, publishing in 1846 a pamphlet supporting that position (*La Réforme parlementaire et la Réforme électorale*). He played an active role in the Banquets campaign of 1847–48 that led to the REVOLUTION OF 1848, and, a member of the Constituant Assembly (1847) and the Legislative Assembly (1849), was detained and then exiled because of his opposition to the coup d'état of December 2, 1851. Author of *Histoire du gouvernement parlementaire en France de 1814 à 1848* (1857–72), Duvergier de Hauranne was elected to the ACADÉMIE FRANÇAISE in 1870.

# E

## Eberhardt, Isabelle (1877–1904)
*writer*

Of Russian origin, Isabelle Eberhardt was born in Meyrin, Switzerland. She led an adventurous life, notably in the Sahara and in ALGERIA, where she married a chieftain, Slimène Ehni, and converted to Islam. She became a journalist for *La Dépêche algérienne* and *Akhbar*. Eberhardt's accounts, which bear witness to her struggles on behalf of the poor, all appeared after her tragic death in a flood at Ain Sefra (*Dans l'ombre chaud de l'Islam*, 1906; *Notes de route*, 1908; *Contes et Paysages*, 1925).

## Effel, Jean (1908–1982)
*political cartoonist*

Born in Paris, Jean Effel (the pen name of François Lejeune) is best known for his political cartoons and satires. While his work is polemical, the humor of his drawings is as poetic as it is satirical. It is often based on a gentle but mocking illustration of certain themes in the republican tradition. Effel published his caricatures in daily newspapers, and some have been put together in collections. He also made an animation, *La Création du monde*, that was produced by a Czech group using his drawings.

## Eiffel, Gustave (1832–1923)
*engineer*

Most famous for his construction of the tower in Paris that bears his name, Gustave Eiffel was born in Dijon and was educated there at the Lycée royal and at the Collège Sainte-Barbe in Paris. He graduated from the École Centrale des Arts et Manufactures (1855) and joined a company that produced steam engines. In 1858, the company was granted a contract to construct a railway bridge at BORDEAUX. Eiffel's achievement of that work allowed him (1866) to begin his own company, and he soon became known for the building of wrought iron structures. In 1877, Eiffel erected a steel arch bridge over the Douro River in Oporto, Portugal (160 m in height) and, in 1884, he completed the Garabit Viaduct in France, which, for a time, was the highest bridge in the world. It demonstrates his expert craftsmanship and graceful sense of design. Eiffel cast FRÉDÉRIC-AUGUSTE BARTHOLDI's colossal statue, *Liberty Enlightening the World* (*Statue of Liberty*), which was dedicated in New York Harbor in 1886. Soon after, he began work on his greatest project, the building of the EIFFEL TOWER. It was completed in 1889 for the celebration of the centennial of the French Revolution. The imposing tower is constructed of 7,000 tons of iron in 18,000 parts, held together by 2,500,000 rivets. Reaching a height of 984 feet (300 m), it dominates the Paris skyline. Eiffel later became interested in the new science of aerodynamics and, in 1912 at Auteil, he opened the first aerodynamic laboratory, which soon contributed to the development of aviation.

## Eiffel Tower (la Tour Eiffel)

The large wrought iron tower in Paris, which is both a city and a national landmark, the Eiffel Tower is an early example of wrought iron construction on a massive scale. It was designed and built (1887–89) by the French civil engineer GUSTAVE EIFFEL for the Paris Exposition, or World's Fair, of 1889. The tower, without its modern broadcasting antennae, is 300 meters high. The lower section consists of four immense arched legs, set on masonry piers. The legs curve inward until they join in a single tapered tower. There are platforms, each with an observation deck, at three levels. The

**Eiffel Tower** *(Library of Congress)*

first also contains a restaurant. The entire tower, constructed of 7,000 tons of iron, has stairs and elevators. It also contains a meteorological station, a radio communications station, and a television transmissions antenna, as well as a suite of rooms originally used by Eiffel located near the top of the tower.

## Elisabeth of Austria (1554–1592)
*queen of France*

Born in Vienna, Elisabeth of Austria was the daughter of the Holy Roman Emperor Maximilian II and Maria of Spain. Elisabeth married King CHARLES IX of France (1570) and played a minor role at the French court, returning to Austria upon her husband's death (1574).

## Elisabeth of France (1545–1568)
*princess, queen of Spain*

Born at Fontainebleau, Elisabeth of France was the daughter of King HENRY II and CATHERINE DE' MEDICI. She married Philip II of Spain, who had requested her in marriage for his son Charles (Treaty of Cateau-Cambrésis, 1559). She died in childbirth.

## Elisabeth of France (1764–1794)
**(Madame)**

*princess, sister of Louis XVI*

Born at VERSAILLES, Madame Elisabeth-Philippine-Marie-Hélène of France was the daughter of the dauphin and Marie-Josèphe of Saxony, and the sister of King LOUIS XVI. Pious, and entirely devoted to her brother, she was, during the REVOLUTION OF 1789, held in the Temple prison with the royal family (1792) after their flight to Varennes. She was then transferred to the Conciergerie before being condemned to death by the Revolutionary Tribunal and guillotined.

## Eluard, Paul (1895–1952)
**(Eugène Grindel)**

*poet*

Born Eugène Grindel in Saint-Denis, Paul Eluard as he was known, had a difficult early life and began writing poetry in 1912 during a long stay in a Swiss sanatorium. He was mobilized during WORLD WAR I (1914) and his pacifist poetry bore witness to the suffering of his comrades (*Le Devoir et l'Inquiétude*, 1917; *Poèmes pour la paix*, 1918). A founder of the surrealist movement, he met the poets ANDRÉ BRETON and LOUIS ARAGON in 1919 and others of their associates. Eluard frequently collaborated with them. In 1930, *L'Immaculée Conception* was written with Breton. During the 1920s and 1930s, Eluard experimented with surrealist poetic techniques, including "automatic writing" (writing done without deliberate intent, often believed to be affected by supernatural forces), transcribing dreams, and imitating insanity. The theme of dream versus reality is reflected in a number of his poems from this period. At this time, Eluard also collaborated with artists such as Max Ernst and Pablo Picasso in an attempt to fuse poetry and painting. In the late 1930s, influenced by the Spanish civil war (*La Victoire de Guernica,* 1936) and membership in the Communist Party, Eluard wrote more political and social poetry, in a more traditional style. During WORLD WAR II, Eluard was a member of the RESISTANCE (he served as director of the writers' committee for the northern zone) and his collections, *Poésie et vérité* (1942), *Au rendez-vous allemand* (1944), and *Dignes de vivre* (1944), were circulated among the Resistance fighters to bolster morale. His postwar poetry includes *Poésie ininterrompue* (1946), *Le Dur Désir et durer* (1946), *Le Temps débordé* (1947), *Corps mémorable* (1947), *Tout dire* (1951), *Le Phénix* (1951), and *Poésie ininterrompue II* (1951). Eluard, in his writings, sought to be a prophet for a humanity seeking to be delivered from agony and hatred.

## Élysée Palace (palais de l'Élysée)

A French government building, the Élysée is a palace in Paris situated north of the Champs-Élysées and serves as the residence of the president of the republic. Originally it was the hôtel d'Évreux (1718), before being rebuilt by Jean Cailleteau (known as Lassurance the younger) for Mme de POMPADOUR (1753). The palace became state property in 1793 and was a place for public entertainments (l'Élysée). It was restored (1805–08) by Percier and Fontaine for CAROLINE MURAT. The residence of NAPOLÉON I, then of NAPOLÉON III, it also served in 1848, and since 1873, as the residence of the president of the republic.

## Empire, First

The government of France from May 18, 1804, to April 4, 1814, and from March 20 to June 22, 1815, which followed the Consulate. On May 18, 1804, the Senate gave First Consul Napoléon Bonaparte, the title of emperor. He was crowned NAPOLÉON I, emperor of the French, in the presence of Pope Pius VII on December 2, 1804. The Empire continued the work of the Consulate government, especially in implementing the new Civil Code (Code Napoléon), the Concordat, and educational reforms. To main-

tain the integrity of his continental blockade of the British, Napoléon practiced a policy of annexation. Territorially, the empire reached its height between 1810 and 1812, comprising at that point France, Belgium, Holland, the Hanseatic cities, Bremen, Hamburg, the left bank of the Rhine, northern Italy, Rome, and the Illyrian Provinces. The king of Spain and the king of Naples were the emperor's vassals, General Charles Bernadotte reigned in Sweden under the name CHARLES XIV, and Denmark was a powerful ally. Napoléon was the mediator of the Helvetic Confederation and protector of the Confederation of the Rhine. The French Civil Code and institutions were introduced in these countries, preparing the way for a transformation of Europe. The Napoleonic Wars, however, cost the lives of a million soldiers, but the economic balance of the period was positive for France, with the blockade favoring the development of certain industries.

## Empire, Second

The government of France from December 2, 1852, to September 4, 1870. Like the FIRST EMPIRE, this regime was the product of a revolution (see REVOLUTION OF 1848), in this case, the one that had established the Second Republic. This was followed by the suppression of the opposition and by the Constitution of January 1852, which strengthened the executive power at the expense of the legislative. A plebiscite (November 21, 1852) allowed the reestablishment of the empire under NAPOLÉON III. It would begin for France a period of great economic development, especially in agriculture, industry, banking, trade, and communications. Important urban transformation occurred (see GEORGE HAUSSMANN) in PARIS, LYON, and other cities.) The development of industrial capitalism and economic liberalism (free-trade treaties, especially with Great Britain in 1860) were accompanied by social changes (the increase in the standard of living of the working classes) and new ideologies (realism, positivism, socialism). From the political point of view, the imperial regime evolved from an authoritarian one during the period 1852 to 1860 (the strengthening of personal powers, limitations of certain public and private freedoms, the oath of loyalty required of officials, control of education, and especially after the assassination attempt on Louis-Napoléon Bonaparte by

FELICE ORSINI, the suppression of the opposition), to a somewhat more liberal one after 1860 (the right of free speech and assembly, the right to strike, etc.), and finally to a parliamentary regime (1869–70). But this political evolution, rather than consolidating the government's power, favored instead the development of a republican and Socialist opposition. The Second Empire had certain military achievements (the CRIMEAN WAR, 1854–56; the campaign in Italy, 1859) and pursued a policy of colonial expansion (North Africa, sub-Saharan Africa, Syria and the Near East, and the Far East), but certain difficulties (the Roman Question concerning the Pope's authority in the Papal States) or military (Mexico, 1860–67) and diplomatic setbacks (notably in relations with Prussia) contributed to growing opposition at home. Finally, the regime collapsed after the initial defeats (Sedan, September 2, 1870) at the beginning of the FRANCO-PRUSSIAN WAR.

See also NAPOLÉON III.

## Enfantin, Prosper-Barthelémy (1796–1864)
*engineer, Socialist*

Born in Paris, Prosper-Barthelémy Enfantin, or "le Père Enfantin" as he came to be known, was one of the principal proponents of Saint-Simonism (see CLAUDE SAINT-SIMON), which developed from a political theory to become a type of religion or sect. Enfantin founded two newspapers, *Le Producteur* and *Le Globe,* and established, at Ménilmontant, a model Saint-Simonian community (1831) that had numerous adaptations. After a period in Egypt (where he tried to establish a company to build a canal at Suez), Enfantin founded and administered a railway company (Compagnie de la ligne de Lyon, 1845). He also influenced AUGUSTE BLANQUI and other thinkers, especially Socialists, of the age.

## Enghien, Louis-Antoine-Henri de Bourbon, duke d' (1772–1804)
*duke of Orléans*

Prince Louis-Antoine-Henri de Bourbon, duke d'Enghien, the oldest son of Louis-Henri-Joseph de Condé and Louise-Marie-Thérèse-Mathilde, the sister of Philippe Egalité, duke of ORLÉANS, was born at Chantilly. Educated privately, he joined the army

in 1788 and, at the outbreak of the REVOLUTION OF 1789, emigrated to Ettenheim in the Grand Duchy of Baden, where he joined the royalist forces. He later fought against the revolutionary forces with his grandfather's Army of Condé until 1797. In 1804, Napoléon Bonaparte (NAPOLÉON I), suspecting him, probably incorrectly, of being part of a conspiracy against him, had him captured in Baden during the night of March 15–16 and tried before a military tribunal. Although innocent, the duke d'Enghien was condemned and shot on March 21 at Vincennes.

## Enlightenment, the

Known in French as L'Âge des lumières, and in German as the Aufklärung, the Enlightenment encompassed European thought throughout the 18th century. Based in the rationalist theories of the 17th century, the Enlightenment, which is also known as the Age of Reason, drew on ideas of BERNARD DE FONTENELLE and PIERRE BAYLE in France and John Locke and Isaac Newton in England. The main representatives of the French Enlightenment, known as the philosophes, are MONTESQUIEU, VOLTAIRE, DIDEROT, ROUSSEAU, D'ALEMBERT, HELVÉTIUS, D'HOLBACH, BUFFON, CONDORCET, and all the Encyclopedists; in England, Toland, Hume, and Smith; in Italy, BECCARIA; and in Germany, C. von Wolff, Lessing, and Immanuel Kant. All, with certain qualifications, shared a faith in reason and the basic goodness of human nature and a belief in tolerance and the perfectibility of society.

## Enragés

During the REVOLUTION OF 1789, Enragés ("enraged ones") was the name given to the revolutionary extremists (e.g., JACQUES ROUX) who demanded not only civil and political but also economic and social equality. They demanded leveling taxation, the requisitioning of commodities, and a redistribution of wealth in favor of the indigent population and the expropriation of profits by the state. Eliminated at the end of 1793 as a result of the TERROR, the Enragés had formulated socialist-inspired programs that would be taken up later by the Hébertists and still later by FRANÇOIS-NOËL BABEUF.

See also HÉBERT, JACQUES; GIRONDINS.

## Entente Cordiale

The name given by FRANÇOIS GUIZOT to the French-British rapprochement that was drafted during the July Monarchy, permitting France to end the diplomatic isolation that occurred after the REVOLUTION OF 1830. This policy, which NAPOLÉON III tried to pursue also (the Franco-British alliance during the Crimean War, 1854–56), was for a long period impeded by the numerous rivalries, in particular the colonial, between the two countries. Meanwhile, faced with growing power in Germany, the French, who had already allied with Italy and Russia, approached Great Britain anew, a move facilitated by Ambassador PAUL CAMBON. The agreements, signed in April 1904, dealt with the various differences between the two countries; in compensation for giving up its rights in Egypt, France obtained rights to Morocco. These accords were strengthened during the Algeciras Conference (1906) and again with the Agadir crisis (1911). Thus at the outbreak of World War I (1914), France and Great Britain were closely allied against the Central Powers led by Germany.

## Entragues (or Entraygues), Catherine-Henriette de Balzac d' (1583–1633)
*nobility*

Born in Orléans, Catherine-Henriette de Balzac d'Entragues was the daughter of François d'Entragues and MARIE TOUCHET, a former mistress of King CHARLES IX. In 1599, she became the favorite of King HENRY IV, with whom she had two children—Gaston-Henri, duke of Verneuil (1601), and a daughter, Gabrielle. She had wanted to marry the king, whose subsequent marriage to MARIE DE' MEDICI led Catherine d'Entragues into a conspiracy (1608) that, however, was foiled.

## Entrecasteaux, Antoine-Raymond-Joseph de Bruni, chevalier d' (1737–1793)
*navigator*

Born at the château d'Entrecasteaux in Provence, Antoine-Raymond-Joseph de Bruni, chevalier d' Entrecasteaux, entered the navy (1754), where he enjoyed a brilliant career, being named commander of the French fleet in the East Indies (1786–89), then governor of the island of Mauritius (1791). He undertook (1791–93) a voyage to search for the explorer the count DE LA PÉROUSE, who had last reported from Botany Bay, Australia, in 1788. During the course of this voyage, Entrecasteaux made important contributions to the geographical knowledge of the South Pacific region and, exploring the coasts of many of Oceania's islands, discovered the D'Entrecasteaux Islands, now part of Papua–New Guinea. He died at sea during the voyage.

## Épernon, Jean-Louis de Nogaret de la Valette, duke d' (1554–1642)
*political figure*

Born in Caumont, Jean-Louis de Nogaret de la Valette, duke d'Épernon, was one of the favorites of King HENRY III. He was devoted to Henry and served him quite faithfully, and, as a consequence, Henry bestowed many honors on him. His influence was reduced under King HENRY IV but, nonetheless, after that monarch's death, he helped to establish the regency of Queen MARIE DE' MEDICI. Épernon was finally removed from power by Cardinal RICHELIEU.

## Épinay, Louise Tardieu d'Esclavelles, marquise d' (1726–1783)
*writer*

Often called Mme d'Épinay, Louise Tardieu d'Esclavelles was born in Valenciennes. After separating in 1749 from her husband, D. J. de la Live d'Épinay, she moved to the château of La Chevrette, Montmorency, where her salons were attended by such leaders of the Enlightenment and notable 18th-century figures as DENIS DIDEROT, Baron F. M. von Grimm, and JEAN-JACQUES ROUSSEAU. In 1756, she provided a rural cottage, l'Hermitage, for Rousseau, from whom she later became estranged. She also carried on an extensive correspondence with various European sovereigns and, in her later years, entertained her literary friends at her small home, la Briche, near La Chevrette. Among these was Grimm, her literary heir with whom she had had a liaison since 1755. D'Épinay's writings include *Les conversations d'Émilie* (1774), in which she prescribed the moral upbringing of her granddaughter, *Lettres à mon fils* (1752), her *Mémoires* (posthumous,

1818), and an *Histoire de Mme de Montbrillant,* an autobiographical work written in collaboration with Diderot (posthumous, 1818).

## Ernst, Max (1891–1976)
*German-born French painter, designer, sculptor, writer*

A seminal figure of 20th-century art, in both dadaism and surrealism, Max Ernst, noted for his extraordinary range of style, technique, and media, was born in Bruhl and studied philosophy and psychiatry at the University of Bonn (1909). During WORLD WAR I (1914–18), he served in the German army. Drawn to the new dadaist movement, which he helped to found, Ernst settled in Cologne after the war, where he began to work in collages (*Fiat Mode,* 1919; *C'est le chapeau qui fait l'homme,* 1920). In 1922, he moved to Paris, where he turned to surrealism. He soon painted pictures with unusual themes, such as solemn humans and fantastic creatures inhabiting precisely detailed Renaissance landscapes, and also more enigmatic works, in collage and tromp l'oeil (*L'Éléphant Célèbes; Oedipus Rex*). In 1925, he invented the frottage technique (pencil rubbings of objects), and later experimented with grattage (scraping or troweling of pigment from a canvas), and also using paint drippings to achieve his image. With the German invasion of France (1940) in WORLD WAR II, he was briefly detained, and in that period worked with decalcomania—a technique of transferring pictures from specially prepared paper to glass or metal. He immigrated to New York City in 1941 with the help of noted art patron, Peggy Guggenheim, whom he soon married. In 1954, Ernst returned to France. His works had already become highly prized, and throughout his remarkably varied career, he was known as a tireless experimenter. In all his works, he sought the ideal method of conveying in two or three dimensions the extradimensional world of dreams and the imagination.

## Escoffier, Auguste (1846–1935)
*chef*

Considered the master of the style of French haute cuisine that had been originated earlier by ANTOINE CARÊME, Auguste Escoffier was born in Villeneuve-Loubet and began his career at age 12 as a kitchen helper in Nice. Before beginning his famous work in England, he spent six years in Paris, where he served as a cook during the FRANCO-PRUSSIAN WAR (1870–71), and later in Monte Carlo as the master chef at the Grand Hotel. From 1890 to 1898, he was chef at the Savoy Hotel in London and then, for 13 years, at the Carlton House there. At the Carlton House, and for brief periods at other great hotels in Europe and New York City. He trained hundreds of chefs in this grand tradition and, after his retirement, wrote on cuisine (*Guide culinaire*). Escoffier is credited with the invention of thousands of recipes, such as the famous Peach Melba.

## Espinasse, Charles-Esprit (1815–1859)
*military figure*

Born in Saissac, Aude, Charles-Esprit Espinasse, after serving in the French army in Africa, took part in the expedition to Rome sent to overthrow the newly proclaimed Roman Republic (1849). He assisted Louis-Napoléon Bonaparte (later NAPOLÉON III) in the coup d'état of December 2, 1851, and was promoted to the rank of general. Named minister of the interior in 1858, after the attempted assassination of Napoléon III by Félice Orsini he helped to put through the law on security (1859). Espinasse was killed at the Battle of Magenta, in Italy.

## Esquirol, Jean-Étienne-Dominique (1772–1840)
*physician*

A noted physician who dealt with mental illnesses, Jean-Étienne-Dominique Esquirol was born in Toulouse. He was a student of PHILIPPE PINEL and was doctor of medicine at La Salpêtrière, and chief inspector for the University of Paris. He is considered one of the founders of modern psychiatry. He was also responsible for setting up the present system of French psychiatric institutions and hospitals, and he fought, as did Pinel, for humane treatment of the mentally ill. Esquirol wrote an important work on the classification of deliria and dementia (*Des Maladies mentales considerées sous le rapport médical, hygiénique, et médico-légal,* 1838), in which he made the first delineation between mental deficiency and insanity.

## Estaing, Jean-Baptiste, count d' (1729–1794)
*admiral*

Born in the château de Ravel, Auvergne, Jean-Baptiste, count d' Estaing, after having served in the Indies and being named vice admiral of the "Asian and African oceans" (1777), fought in the American War of Independence. During that conflict, he was defeated by the British at Newport, Rhode Island, but he then besieged the British post at Grenada (1779). Commander of the National Guard (1789), he was promoted to admiral (1792) and, at the time of the REVOLUTION OF 1789, was arrested during the Terror and executed, despite his republican beliefs.

## Estates General (États généraux)

The national representative body in France before 1789, the basic function of the Estates General, or États généraux, was to give assent to royal taxation. Its members represented the three estates, or classes—clergy, nobility, and third estate, which represented the majority of the population. First convened by King Philip IV in 1302, the Estates General was quite powerful in the 14th and 15th centuries. During the reign of Charles VII, the crown began to develop independent sources of revenue and depended less on the Estates General. After 1614, the estates did not meet again until 1789, when LOUIS XVI summoned it to deal with the major financial crises of his reign. The date for the meeting was set for May 1 of that year. In June, the third estate, joined by members of the clergy and nobility, began a revolution by defying the king and declaring itself a National Assembly

See also REVOLUTION OF 1789.

## Esterhazy, Marie-Charles-Ferdinand-Walsin (1847–1923)
*military officer*

Of Hungarian origin, Marie-Charles-Ferdinand-Walsin Esterhazy was born in Austria. He joined the French military and became an attaché to the general staff. He was accused by GEORGES PICQUART of being the author of the document (bordereau) that caused ALFRED DREYFUS to be found guilty of espionage in 1896. Esterhazy was fully acquitted by a military court (January 1898), but his guilt was later established. He died in self-imposed exile in England.

## Estienne d'Orves, Honoré d' (1901–1941)
*naval officer*

Born in Verrières-le-Buisson, Honoré Estienne d'Orves was a graduate of the École polytechnique and became a naval officer. Joining General CHARLES DE GAULLE in 1940, he organized an intelligence network in German-occupied France. Betrayed by one of his collaborators, however, Estienne d'Orves was arrested by the Gestapo and shot. He left his *Journal de famille* and *Journal de bord* (posthumous, 1950).

## Estienne family
*humanists*

Beginning a family of French humanists, Robert Estienne (1498–1559) was born in Paris and is the author of *Trésor de la langue latine* (1531), he was also a translator. Along with BONAVENTURE DES PRÉIER, CLÉMENT MAROT, and FRANÇOIS RABELAIS, he was part of the literary circle around MARGUERITE DE VALOIS, queen of Navarre, a writer herself and patron of humanism. His son, Henri Estienne (1531–98), was also born in Paris and produced the first edition of Anacreon's *Odes,* then entered into the intellectual debates of the period with *Apologie pour Hérodote* (1566). He crowned his vast philosophical and grammatical output with his *Trésor de la langue grecque* (1572).

## Estrées, House of
*noble family*

The House of Estrées was that of a French noble family of Artois. Gabrielle d'Estrées (1573–99) was the daughter of Antoine d'Estrées, grand master of artillery and governor of the Île-de-France. She became the mistress of King HENRY IV, who made her duchess of Beaufort. He was hoping to marry her, but she died quite young. She left three children by her husband, César de Vendôme. François-Annibal d'Estrées (1573–70), the brother of Gabrielle d'Estrées, was bishop of Noyon, until he left the church to become marshal of France, then ambassador to Rome (1636–48), where he played a decisive role in the election of Pope Gregory XV. Jean d'Estrées (1624–1707) was one of the sons of François-Annibal d'Éstrées. He served as vice admiral and marshal of France and retook Cayenne, in South America, from the Dutch (1677). Victor-Marie, count de Coeuvres, duke d'Estrées (1660–1737), descendant of François, commanded the French navy during the War of the Spanish Succession and became a member of the Regency Council in 1715.

## Étampes, Anne de Pisseleu, duchess d' (1508–1580)

*nobility*

Born in Fontaine-Lavaganne, Anne de Pisseleu, duchess d'Étampes was the mistress of FRANCIS I. She was married by him to Jean de Brosses, who became duke of Étampes and governor of Brittany. She was a woman of great culture and exercised a certain degree of political influence. Her rivalry with DIANE DE POITIERS divided the court, which she had to leave upon the king's death. Anne de Pisseleu converted to Protestantism at the end of her life, and the duchy of Étampes passed in turn to Diane de Poitiers, then to Gabrielle d'Estrées (see HOUSE OF ESTRÉES), and finally to the latter's son, CÉSAR DE VENDÔME.

## Étiemble, René (1909–2001)

*writer, novelist*

Born in Mayenne, René Étiemble, whose early works include *L'Enfant de choeur* (1937) and *Blason d'un corps* (1961), was a literary critic who analyzed in particular *Le Mythe de Rimbaud* (1952–67) and wrote reflections on comparative literature (*Comparison n'est pas raison*, 1963; *Quelques Essais de la littérature universelle*, 1982; *Nouveaux essaiys de littérature universelle*, 1992). He became equally known for his passion for the Far East (*Le Nouveau Singe pèlerin*, 1958) as for his extreme defense of the French language, menaced, he believed, by a "babel" of North American origin (*Parlez-vous franglais?*, 1964). Étiemble's volume of memoirs, *Lignes d'une vie*

(1987), reveal an individual who always kept his life from the prying of the media.

## Eugénie (1826–1920)
### (Eugenia María de Montijo de Guzmán)

*empress of the French*

Born in Grenada, Spain, to a noble family, Eugenia María de Montijo de Guzmán, countess of Téba, who was to become the empress of the French, was educated in Paris at the Convent of the Sacre-Coeur. In 1851, she appeared in Parisian society and was noticed by the future emperor, NAPOLÉON III, whom she married in 1853. She played an important role in the political life of the SECOND EMPIRE, being generally consulted by the emperor on significant matters and acting as a regent during

Empress Eugénie *(Library of Congress)*

his absences. A staunch Catholic, she supported the ultramontane cause and opposed curtailment of the temporal power of the pope. Consequently, she blocked the emperor's plans for the liberation of Italy. Empress Eugénie encouraged the emperor also to declare war on Germany (1870) and, after the French surrender, joined him in England, where she continued to live after his death in 1873.

## European Union (Union européenne)

A political, economic, and monetary union, the European Union (Union européenne), or EU as it is also known, was formally established on February 7, 1993, when the governments of the 12 members states (Belgium, Denmark, France, Germany, Great Britain, Greece, Ireland, Italy, Luxembourg, Netherlands, Portugal, and Spain) signed the Treaty of Maastricht, which was then ratified by the member nations' national legislatures. In 1994, Austria, Finland, and Sweden joined the EU, which brought the total to 15 nations. The EU is the most recent in a series of European cooperative organizations that originated with the European Coal and Steel Community (ECSC) of 1951, which in turn became the European Community (EC) in 1967. The Maastricht treaty transformed the EC into the EU. Among the several objectives of the EU are its efforts to promote and expand cooperation among its members in several areas, including economics and trade, social issues, security, judicial matters, and foreign policy. Another major goal has been to implement the Economic and Monetary Union (EMU), which established a single currency for all EU members, the euro. With the exception of the EMU, which has established a single currency for all EU members, progress toward these other goals has been somewhat slower. The ability of the EU to achieve its objectives has been limited by disagreements among its members, a number of external economic and political issues, and pressure for membership from the new Eastern European democracies. Histori-

cally, the idea of European unity goes back many centuries, but only after WORLD WAR II did proposals for some kind of supranational European organization become more frequent (see JEAN MONNET). By the early 1950s, some steps toward this goal had been achieved. These included the creation of Benelux and the ECSC (see ROBERT SCHUMANN). In 1957, the European Economic Community (EEC), often referred to as the Common Market, was established. In the same year, the treaty was ratified that created the European Atomic Energy Community, known also as Euratom. These treaties, signed in Rome, Italy, paved the way for other cooperative efforts. With the coming to power of nationalist CHARLES DE GAULLE in France, however, progress toward unity was slowed. After 1969, the EC began to expand both its scope and its goals. Presently, the 25 nations of the EU are represented in the European Parliament, whose 626 members are popularly elected by the citizens of the EU states.

See also DELORS, JACQUES.

## Évian Accords

The Évian Accords (Accords d'Évian) were signed on March 18, 1962, by the representatives of the provisional government of the Algerian Republic (GPRA) and those of the French government. The Évian Accords recognized Algerian independence linked to a cease-fire in ALGERIA (March 19) and specified the conditions for a referendum on self-determination, which took place on July 1, 1962. Meanwhile, there was put in place a provisional Algerian executive committee (nine Algerians, the majority to be from the FLN [Front de libération national], and three Frenchmen). The French population of Algeria demonstrated its resistance to the agreement by conducting a two-day general strike (in Algiers and Oran) and by a demonstration that ended with a tragic fusillade on the rue d'Isly in Algiers in which 25 were killed.

See also OAS.

# F

## Fabien, Pierre-Georges (1919–1944)
*Resistance leader*

A celebrated figure of the French RESISTANCE during WORLD WAR II, Pierre-Georges Fabien, or le colonel Fabien as he is known, was born in Paris and was a member of the FRENCH COMMUNIST PARTY. He joined the Resistance early and helped to create the armed youth battalions (batallions armés de la jeunesse). He also organized the action in the Paris subway (Métro) that took the life of a Nazi German officer (August 21, 1941). A RESISTANCE group leadder, then chief of a brigade of FFI (FREE FRENCH) in the Île-de-France, Colonel Fabien was killed during the campaign in Alsace, fighting within the ranks of the First French Army.

## Fabius, Laurent (1946–  )
*political figure*

Born in Paris, Laurent Fabius, in 1984, became the youngest prime minister in French history. A Socialist deputy in 1978, and with the coming of the Left to power, he was named minister of finance (1981–83), then industry (1983–84). Named prime minister (1984–86) by President FRANÇOIS MITTERRAND, Fabius pursued a policy of industrial redevelopment but faced a rise in unemployment and increasing social crises, as well as the *Rainbow Warrior* scandal, involving the international organization Greenpeace, in 1985. As president of the National Assembly (1988–92), he supported a policy of modernization of the Left. He became first secretary of the Socialist Party in 1992, but left that post in April 1993 after the defeat of the Left in that year's legislative election.

## Fabre, Jean-Henri (1823-1915)
*writer, entomologist*

The founder of the study of insect natural history, or entomology, Jean-Henri Fabre was born in Saint-Léon, Aveyron. An amateur scientist, in his 10-volume *Souvenirs entomologiques* (1879–86), Fabre popularized the field and alone set the standards of scrupulous observational patience and accuracy required for entymology. Gifted with a rare popular and humanistic style of writing, Fabre, whose influence cannot be overestimated, became well known and his works widely read. He was made a member of number of scientific societies, received a government pension, and was visited by the president of France.

## Fabre d'Eglantine (1750–1794)
### (Nazaire-François Fabre)
*writer, political figure*

Born in Carcassone, the son of a draper, Philippe-Nazaire-François Fabre, or Fabre d'Eglantine as he is known, was at first a schoolmaster and perhaps an ordained priest, and also an actor. He then turned to literature, and for a sonnet composed for a competition at Toulouse was awarded an eglantine of precious metal, hence his name. He came to Paris in 1787, and there he had a certain success as a playwright (*Philinte de Molière ou la Suite du Misanthrope*, 1790; *Les Précepteurs*, 1749). As a poet, he is the author of a popular romance, *Il pleut, il pleut bergère*. Embracing the ideas of the REVOLUTION OF 1789, he joined the Cordeliers Club, where he became friends with GEORGES JACQUES DANTON (who made him secretary to the minister of justice,

August–November 1792) and with CAMILLE DESMOULINS. A member of the insurrectionist Commune after August 10, 1792, and a Montagnard deputy to the Convention (1792), Fabre d'Eglantine developed the nomenclature for the months of the Republican Calendar adopted in October 1793. A rogue and an opportunist, he denounced the Foreigners' Plot (see JEAN-BAPTISTE CLOOTS) to the National Assembly and especially details of the French Indies Company scandal, in which he was actually involved. Fabre d'Eglantine was sentenced to death and guillotined at the same time as Danton and the Indulgents (April 1794).

## Falconet, Étienne-Maurice  (1716–1791)
*sculptor*

Born in Paris, Étienne Falconet studied under noted sculptors and was accepted into the Academy of Fine Arts in 1754 with a baroque work, *Milon de Crotone devoré par un lion* (Milo of Crotona devoured by a lion). He was a favorite of Mme de POMPADOUR for whom he produced a number of works (*La Musique* (Music), 1751; *L'Hiver* (Winter), 1765), and who placed him in charge of the Sèvres porcelain factory (1757–66). He provided numerous models—lovers, nudes, dancers, children—for manufacture in porcelain in a dainty and intimate style. Falconet triumphed with a *Pygmalion et Galatée* (1763), done in the same mode and which DENIS DIDEROT considered to be a masterpiece. Falconet's *Monument à Pierre le Grand* (1766–78, St. Petersburg, Russia) commissioned by Catherine the Great, is a colossal equestrian statue of Czar Peter the Great and is considered his major later work, prefiguring romanticism in its style. In 1761, Falconet published his *Réflexions sur la sculpture.*

## Falloux, Frédéric-Albert, count de (1811–1886)
*political figure*

Of an aristocratic family, Frédéric-Albert, count of Falloux was born in Angers. In 1846 he was elected a deputy and, after the REVOLUTION OF 1848, was a member of the Constituent Assembly. After having contributed to the closing of the National Workshops (Ateliers nationaux), he supported the candidacy of Louis-Napoléon Bonaparte (later NAPOLEON III) for the presidency of the republic. Named minister of public instruction (1848–49), he composed the first law on freedom of instruction, which, when approved on March 15, 1850, originally favored sectarian education. The Falloux Law, as it is known, was modified several times. It affirmed the role of the laity in primary public education (1882, 1886), abolished congregational teaching (1901, 1902, 1904), and revised the policy of financing of private schools through public funds (1994). Falloux, when elected deputy to the Legislative Assembly (May 1849), opposed the policies of the prince-president, and he was arrested during the coup d'état of December 2, 1851. During the SECOND EMPIRE, he contributed to a liberal Catholic newspaper, *Le Correspondent,* and, after the abdication of Napoléon III, sought reconciliation between the Legitimists and the Orléanists in the hope of restoring the monarchy. He is the author of *Mémoires d'un royaliste* (1888) and was elected to the ACADÉMIE FRANÇAISE in 1856.

## Fanon, Frantz  (1925–1961)
*psychiatrist, political theorist*

Frantz Fanon, whose analysis of colonialism places him among the leading revolutionary thinkers of the modern era, was born in Fort-de-France, Martinique. During WORLD WAR II he served with the Free French forces in North Africa and France, then studied psychiatry in LYON. Appointed chief psychiatrist at the hospital in Blida, ALGERIA, he studied the phenomenon of depersonalization in the population in relation to the colonial situation. At that time, he also supported the Algerian revolution. Expelled from Algeria, he went to Tunis, Tunisia, where he continued his medical work and political activities, especially with the National Liberation Front, and served as diplomatic representative of the provisional government of the Algerian Republic. Fanon was influenced by the writings of ALBERT CAMUS and JEAN-PAUL SARTRE, as well as by those of Karl Marx and G. W. F. Hegel. His own sociological and political analysis of colonialism and the dangers of neocolonialism emphasizes the struggle for liberation in all Africa and the specificity of the revolution in countries of the Third World. He was also a guiding figure in the

American black liberation movement, in particular in the formation of the Black Panther Party. Fanon's principal writings include *Peau noire, masques blancs* (1952); *L'An V de la révolution algérienne* (1959; *Les Damnés de la terre* (1961), his best-known work; and *Pour la révolution africaine* (1969).

## Fantin-Latour, Henri  (1836–1904)
*painter, lithographer*

Born in Grenoble, Henri Fantin-Latour worked in various studios, including that of GUSTAVE COURBET. The influence of naturalism in his works is strengthened by his references to the earlier masters. A friend of the impressionists, and especially of ÉDOUARD MANET, EDGAR DEGAS, and the American James Whistler, he was only superficially influenced by them. In his large formal group portraits, which approach photographic realism but with a certain coldness, he pays homage to the artists of his era (*Hommage à Delacroix*, 1864; *Un Atelier aux Batignolles*, 1870; *Un Coin de la table*, 1872). Fantin-Latour's drawings and lithographs, which later were the inspiration for certain musical works, reveal his symbolist tendencies.

## Fargue, Léon-Paul  (1876–1947)
*poet*

Born in Paris, Léon-Paul Fargue was a disciple of STÉPHANIE MALLARMÉ and a student of the works of PAUL VERLAINE, FRANCIS JAMMES, and JULES LAFORGUE. He brought to his own poetry, prose, and free verse a sense of lyricism, fantasy, a faithfulness to past memories, and melancholy (*Tancrède*, 1895; *Poèmes*, 1912; *Pour la musique*, 1914). A friend of VALÉRY LARBAUD and PAUL VALÉRY, with whom he founded the revue *Commerce* (1923), he was attracted to surrealism but rejected direct confrontation in his writings. Master of a language rich in imagery, he celebrated his native city with a fervid tenderness (*D'après Paris*, 1932; *Le Piéton de Paris*, 1939) and evoked in his brilliant chronicles Parisian society, its artists and artisans, and life from the first years of the century to the immediate post–WORLD WAR II era (*Haute solitude*, 1941; *Refuges*, 1942; *Lanterne magique*, 1944; *Méandres*, 1947; *Portraits de famille*, 1947).

See also TOULET, PAUL-JEAN.

## Fashoda

Fashoda, today Kodok, is a town in the Sudan. It was the site of an incident in 1898 in which France, having tried to compete with British influence in Upper Egypt, sent there a military mission under General JEAN-BAPTISTE MARCHAND, who occupied Fashoda on July 10 of that year. Overtaken by the British commander General Horatio Kitchener in September, Marchand was ordered by the French foreign minister THÉOPHILE DELCASSÉ to leave his position after the British had issued an ultimatum. This setback, which was profoundly resented in France, led to the Franco-British agreement of March 1899 by which France renounced its interests in the Nile region.

See also AFRICA, FRENCH IN.

## Faure, Edgar  (1908–1988)
*political figure, writer*

Born in Béziers, Edgar Faure served as Radical-Socialist deputy (1946–58) and participated in several governments of the FOURTH REPUBLIC as a minister and as premier (January–February 1952, February 1955–January 1956). During his second ministry, Sultan Mohammad V was restored to the Moroccan throne and Tunisia was granted autonomy by France. Placed in the minority by the National Assembly, which he then dissolved (December 1955), he lost power after the Republican Front victory and subsequently directed the leftist coalition upon leaving the Radical Party. Joining General CHARLES DE GAULLE, he was officially charged with establishing diplomatic relations with mainland China (1963). Named minister of national education after the crisis of May 1968, he put through the law for educational reform and reorganization, especially in the universities. From 1973 to 1978, he was president of the National Assembly. Faure wrote on politics and history (*La Disgrâce de Turgot*, 1961) and left his *Mémoires*. He was elected to the ACADÉMIE FRANÇAISE in 1978.

## Faure, Élie  (1873–1937)
*essayist, art historian*

Born in Sainte-Foy-le-Grande, Élie Faure, brought to his career as an art critic (1902) a great curiosity for all the new ideas of the period, notably the role of African art and of the cinema. Influenced by the German philosopher Friedrich Nietzsche, the French political theorist GEORGES SOREL, and the American writers Ralph Waldo Emerson and Walt Whitman, Faure was the author of several works, including *Les Constructeurs* (1914), in which profiles of such diverse individuals as JEAN-BAPTISTE DE LAMARCK, Nietzsche, Feodor Dostoyevsky, and PAUL CÉZANNE are presented along with an analysis of the state of mind of Western civilization in the 19th century. In his *Histoire de l'art* (1909–21) and *L'Esprit des formes* (1927). A well-known scholar in his era, he also had an active political life, supporting the cause of ALFRED DREYFUS (1896) and the Spanish Republicans at the beginning of the Spanish civil war (1936).

## Faure, Félix (1841–1899)
### (François-Félix Faure)
*statesman*

The sixth president of the THIRD REPUBLIC, Félix Faure was born in Paris and, in about 1862, moved to Le Havre, where he became a wealthy leather merchant. He fought in the FRANCO-PRUSSIAN WAR (1870–71) and in 1881 was elected to the Chamber of Deputies. He served as undersecretary of state for French colonies (1882–85) under JULES FERRY and remained in the cabinet until 1894, serving also as naval minister (1885). Upon the resignation of President AUGUSTE CASIMIR-PERIER, Faure was elected to the presidency (1894). He was a popular president, and his term was marked by a strengthening of France's alliance with Russia (he welcomed Czar Nicholas II to Paris in 1896 then met him in Kronstadt, Russia, the following year). He pursued the colonization of Madagascar and encountered certain diplomatic difficulties with Great Britain (FASHODA), but otherwise, he took no significant part in politics until 1898, when he tried to block the retrial of ALFRED DREYFUS during the Dreyfus affair, but he died suddenly of apoplexy during the proceedings.

## Fauré, Gabriel (1845–1924)
*composer*

Born in Pamiers, Gabriel Fauré studied at the Ecole Niedermeyer under CAMILLE SAINT-SAËNS and is considered also a disciple of FRÉDÉRIC CHOPIN. From 1866 to 1905, he was organist in a number of churches in Paris, including the Madeleine and Saint-Sulpice. He became professor of composition at the Paris Conservatoire in 1896, where he later served as director (1905–20). His students included MAURICE RAVEL and others. With Saint-Saëns, Fauré was instrumental in keeping the French musical tradition in the forefront when the tendency at the time was to adopt the style and technique of German romantic music. Fauré wrote within smaller genres, especially short piano pieces and songs. He excelled in melody, piano, and chamber music. As one of the most eminent representatives of French chamber music, he is considered, along with CLAUDE DEBUSSY, a founder of a new musical sensibility. A prolific composer, Fauré's works include a series of *Mélodies* (1868–1900); *La bonne Chanson* (1891), inspired by the poems of PAUL VERLAINE; *La Chanson d'Ève* (1916); *La Requiem* (1887); four *Valses caprices* (1883–1894); six *Impromptus* (1884–1913); 13 *Nocturnes* (1883–22); 13 *Barcarolles* (1883–1921); and nine *Préludes* (1910).

## Faure, Paul (1878–1960)
*political figure*

Born in Périgueux, Paul Faure was a member of the French Worker Party (Parti ouvrier français) of JULES GUESDE and the founder of the newspaper *Le Populaire de Centre* (1914), which he directed until 1914. He was named secretary-general of the SFIO (Section française de l'Internationale ouvrière) after the schism of the Socialists at the Congress of Tours (1920). Minister of state in the Popular Front governments (LÉON BLUM, 1936–37, CAMILLE CHAUTEMPS, 1937–38) and a deputy, Faure signed the Munich Accords (September 1938) and then the armistice after France's defeat by Nazi Germany (1940), for which he was expelled from the SFIO in 1944.

## Faure, Sébastien (1858–1942)
*anarchist*

Born in Saint-Étienne, Sébastien Faure was at first a member of the French Worker Party (Parti ouvrier français) of JULES GUESDE and then, after 1888, an anarchist, founding the anarchist newspaper *Le Libertaire* (1895). Author of *Philosophie lib-*

*ertaire* (1895) and *La Douleur universelle* (1895), Faure edited the *Encyclopédie anarchiste* in collaboration with the Russian anarchist known as Voline (Vsevolod Mikhailovitch Eichenbaum).

## Favras, Thomas de Mahy, marquis de (1744–1790)
*political figure*
Born in Blois, Thomas de Mahy, marquis de Favras, was a first lieutenant (1772) in the Swiss Guard of King LOUIS XVI's brother Monsieur, count of Provence (the future LOUIS XVIII). In 1783, he tried in vain, at the head of a patriotic legion, to bring help to Holland against Prussia. Author of a project on financial reform, which attracted the attention of the count of MIRABEAU and of JACQUES NECKER, Favras was, since the beginning of the REVOLUTION OF 1789, an agent of the count of Provence. Charged with recruiting royalist volunteers to assist in the flight of Louis XVI from Paris, he was denounced by two of his own agents who swore to the marquis de LA FAYETTE that he had asked them also to kill JEAN-SYLVAIN BAILLY, who was serving as the mayor of Paris. Implicated in this plot, the count of Provence denounced Favras, who was sentenced to death and hanged.

## Favre, Jules (1809–1880)
*political figure*
A leader of the republican opposition to NAPOLÉON III and one of the founders of the THIRD REPUBLIC, Jules Favre was born in LYON, where he became a well-known attorney. Coming to Paris, he gained a reputation for successfully defending noted political prisoners. Elected a deputy to the Constituent Assembly (April 1848), then to the Legislative Assembly (May 1849), he took a stand against the coup d'état of December 2, 1851. As a member of the legislature (1857), he joined the republican opposition and defended FELICE ORSINI, the conspirator who had tried to assassinate Napoleon III. This brought Favre to national attention. Opposed also to the Mexican expedition (1861), then to the declaration of war against Prussia (1870), he played a decisive role in the revolutionary day of September 4, 1870, which, after the defeat at Sedan, had as a consequence the fall of the SECOND EMPIRE and the

formation of a government of National Defense in which he served as foreign minister. Having refused to accept the terms presented by German Chancellor Bismarck at their meeting at Ferrières of September 19–20, 1870, he sent LOUIS ADOLFE THIERS on a diplomatic mission to the neutral European powers and then to a new interview with Bismarck (November 1870). This second interview was not successful and the Prussian bombardment of Paris brought a French surrender (the armistice was signed January 24, 1871). Foreign minister in the Thiers government, Favre negotiated the Peace of Frankfurt (May 1871) and resigned shortly after. His writings include *Le Gouvernement de la défense national* (1871–75). He was elected to the ACADÉMIE FRANÇAISE in 1867.

## Fayol, Henri (1841–1925)
*engineer, administrator*
Born in Constantinople (Istanbul) in present-day Turkey, Henri Fayol, who is considered a pioneer in management theory, was the first Frenchman to question the nature of management itself. Director general of the Compagnie de Commentry-Fourchambault-Decazeville (1888), he put forth his theories in *Administration générale et industrielle* (1916), a plan for the administrative reform of business. This program, known as "Fayolism," he believed could be applied to any company; it stresses the need for a hierarchical organization with diverse functions (administrative, technical, commercial, financial, auditing, and controlling) at the center of the enterprise and as the basic role for its administration. Fayol's ideas were influential for much of the 20th century.

## Febvre, Lucien (1878–1956)
*historian*
Born in Nancy, Lucien Febvre was professor of history at the COLLÈGE DE FRANCE. The author of a noted thesis on Philip II and the Franche-Comté (1911), he would, with MARC BLOCH, later be a founder of the *Annales d'histoire économique et social* (1929). In 1922, Febvre published *La Terre et l'évolution humaine,* in which he showed the connections between the studies of history and geography. This was followed by other works, including *Un*

*destin, Martin Luther* (1928) and *Le Problème de l'incroyance au XVIe siècle, la Religion de Rabelais* (1942). Febvre's concept of history, known as the Annales school of historiography, is comprised of a synthesis of political, economic, social, religious, and cultural elements, along with the "mentalité" of its subjects. This thesis is best represented in Febvre's *Combats pour l'histoire* (1953). A prodigious scholar, Febvre directed the editing and writing of *L'Encyclopédie française* (1935).

## Federalist Insurrection

The Federalist Insurrection was a counterrevolutionary movement that took place during the REVOLUTION OF 1789 following the elimination of the GIRONDINS from the Convention (June 2, 1793). After the installation of the insurrectionist Commune of Paris (August 10, 1792), the fear of a Parisian dictatorship provoked in several regions of France the creation of revolutionary departmental committees (end of 1792) that were transformed into revolutionary federalist committees (May 5, 1793). This sectional movement took the form of a real insurrection upon the news of the proscription of the Girondin leaders, several of whom succeeded in escaping and then assuming the leadership of the federalist uprising (JÉROME PETION DE VILLENEUVE, CHARLES BARBAROUX, FRANÇOIS BUZOT, FRANÇOIS REBEQUI). The Federalist Insurrection reached several large centers (Caen, Bordeaux, Lyon, Marseille, Toulon). After July it was suppressed in Normandy and, in September, in Bordeaux but lasted longer in the southeast, where royalists succeeded in dominating the movement (Lyon surrendered on October 9, 1793, Toulon on December 19). Violently suppressed by the representatives sent by the MONTAGNARD Convention, the Federalist Insurrection, like the war in the VENDÉE, constituted one of the most serious domestic threats to the Revolution and contributed to the development of the Terror and the reinforcing of central power.

## Fénelon, François de Salignac de la Mothe (1651–1751)
*prelate, writer, theologian*

François de Salignac de la Mothe Fénelon, whose theories and publications, despite the opposition of church and state, eventually became the basis for profound cultural and political changes in France, was born at the château of Fénelon, Périgord, into a noble family. Educated at the seminary of Saint-Sulpice and the University of Cahors, he was ordained a priest in 1675, and soon was appointed head of the Nouvelles Catholiques, an institute in Paris for the instruction of recent female converts to Catholicism. In 1685, after the revocation of the Edict of Nantes, he was sent to lead a mission among the Protestants in western France. He became a protégé of JACQUES BÉNIGNE BOSSUET and, in 1689, was appointed tutor to the young duke of Burgundy, a grandson of LOUIS XIV. Fénelon wrote a series of moral lessons for this pupil to instruct him in the obligations and duties of a ruler. In 1695, Fénelon was named archbishop of Cambrai, but he soon became involved in a controversy with Bossuet over the quietist doctrines of Mme GUYON. Fénelon himself had been influenced by quietism and its emphasis on the contemplative life, and his *Explication des maximes des saints* (1697) was strongly criticized by Bossuet as inconsistent with church doctrine and teachings. After an appeal to Rome, sections of the book were condemned by Pope Innocent XII. Fénelon was exiled to his archdiocese by Louis XIV, who sided with Bossuet. Also, Louis XIV had been displeased by Fénelon's *Les Aventures de Télémaque* (1699), his best-known work. A political novel, it posits that monarchs are the servants of their subjects and, additionally, denounces war and calls for a fraternity of nations. In another work, the influential *Traité de l'éducation des filles* (1687), Fénelon argued for education for women and later presented a plan for improving the ACADÉMIE FRANÇAISE, of which he had been a member since 1693. His other political work, *Tables de Chaulnes* (1711), is also considered a critique of absolutism. In all his writings, Fénelon can be seen as a precursor of the 18th-century utopians.

## Fermat, Pierre de (1601–1665)
*mathematician*

Born in Beaumont-de-Lomagne, Pierre de Fermat was a magistrate who had a passion for mathematics. In his youth, with his friend BLAISE PASCAL, he made a series of investigations into the properties of figurative numbers. While studying the work of the ancient Greek mathematician Diophantus, Fermat became interested in a chapter on Pythagorean numbers—sets of three numbers for which the equation $a^2 + b^2 = c^2$ is true. He wrote in the margin of the text, "I have discovered a truly remarkable proof which this margin is too small to contain." The result became known as Fermat's Last Theorem. From all his studies, Fermat derived an important method of calculating probabilities. He anticipated differential calculus with his method of finding the greatest and least ordinates of curved lines. He is also a precursor of analytical geometry (independently of RENÉ DESCARTES), and he is the discoverer of Fermat's Principle on the path of light, which is the basis of optical geometry.

## Ferry, Jules  (1832–1893)
*statesman*

A premier of France, Jules-François-Camille Ferry, or Jules Ferry, as he is known, was born in Saint-Dié and began practicing law when he was 19. Extensive travel throughout Europe, however, led him to journalism. In various articles for Paris newspapers and in pamphlets, at first descriptive and anecdotal, he became increasingly political. Between 1868 and 1870, Ferry wrote a number of significant articles, including "Les Comptes fantastiques d'Haussmann," which sharply criticized NAPOLÉON III and his imperial policies. When elected to the legislature, Ferry sat with the opposition in the last imperial chamber. Along with other republicans, he voiced his opposition in July 1870 to the war with Prussia. In the period after the FRANCO-PRUSSIAN WAR (1870–71), he became one of the leading figures among French republicans. In 1879, he entered the government as minister of education and, for the next six years, was almost continually in ministerial office. He served twice as premier: from September 1880 to November 1881, and from February 1883 to March 1885. His expansive colonial policy brought the opposition, especially of GEORGES CLEMENCEAU. Known for his educational reforms (free and secular primary and secondary schools, girls' secondary education), Ferry also was responsible for a broadening of civil liberties and for administrative reforms at the national and local levels. He also pursued an aggressive colonial policy (colonization of Madagascar, conquest of the lower Congo by PIERRE BRAZZA, conquest of

Tonkin, protectorate over Tunisia). Additionally, he served as prefect for the department of Seine and as mayor of Paris, after the fall of the Empire (1870) and when the city was under siege (see COMMUNE, LA).

## Fesch, Joseph  (1763–1839)
*prelate*

Born in Ajaccio, CORSICA, Joseph Fesch was the maternal uncle of NAPOLÉON I. Archdeacon of Ajaccio (1793), he renounced the priesthood and was named commissioner for the French army in Italy. Once again a churchman, after Napoléon gained political power, Fesch was named archbishop of LYON (1802), then was made a cardinal (1803). Ambassador to the Holy See, he encouraged the pope, Pius VII, to come to Paris to crown Napoléon I. Although he was showered with honors and named grand almoner of the empire, count, and then senator (1805), he took a stand against Napoléon's treatment of the pope and was sent away in disgrace. In 1814, he retired to Rome. Fesch amassed an important collection of art.

## Feuillants Club  (Club des Feuillants)

The Club des Feuillants, or Feuillants Club, was born when, after the Affair du Champ-de-Mars (July 17, 1791) in which the National Guard fired upon demonstrators in Paris, moderates opposed to the overthrow of King LOUIS XVI and supportive of a constitutional monarchy left the JACOBIN CLUB. Among them were the marquis de LA FAYETTE, ANTOINE BARNAVE, the LAMETH brothers, Abbé SIEYES, and others who would lead the new club that met in the convent of the Feuillants on the rue Saint-Honoré in Paris. More than 200 deputies from the right wing within the Legislative Assembly joined. The club's position was expressed in the journals *Le Logographe* and *L'Indicateur*. After August 10, 1792, which marked the end of the Bourbon monarchy, the supporters of a bourgeois liberal republic (GIRONDINS) replaced the constitutional monarchists.

## Feuillère, Edwige  (1907–1998)
*actor*

Born in Vesoul, Edwige Feuillère (stage name of Edwige Cunati) made her debut under the name of

Cora Lynn at the COMÉDIE-FRANÇAISE (1931–32). She became famous for her sense of discipline and fine voice and acting in *La Dame aux camélias* (by ALEXANDRE DUMAS, FILS), *Sodome et Gomorrhe* (1943), and *Pour Lucrèce* (1947). She created and interpreted the role of the queen in JEAN COCTEAU's *L'Aigle a deux têtes* (*The Eagle Has Two Heads;* 1946), the character of Ysé in PAUL CLAUDEL's *Partage de midi,* and the title roles in Giraudoux's *La Folle de Chaillot* (*The Mad Woman of Chaillot;* 1965), and in Dürrenmatt's *La Visite de la vieille dame* (*The Visit;* 1976). In cinema, she took on, during the 1940s, comedic roles (*Adorable creatures,* 1952). She was made a member of the LEGION OF HONOR in 1990.

## Fiches, affaire des

The affaire des Fiches occurred because of a system instituted by General LOUIS ANDRÉ, minister of war under the THIRD REPUBLIC (1901–04). It consisted of making the advancement of military officers dependent on their religious and political views, which were noted and kept on cards (*fiches*) compiled by secret societies, particularly Masonic lodges, and sent directly to the ministry. The discovery of this caused violent polemics and an increase in the antiparliamentary opposition. As a result, General André and the premier, ÉMILE COMBES, had to resign.

## *Le Figaro*

A Parisian newspaper, *Le Figaro* was founded in 1826 as a satirical weekly. Taken over by H. de Villemessant in 1854, it became a daily in 1866. At the beginning of the THIRD REPUBLIC, *Le Figaro* expressed the monarchist viewpoint but gradually came over to moderate republicanism, reflecting the view of the Parisian bourgeoisie. Directed successively by F. Magnard, GASTON CALMETTE until his assassination in 1914 (see JOSEPH CAILLAUX), then R. de Flers and A. Capus, *Le Figaro* was owned by and served as the political organ for the perfumer F. Coty from 1922 to 1933, with L. Romier and A. Chaumeix as editors in chief. Taken over by Mme Cotnareanu (the former Mme Coty), *Le Figaro* had P. Brisson as director from 1934 to 1942 and from 1944 to 1964. It was then acquired by the Prouvost-Beghin group. Considered an important political and literary organ of the bourgeoise press, *Le Figaro* has always featured the articles of noted journalists. A weekly, *Le Figaro littéraire,* was published separately from 1946 to 1970, before being integrated into the newspaper as a supplement. *Le Figaro* has been owned by R. Hersant since 1975, and there is now also published a *Figaro magazine* (since 1978) and a *Madame Figaro* (since 1980).

## Fillastre, Guillaume  (1348–1428)
*prelate, scholar*

Born in La Suze, Maine, Guillaume Fillastre was the dean of Reims and endeavored to end the Western Schism. He took part in the Council of Pisa (1409), was made a cardinal in 1411 by the Pisan pope John XXIII and, at the Council of Constance (1414–1418), upheld the sovereignty of a council over the pope. His intervention effectively brought an end to the schism and led to the election of Pope Martin V, who made him legate in France. He served there as intermediary for the peace between the Armagnacs and the Bourguignons. As a scholar, Guillaume Fillastre produced a translation of the *Syntaxe mathématique* (or *Almageste*) of Ptolemy and a map of Europe, the first to show Greenland.

## Fizeau, Hippolyte  (1819–1896)
*physicist*

Born in Paris, Hippolyte Fizeau, who was interested in photography with LÉON FOUCAULT, produced a daguerreotype of the surface of the sun (1845). He also put in place the first method (without recourse to astronomical observation) to measure the speed of light. He did this in 1849 by sending a beam of light between gear teeth in the edge of a rotating wheel. The beam then traveled a distance to a mirror and came back to the rapidly spinning wheel, where a tooth would block the light, allowing the speed to be calculated. He brought, too, to optics the effect discovered by Christian Doppler (Doppler-Fizeau effect) in the case of sonar waves, which allow the measurement of the radical speed of stars (he also discovered double stars). Fizeau, who additionally did work on dilatation and the optical properties of solid bodies, was named to the Academy of Sciences in 1860.

## Flaubert, Gustave (1821–1880)
*writer*

Born in Rouen, Gustave Flaubert is considered by many to be the father of realistic fiction. The son of a prosperous physician, Flaubert was raised in an apartment in the hospital where his father was chief surgeon (an experience that perhaps predisposed the young Flaubert to pessimism about human life). Flaubert was educated in the classics at the Collège Royal in Rouen and, as a youth, was a passionate reader of the works of RENÉ DE CHATEAUBRIAND, VICTOR HUGO, J. W. von Goethe, and Lord Byron. At age 14, he met Mme Elisa Schlesinger, then 26, who influenced his works and became the great love of his life. She inspired, in part, the character of Emma Bovary, that of Madame Renaude in an early version of *L'Éducation sentimentale,* and was immortalized as the lovely Madame Arnoux in the final version of that work (1869). In 1840, Flaubert began the study of law in Paris, but he soon experienced a seizure, perhaps epileptic, that changed his life. Thereafter, he lived as a hermit at Croisset, an estate on the Seine purchased by his father. Flaubert's mother and niece joined him there in 1846, after the death of his father and sister. Only on occasional visits to Paris and a long journey to the Middle East and Greece (1849–51) did Flaubert leave Croisset. He devoted the remainder of his life to literature. But despite his reputation as a realist writer, there is some degree of romanticism in such works as *Salammbô* (1862) and the short story "Hérodias" (1877). His two acknowledged masterpieces, however, reflect the great conscious effort that he exerted to restrain his flights of passion and fantasy. The first of these is *L'Éducation sentimentale,* in which French life is vividly described. The other work, *Madame Bovary,* is the novel through which Flaubert is chiefly known. In it, ordinary, but unforgettable, characters are portrayed, as well as a historical period in its specific reality. The novel's details caused Flaubert to be tried for offenses to public morals. He was acquitted. Because of his literary realism, and innovative narrative, Flaubert was acclaimed by such later modernist novelists as MARCEL PROUST, Henry James, and James Joyce, all of whom acknowledged their indebtedness to him. In his *Bouvard et Pécuchet,* Flaubert anticipated many of the ideas and forms of the novel of the later half of the 20th century.

## Flahaut de la Billarderie, Auguste, count de (1785–1870)
*military figure, diplomat*

Born in Paris, Auguste, count de Flahaut de la Billarderie, the natural son of CHARLES-MAURICE DE TALLEYRAND and the countess de Flahaut, was a staff officer to Napoléon Bonaparte. He had, from his liaison with Queen HORTENSE of Holland, a son who became the duke de MORNY. Living in England from 1815 to 1827 (where he married the daughter of Lord Keith), he regained his rank of division commander under King LOUIS-PHILIPPE, who made him a peer of France (1830), minister plenipotentiary to Prussia (1836), then ambassador to Great Britain (1842–48). A senator in 1853, Flahaut de la Billarderie was made grand chancellor of the LEGION OF HONOR in 1855.

## Fléchier, Esprit (1632–1710)
*preacher, writer*

Born in Pernes, Comtat venaissin, Esprit Fléchier, the almoner to the dauphin, was a worldly priest who frequented the salons held in the Rambouillet mansion in Paris. His lively spirit is evident in his *Lettres, Portraits,* and *Mémoires sur les Grands Jours d'Auvergne* (posthumous, 1844). He is known, too, for his *Sermons,* written and detailed in a simple but expressive style, and above all for his *Oraisons funèbres* (notably those of the viscount of TURENNE, 1672, and Queen MARIA THERESA, 1683), given with ingenious eloquence. Fléchier was elected to the ACADÉMIE FRANÇAISE in 1673.

## Fleurieu, Pierre Claret, count de (1738–1810)
*naval officer, political figure*

Born in LYON, Pierre Claret, count de Fleurieu, who invented the maritime seconds watch (1769), served as director general of arsenals (1776) and set up the plan for naval operations for the American War of Independence. He also planned the voyage of the explorer of the South Pacific, JEAN FRANÇOIS, count de LA PÉROUSE (see 1790–91 ANTOINE ENTRECASTEAUX and JULES DUMONT D'URVILLE). Named minister at the time of the REVOLUTION OF 1789, Fleurieu was imprisoned during the Terror. A member of the Council of Elders until 18 Fructidor (September 4, 1797), he was subsequently named councilor of state and governor of the Tuileries. Fleurieu is the author of *Découvertes des français dans le sud-est de la Nouvelle-Guinée.*

## Fleury, André-Hercule de (1653–1743)
*cardinal, political figure*

Born in Lodève, André Hercule de Fleury was bishop of Fréjus, almoner to the queen, and tutor to LOUIS XV, whose confidence he subsequently enjoyed. In 1726, he was called to replace the duke of Bourbon as minister of state, was made a cardinal, and exercised power with both flexibility and firmness, as well as with prudence and a sense of detachment. His domestic policy was marked by the reestablishment of budgetary equilibrium, owing to economic measures and an improved financial administration. Currency was stabilized (and remained so until the REVOLUTION OF 1789); the system established by JEAN-BAPTISTE COLBERT was reinstated with its problems, but it also gave an impulse to trade and industry. Cardinal Fleury had to deal, too, with a renewal of the Jansenist controversy and could not stop all parliamentary opposition to his policies. Meanwhile, he adopted a critical position regarding the arbitrary use of royal power. In his foreign policy, based on an alliance with Spain, that was also favorable to trade, he tried always to maintain peace. Caught, at this point, in the War of the Polish Succession, he quickly ended that conflict by a compromise (Treaty of Vienna, 1738). In exchange for leaving Poland, Stanislaus I received Lorraine, which would, upon his death, revert to France. Contemporary opinion was critical of this policy, which it viewed as less than aggressive, but Cardinal Fleury's ministry corresponds to one of the most successful periods of the reign of Louis XV, achieved when France's diplomatic prestige was high. Cardinal Fleury was elected to the ACADÉMIE FRANÇAISE in 1717.

## Fleury, Émile-Félix, count de (1815–1884)
*military and political figure*

Born in Paris, Émile Félix, count de Fleury, after taking part in the coup d'état of December 2, 1851 was named aide-de-camp to NAPOLÉON III. He charged Fleury with several diplomatic missions and named him ambassador to Russia (1867). After the fall of the SECOND EMPIRE (September 4, 1870), General Fleury became one of the leaders of the Bonapartist Party during the period of the Third Republic.

## Flon, Suzanne (1918– )
*actor*

Born in Bicêtre, Suzanne Flon, who was secretary to ÉDITH PIAF, began her career at ABC and at Bobino in Paris. Her interpretation of Alvarica in JACQUES AUDIBERTI's *Le mal court* (1947) made her well known. Since then, she played in many contemporary classics (Luigi Pirandello; JEAN ANOUILH; Eugene O'Neill; Loleh Bellon's *Les Dames de jeudi*). The stage left her little time for film, where she worked with some important directors (John Huston, Orson Welles, J. Losey), but generally in supporting roles.

## Floquet, Charles (1828–1896)
*political figure*

Born in Saint-Jean-Pied-de-Port, Charles Floquet was a republican deputy in the National Assembly (1871), president of the Chamber of Deputies (1885–88, 1889–93), and premier (1888) during the period of Boulangism, which he opposed. He is famous for having wounded General GEORGES BOULANGER in a duel. Floquet served as a senator from 1894 to 1896.

## Foch, Ferdinand (1851–1929)
*military figure*

The commander of the Allied forces on the western front during the later campaigns of WORLD WAR I, Ferdinand Foch was born in Tarbes and, after being commissioned in the artillery corps (1873), became professor of strategy at the École supérieure de guerre (1894). His lectures and writings (*Principes de la guerre,* 1903; *Conduite de la guerre,* 1904) established him as a leading military theoretician. In October 1914, shortly after the outbreak of war, he was charged with coordination of the various Allied forces (French, British, Belgian) in northeastern France. Throughout 1915 and 1916, he

Ferdinand Foch *(Library of Congress)*

*Anciens et les Modernes* (1687). He also tried, without success, to compose dramatic works. His originality is apparent in his 24 *Dialogues des mort* (1683), in the manner of the Greek satirist Lucian, as brilliant literary or philosophical paradoxes, and is clearly manifest in his *Entretiens sur la pluralité des mondes* (1686), an elegant work on popular science, and in the *Histoire des oracles* (1687), where he analyzes with ingenious irreverence Christian theology and miracles (*La Dent d'or*). Elected to the ACADÉMIE FRANÇAISE (1691), then the Academy of Sciences (1697), he continues in his *Éloges* on academicians and his *Préfaces*, which are edited in a precise and clear form, this alliance between science and literature. "The ignoramus heard it, the scholar admired it." (VOLTAIRE). Thus, by offering to his readers a synthesis of the scientific achievements of his time (Nicholas Copernicus, RENÉ DESCARTES), and professing a complete faith in science, Fontenelle can well be considered a precursor of the enquiring spirit of the thinkers of the 18th century and the Enlightenment.

## Forain, Jean-Louis  (1852–1931)
*painter, lithographer, engraver*

Born in Reims, Jean-Louis Forain was self-taught except for a year of study with the sculptor JEAN-BAPTISTE CARPEAUX. He was a friend of the writers of the period (PAUL VERLAINE, ARTHUR RIMBAUD, JORIS-KARL HUYSMANS), and also knew and exhibited with the impressionists. He became famous as a caricaturist and, after 1893, produced a large number of works of political satire, and was a cofounder of the satirical journals *Fifre* and *Psst'*. Influenced by HONORÉ DAUMIER and HENRI DE TOULOUSE-LAUTREC, he portrayed scenes of Parisian life with a caustic sense of irony (*Nous, vous, eux,* 1893). His watercolors, pastels, and paintings reveal his admiration for ÉDOUARD MANET and EDGAR DEGAS. In his later years, Forain portrayed religious subjects in a style reminiscent of Rembrandt.

was the commanding general of the Allied armies in the north and, in 1917, became chief of the French general staff. After the German advance in spring 1918, the Allies saw the need for a supreme commander. Foch was named commander in chief of all Allied armies, including the American. After initial setbacks, he launched the series of counteroffensives that led to final Allied victory. Foch was made a marshal of France in August 1918 (Great Britain and Poland also later conferred that honor on him) and, in November, he signed the armistice that ended the war with the Central Powers. Foch was elected to the ACADÉMIE FRANÇAISE and left his account of the war in his *Mémoires de guerre,* published in 1931. He died in Paris.

## Fontenelle, Bernard Le Bovier de (1657–1757)
*writer, philosopher, poet, scientist*

Born in Rouen, the son of an attorney and nephew of PIERRE CORNEILLE, Bernard Le Bovier de Fontenelle was a man of letters who frequented the salons and took the side of the Moderns in his *Digression sur les*

## Forbin, Claude, chevalier, later count (1656–1733)
*naval officer*

Born in Bouches-du-Rhône, Claude, chevalier Forbin served under the command of the duke of ESTRÉES and later the marquis ABRAHAM DUQUESNE in the campaigns of Messina (1675), the Antilles (1680), and Algiers (1682). He then was named high admiral of the king of Siam (1686–88) and subsequently took part in the struggles against England alongside JEAN BART (Plymouth, 1689) and DUGUAY-TROUIN. Ordered to accompany the Stuart pretender to the English throne to Edinburgh, Claude, now count Forbin, failed and was dismissed from his position. His *Mémoires* appeared in 1730.

## Foucauld, Charles-Eugène, viscount de (1858–1916)

*explorer, missionary*

Born in Strasbourg, Charles-Eugène, viscount de Foucauld (later known as "le père Foucauld"), was a military officer who made the first exploratory journey through Morocco and, disguised as a rabbi, charted more than 2,000 kilometers of new routes (1883–84). He had a religious conversion in 1886, left the army, and eventually joined the Trappists of Notre-Dame-des-Neiges, Ardèche (1890). He then made several visits to Palestine, Syria, and Algeria, was ordained a priest (1901), and became a hermit missionary in the Sahara, at first at Bene Abbès, then at Tamanrasset (1905), where he was killed by the Senoussis. Foucauld is the author of *Reconnaissance du Maroc* (1888), works on the Tuaregs: *Grammaire et Dictionnaire français-touareg, touareg-français; Poésies touareg,* and *Écrits spirituels.* A process of beatification for Foucauld was begun in 1926.

## Foucault, Léon (1819–1868)

*physicist*

Born in Paris, Léon Foucault, with HIPPOLYTE FIZEAU, sought to use photography in astronomic studies (1845), and did research in photometrics and spectroscopy, putting in place a method for measuring the speed of light with the help of turning mirrors, applied in both air and water, confirming in turn AUGUSTIN FRESNEL's theory of undulation (1850). Foucault proved the existence of electric currents in conductors placed in variable magnetic fields, a direct consequence of the laws of induction (Foucault's currents). In 1851, in the Panthéon in Paris, he carried out a famous experiment that would prove the rotation of the earth. With a pendulum (Foucault's pendulum) weighing 20 kilograms and suspended from a steel wire 67 meters in length, he demonstrated that its oscillation remained in a fixed plan in relation to a set point. Then, the following year, he invented the gyroscope, an instrument that produced the same result. In 1857, he conceived the idea of replacing the spherical mirror in telescopes with a parabolic one made of silvered glass, eliminating the aberration caused by specificity. Foucault was named to the Academy of Sciences in 1865.

## Foucault, Michel (1926–1984)

*philosopher*

As a philosopher, Michel Foucault attempted to show that the basic ideas usually taken to be permanent truths about human nature and society change in the course of history. His studies challenged the influence of Marx and Freud and offered new concepts that challenged previously held assumptions about criminology, gay rights, welfare, insurance, and care of the emotionally ill. Born in Poitiers, Foucault studied at the École normale supérieure in Paris. He served as chair of philosophy at various universities and, in 1970, was elected to one of the highest French academic posts, as professor of the history of systems of thought at the COLLÈGE DE FRANCE. He subsequently gained an international reputation. Among the many influences on Foucault's thought were the German philosophers Nietzsche and Heidegger. Foucault's thought explored the shifting pattern of power within a society and the ways in which power relates to the self. His ideas developed through three stages. In *Histoire de la folie à l'âge classique* (1961), he traced the evolution of the perception of madness in the Western world. In the second phase of his thinking, Foucault wrote *Naissance de la clinique, une archéologie du regard médical* (1963), and *Les Mots et les Choses* (1966), one of his most important works, in which he explores the relationship of semantics to the nature of things. Foucault argued that each way of understanding things has its advantages and its dangers. His last period was inaugurated by the publication of his monumental and unfinished *Histoire de la sexualité,* which finally comprised three volumes. (Foucault had planned six.) The three complete tomes include *La Volonté de savoir*, 1976; *L'Usage des plaisirs*, and *Le Souci de soi*, 1984. In these books, Foucault traces the stages by which people in Western societies have come to understand themselves as sexual beings, and relates the sexual self-concept to the moral and ethical life of the individual. In all the works of his last period, Foucault seeks to show that Western society has developed what he terms "bio-power"—which is a new system of control that traditional authority is unable to understand and criticize. Foucault describes it as a new power that enhances life by developing individual ethics which allow one to turn one's life into something that can be respected and admired.

## Fouché, Joseph, duke of Otranto (1759–1820)

*administrator, political figure*

Known as the founder of modern political espionage, Joseph Fouché was born in Pellerin, near Nantes. A student of the Oratorians in Paris, then professor at the Oratory (although he never became a priest), Fouché in 1789 embraced the ideas of the REVOLUTION. Elected to the Convention (1792), he sat with the MONTAGNARD deputies and voted for the death of the king. Ordered to suppress the FEDERALIST INSURRECTION in LYON, he organized the TERROR there, earning the name "Assassin of Lyon." An intransigent and unscrupulous individual without any sense of loyalty, he was one of the planners of the events of 9 Thermidor Year II (July 27, 1794), which led to the overthrow of MAXIMILIEN ROBESPIERRE. Nonetheless, he was excluded from the Thermidorian Convention and arrested, but was later pardoned. Thanks to PAUL BARRAS, Fouché was named minister of police in 1799 (30 Prairial Year VII), then joined the service of Napoléon Bonaparte (see NAPOLÉON I) (after waiting to see the outcome of the coup d'état of 18 Brumaire), using the system of agents and spies that he had created. Supported in his work by CHARLES MAURICE DE TALLEYRAND, he was made duke of Otranto (1809) and governor of the Illyrian Provinces. Minister of police during the HUNDRED DAYS, he was a member of the provisional government after Waterloo, and helped to pave the way for the return of the Bourbons. He then again briefly served as minister of police and later ambassador to Saxony (1815), but he was considered a regicide under the Law of 1816 and was exiled. He settled in Prague, then in Linz, before becoming an Austrian citizen and retiring to Trieste.

## Foullon, Joseph-François (1717–1789)

*administrator*

Born in Saumur, Joseph-François Foullon, as intendant general of the army and the navy and an assistant to the minister of war, was charged with supplying military headquarters (July 12, 1789) during the REVOLUTION OF 1789. After the popular revolution in Paris and the fall of the BASTILLE (July 14, 1789), he was condemned to death by the assembly of the electors of the Hôtel de Ville for having "starved" the people. He was executed on July 22, shortly before his son-in-law, the intendant LOUIS-BERTIER DE SAUVIGNY.

## Fould family

*bankers, businessmen*

Bénédict Fould (1792–1858) was born in Paris, the son of the founder of Fould, Oppenheimer, & Co. bank, and contributed to the establishment of the Union Insurance Company (September 1828) and several financial companies. Achille Fould (1800–1867), a banker and political figure, was born in Laloubère, Haute-Pyrénées. The brother of Benedict Fould, he was elected a deputy (1842), and became known through his financial study, *Observations sur la question financière adressées à l'Assemblé nationale* (May 1848). In October 1849, he was named minister of finance by NAPOLÉON III and held that post until January 1852. Founder of a number of old-age and retirement savings plans and of the Crédit Mobilier (with JACOB PEREIRE in 1852), and organizer of the Universal Exposition of 1855, he was a senator, minister of state (1852–60), and a member of the Privy Council under the SECOND EMPIRE. A supporter of economic liberalism, he contributed to the signing of a commercial treaty with Great Britain (1860). Later made minister of finance (1861–67), he tried with little success to limit the regime's expenses.

## Fouquet (or Foucquet), Jean
### (ca. 1420–ca. 1481)
*painter, miniaturist*

The most important French painter of the 15th century, Jean Fouquet was born in Tours and probably developed his technique in Parisian studios, while the style of his miniatures indicated that he was familiar with the LIMBOURG manuscripts. He most likely did the *Portrait de Charles VII* before going to Italy (ca. 1445–48). Already well known, he was commissioned to paint the portrait (lost) of Pope Eugene IV; during his visit he assimilated Leone Alberti's discoveries on perspective, became friends with the Italian architect Antonio Filareti, and adopted the Italian architectural styles and ornamental motifs. Returning to Tours, he worked for King CHARLES VII before becoming the official painter to LOUIS XI (1474). A few of his paintings have survived. The portrait of *Juvenal des Ursins* and the diptych known as *de Melun,* representing *Étienne Chevalier présénte par saint Étienne,* and in the center *La Vierge à l'Enfant,* without doubt figure in the treatises of AGNÈS SOREL (ca. 1450). His portraits are characterized by glowing, clear colors, strong drawing, and characterization and humor. His miniatures are noted for their precision and exquisite technique. Fouquet also painted on enamel (*Autoportrait*) and organized festivals and solemn entrances for the king. In *Heures d'Étienne Chevalier* (between 1450 and 1480), a noted book of hours, he meticulously applied the process of perspective; in *Bocacace* (ca. 1458), the *Grandes Chroniques de France,* and above all the *Antiquités judaïques* (ca. 1467–76), he used diverse perspective techniques in the same composition.

## Fouquet (or Foucquet), Nicolas
### (1615–ca. 1680)
*statesman*

Born in Paris, Nicolas Fouquet, who was associated with Cardinal MAZARIN, became minister of finances in 1653. His personal credit allowed him to regain the confidence of many officials and to face state expenses after the FRONDE. He took advantage of his position to acquire a prodigious fortune, to maintain a large staff, and to build a personal military guard, with a fortress at Belle-Isle. At his château de Vaux, which he had built, he surrounded himself with a personally chosen group of writers and artists (JEAN DE LA FONTAINE, JEAN-BAPTISTE MOLIÈRE, LOUIS LE VAU, NICOLAS POUSSIN, CHARLES LE BRUN). JEAN-BAPTISTE COLBERT, who coveted his success, denounced Fouquet's embezzlement to King LOUIS XIV, and an extremely sumptuous party subsequently held at Vaux, to which he invited the king, caused his downfall. Arrested at Nantes (1661), he was tried in a biased and irregular trial that lasted three years and at the end of which he was confined at Pignerol. The fidelity of his friends (La Fontaine, Mme de SÉVIGNÉ, Mlle SCUDÉRY) was a testimony in his favor. The circumstances of Nicolas Fouquet's death are, however, obscure.

## Fourastié, Jean    (1907–1990)
*economist*

Born in Saint-Benin, Nièvre, Jean Fourastié, like the British economist Colin Clark, and contrary to the more pessimistic analyses of the French sociologist GEORGES FRIEDMANN, saw in technological progress the essential factor for economic and social progress (*Le Grand Espoir du xxe siècle,* 1949; *Machinisme et bien-être* 1950; *Les Trente Glorieuses ou la Révolution invisible,* 1979).

## Fourcroy, Antoine-François, count de
### (1755–1809)
*chemist, political figure*

Born in Paris, Antoine-François, count de Fourcroy helped to establish a rational chemical nomenclature (1787) with a group that included Louis Bernard, baron of GUYTON DE MORVEAU, ANTOINE DE LAVOISIER, and Claude Louis, count of BERTHOLLET. Fourcroy did research on chemical affinities and analyzed the composition of several minerals. Very moderate in his political views, he was a member of the Convention during the REVOLUTION OF 1789. Fourcroy was elected to the Academy of Sciences in 1785.

See also VAUQUELIN, NICOLAS-LOUIS.

## Foureau, Fernand    (1850–1914)
*explorer*

Born in Saint-Barbant, Haute-Vienne, Fernand Foureau, after having taken part in several expeditions in southern ALGERIA as part of a scientific study of the Sahara (1888–96), undertook a crossing of the Sahara and the Sudan regions of Africa, through Ouargia and Chad and reached the Congo (1898–1900). In 1906, he was named governor of Mayotte and the Comoros. He created a map of the Sahara region (1908) and wrote several works (*Rapport sur ma mission au Sahara et chez les Touaregs Azdjers*, 1894; *D'Alger au Congo par le Tchad*, 1902; *Documents scientifiques de la mission saharienne*, 1903–05).

See also AFRICA, FRENCH IN.

## Fourier, Charles (1772–1837)
*philosopher, economist*

The son of a wealthy merchant, Charles Fourier was born in Besançon, where he also studied at the university. In 1799, he began to write on politics and economics, and his first large work, *Théorie des quatres movements et des destinées générales* (1808), expounded his social system and his plans for the cooperative organization of society. In this and in other works (*Traité de l'association domestiques et agricole*, 1822; *Le Nouveau Monde industriel et sociétaire*, 1829) and in his weekly journal, *Le Phalanstère*, his system, known as Fourierism, was presented. It was based on his belief in a universal principle of harmony, displayed in four areas: the material universe, organic life, animal life, and human society. Fourier believed that this harmony could flourish only when the restraints placed upon the gratification of desire by conventional society have been abolished, allowing each person to live a free and complete life. The ideal harmoniousness was to be accomplished by the division of society into cooperative phalanxes, or communities, consisting each of about 1,600 individuals, living in the phalanstary, a vast communal dwelling placed in the center of a highly cultivated area. Elaborate rules were set down for conduct within the phalanx, and assignment of work was based on talent. Private property would still exist, but visible distinctions between rich and poor would be minimized. The phalanx's communal wealth would provide sufficiently for the basic needs of its members. Marriage in the traditional sense would be abolished and replaced by an elaborate system that regulated the community's social behavior. Fourier's utopian

project was not realized, but Fourierism had a number of adaptations.

## Fourier, Joseph (1768–1830)
*mathematician*

Born in Auxerre, Joseph Fourier, who was one of the leading instructors at the École polytechnique, as a scientist took part in Napoléon Bonaparte's (see NAPOLÉON I) expedition to Egypt (1798). His works, concerning the theory of heat, led him to the discovery of the series that bears his name and which allowed the expression of a periodic function as the sum of sines and cosines. Altogether, Fourier's theories constitute one of the most useful applications of mathematics to physics and have assured their author a leading place among the mathematicians of the 19th century. He also developed an important theorem on the roots of algebraic equations, perfecting that of RENÉ DESCARTES. Fourier was elected to the Academy of Sciences in 1817, and to the ACADÉMIE FRANÇAISE in 1826.

## Fourquier-Tinville, Antoine-Quentin (1746–1795)
*magistrate, political figure*

Born in Hérouel, Aisne, Antoine Quentin Fourquier-Tinville embraced the ideas of the REVOLUTION OF 1789 and in 1793 was named public prosecutor of the Revolutionary Tribunal. As such, he became the symbol of the pitiless rigor and cruelty of the Terror. Connected to the CORDELIERS faction and the ultra-revolutionaries, he was denounced under the Thermidorian Convention and, after a long trial, was condemned to death and executed.

## Fragonard, Jean-Honoré (1732–1806)
*painter*

A leading French painter of the rococo age, Jean-Honoré Fragonard was born in Grasse and studied in Paris with JEAN-BAPTISTE CHARDIN and especially FRANÇOIS BOUCHER, from whom he developed his style. In 1752, he won the Prix de Rome with *Jeroboam Sacrificing to the Idols*. He then went to Italy (1756) and was influenced by the works of Francesco Solimena and Giambattista Tiepolo. Befriending HUBERT ROBERT, Fragonard met the

Abbé de Saint-Non, antiquarian and engraver, and with them visited the Roman countryside. He then did numerous sketches and painted landscapes (*The Gardens of the Villa d'Este*) and portraits (*The Abbé de Saint-Non in Spanish Costume*, 1759). In spite of his success through his show at the Academy of Painting and Sculpture (*The High Priest Coresus Sacrificing Himself to Save Callirhoe*, 1765), he quickly abandoned the painting of historical themes. With *The Happy Accident of the Swing* (1766), he acquired the reputation of a painter of libertine scenes that were much sought after (*The Removed Shirt, Young Girl Playing with Her Dog, Le Feu aux poudres*). These sensual and graceful works, always playful and spirited, show the virtuosity of Fragonard's technique. He painted very quickly, often leaving in his picture the appearance of an outline. He expressed all the nuances of amorous sentiments (the four panels of *The Progress of Love*, 1771–72) and was also a sensitive landscapist and alert chronicler (*The Fair at Saint-Cloud*, 1775). He went a second time to Italy (1773) and, after his marriage, painted numerous familiar and sentimental allegorical scenes and portraits of children that recall JEAN-BAPTISTE GREUZE. In his later years, Fragonard was influenced by neoclassicism and did works in a very different vein, sometimes even melancholy, that foreshadow romanticism.

## France, Anatole (1844–1924)
### (Anatole-François-Thibaut)
*writer, Nobel laureate*

Born Anatole-François Thibaut in Paris, Anatole France, as he was known, was a novelist and Nobel laureate and is frequently regarded as the greatest French writer of the late 19th and early 20th centuries. The son of a bookseller who communicated to him his love of literature, France was mostly self-educated and was an insatiable reader. His first published work was a volume of verse, *Les Poèmes dorés* (1873). It was not, however, until the publication of his first novel, *Le Crime de Sylvestre Bonnard* (1881), that he exhibited the subtle stylistic grace, mixed with compassion and irony, that would later become the main characteristics of his work. He soon produced a large body of writings, including dramas, verse, novels (*Thaïs*, 1890; *Le Lys rouge*,

1894) historical works, and philosophical and critical essays. In 1896, he was elected to the ACADÉMIE FRANÇAISE and, in 1921, was awarded the Nobel Prize in literature. In 1883, France formed a liaison with Mme Arman de Caillavet, who inspired his high productivity and helped to promote his works through her various contacts in society. His writings of this period include the critical essays *La vie littéraire* (4 volumes, 1888–92), the novels *Thaïs* (1890); *Le Lys rouge* (1894), and the tetralogy *L'histoire contemporaine* (1897–1901), which was a harsh analysis of the destructive effects of the Dreyfus affair on French life (see ALFRED DREYFUS). France was among the intellectuals who fought for the exoneration of Dreyfus. In his later works, France supported various humanitarian causes. In his writings, he made eloquent appeals for the rights of labor, popular education, and civil liberties.

## France-Soir

A French daily, founded clandestinely in 1940, *France-Soir* was originally a monthly of the RESISTANCE entitled *Défense de la France*. Becoming a daily in 1944, it took the name *France-Soir* in January 1945. Directed by Pierre Lazareff, who revised its format, it became in 1953 the leading French evening newspaper. Bought back by Robert Hachette of the Hachette group in 1976, it has seen its sales decline despite a plan initiated in 1989 to update its format and contents on the model of popular British dailies. It publishes 300,000 copies daily.

## Franchet d'Ésperey, Louis-Felix-Marie-François (1856–1942)
*marshal*

Born in Mostaganem, Algeria, Louis-Felix-Marie-François Franchet d'Ésperey served in Tunisia, Algeria, and then in Tonkin. He was made a member of the army's General Staff and also of the cabinet of CHARLES DE FREYCINET (1886), taking part in the expedition to China against the Boxers, who sought to expel all foreign presence from their country (1900). Subsequently, he was called to Morocco by Marshal LOUIS LYAUTEY (1912). Appointed at the beginning of WORLD WAR I by

General JOSEPH JOFFRE to lead the Fifth Army (after the battle of Guise, 1914), he then commanded the army divisions of the East (1916) and the North (1917). Commander in chief of the Allied armies on the eastern front, he achieved a quick and victorious offensive against the Bulgarians (taking of Dobro Polje), who were then forced to sign the armistice in September 1918. Promoted to the rank of marshal, he became inspector general of the troops in North Africa (1923), where he helped to install the large trans-Saharan communication lines. Franchet d'Ésperey was elected to the ACADÉMIE FRANÇAISE in 1934.

## Francis I (1494–1547)
### (François I)
#### *king of France*
King of France from 1515 to 1547, and remembered for his rivalry with the Habsburg Holy Roman Emperor Charles V, for his governmental reforms, and for his patronage of arts and letters, Francis I was born at Cognac, the son of Charles de Valois, count of Angoulême and Louise of Savoy. His mother and his elder sister, MARGUERITE OF NAVARRE, influenced his upbringing and remained close to him during his reign. His first wife was Claude, daughter of LOUIS XII, whom he succeeded. In 1515, Francis I achieved a spectacular victory over the Swiss at Marignano, which allowed him to seize the duchy of Milan. In 1519, he was a candidate for the Imperial throne but was passed over for Charles of Habsburg. War against Charles then ensued in Italy, where Francis was defeated at Pavia and captured (1525). Imprisoned in Spain, he was ransomed and returned to France (1527). Peace was finally made and, in 1529, Francis married the emperor's sister, Eleanor. Later inconclusive wars were fought against the Habsburgs (1536–38 and 1542–44), during which periods Francis I allied himself with Protestant German princes and with the Ottoman Turks. Earlier, he had gained an alliance with England (Field of Cloth of Gold, 1520). Under his sister's influence, Francis was, for a time, sympathetic to Protestantism, especially in its humanistic form, but later he abandoned his tolerance and persecuted French Protestants (see HUGUENOTS). In 1516, he concluded a concordat with the papacy in which he gained greater control of the Catholic Church in France. His military expenses caused him to undertake financial reforms, and he also began to sell judicial and financial offices, thus creating a new class of ennobled magistrates. An imposing monarch, Francis I centralized the royal government and reinforced royal absolutism. He spent much of his time, however, in liaisons and affairs, leaving the governing power to his mother or one of his favorites. The wealth of his court, derived from the economic prosperity of the kingdom, allowed him to introduce the Italian Renaissance to France and to patronize many artists, including Leonardo da Vinci and Benvenuto Cellini. He employed the scholar GUILLAUME BUDÉ to create a royal library and to found professorships in Greek, Latin, and Hebrew, thus forming the nucleus of the later COLLÈGE DE FRANCE.

## Francis II (1544–1560)
### (François II)
#### *king of France*
Born at Fontainebleau, the eldest son of CATHERINE DE' MEDICI and HENRY II, Francis II was king only briefly (1559–60). In 1558, he married Mary, queen of Scots. Physically and mentally weak, Francis II was dominated by his wife's uncles, François, duke de GUISE, and Charles, cardinal de Lorraine who, during Francis's brief reign, tried to repress the growing power of the Protestants in France. This policy increased especially after the HUGUENOT conspiracy of Amboise in 1560. The death of Francis II ended the ascendancy of the HOUSE OF GUISE, and he was then succeeded by his brother CHARLES IX.

## Franck, César (1822–1890)
#### *composer*
César-Auguste Franck, whose work during the late 19th century significantly influenced the direction of French music, was born in Liège, Belgium. A precocious musician, he made a piano concert tour of Belgium at age 11. He studied music in Liège and, from 1837 to 1842, at the Paris Conservatoire, where he revealed great ability as an organist and

composer. He became a French citizen in 1873 and died in a street accident in Paris. Franck's work is characterized by the use of classical form, including the symphony and sonata, which he imbued with the romantic spirit. He alternated between mystical and brooding themes and those of a more emotional and dramatic type. Somewhat neglected during his lifetime, Franck's compositions are now part of the standard repertoire. A significant work that ranks among the most popular of all symphonies and has served as a model for many important French symphonic works is his symphony in D minor (1886–88). Other of Franck's many compositions include three Trios concertants (1843); the oratorio *Ruth* (1846); six Pièces pour grand orgue (1860); four symphonic poems, Rédemption (1871–72), Le Chasseur maudit (1882), Les Djinns (1884), and Psyché (1887); works for piano and orchestra such as Variations symphoniques (1885); and later works including Quintette avec piano (1880); Prélude, choral et fugue (1884); Sonate pour violon et piano (1886); Prélude, aria et finale pour piano (1887); and Quartuor à cordes (1890). Among his students and disciples, Franck counted many important musicians of the later 19th century, including VINCENT D'INDY and HENRI DUPARC.

## Franco-Prussian War

The underlying causes for this war (1870–71), lost by France to the German states under the leadership of Prussia, was the determination of the Prussian statesman Otto von Bismarck to unify Germany under Prussian control (and also to eliminate French influence over Germany), and the desire of NAPOLÉON III to regain for France the prestige lost as a result of numerous diplomatic reversals. Additionally, Prussian military strength was perceived to constitute a threat to French dominance in Europe. The immediate cause of war was the issue of the candidacy of Leopold, prince of Hohenzollern-Sigmaringen, for the vacant Spanish throne. The French government, alarmed at the possibility of a Prussian-Spanish alliance, demanded a withdrawal. It was Bismarck's editing of a telegram, the Ems dispatch, reworded to make the French demands and the Prussian king's rejec-

tion provocative to both nations, that caused the French declaration of war in 1870. The south German states joined Prussia. The French mobilized about 200,000 troops, the Germans 400,000. All German forces were under the command of the Prussian king Wilhelm and General Moltke. Three German armies drove into France led by General Steinmetz, Crown Prince Frederick Wilhelm, and Prince Frederick Charles. The first engagement at Saarbrücken was won by the French, but in the later battles at Weissenburg, Worth, and Spichern, the French forces, under the command of General EDME MAC-MAHON, were defeated. Command of the French army was assumed by General RENÉ BAZAINE, who was defeated at the battles of Vienville and Gravelotte. The French forces then withdrew to Sedan. The decisive battle of Sedan was fought on September 1, 1870, with the French being commanded by General Emmanuel Wimpffen. Once the situation appeared hopeless, however, NAPOLÉON III surrendered with 83,000 of his troops. Upon news of the surrender, PARIS rose in rebellion, the Legislative Assembly was dissolved, and France was proclaimed a republic. By the end of September, Paris was surrounded by German forces. The new prime minister, LÉON GAMBETTA, escaped by balloon and established a provisional government at Tours. Divisions under his command fought on but were driven into Switzerland. On October 27, Marshal Bazaine surrendered at Metz with 173,000 troops. Paris, meanwhile, was subjected to a terrible siege and bombardment. On January 19, 1871, the city opened negotiations for surrender. The day earlier, Wilhelm I of Prussia was proclaimed emperor of Germany at VERSAILLES. The formal capitulation of Paris took place on January 28. An elected National Assembly, convened at BORDEAUX, chose ADOLPHE THIERS as first president of the THIRD REPUBLIC. In March, the revolutionary government of the Paris COMMUNE was proclaimed but was suppressed in May by government troops. The Treaty of Frankfurt, signed on May 10, 1871, ended the war between France and Germany. It provided that the province of ALSACE (excepting Belfort) and part of Lorraine, including Metz, were to be ceded to the German Empire. France also was to pay a war indemnity of 5 billion gold francs, submitting to German military occupation until it was paid in full. This obligation was discharged in September 1873, and the occupation was then ended. The Franco-Prussian War and the harsh terms of the peace treaty, especially the ceding of the provinces of Alsace and part of Lorraine, would produce in France the rapid rise of nationalism and a spirit of revanchism against Germany.

## French Foreign Legion (Légion étrangère)

A unit of the French army, comprising volunteers of other nationalities, the French Foreign Legion, or Légion étrangère, legally bars Frenchmen from joining as enlisted men (most officers, however, are French). The Foreign Legion was established in 1831, during the reign of LOUIS-PHILIPPE I, as a regiment trained for service in Algeria. The main function of this unit has been to keep order in the French overseas possessions, but it may be sent wherever needed. Until 1962, the legion's head-

quarters were in Sidi Bel Abbès, in ALGERIA. They are now located in Aubagne, France. Physically fit nationals between the ages of 18 and 40 from any country other than France may enlist. Their backgrounds are not investigated and, except for minors, no identification papers are required. War criminals, murderers, and deserters from the armed forces of allies of France, however, are rejected. The initial enlistment term is five years, after which the legionnaire is eligible for French citizenship and promotion to officer. After serving in Algeria, the legion took part in campaigns in many French colonies, including those in North Africa and Indochina. It fought in the CRIMEAN WAR (1854–56), in Italy against the Austrians (1859), in Mexico in support of emperor Maximilian, and in the FRANCO-PRUSSIAN WAR (1870–71). During WORLD WAR I, it served with distinction on many fronts and was the most decorated unit in the French army. The legion fought in Norway and in France at the

French Foreign Legion soldiers *(Hulton/Archive)*

beginning of WORLD WAR II. In 1940, many legionnaires joined the Free French forces of General CHARLES DE GAULLE. In 1942, the legion's heroic defense of Bir-Hakeim brought the unit many honors. Reorganized after World War II, the legion later saw active service in Indochina, North Africa, and Korea. After 1945, large numbers of German war veterans enlisted in the legion.

## Fréron, Élie (1718–1776)
*writer, critic*

Born in Quimper, Élie Fréron was the author of pamphlets critical of VOLTAIRE and the philosophes. He founded *L'Année littéraire,* a revue that was open to the ideas of his time and to foreign literature. His son, LOUIS STANISLAS FRÉRON, continued the revue until the REVOLUTION OF 1789.

## Fréron, Louis-Stanislas (1754–1802)
*publisher, political figure*

Born in Paris, Louis-Stanislas Fréron, the son of ÉLIE FRÉRON, was the director of *L'Année littéraire* from 1776 to 1789, joined the REVOLUTION OF 1789, and founded the journal *L'Orateur du peuple.* A member of the CORDELIERS CLUB, he participated in the great revolutionary events (affair of the Champ-de-Mars, July 17, 1791; August 10, 1792; SEPTEMBER MASSACRES, 1792). Elected to the Convention, where he sat with the MONTAGNARDS, he was sent to MARSEILLE and Toulon to put down federalist and royalist insurrections. Threatened by MAXIMILIEN ROBESPIERRE, he contributed to his downfall and went over to the reaction during the Thermidorian Convention. A friend of PAULINE BONAPARTE, he supported the coup d'état of 18 Brumaire (November 9, 1799) and was named administrator of hospices and later commissioner in Saint-Domingue.

## Fresnel, Augustin (1788–1827)
*physicist*

Born in Chambrais (today Broglie), Augustin Fresnel, after studying the ideas of the British physicist Tomas Young on luminescent interferences, developed, with FRANÇOIS ARAGO, the theory of phenomena. Fresnel also studied light refraction and made a significant presentation of his ideas to the Academy of Sciences in 1819. The creator of modern optics, he expanded on the area of the Newtonian theories of light, establishing the basis, too, for crystalline optics. He studied polarization and discovered the existence of transversal vibrations. After some resistance to his views within the scientific community, his theories were confirmed in 1950 in experiments done by LÉON FOUCAULT. Additionally, Fresnel developed a lighting system that considerably augmented the luminescent power of lighthouses (1821). He was named to the Academy of Sciences in 1823.

## Freycinet, Charles-Louis de Saulces de (1828–1923)
*political figure*

Born in Foix, Charles-Louis de Saulces de Freycinet, as engineer of mines, assisted LÉON GAMBETTA in the efforts of the government of National Defense (September 1870–February 1871) during the FRANCO-PRUSSIAN WAR. A senator (1876–92), he was appointed minister of public works (1877–79), thanks to the support of President JULES GRÉVY, and in that capacity, tried to build a vast program of communications and redevelopment of ports. Premier (1879, 1882, 1886, 1890), he approved the nomination of GEORGES BOULANGER as minister of war (1886), but then took a position against Boulangism and helped to reorganize the military (suppression of exemptions, creation of a Supreme War Council). Freycinet later served as minister of state and wrote *La Guerre en province de 1870 à 1871* (1872), and *Souvenirs* (1912). He was elected to the ACADÉMIE FRANÇAISE in 1891.

## Friedmann, Georges (1902–1977)
*sociologist*

Born in Paris, Georges Friedmann, as a sociologist, addressed in his writings the question of the dehumanizing nature of the organization of work in industrial societies (*Problèmes humains du machinisme industriel,* 1947; *Où va le travail humain?,* 1950; *Le Travail en miettes,* 1956). Friedmann also wrote a sociological study of the Jewish community, *La Fin du peuple juif?* (1966), as well as reflections on the future of moral and philosophical order in civilization (*La Puissance et la Sagesse,* 1971).

## Fronde

A series of revolts against the French monarchy, between 1648 and 1653 during the reign of King LOUIS XIV, the Fronde started initially as a protest by the Parlement of Paris (which was the chief judicial body in France until the late 1780s) and its supporters, against the heavy taxation policies of JULES CARDINAL MAZARIN, the king's chief minister. The Fronde rebellion soon evolved into armed insurrection (1649), and order was restored only when LOUIS II, PRINCE DE CONDÉ, stopped the uprisings and a compromise was arranged between the Parlement and the Crown. In 1650, a second phase of the revolt began with a struggle for power by the nobles against the king (see LOUIS XIV). This unsuccessful attempt on the part of the nobles marked the last insurrection of the French nobility against the Crown, and as a result, royal power was strengthened. Essentially, the Fronde was a reaction to both royal absolutism and the policies established previously during the administration of Cardinal RICHELIEU, chief minister of King LOUIS XIII.

See also LE TELLIER, MICHEL.

## Frontenac, Louis de Baude, count de Palluau and de (1622–1698)
*administrator*

Born in Saint-Germain-en-Laye, Louis de Baude, count de Palluau and of Frontenac was named governor-general of New France (CANADA) in 1672. There, he contributed to the extension and strengthening of French territorial claims and possessions in the New World. But because he governed in such an authoritarian manner, he was recalled to France in 1682. In 1689, Louis de Frontenac was restored to his post, because of the difficult situation that arose owing to attacks from the Iroquois and the English.

## Frossard, Oscar-Louis (1889–1946)
*political figure*

Born in Foussemagne, Belfort, Oscar-Louis Frossard, or Ludovic Oscar as he is known, served as secretary-general of the Section français de l'Internationale ouvrière (SFIO), the French Socialist Party (October 1918), and then, during the Congress of Tours (December 1920), became a supporter of the Third International. Although he then served as secretary-general of the SFIC (French COMMUNIST PARTY, 1921), he was opposed to that party's "bolshevikization" and, in 1923, resigned and returned to the SFIO. Then as a deputy (1928–40) close to the neosocialists, he rejoined the Union of Republican Socialists. Ludovic Oscar was a member of the cabinet several times (1935–40), and voted to give Marshal PHILIPPE PÉTAIN full powers in 1940.

## Frotté, Marie-Pierre-Louis, count de (1755–1800)
*counterrevolutionary*

The leader of the CHOUANNERIE in Normandy, Marie-Pierre-Louis, count of Frotté was born in Alençon and was descended from a noble Protestant family of the region. He converted to Catholicism and was a military officer before the REVOLUTION OF 1789 and, in 1792, emigrated to London. He returned to Normandy in 1795, where he founded the Compagnie des hommes de la Couronne. He then went back to England after the pacification of western France by General LAZARE HOCHE (1796), then returned again to France as a counterrevolutionary agent with the purpose of pursuing an armed struggle against the government. Having obtained a safe-conduct to return to Alençon after having surrendered, he was arrested there and shot on the orders of Napoléon Bonaparte (NAPOLÉON I).

## Furet, François (1927–1997)
*historian*

Born in Paris, François Furet, as a member of the Annales school of historiography, sought to put forth a conceptual history, at once problematic and construed, that gives priority to the study of phenomena over long periods (*L'Alphabétisation des français*, 1976). A specialist in the French REVOLUTION OF 1789 (*Penser la Révolution française*, 1978; *La Révolutions, 1770–1880*, 1988), he opposed giving a Marxist interpretation to that historical event and proposed instead the idea of a "revolution" as a "plurisecular" occurrence, of which the outcome is only an "epiphenomenon." Regarding the view expressed in 1989 at the bicentennial of the Revolution, that left-wing divisions in French society established at the time of the Revolution have largely changed, Furet agreed, stating in a widely quoted phrase, "the Revolution is over." Furet was elected to the ACADÉMIE FRANÇAISE in 1997.

## Fustel de Coulanges, Numa-Denis (1830–1889)

*historian*

Born in Paris, Fustel entered the École normale supérieure in 1850 and, in 1853, attended the French School in Athens, Greece, where he wrote his first thesis on the history of the Greek island of Chios. In 1855, he began his teaching career at the lycée in Amiens, France, and later at the Lycée Saint-Louis in Paris. In 1860, Fustel de Coulanges joined the faculty of the University of Strasbourg, where he became known for his lectures in ancient history. In 1864, he published his first important work, *La Cité antique*, a comparative study of Greek and Roman societies. He later (1870) returned to Paris, where he lectured at the École normale supérieure. In 1875, he became a member of the faculty of the University of Paris and, in 1880, was named director of the École normale supérieure. Fustel de Coulanges's most important work was the six-volume *L'Histoire des institutions politiques de l'ancienne France* (1875–92), in which he contended that the true foundation of European society was more Roman than Germanic. Many of Fustel del Coulanges's writings, including his *Questions historiques,* in which he contended that history was a science and not an art, were edited by Camille Jullian, one of his best students.

# G

## Gabin, Jean (1904–1976)
*actor*

Born Jean-Alexis Moncorgé in Paris, Jean Gabin, as he is known, first appeared in the Folies-Bergère, then in operettas before beginning a long career in film (1930). He acted in more than 100 films, many of them classics (J. Duvier's *Pepé le Moko*, 1937; MARCEL CARNÉ's *Le Quai des brumes*, 1938; JEAN RENOIR's *La Grand Illusion*, 1937; *La Bête humaine*, 1938; and *French Cancan*, 1954). Additionally, he did a series of films in which he played the character Inspector Maigret (*Inspector Maigret*, 1958; *The Sicilian Clan*, 1969). Through his many films, Gabin's characterizations evolved from youthful, generous, restless, and popular to become, without losing their spontaneity and strong presences, those of mature, then old, men, often nonconformist and always energetic and strong, but also gentle.

## Gabriel, Jacques-Ange (1698–1782)
*architect*

Born in Paris, Jacques-Ange Gabriel, who worked with his father, Jacques Gabriel (1667–1742), also an architect and creator of the Biron mansion in Paris, completed some of his father's projects (Place Royale in Bordeaux) and succeeded him in 1742 as first architect to King LOUIS XV and director of the Academy of Architecture. He renovated several royal residences (Fontainebleau, 1749; Compiègne, 1751; Choisy, 1752; Blois) and at VERSAILLES began the rebuilding of a lateral wing on the courtyard. Also at Versailles, he designed the Opéra (1753), and the Petit Trianon (1762–68), characterized by elegance and refinement in proportion and décor. In Paris, he conceived the plans for the Place Louis XV (today the Place de la Concorde) and built the two buildings that border it (1762–70). He also built the Military School (1751–75). Remaining faithful to the spirit of classical French architecture, he had the genius to arrange volume and integrate, in a measured way, decorative aspects. At the same time, the sobriety and amplitude of Gabriel's works foreshadowed neoclassicism.

## Gachet, Paul-Ferdinand (1828–1909)
*physician, painter, engraver, art collector*

Born in Lille, Paul-Ferdinand Gachet was connected with many painters (EDGAR DEGAS, ÉDOUARD MANET, CLAUDE MONET, AUGUSTE RENOIR, CAMILLE PISSARRO, PAUL CÉZANNE, and especially VINCENT VAN GOGH, whom he welcomed to his home at Auvers-sur-Oise). A part of Dr. Gachet's art collection can now be found at the Musée d'Orsay in Paris. Gachet himself exhibited at the Salon des artists independents under the pseudonym of Van Ryssel. His portrait of Van Gogh (1890), whom he served also as physician, is well known.

## Galigaï, Leonora (ca. 1568–1617)
*Italian noblewoman, adventuress*

Eleonora Dori, better known as Leonora Galigaï, was born in Florence, Italy. She traveled to France in the entourage of Queen MARIE DE' MÉDICI, over whom she had a great influence. She used this influence to promote the career of her husband, CONCINO CONCINI, during the minority of King LOUIS XIII. After the assassination of her husband by CHARLES D'ALBERT DE LUYNES on the young king's orders, she was condemned to death and executed.

## Gallicanism

Gallicanism was a combination of political positions and theological doctrines supporting the relative independence of the French Roman Catholic Church and the French government in their relations with the papacy. Three distinct, but closely related, forms of Gallicanism existed. Theological Gallicanism denied the absolute supremacy of the pope, arguing instead for the supremacy of the ecumenical councils. Royal Gallicanism stressed the absolute independence of the French Crown from Rome in all temporal affairs, and parliamentary Gallicanism, a position of the parlements, advocated the complete subordination of the French Church to the state and even the government's intervention in financial and disciplinary matters. Gallicanism can be traced back to the early Middle Ages and was later tied to the conciliar movement of the 14th and 15th centuries, which held that church councils were more powerful than the pope. Thereafter, Gallicanism was strengthened by certain institutional developments such as the Pragmatic Sanction of Bourges (1438) and the CONCORDAT OF BOLOGNA (1516). Then, in 1594, *Les Libertés de l'Église gallicane,* written by PIERRE PITHOU, was published, outlining the position of parliamentary Gallicanism. In response, Rome placed the work on the Index. In the 17th century, Cardinal RICHELIEU attempted to establish an independent French patriarchate within the church, but this effort came to naught. Gallicanism would eventually reach its fullest development and success during the reign of LOUIS XIV, with the Four Gallican Articles of 1682, issued under the direction of JACQUES BOSSUET. These were, immediately rejected by the pope, however, and later officially renounced by Louis, but they would still be taught in French universities and seminaries until the REVOLUTION OF 1789. Gallicanism, which in the late 17th and 18th centuries was also tied to JANSENISM, essentially ended with the CONCORDAT OF 1801, although certain Gallican attitudes lingered among the French episcopate until the mid-19th century.

## Gallieni, Joseph-Simon
## (1849–1916)
*military figure, administrator*

Born in Saint-Béat and educated at SAINT-CYR, Joseph-Simon Gallieni saw his first military service in the FRANCO-PRUSSIAN WAR (1870–71). From 1877 to 1881, he participated in the military campaign and exploration of the upper Niger River region that resulted in the extension of French influence in western Africa. After three years in Martinique, Gallieni became governor of Upper Senegal (1886) and later (1896) served as a military commander in Madagascar, where he then served as governor-general until 1905. There, he reestablished French control and instituted a program of economic development. On his return to France, he was made a general, and soon (1906), military governor of LYON. At the beginning of WORLD WAR I, he was chosen to lead the military government of Paris (1914). General Gallieni played a decisive role in the battle of the MARNE (September 1914), during the course of which he organized the transporting of French troops to the front by taxis and other means, and he was credited with saving Paris. He served as minister of war (1915–16) in the cabinet of Prime Minister ARISTIDE BRIAND and was awarded the title marshal of France posthumously in 1921. Gallieni described his life and military and administrative career in his writings.

## Gallifet, Gaston-Auguste, marquis de
## (1830–1909)
*general*

Born in Paris, Gaston-Auguste, marquis de Gallifet was an ordnance officer in the army of NAPOLÉON III, and was severely wounded in Mexico during the siege of Puebla (1863). Placed in charge of the African Chausseurs in 1870, at the beginning of the FRANCO-PRUSSIAN WAR he was taken prisoner at Sedan (September 2, 1870). Upon returning to France, he took command of the army at Versailles and became known for the violence with which he suppressed the COMMUNE of Paris. Sent shortly after to be commander of a subdivision at Batna, ALGERIA, he led a campaign into southern Algeria. Governor of Paris (1880), he was named minister of war in the cabinet of PIERRE WALDECK-ROUSSEAU at the time of the Dreyfus affair (1899), but he was replaced in 1900.

## Galois, Évariste (1811–1832)
*mathematician*

Born in Bourg-le-Reine, Évariste Galois, who was twice rejected by the École polytechnique, entered the École normale superieure in 1830, from which he was expelled a year later for publishing an article that violently denounced the "reactionary nature of the director." An active republican, who was twice incarcerated, he continued his work in mathematics while in prison. The essence of the work of this genial mathematician is found in his memoir *Sur les conditions de résolubilité des equations par radicaux* (1831), in which he puts forth the theory of substitution sets. The night before the duel in which he was killed, he edited two memoirs on the subjects about which he was most passionate: a manifesto, *À tous les républicains,* and a mathematical testament in which he further explains his theory on algebraic equations, building on the work of the Norwegian mathematician Niels Henrik Abel. The central idea in the works of Galois is the notion of sets that later became fundamental to the study of mathematics.

## Gambetta, Léon (1838–1882)
*political figure*

Born in Cahors, Léon Gambetta, who is considered one of France's most notable orators, statesmen, and patriots, played a leading role in the formation of the THIRD REPUBLIC. A lawyer, he was educated in Paris and, through articles and speeches, soon became known for his opposition to the regime of NAPOLÉON III. In 1868, in a particularly pointed speech, he attacked the coup d'état of 1851. This speech made Gambetta famous. Elected to the Chamber of Deputies in 1869, he at first opposed the French declaration of war in 1870 against Prussia, but once the conflict began, he vigorously supported his nation's cause. On September 4, 1870, after the defeat of French forces at Sedan, he led the Parisian republicans in proclaiming a republic. When the Germans invaded Paris, he escaped in a hot-air balloon and went to Tours. There, as dictated by popular consent, he assumed direction of the nation's affairs and of the war. After the French surrender at Metz, which he considered an act of treason, Gambetta refused to sign the peace treaty and, after the German annexation of ALSACE-LORRAINE, resigned from the provisional government with a number of other deputies, including VICTOR HUGO. One of the most radical members of the National Assembly, Gambetta founded *La République française,* which became an influential newspaper in which he strongly opposed any attempts to restore the monarchy (see EDME MAC-MAHON). In 1879, Gambetta became president of the Chamber of Deputies and, in 1881, premier of France. His ministry lasted only two months, however, because his policies, which were centered on the formation of a strong executive government, were unpopular with almost all political factions.

See also FRANCO-PRUSSIAN WAR.

## Gamelin, Maurice-Gustave (1872–1958)
*military figure*

The commander of the Allied forces at the beginning of WORLD WAR II, Maurice Gamelin was born in Paris and educated at SAINT-CYR. From 1902 to 1911, he served on the staff of General JOSEPH JOFFRE and, during WORLD WAR I, rose to the rank of brigadier general. He was later (1925–27) sent to the Middle East, where he suppressed a Druze revolt in Syria. Named chief of the general staff in 1931 Gamelin directed the extension of the Maginot Line and, in 1935, became inspector general of the army and vice president of the War Council. Commander in chief of Allied forces in September 1939, at the start of World War II, he was replaced in May 1940, when German forces broke through on the western front. In 1942, he was charged by the VICHY government with responsibility for France's entry into the war and interned first at Portalet and later (1943) deported to Germany. He was released and repatriated in 1945. His memoirs were published after the war under the title *Servir* (1946–47).

## Garaudy, Roger (1913–   )
*philosopher, political figure*

Born in MARSEILLE, Roger Garaudy served as a deputy (1945–51, 1956–58), then senator (1959–62), and as a member of the political bureau of the COMMUNIST PARTY. Although he was the formost intellectual theorist within the party, he was expelled in 1970 for criticizing the French party's support of the Soviet-led invasion of Czechoslovakia in 1968. He also had called for a new look at the party's position on the question of the historical role and identity of the working class, and had introduced other theoretical elements, including the ideas of the Italian communist Antonio Gramsci. Garaudy's reappraisal in many ways reflected the discontent within the French party of many left-wing French intellectuals. An academic, Garaudy has authored studies on socialist realism, and Marxism, and sought to establish a dialogue between Marxists and Christians (*De l'anathème au dialogue*, 1965). A convert to Islam, he had published several works on that subject (*L'Islam habité, notre avenir*, 1981) and his memories (*Mon Tour du siècle en solitaire*, 1989). His controversial *Les Mythes fondateurs de la politique israélienne* (1995) has been criticized for restating the ideas of certain negationist historians regarding the Holocaust.

## Garçon, Maurice (1889–1967)
*writer, attorney*

The son of a renowned jurist, Maurice Garçon was born in Paris and was destined for a career in law. He gained a great reputation as a defense attorney in various literary and criminal trials. He was especially interested in historical issues (*Louis XVII ou la fausse Énigme*, 1952; *Histoires curieuses*, 1959) and in cases of witchcraft (*La Vie exécrable de Guillemette Babin*, 1925; *Magdelaine de la Croix, abbesse diabolique*, 1939). Besides important appeals, he wrote an *Essai sur l'éloquence judicaire* (1941) and a *Histoire de la justice sous la IIIe République* (1957). Garçon was elected to the ACADÉMIE FRANÇAISE in 1946.

## Gascony

Gascony (Gascogne) is a former province of France located between the Garonne River and the Pyrenees. Part of the ancient Roman Aquitania, it was conquered by the Visigoths, then the Franks. It takes its name from *Vascones* (Basques), who invaded the region around the middle of the sixth century, before being reunited with the duchy of Aquitaine. Gascony, after a revolt, formed a duchy after 768, passed in 1058 to the house of Poitiers-et-Aquitaine, and subsequently shared its history with Aquitaine. Gascony was finally united with France in 1453, at the end of the HUNDRED YEARS' WAR.

## Gassendi, Pierre (1592–1655)
*philosopher, savant*

Born in Champtercier, near Digne, where he was educated, Pierre Gassend, or Gassendi as he is known, in 1617 was named professor of philosophy at the University of Aix-en-Provence. For several years, he taught and traveled to Holland and Flanders, while continuing his studies in philosophy and in science. In 1634, he was appointed provost of the cathedral at Digne and, in 1645, became professor of mathematics at the College-Royal in Paris. As a philosopher, he first became known through his critiques on Aristotelian theories, and he also disputed the theories of RENÉ DESCARTES concerning the nature of matter that he published in his *Objections aux Méditations* in 1644. Gassendi wrote also two works on Epicurus. His theories are considered forerunners of the modern empirical method, anticipating the ideas of ÉTIENNE CONDILLAC and John Locke. He is mainly responsible for the revival of Epicureanism in the modern age, in that regard influencing also the work of CYRANO DE BERGERAC. In science, Gassendi's work, which supports the theories of Copernicus and Galileo, was mostly in cartography and astronomy.

## Gaston III de Foix (1331–1391)
*soldier, art and literary patron*

Known also as Gaston Phoebus, Gaston, count de Foix, was a renowned soldier and knight, and was the model great lord of the 14th century who was a patron of arts and letters. During the Hundred Years' War during the reign of PHILIP VI, he at first supported the French faction. But King JEAN II having taken sides with his adversary, the count of Armagnac, Gaston de Foix refused to do homage, remained neutral, and went to fight in Prussia alongside the Teutonic Knights (1356). Upon returning to France, he took part in the suppression of the JACQUERIE (1358). Always at war with the count of Armagnac, he fought him with the help of the GRANDES COMPAGNIES, and defeated and took him captive at Lannac (1362), only freeing him in exchange for an enormous ransom. That fund then allowed him to maintain an ostentatious court at Orthez, but he left his domains to the Crown (he had killed his only legitimate son in a fit of anger in 1382). He also had disputes with Jean de France, duke of Berry.

## Gaston de Foix, duke of Nemours (1489–1512)

*king of Navarre*

Born in Mazères, Ariège, Gaston de Foix, duke of Nemours, was the son of Jean de Foix and Marie d'Orléans, sister of LOUIS XII, and the grandson of Eleonor of Aragon, queen of Navarre. He was made a duke and peer in 1505, then assumed the title of king of Navarre. He was 23 when he took command of the army in Italy and revealed his martial talents. In the course of a lightninglike campaign, after having liberated Bologna, he took Brescia, but was killed during the Battle of Ravenna.

## Gauguin, Paul (1848–1903)

*painter, sculptor, engraver*

Born in Paris, Paul Gauguin spent part of his childhood in Peru (1850–55). He served in the merchant marine (1865) before becoming a successful Parisian stockbroker (1871). In 1874, after meeting CAMILLE PISSARO and viewing the first impressionist exhibition, Gauguin became a collector and amateur painter, exhibiting with the impressionists in 1876, 1880, 1881, 1882, and 1886. In 1883, he left his career, as well as his wife and children, to devote himself exclusively to his painting and his art. From 1886 to 1891, he lived mainly in rural Brittany (except for a visit to Panama and Martinique in 1887 and 1888, respectively) where he was the center of a small group of experimental painters known as the school of Pont-Aven. Under the influence of EMILE BERNARD, he turned from impressionism to synthetism, finding inspiration in medieval and indigenous art as well as Japanese prints, to which he was introduced by VINCENT VAN GOGH during a stay in Arles in 1888. In 1891, severely in debt, Gauguin left Europe for the South Pacific. Except for one visit to France (1893–95), he remained there for the rest of his life, first in Tahiti and later in the Marquesas Islands. While his essential style remained the same, under the influence of Polynesian culture his paintings became more powerful, with the subject matter more dis-

tinct and the composition simplified (*Sur la plage* (1891); *Quand te maries-tu* (1892); *L'Esprit des morts veille* (1893). His masterpieces include *Les Seins aux fleurs rouges* (1897) and *D'où venons-nous?* (1897), which he painted before a failed suicide attempt. Gauguin realized the importance of his work, which would have a profound influence on artists of the 20th century (Derain, Picasso, Modigliani, Munch) and would lead directly to the fauvist and expressionist styles and schools of art.

## Gaulle, Charles de (1890–1970)

*military figure, statesman*

The architect of the FIFTH REPUBLIC and its first president (1959–69), Charles de Gaulle was born in Lille and educated at SAINT-CYR. During WORLD WAR I, he served with distinction at VERDUN (1916) and was wounded and taken prisoner. After the war, he served as aide-de-camp to Marshal PHILIPPE PÉTAIN. De Gaulle gained prominence early as a result of his writings (*Vers l'Armée de métier,* 1934), in which he advocated a highly mechanized army. At the beginning of WORLD WAR II, he attained the rank of brigadier general. After the fall of France to Germany (1940), he escaped to London, where he announced the formation of a French National Committee in Exile. In 1942, it was officially recognized by both the RESISTANCE leaders and the Allied governments. As president of the Free French, de Gaulle commanded all French forces. In September 1940, de Gaulle's forces, including French colonials and a part of the French fleet, made an unsuccessful attack on Dakar, Senegal. In 1942, however, they took Madagascar. In June 1943, de Gaulle joined the Committee of National Liberation in Algiers as copresident, with General HENRI GIRAUD. Later, as sole president, de Gaulle moved the committee's headquarters to London (1944), then to Paris (August 1944), after the Liberation. In November 1945, de Gaulle became provisional premier-president, but he resigned two months later because of disputes with the legislature over the issue of executive power. In 1947, he organized a new political movement—the RASSEMBLE-MENT DU PEUPLE FRANÇAIS (RPF)—that in the 1951 elections won the majority in the National Assembly. The party strove to centralize the government

Charles de Gaulle *(Library of Congress)*

and promote private enterprise, but by 1953, the movement had declined and de Gaulle went into retirement. In May 1958, when France was confronted with the threat of civil war because of the Algerian question (see ALGERIA), de Gaulle was recalled to serve as premier. He was granted the power to rule by decree for six months and to supervise the drafting of a new constitution. This new document greatly increased the executive powers. It was overwhelmingly approved in a plebiscite, and de Gaulle was elected president in December 1958 of the newly created Fifth Republic. During his first term, de Gaulle initiated government and economic reforms and negotiated Algerian independence. France also joined the European Economic Community. He sponsored a unilateral nuclear armaments program for France and renewed French ties with the Soviet Union and mainland China, while French influence increased worldwide. In 1965, de Gaulle was elected to a sec-

ond term as president. At this time, he advocated the autonomy of French Canada and the return to an international gold standard. In 1967, he withdrew French forces but not France itself from NATO. In May 1968, de Gaulle faced the greatest crisis of his presidency when striking students and workers brought the nation almost to a complete halt. In the next month, however, de Gaulle won in the presidential elections, but in April 1969, he resigned the presidency following defeat in a national referendum. He retired to his home in Colombey-les-Deux-Églises to continue work on his memoirs until his death. His other writings include *La Discorde chez l'ennemi* (1924), *Le Fil de l'épée* (1932), and *Vers l'armée de métier* (1934). De Gaulle's determination and strength helped to inspire his nation through the world war and occupation and in the difficult postwar years. His brilliant military ability translated into strong political leadership, and his independent stance in foreign affairs enhanced France's position in the world.

## Gautier, Judith (1845–1917)
*writer*

Born in Paris, Judith Gautier was the daughter of THÉOPHILE GAUTIER and the Italian singer Ernesta Grisi. A Chinese mandarin who knew her father introduced her to the cultures of the Far East; she published an adaptation of Chinese poetry (*Le Livre de jade*, signed Judith Walter, 1867), and translations from the Japanese (*Poèmes de la libellule*, 1885). Besides novels inspired by the Orient, she also wrote dramas. Her memoirs, published between 1902 and 1909, are of great interest, as she knew in her childhood and adolescence most of the great French writers of the period (GÉRARD NERVAL, CHARLES BAUDELAIRE, the DUMAS father and son, GUSTAVE FLAUBERT, EDMOND GONCOURT). Briefly married, Gautier was a friend of the German composer Richard Wagner and helped to make his works known in France.

## Gautier, Théophile (1811–1872)
*writer*

Born in Tarbes, Théophile Gautier early in his life was drawn to painting, but opting instead for literature, he became one of the strongest defenders of VICTOR HUGO during the literary debate over *Hernani* (1830). However, in his long and imaginative descriptive poem, *Albertus* (1832), and *Les Jeunes-France* (1833), a collection of ironic stories, Gautier's independence from the romantics is clear. The "Preface" to his novel, *Madamoiselle de Maupin* (1835–36), expresses his exaltation of pure beauty: "All which is useful is ugly." He sought inspiration in place (chronicles of his journeys to the Orient and to Spain) and in time: in a literary essay, *Les Grotesques*, he praises the age of LOUIS XIII, which, in turn, inspired his novel *Le Capitaine Fracasse* (1863). With *Arria Marcella* (1852), he evoked ancient Pompeii, in *Roman de la momie* (1858) ancient Egypt, and finally with *Le Spirite* (1866), he brings his ideal to the plain of the supernatural. Persuaded that art is an end in itself, and that his only chance for fame was technical perfection (*L'Art*, 1857), he constantly worked on his poems, like *Ribeira* (*España*, 1845), or musical variations, like numerous works of *Émaux et Camées* (1852). The precursor and master of Parnassian poetry, Théophile Gautier, who was the father of the writer JUDITH GAUTIER, was hailed by CHARLES BAUDELAIRE (dedication to *Fleurs du mal*) as the "impeccable poet" and the "perfect magician of French letters."

## Gay, Marie-Françoise-Sophie (1776–1852)
*writer*

Born in PARIS, Sophie Gay, as she is known, was the daughter of M. Nichault de la Valette, bursar to the count of Provence (later LOUIS XVIII), and Francesca Peretti, an Italian woman. Through her second marriage, to M. Gay, receiver-general of the department of the Ruhr, Sophie met many distinguished persons, and her salon was frequented by the leading literati and artists of the period. Her first literary effort, published in the *Journal de Paris*, was a defense of Mme de STAËL's novel *Delphine*, followed by her own novel, *Laure d'Estell*. *Lonie de Montbreuse* (1813) is considered by SAINTE-BEUVE to be her best work, but her romance, *Anatole* (1815), is better known. Mme Gay also wrote several comedies and opera libretti and composed a number of musical works. Her daughter is the writer Delphine Gay, Mme de GIRARDIN. Sophie Gay has left a memoir, *Souvenir d'une vieille femme* (1834).

## Gay-Lussac, Louis-Joseph (1778–1850)
*physicist, chemist*

Born in Saint-Léonard-de-Noblat and educated at the École polytechnique and École des ponts et chaussées, Louis-Joseph Gay-Lussac is known for his studies on the physical properties of gases. In 1804, he made balloon ascents to study magnetic forces and the temperature and composition of air at different altitudes. He then (1809) formulated the law of gases that is associated with his name, which states that the ratios of volumes of gases involved in chemical reactions are in small whole numbers. In relation to this work, he studied, with the German naturalist baron Alexander von Humboldt, the composition of water, discovering that it consists of two parts hydrogen and one part oxygen. He also investigated (1809–16) the properties of potassium and boron and of chlorine and hydrocyanic acid. Guy-Lussac served in the Chamber of Deputies and in the Senate and, in 1806, was named to the Academy of Sciences.

## Genet, Jean (1910–1986)
*writer*

An important novelist and dramatist whose works, which dwell upon bizarre aspects of human existence, express profound rebellion against society and its conventions, Jean Genet was born in Paris, the illegitimate son of a prostitute. He was confined (unjustly) at age 10 for theft and from his early adolescence served a number of sentences for theft and homosexual prostitution, over a period of nearly 30 years. He joined the FOREIGN LEGION in 1930 but deserted two years later. In 1947, after his 10th conviction for theft, he was sentenced to life imprisonment. In prison he continued his writing and publishing, while his literary reputation induced a group of leading French writers to petition for his pardon. It was granted by the president of the republic in 1948. Genet's first novel, an autobiographical work about homosexuality and life in the prison underworld, was *Notre-Dame des fleurs* (1943). Later novels include *Le Journal du voleur* (1949), *Miracle de la rose* (1946), and *Pompes funèbres* (1947). His prose is characterized by a mixture of lyricism and use of underworld jargon. In 1947, Genet began to write drama, the genre in which he had the greatest impact. With his first play, *Les Bonnes* (1947), he entered the movement known as the theater of the absurd. In the later plays, he used the techniques of role playing and inversion of good and evil to comment on the absurdity and hypocrisy of traditional values. Later in his career, Genet espoused the causes of such radical groups as the Black Panthers, the Palestine Liberation Front, and the Red Brigade. All of his works reveal his deep sympathy with the outcasts of society. He has been recognized as an existentialist dealing with the problem of identity and alienation and is regarded as one of the 20th century's most influential writers, points revealed in JEAN-PAUL SARTRE's study of Genet, *Saint Genet, comédien et martyr* (1952). Genet, who in 1983 was awarded the Grand Prix National des Lettres, left three unfinished works that were published after his death.

## Gensonné, Armand (1758–1793)
*political figure*

Born in Bordeaux, where he served as an attorney for the Parlement, Armand Gensonné, during the REVOLUTION OF 1789, was one of the principal leaders of the GIRONDINS and sat in the Legislative Assembly, where he helped to pass the vote against the émigré brothers of King LOUIS XVI and the one for a declaration of war on Austria (April 1792). In the Convention, he proved to be one of the most vehement adversaries of the MONTAGNARDS. After the elimination of the GIRONDIN leaders in the Convention during the TERROR (June 1793), Gensonné was arrested, condemned to death, and executed.

## Geoffrin, Marie-Thérèse Rodet, Mme (1699–1777)
*salon hostess*

Born in Paris, Marie-Thérèse Rodet, Mme Geoffrin hosted a famous salon at which she brought together artists, scholars, writers, and philosophers (notably CLAUDE HÉLVETIUS and JEAN D'ALEMBERT). Subsidizing the *Encyclopédie* of DENIS DIDEROT and receiving also notable foreign visitors, Mme Geoffrin and her salon acquired international renown.

## Geoffroy Saint-Hilaire, Étienne (1772–1844)
*naturalist*

Born in Étampes, Étienne Geoffroy Saint-Hilaire was interested in mineralogy before becoming professor of zoology at the Museum of Natural History of Paris (1793), where he later worked with GEORGES CUVIER. In 1798, Geoffroy Saint-Hilaire took part in Napoléon Bonaparte's expedition to Egypt (see NAPOLÉON I), where he made numerous observations on the diverse animal species (especially reptiles and fish). His work in comparative anatomy and paleontology was guided by the theory of a unique plan of organization of living beings and was based on the idea of the subordination of organs within the body and, above all, the anatomical connection and similarity of species that itself is the basis of comparative anatomy. He discovered a dental system in birds, using skeletal evidence to understand the form of living creatures. This work also helped to establish the field of embryology. Geoffroy Saint-Hilaire's studies eventually led him to oppose the theories of Cuvier, and he asserted that the environment could effect changes in species. He was named to the Academy of Sciences in 1807.

## Géricault, Théodore (1791–1824)
*painter*

Considered perhaps the most influential artist of his time and a seminal figure of the romantic movement in art, Théodore Géricault was born in Rouen and worked with noted artists before traveling to Italy (1816–17) to continue his studies. There, he was greatly influenced by the work of Michelangelo and other Italian Renaissance painters, as well as by that of Rubens. Early in his career, Géricault developed a style that set him apart from the French neoclassical artists. He soon was acknowledged as the leader of the French romantics, especially in his paintings *Charging Chasseur* (exhibited at the Paris Salon in 1812) and *The Wounded Cuirrassier* (1814). Both display violent action, dramatic color, bold design, and powerful emotion. These characteristics appeared in heightened form in his immense and overpowering *The Raft of the Medusa*

(1818–19, LOUVRE), inspired by the disturbing details of a contemporary shipwreck. In 1820, Géricault traveled to England, where he painted *The Derby at Epsom* (1821, Louvre). Toward the end of his life he engaged in a series of portraits of mental patients and other works that make him a precursor of realism. Géricault also produced a number of bronze statuettes, a series of lithographs, and many drawings and color sketches.

## Gide, André (1869–1951)
*writer*

Descended on his mother's side from the Catholic bourgeoisie of NORMANDY and on his father's from a Protestant family of LANGUEDOC, André Gide was born in Paris, where he was educated and raised by his strict mother. His novels, plays, and autobiographical works are known for their exhaustive analysis of individual efforts at self-realization and rigid ethical concepts. In his first book, *Les cahiers d'André Walter* (1891), he described the religious and romantic idealism of an unhappy youth. It is also considered a symbolist work, as is his *Le Traité du Narcisse* (1891) and *La Tentative amoureuse ou le Traité du vain désir* (1893). His later works were then devoted to examining the problem of individual freedom and responsibility from several points of view. *L'Immoraliste* (1902) and *La Porte étroite* (1909) are studies of individual ethical concepts in conflict with conventional morality. In *Les Caves du Vatican* (1914) and *La Symphonie pastorale* (1919), which was later made into a motion picture, Gide deals with the issues of love and responsibility and the impossibility of complete personal freedom. Gide's preoccupation with individual moral responsibility led him to seek public office. After serving in various municipal posts in Normandy, he became a special envoy of the colonial ministry (1925–26) and later wrote two works denouncing the excesses of colonialism. Both books, *Voyage au Congo* (1927) and *Retour du Tchad* (1927), were instrumental in achieving reforms in French colonial laws. In the 1930s, Gide expressed admiration for the Soviet system, but after a visit to the USSR, he wrote of his disillusionment in *Retour de l'URSS* (1936) before breaking completely with the communists. Many of

André Gide *(Library of Congress)*

Gide's critical studies appeared in *La Nouvelle Revue française*, a literary periodical that he helped to found in 1909. It would become a dominant influence in French intellectual circles. Besides his verse dramas, Gide translated Shakespeare's *Antony and Cleopatra* and *Hamlet*, as well as works by William Blake and Walt Whitman. In an autobiographical work, *Si le grain ne meurt* (1920 and 1924), and in an early essay, *Corydon* (1911), he made a courageous statement of his homosexuality. His *Journals* (four volumes, 1939–51) and *Correspondances* (with FRANCIS JAMMES, 1948; PAUL CLAUDEL, 1949; and Rainer Maria Rilke, posthumous, 1952; and PAUL VALÉRY, posthumous, 1955) brought worldwide critical interest. Gide received the Nobel Prize in literature in 1947.

## Gide, Charles  (1847–1932)
*economist*

Born in Uzès, Charles Gide was a founder of the Protestant Association for the Study of Social Action (1887) and was one of the principal theorists of cooperativism (Nîmes school). His main works include *Principes d'économie politique* (1884), *La Coopération* (1800), *Histoire des doctrines économiques* (1909), and *Les Sociétés coopératives de consommation* (1910). Gide was the uncle of ANDRÉ GIDE.

## Girardin, Émile de  (1806-1881)
*publisher, political figure*

Born in Paris, Émile de Girardin, who was the husband of the writer Delphine Gay (see GIRARDIN, MME), after numerous successful publications founded *La Presse* (1836), the first moderately priced newspaper, accessible to the general public. This innovation, which made Girardin the founder of the modern press and caused heated debates in the journalistic world, resulted in his fighting a duel with ARMAND CARREL, whom he killed (1836). A political opportunist, Girardin, an elected deputy (1834), was a member of the Legislative Assembly (1849), but was expelled after the coup d'état of December 2, 1851. Upon his return to France, he continued the publication of *La Presse* and founded the newspaper *La Liberté* (1866), in which he was a defender of a liberal Empire, before supporting the government of ADOLPHE THIERS in *Le Moniteur universel* and *Le Petit Journal* (1872). Girardin then attacked General EDME MAC-MAHON and ALBERT, DUKE DE BROGLIE in *La France* (1877).

## Girardin, Mme [Émile] de (Delphine Gay)  (1804–1855)
*writer*

Delphine Gay, or Mme de Girardin, as she is also known, was born in Aix-la-Chapelle and was the daughter of writer Sophie Gay and the wife of the publisher and political figure ÉMILE DE GIRARDIN. Gay was brought up in a literary milieu and in 1824 published her first work, *Essais poétiques*, in which she expressed such noble and poetic sentiments that she was given the name "Muse de la patrie." After a sojourn in Italy (1826–27), where she was given a triumphal welcome, she married

(1831) and wrote novels (*Le Lorgnon*, 1831; *Le Marquis de Pontanges*, 1835), and a charming account, *La Canne de M. Balzac* (1836). Equally a spiritual writer, her *Lettres parisiennes* (published in *La Presse* under the pseudonym of vicomte de Launay, 1836 to 1848) brought her great renown. For the theater, Gay composed tragedies (*Judith*, 1843; *Cléopatra*, 1847) and numerous comedies, including *La Joie fait peur* (1854).

## Giraud, Henri (general)  (1879–1949)
*military figure*

Born in Paris and educated at Saint-Cyr, Henri Giraud served in WORLD WAR I (1914–18) and in Morocco (1923–26). Made commander of the 9th French Army during WORLD WAR II (May 1940), he was taken prisoner but escaped in April 1942. After the assassination of Admiral FRANÇOIS DARLAN (December 1942), he was made, with American support, military and civilian high commissioner in North and West Africa. Despite his hostility to General CHARLES DE GAULLE, he became copresident with him of the French Committee of National Liberation (CFLN), established in Algiers in June 1943, and was named commander in chief of all French forces. Progressively replaced by de Gaulle, General Giraud resigned the copresidency (November 1943), then his post as commander in chief (April 1944). He had meanwhile reconstituted a French army (FFL) in North Africa, reequipped by the Americans, and he played a preponderant role in the victories in Tunisia, in the Italian campaign, and in the liberation of CORSICA.

## Giraudoux, Jean  (1882–1944)
*writer, diplomat*

Born in Bellac, Jean Giraudox, whose impressionistic style of writing helped to change the canons of realism in the French theater, studied in Paris and Munich, Germany. In 1910, he entered the foreign service, became director of information (1929), a post he also held under the VICHY regime. His early novels brought him literary acclaim and show his imagination and humor (*Simon le Pathétique*, 1918; *Siegfried et le Limousin*, 1922; *Bella*, 1925; *Combat avec l'ange*, 1934; *Choix des élus*, 1939). In his works, he expressed a humanistic optimism, but a sense of the tragic too (*Siegfried,* 1928; *Amphitryon 38,* 1929; *Judith,* 1931; *Intermezzo,* 1939). One can trace the evolution to a mood of uneasiness (*La guerre de Troie n'aura pas lieu,* 1935) and to pathos (*Électre,* 1937; *Ondine,* 1939), and even despair (*Sodome et Gomorrhe,* 1943). A satirical and prolific writer, Giraudoux presents his views of an uncertain and disenchanted era in his essay *Pleins pouvoirs.*

## Girondins

During the REVOLUTION OF 1789, the Girondins were a political group, many of whose leaders were deputies to the National Assembly from the Gironde region near Bordeaux (hence the name). The best-known were CHARLES BARBAROUX, JACQUES BRISSOT (the Girondins were also called "Brissotins"), FRANÇOIS BUZOT, the marquis of CONDORCET, ARMAND GENSONNÉ, MARGUERITE ÉLIE GUADET, MAXIMIN ISNARD, JEAN-BAPTISTE LOUVET DE COUVRAY, ROLAND DE LA PLATIÈRE and his wife, MME ROLAND, and PIERRE VERGNIAUD. The Girondins were not a party or the spokespersons for a particular social class but a group of individuals, often journalists, lawyers, or merchants, who held especially to the idea of federalism. They were usually members of the JACOBIN CLUB until September 1792 and sat to the left in the Legislative Assembly, where they were in opposition to the constitutional monarchists (the FEUILLANTS) and where they voted for the declaration of war on Austria (April 1792). August 10, 1792 (the fall of the monarchy), the Girondins would dominate the National Convention, where they sat on the right and where they never ceased to strongly oppose the MONTAGNARDS, early on. The Girondins insisted that the Revolution had achieved its objectives (the end of despotism and the monarchy) and believed that it should be prevented from going further. The trial of King LOUIS XVI, which the Girondins tried to stop, the generalization of the war with aristocratic Europe, the defeats of the Revolutionary armies, the threat of counterrevolution, and the nation's economic and social problems increased the conflict between the Montagnards and the Girondins and led to the fall of the latter under the pressure of the SANS-CULOTTES led by the Hébertists and the ENRAGÉS (May 31–June 2, 1793). Certain Girondin leaders who, because they feared a popular Parisian dictatorship (most of the Montagnard

deputies [the Mountain] were elected from Paris), appealed to local administrations and tried in particular provinces to direct a FEDERALIST INSURRECTION against the Mountain, but without success. Twenty-one of them were condemned to death by the Revolutionary Tribunal and guillotined (late October 1793).

See also DUMOURIEZ, CHARLES-FRANÇOIS DU PÉRIER; HÉBERT, JACQUES-RENÉ.

## Giroud, Françoise (1916–2003)
*journalist, political figure*

Born France Gourdji, in Geneva, Switzerland, Françoise Giroud, a widely admired French journalist, was of Russian and Turkish background. At age 16, she began working as a script girl for several French film directors, including MARC ALLÉGRET and JEAN RENOIR. During WORLD WAR II, she served with the Resistance and was briefly imprisoned. At the time of the Liberation, she was one of the creators of the weekly *Elle* and, in 1953, founded *L'Express* with JEAN-JACQUES SERVAN-SCHREIBER. She later became chief editor, then publisher of that journal (1971–74). A defender of women's rights, Giroud was appointed by Premier JACQUES CHIRAC to serve as secretary of state for women's affairs (1974–76), then as minister of culture in the government of VALÉRY GISCARD D'ESTAING (1976–77). She supported FRANÇOIS MITTERRAND in the presidential elections (1981), but agreed to serve in his government only under the condition that she would have an active role and responsibilities and not merely assume a token post. A prolific writer, Giroud is the author of works on journalism and politics and on the cinema and has published her memoirs (*Leçons particulières,* 1990).

## Giscard d'Estaing, Valéry (1926–  )
*statesman*

The president of France (1974 to 1981) who continued the conservative policies of his predecessors in the Fifth Republic, Valéry Giscard d'Estaing was born in Koblenz, Germany, and educated at the École polytechnique and the École nationale d'administration. He began his career in 1952 in the Ministry of Finance and Economic Affairs, where he served as assistant director of the minister's staff.

Elected to the National Assembly in 1956 and 1958, he was named secretary of state for finance in 1959, and in 1962 became minister of finance. When his policies, which lowered inflation, caused also a slight recession, he left that post (1986) and returned to the National Assembly. In 1969, he joined the government of GEORGES POMPIDOU as minister of finance and economic affairs and, after Pompidou's death in April 1974, was elected president of the republic by 50.81 percent of the vote over FRANÇOIS MITTERRAND (see REPUBLIC, FIFTH). Proposing closer political and economic ties among the European nations, Giscard established personal ties with other world leaders. He also sought to end inflation in France, presenting in 1976 a wide range of economic reforms. He was, however, unable to halt the economy's deterioration caused by worldwide recession. Defeated by Mitterrand in the 1981 election, he later served as president of the regional council of Auvergne (1986) and of the UDF (1988–96). Giscard has outlined his political ideas especially in two works: *Démocratie française* (1976) and *Le Pouvoir et la Vie* (1988–91).

## Gleizes, Albert (1881–1953)
*painter, theorist*

A leading cubist painter and theorist, Albert Gleizes was born in Paris, where he first painted, under the influence of the impressionists. In 1906, he helped to found the Abbaye Group at Créteil. The works of GEORGES BRAQUE and Pablo Picasso, as well as the *Portrait de Jouve* by Henri Le Fauconnier (1909) caused him to modify his technique; he reduced the volume of simple forms to the prismatic while often still maintaining a realistic treatment of focus (*Portrait de Jacques Nayral*). Other of his works have a nonfigurative character (*Brooklyn Bridge*). In 1911, he exhibited at the Salon d'automne in the section called "cubist" and, interested in neoplatonic theories, he attended meetings in the studio of JACQUES VILLON and established, in 1912, the Section d'Or with JEAN METZINGER. Gleizes published the first theoretical work on the cubist movement, which is its manifesto, *Du Cubisme*. After having upheld socialistic and pacifistic ideas, he rediscovered Catholicism and tried to incorporate cubist concepts into traditional religious paintings.

## Gobelins, Manufacture Nationale des

A textile factory located in the 13th arrondissement (zone) of Paris, and named after a family of French dyers, the Gobelin enterprise began in the mid–15th century, when Jean and Philibert Gobelin set up a dye works on the outskirts of the city. Their business flourished and, in the early 17th century, King HENRY IV had the works made into a tapestry factory under Flemish weavers. The Gobelin factory's luxurious products became so famous that in 1662, JEAN-BAPTISTE COLBERT, then minister of finance to LOUIS XIV, incorporated the establishment as part of the Royal Manufactory of Furniture. The noted painter CHARLES LE BRUN was put in charge, and he commissioned the best artists of the day to submit designs. New artisans were also trained, and magnificent tapestries, upholstery, and furniture were all produced in the baroque style. The Gobelins factory was closed briefly (1694–99) because of royal financial problems, then reopened to produce tapestries exclusively. It has remained in operation ever since, with only a brief interruption during the REVOLUTION OF 1789. Through the centuries styles changed from baroque to rococo to neoclassical and finally to modern. In 1825 the factory absorbed the Savonnerie carpet works, founded in 1627, and is now officially known as the Manufacture Nationale des Gobelins.

## Gobineau, Joseph-Arthur, count de (1816–1882)
*diplomat, writer*

A social philosopher whose writings, including those on anti-Semitism, would later become the basis for much of modern racial and racist theory, Joseph-Arthur, count de Gobineau was born to an aristocratic family in Ville-d'Array, near Paris. From 1848 to 1877, he held diplomatic posts in Iran, Germany, Greece, Brazil, and Sweden, and wrote several scholarly books describing his travels (*Trois ans en Asie* 1859; *Traité des écritures cunéiformes*, 1861; *Les Religions et les Philosophies dans l'Asie centrale*, 1865). He also wrote a journal (*Nouvelles asiatiques*, 1876) and novels (*Le Prisonnier chanceux*, 1847; *Les Pléiades*, 1874). His most famous work, however, was *Essai sur l'inégalité des races humaines* (1853–55), in which he stated that the Aryan, or Nordic, race was superior to all others. His ideas of racial superiority later influenced Richard Wagner and Houston Stewart Chamberlain, and were exploited by the pan-Germanists and the National Socialists of Hitler's Germany.

## Godard, Jean-Luc (1930–   )
*film director*

Born in Paris, Jean-Luc Godard is considered the most innovative and influential figure of the Nouvelle Vague (New Wave) movement in French cinema. Of bourgeois background, Godard attended the University of Paris and spent much of his time studying cinema. He also wrote for the influential periodical *Les Cahiers du cinéma*. His first feature-length film, *À bout de souffle* (1959), established him as the leading Nouvelle Vague director. In it, he employed such techniques as jump cuts, unusual camera angles, improvised dialogue, and interspersed philosophical discussions. Godard's prolific film output of the 1960s includes *Une femme est une femme* (1961); *Les Carabiniers* (1963); *Pierrot le Fou* (1965); *Alphaville* (1965); *Une femme mariée* (1964); *Masculin-Féminin* (1966); *Made in USA* (1966); *La Chinoise* (1967); and *Week-End* (1968). Between 1968 and 1973, Godard produced a series of films through the Dziga-Vector Group—a film cooperative dedicated, in Godard's words, to making "revolutionary films for revolutionary audiences." His later films include *Sauve qui peut la vie* (1980); *Prénom Carmen* (1983); *Je vous salue Marie* (1984); *King Lear* (1986); *Nouvelle Vague* (1990); *Hélas pour moi* (1993); and *JLG by JLG* (1994). Godard's films are considered avant-garde works that critique the absurdity of contemporary life.

## Goncourt, Edmond Huot de (1822–1896)
*historian, writer*

Born in Nancy, Edmond Huot de Goncourt became interested in literature quite early. In collaboration with his brother, Jules Huot de Goncourt (1830–70), he developed a critical style of historiography. The brothers were both interested, too, in Japanese art of the 18th century (*Outamaro*, 1891). Other works by the Goncourts include novels (*Soeur Philomène*, 1861, which describes life in a hospital; *Renée Mau-*

*perin*, 1864, a work that evokes the world of bourgeois youth, 1864; and *Germaine Lacesteux*, 1865). After the death of Jules, Edmond Goncourt published *La Fille Elisa* (1877), *La Faustin* (1882), and *Chérie* (1884). He also continued their *Journal* (partially published 1887–96, complete edition, 1956–58), and he later bequeathed his entire estate to establish the prix Goncourt in Jules Goncourt's honor. The prix Goncourt, the most important of the 1,500 French literary awards given each year, is administered by the Académie Goncourt, the group of 10 men and women of letters who select the most imaginative prose work of that year. The prize still consists of the original award of 50 francs, first given in 1903.

## Goscinny, René (1926–1977)
*cartoonist, illustrator*

René Goscinny, who was born in Paris, began the comic strip *Lucky Luke* in 1955. In 1959, he created, with ALBERT UDERZO, *Astérix*, the Gaul and the one of the most famous French comic strips, which appeared in the first edition of *Pilote*, a magazine that Goscinny cofounded with Uzdero and the Belgian cartoonist Jean-Michel Charlier, and in the magazine *Iznogoud* in 1962. Thanks to the worldwide success of *Astérix*, Goscinny could launch in *Pilote* a new generation of artists who addressed their work to an adult audience.

## Gouges, Olympe de (1755–1793)
*writer, feminist*

Born Marie Gouze in Montauban, Olympe de Gouges as she is known, was the daughter of a washerwoman and a butcher. Arriving in Paris some time before the REVOLUTION OF 1789, she married a wealthy older man, became a widow, then supported herself by writing. She soon became a playwright of some note. Although a moderate politically (she defended the king), de Gouges wrote many profoundly revolutionary and feminist pamphlets but also denounced the TERROR. In her now famous *Déclaration des droits de la femme et de la citoyenne* (1792), she was an ardent advocate for women's emancipation, stating that women should be full citizens with full political and personal rights.

Her writings in favor of LOUIS XVI, however, as well as some of her feminist ideas, caused her to be arrested and guillotined.

## Goujon, Jean (1510–ca. 1566)
*sculptor, engraver, architect*

An important artist of the French Renaissance, Jean Goujon was probably of Norman origin, and most likely spent time in Italy, where he studied ancient and contemporary Italian works. Recognized too as an art theorist, he produced a series of engravings for the French translation of *Vitruve*, by Jean Martin (1547). In 1540, Goujon worked in Rouen on the organ gallery of the church of Saint-Maclou and, becoming sculptor to the king (1547), worked also at Écouen for the duke of MONTMORENCY. In Paris (1544), he sculpted, with PIERRE LESCOT, the bas-reliefs of the church of Saint-Germain-l'Auxerrois, then those of the *Quatre Saisons* in the Ligneris mansion (today the Carnavalet Museum), and the six *Nymphes* at the fountain of the Innocents (1549). Additionally, he did allegorical figures for the courtyard of the LOUVRE (1550). His mythological inspiration and the sensuousness and sensitivity of his figures reveal a mannerist aesthetic to which he gives a personal inflection directly linked to the classical, especially the Hellenic, spirit (clinging drapery, etc). The purity also of Goujon's technique and the delicacy of his modeling make him one of the major figures of French Renaissance sculpture.

## Gounod, Charles (1818–1893)
*composer*

Born in Paris, Charles Gounod was a student of JACQUES HALÉVY and other noted artists at the Conservatoire and, in 1839, won the prix de Rome, which allowed him to study in Italy. There, he was inspired by Palestrina and, when he went to Germany, Johann Sebastian Bach, Wolfgang Mozart, Ludwig van Beethoven, and Robert Schumann. At first drawn to sacred music (*Te Deum; Requiem*), as an organist and chapel master, he considered joining the priesthood. But when his first opera, *Sapho* (1851), was produced, Gounod decided to devote himself to musical composition. While some works (*Le Médicin malgré lui*, 1858) had only moderate success, with *Faust* (1859) he gained much notoriety.

Other works also brought him immediate renown (*Mireille*, 1864; *Roméo et Juliette*, 1867), but the poor reception given his last opera (*Le Tribut de Zamora*, 1881), led him to dedicate his later years to religious music (*Rédemption*, 1882; *Mors et Vitae*, 1885; *Requiem*, 1893). Gounod is also the author of two symphonies, 13 masses, motets, canticles, melodies, and choir pieces, as well as works for piano and organ. As a stylist, melodist, and lyricist, he influenced GEORGES BIZET, CÉSAR FRANCK, HENRI DUPARC, GABRIEL FAURÉ, and CLAUDE DEBUSSY. A contemporary of Richard Wagner, Gounod escaped Wagner's ascendancy and found his own unique expressiveness, and his operas are some of the essential contributions of French music and lyric art.

## Gouraud, Henri-Joseph-Eugène (1867–1946)
*general*

Henri-Joseph-Eugène Gouraud, who was born in Paris, graduated from SAINT-CYR and began his military career in the Sudan (1898), where he defeated Samory Touré, the Sudanese leader who fought against French occupation. Gouraud was then called to Morocco by Marshal LOUIS LYAUTEY (1910). During WORLD WAR I, he commanded a division in the Argonne as well as the French expeditionary force in the Dardanelles, where he lost an arm. Named commander of the Fourth Army in Champagne, he halted the last German offensive in that region and subsequently successfully took the counteroffensive (July 1918). High Commissioner in Syria (1919–23), he suppressed uprisings in Damascus and Cilicia. From 1923 to 1937, Gouraud served as military governor of Paris.

## Gourgaud, Gaspard, baron (1783–1852)
*general*

Born at Versailles, Gaspard, baron Gourgaud served as an ordnance officer to NAPOLÉON I, whom he then (1815) followed into exile on Saint Helena. Later, with General CHARLES, COUNT de MONTHELON, he edited Bonaparte's memoirs (*Mémoires pour servir à l'histoire de France sous Napoléon*, 1822–25). Upon Gourgaud's return to Europe in 1818, he tried, in meeting with various European rulers at Aix-la-Chapelle, to ameliorate the conditions of the captive emperor. Named lieutenant general in 1835 by King LOUIS-PHILIPPE, to whom he had become aide-de-camp, Gourgaud participated in the return of Napoléon's remains to Paris in 1840 and was later elected to the Legislative Assembly (1849).

## Gourgues, Dominique de (ca. 1530–1593)
*navigator, adventurer*

Born in Mont-de-Marsan, Dominique de Gourgues, upon the instigation of Queen CATHERINE DE' MEDICI, undertook an expedition to Florida (1567–68) to avenge the colonizers RENÉ DE LAUDONNIÈRE and JEAN RIBAULT and their companions, most of whom had been massacred by the Spanish. Gourgues took several Spanish outposts and killed the survivors. He was then, however, disavowed by the French government, and his victory came to naught.

## Gourmont, Rémy de (1858–1915)
*writer*

Born in Bazoches-au-Houlme, Orne, Rémy de Gourmont was a leader of the symbolist movement and founded the important French journal *Le Mercure de France* (1889). A member of the staff at the Bibliothèque nationale, he was forced to resign because of a subversive article that he supposedly had written. An epicurean in search of beauty, like JORIS-KARL HUYSMANS, he is the author of *Le Latin mystique, Les Poètes de l'antiphonaire et la symbolique au Moyen Âge* (1892), and other works that represent the symbolist ideal (*Esthétique de la langue française*, 1899; *La Culture des idées*, 1900; *Promenades littéraires*, 7 volumes, 1904–13; *Promenades philosophiques*, 3 volumes, 1905–09).

## Gournay, Jacques-Claude-Marie Vincent, seigneur de (1712–1759)
*economist*

Born in Saint-Mâlo, Jacques-Claude-Marie Vincent, seigneur de Gournay, who was influenced by the theories of the Physiocrats, especially those of FRANÇOIS QUESNAY, was a supporter of economic liberalism ("Laissez-faire, laissez-passer"). Gournay recommended freedom in industry and production and the suppression of regulations and monopolies.

## Gournay, Marie le Jars de (1566–1645)
*writer*

Born in Paris, Marie le Jars de Gournay was a friend and inspiration to MICHEL EYQUEM DE MONTAIGNE, and enthusiastically encouraged him in the writing of his *Essais* (which she edited in 1595). Their relationship lasted until his death, and *L'Ombre de Mademoiselle de Gournay* (1626) is a collection, in verse, of writings on morality and polemic texts.

## Gouvion-Saint-Cyr, Laurent, marquis de (1764–1830)
*military and political figure, marshal of France*

Born in Toul, Laurent, marquis de Gouvion-Saint-Cyr, after studying design and painting in Rome and Paris, joined the revolutionary army as a volunteer (1792). Ambassador to Spain under the Consulate (1802), he took part in the campaigns of the FIRST EMPIRE in Prussia (1806–07), Spain, Russia (victory of Polotsk over Wittgenstein, which earned him the field marshal's baton). Sent to defend Dresden (1813), he was forced to surrender, because of lack of supplies. Named minister of war by King LOUIS XVIII (1815–17), he put through a law reorganizing the army (Gouvion-Saint-Cyr Law, March 10, 1818), which regulated conscription and promotion (seniority was recognized, and members of the nobility could no longer directly enter the officer corps). Made a peer in 1815, Gouvion-Saint-Cyr resigned his position because of opposition from the Ultras, extremely conservative monarchists (1819). He is the author of *Mémoires pour servir à l'histoire militaire sous le Directoire, le Consulat et l'Empire* (1831).

## Grafigny (or Graffigny), Françoise d'Issembourg d'Happoncourt, Mme de (1695–1758)
*writer*

Born in Nancy, Françoise d'Issembourg d'Happoncourt, or Mme de Grafigny as she is also known, was married quite young to an abusive husband who caused her to leave and seek refuge with VOLTAIRE at the home of Mme de CHÂTELET at Cirey. Her *Lettres,* which are very revealing, were published in 1820. Mme de Grafigny went to Paris in 1743, where she held a salon and gained much recognition for her *Lettres d'une Péruvienne* (1747), a spirited parody of MONTESQUIEU's *Lettres persanes,* in which she gives a lively critique of the society of her day. One of her plays, *Cénie* (1750), was also well received.

## Gramont, Antoine-Agénor, duke de (1819–1880)
*diplomat, political figure*

Born in Paris, Antoine-Agénor, duke of Gramont, served during the SECOND EMPIRE as minister plenipotentiary to Kassel (1852), Stuttgart, and Turin (1853), then as ambassador to Rome (1857) and to Vienna (1860). He supported French intervention in Italy (1860) while assuring the independence of the pope. He later supported a French rapprochement with Austria (against Prussia). Named foreign minister through the endorsement of Empress EUGÉNIE (May 1870), he was, by his interventions, partly responsible for the declaration of war by France on Prussia (July 15, 1870), bringing about the FRANCO-PRUSSIAN WAR (1870–71).

## Gramont, House of

The House of Gramont originated in Navarre. Its most famous members include the following: Antoine III, duke de Gramont (1604–78), was born in Hagetmou and distinguished himself as a military figure in the service of King LOUIS XIII during the THIRTY YEARS' WAR and remained faithful to the king during the FRONDE. He is the author of *Mémoires.* Philibert, count de Gramont (1621–1707), brother of the preceding, was a military commander. He fought in Franche-Comté and in Holland (1668–71), and his bravery and exploits were made famous by his brother-in-law, the writer ANTOINE HAMILTON, in *Les Mémoires de la vie du comte de Gramont* (1715). Armand de Gramont, count de Guiche (1638–73), also a soldier in the service of King Louis XIV, was the first person known to swim across the RHINE RIVER, during the campaign of 1672.

## Grandes Compagnies

The Grandes Compagnies were groups of mercenaries who fought in the pay of Kings JEAN II and CHARLES V during the HUNDRED YEARS' WAR. Discharged after the Peace of Brétigny (1360), they turned to pillaging France. The menace was ended during the reign of Charles V, who ordered BERTRAND DU GUESCLIN to lead them to fight for King Henry II the Magnificent in Castile in his struggle against Peter the Cruel.

## Grappelli, Stéphane  (1908–1997)
*jazz musician*

Born in Paris to a French mother and Italian father, Stéphane Grappelli, who as a youth studied with Isadora Duncan, became interested in music early and won a number of awards for his talent. By 1927, he had turned to jazz and was a member of the Hot Club de France string quartet since its beginning, along with DJANGO REINHARDT. An excellent improviser, with a lyrical and tender style, Grappelli is considered one of the best jazz violinists. His principal recordings include *Minor Swing* (quintette du HFC, 1937), *Tea for Two* (1970), and *Anniversary Concert* (album, 1983).

## Grave, Jean  (1854–1939)
*anarchist*

Born in Breuil-sur-Couze, Puy-de-Dôme, Jean Grave was a shoemaker and anarchist who edited the newspaper *La Révolte,* founded by the Russian anarchist Peter Kropotkin in Geneva in 1883. He then edited the journals *La Révolte* and *Les Temps nouveaux* in Paris (1894). Grave published several works including *La Société au lendemain de la Révolution* (1882) and *La Société mourante et l'Anarchie* (1893), a book that caused charges to be brought against him by the authorities.

## Gréban, Arnoul  (ca. 1420–1471)
*dramatic poet*

Born in Le Mans, Arnoul Gréban held a degree in theology and was master of the chapel of Notre Dame de Paris. Sometime before 1452, he composed his monumental *Mystère de la Passion,* a work of considerable importance in the history of French theater. Comprising 34,574 verses, it constitutes a most grandiose dramatic summation inspired by

Christianity. Under a form of dialogue interspersed with bits of pure lyricism, Gréban combined the tragic and the comic, and employed all the resources of realism. The work, which is produced over four days, enjoyed a great popularity for over a century. Simon Gréban, Arnoul Gréban's brother, composed, no doubt with his collaboration, *Le Mystère des Actes des Apôtres* (ca. 1465).

## Gréco, Juliette (1927–   )
*actor, singer*

Born in Montpellier, Juliette Gréco made her singing debut in 1946, starring at Le Tabou cabaret in Saint-Germain-des-Prés. Her acerbic and impertinent repertoire evokes, with the help of an unchanging stage technique and props (black robe, immobile stature, play of hands), the sensuality associated with a cynical realism (*Si tu t'imagines, Jolie Môme, Déshabillez-moi*). At the same time, she also has had a successful career in film (*Elena et les hommes* by JEAN RENOIR, 1956), in television (*Belphégor*), and in the theater.

## Grégoire, Henri (1750–1831)
### (Abbé Grégoire)
*ecclesiastic, political figure*

Born in Vého, near Lunéville, Henri Grégoire, or abbot Grégoire as he is known, was a deputy for the clergy to the ESTATES GENERAL in 1789. He joined the Third Estate at the time of the REVOLUTION OF 1789 and was a representative for the extreme Left to the Constituent Assembly. There, he was a supporter not only of the abolition of all privileges, but also favored universal suffrage, and was the first to take the oath of loyalty to the CIVIL CONSTITUTION OF THE CLERGY (November 1790). Constitutional bishop of Blois (1791), he was elected to the Convention, where he helped to pass the decrees that granted civil and political rights to Jews and abolished slavery. He also initiated an inquiry that would lead to a debate about suppressing the use of patois and promoting the French language (1790–91). A member of the Council of Five Hundred (1795), then the Legislative Corps (1800), and senator (1802), abbot Grégoire tried without success to organize a Gallican church (see GALLICANISM) (national councils of 1797 and 1802). Opposed to the First Consul and the CONCORDAT, he supported the overthrow of NAPOLÉON I and, under the Restoration, took his place with the liberal opposition as a deputy for Isère (1819). Abbot Grégoire is the author of, among others, *Histoire des sects religieuses* (1810), and his *Mémoires* (posthumous, 1839).

## Grenoble

A city located in the department of Isère, Grenoble, which is on the Grésivaudan plain, is surrounded by high mountains. It is one of the more important French centers of research and technology (second only to Paris), and to its three universities can be added six national engineering schools. It is also the site of the Installation européenne de rayonnement synchrotron (ESRF). Major sites of Grenoble include the cathedral of Notre-Dame (12th–13th centuries), the Palais de justice (14th century), the Painting and Sculpture Museum, Stendhal Museum, and Museum of the Dauphiné. At first a settlement of the Allobroges, the city took its name from the Roman emperor Gratian in the fourth century. From the ninth to the 11th centuries, it was part of the kingdom of Burgundy-Provence and became part of France, with the rest of the Dauphiné, in the 13th century. The first university was founded there in the 14th century. The city was contested during the WARS OF RELIGION. In 1968, Grenoble was the site of the Winter Olympic Games.

## Greuze, Jean-Baptiste (1725–1805)
*painter*

Born in Tournus, Jean-Baptiste Greuze studied art in Lyon and Paris, where he became a leading genre painter. He recalls in his works the Dutch masters of the 17th century, and he based his paintings on the tastes of his era, being influenced by JEAN-JACQUES ROUSSEAU and the writers Samuel Richardson and Henry Fielding. In 1755, at the Paris Salon, he had a great success with *Un père de famille expliquant la Bible à ses enfants*. His painting, sentimental and edifying, evolved toward a moralizing pathos (*Le mauvais Fils puni*) in accord with bourgeois drama and the comedy of DENIS DIDEROT, who was his enthusiastic admirer. Greuze wanted to bring genre painting to the level of historical painting and produced vigorous and sensitive portraits (*Sophie Arnould; Le Graveur Wille*) and has also done strikingly honest interpretations of children and youths (*La Cruche cassée,* 1789). Greuze had numerous imitators, but his fame was eclipsed by that of JACQUES-LOUIS DAVID.

## Grévy, Jules (1807–1891)
*political figure*

Born in Mont-sous-Vaudrey, Jules Grévy was an attorney with republican sympathies. He was named commissioner of the SECOND REPUBLIC (1848), elected to the Constituent Assembly (April 1848), then to the Legislative Assembly (May 1849). There, he sat with the Left and took a position for freedom of the press and against the expedition to Rome (see NICOLAS OUDINOT). After the coup d'état of December 2, 1851 he temporarily retired from politics. Reelected, he sat as an opposition deputy in the Legislative Corps (1868), where he opposed the declaration of war against Germany (1870) and joined the ranks of the moderate republicans after the fall of the SECOND EMPIRE (September 4, 1870). A deputy for BORDEAUX in the National Assembly in February 1871, then a member of the Chamber of Deputies in 1876, Grévy was elected president of the THIRD REPUBLIC after General EDME MAC-MAHON (1879), and tried to pursue a policy that was opposed to revanchist nationalism and colonial expansion. He kept men like LÉON GAMBETTA and JULES FERRY from power, but the scandal involving the sale of honors and decorations in which his own son-in-law was involved forced Grévy to resign in 1887.

## Griaule, Marcel (1898–1956)
*ethnologist*

Born in Aisy-sur-Armançon, Marcel Griaule, after spending several months in Abyssinia (1928–29), organized an expedition through central Africa from east to west (the Dakar-Djibouti mission, 1931–33), inaugurating an era of ethnographic studies in the region. During this expedition, he made contact with the Dogons in the hills of Bandiagara, Mali, on whom he would do the majority

of his studies: *Les Masques dogons* (1938), *Dieu d'eau,* a work that reveal the structure of Dogon society (1948), and *Renard pale, ethnologie des Dogons,* in collaboration with Germaine Dieterlen (1965).

See also LEIRIS, MICHEL.

## Grignan, Françoise Marguerite de Sévigné, countess de (1646–1705)
*writer*

Born in Paris, Françoise Marguerite de Sévigné, countess de Grignan, maintained, with her mother, Marie du Rabutin-Chantal, marquise de SÉVIGNÉ, a famous correspondence (*Lettres de la comtesse Grignan à la marquise de Sévigné*) that reveals much of the life and mores of their period. The countess de Grignan began this correspondence after her husband, was appointed lieutenant general of Provence.

## Gringore, Pierre (ca. 1475–ca. 1538)
*dramatic poet*

Born in Thury-Harcourt, Pierre Gringore was popularized by VICTOR HUGO in his novel *Notre-Dame de Paris,* in which his name is changed to "Gringoire." The leader of a troop of actors known as "Enfants sans souci" and author of numerous parodies, Gringore put his wit and talent to the service of King LOUIS XII in that monarch's struggle against Pope Julius II by composing satirical poems (*Les folles Entreprises,* 1505; *La Chasse du cerf des cerfs,* 1510). It is, however, especially in *Jeu du prince des Sots et de la mère Sotte,* produced in the Halles of Paris for Mardi-Gras in 1512, that Gringore gives free rein to his strong and joyful style.

## Gros, Antoine, Baron (1771–1835)
*painter*

A romantic painter, best known for his historical paintings chronicling the career of Napoléon Bonaparte (see NAPOLÉON I), Antoine Gros was born in Paris, the son of a miniaturist. He entered the atelier of JACQUES-LOUIS DAVID, who brought him to the attention of JOSÉPHINE de Beauharnais, who then introduced him to Napoléon. Gros's first major work, *Bonaparte at the Bridge of Arcole* (1796), was followed by a succession of enormous canvases, including *Bonaparte Visiting the Pesthouse in Jaffa*

(1804); *The Battle of Aboukir* (1806); and *The Battle-field of Eylau* (1808). All are in the LOUVRE or at VERSAILLES. Gros's paintings, which convey a sense of heroism and action, helped to forge the myth and mystique of the imperial era. Gros also painted several portraits of figures of the imperial court and the heroes of the Empire. Under the RESTORATION, Gros replaced the exiled David as professor at the École des Beaux-Arts and was made a baron. His late work also includes many mythological scenes, but in a formalist neoclassical style. Their unpopularity with both the critics and the public, however, made Gros doubt his abilities and, when his final canvas was badly received at the Salon of 1835, he drowned himself in the Seine. Gros's work was much admired by the romantic painters EUGÈNE DELACROIX and THÉODORE GÉRICAULT.

## Grouchy, Emmanuel, marquis (1766–1847)

*marshal of France*

Born in the château of Villette near Paris, Emmanuel, marquis Grouchy, was an officer of the Guard in 1789, then, joining the REVOLUTION OF 1789, would take part in all the major Napoleonic campaigns (Friedland, Wagram, Borodino, etc). Faithful to NAPOLÉON I during the HUNDRED DAYS, he was made a marshal. At the head of the reserve cavalry in the Army of the North, he could not prevent, after the victory at Ligny, General Gebhard Blucher from joining with General Wellington, making Marshal Grouchy partly responsible for the defeat at Waterloo. He sought refuge in America and returned to France in 1821. King LOUIS-PHILIPPE named him a peer of France in 1832. Marshal Grouchy is the author of *Mémoires* (posthumous, 1873).

## Grousset, Paschal (1845–1909)

*journalist, political figure*

Born in Corte, CORSICA, Paschal Grousset was a member of the Second Executive Commission of the Paris COMMUNE (1871), which, in turn, named him delegate for foreign relations. He was condemned to deportation to New Caledonia (1872), from where he succeeded in escaping with HENRI ROCHEFORT in 1874. Grousset then later served as a deputy for Paris from 1898 to 1909.

## Guadet, Marguerite-Élie (1758–1794)

*political figure*

Born in Saint-Émilion, Marguerite Élie Guadet, an attorney, joined the JACOBIN CLUB shortly after the beginning of the REVOLUTION OF 1789. He became one of the most brilliant of the orators among the GIRONDINS, and sat in the Legislative Assembly and in the Convention, where he voted for the death of King LOUIS XVI and was one of the most bitter adversaries of the MONTAGNARDS. After the elimination of the Girondins (May 31–June 2, 1793), Guadet led the FEDERALIST INSURRECTION in Normandy but was defeated, captured, condemned, and executed.

## Guéhenno, Jean (1890–1978)

*essayist*

Born in Paris, Jean Guéhenno, the son of a seamstress and a shoemaker, understood early in life the concept of "class struggle," which he later expressed in his *Journal d'un homme de quarante ans* (1934). After having denounced cultural inequalities in *Caliban parle* (1928), in *Journal d'une révolution* (1936–38), he gave a testimony to the POPULAR FRONT. It is also as a testimony, but in the form of an indictment, that *Le Journal des années noires, 1940–1941* was written in 1946. Guéhenno did studies, too, on JULES MICHELET (*L'Évangile éternel*, 1927) and JEAN-JACQUES ROUSSEAU (*Jean-Jacques*, 1949–52). He was elected to the ACADÉMIE FRANÇAISE in 1962.

## Guéranger, Prosper-Louis-Pascal, Dom (1805–1875)

*Benedictine*

Born in Sablé, Dom Prosper-Louis-Pascal Guéranger, as he is known, was a reader of the Fathers of the Church and became familiar with the ideas of JOSEPH DE MAISTRE and other Catholic writers. He purchased the monastery of Solesmes (1833) and, in 1837, obtained the approbation of Pope Gregory XVI for his project to reorganize the Benedictine order, making Solesmes the mother abbey of that congregation in France. A supporter of ultramontanism and friend of LOUIS VEUILLOT, with whom he worked on the newspaper *L'Univers,* Dom Guéranger was one of the principal restorers of the Roman liturgical order (*Institutions liturgiques,* 1840–51; *L'Année liturgique,* 1841–66).

### Guérin, Gilles (1606–1698)
*sculptor*

Born in Paris, Gilles Guérin, after studying in various workshops, received commissions to do a number of tombs for the nobility. He worked on the pavilion de l'Horloge at the LOUVRE (*La Renommée*) and did decorative work in several churches, as well as the châteaux of Cheverny and Maisons-Laffitte. Sculptor of the statue of *Louis XIV terrassant la Discorde* in Paris (1654), he was part of the first group of sculptors who worked on the château of VERSAILLES and produced notably *Les Chevaux au Soleil abreuvés par les tritons,* in which his taste for naturalism and movement is apparent.

### Guesde, Jules (1845–1922)
*political figure*

Born Jules Bazile in Paris, Jules Guesde, as he is known, contributed to the popularizing of Marxism in France with the creation of the first French Marxist journal, *L'Égalité* (1877–83). He also helped to form in 1882, with PAUL LAFARGUE, the Worker Party (Parti ouvrier), which became the French Worker Party (Parti ouvrier français) in 1893. Guesde then, with other groups, formed the SOCIALIST PARTY of France (Parti socialiste de France) in 1902 which, in 1905, joined with the FRENCH SOCIALIST PARTY (Parti socialiste français) of JEAN JAURÈS to become the Socialist Party (SFIO). Deputy for Roubaix beginning in 1893, Guesde declared himself to be a collectivist, internationalist, and revolutionary. In contrast to Jaurès, he opposed socialist participation in the "bourgeois" government of PIERRE WALDECK-ROUSSEAU (1899). His ideas were important to the Amsterdam Congress for only a short period, after which Jaurès dominated the French socialist movement. Despite his theoretical views, Guesde accepted the role of minister of state (1914–16) and adopted nationalist policies during World War I.

### Guilbert, Yvette (1867–1944)
*singer*

Born in Paris, Yvette Guilbert, with her exotic silhouette, palid expression, long red hair, and in a green gown with long black gloves, was especially immortalized by HENRI DE TOULOUSE-LAUTREC. At first performing in cabarets her spicy and earthy songs ("Le Fiacre"; "Madame Arthur"), she became, in the course of numerous interviews and tours, the ambassador of popular French song, from the sad ballads of the Middle Ages to the compositions of PIERRE-JEAN DE BÉRANGER and GUSTAVE NADAUD. Her incisive diction, wit, and spirit made these interpretations marvelous to hear. Guilbert published her memoirs (*La Chanson de ma vie*) in 1929.

### Guillain, Simon (1581–1658)
*sculptor, engraver*

Born in Paris, Simon Guillain studied with his father, Nicolas Guillain (known as "Cambray"), and traveled to Rome, where he also studied architecture and engraving. On his return to Paris in 1612, he produced decorative works for several churches (Saint-Eustache, Saint-Germain, les Carmes) and was a founding member of the Royal Academy of Painting and Sculpture (1642). In his major works, the bronze monument at the Port-au-Change (1647, LOUVRE), representing LOUIS XIII, ANNE OF AUSTRIA, and the young LOUIS XIV, Guillain showed a taste for realistic detail, as well as a sense of effect and an expressive, somewhat baroque, spirit.

### Guillaumat, Louis (1863–1940)
*military figure*

Born in Bourgneuf-en-Retz, Louis Guillaumat, during WORLD WAR I, commanded the 2nd French Army at VERDUN (1916). From August to December 1917, he retook the area lost to the Germans on the left bank of the Meuse. Commander of the Army of the East (1917–18) and military governor of Paris (June 1918), General Guillaumat took part, leading the Fifth Army, in the victorious offensive at the end of the war.

### Guillaume de Machaut (or Machault) (ca. 1300–1377)
*musician, poet*

Born in Machaut near Reims, Guillaume de Machaut, after serving various princes of France and Navarre, became canon at Reims. His musical studies inaugurated the polyphonic masses of the 15th and 16th centuries. The principal representative of the Ars nova and concerned with formal perfection, he also assembled the musical and literary rules for the lay, virelay, ballad, rondo, chant royal, and poems known as "fixed form." Additionally, Guillaume de Machaut wrote the first complete polyphonic mass by a single author (*Messe de Notre-Dame*) as well as personal stories in verse and prose, the *Dits*, of which the *Voir Dit* (*Le Dit de la Vérité*) recounts the poet's unrequited love for a young woman.

## Guilleragues, Gabriel de Lavergne, sieur de (1628–1685)
*magistrate, writer*

Born in Bordeaux, Gabriel de Lavergne, sieur de Guilleragues was chief administrator for King LOUIS XIV, who sent him as an envoy to Constantinople (1678). Frequenting the literary milieus of the period, he was friends with JEAN-BAPTISTE MOLIÈRE and JEAN RACINE as well as with Mme de SÉVIGNÉ and Mme de LA FAYETTE. Besides his letters and amorous plays, Gabriel de Guilleragues is the author of the *Lettres portugaises* (1669), which until 1929 were assumed to be the authentic love letters of the nun Mariana Alcoforado.

## Guise, House of

A branch of the House of Lorraine, descended from a younger son of René II of Lorraine. Claude de Lorraine, first duke de Guise (1496–1550), born in Condé-sur-Moselle, served FRANCIS I, was wounded at Marignan, and suppressed a JACQUERIE rebellion in Lorraine. His daughter, queen of Scotland, was the mother of Mary Stuart. François I de Lorraine, second duke de Guise (1519–63), born in Saint-Mesmin, near Orléans, was the son of Claude de Lorraine. Surnamed "le Balafré," after a wound received at Boulogne, he distinguished himself fighting against the emperor Charles V, in particular by his holding of Metz and his victory at Renti (1554) over the Imperial armies. In 1557, he took command of the troops sent to Naples to help Pope Paul IV but was recalled to France after the disaster at Saint-Quentin and, becoming lieutenant general of the kingdom, rectified the situation by taking Calais. The coming to the throne of FRANCIS II, his nephew by marriage, allowed him to exercise

much political power. He employed a policy of repression against the Protestants (suppression of the Amboise conspiracy, 1560; the condemning to death of LOUIS, PRINCE DE CONDÉ). After the death of Francis II, which saved Condé, he eschewed the policy of conciliation of CATHERINE DE' MEDICI and unleashed the first War of Religion with the massacre at Wassy (1562) and won a victory over Condé at Dreux before being assassinated at the siege of Orléans by POLTROT DE MÉRÉ. Henri I de Lorraine, third duke de Guise (1550–88), the son of François I de Lorraine and known also as "le Balafré," served the Holy Roman Emperor Maximillian I in the wars against the Ottoman Turks (1566), then fought the HUGUENOTS (Jarnac, Moncontour). Dissatisfied with the Peace of Saint-Germain, he planned first an attempt on the life of Admiral de COLIGNY, who foiled it, then the SAINT BARTHOLOMEW'S DAY MASSACRE (1572). The Peace of Monsieur (1576), which many considered treasonous, put him at the head of the HOLY LEAGUE and in alliance with Philip II of Spain. He refused also to accept Henry of Navarre as heir to the throne (see HENRY IV). After his victories at Auneau and Vimory over the German Calvinist mercenaries, he entered Paris, where he was very popular and where the League rose up in his support. He left the king and the city, but the former had him assassinated at Blois. Louis II de Guise (1555–88), cardinal of Lorraine and the brother of Henri of Lorraine, was born at Dampierre. He was also involved with the League and was assassinated shortly after his brother. The duchy of Guise then passed to the Condés (1704), then to the House of Orléans (1832).

## Guitry, Sacha (1888–1957)
*actor, playwright, filmmaker*

A leading figure of the French stage and screen, Sacha Guitry, who was born in Saint Petersburg, Russia, was the son of the actor Lucien Guitry. He composed, between 1901 and 1935, more than 130 plays. A fashionable Parisian of the Belle Époque, he had charm, good taste, and a great sense of humor and wit. His works, which often deal with bourgeois adultery, include *Faisons un rêve* (1918), *Mon Père avait raison* (1919), *Mot de Cambronne* (1936), *Quadrille* (1937), and *N'Écoutez pas, mes-*

*dame* (1942). His work as a filmmaker is perhaps as rich as his plays. He produced historical works, such as *Remontons les Champs-Élysées* (1938), and especially *Diable boiteux* (1948), which deal with his favorite historical personage, CHARLES-MAURICE DE TALLEYRAND. Guitry was elected to the Académie Goncourt in 1939 but resigned in 1948.

## Guizot, François (1787–1874)
*statesman, historian*

A leading political figure who dominated the French government in the period before the REVOLUTION OF 1848, François Guizot was born in Nîmes and educated at Geneva and Paris, where he became a professor of modern history at the SORBONNE in 1812. A moderate liberal, he opposed the conservative government of JULES DE POLIGNAC. He lost his university post under the reactionary King CHARLES X, and later would play an active role in his overthrow during the REVOLUTION OF JULY 1830. Under the new king, LOUIS-PHILIPPE I, Guizot served as minister of the interior (1830) then as minister of public instruction (1832–37) and, as such, was responsible for the law that bears his name, which mandated the establishment of primary schools in each commune. After serving as ambassador to Great Britain, he replaced ADOLPHE THIERS as foreign minister (1840–47), during which time he initially pursued a policy of cooperation with Great Britain, achieving the Franco-British Entente cordiale. In domestic affairs, he opposed the liberals, especially because of his insistence on a limited suffrage, and he favored the capitalists and bourgeoisie. Becoming premier in 1847, Guizot saw his unpopularity increase because of economic crises. His ban on opposition meetings, known as the Banquets, in January 1848 led to the revolution that in the next month ended the reign of LOUIS-PHILIPPE I (see REVOLUTION OF 1848). After a year of exile in Belgium and England, Guizot returned to France, where he devoted the rest of his life to scholarly pursuits and writing. His works include *Histoire des origines du gouvernement représentatif* (1821–22), *Histoire de la révolution d'Angleterre* (1826–27), *Histoire de la civilisation en Europe* (1828), *Histoire de la civilisation en France* (1830), and

*Mémoires pour servir à l'histoire de mon temps* (1858–67). Guizot was elected to the ACADÉMIE FRANÇAISE in 1836.

## Guyenne

Guyenne was a former province of France that was associated with Aquitaine until the 11th century. Including the French possessions of the king of England, after the Treaty of Paris (1259), it comprised Limousin, Périgord, Quercy, Agenois, and a part of Saintonge and GASCONY. Finally retaken by France in 1453 (Battle of Castillon), it was given as a fiefdom by King LOUIS XI to his brother Charles (1469), then it reverted to the Crown. With Gascony, Saintonge, Limousin, and Béarn, Guyenne forms a governmental region that has its capital at BORDEAUX.

## Guyon, Jeanne-Marie-Bouvier de la Motte, Mme (1648–1717)
*mystic*

Known as Mme Guyon, Jeanne-Marie-Bouvier de la Motte was born in Montargis and married Jacques Guyon du Chesnoy in 1676. Widowed in 1676, she embraced quietism and helped to bring that philosophy to Savoy and Piedmont (Gex, Thonon, Turin, Grenoble, Vercelli), to other regions of southern France, and to Paris. After an initial confinement in a Visitadine convent (1688), which was due to the intrigue and bribery of the archbishop of Paris, who was critical of her ideas, she was freed through the influence of the wife of King LOUIS XIV, FRANÇOISE D'AUBIGNE, MARQUISE DE MAINTENON. Mme Guyon then met the theologian FRANÇOIS FÉNELON, whom she introduced to the quietist views, and with whom she had an influence over the women enrolled at the school of SAINT-CYR. In 1694, however, after losing the favor of Mme de Maintenon and gaining the hostility of the prelate JACQUES-BÉNIGNE BOSSUET, she saw her writings condemned. She was also arrested (1695) and confined to the BASTILLE (1698–03). Retiring to Blois, she became the center of a Quietist circle (both Catholic and Protestant). Mme Guyon's numerous writings, many in manuscript form, include *Les Torrents spirituels* (1682) and her autobiography, *Vie* (1688).

## Guyton de Morveau, Louis-Bernard, baron (1737–1816)
*magistrate, chemist*

Born in Dijon, where he served as attorney-general to the Parlement (1755), Louis-Bernard, baron Guyton de Morveau was, during the REVOLUTION OF 1789, elected as a deputy to the Legislative Assembly and then to the Convention. He also served as a member of the Committee of Public Safety. As a chemist, he was able to liquefy ammoniac; was the first to have the idea of a radical reform of the chemical nomenclature, which he developed with ANTOINE DE LAVOISIER, ANTOINE DE FOURCROY, and CLAUDE DE BERTHOLLET (1789); and did research on chemical affinities. Guyton de Morveau was elected to the Academy of Sciences in 1795.

# H

## Hachette, Jeanne (ca. 1454–unknown)
### (Jeanne Laisné, Jeanne Fourquet)
*heroic figure*

Born Jeanne Laisné in Beauvais in June 1472, Jeanne Hachette, as she is best known, encouraged and fought alongside her fellow citizens besieged by the Burgundians. By tearing down the Burgundian standard, she galvanized resistance and the attack of CHARLES THE BOLD, duke of Burgundy was repelled. She was honored and granted privileges for her service by King LOUIS XI and, in her city, was given the first place in the procession of Sainte-Angadrême, protectress of Beauvais. Jeanne Hachette entered legend as a popular French heroic figure.

## Halban, Hans (1877–1964)
*physicist*

Of Austrian origin, Hans Halban was born in Vienna. In 1939, with FRÉDÉRIC JOLIOT-CURIE and LEW KOWARSKI, he discovered the production process of neutrons during the fission of uranium, a phenomenon at the basis of chain reactions. In 1940, he succeeded, with Kowarski, in removing from German-occupied territory the world stock of heavy water, needed for the production of an atomic bomb, and transporting the supply to England.

## Halévy family

A family of French composers, writers, and historians. Jacques Fromental Lévy, or Jacques Halévy as he is known, was born in Paris and won second grand prize in the prix de Rome in 1819. Professor at the Conservatoire, he had GEORGES BIZET and CHARLES GOUNOD as his students. Of the 30 operas that he composed, his great success, *La Juive* (1835), is particularly noteworthy. Ludovic Halévy (1834–1908), the nephew of Jacques Halévy, was born in Paris. A dramatic author (*Froufrou,* 1869), and novelist (*L'Abbé Constantin,* 1882), he owes his reputation to the librettos that he composed for the operettas of JACQUES OFFENBACH (*La Belle Hélène,* 1864; *La Vie parisienne,* 1866; *La Grande-Duchesse de Gerolstein,* 1867; *La Périchole,* 1868). Ludovic Halévy also collaborated on the libretto for *Carmen* by Georges Bizet. He was elected to the ACADÉMIE FRANÇAISE in 1884. Élie Halévy (1870–1937), born at Étretat, was the son of Ludovic Halévy. Author of theoretical works (*Théorie platonicienne des sciences,* 1896; *La Formation du radicalisme philosophique,* 1901–04), he also published *Histoire du peuple anglais au xixe siècle* (1913–23). Daniel Halévy (1872–1962), brother of Élie Halévy, who was born in Paris, was also a historian. A friend of CHARLES PÉGUY, he collaborated on *Cahiers de la quinzaine.* Author of articles on Friedrich Nietzsche, Charles Péguy, JULES MICHELET, PIERRE-JOSEPH PROUDHON, and an *Essai sur le mouvement ouvrier en France* (1910), he has also made historical analyses of the beginnings of the Third Republic (*La Fin des notables,* 1936; *La République des ducs,* 1937), as well as an *Essai sur l'accélération de l'histoire* (1948).

## Hamilton, Anthony (1646–1720)
### (Antoine Hamilton)
*writer*

Born in Roscrea, in the county of Tipperary, Ireland, Anthony, or Antoine, Hamilton came to France after the execution of the English king Charles I. He became the biographer of his brother-in-law, the count de Gramont (see GRAMONT, HOUSE OF), published in 1715 under the title *Mémoires de la vie du comte de Gramont,* also known under the name *Histoire amoureuse de la cour d'Angleterre,* written in a style worthy of the great memoirists of the 18th century. Antoine Hamilton has also written a version of *Mille et Une Nuits* (*The Thousand and One Nights*), and diverse poems (*Œuvres mêlées en prose et en vers*, posthumous, 1731).

## Hanotaux, Gabriel (1853–1944)
*statesman, historian*

Born in Beaurevoir, Aisne, Gabriel Hanotaux, as minister of foreign affairs, helped to prepare the Franco-Russian alliance and to strengthen the French presence in the Far East, Tunisia, and the Sudan, where, against Great Britain, he supported the MARCHAND expedition. French delegate to the League of Nations (1918), and ambassador extraordinary to Italy (1920), Hanotaux left a *Histoire du cardinal de Richelieu* (1893–1947, completed by the duke of La Force), *Histoire de la France contemporaine* (1903–08), and *Histoire illustrée de la guerre de 1914* (1915–36), and directed the publication of *Histoire de la nation française* (1920–29). He was elected to the ACADÉMIE FRANÇAISE in 1897.

## Hanriot, François (1761–1794)
*revolutionary*

Born in Nanterre, François Hanriot was, at the time of the REVOLUTION OF 1789, the leader of the sans-culotte groups during the Revolutionary Day of August 10, 1792, and took part in the SEPTEMBER MASSACRES of that year. Named provisional general commander of the Parisian National Guard (May 1793), he directed the SANS-CULOTTE and Hébertist (see HEBERT, JACQUES-RENÉ) riots against the National Convention, causing in turn the elimination of the popular Girondin leadership (May 31–June 2, 1793). Although connected to the ultrarevolutionary Hébertists, he was not condemned with them (March 1794), but was arrested and guillotined at the same time as MAXIMILIEN ROBESPIERRE and his supporters (9–10 Thermidor Year II, July 27–28, 1794).

## Hansi (1872–1951)
*writer, artist, caricaturist*

Born Jean-Jacques Waltz in Colmar, and raised in German-occupied Alsace, Hansi as he is known, studied fine arts in Lyon and Mulhouse, and became recognized through his first work, a satire

on German schoolteachers, *Le Professor Knatschke* (1912). This was followed by *L'Alsace racontée aux petits enfants par l'oncle Hansi* (1912) and *Mon village* (1913), which caused problems with the German authorities. After World War I he published *L'Alsace heureuse* and *Les Clochers dans les vignes*, and assumed, after his father, the directorship of the Unterlinden Museum in Colmar. Read and reread by numerous generations, Hansi's work has become part of Alsatian folklore.

## Hardouin-Mansart, Jules (1646–1708)
*architect*

Jules Hardouin-Mansart, whose work represents the culmination of the Louis XIV style, was born in Paris, the grandnephew of FRANÇOIS MANSART. Hardouin-Mansart was appointed first architect to LOUIS XIV in 1676. Commissioned to enlarge the palace of VERSAILLES, in 1684 he designed the Hall of Mirrors, the Royal Chapel, the north and south wings of the palace, the Orangerie, and the stables. He completed the facade of the palace and gave Versailles its definitive style. Building on the work of his great-uncle François Mansart, he codified the French order, characterized by its grandeur and regularity and its use of fine French products and materials. He also designed the château of Clagny, near Paris, (1675–83) for Mme de MONTESPAN and renovated the Grand Trianon at Versailles. Additionally, he produced many other châteaux, hôtels de ville, churches, municipal buildings, and public squares, including the octagonal Place Vendôme in Paris (1699). Commissioned to complete the INVALIDES, he achieved that building's striking dome, which is considered a masterpiece, by superimposing two drums to create the effect of soaring grandeur (1676–1706, Paris).

## Hardy, Alexandre (ca. 1570–ca. 1632)
*dramatic poet*

Born in Paris, Alexandre Hardy was at first an itinerant actor and poet, and wrote for the Valleran-Lecomte acting troop. He then composed for the Hôtel de Bourgogne acting company some 700 tragedies, tragicomedies, and pastorals, of which only 30 were published (from 1624 to 1628). Although faithful to the forms of humanist tragedy, his work is unique because of the melodramatic treatment of its characters, the richness and freshness of its style, and its violent passions (*Marianne, Didon se sacrifiant, Lucrèce*). Hardy's tragicomedies, inspired by Miguel Cervantes (*La Force du sang*) or J. Hondorff (*Elmire*) also transcend the norms of classicism.

## Harlay de Champvallon, François de (1625–1695)
*prelate*

Born in Paris, where he became archbishop in 1671, François de Harlay de Champvallon, a worldly and ambitious prelate, was one of the principal religious advisers to King LOUIS XIV and leader of the Gallicans (see GALLICANISM). He played a determining role in the "affaire de La Régale," the dispute between the French Crown and the papacy (he was president of the General Assembly of the Clergy), and in the persecutions against Mme GUYON and the Jansenists at Port-Royal, as well as in the revocation of the Edict of Nantes. In 1684, Archbishop Harlay de Champvallon presided at the secret marriage of Louis XIV and Mme de MAINTENON. He was elected to the ACADÉMIE FRANÇAISE in 1671.

See also JANSENISM; GALLICANISM.

## Haussmann, Georges-Eugène, Baron (1809–1891)
*administrator, urban planner*

Georges-Eugène, Baron Haussmann, who extensively redesigned PARIS during the reign of NAPOLÉON III (1852–70), was born in that city and began his administrative career shortly after the REVOLUTION OF JULY 1830. He supported Louis-Napoléon Bonaparte in the coup d'état of December 2, 1851, then the establishment of the SECOND EMPIRE. Haussmann became prefect of the Seine (1853) and remained in that post for 17 years, becoming also a senator and a baron. His plan for the reconstruction of Paris called for new and wider boulevards, new parks, in particular the Bois de Boulogne, and railway stations outside the city. Much of medieval Paris was demolished during his rebuilding. The main part of Haussmann's plans involved grand boulevards punctuated by circular plazas. This also facilitated troop movements and prevented the erection of barricades. Such boulevards provide beautiful vistas of such landmarks as the Opéra and the ARC DE TRIOMPHE. In large part, Haussmann's efforts to embellish and clean up the capital were done to enhance the reputation and prestige of the regime and to eliminate the old quarters of the city that, since 1789 had been places of revolutionary activity. These improvements, however, forced the working-class population to migrate to the suburbs. Haussmann, to realize his project to transform Paris, became involved in some questionable financial matters and was strongly attacked in public opinion and in the national legislature. After the publication of JULES FERRY's critical *Comptes fantastiques d'Haussmann*, Haussmann was replaced (1869). Nonetheless, his innovations had a major influence on later urban design, especially in Europe, Latin America, and many former French colonies.

## Hébert, Jacques-René (1757–1794)
*journalist, political figure*

Born in Alençon, Jacques-René Hébert joined the REVOLUTION OF 1789 and, in 1790, founded the radical journal *Le Père Duquesne*. Replacing PIERRE CHAUMETTE in the insurrectionist Paris Commune after August 10, 1792, and leader of the CORDELIERS CLUB, he carried out, under the Convention, a fierce struggle against the GIRONDINS, who had him arrested by the Commission of Twelve (May 18, 1793). His arrest, by unleashing the popular Sansculottist movement (see SANS-CULOTTES; May 31–June 2, 1793), precipitated the fall of the Girondin leadership. Freed, Hébert adopted the program of the ENRAGÉS, succeeded in having certain radical economic and social measures passed by the Convention, and encouraged the policy of de-Christianization. After denouncing the Indugents' offensive (GEORGES DANTON, CAMILLE DESMOULINS), which had demanded the end of the TERROR (December 1793–January 1794), he accused the Robespierrists of moderation and proposed a more radical social program. Threatened with overthrow by the Left as well as by the Right, the Committee of Public Safety, led by MAXIMILIEN ROBESPIERRE, quickly arrested Hébert and the extremists, or Hébertists (March 12, 1794), who were then condemned to death by the Revolutionary Tribunal.

## Helvétius, Claude-Adrien  (1715–1771)

*philosopher*

An important thinker of the Enlightenment, Claude-Adrien Helvétius was born in Paris. In 1738, he was appointed farmer-general, a post that he held, along with other government appointments, due to the influence of his patron, Queen MARIE LESZCZYNSKA, wife of King LOUIS XV. Helvétius soon devoted himself to writing, collaborating on DENIS DIDEROT's *Encyclopédie* and, in 1758, publishing his most famous work, *De L'Esprit*. In it, he asserted his theory of hedonism, sensualism, atheism, and philosophical materialism. He stated that all human faculties, including judgment, compassion, and memory, are merely attributes of physical sensation and that the only nature of human activity is self-interest. He posited that no true moral choice could exist, with even self-sacrifice only a choice among competitive pleasures. His writings were subsequently condemned by the Royal Council and the theological faculty of the SORBONNE (1759) as affronts to public morals, and were publicly burned.

## Henrietta Anne  (1644-1670)
## (Henriette-Anne )

*queen of France*

The daughter of King Charles I of England and HENRIETTA MARIE OF FRANCE, Henrietta Anne married PHILIPPE D'ORLEANS, brother of King LOUIS XIV of France. Beautiful and spirited, she helped to negotiate the secret Treaty of Dover (1670, between Charles II of England and Louis XIV). The terms of the treaty encouraged Charles to convert to Catholicism, to join the French in the war against the United Provinces, and to uphold Louis's eventual claim to the Spanish throne, especially by giving him financial and military assistance.

## Henrietta Marie  (1609-1669)
## (Henriette-Marie )

*Queen of England*

The daughter of King HENRY IV and MARIE DE' MEDICI, and the sister of King LOUIS XIII, Henrietta Marie of France married King Charles I of England (1625). Her influence contributed to Charles's orientation towards Catholicism and absolutism, which led, in turn, to his downfall.

## Henriot, Émile  (1889–1961)

*writer, literary critic*

Born in Paris, Émile Henriot was a poet (*La Flamme et les Cendres*, 1909; *Les Jours raccourissent*, 1954), and also a novelist (*Valentin*, 1920; *Aricie Brun ou les Vertus bourgeoises*, 1924; *La Rose de Bratislava*, 1948). His literary critiques were collected in *Livres et Portraits* (1923–27), *Épistoliers et Mémorialistes* (1931), and *Portraits de femmes* (1935–37), collections to which one can add *Livres du second rayon* (1925), in which the author focuses on the "secondary" writers of the 17th and 18th centuries. Henriot was elected to the ACADÉMIE FRANÇAISE in 1945.

## Henriot, Philippe  (1889–1944)

*political figure*

Born in Paris, Philippe Henriot was, in the interwar years, a member of extreme rightist organizations, a deputy (1932, 1936), and, after the armistice of June 1940, was an active propagandist for the policy of collaboration with the occupying Germans. Secretary of state for information in the government of PIERRE LAVAL, and one of the leaders of the Milice, Henriot was killed by the RESISTANCE in January 1944.

## Henry II  (1519–1559)
## (Henri II)

*king of France*

Born at Saint-Germain-en-Laye, Henry II was the son of FRANCIS I and Claude de France. He married CATHERINE DE' MEDICI in 1537 and, in 1547, succeeded to the throne. During his reign, he was much influenced by his mistress, DIANE DE POITIERS, and by the duke of MONTMORENCY, constable of France. A staunch Catholic, Henry II persecuted the Protestants (see HUGUENOTS) during the later years of his reign. His foreign policy was a continuation of his father's: he waged war against the Holy Roman Emperor Charles V, seizing from him the bishoprics of Verdun, Metz, and Toul in 1552, and he engaged in war with England (1557–58), winning back Calais, the last English possession in France. From 1556 to 1559, he was involved in war with Philip II of Spain, the French forces being badly defeated at Saint-Quentin (1557). Peace with Spain and England was restored by the Treaty of

Cateau-Cambrésis (1559), by which Henry II gave up French possessions in Italy. The same year, he was mortally wounded in a jousting tournament. From his marriage to Catherine he had 10 children, three of whom reigned: FRANCIS II, CHARLES IX, and HENRY III.

## Henry III (1551–1589)
### (Henri III)
*royalty*

Born at Fontainebleau, the third son of HENRY II and CATHERINE DE' MEDICI, Henry III was the last of the Valois kings. His reign was turbulent and, despite his considerable talent and intelligence, he failed to resolve the religious civil wars in France and, in fact, brought the country close to bankruptcy. This may have been due to his indecisive nature or to the great influence his favorites and lovers (the duke of ÉPERNON and the duke of JOYEUSE) had over him. Henry III was the leader against the HUGUENOTS and took part in the victories over them at Jarnac and Moncontour (1569). He assisted his mother in planning the SAINT BARTHOLOMEW'S DAY MASSACRE in 1572, and the next year, through her influence, was elected king of Poland. He returned after only one year, however, to succeed his brother, CHARLES IX, to the throne of France. Religious wars continued throughout his reign. In 1576, he issued the Edict of Beaulieu, which granted more privileges to the Protestants. The Catholics, displeased with the edict, under the leadership of the duke of Guise, formed the HOLY LEAGUE and renewed the religious conflict. The war ended in 1577 with the Peace of Bergerac, and Henry dissolved the league after revoking some of the concessions he made to the Protestants. The league was revived in 1584 when, upon the death of the king's younger brother, the legal heir to the French throne became Henry III of Navarre (later HENRI IV), a Huguenot, married to King Henry's sister, MARGUERITE DE VALOIS. In 1585, when the league forced Henry to exclude Henry of Navarre from the succession and to repeal the privileges granted to the Huguenots, the so-called War of the Three Henrys began: Henry III leading the royalists; Henry, duke de Guise, the league; and Henry of Navarre, the Protestants. The king was defeated at Coutras in 1587 and, in 1588, on the Day of the Barracades, found that the citizens of Paris, led by the duke de

Guise, had revolted against him, forcing him to flee the city. Henry III subsequently had the leaders of the HOUSE OF GUISE assassinated and allied himself with Henri of Navarre, whom he also declared his successor. Both then became the joint leaders of a Huguenot army. Henry III, however, was assassinated (1589) by a fanatical Dominican friar during the attempt to retake Paris.

## Henry IV (1553–1610)
### (Henri IV)
*king of France and Navarre*

The first of the Bourbon kings, Henry IV was born in Pau, in Navarre, the son of Antoine de Bourbon (see BOURBON, HOUSE OF) and JEANNE D'ALBRET, queen of Navarre. He was raised as a Protestant by his mother but seems to have inherited the religious indifference of his father. In 1572, he married MARGUERITE DE VALOIS, sister of CHARLES IX. A few days later, the SAINT BARTHOLOMEW'S DAY MASSACRE occurred (August 24). Henry saved his own life by converting to Catholicism, but he remained a prisoner at the court until 1576. After his escape, he repudiated the conversion and assumed the leadership of the HUGUENOTS. He was excommunicated when he became the heir to the French throne in 1584. Henry had a successful military career, marked by a brilliant victory at Coutras in 1587 during the War of the Three Henrys (see HENRY III). He formed an alliance with Henry III against the HOLY LEAGUE dominated by the HOUSE OF GUISE. When Henry III was assassinated in 1589, he became king. The league, however, backed by Spain and the pope, refused to acknowledge a Protestant as king of France. Henry won victories over the league at Arques and Ivry, and besieged Paris. He also exploited divisions among members of the league and, in 1593, surprised his opponents by announcing his conversion to Catholicism. (To him is attributed the statement "Paris is worth a Mass.") He then defeated or won over the leaders of the Guise faction and, in 1595, convinced the pope to lift the ban of excommunication. Henry, in turn, agreed to respect church properties and to raise his heirs as Roman Catholics. In 1598, he made peace with Spain and, in the same year, proclaimed the Edict of Nantes, which granted partial religious freedom to the Huguenots. In 1599, he secured papal annulment of his first marriage and, in 1600, married MARIE DE' MEDICI. From their marriage they had four children (LOUIS XIII; GASTON D'ORLÉANS; Elisabeth, who married Philip IV of Spain; and HENRIETTA MARIE, who became the wife of Charles I of England). Henry IV, through his minister, the duke of SULLY, reorganized state finances and promoted the nation's economic recovery after decades of civil war. He encouraged agriculture, commerce, and manufacturing, and reduced taxes on the peasantry. A debt moratorium was issued for the nobility. In 1604, the system of purchasing judicial offices, the "paulette," was instituted. Royal officials also replaced local representative bodies throughout France. In 1609, he began plans to intervene in Germany against the Catholic Habsburg, a move opposed by some French Catholics. In May 1610, as Henry IV was about to join his army, he was assassinated by a Catholic extremist. Henry IV who is known as "the Good king Henry," is credited with restoring order to the kingdom after the ruinous religious civil wars and with ensuring that the French monarchy would be Catholic and absolutist.

## Henry, Hubert-Joseph (1846–1898)
*military officer*

Born in Pogny, Marne, Hubert-Joseph Henry, after serving in Tunisia (1882) and Tonkin (1887), entered the intelligence service of the army as head of counterespionage (1893). Convinced of the guilt of ALFRED DREYFUS, he reedited a letter (dated October 1896), that had been addressed by the Italian military attaché, Alessandro Panizzardi, to his German counterpart, Colonel Max von Schwartzkoppen, and inserted the name of Captain Dreyfus to implicate him. This letter, the existence of which was revealed during the trial of ÉMILE ZOLA (1898), was discovered shortly afterward to have been a forgery. Interned at Mont-Valérien, Colonel Henry committed suicide the next day.

## Henry, Pierre (b. 1927–   )
*composer*

Born in Paris, Pierre Henry studied with OLIVIER MESSIAEN and NADIA BOULANGER. In 1949, he joined the Studio d'essai at RTF (Radio Television Français) and, with PIERRE SCHAEFFER, developed a style known as "concrete music" (*Bidule et ut*, 1949; *Symphonie pour un homme seul*, 1950). Henry never ceased evolving toward a more rigorous style (*Variations pour une porte et un soupir*, 1963; *Messe pour le temps présent*, 1967; *Paris l'Eau*, 1985; *Hugo Symphonie*, 1985; *Le Livre des morts égyptiens*, 1990). He also worked with MAURICE BÉJART on several ballets.

## Hérault de Séchelles, Marie-Jean (1759–1794)
*political figure, magistrate*

Born in Paris, where he served as an attorney, Marie-Jean Hérault de Séchelles joined the REVOLUTION OF 1789 and took his place in the Legislative Assembly with the leftist deputies, then with the MONTAGNARDS in the Convention, where he was president during the proscription of the principal GIRONDIN leaders (June 2, 1793). He helped to write the Constitution of the Year I (adopted by the Convention June 24, 1793) and, as a member of the Committee of Public Safety, helped to organize the TERROR. As a friend of GEORGES DANTON, however, and with connections to the Hébertists, he soon became suspect himself and was accused of having revealed some of the committee's confidential information. Hérault de Séchelles was condemned to death and guillotined with Danton and the Indulgents in April 1794.

## Heredia, José Maria de (1842–1905)
*poet*

Born in La Fortuna, near Santiago, Cuba, to a Cuban father and a French mother, José Maria de Heredia was raised in France and began writing verse in 1862. He contributed to *Parnasse contemporain* and, as a Parnassian poet, rebelled against the romantic style. With the publication of *Trophées* (1893), a collection of 118 sonnets, he was hailed as the master of the Parnassian school. Heredia was elected to the ACADÉMIE FRANÇAISE in 1894.

See also LOUŸS, PIERRE.

## Herriot, Édouard (1872–1957)
*statesman, writer*

One of the most eminent and active French political leaders of his time, and a major figure in the

Radical Socialist Party, Édouard Herriot was born in Troyes and educated at the École normale supérieure in Paris. In 1904, at the time of the Dreyfus affair (see DREYFUS, ALFRED), he entered politics, joining the Radical Socialist Party, which he led from 1919 to 1926, from 1931 to 1936, and from 1945 to 1957. In 1905, he was elected mayor of LYON, a post that he held for a total of 50 years (1905–42 and 1945–57). From 1919 on, Herriot was also a member of the Chamber of Deputies and was premier in the Cartel des Gauches government from 1924 to 1925. He tried to form a second government, but was replaced by RAYMOND POINCARÉ, who named him minister of public instruction (1926). He served again as premier in 1932, then as minister of state (1934–36), before becoming president of the Chamber of Deputies (1936–40). During the 1920s and 1930s, he worked to improve international relations, strongly supporting the League of Nations and calling for official recognition of the Soviet Union, and ordered the evacuation of the Ruhr. In 1940, he refused to collaborate with the Germans or with the VICHY regime. Consequently, he was arrested (1942) and interned in France and Germany until being liberated at the end of the war (1945). Herriot served as one of the deputies who wrote the constitution for the FOURTH REPUBLIC in 1946 and, in the same year, was elected to the first National Assembly to meet under the new constitution. In 1947, he was elected speaker of the National Assembly, holding that post until 1953. As early as 1904, Herriot had also achieved a literary reputation. Among his writings are *Madame Récamier et ses amis* (1904), *La Vie de Beethoven* (1929), *Lyon n'est plus* (1939–40), and his memoirs, published under the title *Jadis* (1948–52). Herriot was elected to the ACADÉMIE FRANÇAISE in 1946.

## Hetzel, Pierre-Jules (1814–1886)
*publisher, writer, political figure*

Born in Chartres, Pierre-Jules Hetzel published novels under the pseudonym P. J. Stahl. He is above all famous as an editor. Beginning as a clerk in Paris in 1836 at the publisher Paulin, he founded, in the following year in association with Paulin, a publishing house. Hetzel then entered politics and, in 1848, became a member of the cabinet of ALPHONSE DE LAMARTINE (foreign affairs and the naval office),

but had to seek exile in Brussels after the coup d'état of NAPOLÉON III on December 2, 1851. It was Hetzel who published VICTOR HUGO's pamphlet, *Napoléon le petit* (1852). Returning to Paris in 1860, he founded the *Bibliothèque illustrée des familles*, which became, in 1864, the *Bibliothèque d'éducation et de recréation*. In the same year appeared the first issue of *Magasin d'éducation et de recréation* for which Hetzel, JEAN MACÉ, and JULES VERNE received a medal from the ACADÉMIE FRANÇAISE in 1867. Besides almost all the works of Verne, Hetzel published works of STENDHAL, GEORGE SAND, ÉMILE ZOLA, and the *Contes* (Tales) of CHARLES PERRAULT.

## Hoche, Lazare-Louis (1768–1797)
*military figure*

Born in Versailles, Lazare-Louis Hoche joined the French Guards in 1784 and, during the REVOLUTION OF 1789, was named brigadier general and commander in chief of the Army of the Moselle (1793). After a defeat by the forces of the Duke of Brunswick at Kaiserslauten (November 28–30, 1793), General Hoche took the offensive, fighting the Austrians near Woerth, reoccupying the area around Wissembourg, freeing Landau (December 28, 1793), and entering Speyer. Denounced, however to the Revolutionary government as a suspect by his rival general CHARLES PICHEGRU, he was imprisoned and held until 9 Thermidor Year II (July 27, 1794). Having resumed his command (September 1794), he was ordered by the Themidorian Convention to pacify the Vendée and the western regions (see CHOUANNERIE), and he fought successfully against the royalist émigrés who had landed at Quiberon with the support of the British (June–July 1975). Placed in charge of the expedition to Ireland (December 1796), he was stopped by a storm. After the victory at Neuwied, near Cologne (April 17, 1797), General Hoche was named minister of war (July 1797), then resumed his command at the head of the army in Germany, but he died shortly after.

## Ho Chi Minh (1890–1969)
*Vietnamese political, revolutionary, and nationalist leader*

Born Nguyn Tat Thanh in Nghe An, in what was then French INDOCHINA, Ho Chi Minh was the founder of the People's Republic of Vietnam. After studying in Hue, he went to France (1911) and, beginning in 1917, became involved in political and patriotic activities. A young nationalist, he hoped in vain that the Paris Peace Conference (1919), which he petitioned, would apply the principle of self-determination to the colonized nations. This setback pushed him towards radical solutions and Leninism. When the French COMMUNIST PARTY (SFIO) was established at the Congress of Tours (1920), he became a member. He traveled to the Soviet Union (1923); Canton (1924), China; then again to the Soviet Union and western Europe (1927) and later Thailand (1928). Arrested in Hong Kong (1931) by the British, he returned to Vietnam (1941), after another sojourn in the Soviet Union (1936–1937). Taking the nom de guerre Ho Chi Minh (He Who Enlightens), and having already established the Vietnamese Communist Party (1931), he formed the Viet Minh Front against the French and the Japanese during World War II. He declared Vietnam's independence at Hanoi, and became the new nation's first president (1946). He led the Viet Minh until the French retreat at DIEN BIEN PHU and, in 1954, after the signing of the Geneva armistice, fought against American policy in South Vietnam, attempting to unite the entire country according to socialist principles, and organized the successful resistance to the American forces.

## Holbach, Paul-Henri, baron d'
## (1723–1789)

*philosopher*

Born in Heidelsheim in the Palatinate, Paul-Henri, baron d'Holbach, who was a contributor to the *Encyclopédie,* presented, in his *Système de la nature* (1770), published under a pseudonym, a materialistic view that was both mechanistic and atheistic. He is also the author of antireligious works (*Le Christianisme dévoilé,* 1767). His Paris salon, where he received JEAN-JACQUES ROUSSEAU and DENIS DIDEROT, was one of the most famous of the period. He challenged Cartesian dualism and Christianity by proposing a radical materialism based on rationalism. The baron d'Holbach insisted on the necessity of morality in politics (*Éthocratie, ou le Gouvernement fondé sur la morale,* 1776).

## Holy League  (Sainte Ligue or Sainte Union)

The Ligue, or Sainte Ligue, was a confederation of French Catholics that played an essential role in the Religious Wars in France after 1576. Formed initially in PICARDY to resist the application of the Peace of Monsieur (1576), the Ligue (or League) quickly spread through the rest of the country. To its avowed purpose, the defense of the Catholic faith, was added the goal of dethroning HENRY III in favor of Henri de Guise (see HOUSE OF GUISE), its leader. Sustained by subsidies from Philip II of Spain, the Ligue became extremely powerful after the DAY OF THE BARRICADES and took action when the succession passed to Henri de Navarre (HENRY IV) upon the death of the duke of Anjou. Henry III had tricked Henry of Guise into coming to Blois, where he was assassinated, along with his brother, the cardinal of Lorraine. This provoked a general uprising. CHARLES DE LORRAINE, DUKE OF MAYENNE, became head of the Ligue and continued the struggle against Henry IV after the assassination of Henry III. Meanwhile, the Ligue had proclaimed the cardinal of Bourbon as king under the name Charles X. In 1590, Mayenne attacked Arques and Ivry, but Paris continued to hold out. The abjuration of his Protestantism by Henry IV added to the discrediting of the Ligue, which had already been weakened by internal conflicts and by the claims of Philip II to the French throne. In 1594, Mayenne and Henry IV signed an agreement that put an end to the religious wars.

## Honegger, Arthur  (1892–1955)

*composer*

Born in Le Havre of Swiss parentage, Arthur Honegger, who is regarded as one of the most important French composers of the early 20th century, began his musical career as an impressionist and gradually evolved a personal style characterized by dissonance, strong rhythms, and an emphasis on counterpoint. He studied at the Zurich and Paris Conservatories. Early in his career he became a member of Les Six, a group devoted to the development of a more robust form of musical composition, inspired often by the music of J. S. Bach and also by the writings of such poets as JEAN COCTEAU and GUILLAUME APOLLINAIRE. Honegger's ability to describe realistically in music various aspects of contemporary life is exemplified by his two orchestral compositions, *Pacific 231* (1923), which is a musical description of a steam engine, and *Rugby* (1928). His other works include the theatrical compositions *Le Roi David* (1925), *Judith* (1925), *Jeanne au bûcher* (1935), and *La Danse des morts* (1938), the last two with texts by PAUL CLAUDEL. He also composed an operetta, *Les Aventures du roi Pausole* (1930); an opera, *L'Aiglon* (1937); and a *Cantate de Noël* (1953). In his later works, Honegger reveals his sense of disillusionment with the barbarity of the modern world and its loss of personal freedom. There are echoes of these sentiments in *Incantation aux fossiles* (1948) and *Je suis compositeur* (1951), a type of autobiographical composition.

## Houdar de la Motte, Antoine (1672–1731)
### (Antoine Lamotte-Houdar)
*dramatic poet*

Born in Paris, Antoine Lamotte-Houdar, or Antoine Houdar de la Motte, as he is known, is the author of comedies and tragedies, including the well-known *Inés de Castro* (1723). A cause of the second Dispute of the Ancients and the Moderns with his adaptation of the *Iliad*, he responded in verse to the arguments of Mme DACIER in his *Réflexions sur la critique* (1715), before submitting to the judgment of FRANÇOIS FÉNELON on this literary matter. Houdar de la Motte's *Réflexions sur la tragédie* (1730) called for abandoning the form of unities and the use of prose in tragedy.

## Houdetot, Élisabeth de la Live de Bellegarde, countess de (1730–1813)
*nobility*

Born in Paris, Élisabeth de la Live de Bellegarde, countess de Houdetot was the sister-in-law of LOUISE D'ÉPIGNAY. Estranged from her husband, she had a long affair with the poet JEAN-FRANÇOIS DE SAINT-LAMBERT, from 1753 until his death, and had a strong influence on JEAN-JACQUES ROUSSEAU during his stay at the Ermitage (1756–57), being the inspiration for Julie, the heroine of *La nouvelle Héloïse*. The countess de Houdetot was described as having "a very natural and very agreeable spirit, gay, stunning, and naïve." Rousseau recalled her also in *Les Confessions*, exalting an evening spent with the presence of her "most lively and tender company" (Book IX).

## Houdon, Jean-Antoine (1741–1828)
*sculptor*

Considered the greatest portrait sculptor of his time, Jean-Antoine Houdon was born in Versailles and trained in the studios of Paris. He won the prix de Rome for sculpture in 1761 and studied in Italy until 1768, being interested in ancient and Renaissance sculpture. He produced *Saint Bruno*, which established his reputation and, on returning to Paris, executed a number of elegant statues with mythological or allegorical themes (*Diane*, 1780, purchased by Catherine II of Russia; *L'Hiver*, 1783; *L'Été*, 1785). With great psychological insight, Houdon also began to produce a long line of sculpture portraits of eminent individuals of his age. The first of these was a bust of *Diderot*, followed by one of *Franklin* (1778) and *Rousseau* (1779) and, in 1781, he exhibited his famous seated statue of *Voltaire*. Producing accurate, expressive, and penetrating portraits, free of ostentation, Houdon sculpted other notable works, including *Sophie Arnould* (1775), *Les Enfants Brongniart* (1777) and *Washington* (1785).

## Hue, Robert (1946–   )
*political leader*

Born in Cormeilles-en-Parisis, Robert Hue has been a member of the French Communist Party since 1962. The mayor of Montigny-les-Cormeilles (1977), he joined the party's central committee in 1987 and its political bureau in 1990, before succeeding GEORGES MARCHAIS as party leader in January 1994. Hue was a candidate in the presidential election of 1995, in which he won 8.69 percent of the vote.

## Hugo, Victor (1802–1885)
*poet, novelist, playwright*

Victor Hugo, whose voluminous works provided the single greatest impetus to the romantic movement in France, was born in Besançon, the son of one of NAPOLÉON's generals. Along with his mother and brothers, Hugo followed his father to Italy and Spain before returning to Paris, where he took up writing ("I want to be Chateaubriand, or nothing"). He married Adèle Foucher, dedicating to her his *Odes et Ballades* (1822–28), in which he attempted to reconcile the classical and romantic styles. This

Victor Hugo *(Library of Congress)*

was followed by his novels *Hans d'Islande* (1823) and *Bug-Jargal* (1824). Then, in his *Préface de Cromwell* (1827), he emerged as the leader of the romantics. In *Orientales* (1829), Hugo defended the principle of artistic freedom, an idea that quickly became the manifesto of the romantic movement and culminated in his poetic drama, *Hernani* (1830), which had a tumultuous premiere and ensured the success of romanticism. It was later adapted by Giuseppe Verdi for his opera *Ernani* (1844). Hugo's social and humanitarian concerns were expressed in *Le Dernier Jour d'un condamné* (1829), and he became a voice for moral and political, as well as literary, ideas. The period from 1829 to 1843 was the most productive of Hugo's career. His great historical novel, *Notre-Dame de Paris* (1831) was a tale set in 15th-century Paris. It made him extremely popular and brought him election

to the ACADÉMIE FRANÇAISE (1841). Another novel of this period, *Claude Gueux* (1834), was an eloquent indictment of the French penal and social systems. Hugo also wrote several well-received volumes of lyric poetry, including *Les feuilles d'automne* (1831), *Les chants du crépuscule* (1837), and *Les Rayons et les Ombres* (1840). His dramatic successes include *Le roi s'amuse* (1832), which was the basis for Verdi's *Rigoletto* (1851); the prose drama *Lucrèce Borgia* (1833); and a melodrama, *Ruy Blas* (1838). The failure of his next work, *Les Burgraves* (1843), and the death of his daughter in that same year caused him to turn from writing and to take a more active role in politics. Raised as a Bonapartist, Hugo had become a royalist and was made a peer in 1845 by King LOUIS-PHILIPPE. But by the time of the REVOLUTION OF 1848, he had become a republican. In 1851, in the aftermath of the unsuccessful revolt against President Louis-Napoleon, Hugo fled to Belgium and, in 1855, began a 15-year exile on the island of Guernsey. While in exile, he composed scurrilous verse satire and also completed his longest and most famous work, *Les Misérables* (1862). Hugo returned to France in 1870 and resumed his role in politics; he was elected to the National Assembly and later to the Senate. Among the most notable of his later works are *L'Art d'être grand-père* (1877) and *Quatre Vents de l'esprit* (1881). All of Hugo's works have set the standard for generations of French youth, and he is still considered one of France's greatest poets. After his death on May 22, 1885, he was given a state funeral, his body lying in state under the ARC DE TRIOMPHE and later borne, in accordance with his wishes, on a pauper's hearse for internment in the Panthéon.

## Huguenots

"Huguenots" is the name given to French Protestants from about 1560 to 1630. Protestantism was introduced in France as early as 1520, and many of its adherents were from the nobility and the intellectual and middle classes. The new religious group at first enjoyed royal protection, especially from Queen MARGUERITE DE NAVARRE and King FRANCIS I. Despite persecution, which began at the end of Francis's reign, French Protestants increased in number. At the first national synod in 1559, 15 churches were represented. Two years later, 2,000 churches sent representatives. This increase in Protestantism alarmed French Roman Catholics, and religious hatred was intensified by the political rivalry between the House of Valois and the House of Guise. CATHERINE DE' MEDICI at the time allied with the Huguenots but generally opposed them. Open civil war broke out and, between 1562 and 1598, eight bitter conflicts were fought between Catholics and Protestants. The Huguenot leaders in the first of nearly four decades of struggle were LOUIS I DE BOURBON, PRINCE DE CONDÉ; Admiral GASPARD DE COLIGNY; and subsequently Henry of Navarre, later HENRY IV. The principal Catholic leaders, besides Catherine de' Medici, were HENRY I of Lorraine, the duke de GUISE, and King HENRY III. Foreign troops also took part in the conflicts. In 1572, after a peace was concluded, the Huguenots in Paris, lulled into a sense of security, were massacred on August 24, St. Bartholomew's Day (see SAINT BARTHOLOMEW'S DAY MASSACRE). Coligny was among those killed. The eighth civil war took place during the reign of King Henry III. The Catholics were defeated and became divided among themselves. When the House of Valois became extinct with the death of Henry III, Henry of Navarre became king. Henry IV, to avoid further strife, converted to Catholicism in 1593. In 1598, he issued the EDICT OF NANTES, by which the Huguenots received almost complete religious freedom. Protestant power in France increased and, to break this, LOUIS XIII and especially LOUIS XIV instigated new persecutions. Civil war again broke out, and in 1628, Cardinal RICHELIEU caused the political downfall of the Huguenots by capturing their principal stronghold, La Rochelle. He then sought reconciliation, however. King LOUIS XIV, instead, persecuted Protestants, revoking the Edict of Nantes in 1685. A massive emigration ensued, with hundreds of thousands of Huguenots fleeing to England, Germany, the Netherlands, Switzerland, and the English colonies in America. About 200,000 emigrated while about 1 million remained in France. Thousands settled in the Cévennes mountain region and became known as CAMISARDS. The government attempted to extirpate them, and the Camisard War broke out (1702–05). During the Enlightenment of the 18th century, French Protestants gradually regained many of their rights. Although King LOUIS XV issued an edict (1752) voiding Protestant baptisms and marriages, it was later recalled under LOUIS XVI. After 1787, Protestant marriages were granted full legal status. Laws passed during and after the REVOLUTION OF 1789 gave full religious freedom to all sects in France. Since then, French Protestants, although comparatively few, have been influential in all areas of French life.

## *L'Humanité*

This French daily, founded by JEAN JAURÈS in 1904, was the newspaper of the SOCIALIST PARTY (SFIO) until the Congress of Tours (1920), when its principal stockholder (Z. Camelinat) joined the Communists and *L'Humanité* became the French COMMUNIST PARTY (PCF) organ. Directed by Marcel Cachin, with Edouard Vaillant as editor in chief, the newspaper was suspended in 1939 but appeared clandestinely during the German Occupation until August 1944, when it again resumed official publication. After the death of Cachin (1958), the direction of the newspaper and of its weekly, *L'Humanité-Dimanche*, was taken over by Étienne Fajon, then by Roland Leroy (1974). Printing at least 100,000 copies, *L'Humanité* had, with the decline of the French Communist Party, a certain loss of readership.

## Hundred Days

The Hundred Days are the last period of the reign of NAPOLÉON I, from March 20 1815 to June 22, 1815, during which time the deposed emperor tried to restore the FIRST EMPIRE. Having escaped from the island of Elba, he landed on March 1, 1815, at Golfe-Juan, rallying the troops sent to arrest him and receiving the enthusiastic response of the people during his passage through France (Laffrey, Grenoble, Lyon, and Auxerre, where Marshal MICHEL NEY joined him). He arrived on March 20 at the Tuileries in Paris; meanwhile, King LOUIS XVIII had fled to Belgium. Napoléon I ordered BENJAMIN CONSTANT to edit the Additional Act to the Imperial Constitution, which favored the bourgeoisie. It was approved by a plebiscite (two-thirds of the electors abstained, however). Napoléon I then named General LAZARE CARNOT as minister of the interior. But the allies had banished Napoléon I from Europe, brought an end to the restoration of his empire at the battle of Waterloo (June 18, 1815), and forced Napoléon to abdicate a second time (June 22, 1815).

## Hundred Years' War

The Hundred Years' War between France and England lasted from 1337 to 1453. It was caused above all by the rivalry between King PHILIP VI of France and King Edward III of England who, upon the death of King Charles IV, the last Capetian in the direct line without an heir, claimed the French Crown because he was the son of Isabelle, daughter of King Philip the Fair. During the reign of Philip VI, the French were defeated at Crécy (1346) and lost Calais (1347). Under JEAN II, the English Black Prince Edward triumphed at Poitiers (1356); France, weakened because of the uprisings in Paris (see ÉTIENNE MARCEL) and devastated by the JACQUERIE, was obliged to sign the disastrous Treaty of Brétigny (1360); as a result, a fourth of Philippe the Fair's kingdom was lost. King CHARLES V and BERTRAND DU GUESLIN rectified the situation, and the English could occupy only Calais and Guyenne. Under King CHARLES VI, the civil war between the Burgundians and Armagnacs, as well as Charles's mistakes, allowed the English, who won the battle of Agincourt (1415), to again gain the upper hand and impose, with the complicity of ISABEAU OF BAVARIA, the shameful Treaty of Troyes (1420), concluded with the English, which gave the French crown to King Henry V. Under King CHARLES VII, JOAN OF ARC revived French patriotism; the heroine delivered Orléans and had the king crowned at Reims, but she was taken at Compiègne and burned at Rouen (1431). Meanwhile, the initiative passed to the French, and, thanks to brave leadership (JEAN XANTRAILLES, JEAN DUNOIS, LA HIRE), the English were defeated at Formigny (1450) and Castillon (1453), then driven from the kingdom except for Calais, which they held until 1558. The events of the Hundred Years' War comprise the first manifestations of French nationalism.

## Huntziger, Charles (1880–1941)
*military and political figure*

Born in Lesneven, Charles Huntziger was commander of French forces in the Levant at Beirut (1933), then a member of the Supreme War Council (1938). He was named commander of the Second Army, then of the Fourth Army Corps at the beginning of World War II, and later was chosen by Marshal PHILIPPE PÉTAIN, after the French defeat by Germany in 1940, to lead the delegation charged with negotiating and signing the armistice with Germany (Rethondes, June 22, 1940) and Italy. General Huntziger then served as minister of war in the VICHY regime (1940).

## Huysmans, Joris-Karl (1848–1907)
**(Charles-Marie-Georges Huysmans)**
*writer*

Of Dutch origin, Charles-Marie-Georges Huysmans, whose pen name is Joris-Karl Huysmans, was born in Paris, where, after a "youth filled with humiliation and trouble," he spent 30 years as a minor government official. Huysmans passed most of his free time writing, however, and after a collection of prose poems, *Le Drageoir aux épices* (1874), he published an article, "L'Assommoir," and a novel, *Les Soeurs Vatard* (1879), which brought him to the attention of ÉMILE ZOLA, with whom he then became good friends. Huysmans worked on a collection, *Les Soirées de Médan* (1880), and then in *En ménage* (1881) and *À vau-l'eau* (1882), he describes with derision a daily life filled with dull existences. His pessimism is apparent in *À rebours* (*Against the Grain;* 1884), in which his hero, Des Esseintes, vainly seeks salvation in art and literature. *À Rebours* is considered the best example of decadence, with Huysmans as one of its leading exponents. The decadent writers had a desire to shock, to cultivate artifice and the abnormal, and sought inspiration in aestheticism (art for art's sake), independent of moral and social concerns. Durtal, a hero of his other novels (*Là-Bas*, 1891; *En route*, 1894; *La Cathédrale*, 1898; *L'Oblat*, 1903), is based on Huysmans's own conversion from the occult to Catholicism. Huysmans's championing of the impressionists (EDGAR DEGAS, CLAUDE MONET, CAMILLE PISSARRO, ODILON REDON), along with naturalism and symbolism in *L'Art moderne* (1883), had a strong influence at the time. He was elected to the Académie Goncourt in 1897.

# I

## Île-de-France

A former land in France that became a province in the 14th century, the Île-de-France is today a French administrative region with its capital at PARIS. By far the most populous region of France (more than 11,000,000 inhabitants), as well as the most densely populated and the wealthiest, it comprises the departments of Paris, Seine-et-Marne, Yvelines, Essonne, Hauts-de-Seine, Seine–Saint-Denis, Val-de-Marne, and Val-de-Oise. Surrounding Paris, the Île-de-France has always been at the heart of French historical developments.

## impressionism

An artistic movement that emerged in France between 1860 and 1865, impressionism became one of the most important and influential artistic styles of the modern age. Following the works of Joseph Turner, the English watercolorists, the painters of the BARBIZON SCHOOL, and CAMILLE COROT and GUSTAVE COURBET, a group of painters from the Swiss Academy, who wanted to shed the constraints of the conventional studio and of the Salon—the only means at the time for official recognition—decided to paint in a more spontaneous style, conveying their impressions of nature. Taking their inspiration and example from ÉDOUARD MANET, whose painting *Le Déjeuner sur l'herbe* shocked many when it was shown at the Salon des Refusés in 1863, CLAUDE MONET, CAMILLE PISSARRO, and ALFRED SISLEY went against the official norm and, with about 20 other painters, including AUGUSTE RENOIR, PAUL CÉZANNE, EDGAR DEGAS, and BERTE MORISOT, formed the Anonymous Society of Painters, which exhibited 165 canvases in 1874 at the former Nadar Studio in Paris. The works provoked public scorn and were considered botched and incomplete. The art critic of the revue LE CHARIVARI, Louis Leroy, inspired by Monet's *Impression, soleil levant* (1872), labeled the new style "impressionist." Despite their diversity, these artists had in common essentially their observation of nature (water, clouds, flowers) in its true state, changing according to the light, as well as objects with all their nuances, especially as observed and reconstructed by the viewer's eye. Manet, Monet, and Degas were also inspired by Japanese art in particular. In a sense, the impressionists had taken up the challenge of the art critic and poet CHARLES BAUDELAIRE, who had called for a "painter of modern life." What set the impressionists apart from their contemporaries was not so much the subject matter of their works but their techniques. The impressionists were willing to replace the artifices of conventional painting—linear perspective and so forth—with the artist's subjective vision and a sense of autonomy in his work. This is especially true of Cézanne and, from him, nearly all the art of the 20th century. Later, the chemist EUGÈNE CHEVREUL and the painter GEORGES SEURAT systematized the optic principles revealed through the intuitive impressionist techniques. Monet applied his ideas of light to paintings of buildings (*La Gare Saint-Lazare*, 1877; *La Cathédral de Rouen*, 1892–1904), painting them in a series according to the changes in light upon them. Despite their poor initial reception and the dispersal of their group, a few impressionists were recognized and appreciated toward the end of their lives. For example, Monet, who left *Nympheas* to the state in 1922, saw his works receive a place of acclaim and prestige with their official permanent installation in the Orangerie des Tuileries in 1927.

## Indochina, French

French Indochina, or L'Union Indochinoise, was the name given in 1887 to the countries of Southeast Asia under the French protectorate and colonized by France. They comprised as first the three parts of Vietnam (Cochin China, Annam, and Tonkin) and Cambodia, then Laos after 1893, and the territory of Guangzhouwan after 1900. The expeditions sent to protect Christian missionaries by NAPOLÉON III were the origin of these conquests. Tourane (today Danang) was taken in 1858, then Saigon (Ho Chi Minh City) and all of Cochin China. The protectorate of Cambodia, while disputed by Siam (Thailand), was established shortly afterward. France then conquered Tonkin after a conflict with China (1882–85). The government, under the authority of a governor-general, had its headquarters at Hanoi and enforced, in spite of native resistance, an economic exploitation of the region that was typical of the period. Cities were created or modernized, the infrastructure improved, and French culture was imposed or adopted by a segment of the population that saw it as an opportunity for change or personal advancement. France finally left the region after the national wars of the 1950s.

See also DIEN BIEN PHU; HO CHI MINH.

## Indy, Vincent d' (1851–1931)
*composer*

Born in Paris into a family of amateur musicians originally from the Cévennes, Vincent d'Indy studied music at the Paris Conservatoire, where he was a student of CÉSAR FRANCK. A friend of HECTOR BERLIOZ and Gioacchino Rossini, he also knew Franz Liszt and Richard Wagner and was a great admirer of German music. His reputation was established in 1883 with his *Chant de la cloche*, which was inspired in turn by the works of the German poet Friedrich von Schiller. Among his other works are operas (*Fervaal*, 1885, inspired by Wagner; *La Légende de saint Christophe*, 1920), *String Quartet* (1890), *Istar* (1896); works inspired by the Mediterranean (*Poème des rivages*, 1921; *Diptyque méditerranéen*, 1926), his masterpiece, *L'Étranger*, a symbolic drama after Ibsen (1898–1901), and other symphonies and sonatas. Indy also published a *Traité de composition musicale*, which is a testament to his love of music and art.

## Ingres, Jean-Auguste-Dominique (1780–1867)
*painter*

A leading figure in the neoclassical movement, Ingres was born in Montauban, the son of an ornamental sculptor who encouraged his son's early skills. Ingres entered the studio of JACQUES-LOUIS DAVID in Paris (1797) and soon won the Prix de Rome (1801). From 1806 to 1820, he painted in Rome, developing his extraordinary talents. He was greatly influenced by the work of Raphael, whose style inspired him as much as David's. In 1820, Ingres left Rome to study in Florence for four years. While in Italy, he executed several portraits. At that time, he also painted a number of important allegorical works, including *Oedipus and the Sphinx* (1807) and *Jupiter and Thetis* (1811). He is also well known for his nudes painted during this period, especially the *Grande Odalisque* (1814). On his return to Paris, Ingres won great acclaim with his *Vow of Louis XIII,* exhibited at the Paris Salon in 1824. He became the recognized leader of the neoclassical school, which contrasted with the romantic movement led by EUGÈNE DELACROIX and THÉODORE GÉRICAULT. At this time, he also painted *The Apotheosis of Homer* (1827). In 1834, angered by the poor reception given his *Martyrdom of Saint Symphorien* (1834), he left Paris to accept the directorship of the French Academy in Rome. Ingres's reputation remained untarnished, however, and in 1841 he returned to Paris to be received as one of France's most celebrated painters. In 1845, he was awarded the rank of commander of the LEGION OF HONOR. In the Universal Exhibition in Paris in 1855, both he and his rival Delacroix were awarded gold medals. Ingres's keen sensitivity, superb draftsmanship, and precise neoclassical linear style were especially suited to portraiture. Ingres continued to paint throughout his life, at age 82 producing his famous *The Turkish Bath* (1863), recognized as the culmination of his superb depiction of female nudes. Ingres's influence has been enormous, and important later painters who acknowledged their inspiration from his style include EDGAR DEGAS, HENRI MATISSE, AUGUSTE RENOIR, and Pablo Picasso.

## Institut de France

The Institut de France is a group of five learned French societies, each fostering a special branch of art, literature, philosophy, or science. As originally organized (1795), the Institut comprised three societies: for physics and mathematics, for the moral and political sciences, and for literature and the fine arts. The five present sections now include the ACADÉMIE FRANÇAISE, founded (1635) by Cardinal RICHELIEU for the principal purpose of standardizing the French language. The first edition of its authoritative dictionary was published in 1694. The dictionary is constantly revised, and volumes are published as they are completed. In 1980, MARGUERITE YOURCENAR became the first woman elected to this academy. The Académie des Inscriptions et Belles-Lettres was organized in 1663 for the purpose of the study of ancient inscriptions and documents, numismatics, and languages. It has 45 members. The Académie des Sciences was established in 1666 to promote work in the mathematical sciences, including geometry and astronomy, and in such physical sciences as chemistry, and also botany, and anatomy. It has 130 members. The Académie des Beaux-Arts was created in 1648 to encourage the fine arts and maintain aesthetic standards. It has 50 members. The Académie des Sciences Morales et Politiques was founded at the same time as the Institut de France (1795). It comprises five divisions: history and geography; legislation and jurisprudence; morals; philosophy; and political economy; it has 50 members. In total, the Institut de France has more than 300 members, each elected for life and receiving a small annuity. There are also about 300 correspondents, many of whom are foreigners. Each section elects its own members when vacancies occur. Since 1805, the Institut has held its meetings in the Palais de l'Institut in Paris. Each section also awards annual prizes to nonmembers who have done notable work in the areas covered by the societies. The Institut possesses a fine artistic and architectural heritage, the result of bequests from benefactors.

## Invalides, Hôtel des

The Hôtel des Invalides is a monumental complex situated in Paris that was conceived by King LOUIS XIV (1670) as a residence for soldiers who had been wounded in his service. Between 1670 and 1676, a quadrilateral 450 meters long by 390 meters wide was built, with six main courtyards, including the Court of Honor with two levels of arcades, and a façade flanked by two pavilions. The entrance to the complex is a central portal dominated by an imposing bas-relief of Louis XIV on horseback. Stately and grand, the Invalides was built by JULES HARDOUIN-MANSARD, who is especially known for the gilded dome (1679 to 1706) of the adjoining Church of Saint-Louis that dominates the vast esplanade that extends to the Seine. Under the cupola have been placed the remains of NAPOLÉON I, alongside, those of his son, NAPOLÉON II. The Hôtel des Invalides, which also contains the tombs of several other great military figures, opens onto the Army Museum.

## Inghelbrecht, Désiré-Émile  (1880–1965)
*orchestra leader, composer*

Désiré-Émile Inghelbrecht, who was a friend of CLAUDE DEBUSSY, was born in Paris, where he was the musical director at the théâtre des Champs-Élysées (1913), orchestra leader at the Opéra-Comique (1924), and then founder of the national orchestra of Radiodiffusion française (1934). An interpreter of Debussy's style and works, he composed in very diverse genres (symphonic, religious, and chamber music, ballet, melodies, piano pieces, and operettas). An essayist, Inghelbrecht published several incisive works on musicology.

## Ionesco, Eugène  (1909–1994)
*dramatic author*

Born in Slatina, Romania, to a Romanian father and a French mother, Eugène Ionesco lived in France until the age of 13. He moved to Romania, where he was a professor of French, then in 1938, returned to reside in France permanently. His first play *La Cantatrice chauve* (*The Bald Soprano;* 1950), a satire of bourgeois society that inspired the Theater of the Absurd movement, was followed by *Les Chaises* (*The Chairs;* 1952), *Victimes du devoir* (1953), and *Amédée ou Comment s'en débarrasser* (1954). His understanding of human suffering (*Tueur sans gages,* 1959), his sense of ideology (*Rhinocéros,* 1958), and death (*Le Roi se meurt*, 1962), is apparent in his works. In his second period of writing, Ionesco produced *Le Piéton de l'air* (1963), *La Soif et la Faim* (1966), and *Jeux de massacre* (1970). He wrote a novel, *Le Solitaire* (1973), and a screenplay (*La Vase*, 1972). His plays reflect the absurdity of life, the human condition, and the universe. Ionesco was elected to the ACADÉMIE FRANÇAISE in 1970.

## Isabeau of Bavaria (1371–1435)
*queen of France*

Born in Munich, Germany, Isabeau of Bavaria was the daughter of Stephen II of Wittelsbach, duke of Bavaria, and Tedea Visconti. She married CHARLES VI of France, after whose dementia she assumed the regency, favoring Louis d'Orléans over JEAN THE FEARLESS, thus provoking the quarrel between the Armagnacs and the Burgundians. Leaving the alliance she made with the Armagnacs, Queen Isabeau allied herself with the Burgundians and with the English and was an accessory to the Treaty of Troyes (1420) that gave Henry V of England a claim to France. Her influence ended with the death of Charles VI. Isabeau of Bavaria was the mother of King CHARLES VII.

## Isabey, Eugène (1804–1886)
*painter, watercolorist, lithographer, designer*

A versatile and romantic painter who worked in many artistic styles, Eugène Isabey was born in Paris, the son of JEAN-BAPTISTE ISABEY. As a leading landscape painter, who followed the colorist experiments of EUGÈNE DELACROIX, Isabey produced many historic scenes, genre paintings, landscapes, and seascapes, which reveal a romantic conception of nature. He was influenced by the English painter Richard Bonington and worked especially in Normandy. Isabey was also a noted printmaker. Toward the end of his life, the style of his watercolors and lithographs presaged impressionism.

## Isabey, Jean-Baptiste (1767–1855)
*painter, miniaturist, designer, watercolorist*

Born in Nancy, Jean-Baptiste Isabey was the student of various artists, including JACQUES-LOUIS DAVID. He gained recognition for producing portraits of the leading members of the Constituent Assembly and of Napoléon Bonaparte (see NAPOLÉON I). He also designed the uniforms and costumes of the Imperial court and was put in charge of organizing Imperial celebrations during the FIRST EMPIRE. Isabey kept this post during the RESTORATION and the SECOND EMPIRE. With his delicate but clearly rendered portraits, he is one of the last representatives of the miniaturist's art.

## Isambert, François (1792–1857)
*magistrate, political figure*

Born in Aunay-sous-Auneau, Eure-et-Loire, François Isambert, during the RESTORATION, was a liberal attorney, and then, under the July Monarchy, also sat in the Constituent Assembly (1848), where he supported General LOUIS CAVAGNAC against the socialists. Isambert is the author of *Recueil des anciennes lois françaises depuis 420 jusqu'à la Révolution de 1789* (1822–1833).

See also REVOLUTION OF 1830; REVOLUTION OF 1848.

## Itard, Jean-Marc-Gaspard (1774–1838)
*physician*

Born in Oraison, Basse-Alps, Jean Itard is considered one of the pioneers in the field of endocrinology (1799–1800) and is known for his work in the teaching and training of deaf-mute children. At first a military surgeon, then a specialist in hearing disorders, Itard, from about 1800, became progressively more interested in the education of deaf-mutes and experimented also with the instruction of mentally retarded children. In 1801, Itard was given the charge of training a feral child, Victor, as he was known, the so-called wild boy of Aveyron, a youth who had been found in the forest and seemed never to have experienced human socialization. The system Itard developed in attempting to socialize and educate Victor led him further to develop methods that would later be used for the instruction of the deaf and mentally challenged. In turn, Itard's methodology influenced many later educators, most notably Maria Montessori.

# J

## Jacob, Max (1876–1944)
*poet*

Of Jewish ancestry, Max Jacob, who was born in Quimper, Brittany, at first led a bohemian existence in the Montmartre district of Paris in the early years of the 20th century. There, he met Pablo Picasso and other artistic and literary figures of the period. After a religious experience (1909), he converted to Catholicism and chose to retire a few years later (1921) to the Abbey of Saint-Benoit-sur-Loire, a retreat where he remained, with the exception of a visit to Paris (1927) and of a few trips abroad. It was at the abbey that he was arrested during WORLD WAR II (1944) by the Gestapo and interned at the concentration camp at Drancy, where he died in a state of exemplary serenity. An exceptional poet, who drew inspiration from dreams and fantasy, Jacob's first works foreshadow surrealism, long before the advent of that movement (*Le Cornet à dés*). Always tinged with humor, but filled also with mysticism, his abundant poetry deals with the ephemeral, and it strips objects and beings of their appearances.

## Jacobins

The Jacobins were a radical political club that played a central role in the REVOLUTION OF 1789. Known also as the Jacobin Club, the group was founded in 1789 as the Friends of the Constitution, which met in a former Jacobin monastery in Paris, hence the name. Both the count de MIRABEAU and MAXIMILIEN ROBESPIERRE were early members. Although it had only 3,000 members in Paris, the club controlled 1,200 related societies throughout France, giving it enormous political power. At first a moderate organization, the club had a diverse membership (besides Mirabeau and Robespierre, who ultimately took control, members included EMMANUEL SIEYÈS, CHARLES DE TALLEYRAND, ANTOINE BARNAVE, the marquis de LAFAYETTE, and others). After the attempted escape of King LOUIS XVI in 1791 and the affair of the Champ-de-Mars, the Jacobins turned against any form of royal government. At the same time, with the formation of the National Convention, the Jacobin Club, which now also used the name Society of the Friends of Liberty and Equality, reached their peak of power. No important action was taken by the National Convention without Jacobin approval. All moderate members had left by 1793, at which point extremists took complete control. Dominating the powerful Committee of Public Safety, they brought the nation into the REIGN OF TERROR. The Jacobins, insisting on the death of the king, destroyed also the moderate GIRONDINS and executed thousands of opponents. Losing much of its power with the downfall of Robespierre, the club was closed during the Thermidorian reaction. It was reorganized under the DIRECTORY (1795–96) without great success and was finally closed in 1799.

## Jacquard, Joseph-Marie (1752–1834)
*inventor*

Born in LYON, the son of a weaver, Joseph-Marie Jacquard developed the Jacquard loom, which enabled a single operator to weave complex patterns. The Jacquard loom began a technological revolution in the textile industry, and the system of punched cards used in its operation became a prototype for the first computers. Because the production of patterned fabrics was so costly, Jacquard, in 1790, began to design a loom that would weave patterns automatically. Finishing the project in 1801, Jacquard demonstrated his automatic loom in Paris and, in 1804, was awarded a patent and medal for his design. By 1812, an estimated 11,000

Joseph-Marie Jacquard *(Library of Congress)*

Jacquard looms were in use in France. By a system of hooks, needles, and perforated thick paper cards, intricate woven patterns could be created. Modern Jacquard looms are still in use and punched cards, similar to those used in Jacquard's loom, were soon applied to other machines, including early information-storage systems.

## Jacquemont de Hesdin  (fl. 1384–1411)
*illuminator*

Jacquemont de Hesdin, who worked for the duke JEAN OF BERRY, imitated in his illuminations the graphism of JEAN PUCELLE and was also influenced by the Italians. This is apparent in his treatment of depth and space, linear characteristics, and picturesque and anecdotal works. His predilection for refined arabesques are characteristic of the international Gothic style. Jacquemont de Hesdin is the author of *Très Belles Heures du duc de Berry* (ca. 1402) and *Grandes Heures du duc de* Berry (ca. 1409), and attributed to him are also the *Petites Heures du duc de Berry* (commissioned 1372).

## Jacquerie

The Jacquerie was an uprising of peasants (Jacques) in the Beauvaisis (1358) during the reign of JEAN II at the time of the HUNDRED YEARS' WAR. The Jacques (or Jacques Bonhommes) taking advantage of the crisis precipitated by the English victory over France at Poitiers attacked the nobles and pillaged their châteaux. Supported for a time by ÉTIENNE MARCEL, and in some places by the burgher classes, the rebellion spread to other areas of the northeast. The Jacquerie was, however, suppressed by an army of nobles led by the king of Navarre, CHARLES II THE BAD. Over a period of two weeks, some 7,000 peasants were killed, with some estimates given at 20,000.

## Jammes, Francis  (1868–1938)
*writer*

Born in Tournay, Hautes-Pyrénées, Francis Jammes is inseparable from his regional birthplace of Béarn in the Basque country, where he set his works. In his first collection, *De l'Angélus de l'aube à l'Angélus du soir* (1898), he established the tone and style of his writings with the same fervid lyricism being present in such subsequent pieces as *Clara d'Ellébeuse* (1899), *Almaïde d'Étremont* (1901), *Le Deuil des primevères* (1901), and *Le Triomphe de la vie* (1902). His close friendship with PAUL CLAUDEL inspired Jammes's return to Catholicism. Becoming over the years a type of rustic patriarchal figure, he was opposed to new literary currents, especially in poetry. Jammes carried on a correspondence with several other writers, including COLETTE and ANDRÉ GIDE, that has been published.

## Janequin, Clément  (ca. 1485–1558)
*composer*

A composer of chansons and psalms whose songs are witty and richly textured, Clément Janequin was born in Chatelleraut and became a protégé of powerful and notable individuals, such as the duke of GUISE and the cardinal of Lorraine, as well as becoming the composer for King HENRY II. Nonetheless, Janequin spent much of his life in poverty. He first served as choirmaster of Angers cathedral (1534–37) and established himself in Paris after 1549. The body of his work consists of 275 songs for three, four, and five voices, and was published after 1520. The incontestable master of the popular music of his day, he wrote in all genres (lyric, narrative, erotic) and employed a style that evoked the imitation of nature and theatrical illusion. Janequin's religious works (motets, masses, psalms, and hymns) are considered unequaled for his time.

## Jansenism

A movement of religious reform, especially in 17th- and 18th-century France, Jansenism takes its name from the Flemish bishop and theologian Cornelius Jansen, whose ideas were summarized in the treatise *Augustinus* (1640). Using the philosophy of St. Augustine, Jansen supported the doctrine of absolute predestination. In this respect, his ideas closely resemble Calvinism, and Jansen and his followers were often accused of being Protestant. The Jansenists always stated their adherence to Catholicism, however, and taught that salvation was possible only inside the Roman Catholic Church. As practiced in France, especially by Jansen's associate JEAN DUVERGIER DE HAURANNE, the abbot of Saint-Cyran, Jansenism entailed an austere form of piety and a rigorous morality. This was in contrast to the more tolerant ethics favored by the Jesuits and others at the time. From the 1640s on, the spiritual center of Jansenism was the convent of Port-Royal-des-Champs, near Paris, where nobles, government officials, and sympathetic thinkers often made religious retreats. Almost from the start, Jansenism aroused the hostility of both the Jesuits and the royal government. In 1635, five of Jansen's propositions were condemned by the pope. Various Jansenist theologians and philosophers, including BLAISE PASCAL, defended the movement while attacking the Jesuits. Finally, in 1713, under pressure from LOUIS XIV, the pope, in his papal bull *Unigenitus,* condemned the remainder of Jansenist writings. Port-Royal had already been closed and razed in 1709 by the king's orders. Nonetheless, during the 18th century, Jansenism continued to have a wide appeal in France, especially among the parish clergy. The movement also spread to other parts of Europe, including Austria, Italy, and Spain. In France, the Jansenists allied themselves with GALLICANISM, and the civil courts often defended Jansenist claims to church rites. The greatest triumph of Jansenism came in the 1760s, when the parlementary courts expelled the Jesuits from France. After the REVOLUTION OF 1789, the Jansenists generally accepted the Civil Constitution of the Clergy but fought against the revolution's later antireligious policies. A small Jansenist Church, founded in 1724, still exists today in the Netherlands.

## Jaurès, Jean (1859–1914)
*political figure, philosopher, historian*

Considered a great French patriot and humanitarian, as well as a Socialist leader, Jean Jaurès was born in Castres, Tarn, and became professor of philosophy at Albi, then at the University of Toulouse. In 1885, he was elected to the Chamber of Deputies but was defeated in the election of 1889. He then returned to teaching and wrote his thesis, *De la réalité du monde sensible: Les Origines du socialisme allemand chez Luther, Kant, Fichte, Hegel* (1891). Elected as a Socialist deputy for Carmaux (1893), Jaurès worked for the unification of the Socialist movement in France. In 1898, he took a position supporting Captain ALFRED DREYFUS (*Preuves,* 1898) and subsequently defended the participation of the Socialist ALEXANDRE MILLERAND in the WALDECK-ROUSSEAU government of 1899 over the opposition of JULES GUESDE and other party leaders. Jaurès took this position to save the threatened republic from its enemies on the Right. In 1904, he founded the socialist daily, *L'HUMANITÉ* and, in 1905, unified the warring factions of French socialism into a single coalition, the Section française de L'Internationale ouvrière (SFIO). Jaurès also continued to speak and write extensively. As a member of the Parlement, he supported laws on public education and workers rights, and strongly criticized French colonialism and imperialism. At the same time, he urged international arbitration of disputes among nations. Just as his socialism was liberal and democratic, his internationalism and pacifism were tied to a democratic patriotism, linked also with his idea for a "new army." Opposed to the coming world war, Jaurès was shot and killed by a nationalist in July 1914, on the eve of WORLD WAR I. As the nation went to war, the government publicly mourned his death. In 1924, his remains were transferred to the

Panthéon. An individual respected for his honesty, idealism, and patriotism, Jaurès has left other writings, including *Action socialiste* (1899); *Études socialistes* (1901); and his major work, *Histoire socialiste de la Révolution française, 1789–1900,* published between 1901 and 1908.

## Jean II the Good  (1319–1364)
### (Jean II le Bon)
*king of France*

Born at the château of Gue de Maulney, near Le Mans, Jean II the Good, who was king of France from 1350 to 1364, was the son of PHILIPPE VI of Valois and Jeanne of Burgundy. In 1332, Jean married Bonne de Luxembourg, and later (1350), Jeanne de Boulogne. As monarch, he debased the currency to deal with court and government expenses, and, in 1353, married his daughter to CHARLES II THE BAD, king of Navarre. Charles then assassinated Charles of Spain, a councilor to Jean II, and his arrest brought about a war with Navarre (1356). Meanwhile, hostilities with England recurred in Guyenne and Languedoc; the son of King Edward III, Edward the Prince of Wales, defeated and captured Jean at Poitier (1356). Jean's son, the dauphin and future CHARLES V, served as regent during his father's captivity and suppressed the JACQUERIE and the uprising of ÉTIENNE MARCEL. The dauphin also agreed to sign the Peace of Brétigny and to pay the ransom of 3 million gold crowns required to free the king. Jean II, having learned that his son, Louis d'Anjou, one of the hostages held by the English, had escaped, remained faithful to his word and returned to London, where he died. Jean II, during his reign, created the Knights' Order of the Star and divided his domains among his sons, giving Anjou to Louis; Berry, Auvergne, and Poitou to Jean; and Burgundy to PHILIPPE II THE BOLD.

## Jean IV the Brave  (ca. 1340–1399)
### (Jean IV le Vaillant)
*duke of Brittany, military leader*

The son of JEAN OF MONTFORT, Jean IV the Brave, duke of Brittany, defeated and killed CHARLES DE BLOIS at Auray in 1364. After being an ally of

England and seeing his lands confiscated (1368), Jean IV renewed his alliance with France.

## Jean de Montfort  (1293–1345)
### *duke of Brittany, political figure*

The son of Arthur II of Brittany and Yolande de Dreux, countess of Montfort-l'Amaury, Jean de Montfort, duke of Brittany, upon the death of his half brother, Jean III, challenged the claims of CHARLES DE BLOIS and took the duchy of Brittany (1341). This action, however, was opposed by PHILIPPE VI, king of France, and Jean de Montfort was captured at Nantes by royal troops led by the king's son, the duke of Normandy. He was kept prisoner in the tower of the LOUVRE (1343) but escaped (1345). Having sworn allegiance to Edward III of England, he died shortly after at the siege of Hennebont. Jean de Montfort was the father of JEAN IV THE BRAVE.

## Jean the Fearless  (1371–1419)
### (Jean Sans Peur)
*nobility*

Born in Dijon, Jean the Fearless, duke of Burgundy was the son of PHILIP II THE BOLD and Marguerite de Mâle. During the incapacity of CHARLES VI, he disputed the power of LOUIS D'ORLÉANS and had him assassinated (1407), provoking the civil war between the Armagnacs and the Burgundians. Leader of the Burgundians, Jean was supported by the SORBONNE and a faction of the bourgeoisie, but he was unable to channel the movement into a force and was driven from Paris (1413). He allied himself with the English, then tried to reconcile with the dauphin (the future CHARLES VII), but was assassinated during their meeting at the bridge at Montereau by one of the dauphin's supporters. Jean the Fearless was the father of PHILIP III THE GOOD.

## Jean Bon Saint-André  (1749–1813)
### *political figure*

Born André Jeanbon, Jean Bon Saint-André as he is known, was, during the REVOLUTION OF 1789, a Montagnard deputy to the Convention and a member of the Committee of Public Safety (July 1793), where, with PRIEUR DE LA MARNE, he helped to organize the navy. He did not take part in the fall of MAXIMILIEN ROBESPIERRE but seems to have supported it. Consul general of France to Algeria (1795), then to Smyrna in the Ottoman Empire (1798) under the DIRECTORY, Saint-André was named commissioner general of the Department of the Left Bank of the Rhine, then prefect, by NAPOLÉON I (1801–02).

## Jean-Baptiste de la Salle (1651–1719)
*cleric, educator, saint*

Born in Reims, Jean-Baptiste de la Salle organized there (1679), then in Paris (1688), and later in the provinces, an association that became (1694) the congregation of the Brothers of the Christian Schools. His feast is celebrated by the Catholic Church on April 7.

## Jean-Baptiste-Marie Vianney (1786–1859)
*cleric, saint*

Born in Dardilly, near Lyon, Jean-Baptiste-Marie Vianney was the priest of Ars in the diocese of Belley (1817), where he restored the practice of Christianity which had greatly declined during the REVOLUTION OF 1789, founded the Work of Providence for poor children, practiced asceticism, and attracted many with his charisma as a priest and confessor. Canonized in 1925, he had, during his lifetime, the reputation of a saint. The Catholic Church celebrates his feast on August 4.

## Jeanmarie, Renée (1924–  )
*dancer, singer*

Born in Paris, Renée Jeanmarie, or Zizi, as she is known, began her career at the Paris Opéra before turning to ballet and becoming the star of the Ballet de Paris, directed by ROLAND PETIT (1949). She danced brilliant and spiritual interpretations of *Carmen*, *La Croqueuse de diamants*, and *La Rose des vents*. Engaged by Hollywood, she appeared in several successful films (*Hans Christian Anderson, Folies-Bergère*) before beginning a career as a music-hall singer, first at the Alhambra, then at the Casino de Paris, where she became director along with her husband, Roland Petit.

## Jeanne II de Navarre (1328–1349)
*queen of Navarre*

The daughter of King LOUIS X of France and Marguerite of Burgundy, Jeanne II de Navarre, although the king's daughter, was not recognized as queen of France in 1317, but in 1328 she was recognized as queen of Navarre. She was the mother of CHARLES II THE BAD of Navarre.

## Jeanne III d'Albret (1528–1572)
*queen of Navarre*

Born in Pau, Jeanne III d'Albret, queen of Navarre (1555–72), was the daughter of Henry II d'Albret, king of Navarre, and MARGUERITE DE VALOIS. After the annulment of her first marriage with the duke of Cleves, she married Antoine of Bourbon (1548). Of great intelligence, she sought energetically to preserve the independence of her kingdom, to which she introduced Calvinism (1567). She also supported her coreligionists, defending La Rochelle in 1568, but died shortly before the marriage of her son (the future HENRY IV) to MARGUERITE DE VALOIS, sister of CHARLES IX.

## Jeanne de Chantal (1572–1641)
*saint*

Born Jeanne-Françoise Frémiot in Dijon, Jeanne de Chantal married Christophe of Rabutin, baron of Chantal. Widowed in 1601, she put herself under the tutelage of Saint François de Sales and with him founded at Annecy the Visitation Sainte-Marie (1610), which became the Order of the Visitation, with cloister and solemn vows, and was established throughout France. Jeanne de Chantal, who was the grandmother of Mme de SÉVIGNÉ, was canonized in 1767. The Catholic Church celebrates her feast on August 21.

## Jeanne de France (1464–1505)
### (Jeanne de Valois)
*princess, saint*

The daughter of King LOUIS XI and Charlotte of Savoy, Jeanne of France (or of Valois), in 1476, married Louis d'Orléans, the future LOUIS XII. Disabled, she was repudiated by her husband on the eve of his accession to the throne (1498) and retired to Bourges, where she founded the Order of the Annunciation (1501). Jeanne of France was canonized in 1951, and the Catholic Church celebrates her feast on February 4.

## Jeanne de Penthièvre (1319–1364)
*duchess of Brittany*

The duchess of Brittany (1319–65), Jeanne de Penthièvre was the niece of Jean III of Brittany and the wife of CHARLES OF BLOIS. Her designation as heiress to the duchy of Brittany caused the War of Succession of Brittany. Jeanne de Penthièvre renounced the duchy (Treaty of Guérande, 1365) in favor of Jean V, son of JEAN IV THE BRAVE.

## Jeannin, Pierre (1540–1623)
*magistrate*

Known as Président Jeannin, Pierre Jeannin was born in Autun. He stood for moderation at the time of the SAINT BARTHOLOMEW'S DAY MASSACRE, but joined the HOLY LEAGUE and was an adviser to the duke de MAYENNE before finally coming over to King HENRY IV. Jeannin was sent on several diplomatic missions (Treaty of Lyon, 1601; negotiated a treaty of 12 years between Spain and the United Provinces, 1609). MARIE DE' MEDICI named him superintendent of finances (1616). His *Négociations* was for a long time considered as an authoritative work on diplomacy.

## Jecker, Jean-Baptiste (1810–1871)
*financier*

Of Swiss origin, Jean-Baptiste Jecker was born in Porrentruy. Employed at the Hottinguer bank in Paris (1831), he joined his brother in Mexico, where he founded a large bank, as well as mining enterprises. The Mexican president Miramón entrusted him with the nation's domestic debt, but his successor, President Juárez, refused to recognize the terms of their agreement. Jecker, who had become a naturalized French citizen (1862), tried to interest the imperial government of NAPOLÉON III, and in particular the duke of MORNY, in this debt issue, which would become one of the motivations for the Mexican expedition (1862–67).

## Joan of Arc (1412–1431)
*national heroine, saint*

Called the Maid of Orleans, who united the nation at the most crucial hour and turned the HUNDRED YEARS' WAR in France's favor, Joan of Arc (Jeanne d'Arc) was born to a peasant family in Domrémy, Lorraine. According to her testimony, when she was 13 she heard celestial voices (St. Michael, St. Catherine, St. Margaret), sometimes also accompanied by visions, which exhorted her to help the dauphin, later CHARLES VII, king of France. In 1428, when the English were about to capture Orléans (see HUNDRED YEARS' WAR), Joan convinced the dauphin (who had not yet been crowned king because of internal strife and the English claim to the throne) that she had a divine mission to save France. A commission of theologians approved her claims, and she was given troops to command. Dressed in armor and carrying the white fleur-de-lys banner, she led the French to a decisive victory over the English at Patay and then took Auxerre, Troyes, and Châlons, thus opening the way to Reims. At the subsequent coronation of the dauphin (1429) at Reims, she was given the place of honor beside the king. Although Joan had unified the French behind Charles, and had put an end to English dreams of hegemony over France, Charles opposed any further campaigns against the English. Thus, it was without royal support that Joan, in 1430, led a military operation against the English at Compiègne, near Paris and was wounded. She was captured by Burgundian soldiers, who sold her to their English allies. She then was turned over to an ecclesiastical court at Rouen to be tried for sorcery and heresy. She defended herself with courage and simplicity as the court, during 14 months of interrogation, accused her of wrongdoing in wearing masculine dress and of heresy. Condemned to death, she confessed, and was sentenced to life imprisonment. Shortly after, she abjured her confession and also resumed masculine dress. She was condemned again and, on May 30, 1431, was burned at the stake. In 1456 however, her case was reinvestigated by the church

Joan of Arc *(Library of Congress)*

and she was pronounced innocent. In 1909, she was beatified and, in 1920, canonized. A symbol of French nationalism, especially in modern times and during the 20th-century world wars, Joan of Arc has also been widely depicted in literature, art, music, and film (VOLTAIRE, Schiller, RUDE, Twain, Audiberti, PÉGUY, Dreyer, DeMille, Preminger, Rossellini, Bresson, Rivette, Shaw, Verdi, CLAUDEL, and HONEGGER).

See also XAINTRAILLES, JEAN POTON.

## Jodelet (ca. 1590–1660)
*actor*

Born Julien Bedeau in Paris, Jodelet as he is known, with his painted and bearded face enjoyed much popularity with the public in the theaters of the Marais and the Hôtel de Bourgogne before joining the acting company of JEAN-BAPTISTE MOLIÈRE. He also acted in the plays of PIERRE CORNEILLE (*Le Menteur,* 1643) and PAUL SCARRON (*Jodelet ou le Valet maître,* 1645), as well as those of Molière (*Les Précieuses ridicules,* 1659).

## Jodelle, Étienne (1532–1573)
*poet, dramatist*

An important literary figure of the French Renaissance, Étienne Jodelle was born in Paris and, at age 20, was the author of the first classic French tragedy, *Cléopatre captive* (1553), which was performed before King HENRY II. He composed other tragedies (*Didon se sacrifiant*) none of which was successful, however. This led to his dismissal (1560) and eventual decline. For Jodelle, the object of tragedy was to put forth a moral lesson, one of a wisdom inspired by the dangers of the passions. Breaking with the comic tradition of the Middle Ages, he is also the author of comedies: *Eugène* (1552) and *La Rencontre* (1556, a lost work).

## Joffre, Joseph-Jacques-Césaire (1852–1931)
*marshal of France*

Known chiefly for his command of the French army during WORLD WAR I, Joseph-Jacques-Césaire Joffre was born in Rivesaltes and educated at the École polytechnique in Paris. Joffre served in French colonies in Africa and Asia and, in 1902, was made brigadier general. Commander in chief of the French armies in the north at the beginning of World War I, he achieved a successful counterattack against the German forces that had invaded France in August 1914. His initial victory, known as the First Battle of the Marne, caused the Germans to abandon their march toward Paris. Joffre became a national hero, but his subsequent failure to break the German lines, and the heavy losses later at Verdun (1916), caused dissatisfaction with his leadership. In December 1916, he was replaced by General GEORGE NIVELLE as active commander of the French forces, although Joffre still retained the title of commander in chief. He was subsequently made a marshal of France and, in 1918, was elected to the ACADÉMIE FRANÇAISE. Marshal Joffre has left his *Memoires* (posthumous, 1932).

## Joinville, François-Ferdinand-Philippe d'Orléans, prince de (1818–1900)
*vice admiral*

Born in Neuilly-sur-Seine, François-Ferdinand-Philippe d'Orléans, prince de Joinville was the third son of King LOUIS-PHILIPPE and Queen MARIE-AMÉLIE DE BOURBON. A naval captain, he was commissioned in 1840 to bring back the remains of Napoléon Bonaparte (see NAPOLÉON I) from St. Helena. He led the expedition against Morocco (August 1844, Tangier, Mogador) and gained a certain popularity by opposing the policies of FRANÇOIS GUIZOT. Exiled to Great Britain (1848), then to the United States, he returned to France in 1870 and served in the FRANCO-PRUSSIAN WAR. Elected to the National Academy in 1871, de Joinville was reinstated to his previous rank of vice admiral in 1872.

## Jolas, Betsy (1926– )
*composer*

Born in Paris, where she studied with DARIUS MILHAUD and OLIVIER MESSIAEN, Betsy Jolas, who also studied in the United States, admired the polyphonists of the 16th century. She puts in her own work a great emphasis on vocalism (*L'Œil égaré*, a cantata after VICTOR HUGO, 1961; *Sonate à 12*, for 12 soloist voices, 1970), as well as music writing and instrumental forms. Jolas was named to the Academy of Fine Arts in 1985 and was awarded the LEGION OF HONOR in 1997.

## Joliet (or Jolliet), Louis (1645–1700)
*explorer*

Born in Quebec, where he studied with the Jesuits, Louis Joliet took minor orders then went to Paris to study cosmography. Upon returning to CANADA (1668), he engaged in trade and exploring the area of the Great Lakes, of which he took possession in the name of the king of France. With JACQUES MARQUETTE, he explored the course of the Wisconsin, the Mississippi (Colbert), and the Illinois Rivers (1672). After having obtained the lordship of Anticosti and being named hydrographer to the king (1688), he also explored the region of Labrador (1694), then taught hydrography at Quebec.

## Joliot-Curie, Frédéric (1900–1951)
*physicist, Nobel laureate*

Born in Paris, where he attended the École normale supérieure de physique et de chimie industrielle, Frédéric Joliet upon graduation took a research position at the Radium Institute at the University of Paris, where he met Irene Curie, the daughter of MARIE and PIERRE CURIE. They married in 1926 and both adopted the surname Joliot-Curie. Frédéric Joliot-Curie is widely credited with bringing France into the atomic age through his research and discovery of artificially induced radioactivity, and later by his appointment as director of the French Atomic Energy Commission. The work of the Joliot-Curies led to the development of nuclear fission, nuclear energy, and atomic power. Their further research eventually led to the discovery of the first artificial isotope, then to artificial radioactivity (see IRENE JOLIOT-CURIE). Frédéric Joliot-Curie's scientific work was always accompanied by social and political activism. A member of various groups and associations dedicated to the pursuit of peace and democracy, he encouraged France, at the beginning of the WORLD WAR II, to purchase the world supply of heavy water (necessary for the production of atomic energy) from Norway and had it transferred to Britain. He was a staunch supporter of the RESISTANCE and a member of the French Communist Party. The first commissioner of the Atomic Energy Commission, he directed the construction of "Zoe," the first major French nuclear research center (1945). Relieved of his post in 1950 because of his political views, he dedicated himself to teaching, research, and serving as president of the World Peace Council. He received the Nobel Prize in chemistry with his wife in 1935 and was named to the Academy of Sciences in 1943.

## Joliot-Curie, Irene (1897–1956)
*physicist, Nobel laureate*

Born in Paris, the daughter of MARIE and PIERRE CURIE, Irene Joliot-Curie did much of her research in collaboration with her husband, FRÉDÉRIC JOLIOT-CURIE. In 1925, she received a doctorate from the University of Paris for her work on alpha particles and continued assisting her mother at the Radium Institute, where she met Frédéric Joliot, whom she married in 1926. They subsequently worked together and both assumed the surname of Joliot-Curie. Specializing in nuclear physics and inspired by the research of the German physicist Walter Bothe, they made the significant discovery that radioactive elements can be artificially prepared from stable elements (1933). In separate experiments, they bombarded aluminum foil and boron with alpha particles, temporarily changing the aluminum into radioactive phosphorus and producing a radioactive form of nitrogen from the boron. This was the first time artificial radioactivity had been created. In 1936, Irene Joliot-Curie became a professor at the University of Paris and also undersecretary of state for scientific research. She was a member of the French Atomic Energy Commission (CEA) from 1946 to 1951, and helped to develop the first French atomic reserve. After 1947, she served as the director of the Institute of Radium. With her husband, she received the Nobel Prize in chemistry in 1935 and became an officer in the LEGION OF HONOR in 1939. She also received many other honors for her contributions to nuclear science. She died in 1956 from leukemia, which she contracted in the course of her work.

## Jolivet, André (1905–1974)
*composer, orchestra leader*

Born in Paris, André Jolivet was the student of EDGAR VARÈSE and was a founding member of Jeune France (1936). Under the influence of dodecaphony, he sought to bring music to its basic and magical origins, through a series of varied works (*Mana,* for piano, 1935; *Cinq Incantations* for flute, 1938; *Cosmogonie,* for orchestra, 1938; *Cinq Danses rituelles,* 1939). He evolved progressively to a modal style with lyrical works (*Trois Complaintes du soldat,* 1940; *Poèmes intimes,* 1944), and then developed a final stage that synthesized all these elements: the

ballet *Guignol et Pandore* (1943), *La Sonate pour piano* (1945), a *Concerto pour ondes Martenot* (1947). In all, Jolivet sought to present, as he stated, the "magical expression and incantations of the religiosity of human groups."

## Jordan, Camille (1771–1821)
*political figure*

Born in Paris, Camille Jordan, a constitutional royalist during the REVOLUTION OF 1789, immigrated to Switzerland after taking part in the royalist insurrection at LYON (1793). Returning to France in 1796, he was a member of the Council of Five Hundred but was proscribed after the coup d'état of 18 Fructidor Year V (September 14, 1797) as a member of the Clichy Club. Jordan served as a deputy during the Restoration (1816).

## Joseph, le Père (1577–1638)
*cleric, political figure*

Born François Joseph Le Clerc du Tremblay in Paris, le Père Joseph as he is known, was the son of a president of parlement and an aristocrat, Marie de La Fayette. He entered the Capuchin Order after a brilliant career in the army and at court (1599), and preaching missions, dedicated himself to the conversion of Protestants. In 1624, he became the close collaborator of Cardinal RICHELIEU (hence his sobriquet, and the term, "Éminence grise"). Le Père Joseph was concerned above all with foreign policy and had a determining influence in France's struggle with the Habsburgs.

## Joséphine (1763–1814)
### (Marie-Josèphe-Rose Tascher de la Pagerie, Joséphine de Beauharnais)
*empress of the French*

Born Marie-Josèphe-Rose Tascher de la Pagerie in Trois-Îlets, Martinique, Joséphine, as she is known, in 1779 married the French army officer Viscount ALEXANDRE DE BEAUHARNAIS. He was sympathetic to the REVOLUTION OF 1789, but in 1793 he was forced to resign as general of the Army of the Rhine because he was a nobleman. He later died in the TERROR, leaving Joséphine with their two children, HORTENSE (later queen of Holland) and EUGÈNE DE

Empress Joséphine *(Library of Congress)*

1965, entered the Foreign Ministry. A member of the Socialist Party since 1971, Jospin was named the party's first secretary in 1981 by President FRANÇOIS MITTERRAND. From 1988 to 1992, he served as minister of education. In 1995, Jospin ran unsuccessfully against JACQUES CHIRAC for president of the republic. Then, in March 1996, he again assumed leadership of the Socialist Party. After the parliamentary elections of April 1997, in which the Socialists had a huge success, Chirac asked Jospin to form a new government. As prime minister, Jospin (who retired from politics in 2002) pursued policies of economic reform and expansion of the European Union's monetary union.

### Josquin des Prés  (ca. 1440–1521)
*composer*
The most influential and highly regarded composer of the Renaissance, Josquin des Prés (Latin, Josquinas Pratensis) was born in Beaucevoir, PICARDY. Musician for the court of Milan (1459), then the pontifical chapel in Rome (1486), he spent time in France at the court of King LOUIS XII (1501), then again as musician for Ercole I, duke of Ferrara (1503). About 1505, he became provost of the church in Condé-sur-l'Escaut in Burgundy, where he died. Known during his lifetime as the "prince of music," he had a considerable effect on the evolution of church music, his masses serving as models for all composers for most of a century. His 32 masses encompass all the techniques of his era, from the strict, structurally ingenious four-part style of the medieval period to late-Renaissance techniques of close melodic imitation, choral writing, and free variations. In his 80 secular compositions, he applied mostly polyphonic French chansons, or songs, and a range of techniques, from simple chordal to highly imitative style. Among Josquin des Prés's most important works are *Messe Hercules dux Ferrariae; Messe L'Homme armé; Messe Pange lingua;* and *Miserere.*

BEAUHARNAIS (later king of Italy). In 1795, through an introduction by PAUL BARRAS, Joséphine met Napoléon Bonaparte (see NAPOLÉON I), whom she subsequently married on March 9, 1796. Much taken with his wife, Napoléon was strongly under her influence. Joséphine was crowned empress in 1804, but, unable to provide her husband with an heir, she was divorced from him in 1809. She retired to Malmaison, while continuing a correspondence with the emperor. During her life at the Tuileries, Joséphine was a popular figure and, as leader of the imperial court, attracted to it the most brilliant of French society.

### Jospin, Lionel  (1937–  )
*political figure, prime minister*
Born into a Protestant Socialist family in Meudon, near Paris, Lionel Jospin was the son of a teacher and a midwife. In 1961, he entered the Ecole nationale d'administration and, upon finishing in

### Joubert, Barthélemy-Catherine (1769–1799)
*military figure*
Born in Pont-de-Vaux, Bresse, Barthélemy-Catherine Joubert was, during the REVOLUTION OF 1789, a

volunteer for the Ain department, was promoted to brigadier general (1795), then to the rank of division commander (1796). He played a brilliant role with NAPOLÉON I in the Italian campaign. General in chief of the armies of Holland, Mainz, then Italy (October 1798), he occupied Piedmont but was dismissed from his command shortly afterward because of his opposition to the civilian commissioners sent by the DIRECTORY. Resuming his post (summer 1799), he was killed at the beginning of the Battle of Novi (August 15, 1799) where his troops were defeated by the Russian army under the command of General Alexander Suvorov. The ABBÉ SIEYÈS, who had considered using General Joubert to foment a coup d'état against the Directory, had to choose instead NAPOLÉON I.

## Jouhandeau, Marcel (1888–1979)
*writer*

Born in Gueret, Marcel Jouhandeau at first considered studying for the priesthood, but then took a degree in literature and became a professor in Paris. Although he destroyed his early writings in 1914, he soon produced an abundant amount of work, which was organized along three themes: himself, God, and others. One of Jouhandeau's important works as an incisive critic of the marital state is *Chroniques maritales* (1935–38). Other works, written in his ironic style, are *La Jeunesse de Théophile* (1921); *Les Pincengrain* (1924); *Monsieur Godeau intime* (1926); and *Monsieur Godeau marie* (1933). In his 28 *Journaliers, 1961–1982*), he deals frankly with the issue that, for him, there are only two sins that count, impiety and murder. A colorful and unusually candid person, Jouhandeau is considered one of the most gifted and versatile of modern writers.

## Jouhaux, Léon (1879–1954)
*labor leader, Nobel laureate*

Born in Paris, Léon Jouhaux left school at age 12 to work in a government match factory. He soon became active in the labor movement and, in 1909, became secretary-general of the CONFÉDÉRATION GÉNÉRALE DU TRAVAIL (CGT). He worked on the labor union journal *La Bataille syndicaliste* and, at the beginning of WORLD WAR I, rallied to the Union sacrée, moderating his radical views and later taking a position against the Russian Revolution (1917). After the war, Jouhaux espoused the cause of state socialism and was instrumental in forming the International Labor Organization (Fédération syndicale mondiale). Before the beginning of WORLD WAR II, he brought the CGT into the center-left coalition government of the Popular Front. The CGT was abandoned, however, when the Germans occupied France in 1940. Jouhaux was put under house arrest by the VICHY regime and was later deported to Germany (1943). After the war, he became secretary-general of the reestablished CGT and also served as vice president of the Fédération syndicale mondiale (1945–48) and as president of the Economic Council. In 1948, he left the CGT and became one of the founders of the reorganized CONFÉDÉRATION GÉNÉRALE DU TRAVAIL–FORCE OUVRIÈRE (CGT-FO), for which he served also as president. In 1951, Jouhaux was awarded the Nobel Peace Prize.

## Jourdan, Jean-Baptiste, count (1762–1833)
*marshal of France*

Born in Limoges, Jean-Baptiste, count Jourdan at age 16 fought in the American War of Independence. A supporter of the REVOLUTION OF 1789, lieutenant colonel of volunteers in October 1791, general in 1793, he distinguished himself at Hondschoote (September 1793) and, at the head of the Armies of the North, was the victor at Wattignies (October 16, 1793) with General LAZARE CARNOT. Relieved of his command in January 1794 for having refused to conduct a winter campaign, he was recalled in March 1794 and won the battle of Fleurus (June 26, 1794), which opened Belgium to the French. Defeated several times later, however, in 1795 and 1796, he was replaced by General LAZARE HOCHE. A member of the Council of Five Hundred (1797), he was the author of the Jourdan Law on conscription (1798). Opposed to the coup d'état of 18 Brumaire (November 9, 1799), he was left by NAPOLÉON I without important posts. Appointed ambassador to the Cisalpine Republic and made marshal (1804), he served as governor of Naples and as military adviser to JOSEPH BONAPARTE (1808). He was defeated by General Arthur Wellesley, duke of Wellington at Vittoria (June 21, 1813), and later went over to the Bourbons and LOUIS XVIII, who made him a count (1816) and a peer of France (1819). After 1830, he served as governor of the Invalides. Marshal Jourdan left his *Mémoires militaires de la guerre d'Espagne*.

## Jouve, Pierre-Jean  (1887–1976)
*poet and novelist*

Born in Arras, Pierre-Jean Jouve was inspired by the tragic aspects of the human condition and was strongly influenced by psychoanalysis and Christian mysticism. His works often have an apocalyptic vision (*Inconscient, spiritualité et catastrophe*, 1933) and a sensuality coupled with sin. In his poems (*Sueur de sang*, 1933–35; *Gloire* 1942; *La Vierge de Paris*, 1944–46) there is also a sense of the tortured and the tragic. His collections (*Diadème*, 1949; *Langue*, 1952; *Mélodrame*, 1957; *Moires*, 1962, *Ténèbre*, 1965) are marked by Taoist philosophy. The prolific Jouve's other works include *Paulina 1880* (1925); *Le Monde désert* (1927); a double work, *Aventure de Catherine Crachat* (*Hécate*, 1928, *Vagadu*, 1931) and *La Scène capitale* (1935), which offers a familiar theme of the union of eros and death. Jouve is also the author of several essays on music (*Le Don Juan de Mozart*, 1942; *Wozzeck ou le Nouvel Opéra*, 1953) and art (*Tombeau de Baudelaire*, 1942; *Défense et Illustration*, 1943).

## Jouvet, Louis  (1887–1951)
*theater figure*

A major figure of 20th-century French theater, Louis Jouvet, who was born in Crozon, made his debut at the Vieux-Colombier acting troop, which he founded with JACQUES COPEAU. He became director of the Comédie des Champs-Élysées en 1924. His first great success was *Knock* (1923), then *Donogoo* (1930). Rejecting the commercialization that he saw in the theater, he was inspired to form the Cartel des Quatres with other actors (1926), and the production of JEAN GIRAUDOUX's *Siegfried* (1928) proved to be a turning point in his theatrical career. This was followed by 11 years of fruitful collabora-

tion with that writer, and from *Amphitryon 38* (1929) to *Ondine* (1939), Jouvet directed some of the great dramatic works of the era. Joining the Athénée in 1934, he there had some of his greatest successes, including *L'École des femmes* of JEAN-BAPTISTE MOLIÈRE (1936). Beginning with the production of one of Giraudoux's posthumous works, *La Folle de Chaillot* (1945), Jouvet returned to France after the war with two daring production of Molière: *Dom Juan* (1947) and *Tartuffe* (1950). Professor at the Paris Conservatoire, lecturer, and essayist, Jouvet also had a wonderful career in films: *Topaze* (1933); *Les Bas-Fonds* (1937); *Drôle de drame* (1937); *Hôtel de Nord* (1938); *Entrée des artistes* (1938); *Volpone* (1939); *Quai des Orfèvres* (1947).

## Joyeuse family
*family of military, political figures*

Anne, duke de Joyeuse (1561–87), admiral of France, was born in Joyeuse, Vivarais. He was a favorite of King HENRY III, who covered him with honors. He was sent to fight the Calvinists in Guyenne and was killed at the Battle of Coutras. François de Joyeuse (1562–1615) cardinal and brother of Anne, duke de Joyeuse, negotiated the reconciliation of HENRY IV with the Holy See and crowned MARIE DE' MEDICI and LOUIS XIII. He served as president of the Estates General (1614). Henri, duke de Joyeuse (1567–1608), brother of Anne, duke de Joyeuse and Cardinal François de Joyeuse, was born in Paris. He became a Capuchin monk upon the death of his wife, Catherine de La Valette, then returning to the secular world, led the armies of the HOLY LEAGUE in the LANGUEDOC, where HENRY IV, to whom he had belatedly made his submission, named him governor and at the same time marshal of France. Henri, duke de Joyeuse returned to the Capuchin order in 1599.

## Juin, Alphonse  (1888–1967)
*marshal of France*

Commander of the French military forces during World War II, Alphonse Juin was born in Bône (now Annaba), ALGERIA. He graduated with honors from SAINT-CYR in 1911 and served in Morocco (1912–17). He was wounded in World War I.

Named to the military cabinet of LOUIS LYAUTEY, he took part in the campaign in Rif in 1924 and helped in the "pacification" of Morocco. Professor of general strategy at the École supérieure de guerre, then head of the general staff of General CHARLES NOGUÈS, commander in chief of the theater of operations in North Africa (1936–39), General Juin (1940) took command of the 15th motorized division that soon distinguished itself at Lille. Taken prisoner by the Germans, he was released in June 1941 and succeeded General MAXIME WEYGAND as leader of the French forces in North Africa (November 1941). After the Allied landing there (November 8, 1942), he commanded the French army detachment that stopped the Axis forces in Tunisia and contributed to the defeat of the Afrika Korps. Promoted to commander in chief of the French Expeditionary Forces in Italy (1943), he successfully intervened in the attempt to make an eastern assault at Cassino (victory of Belvédère, February 1944) and impressed on the Allies his plan for the spring offensive, marked by the victory at Garigliano, which opened the road to Rome (June 5, 1944) and then that of Siena (July 1944). Head of the General Staff for National Defense, then governor-general of Morocco (1947–51), General Juin later served as inspector general of the armed forces (1951–55) and inter-allied commander of the central European Area (1951–56). Raised to the rank of marshal of France in 1952, he opposed the policies of General CHARLES DE GAULLE in Algeria. Marshal Juin was elected to the ACADÉMIE FRANÇAISE in 1952, and his *Mémoires* were published in 1959–60.

## July Monarchy
### (monarchie de juillet)

*July Monarchy* is the name given to the government of King LOUIS-PHILIPPE (r. 1830–48) who came to power after the REVOLUTION OF JULY 1830 (see also CHARLES X). The new regime was truly parliamentary, with the powerful commercial bourgeoisie replacing the nobility as the determinate class. The July Monarchy was nonetheless marked by political agitation: Legitimist, Bonapartist, republican, and socialist. The economic and financial crisis of 1846–47 led to a political one (the Banquets

of 1847–48) and finally to the REVOLUTION OF 1848 that provoked the fall of Louis-Philippe and the proclamation of the SECOND REPUBLIC by the provisional government. The July Monarchy also saw an ENTENTE CORDIALE with Great Britain and French expansion overseas (ALGERIA, sub-Saharan AFRICA, the Far East, the Pacific).

## Junot, Andoche, duke of Abrantès (1771–1813)
### *military figure*

Born in Bussy-le-Grand, Burgundy, Andoche Junot was recognized for his military talents at the siege of Toulon (1793) by Napoléon Bonaparte, who made him his aide-de-camp (1794). Junot followed Bonaparte to Egypt and later was made successively a division commander (1801), governor of PARIS (1804), ambassador to Lisbon (1805), and eventually commander of the French Army in Portugal (1807). There, he won a victory at Abrantes and entered Lisbon in November 1807, but was defeated by General Wellington at Vimeiro (August 1808) and was forced to sign the surrender of Sintra (August 30, 1808). He subsequently fought in Spain, took part in the Russian campaign, and was serving as governor of the Illyrian Provinces when he went mad. General Junot then returned to his family in France and committed suicide shortly afterward. His wife, Laure Permon, Mme Junot, duchess of Abrantès has left their *Mémoires* (*Souvenirs historiques sur Napoléon*, 1831–35).

See also NAPOLÉON I.

## Juppé, Alain (1945–   )
### *political figure, prime minister*

Born in Mont-de-Marsan, Alain Juppé attended the Institut d'études politiques and the École nationale d'administration before becoming, in 1976, assistant to Prime Minister JACQUES CHIRAC. Juppé also served as deputy mayor of Paris (1983), as a member of the European Parliament (1984–86), and as minister of foreign affairs (1993–95). When Chirac won the presidency in 1994, he named Juppé as his prime minister. In 1996, Juppé implemented a number of austerity measures, including a salary freeze for public-sector employees. These measures were widely disliked and, as a consequence, Juppé's popularity declined. After the defeat of the conservatives in the 1997 election, the Socialist leader, LIONEL JOSPIN, replaced Juppé as prime minister.

## Jura

A mountain range straddling the border between France and Switzerland, the Jura begins in coastal France on the northern bank of the RHÔNE RIVER in the department of Ain and extends north, forming the western bank of the river until it reaches the Swiss frontier near Geneva. From that point, it extends through the departments of Jura and Doubs, following the boundary between France and Switzerland in a long curve toward the northeast. The range finally passes into Switzerland, terminating on the south bank of the RHINE RIVER, west of its confluence with the Aare. This is the Jura proper, but the name is also applied to the mountains north of the Rhine and south of the Rhône. South of the Rhône, the chain is known as the Jura Alps and merges with branches of the western ALPS. North of the Rhine, an irregular chain extends east of the Black Forest in the German state of Baden-Württemberg, and through Bavaria to the Main River. This chain, known as the German, or Swabian, Jura, is similar to the Jura proper in the character of rock formation, but different in structure, being entirely formed by faulting. The Jura proper consists of a series of parallel folds in the strata, forming a plateau approximately 320 kilometers long and 32 to 56 kilometers wide. These ridges often show transversal fractures, which, as steep gorges or *cluses*, greatly enhance the picturesque nature of the area. The height of the Jura range is from 910 to 1,520 meters, and its greatest height is at the southern end, west of Lac Leman.

## Jurien de la Gravière

*military figures*

Pierre-Roch Jurien de la Gravière (1772–1849), who was born in Gannat, Bourbonnais, served under NAPOLÉON I and won a naval victory over the British at Sables-d'Olonne (1809). He went over to LOUIS XVIII, who made him a viscount. He was named vice admiral in 1831 and a peer of France in 1832, during the July Monarchy. Jean-Edmond Jurien de la Gravière (1812–92), the son of Admiral Pierre-Roch Jurien de la Gravière, was born in Brest and served in the CRIMEAN WAR (1854–1856) and the campaign in Mexico. He was named aide-de-camp to NAPOLÉON III (1864), then a squadron commander in the Mediterranean (1870). Director of naval maps and plans in 1871, he left numerous works on the history of the French navy (*Guerres maritimes sous la République et l'Empire*, 1864). Admiral Jean-Edmond Jurien de la Gravière was named to the Academy of Sciences in 1806 and to the ACADÉMIE FRANÇAISE in 1888.

## Jurieu, Pierre  (1637–1713)

*cleric, Protestant leader*

Born in Mer, near Blois, Pierre Jurieu, a Calvinist pastor, was professor at the Protestant Academy in Sedan (1674) and then, upon its closing (1681), at Rotterdam, the Netherlands. He carried on the polemic debate against LE GRAND ARNAULD (*Apologie pour la morale des réformés*; 1675), against JACQUES-BÉNIGNE BOSSUET (*Preservatif contre le changement de religion*; 1680), and against Louis Maimbourg. Jurieu serve as adviser to William of Orange, and as an agent for England. After the revocation of the Edict of Nantes, he was the soul of the Calvinist resistance to King LOUIS XIV (*Lettres pastorales aux fidèles de France qui gémissent sous la captivité de Babylone*; 1686–89).

## Jussieu family

*family of botanists, physicians*

Antoine de Jussieu (1686–1758) was born in LYON and was a physician and professor at the King's Garden (today National Museum of Natural History). He is the author of *Traité des virtues des plantes* and was made a member of the Academy of Sciences in 1715. Bernard de Jussieu (1699–1777), brother of Antoine, was born in Lyon and was a director at the King's Garden. In 1734, he imported two cedars of Lebanon from England, one of which has always stood at the Botanical Gardens in Paris. He was made a member of the Academy of Sciences in 1739. Joseph de Jussieu (1704–79), the brother of Bernard and Antoine, was born in Lyon. A botanist and traveler, he visited South America, accompanying CHARLES DE LA CONDAMINE, and introduced numerous varieties of ornamental plants to Europe. Antoine-Laurent de Jussieu (1748–1836), born in Lyon, was the nephew of Antoine, Bernard, and Joseph. He produced a study that serves as the basis for the natural method of the classification of plants (*Genera plantarum secundum ordines naturales disposita*, 1788) and was named to the Academy of Sciences in 1795. Adrien de Jussieu (1797–1853) was born in Paris, the son of Antoine-Laurent. He was a botanist famous for his work entitled *Embroyons monocotyledonés*. He was named to the Academy of Sciences in 1831.

## Juste family

*family of sculptors descended from the Florentine Giusto Betti*

Antoine Juste (1479–1519) was born in Corbignano, Tuscany, and settled in France in 1504. Among others, he produced the dozen alabaster statues of the apostles for the chapel of Cardinal d'Amboise in the château of Guillon (1508–09) and the bas-reliefs on the mausoleum of LOUIS XII and ANNE OF BRITTANY to be placed in the basilica of Saint-Denis. Jean Juste, or Jean I Juste (1485–1549), born in San Martino, was the brother of Antoine Juste, with whom he collaborated on the mausoleum of Louis XII, sculpting the kneeling royal figures with a somber and quiet composition, and the other dramatic figures with an uncompromising realism. By its arrangement and the character of its decoration, this mausoleum was the first monumental tomb of the French Renaissance. Juste de Juste (1505–59), born in Tours, was the son of Antoine Juste and nephew of Jean I Juste, with whom he collaborated and produced the statues of *Vertus* and *Apôtres* for the mausoleum of Louis XII. Named in 1529 sculptor to King FRANCIS I, he participated in the decoration of the Grande Gallerie in the château of Fontainebleau. Jean Juste, or Jean II Juste (1510–79), born in Tours, was the son of Jean I Juste, with whom he collaborated on many works. He also carved several tombs, notably that of Guy d'Espinay. The Juste family contributed to the monumental concepts of the Italian Renaissance.

# K

## Kastler, Alfred (1902–1984)
*physicist, Nobel laureate*

Alfred Kastler, who was born in Guebwiller, ALSACE, developed methods that used light to manipulate and study the energy level of electrons. He studied at the École normale supérieure in Paris, where he later also taught, as well as at Clermont-Ferrand and Bordeaux. From 1968 to 1972, he served as director of the national Center for Scientific Research. Kastler discovered and developed the methods of double resonance and optional pumping in his study of light and action. Both these methods were great improvements over earlier methods and allowed much more detailed studies of atomic structure. Optical pumping, in particular, was later applied to lasers, the magnetometer, and improvements of the atomic clock. For his work, Kastler was awarded the 1966 Nobel Prize in physics.

## Kellermann, François-Christophe, duke de Valmy (1735–1820)
*marshal of France*

Born in Strasbourg, François-Christophe Kellermann, who was an officer during the ancien régime, joined the REVOLUTION OF 1789 and was named lieutenant general in 1792. On September 20 of that year, he won the Battle of Valmy under the command of General CHARLES DUMOURIEZ. General Kellermann suppressed the insurrection of LYON in August 1793, and was later himself arrested as a suspect (November 1793), before being freed in July 1794. He commanded the Army of the Alps (1795–97) and was made a marshal in 1804, and a senator and duke de Valmy in 1808. Marshal Kellermann went over to the Bourbons in 1814 and sat as a member of the Chamber of Peers.

## Kellermann, François-Étienne (1770–1835)
*military figure*

Born in Metz, François-Étienne Kellermann was the son of Marshal FRANÇOIS-CHRISTOPHE KELLERMANN, duke de Valmy. He was one of the best cavalry officers under the command of NAPOLÉON I and distinguished himself at the Battle of Marengo in Italy. In 1803, he signed the surrender at Sintra, Portugal, with General ANDOCHE JUNOT. Kellermann was wounded at the battle of Waterloo (1815).

## Kellogg-Briand Pact

Also called the Pact of Paris and, more formally, the Treaty for the Renunciation of War, the Kellogg-Briand Pact was a multilateral treaty signed by 15 nations in Paris on August 27, 1928, and later almost universally ratified. It was sponsored and drafted by French foreign minister ARISTIDE BRIAND and U.S. secretary of state F. B. Kellogg. The pact had its origins in the international peace and disarmament conference held after WORLD WAR I. It was suggested that France and the United States abolish the possibility of mutual war and extend the proposition to other world powers. As a result, the Kellogg-Briand Pact bound its signatories to renounce war as an instrument of national policy and pledge to settle international disputes by peaceful means.

## Kessel, Joseph (1898–1979)
*writer, journalist*

Born in Clara, Argentina, to a family of Russian-Jewish origin, Joseph Kessel, who became involved with aviation in World War I (1916), used the fraternal military and combat milieu as a central theme in his novels and in a biography. This action-novel literature was also often the material of his reporting. His curiosity was for a world that he knew how to evoke in a realistic and lively fashion: *Fortune carrée* (1955) recalls Yemen; *Le Lion* (1958) takes place in Kenya. Skillful at portraying historical scenes (*Tous n'étaient pas des anges,* 1963, on World War II; *Terre d'amour et de feu,* 1966, on the Israeli experience), Kessel also reveals a sense of individuality (*Belle de jour,* 1929) or that of a community (*Les Cavaliers,* 1967; *Vladivostok, les temps sauvages,* 1975). He was elected to the ACADÉMIE FRANÇAISE in 1962.

## Killy, Jean-Claude (1943–  )
*skier*

Born in Saint-Cloud, Jean-Claude Killy won three titles (downhill, special slalom, and grand slalom) at the 1968 Olympic Games in Grenoble, duplicating the record of Tony Sailor in 1956. Killy served as president, in 1991 and 1992, of the organizing committee for the Winter Olympic Games in Albertville, Savoy, France.

## Kléber, Jean-Baptiste (1753–1800)
*military figure*

A commander who played prominent roles in the War of the First Coalition (1793–97) and in the Egyptian campaign (1798–1800), Jean-Baptiste Kléber was born in STRASBOURG and studied at the military school in Munich, Germany (1776–82), then pursued an architectural career in France. During the REVOLUTION OF 1789, as a French officer in charge of a battalion of Alsatian volunteers, he distinguished himself at Mainz (1792) and was consequently made a general. The next year, he suppressed an uprising in the Vendée, but was recalled after complaints that he showed excessive leniency toward the insurgents. In 1794, he served in campaigns in Belgium and on the Rhine under Marshal JEAN-BAPTISTE JOURDAN, winning the Battle of Fleurus and taking Maastricht. But following a difference of opinion with Jourdan, Kléber resigned and began work on his memoirs (1796). In 1798, however, he was given command of a division as part of the expedition to Egypt undertaken by Napoléon Bonaparte (NAPOLEON I). There,

Kléber was wounded during the capture of Alexandria. He was made governor of that city and the next year won a brilliant victory at Mt. Tabor over the Turks in Syria. After Napoléon's return to France in 1799, General Kléber was left in command of the French Army in Egypt. He defeated Turkish forces at Heliopolis and retook Cairo, where an insurrection against the French had occurred. It was shortly afterward that he was assassinated there.

## Klein, Yves (1928–1962)
*painter*

Yves Klein, who was a leading member of the neo-dadist movement and, with others, founded Nouveau Réalisme, was born in Nice. At the beginning of his career he tried to impose an absolutist vision of color, creating monochromatic surfaces (1946) that excluded all other colors except blue. In this mode, he decorated large panels outside of France (the Opera at Gelsenkirchen, Germany) and did bas-reliefs in the same shade, using overlaid sponge (*Relief-éponge bleue,* 1957). This was followed by controversial exhibits in Paris (where he mostly worked), including female nudes in blue tones (*Anthropométries,* 1958–60). These were produced with "living brushes," as he called them, models covered in paint making imprints on canvas. In other works, he used the natural elements, wind and rain, to produce effects (*Cosmogonies,* 1960) with himself photographed jumping from a window, and burning cardboard, his *Peintures de feu.* A theorist, Klein tried to integrate a universal symbolism into art as well as humanity into the cosmos (*Dépassement de la problématique de l'art,* 1959).

## Klobb, Jean-François-Arsène (1857–1899)
*military officer*

Born in Ribeauville, Colonel Jean-François-Arsène Klobb was sent by the French government to the Sudan (1891–92), where he helped to unite the Meharist groups. He was ordered to remove the officers and explorers CHARLES CHANOINE and PAUL VOULET from their command because of their violent mistreatment of the indigenous people and replace them at their post, but instead he was assassinated by the two. They, in turn, were later killed by their own soldiers.

See also AFRICA, FRENCH IN.

## Klossowski, Pierre (1905–2001)
*writer, artist*
Born in Paris, Pierre Klossowski was the brother of the painter BALTHUS. A talented translator (particularly of Suetonius and Virgil, but also of Hölderlin in collaboration with PIERRE-JEAN JOUVE), he was an essayist too (*Sade mon prochain*, 1974; *Nietzsche et le cercle vicieux*, 1969). Klossowski composed romantic novels describing malaise and anguish (*La Vocation suspendu*, 1950) and a hermetic novel in which the struggle between two opposing currents of the Catholic faith masks an autobiographical work. The sexual adventures of Roberte, Octave her husband, and her nephew Antoine, published in the trilogy *Les Lois de l'hopitalité* (*La Révocation de l'édit de Nantes*, 1959; *Roberte ce soir*, 1953; *Le Souffleur*, 1960) present visions in which the real and the imaginary are combined. In his work, Klossowski tried to overcome forbidden barriers and taboos. After *Le Bain de Diane* (1956), an erotic variation on the myth of Acteon, and *Le Bapomet* (1956), a complex work marked by the perverse, he turned to newer themes, combining the erotic with the mystical.

## Koechlin, Charles (1867–1950)
*composer*
Born in Paris, Charles Koechlin studied at the École polytechnique, then at the Paris Conservatoire (1889), where his teachers were JULES MASSENET and GABRIEL FAURÉ. A complex polyphonist, always in classical form, Koechlin composed symphonic music that includes *La Nuit de Walpurgis classique* (1907), and *Le Livre de la jungle* (1939). He also wrote chamber music (sonatines, quartets for strings, sonatas), numerous melodies (*Rondels, Shéhérazade*), works for chorus and orchestra, and choreographic poems. An eminent pedagogue, Koechlin taught also in the United States (1918–28), was adviser to the Les Six, and counted among his students FRANCIS POULENC and Henri Sauguet.

## Kœnig, Marie-Pierre (1898–1970)
*military figure*
Born in Caen, Marie-Pierre Kœnig was a volunteer in World War I (1917) and, after that conflict, attended the military academy at Saint-Maixent. A captain in 1939, he was part of the French expeditionary corps to Norway in World War II, then, returning to Great Britain, joined General CHARLES DE GAULLE. At the head of a brigade of Free French forces, he fought against Italian, then German, troops at the Battle of Bir-Hakeim in North Africa. Named commander of French Forces of the Interior (1944), then military governor of Paris after the Liberation (August 1944), he later commanded the French zone of occupation in Germany (1945–49). He served as vice president of the High War Council (1950) before entering political life, serving as minister of national defense (1954–55). General Kœnig was granted the title of marshal of France, posthumously, in 1984.

## Kowarski, Lew (1907–1979)
*physicist*
Of Russian origin, Lew Kowarski was born in Saint Petersburg. The author of research on chain reactions, he discovered, with FRÉDÉRIC JOLIOT-CURIE and HANS HALBAN, the emission of neutrons during the fission of uranium. In June 1940, with Halban, he brought to England the world supply of heavy water (necessary for the production of an atomic bomb), after removing it from German Nazis. He took part in the construction of the first (1948) and the second (1952) French atomic pile, as well as the creation of CERN (Conseil européen pour la recherche nucléaire; the European laboratory for the study of nuclear particles established in 1952 at Meyrin, on the French-Swiss border near Geneva). Kowarski is also known for his studies in physical crystallography.

## Koyré, Alexandre (1902–1964)
*philosopher*
Of Russian origin, Alexandre Koyré was born in Taganrog. He studied in Germany with Edmund Husserl and David Hilbert, then in Paris with HENRI BERGSON and LÉON BRUNSCHVICG, but his own stud-

ies on the philosophy of science that he pursued at the École polytechnique des hautes études are profoundly original. He sought to reconstruct the intellectual context that allowed the emergence of new concepts and new scientific doctrines. His best-known work, *Du monde clos à l'univers infini* (1957), analyzes the substitution in modern scientific thought of a limitless universe for a hierarchical and infinite cosmos, and forges a new conception of reason. Koyré's works are close to those of GAS-TON BACHELARD, GEORGES CANGUILHEM, and MICHEL FOUCAULT (*Études galiléennes*, 1940; *Études newtoniennes*, 1964).

## Kundera, Milan (1929–   )
*writer*

Of Czech origin, Milan Kundera was born in Brno. He published poems (*L'Homme, vaste jardin,* and *Monologues,* 1957) then an essay on Roman art dedicated to Czech novelist Vladislav Vancura (1960), a play (*Le Propriétaire des clefs,* 1962), and a lively adaptation of *Jacques le Fataliste* (*Jacques et son maître*). His short stories and his first novel, *La Plaisanterie* (1967), denounced the corruption in his home country and had a wide audience. It was followed by another novel, *La Vie est ailleurs* (1973). Living in France since 1975, Kundera published *La Valse aux adieux* (1976), *Le Livre du rire et de l'oubli* (1979), *L'Insoutenable Légèreté de l'être* (1984), *L'Immortalité* (1990), and an essay, *L'Art du roman* (1986). These works established him as one of the most appreciated representatives of central European literature in the West.

# L

## Labadie, Jean de (1610–1674)
*mystic and reformer*

Born in Bourg, Guyenne, Jean de Labadie, a Jesuit, then an Oratorian priest, was drawn for some time to JANSENISM before converting to Calvinism at Montauban in 1650. As pastor at Middelbourg, the Netherlands (1666), he wanted to return Protestantism to the forms of early Christianity, but he was deposed by the General Synod of the Netherlands because of his mystical tendencies. Nonetheless, his ideas (Labadism) survived until 1732.

## La Barre, Jean-François Lefebvre, chevalier de (1747–1766)
*aristocrat*

Born in Abbeville, Jean-François Lefebvre, chevalier de La Barre, was accused of not uncovering his head when a Catholic religious procession passed by and of mutilating a crucifix. He was condemned by a tribunal to be tortured and then killed. The Parlement of Paris, to which he had appealed, upheld the sentence, which VOLTAIRE sought in vain to have reversed. La Barre was rehabilitated during the REVOLUTION OF 1789, by the Convention. The 19th century saw in him a victim of the all-powerful despotism of the church.

## Labé, Louise (ca. 1524–1566)
*poet*

Born in LYON, Louise Labé, a writer of the French Renaissance, was part of the Lyonnais school of poetry. Named "la Belle Cordière" (she was the daughter and the wife of rope makers), she led a spirited and full life, presiding over a literary salon and composing three *Élégies* and 24 *Sonnets* (1555). In her writings, Labé combines a confident technique with a sincere expression for the love of life

and the sadness of love ("I live, I die, I burn myself, and I drown"). Labé also wrote, in prose, *Débat de Folie et d'Amour* (1555).

## La Bédoyère, Charles-Angélique-François Huchet, count de (1786–1815)
*military figure*

Born in Paris, Charles-Angélique-François Huchet, count de Bédoyère, in 1808, served as aide-de-camp to Marshal JEAN LANNES and, during the HUNDRED DAYS, rallied to NAPOLÉON I. General La Bédoyère was then arrested, tried, and executed after the return of LOUIS XVIII.

## La Boétie, Étienne de (1530–1563)
*writer*

Born in Sarlat, Étienne de la Boétie, who was remarkably precocious, in 1549 edited the *Contr'un*, also called *Discours de la servitude volontaire* (published 1576), a theoretical writing that denounced tyranny. A true "marriage of souls" united him to MICHEL EYQEUM DE MONTAIGNE, whom he met in 1557. The latter considered La Boétie as his teacher. The centerpiece of his first book of essays (*Essais*) contains, among moving pages on friendship, 29 sonnets that Montaigne is said to have still wept over 30 years later.

## La Bruyère, Jean de (1645–1696)
*moralist*

Born in Paris and educated principally at the University of Orléans, Jean de La Bruyère, an attorney, through the influence of JACQUES-BÉNIGNE BOSSUET was appointed tutor then secretary to the duke of Bourbon of the house of CONDÉ. La Bruyère is famous for a particular work, *Les caractères de*

*Théophraste, traduite du grec, avec les caractères ou les moeurs de ce siècle* (1688). It is a translation of the ancient Greek philosopher Theophrastus, combined with maxims, critical comments on French society, and La Bruyère's sharp, incisive, and often satirical literary portraits of eminent contemporaries. Written in a concise, pointed style, this work had immediate popularity, with nine editions published between 1688 and 1696. The book, however, also brought La Bruyère the enmity of those he had ridiculed and, consequently, many of them caused the delay of his election to the ACADÉMIE FRANÇAISE until 1693.

## La Caille, Nicolas-Louis de (1713–1762)
*astronomer, cleric*

Born in Rumigny, Abbé Nicolas Louis de La Caille, after working on geodesics and acoustics, contributed to the verification of the meridian. He took part in an expedition to the Cape of Good Hope (1750–54) during the course of which he made an inventory of the southern (austral) sky, revealing 10,000 stars up to the seventh magnitude. The comparison of his measurements with those of JOSEPH LALANDE in Berlin allowed the establishing of the first determination of the lunar parallax. La Caille assembled a catalog of the precise position of 400 of the brightest stars (1757). He was named to the Academy of Sciences in 1741.

## Lacan, Jacques (1901–1981)
*psychiatrist, psychoanalyst*

Born in Paris, Jacques Lacan came to psychoanalysis after his thesis, *Psychose paronoïaque dans ses rapports avec la personalité* (1932) opened new paths to the study of psychosis. His analysis is of the "mirror" state (or phase) that acts as the mediator of the total self-image in the development of the subject's identity (*Le Stade du miroir comme formateur de la fonction du "je,"* 1936, 1949). For Lacan, it is through the spoken word (method of signification) that the human enters the dialectic of the intersubjective, that is, the area of not just simple needs, but desires. Seeking to bring together psychoanalysis and linguistics, his work recalls the hermetic style of STÉPHANE MALLARMÉ and is contested by numer-

ous psychoanalysts. Lacan left the Freudian school in 1980. A large number of his writings are found together in his *Écrits* (1966), and his seminar on psychoanalysis has been published.

## La Chaise, François d'Aix de (1624–1709)
### (Francois d'Aix de La Chaize)
*cleric*

Born in the Château d'Aix, Forez, François d'Aix de La Chaise served as provincial of the Jesuit order and was called (1675) by King LOUIS XIV to be his spiritual adviser and confessor. He was opposed to the king's liaison with Mme de MONTESPAN, fought against the Jansenists (see JANSENISM), was a moderate Gallican (see GALLICANISM) in the Investiture issue of who should appoint bishops, and was unable to prevent the revocation of the EDICT OF NANTES. In Paris, the Eastern Cemetery, called Père La Chaise, is situated on the former country property of the Jesuits where Louis had La Chaise establish a retreat.

## La Chalotais, Louis-René de Caradeuc de (1705–1785)
*magistrate*

Born in Rennes, where he served as procurator general of the parlement, Louis René de Caradeuc de La Chalotais was drawn to the ideas of the Enlightenment and became famous for his polemics against the Jesuits (*Comptes rendus des Constitutions jésuites,* 1761–62) and for his *Essai d'éducation nationale,* in which he favored the abandoning of Latin for living languages in instruction. In 1764, he led the opposition of Breton parlement members against the king's representative, the duke of AIGUILLON, and defended the special rights of the province. Imprisoned at Saint-Malo (1765), then exiled to Saintes (1768), Louis de La Chalotais was restored to his post in 1775.

## La Chapelier, Isaac-René-Guy (1754–1794)
*political figure*

Born in Rennes, where he served as an attorney, Isaac-René-Guy La Chapelier was a deputy for the

Third Estate to the ESTATES GENERAL and, when the REVOLUTION OF 1789 began, founded, with JEAN LANJUINAIS, the Breton Club, which soon became the JACOBIN CLUB (1789). La Chapelier helped to put through the reforms voted by the National Constituent Assembly, in particular a proposal passed on June 14, 1791, limiting the rights of association, which constituted one of the fundamental bases of liberal capitalism ("Le Chapelier Law"). La Chapelier left for England in 1792, and was condemned as an émigré upon his return (1794) and executed.

## Laclos, Pierre-Choderlos de (1741–1803)
*writer*

Born in Amiens, Pierre-Choderlos de Laclos, a dedicated officer, played a certain role in the REVOLUTION OF 1789 (he was part of the entourage of PHILIPPE ÉGALITÉ, and helped to plan the Battle of Valmy and to develop new artillery). He wrote works on tactics and strategy, poems, and a treatise, *L'Éducation des femmes* (1783). His claim to distinction rests on his epistolary novel, *Les Liaisons dangereuses* (1782), a scandalous and witty treatise on the corrupt aristocracy, which is praised for its style and psychological insight. Through this work, the influence of Pierre Laclos on the romantic literature of the 19th and 20th centuries remains immense.

## La Condamine, Charles-Marie de (1701–1774)
*geodesist, naturalist*

Born in Paris, Charles-Marie de La Condamine made numerous scientific voyages from which he reported his observations. He took part, with PIERRE BOUGUER, in an expedition to Peru (1735–1744) during which they measured the length of an arc of the meridian to one degree. This voyage was also the occasion for the first description of the tree that he called "guinguina" (1738) and of the discovery of rubber. In 1740, La Condamine observed, independently of the Italian Bianconi, that the speed of the propagation of sound depends on temperature. Working on a project for a universal system of measurement, Charles de La Condamine proposed the selection of the length of a pendulum striking

the second at the equator. He was named to the Academy of Sciences in 1735 and to the ACADÉMIE FRANÇAISE in 1760.

## Lacordaire, Henri (1802–1861)
*cleric*

Henri Lacordaire, a Dominican priest who led the Roman Catholic revival in France following the REVOLUTION OF 1789, was born in Recey-sur-Ource, Côte d'Or. He was ordained a priest in 1827, after practicing law in Paris, and soon joined the small group of intellectuals under the influence of FÉLICITÉ ROBERT DE LAMENNAIS, the philosopher, political writer, and priest who was one of the founders of *L'Avenir*. After that journal's condemnation (1832), however, Lacordaire separated from this group and, submitting to the papal decree, turned his energies to preaching. His sermons at the Collège Stanislaus, and especially at Notre-Dame de Paris (1835–36), were considered literary and social events. He entered the Dominican order in Rome in 1839, and was a major force in the order's reestablishment in France (1848). Lacordaire served as the order's provincial (1850–54 and 1858–61) and also as director of the seminary at Sorèze, Tarn (1854). Elected deputy for MARSEILLE in 1848, Lacordaire worked in support of the Christian democratic movement for which he also served as an editor for the journal *L'Ère nouvelle*. He was elected to the ACADÉMIE FRANÇAISE in 1860.

## Lafargue, Paul (1842–1911)
*socialist writer*

Born in Santiago de Cuba, Paul Lafargue was a medical student when he began to follow socialist doctrines, being initially a disciple of PIERRE-JOSEPH PROUDHON. In London he met Friedrich Engels and Karl Marx, whose daughter Laura he married. A member of the First International, Lafargue participated in the Paris COMMUNE (1871) and, after its defeat, went to Spain and Portugal, then to London, where he met JULES GUESDE. Together, they joined the Parti ouvrier français (French Worker Party) in 1880. A deputy for Lille (1885–94), he opposed socialist participation in a bourgeois government.

The author of two pamphlets, *Le Droit à la paresse* (1880) and *La Religion du capital* (1887), Lafargue helped to spread Marxist ideas (dialectical and historical materialism) in France.

## La Fayette, Marie-Joseph-Paul-Yves-Roch-Gilbert du Motier, marquis de (1757–1834)
*general, statesman*

Born into a noted aristocratic family in Chanvaniac and educated at the Collège Louis-le-Grand in Paris, Marie Joseph Paul Yves Roch Gilbert du Motier, marquis de La Fayette served in the French army from 1771 to 1776, rising to the rank of captain. Sympathizing with the American revolutionary cause, he went to America and offered his services to the U.S. Congress. He was commissioned a major general in the Continental Army (1777) and became a member of General George Washington's staff. He was wounded at the Battle of the Brandywine, became a division commander, and fought also at Monmouth. La Fayette returned to France for six months to promote financial and military aid for the American cause and, in 1780, returned to America to fight in the War of Independence. In 1787, in France, he became member of the Assembly of Notables and, in 1789, a supporter of the REVOLUTION OF 1789 and a member of the National Assembly. La Fayette organized and commanded the National Guard and was a founder of the Feuillants. Seeking the reconciliation of the king with the Revolution, he advocated a constitutional monarchy. In 1791, several months after the fall of the BASTILLE, he was put in charge of the National Guard in Paris, but his popularity declined after he ordered the attack on the demonstrators of the Champ-de-Mars (July 1791). He encouraged the king to declare war, was named commander of the Army of the North, and was later held by the Austrians (1792–97), returning to France in 1799. Disapproving of the policies of NAPOLÉON I, he subsequently played little part in politics until 1815. He then served in the Chamber of Deputies (demanding, with others, the abdication of NAPOLÉON I) and the National Guard and took part in the REVOLUTION OF 1830. A moderate liberal, La Fayette, throughout his life, urged popular representation, social equality, freedom of the press, and religious tolerance.

## La Fayette, Marie-Madeleine-Pioche de la Vergne, countess de (1634–1693)
*writer*

A novelist whose book, *La Princesse de Clèves* (1678), is generally regarded as one of the most influential and the earliest French novels, Mme de La Fayette was born in Paris and, in her youth, studied Latin, Greek, and Italian. In 1659, she opened a salon in Paris and mingled with the best society, maintaining friendships with leading writers and thinkers, especially LA ROCHEFOUCAULD. In her masterpiece, *La Princesse de Clèves*, she writes of a married noblewoman who falls in love with another man. She chooses to keep her love a secret, however, and even after her husband dies (having discovered the secret), she does not remarry. The novel is most notable for the level of psychological complexity revealed in it through the character's minds. This realism sets the work apart from other books of the period. Also, by focusing on emotions and thoughts, rather than on physical actions, Mme de La Fayette as a writer departed from traditional adventure prose. The book is significant, too, for its strict sense of historical detail in depicting 16th-century France. Mme de La Fayette's other works include the novels *La Princesse de Montpensier* (1662) and *Zayde* (1670), and a biography, *Histoire de Madame Henriette d'Angleterre* (posthumous, 1720). She also wrote her memoirs (*Mémoires de la cour de France pour les annees 1688 et 1689*, posthumous, 1731), in which she describes especially the later years of her life, during which she played a certain diplomatic role.

## Laffemas, Barthélemy de (1545–ca. 1612)
*economist*

Born in Beausemblant, Dauphiné, Barthélemy de Laffemas, sieur de Beausemblant, who was an ennobled Protestant, served as first valet to King HENRY IV. He contributed to the development of luxury manufacturing in France and was named comptroller general of trade in 1602. A proponent of mercantilist doctrines in France, Laffemas had in particular edited a work on that economic system, entitled *Règlement pour dresser les manufactures de royaume* (1597). His son, Isaac (1584–1657), a magistrate, was known for his severity during the trials of the nobles who had rebelled against Cardinal RICHELIEU.

## Laffitte, Jacques (1767–1844)
*banker, political figure*

Born in Bayonne, Jacques Laffitte began his career in the employ of the banker JEAN FRÉDÉRIC, COUNT OF PERRÉGUAX (1788) and later became his associate (1800), then his successor (1804). Regent of the Bank of France (1809), he was named its governor by the provisional government (1814). A member of the Chamber of Representatives during the HUNDRED DAYS, he served there as a liberal deputy (1816, 1817). In 1830, he financed the opposition newspaper *Le National,* and his home was one of the principal meeting places for the planned uprising of 1830. A representative of the liberal parti du Mouvement, he was called by King LOUIS-PHILIPPE to be minister without portfolio, then minister of finances, then premier (1830). Laffitte proposed a policy of expediency in domestic affairs and one of boldness in foreign matters, and favored intervention in support of the European revolutions (Italy, Poland), but was thwarted in his plans and was forced to resign in 1831.

## Lafitte, Jean (1792–1854)
*pirate*

Born in Port-au-Prince, Saint-Domingue (later Haiti), Jean Lafitte was a smuggler and a corsair in the service of France against the Spanish (1809–10). He then became a pirate who helped the Americans under General Andrew Jackson to repel the British from their blockade of New Orleans during the War of 1812 (1814).

## La Fontaine, Jean de (1621–1695)
*poet*

Jean de La Fontaine, who produced the most famous fables of modern times, was born in Château-Thierry and was educated at the College of Reims. After a carefree provincial bourgeois youth, he gained access, thanks to his position as supervisor of the forests and streams in his district, to the salons where he read both modern and ancient writers. He took the ancients as his model and, in a style of "original imitation," wrote a heroic poem, *Adonis* (1658), inspired by Ovid. He soon won the support of influential patrons of literature, and he had further success with his *Contes et Nouvelles* (1665), which established his literary reputation. He became a member of a noted literary group that included JEAN-BAPTISTE MOLIÈRE and JEAN RACINE. After 1668, his first book of *Fables* (1668–94) appeared, making him one of the most eminent French men of letters of the period. In 1683, he was elected to the ACADÉMIE FRANÇAISE. La Fontaine's work influenced many later writers. He was inspired by ancient writers, such as Aesop and Phaedrus, and also by Boccaccio. La Fontaine wrote many miscellaneous works too, including poems, opera librettos, and plays; the most famous of these are the romantic tale in prose and verse, *Les Amours de Psyché et de Cupidon* (1669).

## Laforgue, Jules (1860–1887)
*poet*

Born in Montevideo, Uruguay, Jules Laforgue, after what he described as a "sad and malnourished youth" in Tarbes and, later, in Paris, subsisted with difficulty but still frequented the literary milieu of the era. A tutor to Princess Augusta of Prussia (1881–86), he edited in Berlin his *Complaintes* (1885), a work of feigned frivolity and irony. He then published *L'Imitation de Notre-Dame de la Lune* (1886), a collection of poems in which he demonstrates his mastery of free verse. Laforgue recapitulated his sentiments in prose, in his stories *Moralités legendaires* (posthumous, 1887).

See also TOULET, PAUL-JEAN; CARCO, FRANCIS; FARGUE, LÉON-PAUL.

## La Grange, Joseph-Louis, count de (1736–1813)
*mathematician*

Born in Turin, Italy, where he was educated at the university, Joseph-Louis, count de La Grange was appointed professor of geometry at age 19 and later (1758) founded a society that was to become the Turin Academy of Sciences. In 1766, he was appointed director of the Berlin Academy of Sciences and, in 1786, was invited to Paris by King

LOUIS XVI. During the REVOLUTION OF 1789, he was in charge of the commmission for establishing a new system of weights and measures, to be known as the metric system. After the Revolution, La Grange became a professor at the newly established École normale supérieure, then at the École polytechnique and, under NAPOLÉON I, was named to the Senate and made a count. As one of the greatest mathematicians of the 18th century, he created the calculus of variations, worked on a theory of numbers, and systematized the field of differential equations. Among his innovations in astronomy were calculation of the movements of the moon and motions of the planets. His greatest work is *Mécanique analytique* (1788). La Grange was nominated to the Academy of Sciences in 1772.

### Lagrange, Léo (1900–1940)
*political figure*
Born in Bourg-sur-Gironde, Léo Lagrange was a Socialist deputy in the Section française de l'Internationale ouvrière (SFIO) from 1932 to 1940, undersecretary of state for sports and leisure (1936–37, 1938) and was the initiator of numerous reforms for the development of sports and popular tourism. In particular, he created the ski schools and a course of study in popular sports. Legrange died in combat at the beginning of World War II.

### La Harpe, Amadée Emmanuel François de (1754–1796)
*military figure*
Of Swiss origin, Amadée Emmanuel François de La Harpe was born in Château des Uttins, Vaud. A member of the Swiss regiment that was in the service of the Dutch (1773), captain in his own country in 1781, he was condemned to death by the Bernois but escaped before being arrested. Coming to France, where he joined the REVOLUTION OF 1789, he was named commander of the volunteers of Seine-et-Oise (1791). He took part as a lieutenant colonel in the siege of Toulon (1793), and as a general, distinguished himself during the course of the Italian campaign. The Swiss political figure Frédéric César de La Harpe was his cousin.

### Lahautière, Richard (1813–1882)
*publisher, political thinker*
Born in Paris, Auguste Richard de La Hautière, or Richard Lahautière as he is best known, with THÉODORE DEZAMY and ALBERT LAPONNERAYE was part of a Neobabouvist communist group (see FRANÇOIS BABEUF) and contributed to several socialist newspapers. He also published *Le petit Catéchisme de la réforme sociale* (1839).

### La Hire (ca. 1390–1443)
*military figure*
Born in Vignolles, GASCOGNY, Étienne de Vignolles, or La Hire as he is known, was a comrade-in-arms to JOAN OF ARC and took part in the defense of Orléans and the victory of Patay (1429). He was taken prisoner in attempting to rescue Joan of Arc from Rouen (1431), escaped, then won a number of victories in the north of France against the English. La Hire became an important adviser to King CHARLES VII.

### Lainé, Joseph, viscount (1767–1835)
*political figure*
Born in BORDEAUX, Joseph, viscount Lainé, a member of the Legislative Corps in 1808, was a political independent. Having taken a position in favor of peace and freedom in 1813, he was accused by NAPOLÉON I of being in the service of Great Britain. President of the Chamber (1815–16), he tried to oppose the reactionary measures of the Ultras (monarchists) and helped to have the Chamber dissolved in 1816. A member of two cabinets of ARMAND RICHELIEU (1816–18, 1820–21), and a peer (1822–30), he was opposed to the Spanish expedition (1823), in support of the Spanish king. Viscount Lainé was elected to the ACADÉMIE FRANÇAISE in 1816.

### Lalande, Joseph-Jérôme-Lefrançois de (1732–1807)
*astronomer*
Born in Bourg-en-Bresse, Joseph-Jérôme-Lefrançois de Lalande, in 1751, with abbot NICOLAS LA CAILLE at the Cape of Good Hope, and himself in Berlin, measured the lunar parallax, calculating it near to

its actual value. He improved Halley's tables (planet, comets, 1759) and identified the positions of 50,000 stars in his *Histoire céleste francaise*. Lalande was admitted to the Academy of Sciences in 1753.

## Lally, Thomas Arthur, baron de Tollendal, count de  (1702–1766)
*military figure*

Thomas Arthur, baron de Tollendal, count de Lally, who was of Irish origin, was born in Romans. After having distinguished himself in the wars of the Polish and Austrian successions, and having supported the English pretender, Charles Edward Stuart, he was sent to India to lead an important expedition. Authoritarian and badly advised, he alienated the indigenous population as well as his own officers. His defeat at Madras (1758) was followed by his surrender at Pondicherry (1761) after a heroic resistance. He was accused of treason and condemned to death. Some years later, VOLTAIRE began the appeal for his rehabilitation and, in 1778, his son, TROPHIME LALLY-TOLLENDAL, obtained a pardon for him from King LOUIS XVI.

## Lally-Tollendal, Trophime Gérard, marquis de  (1751–1830)
*political figure*

Born in Paris, Trophime Gérard, marquis of Lally-Tollendal, who was the son of THOMAS ARTHUR, baron of TOLLENDAL, and count of LALLY, sought, with VOLTAIRE, to rehabilitate the memory of his father, who had been accused of cowardice and treason while serving in India. A deputy to the ESTATES GENERAL at the beginning of the REVOLUTION OF 1789, Trophime Gérard joined the monarchist faction and in 1790 became an émigré. He returned to France in 1792 and was imprisoned, but shortly after he was released and left for England. Named a peer during the RESTORATION, he sat in the upper chamber as a constitutional royalist. He was elected to the ACADÉMIE FRANÇAISE in 1816.

## Lalo, Édouard  (1823–1892)
*composer*

Édouard Lalo, whose work is noted for the richness and clarity of its orchestration and for its melodic charm, was born in Lille to a family of Spanish descent. He studied at the Lille and Paris Conservatories and, in 1855, playing with equal skill on the viola and the violin, joined the Armingaud-Jacquard Quartet, a group organized in Paris to promote the works of German masters. Lalo's compositions include a Violin Concerto in F major (1874); *Symphonie espagnole* (1873); *Rhapsodie norvégienne* (1881); and *Concerto russe* (1883). His ballet, *Namouna* (1882), and his opera, *Le roi d'Ys* (which shows the influence of Richard Wagner), are considered among his greatest works. Lalo also composed other pieces for orchestras (Symphonie en sol mineur, 1886) concertos, melodies, and chamber music. He is considered a belated romantic and a colorful and outstanding folklorist.

## Laloux, René  (1929–  )
*film producer, animator*

Born in Paris, René Laloux, in collaboration with ROLAND TOPOR, produced in 1973 a long animated film with fantastic coloration, *La Planète sauvage,* which put him in the front ranks of French animators. In the same style, Laloux produced, in studios in Hungary, *Les Maitres du temps* (1982) and the *Gandahar* (1988).

## Lamarck, Jean-Baptiste de Monet, chevalier de  (1744–1829)
*naturalist*

Jean-Baptiste Lamarck, who formulated one of the earliest theories of evolution, was born in Bazentin, PICARDY. In 1768, he began his studies in botany, publishing his first work on that subject, *La flore française,* in 1778. As a result of this book and his friendship with the naturalist GEORGES BUFFON, Lamarck was elected to the Academy of Sciences (1779). He became an associate botanist in 1783, but his most significant work was done when he began a career at the Jardin du Roi in Paris in 1788. When the garden was reorganized in 1793, Lamarck's ideas helped to frame the structure of the new Museum of Natural History, where, in that same year, he was appointed professor of the Chair of Invertebrate Zoology. Although Lamarck's contributions to science include work in botany, geology, paleontology, chemistry, and meteorology, he

Jean Lamarck *(Hulton/Archive)*

is best known for his studies in invertebrate zoology and his theoretical work on evolution. He published an important seven-volume work on that subject, *Histoire naturelle des animaux sans vertèbres* (1815–22). Lamarck's theoretical observations on evolution, known in the early 19th century as transformism or transmutation, preceded his extensive observational work on invertebrates. With his colleagues GEORGES CUVIER and ÉTIENNE GEOFFROY SAINT-HILLAIRE, he accepted the idea of the arrangement of life on a "scala naturae," that is, from simple forms come more complex ones. These ideas were presented in Lamarck's major theoretical work, *Philosophie zoologique* (1809). His views, however, were not seriously considered during his lifetime, and his theory, known also as "Lamarckism," was overshadowed by Cuvier's scientific and political influence. Not until the latter part of the 19th century were Lamarck's ideas again seriously considered. In turn, these would then strongly influence Darwin. Lamarck's other important writings

include *Système des animaux sans vertèbres* (1801) and *Recherche sur l'organisation des espèces* (1802). He was named to the Academy of Sciences in 1779.

## Lamarque, Maximilien, count
### (1770–1832)
*general, political figure*

Born in Paris, Maximilien, count Lamarque, enlisted in the army in 1791 and took part in the wars of the REVOLUTION OF 1789 and of the FIRST EMPIRE, where he distinguished himself on the battlefield. A supporter of NAPOLÉON I during the HUNDRED DAYS, he was ordered to suppress the royalist insurrection in the Vendée. Exiled during the Second RESTORATION (1815), he returned to France in 1818. Elected deputy in 1828, Maximilien, count Lamarque was one of the leaders and principal spokesmen of the republican opposition. His funeral services (June 1832) were the occasion for the first republican uprising of the JULY MONARCHY.

## Lamartine, Alphonse de (1790–1869)
*poet, statesman*

A leader in the romantic movement, Alphonse de Lamartine was born in Mâcon to a royalist family. A fervent Catholic in his youth, he became secretary to the French embassy at Naples under King LOUIS XVIII and later served at Florence. Elected to the Chamber of Deputies, he served as minister of foreign affairs in the provisional government of 1848. Remaining deeply religious, Lamartine had his faith shaken by the death of his daughter (*Gethsémani*, 1834), and he became a proponent of a liberal and socially active Christianity (a view that he supported when he served in the government, 1833–51), with 1848 marking the apogee of his political career (a member of the first provisional government; foreign minister), but as a moderate he could please neither the extreme left or right. Lamartine was also interested in literature and took up writing early in life. As a writer, he is known chiefly for his poetry. It is characterized by strong sentiments, expressed with lyrical grace and refinement, as well as with a gentle melancholy and effective descriptions of nature and rural scenery. His most popular and influential volume of poems is *Méditations poétiques* (1820). Other volumes are *Nouvelles méditations poétiques* (1823), *Harmonies poétiques et religieuses* (1830), *Jocelyn* (1836), *La Chute d'un ange* (1838), and *Les Recueillements poétiques* (1839). Lamartine was also a prolific writer of history, biography, critical works, and fiction. His prose writings include *Histoire des girondins* (1847), *Les Confidences* (1849), the autobiographical novels *Raphael* (1849) and *Graziella* (1852), and his *Cours familiar de littérature* (1856–59). Lamartine was opposed to the regime of NAPOLÉON III (1851) but, too poor to go into self-exile, as did VICTOR HUGO, he retired from public life and "sentenced himself," he said, to "forced literary labor." Considered an inspiration to the young romantics because of his lyrical style, Lamartine was honored early in his career, being elected to the ACADÉMIE FRANÇAISE in 1829.

See also REVOLUTION OF 1848.

## Lamballe, Marie-Thérèse-Louise de Savoie-Carignan, princess (1749–1792)
*intimate of Queen Marie Antoinette*

Born in Turin, Marie-Thérese-Louise de Savoie-Carignan, princess Lamballe, who was widowed after only a year of marriage, became the mistress of the household of Queen MARIE ANTOINETTE, to whom she was a devoted friend (1774). Imprisoned at La Force during the REVOLUTION OF 1789, Mme de Lamballe was killed during the SEPTEMBER MASSACRES of 1792.

## Lambert, Anne-Thérèse de Marguenat de Courcelles, marquise (1647–1733)
*writer*

Born in Paris, Anne-Thérèse de Marguenat de Courcelles, marquise Lambert was a woman of letters known for her treatises on morality. She hosted a brilliant salon that was frequented by FRANÇOIS FÉNELON, BERNARD DE FONTANELLE, ANTOINE HOUDAR DE LA MOTTE, CHARLES MONTESQUIEU, and PIERRE DE MARIVAUX. In her writings, the marquise Lambert sought to analyze certain aspects of moral and cognitive philosophy. She wrote "dialogues" with philosophers from Plato to Montesquieu, arguing the aspects of their thought that she believed were based on gender differences. She examined not only the position of women in culture, but also put forth an all-inclusive vision of humanity.

## Lambesc, Charles-Eugène of Lorraine, duke d'Elbeuf, prince de (1751–1825)
*military figure*

Born in Versailles, Charles-Eugène de Lorraine, duke d'Elbeuf and prince de Lambesc, was a member of the HOUSE OF GUISE and was connected to the family of Queen MARIE ANTOINETTE. As commanding colonel of the Royal German Regiment, he ordered the firing on the crowd at the Tuileries during the REVOLUTION OF 1789 on July 12, 1789. Charged but acquitted, he entered the service of the Austrian army against Revolutionary France (1792) and was named field marshal. During the Restoration, he became a peer and was named marshal of France (1814) by King LOUIS XVIII.

## Lamé, Gabriel (1795–1870)
*mathematician, engineer*

Born in Tours, Gabriel Lamé, after having worked on feasibility projects in Russia with ÉMILE CLAPEYRON (1820), on his return to France (1832) took part in the establishment of the Paris–Saint-Germain and Paris-Versailles railroads. In mathematics, he contributed to the development of analytic geometry, introducing algebraic notation and multipliers (*Examen des différentes méthodes pour résoudre les problèmes de géométrie*, 1818). In analytical mechanics, he established general equations of the elasticity of characteristic elements and deformation of internal tensions. He also put forth an important differential equation that he discovered in a problem of propagating heat (Lamé Equation) and the introduction of homofocal quadrics as coordinating surfaces in geometry and in physical mathematics. Lamé was elected to the Academy of Sciences in 1843.

## Lamennais, Félicité-Robert de (1782–1854)
*writer, thinker*

A philosopher who attempted to combine political and theological liberalism, Félicité de Lamennais (or La Mennais) was born in Saint-Malo. He was ordained a priest in 1816 and at first was a royalist and ultramontane (conservative Catholic) who developed his ideas in an early writing, *Essai sur l'indifférence en matière de religion* (1817–23). This work made him famous. He later posited the subordination of temporal power to the spiritual in *De la religion considérée dans ses rapports avec l'ordre politique et social* (1825). Because of these views, he incurred the hostility of the Gallicans (see GALLICANISM). In 1830, with HENRI LACORDAIRE and MARC MONTALEMBERT, Lamennais founded *L'Avenir*, a journal advocating a liberal Christianity and the separation of church and state. After its condemnation by Rome (1832), Lamennais announced his break with the church in *Paroles d'un croyant* (1834) and also in another writing, *Affaires de Rome* (1836–37). He moved toward a form of democratic humanitarianism that he explained in *Le Livre du peuple* (1838), *Le Pays et le Gouvernement* (1838), and *l'Esquisse d'un philosophe* (1841–46), in which he presented his view of a God who must, according to Lamennais, be the basis for all social reforms. In 1848, Lamennais was elected to represent the people as a member of the National Assembly and became editor of the journal *Le Peuple constituent*.

## Lameth family
*military and political figures*

Alexandre Théodore Victor, count of Lameth (1756–1854) was born in Paris and fought in the American War of Independence. A deputy for the Jura to the Legislative Assembly during the REVOLUTION OF 1789, he took his place with the constitutional monarchists (FEUILLANTS) and, with his brothers, spoke against the coalition (1792). A brigadier general, he was dismissed in 1793 for having tried to save the king and remained in exile until the coup d'état of Napoléon Bonaparte (see NAPOLÉON I) on 18 Brumaire (November 9, 1799). Charles, count of Lameth (1757–1832), the brother of Alexandre Victor, was born in Paris, fought in the American War of Independence under General JEAN-BAPTISTE ROCHEAMBEAU, and, in 1789, was elected a deputy for the nobility to the ESTATES GENERAL. Elected during the Revolution to the National Constituent Assembly, he took

a position in favor of reform. After the flight of King LOUIS XVI to Varennes, he rejoined the camp of the constitutional monarchists. A brigadier general, he emigrated after August 10, 1792. Returning to France (18 Brumaire), he served in the republican armies in Spain. In 1829, he became deputy for Seine-et-Oise. Alexandre, count of Lameth (1760–1829), the brother of Alexandre Théodore and Charles, was born in Paris and fought in the American War of Independence. Elected deputy for the nobility of Péronne to the Estates General (1789), he formed with ANTOINE BARNAVE and ADRIEN DUPORT the triumvirate that, within the National Constituent Assembly, took a position in favor of reform and was opposed to strong royal power (in particular to HONORÉ MIRABEAU). Joining the Feuillants after the flight of the king, and named brigadier general, he went over to the enemy with General LA FAYETTE (August 19, 1792) and was imprisoned by the Austrians until 1797. Returning to France after the coup d'état of 18 Brumaire, he served as a prefect and became a baron of the empire (1810), then a peer during the Hundred Days. A liberal deputy during the Restoration, he left a *Histoire de l'Assemblée constituante* (1829).

## Lamoignon, Guillaume de  (1617–1677)
*political figure*

Born in Paris, where he was the first president of the Parlement of Paris, Guillaume de Lamoignon refused to preside over the trial of NICOLAS FOUQUET and spoke out in favor of legislative and judicial procedural and penal reform (the Lamoignon Laws of arrest were introduced in 1702). He envisioned a unification of the laws of the kingdom and institution of a more humane judicial system, with better rights guaranteed for the accused. Lamoignon also protected various writers, such as NICOLAS BOILEAU. His grandson, Guillaume de Lamoignon (1683–1772), was chancellor under King LOUIS XV and was the father of CHRÉTIEN GUILLAUME DE LAMOIGNON DE MALESHERBES and the uncle of Chrétien François de Lamoignon (1735–89), the keeper of the seals who, in 1787, tried to reduce the prerogatives of the parlements, and as a result, was recalled in 1788.

## Lamoricière, Christophe-Louis-Léon Juchault de (1806–1865)

*general, political figure*

Born in Nantes, Christophe-Louis-Léon Juchault de Lamoricière was a graduate of the École polytechnique and took part in the conquest of ALGERIA, distinguishing himself during the siege of Constantine (October 1837) and the Battle of Isly (August 1844). With the duke d'AUMALE, he received as well the surrender of the Emir Abd el-Kader (1847). After the REVOLUTION OF 1848, he entered the Constituent Assembly as a moderate republican and was named minister of war by JEAN-BAPTISTE CAVAIGNAC. Opposed to NAPOLÉON III, he was imprisoned in the fortress of Ham after the coup d'état of December 2, 1851, then banished (1852–57). In 1860, he went over to the service of the pope, reorganizing the papal troops of which he was named general in chief but, defeated at Castelfidardo (September 18) by the Piedmontese, General Lamoricière was forced to surrender at Ancona.

## La Mothe le Vayer, François de (1588–1672)

*writer, philosopher*

Born in Paris, François de La Mothe le Vayer was the tutor of LOUIS XIV and a member of the ACADÉMIE FRANÇAISE (1639). A cultivated and liberal thinker, François de La Mothe demonstrated in his writings on the most varied subjects a critical skepticism (*Cinq dialogues faits à l'imitation des Anciens*, 1631; *La Vertu des païens*, 1641).

## La Motte, Jeanne de Valois, countess de (1756–1791)

### (Jeanne de Valois-St-Rémy)

*nobility*

Born in Fontette, LANGUEDOC, Jeanne de Valois, countess de la Motte was an aristocrat who played an important role, on the eve of the REVOLUTION OF 1789, in the scandalous Affair of the Necklace. In 1786, with the Italian adventurer Alessandro Cagliostro, she persuaded Cardinal LOUIS DE ROHAN, who wished to gain favor with Queen MARIE ANTOINETTE, to serve as an intermediary in the purchase of a necklace worth an enormous sum. A nighttime rendezvous between Cardinal Rohan and the queen was arranged, with a servant girl playing the role of the queen. Meanwhile, the countess de La Motte's lover, who was presented as one of the queen's officers, was given the necklace and sold it. King LOUIS XVI was then badly advised to bring the affair before the Parlement of Paris. The innocent queen was disgraced, as her private affairs and her expenses were made public, as were Rohan and Mme de La Motte, who was confined to La Salpêtrière asylum. She later emigrated during the Revolution and died in England.

## Lamourette, Antoine-Adrien (1742–1794)

*political figure*

Born in Frévent, Pas-de-Calais, Antoine-Adrien Lamourette was vicar general of Arras and, during the REVOLUTION OF 1789, became constitutional bishop of Rhône-et-Loire (February 1791). He was elected deputy to the Legislative Assembly, where he took his place with the political center. Wanting to put an end to the political quarrels between the Right (the FEUILLANTS) and the Left (JACOBINS, CORDELIERS), he gave a impassioned speech (July 7, 1792) that was followed by a general embrace among the delegates. But it was only an ephemeral reconciliation, which became famously known by the ironic name of "baiser [kiss of] Lamourette." Lamourette was opposed to the SEPTEMBER MASSACRES of 1792 and was executed during the Terror.

## Lamy, François-Joseph-Amédée (1858–1900)

*military officer, explorer*

Born in Mougins, François-Joseph-Amadée Lamy led a military escort across the Mediterranean regions to Chad (1899–1900), where he was to meet the mission of PAUL VOULET and CHARLES CHANOINE, who had already been replaced. Commander Lamy, however, was killed during the last offensive of the troops of the Muslim leader Rabah, defeated at Kousseri. Lamy gave his name to the principal city of Chad, Fort-Lamy (today N'Djamena).

## Landais, Pierre (ca. 1440–1485)
*administrator*

Born in Vitré, Pierre Landais, a valet of the wardrobe to François II, duke of Brittany, gained the duke's confidence and became treasurer and receiver-general of Brittany. He signed commercial agreements with Spain, Portugal, England, and the Hanseatic cities and favored the establishment of silk and tapestry workshops. He wanted to arrange a marriage between the duc d'Orléans and the heiress to the duchy of Brittany, with the aim of uniting Brittany with the kingdom of France. In doing so, he alienated the Breton nobles, was accused of embezzlement and murder, and abandoned by the duke, was executed.

## Lang, Jack (1939– )
*political figure, minister of culture, minister of education*

Born in Mirecourt, Jack Lang served as director of the University Theater at Nancy (where he established a World Theater Festival) from 1963 to 1972. He then became the mayor of Bloise (1989) and served at the same time as minister of culture (1981–86; 1988–93) and of education (1992–93). Lang encouraged all forms of creativity and urged the national and regional governments to give their support to artists. He also promoted supportive measures for architects, writers, and cinematographers. Lang was an influential figure in the government of FRANÇOIS MITTERRAND.

## Langevin, Paul (1872–1946)
*physicist*

Paul Langevin, who is credited with the first successful development of sonar, as well as the development of a modern theory of magnetism, was born in Paris. He attended the École Lavoisier and École de physique et de chimie industrielles, and also the École normale superiéure, where he studied with the noted physicist JEAN PERRIN. Additionally, Langevin studied at Cambridge University under the leading British physicist, J. J. Thompson, and at the SORBONNE under PIERRE CURIE. He held professorships in physics at the Collège de France (1904) and at the Sorbonne (1909). Langevin's work on ionized gases led him to studies of magnetism and the properties of magnetic fields. In 1911, he proposed a theory to support Pierre Curie's work on paramagnetic gases, and his studies later influenced the Danish physicist Niels Bohr in that scientist's development of the structure of the atom. During WORLD WAR I (1915), Langevin worked on developing a method for detecting submarines by echolocation (later known as "sonar"), and he also found a method for measuring ultrasonic sound waves. In 1938, he developed a method for slowing fast neutrons. This would later be used by physicists who attempted to develop atomic reactors. During WORLD WAR II, Langevin was an outspoken critic of Nazi Germany, and was imprisoned in a concentration camp after the German invasion of France (1940). He escaped to Switzerland (1944) and, returning to Paris after the war, assumed the post of director of the Collège de France. Langevin was named to the Academy of Sciences in 1934.

## Languedoc

A former province of France, Languedoc lies south of Guyenne and west of Roussillon. Its capital is Toulouse. It takes its name from the language of its inhabitants (langue d'oc, or Occitan—derived from "oc," meaning "oui") that served also to unite the region. Languedoc was formed essentially from the domains of the counts of Toulouse and became a possession of the French Crown in 1271. Languedoc was a center of the ALBIGENSIANS, or Cathars, during the 12th and 13th centuries. Later it was a site of the HUNDRED YEARS' WAR and the WARS OF RELIGION and then the CAMISARD revolt and, in the 19th century, was a center of political radicalism. Today, Languedoc includes the departments of Haute-Garonne, Aude, Tarn, Hérault, Gard, Ardèche, Lozère, and Haute-Loire. Principal cities include Carcassone, Albi, Narbonne, Montpellier, and Béziers. It incorporates part of the Massif Central and borders on the Mediterranean and is an important part of the Midi of France.

## Lanjuinais, Jean-Denis, count (1753–1827)
*political figure*

Born in Rennes, where he was an attorney, Jean-Denis, count Lanjuinais, was a deputy for the Third Estate to the ESTATES GENERAL in 1789. With ISAAC

LE CHAPELIER, he helped to found the Breton Club, which soon became the JACOBIN CLUB (1789), and he played a role in the reforms put forth by the National Constituent Assembly (civil and clerical constitutions, secularization of the civil state) during the REVOLUTION OF 1789. In the Convention, he took a position against the Montagnards and was proscribed with the GIRONDINS (1793). During the Thermidorian Convention, he worked on the development of the Constitution of the Year III (1795). Deputy for Ille-et-Vilaine, senator (1800), and opposed to the consulate for life and the Empire, he was nonetheless made a count (1808). A supporter of the abdication of NAPOLÉON I, Jean-Denis, count Lanjuinais became a member of the Chamber of Peers under the Restoration.

## Lannes, Jean, duke of Montebello (1769–1809)
*marshal of France*

Born in Lectoure, Gers, where he enrolled in a battalion of volunteers during the REVOLUTION OF 1789 (1792), Jean Lannes in 1795 became a brigadier general. He took part in the campaign in Italy and followed Napoléon Bonaparte (see NAPOLÉON I) to Egypt. Having participated in the coup d'état of 18 Brumaire, Year VIII (November 9, 1799), he became commander of the Consular Guard. He contributed to the victory of Marengo and was made a marshal in 1804 and duke of Montebello in 1808. He fought in numerous other battles: Ulm, Austerlitz, Jena, Eylau, Friedland, and in Spain (victory of Tudela, November 1808, siege of Saragossa). Marshal Lannes was mortally wounded at Essling on May 22, 1809, and died after having both legs amputated. He was held in highest esteem by Bonaparte, who had his remains entombed in the Pantheon.

## La Noue, François de (1531–1591)
*military figure, writer*

Surnamed "Bras de Fer" and "le Bayard Huguenot," François de La Noue, a soldier of great repute, was born in Nantes. He converted to Protestantism and was held for five years as a prisoner by the Spanish, during which time he meditated on his *Discours politiques et militaires* (1587), composed and written with rigor and simplicity. Moved by a spirit of tolerance, François de La Noue drew a moral lesson from the events that he took part in (26 discours, called *Mémoires*) and wanted to be known as a "man of good will," more than as a "great soldier" (Henri de Navarre).

## La Palice, Jacques de Chabannes, seigneur de (ca. 1470–1525)
*military figure*

Jacques de Chabannes, seigneur de La Palice, who was one of the most brilliant military figures of his time, fought in the wars in Italy under Kings CHARLES VIII, LOUIS XII, and FRANCIS I. He played a particularly important role in the struggle against the Holy League (Ravenna 1502). Taken prisoner at Guinegatte, he escaped and distinguished himself at Marignan (1515), Le Bicoque (1522), and during the siege of MARSEILLE, which he helped raise. Marshal La Palice was killed at Pavia. The song composed by his soldiers to celebrate his valor ends with this verse: "a quarter hour before his death, he was still alive." This song ("Lapalissade") famous for its naïveté, has been incorrectly attributed to La Palice.

## La Pérouse, Jean-François de Galaup, count de (1741–1788)
*navigator*

Born in Le Guo, near Albi, Jean-François de Galaup, count de La Pérouse joined the navy in 1756 and took part in several campaigns against the British (rejoining the fleet of Admiral JEAN-BAPTISTE D'ESTAING in the Antilles in 1779; seizing two forts in Hudson Bay in 1782). In 1785, he left Brest for an expedition to explore parts of the world. By Cape Horn, Easter Island, and the Sandwich Islands (Hawaii), he reached the northwest coast of North America. North of the Sandwich Islands he discovered Necker Island and the Marianas, reaching Macao. After skirting the Philippines, he reached Japan and discovered the strait separating the islands of Hokkaido and Sakhalin that today bears his name. From there, he went to Kamtchatcka, then sailed toward Samoa, where his second in command was killed by the natives. From Tonga, La Pérouse went to Botany Bay (Australia), where he wrote his last letter (February 7, 1788). The navigator ANTOINE D'ENTRECASTEAUX undertook, without success, an expedition to find La Pérouse in 1791. In 1826, the remains of La Pérouse's ship were found on Vanikoro, where he was probably killed by the inhabitants. The explorer JULES DUMONT D'URVILLE was also sent there in 1828.

## La Place, Pierre-Simon, marquis de (1749–1827)
*astronomer, mathematician, physicist*

Best known for his successful application of Newton's theory of gravitation to account for all planetary motion, Pierre-Simon, marquis de La Place was born in Beaumont-au-Auge, Normandy. In 1767, he became professor of mathematics at the École militaire in Paris. He entered the Senate in 1799, served as its vice president (1803), and was named a count of the Empire by NAPOLÉON I (1806). He later supported King LOUIS XVIII, who made him a marquis and peer of France. La Place's most important work in astronomy concerned a study of the movements of Saturn and Jupiter. It was in describing these movements that La Place made his important mathematical discoveries: that planetary motions are stable, and that perturbations produced by mutual influence of planets or by external bodies, such as comets, are only temporary. He attempted to give a rational theory of the origin of the solar system in his nebular hypothesis of stellar evolution. In his *Traité de mécanique céleste* (five volumes, 1799–1825), he systematized all the mathematical work that had been done on gravitation. His *Exposition du système du monde* (1796) contained a summary of the history of astronomy. La Place also worked on the theory of probabilities in his *Théorie analytique des probabilités* (1812). La Place was named to the Academy of Sciences in 1773 and to the ACADÉMIE FRANÇAISE in 1816.

## Laponneraye, Albert (1808–1849)
*historian, publisher*

Born in Tours, Albert Laponneraye joined the fight for democracy quite young, publishing a *Déclaration des droits de l'homme et du citoyen* (1832), opening a public course on the history of France where he spoke to the workers (*Cours public d'histoire de France de 1789 à 1830*, published from 1832 to 1838), and editing a "newspaper of social reform" (*L'Intelligence*). From 1840, he was part of a Neobabouvist communist group (see FRANÇOIS BABEUF) with THÉODORE DEZAMY and RICHARD LAHAUTIÈRE. Laponneraye also published the *Œuvres de Maximilien Robespierre* (1842).

## Larbaud, Valery (1881–1957)
*writer*

Born in Vichy, Valery Larbaud, after 1898, made long journeys throughout Europe and became like Barnabooth, the hero of his stories, "without horizons." In 1935, he developed aphasia, causing loss of speech, and he ended his life paralyzed. In 1911, his novel on the theme of adolescence, *Fermina Márquez*, appeared, which previews some of the themes in *A. O. Barnabooth. Ses œuvres completes, c'est-a-dire un conte, ses poesies et son journal intime* (1913) and *Amants, heureux amants* (1920–1924). In 1924, Larbaud dedicated himself to literary criticism (*Ce vice impuni, la lecture;* 1941), and translations, making the works of Walt Whitman, Samuel Butler, and James Joyce (he helped in the translation of *Ulysses,* a work from which he borrowed the idea of the interior monologue) more familiar to the French. Laubaud collected his writings, essays, and notes on his travels in *Jaune, bleu, blanc* (1928) and in *Aux couleurs de Rome* (1938).

## La Rochefoucauld, François, duke de (1613–1680)
*moralist, writer*

Born in Paris and destined for a military career, in which he would later gain a reputation for bravery, François, duke de La Rochefoucauld, became involved in intrigues, especially with distinguished noblewomen, against Cardinal RICHELIEU and, as a consequence, was imprisoned in the BASTILLE, then exiled to his estates in Poitou. In 1648, he took part in the FRONDE uprising of the nobles against JULES MAZARIN and, in 1652, was badly wounded (alongside CONDÉ) in the fighting that took place during that rebellion. La Rochefoucauld subsequently abandoned his military activities and political conspiracies and joined the side of the king (his *Mémoires*, 1662, are a useful source for understanding the period 1624–52). Once back in favor, he began a life that centered on the salons, especially those of such eminent literary figures as Mme de LA FAYETTE and the marquise MARIE de SÉVIGNÉ. In his later years, La Rochefoucauld suffered from a serious illness that left him half blind and from personal tragedies. At this point in his life, melancholy, but always with a gentlemanly reserve, he loved "conversation with honest people" and used his incisive mind and psychological insight to analyze his culture and society. Starting to write, probably in 1658, he produced eventually his *Maximes* (1664), which scandalized many by their frankness and lack of pretense and illusion, along with a certain pessimism about human nature. In his maxims he denounced humans' egoistic motives in both emotions and social relationships ("Our virtues are often only our vices disguised"). As a French writer of epigrammatic maxims, he has never been surpassed.

## La Rochefoucauld, Amboise Polycarpe, viscount de, duke de Doudeauville (1765–1841)

*political figure*

Born in Paris, Amboise Polycarpe de la Rochefoucauld, duke de Doudeauville, emigrated at the time of the REVOLUTION OF 1789. He returned to France during the Consulate but, as a royalist, constantly refused to serve under NAPOLÉON I and remained in retirement until the RESTORATION. A member of the Chamber of Peers, where he generally voted with the Right, he became minister of the king's household in 1824. At this time he encouraged CHARLES X to purchase the estate at Grignon for creating an agricultural school there.

## La Rochefoucauld-Liancourt, François-Alexandre, duke de  (1747–1827)

*philanthropist, political figure*

Born in La Roche-Guyon, François-Alexandre, duke de La Rochefoucauld-Liancourt created a model farm on his estates where he tried to apply the agronomic methods that he had studied during a visit to England (1769). In the same period, he founded the École des enfants de la Patrie, later the École des arts et métiers de Châlons. A deputy for the nobility to the ESTATES GENERAL (1789), during the REVOLUTION OF 1789 he presented before the National Assembly his reports on the state of public hospitals and on poverty. He upheld individual freedoms and emigrated to England, then to the United States, after August 10, 1792. He returned to France in 1799 and was a deputy during the HUNDRED DAYS. A peer of France under the RESTORATION and a member of the Council on Hospitals (1816), he was dismissed from his functions because of his liberal views. The duke de La Rochefoucauld-Liancourt wrote *L'État des pauvres en Angleterre* (1800), *Le Bonheur du peuple, almanach à l'usage de tout le monde* (1819), and was named to the Academy of Sciences in 1821.

## La Rochejaquelein family

*aristocratic family of soldiers, political figures*

The La Rochejaquelein family were Vendean nobles, some of whom were renowned for their role in the Wars of the VENDÉE during the REVOLUTION OF 1789. Henri du Vergier, count de La Rochejaquelein (1772–94), born in the château of La Durbellière, near Châtillon-sur-Sevre, was a member of the Constitutional Guard of King LOUIS XVI until 1792. In March 1793, he became one of the principal leaders of the Vendean uprising. After their defeat, he tried to continue the struggle but was killed in battle. Louis du Vergier, marquis de La Rochejaquelein (1777–1815), born in Saint-Auban-de Bourbigne, was the brother of Henri du Vergier. He emigrated shortly after the Revolution of 1789 began and served in the prince de Condé's army, then with the British in Saint-Domingue. Returning to France in 1801, he was named field marshal and commander of the grenadiers of the Royal Guard during the First RESTORATION (1814). He was killed when he tried to lead an insurrection in the Vendée during the HUNDRED DAYS.

## La Rocque, François, count de (1885–1946)

*officer, political figure*

Born in Lorient, François, count de La Rocque, had a brilliant military career that made him, in 1918, the youngest commander in the French army. He retired from the military in 1928 with the rank of colonel to dedicate himself to politics. In 1931, he was elected president of the right-wing Croix-de-Feu. After the disbanding of the Leagues, in 1936, he founded the Parti social français (PSF), another right-wing group. At first supportive of Marshal PHILIPPE PÉTAIN in 1940, he took a position against the policies of collaboration, was arrested, and deported to Germany. His actions in the RESISTANCE were officially recognized in 1961.

## Larousse, Pierre (1817–1875)
*educator, encyclopedist, publisher*
Born in Toucy, Pierre Larousse was a school director who published a series of pedagogical works that would renew the appreciation of the French language (*Traité complet d'analyse grammaticale*, 1850; *Jardin des racines grecques*, 1858; *Jardin des racines latines*, 1860). In 1852, he founded a publishing house, the Librairie Larousse, which quickly grew. His major work was the *Grande Dictionnaire universel du XIXe siècle* (appearing in sections between 1864 and 1876), an encyclopedic collection that was the work of numerous contributors and that collected an enormous amount of erudition in a readable style and format.

## La Sablière, Marguerite Hessein, Mme de (1636–1693)
*writer*
Born in Paris, Marguerite Hessein, Mme de La Sablière, was gifted with a solid education and lived quite freely, separating early from her husband and presiding over a brilliant salon where she gathered together the literary society of the period. She was, beginning in 1672 and for the next 20 years, the attentive patron of JEAN DE LA FONTAINE, who dedicated two of his *Discours* to her (one on the soul of animals, the other on the occasion of his election to the ACADÉMIE FRANÇAISE in 1684). Having abjured Protestantism, Mme de La Sablière retired in 1678 to a convent, taking as her spiritual adviser the abbé de RANCE, a well-known confessor and monastic reformer. She left her *Lettres*.

## La Salle, René Robert Cavelier, sieur de (1643–1687)
*explorer*
Born in Rouen, René-Robert Cavelier, sieur de La Salle, immigrated to CANADA, where he was granted a trading concession on the upper waters of the St. Lawrence, beyond Montreal. He also learned several American Indian languages. Beginning in 1669, accompanied by the Italian explorer Enrico Tonti and a party of French and Native Americans, he followed and explored the course of the Ohio River, the Great Lakes (Ontario, Erie, Huron, Michigan) and their surrounding territory, then followed the Mississippi to the Gulf of Mexico (1681–82). He had already been appointed commander of Fort Frontenac, where he built a trading post. La Salle, as he is also known, returned to France in 1683 and was made viceroy of North America. In 1684, he sailed to the Gulf of Mexico with the plan to establish a colony at the mouth of the Mississippi. Unable to locate that site, he landed on the coast of Texas at Matagorda Bay and set out with a small expedition to find the mouth of the Mississippi. But his men mutinied and he was killed near the Trinity River.

## Las Cases, Emmanuel, count de (1766–1842)
*writer*
Born in Las Cases, near Revel, Emmanuel, count de Las Cases emigrated during the REVOLUTION OF 1789 and returned to France only at the time of the Consulate. In 1802, he published an *Atlas historique* and in 1810, NAPOLÉON I made him chamberlain and a count of the Empire. After the first abdication of Napoléon (1814), Las Cases went to England and returned to France during the HUNDRED DAYS. He accompanied Napoléon to St. Helena, staying with him for 18 months during which he took down the emperor's words and published them in 1823 under the title *Mémorial de Saint-Hélène*. This work contributed to the dissemination of the Napoleonic legend. On the complaint of the governor of Saint Helena, Hudson Lowe, Las Cases was deported in November 1816 to the Cape. He then settled in Germany and in

Belgium and did not return to France until 1821, after the death of Napoléon. Elected deputy for Saint-Denis in 1831, after the JULY REVOLUTION OF 1830, he took his place with the extreme Left in the Chamber of Deputies.

## Lassu, Roland de (1532–1594)
### (Rolando de Lasso)
*composer*

Born in Mons, Flanders, Roland de Lassu, known also by the Italian form of his name, Rolando de Lasso, was a precocious genius and left his homeland very early for Italy (1545). He spent time in Palermo, Milan, Naples, and Rome, where he for a time served as choirmaster at the Church of Saint John in Lateran (1553). It was in Munich, in the service of the duke of Bavaria, for whom he became choirmaster, that he remained until his death, but not without making several journeys in Europe, particularly in Italy, where he met the composer Palestrina and had the future Italian composer Giovanni Gabrieli as a student. His work is vast (more than 2,000 compositions) and includes villanelles, moresques, and Italian madrigals; polyphonic German lieder and French songs; and, in the area or religious music, 53 masses, 180 magnificats, passions, lamentations, and more than 1,000 motets. Lassu's music, with its harmonic innovations, developed concurrently with the Catholic Counterreformation in Germany that occurred after the shock of the Protestant Reformation.

## La Tour du Pin family
*aristocratic family*

A French family originally from the château de La Tour, in Isère, who became the rulers of Dauphiné with the marriage of Hubert to Anne, heiress to that region. The family sided with the Protestant cause during the Wars of Religion. René de La Tour du Pin-Gouvernat (1543–1619), then his son, Hector de La Tour du Pin-Montauban (1585–1630), were brilliant leaders of the Calvinist forces. René de La Tour du Pin-Montauban (1620–87), their descendant, distinguished himself in the service of the Imperial forces at the battle of Saint-Gothard, a

brilliant victory in 1664, in which the Imperial armies—led by Prince Raimondo Montecuculi—defeated the Ottoman forces.

## La Tour du Pin, René, marquis de (1834–1924)
*sociologist*

Born in Arrancy, near Laon, René, marquis de La Tour du Pin was the founder and inspiration for the Catholic workers' circles and was one of the principal representatives of social Catholicism in France. He sought to make the Christian ideal the basis for a corporative and representative social order. His writings include *Les Phases du mouvement social chrétien* (1897) and *Vers un ordre social chrétien* (1907).

## La Tour, Georges de (1593–1652)
*painter*

Born in Vic-sur-Seille, Georges La Tour, who is known for his religious and genre paintings, especially scenes set at night, was for a long period forgotten. There was a renewed interest in him and his work, however, around 1900. Nonetheless, most of his life and also the chronology of his paintings remain obscure or uncertain. La Tour was born into a family of bakers and probably was educated at Nancy and Lunéville, where he became familiar with the work of other artists. He most likely traveled to Italy between 1610 and 1616, and his work reflects the influence of Caravaggio. He went to the Netherlands, too, where he was influenced by the Utrecht school of painting. In 1620, La Tour became the painter for the town of Lunéville and, in 1639, settled in Paris. King LOUIS XIII admired La Tour's painting *Saint Sébastien pleuré par Irène* and made him one of the king's painters. La Tour's works soon became popular. Certain details of his life indicate that, although he painted religious themes, he was personally an opportunistic and unkind individual. La Tour's paintings, whether religious or genre, if set at night were characterized by dramatic lighting effects, with strong colors illuminated by the light of a single candle (*La Madeleine à la vieilleuse; Les Mangeurs de pois* (certainly his earliest work); *Rixe de musiciens,* ca. 1625–30; *Le Tricheur à l'as de trèfle,* ca. 1625–30; *La Deseuse de bonne aventure,* ca. 1632–35; *La Tricheur à l'as de carreau,* ca. 1635). La Tour's paintings exhibit, besides the exquisite use of candlelight illumination, great attention to detail, and he is characterized also by balanced composition, simplified volumetric shape, and a precise, uncluttered realism. All of La Tour's works reflect the classicism of 17th-century art.

## La Tour Maubourg, Marie-Charles-César-Florimond de Fay, count de (1757–1831)
*general*

Born in Grenoble, Marie-Charles-César-Florimond de Fay, count de La Tour Maubourg, was a deputy for the nobility of Puy to the ESTATES GENERAL in 1789, at which time he adopted the ideas of the REVOLUTION OF 1789. After the flight of the king to Varennes (June 20–21, 1791), he was ordered to return him and the royal family to Paris. Brigadier general in 1792, he went with General LA FAYETTE over to the Austrians (August 19, 1792), who imprisoned him until 1797. Joining NAPOLÉON I, he served as senator (1806) and as military commander of Cherbourg. Made a peer of France after having come over to the Bourbons (1814), he was removed from the list of members of the Upper Chamber until 1819, because of his support for NAPOLÉON I during the HUNDRED DAYS.

## Lattre de Tassigny, Jean-Marie-Gabriel de (1889–1952)
*military figure*

Born in Mouilleron-en-Pareds, Vendée, Jean-Marie-Gabriel de Lattre de Tassigny was made a general in 1939 and commanded the 14th Infantry Division in May and June 1940, which distinguished itself at Rethel at the beginning of WORLD WAR II. In November 1942, at Montpellier, where he commanded the 17th Military Division in the armistice forces, he tried to go underground when the Germans invaded the free zone, but he was repudiated by the VICHY government and imprisoned. He escaped and reached Algiers (September 1943) and, at the head of the 1st French Army,

took part in the Allied landing (Provence, Saint-Tropez, August 16, 1944). General Lattre de Tassigny liberated Toulon, Marseille, Lyon, Dijon, and Alsace, crossing the Rhine and taking Karlsruhe, Fribourg, Stuttgart, Ulm, and Constance in Germany. On May 8, 1945, he accepted the German unconditional surrender at Berlin for France. From 1950 to 1952, he served as high commissioner and commander in chief in INDOCHINA. The rank of marshal of France was conferred on General Lattre de Tassigny posthumously in 1952.

## Laudonnière, René de (unknown–1565)
*colonizer*

René de Laudonnière was charged by Admiral GASPARD DE COLIGNY to found in North America a colony for persecuted Protestants. In about 1562, Laudonnière did establish such settlements in Florida and the Carolinas. But, in spite of the reinforcements supplied by the navigator and colonizer JEAN RIBAUT, both were defeated by the Spanish (1565) under the command of Menendez de Aviles, who massacred most of the Protestant settlers.

See also GOURGUES, DOMINIQUE DE.

## Lautréamont, count de (1846–1870)
## (Isidore Ducasse)
*writer*

Isidore Ducasse, who is known by his nom de plume, comte de Lautréamont, was born in Montevideo, Uruguay. Almost nothing else of his early life is known, except that he was the son of a diplomat, studied at the lycée in Tarbes, and prepared to enter the École polytechnique in Paris. In 1868, there appeared anonymously *Chants de Maldoror,* followed by five more versions, signed by the count of Lautréamont, which went rather unappreciated. After having published under the paradoxical title *Poésies* two fragments of prose (1870), Isidore Ducasse died under mysterious circumstances at age 24. Critics such as ANDRÉ BRETON, however, greatly praised his work, calling it "the revenge of the irrational," and Lautréamont is seen as a precursor of the French literary revolution of the 20th century.

## Lautrec, Odet de Foix, viscount de (1485–1528)
*marshal of France*

Odet de Foix, viscount de Lautrec followed King LOUIS XII to Italy, where he served as governor of the Milanese region (1526). He was, however, driven out because of his cruelty. He had been defeated at the Battle of La Bicoque, or Bicocca (1522) and, after the French loss at Pavia (1525), took revenge by pillaging that town. He died during the siege of Naples. Lautrec's career had been advanced by his sister, the countess de Châteaubriand, who was the mistress of King FRANCIS I.

## Lauzun, Antonin-Nompar de Caumont, count, then duke, de (1633–1723)
*marshal of France*

Born in Lauzun, Antonin-Nompar de Caumont, count de Lauzun was an ambitious and unscrupulous courtier who at first was a favorite of LOUIS XIV until his impertinences cost him a stay in the BASTILLE. He succeeded in secretly marrying the Grande Mademoiselle, first cousin of the king (1681), after an imprisonment of nine years at Pignerol. Going to England, he took part in England's Glorious Revolution of 1688 and was commissioned to escort the queen, Mary of Modena, and James Edward, prince of Wales, to France. He fought in Ireland at the Battle of the Boyne. The duke of Lauzun had for his second wife the sister-in-law of the duke de SAINT-SIMON.

## Laval, Pierre (1883–1945)
*political figure*

A member of the Vichy government of German-occupied France and a leader in the collaboration effort, Pierre Laval was born in Châteldon, Puy-de-Dôme and educated in law at Paris. In 1914, he was elected to the Chamber of Deputies for Aubervilliers, a suburb of Paris. He served in WORLD WAR I and was reelected to the chamber in 1924. A year later, he was appointed minister of public works in the cabinet of PAUL PAINLEVÉ and subsequently held many cabinet posts. From 1931 to 1932, Laval was premier and foreign minister. He served as minister of labor (1932), then again as foreign minister

(1934–35) and, in that capacity, arranged a mutual military assistance pact with the Soviet Union. In June 1935, again as premier and foreign minister, he sponsored, with Sir Samuel Hoare, the British secretary for foreign affairs, the Hoare-Laval Treaty, which called for Ethiopia to cede large areas of its territory to Fascist Italy. The treaty, however, aroused great public indignation and was repudiated in both Paris and London. Hoare was forced to resign and the Laval government fell in January 1936. After France's defeat by Germany in 1940, Laval returned to power as vice premier in the VICHY government. He also became the chief aide to the president, Marshal PHILIPPE PÉTAIN. In this capacity, Laval had the Parlement revise the constitution (which put an end to the THIRD REPUBLIC), and engaged France in a policy of collaboration with Nazi Germany, preparing the meeting between Pétain and German chancellor Hitler in 1940. Laval's attitude aroused the hostility of the other ministers, and he was replaced by Admiral FRANÇOIS DARLAN (1941) and arrested. He was released a short time afterward, however, at the insistence of the Germans, who brought him back into the government as minister of the interior, information, and foreign affairs. He declared his desire for a German victory and aided the Nazi cause by sending French laborers to work in Germany as part of the STO (Service du travail obligatoire), and by sending French and foreign Jews there also to their likely death in concentration or extermination camps. Laval also supported the Milice as a force against the RESISTANCE. After the Liberation of France, he fled to Austria, where he was arrested. Returned to France, he was found guilty of plotting against the state and of collaboration and was executed.

## La Vallière, Louise-Françoise de la Baume le Blanc, duchess de (1644–1710)
*mistress of Louis XIV*

Born in Tours, Louise-Françoise de la Baume le Blanc, duchess de La Vallière was a lady-in-waiting to Queen Henriette-Anne of England, sister-in-law to King LOUIS XIV, whose favorite the duchess de La Vallière soon became. Their surviving children were legitimized (Anne of Bourbon, known as

Mme de Blois, the future princess de Conti, and the count de Vermandois). The duchess de la Vallière retired in 1674 to a convent, where she spent her later years.

## Lavardin, Jean de Beaumanoir, marquis de (1551–1614)

*marshal of France*

Born in Lavardin, Jean de Beaumanoir, marquis de Lavardin was raised as a Protestant with Henry of Navarre (the future HENRY IV). He converted to Catholicism after the SAINT BARTHOLOMEW'S DAY MASSACRE and became one of the cruelest adversaries of his former coreligionists. He commanded the Catholics at the battle of Coutras (1587), took the side of the HOLY LEAGUE (1589), and came over to the side of Henry IV when he became king of France. Henry IV made the marquis de Lavardin a marshal of France and governor of Maine. He was in Henry's coach at the time the king was assassinated.

## La Vieuville, Charles, marquis de (ca. 1582–1653)

*political figure*

Born in Paris, Charles, marquis de La Vieuville, served as superintendent of finances (1623) and helped to bring Cardinal RICHELIEU into the Council (1624). Subsequently accused of embezzlement and dismissed, he was confined to the château of Amboise (1624–25), but escaped and left the country. He later obtained permission to reenter France (1628). He conspired against Richelieu and fled to Brussels (1631). After the cardinal's death, he returned to France and obtained from Cardinal MAZARIN the direction of finances (1649), as well as the title of duke and peer.

## Lavigerie, Charles-Martial, Cardinal (1825–1892)

*prelate*

Born in Bayonne, Charles-Martial Lavigerie was professor of ecclesiastical history at the SORBONNE and director of the School of Middle Eastern Studies in Syria. He was named bishop of Nancy (1863), then archbishop of Algiers (1867). Wanting to evangelize the population of North and sub-Saharan Africa, he founded the Society of the White Fathers (Société des pères blancs) in 1868, then that of the Missionary Sisters of Africa (Sœurs missionnaires d'Afrique) in 1869. Head of the church in Africa, cardinal (1882), he also became apostolic administrator of Tunisia (1884) after a French protectorate was established in that country. Cardinal Lavigerie continued his missionary work as well as his struggle against slavery (Brussels Anti-Slavery Conference of 1889). In 1890, at the request of Pope Leo XIII, he gave the famous "toast of Algiers," encouraging loyalty to the government, to show the church's support for the THIRD REPUBLIC.

## Lavoisier, Antoine-Laurent de (1743–1794)

*chemist*

Considered the founder of modern chemistry, Antoine-Laurent de Lavoisier was born in Paris and was educated at the Collège Mazarin. He served as one of the farmers-general and held several other public offices, including those of director of the state gunpowder works (1776), member of a commission during the REVOLUTION OF 1789 to establish a uniform system of weights and measures (1790), and commissary of the treasury (1791). He also attempted to introduce reforms in the monetary and taxation systems. As one of the farmers-general, he was arrested and executed during the TERROR. Lavoisier's experiments were among the first quantitative chemical experiments ever performed. He showed that, although matter changes its state in a chemical reaction, the quantity of matter remains the same. These experiments provided evidence for the law of the conversion of matter (Lavoisier's Principle). Lavoisier also investigated the composition of water, and he named the components "oxygen" and "hydrogen." Some of his most important experiments examined the nature of combustion. He demonstrated that burning is a process involving the combination of a substance with oxygen. He also demonstrated the role of oxygen in animal and plant respiration. Lavoisier's explanation of combustion replaced the phlogiston theory, which postulates that flammable materials contain a substance called phlogiston released when they burn. With the chemist CLAUDE-LOUIS

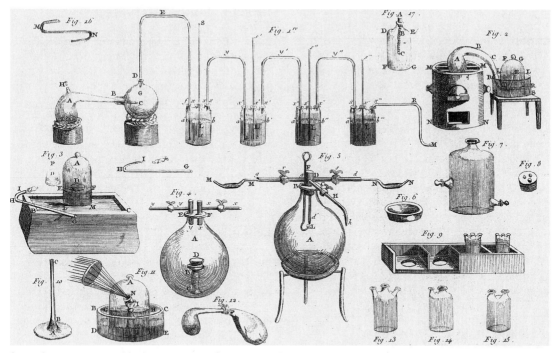

Scientific apparatus used by Lavoisier in studying chemical reactions *(Library of Congress)*

BERTHOLLET and others, Lavoisier devised a chemical nomenclature that is the basis of the modern system (*Méthode de nomenclature chimique,* 1787). In his *Traité élémentaire de chimie* (1789), he clarified the concept of an element as a simple substance, and he devised a theory of the formation of chemical compounds from elements. Lavoisier's other writings include *Sur la Combustion en general* (1777) and *Considérations sur la nature des acides* (1778). He was named a member of the Academy of Sciences in 1768.

## Law, John (1671–1729)
*Scottish-born financier*
Best known as the founder of the notorious Mississippi scheme, John Law was born in Edinburgh, Scotland, and, after having studied banking in various European countries, settled in Paris in 1715. A year later, he secured the patronage of the regent, the duke of Orléans. By royal edict, Law founded the Banque générale, the first bank in France. This new institution produced large quantities of bank-

notes, which, in 1717, were ordered to be received in payment of taxes. That same year, Law originated the Mississippi scheme as a plan to raise revenues for France. His Compagnie de la Louisiane ou d'occident controlled large grants of land around the Mississippi River, where it had exclusive trade rights for 25 years. In 1719, the company absorbed the rival company that controlled trade with China and the East Indies, and the Banque générale became the state bank of France. Law was made comptroller general of finances and councilor of state. When the public was invited to invest in the Mississippi venture, a great speculative wave drove the price of shares upward. The center of speculation was on the rue Quincampoix in Paris. Simultaneously, France was flooded with paper money from Law's bank. A collapse came in 1720 after a royal decree halved the value of the banknotes. Meanwhile, coined money disappeared and there was an extensive price rise. Shares in Law's company, which had been amalgamated with his bank, sank in price and the bank suspended payments. Law had to leave France secretly (1720) and eventually settled in

Venice, where he died, forgotten. His most important writing, in which he explained his theories of finance is *Considération sur le numéraire et la commerce* (1705). The effect of Law's flawed economics would be a crucial factor in the subsequent financial and fiscal developments in France.

## Lazareff, Pierre (1907–1972)
### journalist
Born in Paris, Pierre Lazareff was a reporter for *Soir*, then for *Paris-Midi* (1927). He became director of *Paris-Soir* in 1931, then after the German invasion of 1940 joined the War Information Office in the United States, where he was the chief of French Services. Returning to France, he directed *France-Soir* from 1944 until his death, and contributed to the renewal of the postwar French press. Lazareff also produced for television, from 1959 to 1968, the news program *Cinq colonnes à la une*.

## Léautaud, Paul (1872–1956)
### writer
Born in Paris, Paul Léautaud, who was abandoned as a child, began his literary career in 1895 (*Mercure de France*). Between 1900 and 1929, he published a three-volume anthology, *Poètes d'aujourd'hui*, while at the same time writing articles on the theater (collected in *Théâtre de Maurice Boissard*, 1907–43). In *Le Petit Ami* (1903), he presents a caustic evocation of his unhappy adolescence and in *In Memorium* (1905) recounts other aspects of his family. Léautaud's other writings include: *Passe-Temps* (Vol. I, 1929; Vol. II, 1964) and his articles in *Journal littéraire*, published from 1954 to 1966. He gained notoriety, too, for his radio broadcasts, *Entretiens avec Robert Mallet* (1951).

## Lebaudy, Paul (1858–1937)
### industrialist
Born in Enghien, Paul Lebaudy, with his brother Pierre, devoted a large part of his fortune to the construction of dirigibles, including the first military dirigible (*Jaune*, 1902), and the first English one (*Morning Post*), with which he made the first dirigible crossing of the English Channel (1910).

## Lebœuf, Edmond (1809–1888)
### marshal of France
Born in Paris, where he graduated from the École polytechnique as an artillery officer, Edmond Lebœuf served with distinction in the Italian Campaign (1859) and was named Minister of War in the cabinet of ÉMILE OLLIVIER at the end of the SECOND EMPIRE (January 1870). Major general at the time of the declaration of the FRANCO-PRUSSIAN WAR (1870), he was confident of a victory by the French forces. After their initial defeats, however, he was relieved of his post. Marshal Lebœuf was taken prisoner shortly after the French defeat at Metz.

## Lebon, Philippe (1769–1804)
### engineer, chemist
Born in Brachay, Champagne, Philippe Lebon, beginning in 1797, studied the use of gas given off by the distillation of wood, in lighting and heating. In 1799, he patented his invention, the thermo-lamp. He also worked on a project involving a gas motor supplied and lit by an electrical device (1801). Lebon's work led to the use of gas in urban nighttime illumination.

## Lebourg, Albert (1849–1928)
### painter
Albert Lebourg was born in Montfort-sur-Risle, Eure. After studying architecture, he taught drawing in Algiers, where he took up painting (1872). After 1875, he adopted in his works a free style using fresh colors and a light palette and brushstroke, while seeking to bring out the intensity of the Algerian sunlight. In 1877, he went to Paris and painted landscapes of the ÎLE-DE-FRANCE and the NORMANDY countryside. He began exhibiting in 1883 and, the following year, after a visit to Auvergne, painted numerous canvases (*Pont-du-Château en automne* and *La Neige en Auvergne*, 1886). From 1886 to 1895, he again painted in the Île-de-France (*La Seine à Bougival, Le Bas-Meudon*) and Normandy, and he also traveled to the Netherlands, Belgium, Switzerland, and Great Britain, where he admired the work of Joseph Constable. After 1905, La Rochelle, Paris, and Rouen and its environs constituted his principal subjects. A most sensitive and

spontaneous landscape artist, who could represent the qualities of light and location, Lebourg knew ALFRED SISLEY, CLAUDE MONET, and EDGAR DEGAS and admired all the impressionists without being part of their movement.

## Lebrun, Albert (1871–1950)
### political figure
Born in Mercy-le-Haut, Meurthe-et-Moselle, Albert Lebrun was a graduate of the École polytechnique and became a mining engineer. He sat in the Chamber of Deputies (1900) with the democratic Left, and served as minister of colonies (1911–14), then was in charge of the blockade of liberated territories (1917–20). President of the Senate (1931), he was elected president of the THIRD REPUBLIC (1932–40) and retired after the armistice and the formation of the VICHY government (July 1940). Lebrun was arrested by the Germans and deported (1944–45).

## Le Brun, Charles (1619–1690)
### painter
Born in Paris into a family of artists, Charles Le Brun, whose ornate, baroque designs dominated French art for two generations, was trained in Paris and later Rome, where he worked under the French classicist NICOLAS POUSSIN. Returning to Paris in 1646, Le Brun gradually developed a classical style with a baroque taste for drama, naturalism, and decoration. In 1648, with JEAN-BAPTISTE COLBERT and others, Le Brun helped to found the Royal Academy of Painting and Sculpture, where he also served as secretary (1661) and director (1683). He painted frescoes, too, in such great châteaux as Vaux-le-Vicomte and Sceaux, and in the LOUVRE (Gallery of Apollo). Sponsored by Colbert and by Cardinal MAZARIN, Le Brun was made royal painter and, in 1662, was ennobled. He won King LOUIS XIV's favor in particular with his series *Histoire d'Alexandre*. Responding further to Louis XIV's visions, Le Brun would make VERSAILLES a hymn to the glory of the sovereign and a symbol of absolute monarchy. From 1679 to 1684, he directed the decoration of the palace, including the Ambassador's Stairs, the Hall of Mirrors, and plans for the gardens. He also served as director of the royal GOBELINS factory of tapestry and furniture, for which he provided designs. Le Brun sought to create a series of strict regulations for painting, founded on the ideas of antiquity, and of the artists Raphael and Poussin. Le Brun, describes this codification of art in his *Traité de la physionomie de l'homme comparée a celle des animaux*.

## Lebrun, Charles-François (1739–1824)
### political figure
Born in Saint-Sauveur-Lendelin, Normandy, Charles-François Lebrun served before the REVOLUTION OF 1789 as inspector of Crown domains and as secretary to RENÉ DE MAUPEOU. A member of the Council of Five Hundred, he was chosen by Napoléon Bonaparte as the third consul after the coup d'état of 18 Brumaire Year VIII (November 9, 1799). He created the Government Accounting Office (Cour des comptes) and was named in 1810 lieutenant general in Holland, then governor-general. Made duke of Plaisance, Lebrun was named grand master of the University of France by NAPOLÉON I during the HUNDRED DAYS.

## Lecanuet, Jean (1920–1993)
### political figure
Born in Rouen, Jean Lecanuet, who served in the RESISTANCE, for many years represented Seine-Maritime in the National Assembly and in the Senate. He was mayor of Rouen from 1968 until his death. A Christian Democrat, he led the MOVEMENT REPUBLICAN POPULAIRE (1963–65), created the Democratic Center (Centre démocrate) in 1966, and led the Centre des démocrats sociaux, then the UNION POUR LA DEMOCRATIE FRANÇAISE from 1978 to 1988. A candidate for the presidency of the republic, Lecanuet helped to put General CHARLES DE GAULLE on the ballot (1965) and served as prime minister during the term of VALÉRY GISCARD D'ESTAING.

## Leclerc, Charles-Victor-Emmanuel (1772–1802)
### general
Born in Pontoise, Charles-Victor-Emmanuel Leclerc, who joined the army during the REVOLUTION OF 1789, served with Napoléon Bonaparte during the

siege of Toulon (1793) and during the Italian and Egyptian campaigns. In 1797, he married PAULINE BONAPARTE and later took part in the coup d'état of 18 Brumaire, Year VIII (November 9, 1799). General Leclerc commanded the expedition sent to Santo Domingo in 1802 to repress the Haitian uprising and reimpose slavery. He died there, a victim of yellow fever, after having gained through treachery the surrender of the Haitian liberator TOUSSAINT LOUVERTURE.

## Leclerc, Philippe  (1902–1947)
### (Philippe-Marie de Hauteclocque)
*military leader*

Born in Belloy-Saint-Léonard, Somme, Philippe-Marie, viscount de Hauteclocque, adopted the name Leclerc during World War II. He studied at SAINT-CYR (1922) and at the École de Guerre (1938). Taken prisoner and escaping twice during WORLD WAR II (May–June 1940), he rejoined General CHARLES DE GAULLE in London, then was named governor of the Cameroons, which had come over to Free France, thanks to his efforts in 1940. Military commander of French Equatorial Africa, he left for Chad with a column of Free French forces and conquered Al Kufrah, in Libya, from the Italians (March 1942), then left Chad in December 1942 to join British Marshal Bernard Montgomery in Tripoli (February 2, 1943). He also took part in the Tunisian campaign and then, in 1944, in the Allied landing in Normandy. Entering Paris at the head of the 2nd Armored Division, he received the surrender of the German garrison. General Leclerc liberated Strasbourg on November 23, 1944, and led his troops into Bavaria as far as Berchtesgaden, Adolf Hitler's retreat. Chief commander of the French forces in INDOCHINA (1945), he received, for France, the surrender of the Japanese. He then became inspector of troops in North Africa (1946) and died shortly after in an air accident. The rank of marshal of France was conferred on General Leclerc posthumously in 1952.

## Lecoin, Louis  (1881–1971)
*anarchist*

A militant anarcho-syndicalist, Louis Lecoin was born in Saint-Amand-Montrond, Cher. Secretary of the Anarchist Union (1912), he worked on *Libertaire*, an anarchist newspaper. Profoundly pacifist, he published, in 1916, the tract "Imposons la paix," which caused him to be imprisoned. He was one of the principal leaders in the campaign to free the Italian-American anarchists Nicoló Sacco and Bartolomeo Vanzetti and fought in defense of Domingo Durruti, Nestor Makhno and Camillo Berneri, also anarchists, who were threatened with extradition. In 1936, he founded the Committee for Free Spain and, in 1939, published the tract "Paix immédiate," for which he was again imprisoned. In 1962, after a 23-day hunger strike, he won a vote for the statute on conscientious objection, then dedicated himself to the struggle for peace. Lecoin wrote a memoir, *Le Cours d'une vie* (1965).

## Lecomte, Louis  (1656–1729)
*cleric*

Born in BORDEAUX, Louis Lecomte, a Jesuit, was a member of the group of mathematicians sent to China by LOUIS XIV (1685). He there became involved in the quarrel over indigenous usages in Catholic rites. In his *Nouveaux Mémoires sur l'état présent de la Chine* (1696–1701), he affirmed that the Chinese had revelations of the true faith. This work, however, was censured and ordered burned by the theological faculties of Paris and Rome.

## Le Corbusier  (1887–1965)
### (Charles-Édouard Jeanneret)
*architect, urbanist, painter, theorist*

Charles-Édouard Jeanneret, or Le Corbusier (he adopted his mother's maiden name), as he is known, had a major effect on the development of modern architecture. Born in La Chaux-de-Fonde, Switzerland, he received his early education there, then studied modern building construction in Paris. In 1922, he went into partnership in Paris as an architect with his cousin Pierre Jeanneret. While practicing architecture, Le Corbusier was also active as a painter and writer. In his painting, he was associated with AMADÉE OZENFANT. Together, they published *Après le cubism* (1918), a manifesto of "purism," one of the styles that had grown out of cubism. In 1920, they founded the review *L'Esprit Nouveau*, for which Le Corbusier wrote numerous articles to support his theories on architecture.

Le Corbusier *(Library of Congress)*

He also published *Vers un architecture* in 1923 and, in 1925, *L'Art décoratif aujord'hui* and *Urbanisme*, in which he presented these theories of architecture as an essential part of modern life. Basically a functionalist, Le Corbusier broke with the forms and designs of historic styles and sought a new 20th-century style, to be based on engineering achievements in bridge building and steamship construction; on modern materials, including sheet glass, ferroconcrete, and synthetics; as well as on contemporary urban situations and requirements. Le Corbusier advanced the now-familiar international style of unadorned, low-lying buildings, dependent on functional and simple form and composition. His most notable buildings include the Palace of the League of Nations (Geneva, 1927–28); the Swiss Building (Cité universitaire, Paris, 1931–32); Ville Savoye (Poissey, 1931); Min-

istry of Culture (Rio de Janeiro, 1936–43) Unités d'habitation (Marseille, 1946–52); Notre-Dame-du-Haut (Ronchamp, 1950–55); and the High Courts Buildings (1952–56) in Chandigarh, India. The Secretariat Building of the United Nations in New York City is also primarily his design.

## Ledoux, Claude-Nicolas  (1736–1806)
*architect*

Known for his highly personalized interpretation of the neoclassical style, Claude-Nicolas Ledoux was born in Dormans, Champagne. He studied with JACQUES BLONDEL and, between 1754 and 1764, received his first commissions. From 1762 to 1774, he worked essentially on private commissions, but except for the hôtel d'Hallwy (1766), the majority of the mansions he built were destroyed during the various urban restorations of Paris. For his patron, Mme du BARRY, he built a pavilion at VERSAILLES (1771–72), and he also built the Château de Bénouville, near Caen. In 1774, he began the construction of the vast group of statues at Arc-et-Senans, and in 1785 began his best-known project, the tollhouses for Paris, monumental buildings employing columns, porticos, and pediments of the classical Greco-Roman style, reduced, however, to simple forms. These unpopular structures (now much appreciated) were partially destroyed during the REVOLUTION OF 1789. Ledoux conceived the theater at Besançon, where he introduced the innovative idea of a seating area for the public. Jailed during the Revolution, he dedicated himself to the editing of his theoretical work, *L'Architecture considérée sous le rapport de l'art, des moeurs et de la législation*, published in 1804. Quite imaginative, Ledoux helped to develop the elegant and measured Louis XVI style, while freely interpreting the classical orders.

## Ledru-Rollin, Alexandre  (1807–1874)
## (Alexandre-Auguste Ledru)
*political figure*

Known as Alexandre Ledru-Rollin, Alexandre-Auguste Ledru was born in Paris, where as an attorney, he fought the regime of the JULY MONARCHY and defended the journalists who were condemned after the republican insurrection. Elected deputy (1841), he sat with the extreme Left among the radicals, founded a newspaper, *La Réforme*, with LOUIS BLANC and, during the Banquets campaign (1847–48), he became a proponent of a social-democratic republic. Minister of the interior in the provisional government after the REVOLUTION OF 1848, then a member of the Executive Commission, he was excluded from office after the insurrection of June 1848. An unsuccessful candidate for the presidency of the republic (December 1848) but elected to the Legislative Assembly (May 1849), he was the principal initiator of the failed uprisings of June 13, 1849. In exile in England, Ledru-Rollin made contact with the European revolutionaries Giuseppe Mazzini, Louis Kossuth, and Arnold Ruge. Returning to France (1871), he was elected to the National Assembly but refused to sit; he was elected again in 1874 and took his place as a deputy. Ledru-Rollin's writings include *Du Paupérisme dans les campagnes*, 1847, and *Décadence de l'Angleterre*, 1850.

## Lefebvre, François-Joseph (1755–1820)
*marshal of France*

Born in Rouffach, Haut-Rhine, François-Joseph Lefebvre entered the French Guards in 1773, then went into the Parisian National Guard at the beginning of the REVOLUTION OF 1789. He was named division commander in 1794 and distinguished himself at the Battle of Fleurus. Commandant of the military division of Paris, he gave his support to Napoléon Bonaparte (see NAPOLÉON I) for the coup d'état of 18 Brumaire, Year VIII (November 9, 1799), became a senator (1800), and marshal of the Empire (1804), and took part in several of the emperor's campaigns. He contributed to the victory of Jena (1806), besieged Danzig (1807), a victory that earned him the title duke of Danzig, and fought in the wars in Spain, Austria, and Russia, and in Napoleon's final battles in France. Joining the Bourbons, who made him a peer (1814) under the RESTORATION, then over to Napoléon during the HUNDRED DAYS, he would not be admitted to the Chamber of Peers until 1819. In 1783, Marshal Lefebvre married Catherine Hubscher, a washerwoman for his regiment, who Victor Sardou would later popularize in his comedy entitled *Madame Sans-Gêne* (1893)

## Lefebvre, Georges (1874–1959)
*historian*

A noted and innovative historian, Georges Lefebvre was born in Lille and did his major work in agrarian history, specializing the subject of peasant activity during the REVOLUTION OF 1789 (*Paysans du Nord pendant la Révolution française*, 1924), and on the study of attitude and culture (*La Grande Peur de 1789*, 1932). Lefebvre's work has allowed for important revisions in the historiography of the French Revolution and the social order of the period.

## Lefebvre, Henri (1901–1991)
*philosopher, sociologist*

Born in Hagetmau, Landes, Henri Lefebvre became a Marxist in 1930 and was one of the COMMUNIST PARTY's theoreticians until his expulsion from the party in 1958 because of his emphasis on "permanent revolution." He studied the relationship between philosophy and the proletarian revolutionary praxis, as well as contemporary social structures. He believed that "alienation by bourgeois ideology" could be combated only by a permanent cultural revolution (*La Conscience mystifiée*, 1936; *Lénine*, 1957; *La Somme et la Reste*, 1959). His later works show a great diversity of subject, and are often concerned with the sociology of daily life (*Critique de la vie quotidienne*, 1947–48). Lefebvre's other writings include *La Révolution urbaine* (1970), *La Proclamation de la Commune* (1965), *De l'État* (1976–78), *Contre l'idéologie structuraliste* (1975), *Le Retour de la dialectique* (1988).

## Lefebvre, Marcel (1905–1991)
*prelate*

Born in Tourcoing, Marcel Lefebvre joined the Fathers of the Holy Spirit and for a long time was a missionary in Gabon before becoming the first archbishop of Dakar, Senegal (1948–62). Opposed to the ideas of the Second Vatican Council, he opened in 1970 a traditionalist Catholic seminary in Écône, Switzerland. Several years of negotiations could not end the break, while in 1988 he consecrated four bishops, thus transforming his movement into a schism. He died excommunicated, leaving a community of about 250 priests, six seminaries, and between a few hundred and a few thousand followers.

## Lefebvre-Desnouettes, Charles, count (1773–1822)
*general*

Born in Paris, Charles, count Lefebvre-Desnouettes was aide-de-camp to Napoléon Bonaparte as first consul, then equerry to Bonaparte as Emperor NAPOLÉON I, and commander of the Imperial Guard. He was made a count of the Empire and distinguished himself at Bautzen (1813), then during the campaign in France. He was one of the first to join the emperor during the HUNDRED DAYS and took part in the Battles of Fleurus and Waterloo. Condemned to death during the Second Restoration, he escaped to the United States. Having obtained from King LOUIS XVIII the authorization to return to France, General Lefebvre-Desnouettes was lost on the *Albion,* which sank off the coast of Ireland.

## Lefevre d'Étaples, Jacques (ca. 1450–1537)
*humanist, theologian*

Known also by his Latin names of Fabri, or Faber Stapulensis, Jacques Lefevre d'Étaples was born in Étaples, Picardy, and taught philosophy at Paris. Named vicar to the bishop of Meaux, he created in that city a group who worked on clerical reform and the vulgarization of the Scripture. This "Cenacle of Meaux" was, however, dispersed because of its sympathies for the ideas of Martin Luther. Lefevre d'Étaples sought refuge for a time in Strasbourg, before being called by King FRANCIS I to be tutor to his children. He then retired to Nérac (1530), near MARGUERITE DE NAVARRE. Lefevre d'Étaples did one of the first translations of the Bible, as well as of the works of Aristotle, and is the author of *Commentaires sur les épîtres de saint Paul,* and *Commentaires sur les quatre Évangiles.*

## Legendre, Adrien-Marie (1752–1833)
*mathematician*

Born in Paris, Adrien-Marie Legendre was commissioned by the Convention at the time of the REVOLUTION OF 1789 to work on geodesics and, in doing so, enriched the study of trigonometry, developing a method, for instance, of calculating the area of a spherical triangle and studying geodesic lines. His *Éléments de géométrie* (1794) has historical interest because of his return to the mathematical principles of antiquity. He demonstrated in particular the incommensurability of pi (already known) and that of pi squared. His *Théorie des nombres* (1798) remains a classic, containing remarkable results of the law of reciprocity of quadratic residuals. In 1806, he showed the method of least squares (without being aware of the work of C. F. Gauss). In his most important work, *Traité des fonctions élliptiques et des intégrals eulériennes* (1825), Legendre demonstrated that elliptical integrals can always be reduced to three forms, and he calculated the extended numerical tables. Also, in *Figure des planètes* (1782), he introduced the polynomials that bear his name. Legendre was named to the Academy of Sciences in 1783.

## Legendre, Louis (1752–1797)
*political figure*

Born in Versailles, Louis Legendre was a butcher in Paris who joined the REVOLUTION OF 1789 and took part in the storming of the BASTILLE (July 14) and in the Revolutionary Days of October 5 and 6 of that same year. A member of the JACOBIN and CORDELIERS CLUBS, he helped formulate the petition that was brought to the Champ de Mars and led to the downfall of King LOUIS XVI (July 17, 1791). On June 20, 1792, he took the leadership of the revolutionary movement with ANTOINE SANTERRE and others. A Montagnard deputy to the Convention, he voted for the death of the king. After joining with the Committee of Public Safety, he separated himself from GEORGES DANTON, then in turn opposed MAXIMILIEN ROBESPIERRE and, during the Thermidorian Convention went over to the reaction, closing the Jacobin Club and suppressing the uprising of 1 Prairial Year III (May 20, 1795).

## Leger, Fernand (1881–1955)
*painter*

An influence on cubism, constructivism, and modern commercial poster art, Fernand Leger was born in Argentan and studied art and architecture in

Caen and Paris. Beginning in 1910, he was an important member and exhibitor of the Salon des Independents, in Paris. Most of his early works were cubist (*Nus dans la forêt,* 1910; *La Noce,* 1911; *Les Fumées dans les toits,* 1911; *Paris par la fenêtre,* 1911; *La Femme en bleu,* 1912; *L'Escalier,* 1914). Along with GEORGES BRAQUE and Pablo Picasso, Leger played a significant role in the development and dissemination of the cubist style. Leger's subsequent work was influenced by his experiences in WORLD WAR I. He began to employ symbols from the industrial world and to depict his subjects in machinelike forms (*Les Fumeurs,* 1918; *La Partie des cartes,* 1918). His work had an important effect on the development of neoplasticism in the Netherlands and on that of constructivism in the Soviet Union. He was also highly successful as a sculptor and ceramicist, and a creator of tapestries and mosaics. In his later paintings, Leger separated his figures from color and, in this regard, had an indirect influence on surrealism (*La Jaconde aux clés,* 1940; *Les Plangeurs,* 1940–46; *Adieu New York,* 1947). His *Le Grand Parade* (1954) in the Guggenheim Museum, New York City, is a monumental example also of this original style in which color is laid on the canvas to form a separate composition.

## Legion of Honor (Légion d'honneur)

The Legion of Honor was an order established on May 19, 1802, by NAPOLÉON I with the intention of recognizing outstanding achievements in military or civil life. The first consul was the head of the order, and a decree of July 11, 1804, instituted the Legion of Honor's national decoration. The legion presently comprises five classes of awards. In descending order of distinction, they are grand cross, grand officer, commander, officer, and chevalier. The president of the republic serves as grand master, and the order is conferred on both women and men, either French or foreign.

## Legrand, Michel (1932–  )

*composer, pianist, orchestra leader, arranger*
Born in Paris, Michel Legrand, who had classical musical training, in 1952 began to write arrangements for the string orchestra that accompanied

the American orchestra leader Dizzy Gillespie and then, in 1958, wrote for a recording session with the American jazz artists Miles Davis, John Coltrane, and Bill Evans. He also worked with vocals, as a composer and singer, and wrote the background music for the film musicals of JACQUES DEMY (*Les Parapluies de Cherbourg, Les Demoiselles de Rochefort,* and *Peau-d'Âne*). Working in both France and the United States, Legrand won an Academy Award in Hollywood for the music to the film *The Thomas Crown Affair.*

## Leiris, Michel (1901–1990)

*ethnographer, writer, poet, gallery owner*
Born in Paris, Michel Leiris, a leading ethnographer who initially studied chemistry after having taken part in the dadaist and surrealist movements as a poet (*Simularce,* 1925; *Le Point Cardinal,* 1927), cofounded the Collège de Sociologie as a poet. He then did ethnographic studies of Africa, the Caribbean, and Central America and field work in Sudan and Egypt, and produced a unique autobiographical and travel account of his work in Africa, *L'Afrique fantôme* (1934). His other writings include *De la littérature considéré comme une tauromachie* (1935), *L'Âge d'homme* (1939), and the poems of *Haut-Mal* (1943). He later wrote a four-volume work, *La Règle du jeu* (1955–76), in which he stresses language as means of cultural revelation.

## Le Jeune, Claude (ca. 1530–1600)

*composer*
Born in Valenciennes, Claude le Jeune was a member of the Academy of Music and Poetry founded by JEAN-ANTOINE DE BAÏF, and was devoted to the old style of measured music. Music master for the duke of Anjou, brother of HENRY III (1582), he then entered the service of the duke of Bouillon. His statements hostile to the HOLY LEAGUE forced him to leave Paris and seek refuge in La Rochelle. In 1596, he became chamber music composer to King HENRY IV and wrote psalms, two books of melodies, airs, and numerous songs and motets. Le Jeune's work is in an original harmonic language and is especially remarkable for its rhythm. He took the best part of measured music and, breaking out from the frame-

work of traditional profane music, profoundly influenced the beginnings of the court airs and, in the same sense, prepared the way for the birth of opera.

## Lelouch, Claude (1937–  )
*film director*
Born in Paris, Claude Lelouch wrote, produced, directed, and edited all his films and, in the process, earned a reputation as a complete artist, in the manner of the New Wave (Nouvelle Vague) movement. At the same time, he sought to touch the general public with his often Manichaean stories: *Un homme et une femme* (1966), *Les Bons et les Méchants* (1976), *Les Uns et les Autres* (1981), *L'Itinéraire d'un enfant gâté* (1988).

## Lemaire de Belges, Jean (1473–ca. 1525)
*poet, chronicler*
Born in Bavay, Hainaut, Jean Lemaire de Belges was the historiographer of ANNE OF BRITTANY. His major work in prose, *Les Illustrations de Gaule et singularités de Troye* (1509–13) presents the mythological and scholarly history of the peoples of Europe. In his poetry, he also employed the methods of the great rhetoricians, and heralded the work of the PLÉIADE group (*Concorde des deux langages*, 1513).

## Lemercier, Jacques (ca. 1585–1654)
*architect, sculptor, engraver*
Born in Pontoise, Jacques Lemercier, a major French architectural innovator, came from a family of architects. He went to Rome in 1607 and, in 1618, became the chief architect to King LOUIS XIII and, in 1624, architect of the LOUVRE. He worked on the church of Val-de-Grâce, begun by FRANÇOIS MANSART, on the Oratory, and on the plans for the church of Saint-Roch in PARIS. He built the pavillon de l'Horloge at the LOUVRE (after 1624, and the west and northeast wings of the courtyard). Lemercier laid out the plans for the town of Richelieu (Indre-et-Loire, begun in 1631) and built nearby an immense chateau (today destroyed) for Cardinal RICHELIEU. In Paris, he built the Palais Cardinal (1629–36), which became the Palais-Royal. In the domed church of the SORBONNE (1635–42),

he transposed the Italian forms with such a spirit of balance and strength that he can be considered one of the founders of French classicism.

## Le Muet, Pierre (1591–1669)
*architect*
Born in Dijon, Pierre Le Muet was architect to MARIE DE' MEDICI, LOUIS XIII, and ANNE OF AUSTRIA. Working in Paris, he took part in the building of the church of Val-de-Grâce, begun by FRANÇOIS MANSART and continued by JACQUES LEMERCIER, collaborated with LOUIS LE VAU on the Salpêtrière, and drew up the plans for the church of Notre Dame-des-Victoires. He also built in Paris the Avaux mansion, where he employed the colossal order and was innovative in the roof design. In 1623, Le Muet published *Manière de bien bâtir pour toutes sortes des personnes,* a work that constitutes one of the landmarks of the period of the development of French classical architecture.

## Le Nain family
*noted family of painters*
A family of 17th-century painters consisting of three brothers, Antoine (ca. 1588–1648), Louis (1593–1648), and Mathieu (1607–77). Known especially for their scenes of peasant life, they imbued their works with such affectionate realism that lesser forms of composition are overcome. Born in Laon, they were trained for a year by a "foreign painter," probably Flemish, whose identity remains unknown, then all the brothers moved to Paris by 1630. It is known that Antoine at that point had become the master painter of the church of Saint-Germain-des-Prés. They established a studio that soon acquired a certain renown, and they received commissions from the aldermen of Paris. Although their paintings are signed only with their surname, each of the brothers is thought to have concentrated on one particular type of work. The specific authorship of many paintings, however, remains unclear. Louis, the most talented, used delicate colors, usually with silver and gray-green overtones. Mathieu most likely specialized in individual and group portraits, often of court figures. These portraits depart from his brothers' peasant

scenes. Antoine probably was a miniaturist, painting small works with bright colors on wood or copper. All the works are characterized by dignity, simplicity, and a sense of seriousness, as in *La Famille de Paysans* (1640). The work of the brothers was almost forgotten until the 19th century, when GUSTAVE COURBET revived their reputation and they became known as "painters of reality." Other paintings by the Le Nain brothers include *La Nativité; Anne d'Autriche; Vénus dans la forge de Vulcan; Corps de Garde; Joueurs de trictrac; La Réunion de famille; Le Bénédicité;* and *La Charrette ou le Retour de la fenaison* (1641), an exterior peasant scene.

## Lenclos, Anne (1616–1706)
*literary figure, courtesan*
Born in Paris, Anne Lenclos, or Ninon de Lenclos as she was known, was an educated, cultured, and, for the period, liberated woman (she had as her lovers Admiral GASPARD COLIGNY, LE GRAND CONDÉ, and the MARQUIS D'ESTRÉES). She was highly regarded by Mme de MAINTENON, Mme de la Sablière, and Mme de LA FAYETTE, and she brought together in her salon an intellectual society who, like her, professed libertinage in mores (as followers of Epicurus) and ideas (in reading MICHEL DE MONTAIGNE). A friend of CHARLES DE SAINT-ÉVREMOND, to whom she addressed her *Lettres* (published in 1886), Ninon de Lenclos was the link between the current skepticism of the 17th century and the philosophic movement of the 18th.

## L'Enfant, Pierre-Charles (1754–1825)
*architect, engineer*
Born in Paris, Pierre-Charles L'Enfant was a student of the Royal Academy of Painting (1771) and, in 1776, went to fight in the American War of Independence. He was promoted to major of the Engineering Corps in 1783. After a sojourn in Paris, he returned to the United States, where he renovated the New York City Hall and was then engaged by George Washington to prepare the plans for the new federal capital (1791). He was dismissed, however, in 1792, for having challenged various private interests, but his plans for the city of Washington, D.C., were, on the whole, retained

as the basis for its urban layout. Badly paid for his work, L'Enfant died in poverty.

## Le Nôtre, André (1613–1700)
*landscape architect*
André Le Nôtre, who developed the great French neoclassical style, was born in Paris. The son of the royal gardener of the Tuileries, in 1637, he became gardener to the king (1645) and later was put in charge of royal buildings. In 1649, he redesigned the gardens of the Tuileries and then, thanks to NICOLAS FOUQUET, took over the design of the park of Vaux-le-Vicomte (finished in 1661). The creator of the garden style "à la française," he developed the park of VERSAILLES according to a design approved by King LOUIS XIV. Le Nôtre's work is characterized by highly formal arrangements, using such architectural features as canals, statues, fountains, ornamental urns, trimmed shrubs and trees, geometric floral terraces, and grand axial vistas, some extending for kilometers. He worked also at Clagny (near Versailles), Marly, Sceaux, Choisy, Maintenon, and Dampierre, and received numerous foreign commissions as well. As the epitome of French classicism, his style set the tone for all European landscape architecture until the end of the 18th century.

## Léotard, François (1942–   )
*political figure*
Born in Cannes, François Léotard served as mayor of Fréjus (1977), as a deputy (1978), as president of the Parti républicain (1982–90; since 1995), and of the UNION POUR LA DÉMOCRATIE FRANÇAISE (1996), and was minister of culture and communications (1986–88) in the first government of "cohabitation." He put through the privatization of the main television broadcasting station, TF1, and served as minister of state and as minister of defense in the government of ÉDOUARD BALLADUR (1993–95).

## Le Peletier, Ferdinand-Louis (1767–1837)
*political figure*
Born in Paris, the brother of LOUIS-MICHEL LE PELETIER, Ferdinand-Louis Le Peletier (or Lepeletier

de Saint-Fargeau) was a supporter of the REVOLUTION OF 1789 and its ideals. A member of the Jacobin Club, he was implicated in the Babeuf Conspiracy (see FRANÇOIS BABEUF) (1796), then in the assassination attempt on Napoléon Bonaparte (see NAPOLÉON I) at the rue Saint-Nicaise (1800). He was subsequently interned on the Île de Ré off the French coast, then exiled to Switzerland (1803).

## Le Peletier, Louis-Michel (1760–1793)
*political figure*

Born in Paris, Louis-Michel Le Peletier (or Lepeletier de Saint-Fargeau), the brother of FERDINAND LE PELETIER, was a deputy for the nobility to the Estates General (1789), and was one of the first to join the Third Estate at the onset of the REVOLUTION OF 1789. In 1792, he was reelected to the Convention and voted for the death of the king. He was, however, assassinated the next day by a royalist who was a member of the Royal Guard. Louis Michel Le Peletier was placed among the ranks of the "Martyrs for Liberty," like JEAN-PAUL MARAT, during the Montagnard Convention (see MONTAGNARDS).

## Le Pen, Jean-Marie (1928– )
*political figure*

Born in La Trinité-sur-Mer, Jean-Marie Le Pen served as a Poujadist deputy (1956), then as an independent (1958–62), and has been president of the right-wing Front national since 1972. He served as deputy again from 1986 to 1988 and was a candidate in the presidential elections of 1974, 1988, 1995, and 2002. In that last election, the large percentage of votes that he gained alarmed all moderate and left-wing voters concerned about his extreme, xenophobic political views and proposed policies.

## Lépine, Louis (1846–1933)
*administrator*

Born in LYON, Louis Lépine served as prefect of police (1893–97, 1899–1912) and developed a plan for the regulation of city traffic in Paris. He also created the cyclist patrol to improve the efficacy of that city's police force. Beginning in 1902, he instituted the annual exhibitions organized by the Association of French Inventors and Manufacturers, known as the Concours Lépine.

## Le Play, Frédéric (1866–1882)
*engineer, economist, sociologist*

Born in La Rivière-Saint-Sauveur, Calvados, Frédéric Le Play was a graduate of the École polytechnique and served as a counselor of state (1855) and senator (1867–70). He also created the Société d'économie sociale (1856). Initiator of the monographic method in sociology, he was the main representative of conservative and traditional Catholicism in France, and sought to reform society by restoring the authority of landowners, employers, and fathers of families. His ideas directly influenced the social paternal movement (paternalism) of the second half of the 19th century. Le Play's principal works are *Les Ouvriers européens* (1855) and *La Réforme sociale* (1864).

## Le Prieur, Yves (1885–1963)
*naval officer, aviator, inventor*

Born in Lorient, Yves Le Prieur made the first official flight in the Far East (Tokyo, December 9, 1909) on a glider pulled by an automobile. Inventor of an indicator of air routes (navigraph), used for the first time in an air flight crossing the Sahara (1925), and of a process of cinematographic transparency setting (1928), he is above all known for having conceived the idea of the first practical and portable aqualung. Also, Le Prieur developed an automatic regulator that was adopted by the French navy in 1935.

## Leprince de Beaumont, Jeanne-Marie (1711–1780)
*writer*

Born in Rouen, Jeanne-Marie Leprince de Beaumont separated from her husband and went to live in England (1745–60), where she made her living as a teacher. There, she published *Le Nouveau Magasin français*, a scientific and literary collection compiled for the young. Leprince de Beaumont remains best known for her stories, published together in *Le*

*Magasin des enfants* (1757, featuring *La Belle et la Bête,* or *Beauty and the Beast*), *Le Magasin des adolescents* (1760), and *Le Magasin des pauvres* (1768).

## Leroi-Gourhan, André (1911–1986)
*ethnologist, prehistorian*

Born in Paris, André Leroi-Gourhan completely revised the methods of archaeological investigation. Through his excavations at Arcy-sur-Cure (1946–63) and Pincevent (1964–85), he called attention to the need for a global study of excavation sites to allow an increase in the knowledge available on the way of life and on the thoughts of prehistoric humans. Speaking against the dangers of ethnologic analogies, he sought to present a technological method of explication (*Mileux et techniques*, 1945; *La Geste et la parole*, 1964–65). He also proposed an interpretation of prehistoric art based on sexual symbols (*Préhistoire de l'art occidental*, 1965). Leroi-Gourhan was a professor at the COLLÈGE DE FRANCE from 1969 to 1982.

## Leroux, Pierre (1797–1871)
*philosopher, writer, political figure*

Born in Bercy, Pierre Leroux was admitted to the École polytechnique but had to leave his studies there because of financial difficulties. A mason, then typographer, he became a contributor to the newspaper *Le Globe* (1824) which in great part soon became, because of his influence, the main disseminator of the ideas of HENRI DE SAINT-SIMON (Saint-Simonism). Effectively a Saint-Simonian after 1831, Leroux, during the quarrel in that group between PROSPER ENFANTIN and ARMAND BAZARD, took the part of the latter. An apostle of human solidarity, he put forth, in his principal work (*De l'Humanité, de son principe et de son avenir, où se trouve exposée la vraie définition de la religion*, 1840), the major principles of his religiously oriented socialism. In collaboration with his close friend GEORGE SAND and Louis Viardot, he founded *La Revue indépendente* (1841). To apply his egalitarian ideas, he created in 1845 a print shop in Boussac (Creuse), where he published *La Revue sociale*. During the REVOLUTION OF 1848, he proclaimed the republic from there and was named mayor. Deputy to the Constituent Assembly (1848),

reelected to the Legislative Assembly (1849), he took his place with the extreme Left (la Montagne). The coup d'état of December 2, 1851, forced him to seek refuge in England, then on the island of Jersey. Returning to France (1869), he was no longer directly involved in politics. Leroux left several political works, including *Sept discours sur la situation actuelle de la société et de l'esprit humain* (1841), *De l'humanité, solution pacifique du problème du prolétariat* (1848), and famous socialist poem, *La Grève de Samarez* (1863–64).

## Le Roy, Pierre (1717–1785)
*watchmaker*

Born in Paris, Pierre Le Roy became, in 1737, the master watchmaker in that city. He invented the modern chronometer and, with Ferdinand Berthoud, is also credited with discovering the isochronism of the spiral (1769).

## Le Roy Ladurie, Emmanuel (1929– )
*historian*

Born in Les Moutiers-en-Cinglais, Calvados, Emmanuel Le Roy Ladurie is a professor at the COLLÈGE DE FRANCE (1973) and served as administrator-general of the National Library (1987–94). He is one of the principal representatives of the "new history" associated with the Annales school (MARC BLOCH, LUCIEN FEBVRE, FERNAND BRAUDEL, FRANÇOIS FURET) that seeks an interdisciplinary approach to historical studies. Sensitive to phenomena that have evolved over a long period, Le Roy Ladurie speaks of "histoire immobile," and seeks a holistic and global approach in his research (*Paysans du Languedoc*, 1966). He has in such works explored areas long neglected by historians, such as climate (*Histoire du climat depuis l'an mil*, 1967), and has made accessible to a wide audience the aspects of historical anthropology (*Montaillou, village occitan de 1294 à 1324*, 1975; *Le Carnival des Romans*, 1980).

## Lescot, Pierre (1515–1578)
*architect*

Born in Paris, Pierre Lescot was descended from a noble family of the robe (bureaucracy). He studied architecture and mathematics and enjoyed friendships with humanists and poets. He gained the favor of the royal court at an early age and built a portion of the church of Saint-Germain-l'Auxerrois (1541–44) in collaboration with JEAN GOUJON, who did the sculpture. Lescot is famous for having conceived, under the order of King FRANCIS I, the "new" LOUVRE, with work continuing under HENRY II (southwest wing of the courtyard) until 1558. This work perfectly assimilates the Italian ornamental principles and motifs derived from antiquity. At the same time, the desire to adapt these models to the French tradition yielded an original style, characteristic of the French Renaissance. Also attributed to Lescot, in collaboration with Goujon, is the Fontaine des Innocents and the Ligneris mansion (Musée Carnavalet).

## Lesdiguières, François de Bonne, duke de (1543–1626)
*military figure, magistrate*

Born in Saint-Bonnet, Dauphiné, François de Bonne, duke de Lesdiguières began a career as a magistrate when he enlisted as an ordinary soldier in the HUGUENOT army. He rapidly rose through the ranks and soon became the leader of the Protestants in Dauphiné (1577). Named by King HENRY IV to be lieutenant general of the armies of Piedmont, Savoy, and Dauphiné, he seized Grenoble and defeated the duke of Savoy (Esparron, 1591; Beauvoisin, 1592). He contributed to the economic revival of Dauphiné (rebuilding roads, establishing markets and fairs), as well as the restoration of royal authority in the region. The duke de Lesdiguiéres remained faithful to LOUIS XIII, fought at Saint-Jean d'Angély and at Montauban, and was made constable of France.

## Lespinasse, Julie de (1732–1776)
*writer, salon hostess*

Born in Lyon, Julie de Lespinasse, after having assisted MARIE, MARQUISE DU DEFFAND in her literary salon, herself held a salon where in particular the thinkers JEAN D'ALEMBERT, ÉTIENNE BONNOT DE CONDILLAC, and the marquis of CONDORCET gathered. Julie de Lespinasse's correspondence reveals a sensibility that foreshadows romanticism (*Lettres à Guibert*, posthumous, 1809).

## Lesseps, Ferdinand-Marie, viscount de (1805–1894)
*diplomat, administrator*

Born in Versailles, the son of a diplomat, Ferdinand-Marie, viscount de Lesseps, entered the consular service in 1825 and held many diplomatic posts. While assistant vice consul in Cairo and Alexandria, Egypt (1833–38), he began an association with the crown prince Said and became interested in a project of the Saint-Simonians (see HENRI DE SAINT-SIMON) regarding the building of a canal between the Mediterranean and Red Seas. Lesseps subsequently served as minister plenipotentiary in Spain, (1848–49) then was put in charge of negotiations between the papacy and the Roman Republic (1849) by the commander of the French forces in Rome, General NICOLAS OUDINOT. He was recalled to Egypt in 1854 when Said came to power and began plans for the canal in earnest. Lesseps founded, despite the opposition of the British, the Compagnie universelle du canal maritime de Suez for that purpose. Work began on the Suez Canal on April 25, 1859, and the canal was formally opened on November 17, 1869, in the presence of the Empress EUGÉNIE. Lesseps, who because of this achievement was named to the Academy of Sciences (1873) and the ACADÉMIE FRANÇAISE (1884), in 1880 became the president of a company that planned to build a canal across the Isthmus of Panama. The project was given up for political and financial reasons, however, and Lesseps and his son were tried for mismanagement and misappropriation of the company funds. They were fined and sentenced to prison, but the sentences were never served.

See also PANAMA AFFAIR.

## Le Sueur, Eustache (1617–1655)
*painter*

Born in Paris, Eustache Le Sueur was the favorite student of SIMON VOUET, whose influence is evident in Le Sueur's masterpiece, the 22 paintings of the life of St. Bruno (*Vie de saint Bruno*), done for a

Carthusian monastery. Specializing in religious and mythological works, he was strongly influenced also by the Renaissance classicism of Raphael, and by the baroque classicism of his contemporary NICOLAS POUSSIN (*Les Muses*, 1644). A founding member of the Royal Academy (1648), Le Sueur was also the founder of the style that is today called "Atticism." His works, reflecting a sense of spirituality and sensitivity, as well as classical techniques and composition, include *Agar et l'ange; Portement de croix;* and *Messe de saint Martin.*

## Le Tellier, Michel (1603–1685)
*political figure, administrator*

Born in Paris, Michel Le Tellier was responsible with others for suppressing the FRONDE revolt in Normandy (1639). He owed his rise to Cardinal MAZARIN and served as secretary of state for war and as minister of state (1643). He was also sent on diplomatic missions and played a role in the negotiations leading to the Peace of Rueil, March 1649, which ended the uprising. The founder of the royal army, he prepared the way for the work of his oldest son, FRANÇOIS MICHEL LE TELLIER, MARQUIS DE LOUVOIS, who succeeded to his secretariat when he became chancellor (1677). Michel Le Tellier played an important political role until his death and was, under LOUIS XIV, one of the framers of the revocation of the EDICT OF NANTES. JACQUES-BÉNIGNE BOSSUET gave his funeral oration.

## Le Tellier, Michel (1643–1719)
*cleric*

Born near Vire, Michel Le Tellier was the provincial of the Jesuit order and confessor to King LOUIS XIV after FRANÇOIS LA CHAISE (1709). Le Tellier encouraged and supported the king in his policies against Protestants and Jansenists (destruction of Port-Royal des Champs, obtaining the papal bull *Unigenitus Dei Filius*).

## Le Vau, Louis (1612–1670)
*architect, decorator*

One of the principal designers of the Palace of VERSAILLES, Louis Le Vau was born in Paris. He often worked in collaboration with his brother, François Le Vau, and together they designed and built numerous houses and mansions in Paris and elsewhere, including the châteaux of Vaux-le-Vicomte (built for NICOLAS FOUQUET, it aroused the envy of King LOUIS XIV), Meuden, and Raincy. In 1654, Le Vau also redesigned the facade of the LOUVRE and developed the plans for the main building of the Collège des Quatre-Nations. In 1654, he was named first architect to the king and, in 1669, began work on Versailles. Supervising a brilliant array of artisans, he was responsible for the central building, the garden facade, and the first orangerie at Trianon. His style recalls noble classical proportions and overwhelming scale. Le Vau's interiors are marked also by baroque ornateness and a sense of grandeur. His ideas and forms helped to define the French architecture of the period.

## Le Verrier, Urbain (1811–1877)
*astronomer*

Born in Saint-Lô, Urbain Le Verrier analyzed and compared the early charts of the movements of the planet Uranus with observations that he conducted to support the existence of an unknown mass that was affecting those movements. He determined and confirmed (independently of the British astronomer John Adams) the elements of the orbit of a planet (Neptune), which had been discovered earlier by the German astronomer Johann Gottfried Galle (1846). Le Verrier served as a deputy in the National Assembly (1849), as a senator (1852), and as director of the Paris Observatory. He is responsible also for a revision of the charts of planetary movements. Le Verrier was named to the Academy of Sciences in 1846.

## Lévi-Strauss, Claude (1908– )
*anthropologist*

The leading proponent of structuralism in social anthropology, Claude Lévi-Strauss was born in Brussels, Belgium, and raised in France. He studied at the SORBONNE and, in 1935, became professor of sociology (1935–39) at the University of São Paulo, Brazil. There, he pursued field studies of the Native American tribes. Lévi-Strauss also taught at the New School for Social Research, in New York City

(1942–45), served as associate director of the Musée de l'Homme in Paris (1949), and as director of studies at the École pratique des hautes études (1950–74). In 1959, he became professor of social anthropology at the COLLÈGE DE FRANCE. Lévi-Strauss is preeminent among those scholars who believe that the various cultural traits of all human communities demonstrate a common underlying framework. In this he was influenced by ÉMILE DURKHEIM and others. Lévi-Strauss further believed that such basic structural concepts as time, color and gender became elaborated through culture. He developed the idea of contrasting, but complementary, groups known as "moieties," which exist in each human culture. He also expounded the idea that totemism is merely an anthropological concept that has no objective reality. Lévi-Strauss's other writings include *Structures élémentaires de la parenté* (1949); *Le Totémisme aujourd'hui* (1962); *La Pensée sauvage* (1962); *Le Cru e le Cuit* (1964); *Du miel aux cendres* (1967); *L'Origine des manières de table* (1968); *L'Homme nu* (1971); *Anthropologie structurale* (1973), which is his manifesto. Lévi-Strauss was awarded the LEGION OF HONOR and was made a member of the ACADÉMIE FRANÇAISE in 1973.

## L'Hospital, Michel (1504–1573)
*political figure*
Born in Aigueperse, Puy-de-Dôme, Michel L'Hospital studied at Padua, Italy, and, through his father, who had remained loyal to the Bourbons during their exile, entered the service of MARGUERITE DE NAVARRE, serving as her chancellor. He later served as chancellor to the parlement, president of the Chambre des comptes, then as chancellor of France (1560). He pursued a dual policy of administrative reform and compromise and appeasement in religious matters. He was responsible for the Edict of Romorantin (1560), which prevented the Inquisition from being established in France, the Colloquy of Poissy, which tried to reach a compromise between Catholics and Protestants, the Ordinance of Orléans, which, following the example of the ESTATES GENERAL (1560–61), granted to the Reformed Church, with certain limits, a degree of religious freedom, and undertook administrative reforms followed by the ordinances

of Roussillon (1564) and Moulins (1566). While his administrative reforms succeeded, L'Hospital was not able to achieve his plan of religious reconciliation, and the Ordinance of Orléans had, as a direct consequence, the massacre of Wassy (1562), which began the religious wars in France. Powerless, L'Hospital retired in 1568, escaping the SAINT BARTHOLOMEW'S DAY MASSACRE of 1572. L'Hospital was also a patron of the arts, encouraging the Pléiade group of poets and composing Latin poetry himself. His other writings include a *Traité de la réformation; Harangues;* and *Testament politique.*

## Lhote, André (1883–1962)
*painter, art critic*
Born in BORDEAUX, André Lhote in 1908 settled in Paris and became interested in African art. After having been influenced by fauvism and PAUL CÉZANNE, he was sensitive to the cubist current, while remaining attached to the depiction of the human figure and maintaining a taste for lively and strongly contrasting colors (*L'Escale,* 1913), and sought to reconcile abstraction and reality. Favoring order and method, he exhibited at the Section d'or in 1912. Inspired by the synthetic cubism of ROBERT DELAUNAY, he reorganized forms in an ensemble of colored planes (*Rugby,* 1912), then, around 1920, evolved to a more decorative style. Having founded an art school in 1922, he played an important role as a teacher and a critic (*NRF* chronicles after 1917). A precise and lucid analyst (*Seurat, Bonnard*), he published works on landscape painting (*Traité du paysage,* 1938) and one on human figures (*Traité de la figure,* 1950).

## Lifar, Serge (1905–1986)
### (Sergey Mikhailovych Lifar)
*dancer, choreographer, writer*
Of Russian origin, Sergey Lifar was born in Kiev and was a student of Bronislava Nijinska and Enrico Cecchetti. He was brought into the Ballets russes by Sergey Diaghilev (1923), where he quickly demonstrated his exceptional talent of interpretation (*Le Lac des cygnes, L'Oiseau bleu, Apollon musagéte*) and choreography (*Renard,* by Igor Stravinsky). On the death of Diaghilev, Lifar was called by J. Rouche to

the Opéra de Paris (1929), where he choreographed *Créatures de Prométhée* (music by Beethoven), which earned him the position of first dancer and master of ballet. He then began a brilliant career, marked by numerous creations, like *Bacchus et Ariane* (music by ALBERT ROUSSEL, 1931) *Salade* (music by DARIUS MIL-HAUD, 1935), *Icare*, a "rhythmic" ballet (1935), *Le Chevalier et la Demoiselle* (music by Philippe Gaubert, 1938) *Les Animaux modèles* (music by FRANCIS POULENC, 1943), and *Roméo et Juliette* (music by Sergey Prokofiev, 1955). Lifar also revived numerous works: *Prélude à l'après-midi d'un faune, Le Spectre de la rose, and Giselle*, and composed choreography for various other companies, including the Ballets de Monte-Carlo. Faithful to the academic tradition that he renewed and enlarged, Lifar proclaimed the autonomy of dance in relation to the other arts. He also published numerous works (*La Manifeste du choréographe*, 1935; *Traité de la danse académique*, 1949; *Histoire des Ballets russes*, 1950).

## Ligue du Bien public

The Ligue du Bien public was a feudal coalition that rose in March 1465 against King LOUIS XI and his policy of increasing royal power. Led by the king's brother Charles of Berry, but including at the beginning the dukes of Alençon, Bourbon, and Francis II of Brittany, and joined by CHARLES THE BOLD, this league also had some support among the lesser nobility and the bourgeoisie. After the decisive battle of Montlhéry (July 1465), the king had to agree, by the treaties of Conflans and Saint-Maur (October), to restore the towns of the SOMME to Charles the Bold and to give his brother Normandy, which he took back the following year.

## Limbourg, Pol, and Jean, and Hermann (early 15th-century)

*miniaturists*

Of Flemish origin, the Limbourg brothers, Pol, Jean, and Hermann, studied in illuminating workshops in Paris and, around 1402, Pol and Jean began to work for the dukes of Burgundy. In 1410, texts mention that the three brothers were attracted to the court of Jean, duke of Berry. There, they produced their famous *Belles Heures*, also called *Heures*

*d'Ailly* (between 1403 and 1413) and, in particular, *Les Très Riches Heures du duc de Berry* (1413–16), one of the most remarkable illuminated manuscripts of the early 15th century. The religious scenes, and especially the dozen miniatures of the yearly calendar, evoke a courtly and luxurious worldly universe and show the artists' great attention to detail and interest in landscape. Rendered with intense colors and jewel-like elegance and precision, the whole work is an innovation that sets the stage for later schools of art.

## Linder, Max  (1883–1925)
### (Gabriel Maximilien Leuvielle)

*actor, film producer*

Max Linder (the stage name of Gabriel Maximilien Leuvielle) was born in Saint-Loubès, Gironde. His style, finesse, mischievousness, and playfulness made him a precursor of the British actor and film star Charles Chaplin, who himself recognized Linder as his master. Creator of a type of elegant, yet comic and impertinent persona, he made his character popular through some 300 films made between 1905 and 1925 (*Max et le quinquina, Max toréador*) in France, and in the United States (*Sept Ans de malheur*, 1921; *Soyez ma femme*, 1921; *L'Étroit Mousquetaire*, 1922).

## Lindet, Jean-Baptiste-Robert  (1746–1825)

*political figure*

Born in Bernay, Jean-Baptiste-Robert Lindet was the district attorney for his area (1790) and, during the REVOLUTION OF 1789, was elected to the Legislative Assembly, then the Convention. He took his place first with the deputies for the Plain, then joined the Mountain (MONTAGNARDS). He composed the list of charges against King LOUIS XVI (citizen L. Capet) for his trial and, in April 1793, joined the Committee of Public Safety, to which he was reelected in July of the same year and was in charge of rationing. Under the Thermidorian Convention, he tried to defend the Committee of Public Safety and its members, and was implicated in the Montagnard uprising of 1 Prairial Year III (May 20, 1795). Lindet benefited from the amnesty of the Year IV and, in 1799, served as minister of finance.

## Lissagaray, Prosper-Olivier (1839–1901)

*journalist*

Born in Auch, Prosper-Olivier Lissagaray was the founder of the *Revue des cours littéraires,* who many times took a position against the policies of the SEC-OND EMPIRE. Joining the Paris COMMUNE in 1871, he also published the newspapers *L'Action* and *Le Tribune du peuple.* After the suppression of the Commune, he went into exile in England until the amnesty of 1880. Lissagaray left a work, *Les Huit Journées de mai de derrière les barricades* (1871) and a study, *Histoire de la Commune de Paris,* (1876), on the Commune, both firsthand accounts by an observer and participant that are among the most valuable sources of information on this period.

## Littre, Maximilien-Paul-Émile (1801–1881)

*philosopher, philologist, political figure*

A positivist, Maximilien-Paul-Émile Littre was born in Paris, where he first studied medicine. He translated the works of Hippocrates (1839–61) and David Strauss's *Life of Jesus* (*Vie de Jésus,* 1839–40), and also worked on an *Histoire littéraire de la France* (1838). A disciple of AUGUSTE COMTE, he made that philosopher's ideas known through articles in *Le National* (1844, 1849–51) and by the creation of the *Revue de philosophie positive* (1867). He still declined, however, to get involved in political or mystical aspects of the positivist movement. Littre worked on the *Cours de philosophie positive* and attempted to classify the sciences, through an integration of political economy, philosophic psychology, morality, and esthetics (*A. Comte et la philosophie positive,* 1863; *Des origines organiques de la morale,* 1870; *La Science au point de vue philosophique,* 1873). His numerous philological and lexicographic writings led to the publishing of his principal work, *Dictionnaire de la langue française* (1863–72). A liberal, Littre was elected deputy to the National Assembly (1871) and senator (1875). His election to the ACADÉMIE FRANÇAISE (after an initial rejection) led to the departure of FÉLIX DUPANLOUP. Littre's death was the occasion for great controversy, as his daughter Sophie affirmed that he had been converted to Christianity and had abandoned his positivistic agnosticism.

## Lods, Marcel (1891–1978)

*architect*

Born in Paris, Marcel Lods was an associate of EUGÈNE BEAUDOUIN and is known for having built the housing development of La Muette at Drancy, near Paris (1932–35). There he adopted the formula of apartment towers that subsequently would be widely imitated. With Beaudouin, he built the Maison du peuple at Clichy (1937–39) in which were employed the ingenious prototypes of curtain walls derived from JEAN PROUVÉ. After World War II, Lods built numerous other structures, including the residential complex of Marly-les-Grandes-Terres (1958–60).

## Loisy, Alfred (1857–1940)

*biblical scholar*

Born in Ambrières, Marne, Alfred Loisy, who was ordained a Catholic priest (1879), was professor of Hebrew, then of Holy Scripture, at the Catholic Institute of Paris. He founded the revue *L'Enseignement biblique* and wrote *Histoire critique du texte des versions de l'Ancien Testament* (1892) but had to resign from his chair in 1893. The publication of *L'Évangile el l'Église* (1902), in which he tried to place Christian dogmas within a historical perspective, placed him in the forefront of the Modernist crisis. Modernism, considered revisionist, was a viewpoint condemned by Pope Pius X. Loisy's writings were placed on the Index of books prohibited by the Catholic Church and he was himself excommunicated in 1908. Becoming professor of History at the COLLÈGE DE FRANCE (1909–33), he undertook the study of a "religion of humanity" and published numerous other works, including *La Morale humaine* (1923) and *Mémoires pour servir à l'histoire religieuse de notre temps* (1930–31).

## Loménie de Brienne, Étienne-Charles de (1727–1794)

*prelate and political figure*

Born in Paris, Étienne-Charles de Loménie de Brienne was a friend and associate of the philosophers of the Enlightenment. Despite his own freethinking attitudes, he was made bishop of Condom (1760) and archbishop of Toulouse (1787). He also was an opponent of CHARLES-ALEXANDRE DE CALONNE, whose policies he rescinded when he succeeded him as minister of finance (1787). Not able, however, to have his own measures adopted by the Parlement, Loménie de Brienne had to make successive loans and consider a meeting of the ESTATES GENERAL to discuss the gravity of the fiscal situation in France. He left the ministry after the suspension of payments to the Treasury and was named archbishop of Sens (1787) and cardinal (1788). He was finally dismissed from the government when he took the oath to the CIVIL CONSTITUTION OF THE CLERGY during the REVOLUTION OF 1789, but was nonetheless imprisoned in 1793. Loménie de Brienne was elected to the ACADÉMIE FRANÇAISE in 1770.

### Long, Marguerite (1874–1966)
*pianist*

Born in Nîmes, Marguerite Long was a skilled and sensitive piano soloist and was the interpreter and friend of some of the great musicians of her time (GABRIEL FAURÉ, CLAUDE DEBUSSY, MAURICE RAVEL), for whom she played at the debut of their various works. A renowned teacher, Long taught at the Paris Conservatoire (1906–40) and founded, with the violinist JACQUES THIBAUD, the competition that bears their name (1943) and that, in 1946, became an international event.

### Longueville, Anne-Geneviève de Bourbon-Condé, duchess de (1619–1679)
*nobility*

Born in Vincennes, Anne-Geneviève de Bourbon-Condé, duchess de Longueville was the sister of LOUIS II DE CONDÉ and of the prince de Conti. She married Henry II, duke de Longueville, who had as his mistress the duchess de MONTBAZON, who, in turn, provoked the death of Anne de Longueville's lover, a member of the Coligny family. Anne de Longueville then became actively involved, through her new paramour, FRANÇOIS, DUKE DE LA ROCHEFOUCAULD, in the FRONDE, encouraging also her other lover, HENRY I, VISCOUNT DE TURENNE, to join the rebellion. When the Fronde ended, Anne de Longueville retired to spend the rest of her life in prayer and meditation, at Port-Royal des Champs and the convent of the Faubourg Saint-Jacques.

### Lorrain, le (1600–1682)
### (Claude Lorrain; Claude Gelée)
*painter and engraver*

Born in Champagne, near Mirecourt, Claude Gelée, or le Lorrain as he is better known, is with NICOLAS POUSSIN one of the greatest masters of 17th-century idealized landscape painting. Of peasant origin, he followed his brother, a wood engraver, and settled in Fribourg-en-Brisgau. Impoverished and nearly illiterate, he then left for Italy and probably worked in Naples. In Rome in 1619, he worked for the landscape artist Agostino Tassi, who introduced him to painting. Returning to France in 1625, he worked eventually for the duke of Lorraine but then left again for Rome (1627), where he stayed for the rest of his life. By 1637, his work was being recognized and appreciated by Pope Urban VIII and various French and English architects. He dedicated himself to landscape painting and did numerous scenes of the Roman countryside, with his particular contribution to the idealized landscape genre being his masterly treatment of light. His stylistic evolution falls into three main periods. His early landscapes often feature slanting and other experimental light effects, especially in harbor scenes (*Port de mer au soleil couchant*, 1639, LOUVRE). At this time (1644), he also began compiling his *Liber veritatis*, a collection of sketches of his works, to guard against forgeries. After approximately 1640, his work became more tranquil, as he used warmer and lighter tones (*Les Quatres Heures du jour*). Finally, during the 1660s, although he returned to his earlier themes, Le Lorrain shows in his work a tendency to a more symbolic and visionary style, with a cooler color range (*Psyché devant le palais de l'Amour*, 1664), that often depicts an imagined antiquity.

### Loubet, Émile (1838–1929)
*political figure*

A president of the THIRD REPUBLIC, Émile Loubet was born in Marsanne, Drôme. He began his political life as a moderate republican deputy (1876–85), was a member of the Senate (1885–99), and served as its president (1896). He served as minister of public works (1887–88), then as minister of the interior (1892–93), and was elected to the presidency of the republic upon the death of FÉLIX FAURÉ (1899). Believing in the innocence of ALFRED DREYFUS and, in spite of anti-Dreyfusard threats (he was himself attacked at the Auteuil race course), he pardoned Captain Dreyfus in August 1899. Loubet's term (1899–1906) was marked by the anticlericalism of the PIERRE WALDECK-ROUSSEAU and ÉMILE COMBES ministries, and by important diplomatic activity (visit of Czar Nicholas II to France in 1901; Loubet visited Russia in 1902; King Edward VII of England visited France in 1903), which contributed to a rapprochment among France, Russia, England, and also Italy. After his term ended, Loubet retired from political life.

## Louis XI (1423–1483)
*king of France*

Louis XI, the son and successor of Charles VII and of MARIE OF ANJOU, reigned from 1461 to 1483. Born in Bourges, as king he would continue Charles VII's work of restoring unity and stability to France after the ravages of the Hundred Years' War. In his youth, Louis had joined with discontented nobles in an unsuccessful rebellion (the PRAGUERIE) against his father. In 1440, he was pardoned and made governor of Dauphiné, where he demonstrated great administrative ability. After the death of his first wife, Margaret of Scotland, he defied his father by marrying Charlotte of Savoy (1457). From 1456 to 1461, he lived at the court of Philippe the Good of Burgundy. Louis was known as "the Spider" because of his appearance and the agility with which he outmaneuvered his enemies. As king, his greatest opponent became CHARLES THE BOLD, duke of Burgundy and Philippe's successor. Charles had formed a conspirational league with nobles against the king (1465), and Louis, in response and in his efforts to curb the powers of the French nobility, used the help of the lower nobility and the bourgeoisie. After Charles's defeat and death in 1477, Louis continued the war against MARIE OF BURGUNDY, Charles's daughter. By 1481, Louis had added Anjou, Provence, Maine, and

other areas to his kingdom. In 1482, he divided the Burgundian territories with Maximilian of Habsburg, Marie's husband. A despotic ruler, Louis XI, during the rest of his reign, consolidated power through diplomacy, intrigue, bribery, treachery, and war. In doing so, he laid the foundation for the absolute French monarchy and, by promoting commerce and industry, increased the country's wealth. He was succeeded by his son, who reigned as CHARLES VIII.

## Louis XII (1462–1515)
*king of France*

Born in Blois, the son of CHARLES OF ORLÉANS and Marie of Cleves, Louis (reigned 1498–1515) was imprisoned for a number of years (1487–90) for rebelling against King CHARLES VIII. Earlier, he had been forced by King LOUIS XI to marry JEANNE DE FRANCE, whom the king believed to be sterile, thereby insuring the extinction of Louis's line. On ascending the throne, Louis XII had this marriage annulled and married ANNE OF BRITTANY, widow of Charles VIII. As king, he showed a rare sense of clemency toward former adversaries, but he soon became involved in the wars in Italy (1499–1515), in which he sought to enforce his claims on various inheritances and pursue a policy of French aggrandizement. After the Battles of Milan and Naples, a coalition of powers expelled the French (1504), and by the terms of the Treaty of Blois, Louis had to give as part of his daughter's dowry to her fiancé, the future emperor Charles V, territory in Italy, Burgundy, and Brittany. The treaty, however, was nullified by the Parlement of Tours. This was followed by a period of further military activity, which brought some victories (Ravenna), but ended with the defeat of the French by the Swiss at Novara and by the English at Guinegatte, and Louis's forces were forced to withdraw. The reign ended with further military setbacks, despite a peace signed with England in which Louis married Mary of England, the sister of King Henry VIII. On the domestic level, Louis XII was a popular king, and his various judicial and financial reforms as well as the fairness of his rule earned him the epithet Father of the People (under the administration of Cardinal AMBOISE, the judicial systems was reformed

and traditional laws were codified in the ordinances of 1499). Not having a son, Louis XII was
succeeded by his son-in-law, the future FRANCIS I.

## Louis XIII (1601–1643)
*king of France*

Born in Fontainebleau, the son of HENRY IV, first of
the Bourbon kings, and MARIE DE' MEDICI, Louis,
who reigned from 1610 to 1643, became king at
nine years of age. During his minority (1610–17),
his mother served as regent. She allied France with
Spain and arranged the marriage (1615) of Louis to
Princess ANNE OF AUSTRIA, daughter of Philip III of
Spain. There was a struggle for power between
Louis and his mother during the period of the
regency (Louis, aided by CHARLES DE LUYNES, had
the adventurer CONCINO CONCINI assassinated), but
finally both were reconciled to each other. For most
of his reign, Louis's policies were determined by
Cardinal RICHELIEU, who joined the Council of Ministers (1624) through the efforts of Marie de'
Medici, and served as prime minister until his death
in 1642. Under Richelieu's anti-Hapsburg policy,
France entered the THIRTY YEARS' WAR as an ally of
Sweden and the German Protestant princes. Louis's
reign was also marked by occasional strife between
Catholics and HUGUENOTS, whom he sometimes persecuted. There many conspiracies against Richelieu,
often instigated by the king's brother, GASTON OF
ORLÉANS. Louis was not, however, the puppet king
as he has sometimes been portrayed. No decisions
were made by Richelieu without the king's consent,
and Louis took strong actions against conspiracies.
Also, during his reign, Artois was taken from Burgundy and added to France. Moreover, he was a
patron of the arts and had important additions
made to the palace at Fontainebleau. Louis XIII was
succeeded by his son, the future LOUIS XIV.

## Louis XIV (1638–1715)
*king of France*

King of France from 1643 to 1715, Louis XIV, the
son of LOUIS XIII and ANNE OF AUSTRIA, was born at
Saint-Germain-en-Laye. He was only five years old
when his father died. His mother served as regent
with the help of Cardinal MAZARIN during the
period troubled by the FRONDE. It was these events

Portrait of Louis XIV, by Hyacinthe Rigaud, 1701
*(Library of Congress)*

that impressed on the young Louis a belief in royal
absolutism and his fear of living in Paris. His education, while not neglected, remained rudimentary,
but Mazarin took great care to initiate him in affairs
of state.

The Treaty of the Pyrenees (1659) arranged for
his marriage to the Infanta MARIA THERESA of Spain,
while other terms of this treaty formed much of the
basis for foreign policy for the rest of his reign.
Louis's first political act, when he took power after
the death of Mazarin, was to assume the role and
powers of prime minister. He then began to develop
in France the structure of divine-right state absolutism, already adopted by the Stuarts in England
and as defined by JACQUES-BÉNIGNE BOSSUET in his
*Politique tirée de l' Écriture sainte*. Louis concentrated
all power in his hands, keeping to the side even
his family and mistresses, including Mme de LA
VALLIÈRE, Mme de MONTESPAN, and Mme de MAIN-

TENON, whom he secretly married but who never played an important political role. His ministers were merely executors of his policies and were mostly from the bourgeoisie (JEAN-BAPTISTE COLBERT). The nobility, aside from those in the military, played a purely ceremonial role, while the parlements, too, lost much of their power. The regime was supported by a corps of royal police agents.

Parallel to the development of the theory of absolutism was that of the cult of the Sun King (Roi-Soleil) incarnate in Louis and centered at VERSAILLES, which was the royal residence after 1672. From there, Louis led a regime based on prestige and conquest. The economic policies of Colbert allowed the government the wealth to pursue an aggressive foreign policy based on affirming French supremacy and extending the nation to its natural borders. Soon, however, there were setbacks. During the War of Devolution (1667–68), Louis invaded the Spanish Netherlands. His quick victories prompted Holland, England, and Sweden to check France, but Louis gained 12 fortresses in Flanders and soon isolated Holland by buying English and Swedish neutrality. In 1672, he attacked Holland and, at the Treaty of Nijmegen (1678), gained the Franche-Comté and other territory. Both France and Louis reached their apogee, with Louis being awarded the title "le Grand" by the city of Paris.

Internally, Louis intensified persecution of French Protestants (see HUGUENOTS), and in 1685, he revoked the EDICT OF NANTES, forcing more than 200,000 of his subjects into exile and igniting the CAMISARD revolt. He also aggressively attacked the Jansenist movement within the French Catholic Church (see JANSENISM). Louis also continued his aggressive foreign policy with the invasion of the Palatinate in 1688, in which, however, he gained little at the subsequent Peace of Ryswick. His last major military venture, the War of the Spanish Succession (1701–13), ended in the Treaty of Utrecht, which gave France control in Spain but caused the surrender of several North American territories to the British.

In the arts, Louis's achievements include the performances of the plays of MOLIÈRE and JEAN RACINE at the royal court and the musical presentations of LULLY at the same setting. Louis XIV founded the Academy of Painting and Sculpture (1655), of Science (1666), and Architecture (1671) and, in 1680,

established the COMÉDIE-FRANÇAISE. The great architectural glory of Versailles itself is his monument. But Louis was never able to resolve the tensions between an absolute government and a bureaucracy committed to efficiency. Louis's perpetual pursuit of glory, military expansionism, and underestimation of other powers, especially England, as well as the loss of colonial territory and his indifference to financial excess, all left for his successors in the regency government a weakened nation and eventually grave economic and political crises.

## Louis XV (1710–1774)
*king of France*

Louis XV was born at VERSAILLES, the great-grandson of LOUIS XIV, whom he succeeded at age five. PHILIPPE, DUKE OF ORLÉANS, served as regent until Louis reached his legal majority in 1723. In 1725, Louis married MARIE LESZCZYNSKA, the daughter of Stanislaus I of Poland. The next year, ANDRÉ-HERCULE, Cardinal de FLEURY became Louis XV's chief minister. Under Fleury, France had a stable administration for the next two decades.

An intelligent but skeptical and somewhat weak-willed and erratic king, Louis remained in nominal control but took only a sporadic interest in affairs of state, and he did not follow a consistent policy at home or abroad. Often he was influenced by his mistresses, especially the marquise de POMPADOUR and Mme du BARRY. During Louis XV's reign, France was involved in various wars. Through the War of the Polish Succession (1733–35), France gained the province of Lorraine. The next conflict, the War of the Austrian Succession (1740–48) marked the beginning of a new colonial struggle with Britain, but was indecisive. In the SEVEN YEARS' WAR (1756–63), France lost most of its overseas territories to Britain. During this period, foreign policy, too, was affected by Louis XV's secret diplomacy, in which his agents in other countries at times pursued goals that were in conflict with those of his own ministers.

Through the efforts of a new minister, however, the duke de CHOISEUL, during the 1760s the situation improved to an extent. In the later years of his reign, Louis XV cooperated with RENÉ DE MAUPEAU, his chancellor (eventually in a triumvirate with JOSEPH MARIE, ABBÉ TERRAY, and EMMANUEL, DUKE

D'AIGUILLON), in an attempt to reform the fiscal tax structures. The parlements, which had opposed reform, were reorganized in 1771 and lost their power to oppose royal decrees, as a more authoritarian regime developed. Some efforts were also made to tax the clergy and nobility, but these were halted after Louis XV's death. During Louis XV's reign, criticism against despotism came from the philosophes and the writers of the *Encyclopédie*, and there was a growing interest in reform. Louis left a monarchy somewhat weakened, but with French civilization still at its peak.

## Louis XVI (1754–1793)
### king of France

The king of France from 1774 to 1792, Louis XVI was born at VERSAILLES, the son of the dauphin (the son of LOUIS XV) and Marie-Josèphe of Saxony. He was raised with a strictly religious education and was of middle intelligence, with an indecisive but virtuous character. He took some interest in the natural sciences and geography and in the locksmiths' craft to which he devoted his spare time. In 1770, he married MARIE ANTOINÉTTE of Austria (the marriage was arranged by the chief minister ETIENNE DE CHOISEUL in the interests of an Austrian alliance), and they had four children. Immediately upon his accession to the throne, and aided by capable ministers such as ANN-ROBERT TURGOT, CHRÉTIEN DE MALSHERBES, and CHARLES, COUNT DE VERGENNES, Louis XVI undertook a fiscal and tax reform that had to be reversed because of opposition from the ruling classes and the court. In 1776, Turgot was replaced by JACQUES NECKER. After the French government gave financial aid to the American colonies (1776–81), Necker proposed a drastic taxation program for the French nobility. He was forced to resign in 1781 and was replaced as finance minister by CHARLES DE CALONNE (1783), who borrowed money from the court until 1786, when the limit was reached. Heavy taxation, however, along with the financial excesses of the court, caused popular discontent, resulting in Necker's recall. But he could not prevent the bankruptcy of the government. In 1788, Louis was forced to call a meeting of the ESTATES GENERAL. Once in session, the Estates General (later the National Assembly) assumed power and instituted reforms that Louis

was incapable of accepting (see REVOLUTION OF 1789). On July 14, 1789, the BASTILLE was taken by a Parisian crowd, and shortly after, the king and the royal family were imprisoned in the Tuileries. In 1791, they attempted to escape but were captured and brought back to Paris. Louis XVI swore allegiance to the new constitution but continued to communicate with the émigré community and with counterrevolutionaries. In 1792, the National Convention declared France a republic and condemned the king as a traitor, although many defended him at his trial. He was executed in the Place de la Révolution (now Place de la Concorde) in Paris on January 21, 1793. Louis XVI is considered more a victim of circumstances than a despot like his immediate predecessors. Lacking the qualities of an effective ruler, he preferred to pursue his pastimes while allowing his wife and others at the court to influence him unduly.

## Louis XVII (1785–1795)
### king of France

Born Louis-Charles of France at VERSAILLES, Louis XVII was the second son of LOUIS XVI and MARIE ANTOINETTE. After having borne the title duke of Normandy, he became dauphin in 1789 upon the death of his older brother. Imprisoned in the Temple in August 1792, he was declared king of France by the French Royalists after the execution of his father in January 1793. Taken from his mother shortly after, he died while a prisoner of the republican government in Paris, probably in 1795. Doubts remained about his fate, as numerous personages over the centuries have claimed his identity or to be his heirs. Scientific tests in 1999, however, confirmed that the existent remains in Paris are those of the young Louis XVII, and, per royal tradition, his preserved heart was entombed at St-Denis in 2004.

## Louis XVIII (1755–1824)
### king of France

King of France from 1814 to 1824, Louis XVIII was born at VERSAILLES, the grandson of LOUIS XV and brother to LOUIS XVI and the count of Artois (later CHARLES X). He was first known as the count of Provence and as "Monsieur" on the accession of his brother. Married in 1771 to Marie-Joséphine of Savoy, he had no children. More intelligent than either of his brothers, he was also popular and, after the REVOLUTION OF 1789, remained in Paris. In 1791, however, he was forced to leave France, joining the count of Artois and other émigrés at Koblenz, Germany. After the execution of Louis XVI in January, he took the title of regent and, after the death of the dauphin in 1795, that of king as Louis XVIII. During the course of his exile, and because of the victories of the revolutionary and then the imperial French forces, he was forced to relocate frequently, but he never ceased to work for the restoration of the French monarchy. He sent agents to the Midi and the Vendée and made contact with PAUL BARRAS and NAPOLÉON I to further this end. And he renewed diplomatic efforts after Napoleon's initial defeats. In 1814, with the support of Britain and a provisional government headed by TALLEYRAND, he was recalled to power at the same time that the Senate voted for the overthrow of Napoléon I (April 1814). Landing at Calais in late April, he was installed in the Tuileries and, on June 4, 1814, signed the Constitutional Charter, establishing a constitutional monarchy in France. This first RESTORATION, however, was interrupted by Napoléon's return of the HUNDRED DAYS, during which Louis XVIII again went into exile. Returning after Napoléon's second abdication, Louis XVIII, as king, signed the Constitutional Charter and issued the proclamation of Saint-Ouen, which explained that the charter sought to reconcile the Revolution and the Empire with the restored monarchy, founded on the maxim that he "must not be the king of two peoples." Influenced by his liberal minister ÉLIE DECAZES, he tried to extend the franchise and relax censorship. But after 1820, he was increasingly dominated by his reactionary brother, who succeeded him in 1824 as King Charles X.

## Louis, Joseph-Dominique, baron (1755–1837)
*political figure*
Born in Bry-sur-Marne, Joseph-Dominique, baron Louis, was a priest, adviser to the Parlement of Paris, and had ties to TALLEYRAND. Having taken the oath to the CIVIL CONSTITUTION OF THE CLERGY dur-

ing the REVOLUTION OF 1789, he was excommunicated by the church and left the clergy. Emigrating in 1791, he returned to France after the coup d'état of 18 Brumaire, Year VIII (November 9, 1799). Given various important posts under the FIRST EMPIRE, Louis was made a baron by NAPOLÉON I. Minister of finances in 1814–15 and 1818–19, he helped in the financial restructuring of France at the beginning of the RESTORATION. He also served as minister of finances at the beginning of the July Monarchy (1831–1832), then was made a member of the Chamber of Peers.

## Louise of Lorraine (1553–1601)
*queen of France*
Born in Nomeny, Louise of Lorraine was the daughter of Nicholas of Lorraine, count de Vaudémont, and married King HENRY III of France, over whom she at first had some influence. After her husband's death, Queen Louise retired from public life.

## Louise de Marillac (1591–1660)
*saint*
Born in Paris, Louise de Marillac was the daughter of a counselor to the Parlement and the widow of Antoine Le Gras, secretary to MARIE DE' MEDICI. With VINCENT DE PAUL, Louise of Marillac became a collaborator in that cleric's many charitable endeavors. Beginning in 1633, she organized and became the first superior of the Congregation of the Daughters of Charity (papal confirmation given in 1668). The feast day of Louise de Marillac is celebrated by the Catholic Church on March 15.

## Louise of Savoy (1476–1531)
*queen of France*
Born in Pont-d'Ain, Louise of Savoy was the daughter of Philippe, duke of Savoy, and Marguerite of Bourbon. In 1488, she married Charles of Valois, duke of Angoulême, with whom she had two children: MARGUERITE DE VALOIS and King FRANCIS I. The latter made her regent during his campaign in Italy in 1515 and after Pavia (1525). Beautiful, intelligent, but also ambitious and scheming, she had a sense of politics and kept order after Pavia and in negotiating a peace treaty (paix des Dames, 1529)

with Marguerite of Austria. At the same time, she played a less than glorious role in the condemnation of JACQUES DE SEMBLANÇAY and in the treason of the constable of Bourbon. Well educated, Louise of Savoy was a patron of various scholars and left her *Mémoires.*

## Louis-Philippe I (1773–1850)
*king of the French, first of the House of Orléans*
King of the French from 1830 to 1848, Louis-Philippe I was the son of Louis-Philippe-Joseph, duke of ORLÉANS (known as PHILIPPE ÉGALITÉ), and Louise-Marie de Bourbon-Penthièvre. He bore the titles successively of duke of Valois, of Chartres (1785), and of Orléans (on the death of his father in 1793). Raised with his sister, the future Madame ADÉLAÏDE, by Mme de Genlis, he was, like his father, a fervent supporter of revolutionary ideas. A member of the JACOBINS (see REVOLUTION OF 1789), he distinguished himself as an officer at the Battles of Valmy and Jemappes (1792). After the execution of his father, Louis-Philippe remained in exile, traveling and teaching mathematics and languages in Germany, Scandinavia, the United States, and England. In 1809, he married his cousin, Marie-Amélie, who was King Ferdinand IV of Naples's daughter. They had eight children. He returned to France after the abdication of NAPOLÉON I and was welcomed by LOUIS XVIII, who restored him to the Orléans estates. As the son of a former regicide, however, he was kept out of the court and out of political life. In the late 1820s, he became the favorite of the middle and lower classes, who had grown restive under the reactionary rule of CHARLES X. In the JULY REVOLUTION OF 1830, which overthrew Charles, Louis-Philippe, brought to power by the wealthy bourgeoisie, was proclaimed king of the French by the Chamber of Deputies. At first content to rule as a "citizen-king," he conciliated the republicans who brought him to power, and dispensed with many royal privileges, beginning what is known as the JULY MONARCHY. He had also supported, more or less, such liberal newspapers as *Le Constitutionnel* and later *Le National.* Gradually, however, he became more authoritarian and sought to rule as well as to reign (see FRANÇOIS GUIZOT). The last years of his monarchy were marked by corruption and failures in both domestic and foreign affairs, and he was eventually deserted by both the democratic and the authoritarian elements. He was deposed by the REVOLUTION OF 1848 and, after his abdication, went into exile in England, where he died two years later.

## Louverture, François-Dominique-Toussaint (ca. 1743–1803)
### (Toussaint Bréda)
*Haitian revolutionary leader, military genius*
Born in Haut-du-Cap on the Bréda Plantation in Saint-Domingue, the French colony on the island of Hispaniola that became independent Haiti, François-Dominique-Toussaint Louverture was a freed black slave who formed an insurgent band against French rule on the island (1791) and then entered the service of Spain. He came over to the service of France in 1794, after the proclamation abolishing slavery issued during the REVOLUTION OF 1789 and succeeded in driving British invaders from Saint-Domingue (1798). He proclaimed the island's autonomy within the French Republic (1801). But Napoléon Bonaparte, as First Consul, sent against Saint Domingue a corps of 20,000 troops under General CHARLES LECLERC to restore French authority as well as slavery. Taken by surprise, Louverture was arrested, sent to France, and interned in the Fort de Joux, in the Jura Mountains, where he died from the rigors of the climate. Some scholars attribute his surname Louverture, or "L'Ouverture" ("the opening"), to the breaches that he opened in the ranks of the enemy; some to a gap in his teeth. Very aware of his valor and merit, Louverture did not hesitate to send a letter to Bonaparte with the opening words: "From the First of the Blacks to the First of the Whites."

## Louvet de Couvray, Jean-Baptiste (1760–1797)
*political figure and writer*
Born in Paris, Jean-Baptiste Louvet de Couvray was the author of a famous and licentious 18th-century novel, *Les Amours du chevalier de Faublas* (1787–89) and was also the founder of an antiroyalist newspaper, *La Sentinelle.* At the time of the REVOLUTION OF 1789, he was elected as a deputy to

the Convention, where, as a brilliant GIRONDIN orator, he became one of the most resolute adversaries of MAXIMILIEN ROBESPIERRE. After the elimination of the Gironde leaders (June 2, 1793), Louvet de Couvray was able to escape and hide in the JURA until 9 Thermidor Year II (July 27, 1794). His *Mémoires* were published in 1889.

## Louvois, François-Michel Le Tellier, marquis de (1639–1691)

*political figure*

Born in Paris, François-Michel Le Tellier, marquis de Louvois is, in his achievements, inseparable from those of his father, MICHEL LE TELLIER, with whom he was closely associated. He succeeded his father as secretary of war when the latter became chancellor. Louvois had known how to gain the confidence of King LOUIS XIV by flattering that monarch's desire for glory. He made himself the sole master of the army after the death of HENRI DE TURENNE (1675), and began a series of reforms. The recruitment and training of the army were entirely reorganized. The most outstanding measures were the establishment of the system that opened command positions to commoners, the initiation of provincial militias (the army was thus raised to 300,000 strong), and the foundation of military schools. Louvois achieved this by ceaselessly encroaching on the authority of other government departments, with his growing influence leading to a bitter struggle with JEAN-BAPTISTE COLBERT. Brutal, hard, and authoritarian, Louvois was largely responsible for the devastation of the Palatinate (1679), the bombardment of Genoa (1684), the annexations preceding the League of Augsburg, a coalition formed against the aggressive policies of Louis XIV that included England, Holland, Spain, Sweden, and certain German principalities, and the Dragonnades, persecutions carried out by the Royal Dragoons against the Protestants after the revocation of the EDICT OF NANTES. The Dragonnedes in Languedoc and Béarn were especially brutal.

## Louvre (Musée du Louvre)

The Louvre, known also as the Musée du Louvre, is the national art museum of France and the name of the palace in which it is housed. Located in Paris on the right bank of the SEINE, until 1682 it was a royal residence and is one of the largest palaces in the world, occupying the site of a 13th-century fortress. In 1546, King FRANCIS I began the building of the Louvre based on the plans of PIERRE LESCOT. During the reigns of subsequent monarchs, a number of additions were made. Under HENRY IV, the Grande Galerie was completed; almost three centuries later, under NAPOLÉON III, a north wing was added. The vast complex was completed in the mid-19th century and covers more than 19 hectares (48 acres), making it both a masterpiece of architectural design and the largest museum in the world. In 1793, the Louvre opened as a public museum (a project envisioned by LOUIS XVI), and JACQUES-LOUIS DAVID was made its chief administrator. In 1848, the Louvre became state property. The center of its collection is a group of Italian Renaissance paintings, including several by Leonardo da Vinci that were owned by Francis I. The collection was enriched by acquisitions made by Cardinal RICHELIEU, Cardinal MAZARIN, and LOUIS XIV, including purchases from the collection of King Charles I of England. NAPOLÉON I deposited in the Louvre many artworks seized during his conquests, especially in Italy, and since then a large number of bequests, purchases, and archaeological artifacts have further enriched the Louvre's collection. Its greatest treasures include the *Vénus de Milo*, the *Winged Victory of Samothrace,* and da Vinci's *La Jaconde* (*Mona Lisa*). There are also works by Raphael, Titian, Rembrandt, and Rubens. Several curatorial departments administer the collection. The Department of Egyptian Antiquities was formed in 1826 to study and display the objects brought back during Napoléon Bonaparte's Egyptian campaign. The Department of Oriental Antiquities has a famous Middle Eastern collection. Other departments are the Greek, Etruscan, and Roman antiquities section, Objets d'Art, and Drawings and Prints. The Department of Paintings is considered by many scholars to be the most important in the world. In 1993, President FRANÇOIS MITTERRAND opened the Richelieu gallery in the north wing, which had previously housed the Ministry of Finance. Since 1996, the Rohan Wing has housed the fashion section of the museum. The Louvre complex also includes the Carrousel du Louvre, which has the glass pyramid entrance designed by I. M. Pei.

## Louÿs, Pierre  (1870–1925)
*writer*

Born in Gand, Pierre Louis, or Pierre Louÿs, as he is known, joined the Parnassian writers, who had rebelled against romanticism, rejecting effusive sentiments and the bourgeois values of an increasingly industrialized society. (The name "Parnassian" suggests the objective calm of the Olympian gods, in contrast to the subjective storminess of the romantics. Louÿs married the daughter of the Parnassian poet JOSÉ MARIA HEREDIA). Louÿs published his first poems in *La Conque,* a review that he founded (1891) and, inspired by the eroticism of ancient Greek literature, wrote *Chansons de Bilitis* (1894), prose poems that in turn inspired CLAUDE DEBUSSY to write three musical compositions. Louÿs's *Aphrodite* (1896) was adapted for the stage (1906) and had a notable success, and the author continued his work with *La Femme et le Pantin* (1898) and *Les Aventures de roi Pausole* (1901). Louÿs's other writings include a long poem, *Pervigilium mortis* (1916), and a novel, *Psyché* (posthumous, 1927).

## Luckner, Nicolas, count  (1722–1794)
*marshal of France*

Born in Cham, Bavaria, Nicolas, count Luckner, became a lieutenant general in the French armies in 1763, marshal of France during the REVOLUTION OF 1789, and then commander of the Army of the Rhine, replacing Marshal JEAN-BAPTISTE ROCHAMBEAU in 1792. Suspected of treason and suspended, he was arrested at Metz (1793), condemned to death by the Revolutionary Tribunal, and executed.

## Lully, Jean-Baptiste  (1632–1687)
*composer*

Born in Florence, Italy, Giovanni Battista Lulli, or Jean-Baptiste Lully, as he is known, came to France at age 14 and, in 1652, entered the service of King LOUIS XIV as a violinist and dancer. He later conducted one of the royal orchestras ("bande des petits violons") and, in 1662, became music master to the royal family. Ambitious and a shrewd courtier and businessman, he retained throughout his life the king's favor and dominated French music of the period. He composed ballets, including *Ballet de l'amour malade* (1657) and *Alcidiane* (1658) for the court, often dancing alongside the king in many of them. Lully collaborated with MOLIÈRE on a series of comedy ballets. In 1672, he intrigued to obtain for himself the directorship of the Académie Royale de Musique, a position that gave him the monopoly over opera productions in France. He modeled his operas, known as "tragédies-lyriques," on the classical tragedy of his contemporaries PIERRE CORNEILLE and JEAN RACINE. They are stately, solemn compositions that emphasize clarity of text and the inflections of the French language. Their elaborate dance spectacles and grand choruses are based on the "ballets de cour," the courtly dance pageants staged at VERSAILLES. They stand in contrast to the Italian opera of the period, which emphasized virtuoso solo pieces. Lully's court operas include *Cadmus et Hermione* (1673), *Alceste* (1674), *Thésée* (1675), *Atys* (1676), *Psyché et Ballérophon* (1678–79), *Phaéton* (1683), *Roland* (1685), and *Armide* (1686). Amassing a huge fortune, Lully ended his career by becoming adviser and secretary to the king.

## Lumière brothers
**(Auguste Lumière; Louis Lumière)**

Both the Lumière brothers—Auguste (1862–54) and Louis (1864–1948)—were born in Besançon, and were inventors, photographic manufacturers, and pioneer filmmakers who, in 1895, invented an early picture camera that also functioned as a projector. In contrast to the cumbersome machinery invented by Edison, theirs was portable and lightweight, and suitable for outdoor use. It also used less film, was quieter, and operated more smoothly. They called this device the "Cinématographe," and it allowed the taking of pictures and projection at the same time. On December 28, 1895, in Paris they surprised the public with the showing of their short film, *La Sortie des usines Lumière,* considered to be probably the first true motion picture ever made. They also showed the films *L'Arrivée d'un train en gare de La Ciotat* (1895) and *L'Arroseur arrosé* (1895). In these, their audience was startled by the image of motion and of an oncoming train, and many consider these occasions to be the birth of the cinema industry. The Lumière brothers continued productions, increasing their staff and, by 1898, amassed a film catalog of more than 1,000 motion pictures. In 1903, they also produced the first color photographs. Auguste Lumière, a biologist, additionally studied the therapeutic use of magnesium cells, and was admitted to the Academy of Sciences in 1919. Louis Lumière was interested in photography in relief (photostereosynthesis, 1920), and achieved a method of anaglyphes, or the projection of two complementary colors, in 1935.

## Lustiger, Jean-Marie, Cardinal (1926–  )
*prelate*

Born to a Jewish family in Paris, Jean-Marie Lustiger converted to Catholicism in 1940. Archbishop of Paris (1981), then cardinal (1983), he has always sought to be the representative of a church open to the intellectual debates of the modern era, while still firmly upholding Catholic ethical and moral positions. Cardinal Lustiger, the author of *Le Choix de Dieu* (1987), was elected to the ACADÉMIE FRANÇAISE in 1995.

## Luxembourg, François-Henri de Montmorency-Bouteville, duke de (1628–1695)
*marshal of France*

Born in Paris, François-Henri de Montmorency-Bouteville, duke de Luxembourg, first served under the command of LOUIS II DE CONDÉ, whom he followed during the FRONDE and during the War of Devolution. Luxembourg's successes in the Dutch War, however, were checked by the efforts of William of Orange (1672). But he then distinguished himself at Seneffe (1674), and Kassel (1677), and took Mons (1678) from that Dutch ruler. Implicated in the AFFAIR OF THE POISONS, he was for a short time imprisoned. Marshal Luxembourg regained his command and won great victories during the War of the League of Augsburg—a coalition of European powers including England, Holland, and, later, Savoy—at Fleurus (1690),

Steinkerque (1692), and Neerwinden (1693) and, having taken numerous battle flags, was given the sobriquet *le tapissier de Notre-Dame* (the tapestry maker of Notre-Dame).

## Luynes, Charles d'Albert de (1578–1621)
*constable of France, minister, favorite of King Louis XIII*

Born in Pont-Saint-Esprit to a family of Tuscan origin, Charles d'Albert de Luynes, constable of France, was a favorite of King LOUIS XIII. The king had encouraged Luynes to kill the Italian adventurer and court rival CONCINO CONCINI (1617), who had intrigued his way to power and influence during the regency of Queen MARIE DE' MEDICI. Luynes also played an important role, negotiating with opponents to the royal authority (treaties of Angoulême, 1619; Angers, 1620), and fought against the Protestants (in Béarn, 1620). His defeat at Montauban, however (1621), would leave him in disgrace when he died.

## Lyautey, Louis-Hubert-Gonzalve (1854–1934)
*marshal of France*

Born in Nancy, Louis-Hubert-Gonzalve Lyautey, a graduate of SAINT-CYR (1873) and of the General Staff school, joined the cavalry. Attracted to the social Catholicism of ALBERT DE MUN, he spent most of his career in the colonies. After serving in southern ALGERIA (1879–82), he was sent to INDOCHINA (1894) as chief of staff to General JOSEPH GALLIENI, whom he then accompanied to Madagascar. Recalled to ALGERIA, Lyautey commanded the region of Ain Sefra (1903), was promoted to the rank of general, made division commander of Oran (1906), and occupied Oujda (1907). Named resident general of the French Republic in Morocco (1912) after the events in Fez in 1911 that led to the establishment of a French protectorate in Morocco, he tried to pacify the region, despite the technical difficulties posed at the beginning of WORLD WAR I. Minister of war in the cabinet of ARISTIDE BRIAND (December 1916–April 1917), he returned soon after to Morocco, where he remained during the Rif War (1925). In his colonial policy, General Lyautey discouraged assimilation and tried to promote a truly Moroccan cultural development. He is the author of numerous studies, including *Du Role social de l'officier dans le service militaire universel* (1891), *Du Role colonial de l'armée* (1900), *Dans le sud de Madagascar, pénétration militaire, situation politique et économique* (1903). Marshal Lyautey was elected to the ACADÉMIE FRANÇAISE in 1912.

## Lyon

The third-largest city in France, after PARIS and MARSEILLE, Lyon has a metropolitan area second in size and economic importance only to Paris. At the confluence of the RHÔNE and SAÔNE Rivers, Lyon has diverse manufactures. Nearby, in Saint-Fons and Feyzin, are large petroleum refineries. There are important treatment and research hospitals also. The University of Lyon (1808) is based on three extensive campuses around the city. The center of Lyon and the Fourvière quarter have several interesting buildings and monuments, including the romanesque basilica of Saint-Martin-d'Ainay (12th century), the cathedral of Saint-Jean (12th century), the church of Saint-Nizier (14th century), the church of Saint-Bruno (16th century), the church of Saint-Bonaventure (14th–15th century), and the basilica of Notre-Dame de Fourvière (19th century). The Hôtel-Dieu (17th century) has a museum. Old Lyon has numerous streets and Renaissance mansions on the east bank of the Rhône; there is the Musée Historique des Tissus (with the world's largest collection of textiles), and the Museum of Contemporary Art, which opened in 1995. Lyon has the oldest stock exchange in France, and the city is also considered a center of French gastronomy. In 1981, Lyon was the first city to be connected to Paris by the high-speed "train à grande vitesse" (TGV). Modern highways connect Lyon with major cities in France, Germany, Switzerland, Italy, and Spain. Lyon also has two airports. Lyon was founded in 43 B.C. as the Roman colony of Lugdunum and became the major city of ancient Gaul by the 2nd century A.D. It also was a principal residence of some Roman emperors, who erected various monuments there, and was the birthplace of Claudius and Caracalla. Christianity was introduced into Gaul at Lyon, which for centuries was a leading religious center ruled by archbishops. In the 9th century, Lyon was part of Burgundy, then passed to the Holy Roman Empire (1032). In 1312, it again became part of France and was granted a royal charter. By the 15th century, at the crossroads between northern and southern France, it became a center of trade and famous for its silk industry. Four annual trade fairs were held there. The city also became a center of European business. By the 16th and 17th centuries, the silk industry dominated the city's economy. In 1793, the troops of the Convention (see REVOLUTION OF 1789) attacked the city as it was a center of resistance by supporters of a federal system during the Revolution. Lyon suffered a severe repression from the revolutionary forces and government, but NAPOLÉON I revived and redeveloped the city when he came to power. During the 19th century, parallel to a renewed economic development, a number of social problems arose. The silk workers, suffering from horrendous conditions, revolted in 1831 and 1834. During WORLD WAR II (1939–45), Lyon was an important center of the RESISTANCE. In 1957, the metropolitan area of Lyon was established, and today Lyon is the home to many immigrants from former French colonies in North Africa.

# M

**Mably, Gabriel Bonnot de** (1709–1785)
*philosopher, historian*

Born in Grenoble, Gabriel-Bonnet de Mably, who was the brother of the abbot of CONDILLAC, studied with the Jesuits and then at the seminary of Saint-Sulpice. He soon abandoned ecclesiastical studies and began a diplomatic career, serving on a number of missions, including those involving the negotiations for the Peace of Breda (1746). The author of *Droit public de l'Europe fonde sur les traités* (1748) and *Observations sur l'histoire de France* (1765), Mably held a contrasting theory to the Physiocrats (*Doutes proposés aux philosophes économists sur l'ordre naturel et essentiel des sociétés politiques,* 1766). A figure of the Enlightenment, he affirmed the necessity of reforms (especially in agrarian laws) to establish a more socially just and egalitarian society, and he sought a future society in which all property would be held in common.

**Mac-Mahon, Edme-Patrice-Maurice, count de** (1808–1898)
*military and political figure, marshal of France*

Born in Sully to a family of Irish Jacobite origin, Edme Patrice Maurice, count de Mac-Mahon was educated at SAINT-CYR and took part in the early military campaigns in ALGERIA. For his distinguished service he was made a brigadier general in 1848 and later a division commander in the Crimean War (1854–1856) and in the Algerian Campaign of 1857–58. After the campaign of Magenta (1859) against the Austrians, he was made a marshal of France and duke of Magenta. He was appointed governor-general of Algeria in 1864, a position that he held until 1870. Marshal Mac-Mahon was then given command of the First Army Corps during the FRANCO-PRUSSIAN WAR. Named commander of the army at Versailles by LOUIS-ADOLPHE THIERS, he won the support of the conservatives in the National Assembly by his repression of the Paris COMMUNE (March–May 1871). Backed by the monarchists, he became the second president of the THIRD REPUBLIC in 1873. A conservative and monarchist, Mac-Mahon, during a struggle with the republicans in 1877, dissolved the Chamber of Deputies. When the republicans won the election, he was forced to resign (1879), and he retired from public life.

**Machault d'Arnouville, Jean-Baptiste de** (1701–1794)
*political figure*

Descended from a noble family of the robe, Jean-Baptiste de Machault d'Arnouville was born in Paris and became comptroller-general of finances in 1745. In his efforts to achieve fiscal stability through the reduction of privileges, he met strong opposition from the aristocracy and the clergy. As King LOUIS XV gave in to pressure from these classes, Machault left the office of comptroller-general of finances for that of the navy (1745). To keep France out of any new conflicts, he favored a reevaluation of all foreign alliances. His career ended, and he fell into disgrace, however, when he lost the favor of Mme de POMPADOUR (1757). Arrested during the Terror, Marchault d'Arnouville died in prison.

**Madagascar**

Madagascar, located in the Indian Ocean and separated from Africa by the Strait of Mozambique, is the fourth-largest island in the world. The French presence began in Madagascar in 1642, but ended in 1674, with only a few trading posts being left. The French then returned in the 19th century and, in 1896, the island was occupied and became a French colony. There always was a resistance to French rule, however, that culminated in popular uprising in 1916. The British occupied Madagascar during WORLD WAR II but, in 1943, surrendered the island to the Free French government. In 1946, Madagascar became an Overseas Territory of France but, in 1947, there were a series of armed revolts against the French presence. Self-government was granted by France in 1950, and after a referendum in 1958, Madagascar gained independence in 1960.

## Maginot, André (1877–1932)
### political figure

Born in Paris, André Maginot was a deputy for the democratic Left (1910), and served several times as a minister after World War I, during the course of which he was gravely wounded. He put through the law (January 4, 1930) ordering the construction of fortifications on the northeast corner of France. The Maginot Line, the plan for which had already been formulated by PAUL PAINLEVÉ, did not continue, however, along the French-Belgian border because of opposition from Belgium. Moreover, not adaptable to the new form of mobile warfare, the Maginot Line did not play its anticipated role in World War II, which was a war of movement, making the defensive line obsolete.

## Magny, Olivier de (1529–1561)
### poet

Born in Cahars, Olivier de Magny, after serving as a secretary in Paris to one of his compatriots, made a visit to LYON, where he met and fell in love with the poet LOUISE LABÉ, and then went to Italy. In Rome, he had experiences similar to those of the other poets in the PLÉIADE group (JOACHIM DU BELLAY), which Magny describes in his sonnets (*Soupirs*, 1557) and in which he gives a satirical account of Roman mores. De Magny's debut as a poet featured another brilliant collection of sonnets (*Amours*, 1553), which brought him the praise of PIERRE DE RONSARD and his associates. In 1554 *Gayetez*

appeared, a collection of more profound poems, in contrast to his *Soupirs* and to Du Bellay's *Regrets*. Magny's final work was a volume of *Odes* (1559) inspired by Ronsard. Magny's writings, considered to be filled with erudition, helped to develop an art of the libertine life.

## Maillol, Aristide (1861–1944)
### sculptor, painter

Born in Banyuls-sur-Mer, Aristide Maillol studied at the École des Beaux-Arts, Paris (1882–86), and at first produced paintings, tapestries, and engravings before discovering his talent as a sculptor. Influenced by PIERRE PUVIS DE CHAVANNES and PAUL GAUGUIN, as well as by the art of classical Greece, he restricted himself almost entirely to the female nude, and his figures often portray large, imposing, earthy women. With strong but never contorted poses, the faces of Maillol's figures express relatively generalized emotions of impassive seriousness or severity. Rather than originality, he sought perfection, and his style varied little throughout his career. Examples of this style, in which he reconciled massiveness and heaviness with grace and sensualness, are *Pomone* (1907), *Flore* (1911), *Île-de-France* (1925), *L'Air* (1938), and *La Rivière* (1939–43). Considered the most distinguished sculptor in the period between AUGUSTE RODIN and the moderns, Maillol, through his classically inspired art, essentially marked the end of an earlier tradition, rather than the beginning of a new one.

## Maine, Louis-Auguste de Bourbon, duke of (1670–1736)
### natural son of Louis XIV

The legitimized son of King LOUIS XIV and Mme de MONTESPAN, Louis-Auguste de Bourbon, duke of Maine was born at Saint-Germain-en-Laye. The regent, Philippe d'Orléans, relieved him of most of the prerogatives granted in the will of Louis XIV. He took part in the CELLEMARE PLOT (1718) at the instigation of his wife, Anne-Louise Bénédicte de Bourbon-Condé, duchess of Maine (1676–1753), who held a brilliant court in her château at Sceaux. Imprisoned (1719), then freed in 1720, the duke of Maine then abandoned political life.

## Maintenon, Françoise d'Aubigné, marquise de (1635–1719)

*nobility*

Born in Niort, the granddaughter of AGRIPPA D'AUBIGNÉ, Françoise d'Aubigné, marquise de Maintenon was orphaned early in life and was raised by her grandparents in the Calvinist faith (which she abjured in 1649). Forced by her financial difficulties to marry the poet PAUL SCARRON (1651), she held with him a brilliant salon that attracted many of the leading social figures of the day. The death of her husband in 1660 left her without resources, so she took the position of governess to the children of King LOUIS XIV and his mistress Mme de MONTESPAN. In 1674, she became herself Louis's mistress and purchased the estate of Maintenon, which was made a marquisate in 1678. After the death of Queen MARIA THERESA, she entered a morganatic marriage with Louis (1684). She had a moral, rather than political, influence on the king, and brought to the court an air of austerity. Upon the king's death (1715), she retired to SAINT-CYR, the convent that she had established for the education of girls from poor noble families.

See also FÉNELON, FRANÇOIS DE SALIGNAC DE LA MOTTE.

## Mairet, Jean (1604–1686)

*dramatic poet*

Born in Besançon, Jean Mairet was first the author of a comedy based on *L'Astrée, Chryséide et Arimant* (1625). He then prefaced his tragedy *Silvanire* (1631) with a statement that earned him the title "inventor" of the rules of classical theater. With *Sophonisbe* (1634), he composed the first tragedy in this style. Meanwhile, in *Illustre Corsaire* (1637), *Roland furieux* (1638), and *Sidonie* (1640), Mairet soon abandoned the art of tragicomedy, which, with its extravagant intrigue and multiplication of scenes, and attempt to appeal to sensitive audiences, would be further developed by Italian writers.

## Maistre, Joseph, count de (1753–1821)

*political figure, writer, philosopher*

A leading conservative thinker, Joseph, count of Maistre, was born in Chambéry and served as a member of the senate of Savoy. During the REVOLUTION OF 1789, he emigrated to Lausanne (1793) and soon joined the court of King Charles-Emmanuel of Sardinia, who appointed him minister to Russia. There, he became an adviser to Czar Alexander I. A staunch opponent of the REVOLUTION, DE Maistre affirmed his monarchist views and his support also of papal power in his *Considérations sur la France* (1796) and in *Du pape* (1819). In contrast to the philosophes of the Enlightenment, he replaced the belief in reason with faith and intuition. His view of history is similar to that of JACQUES BÉNIGNE BOSSUET (*Soirées de Saint-Petersbourg*, 1821).

## Malebranche, Nicolas (1638–1715)

*philosopher, theologian*

Born in Paris, Nicolas Malebranche, who developed the metaphysical theory of occasionalism, studied philosophy and theology at the Collège de la Marche and at the SORBONNE. In 1660, he entered the Congregation of the Oratory and was ordained a priest. Some of Malebranche's positions derive from RENÉ DESCARTES, but his own system is profoundly original. His doctrine of occasionalism denies the possibility of any action of matter upon mind. He argues that, since we see all things in God, human knowledge is possible only through interaction between humans and God. Any changes in objects or thoughts are caused by God, not by the objects or individuals. His principal writings include *De la Recherche de la vérité* (1674), and *Traité de la nature et de la grâce* (1675), which was criticized by JACQUES-BÉNIGNE BOSSUET, FÉLIX FÉNELON, and ANTOINE ARNAULD. Malebranche's *Traité de morale* was published in 1683, and *Les Entretiens sur la métaphysique et la religion* in 1688. He also wrote several treatises on the psychology of vision, the nature of light and color, and calculus. A distinguished mathematician, Malebranche was made an honorary member of the Academy of Sciences in 1699.

## Malesherbes, Chrétien-Guillaume de Lamoignon de (1721–1794)

*political figure*

Born in Paris, the son of GUILLAUME DE LAMOIGNON, Chrétien-Guillaume de Lamoignon de Malesherbes served as deputy procurer-general (1741), counselor of state to the Parlement of Paris (1744), and was named first president of the Cour des aides and Director of the Library (1750). In that capacity, he worked to grant freedom of the press, protecting the philosophes and the publication of the *Encyclopédie*. Opposed to RENÉ DE MAUPEOU, he was forced to retire a number of times to Pithiviers (1771). Elected to the ACADÉMIE FRANÇAISE in 1774, he was recalled in 1775, as secretary to the Royal Household and the provinces and attempted some reforms, but had to resign in 1776. A member of the King's Council (1787–88), he helped to gain civil status for Protestants (1787). Emigrating at the beginning of the REVOLUTION OF 1789, he returned shortly after to give support to the king and defend him before the Convention (*Mémoire pour Louis XVI*, published after the king's trial). Malesherbes was executed during the TERROR.

## Malet, Claude-François de (1754–1812)
*general*

Born in Dole to an aristocratic family, Claude-François de Malet joined the REVOLUTION OF 1789 as a captain in the Army of the Rhine (1792) and then, in 1799, became a general. Opposed to NAPOLÉON I, he was arrested in 1808 and confined in a sanitarium. Having conspired against Napoleon, he escaped during the night of October 22–23, 1812, announced the emperor's death, recruited some soldiers from Paris, freed other republican generals, and prepared a provisional government. But the commander of Paris resisted and Malet was arrested and shot on October 29. This event precipitated the return of Napoléon from the Russian campaign.

## Malherbe, François de (1555–1628)
*poet*

François de Malherbe, the critic and poet who set the foundations for classical French literature, was born in Caen and educated at the Universities of Heidelberg and Basel. He was court poet to king HENRY IV and LOUIS XIII and, in his prose and poetry, reacted against the luxuriant style and romantic ferver of the PLÉIADE group (*Les Larmes de saint Pierre*). Instead, Malherbe stressed simplicity and exactness of expression, restraint in emotion, and euphony in style. Through his writings, he was instrumental in making the French spoken in Paris the standard language for all France. Malherbe's own poetry foreshadowed the precise form of verse later developed by the classical French poets and dramatists. His poetic works, which are mainly lyrical, include odes to Queen MARIE DE' MEDICI and to King LOUIS XIII, as well as personal dedications to friends. Among his prose are translations of the works of the Roman historian Livy and the playwright Seneca. Malherbe's other writings include *Remarques sur Desportes* (1605), *Imitation du psaume Lauda anima mea Dominum* (1627), and *Les Œuvres de François Malherbe* (posthumous, 1630).

## Mallarmé, Stéphane (1842–1898)
### (Étienne Mallarmé)
*poet*

One of the founders of the symbolist movement, Étienne, better known as Stéphane, Mallarmé was born in Paris. He taught English at the Lycée Fantanes in Paris and in the provinces and translated literary works in English, notably the poems (1888) of Edgar Allen Poe. Mallarmé used symbols to express truth through suggestion, rather than by narrative, and his poetry and prose are characterized by experimental grammar, musical quality, and refinement through allusion and obscure thought. His best-known poems are *L'Après-midi d'un faune* (1816), which inspired the prelude by the composer CLAUDE DEBUSSY, and *Hérodiade* (1869). Mallarmé was also noted for his conversation, which, while his writings were obscure, was quite lucid. He held a renowned salon on Tuesday nights at his home on the rue de Rome in Paris, where his critiques of literature, art, and music helped to stimulate the creative efforts of the French symbolist writers and the artists and composers of the impressionist school. Moreover, Mallarmé's influence on the modern conception of poetry is fundamental. Among his other poems and writings are *L'Azur* (1864), *Brise marine* (1865), *Igitur ou la Folie d'Elbehnon* (1867–70, posthumous, 1925). The master of the symbolist generation, Mallarmé influenced PAUL VERLAINE, ANDRÉ GIDE,

JORIS-KARL HUYSMANS, and many other writers and artists.

## Malle, Louis (1932–1995)
*film director*

Born in Thumeries, Nord, Louis Malle, a director of influential and often controversial motion pictures, first studied film (1951) at the esteemed Institut des Hautes Études Cinématographiques in Paris. He began his filmmaking career as an assistant to the marine explorer JACQUES COUSTEAU. Together, they filmed *Le Monde du silence* (*The Silent World*), a documentary about undersea exploration that won the prestigious Palme d'Or in 1956. Malle's first feature-length work was *Ascenseur pour l'echafaud* (1957), starring JEANNE MOREAU. His next film, *Les Amants* (1958), cast Moreau as a housewife involved in extramarital affairs and established Malle's reputation for controversy. His portrayal of his characters with grace and sensitivity is apparent in *Zazie dans le métro* (1960) and in *Le Souffle au coeur* (1971), as well as in *Lacombe Lucien* (1973), *Pretty Baby* (1978), and *Atlantic City* (1980). The winner of many other film awards, Malle directed his most autobiographical work, *Au Revoir les Enfants,* with his last film being *Vanya on 42nd Street* (1994), in which, as in some of his other films, he blurs the distinction between life and theatrical performance. Malle was married to the American actress Candace Bergin, with whom he had a daughter.

## Mallet-Joris, Françoise (1930–   )
*writer*

Of Belgian origin, Françoise Mallet-Joris was born in Antwerp. She made her literary debut with *Le Rempart des béguines* (1952), which already showed her ability to describe the adolescent soul as it deals with the world of adults (*Allégra,* 1976). After having written a sequel to this first work, *La Chambre rouge* (1953), Mallet-Joris published a collection of short stories, *Cordélia* (1954), then *Les Mensonges* (1956), a detailed account of the Flemish world. Her sense of irony is apparent in *L'Empire céleste* (prix Femina 1958), and she brings a feminist approach to historical writings such as *Les Personnages* (evoking the period of Cardinal RICHELIEU;

1961), *Marie Mancini* (1965), *Trois Âges de la nuit* (dedicated to sorceresses; 1958), and *Jeanne Guyon* (1978). With *Lettre à moi-même* (1963), *Les Signes et les Prodiges* (1966), and *La Maison de papier* (1970), Mallet-Joris revealed herself through autobiography. She returned to the novel with *Dickie roi* (1980), *Le Rire de Laura* (1985), and *La Tristesse du cerf-volant* (1988). She was named to the Académie Goncourt in 1970.

## Malraux, André (1901–1976)
*writer*

An archaeologist, art theorist, political activist, and public official, as well as a novelist, André Malraux, whose writings are major contributions to 20th-century culture, was born in Paris, where he studied Oriental languages. His early writings were inspired by surrealism (*Lunes en papier,* 1921; *Royaume-Farfelu,* 1928). In 1923, he went to INDOCHINA as an archaeologist and soon became involved in the Annamese revolutionary struggle against French colonial rule. He remained in the Orient until 1927 and used his experiences there as material for three other novels: *Les Conquérants* (1928),

André Malraux *(Library of Congress)*

*La Voie royale* (1931), and *La Condition humaine* (1931), for which he won the prix Goncourt and international repute. In his next novel, *Le Tempts de mépris* (1935), inspired by a visit to Germany, he denounced Nazism. Soon after, he served as a pilot with a Loyalist air squadron in Spain, and his experiences there became the basis for his next work, *L'Espoir* (1937). During World War II, Malraux served in the French army, was captured, and, upon his escape, became a colonel in the RESISTANCE. He was recaptured, but escaped again and in 1945 joined the provisional government of General CHARLES DE GAULLE. He served as minister for cultural affairs (1959–69), and then retired to a suburb of Paris to write until his death.

## Malvy, Louis  (1875–1949)
*political figure*

Born in Figeac, Louis Malvy was a Radical-Socialist deputy for Lot (1906–19) and, in 1914, was named minister of the interior. Criticized during World War I for his lack of firmness in dealing with the strikes of 1917 and for "defeatism," he was dismissed (1917). He demanded to be heard before the Court of High Justice but was accused nonetheless of malfeasance and sentenced to five years' banishment. Amnestied, he was reelected to the Chamber of Deputies (1924–40) and served for a time as minister of the interior in the cabinet of ARISTIDE BRIAND (1926).

## Mancini family
*Franco-Italian family of political figures*

The Mancini family was a Roman family whose most famous members were the nieces of Cardinal MAZARIN, who joined their uncle in France. Laure Mancini (1636–57), born in Rome, married Louis de Vendôme, duke de Mercoeur and brother of FRANÇOIS THE DUKE DE BEAUFORT. Her sons were the marshal and the grand prior of Vendôme. Olympe Mancini (1639–1708), born in Rome, was a mistress to LOUIS XIV and married Eugène Maurice de Savoie-Carignan, count de Soissons. She was the mother of Prince Eugene of Savoy. Compromised in AFFAIRE OF THE POISONS, she took refuge in Flanders. Marie Mancini (1640–ca. 1706), born in

Rome, was also a mistress of Louis XIV, who wanted to marry her but was opposed by Mazarin. She married Prince Colonna of Rome (1661), then separated from him and fled to France, where Louis XIV put her in a convent. She escaped again and led an adventurous life throughout Europe. Hortense Mancini (1646–99), born in Rome, was considered the most beautiful of the five sisters. She married the duke de La Meilleraye, who took the title duke de Mazarin, then left him to become the mistress of the chevalier de Rohan and settled in London. She was for a time the mistress of King Charles II of England, and her salon was a gathering place for such intellectual libertines as CHARLES DE SAINT-ÉVREMOND. Marie-Anne Mancini (1649–1714), born in Rome, married Maurice Godefroy de La Tour d'Auvergne, the duke de Bouillon.

## Mandel, Georges  (1885–1944)
*political figure*

Born in Chatou, Georges Mandel was an aide in the cabinet of GEORGES CLEMENCEAU (1908), and became his main collaborator when the latter was prime minister (1917). Politically moderate as a deputy (1919–24; 1928–40), and serving several times as a minister, Mandel opposed with great vigor the armistice of June 1940. In the hope of being followed by political elements capable of forming a government able to pursue the war overseas, he went to North Africa, but was sent back to France and interned by the VICHY government. Taken by the Nazis, he was shot by the Milice in the forest of Fontainebleau.

## Manet, Édouard  (1832–1883)
*painter*

Édouard Manet, whose work inspired the impressionist style and whose far-reaching influence on painting and the general development of modern art was due to his choice of subject matter and use of color and technique, was born in Paris, the son of a high government official. Manet early gave up the study of law and began a naval career (1848–49). He then returned to Paris to study under the French academic painter Thomas Couture (1850) and subsequently visited Italy, Germany, and the Netherlands to study the styles of the old masters. The Dutch artist Frans Hals and the Spanish painters Diego Velázquez and Francisco de Goya were his principal influences. Manet began to paint genre subjects (including café denizens, street urchins, and beggars), adopting a bold, direct brush technique as he portrayed realistic themes. In 1859, the Paris Salon rejected his *The Absinthe Drinker,* but in 1861 accepted his portrait *M et Mme Manet* and *The Guitar Player,* works that show the influence of GUSTAVE COURBET and of Spanish painters. In 1862, after the arrival of a Spanish troop in Paris, Manet painted *Lola de Valence* (1862), which inspired a poem by his friend and admirer CHARLES BAUDELAIRE. In 1863, Manet showed his *Music in the Tuileries,* and the nonconformism of this painting brought a violent response from the critics. In the same year, his famous *Luncheon on the Grass* (1862), shown at the Salon des Refusés (a new exhibition place opened by NAPOLÉON III in response to the protests of artists rejected by the official Salon), produced an even more bitter attack. Manet was, however, hailed by younger artists as their leader and he became the central figure in the dispute between the academic and the nonconformist factions. In 1864, the official Salon accepted two of his paintings and, in 1865, he exhibited his *Olympia* (1863), inspired by Titian's *Venus of Urbino,* which aroused storms of protest in academic circles because of its unorthodox realism. He left France for a while to visit Spain and, on his return (1866), began meeting at the café Guerbois with CLAUDE MONET, PIERRE RENOIR, PAUL CÉZANNE, CAMILLE PISSARRO, EDGAR DEGAS, Alfred Sisley, and ÉMILE ZOLA, who championed Manet's style of art and became a close friend. In 1868, he met BERTHE MORISOT (*The Blacony; Portrait of B. Morisot,* 1872) who influenced him to do more open-air painting. In 1874, he worked with Monet at Argenteuil, and experimented in the use of natural light (*On the Banks of the Seine at Argenteuil,* 1874). Again rejected and strongly criticized, Manet in the following years painted numerous portraits (*Mallarmé,* 1876; *Nana,* 1876; *Clemenceau,* 1878; *Zola,* 1879), still lifes (*Asparagus,* 1880), and outdoor or particular scenes (*The Waitress,* 1878; *Bar at the Folies-Bergère,* 1881). Ill and partially paralyzed after 1880, Manet, who did not gain recognition until late in life, turned more and more to pastels and

watercolors. There was also a Japanese influence on his work. At the center of the impressionist movement, he was awarded the LEGION OF HONOR in 1882. Manet has left, besides many pastels and watercolors, more than 400 paintings.

## Mangin, Charles (general) (1866–1925)
*military figure*

Born in Sarrebourg, Charles Mangin, after graduating from SAINT-CYR, served for a number of years in Africa (1890–94, 1895–98, 1907–11), in Tonkin (1901–04), and with General LOUIS LYAUTEY in Morocco (1912). During World War I, he took the fortresses of Douaument (October 1916) and Vaux, and was placed at the head of the Sixth Army. Put in the reserves after the failure of the Nivelle offensive (Chemin des Dames, April 1917), he was recalled in December 1917 and, commanding the 10th Army, helped, thanks to his counteroffensive at Villers-Cotterêts, achieve the victory of the Allied forces at the Second Battle of the Marne (July 1918). Entering Metz with his army shortly after the armistice (November 19, 1918), Mangin was named commander of the Army of the Rhine (at Mainz), then sent on a mission to South America (1920–1921). Inspector-general of colonial troops and a member of the Council of War, General Mangin left his *Lettres de guerre* (published 1951).

## Mansart, François (1598–1666)
*architect*

Born in Paris and trained within his family, François Mansart was responsible for the introduction of a purer, more classical mode into the prevailing French baroque style. His style and talent are already evident in his early works, including the hôtel de la Vrillère (1633) in Paris; the Orléans wing (1635–38) of the uncompleted château of Blois (done for GASTON, DUKE OF ORLÈANS; and Maisons (1642), a private estate on the Seine River, known also as Maisons-Laffitte. Mansart's work for the queen mother MARIE DE' MEDICI on a palace and church to be added to the convent of the Val-de-Grâce in Paris was never completed, and he was dismissed, probably because of the project's expenses.

By 1664, however, he was restored to royal favor and, in that year, was asked to submit plans for an extension of the LOUVRE. He refused, nonetheless, to accept the restrictions imposed by King LOUIS XIV on the work. Mansart also worked in Paris on the hôtel d'Aumont and on the hôtel Carnavalet, both in the Renaissance style. In his project for the Bourbon chapel in the church of Saint-Denis, he developed a plan for a cupola that greatly influenced English architect Christopher Wren (who met him in Paris in 1666), and also inspired his own nephew, JULES HARDOUIN-MANSART. He had a significant influence, too, on the Austrian architect Johann Bernhard Fischer von Erlach. Although Mansart is traditionally associated with the mansard style of roof, he did not actually devise the form, which is derived from Italian architecture, but popularized it.

## Manuel, Louis-Pierre (1751–1793)
*political figure*

Born in Montargis, Louis-Pierre Manuel, while working as a tutor, wrote antireligious libels that caused him to be imprisoned (1783). After the taking of the BASTILLE during the REVOLUTION OF 1789, the mayor of the Commune of PARIS, JEAN-SYLVAIN BAILLY, asked him to join the city's security force, and it was at this time that he edited *Police de Paris dévoilée,* which had an instant success. District attorney for the Commune, in 1791, Louis Manuel was removed from office after the insurrection of June 20, 1792, and took, with JÉRÔME PÉTION, the leadership of the Insurrectional Commune (night of August 9–10, 1792) that in turn led to the insurrection of August 10 of that year. A member of the Convention and a republican, Manuel nonetheless voted against the death of the king and was himself guillotined.

## Marat, Jean-Paul (1743–1793)
*physician, publicist, political figure*

A leading figure of the REVOLUTION OF 1789, Jean-Paul Marat was born in Boudry, Neuchâtel, Switzerland. His mother, a Calvinist, was from Geneva, and his father was of Sardinian origin. In

Engraving depicting the assassination of Jean-Paul Marat (in his bath) *(Library of Congress)*

France, Marat studied science and medicine, which he later practiced. He wrote a number of philosophic essays, in particular, *Les Chaînes de l'esclavage* (1774), in which he attacked all forms of tyranny, denounced the corruption of the royal court, and aligned himself with freemasonry. Settling in Paris (1776), he served for a time as physician to the guards of the count of Artois (see CHARLES X). His scientific works on fire, light, and electricity gained the attention of Benjamin Franklin, the American scientist and statesman, and J. W. von Goethe, the German writer. In 1780, he wrote *Plan de législation criminelle*, in which he proposed reforms put forth earlier by Cesare Beccaria. Solitary and bitter, Marat, in September 1789, founded the radical newspaper *L'Ami du peuple*, which became known for its violent tone. In it, he attacked any political moderates. Elected to the Convention, he joined the extreme MONTAGNARDS and called for the end of the monarchy. He contributed also to the violence that would characterize the Revolution after 1792, and achieved the purging of the moderate Girondins from the government, leading to formation of the JACOBIN regime. At the peak of his power, Marat, in July 1793, was assassinated by CHARLOTTE CORDAY. Thereafter, he became enshrined as one of the popular heroes of the Revolution.

## Marceau, François (1769–1796)

*general*

Born in CHARTRES, François-Séverin Marceau-Desgraviers, or François Marceau as he is known, was a lieutenant colonel in the National Guard and, at the time of the REVOLUTION OF 1789, was put in charge of the defense of Mainz (1792). He then was sent with the Army of the West to fight against the Vendéen insurgents. A division commander of the army at Sambre-et-Meuse, he helped to assure the victory of the French forces at Fleurus (June 26, 1794), then seized Koblenz (October 23, 1794). Administrator of Weisbaden, he was mortally wounded at Altenkirchen while assisting in the retreat of French troops under the command of Marshal JEAN-BAPTISTE JOURDAN. The brave deeds and heroic death of General Marceau made him the prototype of the revolutionary hero.

See also VENDÉE, WAR OF THE.

## Marceau, Marcel (1925–  )

*mime*

Marcel Marceau, who is considered to have almost personally revived the art of pantomime, was born Marcel Mangel, in Strasbourg. A student of theater mimes, he first worked with the Compagnie Dullin, then joined the Compagnie Renaud-Barrault (1946–50). He created the character Arlequin in JACQUE PREVERT's *Baptiste* (1946) and founded his own company in 1947. His first productions were efforts to reintroduce mime-drama (*Le Manteau*, 1951; *Pierrot de Montmartre*, 1952; *Monte-de-pieté*, 1956). In the late 1940s Marceau dedicated himself to soloist mime productions and created the personage of Bip, inspired by Charles Chaplin and Buster Keaton. He developed an international reputation by portraying this character as a white-faced little man in culottes, a middy, and a battered top hat with a red flower. He appeared both on stage and on television. In 1978, Marceau opened a school for mimes in Paris. He was named to the Académie des beaux-arts in 1991.

## Marcel, Étienne (ca. 1315–1358)

*political figure*

Born in Paris, Étienne Marcel was the provost of the Parisian merchants and, with ROBERT LE COQ, was one of the leaders of the bourgeoisie in the ESTATES GENERAL of 1355 and 1356. He helped to impose the Grand Ordonnance of 1357 on the dauphin (the future CHARLES V), which anticipated the control of subsidies by the Estates, an advisory council to the dauphin, and the dismissal of the advisers of King JEAN II. In the face of the dauphin's opposition to reform, Étienne Marcel tried to substitute an urban revolution for the one that the Estates General could not achieve. On February 22, 1358, there took place the first Parisian revolution. Marcel and his supporters surrounded the palace, assassinating two of the dauphin's advisers before his eyes, and forcing him to renew the Ordonnance of 1357. The dauphin fled, raised an army, and surrounded Paris. Marcel, compromised by his alliance with CHARLES II THE BAD, to whom he had decided to surrender Paris, was isolated and subsequently was assassinated by a follower of the dauphin.

## Marcel, Gabriel (1889–1973)
*philosopher, dramatist*

Born in Paris, Gabriel Marcel converted from Protestantism to Catholicism (1929) and became one of the proponents of Christian existentialism. Meditating on the concrete existence of the human in the world, in terms of relationships with others, Marcel opposed the idea of the "Avoir," that is, all that one can possess and therefore be alienated from, in contrast to the mystery of the "Être." Rejecting the pessimism of atheistic existentialism, he gave an important place to the transcendent and the encounter between the human and the divine through faith. Besides his philosophical works (*Journal métaphysique*, 1927; *Être et Avoir*, 1935; *Homo viator*, 1946; *Le Mystère de l'Être*, 1951), Marcel also published a number of works for the theater.

## Marchais, Georges (1920–1995)
*political figure*

Born in La Hoguette, Calvados, Georges Marchais became a member of the French COMMUNIST PARTY (PCF) in 1947 and quickly rose through its ranks. He joined its Central Committee in 1956, its Political Bureau in 1959, was named deputy secretary-general in 1970, then became secretary-general in 1972, replacing PIERRE WALDECK-ROCHET, who had resigned because of illness. Marchais helped to develop a common program for the Left with the Socialist Party in 1973. A deputy since that date, he stood as a candidate in the presidential election of 1981 and had to deal with the subsequent electoral decline of the PCF and the development of a struggle at the party's center. A leader of the PCF through the postwar period, Marchais, at the 21st Party Congress (January 1994), ceded leadership of the party to ROBERT HUE.

## Marchand, Jean-Baptiste (1863–1934)
*general*

Born in Thoissey, Ain, Jean-Baptiste Marchand went to the Congo in 1897, where he explored the course of the Oubangui, Ouellé, and the Bahr-el-Ghazal Rivers, reaching Fashoda, Sudan. He occupied that town but was forced to leave by the British. During WORLD WAR I, General Marchand commanded a colonial brigade in Argonne, then a division in Champagne, on the Somme (1916), and at VERDUN (1917).

## Maret, Hugues-Bernard (1763–1839)
### (duke of Bassano)
*political figure*

Born in Dijon, Huges-Bernard Maret joined the REVOLUTION OF 1789 and was initially a member of the JACOBIN Club, then became a founder of the FEUILLANTS Club after the incident in the Champ de Mars (July 17, 1791). Sent as ambassador to Naples, he was then taken prisoner by the Austrians (1793–96) and, following his release, served as secretary-general to the consuls because of his support for the coup d'état of Napoléon Bonaparte (see NAPOLÉON I) on 18 Brumaire, Year VIII (November 9, 1799). Maret, who had been created duke of Bassano by Napoléon, was for a time during the HUNDRED DAYS minister of foreign relations, was exiled from 1816 to 1820, then, after his return to France, was eventually made a peer by King LOUIS-PHILIPPE (1831).

## Marguerite de Valois (1492–1549)
### (Marguerite d'Angoulême, Marguerite de Navarre)
*queen of Navarre, poet, writer*

Marguerite de Valois (or d'Angoulême, or de Navarre, as she is also known) was born in Angoulême, the daughter of Charles de Valois, count of Angoulême, and Louise of Savoy, and was the sister of King FRANCIS I, to whom she was greatly devoted. In 1509, Marguerite married Charles, duke of Alençon and, after his death, married Henri d'Albret, king of Navarre (1527). One of the most educated women of the period, Marguerite de Valois made her court at Navarre a center of humanism. A devout adherent of the Reformation and protector of the Protestants, she supported the work of various Protestant theologians, including JOHN CALVIN, whom she knew. Among the scholars and writers who were part of her circle were Robert Estienne (see ESTIENNE FAMILY), Bonaventure des Préiers, CLÉMENT MAROT, and FRANÇOIS RABELAIS, who dedicated his *Tiers Livre* to her. Marguerite was herself a writer and, besides her *Heptaméron*, her most famous work, her poems

(*Les Marguerites de la Marguerite des princesses*) and some comedies. She was the mother of JEANNE III d'Albret, queen of Navarre.

## Marguerite de Valois (1553–1615)
### (Queen Margot, la reine Margot)
*queen of France and Navarre*

The queen of Navarre and France, Marguerite de Valois, or "la reine Margot" as she is known, was born in Saint-Germain-en-Laye, the daughter of King HENRY II of France and Queen CATHERINE DE' MEDICI. In August 1572, she married the leader of the HUGUENOTS, Henri de Navarre (the future HENRY IV of France). The wedding, which was attended by many prominent Huguenots, far from being an occasion for reconciliation, was one of the causes of the SAINT BARTHOLOMEW'S DAY MASSACRE, in which thousands of Protestants were killed. After estrangement from her husband, and being expelled from the court of King HENRY III because of her involvement in intrigues in favor of her brother François d'Alençon (FRANCIS II), Marguerite retired to Nérac, where she held a brilliant court, with many literary figures in attendance. She then settled at Usson, in Auvergne (1587–1605). Although her childless marriage to Henry IV was annulled with her consent (1599), 10 years after Henry ascended the throne, Marguerite retained the title of queen. She returned to Paris in 1605. Intelligent and cultivated, she left her *Mémoires,* which are held in high regard.

## "Marianne"

"Marianne" is the guiding spirit and the name given to the French Republic, from the time of the REVOLUTION OF 1789. It was also the name of a secret republican society that sought to overthrow the SECOND EMPIRE. The name, which combines those of the Virgin Mary and Saint Anne, and which at first was used by enemies of the republic, has long ago lost any pejorative meaning, and statues of Marianne adorn most public buildings in France and many coins, until the adoption of the euro. The faces of a number of famous and beautiful French women (including BRIGITTE BARDOT and CATHERINE DENEUVE) have served as models for portraits of the Marianne figure.

## Maria Theresa of Spain (queen) (1638–1683)
*Infanta of Spain, queen of France*

The daughter of King Philip IV of Spain and ELISABETH OF FRANCE, daughter of King HENRY IV, Maria Theresa was born in Madrid. She spent a somewhat unhappy childhood at her father's court, until for diplomatic reasons (to secure the Peace of the Pyrenees), she was married in 1660 to LOUIS XIV of France. She then renounced all claims to the Spanish throne. Immediately after the marriage, however, it was apparent that she and the king had little in common and, although they had six children (only one lived to maturity and none survived Louis), he made no pretense of affection. The estrangement between them was ended at the insistence of FRANÇOISE D'AUBIGNÉ, MARQUISE DE MAINTENON, the governess of the royal children and the king's mistress, who, as a deeply moral and religious person, wished the court to be respectable. Queen Maria Theresa always played a self-effacing role, supporting the king even in his infidelities. She died at VERSAILLES shortly after the public reconciliation.

## Marie, Pierre (1795–1870)
*political figure*

Born Pierre-Thomas Marie de Saint-Georges, Pierre Marie as he is known, was a leftist monarchist deputy (Parti de mouvement, 1842) during the JULY MONARCHY, and supported the provisional government after the REVOLUTION OF 1848. Then, as a moderate republican and as minister of public works, he organized the National Workshops (Ateliers nationaux), created in part to counteract the socialist movement. Minister of justice (July–December 1848), Marie took a position against NAPOLÉON III and, from 1863 to 1869, was a member of the opposition in the legislature.

## Marie-Amélie de Bourbon (1782–1866)
*queen of the French*

Born in Caserta, Italy, the daughter of Ferdinand IV, king of the Two Sicilies, and Queen Marie-Caroline, Marie-Amélie in 1809 married the duke de Orléans and, upon his accession as King LOUIS-PHILIPPE, became queen of the French (1830). She had eight children, to whom she gave a liberal education. In 1848, queen Marie-Amélie followed her husband into exile in England.

### Marie of Anjou (1404–1463)

*queen of France*

Born in Châtellier, Poitou, Marie of Anjou was the daughter of Louis II, king of Sicily, and Yolanda of Aragon. Marie married King CHARLES VII of France (1422) and was the mother of King LOUIS XI.

### Marie Antoinette (1755–1793)
### (Marie-Antoinette)

*queen of France*

Marie-Antoinette-Joseph-Jeanne de Lorraine, archduchess of Austria and queen of France, was born in Vienna, the daughter of Empress Maria Theresa and Emperor Francis I. She spent her childhood at the Imperial court, where she received a negligible education. Destined, like her sister Marie-Caroline, to serve the political policies of the House of Habsburg, she was married, thanks to the efforts of the French minister ÉTIENNE DE CHOISEUL, to the dauphin, the future LOUIS XVI (May 1770). From this marriage were born two sons, Louis-Joseph and Louis-Charles (the future LOUIS XVII), and two daughters, MARIE-THÉRÈSE CHARLOTTE (the future duchess d'ANGOULÊME) and Sophie-Hélène-Béatrice. The young queen Marie Antoinette soon became unpopular because of the bad reputation of her friends, her extravagance, which was mistakenly blamed for the government's financial problems, and intrigues, real or imagined, with the king's brother, the count d'Artois (see CHARLES X), and Axel de Fersen, a Swedish nobleman. Especially damaging was her supposed connection with the so-called Affair of the Necklace, a scandal involving the fraudulent purchase of some jewels (1785). Little inclined to the spirit of the Enlightenment, Marie Antoinette, who sided with the intransigents at court and opposed compromise, exercised an increasing influence on the king. In 1789, this influence would make reconciliation between the monarchy and the REVOLUTION OF 1789 impossible. In spite of the advice of HONORÉ DE MIRABEAU, the queen refused to accept the idea of a constitutional

Marie Antoinette *(Library of Congress)*

monarchy and preferred to count on the possibility of foreign intervention to save the royal establishment. Imprisoned in the Temple in Paris after the overthrow of the monarchy (August 10, 1792), she was transferred on August 2, 1793, to the Conciergerie. The king had already been executed and her children had been taken from her. She was subsequently tried before a revolutionary tribunal and, confronted with accusations of conspiring with foreign enemies of France and also with infamous calumnies, brought especially by the ultra-revolutionaries (in particular, JACQUES HÉBERT).

Queen Marie Antoinette nonetheless maintained a dignified and aloft demeanor throughout. Condemned to death, the "Autrichienne," as she was now pejoratively referred to, was executed on October 16, 1793.

## Marie of Burgundy (1457–1482)
*nobility*

Born in Brussels, Marie, duchess of Burgundy (1477–82) was only 20 when her father CHARLES THE BOLD, died, and King LOUIS XI of France annexed Burgundy, invaded Picardy, Artois, and Boulonnais, and wanted to marry her to the dauphin. The Grand Revolt, which he encouraged, forced Marie to sign the Grand Privilège (1477). But Maximilian of Austria, whom she had married, defeated Louis XI at Guingegatte (1479), allowing him to keep Flanders. Marie of Burgundy had two children, Philip the Fair of the Netherlands and Margaret of Austria.

## Marie de l'Incarnation (1566–1618)
*beatified religious figure*

Born in Paris, Barbe-Jeanne Avrillot was educated at the convent of Longchamps. Although she wanted to become a nun, in 1544 she married Pierre Acarie, viscount de Villemare, in obedience to her parents. Known as "la Belle Acarie," she was popular and respected both in Parisian society and among the poor and ill for whom she cared. After her husband was exiled, she dedicated herself to her six children. Greatly influenced by the work of Theresa of Ávila, she sought to introduce the reformed Carmelite order into France. This she succeeded in doing in 1603 with the assistance of Cardinal PIERRE DE BÉRULLE. She also helped to establish the Ursalines. After the death of her husband in 1613, she was received into the convent at Amiens, taking the religious name of Marie de l'Incarnation. Later, she was transferred to Pontoise, where she died. Having acquired a great reputation for holiness, she was beatified in 1794. Because of her position in society, as well as her piety and charity, she had an enormous influence on French Catholicism in the 17th century.

## Marie de l'Incarnation (1599–1672)
*beatified religious figure*

Born in Tours, Marie Guyard entered the Ursaline order after being widowed in 1619. She took the religious name of Marie de l'Incarnation (1631) and became a missionary in Canada (1639). An active woman as well as a mystic, she founded there the first Ursaline convent. Her spiritual work (in particular the two *Relations* of Tours and Quebec, 1677) and her abundant *Correspondance* (1681) made her a leading personage in the religious history of New France. JACQUES-BÉNIGNE BOSSUET referred to her as the "Theresa of the New World."

## Marie Leszczynska (1703–1768)
*queen of France*

Marie Leszczynska was born in Breslau, Poland, the daughter of Stanislaus I Leszcynski, king of Poland, and Queen Marie. Married to LOUIS XV of France (1725), she bore 10 children, seven of whom survived, and was the grandmother of LOUIS XVI. Of a retiring nature and disposition, she made no attempt to rival the king's mistresses (Mme de POMPADOUR, Mme du BARRY). Marie Leszczynska's marriage facilitated French involvement in the War of the Polish Succession (1733–35). After her father renounced his throne (Treaty of Vienna, 1738), he received the duchies of Bar and Lorraine and established his court in France at Lunéville and, especially, at Nancy.

## Marie Louise of Habsburg-Lorraine (1791–1847)
*empress of the French*

Born in Vienna, Marie Louise of Habsburg-Lorraine, archduchess of Austria and, later, empress of the French (1810), was the daughter of the Holy Roman Emperor Francis II and Empress Maria Theresa of Naples. She married NAPOLÉON I in April 1810 and on March 20, 1811, bore him a son, the king of Rome (NAPOLÉON II). When Napoléon I was involved in campaigns in 1813, he named her regent. After her husband's abdication, she rejoined her family in Vienna (April 1814). The Treaty of Fontainebleau (1814) assured her the lifelong sovereignty of Parma, Piacenza, and Guastala, and of the title of imperial majesty. Abandoning Napoléon I to his fate and willing to be separated from her son, Marie Louise, in 1821, married the Austrian field marshal von Neipperg and had two sons. Widowed in 1829, she married in 1834 the count of Bombelles, chamberlain of the court in Vienna.

## Marie de' Medici (1573–1642)
### (Marie de Médicis)
*queen of France*

Born in Florence, Italy, Marie de' Medici was the daughter of the grand duke of Tuscany, Francesco de'Medici, and the grand duchess Giovanna. In 1600, she married HENRY IV of France. They had six children, the eldest of whom became King LOUIS XIII in 1610, when his father was assassinated. As regent during her son's minority, Marie was dominated by her Italian advisers and, unlike Henry IV, pursued a pro-Spanish policy of arranging marriages both for Louis and for his sister ELISABETH into the Spanish royal family. In terms of domestic policy, she was unable to control the restless French nobles and the ESTATES GENERAL. In 1617, she went to war against her son, but her forces were defeated at Ponts-de-Cé (1620). Reconciled with him in 1621, Marie promoted the advancement of ARMAND-JEAN DU PLESSIS DE RICHELIEU, using her influence to have him made a cardinal in 1622 and Louis's prime minister in 1624. When Cardinal Richelieu reversed her policy of alliance with Spain, however, Marie turned against him. Concerned over her former protégé's influence, she tried to overthrow him (1630), but failing, went into permanent exile (Brussels, London, and eventually Cologne). Marie was also a patron to a number of artists, including the Flemish painter Peter Paul Rubens, who illustrated her life in a brilliant series of 21 tableaux (1622–24), for installation in the Luxembourg Palace (today in the LOUVRE).

See also CONCINI, CONCINO; GALIGAÏ, LEONORA.

## Mariette, Auguste (1821–1881)
*Egyptologist*

Born in Boulogne-sur-Mer, Auguste Mariette was employed in 1849 as the curator of the Department of Egyptian Antiquities at the LOUVRE. He was sent the following year to Egypt to purchase Coptic manuscripts. Although he did not accomplish that goal, he took part in the archaeological digs at Saqqara, where he discovered Serapeum, a necropolis complex (1850). Named director of excavations of antiquities in Egypt by the viceroy Saïd Pasha, Mariette organized an archaeological expedition that undertook digs at Tanis, Abydos, Saqqara, Giza, and Thebes. He uncovered the temples of Edfou and Denderah, and brought to light one of the greatest works of ancient Egyptian art: the statue in wood of Cheikh-el-Beled, the seated scribe, as well as the statue in diorite of Khephren. Mariette also launched a campaign against clandestine digs in Egypt and the illicit export of antiquities. In 1863, at Boulaq, he founded a museum whose collection became the basis for the present Cairo Museum. Mariette published the results of his findings in a number of works, among these the *Catalogue du musée de Boulaq* (1864–1876) and *Les Mastabas de l'Ancien Empire* (posthumous, 1889). He was named to the Académie des inscriptions et belles-lettres in 1878.

## Maritain, Jacques (1882–1973)
*philosopher*

Born in Toulouse, Jacques Maritain converted from Protestantism to Catholicism with his wife Raissa and wrote against both materialist philosophy and the ideas of HENRI BERGSON. One of the principal interpreters of Thomism, Maritain, through a humanistic Christianity, approached the problems of existence, religious philosophies, and the esthetic and political realms. He served as French ambassador to the Vatican (1945–48). His principal works include *De la philosophie chrétienne* (1933), *Principes d'une politique humaniste* (1945), *Humanisme intégral* (1936), *Intuition créatrice en art et en poésie* (1962).

## Marivaux, Pierre-Carlet de Chamblain de (1688–1763)
*dramatist and writer*

Born in Paris, Pierre-Carlet de Chamblain de Marivaux, whose distinctive style of writing came to be known as "marivaudage," was the son of the director of the royal mint. He began his writing career early, frequenting the Paris salons (1712) and by 1720 produced his first important comedy, *Arlequin, poli par l'amour*. He also soon founded his own literary journal, *Le Spectateur français* (1722), followed by *L'Indigent philosophe* (1728) and then *Le Cabinet du philosophe* (1734). Outside of two other novels, which are his main genre writings, *La Vie de Marianne* (1731–41) and *Le Paysan parvenu* (1735), Marivaux dedicated most of his energy to writing for the theater. Over a period of 20 years he wrote a large number of works for both the COMÉDIE-FRANÇAISE and the Comédie-Italienne, which was based on the commedia dell'arte and, which had a great influence on Marivaux. Marivaux's incomparable elegance, his use of language, the rustic charm of his characters, and his subtle, analytical style were all critiqued in a lively manner by VOLTAIRE, and his works represent the optimism that was in fashion before the REVOLUTION OF 1789. Marivaux was elected to the ACADÉMIE FRANÇAISE in 1743.

## Marmont, Auguste-Frédéric-Louis-Viesse de (1774–1852)
*marshal of France*

Born in Châtillon-sur-Seine, Auguste-Frédéric-Louis-Viesse de Marmont had been an attaché to Napoléon Bonaparte (see NAPOLÉON I) since the siege of Toulon (1793), was his aide-de-camp in Italy, then accompanied him to Egypt (1798). He was named governor general of Dalmatia (1806), which he subsequently developed; duke of Ragusa (1808), then marshal after the battle of Wagram. He replaced Marshal ANDRÉ MASSÉNA as commander of the army in Portugal (May 1811) and was wounded and defeated in Spain by the duke of Wellington (1812). Marmont campaigned in Germany (Bautzen, Leipzig) and, with remarkable tactics, held back the advance of the coalition forces. In 1814, he fought outside Paris and, with the consent of JOSEPH BONAPARTE, negotiated the surrender of the city with Russian czar Alexander I. On April 3, 1814, ignoring the emperor's abdication plans, he marched his troops into Normandy instead of covering Napoléon at Fontainebleau, which was

considered a betrayal. Meanwhile, he tried to have the king of Rome (NAPOLÉON II) recognized as heir to the throne. King LOUIS XVIII made Marmont a peer of France and, in July 1830, he led the royal troops who fought against the REVOLUTION OF 1830 in Paris. Marshal Marmont accompanied the exiled king CHARLES X to Cherbourg, then went into exile himself. He left his *Mémoires*.

## Marmontel, Jean-François (1723–1799)
*writer*

Born in Bort-les-Orgues, Jean-François Marmontel, who was brought to Paris by VOLTAIRE, acquired great celebrity at the royal court, and, later, in Europe, not only for his tragedies, but for his moral tales (*Contes moraux*, 1761–71) and, above all, for two ideological novels, *Bélisaire* (1767), which upheld the principle of tolerance, and *Les Incas* (1777), which stigmatized slavery. He collected his articles, written for the *Encyclopédie* of DENIS DIDEROT, under the title *Éléments de littérature* (1787) and left unfinished his *Mémoires d'un père* (1804).

## Marne

The Marne River of France, which has its source on the Langres plateau, flows for 525 kilometers through Chaumont, Vitry, Châlons, Epernay, Château-Thierry, and Meaux and empties into the SEINE at Charenton. On the invasion route toward Paris, the Marne was the site of the initial battle of WORLD WAR I.

## Marot, Clément (1496–1544)
*poet*

Born in Cahors, the son of the rhetorician Jean Marot, Clément Marot served as a page to King FRANCIS I and then to the king's sister MARGUERITE OF VALOIS, the future queen of Navarre. He earned their patronage and wrote court poems that followed the style of the period (*D'Anne qui lui jeta de la neige*, 1515; *Temple de Cupido*, 1515; *Adolescence clémentine*, 1532). Sympathetic to the Reformation and to JOHN CALVIN (whom he met in 1535), Marot was exiled for his beliefs and died alone in Turin. His other works, some of which were written in exile, include *Épître à Lyon Jamet* (1526); *Épître au roi, pour le délivrer de prison* (1527), a fierce allegorical satire on the judiciary; *L'Enfer* (composed in 1526, published in 1542); and *Épigrammes* (1527). He also edited a version of the *Roman de la Rose* (1526), an edition of the works of FRANÇOIS VILLON (1533), and did a translation of the psalms (1536). Marot contributed to the literary development of the French language, and his picturesque, clear language inspired such later writers as NICOLAS BOILEAU and JEAN DE LA FONTAINE.

## Marrast, Armand (1801–1852)
*political figure*

Born in Saint-Gaudens, Armand Marrast was the editor of the newspaper, *La Tribune* (1830–35) and *Le National* (1841), in which he put forth his republican views at the time of the JULY MONARCHY. He was one of the organizers of the Banquet of February 22, 1848, the interdiction of which precipitated the REVOLUTION OF 1848. A member of the government as a moderate republican deputy to the Constituent Assembly (April 1848), Marrast assisted in the editing of the constitution of the SECOND REPUBLIC (November 1848).

## Marseillaise, La

"La Marseillaise" is the French national anthem, the words of which (and probably the music) were written in Strasbourg by the French army officer CLAUDE-JOSEPH ROUGET DE LISLE under the title *Chant de guerre pour l'armée du Rhin*. It was sung for the first time in Paris during the REVOLUTION OF 1789 by the federal troops from MARSEILLE, in August 1792, hence the name. Designated the national anthem on July 14, 1795, it remained such until the FIRST EMPIRE. "La Marseillaise" again became the national anthem in February 1879.

## Marseille

Located in southern France, Marseille, the nation's second-largest city after Paris. Situated on a bay on the Mediterranean coast, Marseille has a population of over 800,000. From the Old Port (Vieux-Port), the city extends upward in an irregular hemisphere of hills, with the areas of l'Étoile to the north and l'Estaque to the west. Beyond these areas is an industrial zone with the port of Fos in the west and the area of Berre, and more residential areas like Martiques. Nearby are the airports of Marignane (France's third-largest) and Istres. Marseille is at one end of a metropolitan axis formed with Aix-en-Provence. The southern and central sections of Marseille have been rebuilt, and they contrast with the northern quarters, which are home to a recent immigrant population. There are vestiges of the ancient Greek and Roman city found in various areas. Important buildings include the Basilica of Notre-Dame-de-la-Garde, on a high strip of land projecting into the bay and surmounted by a gilded statue of the Virgin Mary, and the cathedral, both of which were constructed in the 19th century in the Roman-Byzantine style. The Basilica of Saint-Victor stands over a fifth-century abbey. There are several museums including the Museum of Mediterranean Archaeology, Museum of African, Oceanic, and Amerindian Art, Cantini Museum of 20th Century Art, Museum of Fine Arts, Museum of Contemporary Art (MAC), and Museum of Fashion. Marseille's most famous street is La Canebière, a broad boulevard that contains the main shopping district. The noted Cité radieuse, built by LE CORBUSIER, is a residential structure. The port of Marseille-Fos is the largest in France and the third-largest in Europe for trade. The three universities of Aix-Marseille have a relationship with other colleges (physics, petrochemicals, and agrarian studies) and with the 150 research laboratories of the city (biotechnology, electronics, robotics, and artificial intelligence). Connected to Paris by the TGV (Train à Grande Vitesse) railway, Marseille also has an up-to-date highway infrastructure connecting with LYON, Paris, Nice, Toulouse, Italy, and Spain. Marseille was colonized by Greeks from Asia Minor, who called it Massalia. During the Punic Wars the city sided with Carthage and, in 44 B.C.E., it sided with Pompey against Julius Caesar. It was a site of Celtic civilization in Gaul and in the first century B.C.E. was annexed by Rome. In the fourth century C.E. the city was the site of a bishopric. Mar-

The harbor of Marseille *(Library of Congress)*

seille's economic role later declined, but it had a revival during the Crusades. In 1481, with Provence, it was incorporated into the kingdom of France. Its economic development then rivaled that of Genoa. In 1720, Marseille was decimated by the plague, but the city continued to develop until the REVOLUTION OF 1789, in which it played an important role (a battalion of troops from Marseille participated in the August Days of 1792 and introduced the national anthem, "LA MARSEILLAISE," to Paris). Devastated by the revolutionary and Napoleonic Wars (the continental blockade), Marseille's prosperity revived following French colonial expansion and the opening of the Suez Canal. The enlargement of the port began in the early 20th century and continues to the present. The city was dam-

aged during the World War II and was liberated on August 28, 1944, by the First French Army. Many of the city's residents are descendants of immigrants from Italy, Spain, and North Africa.

## Martignac, Jean-Baptiste-Sylvère-Gay, count de (1778–1832)
*political figure*

Born in BORDEAUX, where he served as an attorney general, Jean-Baptiste-Sylvère-Gay, count de Martignac also was the procurator general at Limoges and was elected a deputy in 1821. He replaced JEAN-BAPTISTE DE VILLÈLE after the 1827 elections (which favored the opposition) and was head of the government from 1828 to 1829. His cabinet, relatively liberal, constituted the last attempt of the RESTORATION to reconcile the regime and the Chamber of Deputies. In August 1829, he was replaced by JULES DE POLIGNAC, and had to defend himself during the trial of the ministers who had failed at the time of the July Monarchy.

## Marty, André (1886–1956)
*political figure*

Born in Perpignan, André Marty was a naval machinist officer who, in 1919, fomented the sailors' mutiny of the First Fleet (stationed in the Black Sea), which refused to continue to fight the Russian Bolsheviks. Condemned to 20 years at forced labor, he was amnestied in 1923 and elected deputy (1924), became a member of the Political Bureau of the French COMMUNIST PARTY (1931), then secretary-general of the Communist International (1935). During the Spanish civil war, he took part in organizing the International Brigade, of which he served as commander in chief. Accused of "fractious politics," Marty was expelled from the Communist Party in 1953.

## Masséna, André (1756–1817)
*marshal of France*

Born in Nice, André Masséna was a cabin boy on a ship when he joined the French army in 1775, rising to the rank of general during the REVOLUTION OF 1789. He distinguished himself during the campaigns in Italy, notably at the battle of Rivoli (1797). NAPOLÉON I called him "the beloved child of Victory." General Masséna fought in the battle of Zurich against the Austrians and Russians (September 25, 1799) and helped to prevent an allied invasion of France. In 1800, immobilizing the Austrians near Genoa, he allowed Napoléon to enter Italy and win the victory of Marengo. Made a marshal in 1804, Masséna conquered the kingdom of Naples (1806) and was made the duke of Rivoli (1808). He distinguished himself in the Battles of Essling and Wagram, and was made prince of Wagram by Napoléon (1810), who gave him the command of the army in Portugal (April 1810). But he was pushed back by the British line at Torres Vedras and had to retreat from the region (March 1811). In 1814, Marshal Masséna went over to the Bourbons. He left his *Mémoires*.

## Masson, André (1896–1987)
*painter, engraver, stage designer*

A leader of the surrealist movement, André Masson was born in Balagny, Oise, and studied at the Beaux-Arts in Paris. After a cubist period in his art, he developed a more mysterious and symbolic style. Early in his career, he was attracted to surrealism, and his interest in the unconscious mind led him to experiment systematically with automatic drawing, using pencil and ink and later textured accretions of pigment, sand, and glue. Masson was influenced by other surrealists, especially André Breton, and during World War II (1939–45), he moved to Martinique and then to New York City. He had a notable influence on action painting in the United States and on a number of American artists. In 1947, he settled near Aix-en-Provence and produced a series of landscapes (*Paysages provençaux*). In 1965, he was asked by ANDRÉ MALRAUX to design the stage of the Odéon Theater in Paris and to illustrate his books.

## Matisse, Henri (1869–1954)
*painter, sculptor*

One of the most influential artists of the 20th century, particularly through fauvism, Henri Matisse was born in Cateau-Cambrésis and studied law and worked as a notary before deciding, while convalescing from an illness, to dedicate his life to art. He studied at various studios in Paris and copied works at the LOUVRE, while becoming interested also in Islamic art. During this period, Matisse's style was traditional, but after a visit to Brittany, he became interested in impressionism and was influenced by the works of PAUL GAUGUIN, HENRI DE TOULOUSE-LAUTREC, and PAUL CÉZANNE. In 1898, he painted nude forms at the Carrière Academy and became interested in sculpture. He still showed the influence of Cézanne (*Nus à l'atelier*), but then, after a stay in Saint-Tropez, developed a more individualistic style (*Luxe, Calme et Volupté*, 1905). Matisse soon came to a style noted for the use of strong colors over large areas, and the abandonment of traditional perspective, which were to be his trademarks (*Gypsy*, 1905–06; *The Open Window, Collioure*, 1905). In autumn 1905, at the Paris Salon, he presented with other artists works that were initially pejoratively labeled "fauvist." He soon produced a large painting, *The Joy of Life*, with strong colors, fluid lines, and disregard of proportions (*Bathers with a Turtle*). By 1908, when he opened a studio in Paris, he had achieved international recognition. He traveled to Morocco in 1911–12, and the influence is apparent in his works (*The Moroccans*, 1916). Settling then in Nice, he worked in traditional themes and broadened his range of art (tapestries, pottery) in the same colorful and luxuriant style. The request of the Barnes Foundation for a monumental work (*The Dance*, 1931) marked a new stage in his career. He continued in the use of fluid lines and abstraction (*Rose Nude*, 1935) and, in a series of papiers découpés (*Jazz; Boxeur nègre; Zulma*, 1950), a technique that allowed him to "design in color," Matisse further developed the principles that he had set down earlier and that culminated in his decorations for the chapel at Vence (1951). In all his works, Matisse seems to have achieved, as he said in 1908, "an art of equilibrium, purity, and tranquility."

## Maupassant, Guy de  (1850–1893)
*writer*

Considered one of the masters of the art of the short story, Guy de Maupassant was born in Château de Miromesnil, Seine-Maritime. After a happy and carefree youth, interrupted by the FRANCO-PRUSSIAN WAR, he took a job as a functionary in Paris (some of the bureaucrats with whom he worked can be found in "La Parure," ["The Necklace"] and "L'Heritage" ["The Inheritance"]). Along with leading a fun-loving and sporting life, he did his literary "apprenticeship" with GUSTAVE FLAUBERT, a friend of the family who introduced him to the realist genre and to such writers as JORIS-KARL HUYSMANS, ALPHONSE DAUDET, and ÉMILE ZOLA. "Boule-de-Suif" ("Ball of Fat"; 1880), one of the stories in the collection *Les Soirées de Médan*, decided Maupassant's vocation and assured his success. Devoted to his work, he wrote 300 short stories in 10 years. Evoking in turn Normandy, the FRANCO-PRUSSIAN WAR, and Parisian cynicism, these stories range from the

classic to the comic, from realism to the fantastic. Full of sensual vitality (*Bel ami*, 1885), Maupassant visited Great Britain, Italy, and North Africa (*Au soleil*, 1884; *Sur l'eau*, 1888) on his yacht, but he was progressively suffering from nervous disorders and haunted by death, as is apparent in his works *Une Vie* (1883), *Pierre et Jean* (1888), *Fort comme la Mort* (1889). Suffering from hallucinations, he was eventually hospitalized and, after 18 months, died in a clinic. Whether he speaks in the colorful Norman patois of his peasants or describes with lucid precision his sense of anguish, Maupassant is the master of the short story.

## Maupeou, René-Nicolas-Charles-Augustin de  (1714–1792)
*political figure*

Born in Paris, where he served as president of the Parlement (1763), René-Nicolas-Charles-Augustin de Maupeou was chancellor of finance (1768) and opposed the policies of the minister ÉTIENNE FRANÇOIS DE CHOISEUL, to whose fall he contributed. Called to power, Maupeou formed with EMMANUEL D'AIGUILLON and the abbot JOSEPH TERRAY a true "triumvirate" of power during the reign of King LOUIS XV. Parliamentary unrest was quelled and recalcitrant members exiled, and counsels were created that could be recalled. Meanwhile, reforms were instituted to appease indignant public opinion. This attempt at despotism, however, came to an end with the death of the king.

## Maupertuis, Pierre-Louis Moreau de  (1698–1759)
*mathematician, naturalist*

Pierre-Louis Moreau de Maupertuis, who introduced the theories of Isaac Newton to France, was born in Saint-Malo. In 1736–37, he planned and led an expedition for the Academy of Sciences to Lapland to measure there the length of a meridian arc of one degree; the result, compared with a measurement made in Peru, allowed him to conclude that there was a flattening of the earth at the poles. Revising Fermat's theorem in 1744, Maupertuis presented the "principle of least resistance," which allowed the prediction of the movement of all "material points," and which constituted for him a formulation for all mechanical theory. In the field of biology, he amended the atomic theory and presented the theory of biological mutation. He also elaborated on the theory of particular heredity. Maupertuis was also interested in the origin of languages. From 1741 to 1756, he was at the Royal Prussian Academy of Sciences at the invitation of King Frederick II. Maupertuis was elected to the Academy of Sciences in 1723 and to the ACADÉMIE FRANÇAISE in 1746.

## Maurepas, Jean-Frédéric Phélypeaux, count de (1701–1781)
*political figure*

Born in Versailles, Jean-Frédéric Phélypeaux, count de Maurepas, the grandson of the royal comptroller general LOUIS PHÉLYPEAUX, COUNT DE PONTCHARTRAIN, succeeded his father as minister of the Royal Household, then went into the navy. He improved the city of Paris, encouraged scientific studies (see PIERRE DE MAUPERTUIS, JUSSIEU FAMILY), and reformed the naval administration. But he was disgraced for having been suspected of writing an epigram against Mme DE POMPADOUR, the mistress of King LOUIS XV (1749). Recalled in 1779 by King LOUIS XVI, Maurepas surrounded himself with capable individuals (ROBERT TURGOT, CHRÉTIEN DE MALESHERBES, CHARLES DE VERGENNES), but he could not defend himself against court intrigues. His *Mémoires* have been published.

## Mauriac, François (1885–1970)
*writer*

Born in BORDEAUX, François Mauriac was raised and educated in a strict Christian, almost Jansenist, tradition by his mother, as is reflected in his writings (*Le Jeune Homme*, 1926; *La Province*, 1926; *Commencements d'une vie*, 1932; *Écrits intimes*, 1953). Coming to Paris in 1926, he dedicated himself to literature, but his early writings, a collection of poems (*Les Mains jointes*, 1909) and novels (*L'Enfant chargé de chaînes*, 1913; *La Robe prétexte*, 1914) went unappreciated. He was first recognized for *Le Baiser au lépreux* (1922), which, along with *Génétrix* (1923), won wide critical and popular acclaim. Other works considered among the finest of 20th-century fiction

are *Le Désert de l'amour* (1925). *Thérèse Desqueyroux* (1927), and *Le Nœud des vipères* (1932). He is also the author of a biography, *Vie de Racine* (1928), of critical essays including *Le Rencontre avec Pascal* (1926), and spiritual writings (*La Vie de Jésus*, 1936). Mauriac was also known as an outspoken journalist and incisive polemicist (*Journal*, 1934–51; *Le Cabinet noir*, 1943, written under the pseudonym of Forez; and *Bloc-Notes*, 1958–61). In the postwar period, he took up the cause of colonialism and the ideals of Gaullism. A profoundly religious Catholic, he was chiefly concerned in his novels with basic moral conflicts. Mauriac was elected to the ACADÉMIE FRANÇAISE in 1933, was awarded the Nobel Prize in literature in 1952, and was named to the LEGION OF HONOR in 1958.

## Maurois, André (1885–1967)
### (Émile Herzog)
*novelist, essayist, and historian*

Born Émile Herzog in Elbeuf, André Maurois, as he is best known, was educated at the University of Caen. His first work, *Les Silences du colonel Bramble* (1918), is a fictionalized memoir of his experiences in World War I, in which he served as an officer. This book, with its delicate humor, would launch his career. Five years later, he published the biography *Ariel, ou la vie de Shelley,* which was the first of a number of romanticized biographies. All relied on Maurois's imaginative interpretation, rather than scholarly background, and are written in a popular and engaging style. Maurois was especially interested in describing both creative lives and those of individuals of action. He also wrote philosophical works (*Le Peseur d'âmes,* 1931) and short science-fiction pieces (*Toujours, l'inattendu arrive,* 1943; *La Machine à lire les pensées,* 1943). He was interested, too, in the great developments of history and did a number of large historical studies (*Histoire de l'Angleterre,* 1937; *Histoire des États-Unis,* 1943; *Histoire de la France,* 1947). Maurois was elected to the ACADÉMIE FRANÇAISE in 1938.

## Mauroy, Pierre (1928–  )
*political leader*

Born in Cartignies, Nord, Pierre Mauroy served as a Socialist deputy (1973–92), senator (1992), and mayor of Lille (1973). He was prime minister of the FIFTH REPUBLIC from 1981 to 1984 and undertook several social reforms (retirement at age 60, the 39-hour week, fifth week of paid vacation), but his policies were considered too extreme and the rejection of his reforms in private education forced him to resign. Representing a certain tradition of popular socialism, particularly in the north, Mauroy served as first secretary of the SOCIALIST PARTY (PS) and after 1992 directed the Socialist International.

## Maurras, Charles (1868–1952)
*writer, political figure*

Born in Martigues, Charles Maurras was a Provençal influenced by the writings of FRÉDÉRIC MISTRAL and the ideas of MAURICE BARRÈS, ERNEST RENAN, and ANATOLE FRANCE. In his own writings, he expressed his love for the culture of ancient Greece and the cult of order and reason. His *L'Avenir de l'intelligence* (1900) and *Anthinéa* (1901) are reflections on human nature and the decline of democracy, as well as of art; he was particularly critical of romanticism (*Romanticisme et Révolution,* 1925). His own neoclassicism is expressed in his *Enquête sur la monarchie* (1909), which appeared after the Dreyfus affair (see ALFRED DREYFUS) and inaugurated his Action française movement (1908–44), of which he was the driving force. In all his political writings, done in a forceful dialectical style, Maurras waged a relentless war against the REVOLUTION OF 1789, the 19th century, romanticism, the THIRD REPUBLIC, foreigners in France, Freemasons, and Jews (*Mes Idées politiques,* 1937). An outspoken monarchist, Maurras held a position that is summarized in the motto of the Action française: "Classicism, Monarchy, Catholicism." He even wished to restore Catholicism as the state religion of France. Nonetheless, his writings were put on the Index, the Catholic Church's list of forbidden readings. Maurras, who with his Action française appealed to the most conservative of the French bourgeoisie, supported Benito Mussolini and Francisco Franco, and subsequently collaborated with the VICHY regime. For this, he was sentenced to life imprisonment (1945), but he was released shortly before his death. Maurras was elected to the ACADÉMIE FRANÇAISE in 1938, but he was expelled in 1945.

## Maury, Jean-Siffrein (1746–1817)
*prelate*

Born in Valréas, Jean-Siffrein Maury, a celebrated preacher, was elected as a deputy for the clergy to the ESTATES GENERAL (1789) and during the REVOLUTION OF 1789 was, in the National Constituent Assembly, one of the main defenders of the ancient regime. He opposed the CIVIL CONSTITUTION OF THE CLERGY and demanded that the authority of the pope be recognized in Avignon. An émigré to Rome in 1792, he was named bishop of Montefiascone (1792), and later archbishop of Nicea and cardinal (1794). In favor of the FIRST EMPIRE, he returned to France (1806), where NAPOLÉON I named him archbishop of Paris (1810). He upheld the emperor's policies (1811) and, upon returning to Rome in 1814, was held in the fortress of Sant' Angelo, then freed on the condition of his resignation. Cardinal Maury is the author of *Panégyriques* and *Essai sur l'éloquence de la chaire*. He was elected to the ACADÉMIE FRANÇAISE in 1785.

## May 1873, Day of 24

May 24, 1873, marks the parliamentary day during the THIRD REPUBLIC on which the conservatives in the National Assembly, at the instigation of the duke of BROGIE and others, voted as an order of the day to censure ADOLPHE THIERS, who was judged as too favorable towards the republicans. Thiers had to resign and was replaced by EDMÉ MAC-MAHON.

## May 1958, Crisis of

The Crisis of May 1958 was a series of events that took place in Algiers in May 1958. The resignation of the French government that was in the minority in the National Assembly over the Algerian question on April 15 started the crisis. PIERRE PFLIMLIN was charged on May 8 to form a new government, while tensions increased in Algeria and in France. While Pflimlin was at the Assembly (May 13) to assume office, General RAOUL SALAN and others in Algiers formed a Committee of Public Safety. Faced with the situation that had developed not only in ALGERIA (uprisings, insubordination proclaimed by a faction in the army) but in France (formation of several Committees of Public Safety), and dreading an escalation of the crisis, the president of the Republic, RENÉ COTY, appealed to General CHARLES DE GAULLE to intervene. The crisis led to de Gaulle coming to political power.

## May 1968, Events of

The Events of May 1968 were an economic, social, political, and cultural crisis that cut across France's FIFTH REPUBLIC. The sense of confrontation, existing since 1967 in the student milieu, in France as well as abroad, was openly manifested in early spring 1968, with the birth at the University of Nanterre of the Mouvement du 22 mars (begun by DANIEL COHEN-BENDIT), which violently questioned the role and purpose of higher education. The unrest brought about the closing of the University of Nanterre (May 2) then of the SORBONNE (May 3), provoking confrontations between students and the police (riots and barricades during the night of May 10 and 11 in the Latin Quarter in Paris). The movement won over the workers and, on May 13, on the call of the main labor unions, there was an important demonstration in Paris, accompanied by a general strike that paralyzed the country for a few days. Meanwhile, a break occurred between the "leftist" movements (Trotskyites, Maoists, Anarchists) and the CGT (Confédération générale du travail) and the PCF (Parti communiste française), which, condemning all "adventurism," sought to limit the conflict to social demands. The signing of the Grenelle Accords (May 27) between the government and the representatives of the labor unions was not welcomed by certain elements who staged a demonstration on the same day. After being assured of the support of the army, General CHARLES DE GAULLE announced the dissolution of the National Assembly and reshuffled the government, while his supporters staged a demonstration in his favor on the Champs-Élysées on May 30. Work resumed progressively during the month of June. The crisis in fact strengthened the government, which won a large victory in the legislative elections of June 23–30 that year. Nonetheless, the Events of May 1968, revealed the existence of a profound malaise and, by questioning traditional values, had important consequences for the development of society as a whole.

## Mayenne, Charles of Lorraine, duke de (1554–1611)
*nobility*

Born in Alençon, Charles of Lorraine, duke de Mayenne succeeded his brother Henri, Duke de Guise as head of the HOLY LEAGUE (1589). He had the cardinal of Bourbon crowned, under the name of CHARLES X. Defeated at Arques and at Ivry, he made his submission to King HENRY IV.

## Mazarin, Jules, Cardinal (1602–1661) (Giulio Mazarini)
*cardinal, statesman*

Of Italian origin, Jules Mazarin (Giulio Mazarini), who controlled the French government during the minority of King LOUIS XIV and helped make France the predominant European power, was born in Pescina, in the Abruzzi (Italy). A protégé, like other members of his family, of the Roman Colonna princes, Mazarin went from serving in the papal army to diplomacy. On a mission to Paris (1630), he met ARMAND JEAN DU PLESSIS, CARDINAL DE RICHELIEU, and henceforth he was in the service of France. In 1631, he helped Richelieu gain the Treaty of Pignerol. Nuncio to Paris (1635–36), he was named cardinal by Richelieu (although he was never ordained), and Mazarin soon became his principal collaborator after the death of PÈRE JOSEPH. Because of Mazarin's intelligence and ability, King LOUIS XIII gave him the direction of the Royal Council upon Richelieu's death. Upon Louis's death in 1643, his widow, the regent, Queen ANNE OF AUSTRIA, chose him as her chief minister and tutor to the young king LOUIS XIV. Mazarin, who most likely was the queen's lover (perhaps they even married), continued Richelieu's absolutist policies, asserting royal authority at home and French authority abroad. He successfully concluded the THIRTY YEARS' WAR (Treaty of Westphalia), weakened Habsburg power, and gained ALSACE for France. However, because of his insensitivity to conditions at home, mainly the high taxes and food shortages caused by the war, Mazarin was unpopular. In 1648, his arrest of a dissident magistrate sparked the FRONDE rebellion. Hatred of Mazarin unified the population of Paris and the nobility in a struggle against royal absolutism.

Anne, Louis, and Mazarin were driven out of Paris. Eventually, the royal family returned, but Mazarin went into exile in Germany, from where he directed the suppression of the rebellion. He returned victorious to Paris in 1653 and devoted himself to training Louis XIV in government, diplomacy, and military affairs. The final achievement of his political career was the Treaty of the Pyrenees (1659), which ended long hostilities with Spain, gained the provinces of Roussillon and Artois for France, and acquired a Spanish bride for Louis XIV. Mazarin, who continued the work of Richelieu, remained in power until his death, and left Louis XIV the legacy of absolutist rule. He had also, in his lifetime, amassed a large fortune, enriching himself and his family (see MANCINI FAMILY), acquired a magnificent art collection and a library that he donated to the state (the present Bibliothèque Mazarine), and founded the Collège des Quatre-Nations (the present Institut de France) and the Academy of Painting and Sculpture.

## Méchain, Pierre  (1744–1804)
*astronomer*

Born in Laon, Pierre Méchain, as an astronomer, verified with DOMINIQUE CASSINI and ADRIEN LEGENDRE the differences in longitudes from the observatories of Paris and of Greenwich. With JEAN-BAPTISTE DELAMBRE, he measured, between 1792 and 1798, the arc of the meridian from Dunkerque to Barcelona in order to determine the metric standard adopted as a legal unit of length by the Constituent Assembly during the REVOLUTION OF 1789. Méchain was named to the Academy of Sciences in 1782.

## Méliès, Georges  (1861–1938)
*film producer, director*

Georges Méliès, a pioneer filmmaker whose work had a profound effect on early cinema, was born in Paris. An illusionist by profession (he directed the Théâtre Robert-Houdin) and set designer, he made of cinema, still in its infancy, a true art form by the richness of his poetic and inventive genius. Of some 300 films that he produced between 1896 and 1913, he was inspired by three general themes:

the world of fairy tales and fantasy (*Cendrillon, Le Palais des Mille et Une Nuits, La Fée Libellule*); science fiction—often inspired by the stories of JULES VERNE (*Le Voyage dans la Lune*, 1902, *Le Voyage à travers l'impossible, 20,000 Lieues sous les mers, La Conquête du pole*); and history (*L'Affair Dreyfus, La Civlisation à travers les âges*). The creator of cinematographic direction and founder of the first film studios (at Montreuil), as well as the creator of special effects, Méliès, the pioneer of the seventh art, who had a free sense of imagination and knew poverty during his career and was for a time forgotten, was recognized and acclaimed before his death. In 1931, he was awarded the LEGION OF HONOR. In 1936, the majority of Méliès's works were saved and restored by archivists.

## Mendès France, Pierre  (1907–1982)
*political figure*

Born and educated in Paris, Pierre Mendès France practiced law and, at age 25, was elected as a Radical-Socialist deputy. In 1938, he served as undersecretary of the treasury and, during World War II, after escaping from the prison where he had been held by the VICHY regime, reached Great Britain, where he joined the Free French air force. He was named minister of economics in the provisional government of General CHARLES DE GAULLE, to whom he also served as financial adviser. Following the establishment of the FOURTH REPUBLIC (1946), Mendès France served in the National Assembly as a member of the Radical Party and opposed the government's fiscal policies. He advocated French disengagement in Indochina and, in July 1954, as premier, negotiated the French withdrawal from that region (Geneva Accords). His premiership saw the beginning of the Algerian conflict, and he negotiated the treaty that led to Tunisian independence. In February 1955, after a debate in the National Assembly on North African policy, his government fell. As a leader of the Radical Party and the Radical-Socialists (1955–57), Mendès France was one of the founders of the Republican Front, a noncommunist leftist coalition. Minister of state in the government of GUY MOLLET (1956), he soon resigned in protest over policy toward ALGERIA. After the May 13, 1958, uprising in Algiers, he took a stronger position against the Gaullist administration. Joining the SOCIALIST PARTY after leaving the Radicals, he became known as a main spokesperson for a section of the French Left. Pierre Mendès France's writings include *Gouverner, c'est choiser* (1953); *La Science économique et l'Action* (1954); *La République moderne* (1962); *Pour préparer l'avenir* (1968); and *La vérité guidait leurs pas* (1976).

## Mérimée, Prosper  (1803–1870)
*novelist, historian*

Prosper Mérimée, best known for his lengthy and realistic, yet also fantastic, short stories, was born in Paris. Raised in a cultured milieu in the tradition of the ENLIGHTENMENT, he studied law, then entered the civil service. Through his literary interests, he frequented the Parisian salons and became friends with STENDHAL. He soon successively published two works, *Le Théâtre de Clara Gazul, comédienne espagnole* (1825) and *La Guzla ou Choix de poésies illyriques* (1827), both being literary parodies. In 1830, there appeared an "historic sketch," *La Chronique du règne de Charles IX*, a cloak-and-dagger story set in the period of the Wars of Religion. In 1833, Mérimée grouped, under the title *Mosaïque*, a number of short stories, remarkable for their consistent plots and concise style. The same year, *La Double Mépris* appeared, followed the next year by *Âmes du purgatoire*. Named inspector of historical monuments, Mérimée traveled throughout France to catalog the nation's archaeological treasures, then journeyed through the countries of the Mediterranean (notably Spain), which inspired *La Vénus d'Ille* (1837), his taste for the fantastic, and his novellas, *Colomba* (1840) and *Carmen* (1845). Here, the coldness of his tone contrasts with the violence of his sentiments. Friend to Empress EUGÉNIE and involved in the imperial court of NAPOLÉON III, Mérimée wrote other short stories, such as *Lokis* (1869), in which he displays a precise realism. Mérimée's sober and concise style has been compared to that of Stendhal.

## Merleau-Ponty, Maurice  (1908–1961)
*philosopher*

A leading existential philosopher, Maurice Merleau-Ponty, whose phenomenological studies of the role of the body in perception opened a new area of philosophical discourse, was born in Rochefort and taught at the University of LYON, the SORBONNE, and the COLLÈGE DE FRANCE. His first important writings were *Structure du comportement* (1942), *Sens et Non-Sens* (1948), and *Signes* (1960). Another early major work, *Phénoménologie de la perception* (1945), is a detailed study of perception, influenced by the phenomenology of Edmund Husserl and by Gestalt psychology. In it, he argues that science presupposes an original and unique perceptual relationship to the world that cannot be described or explained in scientific terms. It is a critique of cognitivism and of the existentialism of JEAN-PAUL SARTRE who, unlike Merleau-Ponty, argued that human freedom is total and is not limited by our embodiment. Merleau-Ponty studied Marxism but never accepted its economic and materialistic explanations of the historical process.

## Merlin, Philippe-Antoine, count  (1754–1838)
*political figure*

Known as Merlin de Douai, Philippe-Antoine, count Merlin, who was born in Arleux, was an attorney. During the REVOLUTION OF 1789, he was elected as a deputy for the Third Estate to the ESTATES GENERAL (1789). He was reelected to the Convention (1792), where, with the MONTAGNARDS, he voted for the king's death and was a proponent of the Law of Suspects (September 1793). After the fall of MAXIMILIEN ROBESPIERRE, as a member of the Committee of Public Safety, he encouraged the THERMIDORIAN REACTION and followed an annexationist policy. A member the Council of Ancients and minister of justice in 1795, he was named director, replacing FRANÇOIS BARTHÉLEMY after the coup d'état of 18 Fructidor Year V (September 4, 1797). He was forced to resign after 30 Prairial, Year VII because of his role in the coup d'état of 22 Floréal, Year VI. Procurator general of the Court of Cassation (1806–14) and a count of the Empire, Merlin de Douai was dismissed after the First RESTORATION and proscribed as a regicide (1815). He returned to France in 1830 and was elected to the ACADÉMIE FRANÇAISE that year.

## Merlin, Antoine-Christophe (1762–1833)

*political figure*

Known as Merlin de Thionville, after his birthplace, Antoine-Christophe Merlin, an attorney in Metz, was, during the REVOLUTION OF 1789, elected to the Legislative Assembly (1791), where he supported the confiscation of the properties of the émigrés. Reelected to the Convention (1792), he sat with the MONTAGNARD faction. Sent on a mission to Mainz, he could not prevent the surrender of that city (July 1793). He contributed to the fall of MAXIMILIEN ROBESPIERRE and openly supported the repression of former JACOBINS during the Thermidorian Convention. A member of the Council of Five Hundred and director of the Post (1798), he was opposed to Napoléon Bonaparte (see NAPOLÉON I) as consul for life.

## Mersenne, Marin (1588–1648)
## (Abbé Mersenne)

*philosopher, scholar, cleric*

Born near Oizé, Maine, Marin Mersenne, who had a collective view of, and dedicated himself to, science, favored exchanges between the scholars of his time, visiting and carrying on with them an abundant correspondence (RENÉ DESCARTES, BLAISE PASCAL, PIERRE DE FERMAT, Isaac Beekmann, Evangelista Torricelli). He published *Mécaniques de Galilée*, as well as five smaller works on science (1634), and organized the Academia Parisiensis in 1635. Among the first laboratory scholars, he helped to develop quantitative physics. Before the limits of science he developed a pragmatic philosophical position. The study of Galileo's theories concerning gravity led him to undertake experiments to prove those ideas, notably with the help of a pendulum that he used to discover the law of proportionality of the square root of length. He was also the first to use the pendulum to determine the intensity of weight and gravity (1644). Abbé Mersenne also studied the telescope with a parabolic mirror. But his most important works concerned acoustics; he discovered the laws of sonorous tubes and vibrating cords, observed the existence of superior harmonics, and determined the relationship among the frequencies of notes. Finally, he used the phenomenon of the echo to measure the speed of sound (1636).

## Méry, Joseph (1798–1866)

*writer, polemicist*

Born in Les Aygalades, MARSEILLE, where he founded various antimonarchist newspapers, Joseph Méry became known in Paris as a brilliant chronicler, before collaborating with A. M. Barthélemy on pamphlets in verse in which they expressed their hostility to the Restoration (*Rome à Paris*, 1827; *Napoléon en Égypte*, 1828; *Le Fils de l'homme*, 1829). Their attacks would continue against the July Monarchy, with the satirical newspaper *La Némésis* (1831). The personal work of Joseph Méry includes a number of novels and short stories, notably *La Chasse au chastre* (1853) and *Monsieur Auguste* (1959). He also composed opera librettos and dramatic works, including *Le Chariot d'argile* (1850) and *L'Imagier de Harlem* with GÉRARD DE NERVAL.

## Messiaen, Olivier (1908–1992)

*composer*

Born in Avignon, Olivier Messiaen trained at the Paris Conservatoire. Organist at the church of La Trinité in Paris, he was professor at the École normale de musique, at the Schola Cantorum, then at the Paris Conservatoire (1942). Influenced by CÉSAR FRANCK and CLAUDE DEBUSSY, the music of Messiaen was frequently inspired by religious and mystical symbols. His work is also often characterized by the use of different rhythms of Oriental origin (Bali) or by medieval modes (Gregorian plainsong). An ornithologist, he interspersed his musical notation with the songs of birds and assimilated these into his composition. His orchestration (often including exotic percussion instruments) is considered rich, as is his sonority and use of harmonies and harmonics. All these elements come together in a highly experimental and personal manner. Messiaen's works include pieces for organ (*La Nativité du Seigneur*, 1935; *Les Corps glorieux*, 1939; *Messe de la Pentacoste*, 1950; *Livre d'orgue*, 1952), vocal works (*Poèmes pour mi*, 1936; *Trois Petites Liturgies de la présence divine*, 1943–44); works for piano (*Préludes*, 1929; *Vingt Regards sur l'Enfant Jésus*, 1944), chamber music (*Quatuor pour la fin des temps*, 1941), works for orchestra (*Les Offrandes oubliées*, 1930; *Turangalîlâ-Symphonie*, in 10 parts, 1960; *Chronochromie*, 1960; *Couleurs de la cité céleste*, 1963), and works for choir and orchestra, motets, and melodies. Among these is the opera *Saint François d'Assise* (1983) and *Éclairs sur l'au-delà*, for orchestra (performed in New York City, 1992). Messiaen also wrote a number of texts on musicology. One of the founders of the Jeune France group (1936), Messiaen had a number of notable students, including PIERRE BOULEZ.

## Messmer, Pierre (1916– )
*political figure, prime minister*

Born in Vincennes, Pierre Messmer in 1940 joined the Free French and took part in FOREIGN LEGION operations in Africa and Italy, then in the liberation of Paris with General PHILIPPE LECLERC and his division (August 1944). Parachuted into Tonkin in 1945, he was taken prisoner by the Vietminh; upon his release, he served in various French overseas administrative government posts, then as high commissioner in Africa (1952–59). Minister of armed forces from 1960 to 1969, a Gaullist deputy (1968–88), minister of overseas departments and territories (1971–72), Messmer was prime minister from July 1972 to May 1974.

## Michel, Louise (1830–1905)
*anarchist, feminist*

Born Clémence Louise in Vroncourt-la-Côte, Haute-Marne, Louise Michel as she is known, was a schoolteacher in Montmartre, Paris (1856), who fought in the republican opposition, was a member of the First International, and played an active role in the Paris COMMUNE. Sentenced for her part in that insurrection, she was deported to Nouméa, NEW CALEDONIA (1873), where she befriended the indigenous peoples and the Kabyles (deported after their uprising) from ALGERIA. Amnestied in 1880, "la bonne Louise," as she was also known, never ceased to struggle for those she called the "wretched of the Earth." She also spoke out for women's rights as a component of the class struggle. Michel left important literary works (discourses, poems, novels, and *La Commune, histoire et souvenirs*, 1898).

## Michelet, Jules (1798–1874)
*historian, writer*

Born in Paris, Jules Michelet, a leading French historian, at the end of a poor and laborious ado-

lescence during which he worked in his father's print shop, began his brilliant studies at the École normale supérieure (where he later taught) in ancient history and the philosophy of history. He became a student and disciple of the writings of VICTOR COUSIN, J. G. Herder, and Giambattista Vico. Appointed to the historical section of the National Archives (1831), he directed his research toward the French national past and began his *Histoire de France*, of which six volumes (from the nation's origins until the death of LOUIS XI) appeared between 1833 and 1844. The later volumes (from LOUIS XI to LOUIS XVI, 1855–67) have the power of a political polemic. Breaking with Catholicism, Michelet developed his humanistic and democratic ideas during his lectures, which were popular, at the COLLÈGE DE FRANCE (1838). He also researched and wrote his *Histoire de la Révolution française* (seven volumes, 1847 to 1853), an inspired, engaging, enthusiastic, and remarkably documented work, in which he analyses absolute monarchy and subsequent French governments. During his period of self-imposed semi-exile (he disagreed with the policies of NAPOLÉON III), coupled with his trips to the French countryside, Michelet sought inspiration in nature (*L'Oiseau*, 1856; *La Mer*, 1861), but also continued his concern for humanity (*L'Amour*, 1859; *La Femme*, 1860) and his hopes for the future (*La Bible de l'humanité*, 1864). His death prevented him from finishing *Histoire du XIXe siecle* (three volumes, 1872–75). He left, too, a *Journal intime*. One of the greatest historians of his age Jules Michelet, a literary artist as well as a philosopher, was an eloquent lecturer and writer. In his original, lyrical, and audacious style, he explored not only the events of history but many other aspects, such as geography, that make and define the evolution and development of peoples and nations.

## Michelin brothers
### (André Michelin; Édouard Michelin)
*industrialists*

André Michelin (1853–1931), born in Paris, and his brother Édouard Michelin (1859–1948), born in Clermont-Ferrand, were concerned with matters of travel and transport. In 1891, Édouard conceived the idea for an inflatable removable bicycle tire, and both soon became interested in carriages. They produced the first rubber tire for cabs (1894). In 1895, they patented the first inflatable tire for automobiles. The soon-to-be well-known *Guide Michelin* was created by André in 1900, followed by a series of maps dealing with France and other countries. André worked, too, on the problem of numbering and marking roads (1911). The Michelin Company, the second-largest tire producer in the world, is located in Clermont-Ferrand.

## Mignard, Pierre (1612–1695)
*painter, designer*

Born in Troyes, Pierre Mignard, a leading baroque painter, studied with JEAN BOUCHER in Bourges and with SIMON VOUET in Paris. He then stayed in Italy from 1635 to 1657, where he studied the works of the Carracis, le Dominiquin, Pietro de Cortona, Guido Reni, and Francesco Albani. This period abroad earned him the name "Mignard le Romain." Mignard painted portraits of the aristocracy that became very popular and also small tableaux, inspired by Raphael, that he called "mignardes" (*Virgin of the Grapes*). In 1658, he became the personal painter to the queen mother, ANNE OF AUSTRIA, and produced a number of religious works, decorations for several mansions (hôtel d'Epernon), and had great success as a portraitist. His great rival was CHARLES LE BRUN, and because of this Mignard was named to the ACADÉMIE FRANÇAISE only in 1690. As a portraitist, he never hesitated to flatter his subjects, looking always to express elegance and grace (*Girl Blowing Soap Bubbles*).

## Milhaud, Darius (1892–1974)
*composer*

Born in Aix-en-Provence, where he was descended from an old Jewish family, Milhaud studied under a number of noted music professors, and his earliest inclinations were toward the music of CLAUDE DEBUSSY, Russian music, and the poetry of PAUL CLAUDEL, whom he met in Rio de Janeiro, Brazil, where the latter was serving as secretary to the French ambassador (1917–18). Upon his return to France, Milhaud joined the group of young French composers known as Les Six. His own work was already gaining an international reputation. In 1940, he went to the United States

and became professor of composition at Mills College in Oakland, California. During that time (1940–47), he was both a teacher and a composer. Returning to France (1947), he divided his time between Mills College and the Paris Conservatoire, where he also taught composition. His body of work, which exceeds 400 opera, is one of the largest of the 20th century. He wrote in nearly all genres.

## Millerand, Alexandre (1859–1943)
*political figure*

Born in Paris, where he was also educated, Alexandre Millerand worked with GEORGES CLEMENCEAU in editing and publishing the newspaper *La Justice*. He served as a Radical Party deputy (1885–89) before becoming a Socialist and affirming the need for the socialization of the means of production (1896). Minister of commerce and industry in the PIERRE WALDECK-ROUSSEAU cabinet (1899–1902), he continued to support the passage of several social welfare laws. Nonetheless, his participation as the first Socialist in a bourgeois government was strongly criticized by the majority of Socialists (in particular JULES GUESDE). As a consequence, Millerand more and more distanced himself from the party, especially after the founding of the unified Socialist Party in 1905. Minister of public works (1909–10) under ARISTIDE BRIAND and of war under RAYMOND POINCARÉ, he helped, during World War I, to form the conservative BLOC NATIONAL, maintain the Union sacrée, uphold the provisions of the Treaty of Versailles, and defend private property. After the war, he served in Strasbourg as commissioner general in charge of supervising the return of the Alsace region to France. He also served as president of the Council (January–September 1920) and as president of the republic (1920–24), then resigned after the triumph of the left-wing coalition (Cartel des gauches) in the 1924 elections. Millerand was named to the Academy of Moral and Political Sciences in 1918.

## Millet, Jean-François (1814–1875)
*painter, engraver*

A significant landscape and genre artist of the BARBIZON SCHOOL, Jean-François Millet, the son of peasants, was born in Gréville, Manche. He studied painting at Cherbourg, then at studios in Paris where, at the LOUVRE, he was influenced by the works of NICOLAS POUSSIN, Peter Paul Rubens, and the Spanish painters. To make a living, he painted a number of mythological and amorous subjects inspired by JEAN-HONORÉ FRAGONARD and Correggio. He also painted a number of detailed and finely executed portraits (*Pauline Ono*, 1843; *Naval Officer*, 1845). In 1848, he exhibited *The Winnower* and, at the end of 1849, settled permanently at Barbizon, where in contrast to his fellow landscapists, he devoted himself to painting familiar peasant scenes. Millet had a classic sense of composition and gave his figures a monumental character; his technique was sometimes heavy and strongly worked. From 1860 on, he began to be recognized and, toward the end of his life, gave more emphasis to landscapes, lightening his pallet and searching for the effects of nature (*Spring*, 1873). Some of his paintings, in their sense of pathos and extreme freedom of execution, recall HONORÉ DAUMIER.

## Mink, Paule (1839–1900)
*feminist, political activist*

Born Paulina Mekarska in Clermont-Ferrand, the daughter of Polish nobles who had fled to France after the 1830 Revolution, Paule Minke moved to Paris in her youth and worked as a seamstress. In 1868, she founded a women's mutual aid society and worked with the feminist MARIA DERAISMES. Paule Mink organized the defense of Auxerre during the FRANCO-PRUSSIAN WAR (1870–71), and after trying to raise support for the Paris COMMUNE, she was forced to flee to Switzerland (1871). Returning to France in 1880 after the amnesty, she worked with various socialist groups and on women's rights issues with EUGÉNIE PONTONIE-PIERRE and HUBERTINE AUCLERT. In 1993, she stood as a candidate for the National Assembly and served as editorial secretary of *La question sociale* (1894–97). The effective leader of the Socialist Women's Movement in France, Mink was widely respected and, at her death, there were huge demonstrations in commemoration of her role as a Communard hero.

## Mirabeau, Victor Riqueti, marquis de (1715–1789)
*economist*

Born in Pertuis, Vaucluse, Victor Riqueti, marquis de Mirabeau was a representative of the Physiocratic theory of economics (see FRANÇOIS QUESNAY) and author of *L'Ami des hommes ou Traité sur la population* (1756). He took a position against the method and organization of tax collecting in France (fermiers généraux) in his *Théorie de l'impôt*. Riqueti, marquis de Mirabeau, was the father of HONORÉ-GABRIEL RIQUETI, COUNT DE MIRABEAU.

## Mirabeau, Honoré-Gabriel Riqueti, count de (1749–1791)
*orator, political figure*

The son of the economist VICTOR RIQUETI, MARQUIS DE MIRABEAU, Honoré, Gabriel Riqueti, count of Mirabeau was born in Le Bignon, Loiret. Known for his remarkable intelligence and passionate, even violent nature, he was little attached to his family and was forced into a military career in 1767. He had a stormy youth and was several times imprisoned by lettres de cachet arranged by his father. Thus, after his liaison with the young Sophie, the wife of the marquis de Monnier, with whom he fled to Switzerland and then to the Netherlands, Mirabeau was confined to the château of Vincennes (1777–80), where he wrote the famous *Lettres à Sophie* (published in 1792) and his *Essai sur les lettres de cachet et les prisons d'État* (1782). Upon his release, he wrote pamphlets denouncing royal absolutism and its privileges and abuses. Given a diplomatic mission to the court of Berlin (1786), he published, on his return, *De la Monarchie prussienne sous Frédéric le Grand* (1787), and *Histoire secrète sur la cour à Berlin*, which, when the identity of its author was revealed, caused a scandal (1789). Embracing the ideas of the period and becoming a supporter of constitutional monarchy, Mirabeau was a member of a Masonic lodge and of an abolitionist society (Amis des Noirs). He made contact with the DUKE D'ORLÉANS (PHILIPPE ÉGALITÉ), whom Mirabeau undoubtedly for a time saw as replacing LOUIS XVI on the throne. A delegate to the Estates General, then to the National Assembly, he played a decisive role in the early events of the REVOLUTION OF 1789, establishing freedom of the press with his *Courrier de Provence,* and being celebrated for his famous reply to the royal messenger (June 23, 1789), "If you have orders to remove us from this hall, you must also get the authority to use force, for we shall yield to nothing but bayonets." Mirabeau vigorously defended the principles of the Revolution, taking part in the drafting of the Declaration of the Rights of Man and the Citizen, and proposing to the National Assembly that the property of the church be put at the disposal of the nation. Mirabeau wished to play the role of intermediary between the king and the assembly, a role that was officially recognized (November 7, 1789). After this, Mirabeau distanced himself little by little from the revolutionaries and defended the royal prerogatives and sought to maintain the king's right to the royal veto and his right to declare war and make peace. In both cases, he was only partially successful. Introduced to the royal court, Mirabeau began to play the role of a secret adviser (1790), bringing issues important to the king to the assembly, while at the same time upholding the Revolution's principles. Although accused of treason by some deputies, Mirabeau upheld his reputation and his popularity and was elected president of the National Assembly in January 1791. He died, however, shortly afterward. His personal writings include *Œuvres oratoires* (posthumous); *Correspondence entre le comte de Mirabeau et le comte de La Marck* (posthumous).

## Mistinguett (1875–1956)
*singer, actor*

A star of the music hall, Mistinguett was born Jeanne-Bourgeois in La Pointe-Raguet, near Montmorency. She had a number of successes in the theater and in films, but it was in the café-concert circuit, then on the stage of the Parisian music halls, as the lead in several revues (Moulin-Rouge, Folies-Bergère, Casino de Paris) in the interwar period that she had her greatest triumphs. With her colorful phrasing and voice, mischievous glance, and graceful figure, she was the incarnation of the spirit and charisma of Paris. Mistinguett's best-known song was perhaps "Mon Homme," and she appeared frequently with MAURICE CHEVALIER.

## Mistral, Frédéric (1830–1914)
*Provençal writer, Nobel laureate*

A poet and Nobel laureate, Frédéric Mistral was born in Maillane, Bouches-du-Rhône. In his youth he became the friend of JOSEPH ROUMANILLE, and together they vowed to revive the Occitan language, or langue d'oc. In 1851, Mistral began an epic in 12 sections, *Mireille* ("Mirèio," published in 1859) that evokes the suppressed sentiments and romantic fatalism of PROVENCE. One of seven founders (1854) of the Félibrige, a society dedicated to the revival of Occitan and the Provençal culture, Mistral was an active contributor to *l'Almanach provençal.* In 1866, he began a second rustic epic, *Calendal* ("Calendau"), an allegorical celebration in which the marvels and picturesque wonders of Provence are described. At the same time, Mistral tried to extend the Félibrige from Provence to Catalonia, forming a Latin union. By 1876, a larger, more organized organization was achieved. His richly phrased lyric collection, *Les Îles d'or* ("Lis Isclo d'or," 1875) was followed by a lexicon filled with the various modern Occitan dialects, the *Trésor du félibrige* ("Tresor dóu felibrige", 1878–86). Enjoying considerable popularity that coincided with the expansion of the Félibrige, related to his friendship with CHARLES MAURRAS and his sympathy for the Right, Mistral felt the temptation of regionalism, but refused to become a polemicist and, after *Nerte* ("Nerto," 1884), an "Avignonnais poem," inspired by a medieval legend, and after an historical drama, *La Reine Jeanne* ("La Rèino Jano," 1890), he preferred to present, with *Le Poème du Rhône* ("Lou Pouèmo dóu Rose," 1897), and a collection, *Les Olivades* ("Lis Oulivadou," 1912), an allegorical tableau of a Provence that had to change, but without relinquishing legends and traditions. Mistral was awarded the Nobel Prize in literature in 1904.

## Mitterrand, François (1916–1996)
*statesman*

Born in Jarnac, François Mitterrand, after studying law, literature, and political science in Paris, served in the army in World War II. He was captured but escaped and, for a time, joined the VICHY government (June 1942–January 1943), before becoming involved in the RESISTANCE (and founding the

National Union of Prisoners of War). He served in the postwar government as a Socialist deputy for Niève (1946–58; 1962), as a senator (1959–62), and also was successively minister for war veterans (1947–48), secretary of state to the president of the Council (1948–49; 1953), and minister of overseas territories (1950–51). He left the government for a period, however, because of his disagreement over colonial policy, for which he held a more liberal view. Mitterrand then served as minister of the interior (cabinet of PIERRE MENDÈS-FRANCE, 1954–55), then as minister of justice (cabinet of GUY MOLLET, 1956–57) and, in June 1958, voted against the installation of General CHARLES DE GAULLE and joined the opposition. Mitterrand then became one of the principal leaders of the Socialist Left. In 1965, he ran unsuccessfully for the presidency of the republic against de Gaulle, meanwhile participating actively in the creation of the democratic and Socialist leftist coalition (FGDS, 1966). As secretary of the SOCIALIST PARTY (1971), he supported a common program with the Communists and the radical Left, with the 1973 legislative election in mind. As a candidate again for the presidency in May 1974, Mitterrand obtained 49.19 percent of the vote, as opposed to 50.81 percent for VALÉRY GISCARD D'ESTAING, but was elected May 10, 1988, with 54.01 percent. Mitterrand's two successive presidencies were notable in foreign policy for an increase in the goal toward European unity (European Act, 1986; Treaty of Maastricht, 1991), French participation in the Gulf War (1991), and, in domestic affairs, by the achievement of important reforms (abolition of the death penalty, decentralization of the administration, twice a cohabitation policy with the right, 1986–88; 1993–95, and a response to the acute economic crisis that produced rising unemployment). In May 1991, he appointed ÉDITH CRESSON, the first woman prime minister. At the end of his second term, Mitterrand retired from political life. His writing include *Politique I* (1977), *Ici et Maintenant* (1980), and *Politique II* (1982), among other works.

## Molière (1622–1673)
### (Jean-Baptiste Poquelin)
*playwright, actor*

France's greatest comic dramatist, Molière also produced, directed, and acted in the plays that he wrote. He was born Jean-Baptiste Poquelin in Paris, the son of a well-to-do upholsterer who worked at the royal court. He lost his mother at a young age (1631) and was sent to be educated at the Jesuit College at Clermont (1636)to prepare for a career in law. But after meeting the actors Tiberio Fiorelli (known as Scaramouche) and Madeleine Béjart, he left the study of law for a career in the theater.

With Béjart and her brothers and nine other actors, he founded the Illustre-Théâtre (1643). But the debuts of their company were disastrous, and Molière, as he was now known, was imprisoned for debt at Châtelet (1645). Meanwhile, Madeleine, Joseph, and Geneviève Béjart, who had remained faithful to Molière, rejoined him and together with members of the Dufresne troupe, left Paris for the provinces. Molière became the leader of this group that had gained powerful patrons (the duke d'Epernon, governor of Guyenne, and the prince de Conti, governor of Languedoc). It was at this time, in LYON, that Molière produced his first comedy, *L'Étourdi* (1651).

After these fruitful years of apprenticeship, the troupe returned to Paris (1658) and, in the presence of the king, performed PIERRE CORNEILLE'S *Nicomède* and the farce *Docteur amoureux*, the latter enjoying great success. Monsieur, the King LOUIS XIV's brother, took the actors under his protection and the triumphant reception that the public gave to Molière's *Précieuses ridicules* (1659), one of his first major comedies, established his reputation in Paris. There, at the Palais-Royal, they presented such works as *Sganarelle, ou le Cocu imaginaire* (1660), *Don Garcie de Navarre, L'École des maris*, and his first ballet comedy, *Les Fucheux* (1661). Now married to Armande Béjart, he had another success with *L'École des femmes* (1662), which also caused much jealousy among his rivals. In response, Molière satirized them in *La Critique de l'École des femmes* and *L'Impromptu de Versailles* (1663). Molière, who had the king's favor, then produced plays that were early versions of *Tartuffe*, but before the final work could be presented, members of the church and the court obtained an interdiction, because of the play's critique of religious hypocrisy. Finally, in 1664, the play was presented, as was his new comedy-ballet, *L'Amour médecin*, which pleased the king, who then took the troupe under his protection and granted Molière a pension.

Ill and separated from his wife, Molière left the theater for a while to write his masterpiece, *Le Misanthrope*. The work upset the public, but his next play, *Médicin malgré lui* (1666), was better received. Molière then did other versions of *Tartuffe* (1667–69), which again caused trouble with the church, and wrote in this period his other great works, including *Dom Juan* (1665), *Les femmes savantes* (1672), and *Le Malade imaginaire* (1673). It was directly after Molière had acted in the fourth performance of the latter that he died. Molière's comedy is inseparable from his genius and understanding of human nature, and his many innovations had enormous influence on the French theater (the COMÉDIE-FRANÇAISE is referred to as the "house of Molière"). Later playwrights were much indebted to him, and he has influenced the French language in the way Dante Alighieri, William Shakespeare, and Miguel Cervantes influence theirs.

## Mollet, Guy (1905–1975)

*political figure*

Guy Mollet, a statesman and Socialist leader who served as premier of France, was born in Flers, Pas-de-Calais, and educated in Le Havre. He taught English in Arras and, during World War II, served in the RESISTANCE (Libération-Nord). Mayor of Arras (1945), a deputy (1946), and secretary-general of the Socialist Party (SFIO), he served in a number of governments of the FOURTH REPUBLIC. After the Republican Front's victory (Socialists and Radicals of PIERRE MENDÈS-FRANCE), in the January 1956 legislative elections, Mollet assumed the premiership. During his 16 months in office, he brought France through the Suez crisis (November–December 1956) and the transition in French sub-Saharan Africa and in ALGERIA. He also adopted laws in favor of workers and signed the Treaty of Rome (March 1957). Tax increases in May 1957 forced his resignation. In late 1958, he supported General CHARLES DE GAULLE in his candidacy for the presidency of the republic, a move that forced Mollet to resign his leadership of the SOCIALIST PARTY. He then served as one of the four state ministers in de Gaulle's first cabinet (June 1958), but resigned in January 1959 over disagreements concerning the budget. In 1965, Mollet supported FRANÇOIS MITTERRAND in the latter's unsuccessful bid for the presidency, and at the same time sought to block a proposed alignment of the Socialists with the Christian Democrats. In 1966, in a shadow cabinet formed by de Gaulle's opposition, Mollet was assigned the role of foreign minister. From 1967 to 1969, he served as vice president of a coalition, the Federation of the Left, and in 1973 was again elected mayor of Arras and deputy to the National Assembly.

## Monde, Le

*Le Monde* is a daily, founded in 1944 by Hubert Beuve-Méry, who was succeeded by Jacques Fauvet from 1969 to 1982. A part of the SARL group, *Le Monde*, which since 1987 has added a group of reader stockholders, is the successor to *Le Temps*. After a severe crisis in 1985, the newspaper, which always devoted a great deal of space to political, economic, and cultural news, especially foreign, modernized (a new format in 1989, new headquarters in 1990) under the leadership of André Fontaine. It has been directed since 1994 by Jean-Marie Colombani, who also published a number of monthlies (on diplomacy, education, discussions, philately) and several weeklies, including *Le Monde des livres*. *Le Monde* has a readership of about 500,000.

## Monet, Claude (1840–1926)

*painter*

A leading figure of the impressionist movement, Claude Monet was born in Paris and completed his education in Le Havre. In 1856, EUGÈNE BOUDIN noticed his talent and encouraged him to paint out of doors. Monet met CAMILLE PISSARRO in Paris and, after military service in ALGERIA, where he discovered the Mediterranean light, Monet returned to the studios where he met AUGUSTE RENOIR, FRÉDÉRIC BAZILLE, and Alfred Sisley and went to paint with them at Chailly-en-Bière, near Fontainebleau. He also stayed for a time on the Norman coast with Boudin and the Dutch artist Johann Jongkind. Strongly influenced by the style and vision of ÉDOUARD MANET, Monet painted in 1865 a version of *Luncheon on the Grass* that was critiqued by GUSTAVE COURBET. After an initial success at the Paris Salon of 1866 (*Camille, or Woman in the Green Dress*),

*Waterlilies*, by Claude Monet *(Library of Congress)*

followed by a rejection in 1867 (*Women in the Garden*, 1866), he painted portraits, interior scenes, and especially landscapes, showing a progressive evolution away from Courbet and the Barbizon painters. Staying in London during the FRANCO-PRUSSIAN WAR (1870–71), Monet discovered John Constable and Joseph Turner and sought in his work to convey the foggy atmosphere of the city (*Westminster Bridge*). He then returned to France via Holland and settled at Argenteuil (1872–76). Painting on his studio-boat, he studied the air and light and its reflection on the water, and subtly sought to convey their impression. With other artists, he organized a showing of works rejected by the official Paris Salon. His *Impression: Sunrise* (1872), shown in 1874, inspired a revue in *Charivari* in which the term "impressionist" was (pejoratively) introduced. At Argenteuil, Monet painted some of his most characteristic works (*Régates d'Argenteuil*, 1874; *The Seine at Argenteuil*, 1874). In 1880, Monet declined to show at the fifth impressionist exhibition; after this, to study the variations of form following changes in daylight, he produced a series of paintings (*Haystacks*, 1890; *Rouen Cathedral*, 1892–1904; *Banks of the Thames*, 1899–1904) in which he subtly changed the color of the subject and completed the demolition of the

academic notion of form. Monet, who wanted to show, in his words, "an instant in the consciousness of the world," can be considered, too, a precursor of lyrical abstractionism.

## Monge, Gaspard (1746–1818)
*mathematician, political figure*
Born in Beaume, Gaspard Monge was admitted to the military school at Mézières and was appointed professor of physics at LYON. In 1780, ROBERT TURGOT invited him to teach in Paris, where, joining the REVOLUTION OF 1789, he served as minister of the navy and helped to found the École polytechnique (1794). He then took part in the Egyptian campaign of Napoléon Bonaparte. The recognized inventor of descriptive geometry, Monge established the general theory of figures in space. He was also the author of a number of other theories of analytical geometry, including those dealing with three dimensions. He was professor of descriptive geometry at the École polytechnique for more than 10 years, then discovered pluckerian coordinates. He studied differential equations that he applied to geometry and developed the theories of partial derivatives. Interested also in practical sciences, Monges studied the nature of air and water, and did experiments similar to those of Henry Cavendish and ANTOINE LAVOISIER. Monge's work is characterized by a global vision that unifies analytical, geometrical, and practical aspects. Named count of Péluse, he was, elected to the Academy of Sciences in 1780.

## Monnerville, Gaston (1897–1991)
*political figure*
Born in Cayenne, Gaston Monnerville served as a Radical-Socialist deputy (1932–40), then was a member of the RESISTANCE during World War II. Reelected deputy (1945–46), he helped in the transforming of Guadeloupe, Martinique, Guyana, and Réunion into departments of France (1946). A member of the Council of the Republic (1946), over which he presided (1947), and then president of the Senate (1955–58), a function that he fulfilled by being in the opposition to the executive power of the FIFTH REPUBLIC, Monnerville, in 1974, became a member of the Constitutional Council.

## Monnet, Jean  (1888–1979)
*economist*

An architect of modern Europe, Jean Monnet was born in Cognac and during World War I represented France on the Inter-Maritime Commission, which arranged the purchases and transport of raw materials. From 1919 to 1923, he served as first deputy secretary-general of the League of Nations. From 1923 to 1938, he was in charge of stabilization loans and the economic reorganization of Poland and Romania, as well as the reorganization of railroads in China. At the beginning of World War II, he was appointed by the French and British governments to be president of the coordinating committee of the Allied war effort. In August 1940, as a member of the British council for war supplies, he left for Washington, D.C., to help coordinate the common war effort. In June 1943, he became part of the Committee of National Liberation and served in the Free French movement in Algiers and in London. As president of the French war supplies committee, he signed (1945) the lend-lease agreements with the United States. In 1946, Monnet was involved in the implementation of his plan for French economic recovery through systematic increases in production. A supporter of the concept of European unity, he was the initiator of the Declaration of May 9, 1950, which established the basis for the European Coal and Steel Community (CECA), also known as the Schuman Plan. First president of the High Commission of the CECA (1952–55), Monnet left that post to devote himself fully to the goal of European unity. In 1955, he founded the Action Committee for a United States of Europe, which played a decisive role in implementing the principles of the Treaty of Rome and establishing the European Economic Community. For Monnet, European unity always remained a tangible possibility. His *Mémoires* were published in 1976.

See also EUROPEAN UNION.

## Montagnards

Montagnards (the Mountain) is the name given to the deputies who, during the REVOLUTION OF 1789, sat on the highest benches in the Legislative Assembly and, in doing so, signaled their extremist views. Journalists and lawyers, the Montagnards were generally, like the GIRONDINS, representatives of the bourgeoisie, but, with the difference that the Montagnard leaders (PAUL BARRAS, JEAN-NICOLAS BILLAUD-VARENNE, JEAN-MARIE COLLOT D'HERBOIS, GEORGES COUTHON, JACQUES-LOUIS DAVID, CAMILLE DESMOULINS, FABRE D'ÉGLANTINE, JOSEPH FOUCHÉ, JEAN-PAUL MARAT, MAXIMILIEN ROBESPIERRE, LOUIS-ANTOINE SAINT-JUST), appealed to the most extreme revolutionary elements: the insurrectionist Commune of Paris and the Parisian SANS-CULOTTES, by whom they had, altogether, been elected to the National Convention. After the proscription of the Girondins (June 2, 1793), the Montagnards adopted more radical revolutionary measures (see TERROR). Then, after the fall of Robespierre and his followers (July 27, 1794), the Montagnards tried to oppose the THERMIDORIAN REACTION, of which they were the first targets. The name *Montagnards* is also given to the leftist deputies, during the period of the SECOND REPUBLIC, who sat in the Constituent (1848) and then the National (1849) Assemblies and opposed many of the government's policies.

## Montaigne, Michel Eyquem de (1533–1592)
*writer*

Michel Eyquem de Montaigne, who introduced the essay as a literary form, was born in the château of Montaigne near Libourne, to a wealthy family. Fluent in Latin at an early age, he went to study at the Collège de Guyenne in BORDEAUX. He served as a member of the Parlement of Bordeaux (1557), where he met ÉTIENNE DE LA BOÉTIE. The death of the latter in 1563 did not, however, end the profound friendship and respect of Montaigne who, 15 years later, dedicated an entire chapter of his *Essais* to his friend.

In 1562, Montaigne took an oath of loyalty to the Catholic faith, enabling him to sit in the Parlement of Paris. His literary career began in 1568 when he translated the *Théologie naturelle* of Raimundo Sabunde. Resigning from the Parlement (1572), he began work on his *Essais,* the result of his extensive readings. The ST. BARTHOLOMEW'S DAY MASSACRE (1574) aroused his horror of all violence and his desire for the freedom of expression. After the publication of the first edition of the first two books of *Essais* in 1580 and their presentation to King HENRY III, Montaigne traveled in Italy and Germany. His visits (*Journal de voyage*) were interrupted in 1582, when he was elected mayor of Bordeaux. In 1585, the plague forced him to leave his château. He returned only in 1587 to prepare a fourth edition of his *Essais*. At this time he began his friendship with the writer Mme de GOURNAY, which lasted until his death.

The later years of his life were characterized by his devotion to King HENRY IV, who had stayed several times at his château (1584 and 1587). Celebrated by his contemporaries, the writings of Montaigne were much discussed during the 17th century, and later admirers include VOLTAIRE and DENIS DIDEROT. As a thinker, he is noted for his study of institutions, customs, and opinions, and for his opposition to all forms of irrational dogmatism. He observed life with philosophical skepticism and emphasized the contradictions and inconsistencies inherent in human nature and behavior. His own morality tended toward Epicureanism, and as a scholar and humanist, he refused to be enslaved by passions and desires. As an educator, Montaigne held that the student should be taught the art of living through the development of conversation, observation, and through reading and travel.

## Montalembert, Marc-René, marquis de (1714–1800)
*general*

Born in Angoulême, Marc-René, marquis de Montalembert was a specialist in the art of fortification and developed the prototype for perpendicular or polygonal fortifications (system of detached forts). He fortified the Île d'Oléron and the Île d'Aix and also established the forges at Ruelle, near Angoulême, that furnished cannons and projectiles to the French navy. Montalembert edited *La Fortification perpendiculaire* (1776). He was elected to the Academy of Sciences in 1747.

## Montalembert, Charles Forbes, count de (1810–1870)
*journalist, political figure*

Born in London, the son of an émigré Frenchman and a Scottish Protestant, Charles Forbes, count de Montalembert, went to Paris when he was young

and joined the group of liberal Catholics around HENRI LACORDAIRE and FÉLICITÉ LAMENNAIS, who were collaborating on *L'Avenir* (1830). After the ideas found in this newspaper were condemned in the papal encyclical *Mirari Vos* (1832), Montalembert accepted this and separated from Lamennais. A member of the Chamber of Peers, where he spoke out for religious freedom and freedom in education, he was elected, after the REVOLUTION OF 1848, to the Constituent Assembly, where he took his place with the Right, supporting the policies of NAPOLÉON III. He served in the legislature until 1857. Director of *Correspondant* (a liberal Catholic journal), he left *Histoire de sainte Élisabeth* (1836), a work on *Intérêts catholiques au XIXe siècle* (1852), and a study *Les Moines d'Occident depuis saint Benoît jusqu'à saint Bernard* (1860–67). Montalembert was elected to the ADADÉMIE FRANÇAISE in 1852.

## Montand, Yves (1921–1991)
*actor, singer*

Of Italian origin, Yves Montand was born Ivo Livi in Monsummano, Tuscany. He first became known for his repertoire in music halls, where he performed especially the works of JACQUES PRÉVERT. His movie breakthrough came with the suspense film *Le Salaire de la peur* (1953), followed by *Le Miliardaire* (1960), *La guerre est finie* (1967), *Z* (1968), *L'Avue* (1969), *Le Cercle rouge* (1971), *César et Rosalie* (1972), *Jean de Florette* (1986), and *Manon des Sources* (1886). With his wife, SIMONE SIGNORET, he was, for a time, close to the Communist Party and was often passionately involved in the political and social debates of his time. Very popular in France, Montand also appeared in American films, such as *Let's Make Love* (1960) with the American actress Marilyn Monroe.

## Montbazon, Marie of Brittany, duchess de (1612–1657)
*nobility*

Born in Paris, Marie of Brittany, duchess de Montbazon, was the wife of Hercule de Rohan, duke de Montbazon. She had many amorous adventures and affairs (the duke de Longueville was one of her lovers) and was involved in several intrigues and plots. These included the cabale des Importants, a plot organized by a political faction, mostly victims of Cardinal RICHELIEU, who wanted to take their revenge after the death of King LOUIS XIII by overthrowing Cardinal MAZARIN. The duchess de Montbazon was also involved in other FRONDE conspiracies and was famous for her quarrel with the duchess DE LONGUEVILLE.

## Montcalm de Saint-Véran, Louis Joseph, marquis de (1712–1759)

*general*

Born in the Château de Candiac, near Nîmes, Louis Joseph, marquis de Montcalm de Saint-Véran, as commander of French forces in CANADA in 1756, took several forts from the British (Oswego, 1756; William Henry, 1757). He was mortally wounded, however, on the Plains of Abraham as he tried to defend Quebec from a British attack during the SEVEN YEARS' WAR. The subsequent fall of Quebec (1759), then of Montreal (1760) led to the ceding of all New France (Canada) to Great Britain (Treaty of Paris, 1763).

## Montchrestien, Antoine de (ca. 1575–1621)

*dramatic author, economist*

Born in Falaise, Antoine de Montchrestien, as a writer, conceived of tragedy as a means of teaching wisdom and piety, and he celebrated the virtues of Christian stoicism, often combined with a serene humanism. He was mindful of the lessons offered by FRANÇOIS DE MALHERBE, and his tragedies (*Sophonisbe*, 1596; *L'Écossaise, David, Aman, Hector*, published in a collection in 1601), written in a very unadorned style, are melancholy accounts of violence and crime, reminiscent of the great lyric poems of antiquity. Seeking refuge in England following a duel (1605–11), Montchrestien, upon his return to France, opened a utensil and tool shop at Châtillon-sur-Loire and published his *Traité d'économie politique* (1616). In addition to the expression "political economy," which he created, he was one of the first to affirm the critical importance to society of the economic activities of production and exchange of goods.

## Montespan, Françoise-Athénaïs de Rochechouart de Mortemart, marquise de (1641–1707)

*mistress of King Louis XIV*

Born in Lusac-des-Châteaux, Poitou, Françoise-Athénaïs de Rochechouart was originally known as Mlle de Tonnay-Charente, until she married Pardaillan de Gondrin, marquis de Montespan. Their son was the duke of Antin, who became superintendent of royal fortifications. Mme de Montespan's lively spirit and personality were as celebrated as her beauty. At age 26, she became the mistress of King LOUIS XIV (1667) and held an official position at court. She bore the king eight children, of whom six survived and were legitimized (among them: the duke of MAINE; the future duchess of Bourbon; Mlle de Blois, who married PHILIPPE, DUKE D'ORLÉANS; and the count de TOULOUSE). Like many other prominent individuals, Mme de Montespan was compromised in the AFFAIR OF THE POISONS and little by little was replaced in the king's affections by Mme de MAINTENON. She was allowed to remain at court, however, until 1691.

## Montesquieu, Charles de Secondat, baron de la Brède et de (1689–1755)

*writer, philosopher*

An early leading figure of the ENLIGHTENMENT, Charles de Secondat, baron de la Brède et de Montesquieu, was born in the château de la Brède, near Bordelais. He was the son of a magistrate and became a member (1714) and then president of the Parlement of BORDEAUX (1716–28). Early on, he acquired a reputation as a writer with his *Lettres persanes* (published in 1721 without the author's name), a pleasant satire of the France of his time that also gained him entrance to the leading literary salons. Interested above all in history and political philosophy (he developed the theme of the relationship between forms of government and regional geography and climate), Montesquieu undertook (1728–31) a journey through Europe (especially England) to study the political organizations of diverse countries. Then returning to La Brède, he wrote his *Considérations sur les causes de la grandeur des Romains et de leur décadence* (anonymous, 1734), one of the first works in the philosophy of history, and also his masterpiece, *De l'Esprit des lois* (1748), which made him famous (he wrote, too, *Défense de l'"Esprit des lois"* in 1750, to respond to its critics). In *De l'Esprit des lois,* which he spent 20 years writing, Montesquieu presents his ideas on liberty, forms of government (monarchy, republic, despotism), and his theory of the relationship between governmental forms and the environment. In it, he also holds that governmental powers should be separated to guarantee individual rights and freedoms. He was inspired by the English political philosopher John Locke and Locke's ideas on personal freedom and equitable reform. Montesquieu's theories later had a profound influence, particularly on the leaders of the REVOLUTION OF 1789. Considered also as one of the founders of sociology (although this term was coined only in the 19th century by AUGUSTE COMTE), Montesquieu analyzed the laws that regulate social affairs. His classification of political regimes assigns to each a particular characteristic (for monarchy, honor, for republics, virtue, for despotism, fear) and is both normative and descriptive. Highly regarded as a thinker and writer (he was elected to the ACADÉMIE FRANÇAISE in 1728), Montesquieu wrote personal notes (*Cahiers,* only finally edited and published in 1941) which confirm his regard for the rights of the individual and his respect for personal freedom.

## Montesquiou-Fezensac, François-Xavier-Marc-Antoine, duke de
### (1756–1832)
*political figure*

Born in the château of Marsan, Gascony, François-Xavier-Marc-Antoine, duke de Montesquiou was a representative-at-large for the clergy to the ESTATES GENERAL in 1789. During the REVOLUTION OF 1789, he served in the National Assembly (1791) as one of the "aristocrats," partisans of the ancien régime, and was opposed to the abolition of privileges and to the CIVIL CONSTITUTION OF THE CLERGY. He emigrated in 1792 and, returning to France in 1795, joined the royalist faction (see PIERRE-PAUL ROYER-COLLARD). Exiled to Menton during the FIRST EMPIRE, Montesquiou-Fezensac served as minister of the interior under the RESTORATION (1814–15), was made a peer (1815), a count (1817), and then

a duke (1821). He was elected to the ACADÉMIE FRANÇAISE in 1816.

## Montgolfier brothers
### (Joseph de Montgolfier; Étienne de Montgolfier)
*inventors and industrialists*

Joseph de Montgolfier (1740–1810) and Étienne de Montgolfier (1745–99) managed the family paper business in Vidalon-les-Annonay, where they were born. Étienne introduced the Dutch process of paper milling and vellum to France, and Joseph invented filter paper. Together, after 1782, the Montgolfier brothers invented and experimented with the first practical hot-air balloons, known as *montgolfières.* They made their well-known ascents with paper-lined linen balloons, first at Annonay and then, in September 1783, at VERSAILLES in the presence of King LOUIS XVI and Queen MARIE ANTOINETTE. Ingenious inventors, the Montgolfier brothers also conceived the idea of a hydraulic device (1792) that could convey water. Étienne was named to the ACADEMY OF SCIENCES in 1796, and Joseph was named in 1807.

## Montherlant, Henry Millon de
### (1895–1972)
*writer*

Born in Paris, Henry Millon de Montherlant, a novelist and dramatist, was also an ardent sportsman and nationalist, as well as a sensualist who sought to combine the values of paganism and Christianity. He was known for his literary championing of virile, aristocratic virtues and for his distain for the weaknesses that he perceived in French democracy. His first writings were autobiographical (*La Relève du matin,* 1920; *Le Songe,* 1922) and retraced the writer's Catholic youth, his exhilarating war experiences, and his participation in sports (*Les Olympiques,* 1924 and 1938). In his works, Montherlant celebrated the heroic life from which women were freely absent (*Les Bestiaires,* 1926, which recounted his experiences with bullfighting in Spain), and he also defended sensuality in his *Voyageurs traqués* (*Aux Fontaines du désir,* 1927; *La Petite Infante de Castille,* 1929; *Un Voyageur solitaire est un diable*, 1961). Upon returning from travels in Europe and Africa (*L'Histoire de l'amour de la rose des sables*, 1951, is an extract from an unpublished text dealing with the colonial question), he wrote an incisive study on mores, *Les Célibataires* (1934), and a series of allegorical novels. Monterlant was named to the ACADÉMIE FRANÇAISE in 1960.

## Montgomery, Gabriel de Lorges, count de  (ca. 1530–1574)
*military figure*

Captain of the Scottish Guard, de Lorges, count de Montgomery, accidentally caused the death of King HENRY II during a tournament (1559). After some time spent in England, he returned to France to become the leader of the HUGUENOT forces (1562). Trying to hold La Rochelle (1574), he was defeated at Domfront and was condemned and executed.

## Montholon, Charles-Tristan, count de (1783–1853)
*military figure*

Born in Paris, Charles-Tristan, count de Montholon, served as the chamberlain to Empress JOSÉPHINE (1809) and ambassador to the grand duke of Würzburg (1811). He remained faithful to NAPOLÉON I, who made him general and chamberlain of the palace during the HUNDRED DAYS, and whom he also accompanied to St. Helena in 1815. Upon his return to France after the emperor's death, he published, with Baron GASPARD GOURGAUD, the *Mémoires pour servir à l'histoire de France sous Napoléon par les généraux qui ont partagé à sa captivité* (1822–25). Remaining a Bonapartist, he took part in the attempt on Boulogne by Louis-Napoléon Bonaparte (later NAPOLÉON III) (1840) and was imprisoned at the fortress of Ham (1840–47), where he edited the *Récits de la captivité de Napoléon* (1849). A deputy to the Legislative Assembly (1849), General de Montholon was involved in the coup d'état of December 2, 1851.

## Montmorency family
*noble family of civil and military leaders*

Anne, first duke de Montmorency (1493–1567), born in Chantilly, was a favorite of King FRANCIS I, with whom he had been raised. He distinguished himself at the Battles of Ravenna (1512), Marignan (1515), and La Bicoque (1522) and was taken prisoner with the king at Pavia. In Provence, he successfully carried out scorched-earth tactics against the forces of the Holy Roman Emperor Charles V (1536) and was named marshal, then constable, of France. Until 1540, he had a determining influence in the kingdom. After falling briefly out of favor and being exiled to his estates, he was restored to grace by King HENRY II and was one of those responsible for the Peace of Cateau-Cambrésis (April 1559), which he signed to gain his freedom, having been taken prisoner at the Battle of Saint-Quentin (1557). He allied himself with the duke de GUISE and Marshal SAINT-ANDRÉ in a triumvirate that would approve the policy of appeasement of Queen CATHERINE DE' MEDICI and continue the struggle against the Protestants. Anne de Montmorency was killed fighting the prince de CONDÉ at the Battle of Saint-Denis. François, duke de Montmorency (ca. 1530–79), marshal of France, was the son of Anne I, duke de Montmorency, whom he opposed because of his spirit of religious tolerance. François narrowly escaped the SAINT BARTHOLOMEW'S DAY MASSACRE and supported the moderate faction known as the Politiques or Malcontents. Henri I, third duke de Montmorency (1534–1614), at first called Damville, was the brother of François, second duke de Montmorency. He also was a moderate, which earned him the hostility of the HOUSE of GUISE, and was one of the leaders of the Politiques who favored the accession of King HENRY IV. Henry II, fourth (and last) duke de Montmorency (1595–1632) was born in Chantilly and was the godson of King Henry IV. He was admiral of France and governor of LANGUEDOC and fought against the Protestants at the sieges of Montauban and Montpellier (1622) and the taking of the Île de Ré and the Île d'Oléron, 1625). He distinguished himself in Piedmont, but having intrigued with GASTON D'ORLÉANS and having taken up arms against Cardinal RICHELIEU, he was taken prisoner and condemned to death by the Parlement of Toulouse. Despite many intercessions on his behalf, he was beheaded. The duchy and peerage of Montmorency then passed to the House of CONDÉ.

## Montmorency-Laval, Mathieu-Jean-Félicité, duke de (1766–1826)
*political figure*

Born in Paris, Mathieu-Jean-Félicité, duke de Montmorency fought in the American War of Independence and, in 1789, was elected a deputy for the nobility to the ESTATES GENERAL, then joined the Third Estate. Supporting the REVOLUTION OF 1789, he voted, on the night of August 4, 1789, for the renunciation of all titles and privileges. Becoming an émigré, he settled in Switzerland in 1792 and there became friends with Mme de STAËL. Returning to France after 9 Thermidor (July 27, 1794), he adopted, under the RESTORATION (1815), an ultra-royalist position. Aide-de-camp to the count d'Artois (the future CHARLES X) and later minister of foreign affairs (1821–22), he took part in the Congress of Verona (1822), where he helped to develop the policy of intervention in Spain. Mathieu de Montmorency-Laval was elected to the ACADÉMIE FRANÇAISE in 1825.

## Montpensier, Anne-Marie-Louise d'Orléans, duchess de (1627–1693)
## (La Grande Mademoiselle)
*royal and political figure*

Born in Paris, Anne-Marie-Louise d'Orléans, duchess de Montpensier, or la Grande Madamoiselle as she was known, was the daughter of GASTON D'ORLÉANS and Marie de Bourbon, duchess de Montpensier. La Grande Madamoiselle took part in the FRONDE and, in defense of LOUIS II, PRINCE DE CONDÉ, ordered the cannons of the BASTILLE to fire upon the royal troops during the battle of the faubourg Saint-Antoine (1752). She was one of the wealthiest heiresses in Europe and several times made marriage plans, all of which came to naught. Finally, she secretly married the duke de LAUZUN (1681), from whom she soon separated. La Grande Madamoiselle is the author of *Mémoires*, an account of her life.

## Montpensier, Antoine-Marie-Philippe-Louis d'Orléans, duke de (1824–1890)
*member of French and Spanish royal houses*

The fifth son of King LOUIS-PHILIPPE and Queen MARIE-AMÉLIE, Antoine-Marie-Philippe-Louis d'Or-léans, duke de Montpensier was born in Neuilly-sur-Seine. He became a military officer and took part in the conquest of ALGERIA (1844–46). In 1846, his father arranged for his marriage to Maria Louisa de Bourbon, sister of queen Isabella II of Spain; however the marriage compromised the attempts of a diplomatic reconciliation between France and Great Britain. Of liberal tendencies, the duke de Montpensier tried in vain to convince his father to recall FRANÇOIS GUIZOT as prime minister. After the REVOLUTION OF 1848, he settled in Spain, acquired Spanish nationality, and was named Infante of Spain and captain-general (1859). Exiled to Portugal in 1868 because of his liberal views, he became a candidate for the throne (1870) but, rejected, went into exile in the Balearic Islands after the accession of Amadeus of Savoy (1871). In 1873, however, he succeeded in gaining the Spanish crown for his son-in-law, who became King Alfonso XII.

## Montpensier, Catherine-Marie de Lorraine, duchess de (1552–1596)
*nobility*

Born in Paris, the sister of HENRI DE GUISE ET DE MAYENNE, she married Louis II de Bourbon, duke de Montpensier. One of the most ardent followers of the HOLY LEAGUE, she took part in the Day of the Barricades (May 12, 1588) in support of her brother. Later, she supported king HENRY IV. Her daughter, Marie de Bourbon, would marry GASTON D'ORLÉANS, Henri's son.

## Morand, Paul (1888–1976)
*writer*

Born in Paris, Paul Morand traveled extensively in a diplomatic career that took him to London, Rome, Bucharest, and Bern. He thus became known as the "globe-trotter" of literature. Attempting to "survey the world's disorganization" through his poems (*Lampes à arc*, 1919; *Feuilles de température*, 1920), in his novel (*Lewis et Irene*, 1924), and especially in his lively accounts, he gives a brilliant image of Paris before World War II and of a world about to fall prey to new ideologies. His *Chroniques du vingtième siècle* (1925–30) shows his sensitivity to diverse cultures. In them, he evokes a less superficial world. This development continued after the war (*Le Flagellant de Séville,* 1951; *Hécate et ses chiens,* 1954; *Tais-toi,* 1965), and with these impressionistic writings, Morand earned the title "inventor of the modern style." In his *Vénises* (1971), he presents one of the most original travel journals of the 20th century. Morand was elected to the ACADÉMIE FRANÇAISE in 1968.

## Moreau, Gustave (1826–1898)
*painter*

Born in Paris, where he studied art, Gustave Moreau traveled to Italy (1857–59), where he produced a number of works based on the paintings of Michelangelo, Carpaccio, Mantegna, and Gozzoli. He received notoriety at the Salon of 1869 with *Œdipus and the Sphinx* (Metropolitan Museum of Art, New York City), a painting with a strangely decadent quality. Moreau's esthetic, both refined and sensual, is in contrast to both realism and impressionism. He was admired by the Parnassian poets and the symbolists, and by JORIS-KARL HUYSMANS and MARCEL PROUST. Influenced by Persian and Indian miniatures, and by medieval enamels, he filled his allegorical and mythological subjects with a personal and obscure symbolism, understandable only because of the clarification that he gave in his writings. Professor at the École des beaux-arts after 1892, he had among his students a number, including HENRI MATISSE, who would later become fauvist. Moreau's home in Paris, now transformed into a museum (Musée national Gustave Moreau), contains more than 200 of his paintings and watercolors (including *Apparition,* 1876, a dazzling scene from the legend of Salome, a recurrent theme in his work), and more than 7,000 of his drawings.

## Moreau, Jean-Victor (1763–1813)
*general*

Born in Morlaix, Jean-Victor Moreau joined the army during the REVOLUTION OF 1789 as a volunteer (1791), became a general in 1793, and, under the command of General CHARLES PICHEGRU, took part in the conquest of Holland (1794–95). Commander of the Army of the Rhine and Moselle (1796), he invaded Bavaria, but the defeat of Jean Baptiste at Jourdan, Belgium, forced him to retreat to ALSACE.

In 1797, he retook control of the Rhine but soon after was relieved of his command by the DIRECTORY government. In 1799, however, he again took up a command in the Army in Italy but was defeated by the Russian general Alexander Suvorov at Cassano (April 1799). Having supported Napoléon Bonaparte in the coup d'état of 18 Brumaire (November 9, 1799), General Moreau was named commander in chief of the Army of the Rhine (1800) and won the Battle of Hohenlinden (December 1800). Believing himself to be insufficiently recognized and paid for his services, however, he more openly opposed Bonaparte and allied himself with the royalists GEORGES CADOUDAL and Pichegru. Arrested in 1804, he was allowed to go into exile in the United States. Recalled to Europe as a military adviser to Czar Alexander I of Russia (1813), he was mortally wounded shortly after at Dresden.

See also NAPOLÉON I.

## Moreau, Jeanne (1928– )
*film actor, director*

Jeanne Moreau, who achieved international fame with her enigmatic performances in some of the most influential French films of the 1950s and 1960s, was born in Paris, where she studied acting and drama. She debuted on the stage (COMÉDIE-FRANÇAISE, Théâtre National Populaire) and played in several screen roles (*Touchez pas au grisbi, La Reine Margot*) before becoming the star of the New Wave (Nouvelle Vague) cinema under the direction of LOUIS MALLE (*Ascenseur pour l'échafaud* and *Les Amants,* 1958), ROGER VADIM (*Les Liaisons dangereuses 1960,* 1959), and FRANÇOIS TRUFFAUT, in whose influential *Jules et Jim* she memorably played the role of Catherine. Drawn also to idiosyncratic and unconventional films, she appeared in a number of movies directed by her first husband, Jean-Louis Richard (*Mata Hari, Le Corps de Diane*), and others directed, produced, or written by Orson Welles, MARGUERITE DURAS, Elia Kazan, Joseph Losey, Luis Buñuel (*Le Journal d'une femme de chamber,* 1964), and William Wenders (*Bis ans Ende der Welt,* 1991). She also directed (*Lumière,* 1976) and continued her stage career. In January 2000, Moreau became the first woman inducted into the Académie des beaux-arts.

## Moreno, Marguerite  (1871–1948)
### (Lucie-Marguerite Monceau)
*actress*

Marguerite Moreno (the stage name of Lucie-Mar-
guerite Monceau) was born in Paris and was a
member of the COMÉDIE-FRANÇAISE and then a
cabaret performer before she gained notoriety with
the debut of sound films (1930). In that art form,
she became famous for her comic roles, in which
she portrayed a much older woman. She was the
wife of the scholar Marcel Schwob and had a close
friendship of more than 50 years with the writer
COLETTE. On the stage, Moreno originated the central role in *La Folle de Chaillot* (*The Madwoman of
Chaillot*) by JEAN GIRAUDOUX (1945).

## Morisot, Berthe  (1841–1895)
*painter*

Born in Bourges, Berthe Morisot, an early and
important impressionist, studied at the Lyonnais
Guichard and, from 1862 to 1868, with CAMILLE
COROT. She met ÉDOUARD MANET in 1862 and
became interested in painting out of doors. She also
became Manet's favorite model and married his
brother in 1876. Morisot abandoned her early classical training to pursue an individualistic impressionist style that became distinctive for its subtlety
and delicacy. In 1874, she participated in the first
impressionist exhibition and showed regularly with
the impressionist group. After 1877, her personal
style emerged more in a series of portraits with
freshness of tone, large brush strokes, subtle
nuances, and free expression. Her technique, based
on large touches of paint freely applied in every
direction, gives her works a transparent, iridescent
quality. Morisot worked in oil and in watercolor,
producing mainly landscapes and scenes of women
and children (*Mme Pontillon,* 1873). Around 1889,
under the influence of AUGUSTE RENOIR, she painted
her subjects with more emphasis and definition.

## Morny, Charles-Auguste-Louis-Joseph, count, then duke de  (1811–1865)
*political figure*

Born in Paris, Charles-Auguste-Louis-Joseph,
count, then duke de Morny, was the natural son of
General AUGUSTE DE FLAUHAUT DE LA BILLARDERIE

and Queen HORTENSE DE BEAUHARNAIS of Holland,
and thereby half brother to the future NAPOLÉON III.
Morny served for a while as a military officer in
ALGERIA and, upon returning to France (1836),
became the owner of a sugar refinery near Clermont-Ferrand. He was elected as a deputy (1842)
and took his place with the conservatives who supported the policies of FRANÇOIS GUIZOT. He was
elected to the Legislative Assembly (May 1849) and
played an active role in the planning and carrying
out of the coup d'état of December 2, 1851. Minister of the interior, he was forced to resign after
January 1852, because of his opposition to the
decree ordering the confiscation of the properties
of the Orléans family. He became a member of the
Legislative Corps (1852) and served as its president
(1854). He was named ambassador to Russia
(1856–57), where he married a daughter of the
upper aristocracy (Troubetskoi). Quite sympathetic
to the liberalizing policies of the SECOND EMPIRE, the
duke of Morny was actively involved in the developments of its early period (railroads, mines). He
founded the seaside resort of Deauville, and so as
to recoup, with the banker JEAN-BAPTISTE JECKER,
the debts contracted by Mexico, he played a role in
persuading the French government to undertake
the disastrous Mexican expedition, in which
France tried to support Maximilian of Austria in his
claim to the Mexican throne.

## Mouillard, Louis  (1834–1897)
*engineer*

Born in LYON, Louis Mouillard, inspired at first by
the flight of birds, and then understanding the
principle of rigid wings, constructed several gliders.
He is the author of works that would inspire the
pioneers of aviation: *L'Empire de l'air, essai d'or-
nithologie appliquée à l'aviation* (1881) and *Le Vol sans
battements* (posthumous).

## Moulin, Jean  (1899–1943)
*Resistance leader*

Born in Béziers, Jean Moulin, while serving as
prefect of CHARTRES during WORLD WAR II (1940),
refused to sign a document presented by the German authorities that accused the members of a
Senegalese sharpshooters division of the French

army of certain atrocities. Placed under the control of the VICHY government, Moulin fled and joined General CHARLES DE GAULLE in London. Charged by de Gaulle to organize the French RESISTANCE, he was parachuted into the southern region (1942). After the formation of the Mouvements Unis de Résistance, beginning in 1943, he was named president of the Conseil national de la Résistance. Betrayed shortly afterward, he was arrested at Caluire by the Germans, was tortured, and died during transportation to Germany. Since 1964, Moulin's remains have been enshrined in the Panthéon.

## Mounier, Jean-Joseph (1758–1806)
*political figure*

Born in Grenoble, Jean-Joseph Mounier was elected deputy for the Third Estate to the Estates General (1789), and it was his proposal that led to the swearing of the Oath of the Tennis Court (June 20, 1789), which began the REVOLUTION OF 1789. President of the National Constituent Assembly, he was one of the principal representatives who supported a constitutional monarchy (monarchiens) on the model of Great Britain. Leader of the assembly delegation that was received by King LOUIS XVI on October 5, 1789, he resigned shortly afterward. Unsure what direction the Revolution might take, Mounier emigrated to Switzerland (1790–1801), where he edited his *Appel au tribunal de l'opinion publique.*

## Mounier, Emmanuel (1905–1950)
*philosopher*

Born in Grenoble, Emmanuel Mounier, influenced by HENRI BERGSON, JACQUES MARITAIN, and CHARLES PÉGUY, founded the revue *Esprit* (1932) and played an important role in the intellectual, spiritual, and political movements in France between the two world wars. He denounced the economic, social, and spiritual disorder of the capitalist world, as well as its bourgeois individualism. In its place he proposed his concept of "personnelisme," in which he attempted to synthesize Christianity and socialism and in place of speculation preferred an existential concept based on action. Mounier's principal works include *Révolution personnaliste et communautaire*

(1935), *Introduction aux existentialismes* (1946), *Traité du caractère* (1946), and *Le Personnalisme* (1949).

## Mourguet, Laurent (1769–1844)
*puppeteer*

Laurent Mourguet was born in Lyon. When unemployed in that city, he began to give puppet shows and created the, playful, impertinent, and humorous characters Guignon and his companion, Gnafron (ca. 1808). Mourguet was the founder of a dynasty of puppeteers who have maintained his art until the present day.

## Mouvement républicain populaire (MRP)

The Mouvement républicain populaire, or MRP, was founded in November 1944, inspired by the principles of Christian democracy. The MRP was, with the PARTI COMMUNISTE FRANÇAISE, the great winner in the elections of 1945 and formed, with that party and the Socialists, the system of tripartism (1946–47). The MRP, several of whose members played important roles in the FOURTH REPUBLIC as premiers or ministers (GEORGES BIDAULT, ROBERT SCHUMAN) proposed a program of family social reforms and was the architect of Franco-German rapprochement and the creation of a united Europe. Divided over the Algerian question, its members either joined the Gaullists or JEAN LECANUET to found the Centre démocrate.

## Murat, Joachim (1767–1815)
*military and political figure, marshal of France, king of Naples*

Born in Labastide-Fortunière (today, Labastide-Murat), Joachim Murat joined the army in 1787, became an officer in 1792, and was appointed, during the REVOLUTION OF 1789, to the Constitutional Guard of King LOUIS XVI. As chief of a squadron (1796), he supported NAPOLÉON BONAPARTE on 13 Vendémiaire (October 5, 1795) and became his aide-de-camp during the first campaign in Italy (1796). He was with Bonaparte in Egypt and was made a brigadier general after the Battle of Aboukir. He returned to France with Bonaparte and, playing a role in the coup d'état of

18 Brumaire (November 9, 1799), was made commander of the Consular Guard. In 1800, Murat married CAROLINE BONAPARTE, Napoléon's sister. As emperor, NAPOLÉON I awarded him many honors, making him marshal of France (1804) and prince of the Empire (1805). Possessing remarkable physical courage, Murat took part in many of the major Napoleonic battles, including Austerlitz (1805), Jena (1806), and Eylau (1807). As commander in chief in Spain (1808), he brutally suppressed the popular May 2 uprising in Madrid. Murat accepted the kingdom of Naples in July 1808. He ruled under the name Joachim Napoléon, succeeding JOSEPH BONAPARTE, whose reformist policies, inspired by the Consulate, Murat continued. He kept a court of great pomp and tried also to play a personal political role. He was called by Napoléon for the Russian campaign and took over command of the army (December 1812) on the Emperor's return to France. After a quarrel with some of Napoléon's generals, however, he left and returned to Naples. He was again at Napoléon's side in the campaign against Austria in 1813 (Dresden, Leipzig), but after the emperor's Battle of the Nations defeat, he again returned to Naples and signed a treaty with the Austrians and the British (July 1814) that guaranteed him his throne but obliged him to furnish 30,000 troops for the Emperor's enemies. In 1815, the Congress of Vienna gave his kingdom to the Bourbons. During the HUNDRED DAYS, he rejoined Napoléon and tried in vain to rally Italian nationalists and encourage them to fight for their independence. In his Declaration of Rimini (May 30, 1815), he waged war on Austria and, after Waterloo, sought refuge in CORSICA. Arriving in Calabria in an attempt to regain his throne, Murat was taken prisoner and, on the orders of King Ferdinand IV of Naples, was condemned and executed on October 13, 1815.

## Musset, Alfred de (1810–1857)
*writer*

A leading French romantic poet, Alfred de Musset was born in Paris and, gifted with unusual precocity, was introduced in 1828 into the Cénacle de Nodier, where he met ALFRED DE VIGNY and CHARLES SAINTE-BEUVE and got his first taste of literary success. His *Contes d'Espagne et d'Italie* (1829) show an aggressive romanticism through the use of local color and fantasy and in the description of violent passions. Although his first play was a failure, later works, such as *Les caprices de Marianne* (1833) and *On ne badine pas avec l'amour* (1834), which recalls the author's great love for GEORGE SAND (also recounted in his novel *La Confession d'un enfant du siècle*), are witty, bittersweet comedies that have become part of the classic repertoire of French theater. Musset's other works include plays (*Fantasio*, 1834; *Lorenzaccio*, 1834; *Le Chandelier*, 1835; *Il ne faut jurer de rien*, 1836), poetry (*Nuits*, 1833–37), poetic fantasies (*Sur trois marches de marbre rose*), stories (*Histoire d'une merle blanc*, 1842), his *Lettres à Lamartine* (1836), and *Souvenirs* (1841), and a bitter, troubled work that expressed his frequent sense of disillusionment, *L'Espoir en Dieu* (1838).

# N

## Nabis

Taking their name from *nabi*, Hebrew for "prophet," the Nabis was a group of artists, formed in 1888 by PAUL SÉRUSIER and MAURICE DENIS, that met at the Julian Academy in Paris. It was composed of painters (ÉDOUARD VUILLARD, PIERRE BONNARD, FÉLIX VALLOTTON) and sculptors (ARISTIDE MAILLOL). Their audacity, although measured, shocked the public of the era; they prefigured the extremes of the avant-gardes, especially the fauvists. In their work they rejected academicism, naturalism, and even impressionism and pointillism. Taught by Sérusier and Denis, themselves influenced by PAUL GAUGUIN and VINCENT VAN GOGH and the Pont-Aven school, the Nabis reinterpreted surface with strokes of pure color, suppressed perspective, and rejected the necessity to give way to their feelings. Aspects of Japanese art were also incorporated. WORLD WAR I (1914–18) broke the incentive and spirit of the group, and each one of them then evolved to a more personal style, while retaining, nonetheless, certain of the Nabis principles.

## Nadar (1820–1910)
### (Félix Tournachon)

*photographer, cartoonist, balloonist*

Born Félix Tournachon in Paris, Nadar (the pseudonym by which he is known) studied medicine for a short period but soon left to pursue a career in literature. Under the name Nadar, he began to publish articles and drew cartoons for periodicals. In 1849, he founded the *Revue comique* and the *Petit Journal pour rire* and, having opened a photography studio with his brother, published, beginning in 1854, under the title *Panthéon Nadar,* a series of portraits of celebrated contemporaries, including THÉOPHILE GAUTIER, ALEXANDRE DUMAS, GEORGE SAND, SARAH BERNHARDT, GUSTAVE DORÉ, RACHEL, CHARLES BAUDELAIRE, GÉRARD DE NERVAL, and HONORÉ DAUMIER. The studio soon became the most distinguished in Paris and was a meeting place for intellectuals and artists. As a photographer and portraitist, Nadar sought to record what he described as the "moral intelligence" of his subjects, and sought an interaction between the subject and the photographer. All his portraits were taken in the studio against a plain background, as he sought to produce "an intimate resemblance." Nadar is also known for making the first aerial (1858) and underground (1861) photographs. An ardent balloonist, he patented his aerial photographs for surveying and mapmaking and, in 1861, went into the sewers and catacombs of Paris to take pictures, using a carbon arc light. In 1863, he built his own balloon, *Le Géant* (*Mémoires du Géant,* 1864), and with his son in 1886 pioneered the idea of the photo interview. Nadar later founded the magazine *Paris Photographe* (1891) and wrote a number of books, including his autobiography, *Quand j'étais photographe* (1910).

## Nantes, Edict of

The Edict of Nantes was a decree giving partial religious freedom to the HUGUENOTS, proclaimed by King HENRY IV in 1598, and revoked by LOUIS XIV in 1685. The edict ended the series of religious wars between Catholics and Protestants in France fought from 1562 to 1598. During the course of these wars, a number of ineffectual treaties were concluded, implying various privileges for the Huguenots. The Edict of Nantes included the religious provisions of these treaties and added a number of others. By the terms of the edict, the Huguenots were granted liberty of conscience throughout France. They were permitted to hold religious services and build churches in specified towns and villages, and in the suburbs of any city, except those that were episcopal and archiepiscopal sees, royal residences, or within a certain radius of Paris, while services were permitted in the domiciles of the Huguenot nobility. As a guarantee of protection, 100 sites were designated as fortified cities for a period of eight years. Four schools or universities were also allowed to be Huguenot (Montauban, Montpellier, Sedan, and Saumur). All followers of the faith were granted civil rights, including the right to hold political office, and a special court, the Chambre de l'édit (composed of 10 Catholics and six Protestants), was established to protect Huguenots in the Parlement of Paris, with corresponding courts established in the provincial parlements. Huguenot pastors were to be funded, as were the Catholic clergy, by the government. Although the edict of toleration was unique for its time, its provisions were never fully enforced, even during the reign of Henry IV. In 1629, Cardinal RICHELIEU annulled its political provisions. Persecution of the Protestants, including pressure to convert (1676), resumed during the reign of Louis XIV and culminated in the Dragonnades (persecution of French Protestants by soldiers of the Royal Dragoons) of 1680. When the Edict of Nantes was revoked, more than 200,000 Huguenots (officials, industrialist, merchants, artisans, farmers) were forced to emigrate, settling particularly in Holland and Prussia, while inside France, continued persecution provoked a number of uprisings, including that of the CAMISARDS.

## Napoléon I (1769–1821)

*military genius, emperor of the French*

One of history's greatest military commanders, who conquered, ruled, and influenced much of Europe and instituted many reforms of the REVOLUTION OF 1789, Napoléon Bonaparte was born in Ajaccio, CORSICA, the second son of LETIZIA RAMOLINO and CARLO BUONAPARTE. Bonaparte had three sisters and four brothers, and their parents were both of the Corsican-Italian gentry. Napoléon was educated at the college of Autun and at military schools in Brienne and Paris. In 1785, at age 16, he was commissioned a second lieutenant in the artillery and, in 1791, became a lieutenant colonel in the Corsican National Guard. However, when Corsica declared its independence in 1793, as a republican and French patriot, Bonaparte fled with his family to France. With the rank of captain at the siege of the naval base at Toulon, Bonaparte contributed to a victory (1793) that earned him a promotion to brigadier general.

In 1795, in Paris, he was asked by PAUL BARRAS and others to save the DIRECTORY government from the mob. In 1796, he married JOSÉPHINE DE BEAUHARNAIS and was made commander of the French army in Italy. Defeating four Austrian armies in succession, he forced Austria and its allies to accept the Treaty of Campo Formio, which provided that France maintain most of its conquests. He established the Cisalpine Republic in northern Italy and strengthened his own position in France by sending many treasures back to Paris.

In 1798, he was sent to strike at the British in Egypt, which he conquered. His fleet, however, was destroyed by the British. In Egypt, he reformed the government, while scholars who had accompanied him began the scientific study of ancient Egypt. In 1799, he won a great victory over the Turks at Aboukir. Back in France, he organized a coup d'état (18 Brumaire, Year VIII [November 9, 1799]) with the help of the Abbé EMMANUEL SIEYÈS, CHARLES-MAURICE DE TALLEYRAND, JOSEPH FOUCHÉ, JOACHIM MURAT, and his brother LUCIEN BONAPARTE. In the new regime, the Consulate (JEAN-JACQUES CAMBACÉRÈS and CHARLES LEBRUN), Napoléon held almost dictatorial powers.

As first consul, and then according to a constitutional revision in 1802, as consul for life, he promulgated a new constitution; reformed finances, the justice system, and the administration; established a wide educational system; and created the Bank of France, the LEGION OF HONOR, and a new civil code (Code Napoléon). He also concluded a CONCORDAT with the pope (1801) to appease his Catholic subjects and end the Revolution's conflict with the church. In 1800, he assured his power by crossing the Alps and defeating the Austrians at Marengo, then negotiated a peace establishing the Rhine as France's eastern border.

In May 1804, the Senate declared Napoléon Bonaparte emperor of the French, under the title

Napoléon I, and proclaimed a hereditary monarchy, ratified by a plebiscite. The pope, Pius VII, came to Paris for the coronation, which took place on December 2 of that year in Notre-Dame cathedral and at which Napoléon crowned himself, then Joséphine. Napoléon established an imperial court, and the members of his family were made royalty, while other titles and honors were given to his supporters. The Italian Republic was proclaimed a kingdom, with Napoléon as king and EUGÈNE DE BEAUHARNAIS as viceroy.

After 1805, Napoléon was again at war in Europe. Austrian-Russian forces were defeated at Austerlitz on December 2, 1805, and in 1806 he seized Naples and named his brother JOSEPH BONAPARTE as king. The Dutch Republic was given to his brother LOUIS BONAPARTE and his wife, HORTENSE DE BEAUHARNAIS, as the kingdom of Holland, and the Confederation of the Rhine was established with himself as protector, marking the end of the Holy Roman Empire. The Prussians were defeated at Jena and Auerstadt (1806) and the Russians at Friedland. At Tilsit (July 1807), Czar Alexander I of Russia was made an ally and Prussia was reduced in size. New states were also added to the Empire, including the duchy of Warsaw and the kingdom of Westphalia (under Napoléon's brother JÉRÔME BONAPARTE). At the same time, Napoléon established the Continental System to blockade British goods. In 1807, he seized Portugal and in 1808 made his brother Joseph king of Spain, awarding Naples to his sister CAROLINE BONAPARTE and her husband JOACHIM MURAT (other portions of Italy were given to his sisters ÉLISA BONAPARTE and PAULINE BONAPARTE). The French entrance into Spain, however, brought about the Peninsular War, which eventually caused many French casualties and weakened the Empire in a bloody guerrilla conflict. In 1809, the Austrians were again defeated (at Wagram) and Napoléon annexed the Illyrian Provinces. At the same time, he abolished the Papal States. He also divorced Joséphine, who could not give him an heir, and married (1810) the Habsburg princess MARIE-LOUISE of HABSBURG-LORRAINE, the daughter of the Austrian emperor, thus linking his dynasty to one of the oldest in Europe. A son (NAPOLÉON II) was born in 1811 and was immediately proclaimed king of Rome. The FIRST EMPIRE

Napoléon Bonaparte *(Library of Congress)*

now reached its largest extent with the annexation of Lübeck, Bremen, and other parts of northern Germany, along with the entire kingdom of Holland.

At its height, the Empire was composed of 130 departments, with Sweden having elected French general Bernadotte as King CHARLES XIV. In all the new states created by the emperor, the Code Napoléon was established as law; universal male suffrage was proclaimed; and French judicial and administrative reforms were imposed. In 1812, Napoléon ended his alliance with Czar Alexander and invaded Russia with his Grande Armée. The invasion ended in a disastrous retreat from Moscow, and subsequently all Europe united against the French. Napoléon continued to fight (Leipzig, October 1813) but was defeated by the Allies (Austria, Russia, Prussia, and Sweden), who then entered Paris. He was forced to abdicate (April 1814) and went into exile on the island of Elba in the Mediterranean Sea.

Meanwhile, opposition had grown in France against the regime of the newly installed Bourbon king, LOUIS XVIII. Napoléon arrived back in France and made a triumphant return to Paris (March 20, 1815). During the HUNDRED DAYS, as this period is known, he tried to reestablish his power and make peace with the Allies, which was rejected. He met his final defeat at Waterloo in Belgium (June 18, 1815). Surrendering to the Allies, he was exiled to the remote South Atlantic island of Saint Helena with a few faithful retainers, and he stayed there until his death. His remains were returned to France in 1840 and interred in the INVALIDES in Paris. In his last years, and after his death, the Napoleonic legend was created, as he had dictated his *Mémoires* to EMMANUEL LAS CASES. In them, Napoléon maintained that he had preserved and given the achievements of the Revolution to the world.

## Napoléon II (1811–1832)

*king of Rome, son of Napoléon I*

Born in Paris, the son of NAPOLÉON I and MARIE LOUISE OF HABSBURG-LORRAINE, the young Napoléon had been, since his birth, king of Rome. After the first abdication of Napoléon I (April 4, 1814), the empress Marie Louise took their son to the Imperial court in Vienna. Napoléon abdicated a second time, but in favor of his son (June 22, 1815). The young heir was recognized as Napoléon II by the Napoleonic government that had been set up during the HUNDRED DAYS but was not acknowledged by the Allies. Later, he was recognized as a Habsburg noble by his maternal grandfather, Emperor Francis II of Austria, and given the title duke of Reichstadt. Napoléon II was acclaimed in Paris in 1830, and the Austrian chancellor, Prince Klemens von Metternich, used this fact against the regime of

King LOUIS-PHILIPPE. After 1830, Napoléon II became the friend of Marshal AUGUSTE MARMONT, who told him of his father's glories and achievements. Napoléon II died at age 21 of tuberculosis, and his remains were returned to France in 1940 by Adolf Hitler and interred in the INVALIDES beside those of his father. Napoléon II's life was the inspiration for *L'Aiglon*, a play by EDMOND ROSTAND.

## Napoléon III (1808–1873)

**(Charles-Louis-Napoléon Bonaparte)**

*emperor of the French*

The emperor of the French (1852–70), Charles-Louis-Napoléon Bonaparte was born in Paris, the third son of LOUIS BONAPARTE and HORTENSE DE BEAUHARNAIS. He was raised in Arenenberg, Switzerland, after the fall of the FIRST EMPIRE (1815) and was educated there and in Bavaria. His mother schooled him in the glories of the Napoleonic legend and set his course toward the recovery of family power. After attending the College of Augsburg and the military school at Thoune, Louis-Napoléon Bonaparte became an artillery officer and, in 1831, took part in a liberal uprising in Romagna, Italy. With the death of the duke of Reichstadt (NAPOLÉON II), he was considered the leader of the Bonapartists.

After the failure of the Strasbourg Conspiracy (1836), in which Louis-Napoléon sought to seize power, he went into exile in Brazil, the United States, then England. A second attempt at gaining power in Boulogne in 1840, on the occasion of the return of his uncle's remains to France, also failed. Imprisoned in the fortress of Ham, he escaped to England (1846) disguised as a mason named Badinguet (a surname that he kept). Upon his return to France after the REVOLUTION OF 1848, he was elected to the Constituent Assembly (April 1848). Louis-Napoléon had already outlined his political ideas—"democratic caesarism"—and his economic theories in his writings (*Idées napoléoniennes*, 1839; *L'Extinction du paupérisme*, 1846), largely influenced by the works of HENRI DE SAINT-SIMON. Nostalgia for the Napoleonic legend, but more also the bourgeois fear of the "red peril," after the June Days of 1848, assured that Louis-Napoléon Bonaparte would be able to play his role in maintaining the established order by being a candidate for the presidency of the SECOND REPUBLIC.

On December 10, 1848, he was elected president by a large majority vote. He then moved cleverly, letting the conservatives in the Legislative Assembly carry out reactionary policies (the invasion of Rome, 1849; the Falloux Law, suppressing universal suffrage, 1850), while promoting himself in turn as the champion of universal suffrage and protector of workers and of religion. Unable to obtain the revision of the constitution that would have allowed his reelection in 1852, he carried out the coup d'état of December 2, 1851. The constitution of January 1852, which greatly restricted the legislative powers in favor of the executive, eventually allowed the restoration of the Empire which was proclaimed on December 2, 1852, after a plebiscite. Now known as Napoléon III ("Napoléon le Petit"—VICTOR HUGO), in 1853 he married a Spanish countess, EUGÉNIE DE MONTIJO, who in 1856 gave birth to their son Eugène-Louis-Napoléon (1856–79).

At first, Napoléon ruled as a dictator and, during the SECOND EMPIRE, which was characterized by a growth in finance, industry, and commerce, the Emperor, after initial pacifist declarations ("L'Empire, c'est la paix"), practiced a warlike foreign policy. Abrogating the treaties of 1815, he reaffirmed militaristic Napoleonic policies (CRIMEAN WAR, campaign in Italy, invasion of Mexico). The campaign in Italy far from satisfied his Italian allies and aroused the hostility of French Catholics toward his foreign policy with regard to the papacy. During this period (1859–60), Napoléon III began to make concessions to liberalize his regime. The attempt to establish a parliamentary empire (beginning in 1870) succeeded only in increasing the opposition, despite a plebiscite apparently in favor of the Emperor (May 1870).

Against prudent counsel, Napoléon III decided to declare war on Prussia in July 1870 (see FRANCO-PRUSSIAN WAR). After the initial defeats suffered by the French army, the Emperor ordered a new cabinet (August 9), which could not, however, resolve the military situation. After the French defeat and surrender at Sedan (September 2, 1870), Napoléon III was taken prisoner. On September 4, the National Assembly proclaimed the end of his reign, and he went into exile in England. Viewed as both a tyrant and something of a democrat, Napoléon III embodied certain contradictions in his personality and in his domestic and foreign policies.

## Necker, Jacques (1732–1804)
*financier, statesman*

Born in Geneva, Switzerland, Jacques Necker came to Paris in 1747 as an apprentice to a banking firm. He subsequently improved his financial position and his knowledge of financial operations to such an extent that, in 1763, he established his own bank. In part also because of the influence of his wife, who held a salon frequented by the best individuals of the age, he was able to launch a public career. In 1772, he became known for his *Éloge de Colbert,* recognized by the ACADÉMIE FRANÇAISE and, in 1775, for his notable economic study, *Essai sur la législation et le commerce des grains,* in which he criticized the free-trade policies of ROBERT TURGOT, whom he succeeded as director of the Royal Treasury (1776), then as director of finances (1777). Necker tried to make the best of a financial situation rendered particularly difficult by the considerable expenses of the royal court and such costly and imprudent policies as the loans made to Americans for their War of Independence. He tried to reform the policy on imports, improve provincial administration (the creation of provincial assemblies in 1778), suppress the mortmain (right to own land inalienably) and the personal services on royal estates (1779), and also reform penal policies. A more equitable system of taxation was proposed and a plan for the funding of the national debt. The publication of his *Compte rendu au Roi* (1781) presented a comprehensive analysis of national finances. It was generally well received by the public, but because he recommended the controlling of royal extravagances, he was dismissed and replaced soon after by CHARLES-ALEXANDRE DE CALONNE. The financial crisis, however, led to a political one, and in August 1788, Necker was recalled as minister of state by King LOUIS XVI shortly after the calling of the Estates General. Necker called for a meeting of the Assembly of Notables (November–December 1788) and, in spite of the opposition of the aristocracy, succeeded in getting the representation of the Third Estate doubled in the Estates General. His recall again by the king (July 11, 1789) contributed to the development of the revolutionary movement, and he was reappointed on July 15, a day after the storming of the BASTILLE. Necker never succeeded, however, in redressing the economic and financial situation, and he retired from public life, settling at Coppet, Switzerland, with his daughter, Mme de STAËL, and discussing his economic policies in his work *De la Révolution française* (1796).

## Néel, Louis (1904–2000)
*physicist, Nobel laureate*
Louis Néel, who made significant advances in the understanding of the magnetic properties of solid materials, was born in LYON and studied at the École normale supérieure (1928) and at the University of Strasbourg (1932), where he served as professor from 1937 to 1945. During World War II, he also worked for the French navy, developing methods of protecting warships from magnetic mines. In the late 1920s, when Néel began studies of magnetism, physicists recognized only three types: diamagnetism, paramagnetism, and ferromagnetism. Néel identified two additional types of magnetic materials that were added to the classification scheme; antiferromagnetic and ferrimagnetic. The former act like paramagnetic substances above a certain temperature known as the "Néel point." Néel's pioneering research on magnetics provided new materials for the study of microwave electronics, computer memory, and other applications. Additionally, Néel studied the "magnetic memory" of certain mineral deposits to learn of changes in the earth's magnetic field. Néel was named to the Academy of Sciences in 1953 and, with the Swedish physicist Hannes Alfvén, was awarded the Nobel Prize in physics in 1970.

## Nemours, Jacques d'Armagnac, duke de (ca. 1437–1477)
*nobility*
Born in Paris, Jacques d'Armagnac, duke de Nemours took part in the LIGUE DU BIEN PUBLIC. Governor of the Île-de-France, he conspired against King LOUIS XI and was executed. His son, Louis d'Armagnac, duke de Nemours (ca. 1472–1503),

fought in the wars in Italy, was defeated by Gonzalve de Cordova, and killed at Cerignola, Italy.

## Nemours, Louis-Charles-Philippe d'Orléans, duke de (1814–1896)
*royalty*
Born in Paris, Louis-Charles-Philippe d'Orléans, duke de Nemours was the second son of King LOUIS-PHILIPPE and Queen MARIE-AMÉLIE DE BOURBON. He was put forth as a candidate for the throne of Greece in 1824, then for that of Belgium (1831), which his father, however, rejected, so as not to displease the British. The duke de Nemours took part in the siege of Antwerp (1832), then in the conquest of ALGERIA (1834–42). A peer of France, he went into exile after the REVOLUTION OF 1848. Returning to France in 1871, the duke was restored to his position in the army as a division commander, but he left the ranks in 1886.

## Nerval, Gérard de (1808–1855)
**(Gérard Labrunie)**
*writer*
A leading symbolist writer, Gérard de Nerval (the pen name of Gérard Labrunie) was born in Paris. Orphaned early, he was raised amid the legendary accounts of the Valois region. In Paris, he met THÉOPHILE GAUTIER and spent a carefree youth, evoked in *Les petits Châteaux de Bohème* (1853) and *La Bohème galante* (1855). Fascinated by Germany, Nerval did a celebrated translation of Goethe's *Faust* (1827) and composed stories that were inspired by Ernst Theodore Wilhelm Hoffman, a German writer, composer, and painter who influenced the romantic movement. Already in early poems such as *Fantaisie* (1832) appeared the incarnation of the feminine figure that he pursued throughout his life, the blonde Adrienne who died in a convent. From 1836 to 1841, he pursued an unhappy love for the actress Jenny Colon (referred to as Aurélia or Aurélie in his works). The stories in *Des Filles du feu* (1854) are eerie reminiscences of lost youth and beauty, while his sonnets are dominated by a sense of despair (*Les Chimères*, 1854—Nerval committed suicide a year later). Nerval's use of dreams and fantasies also

influenced surrealism and prefigured the work of CHARLES BAUDELAIRE and STÉPHANE MALLARMÉ.

## Ney, Michel (1769–1815)
### (duke of Elchingen, prince of the Muskowa)
*marshal of France*

Born in Sarrelouis, Michel Ney joined the army in 1788, became a captain during the REVOLUTION OF 1789 (1794), and, two years later, after the capture of Mannheim, was made brigadier general. This intrepid soldier (he was called "the bravest of the brave") distinguished himself again at Hohenlinden and then, from October 1802 to December 1803, undertook the political and military organization of Switzerland. Made a marshal of France in 1804, Ney won a victory at Elchingen, Bavaria (1805) followed by another at Ulm, Württemberg. In 1808, NAPOLÉON I created him duke of Elchingen. Ney's participation in the Battle of Friedland was decisive, and he was subsequently sent to Spain (1808), where he occupied Galicia and Asturia. In 1812, he led the campaign and then the retreat from Russia, achieving many victories during both, and was made prince of the Moscowa. He took part in the campaign of 1813. He encouraged Napoléon to abdicate in 1814, then went over to King LOUIS XVIII, who made him a peer of France and governor of Besançon. The king ordered him to arrest Bonaparte upon his return from Elba, but Ney, with his troops, instead rallied to the emperor (March 13, 1815). Ney showed great courage at the Battle of Quatre-Bras (June 16, 1815) as well as at Waterloo. He was captured, arrested, and tried before the Chamber of Peers for having betrayed the Bourbons. He was condemned to death and shot the next day near the Paris Observatory, where there is now a memorial statue by FRANÇOIS RUDE. Marshal Ney's *Mémoires* were published in 1833.

See also HUNDRED DAYS.

## Niboyet, Eugénie (1797–1883)
*feminist*

An important feminist of the pre-1848 era, Eugénie Niboyet was born in Montpellier into a wealthy bourgeois Protestant family. Her political views were developed through contacts with the Saint-Simonians, and her newspaper, *Le Conseiller des femmes*, founded in 1833 in LYON, was the first feminist journal founded outside Paris. Niboyet was also a pacifist and translator of children's books, and she helped to found the influential feminist journal *La Voix des femmes* in 1848.

See also SAINT-SIMON, CLAUDE-HENRI DE ROUVROY, COUNT DE.

## Nice

The main city of the French Riviera, Nice is the capital of the department of Alps-Maritime. Besides tourism, the major industries are food products (especially olive oil) and perfumes. Built around a bay, Nice comprises the Old and the New Cities. The sea front features the Promenade des Anglais, and there are several museums, including those dedicated to the works of HENRI MATISSE and MARC CHAGALL. Nice, which historically was ruled by the House of Savoy, became part of France in 1793. It was restored to Piedmont in 1814, then in 1860, as a result of the Treaty of Turin, negotiated by NAPOLÉON III, and of a subsequent plebiscite, became a part of France, along with Savoy.

## Niépce, Joseph-Nicéphore (1765–1833)
*physicist, inventor*

Considered the inventor of photography, Joseph-Nicéphore Niépce was born in Chalon-sur-Saône. He began his experiments in photography with his brother Claude in 1793, using light-sensitive compounds of silver (later with silver chloride, 1816, and with silver cells, 1820). Although these early experiments were not successful, he continued in this endeavor while also attempting to develop an improved method of making plates for lithographic printing. In 1827, he successfully made the first surviving permanent photograph, of the courtyard of his home, using a bitumen-coated pewter plate exposed in a camera obsura (a forerunner of the camera). He then did several photographs entitled "points de vue." For a time, he kept the details of his discovery secret but, in 1829, he formed a partnership with LOUIS DAGUERRE, who was inspired by

Niépce's techniques. Earlier, Niépce also had conceived a motor that could propel boats.

## Nivelle, George-Robert (1858–1924)
*general*

Born in Tulle, George-Robert Nivelle became an artillery officer and, in 1900, took part in the military expedition to China, before serving in North Africa. Placed in command of the Fourth Artillery Regiment (1911) at the beginning of WORLD WAR I (1914), he fought in ALSACE and on the Ourcq River. Named commander of the Third Army Corps (1915), then of the Second Army (1916), he took part in a number of counteroffensives launched against the Germans at VERDUN (1916). Replacing General JOSEPH JOFFRE as the commander of the Armies of the North and the Northeast, he was relieved of his command and replaced by General PHILIPPE PÉTAIN after the defeat during the offensive at Chemin des Dames; but the commission that was later charged with discovering the cause of this defeat could not find any tactical errors on the part of General Nivelle. He retired from the military after the war.

## Noailles family
*distinguished family of civil, religious, and military leaders*

The Noailles were a noble family originally from Noailles, Corrèze. Antoine de Noailles (1504–62), admiral of France, was born in Noailles. He distinguished himself at Ceresole Alba, Piedmont (1544), and was ambassador to England. François de Noailles (1519–85), brother of Antoine, was bishop of Dax and served as ambassador to England, the Venetian Republic, and the Ottoman Sublime Porte and was one of the architects of the alliance between France and the Ottoman Empire. Anne-Jules de Noailles, count d'Ayen and duke de Noailles (1650–1708) was born in Paris and served as governor of Languedoc, where he implemented the policy of the dragonnades (persecutions) against the Protestants. He fought in Spain and was made a marshal of France. Louis-Antoine de Noailles (1651–1729), born in Teyssière, near Aurillac, was the brother of Anne-Jules. A fervid supporter of

GALLICANISM, he became archbishop of Paris (1695) and a cardinal (1700). He made attempts at achieving reconciliation between JACQUES BÉNIGNE BOSSUET and FRANÇOIS FÉNELON and for a long time was opposed to the bull *Unigenitus*. ADRIEN-MAURICE de Noailles, count d'Ayen and duke de Noailles (1678–1766), born in Paris, was the son of ANNE-JULES. He married a niece of Mme de MAINTENON, mistress of King LOUIS XIV, which furthered his career. After having fought in the War of the Spanish Succession (1715), he helped the regent to overturn the will of King LOUIS XIV. President of the Council of Finances (1715–18), he was dismissed because of his opposition to JOHN LAW. He reentered the military and again served (Philippsburg, 1734; Dettingen, 1743), became a marshal of France, then foreign minister (1744–45), and concluded an alliance with Prussia. He left his memoirs and correspondence. Philippe de Noailles, duke de Mouchy (1715–94), the son of Marshal de Noailles, was born in Paris and was named governor of Versailles (1740) and of Guyenne (1775–86). Marshal of France, a member of the Assembly of Notables (1787–89), and a royalist during the REVOLUTION OF 1789, he was condemned to death and guillotined under the TERROR. Louis-Marie, chevalier d'Arpajon, viscount de Noailles (1756–1804), born in Paris, the son of Philippe de Noailles. He fought alongside the marquis de LA FAYETTE in the American War of Independence and was made a general. A member of the Assembly of Notables (1787–88), then deputy for the nobility to the ESTATES GENERAL (1789), he voted in favor of the abolition of privileges during the Revolution (August 4, 1789). An émigré, he went to the United States in 1792 and fought with General JEAN-BAPTISTE ROCHAMBEAU at Saint-Domingue and was mortally wounded.

## Noailles, Anna-Elizabeth, countess de (1876–1933)
### (countess Mathieu de Noailles, princess Brancovan)
*poet, writer, society figure*

Born in Paris of Greek and Romanian origin, Anna de Noailles was at the nucleus of a cultured, aristocratic literary circle. Known by her contemporaries for her musical, personal, and often mystical and exotic poetry, first collected in 1901 as *Le Coeur innombrable,* she found through a form of neoclassicism a lyricism abandoned since the romantic period. Her early verses, reveal a passion for light of day and the French countryside. Setting her gaze on wider horizons she celebrated in her later poems the enchantment and beauty of the whole world (*Les Ébouissements,* 1907), while exuding an almost pagan love of life. The themes of the flight of time, the passage of youth, and solitude are found in such collections as *L'Honneur de souffrir* (1927). Also a novelist, Anna de Noailles wrote *La nouvelle Espérance* (1903), *Le Visage émerveillé* (1904), in addition to her memoirs, *Le Livre de ma vie* (1932). She was the first female commander of the LEGION OF HONOR.

## Nodier, Charles  (1780–1844)
*writer*

Born in Besançon, Charles Nodier who made his salon, known as the "Arsenal," the center of literary life in Paris (1824–30) and of the romantic movement, used dreams as inspirations for his writings (*Contes: Trilby ou le Lutin d'Argail,* 1822; *La Fée aux miettes,* 1832). The use of fantasies, at once graceful and terrifying (*Smarra ou les Démons de la nuit,* 1821), also is indicative of his literary style. Nodier inspired GÉRARD DE NERVAL and the surrealists. He was elected to the ACADÉMIE FRANÇAISE in 1833.

See also CÉNACLE.

## Noguès, Charles-Auguste-Paul (1876–1971)
*general*

Born in Monléon-Magnoac, Hautes-Pyrénées, Charles-Auguste-Paul Noguès attended the École polytechnique (1897–99) and later served in the Rif War (1924–26) in North Africa. He was named resident general of Morocco in 1936. Commander in chief of operations in North Africa, in June 1940, after the French surrender to the Germans. He went over to Marshal PHILIPPE PÉTAIN and stopped the ship *Massilia* as it was headed for Morocco with Resistance members of the French parliament. In November 1942, following orders from the VICHY government, he tried to organize a resistance to the

Allies in North Africa. Coming over to Admiral FRANÇOIS DARLAN, he was obliged to leave his post upon the arrival of General CHARLES DE GAULLE in Algiers, and he went into exile in Portugal. Tried in absentia in 1947, General Noguès returned to France, was imprisoned (1954), and then paroled. He returned to Portugal. In 1955, at the request of the government of EDGAR FAURE, he played a decisive role in the negotiations regarding the return of Sultan Mohammad V to Morocco.

## Noiret, Philippe  (1931–   )
*actor*

Born in Lille, Philippe Noiret began his career in cabarets, in the theater, and then in film with AGNÈS VARDA (*La Pointe courte*). His cinematic career was highlighted with such successes as *Zazie dans le métro* (1962), *Thérèse Desqueyroux* (1962), *Alexandre le Bienhereux* (1968), *La Grande Bouffe* (1973), *Les Ripoux* (1984), *Cinéma Paradiso* (1989), and *Tango* (1993). Noiret found in BERTRAND TAVERNIER an author up to his own measure: *L'Horloger de Saint-Paul* (1974), *Que la Fête commence* (1975), *Le Juge et l'Assassin* (1976), *Coups de torchon* (1981), and *La Vie et rien d'autre* (1989).

## Normandy  (Normandie)

Normandy was a former province of France that was given by Charles III the Simple to Rollo, the Norman, or Viking, leader (Treaty of Saint-Clair-sur-Epte, 911), and was retaken from the English by King Philip Augustus in 1204. It was one of the main battlefields during the HUNDRED YEARS' WAR. The capital of Normandy is at Rouen, and the province comprises five departments: Orne, Seine-Maritime, Calvados, Eure, and Manche. It was the site of the Allied landing in 1944 (D Day) and the first province to be liberated, but also suffered great damage during WORLD WAR II. Today, its major industries are textiles and tourism.

## Nostradamus  (1503–1566)
*physician, astrologer*

Born in Saint-Rémy-de-Provence, Michel de Nostre-Dame, or Nostradamus as he is called, is best known for his *Centuries astrologiques* (1555), a famous collection of prophecies. Written in quatrains, these prophecies describe, in vague language, events from the mid-1500s through to the end of the world, which he predicted to be in 3797 C.E. Nostradamus studied medicine in Montpellier and, about 1525, began to treat successfully victims of the plague in communities in southern France, especially in Aix-en-Provence. His success and innovative methods earned him a reputation as an especially gifted healer. Nostradamus's fame brought him to the attention of CATHERINE DE' MEDICI, who asked him to plot the horoscope of her husband, King HENRY II, and their children. In 1560, King CHARLES IX appointed him court physician.

## Noverre, Jean-Georges (1727–1810)
*dancer, choreographer*

Born in Paris, Jean-Georges Noverre debuted at the court of LOUIS XV in 1742. He subsequently traveled to Germany (where he later returned to serve as ballet master in Stuttgart, 1755), then returned to France to stage his first ballets. From 1755 to 1757, he studied in London with the English mime David Garrick, whose techniques influenced Noverre in his efforts to bring innovations and reform to ballet. In LYON, Noverre staged a number of works and published his celebrated *Lettres sur la danse et sur les ballets* (1760). There, he discusses new theatrical forms for the dance, emphasizing plot and incorporating elements of pantomime. Called to Vienna (1767), he collaborated with Christoph von Gluck (*Iphigénie en Tauride, Alceste*) and, returning to France (1776), was named, through the patronage of Queen MARIE ANTOINETTE, director of the Paris Opera. During the REVOLUTION OF 1789, Noverre was in exile in London and, upon his return to France, devoted his later years to editing a dictionary of the dance.

# O

## OAS

The OAS (Organisation de l'armée secrète), formed after the failure of the military putsch in Algiers (April 21, 1961), was begun at the instigation of a number of officers, including General RAOUL SALAN, and various political figures who tried by various means (including terrorism) to oppose the Algerian policy of General CHARLES DE GAULLE. The activities of the OAS intensified during the signing of the ÉVIAN ACCORDS (March 1962), but shortly after, the principal leaders of the organization were arrested.

See also ALGERIA.

## Ocagne, Maurice d' (1862–1938)
*mathematician*

Born in Paris, Maurice d'Ocagne was the inventor of nomography (1884), in which calculus equations are replaced by graphic representations in which the points of intersection give the solution. Nomography has numerous applications in the construction of roads, bridges, and the like, and currently has application in computer graphics. D'Ocagne was named to the Academy of Sciences in 1922.

## Offenbach, Jacques (1819–1880)
*composer*

Of German origin, Jacques Offenbach was born in Cologne, the son of a cantor. He studied the cello at the Paris Conservatory, became a cellist, and, in 1855, opened his own theater, the Bouffes-Parisiens. Beginning in 1866, he had a brilliant career and with his librettist (LUDOVIC HALÉVY), produced many operettas that are considered masterpieces of comic opera, or "opéra bouffe," which reflected the gay Parisian spirit, especially of the SECOND EMPIRE. By 1875, he had composed over 90 works, including *Orphée aux Enfers* (1858), *La Belle Hélène* (1864), *La Vie parisienne* (1866), *La Grande-Duchess du Gérolstein* (1867), *La Périchole* (1868), *Les Brigands* (1869), *Madame Favart* (1878), *La Fille du tambourmajor* (1879). After his death, his *Contes d'Hoffmann* (1881) premiered and, in this masterpiece, which contains the famous "Barcarolle," Offenbach reached the heights of fantastic and whimsical realism.

## Olier, Jean-Jacques (1608–1657)
*cleric*

Known as Monsieur Olier, Jean-Jacques Olier was born in Paris, where he served as the priest for the church of Saint-Sulpice (1642–52). He reformed his parish and created there a seminary that grew and for which he founded the congregation of priest of Saint-Sulpice (Sulpicians). With M de LA DAUVERSIÈRE he also founded the Society of Notre-Dame of Montreal, which, beginning in 1642, sent Sulpicians and colonists to Canada. Olier's writings express a spirituality that is at once severe and warm and, after that of PIERRE DE BÉRULLE, exercised a profound influence on the formation of French clergy (*La Journée chrétienne*, 1665; *Catéchisme chrétien pour la vie intérieure*, 1656; *Introduction à la vie et aux vertus chrétiennes*, 1657).

## Olivétan (1506–1538)
*reformer*

Pierre Robert, or Olivétan as he is known, was a cousin of JOHN CALVIN, upon whom he had a certain influence. He supported the Reformation and taught Greek and Hebrew at Strasbourg, then came to Geneva, Switzerland, where he collaborated on the French translation of the Bible (1535). This translation became the basis for the Geneva Bible. Olivétan was most likely a Waldensian pastor from Italy, to which he returned from Geneva, and there he died.

## Ollivier, Émile  (1825–1913)
*political figure*

Born in MARSEILLE, Émile Ollivier was an attorney before being elected a deputy to the Legislative Corps (1857) where he joined JULES FAVRE and others in forming a republican opposition to the regime of NAPOLÉON III. The increasing liberalization of the regime, however, caused him eventually to support the imperial government of the SECOND EMPIRE. A founder of the Third Party (1863), he took a position against the authoritarian policies of EUGÈNE ROUHER and, after the latter's resignation in 1869, Ollivier was charged by Napoléon III to form a new government (January 1870). He was himself named chief of the ministries of justice and of cults. The attempt to establish a parliamentary regime could not, however, save the Empire, despite the favorable plebiscite of May 8, 1870. Also, the Victor Noir affair, a scandal resulting from the murder of journalist Victor Noir by a relative of Napoléon III; the growth of labor unrest; and the deterioration of relations with Prussia all precipitated the government's fall. After the declaration of war with Prussia (July 1870) that he reluctantly voted for, and after the first defeats of the French army by the Prussians (see FRANCO-PRUSSIAN WAR), Ollivier immigrated to Italy, where he remained until 1873. He left a number of writings on the Second Empire (*Le Ministère du 2 janvier*, 1875; *L'Empire libéral*, 1894–1902). Ollivier was elected to the ACADÉMIE FRANÇAISE in 1870.

## Orléans, House of
*royal dynasty*

Orléans is the name of four princely French families. The first was represented by Philippe (1336–75), duke d'Orléans (1344–75), son of King PHILIP VI of France, who died without heirs. The second issued from LOUIS (1372–1407), DUKE D'OR-LÉANS (1392–1407), the son of King CHARLES V, and whose grandson reigned as LOUIS XII. The third was represented by GASTON, COUNT OF EU, DUKE D'OR-LÉANS (1608–60), brother of LOUIS XIII, who died without male heirs. The fourth was the issue of PHILIPPE, duke d'Orléans (1640–1701), brother of King LOUIS XIV, whose descendant reigned as King LOUIS-PHILIPPE (1830–48).

## Orléans, Gaston, count d'Eu, duke d' (1608–1660)
*political figure*

Born at Fontainebleau, the third son of HENRY IV and MARIE DE' MEDICI, and brother of LOUIS XIII, Gaston, count d'Eu, duke d'Orléans was best known for his bloody, incessant, and unsuccessful intrigues first against Cardinal RICHELIEU, and then against Cardinal MAZARIN. Lacking character but not culture, he became lieutenant general of the kingdom after the death of King Louis XIII and placed himself at the head of the FRONDE against Mazarin. But he soon destroyed his friends and supporters and came to terms with the court. In 1652, Mazarin exiled him to Blois, where he spent his last years. From his first marriage to Mme de MONTPENSIER, he had a daughter, ANNE LOUISE OF ORLÉANS, DUCHESS OF MONTPENSIER, who was known as La Grande Madamoiselle.

## Orléans, Louis, duke d'  (1372–1407)
*royal figure*

The second son of King CHARLES V and brother of King CHARLES VI, Louis, duke d'Orléans was born in Paris. He was protected by Queen ISABEAU OF BAVARIA and fought for power against the dukes of Burgundy PHILIP II THE BOLD, and JEAN THE FEARLESS. Louis d'Orléans's assassination by the soldiers of Duke Jean began the civil war between the Armagnacs and the Burgundians.

## Orléans, Louis-Philippe-Joseph, duke d' (1747–1793)
### (Philippe Égalité)
*royal figure*

Known eventually as Philippe Égalité, Louis-Philippe-Joseph, duke d'Orléans, the cousin of King LOUIS XVI, was born at Saint-Cloud. He married the great-granddaughter of King LOUIS XIV, Adélaïde de Bourbon-Penthièvre, in 1769 and came into a considerable fortune that he used, in part, to advance his political ambitions. A Freemason (grand masonic master in 1786), he adopted the liberal ideas of the period and admired the British political system. His opposition to the ministry of RENÉ MAUPEOU caused him to be briefly exiled (1771–72). After serving as a naval officer, he returned to politics and took every opportunity to express his hostility to the regime and the court. A deputy for the Second Estate to the ESTATES GENERAL, in 1789 he was one of the first to rally to the Third Estate (see REVOLUTION OF 1789). Allied with MIRABEAU, he dreamed perhaps of taking Louis XVI's place, or at least of being named regent. Exiled to England after the uprisings of October 5–6, 1789, he returned to France in 1790. Elected deputy to the Convention in 1792 (he had taken the name Philippe Égalité), he voted for the king's death. His own son, the future king LOUIS-PHILIPPE, had emigrated with CHARLES DUMOURIEZ after this betrayal, and soon the duke d'Orléans was arrested by the MONTAGNARDS, then subsequently sentenced to death and executed.

## Orléans, Philippe, duke d' (1640–1701) (Monsieur)
*brother of Louis XIV*

Born at Saint-Germain-en-Laye, Philippe, duke d'Orléans was the second son of King LOUIS XIII and Queen ANNE OF AUSTRIA and brother of King LOUIS XIV. He was called Monsieur, and his first marriage was to Henriette-Anne of England. His second marriage was to Charlotte Elisabeth of Bavaria, princess of the Palatinate, with whom he had a son (also named PHILIPPE, DUKE D'ORLÉANS), who later became regent for King LOUIS XV. The elder duke d'Orléans was known for his open homosexuality, especially in his relationship with the chevalier de Lorraine, and for his military bravery in war (especially at the Battle of Cassel, 1677).

## Orléans, Philippe, duke d' (1674–1723)
*Regent for Louis XV*

Born at Saint-Cloud, Philippe, duke d'Orléans, who served as regent under LOUIS XV, was the son of PHILIPPE, DUKE OF ORLÉANS (the brother of LOUIS XIV) and Charlotte Elisabeth of Bavaria and, at first, was known by the title of duke of Chartres. Under the influence of his tutor, Cardinal GUILLAUME DUBOIS, he married Mlle de Blois, the daughter of LOUIS XIV and Mme de MONTESPAN. He proved himself early in his career to be a capable military officer, particularly at Neerwinden, and in Spain (Aragon, Catalonia), and led the successful capture of Lerida (1707–08). However, he was accused of plotting to seize the Spanish throne and was exiled from court. Meanwhile, Louis XIV, in his last will, named the duke of Maine to be regent for Louis XV during his minority. But in 1715 this provision was overturned by the Parlement of Paris, and Philippe d'Orléans became regent instead. The rigid ceremony and piety of the last days of the court of Louis XIV was replaced with an atmosphere of moral relaxation, informality, and religious skepticism. Much was a reaction to the rigor imposed by Mme de MAINTENON. The upper aristocracy, for which the duke DE SAINT-SIMON is considered the spokesperson, took its revenge also, attempting to limit the powers that she had exercised (1718). The Parlement, too, gained the right of remonstrance, and it was this concession that would impede the monarchy for the rest of the 18th century. It was at first a handicap for the regent. Intelligent but lazy and debauched, he would come face to face with an especially critical financial situation (1719) when he made JOHN LAW comptroller general of the kingdom. The regent's foreign policy, planned by Cardinal DUBOIS, was often guided by his efforts to secure the succession in the event of Louis XV's death.

## Orry, Philibert (1689–1749)
*administrator*

Born near Nogent-sur-Seine, Philibert Orry served as comptroller general under King LOUIS XV (1730–45) during the ministry of Cardinal FLEURY. Later, as director of fortifications, arts, and manufacturers, he played an important role in the redevelopment of finances, aided by some favorable economic developments of the period. Finances were reestablished by economic and administrative reforms, trade and industry were encouraged, and the construction of roads and canals was begun. Orry's intransigence, however, gained him many enemies and led to his resignation (1745) when, because of his financial policies, credit was taken away from Mme de POMPADOUR.

## Orsini, Felice  (1819–1858)
*Italian revolutionary*

Born in Meldola, near Forli, Italy, Felice Orsini was affiliated with the nationalist Young Italy movement and took part in the liberal insurrection of 1843. Condemned (1844), he was amnestied by Pope Pius IX (1846). One of the main agents of the Italian nationalist Giuseppe Mazzini, he served in the government of the Roman Republic (1849) and fought alongside Giuseppe Garibaldi in the struggle against the invading French forces (see general NICOLAS-CHARLES OUDINOT). Condemned in 1855 for his role in several attempted uprisings, he escaped to England, where, with others, he planned the assassination of NAPOLÉON III. The attempt (January 14, 1858) failed, but it resulted in numerous other victims. Orsini, defended by JULES FAVRE, was sentenced to death and executed. His attempt, on the life of Napoléon III contributed to the reinforcing of repression in France and led to Napoléon III's support for the movement for Italian unification.

## Oudinot, Nicolas-Charles  (1767–1847)
(duke of Reggio)
*marshal of France*

Born in Bar-le-Duc, Nicolas-Charles Oudinot, at the time of the REVOLUTION OF 1789, served as a lieutenant colonel of the Meuse volunteers (1792) and later distinguished himself in Italy (1799), at Austerlitz (1805), and at Ostroleka and Friedland (1807). NAPOLÉON I made him a marshal after his contributions at the Battle of Wagram (1809), and later created him duke of Reggio. Marshal Oudinot also took part in the campaigns in Russia (1812), Germany (1813), and France (1814). Rallying to LOUIS XVIII, Oudinot was made a peer of France and grand chancellor of the LEGION OF HONOR and, in 1842, was named governor of the Invalides.

## Oudinot, Nicolas-Charles-Victor  (1791–1863)
(duke of Reggio)
*general*

Born in Bar-le-Duc, Nicolas-Charles-Victor Oudinot, duke of Reggio, was the son of Marshal NICOLAS-CHARLES OUDINOT. He served as aide-de-camp to General ANDRÉ MASSÉNA in Portugal (1810, and took part in the last military campaigns of the FIRST EMPIRE. Rallying to LOUIS XVIII (1814), he offered his resignation after the REVOLUTION OF 1830, then, resuming various posts (1835), served in ALGERIA. Commander of the French troops sent to overthrow the Roman Republic, Oudinot took Rome in 1849.

## Oudry, Jean-Baptiste  (1686–1755)
*painter, decorator, engraver*

Born in Paris, Jean-Baptiste Oudry studied under noted artists and was initially a religious and portrait painter. He then turned to painting animals, still lifes, and landscapes. Appointed to paint the royal hunting scenes, he also was the director of the tapestry works at Beauvais (1734), then served as superintendent of the GOBELIN works (1736), where he did a series of designs (*Les Verdures fines,* 1736; *Les Chasses de Louis XV,* 1734–45). Oudry continued to paint animal scenes while also producing landscapes and still lifes that show his great technical virtuosity (*Canard blanc,* 1753). Oudry illustrated 230 designs for the *Fables* of JEAN DE LA FONTAINE.

## Ouvrard, Gabriel-Julien  (1770–1846)
*financier*

Born near Clisson, Gabriel-Julien Ouvrard started his career by investing in papermaking during the REVOLUTION OF 1789. Thanks to his friendship with PAUL BARRAS, he was named chief supplier to the navy (1797), which allowed him to make a rapid but questionable fortune that caused a scandal. Imprisoned in 1800, he was freed shortly afterward through the influence of JEAN-JACQUES CAMBACÉRÈS and the Empress JOSÉPHINE. Ouvrard was named banker to the government and subcommissioner of army supplies, which allowed him to increase his fortune even more. At the same time, he controlled the monopoly in trade with the Spanish colonies. NAPOLÉON I, who took umbrage at Ouvrard's power and influence, forced him to dispose of his wealth in 1806. Arrested a number of times, Ouvrard was imprisoned from 1809 to 1814, after having swindled the Finance Ministry. In 1817, his tremendous fortune allowed the duke de RICHELIEU to finance the war debt. Ouvrard was named general supplier to the Spanish army in 1823, but accused of making inflated and fraudulent profits, he was again imprisoned several times. Ouvrard left his *Mémoires* (1826).

## Ozanam, Frédéric (1813–1853)
*writer and historian*

Born in Milan, Italy, Frédéric Ozanam, a French Catholic writer, was one of the founders of the Society of St. Vincent de Paul (1833) and, with HENRI LACORDAIRE, collaborated on the republican Catholic newspaper, *L'Ère nouvelle* (1848). Ozanam's principal writings include *Essai sur la philosophie de Dante* (1839), *Études germaniques* (1847–49), *La civilization au Ve siècle* (1856), *Discours sur la société de Saint-Vincent-de-Paul* (1870).

## Ozenfant, Amadée (1886–1966)
*painter*

Born in Saint-Quentin, Amadée Ozenfant, attracted to architecture and aesthetic theories, founded, with GUILLAUME APOLLONAIRE, a revue, *L'Élan*, and with LE CORBUSIER, in 1928, published the manifesto of "purism." The same year, Ozenfant wrote a work dealing with synthesis entitled *L'Art*. He developed a basic style in which the contours of familiar objects are schematized and forms are put in geometric patterns, while the colors are reduced to some unified areas.

# P

## Pache, Jean-Nicolas (1746–1823)
*political figure*

Born in Paris, Jean-Nicolas Pache was an enthusiastic proponent of the ideals of the REVOLUTION OF 1789 and, originally supporting the GIRONDINS, became minister of war (October 1792–February 1793). Rallying to the MONTAGNARDS, and serving as mayor of the Paris COMMUNE (February 1793–May 1794), Pache had the words "Liberté, Égalité, Fraternité" inscribed on all public monuments.

## Pagnol, Marcel (1895–1974)
*writer, dramatist*

Born in Aubagne, Marcel Pagnol left his career as a professor of English after his debut as a dramatic author (*Les Marchands de gloire,* 1925), then turned to the avant-garde (*Jazz,* 1926), preferring naturalism, with his comedy on morality, *Topaze* (1928). His subsequent sophisticated and melodramatic trilogy about workers on the MARSEILLE waterfront—*Marius* (1931), *Fanny* (1932), and *César* (1936)—brought him international fame and were made into films. Among Pagnol's other works are *Angèle* (1934), *Regain* (1937), and *La Femme de boulanger* (1939). He returned to the stage with *Judas* (1955) and *Fabien* (1956), and published a trilogy on memories of his childhood and youth also made into films. Pagnol was elected to the ACADÉMIE FRANÇAISE in 1946.

## Painlevé, Paul (1863–1933)
*mathematician, political figure*

Born in Paris and educated at the École normale polytechnique, Paul Painlevé worked on differential equations, establishing theories concerning the function of complex variables, the general mechanics of friction, and the mechanics of fluids. Interested in aviation, he was the first passenger of Wilbur Wright, the American inventor and aviator (1908), and of HENRI FARMAN and, in 1910, gained from parliament the first vote for credits for aviation. In the same year, he was elected as an independent Socialist to the Chamber of Deputies. During WORLD WAR I, Painlevé served as minister of public instruction (1915–16) and of war (March–November 1917). He also was prime minister in 1917 (September–November) and again in 1925, and was one of the founders of the CARTEL DES GAUCHES. Painlevé served in several succeeding cabinets as minister of war (1925–29), and made the initial decision concerning the Maginot Line (see ANDRÉ MAGINOT) and the one-year term of military service (1928). He was named to the Academy of Sciences in 1900.

## Palissy, Bernard (ca. 1510–1589 or 1590)
*ceramicist, scholar*

Born in Lacapelle-Biron, near Agen, Bernard Palissy, who would become known for his ceramic pieces with mythological or rustic images (insects, reptiles) in low relief, traveled before settling down as a glassmaker in Saintes. After years of research, he discovered the secret of the composition of enamel, producing from it a smooth glazed pottery. At that time, although he had become a HUGUENOT, he enjoyed the protection of CATHERINE DE' MEDICI, to whom he was royal potter, and of the constable de MONTMORENCY (see MONTMORENCY FAMILY). Much later, however, he was imprisoned in the BASTILLE (1589) for refusing to abjure the Protestant faith. An artist, Palissy was also a scholar, chemist, and geologist and a precursor of paleontology in his observation of fossils.

## Panama affair

The Panama affair was one of the most important financial scandals of the THIRD REPUBLIC. After having obtained from the Colombian government a territorial concession, FERDINAND DE LESSEPS brought together at Paris an international congress with the idea of building an inter-oceanic canal in Panama (1879–81). Underestimating the technical difficulties of the enterprise that the engineers estimated would cost billions of francs and cause the death of many workers, de Lesseps appealed to the public and to leading financiers for funds. A large amount of the monies collected went toward press campaigns for the project. In 1887, de Lesseps abandoned his initial plan and asked GUSTAVE EIFFEL for help. He also had government approval, from various members of parliament and some ministers, to sell bonds. The campaign failed, and nearly 800,000 subscribers went bankrupt. Because of collusion between political and financial figures, the scandal was stifled until 1891, when an inquiry was opened regarding de Lesseps's finances. JACQUES REINACH, a financier also involved, apparently committed suicide as a result of the scandal. De Lesseps was sentenced to five years in prison; the engineers involved, including Eiffel, to two (later reversed); and the scandal caused important political and ideological repercussions (a violent press campaign against Jewish financing started by the anti-Semite ÉDOUARD DRUMONT in his newspaper, *Le Libre Parole*).

## Paoli, Pasquale (1725–1807)

*patriot, political figure*

Born in Morosaglia, CORSICA, Pasquale Paoli was, with his father, exiled to Italy, where he served in the Neapolitan army. Upon his return to his native country in 1755, he was named general-in-chief of the Corsican army and, defeating the Genoese, to whom he left only the littoral coast of the island, tried to organize a democratic government. Paoli helped in the development of Corsican agriculture and trade and founded a university at Corte. When Genoa sold its claims in Corsica to France (1768), Paoli took up arms against the French. CARLO-MARIA BONAPARTE fought at his side, then abandoned the cause and went over to the royal government. Defeated at Ponto-Nuovo (May 8, 1790), Paoli emigrated to England. Recalled by the French National Constituent Assembly (1790) during the REVOLUTION OF 1789, he was named commander of the National Guard and president of the departmental directorate of Corsica. But in 1793, he took a stand against the Convention and appealed to the British for help. Counter to his expectations, the British, once they had taken the island, named an Englishman as viceroy instead of him. Paoli died in exile in London.

## Pape-Carpentier, Marie (1815–1878)

*pedagogue*

Born in La Flèche, Marie Pape-Carpentier, after teaching in the first French *école maternelle* (kindergarten), was placed in charge of the École normale maternelle (1848), then became inspector general of the *salles d'asile* (nursery schools). She published several important works on pedagogy (*Enseignement pratique dans les écoles maternelles*, 1849; *Histoires et leçons et choses pour les enfants*, 1858; *Cours d'éducation primaire*, 1876). Pape-Carpentier is considered a pioneer and innovator in French pedagogy and education.

## Papin, Denis (1647–1714)

*inventor*

Born in Chitenay, near Blois, Denis Papin was the first to discover the elastic power of water vapor and spent the rest of his life inventing and perfecting various machines that employed that power. Forced into exile after the revocation of the EDICT OF NANTES, Papin produced his "kettle" with a safety valve. It was the basis for later inventions and discoveries. Leaving England to live in Kassel, Germany, he developed the idea of a piston engine (1687). This early model was used for pumping water, used cylinders and pistons, and was powered by air pressure. He also invented a waterwheel (1700) that powered a pneumatic transmission. Forgotten, Papin's inventions were never further developed, and he died in poverty in London.

## Paré, Amboise (ca. 1509–1590)

*surgeon*

Born in Bourg-Hersent, near Laval, Amboise Paré was self-taught, became a barber-surgeon in 1536, and served successively as surgeon to kings HENRY II, FRANCIS II, CHARLES IX, and HENRY III. Paré invented the method of binding arteries with ligatures that he substituted for cauterization after amputation; he also discovered ways of extracting projectiles based on the position of the wound. His great practical skills and humaneness distinguished him from his contemporaries and made him famous throughout Europe. Because he had no formal education, and thus discussed his work in his native language, his writings had a wide influence on the public, as well as on medical professionals. In his writings, too, Paré shows a remarkably modern empirical sense, for which reason he is considered the father of modern surgery. Paré is the author of a number of treatises.

## Paris

The capital and largest city of France, Paris is located on the Seine River, about 222 miles (370 kilometers) from its Atlantic outlet at Le Havre. Situated in a low-lying basin, Paris is mostly flat, although the elevation increases gradually from the river to the low hills at the city's edge. The highest natural point within the city proper is the Butte de Montmartre at 396 feet (129 m) above sea level. Having an estimated population of nearly 10 million, the metropolitan area of Paris contains almost 20 percent of the nation's inhabitants and, to an extraordinary degree, dominates the political, economic, and cultural life of France. In 2004, the population of Paris proper was over 2.1 million.

Historically, France's governments have favored the city and made it the central point of national life, although attempts have been made to reduce this influence. Paris is also France's leading industrial center, with nearly one-quarter of the nation's manufacturing concentrated there. Consumer goods production has always ranked high, and high-technology industries are increasing. Preeminent in the arts and culture, Paris has many publishing companies and newspapers (*LE MONDE, LE FIGARO*), luxury manufactures, and is the center of haute couture. Finance and banking are concentrated in Paris, and the city is now one of Europe's most important centers of international commerce and business. Situated in one of Europe's richest agricultural regions, which produces a number of crops, Paris is guaranteed a constant supply of food and is the economic center of the surrounding agrarian areas.

Circular in shape and divided by the Seine, in which there are two islands (Île de la Cité, the original site of the city, and Île Saint-Louis), Paris has no topographical constraints and has grown through the centuries. However, it is densely populated. It has a low skyline (buildings' heights are controlled), with high rises only in the outlying new departments (e.g., La Défense). Paris enjoys mild winters owing to the temperate climate of the nation's west coast, and there is a lively outdoor urban life in its cafés, markets, and boulevards. Its districts each have a distinct character (Left Bank, Latin Quarter, Right Bank, Champs-Élysées, Montmartre, Belleville, Ménilmontant) as the city has steadily grown since the 10th century. Neuilly to the west, has become an important suburb. The Industrial Revolution caused a large population growth and, after World War II, there has been a substantial influx of immigrants from elsewhere in Europe, North Africa, and former colonial territories.

Paris is the principal center of the nation's railway and highway system, and two international airports, Orly and Charles de Gaulle, serve the city, as does a domestic one at Le Bourget. The Paris Métro, or subway, begun in 1900, has 16 main lines connecting the urban areas. The Seine, which is navigable, makes Paris a port, the fourth-largest in France, and connects it to the northern part of the country.

The central area of the city grew early, and open and green spaces developed from areas protected by development, especially those that were royal preserves (Bois de Boulogne, Luxembourg Gardens, Parc Monceau, Bois de Vincennes). Paris's historical and monumental architecture reflects the city's historic and cultural position. These include the cathedral of Notre-Dame, on the Île de la Cité and the nearby Sainte-Chapelle, the LOUVRE, the INVALIDES, the place de la Concorde. In the mid-19th century, the city was redesigned by baron GEORGES HAUSS-

Notre-Dame Cathedral, Paris *(Library of Congress)*

MANN, with the place de l'Étoile (now place Charles de Gaulle) surrounding the ARC DE TRIOMPHE, the Opéra, place de l'Opéra, and the great boulevards—Champs-Élysées, rue de la Paix, rue du Faubourg-Saint-Honoré, boulevard des Italiens, and boulevard du Montparnasse—being constructed. In 1889, the EIFFEL TOWER was built, and in 1910, the basilica of Sacre-Cœur was completed on the summit of Montmartre. Other important buildings are the Panthéon, ELYSÉE PALACE (official residence of the president of the republic), Palais-Bourbon (seat of the National Assembly), Palais-Royal, palais de Chaillot, and palais de Justice. Recent impressive structures include the Grande Arche at La Défense at Nanterre, the Opéra de la Bastille, and the Centre Georges Pompidou. The old markets of Les Halles have been replaced by a multilevel mall.

France's most prestigious educational institutions are located in Paris, the most prominent being the SORBONNE (1257), Collège de France (1530), École polytechnique (1794), and others, and is the site of the Bibliothèque nationale and the ACADÉMIE FRANÇAISE. Theaters include the théâtre de la Comédie-Française, Opéra de Paris Bastille, théâtre de l'Opéra, and the Odéon. Museums besides the Louvre include musée Rodin, musée de l'Art Moderne, and musée d'Orsay.

The history of Paris begins with its founding in the third century B.C.E. by the Parisii, a tribe who settled on the Île de la Cité. The Romans conquered in 52 B.C.E. but Paris was not a center of Roman Gaul. According to tradition, Christianity was introduced in the third century by Saint Denis, and in 451, the city was threatened by the Huns, but was saved, it was said, by the intercession of Saint Geneviève. In 486, the Frankish king Clovis made it his capital. The Capetian kings rebuilt the city, and during the 13th century the population may have reached 100,000. The 14th century was marked by the Hundred Years' War and the plague, but the second half of the 15th century brought peace and prosperity, and in the 16th, King FRANCIS I brought the Renaissance to Paris. A Catholic stronghold, the city was the site of the SAINT BARTHOLOMEW'S DAY MASSACRE in 1572, and only with the reign of HENRY IV did peace return. The Bourbon kings brought classicism to Paris (Invalides, place de la Concorde), illuminated it at night, and made many improvements.

Often a center of rebellion, Paris was at the center of the REVOLUTION OF 1789, and during the reign of NAPOLÉON I, the city's domination over the rest of France increased. The site of the REVOLUTIONS OF 1830 and 1848, Paris, beginning in 1852, was vastly rebuilt. The FRANCO-PRUSSIAN WAR (1870–71) and the Paris COMMUNE uprising (1871) interrupted this process. The THIRD REPUBLIC brought prosperity (Paris Exposition, EIFFEL TOWER, 1889), and during the Belle Époque, the city became a center of modern culture and art. After World War I, Paris enlarged geographically (20 arrondissements) and continued as a center of international culture. Conquered by the Germans in June 1940, Paris was a center of the RESISTANCE. Liberated in 1944, it was fortunately little damaged by the war. In the postwar period, Paris has maintained its reputation as a locus of intellectual, cultural, and artistic life, as well as national (student unrest, May 1968) and international political developments.

See also ÎLE-DE-FRANCE.

## Paris, Prince Henri-Robert d'Orléans, count of (1908–1999)

*pretender to the French throne*

Born in Le Nouvion-en-Thiérache, Prince Henri-Robert d'Orlèans, count of Paris was the son of Jean d'Orléans, duke de Guise (1874–1940) and Isabelle d'Orlèans (1878–1961), both great-grandchildren of King LOUIS-PHILIPPE. Prince Henri-Robert inherited the title "comte de Paris," which had been revived by Louis-Philippe. As claimant to the French throne, the count of Paris went into exile in 1926 upon the death of his uncle, Philippe, duke of Orléans, whose demise made his father heir to the French throne, and settled in Morocco, then Algiers (1942), where he tried to remove Admiral FRANÇOIS DARLAN and assume leadership of the Free French during the war. The opposition of the Americans, however, essentially stopped his plans after Darlan's assassination. The count of Paris returned to France in 1950, following the abrogation of the laws of exile for pretenders to the throne.

## Pâris, Joseph (1684–1770)

*financier*

Born in Moirans, Dauphiné, Joseph Pâris, or Pâris-Duverney as he is known, was entrusted by the count de NOAILLES with the finances of the kingdom of France. Ousted by JOHN LAW, he tried to oppose the latter's "system" in creating a general assembly of stockholders but was finally exiled to Dauphiné. After Law's bankruptcy and flight from France, Pâris-Duverney played an important role in the reorganization of the nation's finances. Also, upon his return from exile, he founded the first French military school, the École Militaire located near the Champ-de-Mars in Paris.

## Parmentier, Antoine-Augustin (1737–1813)

*agronomist, pharmacist*

Born in Montdidier, Antoine-Augustin Parmentier first served as chief apothecary at the INVALIDES, in Paris (1772), and published a work dealing with the chemical aspects of the potato (*Examen chimique de la pomme de terre,* 1773) which he had seen being grown in Germany and recommended its cultivation in France. This study won him a grant from the Besançon Academy to study new forms of vegitation available for human consumption. The author of other studies on the production of wines, grains, chestnuts, and other products, he was named first pharmacist of the army and inspector general of health services (1805–13) and contributed to the promotion of antiviral vaccinations. Parmentier was named to the Academy of Sciences in 1795.

## Parti communiste français See FRENCH COMMUNIST PARTY.

## Parti socialiste See SOCIALIST PARTY.

## Parti socialiste français See SOCIALIST PARTY, FRENCH.

## Pascal, Blaise (1623–1662)

*mathematician, physicist, philosopher*

Considered one of the great minds of Western intellectual history, Blaise Pascal was born in Clermont-Ferrand. His father, who had early recognized his exceptional gifts, oversaw his education and brought the family to live in Paris (1631), where the young Blaise met with scholars. At age 16, he was the author of an "Essai sur les coñiques," in which he put forth what is now known as Pascal's theorem, and invented one of the first adding machines three years later. In 1646, he verified the hypotheses of the Italian physicist Evangelista Torricelli through experiments on barometric pressure and was able to affirm that "Nature abhors a vacuum." (*Expériences nouvelles touchant le vide,* 1647). These principles were later reaffirmed in his treatises *Équilibre des liqueurs* and *Pesanteur de la masse de l'air* (1663). In 1654, in conjunction with the mathematician PIERRE DE FERMAT, Pascal formulated the theory of probability in his famous *Traité du triangle arithmetique.* His methodology always reflected his emphasis on empirical experimentation and his belief that human progress is perpetuated by the accumulation of the knowledge thus gained. Some time before 1647, he came under the influence of JANSENISM and entered the Jansenist community at Port-Royal, where he led a rigorously ascetic life until his death. In 1656, he wrote his famous *18 Lettres provinciales* critiquing that movement. His most positive religious statements appeared posthumously, *Apologie de la réligion chrétienne* (1662), in which he posed the alternatives of potential salvation and eternal damnation ("if you win, you win everything, if you lose, you lose nothing"), and in his last work, *Pensées sur la religion et sur quelques autres sujets* (1670), dealing with original sin, faith, and revelation. His mystical concept of a hidden God appears in his *Lettres à Madamoiselle de Roannez,* and his views on classicism and literature in *L'Art de persuader* (ca. 1657). Pascal, who is ranked among the finest French polemicists, and whose original prose style is much celebrated, is known as one of the most eminent physicists and mathematicians of his age and also as one of the greatest mystical writers in Christian literature.

## Passy, Hippolyte-Philibert (1793–1880)

*economist, political figure*

Born in Garches, Hippolyte-Philibert Passy was elected deputy in 1830 and affirmed his opposition to the colonization of ALGERIA. Minister of finances (1834, 1839–40, 1848–49), and trade (1836), he was a member of the commission that recommended the abolition of slavery (1841). He left public life after the coup d'état of December 2, 1852, which brought Louis-Napoléon Bonaparte (NAPOLÉON III) to full power. In economics, Passy was a proponent of free trade.

## Passy, Frédéric (1822–1912)

*economist, Nobel laureate*

Born in Neuilly-sur-Seine, Frédéric Passy was the nephew of HIPPOLYTE PASSY. Author of works on political economy (*Leçons d'économie politique,* 1861), he is known as the founder of the *Ligue internationale de la paix* (1867) and of the *Société pour l'arbitrage entre les nations* (1870). Passy was awarded the Nobel Peace Prize in 1901.

## Pasteur, Louis (1822–1895)

*chemist, biologist*

Louis Pasteur, the world-renowned scientist who founded the study of microbiology, proved the germ theory of disease, invented the process of pasteurization, and developed important vaccines (rabies), was born in Dole and educated in Paris at the École normale supérieure. His early research was in the area of crystallography, the results themselves forming the basis for stereochemistry. All Pasteur's discoveries, even the most basic, have as their objective some practical application. The first, conducted when he was a professor at Lille, concerned fermentation, the many problems in wine production, and the transformation into vinegar (1863). At this time he discovered the existence of specific microorganisms responsible for all processes of fermentation and decay. He showed that whereas one type could not live without oxygen, the other anaerobic types could be treated by a rapid heating, in a process to become known as pasteurization. The existence of living organisms responsible for chemical reaction and the possibility of life in the absence of oxygen were two hypotheses that were in total opposition to the scientific knowledge of the period. It was also at this

Louis Pasteur *(Library of Congress)*

time that Pasteur's experiments allowed him to refute definitively the prevailing scientific concept of spontaneous generation. Beginning in 1865, because of problems in the silk industry, he became interested in infectious diseases and proved that specific microorganisms were the cause. Studying also sheep (anthrax), then cholera in chickens, and finally rabies, Pasteur discovered with C. É. Chamberland and ÉMILE ROUX that the attenuated bacteria rendered animals immune to diseases: this was the discovery of preventive vaccines. In 1881, assisted by Roux, he gave such vaccines to humans. Pasteur became internationally famous. Convinced that science constituted the way to ameliorate the fate of humankind, Pasteur was an ardent patriot, tireless worker (despite his paralysis), capable experimenter, and gifted with great intuition. Pasteur represents the image of the disinterested, totally devoted scientist. In 1881, he became director of the Institut Pasteur, which still is a center for the study of infectious diseases and other subjects, such as molecular genetics. Pasteur was named to the Academy of Sciences in 1862, and to the ACADÉMIE FRANÇAISE in 1881.

## Pavie, Auguste-Jean-Marie (1847–1925)
*diplomat, explorer*

Born in Dinan, Auguste-Jean-Marie Pavie was a sergeant in the French colonial infantry in Cochin China (1869–70) where he returned, taking part in the construction of the Phnom Penh–Bangkok telegraph line (1879). He served successively as vice consul at Luang Prabang (1886), consul general at Bangkok (1891), and commissioner general of Laos and helped to extend French influence in INDOCHINA, particularly against the claims of Siam (1893, the treaty by which Siam renounced the left bank of the Mekong River). Pavie's explorations enriched knowledge of the regions of Annam, Tonkin, and Yunnan.

## Payen, Anselme (1795–1871)
*chemist*

Born in Paris, Anselme Payen, as a chemist, analyzed numerous food substances, including wheat grain. He isolated the first enzyme, a biological catalyzing agent (1833), and was the first to understand the action of this genre of substances that he called "diastase." His principal work was in industrial chemistry. Payen was named to the Academy of Sciences in 1842.

## Péguy, Charles (1873–1914)
*writer*

Born in Orléans of modest origins, Charles Péguy, who is considered one of the foremost modern Roman Catholic writers, lost his father at a young age (1873) but was able to begin studies on scholarship (1894) at the École normale supérieure, where among his instructors was HENRI BERGSON. Moved by a fervent humanitarianism, Péguy in this period saw the establishment of "a universal socialist republic" as the "only remedy for universal ills." He sided with JEAN JAURÈS during the DREYFUS affair (*Notre Jeunesse*, 1910), but, after 1900, separated from his earlier colleagues as he disapproved of their anticlericalism and antimilitarism. Péguy, in 1900, founded *Cahiers de la quinzaine*, a journal to publish his works along with those of Romain Rolland, Julien Benda, André Saurès, and others and reveal his evolution away from socialism to a mystical nationalism (*Notre Patrie*, 1905). Effectively returning to his Catholic faith, he wrote against modernism and certain French intellectual elements. Suspect to the church, whose conservatism he criticized, and to the Socialists for denouncing pacifism, and somewhat ignored at the time by the general public, Péguy, who appealed in all his writings to the "generation of revenge," was killed in action at the front in World War I, on the eve of the Battle of the Marne.

## Pecqueur, Constantin (1801–1887)
*economist*

Born in Arleux, Constantin Pecqueur initially embraced the ideals of HENRI DE SAINT-SIMON and Saint-Simonism, then those of CHARLES FOURIER, with whom he collaborated on the plan for phalanxes (1832–35). Pecqueur's writings, in which he questions the concept of private property and the concentration of industrial wealth, make him a representative of a spiritually oriented collectivism (*Des Améliorations matérielles dans leurs rapport avec la liberté*, 1939; *Catéchisme communiste*, 1849).

## Pélissier, Aimable-Jean-Jacques (1794–1864)
*marshal of France*

Born in Maromme, Aimable-Jean-Jacques Pélissier, after serving in the military expedition to Spain (1823) and Morea (1828–29) and in the conquest of ALGERIA (1839–54), was named to lead the French army in the Crimea, replacing Marshal FRANÇOIS CANROBERT as French commander in the CRIMEAN WAR (1884–1885). The capture of Sevastopol (September 1855) earned Pélissier the marshal's baton and the title duke of Malakoff. Vice president of the Senate at the beginning of the SECOND EMPIRE and ambassador to Great Britain (1858), he spent his later years as governor of Algeria (1860–64).

## Pelletier, Madeleine (1874–1939)
*political figure, feminist*

Born in Paris to a working-class family, Madeleine Pelletier, because of her intelligence and talent, attended medical school and became a physician specializing in treatment of the mentally ill. A committed feminist, she served as secretary to a feminist organization, Solidarité des femmes (1906), and sought to connect feminism with socialism, working in collaboration with JULES GUESDE and others. She founded a journal, *La Suffragiste* (1908), in which she presented her radical views on sexual liberation and various topics and, after WORLD WAR I, turned to anarchism. Arrested for performing abortions, Pelletier died while in prison.

## Pelletier, Pierre-Joseph (1788–1842)
*pharmacist, botanist*

Born in Clichy-la-Garenne, Pierre-Joseph Pelletier, in his researches, extracted a substance (emetine) from the root of the ipeca plant to be used in the treatment of internal disorders (1817). He also, through his research with Joseph Caventou on cholesterol, discovered strychnine (1818), brucine (1819), veratine, cevadic acid, and quinine (1820). The two also studied vegetal physiology, introducing the word *chlorophyll* (1818). Pelletier isolated the components narceine and thebaine in opium (1832) and did intense work on dyes and coloring agents, techniques of gilding, and the nature of resins. He was named to the Academy of Sciences in 1840.

## Penthièvre, Louis-Jean-Marie de Bourbon, duke de (1725–1793)
*admiral*

Born in Rambouillet, Louis-Jean-Marie de Bourbon, duke de Penthièvre, was the son of the count of Toulouse and served as admiral (1734) and as governor of Brittany, distinguishing himself particularly at the Battle of Fontenoy (1745). Possessed of an immense fortune and known as a patron of the arts, he was the father of LOUISE-MARIE ADÉLAIDE, who married the DUKE D'ORLÉANS (PHILIPPE ÉGALITÉ). He also had a son, the prince of Lamballe (died 1768), whose wife, Marie-Thérèse, was killed in the SEPTEMBER MASSACRES (1792) during the REVOLUTION OF 1789.

## Perdiguier, Agricol (1805–1875)
*worker, political figure*

Born in Morières-les-Avignon, Agricol Perdiguier, known also as Avignonnais la Vertu, was a master carpenter who, as a journeyman, had worked throughout France. He recorded his experiences in *Mémoires d'un compagnon* (1854), a valuable document describing the daily life of French workers in the first half of the 19th century, shortly before the beginning of the industrial era. A committed pacifist, he tried to reconcile the two "duties" (to self and to society) that he believed were in a perpetual, and sometimes armed, conflict. In 1839, he opened in the Faubourg Saint-Antoine in Paris a public school for workers and published his *Livre du compagnonnage*, and fought for the rights of the societies of craftsmen and journeymen (compagnonnages). Elected deputy for the department of Seine in 1848, he had to flee to Switzerland after the coup d'état of December 2, 1851. Perdiguier had support for his ideas from GEORGE SAND and LOUIS BLANC.

## Pereire, Jacob-Émile (1800–1875)
*businessman*

Born in BORDEAUX, Jacob-Émile Pereire came to Paris in 1822 and worked at first as an exchange broker, while adhering for a time to the ideas of HENRI DE SAINT-SIMON and contributing to the Saint-Simonian journals *Globe* and *National*. After dedicating himself to the construction, development, and administration of the first French railroad lines (Paris–Saint-Germain-en-Laye, 1835; North, Lyon, and Midi lines), he formed a company for long-term loans to industries, the Crédit mobilier, an innovation that brought him into competition with the ROTHSCHILD FAMILY. Shortly after, Pereire obtained control of the Compagnie Générale Maritime, which he transformed into the Compagnie Générale Transatlantique. A deputy from 1863 to 1869, he lost his role as a business leader after the failure and liquidation of the Crédit Mobilier, which had financed much of the industrial development during the SECOND EMPIRE.

## Pergaud, Louis (1882–1914)
*writer*

Born in Belmont, Doubs, Louis Pergaud, who was raised in Franche-Comté, where he became a rural schoolteacher, always kept in close touch with the rustic world. Coming to Paris in 1907, he soon became a manager working in the city's fine arts department. His literary career began with his collection of poems, *L'Aube* (1904), and *L'Herbe d'avril* (1908). But it was in his plain, fresh, honest, and humorous stories about the animals and people of the countryside that his talent became evident. His stories of animals, *De Goupil à Margot* (1910) and *Le Roman de Miraut, chien de chasse* (1913) are sensitive studies of an anthropomorphic animal psychology that is at the heart of his realistic descriptions of rural life. In *La Guerre des boutons* (brought to the screen in 1936 by Jack Deroy and in 1962 by Yves Robert), Perraud presents in epic verse the struggles of two groups of street children, from two dif-

ferent villages. Pergaud was killed in battle during WORLD WAR I.

## Perier, Casimir (1777–1832)
*political figure*

Casimir Perier, the son of CLAUDE PERIER, was born in Grenoble. Director of his father's bank and regent of the Bank of France, after 1817 he served a number of times as deputy in the National Assembly. Representing the liberal opposition, he took a position against the policies of the governments of JEAN-BAPTISTE VILLÈLE and then JULES DE POLIGNAC, and supported LOUIS-PHILIPPE during the REVOLUTION OF 1830. President of the Chamber of Deputies and leader of the parti de la Résistance under the JULY MONARCHY, in 1831 he became leader of the cabinet and interior minister. With the hope of favoring the development of business, he followed a policy of repression toward the opposition and manifestations of social unrest (in particular, during the silk-workers' revolt in LYON, November–December 1831). He died of cholera, and his son and grandson took the name of CASIMIR-PERIER.

## Perier, Claude (1742–1801)
*industrialist, banker*

Claude Perier, a cloth manufacturer in Vizille and Grenoble, where he was born, during the REVOLUTION OF 1789 acquired the rights to a mine at Anzin. An associate of the banker JEAN DE PERRÉGAUX, he helped to finance the coup d'état of 18 Brumaire (see NAPOLÉON I) and the establishment of the Bank of France (1801). His sons continued his businesses.

## Perrault, Charles (1623–1703)
*writer, political figure, author of "Mother Goose"*

Born in Paris, the brother of CLAUDE PERRAULT, Charles Perrault, a high-level bureaucrat and protégé of JEAN-BAPTISTE COLBERT, published parodies (*L'Énéide burlesque*, 1648; *Les Murs de Troie ou l'Origine du burlesque*, 1649) and love stories (*Dialogue de l'amour et de l'amitié*, 1660; *Le Miroir ou la Métamorphose d'Orante*, 1660) before taking part in the celebrated debate between the "Ancients" and the

"Moderns" at the ACADÉMIE FRANÇAISE, of which he was a member (1671). His polemic poem, *Le Siècle de Louis le Grand* (1687), then his *Paralleles des Anciens et des Modernes* (1688–89), debated by NICO-LAS BOILEAU, presented and codified his arguments criticizing the principle of authority and affirming that progress is possible in art just as in the sciences, and he stressed the superiority of the "century of Louis" to the "century of Augustus." Perrault's *Histoires ou Contes du temps passé* (called also *Contes de ma mère l'Oye*, "Mother Goose Tales," 1997) guaranteed his fame and contributed to the popularization of fairy tales as a literary genre.

## Perrault, Claude (1613–1688)
*architect, physician, physicist*

Born in Paris, the brother of CHARLES PERRAULT, Claude Perrault, a translator of the works of the ancient Roman architect Vitruvius, has been credited with the plan for the LOUVRE colonnade, the Paris Observatory, and the château of Sceaux for JEAN-BAPTISTE COLBERT. A naturalist, Perrault was a supporter of Italian physicist Giovanni Borelli's iatromechanism (*Mécanique des animaux*). He was named to the Academy of Sciences in 1666.

## Perréal, Jean (ca. 1450–1530)
*painter, miniaturist*

Born in either Paris or Lyon, Jean Perréal, who is also known as Jehan de Paris, worked in the service of that city (1483) before painting for kings CHARLES VIII, LOUIS XII, and FRANCIS I. Perréal made several visits to Italy (1494, 1502, and 1509), before dedicating an important part of his activities to organizing "entrées" and festivals for the royal court. He also participated in a project for building the tomb of Philibert II of Savoy and Margaret of Austria, whom he served as court painter. Considered one of the most representative painters of his generation, Perréal created the medallion portraits of ANNE OF BRITTANY and Louis XII, and it is as a miniaturist (*Portrait de Charles VIII; Portrait de Anne de Bretagne, Portrait de Pierre Sala*) that he excelled, showing a profound sense of naturalism, design, and style. He also produced a noted illustrated frontispiece for the poems of JEAN DE MEUNG (ca. 1516).

## Perrégaux, Jean-Frédéric, count de (1744–1808)
*banker*

Born in Neuchâtel, Switzerland, Jean-Frédéric, count de Perrégaux, set himself up as a banker in Paris and, during the REVOLUTION OF 1789, speculated on the assignats, the new currency issued by the National Assembly. Founder of an accounting fund in Paris and an associate of CLAUDE PERIER, in 1796 he became a senator and regent of the Bank of France.

## Perret, Auguste (1874–1954)
*architect*

Born in Ixelles, Belgium, Auguste Perret, who became one of the most important pioneers of modern French architecture, was the son of a Communard exile. He enrolled in the École des beaux-arts in Paris, where he studied architecture with his brothers Gustave (1876–1952) and Claude (1880–1960), who later became his associates. Perret was one of the earliest advocates of the use of reinforced concrete as a building material, and his apartment building (1903) in the rue Franklin in Paris was the first residential building constructed of that material. He also was preoccupied with classical proportions, a link with earlier architects, as exemplified in his church of Notre-Dame at Le Raincy. As director of the postwar rebuilding of Le Havre (1949–56), Perret designed a gridlike plan based on classical proportions, with a broad central axis, large squares, and stylistically uniform prefabricated houses. In Paris, some of Perret's works include the Théâtre des Champs-Élysées (1911–13), a large building on the rue de Ponthieu (1906), L'École normale de musique (1929), and the Musée des Travaux publics (1937).

## Perret, Jacques (1901–1992)
*writer, Resistance fighter*

Born in Troppes, Seine-et-Oise, Jacques Perret, after spending some adventurous years in Guyana and in the United States (which inspired his exciting *Histoires sous le vent*, 1944), returned to France and made his debut as a novelist with *Roucou* (1936), followed by *Ernest le Rebelle* in 1937. Called to the military in 1939, he was taken prisoner, escaped then joined the RESISTANCE in the *maquis* (underground). In the guise of a novel, he recalls his life as a prisoner and his attempts to escape (*Le Caporal épinglé*, 1947) and his experiences as a Resistance fighter (*Bande à part*, 1951), in which he realistically describes the day-to-day existence living among men who were neither heroes nor villains, but just ordinary individuals. This sensitive and amusing work was followed by other stories and accounts.

## Perrin, Jean (1870–1942)
*physicist, Nobel laureate*

Born in Lille, Jean Perrin was one of the promoters of atomic theory, although more from the conceptual than the experimental viewpoint. His studies (1895) proving that cathodic rays are constituted of corpuscles carrying a negative electric charge put an end to the controversy over the existence of the electron. His research on the sedimentation of colloidal solutions and Brownian motion would yield differing results, all very precise and always in agreement with the determination of the Avogadro number, and offered new and irrefutable proof of the existence of atoms (1908). Perrin also worked on X rays and conduction through gases, and contributed to the development of scientific knowledge by the creation of the Center for Research (palais de la Découverte) in Paris (1937), and his participation in the founding of the Centre nationale de la recherce scientifique. Perrin was named to the Academy of Sciences in 1923 and was awarded the Nobel Prize in physics in 1926.

## Perrot, Jules (1810–1892)
*dancer, choreographer*

Born in LYON, Jules Perrot studied under leading dancers and debuted at the Opéra de Paris, accompanying the celebrated dancer Maria Taglioni (1830). There he demonstrated his exceptional talent, strength, and agility (*Flore et Zéphire*). Having met the dancer Carlotta Grisi in 1833, Perrot made several tours through Europe with her before returning triumphantly to Paris. Following this, he was named first dancer and ballet master at Her Majesty's Theater in London (1842–48), where he choreographed a number of works. But it was at the Imperial Theatre in St. Petersburg, Russia, that he reached the height of his career (1849–59). An incomparable interpretor of dance during the romantic period, Perrot was called by his enthusiastic admirer, THÉOPHILE GAUTIER, "Perrot the airborne."

## Perroux, François (1903–1987)
*economist*

Born in LYON, François Perroux was the founder of the Institut de science économique appliquée (1944), professor at the COLLÈGE DE FRANCE (1955) and, after 1960, served as director of the Institut d'études et de développement économique et social. While critical of simplified economic systems and maintaining his confidence in the dynamic character of the capitalist system, Perroux proposed a third path. He introduced alongside the private capitalist sector a state sector and recognized the necessity of the intervention of certain public powers in economic and social matters. He saw in the "community of work" (an enterprise considered to be completely organized) a way to eliminate the conflict between workers and capitalists and to promote the human element. Perroux published *Le Problème de profit* (1926), *Capitalisme et Communauté de travail* (1938), *Cours d'économie politique* (1939), *La Valeur* (1943), *Théorie générale du progress* (1957), and *Pour une philosophie de nouveau développement* (1981).

## Persigny, Jean-Gilbert-Victor Fialin, duke de (1808–1872)
*political figure*

Born in Saint-Germain-l'Espinasse, Jean-Gilbert-Victor Fialin, duke de Persigny was dismissed from the military because of his republican views and, shortly after, became a Bonapartist, befriending Louis-Napoléon Bonaparte (1834), whom he helped during the failed attempts at Strasbourg (1836) and Boulogne (1840) to seize political control. Imprisoned some time later, then released, he supported Napoléon's candidacy for the presidency (December 1848), was elected to the Legislative Assembly (May 1849), and took part in the coup d'état of December 2, 1851. NAPOLÉON III, as emperor, named Persigny minister of the interior (1852–54, 1860–63) and ambassador to Great Britain (1855–58, 1859–60). The relative liberalization of the regime, however, forced Persigny to leave politics. He left his *Mémoires* (published 1896).

## Pétain, Philippe (1856–1951)
*military and political figure*

A hero of WORLD WAR I who was later condemned as a traitor for having led the pro-German regime at VICHY, Philippe Pétain was born in Cauchy-à-la-Tour and educated at SAINT-CYR and the École supérieure de Guerre in Paris. Named general in August 1914, he took part in the Battles of the Marne (September 1914), at Artois (May 1915), and at Champagne (September 1915) before being called to defend VERDUN (February 1916). Pétain's greatest victory was at Verdun, where the French retained the fortresses against great German odds during World War I. In 1917, he also issued the brutal order condemning to death a large number of mutineers in the French ranks. After Chemin des Dames, he replaced General GEORGES NIVELLE as commander in chief and was subordinate only to Marshal FERDINAND FOCH. Pétain was made a marshal of France in November 1918 and, after the war, held various high-command positions, including command in the Rif war in North Africa (1925). In 1934, he became minister of war and, in 1939, ambassador to Spain. In May 1940, during WORLD WAR II, he was recalled by PAUL REYNAUD to serve as vice president of the Council of Ministers. At that point, Pétain already considered the war to be lost, and thus opposed Reynaud's plan to continue the struggle in the colonies. Becoming president of the Council of Ministers at Bordeaux in June 1940, Pétain ordered an armistice. On July 1, he set up a government at Vichy and, on July 10, was given full powers by the National Assembly there, which declared him head of the French state. Pétain attempted, with his prime minister PIERRE LAVAL, to maintain a French nation within a Europe dominated by Nazi Germany. But their fascist-oriented government became notorious for its collaboration with Hitler, whom Pétain met through the arrangement of Laval, at Montoire in October 1940. The Vichy regime ruled only with Germany's approval, appointing all government officials, con-

Philippe Pétain *(Library of Congress)*

trolling the press, and making arbitrary arrests. The government also passed anti-Semitic laws and rounded up many Jews and others who were deported to German concentration camps. After the Allies landed in France in 1944, Pétain went to Germany, then Switzerland. He returned to France after the war to stand trial for treason. In August 1945, he was found guilty and condemned to death by the High Court, but the sentence was commuted to life imprisonment. He was moved to the Île d'Yeu off the coast of Brittany, where he died.

## Pétion, Anne-Alexandre (1770–1818)
## (Anne-Alexandre Sabès Petion)
*Haitian statesman, general, president*

Born in Port-au-Prince, Anne-Alexandre Sabès, known as Pétion, was a mulatto French officer who joined the insurgents of the French colony of Saint-Domingue against the expedition led by General CHARLES LECLERC (1802). Pétion was, with JEAN-JACQUES DESSALINES and HENRY CHRISTOPHE, one of the principal generals responsible for routing the French in 1803. He contributed to the writing of the republican constitution of Haiti (1806) and was named president in 1807, a position that he held until his death.

## Pétion de Villeneuve, Jérome (1756–1794)

*political figure*

Born in Chartres, where he was an attorney, Jérome Pétion de Villeneuve was elected as a deputy for the Third Estate to the ESTATES GENERAL (1789) and was a member of the antislavery Société des amis des Noirs and the JACOBIN Club. Mayor of the COMMUNE OF PARIS (November 1791–November 1792) during the REVOLUTION OF 1789, first president of the Convention (September 1792), and member of the first Committee of Public Safety, he joined the GIRONDINS. During their elimination (early June 1793), he attempted, with FRANÇOIS BUZOT and CHARLES BARBAROUX, a FEDERALIST INSURRECTION in Normandy and, having failed, committed suicide.

## Petipa, Marius (1818–1910)

*dancer, choreographer*

Marius Petipa, whose works represent the culmination of classical ballet, was born in MARSEILLE, the brother of the dancer Joseph-Lucien Petipa and the son of the dancer and choreographed Jean Petipa, with whom he studied. Marius Petipa debuted in Brussels and soon appeared in Paris at the COMÉDIE-FRANÇAISE (1840) with the noted Carlotta Grisi (1840). He then danced and choreographer in Bordeaux, then in Madrid, where he studied Spanish dance. Invited to be first dancer at the Imperial Theater in St. Petersburg, Russia (1847), he later succeeded JULES PERROT as ballet master (1859). Thereafter began a long career as a choreographer in Russia, which he would never leave. Petipa's works, often inspired by the romantic spirit,

include *Don Quixote, La Bayadère,* and, among his masterpieces, *La Vestale, La Belle au bois dormant* (*Sleeping Beauty*), *Cinderella, Bluebeard, The Seasons,* and *Swan Lake.* Born of the synthesis of French technique, Italian virtuosity, and Russian lyricism, the compositions of Petipa would influence many later artists, including those of Sergey Diaghilev's Ballets-russes.

## Petit, Roland (1924–   )

*dancer, choreographer*

Born in Paris, Roland Petit, who began his career at the Paris Opéra, where he studied under SERGE LIFAR, served successively as the lead of the Ballets des Champs-Élysées (1945) and the Ballets de Paris (1948), where he produced his first choreography (*Les Forains, Le Jeune Homme et la Mort, Le Loup*). Petit then began to work in cinema, choreographing several Hollywood musicals. He returned to France in 1954 and reorganized his troupe, serving as dance director for the Opéra de Paris (1970), then for the Ballet nationale de Marseille. His choice of music (Chopin, Liszt, MILHAUD, Schumann) and designs for his sets reveal his eclecticism. Roland Petit married the dancer ZIZI JEANMAIRE, who with him assumed the direction of the Casino de Paris (1969).

## Peyrefitte, Alain (1925–1999)

*political figure*

Born in Najac, Averyron, Alain Peyrefitte was a Gaullist secretary of state from 1958, secretary-general of the UNION DES DÉMOCRATES POUR LA RÉPUBLIQUE (UDR) (1972–73), several times minister, in particular minister of information (1962–66), national education (1967–May 1968), and justice (1977–1981). In that latter post, he put forth the law of "Sécurité et liberté," which legislated, among other things, the control of personal identification carried by each citizen (1980). During his tenure as minister of national education, the student uprising of MAY 1968 occurred. Peyrefitte authored several essays, including *Quand la Chine s'éveillera . . .* (1973), *Le Mal français* (1976) and *La Tragédie chinoise* (1990). Peyrefitte was elected to the ACADÉMIE FRANÇAISE in 1977 and the Académie des sciences morales et politiques in 1987.

## Peyrefitte, Roger (1907–2000)
*novelist*

Born in Castres, Roger Peyrefitte, after a religious education and a diplomatic career that ended at the close of WORLD WAR II, began his literary career with a novel, *Les Amitiés particulières* (1944), in which was depicted adolescent homosexual evolution among the graduates of a religious school. It was followed by *Les Amours singulières* (1949). After a break in his work, Peyrefitte began his documentary and satirical writings. Dedicated to government institutions (*Les Ambassades*, 1951; *La Fin des ambassades*, 1953), to religious issues (*Les Clefs de Saint-Pierre*, 1955; *Les Chevaliers de Malte*, 1957), or social and moral questions (*Les Fils de la lumière*, a study of freemasonry, 1961; *Les Juifs*, 1965), these successful and also controversial works underscore the ignominies of societies that the author sensed as "marginal." Peyrefitte is also the author of a biographical novel on Alexander the Great (1977–81).

## Peyronnet, Charles-Ignace, count de (1778–1854)
*political figure*

Born in BORDEAUX, Charles-Ignace, count de Peyronnet (or Peyronet) opposed NAPOLÉON I and the FIRST EMPIRE. In 1815, he went over to the Bourbons and became an Ultra deputy (1820). Named guardian of the royal seals in the government of JEAN-BAPTISTE DE VILLÈLE (1831–38), Peyronnet was one of the principal instigators of the most reactionary laws of the Restoration: the limitation on freedom of the press (1822), the law of sacrilege (1825), the law on the right of seniority, and the law of "justice and love" (1827), of which PIERRE ROYER-COLLARD remarked that one could replace these provisions with a single article: "the print-shop is abolished in France." As minister of the interior in the JULES DE POLIGNAC cabinet (1829–30), Peyronnet took part in the editing and signing of the four ordinances of Saint-Cloud (July 25, 1830) that unleashed the REVOLUTION OF 1830. Condemned by the new government, he was amnestied in 1836.

## Pflimlin, Pierre (1907–2000)
*political figure*

Born in Roubaix, Pierre Pflimlin served as a member of two Constituent Assemblies (1945, 1946), as an MRP (MOUVEMENT RÉPUBLICAIN POPULAIRE) deputy to the National Assembly (1946), and was assigned various portfolios under the FOURTH REPUBLIC. President of the MRP (1956–59), he was called to lead the Council of Ministers during the CRISIS OF MAY 1958 in Algiers. He resigned with his government after May 29 and was named minister of state in the cabinet of CHARLES DE GAULLE (June 1958–January 1959) and as minister in charge of cooperation in the first ministry of GEORGES POMPIDOU (April–May 1962). Mayor of STRASBOURG (1959–83), he served as president of the Consultative Assembly of the Council of Europe (1963–66), then of the Assembly of European Communities (1984–87).

## Philip II the Bold (1342–1404)
## (Philippe II le Hardi)
*duke of Burgundy*

Born in Pontoise, Philip II the Bold, duke of Burgundy, was the son of JEAN II, king of France, and Queen Jeanne de Boulogne. His conduct at the Battle of Poitiers (1363) earned him his sobriquet and the duchy of Burgundy (1363), where he founded the second Capetian dynasty. In 1369 he married Marguerite de Mâle (daughter of Louis de Mâle and widow of Philippe de Rouvres), which brought him Flanders, where he ended a revolt with the Peace of Tournai (1385). Upon the death of his brother, CHARLES V of France (1380), Philip the Bold served as one of the regents for CHARLES VI but was forced from power in 1385. In 1392, he returned to the government, where he opposed his nephew LOUIS D'ORLÉANS. Philip the Bold was the patron of the Dutch sculptor Claus Sluter. He was the father of JEAN THE FEARLESS.

## Philip III the Good (1419–1467)
### (Philippe III le Bon)
*duke of Burgundy*

Born in Dijon, Philip III the Good, duke of Burgundy, was the son of JEAN THE FEARLESS, duke of Burgundy, and Margaret of Bavaria. To avenge his father's assassination, he allied himself with the English and signed the Treaty of Troyes (1420), which disinherited the Dauphin (the future CHARLES VII of France). After having fought against the Dauphin, however, Philippe reconciled and signed the Peace of Arras (1435), which gave him the towns of the Somme and the dispensation of vassalage for Flanders. Master of Burgundy, Franche-Comté, Flanders, Artois, and the Belgian provinces, he became one of the most powerful rulers in Europe. He suppressed personal freedoms but was considered a good administrator, as he created the General Estates, a court of justice, and a high council. Philip the Good was a patron of the arts, supporting a number of artists (Van Eyck, Ockeghem).

## Philip VI (1294–1350)
### (Philippe de Valois)
*king of France*

King of France (1328–50) and the first monarch of the Valois dynasty, Philip VI de Valois was born in Nogent-le-Roi, the son of Charles de Valois and Margaret of Sicily, the nephew of King Philip IV the Fair. He married Jeanne of Burgundy and, when King Charles IV died without issue, he was recognized as king by the barons of the kingdom. The barons had rejected Philippe d'Evreux (also a nephew of Philip IV), and especially Edward III of England, grandson, through his mother, of Philip IV. Philip VI was closer because he was the oldest of the claimants as well as a French prince. He recognized the rights to Navarre of Philippe d'Evreux's wife, JEANNE DE NAVARRE, the daughter of Louis X of France (1328). The campaign that Philip VI undertook in Flanders to support his vassal, count Louis de Nevers, against his rebellious subjects ended with his victory at Cassel (1328). Edward III gave him homage for Gascony and Guyenne in 1329, but in 1337, dissatisfied with Philip's encroachments in Guyenne and his intrigues with his Scottish enemies, Edward rose against Philip and renewed his claim to the French throne. This marked the beginning of the HUNDRED YEARS' WAR. Edward III, allied with the Holy Roman Emperor Louis of Bavaria, and especially with Flanders, won the naval battle at L'Ecluse (1340) and subsequently invaded France (1346). Defeated at Crécy (1346), Philip concluded a treaty after the fall of Calais (1347). Besides the war, his reign was marked by a grave economic crisis, famines, and the great plague (1348) that ravaged Europe. He enlarged the royal domains by the additions of the counties of Valois, Chartres, Maine, and Anjou, and by the purchase of Dauphiné and Montpellier (1349). Philip VI was the father of King JEAN II.

## Philippe de Vitry (1291–1361)
*humanist, composer, musical theorist*

Born in Vitry, and known also as Philippus de Vitriaco, Philippe de Vitry was a friend and adviser to the heir to the throne and held important posts at the courts of kings PHILIP VI and JEAN II THE GOOD. He was bishop of Meaux (1351), and being most educated and cultured, had relationships with the intellectual elite of his time, notably with Petrarch, and can perhaps be considered one of the precursors of French humanism. The numerous treatises, transcribed from his lectures (*Liber musicalium, Ars contrapuncti,* and *Ars nova musicae,* ca. 1325) show the importance of his role in the development of a "new art," which, in substituting for the ars antiqua, would revolutionize music at the end of the 14th century. He is known for a theory of notations and counterpoint, and his ideas foreshadow the melodic and rhythmic styles of the Renaissance. A musician and poet, Philippe de Vitry composed only a few works of his own. A dozen of his motets are known, and some parts of the *Roman de Fauvel* are attributed to him.

## Piaf, Édith (1915–1963)
*singer*

Born on a sidewalk in Paris, Édith Giovanna Gassion, or Édith Piaf as she is known, was the daughter of an acrobat and an Italian café singer. Her childhood was difficult and unhappy, and she spent a period of time with her grandmother, who ran a brothel in Bernay, Normandy. Poor diet and meningitis left her blind until age seven, her sight being restored, she claimed, after a visit to the shrine of St. Thérèse of Lisieux. For years she made a living entertaining as a street singer. In 1935, she was noticed by impresario Louis Leplée, who offered her a contract and changed her name to "Piaf" (Parisian slang for sparrow). It was the beginning of a brilliant career (she soon became known through radio, the music hall, and recordings) that led eventually to her becoming a celebrated star in both Europe and the United States. Her powerful, inflected voice, interpretation, and instinct for music make her a great figure in the history of song. Her recordings date from 1936 up to her last recorded song, "L'Homme de Berlin," in 1963. "La Vie en Rose," a song from the film *Neuf Garçons et un Coeur,* is one of her most famous, along with "Les Amants de Paris," "Hymne à l'amour," "Non, je ne regrette rien," "Mon Dieu," and "Milord," several of which she composed. In 1940, she starred in the play *Le Bel Indifférent,* written for her by JEAN COCTEAU. Piaf, who served in the RESISTANCE during World War II, and later inspired such talents as YVES MONTAND, CHARLES AZNAVOUR, and others, had a period of happiness in her marriage to the boxer MARCEL CERDAN, who unfortunately died in an airplane accident in 1949.

## Picabia, Francis  (1879–1953)
*painter and writer*

Born in Paris, Francis Picabia, who is associated with several avant-garde movements, studied at several studios and was especially influenced by ALFRED SISLEY. Up to 1907, he painted impressionist landscapes, then went over to cubism (*Caoutchouc,* 1908, *Udnie ou la danse,* 1913). In 1913, he made his first visit to New York City, where he enjoyed success, but his works, exhibited at the Armory Show, also provoked controversy. He returned again in 1915 with MARCEL DUCHAMP, with whom, along with Man Ray, he had proposed a "pre-Dada" style. At this time, until the early 1920s, Picabia produced another distinctive body of work, in which the human form is drawn in the style of mechanical illustrations (*Paroxysme de la douleur, M'amenez-y*). This iconoclastic spirit is found in *391,* the dadaist

magazine Picaba published between 1917 and 1924. After 1924, he broke completely with the dadaists, including ANDRÉ BRETON, and began a period of expressionism (*La Femme au monocle*), worked on collages (*Les Centimètres*), and helped to create a collaborative performance piece with music by ERIK SATIE. In 1928, he retired to the Midi and returned to figurative painting until 1945. Picaba's writings (*Poèmes et dessins de la fille née sans mère,* 1918; *Pensée sans langage,* 1919) are also expressions of his free, unfettered, and nondogmatic style. A number of Picabia's theories from the dada period became the basis for the tenets of neodadaism, pop art, and conceptual art.

## Picard, Émile  (1856–1941)
*mathematician*

Among the numerous studies that Émile Picard, who was born and educated in Paris, began were those involving uniform and multiform analytical functions and the functions of several complex variables. His theorem (1879), dealing with normal grouping, constitutes the "Picard Cycle," which makes a classification of regular analytical functions. He also worked with differential linear equations (1883) and simple integrals attached to algebraic surfaces (1885), and helped to create algebraic geometry. He discovered the method of successive approximations applied to differential equations (1890), and studied the method, used today in electronics, that consists of the replacement of differential equations by those with finite differences (1899). Picard was named to the Academy of Sciences in 1889 and to the ACADÉMIE FRANÇAISE in 1924.

## Picard, Jean  (1620–1682)
*astronomer, geodesist*

Born in La Flèche, abbot Jean Picard, a scientist, invented, with A. Auzout, the micrometer, which measured the apparent dimensions of celestial bodies and was a great aid in the development of astronomical telescopes. Thanks to this invention, Picard could measure with great precision the arc of the meridian between Paris and Amiens and from it deduce a good estimation of the terrestrial ray, which in turn allowed Isaac Newton to put in place definitively his theory of universal gravitation. Picard was also able to make an estimation of the speed of the movement of sound. Additionally, he worked toward producing a map of France. He was named to the Academy of Sciences in 1666.

## Picardy

Picardy is a former province of France, with its capital at Amiens. It comprises Vermandois, Amiénois, Valois, Santerre, Ponthieu, Boulannais, and Thiérache. Occupied by King Philippe Auguste in 1185, the region was definitively united to the crown in 1477. Picardy is situated in the Paris basin, between the Canche, Oise, Béthune, and Thérain Rivers, and is bordered by the English Channel and NORMANDY. It is still an agricultural region, with various industries. During WORLD WAR I (1914–18), a number of important battles took place in Picardy (Somme, Montdidier).

## Pichegru, Charles  (1761–1804)
*military figure*

Born in Arbois, Charles Pichegru, who fought in the American War of Independence, served during the REVOLUTION OF 1789 as commander in chief of the Army of the Rhine and later of the Army of the North, conquering the Low Countries (1794–95). Coming over to the royalist cause, he lost his command (1796), but then was elected to the Council of Five Hundred in 1797. Deported to Guyana after the coup d'état of 18 Fructidor Year V (September 4, 1797), which brought the republican element of the Directory to power, he escaped to England, then secretly returned to France. In February 1804, he conspired with GEORGES CADADOUL (see CHOUAN-NERIE) in a plot against Napoléon Bonaparte (see NAPOLÉON I), but was denounced and arrested, and later (April 6, 1804) found strangled in his cell.

## Picquart, Georges  (1854–1914)
*military figure*

Born in Strasbourg, Georges Picquart, after serving in ALGERIA, Tonkin, and Annam, was named chief of intelligence on the General Staff (1895). Convinced of the innocence of ALFRED DREYFUS (and the guilt of CHARLES ESTERHAZY), he fought for a reexamination of the case but was ordered to abandon that cause and was transferred shortly after to Tunisia (1896). After Dreyfus was exonerated, Picquart was proven correct and was promoted to general and named minister of war in the cabinet of GEORGES CLEMENCEAU (1906–09).

See also ZOLA, EMILE.

## Pieyre de Mandriagues, André  (1909–1991)
*writer*

Born in Paris, André Pieyre de Mandriagues, after traveling in Europe and the Mediterranean to pursue his interest in Etruscan art and civilization, wrote his accounts in prose poetry (*L'Âge de craie*, 1935; *Dans les Années sordides*, 1943; *Hédéra ou la Persistance de l'amour pendant une reverie*, 1945; *Astyanax*, 1957). He then composed surrealistic collections in which he emerges as a master of the horror story (*Le Musée noir*, 1946; *Soleil des loups*, 1951). Other writings include *Marbre* (1953), a story of pagan Italy; *Les Lis de mer* (1956), set on a Sardinian beach; *La Motocyclette* (1963); and *La Marge* (1967). His *Bona: l'amour et la pienture* is a fascinating and unusual book about his wife, the painter Bona Tibertelli.

## Pigalle, Jean-Baptiste  (1714–1785)
*sculptor*

Known for his lively naturalistic style, Jean-Baptiste Pigalle, whose subjects ranged from the intimate to the formal, was born in Paris, where he studied with some of the leading sculptors of the period. He used his award from the prix de Rome to study in Italy (1734–39) and became later the protégé of Mme de POMPADOUR, who gave him numerous commissions (*L'Amour et l'Amitié*, 1758). He completed the monument in the Place Royale and one in honor of LOUIS XV in Reims (destroyed in 1792, later replaced). In the tomb of the Maréchal de Saxe (1753–76, church of Saint-Thomas, Strasbourg), and of the duke d'Harcourt (1774, Notre-Dame de

Paris), Pigalle demonstrated his taste for grandiose and theatrical effects, as well as a profound tendency towards the baroque. But in his portraits (*Diderot, Voltaire,* nude statue of *Voltaire*), he leaned to a more personal and direct presentation of his subjects.

## Pilâtre de Rozier, Jean-François (1756–1785)
*physicist, aeronaut*

Jean-François Pilâtre de Rozier, the first person to ascend with an untethered balloon, was born in Metz. The author of a work on the nature of gas and a founder of the Musée de Paris, the first museum of science and a meeting place for the leading scientific minds of the period, Pilâtre de Rozier was interested in balloon flight. After the success of the MONTGOLFIER BROTHERS, he convinced King LOUIS XVI to allow him and the marquis d'Arlandes to make this first manned flight (November 1783) between the château de la Muette, in the Bois de Boulogne, and the Butte-aux-Cailles, across the Seine, landing about 8,200 meters from the starting point in about 20 minutes. Two years later, Pilâtre de Rozier attempted to travel across the English Channel in a hot-air balloon attached to a hydrogen one. But when a spark ignited the hydrogen, the balloons exploded and the passengers fell to their death near the French shore.

## Pillot, Jean-Jacques (1809–1877)
*socialist writer, political figure*

Born in Vaux-la-Valette, Charente, Jean-Jacques Pillot was an organizer of workers' movements in Paris, and he published several writings in which he presented his revolutionary ideas in a proletarian spirit. These include *La Communauté n'est pas une utopie* (1841), an exposition of communist ideas from ancient times until the 19th century, and *La Tribune du peuple* (1859), a critique of the Catholic Church. After the suppression of the REVOLUTION OF 1848, he emigrated to Brazil. On his return to France, Pillot was elected a member of the revolutionary Paris COMMUNE (1871). After its suppression, he was condemned and died in prison.

## Pilon, Germaine (ca. 1537–1590)
*sculptor*

Germaine Pilon, considered one of the most important and influential sculptors of the French Renaissance, was born in Paris. He was the preferred sculptor of CATHERINE DE' MEDICI and worked with equal mastery in marble, bronze, wood, and terracotta. His graceful monument *cœur de Henri II* (heart of HENRY II; 1561, LOUVRE) bears the mark of the aesthetic style of the Fontainebleau School, but in the numerous works that he did for the rotunda of Valois in Saint-Denis, other tendencies are apparent: a measured realism derived at once from the French tradition and the Renaissance ideal of Italy, the influence of Michelangelo, and that of the Italian baroque. His portraits attest to his keen sense of observation and vigorous technique. Pilon's works were a strong influence on the following generation of French sculptors.

## Pinay, Antoine (1891–1994)
*political figure*

Born in Saint-Symphorien-sur-Coise, Rhône, Antoine Pinay served as mayor of Saint-Chamond (1929–77), as deputy (1936–38), senator (1938–40), member of the Second Constituent Assembly (1946), deputy to the National Assembly (groupe des Independents, (1946–58), and honorary president of the Center coalition of independents and farmers, and was also a member of several cabinets during the FOURTH REPUBLIC. Premier (March 1952) with the portfolio of finance, Pinay dedicated himself to strengthening the franc and dealt with the social malaise of the period by diverse stabilization measures (the posting of prices, the issuing of a guaranteed gold-backed loan, known as the "Pinay Loan," the creation of a sliding wage scale). In foreign affairs, Pinay's government was marked with the increasing military involvement in INDOCHINA and the signing of the Bonn Accords, which gave sovereignty to the three western sectors of Germany, and arranging for the bases of the European Defense Community. Pinay resigned in 1952, after having been abandoned by the MRP (MOUVEMENT RÉPUBLICAIN POPULAIRE) and being put in the minority over the question of the reform of the property tax and of social security. Foreign minister in the EDGAR FAURE cabinet (February 1955–January 1956), Pinay attended the 1954 Geneva Conference on disarmament and contributed to the granting of autonomy to Tunisia and the return of sultan Muhammad V to the Moroccan throne. A supporter of recalling General CHARLES DE GAULLE during the May 1958 crisis in ALGERIA, Pinay was charged, as minister of finance and economic affairs (June 1958–January 1960) with stabilizing the financial situation (institution of the "new franc"). In 1973–74, Pinay served as a mediator within the government.

## Pinel, Philippe (1745–1826)
*physician*

One of the pioneers of modern psychiatry, Philippe Pinel was born in Saint-André d'Alayrac, Tarn, and practiced medicine at the important hospitals of Bicêtre and Salpêtrière. The teacher of JEAN-ÉTIENNE ESQUIROL, he dedicated himself to the study of mental illnesses and had the great concept of abolishing the brutal therapeutic methods to which the mentally ill were subjected, and replacing them with humane and enlightened treatment. He recommended also that facilities for the mentally ill be changed from institutions to hospitals. Pinel's major writings include *Nostalgie de la philosophie* (1798–1818) and *Traité medico-philosophique sur l'aliénation mentale ou la manie* (1801), in which he classified mental illnesses into four categories: melancholy, mania, dementia, and idiocy. Pinel, a professor at the University of Paris, was named to the Academy of Sciences in 1803.

## Pissarro, Camille (1830–1903)
*painter, lithographer*

Camille Pissarro, an impressionist painter, was born in Saint-Thomas, Antilles, and settled in Paris in 1855. He began a career in business but left to become an artist. He worked with CAMILLE COROT, who gave him much early advice, and was influenced also by the realism of GUSTAVE COURBET. In 1857, at the Académie Suisse, he befriended CLAUDE MONET, PIERRE AUGUSTE RENOIR, and PAUL CÉZANNE, and with them attended the gatherings of the future impressionists. In England (1870), he was greatly impressed by the works of John Constable and

Joseph Turner, and his own style became more airy and clearer, approximating that of Monet. Pissarro later painted at Louveciennes, then at Pontoise, notably with Cézanne, from 1872 to 1874. He sought also to capture the scintillating play of sunlight (*Les Toits rouges,* 1877). Around 1885, he adopted the pointillist technique of GEORGES SEURAT, then evolved to a more systematic style. After 1890, Pissarro painted numerous overviews of the streets of Paris and Rouen. Having an open and generous nature, Pissarro was an ardent spokesperson and active moving spirit of impressionism, and thanks to him, PAUL GAUGUIN, PAUL SIGNAC, Mary Cassatt, and GEORGES SEURAT were able to show with the impressionists.

## Pithou, Pierre (1539–1596)
*jurist*

Born in Troyes, Pierre Pithou, having abjured Protestantism, joined the "political" faction and edited the discourse of the Third Estate in *La Satire Ménippée* (1594), stigmatizing the excesses of the HOLY LEAGUE. A student of JACQUES CUJAS, he was a supporter and apologist for Gallicanism (*Recueil des libertés de l'Église gallicane,* 1594).

## Pléiade

*Pléiade* is the name given in literary history to the groups of seven poets who were considered poetic constellations, by allusion to the seven sons of Atlas (the Pleiades). This designation was applied for the first time to the seven great Alexandrian poets of the third century B.C.E. In 1323, the name was applied to seven poets of the region of Toulouse. The best known use of the term was for those French greats in the mid-16th century who were grouped around PIERRE DE RONSARD: JOACHIM DE BELLAY, PONTUS DE TYARD, JEAN BAÏF, and, after 1553, ÉTIENNE JODELLE, RÉMI BELLEAU, and JACQUES PELETIER DU MANS (who in 1555 replaced GUILLAUME DES AUTELS).

## Poincaré, Henri (1854–1912)
*mathematician*

The last great universal mathematician and one of the foremost mathematicians of the 19th century, who made fundamental contributions to almost all the branches of mathematics and their application to the science of physics, Henri Poincaré was born in Nancy and educated in Paris. His cousin was the statesman Raymond Poincaré. One of his most important discoveries (1881) was that of automorphic functions (which he called "fuchsian" in honor of I. Fuchs, the German mathematician). Poincaré made original contributions, too, to differential equations, linear equations, probability, and analytical mechanics. He did important research involving the electromagnetic theory of light and on electricity, heat transfers, thermodynamics, celestial mechanics, and fluid mechanics, and anticipated the chaos theory. He is likewise considered a founder of analytic geometry and topography. Some of his conclusions can be considered as the first draft of the problem of relativity stated by Albert Einstein some years later. Additionally, Poincaré devoted much of his time to reflection on the philosophy of science (he supported the essential role of intuition in all research), and his book *La Science et l'Hypothèse* (1902) had a great influence on several generations of scientists. He left more than 500 other works. Poincaré was elected to the Academy of Sciences in 1887 and to the ACADÉMIE FRANÇAISE in 1908.

## Poincaré, Raymond (1860–1934)

*statesman*

Raymond Poincaré, the nationalistic statesman who served four terms as prime minister and was president of France from 1913 to 1920, was born in Bar-le-Duc and educated in Paris. He was the cousin of the mathematician HENRI POINCARÉ. A noted lawyer of the Paris bar, deputy (1887–1903), senator (1903–13), minister of public instruction (1893–94), and finance (1894, 1895, 1906), Poincaré began his political career as a moderate. As prime minister with the portfolio of foreign affairs (January 1912–January 1913), he adopted a firm stance vis-à-vis Germany and sought to strengthen France's ties with Great Britain and Russia (which he visited for the first time in 1912). Elected to the presidency of the THIRD REPUBLIC in 1913, he followed a rightist foreign policy and helped to put through the law requiring three years' military service (August 1913), the unpopularity of which contributed to a legislative victory for the left in 1914. After having

asked the Republican-Socialist RENÉ VIVIANI to help him form a government, Poincaré undertook with him a second visit to Russia to strengthen the alliance with France (July 1914). When Austria-Hungary sent its ultimatum to Serbia (30 July), Poincaré assured the czar that he could count on France, thus contributing to encouraging Russia to declare a general mobilization (this caused his opponents to give him the name "Poincaré-la-guerre" upon his return). From the beginning of WORLD WAR I, he was the champion of the "Union sacrée." The military difficulties, however, and especially the failure of General GEORGES NIVELLE's offensive in 1917, as well as the political ones (pacifism or defeatism in parts of public opinion), of a seemingly unending war, obliged Poincaré to entrust his government to GEORGES CLEMENCEAU (November 1917). Reelected to the Senate at the end of his presidential term (1920), named president of the Reparations Commission (February–May 1920), he was recalled to the premiership upon the fall of the ARISTIDE BRIAND government (January 1922–June 1924), with once again the portfolio of foreign affairs. A supporter of the Treaty of Versailles, he ordered the occupation of the Ruhr (1923) because of Germany's late payment of reparations, but the hostility of Great Britain as well as financial difficulties caused him to soften his views and to support the Dawes Plan, a 1923 plan set up to monitor Germany's reparations payments, as decided by the terms of the Treaty of Versailles (1919). After the victory of the CARTEL DES GAUCHES in the 1924 elections, Poincaré resigned, but the financial crisis returned him to power in 1926. He formed a cabinet of national unity (Union nationale) with the Radicals but excluding the Socialists; it included Aristide Briand, LOUIS BARTHOU, ÉDOUARD HERRIOT, PAUL PAINLEVÉ, and ANDRÉ TARDIEU). Invested with full powers in financial affairs, Poincaré governed by decree and, practicing economic politics, created new taxes, establishing the fund for autonomous amortization, and stabilizing to an extent the franc. After the departure of the Radicals from the government (Congress of Angers, 1928), Poincaré had to depend on the center and the right for support. He had to resign shortly after because of illness (1929). He left his memoirs, entitled *Au service de la France* (1926–33). Poincaré was elected to the ACADÉMIE FRANÇAISE in 1909.

## Poisons, affair of the

The affair of the poisons (*affaire des poisons*) involved a series of poisonings that took place between 1670 and 1680 in Paris and Versailles, discovered as a result of facts revealed at the trial of a celebrated poisoner, Marie-Madeleine d'Aubray, marquise de Brinvilliers. A special chamber, or commission, was convened to inquire into the affair, which reached into the highest places (two nieces of Cardinal MAZARIN, the countess of Gramont, the viscountess of Polignac, Marshal de LUXEMBOURG, the playwright JEAN RACINE, and even MME DE MONTESPAN), at which point the public inquest was closed. The principal accused was Catherine Deshayes, known as la Voison, who was accused of having supplied the poison and having practiced sorcery. Thirty-four sentences were imposed as a result of the affair.

## Poisson, Denis (1781–1840)

*mathematician*

Best known for his contributions to the theories of electricity and magnetism, Denis Poisson was born in Pithiviers, and was influenced by the work of JOSEPH LAGRANGE and PIERRE LAPLACE. Named a peer of France in 1837, and called the same year to serve on the Royal Council of the University, he assumed the direction of the teaching of mathematics in all the colleges of France, becoming also the first professor of mechanics at the SORBONNE. Author of works on rational mechanics, the calculus of probability (he discovered the law of distribution in statistics that bears his name), and physical mathematics, Poisson worked on electrical conduction and magnetic potential, gravity, and mathematics applied to astronomy. Poisson, a leading member of the French scientific establishment, was named to the Academy of Sciences in 1812.

## Polignac, Jules-Auguste-Armand-Marie de (1780–1847)

*political figure*

Born in Versailles to a leading aristocratic family, Jules-Auguste-Armand-Marie de Polignac was, early in his career, implicated in the GEORGES CADOUDAL conspiracy against NAPOLÉON I and sentenced to two years imprisonment, but he was con-fined for several more. With his brothers, he succeeded in escaping (1813) and returned to France with the count d'Artois (the future CHARLES X) in 1814, then spent time at Gand with the royal family during the HUNDRED DAYS. A supporter of the restoration of the monarchy and the ancien régime, and hostile to the liberal tendencies of the Charter of 1814, he was made a peer of France in 1920. Ambassador to Great Britain (1823–29), he took part in the negotiations that ended in the treaty of 1827 by which France, Great Britain, and Russia became the mediators between the Ottoman sultan and Greece, which had become independent. After the fall of the liberal cabinet, Charles X named Polignac foreign minister (August 1829), then prime minister (November 1829), but he quickly became unpopular because of his authoritarian and reactionary policies. After launching the Algerian expedition (July 1830), the success of which did little to resolve his domestic political problems, Polignac and his ministry made the blunder, in the face of the liberal opposition's July 1830 election victory, to issue the Four Ordinances of Saint-Cloud, which brought about an uprising in Paris and the fall of King Charles X. The revolution broke out immediately, and Polignac was arrested and condemned by the Chamber of Peers to life imprisonment and the loss of his titles. Amnestied in 1836, he was banished and went to England, returning in 1845. Polignac wrote *Considérations politiques* (1832), *Études historiques, politiques et morales* (1845), and *Réponse à mes adversaires* (1845).

## Polignac, Melchior de (1661–1742)

*cardinal, diplomat*

Born in Le Puy, Melchior de Polignac was brought to Rome by Cardinal de BOUILLON (1689) and began his brilliant diplomatic career by playing a role in preventing a rupture between France and the Holy See. As ambassador to Poland, he contributed, after the death of John III Sobieski (1696), to the election of François-Louis, prince de Conti, for the Polish crown. After the failure of this enterprise, he fell into disgrace and had to wait until 1702 to play an important role again. Later he took part in the Congress of Utrecht (1710–13), negotiations that led to the Treaty of Utrecht, which ended the War of the Spanish Succession.

Compromised under the Regency, however, he was named archbishop of Auch only in 1726. Cardinal Polignac, who was elected to the ACADÉMIE FRANÇAISE in 1704, left his unfinished *Anti-Lucretius . . .* (posthumous, 1745, translated into French in 1813), a Latin poem of nearly 10,000 verses in which he attempts to refute the thinker PIERRE BAYLE and the ideas of materialism.

## Polignac, Yolande-Martine-Gabrielle de Polastron, countess, then duchess de (1749–1793)

*nobility*

Born at Versailles into an aristocratic family, Yolande-Martine-Gabrielle de Polastron married Count Jules de Polignac and made her appearance at the French court, where she soon became a close friend of Queen MARIE ANTOINETTE. The victim of jealousies, calumnies, and slanders, the duchess de Polignac was the object of a farewell letter from the queen that mentioned that the queen would try to obtain favors for the duchess and her family and noting that she had become the intimate friend of the sovereign and of the governess of the royal children. The duchess de Polignac and her husband were thus believed to have a nefarious influence on the court, which in turn, contributed to the unpopularity of the queen herself. Fearing the hatred of the revolutionaries, the duchess emigrated as soon as the REVOLUTION OF 1789 began and died in Vienna. Yolande, duchess of Polignac was the mother of JULES AUGUSTE-ARMAND-MARIE DE POLIGNAC.

## Poltrot, Jean de (ca. 1533–1563)

*assassin of the duke de Guise*

Born in the château de Méré, near Bouex, Angoumois, Jean de Poltrot, sieur de Méré, joined the Reformation and seems to have very early developed a plan to assassinate the duke of GUISE, the leader of the Catholic forces. Poltrot succeeded in mortally wounding Guise during the siege of Orléans and was arrested (1563). He was tortured and stated that he acted with the encouragement and complicity of Admiral COLIGNY, but these allegations could not be proven. Jean de Poltrot was sentenced to death and executed.

## Pompadour, Jeanne-Antoinette Poisson Le Normant d'Etioles, marquise de (1721–1764)

*mistress of Louis XV, arts patron*

The influential favorite of King LOUIS XV, known for her patronage of art and literature, Jeanne-Antoinette Poisson, later the marquise de Pompadour, was born in Paris, the daughter of a financier. She married a government official, Charles-Guillaume Le Normant d'Etioles, and frequenting the leading salons, became acquainted with BERNARD DE FONTENELLE and VOLTAIRE. Becoming the king's mistress in 1745, she was soon installed at VERSAILLES and was able to keep his friendship even through their later years by her ability to amuse and distract. The official favorite, she was more or less tolerated by the royal family but detested by the court, as she was not of aristocratic birth. She was the object of many cabals and plots. She was the patron of many artists who worked also on her several residences (Hôtel d'Evreux, the future Élysée Palace, La Celle, Bellevue, Champs). She influenced Louis XV in transferring the Sèvres porcelain works to Vincennes (1756) and in having her brother, Abel Poisson, marquis de Marigny, placed in charge of the building of fortifications (1751), in which capacity he proved to be a good administrator. She was a friend and sponsor of various writers and thinkers, reconciled VOLTAIRE with the king, and supported the *Encyclopédie* of DENIS DIDEROT. Mme de Pompadour's role was also apparent in affairs of state, and few were appointed to office without her consent, as she acted as an intermediary between the king and his ministers (the duke de CHOISEUL and FRANÇOIS BERNIS owed their influence to her support). It was largely through her encouragement that the diplomatic arrangement was made allying France with Austria during the Seven Years' War.

## Pompidou, Georges (1911–1974)

*statesman*

Born in Montboudif, Cantal, and educated in Paris at the École normale supérieure and the École libre des sciences politiques, Georges Pompidou, the second president of the FIFTH REPUBLIC and a close confidant of CHARLES DE GAULLE, began his career at the Banque Rothschild, where he eventually became general director (1956–62). He had earlier taught literature in MARSEILLE (1939) and served in the Resistance during WORLD WAR II. Pompidou headed de Gaulle's cabinet from June 1958 to January 1959, and was named prime minister on April 14, 1962. In October, however, he and his government resigned after a vote of no confidence in the National Assembly, which was subsequently dissolved by de Gaulle. Following the electoral victory of the UNR-UDR (Union pour la nouvelle République—Union des démocrates pour la République), Pompidou was recalled as prime minister and, following the events of May 1968, his cabinet signed the Grenelle accords with the principal labor unions. After the crushing victory of the UNION DES DÉMOCRATES POUR LA REPUBLIQUE (June 1968) that followed the dissolution of the assembly, Pompidou was placed, according to de Gaulle, "in reserve for the Republic," and replaced by MAURICE COUVE DE MURVILLE. After de Gaulle's resignation, Pompidou, who was a deputy for Cantal, was elected president (June 1969). Wanting to continue de Gaulle's policies, he continued the regionalization of France and an active social policy. But he also personally helped in the negotiations (April 1972) that led to the United Kingdom's entry into the European Community (EUROPEAN UNION), and sought to develop further the modernization of French industry, without completely adhering to the "new society" policy of his prime minister, JACQUES CHABAN-DELMAS (1969–72), who was replaced by PIERRE MESSMER (1972–1974). Pompidou died before the end of his term as president.

## Pompignan, Jean-Georges Lefranc de (1715–1790)

*ecclesiastic, writer*

Born in Montauban, the brother of JEAN-JACQUES LEFRANC DE POMIGNAN, Jean-Georges Lefranc de Pompignan was the bishop of Puy (1743) and became the archbishop of Vienne (Dauphiné) in 1774. He took a strong position against the ideas of the philosophes, in particular VOLTAIRE, in his *Question sur l'incrédulité* (1753–57). Deputy for the clergy to the ESTATES GENERAL (1789), he was one of the first to join the Third Estate at the beginning of the REVOLUTION OF 1789. A member of the government after August 4, 1789, Pompignan was opposed to the CIVIL CONSTITUTION OF THE CLERGY.

## Pompignan, Jean-Jacques Lefranc, marquis de (1709–1784)

*poet*

Born in Montauban, Jean-Jacques Lefranc, marquis de Pompignan served at first as a magistrate then turned to literature. He translated the plays of Aeschylus and composed *Odes* (1741), as well as *Poèmes sacrés* (1734, 1763), lyrical and majestic meditations. He was ridiculed by the philosophes, whom he had attacked in the ACADÉMIE FRANÇAISE (1759), but was appreciated by others for the purity of his writing.

## Poncelet, Jean-Victor (1788–1867)

*military figure, mathematician*

Born in Metz, Jean-Victor Poncelet, upon finishing at the École polytechnique, joined the engineering corps of the army and during the Russian campaign (1812) was taken prisoner and held at Saratov. Without the help of a text, he dedicated himself to mathematical studies and prepared a large revision of geometry. In 1822, he published his *Traité des propriétés projectives des figures,* which marked the beginning of projective geometry. He published also a treatise on mechanics dealing with the propagation of movements. A general in 1848, he served as director of the École polytechnique (1848–50), was elected to the Constituent Assembly and, having refused to serve the SECOND EMPIRE, went into retirement (1852). Poncelet was elected to the Academy of Sciences in 1834.

## Ponge, Francis (1899–1988)

*poet*

Born in Montpellier, Francis Ponge, a leading existentialist poet, recognized in all things a primal ontology, perceiving the autonomy of their existence, which he sought to express in prose and poetry. Considered by JEAN-PAUL SARTRE as the poet of existentialism, Ponge can be seen as a spokesperson for a materialist and linguistic philosophy, as he saw poetry as a means to explore the world and the self and, in his minute description of ordinary things, he came to modify the surrealist techniques and developed his own style of language. Ponge's writings include *Le Parti pris du choses* (1942), *Proêmes* (1948), *Le Grand Recueil* (1961), *Le Savon* (1967), and *Nioque de l'avant printemps* (1983). With *La Fabriqué du pré* (which contains his typical play on words, 1971) and *Comme une Figue de paroles et pourquoi* (1977), he seems to play humorously with text, context, and phrases as a way of perceiving the world.

## Poniatowski, Michel, Prince (1922–2002)
*political figure*

Born in Paris, Prince Michel Poniatowski was descended from Polish royalty (one of his ancestors was a field marshal under NAPOLÉON I). He studied in Paris and at Cambridge and, after the fall of France to Nazi Germany in 1940, he joined the Free French forces in Algiers, where he won the croix de guerre. He sided more with General HENRI GIRAUD than with General CHARLES DE GAULLE, and after the war served as a deputy for Puy-de-Dôme (1959), then as chief of staff to VALÉRY GISCARD D'ESTAING and later as finance minister (1962–66, 1969–74). In 1978, with Giscard d'Estaing, he formed the UNION POUR LA DÉMOCRATIE FRANÇAISE, a loose federation of right and center-right non-Gaullist groups. In 1998, Poniatowski resigned over the UDF's refusal to ally itself with the National Front of JEAN-MARIE LE PEN. Poniatowski planned Giscard d'Estaing's successful campaign to win the presidency after the death of GEORGES POMPIDOU (1974) and became minister of the interior (1974–77). In that capacity, he took some liberal measures, such as abolishing fingerprints on identity cards and relaxing controls on the media. He resigned after a scandal brought on by the death of a rightist political figure.

## Popular Front  (Front populaire)
The Popular Front (Front populaire) was the name given, by analogy to the Spanish Frente popular, to the coalition of leftist parties that came to power in France in June 1936.

See also AURIOL, VINCENT; BLUM, LÉON, DALADIER, ÉDOUARD; RAMADIER, PAUL; THOREZ, MAURICE.

## Portalis, Jean-Étienne-Marie  (1746–1807)
*political figure, jurist*

Born in Le Beausset, Provence, Jean-Étienne-Marie Portalis was an attorney for the Parlement of Aix (1765). During the REVOLUTION OF 1789, he was arrested under the TERROR. A member of the Council of Ancients, he served as its president in 1796. With others, he edited the Civil Code, and as director of cults under NAPOLÉON I, he negotiated the CONCORDAT OF 1801, Napoléon's treaty with the Catholic Church, editing the Organic Articles that reinforced Gallican principles (SEE GALLICANISM). Portalis served again as minister of cults, from 1804 to 1807. He was elected to the ACADÉMIE FRANÇAISE in 1803.

## Portalis, Joseph-Marie, count  (1778–1858)
*political figure*

Born in Aix, the son of JEAN-ÉTIENNE-MARIE PORTALIS, Joseph-Marie Portalis served as secretary-general of cults (1805), then as director general of the press and publishing during the FIRST EMPIRE. Adviser to the Court of Cassation and a peer under the Restoration, he served in the liberal ministry of the count of MARTIGNAC as keeper of the seals, then as foreign minister (1828–29).

## Pot, Philippe  (1428–1494)
*political figure*

Born in La Rochepot, Philippe Pot first served PHILIPPE III of Burgundy, then CHARLES THE FEARLESS, before joining the service of King LOUIS XI, who named him grand sénéchal of Burgundy (1477). He represented the nobility of Burgundy at the Estates General of Tours (1484). Pot's tomb is in the LOUVRE.

## Potonie-Pierre, Eugénie  (1844–1898)
*feminist, political activist*

Born in Paris, where she was the first woman to stand for municipal election, Eugénie Potonie-Pierre was a cofounder of the Union des Femmes.

She worked on various feminist journals (*Le Journal des femmes*) and was responsible for uniting eight Parisian feminist groups to form the Fédération française des Sociétés féministes. In 1893, she ran as a candidate for the National Assembly and, in 1897, led the French delegation to the Feminist Congress in Brussels, Belgium. Eugénie Potonie-Pierre remained a leader of the socialist feminist movement until her death.

## Pottier, Eugène (1816–1887)
*political figure, poet*

Born in Paris, Eugène Pottier was on the side of the insurgents during the REVOLUTION OF 1848 and later would be opposed to the SECOND EMPIRE. In 1867, he founded the Chambre syndicale des ateliers de dessin, which he affiliated with the International Association of Workers (First International). A member of the Central Republican Committee of Twenty Arrondissements of Paris, he played an active role in the Paris COMMUNE and, after Bloody Week (May 22–28, 1871), took refuge in England, then the United States, until the amnesty of 1880. Upon his return to France, he collaborated on *Socialiste*, the newspaper of JULES GUESDE and PAUL LAFARGUE, whose efforts he also supported in the formation of the French SOCIALIST PARTY (Parti ouvrier français). A revolutionary poet, Pottier celebrated the COMMUNE and the struggle of the proletariat (*La Terrier blanche*, June 1871; *Le Monument des fédérés*, May 1883; *L'Insurgé*, 1884), and is the author of the famous revolutionary and socialist hymn, "L'Internationale" (June 1871).

## Pouget, Émile (1860–1931)
*revolutionary syndicalist*

Born in Pont-de-Salars, Aveyron, Émile Pouget took part in the creation of the first workers union in Paris (1879). Imprisoned following a union demonstration (1883), he founded, upon his release, *Le Père Peinard* (1889), where he demonstrated his talents as a pamphleteer, then *La Sociale* (1895). Assistant secretary of the CGT (Confédération générale du travail), Pouget contributed to the publication of *La Voix du Peuple* (1900).

## Poujade, Pierre (1920–2003)
*political figure*

Born in Saint-Céré, Lot, Pierre Poujade, a bookseller and publisher, in 1953 founded the Union de défense des commerçants et artisans de France (UDCA, also called the Poujade, or Poujadist, movement), which took a stand against economic and fiscal controls and various taxes and duties, and supported a French ALGERIA. After a success in the legislative election of 1956, Poujade's movement, which favored the small businessperson, was subject to numerous internal dissensions.

## Poulenc, Francis (1899–1963)
*composer*

Born in Paris, Francis Poulenc, a composer and pianist, studied with several noted musicians but taught himself composition. His first works, *Rhapsodie nègre* (1917) and *Trois mouvements perpétuels* for piano were written while he was serving in WORLD WAR I. In 1920, he founded Les Six (The Six) with five others, including DARIUS MILHAUD, in rebellion against the conservative influence of such composers as VINCENT D'INDY, and CÉSAR FRANCK. Among Poulenc's many compositions are *Le Bestiare*, inspired by the works of GUILLAUME APOLLINAIRE (1919); the ballet *Les Biches* (1923); *Concert champêtre* (1928); *Le Bal masque* (1932); and *Impromptus, Promenades, Toccatas, Improvisations*, and *Villageoises* for piano. Later works were religiously inspired *Litanies à la Vierge noire de Rocamadour* (1936), *Messe en sol majeur* (1937), *Concerto pour orgue et orchestre à cordes avec timbales* (1938), *Petites prière de saint François d'Assise* (1950), a *Stabat Mater* (1950), and a *Gloria* (1959). Poulenc also composed operas (*Dialogues des carmélites* and *La Voix humaine*, after JEAN COCTEAU, 1958); a ballet (*Les Animaux modèles*, 1941), and a comic opera (*Les mamelles de Tirésias*, 1944), again after Apollinaire.

## Poussin, Nicolas (1594–1665)
*painter*

Nicolas Poussin, who was the founder and greatest practitioner of 17th-century French classical painting, was born in Villers, near Les Andelys,

NORMANDY. He studied painting in Paris and probably also Rouen, then in Rome (1624). His early works reflect the influence of Caravaggio and the Mannerists (*Mort de Germanicus, Martyre de Germanicus*, St. Peter's, Rome, 1628). Poussin gained important patrons and in 1631 became a member of the Academy of St. Luke. Returning to France, he was commissioned by Cardinal RICHELIEU to paint *Quatre Bacchanales* and *Triomphe de Neptune*, gaining also wealthy patrons and strengthening his ties to the Royal Academy. Works done in this period include *L'Enlèvement des Sabines, L'Inspiration du poète, Écho et Narcisse, Orphée et Eurydice, L'Empire de Flore, Les Bergères d'Arcadie*, and a series, *Quatre Saisons*, considered the purest embodiment of French classicism. His works are characterized by calm, structured composition, the use of cool colors and clear lighting, and feelings of solemnity. Poussin believed that art should appeal to the mind rather than the eye, and should present noble themes devoid of triviality and sensuality. These principles became the basis of the French academic style of the 17th century, and his work symbolizes the virtues of order, logic, and clarity. Poussin has influenced the course of French art until the present day. Until the 20th century, he remained the dominant inspiration for such classically oriented artists as JACQUES-LOUIS DAVID, JEAN-AUGUSTE INGRES, and PAUL CÉZANNE.

## Poyet, Guillaume (ca. 1474–1548)
*political figure*

Born in Les Granges, near Angers, Guillaume Poyet, an attorney with the Parlement of PARIS, in 1521 was ordered by Queen LOUISE OF SAVOY, mother of FRANCIS I, to plead against the Constable of Bourbon. A presiding judge in 1534 and chancellor of France in 1538, he collaborated on the Ordinances of Villers-Cotterêts (1539). In a calculated move, he supported the constable MONTMORENCY against Admiral PHILIPPE DE CHABOT, but was undone when the constable fell from power. Accused of embezzlement, Poyet was arrested (1542) and removed from all his posts (1545).

## Praguerie

The Praguerie revolt against King CHARLES VIII in 1440 was so called in allusion to the Hussite uprising in Prague. Its leaders were several great feudal lords, including Jean II, duke of Alençon, Louis of Bourbon, La Tremoille, JEAN DUNOIS, and others who resented the reduction of their influence in the royal government. They were joined by the dauphin (later LOUIS XI) and had the support of PHILIP III THE GOOD of Burgundy. The revolt was soon suppressed, however, but the rebellious nobles were given leniency by the monarch, although the dauphin was exiled to Dauphiné.

## Praslin, Gabriel de Choiseul-Chevigny, duke de (1712–1785)
*military officer, diplomat*

Born in Paris, Gabriel de Choiseul-Chevigny, duke de Praslin assisted his cousin the duke de CHOISEUL and succeeded him as foreign minister (Peace of Paris, 1763). He then reorganized the navy and undertook such projects as enlarging the port of Brest and sponsoring the exploratory voyages of the count de BOUGAINVILLE.

## Prévert, Jacques (1900–1977)
*poet*

Born in Neuilly-sur-Seine, Jacques Prévert was a poet who, under the influence of surrealism, sought to dismantle language, freeing it from its conventionality and bourgeois style. Faithful to the anachronistic spirit of the early 20th century, his nonconformism is a sincere expression of his ideals and views. Hostile to all forms of serial oppression, capable of irony and violence, but also charm and tenderness, his celebrated poetry reached a large public, with its themes of liberty, justice, and goodwill. In it, he achieved the height of play with words and phrases through skillful poetic techniques. One can find this also in the scenarios and dialogues that he wrote for some of the films of MARCEL CARNÉ: *Drôle de drame* (1937), *Le Quai des brumes* (1938), *Le jour se lève* (1939), *Les Visiteurs du soir* (1942), *Les Enfants du paradis* (1945), and *Les Portes de la nuit* (1946). Prévert's principal collections include:

*Paroles* (1946), *Histoires* (1946), *Spectacle* (1951), *Le Pluie et le Beau Temps* (1955), *Fatras* (1965), *Imaginaires* (1970), *Choses et autres* (1972), *Hebdomadaires* (1972), and *Arbres* (1976).

## Prévost d'Exiles, Antoine-François (1697–1763)
### (Abbé Prévost)
*writer, cleric*

Antoine-François Prévost d'Exiles, or Abbé Prévost as he is better known, was born in Hesdin and, after having chosen the church over the military as a career, became a preacher (1726). He abandoned that profession two years later, however, then lived in England and Holland before settling in Paris. During his travels, the abbot Prévost wrote numerous novellas and adventure stories, the best known being *Mémoires et aventures d'un homme de qualité* (1728–31), in seven volumes. The seventh volume, *Histoire du chevalier Des Grieux et de Manon Lescaut*, is famous and inspired two popular operas, *Manon* (1884) by JULES MASSENET, and *Manon Lescaut* by Giacomo Puccini.

## Prévost-Paradol, Lucien-Anatole (1829–1870)
*journalist, political figure*

Born in Paris, Lucien-Anatole Prévost-Paradol was a classmate of HIPPOLYTE TAINE at the École normale supérieure and being recognized by the Academy for his *Éloge de Bernadin de Saint-Pierre* (1851), was named professor at Aix. A contributor to the *Journal des débats* and the *Courier du dimanche*, he took a stand against the regime of NAPOLÉON III. A liberal supporter of decentralization and regional and communal self-government, he seems to have favored an English type of political system, more than a republic (*La France nouvelle*, 1868). Nonetheless, he came to support the SECOND EMPIRE and was named ambassador to the United States (1870). Upon the news of France's declaration of war on Prussia, he committed suicide (July 1870). Prévost-Paradol is the author of *Essais de politique et de littérature* (1859–63) and studies on the French moralists. He was elected to the ACADÉMIE FRANÇAISE in 1865.

## Prié, Jeane-Agnès Bertholot de Pléneuf, marquise de (1698–1727)
*nobility*

Born in Paris, Jeane-Agnès Bertholot de Pléneuf, the daughter of a wealthy merchant, married the marquis de Prié, ambassador to Turin. The mistress of LOUIS-HENRI DE BOURBON-CONDÉ, in many ways she governed France through her influence while he was prime minister. She supported the fiscal plans of JOSEPH PÂRIS and arranged the marriage of MARIE LESZCZYNSKA to LOUIS XV. She went into exile after the dismissal of the prince de Condé.

## Prieur of la Côte d'Or (1763–1832)
*political figure*

Claude-Antoine Prieur-Duvernois, or Prieur of la Côte d'Or as he is known, was born in Auxonne. An officer in the army engineering corps, he joined the REVOLUTION OF 1789 and was elected to the Legislative Assembly (1791), later taking his place as a MONTAGNARD deputy in the Convention. Sent on a mission to NORMANDY to suppress a Girondin uprising, he was arrested there by federalist insurgents. Upon his release, he returned to Paris and became a member of the Committee of Public Safety (August 4, 1793–October 1794) and was put in charge of armaments production. He helped to found the École polytechnique, the Conservatoire des arts et métiers, the Bureau des longitudes, and to institute the metric system (*Nouvelle instruction sur les poids et mesures et sur cacul décimal*, 1795).

## Prieur de la Marne (1756–1827)
*political figure*

Pierre-Louis Prieur, or Prieur de la Marne as he is known, was born in Sommesous, Champagne. An attorney, he served as a deputy for the Third Estate to the ESTATES GENERAL (1789) and, during the REVOLUTION OF 1789, became a member of the JACOBIN Club. He sat with the extreme Left in the Constituent Assembly, where his violent statements earned him the sobriquet "Crieur de la Marne." Reelected to the Convention (1792), he helped to put forth the decree ordering the raising of a force of 300,000 for the military (February 24, 1793). He was a member of the Committee of General Defense

(March 1793), then the Committee of Public Safety (July 1793), where, with JEAN BON SAINT-ANDRÉ, he worked on the organization of the navy. After the fall of MAXIMILIEN ROBESPIERRE (9 Thermidor Year II [July 27, 1794]), he was implicated in the MONTAGNARD insurrection of Year III but remained in hiding until the Amnesty Law of Year IV. He was proscribed as a regicide in 1816 and went into exile.

## Proudhon, Pierre-Joseph (1809–1865)
*socialist, anarchist*

Born in Besançon to a working-class family, Pierre-Joseph Proudhon, who is often considered the father of modern anarchism (and to whom Mikail Bakunin, a Russian anarchist, owed much), was successively a typographer, small printer, and journalist. His forceful, audacious, and eloquent attack on the propertied classes in *Qu'est-ce que c'est la propriété?* (1840) aroused strong reactions and alarm among the bourgeoisie. Proudhon continued his criticisms in *De la création de l'ordre dans l'humanité* (1843), in which he defined work as the only true capital. But soon he would nuance his attacks, seeking less to eliminate private property than to attenuate its abuses, and less to eliminate the capitalist system than to reform it and to reconcile the bourgeoisie and the proletariat. In *La Philosophie de la misère*, or *Système des contradictions économiques* (1846), he discussed the basic concepts of communism. This brought a strong reaction from Karl Marx, who wrote *Misère de la philosophie* (1847) in response. A representative for the people in the National Assembly (1848) and the editor of several journals and newspapers, Proudhon was sentenced to prison (1849–50) for his opposition to Louis-Napoléon Bonaparte. But in *L'Idée de la révolution au XIXe siècle* (1851), in which he put forth the principle of anarchism, he seemed to believe in the possibility of a rapproachment between NAPOLÉON III and the cause of social reform (*Révolution sociale démontrée par le coup d'État du 2 décembre 1852*). The publication of *De la justice dans la Révolution et dans l'Église* (1858) forced Proudhon to go into exile to Brussels, Belgium. On his return to France, his work *Du principe fédératif et de la nécessité de reconstituer le parti de la révolution* (1863) appeared and,

after his death, *De la capacité politique de la classe ouvrière* was published. The founder of the mutualist system, worker syndicalism, and federalism, Proudhon seems to be at once a revolutionary and, according to Marx, a conservative. He envisioned a society in which ethical human nature and a sense of moral responsibility would make government unnecessary, and he rejected the use of force to impose any system. His followers opposed Marxist socialism as represented at the First International.

## Proust, Joseph-Louis (1754–1826)
*chemist*

Best known for establishing the chemical law of definitive proportions, sometimes called "Proust's Law," Joseph-Louis Proust was born in Angers. In 1784, he accompanied JEAN-FRANÇOIS PILÂTRE DE ROZIER in a balloon ascent. Later, during a sojourn in Madrid, where he was director of the royal laboratory of Charles IV, he successfully isolated a sugar from grapes (glucose). On his return to France, during Napoléon's continental blockade, he refused to help NAPOLÉON I, who wanted to exploit his findings. He was one of the founders of analytical chemistry and, in 1794, published a paper outlining his work and discoveries. It was not until 1811, however, when the Swedish chemist John Jacob Berzelius gave Proust credit for his discovery, that his findings became widely known. Joseph Proust was elected to the Academy of Sciences in 1816.

## Proust, Marcel (1871–1922)
*writer*

Marcel Proust, the creator of the multivolume *À la recherche du temps perdu* (*In Search of Lost Time*, also known as *Remembrance of Things Past*; 1913–22), the novel regarded as one of the finest achievements in world literature, was born in Paris to a wealthy bourgeois family. Early in life, he manifested extreme intellectual curiosity and, after initially studying law, gave up that pursuit and, mingling in Parisian society, began to write. His first work, *Les Plaisirs et les Jours* (1896, preface by ANATOLE FRANCE) was not so notable, but he would use his experiences gathered in salons for this piece to greater effect in later works. At age 35, after a sojourn in Venice, Proust, who suffered from asthma since youth, became a chronic invalid and remained almost exclusively in his cork-lined room working on his masterpiece, and he died before the final three volumes were published. Written in the first person as an interior monologue, it is in many respects autobiographical and is tied to his homosexuality. In the evolution of French literary genres, the place of Proust's work is fundamental. The importance of his work lies not so much in his descriptions of changing French society as in the psychological development of characters, and in his philosophical preoccupation with time. As Proust traces the path of his hero from happy childhood through romantic attachment to self-awareness as a writer, he is also concerned with seeking eternal truths in a changing world. He writes of time as both a destructive force and as a positive element. In this, he was influenced by HENRI BERGSON, whom he admired and through whose theories he perceived the sequence and passage of time (WORLD WAR I, too, had a pro-

found effect on his writing). *À la recherche du temps perdu* was translated into many languages and established Proust's reputation worldwide, while his techniques and methods of writing (with minute analysis of his characters' development) have greatly influenced 20th-century literary style. Other posthumously published works of Proust include *Chroniques* (1927), *Jean Santeuil* (1952), *Contre Sainte-Beuve* (1954), and his *Correspondance* (20 volumes, 1970–93). He was awarded the prix Goncourt in 1919.

## Prouvé, Jean (1901–1984)
*architect*

Born in Nancy, Jean Prouvé was one of the inventors of the curtain wall (composed of sheet metal and folded steel) and, with EUGÈNE BEAUDOUIN and MARCEL LODS, built the Maison du Peuple at Clichy (1937–39) and the aéro-club of Buc (1935). Prouvé won awards for his work at the International Fairs of Lille (1950–51) and Grenoble (1968) and played a large role in the development of the building

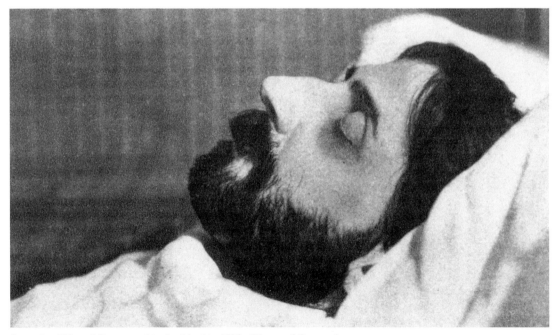

Portrait of Marcel Proust on his deathbed in 1922 *(Library of Congress)*

industry by recognizing the need to standardize and employ light-alloy materials.

## Prouvost, Jean  (1885–1978)
*industrialist*

Born in Roubaix, Jean Prouvost came from a family of textile industrialists and was the owner of several periodicals, including *Paris-Soir, Marie-Clair,* and *Match.* Through these, inspired by the American model, he redeveloped the form, content, and method of the prewar French press. After reorganizing his company at the time of the Liberation, he had to sell his principal titles (*Le Figaro, Paris-Match,* and *Télé 7 Jours*) because of the economic crises of the 1970s.

## Provence

A former province of France, with its capital at Aix-en-Provence, Provence is divided into Upper and Lower Provence. Originally a Roman province, it was at one time ruled by kings, then counts; it was united with France under CHARLES VIII in 1487. Today it comprises the departments of Alpes-de-Haute-Provence, Var, and Bouche-du-Rhône, and parts of Vaucluse and Alpes-Maritime. It is bordered on the east by Italy, on the west by the Rhône River, and on the south by the Mediterranean (MARSEILLE, Toulon). The region abounds in olive groves, vineyards, flower fields, and orchards, and the modern inhabitants preserve a distinct regional character as well as their own language (Provençal).

## Prud'hon, Pierre  (1758–1823)
*painter*

Pierre Prud'hon (known also as Pierre-Paul) was born in Cluny and trained in Paris and Dijon. He traveled to Rome to study (1785–88), where he became friends with Antonio Canova, the famous Italian sculptor. There, he also discovered Alexandrian and Pompeian art and was influenced by the works of Leonardo da Vinci, Raphael, and Correggio. On his return to Paris, he painted a number of portraits and did the decorative panels for the hôtel de Lanois. He was employed by NAPOLÉON I as court painter and decorator and was widely acclaimed for his portrait *L'Impératrice Joséphine à la Malmaison* (1805). Prud'hon expanded into allegorical and mythological themes (*La Justice et la Vengeance divine poursuivant le Crime,* 1808; *Vénus et Adonis,* 1812). If Prud'hon's elegiac grace seems to be a heritage of the 18th century, his melancholy sensuality, the dreaminess of his figures, his taste for diagonal composition, shaded contours, and clear moonlit scenes with silvery chiaroscuro tones announce the coming of romanticism. Prud'hon was named to the Academy of Fine Arts in 1816.

## Puget, Pierre  (1620–1694)
*painter, sculptor, architect*

Born in MARSEILLE, Pierre Puget, the son of a master mason, developed his talent in local workshops before going to Italy, where he became the assistant to Pietro de Cortona, working especially on the Barberini Palace in Rome and the Pitti Palace in Florence. His first important sculpture was the *Atlantes,* for the city hall of Toulon (1656–57). In it, having been influenced by Michelangelo and Bernini, he affirmed his originality. Puget's other important works include *Hercule* (commissioned by NICOLAS FOUQUET) and *Hercule gaulois au repos.* His *Saint-Sébastien* and other pieces made him one of the most imposing baroque sculptors after Bernini. His last two important works, *Alexandre et Diogène* (1671–93) and *Charles Borromée priant* (1690–93) are among his most moving. Arrogant and headstrong, Puget, who is considered a precursor of romanticism, fell victim to the intrigues of fellow artists and saw many of his more ambitious projects rejected.

## Puisaye, Joseph, count de  (1755–1827)
*military figure*

Born in Montagne, Joseph, count de Puisaye was a deputy for the nobility to the ESTATES GENERAL (1789) and initially supported the REVOLUTION OF 1789. After the proscription of the Girondins (June 2, 1793), he took part in the FEDERALIST INSURRECTION of the Eure. Defeated, however, at Pacy-sur-Eure (July 1793), he emigrated to England from where he led, with British support, the disembarking of émigrés at Quiberon, Brittany (June–July 1795). While the majority of the émigrés were killed, Puisaye succeeded in returning to the British squadron offshore. He left his *Mémoires pour servir à l'histoire du parti royaliste* (1808).

## Puvis de Chavannes, Pierre-Cécil (1824–1898)

*painter*

Born in LYON, Pierre-Cécil Puvis de Chavannes worked in the studios of various artists, including EUGÈNE DELACROIX. He admired the work of JEAN-AUGUSTE-DOMINGUE INGRES, THÉODORE CHASSÉREAU, and the Renaissance fresco painters, defending their idealist views and making him the heir to the Nazarenes, a group of German artists who reacted to neoclassicism and academic style. Puvis de Chavannes began exhibiting in 1850, but he was kept out of the Salon until 1858. He then produced a great series of mural compositions on allegorical themes for the museums of Amiens (1865, 1867, 1879), Lyon (1884), Rouen, and for the SORBONNE (*Le Bois sacré*, 1880–89) and the Panthéon (*Sainte Geneviève veillant sur Paris*, 1898). Painted in pale colors and linear rhythms, his noble and saintly subjects do not exclude a sense of sentimentalism (*Le pauvre Pêcheur*, 1881). His work, while still showing aspects of the academic tradition, was admired by PAUL GAUGUIN, who drew stylistic lessons from Puvis de Chavannes's linearism, symbolic conceptions, and sense of composition.

## Pyat, Félix (1810–1889)

*writer, journalist, political figure*

Born in Vierzon, Félix Pyat was an attorney, then journalist. As a founder of the Société des gens des lettres, he published dramatic works that enjoyed a certain success (*Le Chiffonier de Paris*, 1847). Commissioner for the Provisional Government of the SECOND REPUBLIC and elected to the Constituent Legislative Assembly (1848–49), he fled to Switzerland after June 13, 1849, then to Great Britain after the coup d'état of December 2, 1851. On his return to France, he founded the newspaper *Combat* (1870) and was a member of the first Executive Commission and first Committee of Public Health of the Paris COMMUNE, where he became known for his extremist views. Condemned to death for contempt after the failure of the insurrection, Pyat went into exile and, after the amnesty, returned and was elected a leftist deputy for Bouches-du-Rhône (1888).

See also LEDRU-ROLLIN, ALEXANDRE; REVOLUTION OF 1848.

## Pyrenees (Pyrénées)

The Pyrenees are a chain of mountains that extend from the Gulf of Gascony to the Gulf of Lyon. In age the Pyrenees are part of the Alpine system but are different from the FRENCH ALPS in several ways: their highest points are lower, but their valleys are more elevated; the glaciers are smaller than those of the Alps. The Pyrenees chain has three parts: Western, Central, and Eastern. Forming the French border with Spain, the French area of the Pyrenees, like the Spanish, has an agricultural economy and is inhabited by such groups as Basques, Catalans, Béarnais, Andorrans, and Aragonese. There are thermal springs and winter sports facilities.

# Q

## Quarton, Enguerrand (known from 1444–1466)
*painter*

Enguerrand Quarton (also Charonton, Charreton, or Charton) worked in Aix-en-Provence (1444) and settled in Avignon in 1447. Two works that contributed to defining the Provençal style are attributed to him with certainty: *La Vierge de miséricorde* (1452), on which he collaborated with the painter Pierre Vilatte, and *Le Couronnement de la Vierge* (1453–54). The vigor of his forms, the treatment of certain faces inspired by Flemish art, and the elegant stylization of design are subordinated to the image of a very personal ensemble; abstract and monumental character of a complex, but clear composition, an order denoting the pictorial adaptation of the architectural composition of the French tympanum. In his countrysides, the use of perspective attests to the Italian influence, but the nature of light, which is used abundantly, appears typically Provençal.

## Quatremère, Étienne-Marc (1782–1857)
*Orientalist*

Born in Paris, Étienne-Marc Quatremère, who studied Arabic, was the director of the National Library, then, successively, professor of Hebrew, Syriac, and Chaldean at the COLLÈGE DE FRANCE, and Persian at the École des langues orientales. He was the first to identify the relationship between Coptic and ancient Egyptian, preparing the way for the research of JEAN-FRANÇOIS CHAMPOLLION. Quatremère's principal writings include *Recherches critiques et historiques sur la langue et la littérature de l'Égypte* (1808); *Mémoire sur les Nabathéens* (1835); translations (*Histoire des Mongols de la Perse* by Rachid al-Din, 1836, and *Histoire des Ayyabides et des sultans mamelouks* by Maqrizi, 1837–45).

## Quatremère de Quincy (1755–1849)
*archaeologist, political figure*

Born in Paris, Antoine-Chrysostome Quatremère, or Quatremère de Quincy as he is known, was, a deputy to the Legislative Assembly during the REVOLUTION OF 1789, where he joined the constitutional royalists and defended the marquis de LA FAYETTE (1792). Imprisoned under the TERROR, he later served as a member of the Council of Five Hundred but, after the coup d'état of 18 Fructidor (1797), was proscribed as a royalist. Superintendent of public arts and monuments under the RESTORATION (1816), he edited the *Dictionnaire de l'architecture* (1795–1825) for the *Encyclopédie méthodique* and published an *Essai sur l'idéal* (1805), a study on Michelangelo. Quatremère de Quincy served as a deputy from 1820 to 1822.

## Queneau, Raymond (1903–1976)
*writer*

A French surrealist poet and humorous novelist, Raymond Queneau was born in Le Havre and received a degree in philosophy. From 1924 to 1929, he contributed to *Révolution surréaliste*, developing his ideas and writing style. Queneau's prose evokes various insolent and precious characters (*Les Enfants du limon*, 1938), through whom he seeks to denounce the world's absurdity (*Le Chiendent*, 1933; *Pierrot mon ami*, 1942; *Loin de Rueil*, 1944; *Zazie dans le métro*, 1959; *Les Fleurs bleus*, 1965; *La Voi d'Icare*, 1968). He also sought to point out contradictions in language itself and the development of a new type of French, based on the spoken language or argot (*Exercises de style*, 1947 and 1963). For this purpose, he created OuLiPo, the acronym for Ouvroir de Littérature Potentielle, an experimental literary workshop founded by Queneau and other leading writers, where various theoretical writings were developed (*Bâtons, Chiffres et Lettres*, 1950 and 1965). Queneau was named to the Académie Goncourt in 1951.

## Quesnay, François (1694–1774)
*physician, economist*
A surgeon at the Hôtel-Dieu de Mantes and principal founder of the Physiocratic school, François Quesnay was born in Méré, ÎLE-DE-FRANCE. After becoming physician to King LOUIS XV, Quesnay, deeply interested in economics, wrote two articles on that subject ("Fermier," 1756; "Grains," 1757) for the *Encyclopédie* of DENIS DIDEROT and for his own *Tableau économique* (1758), in which he presents his idea of the "natural law" of economics. Affirming that the sole source of wealth is agriculture, and that manufacturing, commerce, and industry, because they derive from it, were essentially nonproductive, Quesnay encouraged free trade in foodstuffs and asserted, with the other Physiocrats (MIRABEAU, CONDORCET, TURGOT), that economic laws must be allowed to act without interference for the prosperity of the nation (the principle of laissez-faire).

## Quesnay de Beaurepaire, Jules (1838–1924)
*magistrate, writer*
Born in Vitrai-sous-l'Aigle, Orne, Jules Quesnay de Beaurepaire was the procurator general of the Court of Appeals in Paris and wrote the statement of accusation against General GEORGES BOULANGER (1889). He also prosecuted the defendants in the PANAMA AFFAIR case (1892). In 1899, he resigned his judicial position in protest against the reversal of the court decision on ALFRED DREYFUS. A novelist, Quesnay de Beaurepaire published several works.

## Quesnel, Pasquier (1634–1719)
*theologian*
Born in Paris, Pasquier Quesnel was an Oratian priest who, upon becoming a Jansenist, left the Oratory (1681) and joined ANTOINE ARNAULD in Brussels (1685). He was, after Arnauld, the leader and main organizer of the Jansenist faction. Imprisoned at Malines (1703), he escaped and settled first in Liège, then in Utrecht. Quesnel's *Réflexions morales sur le Nouveau Testament* (1699) were condemned in the papal bull *Unigenitus Dei Filius* (1713), to which Quesnel responded by "appealing" to a general council of the church.

## Queuille, Henri (1884–1970)
*political figure*
Born in Neuvic-d'Ussel, Corrèze, Henri Queuille served several times as minister (in particular of agriculture) during the THIRD REPUBLIC. He joined General CHARLES DE GAULLE in exile (1943) and, after World War II, served as premier from September 1948 to October 1949. He had to deal with an important series of strikes led by the unions and the PCF (SEE COMMUNIST PARTY, FRENCH) (October–November 1948) and signed the Atlantic Pact for France. Faced with the instability of the FOURTH REPUBLIC, he put to the vote an electoral law called *des apparentements*, whose purpose was to correct the effects of proportionality but that would be rejected by the National Assembly. From 1952 to 1954, Queuille served in various cabinets as vice president of the Council of ministers.

## Quignard, Pascal (1948–    )
*essayist, novelist, translator, screenwriter*
Born in Verneuil-sur-Avre, Pascal Quignard is known for his erudition, enthusiasm, language, and rigorous and elliptical style colored, however, by his sensitivity (*Carus*, 1979; *Les Tablettes de buis d'Apronenia Avitia*, 1984; *Le Salon du Wurtemburg*, 1986; *Les Escaliers de Chambord* (1989), and *Tous les matins du monde*, 1991, successfully adapted to the screen, thus introducing his work to a wider audience). Quignard is equally known for his essays.

## Quinault, Philippe   (1635–1688)

*dramatic poet*

A librettist as well as poet, Philippe Quinault, who was born in Paris, was inspired in turn by Jean de Rotrou (*Les Rivales*, 1653), Pedro Calderón de la Barca (*Le Fantôme amoureux*, 1659), and THOMAS CORNEILLE (*Astrate*, 1655). Quinault's tragedies and comedies (*La Mère coquette*, 1665) all show a cleverness in style and imagination. He took part, along with PIERRE CORNEILLE and MOLIÈRE, in the production of *Psyche* (1671), and also composed the librettos for the operas of JEAN-BAPTISTE LULLY (*Thérèse*, 1675; *Persée*, 1682; *Roland*, 1685), working in close collaboration with the composer. Quinault was elected to the ACADÉMIE FRANÇAISE in 1670.

## Quinet, Edgar   (1803–1875)

*historian*

Born in Bourg-en-Bresse, Edgar Quinet was the translator of J. G. von Herder's major work, *Outlines of a Philosophy of the History of Man* (1825), and later took part in an expedition to Greece (1828), after which he published *De la Grèce moderne et de ses rapports avec l'Antiquité* (1830). Then, influenced by the writings of Mme de STAËL, he developed a deep interest in German history (*Système politique de l'Allemagne*, 1831). Quinet also was, along with JULES MICHELET, one of the strongest opponents of clericalism, and the subject of his lectures at the COLLÈGE DE FRANCE (against the Jesuits, 1843; Ultramontanism, 1844; Christianity and the Revolution, 1845) caused his dismissal in 1846. Elected deputy in 1848, he spoke out for the complete separation of church and state and against the Roman Expedition of 1849, a French campaign against the revolutionary Roman Republic. Proscribed after the coup d'état of December 2, 1851, he went into exile in Belgium and Switzerland, while continuing his studies in history (*Les Révolutions d'Italie*, 1852; *La Révolution*, 1965; *La Création*, 1870). After returning to France, Quinet was elected a deputy (1871) to the National Assembly.

## Quinette, Nicolas-Marie   (1762–1821)
## (baron de Rochemont)

*political figure*

Born in Soissons, Nicolas-Marie Quinette, during the REVOLUTION OF 1789, served as deputy to the Legislative Assembly (1792) and as a member of the Committee of Public Safety (March 1793), and conducted an investigation on the conduct of General CHARLES DUMOURIEZ. The latter then delivered Quinette, along with his fellow commissioners, over to the Austrians, who, in 1795, exchanged him for Madame Royale, the duchess of Angoulême. A member of the Council of Five Hundred, minister of the interior (1799), Quinette went over to NAPOLÉON I in 1799. Successively prefect, counselor of state, baron (of Rochemont) in 1810, and a peer of France during the HUNDRED DAYS, he was banished as a regicide in 1816 and died in exile.

## Quinton, René   (1867–1825)

*physiologist*

Born in Chaumes-en-Brie, Seine-et-Marne, René Quinton in his principal work, *L'Eau de mer, milieu organique* (1904), made the analogy between the internal environment of an organism (plasma) and ocean saltwater, the environment in which life began. From this analogy, he derived his therapeutic applications. He is responsible for developing "Quinton's plasma," sterilized saltwater diluted with distilled water to obtain a concentration equivalent to that of human plasma.

# R

## Rabaut Saint-Étienne, Jean-Paul (1743–1793)
*political figure*

Born in Nîmes, where he served as a Protestant pastor (1785), Jean-Paul Rabaut Saint-Étienne, who was the son of a pastor, was elected as a deputy for the Third Estate to the ESTATES GENERAL (1789). During the REVOLUTION OF 1789, he was elected to the Convention (1792) and, joining the Girondins, voted for a plebiscite and a postponement of the trial of King LOUIS XVI. He was also a member of the Commission of Twelve, established to investigate counterrevolutionary activities. Rabaut Saint-Étienne was proscribed as a moderate, condemned to death with the GIRONDINS, and executed.

## Rabelais, François (ca. 1483–1553)
*writer*

The details of the life of François Rabelais, who was born in La Devinière, near Chinon, are little known. Certain critics think he was born in 1494. In late 1510, he was a novice in the Franciscan monastery of La Baumette, near Angers, and in 1520 or 1521, he became a priest and Franciscan friar minor at the monastery of Puy-Saint-Martin in Fontenay-le-Comte, where he completed his theological studies and, with special permission, also those in law. Joining the Benedictine order in 1524, he accompanied the bishop of Geoffroy d'Estissac on his work at Poitiers. Between 1528 and 1530, he wore the habit of a secular priest and had two children from a liaison with a Parisian widow. Earning a degree in medicine at the University of Montpellier in 1530, he became a physician in LYON in 1532. The same year, Rabelais translated and edited Giovanni Manardi's *Epistolae medicinales,* the *Hippocratis et Galeni libri aliquot,* and the *Testamentum Cuspii,* writing to Erasmus that he recognized him as his "spiritual father," and published his own first great work, *Pantagruel,* under the name Alcofribas Nasier (an anagram of François Rabelais). After the publication of his *Pantagruéline Prognostication* (1533), Rabelais, in the following year, accompanied Cardinal JEAN DE BELLAY to Italy then, returning to Lyon, published consecutively the *Topographia antiquae Romae* of Morliani and his own work, *Gargantua,* the story of Pantagruel's father. Along with *Pantagruel,* this work had a prodigious success, although both were condemned by the SORBONNE. Having regularized his situation in regard to the church, Rabelais made a second journey to Rome with de Bellay (1532–36) and was named chapter canon of the abbey of Saint-Maur-des-Fosses. He then returned to Montpellier (1537), where he practiced medicine. The condemnation of his first two novels did not stop Rabelais from publishing *Tiers Livre* (1546), under royal patronage. But after the death of King FRANCIS I in 1547, Rabelais's writings were again condemned and he had to flee to Metz, where he served as city clerk. When he again visited Rome with de Bellay (1547–49), the first 11 chapters of his *Quart Livre* were published in Lyon (1548), with the entire edition appearing only in 1552, having been censured by the church. During the interval, JOHN CALVIN, in his *Traité des scandales* (1550), vehemently attacked Rabelais. The authorship of a final work, *Cinquième Livre,* published between 1562 and 1564, has been contested, and it seems that the book is not actually the work of Rabelais. In sum, Rabelais's writings are a great expression of 16th-century humanism. A genius, he was an antiquarian, a defender of the spirit of social justice, a pacifist who supported only defensive war, and a physician. He gave satirical expression to the philosophical and political concerns of his contemporaries through an incomparably rich and comic vocabulary, and he filled the French language with neologisms that are still in use today.

## Rachel, Mlle (1821–1858)
*tragedian*

Born in Mumpf, canton of Argovie, Élisabeth Rachel Félix, who is best known by her stage name of Mlle Rachel, was with the COMÉDIE-FRANÇAISE for 17 years, where she successfully acted in and interpreted the roles of heroines from the works of PIERRE CORNEILLE and JEAN RACINE. One of the most celebrated actresses of her day, she also appeared in *Adrienne Lecouvreur,* a popular play written as a vehicle for her by the playwright EUGÈNE SCRIBE.

## Racine, Jean (1639–1699)
*dramatist*

Considered the greatest writer of French classical tragedy, Jean Racine was born in La Ferté-Milon, the son of a tax official. Orphaned at an early age, he was raised and educated at the Jansenist convent of Port-Royal, where his aunt was a nun. Rigorously moralistic and intellectual, Racine accepted JANSENISM as one of the strongest influences in his life, but he was also influenced by the Greek (Sophocles, Euripides) and later classics that he had studied and could read fluently. Failing to gain an ecclesiastical benefice in the provinces, Racine returned to Paris (1663) and became friends with important literary figures, including JEAN DE LA FONTAINE. In 1664, he produced his first play, *Thébaïde,* followed by *Alexandre* (1665), and began a decade-long period that was the most productive of his career, with *Andromaque* (1667), *Les Plaideurs* (1668), *Britannicus* (1669), *Bérénice* (1670), *Bajazet* (1672), *Mithridate* (1673), *Iphigénie* (1674), and *Phèdre* (1677). After *Alexandre,* all his works were produced by the company of players of the Hôtel de Bourgogne and, with *Andromaque,* Racine replaced PIERRE CORNEILLE as the favorite of the young king LOUIS XIV and his court. Very much a figure of the court himself, Racine had several noted liaisons with actresses and was known for a stormy, tormented, and jealous nature. Except for his one comedy, *Les Plaideurs,* a satire on the Parisian language of his day, all of Racine's works deal with the heroic figures of antiquity, with their words and emotions adapted to 17th-century France. At the request of Mme de MAINTENON, Racine wrote his last dramatic works, the biblical tragedies *Ester* (1689) and *Athalie* (1691), for the young girls at her school at SAINT-CYR. In 1672, at the height of his success, Racine was elected to the ACADÉMIE FRANÇAISE and devoted most of his time to writing official history, including Louis XIV's military campaigns. He also wrote religious works, *Cantiques spirituels* (1694) and a history, *Abrégé de l'histoire de Port-Royal* (posthumous, 1767). Regarded as the supreme exponent of French classical poetry in rhymed Alexandrian verse, his most famous tragedies became integral to the repertory of the COMÉDIE-FRANÇAISE, and the interpretations of his characters have been standard tests for French actors. Although Racine's dramas are based on intense human passions, they follow a strict neoclassical formality, with restrained actions and emotions.

## Racine, Louis (1692–1763)
*writer*

Born in Paris, Louis Racine was the last son of the dramatist JEAN RACINE. An attorney, he left the bar to live with the priests of the Oratory, where he wrote a religious poem, *La Grâce* (1720). Ruined by the JOHN LAW financial debacle, he took an administrative post with the government, becoming inspector general of finances and the director of salt taxes (*gabelle*). A scholar, he was, at age 26, a member of the Writers' Academy, but his Jansenist views, which were apparent in his collection of writings (*La Religion,* 1747), were an obstacle to his election to the ACADÉMIE FRANÇAISE. He wrote numerous other works, including the important *Mémoires sur la vie de Jean Racine* (1747), and did a translation of John Milton's *Paradise Lost* (1750).

## Radiguet, Raymond (1903–1923)
*writer*

Born in Saint-Maur-des-Fossés, Raymond Radiguet, whose career was as precocious as it was short, was encouraged by ANDRÉ SALMON before meeting JEAN COCTEAU. Like them, Radiguet wrote novels reminiscent of the traditional psychological works of MARIE DE LA FAYETTE. Having published a collection of poems, *Les Joues en feu* (1920), and a play, *Les Pélicans* (1921), he had a considerable success with his novel, *Le Diable au corps* (1923). With difficulty, Radiguet finished his next novel, *Le Bal du comte d'Orgel* (posthumous, 1924). An admirer of the moral novelists like La Fayette, STENDHAL, and MARCEL PROUST, he wrote also in a restrained and measured style, while evoking human passion and emotion (reminiscent of COLETTE and FRANÇOIS MAURIAC). As COCTEAU said, praising his genius, Radiguet "belonged to that solemn race of men whose lives unfold too quickly to their close."

## Raimu (1883–1946)

*actor*

Born Jules Muraire in Toulon, Raimu as he is known, made his debut in *cafés-concerts* (1914) and gained notoriety for his creation of the role of César in MARCEL PAGNOL's *Marius* (1929), reprised in film in 1931. After the success of Pagnol's trilogy, Raimu appeared in a number of films, including those of MARC ALLÉGRET (*Gribouille*, 1937) and again of Pagnol (*La Femme du boulanger*, 1938; *La Fille du Puisatier*, 1940), and of SACHA GUITRY (*Faisons un rêve*, 1937). On the stage he played, at the COMÉDIE-FRANÇAISE, the role of Argan in *Malade imaginaire* and M. Jourdain in *Bourgeois gentilhomme* (1944). Raimu was known for imparting his powerful personality to the characters he portrayed.

## Ramadier, Paul (1888–1961)

*political figure*

Born in La Rochelle, Paul Ramadier served as the mayor of Decazeville (1919) and as a Socialist deputy (1928), and founded the Socialist and Republican Union (1933). Minister of labor in the cabinets of CAMILLE CHAUTEMPS and ÉDOUARD DALADIER (1938–40), and a supporter of the POPULAR FRONT with LÉON BLUM, he voted against giving full powers to Marshal PHILIPPE PÉTAIN (July 1940) and joined the RESISTANCE. Minister of supplies (1944–45), and of justice (1946–47), then premier (January 1947), he removed the Communist ministers (e.g., MAURICE THOREZ) from the government who were opposed to his social, political, and colonial policies, putting an end also to tripartism (May 1947). Adhering to the Marshall Plan for aid to Europe after World War II, presented to counteract the rise of communism, and putting through the vote on ALGERIA (August 1947), but faced with social unrest, he had to resign (November 1947). Ramadier later served as minister of national defense (1948–49), then of economic affairs (1956–57).

## Rambouillet, Catherine de Vivonne, marquise de (1588–1665)

*salon hostess*

A hostess who presided over one of the most important of the 17th-century French literary salons, Catherine de Vivonne, marquise de Rambouillet, was born in Paris. The salon that she established there, at the hôtel de Rambouillet, exerted a great influence on French literature and language for over a generation and was frequented by such leading writers and intellectuals as PIERRE CORNEILLE, MOLIÈRE, MADELEINE DE SCUDÉRY, Mme de SÉVIGNÉ, JACQUES-BÉNIGNE BOSSUET, FRANÇOIS DE MALHERBE, and others. Molière satirized Mme de Rambouillet's salons in *Les Précieuses ridicules* (1659).

## Rambuteau, Claude-Philibert-Barthelot, count de (1781–1869)

*political figure*

Born in Mâcon, Claude-Philibert-Barthelot, count de Rambuteau served as chamberlain to NAPOLÉON I and as prefect (1811). Keeping his posts during the First RESTORATION (1814), he fought against the royalist insurrectionists during the HUNDRED DAYS and was forced to retire from political life at the time of the Second RESTORATION (1815). A deputy for the opposition in 1827, he gave the "Address of the 221" (March 1830) by members of the opposition in the Chamber after the king's, showing the great distance between the king and the people's representatives. During the JULY MONARCHY, he was named prefect of the Seine (1833–48) and produced numerous works that embellished and renewed the capital (notably the construction of the avenue that today bears his name, the building of the ARC DE TRIOMPHE and the Madeleine, and gas illumination).

See also REVOLUTION OF 1830.

## Rameau, Jean-Philippe (1683–1764)
*composer*

Considered France's greatest 18th-century composer and a highly influential music theorist, Jean-Philippe Rameau was born in Dijon, where he was educated in music by his father, an organist. At age 18, Rameau made a short visit to Italy and, returning to France, was subsequently an organist in Avignon, Clermont-Ferrand, and Paris (1705), where he wrote his first work, *Premier livre de pièces de clavecin*, which at the time went unappreciated. Later, he followed his father as organist at Notre-Dame in Dijon (1709) and then spent some time in LYON. In 1722, his *Traité de l'harmonie réduite à ses principes naturels* was published, followed some time later by another theoretical work, *Génération harmonique* (1737). Settling finally in Paris, Rameau taught harpsichord and music theory and wrote compositions, light theatrical pieces, and religious music. He become director of the private orchestra of a wealthy patron (who introduced him to VOLTAIRE) and devoted himself to composing operas. His approximately 30 operas include such masterpieces as *Hippolyte et Aricie* (1733), *Castor et Pollux* (1737), *Les Fêtes d'Hébé* (1739), *Dardanus* (1739), *Platée* (1745), and *Zoroastre* (1749). Opera-ballets include *Les Indes galantes* (1735) and *La princesse de Navarre*, composed for the marriage of the dauphin (1745). Also at this time, he composed his admirable *Pièces de clavecin* (1741). Rameau was involved, too, in the Bouffons debate over musical styles (1752–1754), with JEAN-JACQUES ROUSSEAU, Melchior de Grimm, and the Encyclopédists, partisans of Italian music, in which he defended the post-Lully style of French opera. Although Rameau's compositions went out of style after his death, his theoretical writings detailed concepts that remained basic to European harmony until the end of the 19th century.

## Rampal, Jean-Pierre (1922–2000)
*flutist*

Jean-Pierre Rampal, who brought the flute to prominence as a virtuoso solo instrument in the 20th century, was born in MARSEILLE, where he studied with his father, also a flutist. Rampal soon left medical school to pursue a musical career and was known for his brilliant technique, warm tone, and sensitive musical style. He performed with many

Jean-Philippe Rameau *(Library of Congress)*

of the world's famous orchestras and chamber ensembles, and edited and performed many hitherto little-known works of the 18th century. Rampal published his memoirs, *Musique, ma vie,* in 1989.

## Ramus (1515–1572)
### (Pierre de la Ramée)
*humanist, mathematician, philosopher*

Born in Cuts, Vermandois, Ramus (the latinized name of Pierre de la Ramée), was opposed to the Scholastic tradition of Thomas Aquinas and wrote two works against Aristotle, which brought a strong reaction from the SORBONNE. Nonetheless, he became the first professor of mathematics at the Collège royal (COLLÈGE DE FRANCE). Joining the Reformation, he had to give up his chair, which he regained after the Peace of Amboise, from 1563 to 1567. In his *Dialectique* (1555), the first philosophic treatise written in French, he upheld the use of the vernacular in debates and discourses. His *Gramere* (1562) is an essay on grammatical structure in which he proposed a reform of French orthography. He translated into French the *Éléments* of Euclid and published *Arithmetica* (1555); his various writings are collected in a work (*Scholarum mathematicorum libri unus et triginta,* (1562) in which he deals with negative numbers. Also, Ramus had a profound effect on methods of teaching and instruction. He was assassinated during the SAINT BARTHOLOMEW'S DAY MASSACRE.

## Rapp, Jean, count (1772–1821)
*general*

Born in Colmar, Jean, count Rapp served as aide-de-camp to Napoléon Bonaparte (see NAPOLÉON I) when he was first consul and, after having fought in the campaign in Egypt and at the Battle of Marengo, was named ambassador extraordinary to Danzig (Prussia) (1807–09). He then served with distinction during the Russian campaign and the siege of Danzig (1813–14). Commander of the Army of the Rhine, charged with defending Strasbourg during the HUNDRED DAYS, he retired at the time of the Second RESTORATION but was nonetheless raised to the peerage in 1817, after going over to the Bourbons.

## Raspail, François-Vincent (1794–1878)
*biologist, political figure*

Born in Carpentas, François-Vincent Raspail came to Paris, where he published several works on animal and vegetal life (1824–28) in which he seems to have developed a preliminary form of the cellular theory of histology and cytology. In particular, he introduced chemical tests in microscopic observations, allowing the identification of several substances. He showed that faint traces of arsenic appear in the human body, a factor brought up in a famous court case of the period (1840), and in medicine he did research in the field of camphor. A supporter of the REVOLUTION OF 1830, Raspail belonged to a number of republican clubs and founded the newspaper *Le Réformateur* (1834–35), while also continuing his scientific studies. His political views, which favored a social-democratic republic, led him to publish works on public health (*Le Médicin des familles,* 1843; *Le Manuel de la santé,* 1845). In 1848, he was one of the first to proclaim the new republic, and he took part in the demonstrations of May 15, causing him to be arrested along with LOUIS BLANQUI and others. The Socialist candidate for president of the republic (1848), Ras-

pail was sentenced to prison (1849), then exiled. He returned to France only in 1863 and served as a deputy in 1869, and again from 1876 to 1878.

## Rassemblement du peuple français (RPF)

The Rassemblement du peuple français (RPF) was a French political movement founded in April 1947 by General CHARLES DE GAULLE, who, encouraged by JACQUES SOUSTELLE, ANDRÉ MALRAUX, and others, brought together former members of the RESISTANCE and members of the traditional right who were opposed to communism and wished for an alliance between labor and capital (see FOURTH REPUBLIC). After a victory in the municipal elections of April 1947, then a strong showing in the legislative elections in 1951, dissension broke out. After 1953, de Gaulle disbanded the party.

## Rassemblement pour la République (RPR)

The Rassemblement pour la République (RPR), a French political party that succeeded the Union des démocrates pour la République (UDR), was founded in December 1976. Led by JACQUES CHIRAC (1976–94), then by ALAIN JUPPÉ, it was the heir to the Gaullist parties.

## Ravel, Maurice (1875–1937)
*composer*

One of the most influential 20th-century composers, Maurice Ravel was born in Ciboure, where his parents encouraged his musical career. He entered the Paris Conservatory in 1889 and had influential teachers, the most important being GABRIEL FAURÉ. Ravel won only second place in the Prix de Rome, but many friends, including Igor Stravinsky and Sergey Diaghilev, saw in him a talent equal to that of his contemporary CLAUDE DEBUSSY. At this point, Ravel had already composed his *Habañera* for two pianos (1895), the overture for *Schéhérazade* (1898), the *Pavane pour une infante défunte* (1898), *Jeu d'eau* (1901), and other important pieces. Other works include *Gaspard de la Nuit* (1908), *Rhapsodie espagnole* (1908), and the celebrated orchestral piece *Boléro* (1928). He also composed impressionistic ballets (*Ma Mère l'Oye,* 1910; *Daphnis et Chloé,* 1912) commissioned by Diaghilev. Besides these, Ravel wrote compositions in all areas except religious music. For voice there are three *Poèmes de Mallarmé* (1913), the *Mélodies hébraïques* (1914), *Chansons madécasses* (1925–26), *Rêves* (1927), and *Don Quichotte à Dulcinée* (1932). For piano, *Menuet sur le nom de Haydn* (1909); for chamber music, *Introduction et Allegro* (1906), *Trio en la mineur* (1914), Sonate (1920), *Berceuse sur le nom de Fauré* (1922); and many other pieces including numerous orchestrations. In 1931, Ravel composed *Concerto pour la main gauche,* his last work, for the Viennese pianist Paul Wittgenstein. Ravel's vivid, transparent orchestral colors rank him as one of the modern masters of orchestration, and his art has found a permanent place in the annals of modern music, with critics noting that he has "reached the limits of the impossible."

## Raysse, Martial (1936–   )

*painter*

Born in Golfe-Juan, Martial Raysse was introduced in 1960 to the group of painters known as new realists, and remained with them until 1963. He developed his own style, approaching pop art with its accumulation of objects (*Hygiène de la vision,* 1960; *Raysse Beach,* 1962), as he sought to use items from the environment while employing new techniques, such as the use of neon tubes (*Peinture haute vision,* 1965), fluorescent paint (*Fait au Japon,* 1964, reproducing a reproduction of JEAN-AUGUSTE-DOMINIQUE INGRES's *Grand Odalisque*), enlarged photographs (*Tableaux à géométrie variable,* 1965). Beginning in 1968, Raysse returned to the use of natural materials and, using film negatives and collages, produced a number of new works (*Homero Presto,* 1968). Later, he turned to historical themes in his paintings, using epic poetry as an inspiration and vast landscapes, saturated with strong colors (*Ceux de maquis,* 1992).

## Réaumur, René-Antoine Ferchault de (1683–1757)

*physicist, naturalist*

Considered the father of the French iron-and-steel industry, René-Antoine Ferchault de Réaumur was born in La Rochelle. He demonstrated that castings can be made into steel by adding metallic iron, and he studied the process of hardening and tempering steel (1722). He also invented an alcohol thermometer and the Réaumur temperature scale (1730). In the natural sciences, he studied invertebrates, especially insects, and devoted a number of works to their habits and development (he opposed the idea of spontaneous generation). He also proved that corals are animals, not plants. Additionally, Réaumur investigated gold-bearing rivers, turquoise mines, and forests, and did research on the composition of Chinese porcelain, which led him to develop an opaque glass. He was named to the Academy of Sciences in 1708, and in 1710 directed the official description of arts and trades in France.

## Rebecqui, François Trophime (1760–1794)
### (François Trophime Rebecquy)

*political figure*

Born in Marseille, François Trophime Rebecqui (or Rebecquy), during the REVOLUTION OF 1789, served as a deputy to the Convention, where he joined with the GIRONDINS. He tried, after the elimination of the Gironde group (June 2, 1793), to raise a FEDERALIST INSURRECTION in Provence. It was suppressed by the royalists, however, and Rebecqui committed suicide.

## Récamier, Jeanne-Françoise-Julie-Adélaïde Bernard, Mme (1777–1849)

*salon hostess*

Born in LYON, at age 15 Jeanne-Françoise-Julie-Adélaïde Bernard married a wealthy banker, Jacques Récamier. Gifted with beauty and wit, she established a salon in PARIS that soon became the favorite rendezvous of the foremost political and literary figures of the age, particularly the opponents of NAPOLÉON I. These included Mme de STAËL, RENÉ DE CHATEAUBRIAND, JEAN-JACQUES AMPÈRE, BENJAMIN CONSTANT, CHARLES SAINTE-BEUVE, and the generals JEAN MOREAU and Charles Bernadotte (see CHARLES XIV). She was exiled from the city in 1811 by Bonaparte for her royalist sympathies, but after his defeat, reestablished her Parisian salon, which continued to attract many notable personages.

There is a famous painting of Mme Récamier by JACQUES-LOUIS DAVID in the LOUVRE and one by INGRES.

## Reclus family
*family of French geographers, scientists, political theorists, and anarchists*

Élie Reclus (1827–1904) was born in Saint-Foy-la-Grande, and was banished in 1851 and again in 1871 for his political beliefs. He wrote an important ethnographic work, *Les Primatifs, Études d'ethnographie comparée* (1885). Elisée Reclus (1830–1905), the brother of Élie Reclus, was born in Saint-Foy-la-Grande, and was also banished because of his opposition to the coup d'état of December 2, 1851. He traveled through Europe and America and, on his return (1857), began his geographic writings, contributing to the *Guides Joanne* and publishing *La Terre, description des phénomènes de la vie du globe* (1867–68). Affiliated with the socialist First International, he took part in the publication of *Cri du peuple* (1869). In 1871, he was sentenced to deportation to New Caledonia for his role in the Paris COMMUNE, but his sentence was commuted to 10 years in exile. Settling in Switzerland, he worked on the journal *La Révolte* with the anarchist Pytor Kropotkin and directed the newspaper *L'Étendard révolutionnaire* (1882). His work on the edition of his *Géographie universelle* earned him a position at the Free University of Brussels. Indefatigable, he never ceased traveling and writing, publishing a work on anarchism, *L'Évolution, la Révolution et l'Idéal anarchiste* (1898) and, in collaboration with his brother Onésime, produced various geographic studies on Africa (*L'Afrique australe*, 1901) and China (*L'Empire du Milieu*, 1902). Onésime Reclus (1837–1916), born in Orthez, was also a traveler and geographer. He explored Europe and Africa and published *La France et ses colonies* (1886–89), while working with his brother on editing studies on Africa and China. Their brother Armand Reclus (1843–1927), born too in Orthez, was likewise a geographer who explored principally Central America. Paul Reclus (1847–1914), another brother, was born in Orthez and did medical research that led to the utilization of cocaine as a local anesthetic, especially for the treatment of tuberculosis and other infections.

## Regnault or Regnaud de Saint-Jean-d'Angély, Michel (1761–1819)
*political figure*

Born in Saint-Fargeau, Michel Regnault (or Regnaud) de Saint-Jean-d'Angély was a deputy to the Estates General (1789) and, during the REVOLUTION OF 1789, joined the monarchists in the National Constituent Assembly (1789–91). Arrested under the TERROR (1793), he escaped and returned to France after Thermidor and the downfall of MAXIMILIEN ROBESPIERRE. Supporting the coup d'état of 18 Brumaire (November 9, 1799), which brought Napoléon Bonaparte (see NAPOLÉON I) to power, Regnault became a member of the Council of State, in which he directed the section for the interior. Prosecutor-general of the High Court and secretary of state to the imperial family, he was highly regarded by NAPOLÉON I, who made him a count (1808). A deputy and minister of state during the HUNDRED DAYS, he convinced the emperor to abdicate after the defeat at Waterloo (1815) and went into exile in America, then Belgium. Elected to the ACADÉMIE FRANÇAISE in 1803, he was excluded in 1816 for having supported Napoléon.

## Regnault or Regnaud de Saint-Jean-d'Angély, Auguste-Étienne (1794–1870)
*marshal of France*

Born in Paris, Auguste-Étienne Regnault (or Regnaud) de Saint-Jean-d'Angély was the son of MICHEL REGNAULT DE SAINT-JEAN-D'ANGÉLY. After serving in the final campaigns of the FIRST EMPIRE, he was aide-de-camp to NAPOLÉON I during the HUNDRED DAYS. Excluded from the military ranks during the Second RESTORATION (1815), he fought in the Greek War of Independence (1825), then was restored to his position in the French military (1829). He was a rightist deputy in the Constituent Assembly, then in the Legislative Assembly (1848, 1849), and a member of the expedition to Rome (1849), sent against the Roman Republic founded and led by Giuseppe Mazzini and other Italian nationalists after the Revolution of 1848. Regnault supported the policies of the prince-president Louis-Napoléon Bonaparte (see NAPOLÉON III), whom he served for a time as minister of war (1851). A senator (1852), he was named a marshal of France after distinguishing himself at the Battle of Magenta (1859).

## Reinach, Jacques, baron de (1840–1892)
*financier*

Of German origin, Jacques, baron de Reinach, was born in Frankfort am Main, Germany. Coming to Paris in 1863, he became involved with republican circles (particularly Gambettist) and obtained French nationality (1871). He was directly implicated in the PANAMA AFFAIR scandal and, accused of having corrupted members of Parlement, then indicted, he was found dead in his home (it was not known whether he committed suicide or was assassinated).

## Reinach, Joseph (1856–1921)
*political figure*

The nephew of JACQUES REINACH, Joseph Reinach was born in Paris. The leader of the cabinet of LÉON GAMBETTA and editor in chief of *La République française*, he was a deputy (1889–98) during the period of the Dreyfus affair. He defended ALFRED DREYFUS and denounced in particular the forgery of Colonel HUBERT HENRY. Reinach was reelected in 1906 and 1910. He is the author of *Histoire de l'affaire Dreyfus* (1901–11).

## Reinhardt, Jean-Baptiste (1910–1953)
**(Django Reinhardt)**

*musician, jazz composer*

Known popularly as Django, Jean-Baptiste Reinhardt was of Romany origin and was born in Liberchies, Belgium. A self-taught guitarist, he performed at the Hot Club de France in Paris, where he formed a string quintet (1934) and developed an original style based on the main currents of black American music. The strength of his harmonic sense and the richness of his improvisations made him one of the greatest jazzmen of his time. Reinhardt's main recordings with the HCF (Hot Club de France) quintet include: *Minor Swing* (1937) and *Nuages* (1940).

## Religion, Wars of

The Wars of Religion were a series of long civil wars, and included various treaties, that took place in France from 1562 to 1598. The success of the Calvinist Reformation and its rapid propagation created little by little a climate of tension, contained for a while by the attempts at reconciliation of CATHERINE DE' MEDICI. The massacre at Wassy (1562), ordered by the duke of GUISE in reaction against the Edict of Saint-Germain (January 1562) opened the conflict that would pit Catholics and Protestants against each other, each side trying to assure by force the triumph of the true faith. The Wars of Religion also had a political aspect; the great lords profited from the situation to gain autonomy in the provinces, while at the national level, the houses of Guise and MONTMORENCY, in rivalry with those of the BOURBONS and Coligny, tried to gain control of the royal power being exercised at the time by the regent, Catherine de' Medici. The two sides appealed to foreign powers for help, one to England and the other to Spain, and brought to France pillaging bands of soldiers, battles, massacres, tortures, and assassinations. The first war ended with the Peace of Amboise (1563) but was soon renewed. Despite the Catholic victories at Jarnac and Moncontour (1569), the subsequent Peace of Saint-Germain (1570) was favorable to the HUGUENOTS. But it also provoked a Catholic reaction, and the ST. BARTHOLOMEW'S DAY MASSACRE (1572) brought a new period of conflict, ended in 1576 by the Peace of Monsieur (1576). This peace, gained through political negotiations, was judged as too moderate. The Catholic League renewed the fighting while dictating its wishes to the king (see HENRY III), and the history of the Wars of Religion became involved with that of the French Crown. The most important subsequent events were the DAYS OF THE BARRICADES (1588), the assassination of the duke of Guise, and then that of Henry III. HENRY IV also had to fight to establish his authority, and gathered around himself a moderate political faction. Peace was already made with the Spanish when he signed the EDICT OF NANTES (1598), which put a final end to the Wars of Religion. The nation was ravaged, however, and royal authority, so strong under the first Valois kings, was challenged. Finally, the discontent of the two religious groups was not ended and resulted in the assassination of Henry IV and the Protestant resistance that would trouble the following reigns.

## Remusat, Charles-François-Marie, count de (1797–1875)

*political figure*

Born in Paris, Charles-François-Marie, count de Remusat, was the son of Auguste de Remusat and the countess, née Claire-Élisabeth Gravier de Vergennes, lady-in-waiting to the empress JOSÉPHINE. He is known for his *Mémoires* (published 1879), which describe life at the imperial court. Remusat was a contributor to several newspapers (*Le Courrier français, Le Globe*) and served as a liberal deputy (1830–47) and as minister of the interior in the cabinet of ADOLPHE THIERS. Remusat supported the republic and was proscribed after the coup d'état of December 2, 1851. He was amnestied in 1859, and later was named foreign minister (1871–73). As a deputy again, he played a part in the editing of the constitutional laws (1875). Besides his memoirs, he left works on history and philosophy. Remusat was elected to the ACADÉMIE FRANÇAISE in 1846.

## Rémy, le colonel (1904–1984)

*Resistance leader*

Born in Vannes, Gilbert Renault, or le colonel Rémy, as he is known, was the founder of the intelligence network, during WORLD WAR II, known as la Confrérie Notre-Dame. After the war, he published works on the RESISTANCE (*Mémoires d'un agent secret de la France libre*, 1946; *La Ligne de démarcation*, 1964–70).

## Renan, Ernest (1823–1892)

*writer*

A leading philologist and historian of religion, Ernest Renan, who was born in Tréguier and had been destined for the priesthood since early youth, began seminary studies and had a serious religious crisis at age 22 (related in *Souvenirs d'enfance et de jeunesse*, 1883), subsequently breaking with the church. In the seminary he had studied Hegel, and that, along with his friendship with other intellectuals like MARCELIN BERTHOLET, led him to take an historical, rather than a theological, view of Christianity and religion in general. In *L'Avenir de la science* (1848, published 1888), he affirmed that religion must be replaced by the "poetry of reality." A dedicated philologist, notably in the field of

Semitic studies, Renan's visit to Lebanon and Palestine (1860–61) inspired his *Histoire des orgines du christianisme* (1863–82), a work of critical and rational philology. The first volume, *Vie de Jésus* (1863), which caused him to lose his chair in Hebrew studies at the COLLÈGE DE FRANCE, had a considerable effect in Europe, as much for its poetic style as for its rationalistic interpretation of Christ. While he rejected Catholic doctrines, Renan continued to admire Judeo-Christian history (*Histoire du peuple d'Israël*, 1887–93), and he always attempted to reconcile religion and science. After 1870, Renan also expressed his skepticism of democracy (*La Réforme intellectuelle et morale*, 1871) and ecclesiastical structures (*Le Prêtre de Némi*, 1885). Elected to the ACADÉMIE FRANÇAISE in 1878, he was named director of the Collège de France in 1883, a post he retained until his death.

## Renard, Charles (1847–1905)

*military officer and engineer*

Born in Damblain, Vosges, Charles Renard constructed a dirigible balloon, *La France,* the first such to make a circuit round trip (about seven kilometer in 1884), powered by an electrically rotated propeller. Interested in aviation, Renard published numerous works dealing with aerodynamics, vertical flight, airship motors, and dirigibles. He also conceived of a series of numbers (Renard Series) constituting a base for normalization, also much used in the air industries.

## Renaud, Madeleine (1900–1994)

*actor*

Born in Paris, Madeleine Renaud, after a successful career at the COMÉDIE-FRANÇAISE (1921–47), founded with her husband, JEAN-LOUIS BARRAULT, the Renard-Barrault Company at the Théâtre Marigny (1947). Since her debut in the classics, Renaud kept a purity of style that also served well her contemporary scripts (*Oh les beaux jours*, Samuel Beckett, 1963; *Les Pavarents*, JEAN GENET, 1966), with a special affinity for those of MARGUERITE DURAS (*Des journées entières dans les arbres*, 1965–75; *Savannah Bay*, 1983). In motion pictures, she appeared notably in *Maria Chapdelaine* (1934), *Remorques* (1941), *Lumière d'été* (1943), *Le Ciel est à vous* (1944), and played a memorable Mme Tellier in *Le Plaisir* (1952).

## Renault, Louis (1843–1918)
*jurist, Nobel laureate*

Born in Autun, Louis Renault, from 1883 to 1918, taught international law at the universities of Paris and Dijon. He served as a legal adviser to the Ministry of Foreign Affairs after 1890 and was a member of the Permanent Court of Arbitration at The Hague (1899–1907). He was also the arbitrator in a number of important international cases. A pacifist, he shared the 1907 Nobel Peace Prize with the Italian pacifist Ernesto Teodoro Monetta.

## Renault, Louis (1877–1944)
*industrialist*

Born in Paris, Louis Renault, after building his first automobile, founded the Renault Frères factory at Billancourt in 1899 with the help of his brothers Marcel (1882–1903, killed during the Paris-Madrid automobile race) and Fernand (1865–1909). Designed at first for the building of racing cars, this plant continued to expand over the years. In 1902, the first Renault engine was built, and in 1905, the company received an order for 250 taxis, for London as well as Paris. In 1911, Renault Frères became the first automobile company to produce airplane engines. During WORLD WAR I, 110 Renault taxis shuttled French troops from Paris to the Battle of the Marne (1914), and in 1916, the company produced airplane engines in Russia. After the war, Louis Renault increasingly took the lead in French automobile production. During WORLD WAR II, the Renault factories produced for the German Wehrmacht and, after the war, Louis Renault was indicted and his factories nationalized (1945), becoming a state-owned company (Régie nationale des usines Renault), which was privatized in 1996.

## René I the Good (1409–1480)
## (René le bon)
*nobility*

Born in Angers, René I the Good was the duke of Bar (1430–80), duke of Lorraine (1431–53) through his marriage with Isabelle of Lorraine, duke of Anjou, count of Provence (1434–80), and titular king of Naples. The son of LOUIS II of Anjou and Yolande of Aragon, he inherited the kingdom of Naples (1453) but could not take it from Alphonse V of Aragon (1438–42). René I gave his support to his brother-in-law CHARLES VII of France during the HUNDRED YEARS' WAR. In his own domains, he created new taxes, centralized the administration, and earned for posterity the name "good king" René for his love of culture. A patron of the arts, he lived an active artistic and literary life in his various possessions, supporting notably the painter NICOLAS FROMENT. Himself a writer of stories (*Le Livre du cœur d'amour épris*, 1457), a treatise (*Traité de la forme et devis comme on fait les tournois*, 1451–52), and poems, he left Provence to his nephew Charles of Maine, who died without issue, thus allowing king LOUIS XI to unite that region with France. René I was the father of MARGUERITE D'ANJOU.

## Renée of France (1510–1575)
*duchess of Ferrara, Protestant leader*

Born in Blois, Renée of France was the second daughter of king LOUIS XII and ANNE OF BRITTANY. In 1528, she married Hercule (Ercole) III d'Este and soon became duchess of Ferrara (1534–59), where she held a brilliant court. A disciple of LEFÈVRE D'ÉTAPLES, she was won over to the Reformation and welcomed Protestant leaders (CLÉMENT MAROT, JOHN CALVIN) but was later imprisoned by her husband. After his death, she returned to Montugis, and formed one of the centers of Protestantism in France.

## Renoir, Jean (1894–1979)
*cinematographer*

One of the masters of French cinema, Jean Renoir, the son of the impressionist painter PIERRE-AUGUSTE RENOIR, was born in Paris. After serving in WORLD WAR I (and receiving the Croix de Guerre), Renoir became a ceramicist, demonstrating his sense of reality, patience, and taste for freedom. In the 1920s, with a small inheritance from his father, he began to write, direct, and produce independent films. A master of poetic naturalism in these works, which featured his wife, Catherine Hessling, Renoir shows the influence of not only the impressionists but also of ÉMILE ZOLA and GUY DE MAUPASSANT (*La*

*Fille de l'eau,* 1925; *Nana,* 1926; *La Chienne,* 1931; *Boudu sauvé des eaux,* 1932; *Une partie de campagne,* 1936). He opened the way to neorealism (*Toni,* 1935) and produced historical works (*La Marseillaise,* 1938) before producing three masterpieces: *La Grande Illusion* (1939), *La Bête humaine* (1938), and *La Règle de jeu* (1939). Audacious for his era, Renoir was an innovator whose greatest contribution was his ability to improvise and resist convention. His work is charecterized by his penchant for long, uninterrupted sequences and deep-focus photography, giving a sense of wholeness to the scene and a full interpretation with the actors. Renoir is also known for exploring the relationship between theater and reality and for his use of water imagery. During and right after the war, Renoir settled in Hollywood, but his films there, with the exception

of *The Southerner* (1945), were less successful. In 1950, he went to India and made *The River,* a beautiful film, then returned to Europe to make *Le Carrosse d'or* (1952), after a play by PROSPER MÉRIMÉE, *French Cancan* (1955), *Elena et les hommes* (1956), and *Le Déjeuner sur l'herbe* (1959). A strong influence on many filmmakers, Renoir was honored by the French government with the LEGION OF HONOR (1977) and received an Academy Award (1975) for his cumulative contributions to film art.

## Renoir, Pierre-Auguste (1841–1919)
*painter*

One of the best-known exponents of IMPRESSIONISM, Pierre-Auguste Renoir was born in Limoges and, as a child, worked in a porcelain factory in Paris,

*Madame Charpentier and Her Children,* by Pierre-Auguste Renoir, 1878 *(Library of Congress)*

painting designs on china. At the LOUVRE, he spent time copying the works of the 18th-century masters. In 1863, studying with the Swiss artist Charles Gleyre, he met CLAUDE MONET, ALFRED SISLEY, and FRÉDÉRIC-JEAN BAZILLE and went to paint with them at Fontainebleau. After initial refusals, Renoir was allowed to show at the 1868 Salon with his *Lise with a Parasol,* a work that shows especially the influence of GUSTAVE COURBET and ÉDOUARD MANET. In 1869, at Croissy, he took up the same themes as his friend Monet (*Les Canotier,* 1868; *La Grenouillère,* 1869) and there developed his particular treatment of color. He also met important art dealers at this time. In 1874, he gained recognition at the first impressionist exhibition and subsequently produced many works (*La Loge,* 1874; *Path Winding through High Grass,* 1875; *Le Moulin de la Galette,* 1876, one of the most famous impressionist paintings; *Madame Charpentier and her Children,* 1878). Renoir also moved away from the other impressionists in terms of color choice and subject, and was as much interested in painting the human form as he was in landscapes (*The Umbrellas,* 1882–84). In 1887, he did a series of studies of the female nude (*The Bathers*) that reveal his extraordinary techniques. Around 1888, he spent some time with PAUL CÉZANNE in the Midi and painted numerous works in the open air as well as intimate scenes (*Girls at the Piano,* 1892). Suffering from arthritis, he continued to paint portraits (*Crouching Venus*) and landscapes. Expressing his own sense of joy and sensuality, Renoir never ceased to convey his love of life in his works, and sought not so much to revolutionize painting as to achieve the quality of the great masters. His interest in the human form allowed him to integrate successfully color with theme and setting, and to present his independent sense of style and technique.

## Republic, First

The First Republic was the government of France from September 1792 to May 1804. Proclaimed during the REVOLUTION OF 1789, on September 23, a day after the revolutionary calendar went into effect (Year I), the First Republic, which replaced the monarchy and the ancien régime, was notable not only for the extension of the principle of universal suffrage, for various popular reforms, and for

military victories abroad, but also for the periods of the TERROR and the rule of MAXIMILIEN ROBESPIERRE (1793–94), the subsequent THERMIDORIAN REACTION, the government of the DIRECTORY (1795–99), which gave the regime a conservative tone, and the coup d'état of 18 Brumaire, Year VIII (November 9, 1799) which brought NAPOLÉON I and the Consulate to power. The First Republic ended with the proclamation of the FIRST EMPIRE.

## Republic, Second

The Second Republic dates from February 25, 1848, to December 2, 1851. Born of the REVOLUTION OF 1848, the Second Republic was founded on a constitution (proclaimed November 1848) that upheld the right to work (*Ateliers nationaux*), freedom of the press and of assembly, and abolition of the death penalty and slavery. A grave economic crisis provoked popular revolutionary agitations (April 16–May 15, 1848) that in turn brought violent repression led by General CAVAIGNAC (June 23–26), who had been given power by the government's Executive Commission to suppress the rebellions. Faced with a "red peril," the conservatives regrouped and, through the parti de l'Ordre, assured the election as president of the republic of Louis-Napoléon Bonaparte (NAPOLÉON III), who then took complete power through his coup d'état of December 2, 1851. A plebiscite was held (November 21–22, 1852), after which the SECOND EMPIRE was proclaimed (December 2, 1852).

## Republic, Third

The Third Republic was the government of France from September 4, 1870, to July 11, 1940, succeeding the SECOND EMPIRE after the defeat at Sedan in the FRANCO-PRUSSIAN WAR. An early act of the Third Republic, under ADOLPHE THIERS, was the suppression of the Paris COMMUNE (May 1871). The republic would also experience in its early years attempts of Bonapartist and monarchist takeovers (1886), the PANAMA AFFAIR (1889), the Dreyfus affair (see DREYFUS, ALFRED) (1896), and WORLD WAR I. Nonetheless, it was also a period marked by economic, scientific, and technological progress. In 1905, the Socialist Party (SFIO) joined the government, and the separation of church and state was achieved. After bringing the nation through World War I, the Third Republic saw, during the 1920s and 1930s, a period both of political unrest and of the formation of political coalitions (Bloc national, 1919; CARTEL DES GAUCHES, 1924; FRONT POPULAIRE, 1936), the rise of right-wing organizations such as the ACTION FRANÇAISE, and a financial scandal (STAVISKY AFFAIR). There were also important gains in terms of labor rights and social welfare during the 1930s. In foreign policy, the Third Republic, while extending the colonial empire, had achieved alliances with Great Britain and Russia in the pre–World War I period (Entente Cordiale), which brought France out of diplomatic isolation and, in the 1930s, sought to increase national defense in the face of the rising threat from Nazi Germany. Soon defeated at the beginning of the WORLD WAR II, the Third Republic ended when the National Assembly gave power to the VICHY regime (1940). The careers of many important French political leaders, including JEAN JAURÈS, JULES FERRY, GEORGES CLEMENCEAU, RAYMOND POINCARÉ, LÉON BLUM, ÉDOUARD DALADIER, and other significant figures were spent during the years of this government.

## Republic, Fourth

The Fourth Republic was the government of France from June 1944 to October 1958. While not officially proclaimed at first, the Fourth Republic came into being with the decree of General CHARLES DE GAULLE that put an end to the VICHY regime. A period of transition followed (1945–46) under a Provisional Government during which time the constitution of the Fourth Republic was adopted and, in January 1947, VINCENT AURIOL was elected as its first president. A Council of Ministers was formed under PAUL RAMADIER and a tripartite government (PARTI COMMUNISTE FRANÇAIS, PARTI SOCIALISTE, and MOUVEMENT RÉPUBLICAIN POPULAIRE) would deal with the critical economic and social issues of the postwar period. By 1947, there existed a Gaullist opposition (RASSEMBLEMENT DU PEUPLE FRANÇAIS), a strong Communist faction, and a centrist coalition (MRP, socialists, liberals). The government of the Fourth Republic signed the North Atlantic Pact establishing the North Atlantic Treaty Organization in 1949, and economic recovery accelerated, particularly because of the policies of JEAN MONNET. Colonial issues became critical during this period and, after the French defeat at DIEN BIEN PHU (May 1954), the government of PIERRE MENDÈS FRANCE ended the war in INDOCHINA and granted autonomy to Tunisia, while that of EDGAR FAURE gave independence to Morocco (1955). The government of Premier GUY MOLLET suffered a setback during the Suez Crisis, brought about by Egyptian leader Gamal Abdel Nasser's nationalization of the French-British–held Suez Canal (October–December 1956), but also signed the Treaty of Rome, which created the European Economic Community (March 1957). Economic problems accelerated the dilemmas of the Fourth Republic, whose end was signaled by the uprising in Algiers in May 1958. The cabinet resigned, and President RENÉ COTY asked General de Gaulle to assume power. In October 1958, the latter's cabinet adopted the constitution of the FIFTH REPUBLIC.

## Republic, Fifth

The Fifth Republic has been the government of France since October 1958. Coming to power in the wake of the events of May 1958, General CHARLES DE GAULLE put through, despite opposition from a faction of the Left, the constitution of the new republic, reinforcing the executive power and guiding France toward a presidential regime. From the Union de la nouvelle République and the Union des démocrates pour la République came the first prime ministers: MICHEL DEBRÉ (1959–62), GEORGES POMPIDOU (1962–68), MAURICE COUVE DE MURVILLE (1968–69), with de Gaulle as president, but who came to power not without difficulty (Algiers putsch, 1961; ÉVIAN ACCORDS, 1962, ending the war in ALGERIA). In foreign policy, de Gaulle sought to gain diplomatic and military independence for France (retreat from NATO; creation of nuclear deterrent powers), and to promote a "Europe des États." In economic and social areas, however, neither the measures of the Pinay-Rueff Plan (1958–59) nor the stabilization policies of VALÉRY GISCARD-D'ESTAING succeeded in halting inflation. After some relative electoral progress of the Left (1965, 1967) and economic, social, and cultural malaise culminating in the widespread strikes and protests of MAY 1968, the government faced a crisis. The resignation of General de Gaulle following a referendum brought political reform as GEORGES POMPIDOU was elected president and his governments (JACQUES CHABAN-DELMAS, 1969–72; PIERRE MESSMER, 1972–74) continued to modify Gaullist policies. Elected president in 1974, Giscard-d'Estaing, a centrist who undertook various reforms, was defeated in the presidential election of 1981 by FRANÇOIS MITTERRAND, marking the first major political change since 1958. Governing with PIERRE MAUROY (1981–84) and LAURENT FABIUS (1984–86), he brought further major reforms (nationalization, decentralization, retirement at age 60). The success of the Right in the 1986 legislative elections forced the president to name JACQUES CHIRAC as prime minister, marking a period of "cohabitation." In 1988 Mitterrand was reelected with a relative legislative election victory for the Socialists as well. The new governments (MICHEL ROCARD, 1988–91; ÉDITH CRESSON, 1991–92) had to face a climate of social malaise and a growing economic crisis. In foreign affairs, Mitterrand followed the policies of his predecessors, notably in terms of European unity, which was greatly encouraged, and he engaged France in the Gulf War (1990–91). The elections of 1993 brought a strong return of the Right, opening again a period of cohabitation (ÉDOUARD BALLADUR, 1993–95), then culminating in the election of JACQUES CHIRAC as president. The Chirac governments also were those of cohabitation (ALAIN JUPPÉ, 1995–97; LIONEL JOSPIN, 1997–2002). Recent developments of the Fifth Republic include the construction of the English Channel Tunnel (1994), nuclear testing in the South Pacific (1995–96), immigration issues, military involvement in Africa (1997–2003), the adoption of the Euro currency (1999), and the pursuit of an independent policy in the Middle East (2003).

## Resistance, French

External resistance to the German occupation during WORLD WAR II was organized after General CHARLES DE GAULLE's appeal from London to continue the war (June 18, 1940) and resulted in the formation of the Forces françaises libres (FFL; Free French Forces) and later the Comité français de libération nationale (National Committee of French Liberation). The interior resistance was formed toward the end of 1940 with the creation of various movements in both the occupied northern area of the country and in the southern area controlled by the VICHY regime (Combat, Libération, Franc-Tireur, OCM, réunion dans les Mouvements unis de Résistance). The actions of diverse networks were coordinated, beginning in 1943, by the Conseil national de la Résistance. While beginning operations for liberation, the military organizations of the Résistance (Armée secrète, Organization de résistance de l'armée, Francs-Tireurs, Partisans francais, and communist groups) were regrouped into the Forces françaises de l'intérieur, which, with the FFL, fought alongside the Allies in the military operations of the Liberation.

See also COMMUNIST PARTY, FRENCH; MOULIN, JEAN; PERRET, JACQUES; RÉMY, LE COLONEL; ROL-TANGUY, HENRI.

## Resnais, Alain (1922– )
### cinematographer

Born in Vannes, Alain Resnais made his debut with short-subject films of rare aesthetic quality: *Van Gogh* (1948), *Guernica* (1950), and the disturbing *Nuit et Brouillard* (*Night and Fog*) (1956). But the strength of his scenes and cinematographic rhetoric of his later works will affirm him as the most original creator of the young French school of film of the 1960s: *Hiroshima mon amour* (1959), *L'Année dernière à Marienbad* (*Last Year at Marienbad*) (1961), *Muriel, ou le Temps d'un retour* (1963), *La guerre est finie* (1966), *Providence* (1977), *Mon oncle d'Amérique* (1978), *La vie est un roman* (1983), *L'Amour à mort* (1984), *Mélo* (1986), *Smoking* and *No Smoking* (1993). In these he developed his most fervid meditations on the themes of love, the times, and the great problems that challenge the contemporary conscience.

## Restif, Nicolas (1734–1806)
### writer

Nicolas Restif, known also as Rétif de Bretonne, was born in Sacy, Yonne. Although he claimed to be self-taught, he received a religious education at

Bicêtre and then was apprenticed as a printer in Auxerre and in Paris. His varied and abundant work shows a keen sense of observation, especially in the two novels, *Le Paysan perverti ou les Dangers de la ville* (1775) and *La Paysanne perverti* (1784), later combined under the title *Le Paysan et la Paysanne perverties* (1787). An autobiographical romance, *La Vie de mon père* (1779), evokes the social conditions of the peasantry under the ancien régime, while his *Nuits de Paris, ou le Spectateur nocturne* (1788–93) gives a detailed picture of the libertine society of the 18th century. While the overall tone of his work is characterized by acute psychological insight, this is most apparent in his autobiographical *Monsieur Nicolas ou le Cœur humain dévoilé* (1794–97). With his *Anti-Justine ou les Délices de l'amour* (1798), Restif took opposition to the marquis de SADE's pornographic style and claimed to have added a moral note to eroticism. At the same time, he proposed a social reform inspired by JEAN-JACQUES ROUSSEAU that also anticipated the ideas of CHARLES FOURIER in a collected work entitled *Les Idées singulières*.

## Restoration

The Restoration (Restauration) is the name given to the period of French history during which, after the abdication of NAPOLÉON I (Treaty of Fontainebleau, April 1814), the monarchy was reestablished in favor of the older branch of the Bourbons and included the reigns of LOUIS XVIII (1814–15, 1815–24) and then of CHARLES X (1824–30). Supported by those who sought peace, the nobility, and the commercial bourgeoisie who hoped for an economic revival, the First Restoration was interrupted by the return of the emperor from Elba (the HUNDRED DAYS). This period ended with the defeat at Waterloo and Napoléon's second abdication, and brought back the Bourbon regime. It was the period of the extreme royalist WHITE TERROR and of a nondemocratic monarchy. Shortly after the accession of Charles X in 1824, the financial, economic, and social situation began to deteriorate, and the political crisis, exacerbated by reactionary policies and ideology, led to the REVOLUTION OF 1830 (July 1830) and Charles's abdication.

## Retz, Jean-François-Paul de Gondi, Cardinal de (1613–1679)
*political figure, satirist, writer*

Born at the château of Montmirail, Jean-François-Paul de Gondi was destined for the church, although, as he said, he "had neither the taste nor the disposition for it." Despite a stormy youth, he was well educated, learned seven languages, and studied both sacred and profane literature. From 1638 to 1642, he took part in plots against Cardinal RICHELIEU, then devoted himself to an ecclesiastical career. In 1644, named coadjutor to his uncle the archbishop of Paris, he became known for his popular sermons, earned the hostility of ANNE OF AUSTRIA and Cardinal MAZARIN, and joined the FRONDE, but then changed sides to the court faction. Made cardinal in 1651 by Pope Innocent X, who detested Mazarin, Cardinal Retz was imprisoned by the latter in 1652, was named archbishop of Paris in 1654, then was exiled to Rome. In 1657, his pamphlet against Mazarin was circulated. Forced to resign as archbishop of Paris (where he never exercised his ministry) in 1662, he was reinstated in 1664. He retired to the abbey of Saint-Denis, where he was buried, with king LOUIS XIV forbidding that even the least monument be erected in his memory.

## Revolution of 1789

The Revolution of 1789, or the French Revolution, includes the events beginning in 1788 and extending to the coup d'état of 18 Brumaire, Year VIII (November 9, 1799), which changed completely the social, political, legal, and religious structures of France, bringing an end to the ancien régime. Beginning with financial and ideological causes (the ideas of the ENLIGHTENMENT and of the philosophes), the Revolution of 1789 was precipitated by the calling of the ESTATES GENERAL the previous year. Marked by the Oath of the Tennis Court and the proclaiming of the Constituent Assembly (June 1789) and the taking of the BASTILLE (July 1789), the Revolution began to reach a critical stage with the flight of LOUIS XVI to Varennes (June 1791) and soon the declaration of war on other European powers. On September 22, a republic (see FIRST REPUBLIC) was proclaimed and, shortly after the execution of the king (January 1793), the TERROR began, with the government under the control the radical JACOBINS. Moderates, such as the GIRONDINS, were proscribed, and only with the overthrow of MAXIMILIEN ROBESPIERRE and his supporters was a moderate and liberal order restored. The instability of the new DIRECTORY government, exacerbated by tension between Left and Right, by financial and social crises, and by the military policy of the period, led the way for the coup d'état that brought NAPOLÉON I to power. The Revolution had brought freedom and political equality, the abolition of feudalism, and the concept of national sovereignty to France.

See also CIVIL CONSTITUTION OF THE CLERGY.

## Revolution of 1830

Known also as the July Revolution, the Revolution of 1830 began with the "Three Glorious" days of July 27, 28, 29, 1830, that put an end to the reign of King CHARLES X and led to the proclaiming of the JULY MONARCHY. The situation in France had already begun to deteriorate in 1826 and was exacerbated by the reactionary policies and ideology of Charles X and his government. The replacing of the moderate government of the count de MARTIGNAC with the conservative cabinet of JULES POLIGNAC reinforced the liberal opposition. Finally, the passing of the four Ordinances of Saint-Cloud (July 25, 1830), which limited the suffrage and abolished freedom of the press, brought the crisis to a peak. Banned newspapers were published, and uprisings, led especially by journalists, workers, and students, occurred throughout PARIS. On July 29, the insurgents proclaimed a republic. The fear of a populist government, however, especially among the bourgeoisie, caused many opposition deputies in the Chamber to seek a compromise by appealing to the Orléans branch of the Bourbon dynasty to assume the throne. After having withdrawn the four Ordinances, Charles X abdicated and the nomination of the duke d'Orléans was accepted (see LOUIS-PHILIPPE) as lieutenant general and regent of the kingdom. Shortly afterward, he was proclaimed king of the French.

## Revolution of 1848

The Revolution of 1848, known also as the Revolution of February 1848, began with the insurrectionist days of February 23 and 24, 1848, that brought an end to the JULY MONARCHY (reign of LOUIS-PHILIPPE), replacing it with the SECOND REPUBLIC. This revolution originated in the financial and economic crisis of 1846 and in the development of an opposition to the authoritarian and conservative policies of FRANÇOIS GUIZOT. This opposition culminated in the celebration of the Banquets (1847–1848) that were held in favor of electoral and parliamentary reform. The banning of such a meeting on February 22, 1848, by Guizot caused a demonstration and the organizing of a revolutionary campaign that led to his recall (February 23). After trying to form a new government (see LOUIS ADOLPHE THIERS), Louis-Philippe abdicated in favor of his grandson, but in the meantime, a provisional government was formed (LOUIS BLANC, DUPONT DE L'EURE, ALEXANDRE LEDRU-ROLLIN, ALPHONSE DE LAMARTINE, and others) that proclaimed the Second Republic. The first political reforms were then instituted: election of a Constituent Assembly by universal manhood suffrage, the formation of the Luxembourg Commission, and the establishment of the *Ateliers nationaux* to resolve the problem of unemployment. Socialist unrest continued, however (April 16 and May 15, 1848), and resulted in brutal suppression the week of June 23–26). Far from representing an isolated event in Europe, the French Revolution of 1848 (like that of 1830), was followed by numerous revolutionary movements in Germany, Austria, Italy (Giuseppe Mazzini), Hungary (Lajos Kossuth), and Poland: the "Springtime of the People," which was followed by a summer of political reaction and repression.

## Reybaud, Marie-Roch-Louis (1799–1879)
*economist and political figure*

Born in MARSEILLE, Marie-Roch-Louis Reybaud was a liberal journalist and the author of *Études sur les réformateurs ou socialistes modernes* (1840–43). In 1843, he published a satirical novel (*Jérôme Parturot à la recherche d'une position sociale*) that, in light of the JULY MONARCHY regime, had a great success. A liberal deputy in 1846, Reybaud moved away from the left after the REVOLUTION OF 1848, joined the Right in the Constituent and Legislative Assemblies (1848, 1849), and published a critique of the new regime in his novel *Jérôme Paturot à la recherche de la meilleure république* (1848). Reybaud retired after the coup d'état of December 2, 1851, and wrote a number of works on economics.

## Reynaud, Émile (1844–1918)

*inventor, cartoonist*

Born in Montreuil, the son of a watchmaker and an artist, Émile Reynaud, who was a teacher of physics and natural sciences, was the inventor of the praxinoscope (1876)—a device conceived for the projection of a strip of his drawings through the use of a drum with a central mirror, a reflector, and lens to enlarge the images. It was an improvement on the zoetrope that had been invented in the 1830s. In 1892, Reynaud began holding public screenings in Paris at the Grévin Museum, his "Théâtre optique," and over the years gave thousands of shows to eager audiences. The true creator of animated cartoons, Reynaud died in poverty.

## Reynaud, Paul (1873–1966)

*political figure*

Born in Barcellonette, Paul Reynaud was the prime minister of France when the German invasion occurred in 1940. Elected to the Chamber of Deputies as a member of the BLOC NATIONALE in 1919, then again from 1928 to 1940, he served also as minister of finance, of colonies, and of justice (1930–32). In April 1938, he became part of the cabinet of ÉDOUARD DALADIER as minister of justice, then of finance, in which role he achieved the devaluation of the franc, the reduction of state expenses, and the raising of tariffs to cover increasing military expenses. Named prime minister in May 1940, he decided, with British prime minister Winston Churchill, to send an expeditionary force to Norway to block Nazi German access to Swedish iron ore and, replacing General MAURICE GAMELIN with General MAXIME WEYGAND as chief of the

French armed forces, named himself minister of defense, appointing Marshal PHILIPPE PÉTAIN to the vice presidency of the Council. Supporting the continuation of the war in the colonies, Reynaud was outnumbered by the supporters of an armistice and resigned (June 16, 1940), leaving Pétain in power. He was subsequently imprisoned by the VICHY government and deported to Germany (1942–45). After the Liberation, he was reelected deputy (1946–62) and became a fervent supporter of the concept of European unity. Reynaud wrote *Le Problème militaire français* (1937), *La France a sauvé l'Europe* (1947), *Au cœur du mêlée* (1951), and his *Mémoires* (1960–63).

## Rhine

The Rhine River (French, Rhin) at ALSACE forms part of the French border with Germany. One of Europe's most historic rivers, the Rhine rises in eastern Switzerland and flows 865 miles (1,390 km) north to the North Sea. It is connected to such rivers as the RHÔNE, SAÔNE, and SEINE by a system of canals.

## Rhône

The Rhône River, which flows in both France and Switzerland (812 kilometers, of which 522 are in France), is one of France's major rivers. Surrounded by mountains, it flows rapidly, being affected by melting glaciers in the spring and summer. It furnishes great quantities of hydroelectric power and is the most navigable of French rivers.

## Ribault, Jean (ca. 1520–1565)

*navigator, colonizer*

Born in Dieppe, Jean Ribault (or Ribaut) was sent by Admiral GASPARD DE COLIGNY to found a colony for Protestants on the eastern coast of North America. He reached Florida in 1562. After returning to France in 1563, he rejoined his fellow colonizer RENÉ DE LAUDONNIÈRE in Florida in 1565 but was killed during an attack by the Spanish under Pedro Menéndez Avilés. His death was avenged by the DOMINIQUE DE GOURGUES.

## Ribot, Alexandre (1842–1923)
*political figure*

Born in Saint-Omer, Alexandre Ribot was an attorney and director of criminal affairs for the Ministry of Justice (1875), and was elected to the Chamber of Deputies as a moderate republican (center left, 1878–85). As foreign minister, he laid the groundwork for the Franco-Russian alliance (1890–93). Premier (December 1892–March 1893), he was forced to resign with his entire cabinet because of the PANAMA AFFAIR. Recalled to lead the government (with the portfolio of Finance, January–December 1895), he contributed to making the African island of Madagascar a French colony and set up the basis for a rapprochement with Germany. Senator (1909) and minister of finance (1914–17), he was named premier during a critical period of WORLD WAR I (March–September 1917). He replaced General GEORGES NIVELLE with General PHILIPPE PÉTAIN and opposed the meeting of ARISTIDE BRIAND with German representatives in Switzerland. He had to resign with his cabinet after the accusations of defeatism brought against the minister of the interior. Ribot left politics after having assumed the portfolio of foreign minister in the cabinet of PAUL PAINLEVÉ (September–November 1917). He was elected to the ACADÉMIE FRANÇAISE in 1906.

## Richelieu, Armand-Emmanuel du Plessis de Chinon, duke de (1766–1822)
*political figure*

Born in Paris, Armand-Emmanuel du Plessis de Chinon, duke of Frosnac (as he was first called) was the grandson of LOUIS-FRANÇOIS-ARMAND DE VIGNEROT DU PLESSIS, DUKE DE RICHELIEU. During the REVOLUTION OF 1789, he emigrated (1790) and served in the Russian army against the Turks. Thanks to the support of Czar Alexander I, he obtained the governorship of the province of Odessa (1803–14). Returning to France during the RESTORATION, he replaced TALLEYRAND as minister of foreign affairs and as prime minister and signed the second Treaty of Paris (November 1815). Under pressure from the Ultras (extreme royalists), he legalized the WHITE TERROR, the bloody reaction of royalists and religious fanatics against the revolu-

tionaries. After gaining the favor of the powers of the Holy Alliance, an 1815 pact among Russia, Prussia, and the Austrian Empire, he gained the removal of Allied forces from French territory and was invited to participate in the Congress of Aix-la-Chapelle in 1818. Replaced in that year by the liberal ministry of the duke DECAZES, Richelieu returned to power after the assassination of the duke of BERRY (1820) and, in the face of liberal opposition, tried to adopt moderately reactionary measures. His policy was judged as insufficient by the Ultras, however, in particular the count of VIL-LÈLE, and too authoritarian by the liberals. This dual opposition brought about the resignation of his cabinet in 1821.

## Richelieu, Armand-Jean du Plessis, Cardinal (1585–1642)
*prelate, statesman*

Armand-Jean du Plessis, Cardinal Richelieu, who more than anyone else promoted absolutism in France, was born in Paris and was destined for a military career. The need to keep the bishopric of Luçon in the family caused him to change to theological studies, and in 1607, he was consecrated a bishop. He zealously administered his diocese and, in 1614, was named a clerical delegate to the ESTATES GENERAL. He soon won the favor of the queen mother, MARIE DE' MEDICI, and in 1616, became secretary of state, but the following year he was banished with the queen from court. During his exile at his priory at Coussay, he wrote *Défense des principaux points de la foi catholique* and an *Instruction pour les chrétiens*. His role in the reconciliation of the queen with her son LOUIS XIII brought him a cardinal's hat (1622), and in 1624 he became the king's chief minister.

More a pragmatic statesman than a reformer, Richelieu remained in power for the rest of his life, pursuing a twofold policy: the restoration of royal power and the preponderance of France in Europe. In domestic affairs, he fought against all who would have inhibited royal authority, opposing even Marie de' Medici, who never ceased to plot against him. He executed many aristocratic opponents of the king. At the same time, he fought

Cardinal Richelieu *(Library of Congress)*

against Protestant power in France, besieging La Rochelle and ending HUGUENOT political and military strength, although assuring them religious freedom. Royal authority was strengthened through centralization and a general reorganization of the state bureaucracy. Legislation and the Royal Council were reformed, the right of remonstrance of the *parlements* was reduced, and intendants were installed. The state also became involved in religious affairs, fighting against the rise of JANSENISM, while Richelieu came into conflict with the Holy See by imposing a tax on the clergy's properties. In 1637 and 1639, Richelieu also undertook several financial reforms throughout the country, while encouraging the creation of a navy, the development of trade, and the growth of a colonial empire. He intervened, too, in the world of the arts, with the founding of the ACADÉMIE FRANÇAISE (1635). He

enlarged the SORBONNE and built the Palais-Cardinal, later the Palais-Royal.

Richelieu's foreign policy rested on his alliances with the Protestant princes against the Hapsburgs. As an alliance was being concluded in 1625 by the marriage of HENRIETTA MARIE of France with Charles I of England, France invaded the Valteline passes through the Alps, cutting off all communication among Austria, Spain, and Italy. He sent military expeditions to Italy (1629–30), while the invasion of duchy of Savoy brought the acquisition of Pignerol for France and the duchy of Mantua for the House of Nevers, which supported France. After having subsidized Gustavus Adolfus II of Sweden and the Protestant princes, France entered into the THIRTY YEARS' WAR (1635). The conquest of Alsace from the Holy Roman Empire and Artois and Catalonia from Spain assured France a preponderant place in Europe and confirmed again the success of the cardinal's foreign policy. Richelieu left a *Testament politique,* and a collection of his letters has been edited.

### Richelieu, Louis-François-Armand de Vignerot du Plessis, duke de (1696–1788)
*marshal of France*

Born in Paris, Louis-François-Armand de Vignerot du Plessis, duke de Richelieu was the great nephew of Cardinal RICHELIEU. He was at first duke de Frosnac. Married at age 15 to a daughter of the duke de NOAILLES, Anne Catherine, who was older than he, he continued his escapades and was confined for his affair with the duchess of Burgundy (1711), then for fighting a duel (1716), and finally for his part in the CELLAMARE PLOT (1719). Ambassador to Austria (1725–1728), thanks to the influence of Mme de PRIE, he sought a rapprochement between Austria and France. After having fought in the Wars of the Polish and Austrian Successions (he served with distinction at Dettingen, Bavaria, and Fontenoy, Belgium, and took Genoa, Italy, in 1747), Marshal Richelieu directed the occupation of Minorca (1756) during the SEVEN YEARS' WAR; seized Port-Mahon (1756), invaded Brunswick and Hanover, and received the capitulation of the Anglo-Hanoverian forces at Kloster Zeven in Lower

Saxony (1757). He was recalled, however, because of the pillaging that he allowed in the defeated areas. Marshal Richelieu then took up the life of a great lord and, libertine and elegant, was quite representative of his era. He was a correspondent and patron of VOLTAIRE and was elected into the ACADÉMIE FRANÇAISE in 1720.

## Richer, Léon (1824–1911)
*political activist*

Born in Paris, Léon Richer was, with MARIA DERAISMES, the founder of the mainstream republican French feminist movement. A notary clerk, he became aware of women's plight and wrote for opposition papers such as *L'Opinion national*. In 1869, he founded the Ligue pour le droit des femmes and began publishing his own newspaper, *Le Droit des femmes,* which lasted until 1891. Richer favored a gradualist approach to women's rights; he sought, first, civil equality, which, he believed, would lead to eventual political equality.

## Richier, Germaine (1904–1959)
*sculptor*

Known for her expressionist sculptures based on animal life, Germaine Richier was born in Grans, Bouche-du-Rhône, and studied at the Beaux-Arts Academy in Montpellier. She trained with the sculptor ANTOINE BOURDELLE and at first produced busts and standing figures. Working in bronze beginning in 1944, she produced animals, including bats, crabs, insects, and spiders (*La Mante religieuse,* 1946; *La Fourmi,* 1953) and, abandoning traditional figurative convention, used her imagination also to create strange beings, either human, animal, vegetable, or mineral, that seemed to incarnate obscure and hostile forces. Richier's inspiration and imaginative repertoire reveal affinities with surrealism (*Tauromachie,* 1953; a series *Hommes-Oiseaux,* 1953; and *La Montagne,* 1956). Mixing inventive forms and elements having a ferocious realism, she submitted anatomies to strange metamorphoses (*L'Aigle,* 1948; *La Feuille,* 1948). Her works can evoke a world of anguish and aggression or grotesqueness and tragedy, often mixed together, showing a powerful expressionist temperament.

Certain of Richier's other sculptures can be placed in an entirely different category, elegant and quiet, characterized by the combination of materials (lead, glass) and revealing a nonfigurative tendency (polychrome plaster, 1957–58).

## Richier, Ligier (ca. 1500–1567)
*sculptor*

Born in Dagonville, Ligier (or Léger) Richier traveled to Italy around 1515, working later in Lorraine and then finally having to go into exile to Switzerland because of his Protestantism. The sculptures he produced, with nature as his inspiration, are at once tragic and profoundly religious, and draw on the late Gothic spirit. His macabre naturalism is seen in the pathetic visages of the *Pietà* of Étain (1528), or in the *Gisant de Philippe de Gueldre* (1548), and is fully expressed in the famous *Transi de René de Chalon,* in the aspect of a nearly skeletal figure offering his heart to God (1544–47). But in the *Sépulcre* at Saint-Mihiel (1533–64), his tendency to the emotional is tempered somewhat by the influence of formal Italian idealism.

## Ricœur, Paul (1913–  )
*philosopher*

Born in Valence, Paul Ricœur was influenced by the existentialism of Karl Jaspers and the phenomenology of Edmund Husserl, whom he helped to make well known in France (*À l'École de la phénoménologie,* 1986, a collection of articles). Ricœur analyzed psychological, ethical, and metaphysical problems of free will in *Philosophie de la volonté* (1950–61) and, as a Christian thinker, tried to elucidate the meaning of prebiblical and biblical myths, questioning the fundamental writings of the great religions (*Lectures III, Aux frontières de la philosophie,* 1993). He sought, too, to develop an interpretive, or hermeneutic, philosophy, supported by psychoanalysis (*De l'interprétation: essai sur Freud,* 1965; *Le Conflit des interprétations: essai d'herméneutique,* 1969; *La Métaphore vive,* 1975; *Soi-même comme un autre,* 1990). His work also has an important place in political ethics (*Lectures I, Autour de la politique,* 1991), and he undertook an interpretation of history (*Histoire et Vérité,* 1955) and of fiction and mystery, with history as a story (*Temps et Récit*, three volumes, 1963–85). Upholding the philosophic tradition, Ricœur is a contemporary author who has pondered the relationship among the state and reason, political experience and human rights, and totalitarian evil. The question of values permeates all his writings on ethics, as does the hope for the improvement of the human condition.

### Rigaud, Hyacinthe (1659–1743)
*painter*

Born in Perpignon, Hyacinthe Rigau y Ros, or Hyacinthe Rigaud, as he is known, settled in Paris in 1681 and, under the guidance of CHARLES LE BRUN, dedicated himself to portrait painting, eventually gaining a success unequaled in that field. The official portraitist of King LOUIS XIV, in 1694 he painted him in his coronation robes and, in 1701, in his robes of state, his best-known work, in which he conveys a convincing image of royal majesty (see page 396). Rigaud had an interest in grand and noble poses that, through expression and costume, portray the social rank of his subjects. The royal courts of Europe, the aristocracy, and the wealthy bourgeoisie all preferred his work, including his large tableaux, which he made with the help of assistants. A master of pomp and ostentation, Rigaud could also show a sense of realism and individuality in his portraits. His style is best shown in his portrait of *Young Louis XV*, and he shows a more sober approach in his portrait of his mother, *Madame Rigaud* (1695), which would serve as a model for the sculptor ANTOINE COYSEVOX. Rigaud's works are well represented in the LOUVRE.

### Rigault, Raoul (1846–1871)
*journalist, political figure*

Born in Paris, Raoul Rigault was a disciple of LOUIS BLANQUI. A journalist for *Démocratie* and *La Marseillaise*, he was arrested in 1866 and again in 1870 after the publication of his pamphlet *Le Grand Complot*. A member of the Second Executive Commission of the Paris COMMUNE, Rigault was killed by the troops sent from Versailles during the Bloody Week of May 24, 1871.

### Rimbaud, Arthur (1854–1891)
*poet*

Born in Charleville, Arthur Rimbaud, a poet of the symbolist school, is the subject of a perennial mythology. Over the image of a precocious genius (he wrote verse at age 10) is superimposed that of an adventurer who, abandoning literature, threw himself into affairs, the details of which are little known, although he always tried to cultivate such an image. An early virtuoso of Latin verse, Rimbaud wrote his first French poem, *Les Étrennes des orphelins*, in 1869. The friendship that he began in 1870 with his French literature professor, G. Izambard, was then decisive; he discovered especially FRANÇOIS RABELAIS, VICTOR HUGO, and THÉODORE DE BANVILLE. Disturbed by the French declaration of war against Russia in 1870 (then later by the defeat of the Paris COMMUNE in 1871), Rimbaud attempted several visits to Paris, each of which ended with his return to Charleville. His poetry at that time shows his feeling against the war (*Le*

Arthur Rimbaud *(Library of Congress)*

*Dormeur du val,* 1870), against power (*L'Orgie parisienne ou Paris se repeuple,* 1871), and the clergy (*Les premières Communions,* 1871). At this point he developed a radical esthetic, particularly apparent in his *Lettre du voyant* (1871), in which he seeks to break with all traditional poetic forms. His works and ideas so impressed PAUL VERLAINE that he invited him to Paris, where Rimbaud attended many meeting of the Cercle Zutique, an avant-garde poetry group. His liaison with Verlaine, which was often stormy, was carried on in Belgium, London, then back to Brussels, where the relationship climaxed with Verlaine twice attempting to take the life of the younger poet, wounding him seriously (July 1873). Rimbaud wrote an allegorical account of this in *Une Saison en enfer* that, along with *Illuminations,* constitutes his literary testament and marks his entrance into modernity. A series of visits followed to Germany, Switzerland, and Italy, then after 1878 to North Africa, where he worked as a trader (1880). Rimbaud then went to Egypt, Aden, and Ethiopia. Verlaine, believing Rimbaud was no longer alive, published *Illuminations* (1886), which contains the famous *Sonnet des voyelles,* in which each of the five vowels is associated with a different color. In 1891, Rimbaud returned to France for medical treatment and died in Marseille.

## Riquet, Pierre-Paul de  (1604–1680)
*engineer*
Born in Béziers, Pierre-Paul de Riquet, an engineer, built the Midi Canal (Canal du Midi, 1666–81) that connects the Mediterranean Sea with the Garonne River. When the funding for this project proved to be insufficient, Riquet used all of his own fortune to finish the enterprise.

## Rist, Charles  (1874–1955)
*economist and administrator*
Born in Lausanne, Charles Rist served as deputy director of the Bank of France (1926–29) and as financial adviser to the National Banks of Austria and Romania. He brought to liberalism his concept of monetary orthodoxy, which was applied to the currency stabilization policies of the post–WORLD WAR I era. Rist's publications include *Histoire des doctrines économiques depuis les physiocrates jusqu'à nos jours* (with CHARLES GIDE, 1909), *Essais sur quelques problèmes économiques et monétaires* (1933), *Défense de l'or* (1955).

## Rivière, Jacques  (1886–1925)
*writer*
A founder in 1910 and the moving spirit of the influential *Nouvelle Revue française,* which he then edited from 1919 onward, Jacques Rivière was born in BORDEAUX. From his student days, he was a friend of ALAIN-FOURNIER, who later became his brother-in-law and with whom he carried on an important *Correspondance* (January 1905–July 1914), along with PAUL CLAUDEL and ANDRÉ GIDE. Rivière is the author of *Études* (1911), a work dealing with his contemporaries (Gide, Claudel, and FRANCIS JAMMES), and a collection of memoirs, *L'Allemand* (1918), of his time as a prisoner of war in WORLD WAR I, and of a novel, *Aimée* (1922). Returning to Catholicism in 1913, he left manuscripts that were reorganized by his wife after his death (*À la trace de Dieu,* 1925). Essays that were published after his death include *Rimbaud* (1933), *De la foi* (1928), and *Moralisme et Littérature* (1933). He also left an unfinished novel, *Florence* (1935).

## Robert, Hubert  (1733–1808)
*painter, engraver*
Known for his landscapes and romantic views of classical ruins, Hubert Robert was born in Paris, where he trained in various studios. In 1759, he began an 11-year visit to Italy (with JEAN-HONORÉ FRAGONARD) and painted a large number of scenes of ruins, Roman monuments, and picturesque scenes. Returning to France, he made the painting of such ruins fashionable, portraying in his works the ancient monuments of Provence (*Le Pont du Gard*), as well as contemporary French scenes and views of historical as well as artistic importance for the glimpses they provide of 18th-century life in and around Paris (*Démolition du pont Notre-Dame*). Robert loved to use diffused light and imbued his views with a sense of melancholy, characterizing a preromantic sensibility.

## Robert-Houdin, Jean-Eugène
## (1805–1871)
*magician*

Born in Blois, Jean-Eugène Robert-Houdin, the son of a clock maker, studied to be a notary. Yet he continued, to be interested in mechanics, especially as applied to slieght of hand and to electricity. The automatons that he invented brought him great renown, and in 1845, he created the Soirées Fantastiques, a theater in which he displayed his repertoire. Considered the "father of modern magic," Robert-Houdin was known for his great showmanship (dressed in evening cloths) and for developing basic stage presentations (identifying objects while blindfolded). Sent by the French government to ALGERIA to dissuade the inhabitants of their credulity toward local sorcerers, he gained there the reputation of a wizard, while in France his illusions became legendary. Robert-Houdin's writings contributed to the development of magicians' techniques, and the American magician Harry Houdini took his professional surname in his honor.

## Roberval, Gilles Personne  (1602–1675)
*mathematician, physicist*

Born in Roberval, Gilles Personne (or Personier de) Roberval for a long time kept his discoveries secret, so it is difficult to date them accurately. He did discover, before Bonaventura Cavalieri, the Italian mathematician, the method of indivisibles, and one can attribute to him a simple and general method for finding tangents. In 1655, he took PIERRE GASSENDI's chair in mathematics at the Collège Royale, but was eclipsed by PIERRE FERMAT, BLAISE PASCAL, and his rival RENÉ DESCARTES. Roberval was a charter member of the ACADÉMIE FRANÇAISE.

## Robespierre, Auguste-Bon-Joseph de
## (1764–1794)
*political figure*

Born in Arras, where he served as a town attorney, Auguste-Bon-Joseph de Robespierre was the brother of MAXIMILIEN DE ROBESPIERRE. He also served as an administrator in Pas-de-Calais and, during the REVOLUTION OF 1789, was elected to the Convention (1792), where he sat with the MONTAGNARDS. As a government representative to the

Army of the Midi, he took part in the siege of Toulon (1793) and befriended Bonaparte (see NAPOLÉON I), whom he had named as head of the army in Italy. On 9 Thermidor Year II (July 27, 1794), he asked to share his brother's fate and to be charged along with him. He was executed the following day.

## Robespierre, Maximilien-Marie-Isadore de  (1758–1794)
*political figure*

One of the most influential figures of the REVOLUTION OF 1789 and one of the principal exponents of the Reign of TERROR, Maximilien-Marie-Isadore de Robespierre was born in Arras to a bourgeois family and was educated in Paris at the Lycée Louis le Grand, where CAMILLE DESMOULINS was his classmate. Through his studies, he became an enthusiastic devotee of the social theories of the philosophes of the 18th century, especially those of JEAN-JACQUES-ROUSSEAU, whom he visited at Ermenonville and whose theory of the general will, as stated in the *Contrat social,* became Robespierre's guiding principle. An attorney, Robespierre was elected in 1789 as a deputy for the Third Estate to the ESTATES GENERAL, and subsequently to the National Constituent Assembly, where his oratory brought him to the attention of his peers. In April 1790, he was elected president of the JACOBIN Club and became popular (particularly after the departure of ANTOINE BARNAVE) as a foe of the monarchy and an advocate for radical reform. He was especially opposed to the moderate Girondin faction then dominant in the government. After the fall of the monarchy (August 1792), he strongly urged the execution of the King LOUIS XVI. In May 1793, with popular support, he forced the GIRONDINS from the National Assembly and in July was elected to the Committee of Public Safety, the chief executive body. Unopposed, he gained control of the government and, in the name of the nation and the revolution, proceeded to eliminate all whom he considered to be its enemies, whether moderate or extremist. The ensuing Reign of Terror led to the execution of many, including the revolutionary leaders JACQUES HÉBERT and GEORGES DANTON. At his insistence, the Convention proclaimed the cult of the Supreme Being, antagonizing both atheists and believers. With the support of the powerful Paris

COMMUNE, however, Robespierre was elected president of the Convention as the Terror intensified, with even many Jacobins fearing for their lives. After a series of military victories in Cholet; Vendée; Fleurus, Belgium; Wattignies, in northern France, made extreme security measures less urgent, a conspiracy was formed to overthrow Robespierre and, on 9 Thermidor, Year II (July 27, 1794), he was banned from speaking at the Convention and placed under arrest. An uprising in his support was suppressed on July 28, and Robespierre was executed along with his close associates GEORGES COUTHON and LOUIS SAINT-JUST and a number of other supporters. The death of Robespierre soon brought an end to the Terror.

## Rocard, Michel (1930– )
*political figure*

Born in Courbevoie, Michel Rocard served as inspector of finances (1958) and participated in the creation of the parti Socialiste unifié (PSU), which he directed from 1967 to 1974. He was a participant in the protests of May 1968 and, in 1969, was a candidate in the presidential election. A deputy for Yvelines (1969–93), he joined the SOCIALIST PARTY in 1974 and became mayor of Conflans-Sainte-Honorine (1977–94). After the left's rise to power in 1981, he served as minister of state charged with the Plan for Territorial Development (1981–83), then as minister of agriculture (1983–85). Prime Minister from 1988 to 1991, he reestablished peace in New Caledonia (1988) and put through unified social reform policies (Revenue minimum d'insertion; Contribution sociale généralisée) and various economic reforms as well. Rocard became first secretary of the Socialist Party after the defeat of the Left in the legislative elections of 1993, but the day after the defeat of the list that he led in the elections for the parliament of the European Union, he had to resign his post.

## Rochambeau, Jean-Baptiste-Donatien de Vimeur, count de (1725–1807)
*marshal of France*

Born in Vendôme, Jean-Baptiste-Donatien de Vimeur, count de Rochambeau, became an officer in 1742 and, as lieutenant general, commanded

60,000 men sent by the French government to help the Americans during the War of Independence. He succeeded in joining with General George Washington and contributed to the taking of Yorktown from the British under General Cornwallis (1781). Returning home, Rochambeau became governor of Picardy and Artois and a marshal of France in 1791. During the REVOLUTION OF 1789, he was appointed (1792) to lead the Army of the North, but was soon replaced by General NICOLAS LUCKNER. Imprisoned under the Terror, he escaped the guillotine thanks to the fall of MAXIMILIEN ROBESPIERRE on 9 Thermidor, Year II (July 27, 1794).

## Rochambeau, Donatien-Marie-Joseph de Vimeur, viscount of (1750–1813)
*general*

Born in Vendôme, Donatien-Marie-Joseph de Vimeur, viscomte de Rochambeau was the son of JEAN-BAPTISTE DONATIEN DE VIMEUR, COUNT DE ROCHAMBEAU. After having served with his father in the American War of Independence, he was sent to Saint-Domingue, then to Martinique, which he retook from the British (1793), but then soon lost (1794). After serving in the campaigns in Italy, he had to surrender to the British in 1803 and was imprisoned until 1811. Rochambeau was killed at Leipzig during the campaign in Germany.

## Rochefort, Henri (1831–1913)
## (Henri, marquis de Rochefort-Luçay)
*political figure*

Born in Paris, Henri, marquis de Rochefort-Luçay, or Henri Rochefort as he is known, began his political journalism career early and held republican views hostile to the SECOND EMPIRE. Forced to leave *LE FIGARO*, he founded *La Lanterne* (1868), and, after a brief exile in Brussels, Belgium, *La Marseillaise* (1869). He took a position in favor of the Paris COMMUNE (1871) and was condemned to deportation to New Caledonia (1872). He escaped with some comrades in 1874 and settled in Geneva, Switzerland, until the amnesty of 1880. Upon returning to France, he founded *L'Intransigeant*, a republican journal. A deputy (1885), he became a nationalist and a supporter of General GEORGES BOULANGER, whom he followed to Brussels before going to London. Rochefort's principal writings include *Les Français de la décadence* (1866), *Les Dépravés* (1875), *L'Évadé* (1880), *L'Aventure de ma vie* (1895–96).

## Rochet, Waldeck (1905–1983)

*political figure*

Waldeck Rochet, or Waldeck-Rochet as he is known, was born in Sainte-Croix, Saône-et-Loire, and, as a worker on a truck farm, joined the French COMMUNIST PARTY in 1923. A Communist deputy (1936–39), he represented his party with General CHARLES DE GAULLE in London during WORLD WAR II. Reelected after the Liberation, he led the party faction in parliament (1958–59, 1962–64). He succeeded MAURICE THOREZ as secretary-general of the PCF party (1964), but illness ended his political activity in 1969, and GEORGES MARCHAIS became, in turn, secretary-general in 1972.

## Rodin, Auguste (1840–1917)

*sculptor, watercolorist*

Regarded as the foremost sculptor of the 19th and early 20th centuries, Auguste Rodin was born in Paris. He studied art in a free school for artists and on his own at the LOUVRE, after his *L'Homme au nez casié* (1864) was rejected and he was refused admittance to the École des beaux-arts. To earn a living, he worked with other sculptors in France and Belgium until 1871. In 1875, he traveled to Italy, where he was greatly influenced by the works of Donatello and Michelangelo. Rodin finally gained recognition when his male nude figure, *L'Âge d'airain*, was exhibited at the Salon of 1877. The work aroused controversy and provoked the accusations that Rodin had made plaster casts from living models. But in 1879, with his *Saint Jean-Baptiste*, his talent was fully recognized. In 1880, he received a commission from the Musée des arts décoratifs to do a monumental bronze door with the theme *Gates of Hell*, inspired by Dante. But he found it difficult to integrate his sculpture into the architectural setting and finally left the work unfinished. Although he did not complete *Gates of Hell*, he created models or studies of many of its components, all of which were acclaimed as independent achieve-

*The Thinker*, by Auguste Rodin *(Library of Congress)*

ments. These include the most famous *The Thinker*, *The Kiss*, *Fugit amor*, *Adam*, *Eve*, *Paolo and Francesca*, and *Les Océanides*. In 1884, he completed a separate work, *Bourgeois de Calais*, a monumental bronze group in which the historical figures are represented with great psychological insight. Rodin also produced numerous portraits, including monuments to *Claude Lorrain* (1889), *Victor Hugo* (1890), and *Honoré de Balzac* (1891–97), as well as several busts of the artist *Jules Dalou* (1883), the political figure *Georges Clemenceau* (1911), and others. Rodin's work was always done with great personal force, expressed largely through modeling, and he sought to show a truthful representation through his technique of often subtly disturbing anatomy, most characteristically shown by a roughness of texture and surface.

See also BOURDELLE, ANTOINE; CLAUDEL, CAMILLE.

## Roederer, Pierre-Louis, count
## (1754–1835)

*political figure*

Born in Metz, where he was an adviser to the parlement (1780), Pierre-Louis, count Roederer was elected a deputy for the THIRD ESTATE to the Estates General in 1789. A member of the JACOBIN Club at the beginning of the REVOLUTION OF 1789, and district attorney for the department of Seine (1791), he gave his support to King LOUIS XVI after June 20, 1792, and counseled him to seek refuge after the events of August 10 of that year. Retiring from political life during the Convention, he taught political economy in the DIRECTORY period and founded the *Journal d'économie publique, de morale et de législation* (1796). After he supported the coup d'état of 18 Brumaire, Year VIII (November 9, 1799), he served successively as a counselor of state, senator (1802), minister of finances for the kingdom of Naples (1806), minister secretary of state for the grand duchy of Berg, Germany (1810), and commissioner to Strasbourg (1814). Count of Roederer wrote works on political economy and on history and was elected to the ACADÉMIE FRANÇAISE in 1803.

## Rohan-Guémené, Louis-René-Édouard, prince de (1734–1803)
## (Cardinal de Rohan)

*prelate*

Born in Paris, Louis-René-Édouard, prince of Rohan-Guémené, or Cardinal de Rohan, as he was eventually known, was coadjutor to his uncle, the bishop of Strasbourg. He was sent to Vienna as ambassador to Empress Maria Theresa of Austria but was recalled because of his diplomatic ineptitude and his scandalous behavior. He was made grand almoner (1777), cardinal (1778), and was given the bishopric of Strasbourg (1779). In his efforts to gain favor with Queen MARIE ANTOINETTE, he became a dupe of the Italian adventurer Count A. Cagliostro and the countess de LA MOTTE, in what would become the Affair of the Necklace. More naïve than guilty, Cardinal de Rohan benefited during his trial from the unpopularity of the queen and was viewed as a victim. He was sent away from the court and exiled to La Chaise-Dieu (1786). During the REVOLUTION OF 1789, he emigrated and went to Baden.

## Roland, Marie-Désirée-Pauline
## (1805–1852)

*socialist*

Born in Falaise, where her mother was postmistress, Marie-Désirée-Pauline Roland, or Pauline Roland, as she is known, was a schoolteacher who adopted the ideas of Saint-Simonianism (see SAINT-SIMON, COUNT DE). She fought a dual political battle for popular education and women's equality, and wrote for *La Femme libre* and *La Tribune des femmes*. A close associate of GEORGE SAND and PIERRE LEROUX, she served as director of the Women's Republican Club (Club républicain des femmes) in 1848 and, with JEANNE DEROIN, founded the Association of Socialist Professors and Schoolteachers (1849). After the death of the feminist FLORE TRISTAN, Roland adopted her daughter Aline, who later became the mother of PAUL GAUGUIN. Opposed to the SECOND EMPIRE and convicted as a Socialist, Roland was deported to ALGERIA (1852), was pardoned, and died shortly after her return.

## Roland de la Platière, Jean-Marie
## (1734–1793)

*political figure*

Born in Thizy, Beaujolais, Jean-Marie Roland de la Platière adopted the ideas of the REVOLUTION OF 1789 and sat as a notable on the Council of the Commune of LYON (1790), where he also helped to found a JACOBIN Club. Coming to PARIS in 1791, he allied himself with JACQUES BRISSOT and became one of the leaders of the GIRONDIN, or Brissotin, movement with his wife, JEANNE-MARIE ROLAND. Under the Legislative Assembly, he was named minister of the interior in the Girondin cabinet formed in March 1792. Having taken a position against the SEPTEMBER MASSACRES, and above all having voted against the execution of the king, his popularity plummeted, and, on January 22, 1793, he tendered his resignation. During the elimination of the Girondins (May 31–June 2, 1793), he was outlawed and fled to Normandy, committing suicide after learning of the execution of his wife.

## Roland de la Platière, Jeanne-Marie (1754–1793)
### (Mme Roland, Manon Philipon)
*political figure*

Known as Manon Philipon, and especially as Mme Roland, Jeanne-Marie Roland de la Platière was born in Paris. She received a better education than most of the young women of her time. She studied mathematics and was a passionate reader of Plutarch, the ancient Roman biographer. Early on, she enthusiastically embraced the ideas of the REVOLUTION OF 1789 while also editing articles for the *Courier de Lyon*. Settling in Paris in 1791 with her husband, JEAN-MARIE ROLAND DE LA PLATIÈRE, she was, more than he, the guiding spirit and adviser to the GIRONDIN movement, whose members (such as JACQUES BRISSOT, CONDORCET) met in her salon. Her influence and her role were considerable during the Girondin minority (March–June 1793). Imprisoned after the fall of the Gironde (May 31–June 2, 1793), she wrote her *Mémoires.* Condemned to death by the Revolutionary Tribunal (November 8, 1793), she was guillotined. The statement, "Liberty, Oh Liberty, what crimes are committed in thy name," addressed to a large statue of Liberty nearby, is attributed to her at the time of her execution.

## Rolland, Romain (1866–1944)
*writer, Nobel laureate*

Born in Clamecy, during a sojourn at the École française de Rome (1889–91), Romain Rolland met Malwilda von Meysenbug, who introduced him to Germanic culture. Passionate about music as well as art history, he published *Vies des hommes illustres* (1903–11) and *Vie de Beethoven* (1903), in which he presented his idea of a humanitarian heroism. Divided between the thought of German philosopher Friedrich Nietzsche and Russian writer Lev Tolstoy, Rolland imagined a nonviolent hero who would seek to "understand all so as to love all." His *Au-dessus de la mêlée* (1915), a series of articles written during a self-imposed exile in Switzerland (he was a pacifist), won him the Nobel Prize (1916) but also enemies on both sides of the Rhine. In contact with some noted world figures (he met Mohandas Gandhi and Maxim Gorky), Rolland wrote two vast novel series, *Jean-Christophe* (1903–12) and *L'Âme enchantée* (1922–33), works on the theater, and later published his autobiography, *Voyage intérieur* (1942).

## Rol-Tanguy, Henri (1908–2002)
*Resistance leader*

One of France's most decorated RESISTANCE fighters and heroes, Henri Tanguy (he took as his nom de guerre the name of a comrade, Théo Rol, who was killed in combat) was born in Morlaix, Brittany. He left school at age 14 to become a metallurgical worker in Paris and, at age 17, joined the COMMUNIST PARTY. In 1936, he was named secretary of the Union of Metallurgical Workers of the Paris region, and in 1939 he married Cécile Le Bihan, who joined him in his political and Resistance activities. A lifelong Communist, Rol-Tanguy became, at the beginning of WORLD WAR II, the leader of the Communist-led Francs-Tireurs et Partisans. From October 1940 to August 1941, he and other Communist leaders helped to organize resistance to the German occupation in the Paris region. He then went to Anjou before returning to Paris in 1943 and was named a captain, then a colonel, in the Forces Françaises de l'Interieur. Working from a base in the catacombs of Paris, he called on Parisians to take up arms and was alongside General PHILIPPE LECLERC when the German governor of Paris surrendered to Leclerc (August 1944). Rol-Tanguy remained in the military until 1962, then served as a member of the Central Committee of the French Communist Party (1964–87). He received the croix de guerre and Grand Croix of the LEGION OF HONOR, and is the author of books on the French Communist Party and on the Resistance.

## Romains, Jules (1885–1972)
### (Louis Farigoule)
*writer*

Jules Romains (the pseudonym of Louis Farigoule), a leader of the unanimist movement, was born in Saint-Julien-Chapteuil, Haute-Loire, and educated in Paris at the École normale supérieure. He taught philosophy (1909–19) before devoting his life to writing, eventually publishing almost 100 titles. His ideas (first expressed in *La vie unanime,* 1908, a collection of poems) were based on the unanimist philosophy that humans must be regarded as social creatures, not as individuals. His works are distinguished by a broad vision, in which he describes with satire and irony, as well as charity and detail, different social structures. Like the works of VICTOR HUGO and HONORÉ DE BALZAC, he depicted completely the society of his time (*Les Copains,* 1913; *Knock ou le Triomphe de la médicine,* 1923; *Monsieur Le Trouhadec saisi par la débauche,* 1923; *Le Mariage de Monsieur Le Trouhadec,* 1925; *Donagoo Tonka,* 1929; *Psyché,* 1922–29). Romains was elected to the ACADÉMIE FRANÇAISE in 1946.

## Romme, Charles-Gilbert (1750–1795)
*political figure*
Born in Riom, Charles-Gilbert Romme was a professor of mathematics, then tutor to Count Gregory Stroganov (1771) before the REVOLUTION OF 1789. In 1791, he was elected to the Legislative Assembly, then, in 1792, to the Convention, where after sitting with the deputies from the Plain, he joined the MONTAGNARDS. Sent on a mission to Cherbourg, he was held for a time by federalist insurgents at Caen (June–July 1793). He later helped FABRE D'EGLANTINE in the development of the revolutionary calendar. Implicated in the Jacobin and popular uprising of 1 Prairial, Year III (May 20, 1795) against the Thermidorian Convention, he was sentenced to death but committed suicide before the sentence was carried out.

## Ronsard, Pierre de (1524–1585)
*poet*
Born near Vendôme and trained as a royal page and then a squire, Pierre de Ronsard, upon becoming deaf, became a cleric and turned to books and poetry (1543). In 1544, he went to Paris, where he studied with classicists, including DORAT (1544–50). With JOACHIM DU BELLAY and others, he founded the famous PLÉIADE, a group of seven writers dedicated to reforming the French language and literature. Remaining faithful to the principles set out in *Défense et Illustration de la langue française,* Ronsard first published his *Odes* (1550–52), scholarly poems modeled after the classical poets Pindar and Horace, which brought him the favor of King HENRY II. In 1525, he wrote *Amours de Cassandre,* a series of love sonnets influenced by Petrarch. Ronsard's fame increased as he published *Continuation des amours* (1556) and *Hymnes* (1555–56), and he would enjoy the friendship of King CHARLES IX, whom he praised, along with the Catholic faith, in his *Discours* (1562–63). Ronsard's best-known love poetry is his *Sonnets pour Hélène* (1578), and he also began an epic, *La Franciad* (1572), on the origin of the French nation, which remained unfinished. During his lifetime called "Prince of Poets," Ronsard would later be criticized by FRANÇOIS DE MALHERBE and NICOLAS BOILEAU and remained out of favor for two centuries, until being rediscovered by CHARLES SAINTE-BEUVE and the romantics, who recognized him as the founder of a school of poetry and as a great lyric poet.

## Ronsin, Charles-Philippe (1752–1794)
*general, writer*
Born in Soissons, Charles-Philippe Ronsin joined the REVOLUTION OF 1789 early on and was the author of patriotic plays that enjoyed a certain success. A member of the CORDELIERS CLUB, he served as commissioner of war (1792) and was sent on a mission to Belgium, then named general during the campaign in the VENDÉE. General Ronsin was guillotined with the Hébertists (March 24, 1794).

## Roquelaure family
A noble French family from Armagnac. Antoine, baron de Roquelaure (unkown–1625) fought alongside King HENRY IV at Moncontour, Coutras, Arques, and Ivry. He was master of the king's wardrobe and was in Henry IV's carriage when the king was assassinated. Roquelaure was made a marshal of France in 1614. Jean-Baptiste-Gaston, marquis (then) duke de Roquelaure (ca. 1617–83), the son of Antoine, baron de Roquelaure, served as a captain in the king's army (1635) and became a field marshal after the siege of Courtrai (1646). He served as governor

of Guyenne (1676). Antoine Gaston, duke de Roquelaure (1656–1738), the son of Jean-Baptiste-Gaston, duke de Roquelaure, served as governor of Languedoc, fought the CAMISARDS and was made a marshal of France (1724).

## Rossignol, Jean-Antoine (1759–1802)
*general*

Born in Anjouan, Jean-Antoine Rossignol joined the REVOLUTION OF 1789 early on and, in 1793, was made a general in the revolutionary armies. He took part in the fighting against the Vendean counterrevolutionaries and eventually took command in that region. Denounced and charged by the Thermidorian Convention and removed from his post (1795), he was implicated in the Conspiracy of Equals of FRANÇOIS BABEUF (1796) but was acquitted. Implicated (wrongly) in the assassination attempt against NAPOLÉON I at the rue Saint-Nicaise in Paris, General Rossignol was deported to the Comoro Islands (1801), where he soon died.

## Rostand, Edmond (1868–1918)
*playwright, dramatic poet*

Born in MARSEILLE, Edmond Rostand, whose romantic plays, mostly in verse, were a contrast to the naturalism and symbolism of the era, produced his first drama, *Les Romantiques,* in Paris in 1894 (the story was adapted as the long-running American musical *The Fantasticks* in 1960). *Les Romantiques* was followed in 1897 by *Le Samaritaine,* a play with a religious theme, and *Cyrano de Bergerac,* a heroic comedy in five acts that brought Rostand international fame and whose title role has been played by many famous actors, and by *L'Aiglon* (1900), the story of the duke of Reichstadt (see NAPOLÉON II), the unfortunate son of NAPOLÉON I. Like previous works, this drama, whose original title role was played by SARAH BERNHARDT, had an immediate success and is still produced today. Rostand's last work was *Chantecler* (1910), with the noted actor SACHA GUITRY playing the title role. Rostand, who was elected to the ACADÉMIE FRANÇAISE in 1901, also left a drama, *La Dernière Nuit de Don Juan* that was published posthumously in 1912.

## Rostand, Jean (1894–1977)
*biologist, writer*

Born in Paris, Jean Rostand was the son of the dramatist EDMOND ROSTAND. Known for his works on parthenogenesis and teratogenesis (in particular, among bacteria), Rostand published popular works on science and philosophy that brought him the Kalinga Prize (international award for popularization of science). Rostand was elected to the ACADÉMIE FRANÇAISE in 1959.

## Rothschild family
*family of financiers, public figures*

The French branch of the Rothschild family was founded in 1817 by Jacob Rothschild (1792–1868). He was the son of Meyer Rothschild (1743–1812), who started the family banking business in Frankfurt, Germany, whose other sons opened branches in London, Vienna, and Naples, while one continued the business in Germany. Jacob, at the Paris branch, was the banker to kings LOUIS XVIII, CHARLES X, and LOUIS-PHILIPPE and served as French consul in Austria. All five Rothschild brothers were ennobled (1816) and made barons (1822) by the Austrian emperor Francis II. The French branch of the family had considerable success. Alphonse de Rothschild (1827–1905), the son of Jacob, made Paris the center of the family business, served as regent of the Bank of France (1855), and greatly increased the family fortune. Gustave de Rothschild (1829–1911), Alphonse's brother and a partner in the business, served as Austro-Hungarian consul in Paris. Edmund de Rothschild (1845–1934), their brother, was the director of the Chemin de fer de l'Est for the French Railways. Édouard de Rothschild (1868–1949), the son of Alphonse and head of the French branch of the family upon the death of his father, played an important role in the early Zionist movement. Maurice de Rothschild (1861–1957), the son of Edmund, served as a senator from 1929 to 1945. Robert de Rothschild (1880–1946), in 1911, followed his father Gustave in the business. Upon the death of Édouard, the directorship of the French branch of the Rothschild bank was given to his son Guy de Rothschild (b. 1909), and to two of Robert's sons, Alain (1910–82) and Élie (b. 1917).

## Rotrou, Jean de  (1609–1650)

*dramatist*

Born in Dreux, Jean de Rotrou enjoyed the protection of Cardinal RICHELIEU and was thus able to dedicate himself to dramatic writing. Thirty of his works survive, among them comedies (*Les Sosies,* 1637), tragie-comedies (*Venceslas,* 1647), and tragedies (*Antigone,* 1637; *Iphigénie,* 1639; *Bélisaire,* 1643; *Saint Genest,* 1646; *Cosroès,* 1648).

## Rouault, Georges  (1871–1958)

*painter, engraver*

Known for his somber portraits and sorrowful, spiritual images, Georges Rouault, considered perhaps the greatest religious painter of the 20th century, was born in Paris. Introduced to paintings by his grandfather, who was an admirer of GUSTAVE COURBET, ÉDOUARD MANET, and HONORÉ DAUMIER, in 1885 Rouault was apprenticed to a master stained-glass maker. He then studied with various artists who recognized his talent. His early work shows the influence of HENRI DE TOULOUSE-LAUTREC, while later pieces reflect that of the fauvists, with whom he exhibited. He differed, however, from the fauvists in technique and theme, being deeply inspired by Christianity (*L'Ivrognesse,* 1905; *L'Entremetteuse,* 1906, *Les Juges,* 1908, *Faubourg des langues pienes,* 1911). Rouault later produced a series of *Pierrots* (1937–38), but at the same time a large number of religious themes were also painted (*La Sainte Face,* 1933; *Le Vieux Roi,* 1937; *Nocturne chrétien*), often reminiscent of medieval icons and mosaics. A remarkable engraver, Rouault produced a monumental *Miserere* (1917), a *Passion* (1939), and the illustration for AMBOISE VOLLARD's *Réincarnations du père Ubu.* Rouault also designed theater sets and stained-glass windows (church at Assy), and worked in ceramics and tapestries.

## Rouget de Lisle, Claude-Joseph  (1760–1836)

*composer, officer*

Born in Lons-le-Saunier, Claude-Joseph Rouget de Lisle served as an engineering officer in Strasbourg. During the REVOLUTION OF 1789, he composed the "Chant de guerre pour l'armée du Rhin" (1792), which became "LA MARSEILLAISE." Sung first in Strasbourg and soon adopted as the marching song of the troops from MARSEILLE, it became the most popular hymn of the Revolution and eventually became the national anthem. Imprisoned during the Terror, he wrote, after his release, *Hymne dithyrambique sur la conjuration de Robespierre* (1794), *Chant des vengeances* (1798), *Chant des combats* for the army in Egypt (1800), the melody of *Cinquante chants français,* and librettos and romances.

## Rouher, Eugène  (1814–1884)

*political figure*

Born in Riom, Eugène Rouher entered politics during the REVOLUTION OF 1848. A candidate in the elections to the Constituent Assembly (April 1848) as a republican, he joined the parti de l'Ordre, was reelected to the Legislative Assembly (May 1849), and was twice named minister of justice between 1849 and 1851. Recalled to that ministry after the coup d'état of December 2, 1851, he resigned in January 1852 in opposition to the decree confiscating the properties of the House of Orléans (like that of the duke de MORNY). Rouher, as minister of trade, agriculture, and public works (1855–63), contributed to implementing several important measures (development of the railroad, navigation routes, improvement of the Landes region, signing the free-trade treaty with Great Britain). Minister of state (1863), he never ceased to oppose all attempts at liberalizing the regime and, in foreign policy, supported the disastrous expedition to Mexico. After the elections of 1869, which assured a victory for a majority opposed to the exercise of personal power, Rouher was forced to resign. President of the Senate (1870), he took refuge in London after the abdication of NAPOLÉON III before becoming, during the THIRD REPUBLIC, one of the leaders of the Bonapartist Party in the National Assembly, where he served from 1872 to 1879.

## Roumanille, Joseph  (1818–1891)

*Provençal-French writer*

Born in Saint-Rémy-de-Provence, Joseph Roumanille, as a tutor in Avignon, imparted to the young FRÉDÉRIC MISTRAL his passion for a revival of

Provençal literature. Together, they became the chief members of the literary school known as Félibrige, dedicated to the renaissance of the Provençal language, or "langue d'oc," and culture. Roumanille played a significant role in this revival with his personally inspired collection of verses, *Les Pàqerettes* (1847), and later with his story in octosyllabic verse, *Les Songeuses* (1851). All his poetry appeared in a collected version, *Les Œuvrettes en vers* (1860). An energetic prose writer, Roumanille, after the REVOLUTION OF 1848, wrote legitimist pamphlets that would later be collected in *Les Ocunettes en prose* (1859). Dedicated to gathering together the works of the langue d'oc writers, he published a compilation, *Les Provençales* (1851), organized the linguistic congresses at Arles (1852) and Aix (1853), and took part in the development of the Félibrige (1854). In 1884, he succeeded Mistral as the "capoulié" of that movement and published the *Almanach,* which served as the organ of linguistic revival and in which *Les Contes* appeared, a realistic work that made Roumanille the creator of modern Provençal prose.

## Rousseau, Henri (1844–1910)
*painter*

Known as "Le Douanier," (customs agent) Henri Rousseau, who was born in Laval, is recognized especially for his bold colors, flat designs, and imaginative subject matter, all much praised and imitated by modern artists. After serving in the army in Mexico, in 1868 he obtained a position at the Paris tax office (not the customs office, contrary to his sobriquet). Totally self-taught, Rousseau, when he retired in 1884, began painting and copying at the LOUVRE, and soon demonstrated his talent. He also became friendly with artists associated with the Salon des Indépendants, where he began to show regularly after 1886. There he won the admiration of such contemporaries as PAUL GAUGUIN, GEORGES SEURAT, and Pablo Picasso. After painting mainly portraits (*Pierre Loti; Moi-même*), Parisian scenes (*Scieries aux environs de Paris; L'Octroi,* ca. 1890), he turned during the 1890s to highly original depictions of fantasy, typically showing tropical scenes with human figures resting or playing with animals, often mysteriously charmed to an alert

stillness (*Forêt vierge au soleil couchant; Joyeux farceurs,* 1906; *La Charmeuse de serpents; Les Flamants,* 1907). Rousseau also painted flowers and still lifes and what he called "creations," taken from romantic themes (*Rendez-vous dans la forêt,* ca. 1890), patriotic, or "modern," works (*Centenaire de l'Indépendence,* 1892; *Les Joueurs de football,* 1908), and those with exotic themes (*La Bohémienne endormie,* 1897).

## Rousseau, Jean-Jacques (1712–1778)
*writer, philosopher*

One of the greatest figures of the ENLIGHTENMENT, Jean-Jacques Rousseau was born in Geneva, Switzerland, to a Protestant family of French origin. Raised by relatives after the death of his mother and educated by his father, he acquired a taste for romantic writings as well as the works of the Roman writer Plutarch. After three years of an unhappy apprenticeship to an engraver, at age 16 he ran away to Chambéry and became secretary and companion to Mme Louise de Warens, a wealthy woman who had a profound influence on his life and writings. In Paris (1742–49), Rousseau earned his living as a music teacher and copyist and became a close friend of DENIS DIDEROT, with whom he collaborated on the *Encyclopédie.* Rousseau's literary fame came with his controversial theses, *Discours sur les sciences et les arts* (1750) and *Discours sur l'origine et les fondements de l'inégalité parmi les hommes* (1755), which has had considerable influence on modern political thought.

Following the arguments he had already set forth, Rousseau criticized the trappings of civilization and condemned luxuries and the theater, a school for bad morals, as he put it in his *Lettre à d'Alembert sur les spectacles* (1758), which alienated him from the philosophes, who had already opposed his break with Diderot and Mme d'ÉPINAY. Befriended by M and Mme de Luxembourg, Rousseau completed *Julie ou la nouvelle Héloïse* (1761), an epistolary novel that extols the benefits of a return to the state of nature while pointing out the aspects of human happiness. This work enjoyed an immense success. Then, always eager to put forth his political ideas tied to his theories on education, Rousseau published his *Contrat social* at the same time as *Émile* (1762), a pedagogic work in

Jean-Jacques Rousseau *(Hulton/Archive)*

as sources of totalitarian ideology (see REVOLUTION OF 1789). His theories on education led to more psychologically oriented methods of pedagogy, influencing the German Friedrich Fröbel, Johann Pestalozzi of Switzerland, Maria Montessori in Italy, and other educators. His various writings introduced a new style of extreme emotional expression that profoundly influenced romanticism, of which Rousseau was a forerunner. And he affected the development of psychological literature and psychoanalytic theory and the philosophy of existentialism through his emphasis on free will and rejection of original sin. Rousseau, in his spirit and ideas, stands at the midpoint between rationalistic Enlightenment thought and the subjectivism of the early 19th century.

### Rousseau, Théodore (1812–1867)
*painter*

Théodore Rousseau was born in Paris, where he studied with academic and landscape artists. In 1830, he began a journey through southern France, to paint out of doors and, using natural light, faithfully represent nature. An admirer of the Dutch landscapists, Rousseau, beginning in 1833, often painted in the forest of Fontainebleau. But little appreciated and rejected a number of times by the Salon, he settled eventually at Barbizon (1848) and was joined by JEAN-FRANÇOIS MILLET, CHARLES DAUBIGNY, and other painters who together formed the group known as the BARBIZON SCHOOL. They sought to achieve simple and faithful representations of nature, while portraying with passion and vigor its various aspects.

### Roussel, Albert (1869–1937)
*composer*

One of the leading French composers of the post–WORLD WAR I era, Albert Roussel was born in Tourcoing and was a career naval officer when he began his pursuit of music. He studied in Paris with VINCENT D'INDY and at the Scola Cantorum, where he later taught counterpoint (1902–14). In his first compositions, the influence of Indy, CLAUDE DEBUSSY, and CÉSAR FRANCK, as well as of impressionism, is evident (*Poème de la forêt,* for orchestra,

which he presented a new educational view, emphasizing experiences over repression to produce a well-balanced and freethinking child. Because of his controversial ideas, Rousseau left France and began work (1765–70) on his autobiographical *Confessions* (posthumous, 1782 and 1789). His autobiographical works reveal his complex personality and further explain his views on society, politics, and education. Hostile also to dogmatic faith, Rousseau put faith instead in spiritual views, as he stated in *Profession de foi du vicaire Savoyard* (1758–62), an apology for the love of nature and for a natural religion. Rousseau's themes are controversial because, while he made a great contribution to the modern movement for individual freedom and against absolutism in church and state, his idea of the state as the embodiment of the abstract will of the people and his arguments for political and religious conformity are often regarded

1909). As a result of a long stay in the Far East (1909–11), he also brought to his music an intense color (*Évocations,* 1912; *Le Festin de l'araignée,* 1912, a ballet). Although disabled, he served during World War I and at that time began the composition of an opera-ballet, *Padmavâti* (1914), which reflects his fascination with Oriental culture. After the war, Roussel found his way to a more classical form of music composition, and works from this period are also characterized by spontaneity, intensity of rhythm, and dynamism (*Concerto pour piano,* 1927; *Suite en fa;* 1927; *Psaume LXXX,* 1929). Other of Roussel's works include *Troisième* and *Quatrième* symphonies (1930–34), the ballets *Bacchus et Ariadne* (1931) and *Aeneas* (1935), and *Trio pour alto, violon et violoncelle* (1937).

## Roussel, Raymond (1877–1935)
*writer*

Born in Paris to a wealthy bourgeois family, Raymond Roussel studied at the Paris Conservatory until, at age 17, he felt himself called to be a poet. He began a large work in Alexandrian verse, *Les Doublure* (published 1897), a detailed description of the Carnival in Nice. The writing put him in an ecstatic state, but it was not the success he had hoped it would be. He continued, nonetheless, to write, composing poems (*La Vue,* 1903; *Le Concert,* 1904; *La Source,* 1904) before beginning his important prose work, *Impressions d'Afrique* (published 1910), an imaginary description of Africa filled with strange devices. A play that he developed from it caused a scandal. This was followed by *Locus Solus* (1914), written in a similar way, the two plays *L'Étoile au front* (1924) and *La Poussière de soleils* (1927), as he continued to work on a large poem also in Alexandrian verse, *Nouvelles Impressions d'Afrique* (published 1932), in which the text is interspersed with a play in parentheses. From 1920 to 1921, Roussel traveled widely, but he said that this period failed to inspire him and he ceased writing in 1932. He died mysteriously in a palace in Palermo, Italy, poisoned by barbiturates. In 1989, a great amount (10,000 pages) of his manuscripts were discovered. Considered one of the most extraordinary writers of the 20th century, Roussel, for his bizarre works

and eccentric lifestyle, drew a critical response from many of his illustrious contemporaries, and he has been claimed as a precursor by authors associated with the surrealists (ANDRÉ BRETON), the OuLiPo, and semioticians and poststructuralists. MARCEL PROUST, JEAN COCTEAU, and MICHEL FOUCAULT all recognized his genius and influence.

## Rouvier, Maurice (1842–1911)
*political figure*

Born in Aix-en-Provence, Maurice Rouvier was a journalist for LÉON GAMBETTA's *La République française,* served as a deputy (1871–1903), senator (1903–11), minister of commerce (1881–82, 1884–85), and specialized in financial issues. Premier in 1887, he retired during the scandal over trafficking in government awards, then as minister of finances (February 1889–December 1892) had to resign again during the PANAMA AFFAIR. Recalled to the Ministry of Finances in the ÉMILE COMBES cabinet (1902–05), he succeeded the latter as premier (January 1905–March 1906) and put through the Law of Separation of Church and State. After the Tangiers Speech (1905), he supported negotiations with Germany and arranged for the Algeciras Conference.

## Roux, Jacques (1752–1794)
*revolutionary*

Born in Pransac, Charente, Jacques Roux was ordained a priest after studies in the seminary at Angoulême, where he later taught. During the REVOLUTION OF 1789, he greeted the taking of the BASTILLE (July 14, 1789) as the end of "despotism" and, after 1790, seems to have leaned toward socialistic views, preaching equal distribution of property. He was, no doubt, responsible for the peasant uprising in Saint-Thomas-de-Conac (Charente). Having taken the oath to the CIVIL CONSTITUTION OF THE CLERGY, he was named vicar of Saint-Nicolas-des-Champs in Paris and quickly became known as the "SANS-CULOTTE priest," the moving spirit of the Gravilliers, and the leader of the ENRAGÉ movement. After taking part in the Revolutionary Day of August 10, 1792, which marked the fall of the monarchy following the insurrection of August 9, and mistrusting the Conventionals, Roux preferred an economic and social struggle and proclaimed a veritable "economic terrorism." On June 25, 1793, he gave before the Convention a speech known as the "Manifesto of the Enragés," which criticized the apathy of the public authorities and advocated quick and severe measures against speculators and monopolists. The speech brought violent reactions from the MONTAGNARD deputies. Attacked by the JACOBINS and the CORDELIERS (the Hébertists, however, adopted his program), he was equally criticized by JEAN-PAUL MARAT. Arrested on the orders of the Commune on August 22, 1793, then released on August 27, he was again imprisoned at Bicêtre, where he stabbed himself to death upon learning of his sentence by the Revolutionary Tribunal.

## Roux, Émile (1853–1933)
*bacteriologist*

Born in Confolens, Émile Roux was a colleague of LOUIS PASTEUR, with whom he worked on the study of forms of cholera and rabies, and on a preventive vaccination for infectious diseases. Roux also did research on toxins, discovering the diphtheritic variety, and with Emil von Behring, a German bacteriologist, produced the first antidiphtheritic serum (1894). He developed the course of study in microbiology at the Pasteur Institute in Paris, where he served as director after ÉMILE DUCLAUX. Roux was named to the Academy of Sciences in 1899.

## Royer-Collard, Pierre-Paul (1763–1845)
*political figure, philosopher*

Born in Sompuis, Champagne, Pierre-Paul Royer-Collard, during the REVOLUTION OF 1789, was a member of the Paris Commune (until August 10, 1792), then served as a deputy to the Council of Five Hundred. From 1797 to 1803, he was part of a secret royalist council and an advocate of a constitutional monarchy. In the Chamber of Deputies, he was, after 1816, leader of the "doctrinaire" faction. An adversary of the Ideologues, he developed a spiritualist philosophy that would influence VICTOR COUSIN. Royer-Collard was elected to the ACADÉMIE FRANÇAISE in 1827.

## Rude, François (1784–1855)
*sculptor*

Born in Dijon, François Rude studied in Paris with noted sculptors. Exiled to Brussels, in 1826 he carved a bust of *L. David* and, at the Salon in Paris in 1827, exhibited his *Mercure rattachant son talonnière*, done in classical style. In 1833, he produced a small *Pecheur napolitain*, known for its lively and intimate workmanship. Commissioned by ADOLPHE THIERS to decorate one of the piers of the ARC DE TRIOMPHE, Rude produced in low relief *Le Départ des volontaires*, also known by the name *La Marseillaise* (1835–36). Although this work shows a proximity to the academic tradition, it was strongly criticized by many officials because of the violent expression of its central figure, the intense movement of the composition, and its realistic appearance. Rude shows his more romantic temperament in works such as *Jeanne d'Arc écoutant ses voix* (1845–52) or *Napoléon s'éveillant à l'immortalité* (1847). Rude had a great sense of expression and a feel for movement in both individual figures and in groupings, all without losing a sense of precision and restraint (*Gaspard Monge*, 1848; *Le Maréchal Ney*, 1852–53).

## Ruyer, Raymond (1902–1987)
*philosopher*

Born in Plainfaing, Vosges, Raymond Ruyer as a thinker supported the concept of the spatial-temporal structure of "the real" or the actual (*Esquisse d'une philosophie de la structure*, 1930). He deepened the study of living beings, their organization, and their development. In affirming the nature of life and the psychical, he redefined the primary original awareness of all organisms and the secondary original conscience of the human through symbolic thought and function (*Éléments de psycho-biologie*, 1946). His thoughts extended also to problems of finality (*Le Néo-finalisme*, 1952), and questions posed by the development of cybernetics (*La Cybernétique et l'Origine de l'information*, 1954).

# S

## Sablé, Madeleine de Souvré, marquise de (ca. 1598–1678)
*writer, salonist*

Born in Touraine, Madeleine de Souvré, marquise de Sablé was a frequent guest at the salon of CATHERINE DE RAMBOUILLET and received in her own salon FRANÇOIS DE LA ROCHEFOUCAULD and Mme de LA FAYETTE. She is the author of *Maximes* (posthumous, 1678), a genre she helped popularize. Mme de Sablé's *Traité de l'amitié* was published in 1859 through the efforts of VICTOR COUSIN.

## Saboly, Nicolas (1614–1675)
*French-Provençal composer*

Born in Carpentras, where he studied at the Jesuit College, Nicolas Saboly was ordained a priest in 1635. Chapel master at the cathedral of Carpentras (1640–43), then at Saint-Trophime d'Arles (1643–46), he became the music master at Avignon. Saboly composed several *Nouvé* (*Noéls*), with words (in Provençal) and music (published 1671), trio motets, and two masses in plainchant.

## Sade, Donatien-Alphonse-François, count de (1740–1814)
**(marquis de Sade)**
*writer*

Born in Paris, Donatien-Alphonse-François, count de Sade (or the marquis de Sade as he is better known), is best recognized for his erotic works. After spending a number of years in the military, he married Renée Pelagie de Montreuil (1763) and succeeded his father as lieutenant general of several provinces (1764). His libertinage, in part seen as an aristocratic privilege, increased and, in 1768, he was sentenced to prison and fined 100 livres following a morals scandal. After imprisonment for debt (1771), a new scandal broke, connected with an orgy in Marseille (1772). Sade and his servant were condemned to death for contempt and the marquis was finally incarcerated in the fortress of Moilans, from which he escaped in 1775. Recaptured in Paris, he was imprisoned at Vincennes (1777). After another escape, he was caught and jailed until 1778. Subsequently, he was imprisoned at various places, including the BASTILLE (until July 4, 1789). During the REVOLUTION OF 1789, Sade divorced and again served in the military. In 1791, he published *L'Adresse d'un citoyen de Paris au roi des Français,* as well as *Justine ou les Malheurs de la vertu* and produced *Oxtiern ou les Effets du libertinage* (1791, published 1797). Arrested as a moderate by the Committee of Public Safety, his life was saved by the fall of MAXIMILIEN ROBESPIERRE. In 1795, he published *La Philosophie dans le boudoir,* then, in 1797, *La nouvelle Justine ou les Malheurs de la vertu, suivie del l'Histoire de Juliette, sa soeur,* better known as *Juliette ou les Prospérities du vice.* Imprisoned in 1801 at Saint-Pélagie, then moved to Bicêtre after having seduced some inmates, he was finally put in the insane asylum at Charenton, where he died, receiving a religious burial against his wishes as stated in his will. His other writings include *Les Journées de Florbelle ou la Nature dévoyée* (1804), a work seized by the police, *Adélaïde de Brunswick, princesse de Saxe* (1812, published 1964), and *L'Histoire secrète d'Isabelle de Bavière* (1813, published 1953). As a materialist poet, Sade must be read in the context of all the philosophic literature of the 18th century. Radically subversive, he questioned all systems of authority but stands apart from other libertine writers of the age because of his emphasis on violence more than pleasure, hence the term *sadism.*

## Sagan, Françoise (1935– )
*writer*

Born Françoise Quoirez in the village of Cajarc, Lot, Françoise Sagan (she took as her nom de plume the name of a character in one of MARCEL PROUST's works), whose elegant comedies and glamorous lifestyle have made her a best-selling author and celebrity, had an early success with her first novel *Bonjour Tristesse* (1954), a bittersweet story of the loves of its 17-year-old protagonist, Cécile. The work won Sagan the prix des Critiques and enthralled the postwar generation. Sagan continued its themes in her next work, *Un certain Sourire* (1956), and her style and theme of a fictional upper-middle-class world and its sexual life and hypocrisies are apparent in works that followed: *Dans un Mois, dans un an* (1957) and especially *Aimez-vous Brahms* (1959). Among other writings that cross between popular and serious literature and between fiction and autobiography, written in her characteristic detached style, are *La Chamade* (1965), *Le Lit défuit* (1977), and *La Femme fardée* (1981). At the same time, Sagan has also written for the stage (*Château en Suède*, 1960; *Bonheur, impair et passé*, 1964; and *Un piano dans l'herbe*, 1970), and has published her memoirs (*Avec mon meilleur souvenir*, 1985). A number of her works have been adapted to the screen.

## Saint-Amant, Marc-Antoine-Girard, sieur de (1594–1661)
*poet*

Born in Quevilly to a bourgeois family from Rouen, Marc-Antoine-Girard, sieur de Saint-Amant, studied at the Collège de la Marche in Paris where, at the same time, he became part of the literary and libertine milieus. He also lived the life of a traveler and sailor, and journeyed as far as Senegal in Africa. Later, as a soldier, he served in a number of military campaigns. His works, which appealed to the baroque tastes of the period, were collected in 1629, then augmented in 1645, 1651, and 1661. Saint-Amant's rhetorical style puts him in the class of the greater French poets. Like his contemporary, THÉOPHILE DE VIAU, his work often disregarded moral and sexual codes, and religious and social conventions, and prepared, with those of others,

the way for the critical and questioning spirit of VOLTAIRE and the Encyclopedists of the 18th century by transmitting the reasoning of the Renaissance. Saint-Amant's works include his "heroic idyll," *Moïse sauvé* (1647–53) in 12 parts; his satirical poems (*L'Albion, Le Poète crotté*); comic pieces (*Le Fromage*); and more fanciful writings (*Les Visions*). Unjustly forgotten, his theoretical work, *Le Passage de Gibraltar* (1640), is one of the first reflections on the pleasure of reading and is considered an essential component in the study of literature. Saint-Amant was elected to the ACADÉMIE FRANÇAISE in 1634.

## Saint-André, Jacques d'Albon, seigneur de (ca. 1505–1562)
*marshal of France*

Born in Albon, Dauphiné, Jacques d'Albon, seigneur de Saint-André, was one of the principal Catholic military leaders in the French WARS OF RELIGION. Made a marshal of France, he joined with the constable MATHIEU DE MONTMORENCY and the duke de GUISE to form a triumvirate directed against the Calvinists in 1561. Marshal Saint-André was killed the following year at the battle of Dreux, Eure, in the Wars of Religion between Catholics and Protestants.

## Saint-Arnaud, Achille-Leroy de (ca. 1800–1854)
*marshal of France*

Born in Paris, Armand-Jacques Arnaud, or Achille, Leroy de Saint-Arnaud as he is known, was a member of the guard of King LOUIS XVIII but had to leave the army after falling into debt. He spent some time in Greece (1827), then, restored to his rank in 1831, was named an ordinance officer. He served with distinction in ALGERIA, and was promoted to the rank of general in 1847. Named minister of war by NAPOLÉON III (October 1851), he was actively involved in the preparations for the coup d'état of December 2, 1851, which brought Napoléon III to power and began the Second Empire, earning him the marshal's baton (1852). A senator and a great cavalry officer, he took command of the French forces in the Crimea in 1854 (see

CRIMEAN WAR) and, with the British commander Lord Raglan, won the victory at Alma (September 1854) in the Crimea that began the Crimean War. Replaced by General FRANÇOIS CANROBERT for reasons of health, he died abord the ship that was taking him back to France.

## Saint Bartholomew's Day Massacre

The Saint Bartholomew's Day Massacre was a massacre of the Huguenot leaders in PARIS on August 23–24, 1572. To increase her power, Queen CATHERINE DE' MEDICI intrigued with the Catholic faction, led by the House of GUISE, against the Protestants, led by the House of CONDÉ. Jealous of the power of the Huguenot leader Admiral GASPARD DE COLIGNY, the adviser to her son, King CHARLES IX, she ordered his assassination. The plot failed, however, and the Huguenot leaders who had gathered in Paris for the wedding of Catherine's daughter, MARGUERITE DE VALOIS, to Henri de Navarre (HENRY IV), demanded an investigation. Instead, the Huguenot leaders and many of their followers, numbering in the thousands, were murdered. The first to be killed was Coligny. The massacre then spread from Paris to the provinces, with many more victims (see WARS OF RELIGION).

## Saint-Cyr

Saint-Cyr, located near Versailles, was originally an educational center for young women, established by MME DE MAINTENON in 1668. In 1808, NAPOLÉON I transformed it into a military academy. The national French military academy, the facility was closed in 1944 and the school transferred to Coëtquidan, where it is now located. Most of France's leading military figures since the Napoléonic era have graduated from Saint-Cyr.

## Sainte-Beuve, Charles-Augustin (1804–1869)

*writer and literary critic*

Born in Boulogne-sur-Mer, Charles-Augustin Sainte-Beuve was educated in Paris. At age 20 he was a journalist for the *Globe,* a philosophic, literary, and political newspaper founded in 1824, one of the opposition newspapers during the RESTORATION. Already a literary critic, he became friends with VICTOR HUGO and a member of the CÉNACLE group of romantics. In his *Tableau historique et critique de la poésie française et du théâtre au XVIe siécle* (where he notably discovered PIERRE DE RONSARD), he described romanticism as the continuation of a national tradition beginning in the Renaissance. He published a work that mixed prose and verse, *Vie, poésies et pensées de Joseph Delorme* (1829), followed by a collection of poems, *Les Consolations* (1830), in which his style can be seen as a precursor to that of CHARLES BAUDELAIRE and PAUL VERLAINE. Disappointed by the lack of success of his writings and of his novel *Volupté* (1834), Sainte-Beuve turned to the study of literary history and published *Port-Royal* (1840–59), a serried critique on JANSENISM, and later *Chateaubriand et son groupe littéraire* (1860) before collecting his articles in a series, *Critiques et portraits* (1836–46) in the *Causeries du Lundi* (1851–62), followed by the *Nouveaux Lundis* (1863–69). At the time of his death, he left important correspondences and personal notes, *Mes poisons* (published 1926). Sainte-Beuve wrote about all literary genres as he sought to replace unqualified subjectivity with precise and solid scholarship and a sensitivity and intuitiveness for his subject matter, which he then introduced to the literary criticism of his day. Widely admired, especially because he changed the techniques of French literary criticism, his methodology was severely criticized, however, by MARCEL PROUST (*Contre Sainte-Beuve*). Sainte-Beuve was elected to the ACADÉMIE FRANÇAISE in 1843.

## Saint-Évremond, Charles de Marguetel de Saint-Denis de (ca. 1615–1703)

*moralist, critic*

Born in Saint-Denis-le-Gast, near Coutances, Charles de Marguetel de Saint-Denis de Saint-Évremond, after a successful military career during which became known for *La Comédie des académistes* (published anonymously in 1650), was forced, because of his Frondist writings against Cardinal MAZARIN, to go into exile in London. He remained there for the rest of his life, refusing a pardon granted by King LOUIS XIV. In London, Saint-Évremond frequented the leading salons, especially that of HORTENSE MANCINI. His writings, which circulated in France as well as in England, show, through diverse subject matter, his libertine spirit. In historiography, his *Réflexions sur les divers génies du peuple romain dans les différents temps de la République* (1663) foreshadows the ideas of MONTESQUIEU, while his *Conversation du maréchal d'Hocquincourt avec le Père Canaye* upholds natural morality based in a measured Epicureanism. Finally, in literature, Saint-Évremond's writings (particularly those on the theater) and his voluminous correspondence reveal his independent spirit and incisive views on the necessary evolution of the arts (*Sur les poèmes des Anciens*, 1685).

## Saint-Exupéry, Antoine de (1900–1944)
*writer, aviator*

Born in LYON, Antoine de Saint-Exupéry joined the French air force in 1921 and in 1926 became a commercial pilot flying the Toulouse-Casablanca route and later flew in Patagonia, at the southern end of South America. He then took part in important missions as a test pilot and as a military aviator. A man of action with a humanistic spirit, Saint-Exupéry sought to uncover the spiritual and moral significance in human activity, and his writings poetically evoke the romance and discipline of flying and its needs for devotion and the taking of great risks (*Courrier Sud*, 1928; *Vol de nuit*, 1931). He sought through his personal experience a sense of the universal, and found the peace of meditation through the dangerous solitude of the solo flyer or in desert terrains. In a classic work, *Terre des hommes* (1939), he insisted on a rigorous self-examination to become a full human being. In works such as *Pilote de guerre* (1942) and *Lettre à un otage* (1943), Saint-Exupéry underscores the need to link individual courage with sacrifice for the human community and exalted love for the Earth itself. The same spirit is found in *Écrits de guerre* (reedited in 1982). Emphasizing the virtue of love over intellect, he translated these thoughts in *Le Petit Prince* (1943), a popular children's book read by adults for its allegorical meanings, and later in *Citadelle* (posthumous, 1948). During WORLD WAR II, Saint-Exupéry was shot down by Germans and later joined CHARLES DE GAULLE's Free French

Antoine Saint-Exupéry, ca. 1935 *(Hulton/Archive)*

forces in North Africa. On a reconnaissance mission near Corsica, his plane was lost and never recovered.

## Saint-Gelais, Mellin de (1491–1558)
*writer*

Born in Angoulême, Mellin de Saint-Gelais was named "Merlin" or "Melusin" by his friends, including FRANÇOIS RABELAIS. Mellin de Saint-Gelais served as the official poet of the royal court after CLÉMENT MAROT was exiled. Author of courtly poems and epigrams, he had a tenuous relationship with the PLÉIADE group, despite an official reconciliation in 1553. The complete works of Mellin de Saint-Gelais were published in 1873.

## Saint-Georges, Joseph Boulogne, chevalier de (ca. 1739 –1799)
*composer, violinist, conductor*

The mulatto son of a French nobleman and a former slave, Joseph Boulogne, chevalier de Saint-

Georges was born in Basse-Terre, Guadaloupe. Brought to Paris by his father, Saint-Georges studied the violin with noted artists and composers. An acclaimed musician, he then directed the Concert des amateurs and was one of the founders of the Concert de la Loge olympique. The majority of his compositions (sonatas, quartets for strings, concertos) were written between 1772 and 1779. The composer Wolfgang Amadeus Mozart had seen him play and conduct some of these pieces that, in turn, may have influenced his own work (Saint-Georges has been called the Black Mozart). Favored by King LOUIS XVI, Saint-Georges was considered for a time for the position of director of the Paris Opéra. During the REVOLUTION OF 1789, he served as a captain of the National Guard and led a battalion composed of many of black volunteers known as Saint-Georges's Legion. An outspoken proponent of equality and human rights, he was imprisoned under the TERROR because of his aristocratic background. Released in 1794, he died in relative obscurity.

## Saint-Germain, Claude-Louis-Robert, count de (1701–1778)
*political figure, general*

Born near Lons-le-Saunier, Claude-Louis-Robert, count de Saint-Germain, served with distinction as a military officer for the elector of Bavaria and the kings of Prussia, France, and Denmark. He was made secretary of war by ROBERT TURGOT (1775) and reorganized the French army through a series of important reforms, including the suppression of privileged companies (musketeers and king's grenadiers) and the sale of military positions, restoration of discipline, augmentation of personnel, and a preferred placement to officer positions for the lower nobility.

## Saint-Germain, count de (unknown–1784)
*adventurer*

Of unknown origin, the count de Saint-Germain, as he was known, was famous in France between 1750 and 1760. He astonished the salons and the royal court by his prodigious memory, his talent at storytelling, and his spiritualist practices. He claimed to have been living since the time of Christ. The count de Saint-Germain died in Eckernförde, Schleswig-Holstein.

## Saint-John Perse (1887–1975)
*diplomat, poet, Nobel laureate*

Born in Point-à-Pitre in the overseas department of Guadeloupe, Alexis Leger, who was known as Alexis Saint-Leger Leger and then as Saint-John Perse, was the descendant of French colonists who had lived in the Antilles since the end of the 17th century. He began his studies in Point-à-Pitre, then continued at Pau and at BORDEAUX. There, he wrote *Images à Crusoë* (1904), soon followed by *Éloges*, in which he speaks of his nostalgia for his childhood on the family plantation. A meeting with PAUL CLAUDEL at the home of FRANCIS JAMMES in 1905 encouraged Saint-John Perse to write his first poetic essays and also directed him toward a diplomatic career. Meanwhile, he became friends with a group of writers of the NRF (*Nouvelle Revue française*), including PAUL VALÉRY and ANDRÉ GIDE, who would edit *Éloges* (1911). Joining the Foreign Ministry (1914), Saint-John Perse served successively as secretary to the ambassador to China (1916–21), director of the diplomatic cabinet of ARISTIDE BRIAND (1925–32), then secretary-general of the Foreign Ministry (1933–40). A great opponent of fascism, he was removed from his post by the VICHY regime and went to the United States. He returned to France in 1957 and was given the rank of ambassador. A philosopher and historian, but also a geologist, naturalist, and ethnologist, he studied as well archaeology and music, and brought much knowledge to his poetic writings. Awarded the Nobel Prize in literature in 1960, he was much admired by critics and other poets for his complexity of style. Among his other works, which also deal with the themes of solitude and exile, are *Anabase* (1924); *Exil* (1942), later enlarged; *Oiseaux* (1962), which recalls his collaboration with GEORGES BRAQUE; and the collection *Chant pour un équinoxe*, published in 1975.

## Saint-Just, Louis-Antoine-Léon (1767–1794)
*political figure*

Born in Decize, Louis-Antoine-Léon Saint-Just studied at the Oratian College in Reims and quite early supported the REVOLUTION OF 1789, publishing a satirical poem, "Organt" (1789) and a work entitled *Esprit de la Révolution et de la Constitution de France* (1791), making him one of the youngest theoreticians of the French Revolution. A deputy for Aisne to the Convention (1792), he sat with the MONTAGNARDS and became known for his violent views, unceasingly demanding the king's death and opposing the GIRONDINS' plan for a federalist constitution as outlined by CONDORCET (April 1793). A member of the Committee of Public Safety (where with MAXIMILIEN ROBESPIERRE and GEORGES COUTHON he formed the "Triumvirate"), he devoted himself to domestic issues and organized the armies of the Rhine in taking measures against guilty officers and deserters. As president of the National Convention (February 1794), Saint-Just contributed to the strengthening of dictatorial revolutionary powers and used his authority to confiscate the property of émigrés, redistributing it to the indigent, and helped Robespierre to suppress various opposing factions (Hébertists, Indulgents, Dantonists, moderates, and ultrarevolutionaries). He was arrested with Robespierre, with whom he was executed the next day (9 and 10 Thermidor Year III, July 27–28, 1794). Saint-Just's writing, *Institutions républicaines,* was published only after his death. A notorious figure of the Revolution, and especially of the TERROR (he played a major role in the conviction of GEORGES DANTON), his phrases and statements were often quoted.

## Saint-Lambert, Jean-François de (1716–1803)
*writer*

Born in Paris, Jean-François de Saint-Lambert was the friend of the writers Mme du CHÂTELET and Mme de HOUDETOT, with whom he also had a long liaison. He mirrored the concepts of the Encyclopedists in his *Principes des mœurs ou Catéchisme universel* (1798). He also wrote descriptive poetry (*Les Saisons,* 1764). Saint-Lambert was elected into the ACADÉMIE FRANÇAISE in 1770.

## Saint Laurent, Yves-Henri-Donat-Mathieu (1936–  )
*couturier*

Born in Oran, ALGERIA, Yves Saint Laurent, as he is known, the successor to CHRISTIAN DIOR, was immediately recognized for his talent in 1958 at the showing of his first collection. The founder of his own fashion house (1961), Saint Laurent became known for his original designs of everyday wear and for his knowledge of color, inspired by sources from his North African birthplace. He has given his name to an internationally recognized brand of luxury goods, although he retired in 2002.

## Saint-Léon, Arthur (1821–1870)
*dancer, choreographer*

Born in Paris, Arthur Saint-Léon was the son of the ballet master of the ducal theater of Stuttgart. He was also an excellent violinist as well as a brilliant choreographer, and occasionally composed the music for some of his ballets. Having married the Italian dancer Fanny Cerrito, he created for her *La Vivandière* (1844). He made numerous visits to St. Petersburg, Russia to study dance (1859–69) and became ballet master for the Opéra de Paris (1863–70). Several of his choreographies are still quite well known: *La Fille de marbre* (1847), *Le petit Cheval bossu* (1864), *La Source* (1866), and especially *Coppélia* (1870). Saint-Léon also took part in the revival of the great romantic ballets and created a system of dance notation known as stenochoreography (1852).

## Saint-Marc Girardin (1801–1871)
*critic*

Born in Paris, François-Auguste-Marc Girardin, or Saint-Marc Girardin, as he is known, was named professor of rhetoric at the lycée Louis-le-Grand in 1826, the same year that he joined the editorial staff of *Journal des débats*. From then on, he pursued an active career as a journalist (*Souvenirs et Réflexions d'un journaliste,* 1859), while continuing to teach. Because of his liberal views, he became, after the REVOLUTION OF 1830, a member of the Council of State, then served as a deputy from 1834 to 1848. In 1871, he joined the center-right and contributed to the overthrow of ADOLPHE THIERS. The successor to FRANÇOIS GUIZOT at the SORBONNE, he taught during the JULY MONARCHY and the SECOND EMPIRE a popular course in French literature in which he proved himself to be the spiritual adversary of the romantics. Saint-Marc Girardin's principal work is his *Cours de littérature dramatique ou De l'usage des passions dans le drame* (five volumes, 1843–63). He was elected to the ACADÉMIE FRANÇAISE in 1844.

## Saint-Phalle, Niki de (1930– )
*painter and sculptor*

Recognized for her brightly colored and fanciful sculptures, as well as for her performance art, Marie-Agnès Fal de Saint-Phalle, or Niki de Saint-Phalle, as she is known, was born in Paris. She staged her first performance art in 1961 with "tableaux surprises," in which participants were invited to shoot mixed-media constructions at her, releasing bursts of color in expressionist patterns. In 1963, she was invited to join the group of Nouveaux Reálistes artists (YVES KLEIN, Christo, and others), and, in 1964, she sculpted the first of her *Nanas*, large female figures—the largest being the *Hon* figure (1966) and, after 1969, her "maisons-sculptures" and the "sculptures-jeux" (*Golem*, for Rabinovitch Park in Jerusalem, 1972; *Nana-piscine*, in Saint-Tropez, 1973). Niki de Saint-Phalle created a fantasy garden in Tuscany (Giardino dei Tarrochi, 1980), then in 1983, in collaboration with her husband, Jean Tinguey, the Fontaine Stravinsky near the Centre Georges Pompidou in Paris. Her works are often considered as feminist statements against what was once the male-dominated art movement.

## Saint-Pierre, Bernardin de (1737–1814)
*writer*

Bernardin de Saint-Pierre, whose writings foreshadowed those of RENÉ DE CHATEAUBRIAND and the romantics, was born in Le Havre and worked first as a government engineer. He was known for his brusque, unstable nature but also for his utopian dreams (his ideal republic is described in *L'Arcadie*, 1781) and for his many travels (to Malta, Russia, Poland, and Germany). After a sojourn on the Île de France (now Mauritius) from 1768 to 1770, he returned to Paris and became a disciple of JEAN-JACQUES ROUSSEAU. He expressed his nostalgia for a lost paradise in *Voyage à l'Île de France* (1775) and later in his *Études de la nature* (1784–88), which brought him instant celebrity. This success continued with the publication of *Paul et Virginie*, a part of the last volume of *Études de la nature* (1788), and was followed by *La Chaumière indienne* (1790), then *Harmonies de la nature* (1796). Appointed director of the Paris Botanical Gardens (1792) and named to the Institut de France (1795), he also received many honors during the FIRST EMPIRE and was elected to the ACADÉMIE FRANÇAISE in 1814. The writings of de Saint-Pierre reveal his imaginative love of nature and the sentimental, in contrast to the emphasis on external form and wit that characterized most of the French literature of the period.

## Saint-Pol Roux (1861–1940)
### (Saint-Pol Roux the Magnificent)
*poet*

Born in Saint-Henry, near Marseille, Paul-Pierre Roux, or Saint-Pol Roux the Magnificent, as he is known, was a disciple of STÉPHANIE MALLARMÉ and, like him, was devoted to a cult of beauty. A symbolist, he is recognized for his baroque style (*Manifeste du magnificisme*, 1895), and he sought to be more of a dramatic writer than a poet (*La Dame à la faulx*, 1899), but none of his works was ever performed. It was above all for his recognition of the liberating power of the image and for his unique style that he emerged as a precursor of later traditions (*De la colombe au corbeau par le paon*, 1885–1904; *Les Féeries intérieures*, 1907). His talent was only later, and paradoxically, appreciated: A banquet given in his honor in a lilac grove became one of the greater scandals of the surrealist movement (1925). Saint-Pol Roux was killed during the first days of the Nazi occupation in his home near the Île-de-Camaret, where he had lived in retirement since 1905.

## Saint-Saëns, Camille (1835–1921)
*composer*

Born in Paris and gifted with an exceptional musical precocity, Camille Saint-Saëns, a piano virtuoso since early childhood, was the pupil of several noted musicians. Organist at Saint-Merri (1853) and at the church of the Madeleine in Paris (1857–77), where he gained a reputation as a remarkable improvisor, he later was professor at the Niedermeyer School in Paris (1861–65), where he taught GABRIEL FAURÉ and ANDRÉ MESSAGER. Encouraged by Franz Liszt, Saint-Saëns pursued a career as a composer, while remaining a virtuoso and conductor. Cofounder with CÉSAR FRANCK, ÉDOUARD LALO, JULES MASSENET, GEORGES BIZET, HENRI DUPARC, and GABRIEL FAURÉ of the Société nationale de musique (1871), he became an outspoken opponent of Richard Wagner, a German composer whom he had originally admired. Written in the French classical tradition, Saint-Saëns's music is elegant and precise in detail and his work would have a great influence on CLAUDE DEBUSSY and MAURICE RAVEL. His compositions include the opera *Samson et Dalila, Messe solonnelle* (1856), Requiem (1878), and about 100 melodies.

## Saint-Simon, Claude-Henri de Rouvroy, count de (1760–1825)
*philosopher, economist*

A distant cousin of LOUIS DE ROUVROY, DUKE DE SAINT-SIMON, Claude-Henri de Rouvroy, count de Saint-Simon was born in Paris and served as a military officer in the American War of Independence. Returning to France, he supported the REVOLUTION OF 1789 but was imprisoned (1793–94) during its radical stage. Reduced to working as a copier in a pawnshop, he rallied to the Empire during the HUNDRED DAYS and, opposed to the RESTORATION, was arrested (1820) and later attempted suicide (1823). Only because of the support of one of his disciples did he not sink into complete poverty. Saint-Simon's first works make him the precursor of positivist philosophy and the social sciences (*Lettres d'un habitant de Genève à ses concitoyens,* 1803; *Introduction aux travaux scientifiques du XIXᵉ s.,* 1807). With the creation of his revue, *L'Industrie* (1816), the publication of *L'Organisateur* with AUGUSTE COMTE (1819–20), and the editing of two other works (*Du Système industriel,* 1821–22; *Le Catéchisme des industriels* 1823–24), he affirmed the theses of his optimistic industrialism, the end of the old order, and the future of an industrial society led by scientists, which would automatically bring together the interests of the owners and the workers. *Le nouveau Christianisme* (published posthumously in 1825), formulated the morality for this new society by using presocialist themes. It would, in turn, serve as the basis for the Saint-Simonian school of socialism, founded by his disciples (PROSPER ENFANTIN, ARMAND BAZARD, and PIERRE LEROUX). A number of economists, industrialists, and bankers (FERDINAND DE LESSEPS, MICHEL CHEVALIER), who subsequently played important roles in 19th-century economic developments, were all influenced by Saint-Simonian ideas.

## Saint-Simon, Louis de Rouvroy, duke de (1675–1755)
*writer*

Known for his memoirs, Louis de Rouvroy, duke de Saint-Simon was born in Paris. Because his father had been created a duke and a peer, he received an exceptional education and upbringing, during which he became friends with the future regent, PHILIPPE D'ORLÉANS. He began his military career early, distinguishing himself at the Battle of Neerwinden (1692) against William of Orange, which he describes in his *Relation* (written for his mother) and in which can be seen the origins of his noted *Mémoires*. In 1702, he left the army and established himself at the court of LOUIS XIV at VERSAILLES, spending time also at his château at La Ferté-Vidame, Eure-et-Loire. He had tied his political ambitions to the career of the duke of Burgundy, who died in 1712. Although he was close to the regent, Saint-Simon was eclipsed by others. Nonetheless, he held some positions, namely, as part of a diplomatic mission to Madrid, Spain (1712–22), which allowed him to write a *Tableau de la cour d'Espagne*. The death of the regent in 1723 put a definite end to his political hopes, and he returned to his château and his *Mémoires,* which he had begun in 1694. Written mostly between 1739 and 1750, they particularly describe his experiences between 1691 and 1723. The final years of the reign of LOUIS XIV and the period of the regency are evoked in a series of descriptions and portraits in which the author discusses the royal court and his own life. Much admired by RENÉ DE CHATEAUBRIAND, STENDHAL, and MARCEL PROUST, the *Mémoires,* while digressive and partisan, are considered classic and eloquent masterpieces of French prose. A nearly complete edition appeared in 1829, with the complete (41 volumes) work appearing later.

## Salacrou, Armand (1899–1989)
*dramatist*

Born in Rouen, Armand Salacrou, despite praise for his early works (*Tour à terre,* 1925; *Patchouli,* 1930), had difficulty becoming known and had his first success only with *Une femme libre* (1934). With *L'Inconnue d'Arras* (1934), he emerged as one of the creators of the most original form of avant-garde theater. From surrealism to bourgeois comedy and from Pirandellisms to other involved works, his theater covers all genres. Considering dramatic work as a meditation on the human condition, Salacrou expressed the suffering and anguish of life as an adventure whose meaning escaped him. He published his memoirs under the title *Dans la Salle des pas perdus* (1974–76). Salacrou was named to the Académie Goncourt in 1949.

## Salan, Raoul (1899–1984)
*general*

Born in Rocquecourbe, Tarn, Raoul Salan was named a division commander during the 1944–45 campaign during World War II and later was made commander of French forces in chief in INDOCHINA (1952–53). He then was placed in command of the French forces of the 10th military region of ALGERIA (1956). After the events of May 1958, he rallied to General CHARLES DE GAULLE, but as a supporter of a French Algeria. Salan subsequently broke with de Gaulle and took part in the generals' putsch of April 1961, then took over the leadership of the Organization de l'armée secrète (OAS). Arrested in 1962, he received a death sentence for contempt that was commuted to life imprisonment. He was amnestied in 1968 and was rehabilitated in 1982.

## Saliceti, Antoine-Christophe (1757–1809)
*attorney, political figure*

Born in Saliceto, CORSICA, Antoine-Christophe Saliceti (or Salicetti) served, during the REVOLUTION OF 1789, as a deputy for Corsica to the Constituent Assembly and the Convention. He put the young Napoléon Bonaparte (see NAPOLÉON I) in charge of artillery under the command of General JACQUES DUGOMMIER at the siege of Toulon (1793). Saliceti also served a member of the Council of Five Hundred (1797), then as minister of police and of war under JOSEPH BONAPARTE in Naples.

## Sallé, Marie (1707–1756)
*dancer, choreographer*

Born in Paris, Marie Sallé enjoyed her first successes at the Foire theaters and then at the Paris

Opéra (1727), where she appeared in the opera-ballets of JEAN-BAPTISTE LULLY. She performed for the royal court and danced in several of MOLIÈRE's comedies, then appeared in London for three seasons. In *Pygmalion* (1734), when she danced the role of Galatea, she abandoned the traditional heavy robe and collar and, substituting a simple tunic, introduced a modification to the style of ballet costuming. Returning to Paris (1737), she danced *Les Indes galantes* and created the main role in *Castor et Pollux* by JEAN-PHILIPPE RAMEAU. A friend of VOLTAIRE, David Garrick, and JEAN-GEORGES NOVERRE, Sallé played a definitive role in the evolution of classical ballet to a more active form.

## Samain, Albert (1858–1900)
*poet*

Born in Lille, Albert Samain slowly gained fame with his first collection of lyrical poetry, *Au jardin de l'infante* (1893). Because of his love of musical nuances, he was attracted to the symbolist movement and was an admirer of CHARLES BAUDELAIRE and PAUL VERLAINE. A romantic because of his deep sense of melancholy, Samain was equally sensitive to the realistic and naturalistic style of the Parnassian school, a reaction against Romanticism includes Baudelaire, Verlaine, STÉPHANE MALLARMÉ. In his collection of poems, *Aux flancs du vase* (1898), he exhalts a peaceful and bright paganism. *Le Chariot d'or* (posthumous, 1901) best expresses the languorous style that characterizes Samain. His somewhat troubled sexuality is also expressed in his *Contes* (posthumous, 1901) and in his lyrical drama, *Polyphème* (posthumous, 1901, set to music in 1922).

## Sambin, Hugues (1515–1601)
*architect, sculptor, furniture designer*

Born in Gray, near Versoul, Hugues Sambin, through his various works, demonstrates a strong interest in the Italian Renaissance. His originality rests in the combination of the Italianate style, which was inspired by the designs of antiquity and Burgundian motifs (notably that of a cabbage within a Greek palmette). He worked especially in Dijon (the entrance to the Palace of Justice and to the Compasseur residence). A major figure among

16th-century French cabinetmakers, Sambin published an influential folio of designs, presaging a new classicism that inspired many who came later.

## Sand, George (1804–1876)
## (Amandine-Aurore-Lucille Dupin, baroness Dudevant)
*novelist*

A leading romantic novelist, George Sand (the pen name of Aurore Dupin, baroness Dudevant) was born in Paris. After a carefree rural childhood, she led an independent life after separating from her husband, becoming the mistress of JULES SANDEAU (hence the pseudonym). Having strong feminist convictions, George Sand, in her early autobiographical novels, insisted on women's rights of passion and sought to assimilate personal happiness with a moral regeneration. Thus *Indiana* (where she used her pseudonym for the first time, 1832) and *Leila* (1833), are the romantic and lyrical works in which love confronts worldly conventions and social prejudices, just as George Sand did in her successive love affairs, notably with ALFRED DE MUSSET and FRÉDÉRIC CHOPIN. Beginning in 1836, inspired by the ideas of JEAN-JACQUES ROUSSEAU, she became an advocate for social reforms and humanitarian ideals: *Le Compagnon du tour de France* (1840) and *Consuelo* (1842–43) are statements against society, mixed with the romantic theme of sovereign love. Disillusioned with politics after the failure of the REVOLUTION OF 1848, she returned to her country house in Nohant (1845) and wrote the novels of her third period, which dealt with rustic life and the peasantry, still expressing her sentimental optimism (*La Mare au diable*, 1846; *François le Champi*, 1847–48; *La petite Fadette*, 1849; *Les Maîtres sonneurs*, 1853), in each presenting her ideals regarding art, literature, and humanitarianism. Called "la bonne dame de Nohant," she also began a voluminous correspondence with GUSTAVE FLAUBERT (25 volumes, published 1967 to 1991). George Sand continued her romantic and dramatic writing up to the time of her death and continued to edit her lengthy autobiography, *Histoire de ma vie*, begun in 1854. While George Sand's effusive style and humanitarian declarations might seem excessive by today's standards, one is still struck by her generosity of spirit and sincerity of narrative.

George Sand *(Library of Congress)*

## Sandeau, Julien (1811–1883)
*writer*

Born in Aubusson, Julien Sandeau, also known as Jules Sandeau or Jules Sand, left his law studies to write in collaboration with the baroness Dudevant (who became GEORGE SAND, whose nom de plume is an adaptation of his). Their first work was the novel *Rose et Blanche* (1831). After the end of their liaison (1833), he henceforth led a self-effacing life, writing *Sacs et Parchemins* (1851) and *Madamoiselle de la Seiglière* (1848), an idealistic novel that had a great success for more than half a century; it was also adapted to the stage. Jules Sand's theatrical works, written in collaboration with ÉMILE AUGIER, include *Le Gendre de M. Poirier* (1854). Jules Sand was elected to the ACADÉMIE FRANÇAISE in 1859.

## Sangnier, Marc (1873–1950)
*journalist, political figure*

Born in Paris, Marc Sangnier was the founder of the social and religious movement known as Le Sillon, which sought to reconcile Christian values with the republic and with social democracy. Its ideas were expressed especially in *L'Éveil démocratique* (1904). Condemned by Pope Pius X (1910), Sangnier submitted to Rome and founded a new newspaper, *La Démocratie*, then the Jeune République movement (1912). As a deputy (1919–24), he struggled for peace and against racism, and created the Ligue française des auberges de juenesses (1930). The Jeune République merged with the MRP after the Liberation.

## Sans-culottes (sanculottes)

During the REVOLUTION OF 1789, *Sans-culottes* was the name given at the time of the Convention (1792) to the revolutionaries who considered the *culottes* (knee-britches) worn by the former aristocracy as a sign of the ancien régime. As such, they wore instead long pants, as well as workers' smocks and the red bonnet of revolution. Formed in the districts of Paris, the Sans-culottes were led by the ENRAGÉS (JACQUES ROUX) and then by the Hébertists and were responsible for the days of revolutionary uprising (May 31 and June 2, 1793) that led to the fall of the GIRONDINS and also the uprisings on September 4 and 5 of that year. It was generally because of pressure from the Sans-culottes that the revolutionary government (the MONAGNARD Convention) introduced various radical political (the TERROR), social, and economic measures.

See also HÉBERT, JACQUES-RENÉ.

## Santerre, Antoine-Joseph (1752–1809)
*political figure*

Born in Paris, where he was a brewer in the faubourg Saint-Antoine (and where he was called "le Père du faubourg" because of his generosity), Antoine-Joseph Santerre, during the REVOLUTION OF 1789, took part in all the major revolutionary events and was one of the leaders of those that occurred on June 20, 1792. He was put in charge of guarding the Temple, where the royal family was imprisoned, and he led King LOUIS XVI to the scaffold. A division commander in the VENDÉE in 1793, he was defeated at Coron. A suspect, Santerre was imprisoned in the Carmes, but was freed after 9 Thermidor, Year II (July 27, 1794).

## Sarazin, Jacques (1588–1660)
*sculptor*

Born in Noyen, Jacques Sarazin (or Sarrazin) worked for 18 years in Rome for Cardinal Aldobrandini and decorated the fountains of his villa at Fracasti. Upon returning to France, he collaborated with SIMON VOUET, whom he had met in Italy. He worked on the *nymphée* (lily pond) (1630–32) of Widewille, made the models for the caryatids for the pavilion de l'Horloge at the LOUVRE, and, with other painters, decorated the château des Maisons. In bronze he produced four bas-reliefs (*Les Vertus*). Commissioned by Henri de Bourbon, for whom he carved a funerary monument, Sarazin also sculpted the tomb of Cardinal de BÉRULLE (Louvre).

## Saône

The Saône River, which has its source at Viomenil, flows for 418 kilometers through Gray, Châlon-sur-Saône, Mâcon, and into the RHÔNE at LYON. The Saône regularizes the course of the lesser Rhône. It is connected to the RHINE and the SEINE Rivers by a system of canals and is fed by flows from the JURA Mountains.

## Sarkis (1938– )
*artist*

Of Armenian origin, Sarkis Zabunyan, or Sarkis, as he is known, was born in Istanbul, Turkey, and settled in Paris in 1964. He painted works close to the figurative narrative style, then, after discovering conceptual art and the works of German artist Joseph Beuys, created installations with solid materials (spools, felt) that are charged with energy. Sarkis has willingly adapted the military aesthetic (going as far as to paint water tanks with camouflage colors), archaeology (rearranging archaeological labels to contradictory places), the cinema, and music. His series *Kriegshatz*, begun in 1976, represents his synthesis of research done on the memory of locations.

## Sarrault, Albert (1872–1962)

*political figure*

Born in BORDEAUX, Albert Sarrault served as a Radical-Socialist deputy (1902–24) and as a senator (1926–40). He was named governor-general of INDOCHINA (1911–14, 1916–19) and was a minister several times, carrying successively the portfolios of public instruction (1914–15), colonies (1920–24, 1932–33), interior (1926–28, 1934–35), and navy (1930). Premier (October–November 1933), he was recalled in January 1936 to lead the government, but social upheavals such as strikes and political problems (German occupation of the Rhineland) obliged him to retire and give the government to the POPULAR FRONT (June 1936). Minister of state (1937–38), interior (1938–40), and national education (March–June 1940), he was deported to Germany late in the war (1944–45). Sarrault served as president of the Assemblée de l'Union française (1951).

## Sarrault, Maurice (1869–1943)

*political figure*

Born in Toulouse, Maurice Sarrault was the brother of ALBERT SARRAULT. A Radical-Socialist deputy (1913–32), he was the owner and director of *La Dépêche de Toulouse*. An outspoken opponent of the VICHY regime, Sarrault was assassinated by the French Milice in Toulouse.

## Sarrault, Nathalie (1900–  )

*writer*

Born in Invanoe, Russia, Nathalie Sarrault lived in Paris since her childhood and, in 1941, left the practice of law to dedicate herself to writing. Best known for her innovations associated with the "nouveau roman," in an important essay, *L'Ère de soupcon* (1956), she broke with the conventions of traditional realistic novel writing. Her writing would subsequently influence the conception of modern fiction. An admirer of MARCEL PROUST and British writer Virginia Woolf, she portrayed her characters minutely, as in *Tropismes* (1939) and *Portrait d'un inconnu* (1948). The novel *Planétarium* (1950), generally considered her masterpiece, was followed by *Les Fruits d'or* (1963), the play *Le Silence* (1967), and many other works, in which the narrative voice and viewpoint derive from the mind, sensibilities, and fleeting emotions, as Sarrault argues that truth is entirely subjective.

## Sarrien, Jean-Marie-Ferdinand (1840–1915)

*political figure*

Born in Bourbon-Lancy, Jean-Marie-Ferdinand Sarrien served as a radical leftist deputy (1876) and later headed various ministries. As premier (March–October 1906) his ministry saw, on the domestic level, passage of the law on a weekly day of rest—an attempt to appease Catholics after the law of separation of church and state (in particular regarding the question of the inventories)—and the overturning of the verdict condemning ALFRED DREYFUS, and, on the foreign level, the Algeciras Conference, convened to mediate a dispute between France and Germany over Morocco.

## Sartre, Jean-Paul (1905–1980)

*philosopher, writer, critic*

The leading exponent of existentialism, Jean-Paul Sartre was born in Paris to a liberal Protestant bourgeois family and was raised by his mother and grandfather, a relative of ALBERT SCHWEITZER. Early in his life, Sartre developed his attitudes about himself, life, and society, and his vocation as a writer (*Les Mots*, 1964). While attending the École normale supérieure, he questioned with several of his classmates, including PAUL NIZAN, the values, privileges, and traditions of the bourgeoisie. He taught for a time at the lycée in Le Havre then, while a resident student at the French Institute in Berlin (1933–34), he developed his philosophy, combining the phenomenology of German philosopher Edmund Husserl, the metaphysics of Hegel and Heidegger, and the social theory of Marx into the single view of existentialism. His first philosophical writings (*L'Imagination*, 1936; *Esquisse d'une théorie des émotions*, 1939) made these thinkers, especially Heidegger, better known in France. During the World War II, Sartre served in the military and was cap-

Jean-Paul Sartre *(Library of Congress)*

*tique* (1960, 1980, second edition), moved his emphasis from existential freedom and subjectivity to Marxist social determinism. Never joining the Communist Party, he remained free to criticize it and the action of Communist regimes. Sartre profoundly influenced the intellectual youth of the postwar era. He never ceased to question the contemporary world in the name of humankind and freedom participating in Bertrand Russell's tribunal, taking part in anticolonial struggles, refusing the Nobel Prize in literature in 1964, acting as director of *La Cause du peuple,* then of *Libération* until 1974. His last great work is an attempt at an integral biography of GUSTAVE FLAUBERT (1971–72), and his correspondence revealed invaluable documents on the details of his life and relationships, notably with his companion SIMONE DE BEAUVOIR (*Lettres au Castor et à quelques autres,* 1983).

## Satie, Alfred-Erik-Leslie (1866–1925)
*composer*

Born in Honfleur, Alfred-Erik-Leslie Satie, or Erik Satie, as he is known, came to Paris in 1879 and studied at the Paris Conservatoire. Rebelling against its academic discipline, he enlisted in the army, which he soon left as well. He then worked as a conductor and pianist in the cabarets of Montmartre (Le Chat noir, L'Auberge du Clou) where he met CLAUDE DEBUSSY, who became his lifelong friend. An innovator as well as a rebel, Satie anticipated the future of French music, and many younger composers hailed him as a master, particularly the innovative group of Les Six. Older composers such as Debussy and MAURICE RAVEL were influenced also by his compositions. Satie studied counterpoint at the Schola cantorum with VINCENT D'INDY and ALBERT ROUSSEL (1905–08), after which he composed works with ironic titles, often inspired by impressionism (*Aperçus désagréables, En habit de cheval, Véritables préludes flasques pour un chien, Descriptions automatiques, Embryons désséchés, Heures séculaires et instantées*). During WORLD WAR I, he was connected with Russian impressario Sergey Diaghilev, Spanish artist Pablo Picasso, and JEAN COCTEAU. Fame came to Satie with his ballet *Parade,* with a prologue by Cocteau, choreography by JULES MASSINE, and costumes and sets by Picasso. This first "cubist" spectacle caused a scandal that in turn pro-

tured, then released. He taught for a while and served in the RESISTANCE. At that time, his major philosophic work, *L'Être et le Néant (Being and Nothingness),* was published (1943). He also wrote a play, *Huis clos* (1944), in which he states "Hell is others," affirming the existentialist view presented in earlier works. He continued to develop his philosophy in such works as *L'existentialisme est un humanisme* (1946). Sartre's writing include *La Nausée* (1938), *Le Mur* (1939), *Les Chemins de la liberté* (1945–49), *Réflexions sur la question juive* (1946), *Baudelaire* (1947), *Saint Genet, comédien et martyr* (1952), and *Situations,* a collection of articles (1947–65). His plays and adaptations have also known a wide audience (*Les Mouches,* 1943; *Morts sans sépulture,* 1946; *La Putain respectueuse,* 1946; *Les Mains sales,* 1948; *Le Diable et le Bon Dieu,* 1951; *Kean,* 1954; *Nekrassov,* 1955; *Les Séquestres d'Altona,* 1959; and an adaptation of Euripides' *Trojans,* 1965). Sartre, in a later philosophic work, *Critique de la raison dialec-*

duced the Arcueil school of music. Satie then wrote his masterpiece, *Socrate,* a "symphonic drama" based on the writings of Plato as translated by VICTOR COUSIN (1918). Satie made an indelible mark on the stylists of his times, including Russian composer Igor Stravinsky.

## Saumaise, Claude  (1588–1653)
*scholar, philologist*

Known also as Claudius Salmasius, the Latinized form of his name, Claude Saumaise was born in Auxeis. Besides his studies in law, theology, medicine, and history, he acquired a good knowledge of Greek, Latin, Arabic, Hebrew, and Persian. Joining the Reformation, he settled in Leyden, Netherlands where he taught philology. An encyclopedic scholar, Saumaise left a number of erudite works, especially on juridical and theological matters. In his writings, he attempts to show the compatibility of usury with the precepts of Christianity.

## Saumoneau, Louise  (1875–1949)
*socialist, feminist*

Born in Paris, Louise Saumoneau founded in 1899 the first feminist socialist organization (Groupe des femmes socialistes) in France. She sought both the right to vote and political equality for women. On July 5, 1914, she organized a great demonstration in Paris that was the first Women's Day (Journée des Femmes). She believed that social and economic justice must accompany the achievement of women's rights. Saumoneau is the author of *Principes et action féminists socialistes* (1923).

## Saumur

The site of a famous French cavalry school, Saumur was originally an abbey, founded in the ninth century. In 1599, DUPLESSIS MORNAY established a Protestant theological academy there. The revocation of the Edict of NANTES, however, caused a large portion of the population to emigrate and brought about the town's decline, which lasted until the founding of the School of Cavalry (École de cavalerie) in 1764. HONORÉ DE BALZAC, in his novel *Eugénie Grandet,* evokes the lethargic life at Saumur at the beginning of the 19th century. During World War II, the students of the École de cavalerie defended the passage to the Loire for 20 kilometers against the advance of the German armies.

## Sauvage, Henri  (1873–1932)
*architect*

Born in Rouen, Henri Sauvage, after following the Art Nouveau style, moved toward functionalism, becoming a precursor in the use of prefabricated materials. One of the best examples of this is the apartment building at 28, rue Vavin in Paris (1912), on which the facade of white and blue squares gives the building a clean and clear aspect, while the graduated stories recall a pyramid or an urban hanging garden, allowing for maximization of light. Sauvage employed these principles again in Paris in his apartment building on the rue des Amiraux (1925), and in his Project d'immeubles en front de Seine (1928). In Nantes, he built the Decré department store, whose facade consisted of a large glass panel (1931, destroyed in 1943). An innovator and utopian, Sauvage was the inspiration for the Italian architect Antonio Sant'Elia in his project Città Nuova in Rome (1914) and perhaps also for the American "Babylonian" skyscrapers, such as the Paramount Building in New York City.

## Savary, Anne-Jean-Marie-René (1774–1833)
*general, political figure*

Born in Marcq, Ardennes, Anne-Jean-Marie-René Savary enlisted in the army in 1789 and became aide-de-camp to General Desaix during the Napoleonic Wars (campaigns in Egypt and Italy), then served as colonel of the elite Consular Police, effectively heading the secret police of the first consul. He was put in charge of the execution of the duke d'ENGHIEN (1804). Named division commander in 1805, he distinguished himself at the Battle of Ostroleka, Poland, and, in 1808, was made duke of Rovigo. Sent as an envoy to Spain, he convinced Kings Charles IV and Ferdinand VII to come to the meeting at Bayonne for victory of Ostroleka (1808). He succeeded JOSEPH FOUCHÉ as minister of police (1810–14) and, remaining faithful to NAPOLÉON I, wanted to follow him into exile, but instead was arrested. Savary later served as commander in chief in ALGERIA (1831–33) and left his *Mémoires pour servir à l'histoire de Napoléon.*

## Saxe, Maurice, count de (1696–1750)
**(Marshal Saxe)**
*military figure*

Born in Goslar, Maurice, count de Saxe, or Marshal Saxe, as he is known, was the son of the elector of Saxony, August II, the future king of Poland, and Aurora of Königsmarck. He served successively Prince Eugene of Savoy, Peter the Great of Russia, then his father (who recognized him in 1711), and finally the king of France, Louis XIV. Elected duke of Courland (1726), he was unable to take possession of his duchy and so returned to France. He demonstrated his exceptional tactical and strategic skills during the War of the Austrian Succession (taking Prague and Eger, victories at Fontenoy and Lawfeld). Marshal Saxe can be considered the last of the condottieri not only because of his military talents, but also for his actions in his private life.

## Say family
*family of economists, industrialists, political figures*

Born in LYON, Jean-Baptiste Say (1767–1832), who was influenced by the theories of Adam Smith, the English philosopher, published his first work, *Simple exposé de la manière dont se forment, se distribuent et se consomment les riches,* in 1813. The manager of a cotton mill in Pas-de-Calais (1807–13), after the RESTORATION he taught political theory and wrote on political economy (*Catéchisme d'économie politique,* 1815; translation of the works of David Ricardo, an English economist, 1819; *Lettre à Malthus,* 1820; *Cours complet d'économie politique pratique,* 1829–30), in which he argued for industrialization and free trade. His brother, Louis-Auguste Say (1774–1840), born in Lyon and also an economist, was the director of a sugar refinery at Nantes, was opposed to his economic theories, and, in his own work, *Études sur les richesses des nations,* argued that labor, as the productive force, was the source of wealth. Horace-Émile Say (1794–1860), born in Noisy-le-Sec, was the son of Jean-Baptiste Say. He served as the president of the Chamber of Commerce of Paris and undertook an inquiry into that city's industries. He founded the Société d'économie politique, the *Jour-*

*nal des économists,* and the *Journal du commerce.* Léon Say (1826–96), born in Paris, was the son of Horace-Émily Say. He served as prefect of the Seine (1871), minister of finances (1872–73, 1875–79), opposed socialism, and supported a policy of free exchange. He was elected to the ACADÉMIE FRANÇAISE in 1886.

## Scarron, Paul (1610–1660)
*writer*

Born in Paris, Paul Scarron, a bohemian, became a canon and was attached to the bishop of Mas. He became infirm but still continued to frequent the literary salons, and had married Françoise d'Aubigné, who would become Mme de MAINTENON. Scarron is the author of comedies that were much prized for their intrigue-filled buffoonery and for their verbal play—*Jodelet ou le Maître valet* (1645) and *Don Japhet d'Arménie* (1653). He also wrote a burlesque parody in octosyllables, *Virgile travesti* (1648–52), and *Le Roman comique* (1651–57).

## Scève, Maurice (1501–1564)
*scholar, poet*

Born in LYON, where he was, like PONTUS DE TYARD and SÉBILLET, a member of the Lyonnais school, Maurice Scève, a friend of CLÉMENT MAROT (after 1536), took part in the Barbe festivals, poetic celebrations dedicated to the veneration of the relics of St. Ann, for which he wrote two works praising the feminine ideal. His collection, *Délie, objet de plus haute vertu* (1544), composed of verses in decasyllables, is a work of lyric praises of beloved women and mystical symbols ("Délie" is the anagram for *idéel*—"ideal"). In *Microcosme* (1562), a biblical epic of 3,003 elaborately constructed verses, Scève describes the human as a microcosm of the universe. He also did verse translations of Psalms 26 and 83 from the Vulgate (1542). An avid reader of Petrarch and Sannazaro, Scève was highly regarded by the symbolists of the 20th century.

## Schaeffer, Claude (1898–1982)
*archaeologist*

Born in Strasbourg, Claude Schaeffer took part in the archaeological excavations at Ras Shamra (Ougarit) in 1929 in Syria, where he discovered thousands of tablets written in the cuneiform script. He also found five levels of civilization, from the Neolithic to the 13th-century B.C.E., as well as temples to Dagon and Baal, palaces, fortifications, and votive tombs. The tables included the ancient poems *Baal and Anat, The Epic of Yam, The Legend of Keret, The Legend of Danil,* and a version of *The Legend of Gilgamesh,* and make up the only known Canaanite literary texts, all dating from the 14th century B.C.E. Schaeffer also excavated at Engomi, on Cyprus. In 1954, he was named professor at the COLLÈGE DE FRANCE.

## Schaeffer, Pierre (1910–1995)
*engineer and composer*
Born in Nancy, Pierre Schaeffer, a graduate of the École polytechnique, was a sound engineer at RTF (Radiodiffusion-télévision française) With PIERRE HENRY, he founded the *Studio d'essai* and was one of the inventors of "concrete music, a new composition technique consisting of separating heavy recorded natural sound materials. Concrete sound is prerecorded natural sound used in electronic music, as opposed to purely synthesized noises or tones. Their electro-acoustic manipulations are the basis for several of Schaeffer's compositions, including *Études de bruits* (1948), *Suite pour 14 instruments, Variations sur un flute mexicaine* (1949) and in collaboration with Pierre Henry: *Bidule et ut* (1949), *Symphonie pour un homme seul* (1950), and *Orphée,* the first opera in concrete music (1953). He served as director of the music research group for ORTF and was professor at the Conservatoire de Paris. As a philosopher, he was also interested in popular culture and in communication in general.

## Schélandre, Jean de (1584–1635)
*dramatist*
Born in Soumazannes, Lorraine, Jean de Schélandre is the author of an irregular tragedy, *Tyr et Sidon ou les Funestes Amours de Belcar et de Méliane* (ca. 1608), which he later transformed into a tragicomedy (1628). In the preface of this work, Schélandre made a veritable declaration of war against the traditional rules of tragedy in that he presented the mixture of comedy and tragedy as the only true way to portray theatrically the diverse aspects of life.

## Scheurer-Kestner, Auguste (1833–1899)
*industrialist, political figure*
Born in Mulhouse, Auguste Scheurer-Kestner, as a liberal, was opposed to the SECOND EMPIRE and served as a deputy for the Union républicaine in the National Assembly (1871). A permanent senator and the director of *La République française* (1879–84), Scheurer-Kestner was among those who, persuaded of the innocence of captain ALFRED DREYFUS, fought for a review of that officer's trial and a reversal of his sentence.

## Schlumberger, Jean (1877–1968)
*writer*
Born in Guebwiller, Jean Schlumberger was a friend of ANDRÉ GIDE, with whom he founded and sustained *La nouvelle Revue française,* and also of JACQUES COPEAU. Schlumberger, who was raised in a Protestant milieu and was interested in the history of religions, wrote a work that identified him as a foremost a moralist and henceforth an agnostic, concerned with the dramas that took place within the family or in social groups, when individuals are forced to deal with generational conflicts. *Le Lion devenu vieux* (1924), an evocation of the final weeks of Cardinal RETZ and the bitter constraints on his life, is a study of the tragedy of aging, which is also the main theme in *Saint-Saturnin* (1931), a book about the attachment to a house and faithfulness to a tradition, as well as being a study of the self-betrayal that old age might bring. This taste for psychological analysis as well as a rigorous self-examination is found in Schlumberger's other stories, such as *Passion* (1956); in his critical studies, like *Plaisir à Corneille* (1936) or *Madeleine et André Gide* (1956); and in his plays and essays.

## Schmitt, Florent (1870–1958)
*composer*
Born in Blâmont, Meurthe-et-Moselle, Florent Schmitt was the student of both JULES MASSINET and GABRIEL FAURÉ at the Conservatoire de Paris. Winner of the Grand prix de Rome (1900), he gained his celebrity with *Psaulm XLVII,* for orchestra, choir, organ, and soprano (1904). From his travels throughout Europe, the Mediterranean,

and the Middle East, he brought back sparkling inspirations that are evident in his *Feuillets de voyage* (1903–13), *Reflets d'Allemagne* (1905), and in a nostalgia for the East that, joined with his intense romanticism and his complex writing, would characterize his major work, especially orchestral compositions (*Le Palais hauté*, 1907; *Antoine et Cléopâtre*, 1920; *Mirages*, 1921; *Salammbó*, based on GUSTAVE FLAUBERT, 1925; *Danse d'Abisag*, 1925), ballets (*La Tragédie de Salomé*, 1910; *Oriane et le Prince d'amour*, 1938), a *Symphonie concertante*, for piano and orchestra (1928), a second *Symphonie* (1957), and chamber music (*Quintette*, 1908; *Trio*, 1944; *Quatuor*, 1947).

## Schneider family
### family of industrialists

Eugène Schneider (1805–75), born in Bidestroff, was the owner of the Bazeilles (Ardennes) steel mill. In 1836, with his brother Adolf Schneider (1802–45), he took over the steel works of Creusot (founded in 1788 by IGNACE WENDEL) and established the Société Schneider Frères et Cie, whose factories were considered among the most advanced of the era (they built the first steam locomotive in 1838). A liberal deputy in 1845, minister of trade and agriculture in 1851, and member of the Legislative Corps during the SECOND EMPIRE, Schneider was responsible for several pieces of social legislation. Henri Schneider (1840–98), his son, was born in La Creusot and served as director of the Société Schneider Frères et Cie. He developed the manufacturing of mechanical engineering devices and armaments, while pursuing the social works of his father. Eugéne Schneider (1868–1942), the son of Henri Schneider, with his own son Charles Schneider (1898–1960), helped to develop and modernize the Creusot factories.

## Schneider, Hortense (1833–1920)
### singer

Born in BORDEAUX, Hortense Schneider was a popular interpreter of the works of JACQUES OFFENBACH, who brought her to the Bouffes-Parisiens in 1855 and wrote most of his masterpieces for her, which she performed at Variétés (*La belle Hélène, Barbe-Bleue, La Perichole, La Diva*). Schneider was

one of the most famous and celebrated operetta sopranos of the Belle Époque.

## Schoelcher, Victor (1804–1893)
### political figure

Born in Paris, Victor Schoelcher, after the REVOLUTION OF 1848, served as undersecretary of state in the Provisional Government and helped in passing the decree abolishing slavery in the colonies, an objective that he had sought since 1840. A leftist deputy for Guadeloupe and Martinique (1848–51), he went into self-imposed exile in England during the SECOND EMPIRE. After the abdication of NAPOLÉON III (September 1871), he was reelected deputy for Martinique to the National Assembly (1871), then was named senator for life (1875). In 1949, Schoelcher's remains were transferred to the Panthéon.

## Schöffer, Nicolas (1912–1992)
### sculptor

Considered the founder of cybernetic art and one of the more important artists of the second half of the 20th century, Nicolas Schöffer, who was also a painter, architect, and art theorist, was born in Kalocsa, Hungary. He came to France after the war and, in 1948, created "spatio-dynamic" sculpture, made from geometric metal frameworks comprised of small pieces. Later mobile sculptures were done with sound-and-light effects (*Cysp I*, 1956). With their "lumino-dynamism" (*Lux I*, 1957), Schöffer's sculptures, because of their reflectors and other optic aspects, produce the effect of mobile luminosity. His *Reliefs anamorphoses* (1961) create anamorphoses by movement of elements in plexiglass, and his *Mer-lumière* (1962) and *Telelumino-scope* produce abstract forms using the power of light-sensitive cells.

## Schomberg family
### family of military figures

Of German origin, Gaspard de Schomberg (1540–99) was born in Meissen, Saxony, and fought at first in France on the side of the HUGUENOTS before entering the service of Kings HENRY III and HENRY IV. His brother Georges de Schomberg (1543–78), the favorite of Henry III, was killed in a duel. Gaspard de Schomberg's son, Henri Schomberg, count of Nanteuil (1574–1632), who captured the pass at Susa, was named a marshal of France, as was his grandson, Charles Schomberg, duke d'Halluin (1601–56).

## Schomberg, Frédéric-Armand, duke de (1615–1690)
*marshal of France*

Of German origin, Frédéric-Armand, duke de Schomberg (or Schonberg), was born in Heidelberg, Germany. He fought in the service of William of Orange, then of France, and took part in the Battle of the Dunes (1658). He won a victory over Portuguese forces at the Battle of Viçosa (1658) and was made a marshal of France. Forced to flee because of the revocation of the EDICT OF NANTES, marshal Schomberg became an adviser to William III of Orange-Nassau. He was killed at the battle of the Boyne.

## Schuman, Robert (1886–1963)
*political figure*

Born in Luxembourg, Robert Schuman served as a Démocrate-populaire deputy from 1919 to 1940, and as undersecretary of state for refugees from March to July 1940. Deported at the beginning of WORLD WAR II, he escaped and, after the war, served as an MRP (MOUVEMENT RÉPUBLICAIN POPU-LAIRE) deputy (1945–62) and minister of finances (June 1946–November 1947), then became premier (November 1947–48). He subsequently held the portfolio for foreign affairs (July 1948–January 1953). His ministry was marked by the beginnings of the Marshall Plan (1948) and by the rapprochement between France and the German Federal Republic (France gave up control of the Ruhr). Schuman was, with JEAN MONNET, one of the major proponents of the reconstruction of Europe, helping to establish, through the Schuman Plan, the European Coal and Steel Community and the European Defense Community (Paris Accords, 1952). Faced with the strong opposition of the RPF and the Communists to this latter project, he resigned. As minister of justice (February 1955–June 1956), Schuman dedicated himself to the European move-

ment (1955), then to the European Parliament at Strasbourg (1958). He is the author of *Pour l'Europe.* See also EUROPEAN UNION.

## Schumann, Maurice (1911–1998)
*political figure*

Born in Paris, Maurice Schumann, having rejoined General CHARLES DE GAULLE in London in 1940 during WORLD WAR II, was the spokesperson for Free France (France libre) on the BBC. A member of the Consultative Assembly (provisional) from 1944 to 1946, he served as deputy (beginning in 1945), then senator (1974–98), and contributed to the founding of the MOUVEMENT RÉPUBLICAIN POPULAIRE, for which he served as president from 1945 to 1949. Secretary of state for foreign affairs (1951–54), minister in charge of the development of territory (1962), minister of state from 1967 to 1969, he was minister of foreign affairs from 1969 to 1973. Schumann was elected into the ACADÉMIE FRANÇAISE in 1974.

## Schweitzer, Albert (1875–1965)
*theologian, philosopher, musician, musicologist, physician, missionary, Nobel laureate*

Born in Kaysersberg, Alsace, Albert Schweitzer studied at the Universities of Strasbourg, Paris, and Berlin. He was ordained a curate for the Church of St. Nicolas in Strasbourg (1900) and a year later became principal of its theological seminary. He then undertook medical studies and, in 1913, went to Lambarene, Gabon, to establish a hospital where, as a medical doctor, he would treat thousands of patients each year. He settled there permanently after WORLD WAR I (1924) and traveled to Europe and America only to give organ concerts. As a theologian, he did research on Jesus and Saint Paul and, as a philosopher, is the author of such works as *Philosophie de la culture, Culture et Éthique,* and *Les Grandes Penseurs de l'Inde.* As a musicologist, he wrote a study of Bach (*J.-S. Bach, le musicien poète,* 1905). Concerned always with ethics, Schweitzer put forth a philosophy based on a "reverence for life," embracing compassion for all forms of life. His ideals have had considerable influence in on modern thought and ethics. A world-renowned humanitarian, as well as an ethical philosopher of the modern age, he outlined his own life and thought in *À l'orée de la forêt vierge, Ma vie et mes pensées* (1960), in which it is apparent that the scope of his interests were unified especially by the profound spiritual meaning that he found in the natural world. Schweitzer was awarded the Nobel Peace Prize in 1952.

## Scribe, Eugène (1791–1861)
*playwright*

Born in Paris, Eugène Scribe was not well received initially, during the early years of the RESTORATION. However, his comedies, influenced by Goldoni and DIDEROT, soon gained great popularity, especially among the bourgeoisie, because of their praise of social success and wealth. A great creator of comic and theatrical effects, Scribe, who was also criticized for lack of taste and originality, was acknowledged as a master of his craft and eventually composed more than 350 plays and other works. Among the best known are *Bertrand et Raten* (1833), *Le Verre d'eau* (1840), *Une Chaîne* (1841), *Le Puff ou Mensonge et Vérité* (1849), and *Bataille des dames* (1851). He also wrote himself, or in collaboration, a number of librettos and comic operas, including *La Muette de Portici* (1828), *La Juive* (1835), *Les Huguenots* (1836), *La Favorite* (1840), and *Le Prophète* (1849). Scribe was elected to the ACADÉMIE FRANÇAISE in 1836.

## Scudéry, Madeleine de (1607–1701)
*writer*

Known for her lengthy sentimental novels, Madeleine de Scudéry, who was one of the most popular authors of her time, was born in Le Havre. She eventually settled in Paris and became part of the literary salon of CATHERINE DE VIVONNE, marquise de RAMBOUILLET, before hosting her own salon, which was also frequented by leading social and intellectual figures. Her major writings (romans à clef and dissertations on morality and love) include *Artemené ou la grand Cyrus* (10 volumes, 1649–53), *Clélie, histoire romaine* (10 volumes, 1654–61), and *Conversations morales* (1686 and 1688). De Scudéry wrote in the literary style of preciosity, which emphasized refined over course language and presentation. It

would play an important role in encouraging the tendency toward psychological realism that would later become prominent in French fiction. The adherents of preciosity, like de Scudéry, sought in their salon gatherings and in their writings to advance women's personal and social status. Her brother, Georges de Scudéry (1601–67), an author and critic, collaborated on some works.

## Sébillet, Thomas (ca. 1512–1589)
*humanist, translator*

Born probably in Paris, Thomas Sébillet (or Sibellet) is the author of *Art poétique français* (1548), which advocated the study of the ancient virtues but also proposed an emulation of the style of the moderns (CLÉMENT MAROT, MAURICE SCÈVE). Sébillet drew a response from JOACHIM DU BELLAY in his *Défense et illustration de la langue française* (1549).

## Sée, Camille (1827–1919)
*political figure*

Born in Colmar, Camille Sée was a deputy for the republican left (1876–81) and, joining with JULES FERRY, helped to put forth the reformist principles concerning public education: the establishment of girls' high schools (Camille Sée Law, 1880) and the École normale supérieure at Sèvres (1881).

## Segalen, Victor (1878–1919)
*writer*

A naval doctor, Victor Segalen, who was born in Brest, left for Tahiti (1903) and collected the later works of PAUL GAUGUIN (*Hommage à Gauguin*), while also praising the comfortable and sensual life there in a poetic novel, *Les Immémoriaux* (1907), in which the author recounts in poetic style the various myths of the islands, already in danger of being forgotten. Returning to France, he composed a drama, *Orphée-Roi* (posthumous, 1921) for CLAUDE DEBUSSY, which, however, the composer never set to music. Segalen went to China where he met PAUL CLAUDEL, journeyed to Tibet, took part in an archaeological expedition (discovering the funerary monuments of the Han dynasty), and treated victims of the plague in Manchuria, before being called back to France by WORLD WAR I. His novel, *René Leys* (posthumous, 1921), takes its inspiration from China and the Forbidden City of Beijing. After a final mission to Nanjing, he died in Brittany, either by accident or as a suicide. As a poet, Segalen influenced ARTHUR RIMBAUD and STÉPHANE MALLARMÉ. His works, filled with Oriental mysticism, present a wide geographic and personal viewpoint (*Stèles*, 1912; *Pientures*, 1916). It was only in 1975 that his last novel, *Le Fils du ciel*, was published.

## Séguier family
*family of French magistrates who served from the 16th to the 19th centuries*

Antoine Séguier (1552–1626), born in Paris, where he served as president of the Parlement, was an opponent of the HOLY LEAGUE. Pierre Séguier (1586–1672), born in Paris and nephew of Antoine Séguier, served as chancellor under Kings LOUIS XIII and LOUIS XIV, presided over the Cinq-Mars proceedings and at the trial of NICOLAS FOUQUET. He was one of the protectors of the ACADÉMIE FRANÇAISE, to which he was elected in 1635. Antoine-Louis Séguier (1726–92), born in Paris, where he served as attorney general of the Parlement, was an opponent of both the Jesuit and the Encyclopedists. He emigrated during the REVOLUTION OF 1789. His son, Antoine-Mathieu, baron Séguier (1768–1848), born in Paris, had a successful career during the FIRST EMPIRE, then rallied to king LOUIS XVIII, took part in the proceedings against MICHEL NEY, and later served under king LOUIS-PHILIPPE.

## Séguin, Philippe (1943–    )
*political figure*

Born in Tunis, Philippe Séguin served as a deputy for the RPR (RASSEMBLEMENT POUR LA RÉPUBLIQUE) (1978) and as mayor of Épinal (1983). He was minister for social affairs and employment from 1986 to 1988. Opposed to the Maastricht Treaty on European redevelopment, he is a proponent of Gaullist nationalistic, populist, and social traditions. In 1993, Séguin became president of the National Assembly.

## Ségur, Henri-Philippe, marquis de (1724–1801)
*marshal of France*

Born in Paris, Henri-Philippe, marquis de Ségur served as secretary of state for war under king LOUIS XVI. He improved the education of officers and founded the light artillery and headquarters corps, thus preparing the way for the future success of the French armies during the REVOLUTION OF 1789. A marshal of France, de Ségur was imprisoned during the TERROR, then restored to his rank by NAPOLÉON I. His *Mémoires* were published in 1895.

## Ségur, Philippe-Paul, count de (1780–1873)
*general, historian*

Born in Paris, Philippe-Paul, count de Ségur was the grandson of HENRI PHILIPPE, marquis de SÉGUR. He took part in the campaigns of the First Empire (in particular in Russia, Germany, and France) and, in 1824, published *Histoire de Napoléon et de la Grande Armée de 1812*, in which he was one of the first to deduce the causes and analyze the disastrous French retreat from Russia. This work enjoyed great success and provoked violent polemics, culminating in a duel between Ségur, who was wounded, and general Gourgaud, who had tried to refute his theses (1825). The count of Ségur was elected into the ACADÉMIE FRANÇAISE in 1830.

## Ségur, Sophie Rostopchine, countess de (1799–1874)
*writer*

The daughter of Count Rostopchine, Sophie Rostopchine was born in St. Petersburg, Russia, and left Russia with her father, who had fallen into disgrace, to settle in France (1817). There she married Count Eugène de Ségur (1819). Ignored by her husband, she spent a large part of her life on her estate at Nouettes (Orne), which must have inspired her stories, which were written essentially for her grandchildren but which soon became well known. In them, she created a dualistic world in which morality triumphs, and the characters are set out clearly as good or evil. The most famous of her stories are *Les petites Filles modèles* (1858), *Les Mémoires d'une âne* (1860), *Les Malheurs de Sophie* (1864), *Le Général Dourakine* (1864), and *Un bon petit Diable* (1865).

## Ségur, Georges (1927–  )
*labor union leader*

Born in Toulouse, Georges Ségur enrolled in the Communist Party in 1942 and fought in the RESIS- TANCE. He was deported to Mauthausen in 1944. After the war, he served as secretary-general (1961–65) of the Fédération des cheminots CGT (CONFÉDÉRATION GÉNÉRALE DU TRAVAIL), then became secretary-general of the CGT itself (1967–82). Ségur was a member of the Communist Party's Central Committee (1954–94) and of its Political Bureau.

## Seine

The Seine River of France, draining a part of the Parisian basin, flows for 776 kilometers. Beginning on the Langres Plateau, the Seine traverses Cham- pagne and the ÎLE-DE-FRANCE. Before entering Paris, it connects with the MARNE. A somewhat navigable river, the Seine also supplies hydroelectric power to adjacent regions.

## Sembat, Maurice (1862–1922)
*political figure*

Born in Bonnières-sur-Seine, Maurice Sembat was a member of the SFIO (Section française de l'inter- nationale ouvrière), served as a Socialist deputy (1893–1922), and was the author of a pacifist pam- phlet, *Faites un roi, sinon la paix* (1913). He served, nonetheless, as minister of public works during the period of the Union sacrée (1914–17) and adopted a nationalist position. A reformist, he voted against adhering to the Third International during the Congress of Tours (1920).

## Semblançay, Jacques de Beaume, seigneur de (1445–1527)
*political figure*

Born in Tours, Jacques de Beaume, seigneur de Semblançay served as one of the principal bankers of Kings CHARLES VIII, LOUIS XII, and FRANCIS I. After

View of the Seine River looking toward the cathedral of Notre-Dame *(Library of Congress)*

1518, he served as superintendent of finances. Queen LOUISE DE SAVOIE, after having accused him in vain of embezzlement, had him condemned to death in the king's absence without, however, destroying his reputation.

## Senac de Meilhan, Gabriel (1736–1803)
*administrator, writer*

Born in Paris, Gabriel Senac de Meilhan served as intendant general and as a sometimes aide and collaborator of the count of SAINT-GERMAIN in the War Ministry (1776). He became known in the world of letters through the publication of his apocryphal *Mémoires d'Anne de Gonzague, princesse Palatine* (1786). He then wrote *Considérations sur le luxe et les richesses* and *Considérations sur l'esprit et les mœurs* (1787), in which he deals with JACQUES NECKER. Leaving France as a émigré in 1791, he became friends with Catherine II of Russia, then settled in Vienna. Besides an historical novel, *L'Émigré* (1797), Senac de Meilhan published a work that traces the social and political conditions in France before the REVOLUTION OF 1789 entitled *Du gouvernement, des mœurs, et des conditions en France avant la Révolution* (1797).

## Senacour, Étienne Pivert de (1770–1846)
*writer*

Born in Paris, Étienne Pivert de Senacour led a solitary and errant existence, finding in the theories of JEAN-JACQUES ROUSSEAU, then in the doctrines of the Enlightenment, the basis for disenchantment and an unsatisfied need that could not be resolved by Christianity. In his *Rêveries sur la nature primitive de l'homme* (1799) and in his autobiographical, epistolary, and pre-romantic novel, *Oberman* (1804), there appeared a sense of an existential malaise that was translated into the incurable sadness and melancholy of his heroes. Senacour knew no success until after 1830; his principal works were reedited and he wrote a new novel, *Isabelle* (1833).

## Senghor, Léopold Sédar (1906-2002)
*Senegalese statesman and poet*

Born in Joal, Senegal, Léopold Sédar Senghor studied in Dakar and in Paris, where he met the poet AIMÉ CÉSAIRE, who at that time was formulating his concept of negritude, or black indentity. Senghor received his degree in 1935 and in 1945 was elected to the Constituent Assembly. He took part in the writing of the constitution of the FOURTH REPUBLIC and served as secretary of state in the EDGAR FAURE cabinet (1955–56). A founder of the Union progressiste sénégalese, he became, after the breakup of the Federation of Mali, president of the Republic of Senegal (1960). He strongly supported intercultural dialogue and retired from politics in 1980. Senghor's poetry expresses his love for his native country and the traditions of its people and, while celebrating negritude, the hope, too, for a universal reconciliation of the races. In 1966, he organized in Dakar the first World Festival of Black Arts. Senghor's works include poems as well as several literary and political essays. He was elected to the Academy of Moral and Political Sciences in 1969 and to the ACADÉMIE FRANÇAISE in 1983.

## September Massacres

During the REVOLUTION OF 1789, the September Massacres were summary executions that took place between September 2 and 6, 1792 in Paris (in the Abbaye prison, at the Bernardins, at Bitêtre, at the Carmes, at Châtlet, at the Conciergerie, and at la Salpêtrière) and in several provincial cities. With the suspension of the monarchy in August 1, 1792, the threat of an aristocratic conspiracy again haunted the revolutionaries at the same time that there was the danger of a foreign invasion. After the surrender of Longwy (August 25) and then of Verdun (September 2) to the Prussians, the insurrectional Commune issued a proclamation to the Parisians sounding the alarm and raising volunteers. It was in this atmosphere of general excitement that popular rage exploded, that the authorities (in particular GEORGES DANTON), could not calm, and the certain revolutionary leaders, like JEAN-PAUL MARAT, undoubtedly incited by appealing to the people to themselves take justice on their enemies. More than 1,200 detainees were massacred in Paris: refractory priests, nobles, but also simple prisoners who were held for ordinary offenses. The September Massacres, which mark the beginning of the TERROR, meant for many a struggle for liberty.

## Serre, Pierre, count de  (1776–1824)
*political figure*

Born in Pagny-sur-Moselle, Pierre, count de Serre served as president of the imperial court of Hamburg, Germany (1811), then of Colmar. After the abdication of NAPOLÉON I, he rallied to the Bourbons. He served as a deputy, then as president of the Chamber of Deputies (1817–18), joining the doctrinaire constitutionalists. Minister of justice in ÉLIE DECAZES cabinet (1818), he put through the liberal law on the press but refused a law allowing an amnesty for the banished regicides. At the Congress of Verona (1822), Serre upheld the interests of king Ferdinand VII.

## Serres, Jean de  (1540–1598)
*cleric*

Born in Villeneuve-de-Berg, Ardèche, Jean de Serres was the brother of the agronomist OLIVIER DE SERRES. While serving as a Calvinist pastor at Nîmes, de Serres was appointed the official historian of France by king HENRY IV, who also placed him in charge of negotiations with foreign Protestants. De Serres wrote *Recueil des choses mémorables advenues en France depuis Henri II jusqu'à Henri IV* and *Inventaire de l'histoire de France* (1597).

## Serres, Michel  (1930–   )
*philosopher, writer*

Born in Agen, Michel Serres served as a naval officer and then became a university professor (the SORBONNE and Stanford University in the U.S. State of California). He wrote his thesis on Leibnitz (*Le Systéme de Leibnitz et ses modèles mathématiques*, 1968), and has written works on the history of science and of ideas (*Hermes*, five volumes, 1969–80; *Les Origines de la géométrie*, 1933), texts on art, such as *Esthétiques sur Carpaccio* (1975), as well as more general essays in which he demonstrated his talents as a writer (*Le Contrat naturel*, 1990; *Le Tiers instruit*, 1991). His views, inspired by the structures

of logical thought (Leibnitz), examine the paths of knowledge and end up with studies or readings such as *Jouvences sur Jules Verne* (1974). Identifying with the 18th-century French tradition, he added to the intellectual heritage with a sensualist reflection on the wisdom of the body (*Les Cinq Sens*, 1985). Insisting on the importance of communication (sometimes with humor and brio, as in his analysis of Belgian artist Hergé's *Bijoux de la Castafiore* in *Hermes*), Serres ascribes to the subject a function of transcendence by a rapport between theory and practice. He was elected to the ACADÉMIE FRANÇAISE in 1990.

## Serres, Olivier de  (ca. 1539–1619)
*agronomist*

Born in Villeneuve-de-Berg, Ardèche, Olivier de Serres, on his estate at Pradel, established a model farm where he practiced crop rotation and the cultivation of sugar beets, maize, hops, rice, and other grains. Summoned to Paris by king HENRY IV, he planted 20,000 white mulberry trees in the garden of the Tuileries and, at the king's request, wrote *Traité de la cueillette de la soie par la nourriture des vers qui la font* (1599). In 1600, de Serres wrote his major work, *Théâtre d'agriculture et mesnage des champs*. His brother was the Huguenot pastor JEAN DE SERRES.

## Sérurier, Jean-Matthieu-Philibert, count  (1742–1819)
*marshal of France*

Bon in Laon, Jean-Matthieu-Philibert, count Sérurier was an officer in the royal army and fought in the SEVEN YEARS' WAR (1756–1763). Supporting the REVOLUTION OF 1789, he was named a division commander in 1795 and served with distinction during the Napoléon Bonaparte's first campaign in Italy (1796), then as governor of Venice. He took part in the coup d'état of 18 Brumaire, Year VIII that brought Napoléon Bonaparte to power (November 9, 1799) and was named governor of the INVALIDES, then marshal (1804). Marshal Sérurier voted nonetheless for NAPOLÉON I's abdication. King LOUIS XVIII made him a peer, but

Sérurier rallied to Napoléon Bonaparte during the Hundred Days and was subsequently disgraced.

## Sérusier, Paul (1864–1927)
*painter, theorist*

Born in Paris, Paul Sérusier studied painting at the Académie Julian in Paris while pursuing his interests in music, philosophy, and Oriental languages (Arabic and Hebrew). In 1888, at Pont-Aven, he joined with PAUL GAUGUIN and, under Gauguin's guidance, painted *Le Talisman,* a small landscape on wood composed with splashes of pure color to demonstrate the idea of synthesis and to serve as reference points. With his friends from the Académie Julian, Sérusier founded the NABIS group (1888), painters who practiced a colorful, postimpressionist style with symbolic overtures, influenced primarily by Gauguin. Sérusier worked again with Gauguin in 1889 and 1890, decorating the theater of l'Œuvre de Lugné-Poe, using many symbolist designs. The spirit of these styles is manifest in Sérusier's writings, which include *Esthétique de Beuron* (1905) and *ABC de la peinture* (1921). He returned to Brittany in 1923, where he decorated the church at Châteauneuf-du-Faou. His works—Breton scenes, portraits, and landscapes—show an artist with a great sense of delicacy and personal spirituality, who presages aspects of modern art, especially that of the Italian and German primitivists.

## Servan de Gerbey, Joseph (1741–1808)
*general*

Born in Romans, Dauphiné, Joseph Servan de Gerbey was a contributor to the Diderot's *Encyclopedia* and author of *Projet de constitution pour l'armée française* (1790). During the REVOLUTION OF 1789, he was named minister of war in the GIRONDIN cabinet formed in March 1792 under the National Legislature, and he proposed the formation of a camp of 20,000 National Guards at Paris. Approved by the Assembly, this decree was not sanctioned by King Louis XVI, who dismissed the Girondin ministry (June 13, 1792). A member of the Executive Provisionary Commission, constituted after the Revolutionary day of August 10, 1792, marking the end of the monarchy, Servan de Gerbey commanded the Army of the Western Pyrenees, then was interned, under the TERROR, at the Abbey prison as a Girondin and released after the fall of MAXIMILIEN ROBESPIERRE.

## Servan-Schreiber, Jean-Jacques (1924– )
*journalist, political figure*

Born in Paris, Jean-Jacques Servan-Schreiber was the founder of *L'Express* (1953) and served as a deputy (1970–79) and as president of the Radical Party (1971–79). At that time, he took a position in favor of regionalism and a supranational Europe. Named minister for reform in 1974, he was dismissed after 13 days because of his criticism of French foreign and military policy. Director of the World Information Center (1982–85), Servan-Schreiber published his *Défi américain* (1967), *Le Défi mondial* (1980), as well as political autobiographies (*Passions,* 1991; *Les Fassoyeurs,* 1993).

## Seuphor, Michel (1901–1999)
*writer, artist*

Of Belgian origin, Michel Seuphor, was born Ferdinand Louis Berckelaers, in Antwerp. After 1918, he played an active role in the movement for Flemish claims and founded at Antwerp the revue *Het Overzicht* (*Panorama,* 1921–25), an organ of cultural and political struggle before it became one for avant-garde intellectuals. Settling in Paris in 1925, he established the revues *Les Documents de l'esprit nouveau* (1927) and *Cercle et Carré* (1930), journals for a group he had founded the preceding year with fellow artists Torres-Garcia and Van Doesburg. Besides romantic and poetic writings, Seuphor published a number of critical works and became, after 1945, one of the principal theorists of modern art (*L'Art abstrait, ses origines, ses premiers maîtres,* 1949; *Dictionnaire de la peinture abstraite,* 1957; *La Sculpture de ce siècle,* 1959; *La Pienture abstraite, sa genèse, son expansion,* 1962; *Le Style et le Cri,* 1965). He also edited studies of the Dutch artist Mondrian (1956) and Jean (Hans) Arp. Seuphor's graphic work after 1951 consists of designs that are often done in black and white, in which the horizontal aspects reveal various symbols or forms (*La Mort d'Orphée*, 1964).

## Seurat, Georges (1859–1891)
*painter*

Georges Seurat, who along with PAUL SIGNAC developed the theories and techniques of neoimpressionism, was born in Paris, where he studied painting and drawing with a student of JEAN-AUGUSTE-DOMINIQUE INGRES. Greatly interested in research on color and theories of vision, he did his earliest works at Brest, where he painted a number of landscapes and figure studies. Returning to Paris in 1880, he dedicated himself exclusively to drawing (1882–83) and proved to be an exceptional master in the technique of replacing line for mass. Accepted by the Paris Salon the official exhibition in 1883 with his *Portrait of Aman-Jean*, he painted, after a number of preparatory studies, *Bathing at Asnières*, which was rejected by the Salon in 1884. He then founded with other painters who had been rejected la Société des artistes indépendants and there showed his works. Joining with Signac, Seurat also parted with the style of several painters, rejecting the techniques of CLAUDE MONET. Seurat seems to have convinced CAMILLE PISSARRO of his new techniques and, thanks to him, was able to show at the last impressionist exhibition (*Sunday Afternoon on the Island of the Grand-Jatte,* 1884–86), which appeared as the manifesto of the new school of neoimpressionism, or pointillism, so named for his technique of applying small, closely packed dots of unmixed color to create a solid form on a white background. Always a scientist, Seurat enunciated the principles on which his art was founded, studying also the effects of artificial light (*Le Chahut,* 1889–90; *Le Cirque,* 1890–91). He had a notable influence on PAUL GAUGUIN, VINCENT VAN GOGH, and Pissarro, as well as on the fauvists, cubists, and futurists.

## Seven Years' War

The Seven Years' War (1756–63) was a conflict that broke out during the reign of LOUIS XV between France, Austria, and Russia on one side, and England, Hanover, and Prussia on the other. Its causes were the Austrian desire to retake Silesia and Franco-British colonial rivalry. Marked by great French losses on land (Rossbach), the sea, and in the colonies (the loss of French territory in India and CANADA), it cost France, by the terms of the Treaty of Paris, some of its most flourishing colonies. The war gave Silesia to Frederick II of Prussia under the terms of the Treaty of Hubertsbourg. In America, where the fighting had begun earlier in 1754, the conflict was known as the French and Indian War.

## Sévigné, Marie de Rabutin-Chantal, marquise de (1626–1696)
*writer*

The author of one of the most celebrated epistolary collections, Marie de Rabutin-Chantal, marquise de Sévigné was born in Paris, where she was educated by tutors. Quite cultivated, lively, and talented, in 1644 she married the marquis de Sévigné, who was killed in a duel in 1651. Widowed at age 25, she reestablished herself at Rochers, in Brittany, with visits to Paris, where she frequented the court and the social and intellectual circles of the salons, especially that of Mme de LA FAYETTE. Mme de Sévigné left a vast correspondence (more than 1,500 letters) written to her by friends, and, above all, by her daughter, the countess de GRIGNAN, who lived in Provence and whom she missed very much. These *Lettres* (posthumous, 1726) are spontaneous and detailed chronicles of the events and personages at the court and life among the high society of 17th-century France. Sprinkled with sparkling and humorous anecdotes, the letters also tell of Mme de Sévigné's life and her relationship with her daughter. Long seen as a valuable tableau of the era, this correspondence is written with a freedom of style exceptional in the classical age.

## Sicard (1742–1822)
*educator*

Born in Le Fousseret, Roch Ambroise Cucurron, or Sicard as he is known, took holy orders and assumed the direction of the school for deaf-mutes in BORDEAUX (1786), then became the director of a well-known similar school in Paris founded by the abbot of l'Epée, who had developed a system of communication with deaf-mutes. Imprisoned as a suspect during the TERROR (1792) at the time of the REVOLUTION OF 1789, he was, upon his release, named professor at the École normale in 1794 and a member of the INSTITUT of France in 1795, escaping deportation after the coup d'état of 18 Fructidor, Year V (September 4, 1797), he had opposed the government but then later aroused the hostility of NAPOLÉON I. For that reason, he did not serve in important posts until the RESTORATION. Sicard is the author of several works on deaf-mutes (*Mémoire sur l'art d'instruire les sourds-muets de naissance*, 1789; *Cours d'instruction d'un sourd-muet de naissance*, 1800; *Théorie des signes pour l'instruction des sourds-muets*, 1808).

## Sieyès, Emmanuel-Joseph (1748–1836)
## (Abbé Sieyès)

*political figure*

Born in Fréjus, Emmanuel-Joseph Sieyès, or Abbé Sieyès, as he is known, was an avid reader of the 18th-century philosophers. He took holy orders in 1787 and was named vicar general of CHARTRES. Coming to Paris in 1788, he published shortly after his *Essai sur les privileges* and, at the beginning of the REVOLUTION OF 1789, his celebrated pamphlet *Qu'est-ce que le tiers état?* (1789), in which he upholds the principles of the Revolution. A deputy to the ESTATES GENERAL, he played a decisive role in the transformation of that body into the National Assembly (June 1789) and stood with MIRABEAU against any attempts to disband it. An early member of the JACOBIN Club, he contributed to the decision to divide France into 83 departments and to expand the suffrage in the constitution of 1791. A constitutional monarchist, he joined the moderates and was elected to the Convention, where he voted, however, for the death of the king. Although he is seen as one of the instigators of the TERROR because of his support for the idea of the General Will, Sieyès played only a small role during that period. But later, as a member of the Committee of Public Safety after 9 Thermidor, Year II (July 27, 1794), he was involved in diplomacy and as a proponent of

annexation signed the Treaty of The Hague (1795) with Holland. Elected a Director in 1795, he resigned in favor of LAZARE CARNOT and took his place on the Council of Five Hundred, over which he presided after the coup d'état of 18 Fructidor, Year V (September 4, 1797). Minister plenipotentiary to Prussia, Sieyès returned to Paris in May 1799 to join the Directory again and, in November, helped prepare the way for the coup d'état of 18 Brumaire, Year VIII (November 9, 1799), which launched the political career of Napoléon Bonaparte. Together with Bonaparte and PIERRE DUCOS, he became a member of the Consulate and helped to frame the Constitution of the Year VIII, which NAPOLÉON I then revised. Sieyès subsequently resigned from politics. He was made a count of the Empire in 1809 and, during the HUNDRED DAYS, a peer of France. Seeking refuge in Brussels, in Belgium, after Bonaparte's defeat, he was proscribed as a regicide (1816) and did not return to France until 1830. Abbé Sieyès was elected into the ACADÉMIE FRANÇAISE in 1803.

## Signac, Paul (1863–1935)

*painter, watercolorist, art critic*

Paul Signac, a neoimpressionist artist who, with GEORGES SEURAT, originated the technique of pointillism, was born in Paris, where he also studied art. He was an admirer of CLAUDE MONET and his associates, whose influence can be seen in his works. Not adhering to the official Salon style, Signac, in 1884, exhibited with the groupe des Artistes indépendants and, befriending Seurat, helped him to develop the basic theories of neoimpressionism. He later became that style's foremost spokesperson (*De Delacroix au néo-impressionisme*, 1899). Seeking to find the greatest luminosity in his paintings, he developed a technique of showing glittering sunlight through placement of colored dots to achieve a prismatic effect. He painted seascapes (*Port de Collioure*) but also interiors (*Le petit Dejeuner*, 1886–87; *Femme se peignant*, 1892), portraits (*Félix Fénélon*, 1890), characterized by hieratism and arabesques and other symbolist traits. After 1895, Signac moved away from pointillism and chose to work with larger touches of paint, creating mosaiclike effects. An avid sailor, he also made several trips during which he produced a large number of watercolors depicting views of ports and harbors. At the end of this period, he returned to studio painting and did large compositions in which he remained faithful to the division of tones and the simultaneous contrast of colors. After 1908, Signac served as president of the Société des indépendents.

## Signoret, Simone  (1921–1985)
*actor*

Born Simone Kaminker in Wiesbaden, Germany, to French parents, Simone Signoret, through her exceptional talent, went beyond the limits of theater and film to embrace social and political activism (alongside her husband YVES MONTAND), and literature (*La nostalgie n'est plus qu'elle était,* 1976; *Adieu Volodia,* 1985). Among her more than 50 films, a masterpiece, *Casque d'or* (1952), stands apart, but also commendable are *Manèges* (1950); *La Ronde* (1950); *Thérèse Raquin* (1953); *Room at the Top* (Great Britain, 1958), which won her an Oscar for Best Actress; and later in her career, *L'Armée des Ombres* (1969), *Le Chat* (1971), *La Veuve Couderc* (1971), *La vie devant soi* (1977), and *Mama Rosa* (1977), which won an Academy Award for best foreign film. In 1960, Signoret signed, with many other highly regarded intellectuals and artists, the manifesto appealing for an end to the Algerian War (see ALGERIA).

## Silvestre, Israël  (1621–1691)
*designer, engraver*

Born in Nancy, Israël Silvestre was raised in Paris by his uncle, Israël Henriet, the friend and publisher of JACQUES CALLOT. Silvestre entered the engraving business and, in 1692, was named designer and engraver to the king Louis XIV. His large amount of work includes as its subject matter scenes of Italy and France, which are interesting from the historical viewpoint. At the request of LOUIS XIV, he produced engravings that are solemn or ostentatious (notably the *Plaisirs de l'île enchantée,* 1664). Commissioned to decorate the royal residences, Silvestre gave his work a sense of space and airiness that has the look of charming landscapes.

## Silvestre de Sacy, Antoine-Isaac  (1758–1838)
*Orientalist*

Born in Paris, Antoine-Isaac Silvestre de Sacy was professor of Arabic at the École des langues orientales (1795) and also, after 1806, of Persian at the COLLÈGE DE FRANCE, where, in 1823, he was named director. Created a baron during the RESTORATION, which he supported, he encouraged Arabic studies in France and published a *Mémoire sur l'histoire des Arabes avant Mohomet* (1785), *Chrestomathie arabe* (1806), and an important *Grammaire arabe* (1820).

## Simon, Claude  (1913–   )
*writer, Nobel laureate*

Born in Tananarive, Madagascar, Claude Simon, the son of a French army officer, was brought up by his mother in Perpignan and educated in Paris and England. Using a stream-of-consciousness effect, with extremely long sentences (sometimes up to a thousand words), Simon, who served in the French cavalry in WORLD WAR II and then the RESISTANCE, downplays character development and plot in his novels (*Le Tricheur,* 1945, his first novel; *Le Vent,* 1957; and *L'Herbe,* 1958), but recounts instead the complexity of human life (*La Route des Flandres,* 1960; *Le Palace,* 1962). One of the best exponents of the nouveau roman, Simon attempted to reconcile various fractured views of the world and of life as he sought to create the illusion of permanence in a turbulent society. He drew upon own military experiences and upon the theme of solitude and fragmentation, but he is less theoretical than other writers of the nouveau roman school. Simon's later works include *Histoire* (1967), *Les Géorgiques* (1981), *La Bataille de Pharsale* (1969), *Les Corps conducteurs* (1971), *Triptique* (1973), *Leçon de chose* (1975), and *L'Acacia* (1989). He was awarded the Nobel Prize in literature in 1985.

## Simon, François  (1895–1975)
*actor*

Of Swiss origin, François Simon, known popularly as Michel Simon, was born in Geneva. A photographer, singer, and huckster, he became an actor in

Paris, joining the Pitoeff troupe (1922–25) then playing at Charles Dullin's théâtre d'Atelier (1925–26). He portrayed his characters as rough, rude, but warm and is particularly remembered for his stage roles in *Jean de la Lune* by Marcel Achard (1929), *Fric Frac* by E. Bourdet (1936), and in a number of films, notably of JEAN VIGO (*L'Atalante*), JENN RENOIR (*Boudu sauvé des eaux*), CARNÉ (*Drôle de drame*), CLAIR (*La Beauté du diable*).

## Simon, Jules  (1814–1896)

*political figure, philosopher*

Born in Lorient, Jules François Simon Suisse, or Jules Simon as he is known, a professor of philosophy, was recognized for his *Histoire critique de l'école d'Alexandrie* (1844–45). In 1851, he was suspended from his post at the University of Paris for having refused to take an oath of loyalty to the SECOND EMPIRE. A republican deputy (1863–70), he published several studies on the condition of workers (*L'Ouvrière*, 1863; *Le Travail*, 1860) and, after the fall of the SECOND EMPIRE, was appointed minister of public instruction (September 1870). As head of the government, he had to resign because of the crisis of May 16, 1877. Simon took a position against the educational policy of JULES FERRY and against Boulangism. He was elected to the ACADÉMIE FRANÇAISE in 1875 (see GEORGE BOULANGER).

## Simon, Pierre-Henri  (1903–1972)

*writer*

Born in Saint-Fort-sur-Gironde, Pierre-Henri Simon is known for his critical work (*L'Homme en process,* 1949; *Procès du heros,* 1950; *Témoins de l'homme,* 1951; *Théâtre et Destin,* 1959), which affirms the values of humanism that he combined with Christian morality. In his political essays (*Contre la Torture,* 1957), as well as his novels, Simon in seeking to uphold "a positive concept of the dignity of the essence of and sense of life" in humankind, made his characters incarnations of a system of values that are presented in a positive light (*L'Affût,* 1946; *Les Raisins verts* (1950); *Les Hommes ne veulent pas mourir* (1953), *Elsinfor* (1956), and *Histoire d'un bonheur* (1965). Simon was elected to the ACADÉMIE FRANÇAISE in 1966.

## Simon, Richard  (1638–1712)

*scholar*

Born in Dieppe, Richard Simon, an Oratorian priest, was one of the founders of biblical criticism and was the first to present that topic in French. Solicitous, in his *Histoire critique du Vieux Testament* (1678), in reevaluating a tradition that previously was based only on text, he was more violently attacked by JACQUES BOSSUET and by the Jansenists than by the Protestants, with whom he considered doing a translation of the Bible. Put on the Index of forbidden books issued by the Catholic Church and expelled from the Oratory, he left a *Histoire critique de texte* (1689), *des versions* (1690), and *des principaux commentateurs* (1693) *du Nouveau Testament.*

## Simon, Théodore  (1873–1961)

*psychologist*

Born in Dijon, Théodore Simon developed and perfected, with ALFRED BINET, a metric intelligence scale (in 1904, 1908, 1911) to study the intelligence level of children (especially those of school age). This scale was improved upon by the American psychologist Lewis Terman.

## Simonin, Albert  (1905–1980)

*writer*

Born in Paris, Albert Simonin had a number of jobs, including that of taxi driver, and used his knowledge of Parisian nightlife to create the setting for his police and mystery novels. In a literary style, using the local argot, the stories of the common people who inhabit his world are told with all their rivalries and travails in *Touchez pas au grisbi!* (1953) *Le cave se rebiffe* (1954), and *Le Hotu, chronique de la vie d'un demi-sel* (three volumes, 1968–71). Simonin is also the author of *Du mouron pour les petits oiseaux* (1963) and his reminiscences, *Confessions d'un enfant de la Chapelle* (1977).

## Siné  (1928–   )

*caricaturist, poster artist*

Born Maurice Sinet in Paris, Siné as he is known, worked for a number of newspapers and journals (*Paris-Match, France-Soir, Le canard enchaîné,* and especially *L'Express* and then *Charlie-Hebdo*, 1980). He won the prize for black humor in 1954 and founded his own revue, *Siné Massacre*, in 1962. In his witty and summary drawings, he lampoons the bourgeoisie and its representatives (police, military, business owners, and churchmen). Siné's principal published collections include *Complaints sans paroles*, *Portée des chats*, and *Le Code penal*.

## Sirven, Pierre-Paul  (1709–1777)
*Protestant figure*

Pierre-Paul Sirven, a Protestant who was born in Castres, was accused of having killed one of his daughters, who, in fact, had actually committed suicide. As a result of the accusation, and fearing also that religious prejudice would not allow him have a fair trial, he fled to Switzerland. He was sentence to death in absentia but, thanks to the intervention of VOLTAIRE, he was rehabilitated by the Parlement of Toulouse (1771).

## Sisley, Alfred  (1839–1899)
*painter*

Born in Paris to English parents, Alfred Sisley studied there in the studio of the Swiss painter Charles Gleyre and became a friend of FRÉDÉRIC BAZILLE, CLAUDE MONET, and PIERRE-AUGUSTE RENOIR. Rejecting the academic style, rent to paint with them at Chailly, in the forest of Fontainebleau. His early works were influenced by the realism of GUSTAVE COURBET and the style of CAMILLE COROT and Charles Daubigny. Refused several times by the Paris Salon, Sisley moved, thanks to Monet, closer to IMPRESSIONISM, to which he remained faithful in spite of the poverty that he suffered after 1870. He painted exclusively landscapes, which were done at Marly, Louveciennes, Bougival, and Moret, which became his home in 1879. He traveled to London (1879), where he became familiar with the works of Constable and Turner, and later went to Normandy (1894). Especially skillful at showing the effects of fog, rain, or snow, and the transparency of reflections and the fluidity of water, he used a refined palette with overtures of gray. Showing a poetic and discrete use of fleeting light, and a coming together

of colors rather than a clearly set juxtaposition on canvas, his compositions have unity (*Inondations à Port-Marly*, 1878; *La Neige à Louveciennes* 1878). Sisley's genius and his works were recognized only after his death.

## Socialist Party  (Parti socialiste)

The Parti socialiste (PS) developed principally from the SFIO (Section française de l'internationale ouvrière) in 1969. Further developed during the Congress of Épinay (1971), it adopted the strategy of creating the Union de la gauche, which, in 1972, ended with the signing of a common government program with the French COMMUNIST PARTY. Despite the break in the Union in 1978 and the development of divergent currents, the party, under the leadership of FRANÇOIS MITTERRAND, won the presidential and legislative election of 1981. Becoming the majority party, the PS, led by LIONEL JOSPIN (1981–88), during the 1980s underwent an important evolution that included the adoption of a rigorous economic policy and the abandonment of all Marxist references. Defeated in the legislative elections of 1986, the PS remained the first party of France and regained seats in 1988. But confronted with internal strife and political and financial scandals, as well as the worsening economic crisis and growing unemployment, the party, led by PIERRE MAUROY (1988–92), then LAURENT FABIUS (1992–93), suffered a serious reversal in the legislative elections of March 1993. The PS, profoundly affected by this defeat, sought new leadership, culminating in 1995 with Lionel Jospin, who resigned in 2002. Subsequently, the PS remains a leading party and has undergone positive reorganization.

## Socialist Party, French  (Parti socialiste français)

The Parti socialiste français, or the Section française de l'internationale ouvrière (SFIO) as it was known (1905–69), evolved from several socialist political organizations after 1877, including the Parti ouvrier français of JULES GUESDE and PAUL LAFARGUE, which of a Marxist orientation proclaimed the taking of political power by the proletariat, and the

Fédération des travailleurs socialistes (or Parti pos-
sibiliste), which, created by PAUL BROUSSE, envisioned a progressive realization of socialism by
transitional measures. It separated itself from the
Parti ouvrier socialiste révolutionnaire (which
favored the subordination of electoral and political
actions to revolutionary syndicalist ones). After
1901, the Parti ouvrier français and the Parti socialiste révolutionnaire formed the Parti socialiste de
France (PSDF); the independent Socialists, the
Broussistes, and others formed the Paris socialiste
française (PSF) with JEAN JAURÈS. After the International Socialist Congress of Amsterdam (1904),
French socialist unity was realized (Congress of
Paris, 1905) by the joining of the PSDF, the PSF,
and several autonomous federations, all under the
SFIO (led by Jules Guesde, Jean Jaurès, and
ÉDOUARD VAILLANT). The new party, in which the
Guesdist faction was in the minority after 1906,
took a position against the government's colonial
policy (especially in Morocco) and against the militant nationalists. But after WORLD WAR I, party
unity was ended at the Congress of Tours (1920).
The majority Socialists, who favored the Russian
Revolution of 1917, left the SFIO (their organ
would henceforth be *Le Populaire*) to form the Sec-
tion française de l'internationale communiste
(SFIC), or Parti communiste français; this political
schism was replicated by a labor union schism
(Confédération générale du travail). Led by LÉON
BLUM and PAUL FAURE, the SFIO was the driving
force behind the reorganization of the leftist parties
(CARTEL DES GAUCHES) and their victory in 1924.
After the exclusion in 1933 of the supporters of
ministerial participation, the Parti socialiste de
France was formed, which joined with the Communists (1934) and became the main basis for the
leftist coalition Front populaire (1936), before a
Trotskyite group broke away and formed the Parti
socialiste ouvrier et paysan (1938). During WORLD
WAR II, while some Socialists supported the VICHY
regime, the majority joined the RESISTANCE. After
the Liberation, the SFIO played an important role
in the French government, with the Communists
and the MRP (MOUVEMENT RÉPUBLICAIN POPULAIRE)
(1946–47), then, after the exclusion of the Communists, with the MRP and the liberals (1947–50).

Joining the opposition, the Socialists returned to
power in the cabinet of GUY MOLLET (reversed in
May 1957). The Suez affair, financial difficulties,
and the Algerian War brought new divisions within
the SFIO, resulting in the formation of the Union
de la gauche socialiste (UGS) and the autonomous
Parti socialiste, which became the Parti socialiste
unifié (PSU) in 1960. In the opposition since
1958–59, the Socialists regrouped (under the leadership of FRANÇOIS MITTERRAND) to form the Fédération de la gauche démocrate et socialiste (1965). At
the Congress of Issy-les-Moulineaux (July 11–13,
1969), the SFIO was replaced by the Parti socialiste.

## Soissons family

The Soissons was a French noble family. Charles de
Bourbon, count de Soissons (1566–1612), born in
Nogent-le-Routrou, was the son of the prince de
CONDÉ, LOUIS I, and Françoise d'Orléans Longueville. He successively joined, then abandoned, each
faction in the WARS OF RELIGION and, although
Catholic, fought at the Battle of Coutras on the side
of the Protestant princes. He tried in vain to con-
vince HENRY IV to marry his sister Catherine. Dur-
ing the minority of King LOUIS XIII, he opposed the
regency of MARIE DE' MEDICI, along with his nephew
HENRI, prince de CONDÉ, but was appeased by being
offered the governorship of Normandy. Louis de
Bourbon, count de Soissons (1604–41), born in
Paris, was the son of Charles de Bourbon, count de
Soissons and Anne, countess de Montafie et de
Clermont. He conspired with GASTON D'ORLÉANS
against Cardinal RICHELIEU, then went over to the
Spanish, fighting the French at La Marfée, where
he was killed. Eugène Maurice de Savoie-Carignan,
count de Soissons (1633–73), born in Chambéry,
was the nephew of Louis de Bourbon, count de
Soissons and the son of Marie de Soissons and
Thomas of Savoy, prince de Carignan. A military
commander, he married Olympe MANCINI, the niece
of Cardinal MAZARIN, and they became the parents
of Prince Eugène de Savoie-Carignan (Prince
Eugene of Savoy), who, halted in his ambitions by
LOUIS XIV, went on to serve the Austrians. The governor of Champagne, Eugène, count de Soissons,
served with distinction at the Battle of the Dunes,

in Spain, in Franche-Comté, and in Holland and was made a general in 1672.

## Sollers, Philippe (1936– )
*writer*

Born in BORDEAUX, Philippe Soller (the pen name of Philippe Joyaux) wrote his first work, "Le Défi," a short story, in 1957 and was then recognized for his psychological account, "Une curieuse solitude" (1958), which was praised by FRANÇOIS MAURIAC and ANDRÉ BRETON for its elegant style. In 1960, the *revue Tel Quel* was founded, to which Sollers's name remains attached. Sollers wrote *Le Parc* (1961), which won the prix Médicis; *l'Intermédiare* (1963); *Drames* (1965); *Logiques* (1968); and *Lois* (1972), works that show both a psychological tone and a political orientation to Marxism. After 1976, following an experimental period, Sollers seems to have gone toward a type of romantic epic of which *H* (1973) and *Paradis* (1981) constitute the best examples. With *Femmes* (1983), he wrote a baroque novel filled with contemporary happenings. Sollers wrote an autobiographical work, *Portrait de joueur* (1984), and, as a moralist, tried in his later novels to present a progressivist viewpoint and a defense of civilization (*Le Cours absolu*, 1987; *Les Folies françaises*, 1988; *Le Lys d'or*, 1989; *La Fête à Venise*, 1991; *Le Secret*, 1993).

## Somme, Battles of

The Battles of the Somme occurred between France and Germany during WORLD WAR I and WORLD WAR II. The battle of 1916, a Franco-British offensive, began in January and continued during the battle of VERDUN. This enormous battle, at which armored tanks first appeared, resulted in a huge number of casualties on both sides. The battle of 1940 was a defensive undertaken by General MAXIME WEYGAND to contain the German advance during the evacuation of Allied troops at Dunkirk.

## Sorbonne, La

One of the world's most famous universities, the Sorbonne is a public institution of higher learning in the Latin Quarter of PARIS. The site of five colleges of arts and sciences, the Sorbonne essentially directs the policy for the administration of the rectorate of Paris, which includes the École de Chartres; some sections of the École pratique des hautes études; the Universities of Paris I (Panthéon-Sorbonne), Paris IV (Paris-Sorbonne), Paris V (René-Descartes); and is the seat of the Academy of Paris. Established by Robert de Sorbon (1257) to allow poor scholars to continue their education, the college of the Sorbonne became the center of theological studies and, serving as an ecclesiastical tribunal, was the highest religious authority in the Christian West after the pope. The Sorbonne opposed the Jesuits in the 16th century, the Jansenists in the 17th, and the philosophes in the 18th before being suppressed in 1790. Its buildings were given to the University of Paris in 1808. From 1626 to 1642, they were rebuilt by JACQUES LEMERCIER on the orders of Cardinal RICHELIEU, whose tomb is in the chapel. From 1885 to 1901, the Sorbonne was considerably rebuilt or renovated. In the large auditorium is *Le Bois sacrée by* PUVIS DE CHAVANNES.

## Sorel, Agnès (1422–1450)
*nobility*

Born in Fronenteau, Touraine, Agnès Sorel was the favorite of king CHARLES VII, with whom she had five sons. Patriotic, she had a good political influence on the king. Charles VII gave her the château of Beauté-sur-Marne, from which she got the sobriquet "dame de Beauté." JEAN FOUQUET portrayed her in his painting *La Vierge à l'enfant*, now in the Royal Museum of Fine Arts in Antwerp.

## Sorel, Albert (1842–1906)
*historian*

Born in Paris, Albert Sorel was professor of diplomatic history at the École des sciences politiques (1872), then served as secretary-general of the Senate (1876–1902). He is the author of novels and a number of historical studies, of which the best known are *Histoire diplomatique de la guerre franco-allemande* (1875), *La Question d'Orient au XVIIIe siècle* (1878), and *L'Europe et la Révolution française* (1885–1906). Sorel was elected to the ACADÉMIE FRANÇAISE in 1894.

## Sorel, Charles, sieur de Souvigny (ca. 1600–1674)
*scholar, novelist*

Born in Paris, Charles Sorel, sieur de Souvigny demonstrated a critical and perspicacious sense of judgment in his *Bibliothèque française* (1664) and, above all, an astonishingly realistic style in his picaresque novel, *La Vraye Histoire comique de Francion* (1623), comprising a dozen books, with colorful and comic scenes of society during the reign of LOUIS XIII. Such scenes are found also in his parody novel, *Le Berger extravagant* (1627).

## Sorel, Georges (1847–1922)
*social philosopher, journalist*

Born in Cherbourg and educated at the École polytechnique in Paris, Georges Sorel was a civil engineer until 1892, when he became a contributor to several socialist journals. Denouncing the economic, social, and moral decadence of the capitalistic bourgeoisie, he formulated, under the influence of the theories of PIERRE-JOSEPH PROUDHON, Karl Marx, Friedrich Nietzsche, HENRI BERGSON, and William James a type of ethical socialism. In place of liberalism and democratic reformism, he proposed an anarchosyndicalist view, using violence and, in particular, the general strike, the crystallization of the class struggle, and the social ideas of "myths," expressing the aspirations of the proletariat (*Réflexions sur la violence*, 1908). Recognized as the leader and principal theoretician of the revolutionary syndicalist movement, Sorel had a great influence, but the most reactionary movements, particularly Italian fascism, also appropriated his theories. Sorel's other writings include *Introduction à l'économie moderne* (1903) and *Matériaux pour une théorie du proletariat* (1919).

## Soubise, Benjamin de Rohan, seigneur de (1583–1642)
*military figure*

Born in La Rochelle, Benjamin de Rohan, lord of Soubise was the brother of HENRI DE ROHAN, and with him was one of the leaders of the Protestant party during the reign of LOUIS XIII. During the siege of La Rochelle, with the help of the duke of Buckingham, he tried to rescue the city. He died in England, not wanting to take advantage of the Peace of Alès which granted freedom of worship to the HUGUENOTS (1629).

## Soubise, Charles de Rohan, prince de (1715–1787)
*marshal of France*

Born in Paris, Charles de Rohan, prince de Soubise was a favorite of King LOUIS XV and was given the command of an army. In 1757, his troops suffered a terrible defeat from the forces of King Friedrich II of Prussia at Rossbach during the SEVEN YEARS' WAR. The following year, however, Marshal Soubise seized the landgraviate of Hesse, leading to a French ascendency during that period of the conflict.

## Soufflot, Germain (1713–1780)
*architect*

Germain Soufflot, who was a precursor of the neoclassical movement, was born in Irancy, near Auxerre. He was in Rome from 1735 to 1737, then worked in LYON (facade of the hôtel-Dieu, 1748). In 1750, at the request of Mme DE POMPADOUR, he accompanied her brother, M. de Vandières (later the marquis de Marigny), who was the superintendent of royal buildings, to Italy. There, Soufflot sketched the ruins at Paestum and, upon his return to France, obtained a number of official commissions. LOUIS XV entrusted him with the construction of the church of Saint-Geneviève in Paris (1756–80), which later would become the Panthéon. Inspired by the facades of Roman temples, he carefully opened the base of the cupola of the church to gain elegance and light, while resting the weight on four groups of columns. Soufflot had a profound influence on the neoclassical movement in architecture, heralded by his colossal style, a tendency that would later be developed by other noted architects.

## Soulages, Pierre (1919–  )
*painter*

A leading abstract expressionist, Pierre Soulages was born in Rodez. After painting sparse landscapes (1938–46), he developed a powerful and balanced abstract style. He painted, at the same time, strong compositions dominated by rectangular black forms, constructed on the play of horizontals and verticals, and often animated by light or rare bursts of color. Paradoxically, this extremely abstract painter was dedicated to the rigorous techniques of the artists he had known in his childhood at Rodez. Giving a great importance to the material aspects of his art, he did not hesitate to use the tools of building painters or even the soles of shoes. At the same time, he often gave his works identical titles (*Pienture,* date, size), thereby eliminating all anecdotal aspects. After 1979, his paintings have been done entirely in black, and are given movement by large stripes transversed by streaks that hold the light.

## Soult, Nicolas-Jean de Dieu (1769–1851)
*marshal of France*

Born in Saint-Amans-la-Bastide, Nicolas-Jean de Dieu Soult joined the military in 1785 and later, during the REVOLUTION OF 1789 and the FIRST EMPIRE, served with distinction in a number of campaigns. He took part in the victory at Saxony, Austerlitz (1805) and the capture of Königsberg (1807), after which he was made governor of Prussia and duke of Dalmatia by NAPOLÉON I. Sent to Spain, Soult eventually forced the British to give up the siege of Badajoz (1811). Returning to France because of his differences with JOSEPH BONAPARTE, he soon took part in the victory of Bautzen, Saxony, then was sent back to Spain, where he stopped Wellington's advance. Rallying to the Bourbons in 1814, he was made a peer of France and named minister of war (1814–15). During the HUNDRED DAYS, he joined Napoléon and was banished under the Second RESTORATION. He returned to France in 1819 and was restored to the Chamber of Peers in 1827. A supporter of the JULY MONARCHY, Marshal Soult suppressed the insurrection at LYON (1831); as minister of war, planned the expedition to Antwerp (1832); and as president of the Council of Ministers, was sent to London as part of the French delegation to the coronation of Queen Victoria (1838). He later again served as president of the Council of Ministers (1840–47), but power at that time was held by FRANÇOIS GUIZOT.

## Soupault, Philippe (1897–1990)
*writer*

Born in Chaville, Philippe Soupault was active in the dadaist movement (1918–20) before becoming involved in surrealism alongside ANDRÉ BRETON and LOUIS ARAGON. He participated in its most controversial aspects as well as in the founding of the revue *Littérature.* The publication of the collection *Champs magnétiques* (in collaboration with Breton, 1920) was followed by his works done in "automatic writing," marking an important date in the history of contemporary poetry. Soupault left Paris and his friends for long trips around the world. Becoming a journalist and novelist (*Le Bon Apôtre,* 1923; *Les Frères Durandeau,* 1924; *Le Nègre,* 1927; *Les Dernières Nuits de Paris,* 1928; *Le Grand Homme,* 1929), he sought to bear witness to his age and to his new experiences (*Voyages en URSS,* 1930) and gave a modernist interpretation also to music (jazz) and to film (*Charlot,* 1930). Altogether, Soupault's curiosity brought him back to poetry (essay on *Lautréamont,* 1927; *William Blake,* 1928) and painting (*Jean Lurçat,* 1928; *Paolo Uccello,* 1929). He published several collections: *Odes* (1946) and *Sans phrases* (1953). His activities extended also to the theater (*Tous ensemble autour du monde,* 1943) and radio, where he produced a number of broadcasts (Paris, 1928; Tunis, 1938–40; Paris, 1945–57). A tireless traveler, most inquisitive and possessing a free and easy spirit, Soupault lived always faithful to the joyful fantasies of his youth.

## Soustelle, Jacques (1912–1990)
*ethnologist, political figure*

Born in Neuilly-sur-Seine, Jacques Soustelle, was a specialist on pre-Columbian Mexico (*La Famille Otoni-Pame,* 1937; *L'Art du Mexique ancien,* 1966; *Mexique et les Quatre Soleils,* 1967). He served as assistant director of the musée de l'Homme (1937) and was a founding member of the Union of Intellectuals against Fascism and War. In 1940 he joined the Free French forces. Director general of Special French Services in London, then in ALGERIA (1943), after the Liberation he served as minister of information (1945) and of colonies (1945–46) and took part in the establishment of the Gaullist movement, the RASSEMBLEMENT DU PEUPLE FRANÇAIS (RPF) (April 1947). A deputy (1951–58), he served as governor-general of Algeria (1955–56) and became a leading spokesperson for an integrated French Algeria. A leader of the May 1958 civil and military rebellion there that led to the appointment of General CHARLES DE GAULLE as premier, he subsequently opposed the policy of Algerian self-determination and went into exile in Italy. Returning to France in 1968 after a general amnesty, he was elected deputy (1973–78). Besides his ethnological works, Soustelle wrote his memoirs of the RESISTANCE (*Envers à contre tout,* 1947–50) and published works on the Algerian problem (*L'Espérance trahie,* 1962) and on Gaullism (*Vingt-huit Ans de gaullisme,* 1968). He was elected to the ACADÉMIE FRANÇAISE in 1983.

## Soutine, Chaim   (1894–1943)
*painter*

Born in ghetto in Smilovitchi, Lithuania, the 10th child of a poor family, Chaim Soutine worked for a photographer and studied art in Minsk and Vilna, Russia (1910) before leaving for France. Arriving in Paris (1913), he frequented the Cormon Studio but soon left this academic environment for Ruche, where MARC CHAGALL and others already lived. During this period (1919–25) of great poverty, which Soutine saw as a necessary circumstance, he met dealers through Amadeo Modigliani who helped him sell many of the 200 canvases (usually landscapes) that he had painted, and he produced some series (*Bœufs ecórchés, Volailles plumées, Enfants de chœur*). His style was based on a highly personal vision and technique, in which he sacrificed careful composition and drawing for a fervid intensity and the use of pigment in vivid and sometimes ugly colors, resulting in brutal psychological portraits or shocking still lifes. An expressionist painter, Soutine often reworked or destroyed his earlier paintings, while those that remain convey his inner turmoil.

## Sperber, Manès   (1905–1984)
*writer*

Born in Zablotov, in Austrian Galicia, Manès Sperber came to Vienna with his family during WORLD WAR I. He discovered Marxism at the same time as philosophy, which he then taught as a professor at Berlin (1927). Fleeing the anti-Semitic persecutions that began in 1933, he sought refuge in Paris, where, in 1939, he joined the army. His work, part of which is written in German and part in French, is entirely dedicated to the denunciation of totalitarianism and the upholding of human dignity. Notable among his writings are essays (*Analyses de la tyrannie,* 1938; *Sept questions sur la violence,* 1972), autobiographical works (*Les Porteurs d'eau,* 1974; *Le Pont inachevé,* 1975; *Au-delà de l'oubli,* 1977), as well as novels that evoke Central Europe during the years 1930–40 (*Et le buisson devint cendres,* 1944; *Qu'une larme dans l'océan,* 1952; *Le Baie perdue,* 1953).

## Staël, Mme de   (1766–1817)
### (Anne-Louise-Germaine Necker, baroness de Staël-Holstein)
*writer, salon hostess*

Mme de Staël was born in Paris, the daughter of the financier and statesman JACQUES NECKER. In 1786, she married the Swedish minister to France, baron de Staël-Holstein. Raised on the works of the philosophes (her first work was a eulogy to JEAN-JACQUES ROUSSEAU), she enthusiastically supported the REVOLUTION OF 1789. Leaving France at the beginning of the TERROR (1793), but still wishing to play a political role, she took refuge in Switzerland, where she held a brilliant salon that drew many opponents to the French Revolutionary regimes, including the Directory. Returning to France in 1800, she incurred the hostility of Napoléon Bonaparte and was forced to leave again. Traveling throughout Europe, sometimes with BENJAMIN CONSTANT, she lived what would become the romantic ideal, through the example of her passionate life and her writings. After 1800, her *De la Littérature considérée dans ses rapports avec les institutions sociales* underscores the importance of the heart and the imagination and asks for a new literature for a new age, presaging the ideas she would later develop in *De l'Allemagne* (1813), which show the aesthetic relativity and the fruitful contribution of cosmopolitan literature. The author calls for renewal of genres, and exalts sensibility and individualism, as is also found in her two novels, *Delphine* (1802) and *Corinne, ou l'Italie* (1807). In the latter work, one of her best known, Mme de Staël exerted enormous influence on literary women in Europe and the United States, challenging *them* to fulfill their hopes and aspirations for fame as it focused on the

Mme de Staël *(Library of Congress)*

triumphant literary and artistic career of its heroine. Mme de Staël believed that through poetry also, one could experience the feelings of "souls at once exalted and melancholy." Her writings disseminated the themes and spirit of romanticism and, in her studies of German culture of the period, the aspects of *Sturm und Drang.*

## Staël, Nicolas de (1914–1955)
*painter*

Of Russian origin, Nicolas de Staël was born in St. Petersburg to a noble family who left during the Russian Revolution (1917). He was raised in Brussels, Belgium, where he studied art, before settling in Paris. In 1936, he left for Morocco, where he began to paint from nature. After serving in the FOREIGN LEGION (1940), he moved to Nice, where he did his first still lifes and portraits of his companion, Jeannine (1941–42), which have been compared to the rose period of Pablo Picasso. Returning to Paris (1943), he developed a friendship with GEORGES BRAQUE and had his first shows. Retiring to the Vaucluse and then Antilbes, de Staël developed a style

with more nuance (*Ciel à Honfleurs,* 1954). He also created tapestries and illustrations.

## Stavisky, Serge-Alexandre (1886–1934)
*businessman*

Of Ukrainian origin, Serge-Alexandre Stavisky, the financier who caused a scandal that resulted in a major upheaval in the French government, was born in Slobodka, Ukraine. He was the founder and director of the Crédit municipal de Bayonne (1931), through which he issued a large number of bonds that were based on false or stolen gems. The discovery of this financial fraud (late 1933) contributed to the discrediting of the regime as many government officials were more or less directly implicated in the scandal. Sought by the police, Stavisky, who used his charm to befriend many well-placed political and social figures, was found dead from a pistol shot in Chamonix. The extreme right-wing leagues accused the government of his death and, after the resignation of the cabinet (which was replaced by that of ÉDOUARD DALADIER), held demonstrations on February 6, 1934. The Stavisky affair, which resulted in many being swindled out of their savings, caused one of the major political crises of the decade.

## Steinlen, Théophile-Alexandre (1859–1923)
*painter, lithographer*

Of Swiss origin, Théophile-Alexandre Steinlen was born in Lausanne, Switzerland, and settled in Paris in 1878. He began his career as an industrial designer and worked on several journals: *Le Chat noir, Gil Blas, L'Assiette au buerre.* His drawings of cats soon brought him fame; he illustrated a number of works (*Dan la rue,* ARISTIDE BRUANT), making posters strongly influenced by the "Japanese style" (japonisme) then in vogue, and tableaus in sometimes muted tones, evoking popular customs through which Steinlen expressed his social concerns and humanitarian hopes. Sensitive to the examples of HONORÉ DAUMIER and HENRI DE TOULOUSE-LAUTREC, he had a keen curiosity and sense of observation that makes him one of the most interesting commentators on the fin de siècle period.

## Stendhal (1783–1842)
### (Henri Beyle)
*writer*

Stendhal (the pseudonym of Henri Beyle), whose works reflect the turbulent era and extreme individualism of the author, was born in Grenoble. After a rebellious adolescence during which he declared himself an atheist and a Jacobin, Stendhal developed an interest in the works of the philosophers and of the romantics. While serving as an officer in the army of NAPOLÉON I, he became fascinated by Italian culture. He then edited his *Journal* (later published 1881–1935) to reflect his views. Settling in Milan, Italy, (1814–1821), he wrote an essay entitled *Rome, Naples, et Florence* (1817, signed with the name Stendhal). After a stay in Germany, he returned to Paris, where he was well received in worldly Parisian society and published *De l'amour* (1822) and a manifesto for liberal literary romanticism (*Racine et Shakespeare,* 1823, 1825) and two novels, *Armance* (1827) and his famous *Le Rouge et le Noir* (1830). Hampered, however, by his relative poverty and limited literary success, he returned to Italy (serving as consul in Trieste, then Civitavecchia, from 1830 to 1842). In 1834, he began *Lucien Leuwen* (unfinished, 1855) and, from 1836 to 1839, he stayed in Paris and published *Les Mémoires d'un tourist* (1838), then *La Chartreuse de Parme* (1839) and *L'Abbesse de Castro* (1939), a collection of short stories that would become the *Chroniques italiennes* (posthumous, 1855), accounts in which he presents his "cult of the self." Before returning to Italy, he wrote *Lamiel* (1842), an unfinished novel in which all his aspirations are expressed through a fascinating female character. After his death, besides his *Journal,* were published *Vie de Henry Brulard* (reminiscences of his childhood and adolescence, 1890) and *Souvenirs d'égoïsme* (1821–30, published 1892). Developing a theory that he called "beylism" (a combination of knowledge and a method of living that bases mental experiences in sensations), Stendhal believed that he would actually not be understood until the 20th century. Nonetheless, his writings, style, and literary concepts have had a great effect, influencing such writers as MARCEL PROUST, ANDRÉ GIDE, and ALBERT CAMUS, as well as the German philosopher Friedrich Nietzsche.

## Strasbourg

Located in the department of Bas-Rhin, region of ALSACE, on the Ill River, near the Rhine, Strasbourg is a French city with over 250,000 inhabitants. The see of a bishop, it has numerous famous monuments, including the cathedral in red sandstone, built from the 11th to 14th centuries. Having only one tower, it is decorated with Gothic carvings, stained glass, and tapestries, and has a beautiful astronomical clock. The maison de l'Œuvre Notre-Dame, from the 14th to 16th centuries, contains a museum. Other churches include Saint-Thomas, from the 13th to 14th centuries, with the masoleum of Marshal SAXE, BY JEAN-BAPTISTE PIGALLE, Saint Pierre-le-Jeune (13th century), Saint-Guillaume (15th century), and Saint-Pierre-le-Veiux (15th century). A famous building is the château des Rohan, dating from the 18th century. Strasbourg's museums include the Archaeologic, Modern Art, Alsatian, Historic, Fine Arts, and Decorative Arts, and in its picturesque quarter, "Old France," are mansions, covered bridges, and three important towers. The main squares are Place Kléber (statue of General KLÉBER) and Place Broglie. As a city on the Rhine (France's second-largest river port, after Paris), situated near the great European economic and urban centers, Strasbourg takes full advantage of its strategic position as a central border city. It is the headquarters of the European Council since 1950 and of the EUROPEAN UNION and Human Rights Commission since 1966; in 1992, Strasbourg became the seat of the European Parliament. There is a university, particularly noted for medical and biological studies, other large schools, and, since 1992, the École nationale d'administration (ENA). Historically the site of the Oath of Strasbourg, taken by Charles the Bald and Louis the German in 842, Strasbourg, with all of Alsace, became part of the Holy Roman Empire beginning in 855. The German inventor of printing, Johann Gutenberg, resided there from 1434 to 1447, where he began his invention of typography. In 1681, the city was reunited with France, and a citadel was constructed in 1687. J. W. Goethe and prince Klemens von Metternich both studied at the university. In 1792, it was at Strasbourg that ROGER DE LISLE first sang LA MARSEILLAISE ("Chant de guerre pour l'armée du Rhin"). Besieged by the Germans in 1870, the city surrendered after a heroic resistance. It remained part of Germany until 1918. Strasbourg also suffered much during WORLD WAR II and was liberated by General PHILIPPE LECLERC in November 1944.

## Subleyras, Pierre-Hubert (1699–1749)
*painter*

Born in Saint-Gilles-du-Gard and trained in studios in Toulouse and Paris, where he won the first prize at the Academy of Fine Arts in 1728, Pierre-Hubert Subleyras in 1728 settled in Rome. There, he was in demand among the religious establishment and the aristocracy. In 1740, he became a member of the prestigious Roman Academy of Saint Luke. The following year, pope Benedict XIV commissioned his portrait and, in 1747, *Une messe de saint Basile* for Saint Peter's. Subleyra's work stands between portraiture and historic themes, although he also did landscapes, still lifes, nudes, and street scenes. While the influence of other artists is evident in the formation of Subleyras's style, he cannot be assigned to any particular school and remains a unique figure who used contrasting colors with a great sense of refinement.

## Sue, Eugène (1804–1857)
*novelist*

Born in Paris, Eugène Sue (the pen name of Marie-Joseph Sue) was the son of a noted physician. A naval physician himself, after many travels he took up the life of a dandy. An admirer of American author Fenimore Cooper, Sue started in literature with novels about the sea (*La Salamanche*, 1832), then wrote novels about everyday life and customs (*Mathilde*, 1841), and became successful with *Les Mystères de Paris*, the first of his serialized works, that augured the humanitarian ideals later found in those of VICTOR HUGO. Sue's *Le Juif errant* (1844–45), directed against the Jesuits, and his *Sept Pêches capitaux* (1847–49) were also well received. By the power and exactness of his description of the world of the working classes and the downtrodden, the portrayal of innumerable characters who animate his works, Sue can perhaps be considered the initiator of realism. Often rich in detail, his work is also

an expression of a basic, Manichean morality and, to a certain degree, social conservatism.

## Sully, Maximilien de Béthune, baron de Rosny, duke de (1560–1641)
*statesman*

Born to a Protestant family at their château at Rosny, Maximilien de Béthune, baron de Rosny, duke de Sully was a childhood friend of king HENRY IV. A trusted adviser, his talents were first used as a military engineer (he was wounded at the Battle of Ivry), then he was put in charge of royal finances (1598) and remained in complete control of the royal funds until the king's death (1610). Among his economic achievements was the successful reorganization of the national system of taxes and revenues. His rigorous policies allowed the reestablishment of an economic equilibrium as he reformed the system of taxes, tolls, and duties. He instituted policies in favor of trade and agriculture (encouraging the work of OLIVIER DE SERRES) and abolished many ordinances that hindered production in those areas. He retired after the death of Henri IV but continued to support the Crown, encouraging his coreligionists to give their loyalty to King LOUIS XIII. The duke de Sully left his memoirs, *Économie royale* (1638–62).

## Sully Prudhomme (1839–1907)
### (René-Francois-Armand Prudhomme)
*poet, Nobel laureate*

Born in Paris, Sully Prudhomme (the pen name of René-François-Armand Prudhomme) was an engineer at the Creusot firm and completed his education with studies in law. He soon decided, however, to devote himself to his first love, poetry. He was part of the Parnassian movement, but, with *Stances et Poèmes* (1865), his poetry became less impersonal. Elegiac with a sense of nuanced intimacy, he expressed melancholy and amorous anguish in *Les Solitudes* (1869) and *Les vaines Tendresses* (1875). A translator of Lucretius, Sully Prudhomme hoped to unite poetry and science, and composed long philosophic poems like *La Justice* (1878) and *Le Bonheur* (1888), in which he dealt with issues of conscience and the modern universe. He also wrote essays on aesthetics, philosophy, and criticisms. Sully Prudhomme was elected to the ACADÉMIE FRANÇAISE in 1881 and was awarded the first Nobel Prize in literature in 1901.

## Supervielle, Jules  (1884–1960)
*poet, novelist*

Of Basque origin, Jules Supervielle, who was born in Montevideo, Uruguay, spent his entire life in France or South America. All his work is filled with memories of the vast empty spaces of the pampas and the ocean, the frequency of which he often uses to give a sense of distance and isolation. But his first publications, the *Poèmes de l'humour triste* (1919) and *L'Homme de la pampa* (1925), a free essay and a whimsical novel, respectively, hid the poet's feeling of anguish. It was only when, at age 40, with *Gravitations* (1925), that Supervielle found his true style. After this, he composed a number of poetry collections, like *Le Forçat innocent* (1930), *Les Amis inconnus* (1934), *Oublieuse Mémoire* (1949), *Naissances* (1951), *Le Corps tragiques* (1959); some stories, the genre that demonstrates most profoundly his talent (*Le Voleur d'enfants*, 1926; *L'Enfant de la haute mer*, 1931; *Le Jeune Homme de dimanche et des autres jours*,

1952); and plays (*La Belle au bois*, 1932; *Bolivar*, 1936; *Schéhérazade*, 1949). Supervielle chose to remain apart from the surrealist movement. His work, presented in a clear vocabulary and populated essentially with flora and fauna, describes a recognizable and attainable world.

## Survage, Léopold  (1879–1968)
*painter*

Of Russian origin, Léopold Frédéric Sturzwage, or Léopold Survage as he is known, was born in Moscow to a Finnish mother and a Danish father. He was introduced to Western art by the collector Chtchoukine, then in 1908 went to Paris. His first works show the influence of PAUL CÉZANNE and cubism, which he interpreted, with the encouragement of GUILLAUME APOLLINAIRE, in his *Rythmes colorés* (1912–13). He joined with other artists in the Section d'Or and served as that group's secretary. He moved stylistically toward a synthesis of forms, with urban landscapes (*Villefranche-sur-Mer*, 1915) and a return to the human figure (*Le Paysan*, 1915). In 1922, Survage created the sets for Sergey Diaghilev's ballet *Mavra* and, in 1937, received a gold medal for his three panels done for the palais de Chemins de fer at the Paris Universal Exposition.

# T

## Tailhade, Laurent (1854–1919)
*writer*

Born in Tarbes, Laurent Tailhade, who became a friend of PAUL VERLAINE and other symbolists, began his writing career with a collection *Le Jardin des rêves* (1880), done in the Parnassian style, then wrote *Vitraux* (1892), and finally *Poèmes élégiaques* (1907). *Au pays du muffle* (1891) followed by *À travers les groins* (1899) revealed a virulent poet who put his satirical verve in the service of the anarchistic ideals that he held. One can find "Aristophanian" tendencies in his poetry and his writings (*Imbéciles et Gredins*, 1900) and in the articles that he wrote for *Libertaire* and *L'Aurore*. Tailhade also did translations of Plautius and Petronius.

## Taille

The Taille was a tax collected under the French monarchy, and before the REVOLUTION OF 1789, on the estimated value of properties. As a direct tax, and because its method of assessment was quite arbitrary, varying from province to province, and even district to district, it was much resented. The Taille and its arbitrary methods of valuation and collection were among the grievances collected and brought by the Third Estate to the ESTATES GENERAL of 1789.

## Taine, Hippolyte (1828–1893)
*literary critic, philosopher, historian*

One of the leading exponents of positivism, Hippolyte Taine was born in Vouziers, Ardennes, and was educated in Paris at the Collège Bourbon and the École normale. In one of his first works, *Les Philosophes français du xixe siècle* (1857), he questioned the eclectic approach of VICTOR COUSIN and proposed instead the application of scientific methodology to the study of history and human nature. Taine's works have a coherent unity based on rigorous and systematic research, in which he sought to uncover in human groups, milieus (geographic and social), and time (historical evolution), the most important factors in explaining literary and artistic expression, As a literary critic and philosopher, he wrote *La Fontaine et ses faibles* (1853–1861), *Essais de critique et d'histoire* (1858), and *Histoire de la littérature anglaise* (1864), in which he applied his theories to the psychological and physical factors affecting the development of English literature. Taine's lectures on aesthetics and art history, collected in *Philosophie de l'art* (1882), applied the same methodology. Influenced by ÉTIENNE CONDILLAC, J. S. Mill, and A. Bain, he presented in *De l'intelligence* (1870) a sensualist and associationalist theory. Finally, in *Les Origines de la France contemporaine* (1876–93), he attempted, in the aftermath of the FRANCO-PRUSSIAN WAR and the Paris COMMUNE, to discover the causation for those events and for the extreme centralization of political power in France, which he believed to be the cause of its modern political instability. Taine was elected to the ACADÉMIE FRANÇAISE in 1878.

## Tallemant des Reaux, Gédéon (1619–1692)
*writer*

Born in La Rochelle, Gédéon Tallemant des Reaux, after having accompanied the future Cardinal de RETZ to Italy (where he also befriended VOLTAIRE), returned to Paris and frequented the salon CATHERINE DE RAMBOUILLET, who encouraged him to write *Historiettes* (1657, published 1834–35). Filled with lively accounts of the royal court as well as city life during the reigns of HENRY IV and LOUIS XIII, as well as of the FRONDE, they comprise a realistic portrait of the mores of the 17th century and offer valuable testimony to the changes within the social classes, especially the bourgeoisie.

## Talleyrand-Périgord, Charles-Maurice de (1754–1838)
*statesman*

Born in Paris, Charles-Maurice de Talleyrand-Périgord, one of French history's most important statesmen and better known as Talleyrand, became lame as the result of a childhood accident and could not therefore enter the military. While not having a religious vocation, he was still destined for an ecclesiastical career. Educated at the seminary of Saint-Sulpice and ordained a priest, his aristocratic background allowed him to obtain an abbey in the diocese of Reims, and in 1780 he became an agent-general for the French clergy and in 1788, bishop of Autun. He was elected deputy for his class to the ESTATES GENERAL in 1789 and, acquainted with the writings of the philosophes and open to their ideas, at the beginning of the meetings (and of the REVO-LUTION OF 1789) supported the joining of the three Estates, and subsequently played a preponderant role in the National Constituent Assembly, where he voted to put the church's property at the disposal of the nation. During the festival of the National Federation, he celebrated mass on the Champ du Mars (July 14, 1790). While he did not take a direct role in the drafting of the CIVIL CON-STITUTION of the Clergy, he was one of the first to take an oath to it and became the leader of the constitutional clergy, after resigning from his see at Autun. Condemned as a schismatic by the pope, he left the church shortly thereafter. Under the new Legislative Assembly, he began what would be a long diplomatic career. Sent to Great Britain to secure that country's neutrality, he was accused, after August 10, 1792, of having intrigued in London for the duke of ORLÉANS. After trying to defend himself, left again for Great Britain in September 1792 and was put on the list of émigrés. After spending time in the United States, he returned to France with his mistress, Mme Grand (whom he married in 1803) after the fall of MAXIMILIEN ROBE-SPIERRE. Thanks to PAUL BARRAS, Talleyrand was made minister of foreign relations, a post that he kept after the coup d'état of 18 Brumaire (November 9, 1799), which he helped to carry out, and in

spite of the charges of embezzlement that were made against him during the DIRECTORY period. The inspiration for the Organic Articles in the CONCOR-DAT OF 1801 and for the treaties negotiated at Lunéville, Amiens, Pressburg, and Tilsit, he was successively grand chamberlain (1804), prince of Benevento (1806), then vice-grand elector (1807), giving up his ministerial post. Having plotted with JOSEPH FOUCHÉ against NAPOLÉON I, in 1809 he fell into disgrace. Leader of the provisional government in 1814, he helped to gain the Senate vote that removed Napoléon and called LOUIS XVIII to power. Restored to his position as foreign minister, he negotiated the Treaty of Paris (May 1814) and took part in the Congress of Vienna, where he was able, through his intrigues, to divide the Allies and limit the excessive demands of Prussia and Russia on France, diplomatic efforts that were in a great part rendered in vain by the episode of the HUNDRED DAYS. President of the Council at the beginning of the Second RESTORATION (July 1815), he was forced to resign shortly after because of the opposition of the ultraroyalists. As a member of the House of Peers, he played only a minor role, siding with the opposition to the government. Supporting the Orléans branch during the REVOLUTION OF 1830, he was named ambassador to Great Britain by king LOUIS-PHILIPPE and took part in the Conference of London (1830–31, dedicated in large part to the Belgian question) and in meetings regarding issues in Iberia. Intelligent and cultivated but greedy for gain and apparently little bothered by moral scruples, in diplomacy Talleyrand kept the impassive face of a great lord and the bearing of his ecclesiastical background. Gifted with prodigious foresight, it was said that although he "often changed his party, he never changed his opinion."

## Tallien, Jean-Lambert (1767–1820)
*political figure*

Born in Paris, Jean-Lambert Tallien was a member of the JACOBIN Club since the beginning of the REVOLUTION OF 1789 and, in 1791, published a popular newspaper, *L'Affiche des citoyens*. Recording secretary of the insurrectionist Commune of Paris after August 10, 1792, he was elected to the Convention, where, joining with the MONTAGNARDS, he opposed GIRONDIN policies and voted for the king's death. A member of the Committee of Public Safety, he was sent on a mission to BORDEAUX to organize the TERROR there. In Bordeaux, among the prisoners, he met Theresa de Cabarrus (MME TALLIEN), whom he married in 1793. Under her influence, he adopted a more moderate position and, seeing a new opportunity, contributed decisively to the fall of MAXIMILIEN ROBESPIERRE. Tallien played an active role in the Themidorian reaction (closing the Jacobin Club, suppressing the Revolutionary Tribunal and the Montagnard insurrection of Year III—May 20, 1795). A member of the Council of Five Hundred, he accompanied Napoléon Bonaparte (see NAPOLÉON I) to Egypt.

## Tallien, Mme (1773–1835)
### (Theresa de Cabarrus)
*style setter*

Born near Madrid, Theresa de Cabarrus, Mme Tallien, was the daughter of a Spanish financier of French origin, François, count de Cabarrus, who later served as minister of finance to JOSEPH BONAPARTE. Mme Tallien, as she is known, married an adviser to the Parlement of BORDEAUX, Davis de Fontenoy, whom she divorced in 1793. Although she had at first some sympathy for the REVOLUTION OF 1789, she was disturbed by the events leading to the TERROR and tried to cross over to Spain but was arrested and imprisoned at Bordeaux. There she became the mistress and then the wife of JEAN-LAMBERT TALLIEN and subsequently gained the sobriquet "Notre-Dame de Thermidor" because, during the Thermidorian Convention, and especially the DIRECTORY, she became one of the most famous women of the period, in particular inspiring the fashion of returning to the styles of antiquity. Divorced in 1802, in 1805 she married the count of Caraman, later prince of Chimay.

## Talma, François-Joseph (1763–1826)
*tragedian*

One of France's most celebrated actors, François-Joseph Talma was born in Paris, where he debuted at the COMÉDIE-FRANÇAISE in VOLTAIRE's *Mohamet*, then created the title role in *Charles IX* by MARIE-JOSEPH CHÉNIER (1789). The scandal evoked by the latter play's production caused a division among the actors at the Comédie-Française, and Talma subsequently founded a dissident theater that would become the théâtre de la République (1793). There, Talma played in *Othello, Macbeth,* and *Hamlet* in adaptations by Jean-François Ducis. He returned to the Comédie-Française in 1799, where he played the lead roles in the works of CORNEILLE with such an unequaled grandeur that he gained the respect, friendship, and beneficence of Napoléon Bonaparte who took the actor under his protection and showered him with many favors and gifts. Talma brought to the stage a profound reform in speech and costuming and, especially, a naturalism and verisimilitude that presaged the romantic style.

## Talon, Jean (1625–1694)
*administrator*

Born in Châlons-sur-Marne, Jean Talon served as a military commissioner (1654) and as intendant of Hainault, Belgium (1655), then was sent by JEAN-BAPTISTE COLBERT to be intendant of Nouvelle-France (CANADA). There, from 1665 to 1668 and again from 1670 to 1672, he contributed to the development of colonization by exploiting the resources of the region's forests and wildlife and increasing its maritime trade with the Antilles, as well as by his administrative organization. Upon his return to France, Talon was named secretary to the king's cabinet (1681).

## Tarde, Gabriel (1843–1904)
*sociologist*

Born in Sarlat, Dordogne, Gabriel Tarde, a noted criminologist and sociologist, as well as the author of works on problem of criminality, was the principal French representative of the psychological school of sociology. After serving as a provincial magistrate, he was appointed director of criminal statistics at the Ministry of Justice (1894), and later (1900) became professor of modern philosophy at the COLLÈGE DE FRANCE. In *La Criminalité comparée* (1886), he challenged the theories of Cesare Lombroso and developed the thesis that social phenomena are the main causes of crime. Tarde, in his social philosophy, posited that historical progress is the result of a conflict between the inventive and the conservative aspects of society and distinguished three recurring phases of social development: repetition, opposition, and adaptation. His other works include *Études pénales et sociales* (1892), *Études de psychologie sociale* (1898).

## Tardieu, André (1876–1945)
*political figure*
Born in Paris and educated at the École normale supérieure, André Tardieu served as leader of the PIERRE WALDECK-ROUSSEAU cabinet foreign news editor of *Le Temps* (1902). He was elected deputy (1914) and was chosen by GEORGES CLEMENCEAU to be the special commissioner of France to the United States (1917–18). He took part in the Paris Peace Conference (1919) and served as minister for the liberated regions of Alsace-Lorraine (1919–20). At the peace conference, he played a leading role in drafting the political and territorial claims of the Treaty of Versailles. A founder of *L'Echo national*, in 1924 he lost in the general election (during the victory of the CARTEL DES GAUCHES), but was reelected in 1926 and appointed successively by RAYMOND POINCARÉ as minister of public works (1926–28) and the interior (1928–29). As prime minister (November 1929–December 1930), during a time of international economic and financial crises, he carved out a policy of optimistic politics, making important economic decisions (social security, free education, military pensions, major public work, and the like. Losing power for a time, Tardieu later became minister of agriculture and then of war in the PIERRE LAVAL cabinets (1931–32). He was recalled to be premier (February–May 1932) and served for a final time as a minister in the GASTON DOUMERGUE cabinet (1934) and was charged with the study of constitutional reform. Tardieu retired from public life in 1935. His writings include *La Paix* (1921), *Sur la pente* (1935), *La Révolution à refaire* (1936–37).

## Target, Guy-Jean-Baptiste (1733–1807)
*magistrate*
Born in Paris, where he served as an attorney for the Parlement, Guy-Jean-Baptiste Target is noted for his opposition to the policies of RENÉ DE MAUPEOU and for his *Mémoire sur l'état des protestants en France* (1787). Elected deputy for the Third Estate to the ESTATES GENERAL (1789), during the REVOLUTION OF 1789 he served as an adviser to the Tribunal de cassation under the DIRECTORY (1798) and was involved in the editing of the civil and criminal codes. Target was elected to the ACADÉMIE FRANÇAISE in 1785.

## Tati, Jacques (1908–1982)
*cinematographer*
Born Jacques Tatischeff in Le Pecq, Jacques Tati began his career in the music halls of Paris, where he pantomimed various characters before becoming a celebrated personality of French comic cinema, best known there as the clumsy, good-natured "Monsieur Hulot." Tati was gifted with a keen sense of observation of everyday life, and his art is the effect of a slow and determined characterization of various scenarios: the peasant life (*Jour de fête*, 1949), the world of the petite bourgeoisie (Les Vacances de M. Hulot, 1953; *Mon oncle*, 1958), and more ambitious works. As a director (*Playtime*, 1957; *Trafic*, 1969), Tati sought to present parodies of mechanization being done at the expense of human dignity. Because he often worked with limited budgets, he produced relatively few films, but these remain landmark comedies.

## Tavernier, Bertrand (1941– )
*critic, cinematographer*
A leading motion picture director and screenwriter known for his studies of complex interpersonal relationships, Bertrand Tavernier was born in LYON and studied law before beginning a career as a film critic. He was attracted to the film industry early in his youth, attending film clubs and working in the industry's press in various capacities, especially as a publicist promoting various unknown or unappreciated directors. Even today, with his own film career well advanced, he still sought to bring to the fore overlooked writers and directors, especially American, and has edited a monumental *Dictionnaire du cinéma américain* (1991). His first work as a director was on a short segment of the film *Les*

*Baisers* (1964), and his best works have a warm aspect, colored by a sense of seriousness, along the lines of JEAN RENOIR: *L'Horloger de Saint-Paul* (1974), which won a number of awards.

## Tavernier, Jean-Baptiste (1605–1689)
*traveler*

Born either in Paris or Copenhagen, Jean-Baptiste Tavernier was ennobled by king LOUIS XIV in 1669 and was given the barony of Aubonne (canton of Vaud) in 1676. His first travels brought him to England, the Low Countries, and central Europe (Hungary and Poland). Following this, he visited Turkey, Palestine, Persia, the Indies, Sumatra, and Java. Brought to ruin by his nephew, he was constrained, as a Protestant, to go into exile after the revocation of the EDICT OF NANTES (1685). Named director of a new commercial company by the elector of Brandenburg, he died while traveling through Russia en route to Asia. His account, *Les Six Voyages de Jean-Baptiste Tavernier* (Paris, 1681), is a descriptive and valuable document of the period.

## Teilhard de Chardin, Pierre (1881–1955)
*theologian, philosopher, paleontologist*

Known for his evolutionary interpretation of humanity and the universe, Pierre Teilard de Chardin was born in the château of Sarcenat, Orcines, Puy-de-Dôme. Entering the Jesuit order in 1899, he soon became interested in geology. After he wrote his thesis on prehistoric mammals (*Les Mammifères de l'Écocene inférieur en France*, 1922), he was appointed professor at the Institut catholique de Paris. Beginning at that time, he participated in a number of scientific expeditions to the Far East: the Gobi Desert (1928); excavations of deposits of prehistoric cultures at Zhoukoudian, near Beijing (1926); an automobile trip organized by ANDRÉ CITROËN across central Asia to follow the Silk Road (1931–32); American expeditions to India (1935–36); and excavations of artifacts of *Pithecanthropus* in Java (1937–38). From this point on, the study of the stages of human development dominated the work of Teihard de Chardin, as he formulated his global vision, an optimistic evolutionism that sought to reconcile scientific theories

with those of Catholicism. Cosmogenesis, biogenesis, and noogenesis are the basic stages in this thesis, which sees a progressive spiritualization of all matter and in which humankind is the key to God, who is the initial and final point (the alpha and the omega). Giving Christ a cosmic dimension, without denying grace or the supernatural, Teihard de Chardin can perhaps be construed as seeming to adopt an almost pantheistic position and, for this reason, the Holy Office sent a notice (1962) to those responsible for religious education to avoid or cautiously approach his writings. Teihard de Chardin's principal works include *Le Phénomène humain* (1955); *L'Apparition de l'homme* (1956); *Le Milieu divin* (1957); *L'Avenir de l'homme* (1959); and *Lettres*. He was named to the Academy of Sciences in 1950.

## Tencin, Claudine-Alexandrine-Guérin, marquise de (1682–1749)
*writer*

Born in Grenoble, Claudine-Alexandrine-Guérin, marquise de Tencin was the mother of JEAN LE ROND D'ALEMBERT. Her renown came from the salon that she held, where a quite eclectic group would meet (CHARLES PINOT DUCLOS, Abbe PRÉVOST, JEAN-FRANÇOIS MARMONTEL, GABRIEL-BONNOT DE MABLY, CLAUDE ADRIEN HELVÉTIUS, and other writers and philosophers) to discuss ideas and philosophies. Mme Tencin's own writings, including her novels (*Les Mémoires du comte de Comminges*, 1735; *Le Siège de Calais*, 1737; and *Les Malheurs de l'amour*, 1747) inaugurated the genre of "sensibility" and were quite successful.

## Tennis Court, Oath of the

The Oath of the Tennis Court (Serment du jeu de paume) marks the beginning of the REVOLUTION OF 1789. After the threats of King LOUIS XVI (influenced by the court) to stop the deliberations of the Third Estate and to close the hall (Menus-Plaisirs) where the ESTATES GENERAL was meeting, the deputies of the Third Estate reconvened at an indoor tennis court. There, on June 20, 1789, on the proposal of JEAN-JOSEPH MOUNIER and following the example of their president, JEAN-SYLVAN BAILLY, swore a solemn oath "to never disband and to continue to meet until the constitution of the kingdom was established and affirmed on solid bases." The famous scene was portrayed by the artist JACQUES-LOUIS DAVID.

## Tenon, Jacques-René (1724–1816)
*surgeon, physician*
Born in Sépeaux, Burgundis, Jacques-René Tenon, while serving as first surgeon to the king (1759), submitted a plan to reform hospital service that would eventually bring about a new type of institution. In 1785, he was commissioned by LOUIS XVI to investigate the Hôtel-Dieu, where mortality was particularly high; his report opened an important debate. A deputy to the Legislative Assembly (1791) during the REVOLUTION OF 1789, where he chaired the committee on health, he left political life after August 10, 1792, to pursue his anatomical research. Tenon was elected to the Academy of Sciences in 1759.

## Terray, Joseph-Marie (1715–1778)
*political figure*
Born in Boën, Forez, Joseph-Marie Terray, or abbot Terray as he is known, was a protégé of Mme de POMPADOUR. He became comptroller general of finances in 1769 and formed, with MAUPEOU and d'AIGUILLON, a "triumvirate." He sought to reduce the public debt but resorted to authoritarian measures (new taxes, suspension of payments), that made him unpopular. He was accused of trying to speculate on grain (pacte de Famine) when he established a royal monopoly on that commodity. King LOUIS XVI, upon his accession, replaced Terray with ANNE ROBERT TURGOT.

## Terror
The Terror is the name given to a period of the REVOLUTION OF 1789. After August 10, 1792, the fear of an aristocratic conspiracy and the defeats of the French army brought about, with the impetus of the insurrectional COMMUNE OF PARIS, the creation of an extraordinary criminal tribunal (August 17, 1792) to judge suspects and the SEPTEMBER MASSACRES (the first Terror). After the elimination of the GIRONDINS (June 2, 1793), the external and internal threats (FEDERALIST INSURRECTION, war in the VENDÉE, CHOUANNERIE) and financial and economic difficulties favored the development of the popular revolutionary movement of the SANS-CULOTTES and the ENRAGÉS, who gained, after the riots of September 4 and 5, 1793, the legislation of the Terror (Law of Suspects, September 17, 1793). It targeted the nobles and the refractory priests, the émigrés and their families, officials suspected of treason, speculators, and monopolists. The main organs of the Terror were the Committee of Public Safety the Committee of General Security, the Revolutionary Tribunal, the Surveillance Committees, and the representatives of missions sent to the nation's departments. It is estimated that 17,000 persons were executed after being tried, and 25,000 on a simple affidavit of identity. The first wave struck down the leaders of the Girondins and Queen MARIE ANTOINETTE (October 1793). After the end of the war in the VENDÉE and external military successes (Hondschoote, Watignies) the continuation of the Terror was not justified. The Terror, transformed into a method of government (execution of the Hébertists and the Indulgents), was again strengthened by the law of 22 Prairial, Year II (June 10, 1794) that suppressed preliminary interrogation. A manifestation of an extreme political will founded on the idea of absolute and indivisible popular sovereignty, the Terror came to an end with the fall of MAXIMILIEN ROBESPIERRE (July 27, 1794). Under the Thermidorian Convention, the Terror was abolished and the form terrorists were deported or executed.

## Teste, Jean-Baptiste (1780–1852)
*political figure*
Born in Bagnols-sur-Céze, Jean-Baptiste Teste served as director of police and as a deputy during the HUNDRED DAYS of NAPOLÉON I and was subsequently proscribed under the Second RESTORATION. Returning to France in 1830, he served several times as minister under the JULY MONARCHY (1834–43), then was made a peer and president of the Cour de cassation. In 1847, he was accused, with others, for having given away the concession to a salt mine in exchange for bribes, causing one of the great

scandals of the later years of the July Monarchy. He was sentenced to three years in prison.

## Théot, Catherine (ca. 1725–1794)
*visionary*

Born in Barenton, Manche, Catherine Théot, who suffered since adolescence from hallucinations, believed herself to be chosen by God to be the mother of a new messiah. As a consequence, she was placed in a convent until 1782 and then was confined until the beginning of the REVOLUTION OF 1789. When MAXIMILIEN ROBESPIERRE in May 1794 instituted the Cult of the Supreme Being, Théot declared that he was the precursor of the Divine Word. The subsequent "affair of Catherine Théot" was denounced in the National Assembly and, despite Robespierre's protection, she was interned in the Conciergerie, where she soon died. This affair, which exposed Robespierre and the Cult of the Supreme Being to ridicule, contributed to his downfall.

## Thérèse de l'Enfant-Jésus et de la Sainte-Face (1873–1897)
## (Saint Thérèse of Lisieux)
*saint*

Born Thérèse Martin in Alençon, St. Thérèse of Lisieux, as she would be known, entered the Carmelite convent at Lisieux in 1888, following her two sisters, and died there of tuberculosis after nine years of an apparently ordinary religious life. Her autobiography (*Histoire d'une âme,* 1897), however, which was edited at the request of her superiors, caused a great interest in the "little way" of humility and abandonment to God that brought her to sainthood. Thérèse was canonized in 1925; a pilgrimage takes place on October 1 to her tomb at the basilica of Lisieux.

## Thermidorian Reaction

The Thermidorian Reaction, a stage in the REVOLUTION OF 1789, was a consequence of the fall of MAXIMILIEN ROBESPIERRE and the end of the MONTAGARD Convention (July 1794). It was directed against the ultra-revolutionary forces and representatives of the JACOBIN dictatorship. After the strictures of the governments during the TERROR (Committee of Public Safety), a period of relief and even indifference in France set in, to be followed by the government of the DIRECTORY.

## Thibaud, Jacques (1880–1953)
*violinist*

Born in BORDEAUX, Jacques Thibaud studied under leading musicians at the Paris Conservatory and won his first prize for music in 1896. Soon he was engaged as a concert soloist. His style and technique brought him a brilliant international career and reputation and, in 1905, he joined ALFRED CORTOT and Pablo Casals to form a trio that was celebrated for its exceptional interpretation of classical and romantic music (Mozart, Beethoven). In 1943, with MARGUERITE LONG, Thibaud established the competition that bears their names and that soon became international (1946).

## Thibaudet, Albert (1847–1936)
*literary critic*

Born in Tournas, Albert Thibaudet was greatly influenced as a philosopher by HENRI BERGSON and taught French literature at the University of Geneva, Switzerland, from 1925 until his death. His articles for *La nouvelle Revue française* (1912–14, 1919–34) put together later in *Réflexions sur le roman* (1938), *sur la littérature* (1938 and 1941), and *sur la critique* (1939), as well as his numerous essays, had a considerable influence on critical thought in the period between the two world wars. The effect he brought to the most diverse intellectual and cultural currents was apparent with his first essays, *La Poésie de Stéphane Mallarmé* (1912; revised 1926), in which he proved himself to be an incisive theorist of symbolism, and *Les Heures de l'Acropolis* (1913). Able to apply a Bergson-like interpretation to writers as different as *Flaubert* (1922; revised 1935), *Stendhal* (1931), or *Paul Valéry* (1924), Thibaudet collected his studies in the three volumes that constitute *Trente Ans de vie française, Les Idées de Charles Maurras* (1920), *La Vie de Maurice Barrès* (1921), and *Le Bergsonisme* (1923) before analyzing them more personally in *Les Idées politiques de la France* (1931). A significant demonstration of the extent and eclecticism of his knowledge, his *Histoire de la littérture française de 1789 à nos jours* (1936) was put together, posthumously, from his notes.

## Thierry, Augustin (1795–1856)
*writer, historian*

Born in Blois, Augustin Thierry was the secretary to the count of SAINT-SIMON before collaborating on his liberal journals. Having felt early the vocation of historian (after reading the *Martyrs* of RENÉ DE CHATEAUBRIAND), he dedicated himself in 1821 to writing his *Histoire de la conquête de l'Angleterre par les Normands* (1825), in which he demonstrated his theory of a people's (conquering and conquered) secular struggles explaining their history. The same struggle, this time between the Romans and the Franks, between "the spirit of civil discipline and the violent instincts of the barbarian," appeared in his *Récits des temps mérovingiens* (1840), an evocative tableau of sixth-century Gaul that reached a wide audience with its skilled combination of erudition and imagination. Although he became blind in 1833, he continued his historical writings and published his essay *Histoire de la formation et des progress du tiers état* (1850), in which he presented his ideas on exactitude and precision in research methodology. A master of the lively narrative of events, Thierry through his care in reconstructing local color as well as the psychology of his evocative characters, remains a great literary historian.

## Thiers, Louis-Adolphe (1797–1877)
*statesman, journalist, historian*

Born in MARSEILLE, Louis-Adolphe Thiers was an attorney in Aix-en-Provence before coming to Paris, where he frequented literary circles. There, he contributed to a journal, *La Constitution*, and published, between 1823 and 1827, his *Histoire de la Révolution*. A founder, with ARMAND CARREL and others, of the opposition newspaper *Le National* (January 1830), he became the defender of a constitutional monarchy based on the English model and, on July 26, 1830, took part in the drafting of the journalists' protest to the Ordinances of Saint-Cloud, thus beginning the REVOLUTION OF 1830. Having supported the Orléanists, Thiers served successively as councilor of state, deputy for Aix, secretary-general to the minister of finances in the leftist cabinet, min-

ister of the interior (1832), then of agriculture and trade (1834). Carrying the portfolio of the interior and of foreign affairs (1834–36), he took a strong stand against the legitimist-royalist opposition (the affair of the duchesse of Berry, 1839), as well as against the republican riots of April 1834. After King LOUIS-PHILIPPE refused to intervene in Spanish affairs, as Thiers had wished, he was dismissed (1836) but returned to the government in 1840 as foreign minister. In that role, Thiers pursued an aggressive policy, intervening in North Africa and almost causing a war with Great Britain after signing the Treaty of London (July 1840). Forced to resign again, he began work on his *Histoire du Consulat et de l'Empire* (1845–62) while remaining as a center-left deputy in the opposition and taking part in the fall of the government of FRANÇOIS GUIZOT. On February 23, 1840, Louis-Philippe recalled Thiers to form a new ministry, but it was too late. Thiers sided with the provisional government and, as deputy, consistently voted with the conservative right against the socialists. After having supported the candidacy of Louis-Napoléon Bonaparte (see NAPOLÉON III) for the presidency, he then fought against the creation of the SECOND EMPIRE, was arrested, and, after the coup d'état of December 2, 1851, went into exile in Switzerland. Returning to France in 1852, he remained out of politics until 1863. He became leader of the liberal opposition and roused the National Assembly by his speech on "necessary freedom" (personal, electoral, and press), and through his opposition to the emperor's foreign policy. After the defeat at Sedan and the surrender of Napoléon III, he was sent by JULES FAVRE to various European capitals to plead the French cause (September–October 1870). After this fruitless effort, he was sent to negotiate with Bismarck at Versailles (November 1870). Elected to the National Assembly, which since February 12, 1871, had been meeting at BORDEAUX, Thiers was named chief executive (February 17) and formed a government of national unity that chose Versailles as its headquarters. The signing of the preliminaries with Bismarck (February 28), by which Thiers obtained a reduction of France's war indemnity and kept Belfort as French territory, and then the Bordeaux Pact (March 10, 1871), which left in suspension the question of national institutions until an administrative reorganization took place, angered Parisians, whose economic, social, and military situation was a catastrophe. Thiers's subsequent attempt to confiscate artillery from Paris caused the Paris COMMUNE uprising. Having made the decision to leave the city (March 25), Thiers signed the Treaty of Frankfurt with Prussia (May 10) and shortly after violently suppressed the Commune ("Bloody Week," May 22–28). As president of the republic, he sought to pay off the French indemnity, reform finances and the military (institution of five years' obligatory service), and secure the total German evacuation of French territory by 1873. Nonetheless, he was defeated in May 1873 by the conservative majority and replaced by marshal EDME MAC-MAHON. Elected deputy, he again served as a leader of the republican opposition. Thiers was elected to the ACADÉMIE FRANÇAISE in 1833.

### Thimonnier, Barthélemy (1793–1857)
*inventor*

Born in L'Arbresle, Rhône, Barthélemy Thimonnier was the inventor of the first practical sewing machine (patented in 1830). It employed a hook-type needle that was moved downward by a foot treadle and returned by a spring, producing a chain stitch. He went to Paris in the hope of popularizing his invention but encountered the opposition of the tailors there, who, when Thimonnier installed 80 of his machines in a clothing factory, wrecked them. He then went to Amplepuis, where he worked as a tailor himself, he perfected his machine then sold the patent in 1848 to a company in Manchester, England.

### Thirty Years' War

The Thirty Years' War was a religious political conflict that began in 1618 and ended in 1648 with the Treaty of Westphalia. Its causes were essentially the antagonism between Protestants and Catholics and the unrest that developed in Europe owing to the ambitions of the house of Austria. The war broke out in Bohemia, following the Defenestration of Prague and is divided into four periods. The first was the Palatine period (1618–24), during the course of which Frederick, the elector of the Palatinate who was elected king of Bohemia, was defeated at White Mountain (1620) and subsequently deprived of his territories. The second

period was the Danish (1624–29), during which King Christian IV of Denmark became the leader of the Lutherans. The third was the Swedish period (1630–35), during which King Gustavus Adolphus of Sweden, the victor at Breitenfeld and at Lech, was killed at Lützen. The fourth, or the French period (1635–48), so called because Cardinal RICHELIEU, after having secretly supported the enemies of the house of Habsburg, intervened directly against Austria by declaring war on Spain. After initial setbacks, the French victories at Rocroi (1643) and at Fribourg and Nordlingen in 1645 (see HENRI DE TURENNE), at the same time as the Swedish taking of Prague, forced Austria to negotiate and subsequently to sign the Peace of Westphalia. The Thirty Years' War left Germany devastated. The beneficiaries of the war were France, Sweden, the United Provinces, and Switzerland, as well as the electorate of Brandenburg, which then began its rise.

### Thom, René (1923–2002)
*mathematician*

Born in Montbéliard, René Thom studied at the École normale superieure and taught at the Universities of Grenoble and STRASBOURG before moving to the Institut des Hautes études scientifiques (1961). Thom contributed to the field of algebraic topology, but he is best recognized as the author of the theory of cobordism (dealing with differentials) and studies on layered spaces and stratified morphisms (*Stabilité structurelle et morphogenèse*, 1973). He is known especially, however, for his catastrophe theory, which emphasizes the discontinuities of phenomena and focuses on the qualitative aspects that determine general form. Thom's theory had been applied to physical, social, and biological problems, as well as to linguistics. In 1958, he received the Field's Medal, the highest award in mathematics and, in 1976, was named to the Academy of Sciences.

### Thomas, Albert (1878–1932)
*political figure*

Born in Champigny-sur-Marne, Albert Thomas was a professor of history and author of a study on German trade unionism (*Le Syndicalisme allemand*, 1903). He worked with JEAN JAURÈS as an editor on

*L'Humanité* (1904) and served as a Socialist deputy (1910). During WORLD WAR I he was undersecretary of state, then minister of armaments (1915–17) and supported a policy of industrial mobilization (tax benefits and high salaries for metallurgical workers). Immediately after the war, he was one of the founders of the International Workers Bureau (BIT), on which he served as president from 1920 to 1932.

## Thomas, Henri  (1912–1993)
*poet, essayist, novelist, translator*

Born in Anglemont, Vosge, Henri Thomas wrote autobiographical novels centered on heroes who are "free of attachments, but who have a past" (*Le Seau à charbon*, 1940; *La Nuit de Londres*, 1956; *Une saison volée*, 1986; *Le Goût de l'éternel*, 1990). *Le Promentoire* (1961, prix Femina) is a reflection on writing. In easygoing short stories (*La Cible*, 1955; *Les Tours de Notre-Dame*, 1979), as well as in his essays, Thomas wrote in the first person, in a simple, clear, almost ascetic, style. For this reason, he is first of all a poet (*Travaux d'aveugle,* 1941), as he continued to be in his best translations (Goethe; Jünger; Kleist; Melville; Pushkin; *Le Convive de Pierre*, 1947; Shakespeare, *Sonnets*, posthumous, 1995).

## Thorez, Maurice  (1900–1964)
*political figure*

Born in Noyelles-Godault, Pas-de-Calais, Maurice Thorez worked for a mining company and became a member of the Section française de l'internationale ouvrière (SFIO). During the schism at the Congress of Tours (1920), he was among the majority who formed the French COMMUNIST PARTY. A member of the French Communist Party's Political Bureau (1925), he became secretary-general of the party in 1930. Elected deputy (1932, 1936), he worked for the alliance with the Socialists in the POPULAR FRONT (July 1934). Mobilized shortly after the signing of the German-Soviet Pact in 1939, he left his regiment and went to the USSR (October 1939–44). Condemned to death in absentia, he was amnestied after the Liberation. Elected deputy in October 1945, he was called by General CHARLES DE GAULLE to be minister of state in charge of public service (November 1945–January 1946) and served as vice president of the cabinet in following gov-

ernments. In May 1947, he left the government with the other Communist ministers who were excluded by PAUL RAMADIER. In 1964, PIERRE WALDECK ROUSSEAU succeeded him as secretary-general of the Parti communiste française. Thorez wrote *Fils du peuple* (1937) and *Une politique grandeur française* (1949).

## Thouret, Jacques-Guillaume  (1746–1794)
*political figure*

Born in Pont-l'Évêque, Jacques-Guillaume Thouret was an attorney for the Parlement of Rouen and a deputy for the Third Estate to the ESTATES GENERAL (1789), where he adopted a moderate stance. President of the Tribunal de cassation during the REVOLUTION OF 1789, he contributed to the institution of jury trials in criminal matters and spoke out strongly against the excesses of the TERROR regime. He was guillotined shortly after the Indulgents. Thouret left *Projet de déclaration des droits de l'homme en société* (1789) and *Projet de l'organisation judicaire* (1790).

## Thuriot de la Rozière, Jacques, chevalier  (1753–1829)
*political figure*

Born in Sézanne, Jacques Thuriot de la Rozière, who was a deputy (1791) to the Legislative Assembly during the REVOLUTION OF 1789, took part in the revolutionary day of August 10, 1792, and then in the creation of the Revolutionary Criminal Tribunal. Reelected to the Convention (1792), he sat with the MONTAGNARDS, but, as president of the Assembly on 9 Thermidor, Year II (July 27, 1794), he opposed MAXIMILIEN ROBESPIERRE, whom he prevented from making a speech. Accused of being involved in the popular uprising of Germinal Year III (April 1795), he went into exile. Returning to France, he presided as judge at the trial of GEORGES CADOUDAL (1804). Thuriot de la Rozière was proscribed as a regicide in 1818.

## Tillon, Charles  (1897–1993)
*political figure*

Born in Rennes, Charles Tillon was the organizer with ANDRÉ MARTY of the mutiny in 1919 of the French fleet in the Black Sea. Amnestied in 1922, he joined the French COMMUNIST PARTY the same year and later became a member of its Central Committee (1931) and a deputy (1936–40). During the Spanish civil war, he served as a volunteer in the International Brigade and, in WORLD WAR II, he was part of the clandestine secretariat of the Communist Party. He took the lead in the organization of the armed resistance forces, the Francs-Tireurs and the French Partisans (1942–44). Minister of air in the cabinet of General CHARLES DE GAULLE (1944), he was excluded from the leadership of the Communist Party in 1952 because of "fractional politics," then from the party itself in 1970.

## Tiraqueau, André (ca. 1480–1558)
*humanist, jurist*

Born in Fontenay-le-Comte, where he was the seneschal and the patron and friend of FRANÇOIS RABELAIS, André Tiraqueau became an adviser to the Parlement of Paris in 1541. Well versed in common and popular law, he is the author of *De legibus connubialibus* (1513) and *De nobilitate et jure primogenitorum* (1549).

## Tirard, Pierre-Emmanuel (1827–1893)
*political figure*

Born in Geneva, Switzerland, Pierre-Emmanuel Tirard was a deputy in the National Assembly in 1871, where he tried to avoid a confrontation between the Versailles government and the Paris COMMUNE. He sat with the republican left in the Chamber of Deputies (1876) and served several times as a minister. Premier (December 1887–March 1888, February 1889–March 1890), he took a position against Boulangism, whose leaders he brought before the High Court of Justice.

See also BOULANGER, GEORGES.

## Tisserand, Eugène (1830–1925)
*agronomist, administrator*

Born in Flavigny-sur-Moselle, Eugène Tisserand reestablished the Institut agronomique and was named its director in 1876. Called to direct agriculture in the cabinet (1879), he helped in the development of scientific research and agricultural education, and is the author of studies on the agriculture and economies of Holstein, Schleswig, and Denmark (*Considérations générales sur l'agriculture*, 1867), and of *Rapport sur l'enseignement agricole en France* (1894). Tisserand was elected to the Academy of Sciences in 1911.

## Tisserant, Eugène, Cardinal (1884–1972)
*prelate*

A noted Vatican figure and scholar, Eugène Tisserant was born in Nancy and specialized in the study of Oriental languages and early Christian literature. He was director of the Vatican library and became a cardinal in 1936. Titular archbishop of Iconium (1937) and dean of the Sacred College (1951), he was prefect of the Congregation for Eastern Churches (1936–59). Bishop of Ostia (1951–66), he was named librarian archivist of the Roman Church (1957). Cardinal Tisserant was elected into the ACADÉMIE FRANÇAISE in 1961.

## Titelouze, Jehan (ca. 1563–1633)
*organist, composer*

Born in Saint Omer, Jehan Titelouze was organ master at the church of Saint-Jean de Rouen (1585), then at the Rouen Cathedral (1588), where he soon earned a reputation as an improvisor. His work, exclusively for the organ, was influenced by the English virginalists and organists and the Franco-Flemish polyphonists. Somewhat austere, but with an admirable perfection in composition, his work marks the transition from the modal structure of the beginning of tonal music. Titelouze's compositions include *Hymnes de l'Église pour toucher sur l'orgue avec les fugues et recherches sur leur plainchant* (1623), the *Magnificat ou cantique de la Vierge pour toucher sur l'orgue suivant les huit tons de l'Église* (1626), and several masses.

## Tocqueville, Charles-Alexis-Clérel de (1805–1859)
*historian, political figure*

Charles-Alexis-Clérel de Tocqueville, who wrote a classic study of the United States, was born in Paris, where he studied law. A magistrate during the

Alexis de Tocqueville *(Library of Congress)*

RESTORATION, he was commissioned by the JULY MONARCHY to travel to the United States to do a study of the American penal system. He expanded on that subject and wrote *De la Démocratie en Amérique* (*Democracy in America*; 1835–40), for which he is famous. Even in the United States, this work has always been considered the most incisive and prophetic analysis of American culture and civilization. A deputy, then foreign minister (1849), Tocqueville left political life after the coup d'état of December 2, 1851, and dedicated himself to historical studies; his work *L'ancien Régime et la Révolution* (1856) was widely received. As in his other writings, Tocqueville, through a penetrating analysis of the principal political and social ideas of his age, emphasized the evolutionary aspects underlying all social changes. He interpreted the French REVOLUTION OF 1789 as the result of gradual changes in the structure of government and in political attitudes toward freedom and equality. The great danger, as he stated, is the loss of freedom in the name of the popular will, and he concluded that the remedies to avoid such a despotism of the majority are at once political (decentralization, freedom of the press, defense of local liberties), social (development of associations), and judicial (independence of judiciary power). This presentation, based on historical facts, uses a methodology that evokes that of MONTESQUIEU, whom Tocqueville approaches in his rigorous logic and his clear and austere style. Tocqueville was elected to the ACADÉMIE FRANÇAISE in 1858.

### Tomasi, Henri (1901–1971)
*composer, orchestra leader*
Born in MARSEILLE, Henri Tomasi was a student of VINCENT D'INDY at the Conservatoire de Paris and, in 1927, won first prize in the prix de Rome. He directed the orchestra of the Opéra de Monte Carlo from 1946 to 1950 and, besides his concertos, symphonic pieces, and an oratorio (*François d'Assise*), also composed ballets (*La Rosière du village; Les Santons; Noces et cendres*) and operas (*Miguel de Mañara; Sampiero Corso; Le Triomphe de Jeanne*) in a lively and colorful style often inspired by themes from Corsican or Provençal folklore.

### Topinard, Paul (1830–1911)
*physician, anthropologist*
Born in L'Isle-Adam, Paul Topinard studied with and was influenced by the work of the anthropologist PAUL BROCA. Topinard was concerned essentially with biological anthropology (studies on pigmentation, on the classification of different types of prognathism, on variations in body size and weight). His main works are *Éléments d'anthropologie générale* (1885) and *L'Homme dans la nature* (1891).

### Topor, Roland (1938–1997)
*artist, writer*
Born in Paris, Roland Topor collaborated on various revues, including *Hari-Kiri*, and in 1961 was a founder of the Panique group that also gives its title to one of his albums of ink drawings (*Panic*, 1965).

The creator of color drawings, seriographs, and text illuminations (*La Vérité sur Max Lampin*, 1968), Topor also wrote novels and short stories (*La Princesse Angine*, 1967; *La Cuisine cannibale*, 1971; *Mémoires d'un vieux con*, 1975). With RENÉ LALOUX, he produced an animated film, *La Planète sauvage* (1973). One can find, in all Topor's works, a black humor that blends the absurd with the cruel, while leaving the appearance of poetry that is reinforced in his drawings through a style that evokes the engravers of the 19th century.

## Tory, Geoffroy (ca. 1480–after 1533)
*typographer, writer, engraver*
Born in Bourges, Geoffroy Tory traveled in Italy and, around 1518 became a bookseller. King FRANCIS I appointed him royal printer in 1530. In his printing, Tory used accents, apostrophes, cedillas, and expanded the use of Roman characters in France. His *Livre d'heures* (1525) is one of the masterpieces of Renaissance decorative printing, and in his *Champfleury* (1529), he presented his ideas on grammar, orthography, writing, and typography.

## Touchet, Marie (1549–1638)
*mistress of King Charles IX*
Born in Orléans, Marie Touchet was the mistress of King CHARLES IX, with whom she had a son, Charles de Valois, duke of Angoulême. After the king's death, she married François de Balzac d'Entragues, governor of Orléans, and was the mother of the marquise CATHERINE HENRIETTE DE BALZAC D'ENTRAGUES, who became the favorite of HENRY IV.

## Toulet, Paul-Jean (1867–1920)
*writer*
Born in Paris, Jean-Paul Toulet had a rare technical virtuosity and a charming imagination and precocity mixed with a sense of modesty in his poetry collection, *Les Contrerimes* (1921), a serious and often bitter and poignant work. Similar to JULES LAFORGUE and PAUL VERLAINE, he was the initiator of a style of poetry that had among its best representatives LÉON-PAUL FARGUE and FRANCIS CARCO. A novelist, Toulet wrote, in the same ironic and tender vain, *Mon Amie Nane* (1905) and *La jeune Fille verte* (1920).

## Toulouse, Louis-Alexandre de Bourbon, count of (1678–1737)
*admiral*
Born at VERSAILLES, Louis-Alexandre de Bourbon, count of Toulouse was the third legitimized son of king LOUIS XIV and Mme de MONTESPAN. He served in the War of the Spanish Succession, fighting the British fleet commanded by Admiral Rooke (1704) at Málaga. The count of Toulouse held a small court at Rambouillet that rivaled that at Sceaux.

## Toulouse-Lautrec, Henri de (1864–1901)
*painter, illustrator, lithographer*
The postimpressionist artist best known for his depictions of late-19th-century bohemian Parisian nightlife, Henri de Toulouse-Lautrec was born in Albi to an old aristocratic family. He studied at the lycée Condorcet and, because of a congenital deficiency and aggravated by two falls from horses (1878, 1879), remained stunted fro the rest of his life. Encouraged by his mother to paint and talented at drawing, he received tutoring in those areas and began to paint equestrian and military scenes (*Artilleur sellant son cheval*, 1879). Beginning in 1882, he studied in Paris with LÉON BONNAT and became friends with ÉMILE BERNARD and VINCENT VAN GOGH (1886). Settling in Montmartre, he assiduously frequented and was fascinated by that district's cabarets (including the Moulin-Rouge), cafés, dance and music halls, and theaters. He illustrated the songs of ARISTIDE BRUANT and, with an initially somber palette, painted realistic female portraits and dance scenes. Under the influence of impressionism, his palette became lighter, but he always put his own emphasis on his figures and remained entirely independent. He learned from ÉDOUARD MANET but above all assimilated the art of EDGAR DEGAS while influenced, too, by Japanese prints, with their bright colors and lines. The development of these aspects is evident in the series of posters that he produced beginning in 1891 (*Le Bal du Moulin-Rouge*), remarkable for their concise lines and liveliness. In his prints (more than 500) and humorous drawings, Toulouse-Lautrec shows his virtuosity and keen and often caustic sense of observation, and demonstrates his use of sharp delineation. His paintings and chalk drawings done on cardboard and enhanced by color (*Femme qui tire*

*son bras,* 1894) evoke, with a rare and expressive intensity, the entertainers, celebrities, and familiar personages of Montmartre (*Au bal du Moulin de la Galette,* 1889; *Jane Avril sortant du Moulin-Rouge,* 1892; *Yvette Guibert,* 1894). He found inspiration, too, in the world of horse racing and domestic themes (*Au salon,* 1894), but also at the courts of justice and in hospitals. Excessive drinking, however, would destroy his sanity and eventually paralyze him. In his work the dominance of the graphic element and the audacious use of color, chosen above all for its expressive value, made Toulouse-Lautrec a much admired favorite of the Fauvists and expressionists. The town of Albi has an important museum dedicated to his works.

## Touraine, Alain (1925– )
*sociologist*

Born in Hermanville-sur-Mer, Calvados, Alain Touraine, at the beginning of his career, established the foundation for an industrial sociology based on

the practice of studying the place of work relationships in the wider social context. He emphasized not social class but social movements (*Production de la socieété,* 1973) and the possibility of social transformation (*Le Retour de l'acteur: essai de sociologie,* 1964). Director of the Centre d'analyse et d'intervention sociologique, he supported the necessary connection between sociological awareness and social action. He also did a number of studies of Latin America (*La Parole et le Sang: politique et société en Amérique latine,* 1988), where he is particularly well known. In *Critique de la modernité,* Touraine questions the validity of reason and the rational.

## Tour de France, Le

The world's most famous and popular cycling race, the Tour de France was organized in 1903 to promote cycling, health, and tourism. The first winner that year was the Frenchman Maurice Garin. The Tour, which takes place each year in July (it was canceled only during the WORLD WAR I), covers

Belgian cyclist Eddy Merckx on his way to winning the final stage of the Tour de France that led to his overall victory for the second consecutive year, 1970 *(Hulton/Archive)*

more than 3,400 kilometers through almost all France's major cities and regions and ends on the Champs-Élysées in Paris. It is conducted in stages with teams and support staff. Winners have come from many different countries, including Belgium (Eddy Merckx), Spain (Miguel Indurain), the United States (Lance Armstrong), Italy, Germany, Switzerland, Luxembourg, Denmark, and the Netherlands, as well as France (Bernard Hinaut, Jacques Anquetil).

## Tournefort, Joseph Pitton de
## (1656–1708)
*botanist, traveler*

Born in Aix-en-Provence, Joseph Pitton de Tournefort was professor of botany at the Royal Gardens (later the Museum of Natural History) and was sent on scientific trips through Europe and Asia Minor. His classification of plants makes him a precursor of Linnaeus (*Éléments de botanique, ou Méthode pour connaître les plantes*, 1694). De Tournefort was elected to the Academy of Sciences in 1691.

## Tourneur, Maurice  (1878–1961)
*cinematographer*

Born in Paris, Maurice Tourneur, a spirited and cultivated former actor and stage director trained in the European avant-garde school of theater, introduced to Hollywood between 1914 and 1926 a number of high-quality productions: *L'Oiseau bleu,* based on Maeterlinck's *The Blue Bird* (1918); *The Last of the Mohicans,* with Clarence Brown (1922); and *The Island of the Lost Ships* (1924). In France, he was known for a number of "films d'atmosphère" such as *Justin de Marseille* (1935) and *La Main du diable* (1943).

## Tournier, Michel  (1924–  )
*writer*

Born in Paris, Michel Tournier in *Le Vent paraclet* (1977), an intellectual autobiography as well as an aesthetic literary essay, relates the stages of his late introduction to literature (age 43). Seeking to teach philosophy, he wanted to find a path between that

study and the novel, by way of the great myths that are always culturally alive. His major novels are at the same time meditations on civilization (*Vendredi ou les Limbes du Pacifique,* 1967) or studies on free will and the power of the imagination (*Le Roi des aulnes,* 1970, prix Goncourt). *Les Météores* (1975) retells the story of twins in mythology while *Gaspard, Melchior et Balthasar* (1980) and *La Goutte d'or* (1985) follow the dream of a classical writer. Tournier has also written stories and short stories (*Coq de bruyère,* 1978; *Le Medianoche amoureux,* 1989) and has demonstrated his love of photography in *Des clefs et des serrures* (1979) and *Journal de voyage au Canada* (1984). Tournier was elected to the Académie Goncourt in 1972.

## Tournon, François de, Cardinal
## (1489–1562)
*prelate, political figure*

Born in Tournon, Ardèche, François de Tournon successfully negotiated the Peace of Madrid (1526) but was diplomatically defeated when he tried to obtain a divorce for Henry VIII of England from the pope. With MONTMORENCY, he defended Provence against the emperor Charles V (1536) and directed French politics until the death of king Francis I (1530). Cardinal (1530) and archbishop of LYON (1551), he founded, in 1536, the Collège de Tournon.

## Trauner, Alexandre  (1906–1993)
*film set designer*

Of Hungarian origin, Alexandre Trauner was born in Budapest and studied with Lazare Meerson, after which he made his debut with *À nous la liberté* and *La Kermesse héroïque.* He came into his own on the eve of WORLD WAR II with MARCEL CARNÉ, who commissioned him to build the famous film set complexes for *Hôtel du Nord* and *Quai des brumes.* The collaboration culminated in the "Boulevard du Crime" set for *Enfants du paradis* and the "métro Barbès" set for *Ports de la nuit,* both done in a realistic stylization. Trauner's career developed as he worked with Orson Wells (*Othello,* 1952), Howard Hawks (*Land of the Pharoahs,* 1955) and Billy Wilder (eight films, one of which, *The Apartment*, 1960, won Trauner an Academy Award). His later outstanding work is evident in such French films as *Subway* (1985) and *Autour de minuit*, with BERTRAND TAVERNIER (1986).

## Treilhard, Jean-Baptiste (1742–1810)
*political figure*

Born in Brive-la-Gaillarde, Jean-Baptiste Treilhard was an attorney for the Parlement of PARIS and, during the REVOLUTION OF 1789, served as a deputy to the Constituent Assembly. He helped in the editing of the CIVIL CONSTITUTION OF THE CLERGY and later (1792), was reelected to the Convention, where he sat with the MONTAGNARDS. He was a member of the Committee of Public Safety (April 1793), plenipotentiary to the Congress of Rastatt (1797–99), a member of the DIRECTORY (1798–99), and then counselor of state after the coup d'état of 18 Brumaire, Year VIII (November 9, 1799). Treilhard helped NAPOLÉON I in editing the Civil Code, and was made a senator, count of the empire, and, in 1809, minister of state.

## Trenet, Charles (1913–2001)
*author, composer, singer*

Born in Narbonne, Charles Trenet is considered a true son of the Catalan region who brought poetry to French song, with his nearly 500 works filled with inspiration, humor, and melodic creativity—all of which accounted for his success. Influenced by MAX JACOB, JEAN COCTEAU, and the surrealists, his poetic universe, full of freedom and imagination, is a celebration of the joy of life ("Je chant," "Y'a d'la joie," "Fleur bleue," "Boum," "La vie qui va," "C'est bon") and the mystery of the appearances of things ("Une noix"). This familiarity with the invisible, often funny ("Mam'zelle Clio"), and sometimes disconcerting ("La Folle Complainte," "Papa pique et maman coud") is connected to the sense of melancholy in the passage of time ("Coin de rue," "Mes jeunes années," "Fidèle," "Que reste-t-il de nos amours?"). Finally, in his most popular work, "La Mer," Trenet celebrated the beauty and mystery of the sea.

## Triolet, Elsa (1896–1970)
*novelist*

Of Russian origin, Elsa Triolet was born in Moscow. The sister-in-law of Vladimir Mayakovsky (for whom she translated a volume, *Vers et Prose*), she was encouraged to write by Maxim Gorky. After a trip to Tahiti, then to Berlin (with her first husband, André Triolet), she met, in Paris (1928), LOUIS ARAGON and became his companion and muse. Since her first work in French, *BONSOIR THÉRÈSE* (1938), Triolet wrote numerous published pieces, "in dialogue" with those of Aragon (*Œuvres romanesques croisées*, 1964). In her novels, she sought to understand man and his issues (*Le premier Accroc coûte deux cents francs*, 1944, a collection of short stories filled with the adventures of the RESISTANCE), as she does in other works with the same quest (*Le Cheval blanc*, 1943). Very much of the 20th century and written in the style of socialist realism, in which the image of the capitalist world seems to justify the revolution, *L'Âge de Nylon* reveals the author's concern with the fascination that the modern mechanized world holds for many (*Roses à crédit*, 1959), and also her confidence and wonder at the progressive developments of science (*Luna-Park*, 1959), but above all her sense of the mysterious nature of the human soul (*L'Âme*, 1963). This mystery of humankind is again the theme in Triolet's *Le Grand Jamais* (1963), a reflection on historical truth, time, love, and death that will be echoed in Aragon's *La Mise à mort* (1965).

## Tristan, Flora (1803–1844)
*political figure, feminist*

Born Flore-Célèstine-Thérèse Tristan-Moscoso in Paris, Flora Tristan, as she is known, the daughter of a Peruvian noble and a Frenchwoman, married an engraver, André Chazal, in 1821. The grandmother of the artist PAUL GAUGUIN, she was one of the founders of French feminism and fought for the right to divorce and to practice free love. Besides her work, *Pérégrinations d'une paria* (1838), Tristan, who was an associate of GEORGE SAND, JEANNE DEROIN, and PIERRE LEROUX, published *Unité ouvrière*, which helped to open the way for an internationalist socialism.

## Tristan l'Hermite  (ca. 1601–1665)
*poet, dramatist, novelist*

Born in the château du Solier, Marche, François l'Hermite, or Tristan l'Hermite, as he is known, recounts his youthful adventures in a spirited autobiographical novel, *Le page disgracié* (1643). He also wrote collections of poetry, including *Les Plaintes d'Acante* (1633), rich in lyricism inspired by nature, and *Les Amours de Tristan* (1638), in which one can find the famous ode "Le Promenoir des deux amants" that was set to music by CLAUDE DEBUSSY. This collection is one of varied inspirations: burlesque pieces, descriptive poetry, but above all amorous sentiments delicately expressed in musical verse. Tristan l'Hermite's dramatic works include notably a comedy, *Le Parasite* (1656), and the tragedy in verse, *Marianne* (1636), a melancholy portrait of passion, which deserves comparison with CORNEILLE's *Cid*. Tristan l'Hermite was elected to the ACADÉMIE FRANCAISE in 1649.

## Tronchet, François-Denis  (1726–1806)
*jurist, political figure*

Born in Paris, François-Denis Tronchet, before the REVOLUTION OF 1789, was involved in judicial reform and, in 1789, was elected as a deputy for the Third Estate to the ESTATES GENERAL. A member of the commission that dealt with reform of criminal jurisprudence, he defended king LOUIS XVI before the Convention (December 1792–January 1793) and succeeded in remaining in hiding during the TERROR. Later, as a member of the Conseil des anciens (1795) and president of the Tribunal de cassation, he was chosen by NAPOLÉON I to be part of the commission involved in the planning of the Civil Code (1800). A senator (1801), he was opposed to the consulate for life.

## Truffaut, François  (1932–1984)
*cinematographer, director, producer*

A leader of the Nouvelle Vague movement in filmmaking (in which the director serves as auteur), François Truffaut was born in Neuilly and, after a troubled youth, began his career as a writer for the influential journal *Cahiers du cinéma*. In large part autobiographical, his work is personal and characterized by sensitivity, restlessness, and compassion. It shows, under the guise of irony, nostalgia for the times of quickly fleeting youth. Throughout his filmmaking career, he wrote or coauthored, as well as directed, all his films, which beautifully combine pathos, comedy, melodrama, and suspense. These include *Les quatre cent Coups* (1959), *Tirez sur le pianiste* (1960), *Jules et Jim* (1962), *Fahrenheit 451* (1966), *Baisers volés* (1968), *L'Enfant sauvage* (1970), *La Nuit américaine* (1973), *La Chambre verte* (1978), *Le Dernier Métro* (1980), and *La Femme d'à coté* (1981). Truffaut was strongly influenced by the French filmmakers JEAN RENOIR and JEAN VIGO, and by the English director Alfred Hitchcock, who is also the subject of his book *Hitchcock/Truffaut* (1983).

## Turenne, Henri de la Tour d'Auvergne, viscount de  (1611–1675)
*marshal of France*

Born in Sedan, Henri de la Tour d'Auvergne, viscount de Turenne was the second son of the duke de BOUILLON and the grandson, on his mother's side, of William I, prince of Orange. He began his military career under Prince Maurice de Nassau and prince Frederick Henry. Joining the French army (1630), he fought in the THIRTY YEARS' WAR in Flanders, on the Rhine, and in Italy (where he distinguished himself by taking Turin from the Spanish in 1640). Returning to Germany, he avenged his defeat at Marienthal in 1645 by his victory at Nördlingen, which he won with CONDÉ, that same year. After being defeated by the Spanish at Rethal (1650), he joined the FRONDE, but then went over to the Crown and defeated Condé at the faubourg Saint-Antoine, in Paris in 1652. He then defeated the Spanish, led by Condé, at the Battles of Arras (1654) and the Dunes, near Dunkerque (1658), for which he was named marshal of France (1660). Marshal Turenne fought in the War of Devolution and, in three months, took Flanders from Spain (1667). He played a determinant role in the war with Holland and, after taking the Palatinate, invaded Alsace, which he reconquered in the most audacious of his campaigns (victory at Turckheim, 1675). Marshal Turenne was killed during the Battle of Sasbach, Baden, fighting against the Imperial forces under the command of General Montecuccoli. A Protestant, he converted to Catholicism in 1668.

## Turgot, Anne-Robert-Jacques (1727–1781) (baron de l'Aulne)
*statesman, economist*

Born in Paris and educated at the SORBONNE, Anne-Robert-Jacques Turgot, baron de l'Aulne was initially destined for an ecclesiastical career. He frequented the milieu of the philosophes, published *Lettres sur la tolérance* (1754), and contributed to the *Encyclopedia*, writing a remarkable article on etymology. After holding several minor government posts, he was appointed intendant of Limousin (1761–74) and, under the influence of the Physiocrats, instituted a number of financial reforms, including the substitution of a monetary tax for the corvée. Shortly after, Turgot edited an outstanding work on political economy, *Réflexions sur la formation et la distribution des richesses* (1776). He became comptroller-general of finances in 1774, and immediately instituted wide reforms dealing with taxation and expenses, encouraging free trade, and promoting the circulation of grain (a Physiocratic idea), as well as of labor (1776), through the suppression of corporations and the guild structure. His reforms earned him the hostility of important political and commercial interests, however, and he was forced to resign (1776). While his theories were influenced by those of the Physiocrats (see FRANÇOIS QUESNAY), Turgot nevertheless went beyond these as he emphasized the importance of industry and trade.

See also LOUIX XV.

## Tyard, Pontus de (1521–1605)
*poet, scholar*

Born in the Château of Bissy, near Mâcon, Pontus de Tyard (or Thiard) was consecrated bishop of Chalon-sur-Saône in 1578. A friend of MAURICE SCÈVE, he was at first a follower of the Lyonnais school, with his collection *Erreurs amoureuses* (1549). Then, introduced to the Pléiade group by PIERRE DE RONSARD, he wrote *Livre des vers lyriques* (1555) before dedicating himself to scientific and philosophic works (*L'Univers ou Discours des parties et de la nature du monde*, 1557; *Ephemerides octavae spherae*, 1562).

## Tzara, Tristan (1896–1963)
*writer*

Of Romanian origin, Tristan Tzara (the pen name of Samy Rosenstock) was born in Moinesti, Romania. Resolutely opposed to all literary and artistic pretension, he identified with poetic revolt and social revolution, and the dadaist movement, which he founded in Zurich in 1916, and which he put forth as a reaction to the violence of war, which he saw as useless and devastating. The movement was widely supported by Europe's young intellectuals. Determined to dismantle all aesthetic, moral, philosophical, and religious values of Western civilization, Tzara and his friends (LOUIS BRETON, PAUL ÉLUARD, Adolf Fraenkel, PHILIPPE SOUPAULT, and others) initially expressed their revolt through a nihilistic critique, founding a revue (*Dada*) and organizing in most of Europe's capitals, and particularly in Paris (*Sept manifestes dada*, 1924), "artistic" and literary soirees that shocked many in their praise of the illogical and the absurd. Their quest for authenticity and absolute freedom and the resurgence of romanticism was centered around Tzara and Breton. Tzara's writings include *La première Aventure céleste de M. Antipyrine* (1916), *L'Anti-tête* (1933), *La deuxième Aventure céleste de M. Antipyrine* (1938), *Midis gagnés* (1939), *Le Cœur à gaz* (a play, conceived 1923, published 1946). After WORLD WAR II, having renounced the most provocative of his ideas and actions, and becoming concerned about humanity's future, Tzara published *Entre-temps* (1946), *De mémoire d'homme* (1951), *Le Fruit permis* (1956), and *La Rose et le Chien* (1957).

# U

## Uderzo, Albert (1927– )
*cartoonist*

Born in Fismes, Marne, Albert Uderzo is the founder, with RENÉ GOSCINNY, of *Pilote* (1959) and, as a cartoonist, is best known for his character *Astérix*. Through a traditional yet truculent style of drawing, Uderzo contributed to the exceptional success of this comic strip series.

## Unified Socialist Party (Parti socialiste unifié)

The Parti socialiste unifié (PSU), was a French political party that was founded in April 1960 and dissolved in November 1989. It was formed from two groups, the Union de la gauche socialiste and the Parti socialiste autonome, and was composed of former members of the Section française de l'internationale ouvrière who refused to accept the agreement between that party and CHARLES DE GAULLE following the EVENTS OF MAY 1958 in ALGERIA. The PSU was joined by some former Communists and by political figures such as PIERRE MENDÈS FRANCE. Led by MICHEL ROCARD from 1967 to 1974, the PSU, which endorsed an independent path to socialism, supported the movement of MAY 1968. After 1974, the PSU worked with the Socialist Party and was part of the government from 1981 to 1984.

## Union des démocrates pour la République (UDR)

The Union des démocrates pour la République (UDR) was the name adopted by the Gaullist party (Union pour la défense de la République) in 1971. The UDR went through some dissension with the coming of GEORGES POMPIDOU to power, but held the majority in the legislative elections of 1973. In December 1976, its secretary-general, JACQUES CHIRAC, transformed the movement into the RASSEMBELMENT POUR LA RÉPUBLIQUE (RPR).

## Union française

The Union française was the name given by the constitution of 1946 to the union formed by France and various countries overseas. France granted citizenship to all inhabitants of the Union française but made a distinction between the citizen of the metropolitan region and others. The overseas countries were divided into four groups: certain colonies (Martinique, Guadeloupe, Guyane, and Réunion) became overseas departments; ALGERIA had a special status; the other colonies became overseas territories; the former mandate areas (Cameroun, Togo) became associated territories; the former protectorates (Vietnam, Laos, Cambodia, Tunisia, Morocco) became, if they wished, associated states. The Union française had as its head the president of the French republic, who was assisted by a High Council and Assembly of the Union française comprised of equal members from France and the overseas countries. The Union française was replaced in 1958 by the COMMUNAUTÉ.

## Union pour la démocratie française (UDF)

The Union pour la démocratie française (UDF) is a political formation, or party, that groups the Parti républicain, the Centre des démocrates sociaux (which became in 1995 the Force démocrate), the Parti radical, the Parti social-démocrate, and the Perspectives and Réalités Clubs (which had become the Parti populaire pour la démocratie française in 1995). It was created in 1978 and led by JEAN

LECANUET (1978–88), VALÉRY GISCARD D'ESTAING (1988–96), then FRANÇOIS LÉOTARD (1996). Formed with the idea of maintaining the gains in the legislative elections of 1978, the UDF, supporting the policies of Giscard d'Estaing as president of the republic, nonetheless lost ground in the 1981 elections. Part of the opposition from 1981 to 1986 and 1988 to 1993, the UDF drew closer to the Rassemblement pour la République (RPR) beginning in 1984. The parties merged briefly (1990–93) to form the Union pour la France (UPF). The second-largest group on the right with 200 deputies in 2003, the UDF is a centrist and liberal party that supports European integration.

**Union pour la France**  See UNION POUR LA DEMOCRATIE FRANÇAISE

## Urbain, Georges  (1872–1938)
*chemist*

Born in Paris, Georges Urbain was a specialist on the family of elements known as rare earth. He was successful in separating the principals between them, identifying lutetium, and demonstrating that the role of luminogen in natural florins is achieved by certain of these elements (europium, samarium, etc). Urbain was named to the Academy of Sciences in 1921.

## Urfé, Honoré d'  (1567–1625)
*writer*

Born in MARSEILLE, Honoré d'Urfé was a politically active individual, as well as a writer, who took part in the LIGUE and various military campaigns (he fell ill and died during the war in the Valteline, in which France and Savoy were allied against Spain). His *Épîtres morales* (1598, 1603) established the discourse on love that one can find in the poem *Sireine* (1604), in the drama *Silvanie ou la morte vive* (1625), and in his great pastoral novel *L'Astrée*, a work much discussed in the literary salons of the period. After the first three sections of this novel (1607, 1610, and 1619) were completed, fourth was added, published in 1627, through the efforts of d'Urfé's secretary, Balthazar Baro, who, in 1628, added to it *La Conclusion et Dernière Partie d'Astrée*. The entire work is a summary of caustic love, but it is also a story of national origins through which the author establishes the moral ideal for the 17th-century classics.

## Utrillo, Maurice  (1883–1955)
*painter*

Born in Paris, Maurice Utrillo was the son of SUZANNE VALADON (who was his only art teacher) and probably an individual, known as Boissy, but was acknowledged by the Catalan critic Miguel Utrillo in 1897. Becoming an alcoholic quite young, Utrillo had to undergo early treatment for detoxification. His mother, to keep him occupied, encouraged him to draw and paint. Committed several times, he soon became known as the classic "troubled artist" (*peintre maudit*) and a legend grew up around him. Admired by other artists and critics alike, he became popular with the public and, in 1928, was awarded the LEGION OF HONOR. Practically self-taught, he began with a realistic and somber style (*Roofs of Montmagny*, 1906–07) but quickly evolved toward a lighter and airier technique that shows the influence of CAMILLE PISSARRO and ALFRED SISLEY. Beginning in 1907, his townscapes of the Parisian suburbs and of Montmartre show personal touches and are part of what is known as his "white period" (1906–16), a time of experimentation in which he worked with a palette knife instead of a brush. The harmony of varied nuances in his paintings confers a poetic, often melancholy character to these urban locales, cafés, churches, town squares, and often snowy and deserted streets. Utrillo also found a source of inspiration in postcards, and he had a tendency to use the most vivid colors, stressing line and minute detail, recalling in his paintings the naive style.

# V

## Vacquerie, Auguste (1819–1895)
*writer*

Born in Villequier, Seine-Maritime, Auguste Vacquerie was a member of a group of romantics and was an admirer of VICTOR HUGO, being the brother of Charles Vacquerie, who was married to Hugo's daughter Léopoldine. A contributor to the *Globe, L'Époque,* and *L'Événement* (which became *L'Avènement du peuple* in 1851), he wrote romantically inspired collections of poetry (*L'Enfer de l'esprit,* 1840; *Les Demi-Teintes,* 1845) and plays (*Tragaldabas,* 1848; *Les Funerailles de l'honneur,* 1861). After the coup d'état of December 2, 1851, he accompanied Hugo for a time in his exile on Jersey. A democrat and a liberal, Vacquerie never ceased to oppose the SECOND EMPIRE, especially through his articles in *Le Rappel.*

## Vadier, Marc-Guillaume (1736–1828)
*political figure*

Born in Pamiers, Marc-Guillaume Vadier was a deputy for the Third Estate to the ESTATES GENERAL in 1789. Reelected, during the REVOLUTION OF 1789, to the Convention (1792), where he sat with the MONTAGNARDS, he was also a member of the Committee of Public Safety and became one of the main opponents of MAXIMILIEN ROBESPIERRE. Condemned, nonetheless, after 9 Thermidor, Year II (July 27, 1794) and following the days of 12 and 13 Germinal, Year III (April 1 and 2, 1795), he succeeded in hiding but was implicated in the Conspiracy of the Equals of FRANCOIS-NOËL BABEUF (1796). A deputy during the HUNDRED DAYS, Vadier was proscribed as a regicide in 1816.

## Vadim, Roger (1928–2000)
*film director*

Born Roger Vadim Plemianikov in Paris, Roger Vadim, as he is known, worked briefly as a stage actor in the 1940s before beginning his cinematic career as a film assistant to MARC ALLÉGRET on *Juliette* (1953). He directed and cowrote the successful *Et Dieu créa la femme* (196), starring BRIGITTE BARDOT followed by *Les Liaisons dangereuses* (1959), with JEANNE MOREAU. Vadim also directed *Vice et virtu* (1962), featuring CATHERINE DENEUVE, and *Barbarella* (1968), starring Jane Fonda.

## Vailland, Roger (1907–1965)
*writer*

Born in Acy-en-Multien, Oise, Roger Vailland, with others, was a founder of the revue *Le grand Jeu* (1928), in which they launched a revolt similar to that of surrealism. Vailland began as a journalist and later served in the RESISTANCE (1942) while beginning his career as a writer (*Drôle de jeu,* 1945) and also entered politics as a member of the French COMMUNIST PARTY (1952). Writings from this period include *Bon pied, bon œil* (1950), *Beau masque* (1954), and *325,000 francs* (1955). In publishing *Esquisses pour un portrait du vrai libertin* (1946), *Le Mauvais Coups* (1948), and *Laclos par lui-même* (1953), Vailland showed his attachment to one of his major themes, libertinage, and his rejection of moral and religious constraints in a quest for absolute freedom. This attempt to reconcile individual revolt and revolutionary action brought him disillusionment after the publication of the Soviet leader Nikita Khrushchev's report on Stalinism in 1956. Thereafter, Vailland distanced himself from the world, spending his time in travel or often in bitter meditation on the futility of commitment. In this last period, he produced *Éloge du cardinal de Bernis* (1956), *La Loi* (prix Goncourt, 1957), *La Fête* (1960), and *La Truite* (1964). The publication of *Écrits intimes* (1968) brought to light a new side to his personality, especially through the protagonists and their lucidity and strength of character, often evoking those of PIERRE LACLOS and STENDHAL.

## Vaillant, Jean-Baptiste-Philibert (1790–1872)

*marshal of France*

Born in Dijon, Jean-Baptiste-Philibert Vaillant, after graduating from the École polytechnique, during the period of the FIRST EMPIRE took part in the Russian campaign and the battle of Waterloo. Later, after serving with distinction at the siege of Algiers (July 1830), he helped develop the plans for the fortification of Paris. Minister of war (1854), he was made a marshal by NAPOLÉON III and became minister of the emperor's household (1860–70). After the surrender at Sedan (September 1870) and the fall of the SECOND EMPIRE, he immigrated to Spain (September 1870–1871).

## Vaillant, Édouard (1840–1915)

*socialist*

Born in Vierzon, Édouard Vaillant was a member of the First International and of the Paris COMMUNE, after whose fall he was forced to seek refuge in Great Britain (1871–80). One of the directors of the Second International, he moved from Blanquism to Marxism, then to reformist socialism. An associate of JEAN JAURÈS, Vaillant, at the beginning of WORLD WAR I, gave his support to the Union sacrée.

## Vaillant-Couturier, Paul (1892–1937)

*political figure, journalist*

Born in Paris, Paul Vaillant-Couturier served as a member of the Central Committee of the French COMMUNIST PARTY (1921), a deputy (1919–28, 1936), and editor in chief of *L'Humanité* (1928). He was one of the founders of the Association des écrivains et artistes révolutionnaires, and directed that organization's revue, *Commune* (1933). Vaillant-Couturier published *Lettres à mes amis* (1920), *Le Bal des aveugles* (1927), and *Défendons l'URSS* (1929).

## Vaïsse, Claude-Marius (1799–1864)

*political figure, administrator*

Born in MARSEILLE, Claude-Marius Vaïsse, after participating in the liberal movement and the REVOLUTION OF 1830, began his administrative career under the JULY MONARCHY. Rallying to Bonapartism after the REVOLUTION OF 1848, he served as minister of the interior (January–July 1851), then, as a deputy in the Legislative Assembly. He was a supporter of the coup d'état of December 2, 1851. Named prefect of the Rhône (1854–63), he undertook important renewal works in the city of LYON.

## Valadon, Suzanne (1867–1938)

*painter*

Born in Bessines-sur-Gartempe, Haute-Vienne, Marie-Clémentine Valadon, who would be known as Maria, and then Suzanne Valadon, was the daughter of a mason and a laundress and came to Paris as a youth with her mother. She had to give up a career as an acrobat after a fall and became an artist's model. At age 18 she had a child (MAURICE UTRILLO) who, a few years later, was recognized by the critic Miguel Utrillo. She posed for a number of outstanding painters, including PUVIS DE CHAVANNES, AUGUSTE RENOIR, HENRI DE TOULOUSE-LAUTREC, and EDGAR DEGAS. The latter, after seeing her drawings, encouraged her to continue, and, around 1908, she began to paint, producing still lifes, landscapes, and portraits and female nudes. Her portraits show the influence of PAUL GAUGUIN, while her realistic portrayals of life in the Montmartre district of Paris draw on hers and her mother's working-class life, with often a sense of despair or loneliness, even in her drawings and paintings of children. The decorative aspects of her work recall HENRI MATISSE (*Nu à la couverture rayée*, 1922; *La Chambre bleue*, 1923).

Valadon's works clearly demonstrate a deep sense of personal vision (*Portrait d'Érik Satie*), and she regularly exhibited in the Parisian salons and galleries and later with the group Femmes Artistes Modernes.

## Valette, Aline (1850–1899)
*socialist*

Born in Paris, Aline Valette was a schoolteacher and served as secretary to the newly formed Teacher's Union in 1878. Widowed, she became a writer and published a successful home-management book, *La Journée de la petite ménagerè* (1883). She was one of the first voluntary labor inspectors in Paris during the 1880s, and became a Socialist, founding with EUGÉNIE PONTONIE-PIERRE the Fédération française des sociétés feministes (1892). She was also a member of the national council of the Parti ouvrier français (1893). Valette struggled for both the civil and the political rights of women, while continuing in her conviction that women's ultimate role was as a homemaker.

## Valentin de Boulogne (1594–1632)
*painter*

Born in Coulommiers, Valentin de Boulogne (or de Boulongne) traveled to Rome around 1620 and came under the influence of Manfredi and especially Caravaggio, as well as later the works of SIMON VOUET and Guido Reni. Valentin de Boulogne painted allegorical and religious subjects (*Le Martyre des saints Procés et saint Martinien*, 1630) and also popular subjects—tavern scenes with musicians and entertainers, and soldiers in which the figures are presented in various poses. Becoming more deeply involved in his art, Valentin de Boulogne is recognized as among the most faithful to the style of Caravaggio, while at the same time giving to his own work a personal lyrical and melancholy emphasis (*Concert dans un intérieur*).

## Valéry, Paul (1871–1945)
*writer*

One of the most important modern philosophical writers, in both prose and verse, Paul Valéry was

Paul Valéry  *(Library of Congress)*

born in Sète. Early in his life, he planned to enter the Naval Academy but soon abandoned that goal to pursue a career in letters and painting. A lover of poetry, he studied the sciences and music in Paris. When he was about 21, he met PIERRE LOUŸS, who became his friend, corresponded with STÉFANE MALLARMÉ, whom he admired, then met ANDRÉ GIDE. The conflict between a narcissistic intellectual life and the detachment needed to measure his potentialities provoked a crisis. In 1892, he abandoned his earlier artistic passions and, by 1894, began to write on new themes. He also began to keep a daily journal that he continued throughout his life. At this time, too, he wrote on the great intellectual influences of his life: Mallarmé, Edgar Allan Poe, Leonardo da Vinci (*Introduction à la méthode de Léonard de Vinci*, 1895, and later *Europlinos ou l'Architecte*, 1921). In 1900, he published the first of his journals, *Cahiers*, which eventually would total 261. A perfectionist, in 1922 he began an edition of a volume of his works (*La jeune Parque*, 1917; *Le*

*Cimitière marin*, 1920; *L'Album de vers anciens*, 1920; *L'+me et la Danse*, 1921; and *Charmes*, 1922). Achieving fame with *La Jeune Parque*, he was much sought after in intellectual circles, was invited abroad (he was received by Gabriele D'Annunzio and Ranier Maria Rilke) and, in 1925, was elected the ACADÉMIE FRANÇAISE. Named professor of poetry at the COLLÈGE DE FRANCE in 1937, he published *La Cantate du Narcisse* (1938) and edited *Variété IV*. During the German Occupation, he finished *Mon Faust* (1940), and began to publish *Mauvaises pensées et autres*. When he died in 1945, he was given a state funeral.

## Vallès, Jules (1832–1885)

*writer, journalist*

Born in Puy, Jules Vallès came to Paris to dedicate himself to a career in letter, but soon took up other diverse professions. As an uncompromising polemicist, he collected his various articles (written between 1861 and 1865) in *Les Réfractaires* (1865) and *La Rue* (1866), in which he demonstrated his enthusiasm for the proletarian cause. In 1871, he became a member of the Paris COMMUNE, which he defended in his journal *Cri du peuple*. Condemned to death at the end of the insurrection, he sought refuge in London and did not return to Paris until 1880. His romantic trilogy, *Jacques Vingtras* (1879–86), which includes *L'Enfant* (1979), *Le Bachelier* (1881), and *L'Insurge* (posthumous, 1886), evokes the author's youth and struggles, as well as the tragedy of the Commune. Outraged by the injustices of bourgeois society (and the ideas that it put forth), Vallès never claimed to be objective but wrote in a lively style, full of unexpected images and in a sometimes disconcerting syntax. He also resorted to an often shocking realism enlivened by his revolutionary lyricism and rhetoric.

## Vallotton, Félix (1865–1925)

*painter*

Of Swiss origin, Félix Vallotton was born in Lausanne and studied at the Julian Academy. He became a friend of the NABIS painters (ÉDOUARD VUILLARD and others), who practiced a colorful and symbolic postimpressionist style and, while exhibit-

ing with them, continued to remain independent. He became a master of xylography, producing illustrations for *La Gazette de Lausanne, La Revue blanche, Rire*, and *Courrier français*. In his series of large works (*C'est la guerre, Intimités, Crimes et châtiments*), he demonstrated a caustic spirit. Having assimilated the Japanese style, he produced works with audacious foreshortenings, elliptical graphics, and a play of white against large dark, uniform masses. His paintings depict interior scenes graphically and with an occasional angular composition and elaborate colors. In his maturity, he painted female nudes with taut forms, revealing his acerbic viewpoint. Vallotton also wrote several pessimistic works, including a novel, *La Vie meurtrière*, that was published posthumously.

## Valois, Georges (1878–1945)

*political figure*

Born in Paris, Alfred-Georges Gressent, or Georges Valois as he is known, was self-educated and developed his ideas by reading PIERRE-JOSEPH PROUDHON, GEORGES SOREL, and Friedrich Nietzsche. Drawn for a time to revolutionary syndicalism, he followed the ACTION FRANÇAISE then founded the Faisceau movement (1925), modeled on Italian fascism, from which he separated in 1935. A member of the RESISTANCE, he died in deportation. Valois's principal writings are *L'Économie nouvelle, La Monarchie et la Classe ouvrière, La Réforme économique et sociale*, and *La Fin du bolchevisme*.

## Van der Meersch, Maxence (1907–1951)

*writer*

Born in Roubaix, Maxence Van der Meersch wrote *La Maison dans la dune*, which was an immediate success (1932). This story of a smuggler was followed in 1933 by *Quand les Sirèens se taisent*, an account of a textile strike in Roubaix. In 1936, Van der Meersch won the prix Goncourt for his *Empreinte du dieu* and in 1943 the grand prix of the ACADÉMIE FRANÇAISE for *Corps et Âmes*. Among the other works of this Catholic writer are *Pêcheur d'hommes* (1940), *Vie du curé d'Ars* (1942), and *La petite Sainte Thérèse* (1947).

## Van Dongen, Kees (1877–1968)

*painter*

Of Dutch origin, Cornelius Theodorus Marie Van Dongen, or Kees Van Dongen as he is known, was born in Delfthaven. His talent was evident early, as he painted at first in a progressively realistic style, marked by an impressionist influence. Van Dongen became a sketch artist and reporter for a Dutch newspaper, then in 1897 settled in Paris, where he worked at various jobs while submitting his satirical sketches to different journals. He became interested for a while in neoimpressionist theories and soon began experimenting with form and strong colors. Settling at Bateau-Lavoir in 1905, he became familiar with the group of artists that critics would call "fauvists" and exhibited with them at the Salon d'automne of 1905. Some of his works were also shown in Germany by Die Brücke group, thus contributing to the connection between the fauvists and the German expressionists. His landscapes, scenes of society and of music halls, and female figures with heavily made-up faces are distinguished by their audacious treatment, stylization of form, with the accentuation of certain more expressive features and an often arbitrary richness of color. After causing a scandal at the Salon with a nude that was judged as indecent Van Dongen became one of the favorite portraitists of the aristocratic and theatrical worlds.

## Van Gogh, Vincent Willem (1853–1890)

*painter*

Vincent Willem Van Gogh, one of the most famous of the impressionists and a precursor of fauvism and expressionism, was born in Groot-Zundert, Brabant, Holland. The son of a Calvinist pastor, he worked at the Goupil art gallery in The Hague (1869), in London (1873–74), then in Paris (1874–75). Of a tormented, mystical nature, he undertook an evangelizing mission among the miners of Borinage that ended in disappointment. In 1880, he studied drawing at Antwerp and did sketches of miners that were inspired by JEAN-FRANÇOIS MILLET, whom he admired. In 1882, he went to work with his cousin, the painter Mauve. He produced several drawings and watercolors and was introduced to the use of oils. Back at his fam-

ily home in Nuenen (December 1883–85), he worked furiously, producing landscapes, still lifes, and peasant scenes with a somber realism that already revealed his restless, uneasy spirit (*Les Mangeurs de pommes de terre,* 1885). During a stay at Antwerp, Belgium (1885–86), he became familiar with Rubens and discovered Japanese prints that inspired him to modify his view of color. After several works done in the same realistic vein (*Les Souliers avec lacets,* 1886), he joined his brother Theo in Paris, who never failed to encourage him and give him material support (their correspondence has been published: *Lettres à Théo*). He studied at the Cormon studio where he met HENRI DE TOULOUSE-LAUTREC and ÉMILE BERNARD, who introduced him to PAUL GAUGUIN. Influenced above all by the impressionist canvases, he also adopted clear colors and fragmented brushstrokes (*Tournesols,* summer 1887). During this very personal period (self-portraits, *Le Père Tanguy,* 1888), he settled at Arles (February 1888) and, in a time of intense creativity, painted many landscapes (*Vue d'Arles aux iris, La Plaine de Crau, Les Barques sur la plage,* the series of "Sunflowers"), and portraits, (*L'Arlésienne, Mme Ginoux*). Abandoning traditional representation and illusionist perspective, he simplified forms and used a bright colorization that expressed his strong sentiments and emotions. He wanted to create a community of artists and persuaded Gauguin to join him (October 1888). But following a violent argument, the latter left and Van Gogh, in a state of despair, cut off his left ear (*Autoportrait à l'oreille coupée, Portrait du docteur Rey, Berceuse*). Suffering from hallucinations, he was institutionalized at Arles, then at Saint-Rémy-de-Provence (1889–90). In between his crises he continued to work (*Les Blés jaunes au cyprès, La Nuit étoilée, Champ d'oliviers*), modulating volume with a clearly strong brushstroke and producing startling forms with intense colors. Returning to Paris in May 1890, he finally settled at Auvers-sur-Oise, looked after by Doctor Paul GACHET, the friend of CAMILLE PISSARRO and Gauguin. In certain works his style intensifies (*L'Église d'Auvers,* 1890), but at the same time his work seems to loose its tormented character and expresses a dramatic lyricism (*Le Champ de blé aux corbeaux*). On July 27, 1890, he shot himself and died the next day, mostly unknown.

## Van Loo, Carle  (1705–1765)
*painter*

Born in Paris, Charles-André Van Loo, or Carle Van Loo, as he is known, was the student of his brother JEAN-BAPTISTE VAN LOO, with whom he worked at the château of Fontainebleau. After winning the prix de Rome (1723), he left for Italy and worked in Turin at the palace of the duke of Savoy. Returning to Paris in in 1734, he was named painter to King LOUIS XV in 1762; his renown was comparable to that of FRANÇOIS BOUCHER, and he was considered for a time the master of the French school. Remaining attached to the tradition of the "grande manière" (historical, biblical, and mythological subjects), he painted oblique compositions, with declamatory effects, particularly in his religious works (*L'Adoration des bergers* for the church of Saint-Sulpice, Paris); he imitated Rubens and Van Dyck but often omitted their luminosity. Carle Van Loo is less conventional in his mythological scenes, gallant paintings, genres, "turqueries," and portraits (*Louis XV*).

## Van Loo, Jean-Baptiste  (1684–1745)
*painter*

Jean-Baptiste Loo was born in Aix-en-Provence. He studied art there and in Toulon, as well as being taught by his father. He worked in Genoa, Rome, and Turin, in Italy, and beginning in 1719 in Paris, becoming a sought-after portrait painter (*Portrait de Louis XV à cheval*, 1723). He was commissioned to restore the Primatrice Gallery at Fontainebleau, where he worked with his brother CARLE VAN LOO. From 1737 to 1741, he worked in London (*Portrait of Walpole.*) A painter of religious and mythological scenes (*Triomphe de la Galatée*), Jean-Baptiste Loo painted elegant, often mannered, portraits.

## Varda, Agnès  (1928–  )
*film producer, director*

Born in Ixelles, Belgium, Agnès Varda, who was at first a photographer, formed a production company to produce her first film, *La Pointe courte* (1956), which was a precursor to the Nouvelle Vague (New Wave) film genre. She then produced three short subject films: *Ô saisons, ô châteaux* (1957); *Opéra Mouffe*, on the rue Mouffetard); and *Du côte de la côte* (1958). Her second full-length film, *Cléo de cinq à sept* (1961), brought her to public attention. This film, with its tragic scenario, is presented in an intimate, delicate, and warm style, with great freedom in its direction. Following this *Cléo* were *Le Bonheur* (1964), *Daguerréotypes* (documentary, 1975), *L'une chante, l'autre pas* (1977), *Sans toit ni loi* (1985) and, in a poignant homage to her late companion, JACQUES DEMY, *Jacquot de Nantes* (1991).

## Varese, Edgar  (1883–1965)
*composer*

Born in Paris, Edgar Varese was a student of VINCENT D'INDY at the Schola Cantorum and studied also at the Paris Conservatory and in Berlin. He received the advice and encouragement of the Austrian composers Gustav Mahler and Richard Strauss. He was mobilized and later discharged from the French army during WORLD WAR I and then settled in New York City (1916). Orchestra leader and founder of the New Symphonic Orchestra and the International Guild of Composers, he soon established himself as one of the most original personalities in contemporary music (*Amériques*, for full orchestra, 1920–21; *Hyperprism*, for small orchestra and percussion, 1923; *Octandre*, for six wind instruments and counterbase, 1923; *Intégrales*, for small orchestra and percussion, 1925; *Arcana*, for full orchestra, 1927; *Ionisation*, for 13 percussionists, 1931; *Ecuatorial*, for choir, trumpets, trombones, piano, and percussion, 1934). Varese, through his compositions, prefigured electro-acoustic music, especially after tape-recording (*Tape Music*) allowed him to experiment in "concrete" music and electronic amplification (*Déserts*, 1954; *Poème électronique*, 1958).

## Varin, Jean  (1604–1672)
*sculptor, medallion maker*

Of Walloon origin, Jean Varin (or Warin) was born in Liège (Belgium) and settled in Paris, where he obtained the position of general engraver of the mint. He sculpted busts of RICHELIEU, LOUIS XIII, and the young LOUIS XIV, as well as that same king as a Roman emperor. Varin became one of the most famous medallion makers of his time, producing effigies with an incisiveness and technical mastery (*Louis XIII, Christine de Suède, Richelieu, Colbert*).

## Varlin, Eugène (1839–1871)
*revolutionary*

Born in Claye-Souilly, Eugène Varlin worked as a bookbinder and served as secretary-general of the French section of the International Association of Workers (First International, 1865). He sought to organize the workers' struggle and supported the strikes at Creusot and Roubaix (1870). A member of the Central Committee of the National Guard, where he represented the Workers Association, he was elected to the Paris COMMUNE as a representative for the sixth, 12th, and 18th arrondissements, and was named to the finance, then the supplies commissions. Varlin was shot by the troops sent from Versailles on May 28, 1871.

## Vasarely, Victor (1908–1997)
*painter*

Of Hungarian origin, Victor Vasarely, the creator of Op Art and one of its most successful proponents, was born in Pecs, Hungary, where he studied the principles of the Viennese Bauhaus school. He settled in Paris in 1930 and, while working there as a graphic artist, developed his theories on axonometric perspective and linear derivations. His series of geometric abstractions (*Arlequins, Échiquiers, Zèbres, Improvisations sur calques*) were the result of his research. After 1937, he organized inspired forms based on the patterns of the tiling views of the Denfert-Rochereau metro station (his "Denfert period") and began to study light and the illusion of movement created by optical processes which he eventually termed "cinétisme" (1955). He also developed art based on the repetition of a cell (a square containing a figure or a geometric plane), and later introduced vibrant colors that further enhanced these optical illusions. In their fully developed form, his geometric abstractions produce mesmerizing, almost hallucinatory effects through the manipulation of perspective and foreshortening. His art, based on both mathematical precision and joyful expression, seeks to reconcile modern technology with art. He redefined the latter through his efforts to ameliorate the human environment. Vasarely, who had an enormous influence on younger op artists, established the Foundation Vasarely near Aix-en-Provence. He also collaborated with other artists on such projects as the French Pavillion at Expo '67 in Montréal.

## Vauban, Sébastien Le Prestre de (1633–1707)
*marshal of France*

A military engineer who revolutionized fortification and siege strategies during the reign of LOUIS XIV, Sébastien Le Prestre de Vauban was born in Foucheret (today Saint-Léger-Vauban), Burgundy. As commissioner of fortifications (1678), he made great efforts to encircle the kingdom with fortresses, in particular along the Escaut, the Meuse, and the Rhine Rivers. He also constructed large ports, canals, and the aqueduct at Maintenon. Vauban was interested in offensive techniques, too, and his methods allowed him to win a number of sieges; he was particularly successful during the War of the League of Augsburg in taking Mons, Namur, and Steinkerque. Vauban not only wrote works on the art of warfare but also on politics, yet his freethinking attitude brought about his disgrace (his *Project d'une dime royale* was banned in 1703).

## Vaublanc, Vincent-Marie-Vienot, count de (1756–1845)
*political figure*

Born in Saint-Domingue, Vincent-Marie-Vienot, count de Vaublanc, after leaving the army during the REVOLUTION OF 1789, was elected to the Legislative Assembly, where he took a royalist position. Condemned to death for contempt for having taken part in the uprising of 13 Vendémiaire, Year IV (October 5, 1795), and exiled after the coup d'état of 18 Fructidor, Year V (September 4, 1797), he supported the First Empire, then the Bourbons, becoming minister of the interior (1815). His extremist policies, however, forced him to resign in 1816.

## Vaucanson, Jacques de (1709–1782)
*mechanical engineer*

Born in Grenoble, Jacques de Vaucanson conceived the idea for a number of machines, including a water pump, the first entirely automatic loom (which was later perfected by JOSEPH JACQUARD), and an industrial lathe with a sliding tool holder, the basis for the modern machine tool. He also invented his famous automatons, the "Flute Player" (1737), the "Drummer," and the "Duck" (1738). He foresaw the development of moving automatons to be used in medicine. His collection of machines became, in 1794, the basis for the collection at the Conservatoire national des arts et métiers in Paris. Jacques de Vaucanson was named to the Academy of Sciences in 1746.

## Vaudreuil, Pierre de Rigaud de Cavagnal, marquis de (1698–1778)
*administrator*

Born in Quebec, Pierre de Rigaud de Cavagnal, marquis de Vaudreuil, was the son of the governor-general of CANADA. Later the governor himself of Trois-Rivières, then of Louisiana (1743–55), he then became the administrator of Canada (1755–60). Vaudreuil had a bad relationship with the French military commander there, however, so much so that it compromised French control of the region. During the SEVEN YEARS' WAR, Vaudreuil ordered the surrender of Montreal (1760) and was then imprisoned and tried in France, but he was acquitted.

## Vaugelas, Claude Favre, seigneur de (1585–1650)
*grammarian and linguist*

Born in Meximieux, in Bresse, Claude Favre, seigneur de Vaugelas, directed the activities of the ACADÉMIE FRANÇAISE and published, in 1647, the *Remarques sur la langue française,* not so much to regulate but to guide the development of the French language. Reacting against the "Latinists," he built his theories of language on usage, based on the "good taste" of the royal court and the city. Vaugelas was elected to the Académie française in 1634.

## Vauquelin, Nicolas-Louis (1763–1829)
*chemist*

The discoverer of beryllium and chromium (which he named for the varied colors—from Greek, "chrome"—of its components), Nicolas Louis Vauquelin was born in Saint-André d'Hebertot, near Pont-l'Évêque. With ANTOINE DE FOURCROY, he analyzed various chemical products of animal or vegetable origin and identified the chemical composition of aragonite and calcite (1804). He also discovered the almost constant presence of chromium in meteorites. Vauquelin, who was named to the Academy of Sciences in 1795 was the teacher of the chemist ANSELME PAYEN.

## Vauquelin de la Fresnaye, Jean (ca. 1536–1606)
*poet*

Born in Fresnaye-au-Sauvage, near Falaise, Jean Vauquelin de la Fresnaye is the author of *Art poétique français* in verse (1574; published with *Les diverse Poéies* in 1605), in which he is clearly the student of PIERRE DE RONSARD, while still showing an appreciation for modern poetry. A friend of JEAN DE BAÏF and the humanists, Vauquelin found inspiration in Horace for his bucolic poems, the *Foresteries* (1555).

## Vauvenargues, Luc de Clapiers, marquis de (1715–1747)
*moralist*

Born in Aix-en-Provence, Luc de Clapiers, marquis de Vauvenargues was forced to abandon his plans for a military career because of illness and so turned to letters. He wrote *Caractères,* inspired by JEAN DE LA BRUYÈRE, in which he criticized the follies of the era. He also published *Introduction à la connaissance de l'esprit humain,* and *Maximes et Réflexions* (1746), in which he expressed his optimistic confidence in humankind. Believing that the essential human instinct is to do good, he questioned the belief in the supernatural and stated that human nature can be improved in and of itself. Exalting also the goodness of nature, Vauvenargues put his faith in reason and the belief that altruistic sentiments could be put to the service of society. In this moral doctrine, he challenged the theses of BLAISE PASCAL and FRANÇOIS DE LA ROCHEFOUCAULD.

## Védrines, Jules (1881–1919)
*aviator*

An important early French aviator, Jules Védrines, who was born in Saint-Denis, in 1911 won the Paris-Madrid air race. During WORLD WAR I, he took part in a number of dangerous missions in his Bleriot airplane, named *La Vache*. In 1919, Védrines (who was the first to fly an airplane at more than 160 kilometers/hr (100 miles per hour) landed on the roof of the Galeries Lafayette in Paris. Shortly after, he was killed during the Paris-Rome run.

## Veil, Simone (1927–  )
*political figure*

Born Simone Jacob in Nice, Simone Veil and her family were deported to the German death camps of Auschwitz and Bergen-Belsen during WORLD WAR II. A magistrate after the war, she was the first woman to serve as secretary-general of the Supreme Magisterial Council (1970). Minister of health (1974–79), she helped in the passage of the law that allowed voluntary abortions (1975). A centrist who supported the political and economic union of Europe, she served as a deputy to the EUROPEAN UNION (1979) and was president of the European Parliament from 1979 to 1982, where she later led the liberal faction (1984–89). Veil served as minister of state, of social affairs, and of health and urban affairs in the ÉDOUARD BALLADUR government (1993–95).

## Vendée, War of the

The War of the Vendée was a counterrevolutionary insurrection during the REVOLUTION OF 1789 that developed in the Vendée region of western France, in Maine-et-Loire and within the confines of Poitou and Anjou. Precipitated by the February 24, 1793, decree of the Convention calling for the military conscription of 300,000 men and more profoundly by economic difficulties and Revolutionary religious policies (CIVIL CONSTITUTION OF THE CLERGY), it was born among the peasant populations and led by nobles (LOUIS DE LA ROQUEJACQUELEIN and FRANÇOIS-ATHANASE CHARETTE DE LA CONTRIE.), numerous refractory priests, and others. The large army of Vendée insurgents (or "Whites") included 40,000 men and, in 1793, had several victories before being stopped at Nantes (June 1793). To crush the revolt, the Committee of Public Safety adopted the stronger measures and sent more republican troops, who formed the Army of the West, under the command of General JEAN-BAPTISTE KLÉBER, into the region. The massacre of republicans by the insurgents led to the establishment of the TERROR. Collective drowning of the insurgents was ordered by the government, and the Revolutionary commanders were ordered to devastate the Vendée. The revolt continued, however, with an army of émigrés landing at Quiberon in June 1795, but they were defeated. In 1815, the Vendée rose up again but this uprising, too, was suppressed.

## Vendôme, César de Bourbon, duke de (1594–1665)
*nobility*

Born in Coucy-le-Château, César de Bourbon, duke de Vendôme was the natural son of King HENRY IV and Gabrielle d'ESTRÉES. He joined in the conspiracies of the nobility during the reign of LOUIS XIII and was implicated in the Chalais plot against Cardinal RICHELIEU. Remaining loyal during the FRONDE, he became tutor to the duke of Burgundy (1651). His youngest son was FRANÇOIS DE BOURBON-VENDÔME, DUKE DE BEAUFORT.

## Vendôme et Penthièvre, Louis-Joseph, duke de (1654–1712)
*nobility and military figure*

Born in Paris, Louis-Joseph, duke de Vendôme et Penthièvre, the grandson of FRANÇOIS DUKE DE BEAUFORT, was one of the most outstanding French commanders in the War (1701–14) of the Spanish Succession. He campaign in Italy and in Flanders (the Battle of Oudenaarde, 1708), and defeated King Philip V of Spain at Madrid (Battle of Villaviciosa, 1710).

## Ventura, Raymond  (1908–1979)
*composer, orchestra leader*

Born in Paris, Raymond, or Ray Ventura, as he is known, formed an orchestra called les Collégiens in 1930. Mixing pieces of music with comedic sketches, the Collégiens helped to popularize swing in France and gave birth to to a new light and lively style of singing (*Tout va très bien, madame la Marquise; Ça vaut mieux que d'attraper la scarlatine; Qu'est-ce qu'on attend pour être heureaux*). Ray Ventura and his Collégiens also appeared in a number of films.

## Verdun, Battle of

The Battle of Verdun, which began February 1916 and lasted until November of that year, was the greatest of WORLD WAR I. The defense of this French fortress on the Meuse was believed to be vital to France's winning the war. It was, therefore, also believed that it had to be held at all costs. Likewise, the Germans, under the command of General Erich von Falkenhayn and Crown Prince Frederick William, realizing the significance of Verdun, were determined to take it at all costs. The French defense was entrusted to Generals PHILIPPE PÉTAIN, who would later be recognized as the hero of Verdun, and GEORGES NIVELLE. An immense artillery battle, but also one of great individual sacrifice on both sides—the "hell of Verdun"—the largest German offensive of the war, cost the French 360,000 casualties and the Germans 335,000. Verdun was held, but at an enormous price.

## Vergennes, Charles Gravier, count de (1719–1787)
*diplomat*

One of the most capable of King LOUIS XVI's diplomats, Charles Gravier, count de Vergennes was born in Dijon. He first served as ambassador to Turkey (1755–68) then to Sweden (1771–74), where he supported the coup d'état of Gustavus III. Recalled to become foreign minister, he followed ETIENNE DE CHOISEUL's policy of hostility toward Great Britain, which was opposed by TURGOT, who saw in the war the signs of bankruptcy. Having also contributed to the fall of Turgot, Vergennes involved France in the American War of Independence (1778). His initial policy in that conflict was to keep France officially neutral until the appropriate moment, while offering covert aid to the American rebels. In 1782, he sent DUPONT DE NEMOURS to negotiate with Great Britain, and this led to British recognition of American independence the following year. Through his diplomacy, Vergennes also sought to preserve peace in Europe while invoking the Teschen conventions (1779) when Emperor Joseph II of Austria wanted to annex Bavaria. After the Treaty of Versailles (1783), he realized that while France had achieved military success, the war had drained the nation's finances, and he preferred then to work for a rapprochment with Great Britain. In 1786, he signed an advantageous commercial treaty with that nation.

## Vergniaud, Pierre-Victurnien (1753–1793)
*political figure*

Born in Limoges, Pierre-Victurnien Vergniaud served as an adviser to the Parlement of BORDEAUX, then as administrator of the Gironde and, during the REVOLUTION OF 1789, was one of the most remarkable leaders and speakers of the Girondins in the Legislative Assembly. There, he took a position against the refractory clergy and the émigrés. President of the Convention (January 1793), he voted for the death of the king without reprieve. He tried to oppose the first public safety measures proposed by the MONTAGNARDS (creation of the Revolutionary Tribunal, March 1793) and was himself sentenced and condemned with the principal GIRONDIN leaders after the populist riots of May 31–June 2, 1793.

## Verlaine, Paul  (1844–1896)
*poet*

A leader of the symbolist movement, Paul Verlaine was born in Metz and became interested in poetry at an early age. He was involved in the literary movements of the period. His first collection, *Poèmes saturniens* (1866), shows his affinity for the Parnassian movement. His *Fêtes galantes* (1869) evokes a scene from a painting by ANTOINE WATTEAU, and its sensual and affected subjects. Engaged to Mathilde Mauté, Verlaine described his thoughts on impending marriage in *La bonne Chanson* (1870), and expressed his hopes for a simple and tranquil life. His meeting with ARTHUR RIMBAUD (September 1871) ended those plans, and his subsequent life together with Rimbaud in Paris, London, and in Belgium was a long series of altercations and separations. For firing two revolver shots at his companion (1873), Verlaine was imprisoned for two years at Mons. There, he wrote his collection, *Romances sans paroles* (1874), recalling his adventures with Rimbaud. Shortly after his release, he underwent a religious conversion that inspired his mystical poems *Sagesse* (1880) and *Amours* (1888). He also tried unsuccessfully, with a young protégé, to be a farmer and then, for the rest of his life alternated between periods of intoxication and debauchery and ascetic repentance. With the publication of *Poètes maudits* (dedicated to Rimbaud, TRISTAN CORBIÈRE, and STÉPHANIE MALLARMÉ) and *Jadis et Naguère*, a collection of verse, Verlaine emerged as a symbolist poet. An erotic work, *Parallèlement* (1889), was followed by *Liturgies intimes* (1892), and *Épigrammes* (1894). Verlaine, who also wrote autobiographical prose (*Mes Hôpitaux*, 1892; *Mes prisons*, 1893; *Confessions*, 1893), not only exerted an influence on the French poets who followed him, but on various composers as well (GABRIEL FAURÉ, HENRI DUPARC, CLAUDE DEBUSSY, MAURICE RAVEL, and Igor Stravinsky).

## Vernant, Jean-Pierre (1914– )

*historian, Hellenist*

Born in Provins, Jean-Pierre Vernant was a professor at the COLLÈGE DE FRANCE (1975–84). He studied the development of knowledge and the formation of ideas and analyzed the emergence in Greece during the sixth century of positive reason, which he connects in his writings with the evolution of mythic thought and the birth of the city-state. This philosophical and psychological history of thought, based on the structural analysis of myth, emerged, he posits, along with political history. Vernant published *Les Origines de la pensée grecque*, 1962; *Mythe et pensée chez les Grecs*, 1965; *Mythe et tragédie en Grèce ancienne*, 1972.

## Verne, Jules (1828–1905)

*writer*

Regarded as the father of the science fiction genre, Jule Verne was born in Nantes and, while studying law in Paris, decided to pursue a career in letters. Toward the end of 1851, he began to write plays and librettos and also his first short stories (*Les Premiers Navires de la marine mexicaine* and *Un voyage en ballon*, 1851), followed in 1854 by a historical novel, *Martin Paz* and, in 1855, *Un hivernage dans les glaces*. Numerous visits at this time to the National Library allowed him to acquire a scientific vocabulary and knowledge so that he could take advantage of the popular interest in the science of the period. Influenced by Edgar Allan Poe's use of fantasy in his writings, Verne published a novel, *Maître Zacharius ou l'horloger qui a perdu son âme*, and began work on the first manuscripts by *Cinq semaines en ballon*, which, when published in 1863, was an immediate success. It is the first volume of a series, *Les Voyages extraordinaires*, which includes also *Les Aventures du capitaine Hatteras* (1864), *Les Enfants du capitaine Grant* (1867–68), the famous *Vingt-mille lieues sous les mers* (*20,000 Leagues under the Sea*; 1870), *Une ville flottante* (1871), *Au pays des fourrurers* (1873), the celebrated *Le Tour du monde en 80 jours* (*Around the World in Eighty Days*; 1873), *Une capitaine de quinze ans* (1878), *Deux ans de vacances* (1888), *Mrs. Branican* (1891), *L'Île à hélice* (1895), *Le Sphinx des glaces* (1897), and *L'Étonante Aventure de la mission Barsac* (1910). Fascinated by aeronautics, Verne founded in 1862 with NADAR a society for research into the possibility of air flight. Nadar did achieve a number of balloon ascensions, and the heroes in Verne's novels imitated him in both lighter- and heavier-than-air flights, as in the well-known *De la Terre à la Lune* (*From the Earth to the Moon*; 1865). Along with exploration of outer and interplanetary space was that of earthly or oceanic realms, as in *Voyages au center de la Terre* (1864). Although much interested in inventions of the future, many of which he anticipated (space flights, helicopters, submarines, guided missiles, air conditioning, motion pictures), Verne was no less concerned with contemporary events, which inspired many of his other works and, through his humanistic and scientific optimism, represent the positivistic spirit of his age. His inventions reveal, too,

Jules Verne *(Library of Congress)*

of general CHARLES DE GAULLE and took part in the staffing of the maquis. Arrested by the Germans (October 1943), he was deported and died in Buchenwald concentration camp.

## Vernet, Joseph (1714–1789)
*painter, engraver*

One of the leading landscape and seascape artists of his era, Joseph Vernet, who was born in Avignon, was the son of a painter and engraver. He began his career by decorating various works, then traveled and studied in Italy. An admirer of NICOLAS POUSSIN and LE LORRAIN, he painted views of Rome, Naples, and their environs. Combining landscapes and genre scenes, he depicted small figures going about their daily activities. His carefully planned paintings, rendered with finesse the limpidity of the atmosphere and the particular quality of Mediterranean light (*Château Saint-Ange, Pont Rotto*), presaging the Italian landscapes of CAMILLE COROT. In 1753, Vernet was commissioned to paint a series of 24 French ports. Between 1753 and 1762, he produced 14, skillfully meeting the requirements of the commission with topographic precision. He then painted alpine landscapes and, for the public, maritime scenes—moonlights, storms, tempests, shipwrecks—with slight nuances and widely chromatic formats, but ones that reveal a personalized view of nature.

a sense of fantasy and subtle ambiguity, the relationship between space and time, matter and energy, with heroes who are more ambiguous than they appear. All these factors demand a new reading of his works, which are much less naive than they first appear.

## Verneau, Jean (1890–1944)
*general*

Born in Vignot, Meuse, Jean Verneau graduated from the École polytechnique as an engineering officer. During WORLD WAR II, he served as chief of staff of the armistice army until 1942, then joined the RESISTANCE, helping to organize the Organisation de résistance de l'armée (ORA), of which he eventually became the commander. He concerned himself with coordinating the ORA with the army

## Versailles, Palace of

The palace of Versailles, perhaps the most famous in Europe, is closely associated with king LOUIS XIV. Beginning in 1624, king LOUIS XIII had additions made to a royal lodge that already existed at Versailles, and in 1631 construction began on a château on the site of the present palace. In 1661, Louis XIV began modifications following the design of LOUIS LE VAU. An Orangerie and Menagerie were designed by ANDRÉ LE NÔTRE, and a second building phase (1668–71) transformed the château entirely, creating a palace oriented around the new royal court, with interiors done under the direction of CHARLES LE BRUN. The third phase began in 1678 under the direction of JULES HARDOUIN-MANSART. As part of this, the north and south wings of the palace were constructed and the Hall of Mirrors, the work of both Le Brun and Hardouin-Mansart, was completed. It measures 75 meters by 10 meters and is illuminated by 17 great windows to which correspond 17 panels of mirrors on the opposite wall (the 400 accompanying glass panels were the greatest collection of the period). Le Brun did the paintings on the ceiling. Shortly after, Hardouin-Mansart completed his work at Versailles with the building of the new Orangerie (1684–86), the Grand Trianon, and the Chapel. Louis XIV had already moved the government from Paris to Versailles in 1682. Under LOUIS XV, the right wing (where the Ambassadors' Staircase had been) was torn down and in its place was built the present structure with its colonnaded facade. The Opera House at Versailles was built in 1770 for the occasion of the marriage of the dauphin to MARIE ANTOINETTE. Until the end of the Bourbon monarchy, Versailles was associated with all major French political developments. Under LOUIS-PHILIPPE, a part of the left wing was rebuilt and the Hameau, built originally for queen Marie Antoinette by HUBERT ROBERT, was made into a historical museum. The gardens of Versailles are considered the prototype of the French garden style and were the masterwork of Le Nôtre, who created them between 1661 and 1668. There, simplified lines are complemented by fountains and classical statues and by an equestrian figure of Louis XIV by Italian sculptor and architect Gian Lorenzo Bernini. The Grand Canal at the gardens' center was completed in 1671.

## Versailles, Treaty of

The Treaty of Versailles was signed on June 28, 1919 in the Hall of Mirrors, at the PALACE OF VERSAILLES, between France (GEORGES CLEMENCEAU), its allies (United States: Woodrow Wilson; Italy: V. E. Orlando; Great Britain: David Lloyd George) and Germany. It brought an end to WORLD WAR I. The negotiations, from which Germany was excluded, were not without difficulties. Clemenceau, eager to affirm French hegemony in Europe, encountered the opposition of Great Britain and the United States; the Japan had claims based on a conflict with China; the refusal to recognize Italy's right to annex Fiume and Dalmatia provoked the momentary departure of Orlando. Preceded by the League of Nations pact, the treaty included territorial, mil-

itary, and financial clauses. The first consisted of the restoration of Alsace-Lorraine to France; the ceding of the districts of Eupen and Malmédy to Belgium; the areas of Posnania and part of West Prussia to Poland, which also gained access to the sea (Polish Corridor); the administration of the Saar by the League of Nations for a period of 15 years (after which a plebiscite would be held), as well as in Silesia and East Prussia; the abandonment by Germany of its colonies, the mandates of which would be given to France, Belgium, Great Britain, the Union of South Africa, and Japan. The military clauses of the treaty stipulated that the German army could not exceed 100,000 troops and 16,000 for the navy (with no submarines), and the air force would be disbanded. The financial clauses outlined the reparations to be paid by Germany in goods and supplies as well as in money in installments. Finally, to guarantee the application of the treaty, which would become effective in January 1920, it was determined that the left bank of the Rhine River (the Rhineland) would be occupied by Allied forces (as well as three bridgeheads on the right bank: Mainz, Coblenz, and Cologne) for a period of 15 years, after which the Rhineland would be demilitarized. This treaty, which was imposed on Germany, was never accepted by that nation. To erase the diktat of Versailles became one of the political goals of Adolf Hitler and his Nazi followers.

## Vestris, Auguste (1760–1842)
*dancer*

The son of the Italian dancer Gaetano Vestris and the French dancer Marie Allard (Vestr' Allard), Marie-Jean-Augustin Vestris or Auguste Vestris, as he is known, was born in Paris, where he made his early debut at the Opéra. Following this, he appeared in various ballets, including Mozart's *Les Petits Riens*. Acclaimed for his exceptional virtuosity, the speed of his pirouettes, the subtlety of his musicality, but disliked because of his difficult nature, Vestris brought a style to dance that, by its free character, heralded the romantic school. Celebrated in London as well as in Paris, he had a long career, marked by numerous creative ballets by noted composers. He then dedicated himself to teaching, counting JULES PERROT among his students.

## Veuillot, Louis (1813–1883)
*journalist*

Born in Boynes, Gâtinais, Louis Veuillot was an important French Catholic journalist. Contributor to, and then editor in chief of, *L'Univers*, he made it a powerful organ in the service of the Ultramontane Party, which caused the newspaper to be suppressed when it opposed the Italian policy of NAPOLÉON III (1860). Veuillot, who carried on heated polemics in favor of papal infallibility (promulgated in 1870), is the author of *Rome et Lorette* (1841), *Les Odeurs de Paris* (1866), *Paris pendant deux sièges* (1871), and *Rome pendant le concile* (1872).

## Vian, Boris (1920–1959)
*writer, playwright, poet*

Born in Ville-d'Avray, Boris Vian was a bohemian poet, science fiction writer, popular novelist, actor, trumpet player, singer, translator, engineer, inventor, and anarchist who, because he neglected a serious heart condition, died early. He wrote some of his popular fictions (*J'irai cracher sur les tombes*, 1946) under the name Vernon Sullivan in the style of the American crime novel. His best writing (under his own name) includes novels (*Vercoquin et le Plancton*, 1946; *L'Écume des jours*, 1947; *L'Automne à Pékin*, 1947; *Les Fourmis*, 1949; *L'Herbe rouge*, 1950; *L'Arrache-cœur*, 1953), plays (*L'Équarrissage pour tous*, 1950; *Le Goûter des généraux*, *Les Bâtisseurs d'empire*, 1959), and poetry collections (*Cantilènes en gelée*, 1950; *Je voudrais pas crever*, 1959). A tragic comic writer who protested against the absurdity of death, Vian was also a music critic for a number of reviews, played the trumpet and sang in Parisian clubs, acted in films, and was an artistic director for a recording studio. An influential figure of postwar literature, especially during the 1970s, he had a wide following, particularly among the young.

## Viau, Théophile de (1590–1626)
*poet*

Of Protestant background, Théophile de Viau (or Théophile Viau) was born in Clairac. Under the influence of the Italian philosopher Giulio Cesare Vanini, he embraced the growing pessimism regarding human nature and destiny that arose among 17th-century skeptics and "libertines." This caused him to be banished for impiety and dissipated living, then condemned to death (1623), although he escaped that sentence. His *Œuvres* (published in 1621 and augmented in 1622, 1623, and 1626) comprise two plays (*Pyrame et Thisbé*); satirical, sometimes licentious writings; sonnets; elegies; and personal odes (*La Solitude*) in which he eloquently expresses his epicurean naturalism. Opposed by FRANÇOIS DE MALHERBE because of his disdain for classical rules, Viau, who disregarded prevailing moral codes and went against religious doctrine and social convention, was popular during the 17th century because of his melodious poetry. Rediscovered by the romantics and admired by STÉPHANE MALLARMÉ, he is regarded today as the most modern poet of his era.

## Vichy, government of

The Vichy government was the name given to the executive power of the État français (French state) installed at Vichy from July 10, 1940, to August 1944. After the signing of the armistice at the beginning of WORLD WAR II (June 22, 1940), the majority in parliament voted, on July 10, full powers to Marshal PHILIPPE PÉTAIN to form a new constitution for the État français. Invested the next day with complete legislative and executive power, Pétain, who chose PIERRE LAVAL as his vice president and successor, launched a campaign for a "National Revolution" with the slogan "Travail, Famille, Patrie," that expressed the most conservative and reactionary principles. Several exceptional measures were immediately adopted: dissolution of secret societies, special statutes for French Jews, suppression of labor unions, administrative internments, and judicial charges against several political and military figures of the THIRD REPUBLIC. The arrest of Laval (December 1940), who had arranged the Hitler-Pétain meeting at Montoire (October 24, 1940), offered some hope of a Vichy resistance to the Nazis, but the policy of collaboration (see Admiral DARLAN) regarding the question of the East (Darlan-Warlimont Accords) and the return of Laval to the Vichy government (April 1942), as well as the German occupation of southern France (November 1942), made that impossible. The policy of collaboration and discrimination only intensified, with the Jews being key victims of the mass arrests and deportations. The Légion des volontaires, which was created in 1941 (to fight alongside German troops against bolshevism), was followed by the Milice français (January 1943) and the institution of Service du travail obligatoire (February 1943), while Vichy continued the struggle against the RESISTANCE. After the collapse of the Wehrmacht (Summer 1944), the Vichy government fled to Belfort, then Sigmaringen.

## Victor, duke de Bellune (1764–1841)
### marshal of France

Born Claude Perrin in Lamarche, Vosges, Victor, duke de Bellune, as he would become known, at the time of the REVOLUTION OF 1789 was a volunteer with the Drôme battalion (1792), was with the Army of the Alps, and was named brigadier general at the siege of Toulon (1793). He took part in the Italian campaign and played an important role at the Battle of Marengo (1800). Named ambassador to Denmark (1805), he served with distinction at Friedland (1807) and was named marshal and then duke de Bellune (1808). He served brilliantly in Spain, then in Russia, where he protected the crossing at the Bérésina River (1812). He took part in the campaign in France, distinguishing himself at La Rothière, Mormant, and Montereau (1814). After the RESTORATION, he went over to the Bourbons and voted for the execution of Marshal NEY. Minister of war (1821–23), he organized the Spanish campaign, then served as minister of state and as a member of the War Council (1823), before going over to the regime of King LOUIS-PHILIPPE.

## Victor, Paul-Émile (1907–1995)
### explorer

Born in Geneva, Switzerland, Paul-Émile Victor was an engineer, naval officer, and ethnologist. He explored the polar region, traveled among the Eskimos of Angmassalik (east coast of Greenland, 1934–35, 1936–37) and in Lapland (1939). After WORLD WAR II, he led French expeditions to Greenland and the Adelaide Peninsula. He is the author of a number of works including accounts (*Banquise*, 1939), memoirs (*La Mansarde*, 1981; *L'Iglou*, 1987); a translation (*Poèmes Eskimos*, 1951); and ethnographic studies (*La Civilisation du phoque: jeux, gestes et techniques des Eskimos d'Ammassalik*, 1989).

## Vidal de la Blache, Paul (1845–1918)
### geographer

Born in Pézenas, Paul Vidal de la Blache was the founder of the *"Annales de géographie"* (1891) and the French school of geography. He assigned a particular importance to regional monographs, always stressing the relationship of physical geography to the human. His best-known work is *Tableau de la géographie de la France* (1903), first published as an introduction to *Histoire de France* and later published separately. He also wrote *Principes de géographie humaine* (unfinished). Under his direction was later edited and published *Géographie universelle* (1927–48), which is a collaboration with a number of other noted geographers.

## Vidocq, François-Eugène (1775–1857)
### police official

Born in Arras, François-Eugène Vidocq was sentenced to eight years at Brest for counterfeiting, but escaped after three years. He was imprisoned a number of other times for robbery and then, in 1809, turned police agent and became the first chief of the Sûreté, the famed Parisian detective bureau. He retired in 1827 to establish a paper factory but, unsuccessful, he returned to the police in 1832. He was forced to resign because he was involved in a theft. His *Mémoires*, which were perhaps the most important stimulus for the development of detective fiction, appeared in an initial volume in 1828. In this and subsequent installations, Vidocq describes his exploits and his methods of investigation in great detail and gives remarkable accounts of the criminal world of the period and its mores, language, and argot. Vidocq was the inspiration for the character Vautrin in several novels by HONORÉ DE BALZAC, including *Splendeurs et Misères des courtisanes*.

## Vieira da Silva, Maria-Elena (1908–1992)
### painter

Of Portuguese origin, Maria-Elena Vieira da Silva, who was born in Lisbon, settled in Paris in 1928, and, except for a brief period in Brazil during WORLD WAR II (1940–47), spent most of her life in France. Vieira da Silva began her art training by studying sculpture and then turned to painting, being tutored by FERNAND LÉGER and ROGER BISSIÈRE (1932). Progressively, her works lost all descriptive character and, in the late 1930s, she achieved critical recognition with semiabstract pieces, which are suggestive of landscapes reduced to geometric and linear formations. The illusion of space is achieved without traditional perspectives by utilizing flecks of color on neutral background. Her works often evoke urban spaces that employ horizontal and vertical elements to produce structured and luminous cityscapes. She also painted interior scenes (*La Bibliothèque,* 1949) or panoramic views with imprecise limits. Vieira da Silva's graphic talent is also apparent in her engravings and drawings for the tapestries that she produced.

## Viète, François  (1540–1603)
### *mathematician*
Born in Fontenay-le-Comte, François Viète was a magistrate for whom mathematics was originally just a pastime. Although regarded by his contemporaries as more of a decipherer than a mathematician, he influenced through his work, especially on equations, many later mathematicians, including PIERRE DE FERMAT and Isaac Newton and was the founder of algebra. In 1579, he published a table of trigonometric functions (*Canon mathematicus*), in which he introduced the polar triangle into spherical trigonometry and stated the multiple-angle formulas for sine and cosine in terms of their separate powers. Regarding equations, he demonstrated the relationship between the roots of an algebraic equation and its coefficients. Viète also contributed important numerical methods for approximating the roots of equations (1600) and introduced various symbols of aggregations used as bases in modern mathematics.

## Vigée-Lebrun, Élisabeth  (1755–1842)
### *painter*
A much-sought-after portraitist, Élisabeth Vigée-Lebrun was born in Paris and studied painting with her father, JOSEPH VERNET, and JEAN-BAPTISTE GRUEZE. Her portrait of MARIE ANTOINETTE, done in 1779, established her reputation and was the first of

many that she would do for the queen (*La Reine et ses enfants,* 1787). In her paintings, Vigée-Lebrun conveys great sense of personal dignity and royalty, and her compositions show the influence of the artistic theories of JEAN-JACQUES ROUSSEAU and DENIS DIDEROT. She often gave her subjects compassionate, soft expressions and underscored their grace and style. Around 1785, inspired by JACQUES-LOUIS DAVID, she purified her style using more profiles and giving a more studied and traditional appearance to her models, as reflected in her well-known self-portrait with her daughter (*Mme Vigée-Lebrun et sa fille,* 1789). In 1783, she became a member of the Royal Academy and in 1789 left France to travel throughout Europe. She returned in 1802 and 1810 settled in Louveciennes. Between 1835 and 1837, she published her memoirs (*Souvenirs*). Vigée-Lebrun is considered a prodigious painter, producing perhaps more than 800 canvases, with many of her subjects being members of the nobility. Her style is a combination of rococo delicacy combined with the neoclassical ideals of purity and simplicity.

## Vigny, Alfred, count de  (1797–1863)
### *writer*
Born in Touraine to an old noble family, Alfred, count de Vigny was raised in the cult of arms and honor. He had dreams of military glory (1814) but became disillusioned by garrison life. In 1822, he wrote his poem *Moïse,* followed by *Éloa ou la Sœur des anges,* an epic that had great success. He often frequented the literary milieu, especially the CÉNACLE (where he met VICTOR HUGO) and, between 1822 and 1826, put together a collection, *Poèmes antiques et modernes* (completed in 1837) while writing *Cinq-Mars,* an historical novel that evokes the nobility that had been humbled by absolute monarchy. His religious pessimism, already apparent in *Daphne* (1837), was intensified by personal tragedies. Disappointed further (a reserved welcome into the ACADÉMIE FRANÇAISE in 1845 and a political defeat in 1848), he meanwhile proclaimed his humanistic optimism in the poems *Destinées* (posthumous, 1864). His personal writings were also published posthumously (1867) and reveal his thoughts haunted by destiny, the silence of God, and the

indifference of Nature, as well as his sense of deep spiritual isolation. A passionate reader of the Bible, he placed powerful yet simple symbols in his work, as he speaks of the divine and the supernatural. An intellectual and philosophical writer who would later be eclipsed by his contemporaries (Victor Hugo and ALFRED DE MUSSET), Vigny was regarded as the initial leader of the early years of romanticism.

## Vigo, Jean (1905–1934)
*film director*

Born in Paris, Jean Vigo, whose innovative style of cynicism, stark realism, and dramatic imagery would profoundly influence French cinema, began his life with both medical and social difficulties. An asthmatic, both his parents were political activists often in conflict with the authorities (his father, the anarchist Almereyda, died in prison in 1917 under mysterious circumstances). In 1929, after studying at the SORBONNE, he married Elizabeth Losinka and began his directing career. His first film, *À propos de Nice* (1930), a satire on the egotism and vanity of the bourgeoisie, was followed by *Taris champion de natation* (1931) and *Zéro de conduite* (1933), a sharp criticism of the educational system and a strong antiauthoritarian statement that was banned shortly after its premiere and rereleased only in 1945. Vigo's last film was *L'Atalante* (1934), a proletarian love story set on a barge on the Seine is generally considered his masterpiece. Notable for its combination of surrealistic imagery and dreamlike romanticism, combined with a great naturalism, the film had been released for only a few days when he died. Although his promising career was cut short too early, Vigo's few works are greatly appreciated and have considerably influenced such later filmmakers as FRANÇOIS TRUFFAUT and JEAN-LUC GODARD.

## Vilar, Jean (1912–1971)
*film director, actor, stage manager*

Born in Sète, Jean Vilar decided on a theatrical career after a meeting with CHARLES DULLIN. He received favorable revues for his first productions (Synge, Strindberg, MOLIÈRE) and, after the success

of his productions of T. S. Eliot's *Murder in the Cathedral* (1945), he established the Festival d'art dramatique, the first Festival d'Avignon, and he was named director of the Théâtre national populaire (TNP). Vilar was drawn to the beautifully proportioned courtyard of the Palais des Papes at Avignon and felt that it would be a perfect site for an open-air public celebration of theater performances. He also led an ambitious theater group that worked with the public through his Association des Amis du Théâtre populaire and through the journal *Bref.* Under his direction, the TNP performed for nearly 5 million spectators.

## Vildrac, Charles (1882–1971)
**(Charles Messager)**
*writer*

Born in Paris, Charles Vildrac (the pen name of Charles Messager), who founded, along with his brother-in-law GEORGES DUHAMEL and some friends, the Abbaye group (1903–08), was known as a modest and sensitive poet (*Poèmes, 1905.* 1906; *Livre d'amour,* 1910). After WORLD WAR I, he became a poet of sorrow and rebellion (*Chants du désespéré,* 1920). He contributed to the theater through works such as *Pèlerin,* 1921; *Michel Auclair,* 1922; *Madame Béliard,* 1925; and *La Brouille,* 1930. Vildrac is also the author of charming works for children, *Les Lunettes du lion* and *La Famille Moineau,* 1952).

## Villars, Claude-Louis-Hector, duke de (1653–1734)
*marshal of France*

Born in Moulins, Claude Louis Hector, duke de Villars, as a military commander during the War of the Spanish Succession, won a great victory at Friedlingen, Baden, over the Imperial armies (1702). Sent to the Cévennes against the CAMISARDS, he forced the surrender of the Camisard leader JEAN CAVALIER. Defeated by the Austrian commander, Prince Eugene of Savoy, and by the English commander, the duke of Marlborough, at Malplaquet (1709), he nonetheless inflicted losses on the enemy that prevented an invasion of France. His victory at Denain with France's sole remaining army saved the kingdom and allowed King LOUIS XIV to gain better terms at the peace signed in 1713. Villars is said to have made many enemies by his cupidity and many friends by his audacity. He was elected to the ACADÉMIE FRANÇAISE in 1714.

## Villèle, Jean-Baptiste-Guillaume-Joseph, count de  (1773–1854)
*political figure*

A naval officer, Jean-Baptiste-Guillaume-Joseph, count de Villèle was born in Toulouse and spent most of the period of the REVOLUTION OF 1789 on the islands of Mauritius and Réunion, where he married the daughter of a wealthy Creole landowner. Returning to France in 1807, he joined during the First Empire an ultraroyalist group, Chevaliers de la foi. Rallying to the Bourbons, he questioned the liberal tendencies of the Charter of 1814 in his *Observations sur le projet de Constitution* (1814). A deputy during the Second RESTORATION, he was one of the leaders and main speakers in the "Chambre introuvable" (1815–16). Reelected after its dissolution, he helped to found the newspaper *Le Conservateur.* Minister without portfolio in the RICHELIEU cabinet (1820), which he criticized for its moderation, he was dismissed in 1821. Minister of finance (October 1821), then prime minister (1822), he was forced to accept, after the Congress of Verona, the sending of French troops to Spain (1822), an expedition that he had opposed. After the election of the chamber known as the "retrouvée" (1824), his term was extended to seven years. Under pressure from the Ultras, it passed a number of reactionary laws (extremely large indemnities for the émigrés; laws on the congregations) but met opposition when he tried to reestablish the right of seniority and the law limiting the freedom of the press. After the dissolution of the chamber and the subsequent electoral victory of the liberal opposition, Villèle resigned and was replaced by the MARTIGNAC cabinet. Elevated to the peerage, he retired from politics after the REVOLUTION OF 1830 and returned to Toulouse, where he remained an adviser to the Legitimists and a critic of the fiscal policies of the JULY MONARCHY. Villèle's *Mémoires* were published between 1887 and 1890.

## Villemain, Abel-François  (1790–1870)
*professor, political figure*

Born in Paris, Abel-François Villemain, who was professor of literature at the SORBONNE (1816–30), published his *Cours de littérature française* (1828–29), which helped to revive French literary studies by introducing historical criticism and insisting on the role of social interpretations in the study of foreign literature (*Études de littérature ancienne et étrangère*, 1846). Elected deputy shortly before the REVOLUTION OF 1830, a peer of France in 1832, member of the NICOLAS SOULT ministry (1839–40), Villemain was named minister of public instruction (1840–44) and fought for reforms in secondary schooling, in particular for its secularization. He was elected to the ACADÉMIE FRANÇAISE in 1821.

## Villeneuve, Pierre-Charles-Jean-Baptiste-Silvestre de  (1763–1806)
*admiral*

Born in Valensoie, Pierre-Charles-Jean-Baptiste-Silvestre de Villeneuve, during the REVOLUTION OF 1789, became a vice admiral (1896). He took part in the Egyptian campaign and escaped the disaster at Aboukir (August 1798) by seeking refuge in Naples. In 1804, NAPOLÉON I, who wanted to invade England, ordered Villeneuve to draw the British fleet, under Admiral Nelson, toward the Antilles and then return quickly accompanied by Spanish ships. Villeneuve arrived in Martinique in May 1805, and set sail in June, but was followed by Nelson. Villeneuve took refuge at Cadiz, Spain, on August 18 to protect his fleet instead of going to Brest, as Napoléon had ordered. Nelson was waiting for him and Villeneuve was caught in the Battle of Trafalgar. It was a disaster for France. Captured by the British, de Villeneuve committed suicide upon his release.

## Villeneuve-Bargemont, Jean-Paul-Alban, viscount de  (1784–1850)
*administrator, economist*

Born in Saint-Alban, Provence, Jean-Paul Alban, viscount de Villeneuve-Bargemont is the author of *Économie politique chrétienne ou Recherches sur les causes du paupérisme* (1834). It is considered one of the first works on social Catholicism. Villeneuve-Bargemont, who was elected a deputy in 1830, and served again from 1840 to 1848, sat with the representatives in the Chamber of Deputies who had legitimist leanings.

## Villermé, Louis-René (1782–1863)
*physician, sociologist*

Born in Paris, Louis-René Villermé was a surgeon in the imperial army until 1814, then a private physician until 1830, after which he did economic and social research. Author of a work on political economy and society, he is known for his *Tableau de l'état physique et moral des ouvriers dans les fabriques de cotton, de laine et de soie* (1840), which resulted in an inquiry into working conditions, particularly in the regions of Lille and Rouen. This work also contributed to the adoption of social legislation limiting child labor (1841).

## Villiers de L'Isle-Adam, Auguste, count de (1838–1889)
*writer*

Born in Saint-Brieuc, Auguste, count de Villiers de L'Isle-Adam was descended from an old and illustrious Breton family. Having a disdain for contemporary mores, he lived a precarious bohemian life in Paris and was a friend of CHARLES BAUDELAIRE, who introduced him to the works of Edgar Allen Poe. He was also influenced by Hegel, whose writings verified for Villiers his own sense of mystical idealism. His philosophical novel, *Isis* (1862), then his dramas, *Elën* (1865) and *Morgane* (1866; second version entitled *Le Prétendant*, 1875), were ignored by the public; he turned to a romantic work, published first in serialized form: *L'Ève future* (1886), *Akëdyssérie* (1886), *L'Amour supreme* (1886), and *Tribunat Bonhomet* (1887) and denounced the pretensions of science, while his sardonic *Les Contes cruels* (1883), for which he is best known, also rejected the prevailing naturalism and materialism of the age. This idea reoccurs in Villiers's work, *Axël* (posthumous, 1890), which made him a symbolist and admired by STÉPHANE MALLARMÉ. All of Villiers's writings reflect a romantic and symbolist interest in fantasy and express his own idiosyncratic philosophical views. Villiers died alone and in poverty, without having known the fame and glory for which he believed he was destined.

## Villon, François (ca. 1431–ca. 1463)
*poet*

François Villon, whose works reflect his controversial life and who is often considered France's outstanding lyric poet, was born in or near Paris. His original name was probably either de Montcorbier or des Loges, but he assumed the name Villon in honor of his professor Guillaume de Villon. While earning a bachelor of arts (1449) and a master of arts (1452) at the SORBONNE, Villon was involved in the boisterous academic life of the age and, in 1455, killed a priest in a street brawl. A year later, he was involved in a theft and consequently was banished. During the next four years (1456–60), he wandered throughout France and was arrested but pardoned because of the influence of CHARLES D'ORLÉANS and King LOUIS XI. Villon's poems, often octosyllabic, like *Les Lais* (or *Petit Testament,* 1456) and *Le Testament* (or *Grand Testament,* 1461), sometimes in decasyllables, as in *L'Épitaphe Villon* (called also *Ballad des perdus,* 1463), express the originality, beauty, and evocativeness of his verse. Moving between sensual aspirations and poignant pessimism, between immorality and profound religious faith (*Le Débat du corps et du Cœur,* 1461), between irony and a sense of the tragic, and between realism and lyricism, Villon's writings reveal him to be a master of language and, as some have described him, "the first modern poet."

## Villon, Jacques (1875–1963)
*painter, engraver*

Born in Danville, Gaston Duchamp, or Jacques Villon, as he is known (he adopted his pseudonym in honor of FRANÇOIS VILLON), was the brother of the artists MARCEL DUCHAMP, SUZANNE DUCHAMP, and RAYMOND DUCHAMP-VILLON. He studied in Rouen before coming to Paris in 1892 and worked as an engraver, making posters and drawings of Parisian scenes in a style similar to that of HENRI DE TOULOUSE-LAUTREC. He also did sketches for *Rire* and *L'Assiette au buerre*. After producing works similar to the impressionists and fauvists, he found his own style in cubism, and around 1911, his studio became one of the principal cubists' gathering places. Seeking to base his own compositions on mathematical concepts, he reduced the subjects to an abstract play of lines and colored surfaces (*Soldats en marche,* 1913), or bright tones (*Jeu,* 1919), a style that continued through the 1920s. After 1935, he sought to produce a pictorial transposition of more traditional subjects and, after 1940, landscapes (*Homme dessinant,* 1935; *Le Nageur,* 1936; a series of *Potagers,* 1941–42; *Les Moissons,* 1943), while also producing completely nonfigurative works (*Les grands Fonds,* 1945).

## Vincent, Jean-Paul (1942–   )
*stage director*

Born in Paris, Jean-Paul Vincent, after working in Sartrouville with noted directors, established the Théâtre de l'Espérance (1968). He is known for staging and direction marked by its intellectual clarity and central spacing, and he extols a theater of political and social comment, affirming the theories of both the artist and the audience. Director of the Théâtre national de Strasbourg (1975–83), he later was general manager of the COMÉDIE-FRANÇAISE (1983–86). Professor at the Conservatoire supérieure d'art dramatique and an independent stage director, he achieved his goal of creating a theater where joy and humor are catalysts for self-reflection (*Le Mariage de Figaro* by Beaumarchais, 1987; *Œdipus Rex* and *Œdipus à Colonna* by Sophocles, 1989; *On ne badine pas avec l'amour* by MUSSET, 1988, 1993; *Les Fourberies de Scapin* by MOLIÈRE, 1990). Jean Vincent has directed the théâtre des Amandiers at Nanterre since 1990.

## Vincent de Paul  (1581–1660)
*cleric, saint*

The founder of the charitable Congregation of the Missions, known also as the Vincentians or the Order of the Lazarists, Vincent de Paul was born in

Pouy (now Saint-Vincent de Paul) in Gascogny. He studied at the Universities of Dax and Toulouse and, in 1665, was captured and held as a slave by the Barbary pirates. Upon his release, he served as a priest among the poor of Paris and became almoner to MARGUERITE OF VALOIS (1610), pastor of the parish of Clichy (1611), and tutor to the children of Emmanuel de Gondi (1613). He then began his charitable missions, preaching among the poor and, in 1617 at Châtillon-des-Dombes, organized the first Confraternity of Charity, from which developed the Daughters of Charity, to be led by LOUISE DE MARILLAC (1633). Chaplain general of the galleys in France (1619), superior of the Order of the Visitation (see JEANNE DE CHANTAL), in 1624 he organized rural missions, developed other charitable institutions (charité de l'Hôtel-Dieu, 1634; œuvre des Enfants trouvés, 1638) and, during the regency of ANNE OF AUSTRIA, was made a member of the Conseil de conscience (1643–52), in which capacity he strongly influenced episcopal nominations, and, with his opposition to JANSENISM, it is believed, was responsible in part for its suppression. He was canonized in 1737 and his *Correspondence* was published in 1920–25.

## Viollet-le-Duc, Eugène-Emmanuel (1814–1879)
*architect, theorist*

Born in Paris, Eugène-Emmanuel Viollet-le-Duc was self-taught and, with great enthusiasm for medieval architecture, visited Italy in 1836. He then traveled through France accompanied by his friend PROSPER MÉRIMÉE while the latter was inspector of historical monuments. In 1839, Mérimée commissioned Viollet-le-Duc to restore the basilica of Vézelay, and he soon began the restoration of other important medieval religious and civil structures (Saint-Germain-des-Prés, Saint-Séverin, Notre-Dame de Paris, the walled city of Carcassone). His rationalist concept of Gothic architecture and his ideas of restoration (alterations of what were considered characteristic aspects of the medieval style) were strongly criticized. In the rebuilding of the château of Pierrefonds (1859–70), he applied his ideas of feudal architecture most obviously and, in his buildings, he based his plans on stylized medieval and classical formulas, often using floral decorative motifs that foreshadow those of Art Nouveau. He was an audacious theorist, extolling the use of functional forms and of metal. Viollet-le-Duc is the author of a number of works of which his *Dictionnaire raisoné de l'architecture française du xie au xvie siècle* (1854–68) and *Entretiens sur l'architecture* (1863–72) influenced the majority of architectural innovations of succeeding generations.

## Vitez, Antoine (1930–1990)
*actor, stage director*

Born in Paris, Antoine Vitez, who held a degree in Oriental languages and served as secretary of LOUIS ARAGON, collaborated on the revue *Théâtre populaire* before beginning his career as a stage director of Sophocles' *Electra* in 1966. Drawn at first to Russian (*Les Bains,* by Vladimir Mayakovsky) and German (*Le Precepteur,* by Jacob Lenz; *Faust,* 1981) plays, he took on contemporary French scripts (*m=M,* by Xavier-Agnan Pommeret; *Le Picque-Nique de Claretta* by René Kalisky; *L'Échange,* by PAUL CLAUDEL) and classics (*Phèdre* by JEAN RACINE; *Le Misanthrope* by MOLIÈRE; *Hernani* by VICTOR HUGO). Vitez saw stage directing and writing as a way of presenting his views of society and history. After founding and directing the Studio-Théâtre d'Ivry (1972–81), he took over the direction of the Théâtre national de Chaillot (1981–88). He was named general manager of the COMÉDIE-FRANÇAISE in 1988 and produced works for the Festival d'Avignon.

## Viviani, René (1863–1925)
*political figure*

A leading political figure during WORLD WAR I, René Viviani was born in Sid-Bel-Abbés in French ALGERIA. As a journalist, he contributed to a number of newspapers, *La petite République, La Lanterne,* and *L'HUMANITÉ,* then was elected to the Chamber as a Socialist deputy (1893–1902), then as an independent Socialist (1906–22), before helping found the Parti républicain socialiste. Minister of labor (1906–10) and of education (1913–14), he was

named prime minister in June 1914 and soon ordered the general mobilization for WORLD WAR I (August 1, 1914). The early French military setbacks forced him to reshuffle his government and form a mixed cabinet—the Union sacrée (THÉOPHILE DELCASSÉ, ARISTIDE BRIAND, GASTON DOUMERGUE, AND ALEXANDRE MILLERAND). Replaced in October 1915 by Briand, Viviani was named minister of justice (September 1915–17). After the war, he represented France at the League of Nations (1920–21) and was elected senator (1922).

## Viven, Louis (1861–1936)
*painter*

Of humble origin, Louis Viven was born in Hadol, Vosges, and came to Paris in 1880. Self-taught, he exhibited at the Foire aux croûtes in Montmartre in 1922, but remained a postal employee until he retired. His style is naive, with meticulous attention to detail, and he is academic in his use of luminous colors applied in a flat manner. But he often dabbled in an unreal style, especially in his depiction of Parisian buildings (*Le Sacre-Cœur,* 1930; *Notre-Dame,* 1935). For his landscapes, which are deprived of perspective, he composed a succession of simplified planes, of which the critic Wilhelm Uhde said that they "seemed to be facades of another landscape." Viven's scenes of wildlife (*Le Cerf et les loups,* 1925) express a feeling of anguish and solitude. Recognition of Viven's work came late, his first show having been in 1927.

## Vivonne, Louis-Victor de Rochechouart, duke de Mortemart et de (1636–1688)
*marshal of France*

Born in Paris, Louis-Victor de Rochechouart duke de Mortemart et de Vivonne, who was the brother of FRANCOISE DE MONTESPAN, in 1664, after having served in Flanders under HENRI DE TURENNE, was named a field marshal. He joined the navy and took part in the expedition against the Barbary pirates (1664), then was appointed general of the galleys (1669). He fought in the war against Holland and was gravely wounded during the crossing of the Rhine (1672). Governor of Champagne and

Brie (1674), he became viceroy of Sicily (1675), and in 1676 defeated the Spanish-Dutch fleet at Palermo. Recalled to France, he again took part in the war against Holland (1678). An aristocrat, educated and spirited, he spent the later years of his life at the royal court, where he was patron to a number of writers.

## Vlaminck, Maurice de (1876–1958)
*painter, engraver, writer*

One of the founders of fauvism, Maurice de Vlaminck was born in Paris and was largely self-taught (he once boasted that he had never been inside the LOUVRE). A professional bicyclist, he also worked as a violinist in Gypsy orchestras before becoming an amateur painter. Around 1890, he met ANDRÉ DERAIN and opened a studio. A rebellious artist, he sought to create by instinct and subjectivity. In 1907, he met HENRI MATISSE and was impressed by the work of VINCENT VAN GOGH. He painted landscapes, urban views, and street scenes in often violent tones and unreal colorations, accentuating his expressive powers (*La Péniche*, 1905; *Les Arbres rouges*, 1906). His work eventually caught the attention of PAUL CÉZANNE (*Nature morte*, ca. 1907), after which he abandoned his audacious techniques and returned to a more traditional configuration. Vlaminck is the creator of a number of book illustrations, wood block engravings, and lithographs and published various works on art.

## Voisenon, Claude-Henri Fuzée de (1708–1775)
*writer*

Born in Voisenon, near Melun, Claude-Henri Fuzée de Voisenon was a protégé of Étienne-François, duke de CHOISEUL and of VOLTAIRE, who called him "dear friend Greluchon." An ecclesiastic who was well known among the salons of the period, he was, because of his literary spirit and dissipated lifestyle, typical of the worldly clergy of the 18th century. He wrote libertine stories (*Le Sultan Misapouf et la Princesse Grisemine ou les Métamorphoses*, 1746; *Zulmis et Zelmaïde*, 1747; *Histoire de la félicité*,

1751), amorous poetry, and comedies that were staged between 1738 and 1756 (*L'Heureuse Ressemblance*, 1738; *Les Mariages assortis*, 1744; *La Coquette fixée*, 1746). Voisenon's complete works were published in 1781.

## Voisin brothers

The Voisin brothers, Charles (1882–12), who was born in LYON, and Gabriel (1880–72), born in Ozenay, Saône-et-Loire, became in 1908 the first French airplane manufacturers to build on an industrial scale. Charles Voisin, who was killed in an automobile accident at Corselles, Rhône, was the first French pilot to fly in Europe in a motorized airplane (1907). Gabriel Voisin, who after 1918 dedicated himself to building automobiles, contributed greatly to the field of aerodynamics.

## Volland, Louise-Henriette (1717–1784)
*writer*

Known as Sophie Volland, Louise-Henriette Volland was born in Paris. She was, from 1755 to 1784, the principal correspondent of DENIS DIDEROT, in whom she inspired a lasting passion. The *Lettres* that he addressed to her are rich in insights into his literary works and his difficulties regarding the *Encyclopédie* and are remarkable for their spontaneity and freshness.

## Vollard, Ambroise (1868–1939)
*art dealer, writer, editor*

Born in Saint-Denis, Île de la Réunion, Ambroise Vollard, who played an important role in the history of painting, organized the first exhibitions of ÉDOUARD MANET, PAUL CÉZANNE (1893), VINCENT VAN GOGH and the NABIS (1899), Pablo Picasso (1901), HENRI MATISSE (1904), MAURICE DE VLAMINCK and ANDRÉ DERAIN (1906), and GEORGES ROUAULT, while going against the popular tastes of the period. He also helped make AUGUSTE RODIN and ARISTIDE MAILLOL well known. From 1900 to 1910, Vollard had his shop at 6, rue Lafitte; it became a celebrated meeting place of artists of the period and their patrons. Cézanne, AUGUSTE RENOIR, RAOUL DUFY,

PIERRE BONNARD, Picasso, and Rouault all painted Vollard's portrait. Vollard wrote several works on the painters whom he knew, in particular, *Paul Cézanne* (1914), *Renoir* (1920), and *Degas* (1924). He is the author of *Souvenirs d'un marchand de tableaux* (1939).

## Volney, Constantin-François de Chassebœuf, count de (1757–1820)
*philosopher, writer*

Born in Craon, Anjou, Constantin-François de Chassebœuf, count de Volney, after finishing his studies in law and medicine, visited the Near East and upon his return soon became known for his descriptions of that region through his *Voyages en Égypte et en Syrie* (1787). A representative of the Third Estate, then secretary to the National Assembly (1790), he edited his most famous work, *Les Ruines ou Méditations sur les révolutions des empires* (1791). During the REVOLUTION OF 1789, he was imprisoned under the TERROR, then served as a member of the education committee under the Directorate. Volney can perhaps be considered through his writings as the moralist and sociologist for the "Ideologues"—the group of late-18th-century French philosophers who sought the practical application of the ideas of the ENLIGHTENMENT (*Recherches nouvelles sur l'histoire ancienne*, 1814; *Discours sur l'étude philosophique des langues*, 1819). Volney was elected to the *académie française* in 1803.

## Voltaire (1694–1778)
### (François-Marie Arouet)
*writer, philosopher*

One of the leading figures of the ENLIGHTENMENT, Voltaire (the pen name of François-Marie Arouet) was born into the Parisian bourgeoisie and, having chosen a literary career, soon became known in the salons of Paris as a brilliant, sarcastic, and critical poet. While writing his epic poem, *La Henriade* (1725–28), he was incarcerated for a brief time in the BASTILLE for impertinence, then released on his promise to leave for England. It was a visit from which he greatly profited (1726–29), as he met the philosopher John Locke, conceived the idea for *L'Histoire de Charles XII* (1731), and wrote tragedies

inspired by Shakespeare (*Zaïre,* 1732). His admiration for the liberal English regime is apparent in his *Lettres philosophiques* (1734), but his criticism of the French political and ecclesiastical institutions forced him to seek refuge at the château of MME DU CHÂTELET at Cirey. She later became an intimate friend who exerted a strong intellectual influence on him. This was a period of intense activity for Voltaire; he wrote new tragedies (*La Mort de César,* 1735; *Mahomet,* 1741; *Mérope,* 1734), engaged in scientific studies, and expressed his epicureanism in poems such as *Le Mondain* (1736) or the *Discours sur l'homme* (1738).

Once back in grace (1744), Voltaire traveled to Paris, Sceaux, and Versailles, where, owing to the influence of Mme de POMPADOUR, he became a court favorite. He wrote of his misadventures as a courtier in the critical story *Zadig* (1747), originally published under the title *Memiron, histoire orientale*. In 1749, he accepted a long-standing invitation from King Frederick II of Prussia to reside at his court (1750–53), where his acidulous wit clashed with the king's autocratic nature. He completed his great historical work, *Le Siècle de Louis XIV,* and an important philosophical writing, *Micromégas* (1752), before he left. Unwelcome as much in Paris, however, he had been in Berlin, Voltaire settled at Délices, near Geneva, and edited his history of civilization, *L'Essai sur les mœurs et l'esprit des nations* (1756), along with a philosophical poem, *Sur le désastre de Lisbonne* (1756), the pessimistic theme of which (in contrast to the optimistic views of JEAN-JACQUES ROUSSEAU) was reaffirmed in *Candide* (1759).

Moving to Ferney, he made that village prosperous by undertaking a vast correspondence and welcoming innumerable visitors. The essential part of Votaire's literary activity was dedicated to disseminating his philosophical ideas, particularly through new stories (*Jeannot et Colin,* 1764; *L'Ingénu,* 1767) and antireligious pamphlets. He courageously intervened on behalf of victims of religious intolerance or of unjust judicial practices (JEAN CALAS, PIERRE-PAUL SIRVEN, CHEVALIER LA BARRE, LALLY-BARON TOLLENDAL, and others). In his efforts against all forms of "superstition," he wrote two works: *Traité sur la tolérance* (1763) and *Dictionnaire philosophique portatif* (1764), and works of literary, social, and religious

Bust portrait of Voltaire  *(Library of Congress)*

criticism. Considered the "universal man" and the champion of tolerance, he made a triumphant return to Paris and was elected director of the ACADÉMIE FRANÇAISE.

Voltaire, who died at the height of great popularity, wrote in all genres and on all subjects with remarkable intelligence, if not equal success. An enlightened admirer of classical perfection, he developed modern themes. His historical work was done after scrupulous research and gives new insight into the historical process. But the greatest part of Voltaire's work lies in his philosophical stories (*Contes*), which illustrate the themes dear to the philosophes. Professing a deism based on reason and its usefulness to society, he proposed an earthly happiness "as much as human nature allowed," and affirmed his faith in a moral altruism and perfectible civilization.

## Vouet, Simon (1590–1649)
*painter*

Simon Vouet, who brought Italian influences to French baroque painting, was born in Paris and studied with his father, Laurent Vouet, who was the painter of the royal stables of King HENRY IV.

The younger Vouet's talents were evident early on and, after 1604, he became known as a portrait painter during a visit to England. In 1611, he accompanied the French ambassador to Turkey on a visit to Constantinople (*Portrait du sultan Mustafa I*), and then traveled for 15 years throughout Italy. In Rome, he gained great repute, becoming the protégé of Cardinal Barberini and, in Genoa, of the Dorias. He opened a school using live models and, in 1624, became the "prince" of the Academy of Saint Luke. Vouet painted genre scenes and religious subjects (*La Cène,* 1625) and evolved from an initial Caravaggio-like style, which manipulated light and shadow, to a clear and elegant mannerism that shows diverse influences (Bolognese and Venetian), which he easily assimilated. Recalled to France in 1627 and named first painter to the king, he received a multitude of commissions, notably to decorate the châteaux of Chilly, Saint-Germain, and Wideville and the mansions of Bullion and Saguier. But his glory faded with the arrival of NICOLAS POUSSIN in Paris. Vouet, who loved brilliant colors and studied poses brought to France the taste for large compositions and an expressiveness that would become the basis of the academic style.

## Voulet, Paul (1866–1899)
*officer, explorer*

Born in Paris, Paul Voulet explored the course of the Niger River in Africa and, along with CHARLES CHANOINE, contributed to the annexation of the Mossi states in West Africa (1896–97). He was sent to the Sudan and was ordered to establish a liaison with various missions (1898–99). Having carried out violent reprisals against the indigenous peoples, he was killed by his troops before Colonel JEAN-FRANÇOIS KLOBB could investigate charges of cruelty brought against him.

## Vuillard, Édouard-Jean (1868–1940)
*painter, watercolorist, scenery designer, engineer*

Known for his intimate interiors and individualistic techniques, Édouard-Jean Vuillard was born in Cuiseaux, Saône-et-Loire and studied art in Paris.

A member of the NABIS group, he was part of the symbolist milieu and, interested in the decorative arts, worked for the Théâtre-Libre and the théâtre de l'Œuvre. His main inspiration, however, was not the Nabis but Japanese prints and the paintings of PUVIS DE CHAVANNES (*Le Lit*, 1891). As a symbolist, he preferred intimate scenes in calm, bourgeois settings (*Femme au corsage bleu*), painted with a discreet charm and refined palette of muted tones (*La Mère d'Artiste*, 1893). He painted on cardboard, mixing media—oil, gouache, and pastel—and his decorative style is characterized by the lavish use of pattern, with fabrics, wallpaper, and upholstery often juxtaposed to create a collagelike effect (*La Soupe d'Annette*, 1900). He produced great decorative murals. Although extremely popular in his time, Vuillard's style was too far from the mainstream of modern art to be of significant influence.

## Vulpian, Alfred (1826–1887)
*physician, physiologist*

Born in Paris, Alfred Vulpian was a professor of anatomy and comparative pathology and was interested in the physiology of the nervous system. In 1866, he identified sclerosis in platelets and gave his name to the condition of progressive muscular atrophy. In discovering an active agent in the veins (1856), he made the first biomedical confirmation of a hormonal secretion as well as demonstrating functional anatomy. Vulpian was named to the Academy of Sciences in 1867.

# W

## Waldeck-Rousseau, Pierre (1846–1904)
*political figure*

The son of a moderate leftist deputy in the SECOND REPUBLIC, Pierre Waldeck-Rousseau was born in Nantes. He was elected to the Chamber of Deputies as a member of the Union républicaine (1879–89) and, named minister of the interior (November 1881–January 1882; February 1883–March 1885), he put through the law on professional associations that favored the development of the labor union movement (1884). Returning occasionally to his profession as an attorney, he defended GUSTAVE EIFFEL during the PANAMA AFFAIR. As a senator (1894–1904), he was called to serve as prime minister (1899–1902) and, faced with the right-wing nationalist movement, formed a cabinet that would defend the republic and its principles (GASTON GALLIFFET, ALEXANDRE MILLERAND) and that reversed the sentence of captain ALFRED DREYFUS. Waldeck-Rousseau put through the law on associations (1901), aimed particularly at religious congregations, which would bring about the separation of church and state in France. In 1900, responding to the Boxer Rebellion, he sent a French military expedition to China.

## Walewski, Alexandre-Florian-Joseph Colonna, count (1810–1868)
*political figure*

The natural son of NAPOLÉON I and Marie, countess Walewska, Alexandre-Florian-Joseph Colonna, count Walewski was born in Walewice, near Warsaw, Poland. A Pole, he was sent to London to support the cause of Polish independence from Russia after the insurrection of 1830. That uprising having been checked, Walewski went to France, where he was naturalized and, joining the military, took part in the conquest of ALGERIA (1834). He then left his military career for the theater and journalism and started a newspaper, *Le Messager.* Charged with diplomatic missions by the JULY MONARCHY government, he continued in the diplomatic service during the SECOND REPUBLIC and the SECOND EMPIRE. Minister plenipotentiary to Florence, then to Naples, ambassador to Spain then to Great Britain, he was named foreign minister (1855–60) and presided over the Congress of Paris (1856). Count Walewski broke with NAPOLÉON III over the issue of the latter's policy toward Italy (the Italian question, 1859).

## Wallon, Henri (1879–1962)
*psychologist*

Born in Paris, Henri Wallon was a founder of the society for a new French educational system and served as secretary-general of national education and as a Communist deputy (1945–46). He presided over the commission for educational reform (Langevin-Wallon, project, 1945). An authority on infant psychology, he emphasized the interdependence of biological (maturation of the nervous system) and social factors in psychological development. In contrast to Jean Piaget, he affirmed that this was achieved by a discontinuous succession of stages, the passage from one to the other not being a simple amplification but a revision or brusque transformation. This idea was of the development of thought was itself based on observation. It was in agreement with the principles of dialectical and historical materialism. Wallon's principal writings include *L'Enfant turbulent,* 1925; *L'Évolution psychologique de l'enfant,* 1941; *De l'Acte à la pensée,* 1942; and *Les Origines de la pensée chez l'enfant,* 1945.

## Wallon, Henri-Alexandre  (1812–1904)
*historian, political figure*

Born in Valenciennes, Henri-Alexandre Wallon was professor of history at the SORBONNE, where he succeeded FRANÇOIS GUIZOT. He served as a deputy in the Legislative Assembly (1849–50) and sat with the center-right in the National Assembly (1871), where, at first supportive of ADOLPHE THIERS, he voted against him on May 24, 1873. The amendment that bears his name (January 1875) stipulated that the president of the republic would be elected by an absolute majority of votes in the Senate and Chamber of Deputies sitting together in the National Assembly for a term of seven years, and that there can be reelection. This amendment, which was unanimously approved, thus confirmed the republican regime, and is considered the official "baptism" of the THIRD REPUBLIC. For this, Wallon would be called "father of the Republic." As minister of education and of cults (1875–76), he put through the law on the freedom of higher education (1875). Wallon's principal, writings include *L'Esclavage dans les colonies*, 1847; *La Terreur*, 1873; *Du Monothéisme chez les races sémitiques*, 1875; *Saint Louis et son temps*, 1875, *Histoire du Tribunal révolutionnaire de Paris*, 1880–82.

## Walras, Léon  (1834–1910)
*economist*

Born in Évreux, Léon Walras was professor of political economy at Lausanne, Switzerland. Seeking to construct an economic theory that would reconcile the free market and social justice, he developed, at the same time as William Stanley Jevons-British economist and Carl Menger- Austrian economist, a new theory of value based on the principle of marginal utility. Adept at statistical economics, he demonstrated this theory mathematically. Walras's principal works include *La Théorie mathématique de la richesse sociale*, 1873–83; *Éléments d'économie pure*, 1874–87; *Études d'économie politique appliquée*, 1898.

## Warens, Louise-Éleonore de la Tour du Pil, baroness de  (1700–1762)
*aristocrat, literary patron*

Born in Vevey, Vaud, Switzerland, Louise Éleonore de la Tour du Pil, baroness de Warens welcomed

and took in the young JEAN-JACQUES ROUSSEAU at her home in Chaumettes, where the philosopher stayed with her from 1728 to 1742. A great influence on, and supporter of, that writer and thinker, Mme Waren and her relationship with Rousseau are described in Books I to VI of his *Confessions*.

## Watteau, Antoine  (1684–1721)
*painter*

One of the greatest rococo artists, Antoine Watteau was born in Valenciennes, where he was apprenticed to a local painter. He began by drawing street scenes. In 1702, he went to Paris, where a merchant hired him to paint religious pictures and scenes done in the Dutch style. By 1704, he was painting genre scenes and actors and scenes from the commedia dell'arte, from which he gained an interest in theatrical costumes. In 1708, he began to work with master rococo artists and also discovered the collection of Ruben's painting in the Luxembourg Palace gallery and became interested in landscapes. Winning second prize in the prix de Rome, he sold his painting *La Recrue* so he could return to Valenciennes and was at the same time commissioned to paint *La Halte*. In his native town, he continued to paint and draw military scenes, in which he further developed his own style and techniques (*Les Délassements de la guerre*). Returning to Paris in 1710, he was named an associate of the Academy of Art in 1712. Around 1715, he became known in the salons, where he met the intellectual and artistic elite of the period and could further study the collections of the Flemish and Italian masters, especially the Venetians. Given the title of "painter of fêtes galantes" by the academy, he was also interested in nudes and mythological scenes (*Jupiter et Antiope*). In 1717, he presented his masterpiece, *L'Embarquement pour Cythère* at the academy, having also done a second version for the king of Prussia. While Watteau's canvases reflect the influence of previous masters, his own distinctive style dominates and demonstrates his feeling for light and color, sensuousness, and lyrical grace. Other rococo painters would imitate Watteau but failed to replicate his dreamlike qualities. Besides *fêtes galantes*, clowns, and harlequins (*Pierrot, Harlequin et Columbine*), as an acute observer, he made a signboard

(*L'Enseigne de Gersaint*, 1720) for a art dealer's shop, which is a masterpiece of realism in its design and composition; its coloration would later influence the impressionists. Because he has been widely copied, there are often problems in the authentication of Watteau's works.

## Weil, Simone (1909–1943)
*philosopher, writer*

Born and educated in Paris, Simone Weil, whose writings would influence French and British social thought, in 1934 worked at the Renault plant, then taught secondary school while becoming a social activist. In 1936, she joined the International Brigade and fought in the Spanish civil war. After returning to France (1941), she left for New York and London, where she worked in the offices of the RESISTANCE in exile. Disagreeing, however, with certain of general CHARLES DE GAULLE's political policies, she resigned in 1943. She died in August of that year in England while trying, despite her tuberculosis, to subsist on the same rations as her French compatriots living under the German Occupation. Opposed to violence, she always took the side of the weak, vanquished, and oppressed, with whom she identified in her passionate and unrelenting quest for truth and justice. While her mysticism has a Christian inspiration (of Jewish origin, she never converted to Christianity), her views were also drawn from Hellenism, Gnosticism, and Hinduism. The writings of Weil, published after her death, include *La Pensateur et la Grâce*, 1947; *La Connaissance surnaturelle*, 1949; *L'Enracinement*, 1950; *Lettre à un religieux*, 1951; *La Condition ouvrière*, 1951; *La Source grecque*, 1953; *Oppression et Liberté*, 1955; *Écrits historiques et politiques*, 1960.

## Weiss, Louise (1893–1983)
*political figure, writer*

Born in Arras, Louise Weiss founded in 1918 the weekly *L'Europe nouvelle*, which she directed until 1934. She dedicated herself to the promulgation of the European idea as well as to the struggle for women's rights and was one of the founders of the Institut de polémologie (1945). The author of nov-els (*Délivrance*, 1938), Weiss published her memoirs (*Mémoires d'une Européenne*, 1970) and served as the dean of the European Parliament in 1979.

## Wendel family

A family of French industrialists originally from Bruges, the Wendels settled in Coblenz in the 16th century, and, beginning of the 18th century, at Hayange, where Jean-Martin Wendel obtained the rights to the forges. His son, Charles Wendel (1708–84), became one of the principal suppliers of artillery to the state. Ignace Wendel (1741–95), the son of Charles, became the commissioner of royal forges and the director of numerous factories, and was one of the first to substitute coke for charcoal in the manufacturing of iron (1769). He established the forge at Creusot (1785) before emigrating during the REVOLUTION OF 1789. François de Wendel (1778–1825), the son of Ignace, regained the forges at Hayange after the Revolution and also acquired those at Moyeuvre. In 1871, Les Petits-Fils de François de Wendel et Cie was founded, directed by his grandsons, Henri and Robert de Wendel. This company expanded greatly in the late 19th and early 20th centuries. During WORLD WAR I and WORLD WAR II, as the factories were located in German-occupied areas, they were confiscated and made part of German consortia. After the war, the Société de Wendel et Cie, which in 1952 went public, became one of the largest French iron and steel companies.

## Weygand, Maxime (1867–1965)
*general*

Born in Brussels, Belgium, Maxime Weygand was educated at SAINT-CYR and, at the beginning of WORLD WAR I, served as chief of staff for general FERDINAND FOCH and was his close adviser for the rest of that conflict. He was sent to Poland in 1920 as a military adviser during the Polish-Soviet War, then, in 1923, served as high commissioner in Syria. A member of the Supreme War Council (1924) and director of the Center for Military Studies (Centre des hautes études militaires), he was named as chief of the French Army General Staff and left military service in 1935. In 1939, with war imminent, general Weygand was named commander in chief of the Mediterranean theater of operations and, in May 1940, was called by PAUL REYNAUD to replace general MAURICE GAMELIN as supreme commander. He tried to oppose the enemy invasion with a resistance at the Somme and at the Aisne Rivers, and then was advised to accept an armistice for which the government accepted full responsibility. Named minister of national defense in the VICHY government (June–September 1940) and delegate-general of Marshal PHILIPPE PÉTAIN in North Africa (1940–41), he signed the agreements with the Americans that would facilitate the Allied landing of 1942 (Weygand-Murphy Accords, 1941) and succeeded in preventing the application of the Darlan-Warlimont agreements. Recalled to France on the orders of the Germans, he was arrested and interned in Germany (1942). Freed (1945), he was tried before the High Court of Justice by the government of General CHARLES DE GAULLE, but in 1948 he was exonerated of all the main charges against him. Besides his *Mémoires* (1950–57), general Weygand left *Histoire de l'armée française* (1938) and a biography, *Foch* (1947). He was elected to the ACADÉMIE FRANÇAISE in 1931.

## White Terror

The White Terror is the name given to the bloody reprisals of royalists and religious fanatics against the revolutionaries in the latter part of and after the REVOLUTION OF 1789. The first White Terror occurred especially in the southeast of France after the failure of Jacobin insurrections (April and May 1795). Royalist bands of the Compagnies de Jéhu, Jésus, or Soleil, as they called themselves, pursued and massacred JACOBINS, republicans, constitutional priests, Protestants, and political detainees in Lons-le-Saunier, Bourg, Lyon, Saint-Étienne, Aix, Marseille, Toulon, Tarascon, etc., generally with the complicity of the authorities. After the failed landing of émigrés at Quiberon, on France's west coast (June–July, 1795), and the failure of the uprising of 13 Vendémiaire, Year IV (October 5, 1795), the White Terror was partially suppressed. It began again after the Conspiracy of the Equals, a plan to overthrow the DIRECTORY and establish a communist social order, led by FRANÇOIS-NOËL BABEUF and others, was checked. Just as violent, the second

White Terror took place after the defeat of NAPOLÉON I at Waterloo (June 18, 1815). In the west and southeast, bands of "greens" (*verdets*), wearing the green cockade of the count of ARTOIS, killed former revolutionaries, Jacobins, Bonapartists, and some military figures. The RESTORATION government partly condoned this terror and itself executed Marshal MICHEL NEY and banned the regicides.

## Willette, Adolphe (1857–1926)
*artist, lithographer*

Born in Châlons-sur-Marne, Adolphe Willette studied at the École des beaux-arts and in studios in Paris. He dedicated himself especially to drawing and lithography and, in particular, designed and produced posters. He did numerous illustrations for *Chat-noir, Courrier français, Boulevard,* and *Rire,* as well as for *Pierrot* and *Pied-de-nez.* Having a sense of spirit and verve, he also had a feeling for nature and became popular through his representations of Pierrot and Columbine, which were at once lighthearted and sentimental. His work, which he published in an anthology (*Cent Dessins de Willette*), reflects one of the characteristic aspects of the Belle Époque.

## World War I

Known also as the First World War, World War I dates from July 28, 1914 to November 11, 1918. It was a conflict between the Allies (France, Great Britain, Russia, Belgium, Serbia, and, later, the United States) and the Central Powers (Germany, Austria-Hungary, Ottoman Empire). There were several causes, including an intense naval rivalry between Great Britain and Germany; a rise in nationalism, imperialism and colonialism; and the system of secret alliances (Triple Alliance, Triple Entente, Russian-Serbian Defense Treaty, Treaty of Belgian Neutrality). The immediate cause was the assassination in Sarajevo, Bosnia, of the archduke Francis-Ferdinand, heir to the Austrian throne, by a Serbian nationalist, in June 1914.

### POLITICAL, DIPLOMATIC, AND MILITARY DEVELOPMENTS

1914: June 28—Assassination at Sarajevo; July 28—Austrian declaration of war on Serbia and Russia (August 6); August 1—German declaration of war on Russia and France (August 3); August 4–British declaration of war on Germany; August 23–Japanese declaration of war on Germany after German violation of Belgian neutrality. Italian declaration of neutrality. October 29–Turkish declaration of war on the Allies. Western-front: August—German invasion of Belgium and northern France; September 6–13—Victory of JOFFRE at the MARNE. September–November—Beginning of sea war and war in Flanders. Front at Ypres. Eastern front: August–October—Russian offensives in East Prussia (September 26—Russian defeat at Tannenberg) and in Galicia. Stabilization of front at Niemen. Other Fronts: September–December—Austrian setbacks in Serbia; October–December—British entrance in Mesopotamia.

1915: April 25—Italy signs the Treaty of London with the Allies; October 5—Bulgaria joins the side of the Central Powers; Greece remains neutral; Allies put in place naval blockade of Central Powers. Western front: May–September—unsuccessful French attempts to break through in Champagne and Artois (Germans use poison gas). Eastern front: February–September—German offensives in East Prussia and Poland; February–April—Allied setbacks in the Dardanelles (Galipoli) and landing in Salonika; October—Bulgaria invades Serbia; other fronts: July—Italian offensive in Trentino; occupation of German South-West Africa.

1916: Arab uprising against the Turks; August 27—Italy and Romania declare war on Germany; November 21—death of emperor Francis-Joseph and accession of Charles I of Austria. Western front: February 21–December—Battle of VERDUN (la Voie sacrée); July 1–October—Allied offensive on the Somme (British introduce tanks). Eastern front: February—Russian offensives in Armenia and Galicia; October–December—German conquest of Romania. Other fronts: January—Allied occupation of the Cameroons. April 28—British defeat at Kut el-Amara. May 31—Battle of Jutland.

1917: February 1—German emperor William II declares unrestricted submarine warfare. March– November—Russian Revolution. April 6—United States enters on the Allied side. November 17—government of GEORGES CLEMENCEAU. Western front: April 17—Failure of the NIVELLE offensive at Chemin des Dames. Crisis in the French army. PÉTAIN is supreme commander. August—French assaults at Verdun, Ailette (October). November 20—British assault at Cambrai. Eastern front: October 3—Germans take Riga and occupy Bukovina (July–September). December 15—Russian-German armistice of Brest-Litovsk. Other fronts: October 24—Italian defeat at Caporetto. March 10—taking of Baghdad and Jerusalem (December 9) by the British.

1918: January 8—U.S. president Wilson announces the 14 Points. March 3—Treaty of Brest-Litovsk between Germany and Russia. March 26—FOCH is commander in chief of Allied forces on the western front. June 7—Treaty of Bucharest. October—Independence of Hungarians, Czechs, and Yugoslavs. November 9—abdication of William II of Germany. November 11—Austria proclaimed a republic. Western front: March 21—German offensives in Picardy and the Marne (June 27) and Champagne (July 18). July–November—Foch's counteroffensives in Champagne and Picardy (August) and the Meuse (September), German retreat at Gand, Mons, and Sedan. November 11—armistice. Other fronts: September 15—offensive of Franchet d'Esperey in Macedonia. September 29—Armistice with Bulgaria. September–October—taking of Beirut, Damascus, and Aleppo by the British. October 24—Italian victory at Vittorio Veneto. October 30—armistice with Turkey and Austria (November 3). November 13—surrender of the Germans in South-East Africa.

The results of World War I were the fall of the empires (German, Austrian, Russian, and Ottoman), technological and social changes, and the redistribution of the balance of power. For France, which emerged victorious but with demographic and economic setbacks (the war cost 1,350,000 casualties), the period was marked by such political events as the formation of the Union sacrée and the advent and fall of a number of governments (Clemenceau), under the presidency of RAYMOND POINCARÉ.

## World War II

Known also as the Second World War, World War II dates from September 1, 1939 to September 2, 1945, and involved the Axis Powers (Germany, Italy, Japan) and the Allies (France, Great Britain, USSR, United States, and China). The war was caused by the expansion and conquests of the fascist Axis powers, in particular the German invasion of Poland on September 1. The rise of fascism, or National Socialism, in Germany was the result, in large, part of the diktat of Versailles of 1919, which intensified German resentment, thus making World War II, in a real sense, a direct result of WORLD WAR I.

### POLITICAL, DIPLOMATIC, AND MILITARY

1939: September 3—French and British declaration of war on Germany (Italian nonbelligerent status; U.S. neutrality). September 28—German-Soviet Treaty and partition of Poland. Front: September 1–27—Campaign in Poland. September–October—French operations in the Saar. November 30—Russian attack on Finland. September–November—Japanese invasion of China, taking of Nanjing (Nanking).

1940: June 10—Italy declares war on France and Great Britain. June 17—PÉTAIN requests an armistice. June 18 Appeal of General DE GAULLE from London. June 22–25—Franco-German and Franco-Italian armistices. July 10—Pétain invested with constituent power. September 27—Tripartite Pact (German-Italy-Japan). August–September—Romanian territory given to Hungary and Bulgaria. October 24—meeting of Hitler and Pétain at Montoire. Western front: April 9–June 10—Campaign in Norway. May 10–June 25—Campaign in France. May 15–18—Dutch and Belgian capitulations. May 28–June 4—Battle of Dunkerque. June 14—Germans arrive in PARIS. August–October—air Battle of Britain. Eastern front: June 15–29—Soviet occupation of the Baltic states and other areas. October 7—German invasion of Romania. October 28—Italian invasion of Greece. Africa: July 3—French fleet taken at Mers el-Kébir. August–December—Italian attack on Somalia and Libya.

1941: April 13—Soviet-Japanese Treaty. May 28—Darlan-Warlimont Accords on Africa. July 29—Franco-Japanese accord on Indochina. August 14—Atlantic Charter. September 24—creation of the Comité national français in London. November 18—General WEYGAND recalled from Africa. December 7—United States, then China, declares war the Axis powers. Eastern front: April—German intervention in Greece. June 22—German offensive against the USSR. Other fronts: June 8—Campaign in Syria. December 7—Japanese attack on Pearl Harbor. German (March) offensive, then British (November) in Libya.

1942: January 1—formation of the United Nations. April 18—LAVAL head of VICHY government. August 8—Indian Congress asks Britain to leave India. May–July—beginning of deportations and of the French RESISTANCE. November 8—Pétain orders resistance to the Allies in Africa. November 10—Franco-Allied armistice in Africa. November 11—Germans invade the French nonoccupied zone. November 13—DARLAN brings French Africa to the Allied side. December 26—GIRAUD replaces Darlan, who was assassinated. African front: Rommel attacks Libya. October 23—El Alamein. Russian front: German offensives. Far East: Japanese take the Philippines and Singapore (January–February). France: November 27—Scuttling of the French fleet at Toulon. Dissolution of the armistice army.

1943: January 14—Casablanca Conference. May 12—Giraud in Tunis. May—Constitution of the National Council of the French Resistance. June 3—formation in Algiers of the French Committee of National Liberation. July 27—dismissal of Mussolini; Badoglia government. September 17—creation of the Consultative Assembly in Algiers. November 8—Lebanon abolishes the French mandate. October 13—Badoglio declares war on Germany. December 2—Teheran Conference. Fronts: Africa: January 23—British take Tripoli, rejoin French-American forces in Tunisia (April). Italy: December 10—Allies land in Sicily. September 8—Italian surrender. Russia: February 2—Stalingrad. Far East: Allied counteroffensive in Gilbert and Solomon islands (June–December).

1944: January 3—France recognizes sovereignty of Syria and Lebanon. June 3—CFLN proclaimed provisional government. June 10—Massacre at Oradour. Fronts: Italy: February–May—Battle of Cassino. France: March–April—Battles of Glières and Vercors. June 6—Normandy landing. August 15—invasion of Provence. August 25—Liberation of PARIS. August 31—transfer of government form Algiers to Paris. September 5—Benelux Constitution. Fronts: eastern: February–April—Russian offensive. Far East: Battles of New Guinea (January–July), Marianas, and Philippines.

1945: February 12—Yalta Conference. July 26—Potsdam Conference. Fronts: west: March—Allies cross the Rhine. East: Soviets take Warsaw (January) and enter Berlin (May). France: May 7—German surrender at Reims. Far East: Bombing of Hiroshima and Nagasaki (August), Japanese surrender (August 15).

After the Munich Pact in September 1939 (DAL-ADIER), Germany continued its policy of annexation and war broke out, leading to the invasion and occupation of France. The THIRD REPUBLIC came to an end when the armistice was signed (June 22, 1940) and the National Assembly voted full powers to Marshal Pétain. While the Vichy government followed a policy of collaboration with the Germans, RESISTANCE was organized after de Gaulle's appeal, and fought against the Occupation. By 1944, most of France was liberated and after the war (1946), the new government of the FOURTH REPUBLIC was formed.

# X, Y

## Xaintrailles, Jean Poton, seigneur de (unknown–1461)
*military figure*

A companion-in-arms to JOAN OF ARC, Jean Poton, seigneur de Xaintrailles began as a mercenary (1424) in the service of the duke of Burgundy, then went over to fight for King CHARLES VII. Captured by the Burgundians at Mons-en-Vimeu (1421), then ransomed, he became a comrade-in-arms to Joan of Arc and took part in the victory at Patay over the English commander Talbot, whom he took as a prisoner (1429). He also apparently attended the coronation of the dauphin at Reims (July 1429), and fought at Compiegne. Captured in 1431, he was exchanged for Talbot and, in 1444, fought under the dauphin Louis in a campaign against the Swiss. He served as a leader of the French armies (1450), reconquered Normandy, and led the victorious procession of Charles VII into Rouen (1451). In 1455, Xaintrailles conquered Guyenne and was named a marshal of France.

## Yersin, Alexandre (1863–1943)
*microbiologist*

Of Swiss origin, Alexandre Yersin was born in Lavaux, Switzerland, and in 1886 joined the Pasteur Institute and worked with ÉMILE ROUX on research on diphtheria toxins. He is recognized as the discoverer of the specific plague bacillus that infected Hong Kong (1894), the Yersin and Kitasato bacillus (named also for the Japenese physician who discovered it at the same time). Yersin also authored several geographic works dealing with the coast of Annam, which he explored during his travels.

## Yourcenar, Marguerite (1903–1987)
*novelist, essayist*

Born in Brussels, Belgium, Marguerite Yourcenar (the pen name of Marguerite de Crayencour) was raised in a humanistic environment that explains her love of classical Greece (she authored an anthology of ancient Greek poets, *La Couronne et la Lyre*, 1979). She translated Pindar but also the *Poèmes* of Constantin Cavafy, for which she received a Présentation critique in 1958. Marguerite Yourcenar traveled to Switzerland and Italy before visiting the United States, where she settled with her companion, Grace Frick, in 1949. She did a translation of black spirituals, collected in *Fleuve profound, sembre rivière* (1964), and later in *Blues et Gospels* (1984). A translator of Virginia Woolf (*Les Vagues*, 1937) and of Henry James (*Ce que Maisi savait*, 1947), author of essays (*Les Songes et les Sorts*, 1938; *Sous bénéfices d'inventaire*, 1962), of poems in prose and verse (*Feux*, 1936; *Les Charités d'Alcippe*, 1956 and 1974), memoirs (*Souvenirs pieux*, 1974; *Archives du Nord*, 1977; *Quoi? L'éternité*, posthumous, 1938). Marguerite Yourcenar is above all known for her novels. After writing, in a style similar to that of ANDRÉ GIDE, *Alexis ou le Traité du vain combat* (1929), she composed *Le Coup de grâce* (1939), in which her sophistication as a writer is also evident. In 1951, with *Mémoires d'Hadrien*, she again demonstrated her broad knowledge of ancient civilization and historical periods. Other of her writings include a semi-historical novel, *L'Œuvre au noir* (1968), which won her the prix Femina, a series about her life and work entitled *Le Yeux ouverts* (1980), a biography, *Mishima: ou la vision du vide* (1981), and a collection of essays, *Le Temps, ce grand sculpteur* (1983). In

1980, Marguerite Yourcenar became the first woman to be elected into the ACADÉMIE FRANÇAISE.

## Yvain, Maurice (1891–1965)
*composer*

Born in Suresnes, Maurice Yvain was, during the interwar period, one of the revivers of the French operetta, to which he introduced, with rhythms inspired by jazz, a lively and spiritual melodic style. Many of his works, especially those with Yves Mirande and Albert Willemetz as librettists, enjoyed a long success: *Ta bouche* (1922), *Là-haut* (1923), *Gosse de riche* (1924), *Pas sur la bouche* (1925). He composed numerous songs, many of which were for MISTINGUETT (*Mon homme, J'en ai marre, En douce*), as well as several musical selections for film and for two ballets: *Vent* (1937) and *Blanche-Neige* (1951).

## Yvon, Adolphe (1817–1893)
*painter*

Born in Eschwiller, Lorraine, Adolphe Yvon is known for his historical tableaus: *La Bataille de Koulikovo* (1850), *Le premier Consul descendant le mont Saint-Bernard* (1850, in the Hermitage Museum, St. Petersburg), *Le Maréchal Ney à la retraite de Russie, Portrait du Prince impérial* (1864), and *Les États-Unis d'Amérique* (1870, Washington, D.C.).

# Z

## Zadkine, Ossip (1890–1967)
*sculptor, engraver*

Of Russian origin, Ossip Zadkine was born in Smolensk and studied in London and Paris (1909), where he became interested in the work of AUGUSTE RODIN and in African sculpture. The cubist experience determined his development, as he experimented with form and space (*Tête d'homme; Le Prophète*). After WORLD WAR I, in which he served as a volunteer and was severely gassed, he continued his artistic experimentation and eventually produced works with mythological themes (*Ménades; Prométhée; Orphée*, 1945). He also dealt with allegorical (*Homo sapiens*, 1955) and religious (*Saint Sébastien*) subjects and produced symbolic monuments honoring various artists (*Hommage à Rimbaud, Lautrémont, Apollinaire, Jean-Sébastien Bach*). He worked in wood, which he sometimes painted, and in clay and bronze, and developed an expressionist orientation evident in some of his works (*Monument pour une ville détruite*, Rotterdam, 1948–51). His studio in Paris now the Zadkine Museum.

## Zamet, Sebastiano (ca. 1549–1614)
*financier*

Of Italian origin, Sebastiano Zamet was born in Lucca and came to Paris, as a simple rope maker in the entourage of CATHERINE DE' MEDICI. He quickly made a fortune, however, and became one of the richest bankers of the time. He gained the favor of king HENRY IV and became captain of the château of Fontainebleau and superintendent of the queen's household.

## Zamet, Sébastien (1588–1655)
*cleric*

Born in Paris, Sébastien Zamet was the son of SEBASTIANO ZAMET and became bishop of Langres.

In 1625, he became director of the abbey of Port-Royal and hence involved in its Jansenist activities. With Jacqueline Marie Angelique ARNAUD (Mère Angelique), abbess of Port-Royal, he founded the Institut du Saint-Sacrement.

## Zay, Jean (1904–1944)
*political figure*

Born in Orléans, Jean Zay was a Radical-Socialist deputy (1932–40) and held the portfolio for national education from 1936 to 1939, contributing to the adoption of the POPULAR FRONT government's educational reforms (increase in scholarships for primary students; raising the age of obligatory education to 14). A partisan in the RESISTANCE since the signing of the armistice, Zay left France on the *Massilia* but was arrested in Morocco and interned on the orders of the VICHY regime. In 1944, he was taken from his prison in Riom and assassinated by members of the Milice.

## Zazzo, René (1910–1995)
*psychologist*

Born in Paris, René Zazzo was a specialist in infant psychology in the tradition of Arnold Gesell and HENRI WALLON. His best-known work was on twins, which allowed him to study the problems of learning and hereditary mechanisms as well as the effects of pairing (*Les Jumeaux, le couple et la personne*, 1960; *Le Paradoxe des jumeaux*, with an introduction by MICHEL TOURNIER, 1984). Zazzo was also interested in psychomotor development (*Des garçons de six à douze ans*, 1969).

## Zédé, Gustave (1835–1891)
*naval engineer*

Born in Paris, Gustave Zédé developed the plans for the *Gymnote*, the first operational French submarine

(1887). It was powered by electrical propulsion and carried two large torpedoes.

## Zehrfuss, Bernard (1911–1996)
*architect*

Born in Angers, Bernard Zehrfuss built the National Center of Industry and Technology (Cnit) at la Défense (1958) and the UNESCO headquarters in Paris. He also built the Renault plant at Flins and the Museum of Gallo-Roman History in LYON (1972–75). Elected to the Académie des beaux-arts, he was named its permanent secretary in 1994.

## Zervos, Christian (1889–1970)
*art editor, collector, art critic, historian*

Of Greek origin, Christian Zervos was born in Argostoli and, coming to France, founded the revue *Cahiers d'art* (1926–60), which supported and popularized avant-garde European art (GEORGES BRAQUE, HENRI, MATISSE, Pablo Picasso, V. Kandinsky, Juan Gris) and opened an art gallery and publishing house. Zervos published books on prehistoric as well as contemporary art and produced a 33-volume catalog on the works of Picasso. He also followed surrealism, abstractionism and, starting in the 1950s, the return of figuration. A Zervos Museum was opened in Vézelay in 1994.

Émile Zola *(Library of Congress)*

## Zola, Émile (1840–1902)
*writer*

Born in Paris, Émile Zola spent his formative years, raised by his mother, in Aix-en-Provence. After returning to Paris, he soon abandoned his studies and took a number of jobs before becoming a journalist. At first an ardent romantic (*Contes à Ninon*, 1864) and critic of modern art (*Édouard Manet*, 1867), he moved to naturalism with *Thérèse Raquin* (1867) and, an enthusiast of CLAUDE BERNARD, sought to write an "experimental novel" based on theories of heredity and the environment. In 1868, he outlined the genealogy of *Rougon-Macquart* and, from 1871 to 1893, the 20 volumes of *Histoire naturelle et social d'une famille sous le Second Empire* appeared. It was then *L'Assomoir* (1877) that assured Zola his success. Henceforth a leader of the naturalist writers (GUY DE MAUPASSANT and JORIS-KARL

HUYSMANS), he defined his style in *Le Roman expérimental* (1880) and continued his cyclical work: *Nana* (1880), which harshly denounced the foibles of the wealthy and elite, and *Germinal* (1885), a powerful evocation of a miners' strike that was extremely successful and controversial. His preoccupation with social issues (he was a reader of CHARLES FOURIER, PIERRE-JOSEPH PROUDHON, and Karl Marx) was already apparent in *Au Bonheur des dames* (1883), and his emerging socialist sympathies were soon strongly reinforced. Converted, he followed these inquiries into the world of workers to the doctrines of socialism and, from that point on, had a humanitarian character (*Les quatre Évangiles*, 1899–1903 ar hymns to human progress) and sense of political commitment, especially after the Dreyfus affair (see DREYFUS, ALFRED), during which he issued his resounding statement, "J'accuse," published in

*L'Aurore* (1898). Zola's death was perhaps due to a criminal attempt and a huge assemblage of people attended his funeral, at which time, ANATOLE FRANCE, in his eulogy, described Zola as "the conscience of mankind." A naturalist to the extent that he employed scientific methods to his background research and he wanted his experimental novels to be stories in which psychology is subordinated to physiology (the influence of AUGUSTE COMTE and Positivism), Zola set for himself a dual task: to observe facts and to see how they can be interpreted and used in his storytelling. However, he transcended even this simplified doctrine with a powerful imagination and an epic sense complemented by lyrical prose and an extremely abundant vocabulary.

# CHRONOLOGY

**751**
Pippin crowned king of the Franks

**768–814**
Reign of Charlemagne (sole ruler of 771)

**794**
Permanent capital at Aachen

**802**
Major administrative reforms; *missi domini*

**842**
Oath of Strasbourg

**843**
Treaty of Verdun; Assembly of Coulaines

**858**
Quierzy agreement of Charles the Bald and his magnates

**877**
Capitulary of Quierzy; Coronation oath of Louis the Stammerer

**885–887**
Siege of Paris by Vikings

**887**
Charles the Fat deposed as emperor

**888**
Charles the Fat dies; Eudes elected king of the Franks

**893**
Charles III the Simple, crowned king of the Franks

**910**
Founding of abbey at Cluny

**911**
Charles the Simple gives Normandy to Rollo the Viking

**918**
Richard the Justiciar, duke of the Burgundians

**922**
Election of Robert as king of the West Franks

**923**
Death of Robert; election of Raoul of Burgundy as king

**929**
Death of Charles the Simple

**936**
Return of Carolingian Louis d'Outremer

**987**
Hugh Capet elected king of the Franks

**996**
Robert II succeeds Hugh Capet

**1002**
Burgundian civil war; Robert II seizes the duchy

**1031**
Independent Capetian duchy of Burgundy; accession of Henry I

**1031–1033**
Great famine in France

**1037**
William the Bastard inherits Normandy

**1060**
Accession of Philippe I

**1066**
William, duke of Normandy, conquers England; becomes its king

**1071**
Norman conquest of southern Italy

**1085**
Christians capture Toledo; Robert Guiscard dies in Greece

**1061–1091**
Norman conquest of Sicily

**1095**
Urban II preaches the First Crusade at Clermont

**1096–1099**
First Crusade; Christians take Jerusalem, July 15, 1099

**1106**
Court of Anjou again does homage to king of France

**1107**
Concordat between King Phillip I and Pope Paschal II on investiture of bishops

**1108**
Louis VI crowned at Orléans

**1127**
Count of Flanders again does homage to king of France

**1137**
Louis VII becomes king, marries Eleanor of Aquitaine

**1147**
Louis VII goes on the Second Crusade; fails to take Damascus
Second Crusade fails at Damascus

**1152**
Eleanor and Louis divorce; Eleanor marries Henry Plantagenet

**1169**
Plantagenets do homage for Normandy, Anjou, Maine, and Poitou

**1180**
Accession of Philip Augustus

**1183**
Death of the young Henry Plantagenet

**1186**
Death of Duke Geoffrey of Burgundy

**1187**
Saladin routs Christians at Springs of Cresson and at Hattin; takes Jerusalem

**1189**
Death of Henry II of England; Richard I, king of England

**1190**
Richard I and Philip Augustus leave on Third Crusade

**1191**
Death of Philip, count of Flanders; deaths of Thibaud, count of Blois, and Henry, count of Troyes, at siege of Acre

**1192**
Philip Augustus returns from Third Crusade

**1194**
Richard defeats Philip Augustus at Freteval; captures royal archives

**1199**
Death of Richard the Lion-Hearted; John Lackland, king of England

**1202–1204**
Fourth Crusade. Crusaders sack Constantinople, 1204, and establish the Latin Empire of Byzantium

**1204**
Philip Augustus confiscates fiefs of John Lackland

**1214**
Philip defeats count of Flanders and the emperor at Bouvines (July 27); Crown Prince Louis defeats John in the Loire valley

**1215**
King John issues the Magna Carta

**1216–1217**
French invade England, defeated at Lincoln (1217)

**1223**
Accession of Louis VIII

**1226**
Accession of Louis IX (Saint Louis); persecution of Albigensians

**1243**
Massacre at Montségur

**1248–1254**
Louis IX on crusade; defeated at Mansurah (1250)

**1254**
First surviving *Olim* (records of the Parlement of Paris)

**1257**
Sorbonne founded

**1261**
End of Latin Empire of Byzantium

**1270**
Louis IX dies at Tunis; accession of Philippe III

**1271**
Poitou and Toulouse revert to the French Crown

**1285**
Accession of Philippe IV

**1314**
Accession of Louis X

**1316**
Accession of Jean I; accession of Philippe V

**1322**
Accession of Charles IV

**1328**
Philip VI of Valois chosen king of France; Battle of Cassel

**1329**
Edward III does homage for Guyenne

**1337**
Philip VI confiscates Guyenne from Edward III of England; war starts

**1340**
Breton civil war starts

**1346**
English rout the French at Battle of Crécy

**1348**
Black Death arrives in France

**1349**
Death of Humbert of Dauphiné; province passes to French royal family; purchase of Montpellier

**1350**
Accession of Jean II

**1356**
English destroy French army at Poitiers; King John captured

**1358**
Jacquerie uprising

**1359**
Peace of Brétigny

**1360**
Estates General of Langue d'Oil imposes long-term taxation to pay John II's ransom

**1363**
Estates Generals create standing army and taxes to pay for it

**1364**
Accession of Charles V

**1367–1374**
Du Guesclin defeats the English; France regains lost provinces

**1378**
Battle of Roosebeke; French defeat Flemish militias

**1378–1382**
Rebellions at Paris, Rouen, and in rural south (Tuchins)

**1380**
Death of Charles V; "abolition" of taxes

**1392**
Onset of madness of Charles VI

**1396**
Disaster at Nicopolis

**1405**
Christine de Pisan's *Le Livre de la Cité des Dames*

**1407**
John of Burgundy has Louis of Orléans murdered

**1413**
Cabochien rising at Paris

**1415**
Battle of Agincourt: Henry V annihilates French army

**1419**
Entourage of the dauphin Charles murders John of Burgundy

**1420**
Treaty of Troyes

**1422–1423**
Death of Henry V and Charles VI

**1428–1429**
Joan of Arc delivers Orléans, Charles VII crowned at Reims

**1435**
Treaty of Arras: Charles VII and Philip of Burgundy make peace

**1436**
Charles regains Paris

**1445**
Charles regains Normandy; creation of the Compagnies d'ordonnance

**1449–1453**
Charles conquers Guyenne; end of the Hundred Year's War

**1461**
Accession of Louis XI

**1483**
Accession of Charles VIII

**1491**
Brittany united with the French Crown

**1498**
Accession of Louis XII

**1509**
Jean Lemaire de Belge's *Les Illustrations de Gaule et singularités de Troye*

**1516**
Concordat of Bologna

**1515**
Accession of Francis I; French victory at Marignan

**1525**
French defeat at Pavia

**1530**
Collège de France founded

**1533–1549**
Rabelais's *Gargantua et Pantagruel*

**1534**
Jacques Cartier reaches Canada

**1536**
John Calvin's *Institution de la Religion chrétienne*

**1547**
Accession of Henry II

**1549**
Du Bellay's *Défense et illustration de la langue française*

**1550**
Ronsard's *Odes*

**1552**

J. de Baïf's *Amours de Méline;* occupation of Metz

**1557**

Du Bellay's *Les Regrets*

**1559**

Death of Henry II; Francis II king at 14; Treaty of Cateau-Cambrésis

**1560**

Tumult of Amboise (February); death of Francis II (12/5); Estates General of Orléans opens (12/3); Jeanne d'Albret declares for Protestantism (12/25); accession of Charles IX

**1561**

Estates General of Pontoise (August), Colloquy of Poissy (September)

**1562**

Edict of Saint-Germain (March), Massacre of Wassy (3/1); Protestants seize major towns (March–April); Catholics take Rouen (10/26); death of Antoine de Bourbon (11/17); Battle of Dreux (12/19)

**1563**

Assassination of François de Guise (February); peace of Amboise (3/19)

**1564**

Edict of Paris, first day of the year set as January 1, not Easter; Charles IX and Catherine de' Medici begin their two-year trip around France

**1566**

Ordinance of Moulins (February); iconoclasm in the Low Countries

**1567**

**September 26:** Attempted seizure of Meaux by Condé

**September 30:** *Michelaude* at Nîmes

**November 10:** Second War of Religion begins; deaths of Anne de Montmorency and Marshal Saint-André

**1568**

**March 23:** Peace of Longjumeau

**June:** De L'Hopital removed from royal council

**June 5:** Duke of Alba executes counts Egmont and Hoorn

**August 1:** Third War of Religion starts

**1569**

**March 13:** Battle of Jarnac

**September 13:** Death of Condé; Parlement of Paris sentences Coligny to death

**1570**

Peace of Saint-Germain

**1571**

**September:** Coligny returns to court

**December 20:** Gastines riot

**1572**

**April 1:** Dutch "Sea Beggars" take Brill

**June 9:** Death of Jeanne d'Albret

**August 18:** Marriage of Henry of Navarre and Marguerite de Valois

**August 22:** Attempted assassination of Coligny

**August 24:** Saint Bartholomew's Day Massacre

**August 26:** Massacres of Protestants at Orléans, Lyon (8/31), Rouen (9/17), and Toulouse (10/3)

Siege of La Rochelle begins

**1573**

**May:** Henry of Valois elected king of Poland-Lithuania

**July:** Peace of Boulogne

**1574**

**March:** Fifth War of Religion starts

**March 30:** Death of Charles IX; accession of Henry III

**June 18:** Henry III leaves Cracow

**June 9:** Henry III reaches Lyon

**December 26:** Death of cardinal of Lorraine

**1575**

**February 13:** Henry III crowned and married to Louise of Vaudemont

**September 15:** Duke of Alençon flees court

## 1576

January: First organization of the Holy League
February 2: Henry of Navarre flees court
May: Edict of Beaulieu/Peace of Monsieur
December 6: Opening of Estates General
Henry III calls for the extirpation of Protestants

## 1577

January: Start of the Sixth War of Religion
February: Estates General endorses toleration
September 14: Peace of Bergerac
September 17: Edict of Poitiers

## 1579

January 23: Union of Utrecht creates United
  Provinces of the Netherlands
November: Start of the Seventh War of Religion

## 1580

Peace of Fleix

## 1583

March: White penitent movement begins
November: Assembly of Notables at Saint-Germain-
  en-Laye

## 1584

June 10: Death of duke of Anjou
July 10: Assassination of William of Orange
Autumn: Holy League reconstituted

## 1587

October 20: Navarre routs royal army at Coutras
October–November: Duke de Guise destroys German mercenary armies

## 1588

May 9: Guise enters Paris
May 12: Day of the Barricades; duke de Guise takes
  Paris
July 15: Henry III flees Paris; Edict of Union de-
  clares Protestantism to be treason
Summer: Invincible Spanish Armada destroyed off
  England
September 9: Pope bars Henry of Navarre and prince
  de Condé from throne of France
October 16: Estates General at Blois

October 18: Henry III declares Edict of Union a fun-
  damental law
December 23: Assassination of duke de Guise
December 24: Assassination of cardinal de Guise

## 1589

January 5: Death of Catherine de' Medici
January: Antiroyal riots in Paris
April 3: Alliance of Henry of Navarre and Henry III
May 26: Pope Sixtus V excommunicates Henry III
August 1: Jacques Clement stabs Henry III
August 2: Death of Henry III; Henry of Navarre
  (Henry IV) becomes king of France
September 21: Henry IV defeats Mayenne at Arques

## 1590

March 14: Henry defeats Mayenne at Ivry
May 14: Death of Charles, cardinal of Bourbon,
  "Charles X"

## 1593

July 25: Estates General meet to elect a "king";
  Henry abjures Protestantism

## 1594

February 27: Henry crowned at Chartres
September: Brissac sells Paris to the king

## 1595

September 17: Pope Clement VIII accepts Henry's
  conversion
Mayenne agrees to terms

## 1596

December: Assembly of Notables at Rouen

## 1597

February: Spanish seize Amiens
September 19: Henry retakes Amiens

## 1598

April: Mercoeur surrenders in Brittany; Edict of
  Nantesµ
May 2: France and Spain sign Peace of Vervins

## 1600–1601

War with Savoy; France gains Bresse and surrounding area; execution of Biron

**1608**
Founding of Quebec by Samuel Champlain

**1610**
**May 10:** Assassination of Henry IV by Ravaillac

**1614**
**October:** Estates General meets in Paris

**1615**
Marriage of Louis XIII and Anne of Austria

**1616**
Agrippa d'Aubigné's *Histoire universelle depuis 1550 jusqu'en 1601*

**1617**
Assassination of Concini; war breaks out with Protestants

**1618**
Thirty Years' War begins

**1620**
Marie de' Medici defeated; Catholicism restored in Béarn

**1621–1622**
Failed siege of Montauban; Montpellier taken

**1624**
Richelieu rejoins the royal council

**1626**
Assembly of Notables leads to reform; notable Code of Michau (1629); Chalais conspiracy; Michel de Marillac given the Seals

**1627–1628**
Siege and capture of La Rochelle

**1629**
**June:** Grace of Ales eliminates Protestant rights to fortified towns

**1629–1630**
Mantuan Wars

**1630**
**November 10–11:** Days of the Dupes

**1632**
Death of Michel and Louise de Marillac and of d'Effat

**1635**
France enters the Thirty Years' War; Académie française established

**1635–1640**
Endemic rebellions of the Croquants in the Southwest

**1636**
Nu-Pieds rebellions in Normandy

**1637**
Corneille's *Le Cid;* Descarte's *Discours de la méthode*

**1642**
**December 4:** Death of Richelieu

**1643**
**May 14:** Death of Louis XIII; ministry of Mazarin
**May 19:** Victory at Rocroi

**1648**
Peace of Westphalia; August 26—Day of the Barracades; Paris rises against Anne of Austria

**1648–1649**
Parlementary Fronde

**1649–1653**
Fronde of the Princes

**1651**
Le grand Arnauld's *Apologie pour les Saints-Pères*

**1654**
**June 7:** Louix XIV crowned

**1656–1657**
Pascal's *Provinciales*

**1658**

June 14: Turenne's victory at the Battle of the Dunes

**1659**

November 9: Peace of the Pyrenees

**1661**

March 9: Death of Mazarin; Louis XIV assumes personal power

**1664**

Colbert becomes superintendent of arts and manufactures

**1665**

La Rochefoucauld's *Maximes*

**1666**

Molière's *Misanthrope*

**1667–1668**

War of Devolution; France seizes Franche-Comté, Artois, and part of Flanders

**1668**

Peace of Aix-la-Chapelle; France returns Franche-Comté to Spain; keeps major towns of Artois, such as Lille

**1669**

Molière's *Tartuffe*

**1672–1673**

Unsuccessful siege of Amsterdam; capture of Maastricht; emperor allies with Dutch

**1672–1678**

Dutch War

**1675**

Death of Turenne; retirement of Condé

**1677**

Racine's *Phèdre*

**1678**

Capture of Ghent; Peace of Nijmegen: annexation of Franche-Comté; Mme de la Fayette's *Princesse de Clèves*

**1679**

Treaty of Nijmegen; France keeps Franche-Comté; gives up Flanders; Port-Royal closed

**1680**

Comédie-Française established

**1681**

Louis XIV seizes Strasbourg; Four Gallican Articles

**1682**

Royal Court established at Versailles; Louisiana founded

**1684**

France takes Luxembourg; Truce of Regensberg

**1685**

Revocation of the Edict of Nantes (Edict of Fontainebleau); death of elector of the Palatinate

**1688**

Death of archbishop-elector of Cologne; French troops pillage the Rhineland; English depose James II and call in William and Mary

**1689–1696**

War of the League of Augsburg

**1692**

French navy destroyed at La Hougue

**1693–1694**

French victory at Neerwinden; capture of Namur; famine kills 1.3 million French people

**1697**

Peace of Ryswick; Louis XIV relinquishes Luxembourg; Bayle's *Dictionnaire*

**1701**

Death of Charles II of Spain; Philip of Anjou (Philip V) king of Spain

**1702–1713**

War of the Spanish Succession

**1704–1705**

French routed at Blenheim and Ramillies

**1709–1710**
Famine kills 600,000 French people; winter freeze destroys olive trees and vines of all southern France; Battle of Malplaquet

**1711**
Death of the dauphin

**1712**
Villar's victory at Denain; deaths of duke of Burgundy and his oldest son

**1713–1714**
Treaties of Utrecht and Rastatt

**1715**
Death of Louis XIV; five-year-old Louis XV is king; Philip d'Orléans is regent, the regency administration of Dubois

**1716–1720**
John Law's System

**1721**
Treaty of Nystadt

**1725–1743**
Ministry of Cardinal Fleury

**1726**
Mme de Sévigné's *Lettres* published

**1731**
Prévost's *Manon Lescaut*

**1733**
Montesquieu's *Lettres persanes* published

**1734**
Voltaire's *Lettres philosophiques* published

**1738**
Treaty of Vienna

**1741–1754**
Dupleix in India

**1743**
Jean Le Rond d'Alembert's *Traité de dynamie*

**1748**
Montesquieu's *Esprit des lois;* Treaty of Aix-la-Chapelle

**1751–1772**
Publication of Diderot's *L'Encyclopédie*

**1754**
Start of the French and Indian War in North America

**1755**
Start of Seven Years' War in Europe

**1757**
French routed at Rossbach; French victories in North Africa

**1758**
François Quesnay's *Tableau économique*

**1759**
British forces drive French from North America (Plains of Abraham); British navy annihilates French at Quiberon Bay; Voltaire's *Candide* published

**1760**
Loss of Quebec and Montreal

**1762**
Rousseau's *Émile* and *Contrat social*

**1763**
Peace of Paris; France loses Canada, Louisiana, and Senegal

**1764**
Suppression of the Jesuit Order

**1765**
Treaty of Paris and Hubertsbourg

**1766–1768**
Annexation of Lorraine and Corsica

**1770**
Marriage of the future Louis XVI to Marie Antoinette of Austria

**1772**

First partition of Poland

**1774**

Ascension of Louis XVI; Lavoisier's analysis of air

**1776**

Turgot's *Réflexions sur la formation et la distribution des richesses* published

**1778**

French ally with the United States of America in the War of American Revolution; Russian War with Ottoman Empire

**1781**

French navy defeats British at Yorktown and in India; dismissal of Necker

**1782**

Laclos's *Les Liaisons dangereuses*

**1783**

Peace of Paris; United States becomes independent; French regain Senegal; Russia attacks the Ottoman Empire; Montgolfier Brothers' balloon flight

**1787**

**Spring:** Meeting of the first Assembly of Notables
**May:** Resignation of Calonne; Brienne replaces him
**May 21:** Lafayette calls for an Estates General
**June–July:** Court of Peers registers reform edicts—provincial assemblies, revised tax and fiscal system
**July:** Louis XVI announces he will summon the Estates General by 1792; Parlement of Paris exiled
**November:** Parlement recalled

**1788**

**January:** Parlement registers tax-reform edicts; limited tolerations for Protestants
**May:** Louis XVI sends judicial reform edicts to parliament
**June 7:** Day of the Tiles in Grenoble
**August:** Louis XVI dismisses Brienne; announces Estates General for May 1, 1789; Necker returns to the government

**September:** Parlement of Paris rules that Estates General will follow rules of 1614
**Fall:** Second Assembly of Notables
**December:** Louis XVI issues edicts on rules for the Estates General

**1789**

**January:** Estates General formally summoned
**March–April:** Electoral campaign for the Estates General; redaction of the cahiers
**April:** Reveillon riots in Paris
**May 5:** Estates General open at Versailles
**August 4–11:** Abolition of the ancien régime
**August 26:** Declaration of the Rights of Man and of the Citizen
**September 11:** Debate on king's veto power; he receives suspensive veto only
**October 5–6:** Parisian women, followed by the National Guard, march to Versailles; forcibly bring royal family to Paris (Tuileries Palace)
**November 2:** Confiscation of church property
**November 3:** Louis XVI signs August Decrees
**December 14:** Reorganization of municipal and local governments

**1790**

**January–February:** Municipal elections
**April 17:** *Assignats* become legal tender
**June:** Bagarre de Nîmes
**July 12:** Civil Constitution of the Clergy
**July 14:** Feast of the Federation
**August 31:** Repression of mutineers at Nancy

**1791**

**February:** Second Camp de Jalès; municipal elections
**March 2:** Guilds suppressed
**March–April:** Pope condemns the Civil Constitution of the Clergy; district elections
**April 2:** Mirabeau dies
**June 14:** Le Chapelier Law
**June 20–21:** Royal family flees Paris; arrested at Varennes

**1792**

**August 10:** Storming of the Tuileries; end of the monarchy

**August:** Decrees establishing new government; mandatory house searches

**September 2–6:** September Massacres

**September 20:** Battle of Valmy; French defeat the Prussians

**September 21:** First meeting of the Convention; declaration of the republic

**November 6:** Battle of Jemappe, Dumouriez defeats Austrians

**December:** Trial of Louis XVI begins

Olympe de Gouge's *Déclaration des droits des femmes et de la citoyenne;* Condorcet's *Esquisse d'un tableau des progrès de l'esprit humain*

## 1793

**January 21:** Execution of Louis XVI

**February 1:** Declaration of war against Great Britain and Holland

**March 10–11:** Massacre at Machecoul, start of Vendée uprising

**May 31–June 2:** June days; riots in Paris, collapse of the Girondin government

**June:** Vendéans capture Saumur and Angers; are repulsed at Nantes; Jacobins gradually take over the government

**June 24:** Convention approves the Constitution of the Year II

**July 13:** Assassination of Marat by Charlotte Corday

**July 27:** Robespierre joins the Committee of Public Safety

**August 23:** *Levée en masse* (Mass conscription)

**August 27:** British capture Toulon

## 1794

**October:** French victories in the German Rhineland

**November 12:** Convention closes Paris Jacobin Club

**December 8:** Banned Girondin deputies restored to Convention

**December 24:** Wage and price controls (General Maximum) relaxed

**December 27:** Barère, Billaud-Varenne, Collot d'Herbois, and Vadier impeached

## 1795

**January:** French troops enter Amsterdam; Dutch renounce the House of Orange and create the Batavian Republic

**February 8:** Marat's remains removed from the Panthéon

**March 8:** Federalists pardoned; Federalist deputies restored to their seats

**April 1:** Sansculottes demonstrations (Germinal) in Paris; artisans invade the floor of the Convention but movement fails; Billaud-Varenne Collot d'Herbois, and Vadier sent to French Guiana

**April 5:** Treaty of Basel; Prussia officially recognizes the French republic

**April 20–24:** Prairial uprising in Paris; Sansculottes again invade the Convention and again are defeated and disarmed (May 24)

**June 8:** Death of Louis XVI's son; count of Provence becomes heir to the throne

**August 22:** Adoption of constitution of 1795

**October 1:** Annexation of Belgium

**October 5:** Royalist uprising in Paris is crushed; General Napoléon Bonaparte distinguishes himself in the fighting

**October 16–21:** Legislative elections under the "two-thirds" decree

**November 3:** Directory officially takes power

**April 1796:** Bonaparte defeats Austrians and their allies in Italy

**October:** Napoléon Bonaparte creates Cisalpine Republic

**May 10:** Arrest of members of the Conspiracy of the Equals

## 1797

**December–January:** Bonaparte's expedition to Ireland fails

**March–April:** Royalist success in legislative elections

**April 18:** Leoben agreement between Bonaparte and Austrians, later ratified as Peace of Campo Formio in October

**May 26–27:** Trial of the "Equals" ends; execution of Gracchus Babeuf

**July:** Cisalpine and Ligurian Republics created by Bonaparte

**July 15:** Decrees against refractory clergy repealed

**September 4:** Elections invalidated, royalist deputies removed from legislature; local elections overturned, Carnot and Barthelemy removed (18 Fructidor)

**September 5:** Draconian laws against refractory clergy reinstated

**1798**

**January:** French troops intervene against the pope; Roman republic declared; annexation of Mulhouse; de facto annexation of left bank of the Rhine

**March:** Declaration of Helvetian (Swiss) Republic

**April:** Jacobins successful in legislative elections

**May–July:** Bonaparte's victories in Egypt (Battle of the Pyramids, July)

**May 11:** Election results invalidated, new deputies removed

**August:** Admiral Nelson annihilates French fleet at Aboukir, European War. Fighting in Germany, Italy and Switzerland; France against the Second Coalition: Great Britain, Austria, Spain, Italian states, and Russia

**1799**

**January:** French defeat Neapolitan troops; occupy mainland portion of Kingdom of Naples; declares the Republic of Naples

**April:** French evacuate Milan; Cisalpine Republic collapses

**May:** Royalist forces retake Naples; Neapolitan Republic disintegrates

**June–August:** French defeats in Italy; withdrawal of French troops, end of Roman Republic

**July:** Jacobin Club reopens

**August 13:** Jacobin Club closed again

**August 23:** Napoléon abandons his troops in Egypt and secretly sails for France

**October 9:** Napoléon arrives in France

**November 9–10:** Coup d'etat of 18 Brumaire; Napoléon becomes effective ruler of France

**1799–1804**

Le Consulat; Constitution of the Year VIII

**1800**

Battles of Marengo and Hohenlinden

**1801**

Concordat; Treaty of Luneville with Austria; Pinel's *Traité médico-philosophique*

**1802**

Treaty of Amiens with Britain

**1804**

Civil Code; Napoléon declared emperor; Legion of Honor established; Haiti declares independence

**December 2:** Napoléon's coronation

**1804–1814**

First Empire

**1805**

Third coalition, Trafalgar, Austerlitz, Treaty of Pressburg

**1806**

Fourth coalition; Jena and Auerstadt, continental blockade

**1807**

Eylau, Friedland, Treaty of Tilsit

**1808**

War with Spain; founding of the Imperial University

**1809**

Fifth coalition; Wagram

**1810**

Treaty of Varenne

**1811**

Birth of the king of Rome (Napoléon II)

**1812**

Beginning of the Russian campaign

**1813**

Seventh Coalition; Leipzig; Mme de Staël's *De L'Allemagne*

**1814**

Allies invasion of France, Napoléon abdicates

**1814–1830**

Restoration

**1814**

First Restoration; monarchy reinstated with Louis XVIII; Treaty of Paris; Jean Ingres's work debuts in Paris

**1815**

Congress of Vienna; Napoléon's exile to Elba, One Hundred Days, Second Restoration, Second Treaty of Paris; Holy Alliance
**June 18:** Battle of Waterloo

**1815–1816**

White Terror

**1816–1820**

Moderate government

**1818**

Congress of Aix-la-Chapelle, evacuation of French territory

**1819**

Henri de Saint-Simon and Auguste Comte publish *L'Organisateur*

**1820**

Assassination of the duke of Berry; Ampère formulates laws of electromagnetism

**1820–1828**

Rightist government

**1823**

Expedition in Spain

**1824**

Niépce debuts photography

**1824–1830**

Reign of Charles X

**1827**

Battle of Navarin

**1830**

Algiers expedition
**July 27–28–29:** "Les trois glorieuses"—Revolution of Paris; Louis-Philippe I crowned king the French; Belgian uprising

**1830–1848**

July Monarchy, Realism school of painting begins, led by Gustave Courbet and Honoré Daumier

**1831**

Belgian independence; Victor Hugo's *Notre-Dame de Paris* published; French Foreign Legion created

**1833**

Guizot Law establishes primary education system; George Sand's *Lélia* published

**1834**

Félicité de Lamennais's *Paroles d'un croyant*

**1835**

Honoré de Balzac publishes first successful novel, *Perè Goriot*

**1836**

Alexis de Tocqueville publishes *La démocratie en Amérique*

**1837**

Treaty of Tafna

**1839**

Stendhal's *La chartreuse de Parme* (*Charterhouse of Parma*) published; first daguerreotype

**1840**

Eastern question; J. Proudhon's *Qu'est-ce que c'est la propriété?*

**1840–1848**

Guizot Ministry

**1842**

Train laws enacted; Étienne Cabet's *Voyage en Icarie*

**1844**

Victory of Isly

**1846**

Establishment of free trade with England

**1847**

Surrender of Abd-el-Kader

**1848**

February revolution, Second Republic proclaimed
**June:** Workers' insurrection in Paris

**1848–1849**

Revolutions in Europe; French troops occupy Rome

**1848–1852**

Second Republic
The days of June
**December:** Louis-Napoléon Bonaparte made president of the republic

**1850**

Falloux Law; Electoral Law

**1851**

**December 2:** Coup d'état of Louis-Napoléon Bonaparte, proclaimed as Napoléon III
**December 3:** Days of the Barracades in Paris—protest against the coup d'état

**1852–1870**

Second Empire; Constitution of 1852; Napoléon III emperor; Georges Haussmann redesigns city of Paris

**1854**

Faidherbe in Sénégal

**1854–1855**

Crimean War, siege of Sevastopol

**1854–1862**

Berthelot discovers organic synthesis

**1856**

Congress of Paris

**1857**

Gustave Flaubert's *Madame Bovary* and Charles Baudelaire's *Les fleurs du mal* published

**1858**

Orsini assassination attempt; Mont Cénis Tunnel begun

**1858–1863**

Occupation of Cochin China and Kampuchea (Cambodia)

**1859**

Italian War, Magenta, Solferino, Central Italy votes for annexation to Piedmont

**1860**

Beginning of liberal period of Second Empire
Start of impressionist school of painting led by Édouard Manet

**1862**

Victor Hugo's *Les Misérables* published

**1862–1867**

Expedition to Mexico

**1864**

Right to strike given to French workers

**1865**

Jules Verne's *Voyage au center de la terre* (*Journey to the Center of the Earth*) published

**1866**

Austria-Prussian War, Battle of Sadowa, Confederation of North Germany

**1867**

Establishment of Austria-Hungarian dualism

**1869**

Parliamentary period of empire; Paul Verlaine's *Fêtes galantes* published; Suez Canal opened

**1870–1871**

Franco-Prussian War
**September 2:** Defeat at Sedan

**1871**

**January 18:** Proclamation of German Empire
**May 10:** Uprising of the Paris Commune, Treaty of Frankfurt

**1872**

German annexation of Alsace-Lorraine

**1873**
Thiers replaced as president by Mac-Mahon; attempt to restore the monarchy

**1874**
Paul Verlaine's *Romance sans paroles* published

**1875**
Vote on the republican constitution; George Bizet's *Carmen*

**1876**
Stéphane Mallarme's *L'Après-midi d'un faune* published; Hubertine Auclert founds Le Droit des femmes; H. Taine begins *Les Origines de la France contemporaine*

**1877**
Failed monarchist coup against republic; beginning of gradual consolidation of control by pro-republican parties

**1878**
French feminist delegates attend the International Women's Conference in Liverpool

**1879**
Resignation of Mac-Mahon and republican victory (Jules Grévy becomes president)

**1880–1901**
French expansion in West and Equatorial Africa

**1881**
Protectorate of Tunisia

**1881–1886**
Education Laws of Jules Ferry

**1882**
Triple Alliance

**1883–1885**
Tonkin War

**1884**
Law on labor unions

**1885**
Beginning of the automobile, Louis Pasteur discovers antirabies vaccine

**1887**
Sadi Carnot becomes president of the republic; Pierre de Brazza begins colonial administration in Congo

**1888**
Statue of Liberty dedicated

**1889**
Eiffel Tower built

**1893**
Franco-Russian alliance

**1894**
Dreyfus affair begins; Jean Casimir-Perier elected president

**1895**
Expedition to Madagascar, invention of the cinema by the Lumière brothers; CGT founded; Félix Faure elected president

**1896**
Becquerel demonstrates radioactive phenomena

**1897**
Edmond Rostand's *Cyrano de Bergerac* produced

**1898**
Émile Zola publishes *J'accuse*—successful mobilization of pro-republican forces in the Dreyfus affair; Law on Workers' Compensation

**1899**
Émile Loubet becomes president of the republic

**1900**
Marie and Pierre Curie discover radium; Colette begins the *Claudine* series

**1901**
Law on Free Assembly

**1903**
Prix Goncourt established

**1904**
Franco-English accords—the Entente Cordiale; *L'Humanité* founded by Jean Jaurès and others

**1905**
Law of separation of church and state in France; fauvism movement started in Paris, Henri Matisse and Georges Rousseau exhibit their work; Section française de l'internationale ouvrière founded

**1906**
Armand Fallières becomes president of the republic; Paul Claudel's *Partage du midi* published

**1907**
Triple Entente

**1908**
Charles Maurras founds the Action française movement

**1909**
Sergey Diaghilev's Ballets-russes in Paris

**1911**
Agadir; France cedes part of French Congo

**1912**
Protectorate over Morocco

**1913**
Raymond Poincaré becomes president of the Republic; first part of Marcel Proust's *À la Recherche du temps perdu* (*In Search of Lost Time*) published

**1914**
**September:** Battle of the Marne

**1914–1918**
World War I

**1916**
Battle of Verdun

**1917**
Entrance of United States; Russian Revolution

**1918**
Battle of France
**November 11:** Armistice

**1919**
Paris Peace Conference; League of Nations; Treaty of Versailles

**1920**
Alexandre Millerand replaces Paul Deschanel as president; Congress of Tours, two-thirds of Socialists form French Communist Party

**1921**
André Breton's *Les Champs magnétiques* published

**1923–1925**
French occupation of the Ruhr

**1924**
Gaston Doumergue elected president; Cartel des gauches formed; André Breton's *Manifeste du surréalisme*

**1925**
André Gide's *Les faux Monnayeurs* (*The Counterfeiters*) published

**1928**
Law on Social Security; Maurice Ravel's *Boléro*

**1930**
Maginot Line begun

**1931**
Paul Doumer becomes president of the republic; France feels effects of the Great Depression
François Mauriac's *Le Nœud des vipères* (*Nest of Vipers*) published

**1932**
Albert Lebrun becomes president

**1933**
**February:** Failed right-wing coup leads to "unity" of left-wing parties: Radicals, Socialists, Communists; Stavisky affair; André Malraux's *La Condition humaine* published

**1934**
Foreign Minister Louis Barthiou assassinated

## 1936

**June:** Victory of Popular Front; Socialist Party takes power for the first time with Léon Blum as premier

Forty-hour week and collective bargaining established

German remilitarization of the Rhineland

## 1936–1939

Spanish civil war

## 1937

Malraux's *L'Espoir* published

## 1938

**June:** Blum resigns as prime minister, ending the Popular Front

## 1939

German invasion of Czechoslovakia, Poland, World War III begins

Jean Renoir's *La Règle du jeu* (*Rules of the Game*)

## 1940

France overrun by Nazi Germany and surrenders. Northern third of France "occupied" by the Germans; government relocates to Vichy, and World War I hero Marshall Pétain with Pierre Laval establishes a new government that will "collaborate" with Germany. De Gaulle flees to London and begins organizing Free French forces; Resistance movement begins

## 1940–1944

French State, known as "Vichy"; Germany directly administers formerly occupied sector; pockets of resistance spread across France.

## 1942

Albert Camus's *L'Etranger*

Cave paintings at Lascaux discovered

## 1943

Jean-Paul Sartre's *L'être et le néant* (*Being and Nothingness*)

## 1944

**June 6:** Allied landings in Normandy
**August 25:** Liberation of Paris

**December 10:** Signature of Franco-Soviet pact in Moscow

Jean Genet's *Notre-Dame des Fleurs* (*Our Lady of the Flowers*)

## 1945

**March 31:** French forces cross into Germany
**April 29–May 13:** Municipal elections—French women vote for the first time
**May 8:** German capitulation; suppression of riots in Algeria

Sartre's *Huis-clos* produced

**May 29–31:** Bombardment of Damascus
**September 2:** Proclamation of independent Vietnamese Republic
**October 21:** Constitutional referendum and elections to first Constituent Assembly
**November 13:** De Gaulle elected head of provisional government

## 1946

**January 20:** Resignation of General de Gaulle
**January 23:** Gouin government
**March 6:** French recognition of Vietnamese Republic
**May 5:** Referendum rejects first constitutional project
**May 28:** Blum-Byrnes agreement
**June 1:** Proclamation of Republic of Cochin-China
**June 26:** Bidault government
**October 13:** Referendum endorses second constitutional project
**November 23:** Bombardment of Haiphong
**December 16:** Blum government

## 1947

**January 16:** Auriol becomes president of the republic
**January 28:** Ramadier government
**May 4:** Dismissal of Communist government
**June 17:** France accepts Marshall Plan aid
**November:** Wave of strikes and demonstrations
**November 22:** Schuman government

## 1948

**March 17:** Signature of Brussels Act
**July 27–August 27:** Marie government
**September 11:** Queuille government

**1949**

Simone de Beauvoir's *Le Deuxième Sexe* (*The Second Sex*) published
**April 4:** Signature of NATO Pact
**October 27:** Bidault government

**1950**

**March 3:** Franco-German agreement on the Saar
**May 9:** Schuman declaration on Coal and Steel Community
**July 13:** Pleven government
**October 24:** Pleven plan on European Army

**1951**

**June 17:** Legislative elections

**1952**

**March 6:** Pinay government
**May 27:** Signature of EDC treaty
**May 28:** Ridgeway riots

**1953**

**January 12:** Opening of Oradour trial
**January 7–May 21:** Mayer government
**June 26:** Laniel government
**July:** Launch of Poujadist movement

**1954**

**May 7:** Fall of Dien Bien Phu
**June 18:** Mendès France government
**August:** National Assembly rejects EDC
**November 1:** Beginning of rebellion in Algeria
René Coty becomes president of the republic
Françoise Sagan's *Bonjour Tristesse*

**1955**

**February 6:** Fall of Mendès France government
**February 25:** Faure government
**June 1–3:** Messina conference
**November 23:** Referendum in the Saar

**1956**

**January 2:** Legislative elections
**February 5:** Mollet government
**November 4:** Soviet Union suppresses Hungarian Revolution
**November 5–7:** Franco-British raid in Suez Canal

**1957**

**January 7:** Full powers given to General Massu in Algiers
**March 25:** Signature of the Treaty of Rome
**May 21:** Fall of Mollet government
**June 21–September 30:** Bourges-Maunoury government
**November 5:** Gaillard government

**1958**

**May 13:** Pflimlin government; coup by extremists in Algiers
**June 1:** Investiture of de Gaulle
**June 2:** Full powers voted to de Gaulle
**September 14:** Visit of Adenauer to de Gaulle
**September 28:** Referendum on constitution of the Fifth Republic
**November 23–30:** Legislative elections
**December 21:** De Gaulle elected president of Fifth Republic and French Community
Beginning of Nouvelle Vague (New Wave) cinema

**1959**

**January 9:** Formation of Debré ministry
**March:** Withdrawal of French Mediterranean fleet from control of NATO
**September 16:** Speech of de Gaulle on self-determination of Algeria
Nathalie Sarraute's *Le Planétarium* published

**1960**

**January 24–February 1:** Week of the Barricades in Algiers
**February 13:** Explosion of the first French atomic bomb in the Sahara
**January–July:** Independence of French colonies in sub-Saharan Africa
**September 5:** Opening of Jeanson network trial; manifesto of 121 intellectuals on the Algerian cause

**1961**

**January 8:** Referendum on principle of Algerian self-determination
**April 22–25:** Putsch of generals in Algiers—OAS founded

October 17: Repression of Arab demonstration in Paris, scores of deaths; Franz Fanon's *Les Damnés de la terre* published

## 1962

February 8: Anti-OAS demonstration in Paris; eight deaths at Métro Charonne
February 13: Demonstration for funeral of victims of Métro Charonne
March 17: Evian agreement resulting in cease-fire in Algeria
March 26: French army shoots at French Algerian demonstrators in Algiers
April 8: Referendum on Algerian independence in metropolitan France
April 14: Pompidou replaces Debré as prime minister
July 1: Referendum of Algerian independence in Algeria
August 22: Assassination attempt on de Gaulle at Petit-Clemart
September 12: De Gaulle decides to hold referendum on direct elections to the presidency of the republic
October 5: Censure of Pompidou voted by National Assembly
October 28: Referendum on direct elections to the presidency of the republic
November 18–25: Legislative elections
François Truffaut's *Jules et Jim*

## 1963

January 14: De Gaulle vetoes British application to join the Common Market
January 22: Franco-German treaty of cooperation
June 22: Birth of French rock, Place de la Nation

## 1964

January 27: French recognition of People's Republic of China
June 7: Creation of Convention des Institutions Republicaines

## 1965

July 1: French boycott of European Council of Ministers
September 10: Creation of Fédération de la Gauche Démocrate et Socialiste

December 5–19: Presidential elections; reelection of de Gaulle

## 1966

February 2: Foundation of Centre Démocrate
March 4: France leaves integrated military command of NATO
September 1: De Gaulle's speech at Phnom Penh

## 1967

March 12: Legislative elections; setback for Gaullists
June 5–10: Six-Day War
July 26: De Gaulle's speech at Montreal: "Long live free Quebec!"
December 19: Neuwirth law on contraception

## 1968

March 22: Student occupation at University of Nanterre
May 3: Beginning of student unrest in Latin Quarter
May 10–11: Night of the Barricades in Paris
May 13: One-day strike; march of students and trade unions in Paris
May 14–18: Official visit of de Gaulle to Romania
May 27: Grenelle agreements with trade unions; rally in Charlèty stadium
May 29: Disappearance of de Gaulle
May 30: Broadcast of de Gaulle; Gaullist rally in Paris
June 23–30: Legislative elections; triumph of Gaullists
July 10: Couve de Murville replaces Pompidou as prime minister
August 21: Soviet-led invasion of Czechoslovakia

## 1969

April 27: De Gaulle loses referendum on reform
April 28: Resignation of de Gaulle
June 1–15: Presidential elections; Pompidou elected
June 20: Chaban-Delmas appointed prime minister
September 16: Chaban-Delmas's speech on the New Society

## 1970

February: Visit of Pompidou to the United States

## 1971
**April:** Manifesto demanding the right to abortion
**April 5:** First screening of *Le Chagrin et la Pitié* (*The Sorrow and the Pity*)
**June:** Foundation of Socialist Party at Épinay

## 1971–1974
François Mitterrand unifies centrists and leftist parties

## 1972
**April 23:** Referendum on British entry into European Common Market
**June 27:** Common Program of Government
**July 5:** Mesmer replaces Chaban-Delmas as prime minister

## 1973
**October:** Beginning of oil crisis
**December:** Solzhenitsyn's *Gulag Archipelago* published in Russian edition in Paris

## 1974
**April 2:** Death of Georges Pompidou
**May 5–19:** Presidential elections; election of Giscard d'Estaing
**May 27:** Jacques Chirac appointed prime minister
**November:** PSU joins Socialist party

## 1975
**January 17:** Law on abortion promulgated
**November:** Arms deal with Iraq

## 1976
**February:** French Communist Party abandons doctrine of the dictatorship of the proletariat
**August 25:** Resignation of Jacques Chirac; replaced as prime minister by Raymond Barre
**December 5:** Foundation of RPR

## 1977
**March:** Municipal elections; success of the Left; election of Chirac, mayor of Paris
**May:** Foundation of RPR
**May:** Communist Party endorses French nuclear deterrent

**September 14:** Rupture of Union of the Left
**December 4:** Coronation of Bokassa as emperor of the former Central African Republic

## 1978
**January:** Socialist Party endorses French nuclear deterrent
**February:** Foundation of the UDF
**March 12–19:** Legislative elections; defeat of the Left

## 1979
**March 13:** France joins European Monetary System
**June 10:** European elections

## 1980
**May 19:** Giscard d'Estaing meets Brezhnev in Warsaw; Marguerite Yourcenar first woman elected to the Académie française

## 1981
**April 26–May 10:** Presidential elections; victory of François Mitterrand
**June 14–21:** Legislative elections; PS and MRG win absolute majority
**June 22:** Mauroy government includes four Communists

## 1982
**March 2:** Law on decentralization
**March:** Official visit of Mitterrand to Israel
**December 8:** Resignation of Jean-Pierre Cot
First manned French space flight (Jean-Loup Chrétien)

## 1983
**January 20:** Mitterrand addresses the West German Bundestag
**March 6–13:** Municipal elections; setback for Socialists
**March 25:** Austerity plan marks U-turn in Socialist economic policy
**July 13:** Law on occupational equality

## 1984
French intervention in Chad
**January:** Foundation of Greens as a united party

June 17: European elections

June 24: Demonstration by Catholics against school reform

July 15: Resignation of Pierre Mauroy as prime minister; replaced by Laurent Fabius

November: Launch of SOS-Racisme

## 1985

January: Jacques Delors takes up presidency of European Commission; idea of single European Market launched

July 10: Sinking of the *Rainbow Warrior*

## 1986

January 17–19: First summit of Francophone countries

March 16: Legislative elections; victory for Right; Jacques Chirac appointed prime minister; first "cohabitation" government

July: Dispute between Mitterrand and Chirac over privatization

November–December: Students protest against university reform

## 1987

May–July: Trial of Klaus Barbie

## 1988

April 24–May 8: Presidential elections; reelection of Mitterrand

May 10: Rocard replaces Chirac as prime minister

May 14: Mauroy defeats Fabius for the first secretaryship of Socialist Party

June: Legislative elections; return of Socialists with reduced majority

November: Referendum on New Caledonia

## 1989

January: Pechiney affair discredits Socialist government

June: European elections

July 14: Celebration of bicentennial of French Revolution of 1789

October: Muslim head-scarf affair

November 10: Fall of Berlin Wall; reunification of Germany begins

## 1990

March: Rennes congress of PS; Maurey holds off challenge of Fabius for first secretaryship

May: Foundation of Génération Écologie

## 1991

January 29: Resignation of Chevenement as foreign minister over Gulf War

May 15: Rocard replaced as prime minister by Édith Cresson

August 19: Mitterrand slow to condemn military coup against Gorbachev in Soviet Union

December 10: Treaty of Maastricht

## 1992

April 2: Cresson replaced as prime minister by Bérégovoy

September 20: Referendum on Maastricht Treaty

## 1993

March: Legislative elections; landslide of Right; Balladur prime minister

May 1: Suicide of Pierre Bérégovoy

May 13: Revision of law on French nationality

October: Bourges congress of PS; Rocard secretary of the party

November 19: Revision of constitution on right of asylum

December: Conclusion of GATT talks

## 1994

January 16: Demonstrations against reform of Falloux law

January: Resignation of Georges Marchais as secretary-general of PCF; PCF abandons doctrine of democratic centralism

March: Demonstrations against "SMIC-Jeunes"

March–April: Trial of Paul Touvier

June 12: European elections; setback for mainstream parties; resignation of Rocard as first secretary of PS

September: Mitterrand affair

Foundation of Independent Ecologist Movement

December: Law against political corruption

## 1995

**April 23–May 7:** Presidential elections; election of Jacques Chirac

## 1997

**May–June:** Chirac dissolves National Assembly; Socialist-Communist-Green coalition wins in assembly. Lionel Jospin is prime minister— "cohabitation" government

## 1998

Farmer José Bové protests against globalization and genetically modified food

## 2001

**January:** The euro currency replaces the franc

## 2002

**April:** Far right National Front of Jean-Marie Le Pen finishes ahead of Lionel Jospin

**May:** Chirac wins national election, largest peacetime rally in French history
Jean-Pierre Raffarin is prime minister

## 2003

France declines to enter U.S.-led coalition against Iraq, favors instead negotiations and inspections; France hosts summit talks at Évian

## 2004

National Assembly adopts a law banning in public schools "symbols and clothing that ostentatiously show students' religious membership"
Several people killed as roof collapses at terminal building at Charles de Gaulle Airport

# APPENDIXES

APPENDIX I
Maps

APPENDIX II
Statesmen of France

# APPENDIX I

## MAPS

France, 2003

French Local Government, 2003

Division of the Carolingian Empire, 843

Hundred Years' War, 1337–1453

Renaissance France, 1400–1600

Expansion of the French Kingdom, 1678–1697

Ancien Régime

Revolutionary France, 1789–1794

Napoleonic Wars, 1792–1815

French Colonial Empire, 1700 to the Present

World War I, the Western Front, 1914–1918

France in World War II

Indochina War, 1946–1954

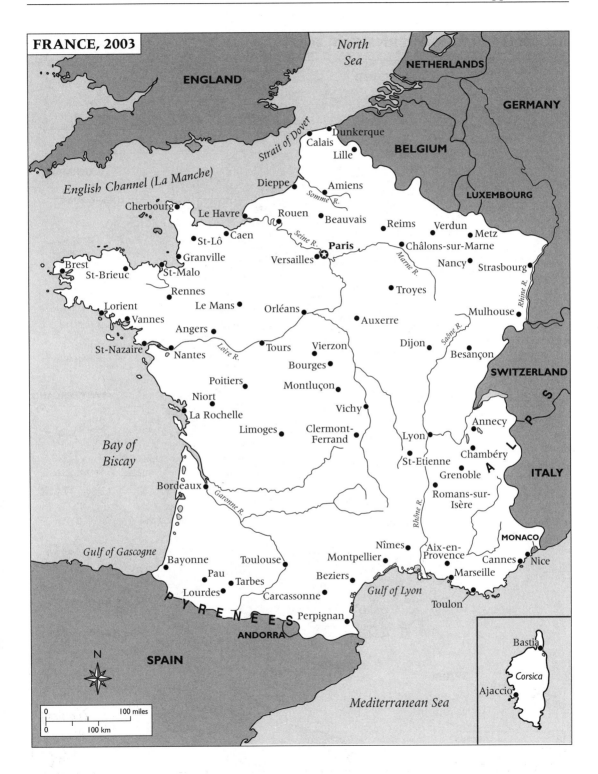

FRANCE, 2003

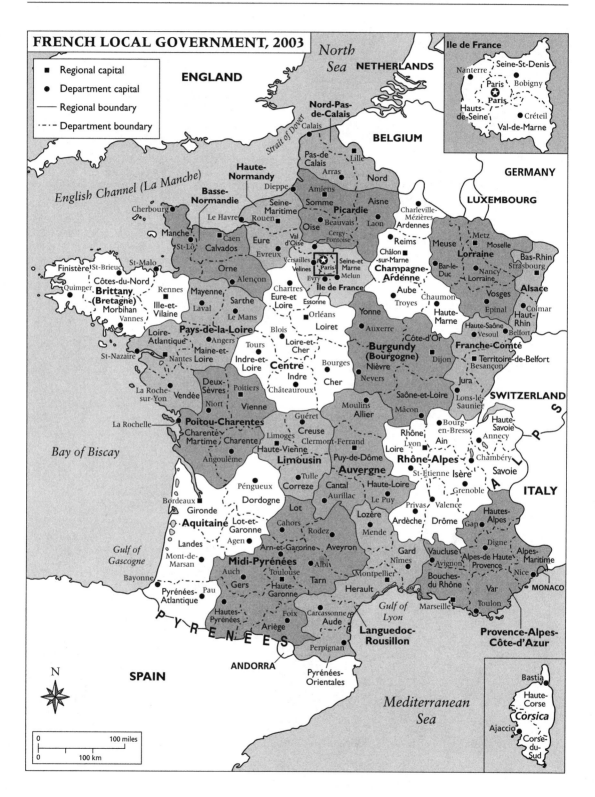

# FRENCH LOCAL GOVERNMENT, 2003

- ■ Regional capital
- ● Department capital
- — Regional boundary
- –·–· Department boundary

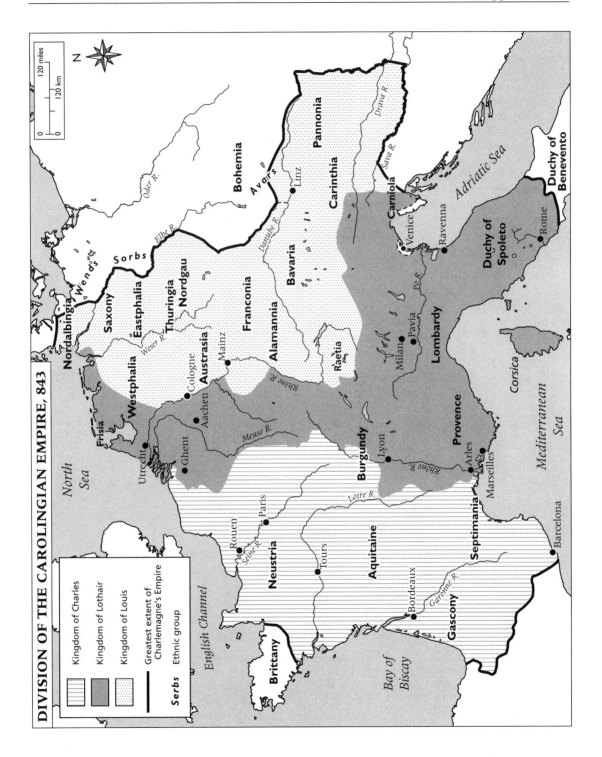

**DIVISION OF THE CAROLINGIAN EMPIRE, 843**

Kingdom of Charles

Kingdom of Lothair

Kingdom of Louis

Greatest extent of Charlemagne's Empire

*Serbs* Ethnic group

North Sea

Nordalbingia

Wends

Sorbs

Oder R.

Bohemia

Avars

Elbe R.

Saxony

Westphalia

Eastphalia

Thuringia

Nordgau

Linz

Pannonia

Carinthia

Drava R.

Sava R.

Carniola

Adriatic Sea

Duchy of Benevento

Frisia

Utrecht

Ghent

Cologne

Aachen

Austrasia

Mainz

Weser R.

Franconia

Alamannia

Bavaria

Danube R.

Raetia

Rhine R.

Meuse R.

Venice

Ravenna

Milan

Pavia

Lombardy

Po R.

Duchy of Spoleto

Rome

Corsica

Mediterranean Sea

English Channel

Brittany

Rouen

Paris

Seine R.

Neustria

Tours

Loire R.

Aquitaine

Bordeaux

Gascony

Garonne R.

Burgundy

Lyon

Rhône R.

Arles

Marseilles

Provence

Septimania

Barcelona

Bay of Biscay

N

120 miles

120 km

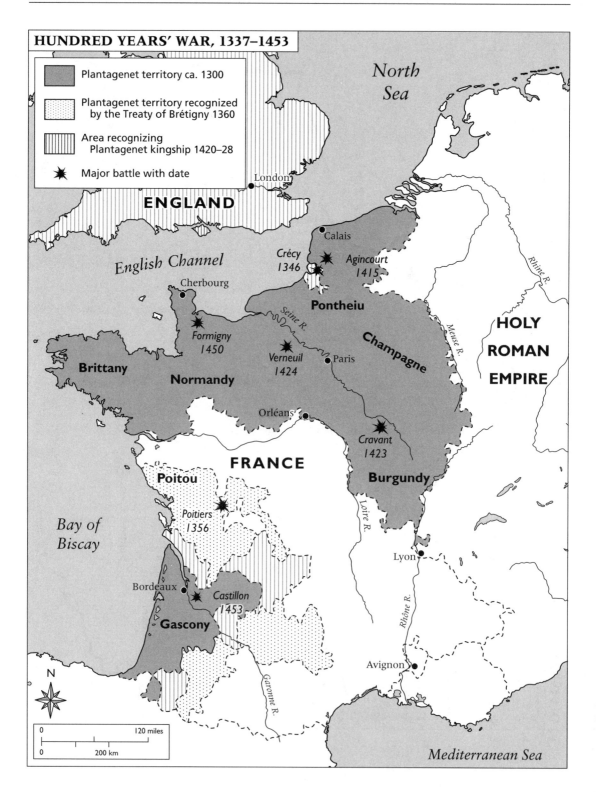

**HUNDRED YEARS' WAR, 1337–1453**

- Plantagenet territory ca. 1300
- Plantagenet territory recognized by the Treaty of Brétigny 1360
- Area recognizing Plantagenet kingship 1420–28
- ✳ Major battle with date

*North Sea*

London

**ENGLAND**

*English Channel*

Calais

Crécy 1346

Agincourt 1415

Cherbourg

**Pontheiu**

*Seine R.*

**Champagne**

*Meuse R.*

*Rhine R.*

**HOLY ROMAN EMPIRE**

Formigny 1450

**Brittany**

**Normandy**

Verneuil 1424

Paris

Orléans

**FRANCE**

Cravant 1423

**Poitou**

**Burgundy**

*Bay of Biscay*

Poitiers 1356

*Loire R.*

Lyon

Bordeaux

Castillon 1453

**Gascony**

*Rhône R.*

*Garonne R.*

Avignon

N

0        120 miles
0        200 km

*Mediterranean Sea*

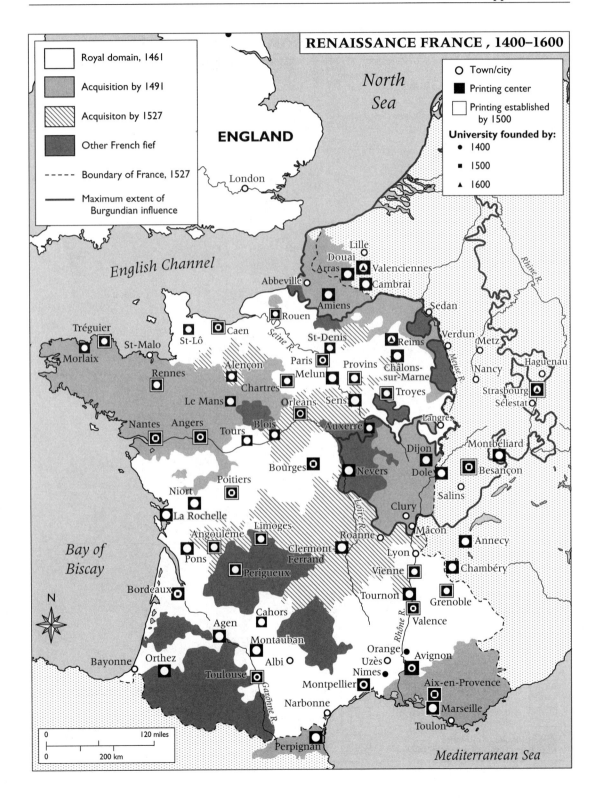

**RENAISSANCE FRANCE , 1400–1600**

Royal domain, 1461

Acquisition by 1491

Acquisiton by 1527

Other French fief

- - - Boundary of France, 1527

— Maximum extent of Burgundian influence

○ Town/city
■ Printing center
□ Printing established by 1500

**University founded by:**
● 1400
■ 1500
▲ 1600

*North Sea*

ENGLAND

London

*English Channel*

*Bay of Biscay*

*Mediterranean Sea*

Lille
Douai
Arras
Valenciennes
Cambrai
Abbeville
Amiens
Sedan
Rouen
St-Denis
Verdun
Tréguier
St-Malo
Caen
St-Lô
Reims
Metz
Morlaix
Paris
Provins
Châlons-sur-Marne
Nancy
Haguenau
Rennes
Alençon
Melun
Troyes
Strasbourg
Chartres
Sens
Sélestat
Le Mans
Orleans
Auxerre
Langres
Nantes
Angers
Tours
Blois
Dijon
Montbéliard
Bourges
Nevers
Dole
Besançon
Salins
Poitiers
Clury
Niort
Limoges
Roanne
Mâcon
La Rochelle
Angoulême
Clermont Ferrand
Lyon
Annecy
Pons
Périgueux
Vienne
Chambéry
Bordeaux
Tournon
Grenoble
Cahors
Valence
Agen
Montauban
Orange
Avignon
Bayonne
Orthez
Albi
Uzès
Nimes
Aix-en-Provence
Toulouse
Montpellier
Marseille
Narbonne
Toulon
Perpignan

*Seine R.*
*Rhine R.*
*Meuse R.*
*Loire R.*
*Rhône R.*
*Garonne R.*

N

0          120 miles
0     200 km

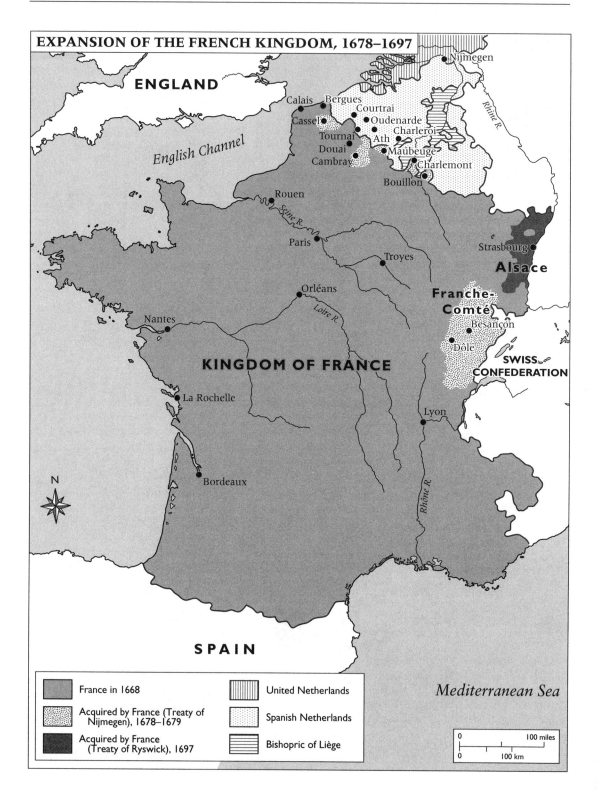

# EXPANSION OF THE FRENCH KINGDOM, 1678–1697

ENGLAND

*English Channel*

Calais
Bergues
Cassel
Tournai
Douai
Cambrai
Courtrai
Oudenarde
Charleroi
Ath
Maubeuge
Charlemont
Bouillon

Nijmegen

*Rhine R.*

Rouen

*Seine R.*

Paris

Troyes

Strasbourg

**Alsace**

Orléans

*Loire R.*

**Franche-Comté**

Besançon

Dôle

Nantes

**KINGDOM OF FRANCE**

**SWISS CONFEDERATION**

La Rochelle

Lyon

*Rhône R.*

Bordeaux

N

SPAIN

*Mediterranean Sea*

| | France in 1668 | | United Netherlands |
| | Acquired by France (Treaty of Nijmegen), 1678–1679 | | Spanish Netherlands |
| | Acquired by France (Treaty of Ryswick), 1697 | | Bishopric of Liège |

| 0 | 100 miles |
| 0 | 100 km |

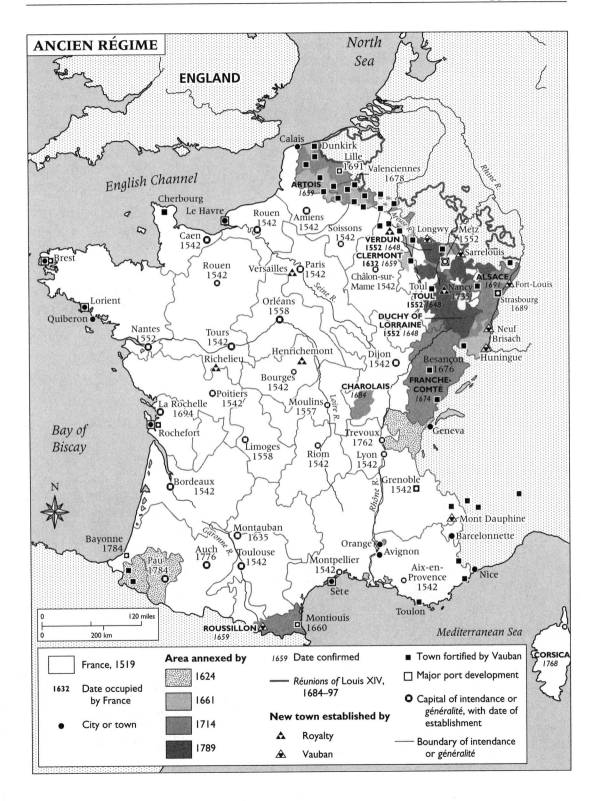

ANCIEN RÉGIME

North Sea

ENGLAND

English Channel

Calais
Dunkirk
Lille 1691
Valenciennes 1678
ARTOIS 1659

Rhine R.

Cherbourg
Le Havre
Rouen 1542
Amiens 1542
Soissons 1542
Longwy
Metz 1552
Verdun 1552 1648
CLERMONT 1632 1659
Sarrelouis

Caen 1542
Brest
Rouen 1542
Versailles
Paris 1542
Châlon-sur-Marne 1542
Toul
TOUL 1552 1648
Nancy 1735
Fort-Louis
ALSACE 1691
Strasbourg 1689

Lorient
Quiberon
Orléans 1558
DUCHY OF LORRAINE 1552 1648
Neuf Brisach

Nantes 1552
Tours 1542
Richelieu
Henrichemont
Dijon 1542
Besançon 1676
Huningue

Bay of Biscay
Poitiers 1542
Bourges 1542
Moulins 1557
CHAROLAIS 1684
FRANCHE-COMTÉ 1674

La Rochelle 1694
Rochefort
Limoges 1558
Riom 1542
Trevoux 1762
Lyon 1542
Geneva

N
Bordeaux 1542
Grenoble 1542

Mont Dauphine
Barcelonnette

Bayonne 1784
Montauban 1635
Auch 1776
Toulouse 1542
Montpellier 1542
Orange
Avignon
Aix-en-Provence 1542
Nice

Pau 1784
Sète
Toulon

Garonne R.

ROUSSILLON 1659
Montiouis 1660

Mediterranean Sea

CORSICA 1768

Seine R.
Loire R.
Rhône R.
Meuse R.

0    120 miles
0    200 km

France, 1519

1632 Date occupied by France

● City or town

Area annexed by
1624
1661
1714
1789

1659 Date confirmed

—— Réunions of Louis XIV, 1684–97

New town established by
△ Royalty
△ Vauban

■ Town fortified by Vauban

□ Major port development

◉ Capital of intendance or généralité, with date of establishment

—— Boundary of intendance or généralité

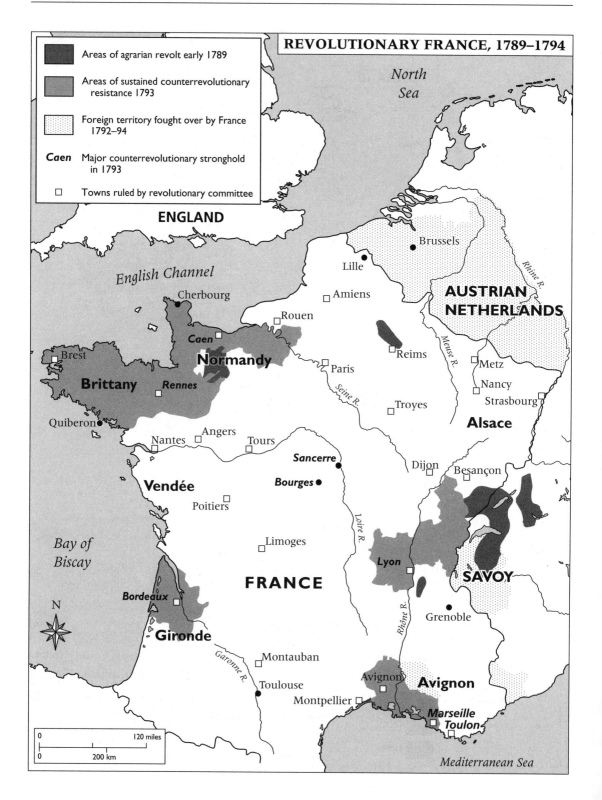

REVOLUTIONARY FRANCE, 1789–1794

Areas of agrarian revolt early 1789

Areas of sustained counterrevolutionary resistance 1793

Foreign territory fought over by France 1792–94

*Caen* Major counterrevolutionary stronghold in 1793

☐ Towns ruled by revolutionary committee

North Sea

ENGLAND

English Channel

Brussels

Lille

AUSTRIAN NETHERLANDS

Cherbourg

Amiens

Rouen

Rhine R.

*Caen*

Reims

Meuse R.

Metz

Brest

Normandy

Paris

Nancy

Strasbourg

Brittany

Rennes

Seine R.

Troyes

Alsace

Quiberon

Angers

Tours

Nantes

*Sancerre*

Dijon

Besançon

Vendée

*Bourges*

Poitiers

Loire R.

Bay of Biscay

Limoges

FRANCE

*Lyon*

SAVOY

N

*Bordeaux*

Rhône R.

Grenoble

Gironde

Garonne R.

Montauban

Avignon

*Avignon*

Toulouse

Montpellier

*Marseille*

*Toulon*

Mediterranean Sea

0        120 miles
0        200 km

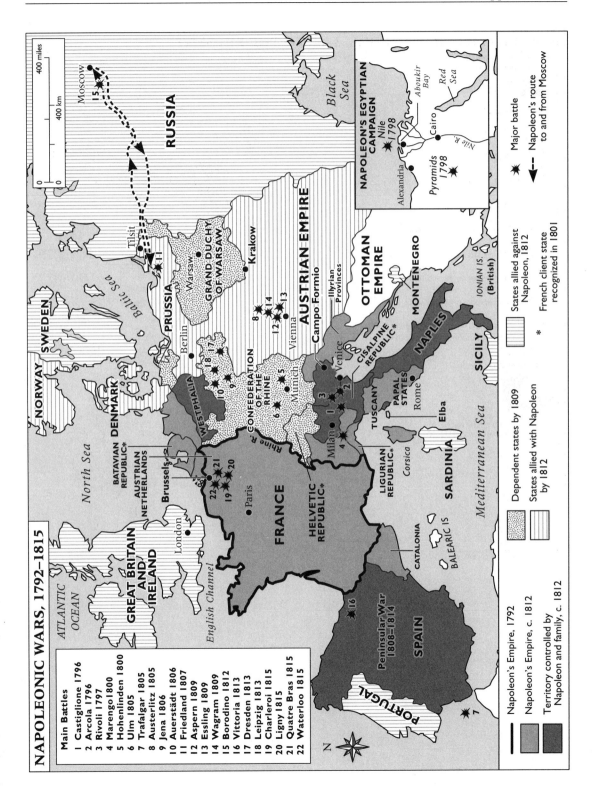

NAPOLEONIC WARS, 1792–1815

Main Battles
1 Castiglione 1796
2 Arcola 1796
3 Rivoli 1797
4 Marengo 1800
5 Hohenlinden 1800
6 Ulm 1805
7 Trafalgar 1805
8 Austerlitz 1805
9 Jena 1806
10 Auerstädt 1806
11 Friedland 1807
12 Aspern 1809
13 Essling 1809
14 Wagram 1809
15 Borodino 1812
16 Vittoria 1813
17 Dresden 1813
18 Leipzig 1813
19 Charleroi 1815
20 Ligny 1815
21 Quatre Bras 1815
22 Waterloo 1815

Napoleon's Empire, 1792
Napoleon's Empire, c. 1812
Territory controlled by
Napoleon and family, c. 1812

Dependent states by 1809
States allied with Napoleon
by 1812

States allied against
Napoleon, 1812
French client state
recognized in 1801

Major battle
Napoleon's route
to and from Moscow

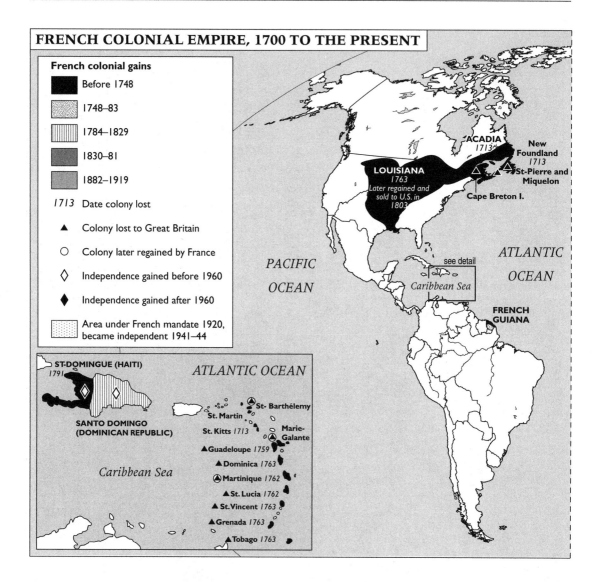

# FRENCH COLONIAL EMPIRE, 1700 TO THE PRESENT

**French colonial gains**

- Before 1748
- 1748–83
- 1784–1829
- 1830–81
- 1882–1919

*1713*   Date colony lost

▲   Colony lost to Great Britain

○   Colony later regained by France

◇   Independence gained before 1960

◆   Independence gained after 1960

Area under French mandate 1920, became independent 1941–44

ACADIA *1713*

New Foundland *1713*
St-Pierre and Miquelon

Cape Breton I.

LOUISIANA *1763* *Later regained and sold to U.S. in 1803*

*PACIFIC OCEAN*

see detail

*Caribbean Sea*

*ATLANTIC OCEAN*

FRENCH GUIANA

ST-DOMINGUE (HAITI) *1791*

SANTO DOMINGO (DOMINICAN REPUBLIC)

*ATLANTIC OCEAN*

St- Barthélemy
St. Martin
St. Kitts *1713*
Marie-Galante
▲ Guadeloupe *1759*
▲ Dominica *1763*
▲ Martinique *1762*
▲ St. Lucia *1762*
▲ St. Vincent *1763*
▲ Grenada *1763*
▲ Tobago *1763*

*Caribbean Sea*

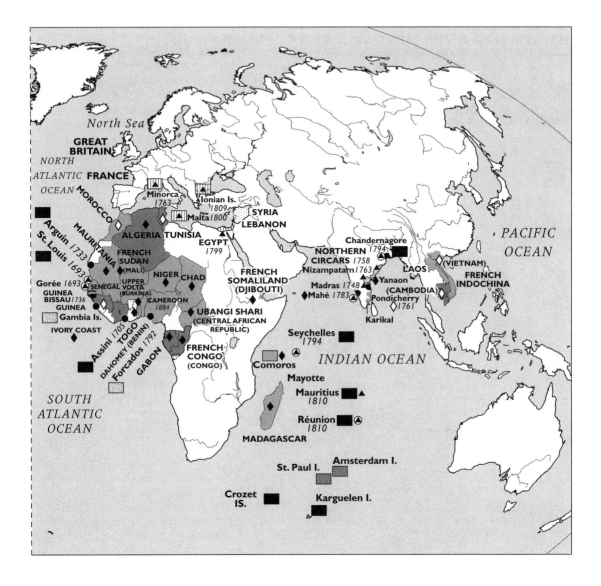

North Sea

GREAT
BRITAIN

NORTH
ATLANTIC **FRANCE**
OCEAN

MOROCCO

Minorca
*1763*

Ionian Is.
*1809*

Malta *1800*

SYRIA
LEBANON

PACIFIC
OCEAN

Arguin *1733*
St. Louis *1693*

MAURITANIA

ALGERIA TUNISIA

FRENCH
SUDAN
(MALI)

EGYPT
*1799*

Chandernagore
*1794*

NORTHERN
CIRCARS *1758*
Nizampatam *1763*

NIGER CHAD

FRENCH
SOMALILAND
(DJIBOUTI)

LAOS

(VIETNAM)

Gorée *1693*

GUINEA
BISSAU *1736*
GUINEA

SENEGAL

UPPER
VOLTA
(BURKINA)

CAMEROON
*1884*

Madras *1748*
Mahé *1783*

Yanaon

Pondicherry
*1761*

(CAMBODIA)

FRENCH
INDOCHINA

Gambia Is.

IVORY COAST

Assini *1705*

TOGO

DAHOMEY (BENIN)

Forcados *1792*

GABON

UBANGI SHARI
(CENTRAL AFRICAN
REPUBLIC)

Karikal

FRENCH
CONGO
(CONGO)

Comoros

Seychelles
*1794*

INDIAN OCEAN

SOUTH
ATLANTIC
OCEAN

MADAGASCAR

Mayotte

Mauritius
*1810*

Réunion
*1810*

St. Paul I.

Amsterdam I.

Crozet
IS.

Karguelen I.

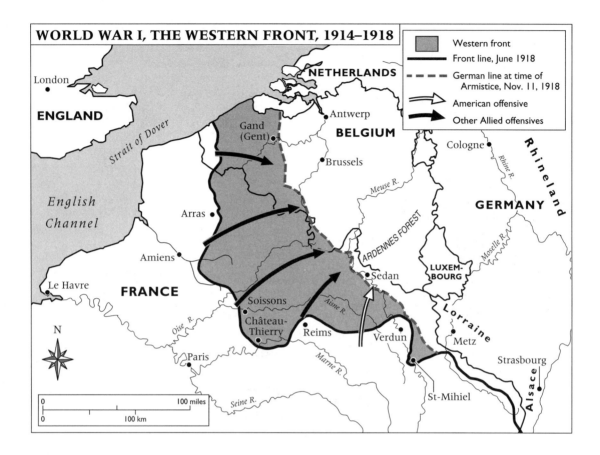

**WORLD WAR I, THE WESTERN FRONT, 1914–1918**

Legend:
- Western front
- Front line, June 1918
- German line at time of Armistice, Nov. 11, 1918
- American offensive
- Other Allied offensives

London

ENGLAND

Strait of Dover

English Channel

NETHERLANDS

Antwerp

BELGIUM

Gand (Gent)

Brussels

Meuse R.

Cologne

Rhine R.

Rhineland

GERMANY

Arras

ARDENNES FOREST

Amiens

Moselle R.

LUXEM-BOURG

Le Havre

FRANCE

Sedan

N

Soissons

Aisne R.

Lorraine

Château-Thierry

Reims

Verdun

Metz

Oise R.

Paris

Marne R.

Strasbourg

Seine R.

St-Mihiel

Alsace

0          100 miles
0          100 km

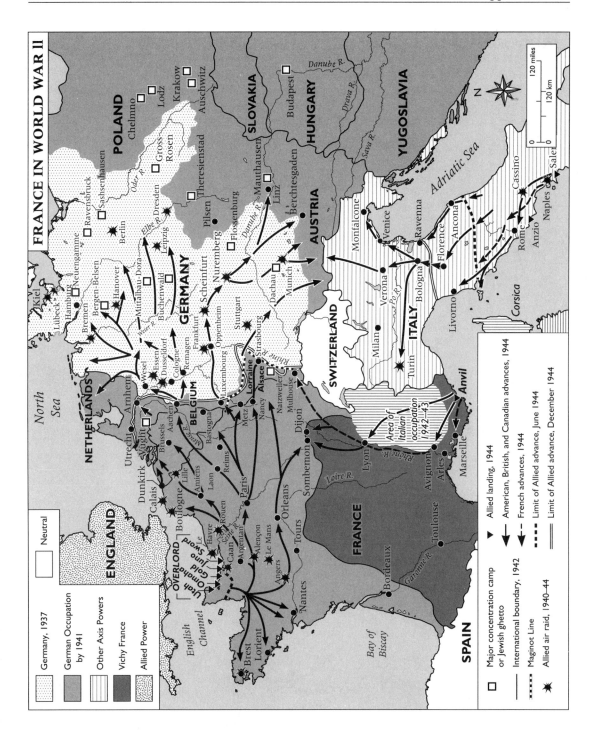

FRANCE IN WORLD WAR II

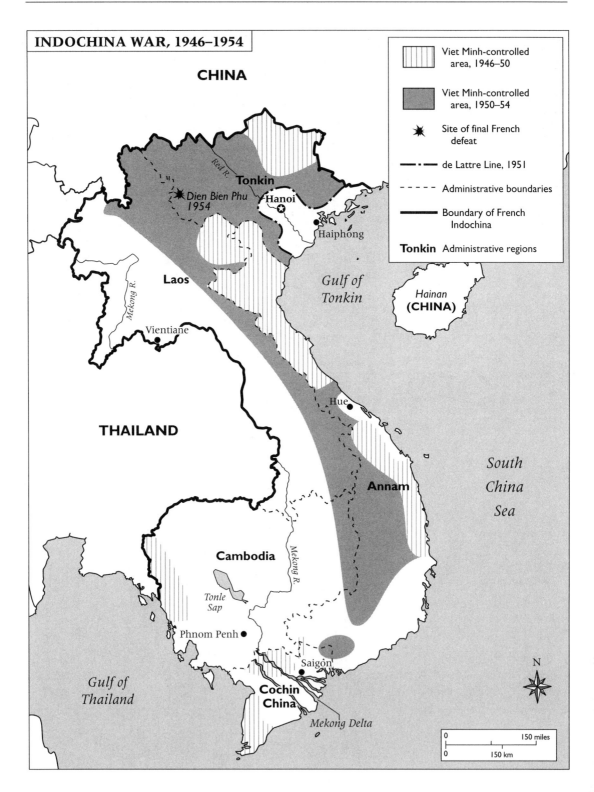

## INDOCHINA WAR, 1946–1954

CHINA

Red R.

Tonkin

Dien Bien Phu
1954

Hanoi

Haiphong

Laos

Gulf of
Tonkin

Hainan
(CHINA)

Mekong R.

Vientiane

THAILAND

Hue

South
China
Sea

Annam

Cambodia

Mekong R.

Tonle
Sap

Phnom Penh

Saigon

Gulf of
Thailand

Cochin
China

Mekong Delta

N

**Legend:**

- Viet Minh-controlled area, 1946–50
- Viet Minh-controlled area, 1950–54
- ✳ Site of final French defeat
- —·—·— de Lattre Line, 1951
- – – – – Administrative boundaries
- Boundary of French Indochina
- **Tonkin** Administrative regions

0        150 miles

0        150 km

# APPENDIX II

| Reign | Name |
|---|---|
| Later Carolingian Transition | |
| 814–840 | Louis I (not a king of "France") |
| 840–877 | Charles II the Bald |
| 877–879 | Louis II the Stammerer |
| 879–882 | Louis III (joint with Carloman below) |
| 879–884 | Carloman (joint with Louis III above, until 882) |
| 884–888 | Charles the Fat |
| 888–898 | Eudes (Odo) of Paris (non-Carolingian) |
| 898–922 | Charles III the Simple |
| 922–923 | Robert I (non-Carolingian) |
| 923–936 | Raoul (Rudolf, non-Carolingian) |
| 936–954 | Louis IV (d'Outremer, or The Foreigner) |
| 954–986 | Lothar (Lothaire) |
| 986–987 | Louis V the Do-Nothing |
| | |
| Capetian Dynasty | |
| 987–996 | Hugh Capet |
| 996–1031 | Robert II the Pious |
| 1031–1060 | Henry I |
| 1060–1108 | Philip I |
| 1108–1137 | Louis VI the Fat |
| 1137–1180 | Louis VII the Young |
| 1180–1223 | Philip II Augustus |
| 1223–1226 | Louis VIII the Lion |
| 1226–1270 | Louis IX (St. Louis) |
| 1270–1285 | Philip III the Bold |
| 1285–1314 | Philip IV the Fair |
| 1314–1316 | Louis X the Stubborn |
| 1316 | John I |
| 1316–1322 | Philip V the Tall |
| 1322–1328 | Charles IV the Fair |

## RULERS OF FRANCE: 840 TO THE PRESENT *(continued)*

| Reign | Name |
|---|---|
| **Valois Dynasty** | |
| 1328–1350 | Philip VI |
| 1350–1364 | John II the Good |
| 1364–1380 | Charles V the Wise |
| 1380–1422 | Charles VI (the Mad, Well-Beloved, or Foolish) |
| 1422–1461 | Charles VII (the Well-Served or Victorious) |
| 1461–1483 | Louis XI (the Spider) |
| 1483–1498 | Charles VIII (Father of His People) |
| 1498–1515 | Louis XII |
| 1515–1547 | Francis I |
| 1547–1559 | Henry II |
| 1559–1560 | Francis II |
| 1560–1574 | Charles IX |
| 1574–1589 | Henry III |
| **Bourbon Dynasty** | |
| 1589–1610 | Henry IV |
| 1610–1643 | Louis XIII |
| 1643–1715 | Louis XIV (Sun King) |
| 1715–1774 | Louis XV |
| 1774–1792 | Louis XVI |
| **First Republic** | |
| 1792–1795 | National Convention |
| 1795–1799 | Directory (Directors) |
| 1795–1799 | Paul-François-Jean-Nicolas de Barras |
| 1795–1799 | Jean-François Reubell |
| 1795–1799 | Louis-Marie La Revellière-Lépeaux |
| 1795–1797 | Lazare-Nicolas-Marguerite Carnot |
| 1795–1797 | Étienne Le Tourneur |
| 1797 | François, marquis de Barthélemy |
| 1797–1799 | Philippe-Antoine-Merlin de Douai |
| 1797–1798 | François de Neufchâteau |
| 1798–1799 | Jean-Baptiste, count de Treilhard |
| 1799 | Emmanuel-Joseph, count de Sieyès |
| 1799 | Roger, count de Ducos |
| 1799 | Jean-François-Auguste Moulins |
| 1799 | Louis Gohier |
| 1799–1804 | Consulate |
| 1st Consul: 1799–1804 | Napoléon Bonaparte |
| 2nd Consul: 1799 | Emmanuel-Joseph, count de Sieyès |
| 1799–1804 | Jean-Jacques Régis Cambacérès (duke of Parma) |

## RULES OF FRANCE: 840 TO THE PRESENT *(continued)*

| Reign | Name |
|---|---|
| 3rd Consul: 1799 | Pierre-Roger Ducos |
| 1799–1804 | Charles-François Lebrun |
| **First Empire (emperors)** | |
| 1804–1814 | Napoléon I |
| 1814–1815 | Louis XVIII (king) |
| 1815 | Napoléon I (second time) |
| **Bourbons (restored)** | |
| 1814–1824 | Louis XVIII |
| 1824–1830 | Charles X |
| **Orléans** | |
| 1830–1848 | Louis Philippe |
| **Second Republic (presidents)** | |
| 1848 | Louis-Eugène Cavaignac |
| 1848–1852 | Louis-Napoléon Bonaparte (later Napoléon III) |
| **Second Empire (emperors)** | |
| 1852–1870 | (Louis-Napoléon Bonaparte) Napoléon III |
| **Third Republic (presidents)** | |
| 1870–1871 | Louis-Jules Trochu (provisional) |
| 1871–1873 | Adolphe Thiers |
| 1873–1879 | Edme de MacMahon |
| 1879–1887 | Jules Grévy |
| 1887–1894 | Sadi Carnot |
| 1894–1895 | Jean Casimir-Périer |
| 1895–1899 | Félix Faure |
| 1899–1906 | Émile Loubet |
| 1906–1913 | Armand Fallières |
| 1913–1920 | Raymond Poincaré |
| 1920 | Paul Deschanel |
| 1920–1924 | Alexandre Millerand |
| 1924–1931 | Gaston Doumergue |
| 1931–1932 | Paul Doumer |
| 1932–1940 | Albert Lebrun |
| **Vichy Government (Chief of State)** | |
| 1940–1944 | Henri-Philippe Pétain |
| **Provisional Government (presidents)** | |
| 1944–1946 | Charles de Gaulle |
| 1946 | Félix Gouin |

## RULERS OF FRANCE: 840 TO THE PRESENT *(continued)*

| Reign | Name |
|---|---|
| 1946 | Georges Bidault |
| 1946 | Léon Blum |

**Fourth Republic (presidents)**

| | |
|---|---|
| 1947–1954 | Vincent Auriol |
| 1954–1959 | René Coty |

**Fifth Republic (presidents)**

| | |
|---|---|
| 1959–1969 | Charles de Gaulle |
| 1969–1974 | Georges Pompidou |
| 1974–1981 | Valéry Giscard d'Estaing |
| 1981–1995 | François Mitterrand |
| 1995–Present | Jacques Chirac |

## LEADING STATESMEN OF FRANCE

This is a chronological list of France's leading statesmen; the dates given are the periods of said rule. Although the title "prime minister" was officially introduced only with the Fifth Republic, it can— and normally is—used to describe all these individuals.

| Term | Name |
|---|---|
| Third Republic | |
| 1871–1873 | Armand Dufaure |
| 1873–1874 | Albert de Broglie (two terms) |
| 1874–1875 | Ernest-Louis-Octave Courtot de Cissey |
| 1875–1876 | Louis-Joseph Buffet |
| 1876 | Armand Dufaure (second and third terms) |
| 1876–1877 | Jules Simon |
| 1877 | Albert de Broglie (fourth term) |
| 1877 | Caétan de Grimaudet de la Rochebouet |
| 1877–1879 | Armand Dufaure (third term) |
| 1879 | William Henry Waddungton |
| 1879–1880 | Charles de Freycinet |
| 1880–1881 | Jules Ferry |
| 1881–1882 | Léon Gambetta |
| 1882 | Charles de Freycinet (second term) |
| 1882–1883 | Charles du Clerc |
| 1883 | Armand Fallières |
| 1883–1885 | Jules Ferry (second term) |
| 1885 | Henri Brisson |
| 1886 | Charles de Freycinet (third term) |
| 1886–1887 | René Goblet |
| 1887 | Maurice Rouvier |

## LEADING STATESMEN OF FRANCE *(continued)*

| Term | Name |
|------|------|
| 1887–1888 | Pierre-Emmanuel Tirard |
| 1888–1889 | Charles-Thomas Floquet |
| 1889–1890 | Pierre-Emmanuel Tirard (second term) |
| 1890–1892 | Charles de Freycinet (fourth term) |
| 1892 | Émile Loubet |
| 1892–1893 | Alexandre-Félix-Joseph Ribot (two terms) |
| 1893 | Charles du Puy |
| 1893–1894 | Jean-Paul Casimir-Périer |
| 1894–1895 | Charles du Puy (second and third terms) |
| 1895–1895 | Alexandre-Félix-Joseph Ribot (third term) |
| 1895–1896 | Léon Bourgeois |
| 1896–1898 | Jules Méline |
| 1898 | Henri Brisson (second term) |
| 1889–1899 | Charles du Puy (fourth and fifth terms) |
| 1899–1902 | Pierre Waldeck-Rousseau |
| 1902–1905 | Émile Combes |
| 1905–1906 | Maurice Rouvier (second and third terms) |
| 1906 | Ferdinand Sarrien |
| 1906–1909 | Georges Clemenceau |
| 1909–1911 | Aristide Briand (two terms) |
| 1911 | Antoine-Emmanuel-Ernest Monis |
| 1911–1912 | Joseph Caillaux |
| 1912–1913 | Raymond Poincaré |
| 1913 | Aristide Briand (third and fourth terms) |
| 1913 | Louis Barthou |
| 1913–1914 | Gaston Doumergue |
| 1914 | Alexandre-Félix-Joseph Ribot (fourth term) |
| 1914–1915 | René Viviani (two terms) |
| 1915–1917 | Aristide Briand (fifth and sixth terms) |
| 1917 | Alexandre-Félix-Joseph Ribot (fifth term) |
| 1917 | Paul Painlevé |
| 1917–1920 | Georges Clemenceau (second term) |
| 1920 | Alexandre Millerand (two terms) |
| 1920–1921 | Georges Leygues |
| 1921–1922 | Aristide Briand (seventh term) |
| 1922–1924 | Raymond Poincaré (second and third terms) |
| 1924 | François-Marsal |
| 1924–1925 | Édouard Herriot |
| 1925 | Paul Painlevé (second and third terms) |
| 1925–1926 | Aristide Briand (eight, ninth, and tenth terms) |
| 1926 | Édouard Hérriot (second term) |
| 1926–1929 | Raymond Poincaré (fourth and fifth term) |

## LEADING STATESMEN OF FRANCE *(continued)*

| Term | Name |
| --- | --- |
| 1929 | Aristide Briand (eleventh term) |
| 1929–1930 | André Tardieu |
| 1930 | Camille Chautemps |
| 1930 | André Tardieu (second term) |
| 1930–1931 | Théodore Steeg |
| 1931–1932 | Pierre Laval (three terms) |
| 1932 | André Tardieu (third term) |
| 1932 | Édouard Herriot (third term) |
| 1932–1933 | Joseph Paul-Boncourt |
| 1933 | Édouard Daladier |
| 1933 | Albert Sarraut |
| 1933–1934 | Camille Chautemps (second term) |
| 1934 | Édouard Daladier (second term) |
| 1934 | Gaston Doumergues (second term) |
| 1934–1935 | Pierre-Étienne Flandin |
| 1935 | Fernand Buisson |
| 1935–1936 | Pierre Laval (second term) |
| 1936 | Albert Sarraut (second term) |
| 1936–1937 | Léon Blum |
| 1937–1938 | Camille Chautemps (third and fourth terms) |
| 1938 | Léon Blum (second term) |
| 1938–1940 | Édouard Daladier (third, fourth and fifth terms) |
| 1940 | Paul Reynaud |

### Second World War

| Term | Name |
| --- | --- |
| 1940–1942 | Henri-Philippe Pétain |
| 1942–1944 | Pierre Laval (third term) |
| 1944–1946 | Charles de Gaulle |
| 1946 | Félix Gouin |
| 1946 | Georges Bidault |
| 1946–1947 | Léon Blum (third term) |

### Fourth Republic

| Term | Name |
| --- | --- |
| 1947 | Paul Ramadier (two terms) |
| 1947–1948 | Robert Schuman |
| 1948 | André Marie |
| 1948 | Robert Schuman (third term) |
| 1948–1949 | Henri Queuille |
| 1949–1950 | Georges Bidault (second and third term) |
| 1950 | Henri Queuille (second term) |
| 1950–1951 | René Pleven |
| 1951 | Henri Queuille (third term) |

## LEADING STATESMEN OF FRANCE *(continued)*

| Term | Name |
|------|------|
| 1951–1952 | René Pleven (second term) |
| 1952 | Edgar Faure |
| 1952 | Antoine Pinay |
| 1953 | René Mayer |
| 1953–1954 | Joseph Laniel (two terms) |
| 1954–1955 | Pierre Mendès-France |
| 1955 | Christian Pineau |
| 1955–1956 | Edgar Faure (second term) |
| 1956–1957 | Guy Mollet |
| 1957 | Maurice Borgés-Maunory |
| 1957–1958 | Félix Gaillard |
| 1958 | Pierre Pflimlin |
| 1958–1959 | Charles de Gaulle (second term) |

| Fifth Republic | |
|------|------|
| 1959–1962 | Michel Debré |
| 1962–1968 | Georges Pompidou |
| 1968–1969 | Maurice Couve de Murville |
| 1969–1972 | Jacques Chaban-Delmas |
| 1972–1974 | Pierre Messmer |
| 1974–1976 | Jacques Chirac |
| 1976–1981 | Raymond Barre (three terms) |
| 1981–1984 | Pierre Mauroy (three terms) |
| 1984–1986 | Laurent Fabius |
| 1986–1988 | Jacques Chirac (second term) |
| 1998–1991 | Michel Rocard |
| 1991–1992 | Édith Cresson |
| 1992–1993 | Pierre Bérégovoy |
| 1993–1995 | Édouard Balladur |
| 1995–1997 | Alain Juppé (two terms) |
| 1997 | Lionel Jospin |
| 2002–Present | Jean-Pierre Raffarin |

# SELECTED BIBLIOGRAPHY

Adamthwaite, A. P. *Grandeur and Misery: France's Bid for Power in Europe 1914–1940.* London: Arnold, 1995.

Alexander, M., ed. *French History since Napoleon.* London: Arnold, 1999.

Allmand, C. *The Hundred Years War.* London: Clarendon, 1987.

———, ed. *Power, Culture and Religion, c. 1350–c. 1550.* London: Clarendon, 1989.

Aldrich, R., and J. Connell. *France's Overseas Frontier. Départements et Territoires d'Outre-Mer.* Cambridge: Cambridge University Press, 1992.

Agrippa d'Aubigné, T. *Oeuvres complètes,* ed. E. Reaume de Caussade. Geneva: Slatkin Reprints, 1967.

Ambler, J. *The French Army in Politics 1945–1962.* Columbus: Ohio State University Press, 1966.

Antoine, M. *Louis XV.* Paris: Fayard, 1989. Antoine has many other fine books, essential reading for any serious student of 18th-century France.

Asselain, J. C. *Histoire économique de la France du XVIIe siècle à nos jours.* Paris: Éditions du Seuil, 1984.

Aulard, A. *Histoire politique de la révolution française,* 4 vols. Paris: Colin, 1901.

Avril, P., et al. *Personnel politique français, 1870–1988.* Paris: Éditions du Seuil, 1989.

Babelon, J. P. *Henri IV.* Paris: Fayard, 1982.

Baker, K. *The Political Culture of the Old Regime.* 1987.

Barbiche, B. *Les Institutions de la monarchie française à l'époque moderne.* Paris: PUF, 1999.

Barbiche, B., and S. Barbiche. *Sully, l'homme et ses fidèles.* Paris: Fayard, 1997.

Bard, C. *Les Filles de Marianne: histoire des feminisms 1914–1940.* Paris: Fayard, 1995.

Baudouin-Matuszek, M.-N., ed. *Marie de Médicis, et le Palais du Luxembourg.* Paris: Foundation Septention, 1991

Baumgartner, F. *Change and Continuity in the French Episcopate: The Bishops and the Wars of Religion 1547–1610.* Durham, N.C.: Duke University Press, 1986.

———. *Henry II.* Durham, N.C.: Duke University Press, 1988.

Bayard, F. *Le Monde des financiers au XVIIe siècle.* Paris: Flammarion, 1988.

Beauvoir, S. de. *The Second Sex.* London: David Campbell, 1953.

Bedos-Rezak, B. *Anne de Montmorency: seigneur de la Renaissance.* Paris: Éditions Publiard, 1990.

Beik, W. *Absolutism and Society in Seventeenth Century France.* Cambridge: Cambridge University Press, 1985.

———, ed. *The French Revolution.* New York: Walker, 1970.

———. *Louis XV and Absolutism: A Brief Study with Documents.* Boston: St Martin's, 2000.

———. *Urban Protest in Seventeenth Century France.* Cambridge: Cambridge University Press, 1997.

Benedict, P., *Rouen during the Wars of Religion.* Cambridge: Cambridge University Press, 1981.

Bernard, P., and H. Dubief. *The Decline of the Third Republic.* Cambridge: Cambridge University Press, 1988.

Berce, Y.-M. *Histoire des Croquants: Étude de soulèvements populaires au XVIIe siècle dans le Sud-Ouest de la France,* 2 vols. Geneva: Droz, 1974.

Bergeron, L. *France under Napoleon.* Cambridge: Cambridge University Press, 1981.

———. *Les Capitalistes en France, 1780–1914.* Paris: Gallimard, 1978.

Bergin, J. *Cardinal Richelieu: Power and the Pursuit of Wealth.* New Haven, Conn.: Yale University Press, 1985.

———. *The Making of the French Episcopate, 1598–1661.* New Haven, Conn.: Yale University Press, 1996.

Berstein, S. *The Republic of de Gaulle, 1958–1969.* Cambridge: Cambridge University Press, 1993.

Bertaud, F. (Mme de Motteville). *Memoirs of Madame de Motteville on Anne of Austria and her Court,* 3 vols., ed. C.-A Saint Beuve, trans. K. Prescott Wormeley. Boston: Hardy, Pratt and Co., 1901.

de Bertier de Sauvigny, G. *The Bourbon Restoration.* Philadelphia: University of Pennsylvania Press, 1966.

Betts, R. *France and Decolonization, 1900–1960.* Basingstoke: Macmillan, 1991.

Birke, E. *Frankreich und Ostmitteleuropa im 19 Jahrhundert.* Cologne: Bohlau, 1960.

Bloch, M. *Strange Defeat.* New York: Oxford University Press, 1949.

Bluche, P. *Louis XIV,* trans. M. Greengrass. Oxford: Basil Blackwell, 1990.

Bodin, J. *Les Livres de la République.* Paris, 1583; reprinted in Geneva. One should also consult, if possible, the original Paris edition of 1576. The 1606 English translation by Richard Knolies, *The Six Books of the Commonweal,* is available in a modern reprint (Harvard, 1962). For a brief taste of Bodin in English, one can turn to Julian Franklin's excellent edition, *On Sovereignty: Four Chapters From Six Books on the Commonwealth* (Cambridge, 1992).

Bodin, L. *Les Intellectuels.* Paris: PUF, "Que sais-je?", 1962.

Bonney, R. *Political Change in France under Richelieu and Mazarin.* Oxford: Oxford University Press, 1976. Bonney has written several other important works on state finance.

Boucher, J. *La vie de Bayard,* ed. D. Crouzet. Paris: Imprimerie Nationale, 1992.

Bouloiseau, M. *The Jacobin Republic 1792–1794,* trans. J. Mandelbaum. Cambridge: Cambridge University Press, 1983.

Braudel, F., and E. Labousse, eds. *Histoire économique et sociale de la France,* 4 vols. Paris: Presses universitaires, 1976.

Briggs, R. *Early Modern France, 1560–1715.* Oxford and New York: Oxford University Press, 1977.

Brodhag, C. *Objectif Terre: Les Verts, de l'écologie à la politique.* Paris: Éditions du Félin, 1990.

Brogan, D. W. *The Development of Modern France (1870–1939).* London, 1940.

Bruhat, J. *Histoire du mouvement ouvrier français.* Paris: Ed. Sociales, 1952.

Bryant, L. *The King and the City in Parisian Royal Entry Ceremony.* Geneva: Droz, 1986.

Burke, E., and T. Paine. *Reflections on the Revolution in France and the Rights of Man.* Garden City, N.Y.: Anchor Books, 1973.

Burley, P., ed. *Witness to the Revolution: American and British Commentators in France, 1789–94.* London: Weidenfield and Nicholson, 1989.

Cabantous, A. *Les Citoyens du large: les identités maritimes en France. XVIIᵉ–XIXᵉ siècle.* Paris: Aubier, 1995.

Cameron, R. *France and the Economic Development of Europe 1800–1914.* Princeton, N.J.: Princeton University Press, 1961.

Capdevieille, Jacque, and René Mouriaux. *Mai 68, L'Entre-deus de la modernité. Histoire de trente ans.* Paris: FNSP, 1988.

Carroll, S. Noble. *Power during the French Wars of Religion.* Cambridge and New York: Cambridge University Press, 1998.

Castan, N. *Justice et répression en Languedoc à l' époque de Lumières.* Paris: Flammarion, 1980.

Charle, C. *A Social History of France in the Nineteenth Century.* Oxford: Berg, 1994.

Charlton, D. G. *Positivist Thought in France during the Second Empire.* Oxford: Clarendon, 1959.

Chartier, R. *The Cultural Uses of Print in Early Modern France,* trans. L. Cochrane. Princeton, N.J.: Princeton University Press, 1987.

Chassin, Ch.-L. *Les Élections et les Cahiers de Paris en 1789.* Paris: Jouast et Sigaux, 1888, 4 vols. Geneva, reprint edition of 1967.

Chatellier, L. *La religion des pauvres: Les sources du christianisme modern, XVIᵉ–XIXIᵉ siècles.* Paris: Aubier, 1993.

Chebel d'Appollonia, A. *Histoire politique des intellectuels en France, 1944–1954.* Paris: Complexe, 1991.

Chevalier, P. *Louis XIII: Roi Cornélien.* Paris: Fayard, 1979.

Chipman, J. *French Power in Africa.* Oxford: Blackwell, 1989.

Church, W. *Constitutionalism and Resistance in Sixteenth Century France.* New York: Octagon, 1941.

Clark, T. N. *Prophets and Patrons: The French University and the Emergence of the Social Sciences.* Cambridge, Mass.: Harvard University Press, 1973.

Clout, H. D. *Themes in the Historical Geography of France.* Oxford: Oxford University Press, 1977.

Cobban, A. *The Social Interpretation of the French Revolution.* Cambridge: Cambridge University Press, 1964.

———. *History of Modern France,* 3 vols. Baltimore: Penguin, 1957–65.

Collins, J. B. *From Tribes to Nation: The Making of France 500–1799.* Washington, D.C.: GUP, 2001.

———. *Classes, Estates, and Order in Early Modern Brittany.* Cambridge: Cambridge University Press, 1994.

———. *The Fiscal Limits of Absolutism.* Berkeley: University of California Press, 1988.

———. *The State in Early Modern France.* Cambridge: Cambridge University Press, 1995.

———. *Constitutionalism and Resistance in the Sixteenth Century,* ed. J. Franklin. New York: Pegasus, 1969.

Corvisier, A. *Louvois.* Paris: Fayard, 1983.

Crespelle, J. P. *Les Maîtres de la Belle Époque.* Paris: Libraire Hachette, 1966.

Croix, A. *La Bretagne aux xvie et xviie siècles: la vie, la foi, la morte,* 2 vols. Paris: Malouine, 1981.

Croix, A., A Lespagnol, and G. Provost, eds. *Église, Éducation, Lumières . . . Histoires Culturelles de la France (1500–1830).* Rennes: Presses Universitaires de Rennes, 1999.

Croix, A., and J. Quéniart. *Histoire culturelle de la France, vol. 2., De la Renaissance l'Aube des Lumières.* Paris: Éditions du Seuil, 1997.

Cronin, V. *Napoleon Bonaparte, An Intimate Biography.* New York: Morrow, 1971.

Crouzet, D. *Jean Calvin.* Paris: Fayard, 2000.

———. *Les guerrières de Dieu: la violence au temps des troubles de la religion, vers 1525–vers 1610,* 2 vols. Seyssel: Champ Vallon, 1990.

———. *La nuit de la Saint Barthélemy: un rêve perdu de la Renaissance.* Paris: Fayard, 1994.

———. *La sagasse et le malheur: Michel de l'Hôpital, chancelier de France.* Paris: Seyssel, 1998.

Cruickshank, J. *French Literature and Its Background,* 4 vols. London: Oxford University Press, 1969.

Dansette, A. *Religious History of Modern France,* 2 vols. New York: Herder and Herder, 1961.

———. *Mai 1968.* Paris: Plon, 1971.

Dautry, J. *1848 et la IIe république.* Paris: Ed. sociales, 1957.

Dejean, J. *Ancients against Moderns: Culture Wars and the Making of a Fin de Siècle.* Chicago: University of Chicago Press, 1997.

Delameau, J. *Catholicism between Luther and Voltaire.* London: Burns and Oates, 1977; Philadelphia: Westminster Press, 1977; trans. of French edition of 1971. Delameau has written a wide range of other books examining early-modern religion.

Descartes, R. *Discourse on Method and Meditations,* trans. L. Lafleur. Indianapolis, Id.: Bobbs Merrill, 1960.

Descaux, A. *Histoire des françaises,* 2 vols. Paris: Perrin, 1972.

Descimon, R., ed. *Discours pour la majorité de Charles IX et trois autres discours.* Paris: Imprimerie Nationale, 1993.

Descimon, R., and C. Jouhad. *La France du premier XVIIe siècle, 1594–1661.* Paris: Belin, 1996.

Desmoulins, C. *Oeuvres de Camille Desmoulins.* Paris: Ebrard, 1838, reprinted in New York: AMS, 1972.

Dessert, D. *Argent, pouvoir et société au Grand Siècle.* Paris: Fayard, 1984.

———. *Fouquet.* Paris: Fayard, 1987.

———. *La Royale: Vaisseaux et marins du Roi-Soleil.* Paris: Fayard, 1996.

Dewald, J. *Aristocratic Experience and the Origins of Modern Culture; France 1570–1715.* Berkeley: University of California Press, 1993.

———. *Pont St.-Pierre, 1398–1789, Lordship, Community and Capitalism in Early Modern France.* Berkeley: University of California Press, 1987.

———. *The Formation of Provincial Nobility: The Magistrates of the Parlement of Rouen, 1499–1610.* Princeton, N.J.: Princeton University Press, 1980.

Diefendorf, B. *Beneath the Cross: Catholics and Huguenots in Sixteenth Century Paris.* New York: Oxford University Press, 1991.

Digeon, C. *La Crise allemande de la pensée française, 1870–1914.* Paris: Presses universitaires, 1959.

Donnat, O. *Les Français face à la culture: de l'exclusion à l'éclecticisme.* Paris: La Découverte, 1994.

Doyle, W. *The Origins of the French Revolution.* Oxford and New York: Oxford University Press, 1980.

————. *The Oxford History of the French Revolution.* Oxford and New York: Oxford University Press, 1989.

Dubost, J.-F. *La France italienne XVIe–XVIIe siècle.* Paris, Aubier, 1997.

Duby, G. ed. *Histoire de la France urbaine,* 5 vols. Paris: Éditions du Seuil, 1976.

————, and A. Wallon, eds. *Histoire de la France rurale,* 4 vols. Paris: Éditions du Seuil, 1976.

————. *France in the Middle Ages, 987–1460.* Oxford: University Press, 1991.

Duchen, C. *Women's Rights, Women's Lives in France 1944–1968.* London: Routledge, 1994.

Du Roy, A. and N. *Citoyennes! Il y a cinquante ans, le vote des femmes.* Paris: Flammarion, 1994.

Eichengreen, B., ed. *Europe's Post-War Recovery.* Cambridge: Cambridge University Press, 1995.

Ehrmann, H. W. *Politics in France.* Boston: Little, Brown, 1971.

Elgey, G. *Histoire de la IVe république,* 2 vols. Paris: Fayard, 1965–70.

Elias, N. *The Civilizing Process,* trans. E. Jephcott. New York: Urizen, 1978.

Élisabeth Charlotte, duchess of Orléans. *A Woman's Life in the Court of the Sun King: The Letters of Liselette von der Pfalz, 1622–1722,* ed. and trans. E. Fortser. Baltimore: John Hopkins University Press, 1984.

Étienne, B. *La France et l'Islam.* Paris: Hachette, 1989.

Farge, A. *Subversive Words: Public Opinion in Eighteenth Century France,* trans. R. Morris. University Park: Pennsylvania State University Press, 1995. Farge has written many superb books on eighteenth-century Paris.

Farr, J. *Authority and Sexuality in Early Modern Burgundy (1550–1730).* New York: Oxford University Press, 1995.

Ferro, M. *The Great War, 1914–1918.* London: Routledge, 1973.

————. *Hands of Glory: Artisans and Their World in Dijon, 1550–1650.* Ithaca, N.Y.: Cornell University Press, 1995.

Fohlen, C. *La France de l'entre-deux-guerres.* Paris: Casterman, 1966.

Foisil, M. *La révolte des Nu-Pieds.* Paris: PUF, 1970.

Fourastié, J. and J. *D'une France à une autre: avant et après les Trente Glorieuses.* Paris: Fayard, 1987.

Foucault, M. *Les mots et les choses, une archéologie des sciences humaines.* Paris: Gallimard, 1965.

Franklin, J. *Jean Boudin and the Rise of Absolutist Theory.* Cambridge: Cambridge University Press, 1973.

Furet, F., *Revolutionary France, 1770–1880,* trans. A. Nevill. Oxford: Basil Blackwell, 1992; Paris-Hachette, 1988.

Furet, F. and M. Ouszof. *Dictionnaire Critique de la Révolution Française.* Paris: Flammarion, 1988.

Gérard, A. *La Révolution française: mythes et interprétations, 1789–1970.* Paris: Flammarion, 1970.

Geyl, P. *Napoleon: For and Against.* New Haven, Conn.: Yale University Press, 1949.

Gildea, Robert. *France Since 1945.* Oxford: Oxford University Press, 1997.

————. *The Past in French History.* New Haven, Conn.: Yale University Press, 1994.

Gilpin, R. *France in the Age of the Scientific State.* Princeton, N.J.: Princeton University Press, 1968.

Girard L. *La Politique des travaux publics sous le second empire.* Paris: Colin, 1951.

Giradet, R. *La société militaire dans la France contemporaine.* Paris: Plon, 1953.

Giroud, F., and B.-H. Lévy. *Les Hommes et les Femmes.* Paris: Olivier Orban, 1993.

Godineau, D. *Citoyennes tricoteuses: les femmes du peuple à Paris pendant la Révolution française.* Aix-en-Provence: Alinéa, 1988.

Gorce, P. de la. *Histoire du second empire.* Paris: Plon, 1899–1905.

Goubert, P. *Mazarin.* Paris: Fayard 1990. Goubert has authored many other essential works, beginning with his magisterial thesis on Beauvais and its region.

Goubert, P., and D. Roche. *Les Français et l'Ancien Régime,* 2 vols. Paris: Armand Colin, 1984.

Grosser, Alfred. *Affaires extérieures. La Politique de la France, 1944–1984.* Paris: Flammarion, 1984.

Guillemin, H. *Les origines de la Commune,* 3 vols. Paris: Gallimard, 1956–60.

Guittart de Floriban, C. *Journal de Célestin Guittard de Floriban, Bourgeois de Paris sous la Révolution,* ed. R. Aubert. Paris: Éditions France-Empire 1974.

Habermas, J. *Structural Transformation of the Public Sphere,* trans. T. Berger. Cambridge, Mass.: MIT Press, 1989.

Hall, H. *Richelieu's Desmarets and the Century of Louis XIV.* Oxford: Clarendon Press 1990.

Hamon, P. *L'Argent du roi.* Paris: Comité pour l'histoire économique et finacière de la France, 1994. See also his fine book on the financiers, *Messieurs des finances,* published in 1999.

Hanley, S. *The Lit de Justice of the Kings of France.* Princeton, N.J.: Princeton University Press, 1983.

Hargreaves, A. *Immigration in Post-War France: A Documentary Anthology.* London: Methuen, 1987.

Haudrere, P. *L'Empire de Rois, 1500–1789.* Paris: Denail, 1997.

Hause, S. C., with A. R. Kenney. *Women's Suffrage and Social Politics in the French Third Republic.* Princeton, N.J.: Princeton University Press, 1984.

Haute Conseil de la Francophonie. *État de la Francophonie dans le monde.* Paris: Presses universitaires, 1994.

Havelange, C. *De l'oeil et du monde: Une histoire du regard au seuil de la modernité.* Paris: Fayard, 1998.

Hazareesingh, S. *Political Traditions in Modern France.* Oxford: Oxford University Press, 1994.

Heller, H. *Labour, Science and Technology in France, 1500–1620.* Cambridge: Cambridge University Press, 1986.

Hemmings, F. W. J. *Culture and Society in France 1848–1898.* New York: Scribner, 1971.

Herbert, R. L. *Impressionism: Art, Leisure, and Parisians Society.* New Haven, Conn.: Yale University Press, 1988.

Heroard, J. *Journal de Jean Heroard,* ed. M. Foisil, 2 vols. Paris: Fayard, 1989, Heroard was Louis XIII's private physician; this journal is an invaluable source of both royal family life and early-modern childhood.

Hickey, D. *The Coming of French Absolutism; The Struggle of Tax Reform in the Province of Dauphiné 1540–1640.* Toronto: University of Toronto Press, 1986.

Higonnet M., J. Jenson, S. Michel, and M. C. Weitz, eds. *Behind the Lines: Gender and the Two World Wars.* New Haven, Conn.: Yale University Press, 1986.

Hoffmann, P. *Growth in a Traditional Society: The French Countryside 1450–1815.* Princeton, N.J.: Princeton University Press, 1996.

Holt, M. *The French Wars of Religion 1562–1629.* Cambridge and New York: Cambridge University Press, 1995.

———. *Sport and Society in Modern France.* Hamden, Conn.: Archon Books, 1981.

Huard, R. *La Naissance du parti politique en France.* Paris: Presses de la Fondation Nationale des Sciences Politiques, 1996.

Huppert, G. *The Style of Paris: Renaissance Origins of the French Enlightenment.* Bloomington: Indiana University Press, 1999.

Hurault, P. *Mémoires de Mesieur Phillipe Hurault, comte de Cheverny, Chancelier de France in Collection complète des mémoires relatifs à l'Histoire de France,* v. XXXVI, ed. M. Petitot. Paris: Foucault, 1819.

Ingram, N. *The Politics of Dissent: Pacifism in France 1919–1939.* Oxford: Clarendon Press, 1991.

Jackson, R. *Vive le Roi!: A History of the French Coronation from Charles V to Charles X.* Chapel Hill: University of North Carolina Press, 1983.

James E. *The Origins of France, From Clovis to the Capetians, 500–1000.* Cambridge: Cambridge University Press, 1982.

Jaurès, J. *Histoire socialiste de la révolution française,* 8 vols. Paris: 1901–04.

Jones, C. *The Cambridge Illustrated History of France.* Cambridge: Cambridge University Press, 1994.

Jouanna, A. *Histoire et dictionnaire des guerres de religion.* Paris: Laffont, 1998.

———. *Le Devoir de révolte.* Paris: Fayard, 1988.

Joughin, J. *The Paris Commune in French Politics, 1871–1880.* Baltimore: Johns Hopkins University Press, 1955.

Judt, T. *A Study of the Origins of the Modern French Left.* Cambridge: Cambridge University Press, 1979.

Julliard J., and M. Winock. *Dictionnaire des intellectuels français.* Paris: Éditions du Seuil, 1996.

Kemp, T. *Economic Forces in French History.* London: Dobson, 1971.

Kennedy, E. *Cultural History of the French Revolution.* New Haven, Conn.: Yale University Press, 1989.

Keohane, N. *Philosophy and the State in France.* Princeton, N.J.: Princeton University Press, 1980.

Kepel, G. *Les Banlieues de l'Islam.* Paris: Éditions du Seuil, 1987.

Kettering, S. *Judicial Politics and Urban, Revolt in Seventeenth Century France. The Parlement of Aix 1629–1659.* Princeton, N.J.: Princeton University Press, 1978.

————. *Patrons, Brokers, and Clients in Seventeenth-Century France*. New York and Oxford: Oxford University Press, 1986.

————. *French Society, 1589–1715*. Harlow: Longman, 2001.

Kim, S.-H. *Michel de l'Hôpital: The Vision of a Reformist Chancellor during the French Revolution Wars*. Kirksville, Mo.: Sixteenth Century Journal Publishers, 1997.

Kingdon, R. *Myths about the Saint Bartholomew's Day Massacre*. Cambridge, Mass.: Harvard University Press, 1988.

Kley, D. van. *The Religious Origins of the French Revolution*. New Haven, Conn.: Yale University Press, 1996. Van Kley has written several important books on eighteenth-century Jansenism.

Knecht, R. J. *Catherine de Medici*. New York and London: Longman, 1998.

————. *Francis I*. Cambridge and New York: Cambridge University Press, 1982.

Kriegel, A. *Aux origines du communisme française*. Paris: Flammarion, 1969.

Kuisel, R. F. *Capitalism and the State in Modern France: Renovation and Economic Management in the Twentieth Century*. Cambridge: Cambridge Univeristy Press, 1981.

Labe, L. *Oeuvres complétes*, ed. E Guidici. Geneva: Droz, 1981.

Ladurie, E. La Roy. *The Beggar and the Professor: A Sixteenth Century Family Saga*, trans. A. Goldhammer. Chicago and London: University of Chicago Press, 1997.

————. *Carnival in Romans*, trans. M. Feeney. New York: George Braziller, 1979.

————. *The Peasants of Languedoc*, trans. J. Day. Urbana, Chicago, and London: University of Illinois Press, 1974, 1980. Only the French edition of 1966, *Les paysans de Languedoc*, 2 vols., contains the full text and the appendixes.

Landes, J. *Women and the Public Sphere in the Age of the French Revolution*. London: Routledge, 1988.

Larkin, M. *France Since the Popular Front, 1936–1996*. Oxford: Clarendon Press, 1997.

Lefebvre, G. *The French Revolution*, 2 vols. London: Routledge & Kegan Paul, 1962–64.

————. *The Coming of the French Revolution*, trans. R. R. Palmer. Princeton, N.J.: Princeton University Press, 1947, 1948.

Lefranc, G. *Histoire du Front Populaire*. Paris: Payot, 1965.

Lequin Y. ed. *La Mosaïque France. Histoire des étrangers et de l'immigration*. Paris: Larousse, 1988.

Leymarie, J. *Impressionism*, 2 vols. Geneva: Éditions d'Art Albert Skira, 1955.

L'héritier, M., ed. *Les débuts de la Révolution à Bordeaux d'après les Tablettes manuscrites de Pierre Bernadau*. Paris: Société d'histoire de la Révolution Française, 1919.

Loschak, D. *La Convention des institutions républicaines. François Mitterrand et le socialisme*. Paris: PUF, 1971.

Louis XIV. *Memoirs for the instruction of the Dauphin*, trans. P. Sonnino. New York: Fress Press, 1970.

————. *Mémoires pour l'instruction du dauphin*, ed. P Goubert. Paris: Imprimerie Nationale, 1992.

Maistre, J. de. *Considerations on France*, trans. and ed. R. Lebrun. Cambridge: Cambridge University Press, 1994.

Major, J. R. *Representative Government in Early Modern France*. New Haven, Conn.: Yale University Press, 1980. Major has written a number of other works on the representative institutions of the 16th and 17th centuries; all are worth reading.

Malherbe, F. de, *Oeuvres*, ed. A. Adam. Paris: Gallimard, 1971.

Mallet, S. *La nouvelle Class ouvrière*. Paris: Éditions du Seuil, 1969.

Mandrou, R. *Des humanists aux hommes de science (XVIe et XVIIe siècles)*, vol. 3 of *Histoire de la pensée européene*. Paris: Éditions du Seuil 1973.

————. *Introduction to Modern France, 1500–1640. An Essay in Historical Psychology*, trans. R. E. Hallmark. New York: Harper and Row, 1975, 1977.

Marat, J.-P. *Oeuvres Politiques*, 5 vols., ed. J. de Cock and C. Goetz. Brussels: Pole Nord, 1989–93.

Marseille, J. *Nouvelle Histoire de la France*. Paris: Perrin, 1999.

Massip, Roger. *De Gaulle et l'Europe*. Paris: Flammarion, 1963.

Mayeur A. J., and M. Réberioux. *The Third Republic from Its Origins to the Great War 1871–1914*. Cambridge: Cambridge University Press, 1982.

McMillan, James. *Twentieth Century France: Politics and Society 1898–1991*. London: Arnold, 1992.

Melzer S. E., and L. Rabine. *Rebel Daughters: Women and the French Revolution*. New York: Oxford University Press, 1992.

Mendras Henri, with Alistair Cole. *Social Change in Modern France: Towards a Cultural Anthropology of the Fifth Republic.* Cambridge and Paris: Cambridge University Press/Maison des Sciences de l'Homme, 1991.

Mettam, R. *Power and Faction in Louis XIV's France.* Oxford and New York: Basil Blackwell, 1988.

Michel, H. *Histoire de la résistance.* Paris: Presses universitaires, 1950.

Michelet, J. *Histoire de France,* 6. vols. Paris: Plon, 1855–67.

Minard, P. *La fortune du colberstisme: État et industries dans la France des Lumières.* Paris: Fayard, 1998.

Miquel, P. *L'Affaire Dreyfus.* Paris: Presses universitaires, 1959.

Monnet, Jean. *Mémoires.* London: Collins, 1978.

Montaigne, M. De. *The Complete Works of Montaigne: Essays, Travel Journal, Letters,* trans D. Frame. Stanford, Calif.: Stanford University Press, 1958, 1967.

Montluc, B. de. *Commentaires.* Paris: Gallimard, 1951.

Moote, L. *Louis XII. The Just.* Berkeley and Los Angeles: University of California Press, 1989.

———. *The Revolt of the Judges.* Princeton, N.J.: Princeton University Press, 1968.

Moriceau, J. M. *Les fermiers de l'Île-de-France $XV^e$-$XVIII^e$ siècle.* Paris: Fayard, 1994.

Morris, G. *A Diary of the French Revolution,* 2 vols., ed. B. Cary Davenport. Boston: Houghton Mifflin, 1939.

Mousnier, R. *La Venalité des offices.* Paris: PUF, 1945, 1970. Mousnier is the author of many books and articles. Although few current historians accept his views on early-modern French society, his model of that society continues to have an important influence on sociologists, and had a great influence both on sociologists and on historians from the 1960s through the 1980s.

Muchembled, R. *L'invention de l'homme moderne.* Paris: Fayard, 1988.

Mukerji, C. *Territorial Ambitions and the Gardens of Versailles.* Cambridge: Cambridge University Press, 1997.

Neuschel, K. *Word of Honor: Interpreting Noble Culture in Sixteenth Century France.* Ithaca, N.Y.: Cornell University Press, 1989.

Noin D., and Y. Chauviré. *La Population de la France.* Paris: Masson, 1987.

Noiriel, G. *Le Creuset français. Histoires de l'immigration, $XIX^e$–$XX^e$ siècles.* Paris: Éditions du Seuil, 1988.

Nora, P., ed. *Realms of Memory: Rethinking the French Past.* New York: Columbia University Press, 1996.

Noue, F. de la. *Mémoires de sieur François de la Noue,* in *Collection complète des mémoires relatifs à l'histoire de France,* v. XXXIV, ed. M. Petitot. Paris: Foucault, 1823.

Novotny, F. *Painting and Sculpture in Europe, 1780–1880.* New York: Penguin Books, 1960.

Ory, P. *L'Aventure culturelle française, 1945–1981.* Paris: Éditions du Seuil, 1983.

———, and J.-F. Sirinelli. *Les Intellectuels en France, de l'Affaire Dreyfus à nos jours.* Paris: Armand Colin, 1996.

Palmer, R. R. *Twelve Who Ruled.* Princeton, N.J.: Princeton University Press, 1969.

Pascal, B. *Oeuvres Complètes,* ed. L. Lafuma. Paris: Éditions du Seuil, 1963.

Paxton, Robert O. *Vichy France: Old Guard and New Order, 1940–1944.* London: Routledge, 1972.

Perry S., ed. *Aspects of Contemporary France.* London: Routledge, 1997.

Petitfils, J.-C. *Le Régent.* Paris: Fayard, 1986.

Peyre, H. *French Novelists of Today.* New York: Oxford University Press, 1967.

Pickles, D. *The Government and Politics of France,* 2 vols. London: Methuen, 1972–73.

Pillorget, R. and S. *France Baroque, France Classique, 1589–1715, 2 vols.* Paris: R. Laffont, 1995.

Planhol, X. de. *An Historical Geography of France.* Cambridge: Cambridge University Press, 1994.

Plessis, A. du. Cardinal Richelieu. *Les papiers de Richelieu,* ed. P. Grillon. Paris: Pedone, 1980, multiple volumes.

———. *Testament politique de Richelieu,* ed. F. Hildesheimer. Paris: Société de l'Histoire de France, 1995. Selections have been translated and edited by H. Hill, Wisconsin, 1961.

Pointrineau, A. *Ils travaillaient la France: Métiers et mentalités du $XVI^e$ au $XIX^e$ siècle.* Paris: Armand Colin, 1992. Pointrineau's other works and above all his thesis on the Auvergne provide an important contribution to eighteenth-century studies.

Ponteil, F. *Les institutions de la France de 1814 à 1870.* Paris: Presses Universitaires, 1966.

Poole, P. *Impressionism.* New York: Praeger, 1967.

Porshnev, B. *Le soulèvements populaires en France avant la Fronde, 1623–1648.* Paris: SEVPEN, 1963.

Prendiville, B. *L'Écologie. La Politique autrement?* Paris: L'Harmattan, 1993.

Price, R. *An Economic History of Modern France, c. 1730–1914.* Oxford: Oxford University Press, 1981.

Prost, Antoine. *L'Enseignement, s'est-il démocratisé?* Paris, PUF, 1986.

Quilliet, B. *La France du Beau XVIe Siècle, 1490–1560.* Paris: Fayard, 1998.

Rabelais, F. *The Complete Works of François Rabelais,* trans. D. Frame. Berkeley: University of California Press, 1991.

Racine, J. *Ouevres complètes,* ed. L. Estang. Paris: Éditions du Seuil, 1962.

Ranum, O. *Artisans of Glory: Writers and Historical Thought in Seventeenth Century France.* Chapel Hill: University of North Carolina Press.

———. *The Fronde: A French Revolution.* New York: Norton, 1993.

Rapley, E. *The Dévotes: Women and Church in Seventeenth-Century France.* Montreal: McGill-Queen's University Press, 1990.

Rebérioux, M. *L'extrême Droite en questions.* Paris: Études et Documentation Internationales, 1991.

Rémond, R. *La Vie politique en France,* 3 vols. Paris: Colin, 1965–70.

———. *The Right Wing in France: From 1815 to de Gaulle.* Philadelphia: University of Pennsylvania Press, 1969.

Renouvin, P. *Histoire des relations internationales: le XIXe siècle.* Paris: Hachette, 1954.

Retif de la Bretonne, N. *Les Nuits révolutionnaires, 1789–1793,* ed. M. Dorigny. Paris: Les Éditions de Paris, 1989. Excerpts taken from *Les Nuits de Paris.*

Reynolds, S. *France Between the Wars: Gender and Politics.* London: Routledge, 1996.

Rioux, J.-P., ed. *La Guerre d'Algérie et les français.* Paris: Fayard, 1990.

———. *The Fourth Republic, 1944–58.* Cambridge: Cambridge University Press, 1987.

Roelker, N. *One King, One Faith.* Berkeley: Univesity of California Press, 1996.

———. *Queen of Navarre, Jeanne d'Albret, 1528–1572.* Cambridge, Mass.: Belknap Press, 1968.

Ronsard, P. *Œuvres complètes,* ed. G. Cohen. Paris: Gallimard, 1950.

———. *Poems of Pierre Ronsard,* trans. N. Kilmer. Berkeley: University of California Press, 1979, bilingual edition.

Rosanvallon, P. *Le Sacre du citoyen: histoire du suffrage universel en France.* Paris: Gallimard, 1992.

Ross, G., S. Hoffmann, and S. Malzacher, eds. *The Mitterrand Experiment: Continuity and Change in Modern France.* Cambridge: Polity Press, 1987.

Roudy, Y. *À cause d'elles.* Paris: Albin Michel, 1985.

Rousso, H. *The Vichy Syndrome. History and Memory in France since 1944.* Cambridge, Mass.: Harvard University Press, 1991.

Ruault, N. *Gazette d'un Parisien sous la Révolution. Lettres à son frère, 1783–1796,* ed. A Vassal and C. Rimbaud. Paris: Librairie Académique, 1976.

Rudé, G. *The Crowd in the French Revolution.* Oxford: Oxford University Press, 1959.

Sahlins, P. *Boundaries: The Making of France and Spain in the Pyrenees.* Berkeley: University of California Press, 1989.

Saint-Simon, The duke of. *Mémoires,* 8 vols., ed. Y. Coirault. Paris: Gallimard, 1983–88.

Sauvy, A. *Histoire économique de la France entre les deux guerres,* 2 vols. Paris: Fayard, 1965–67.

Schaeper, T. *The French Council of Commerce, 1700–1715.* Columbus: Ohio State University Press, 1983.

Schmidt, V. A. *From State to Market? The Transformation of French Business and Government.* Cambridge: Cambridge University Press, 1996.

Scott, J. W. *Paradoxes to Offer: French Feminists and the Rights of Man.* Cambridge, Mass.: Harvard University Press, 1996.

———. *Gender and the Politics of History.* New York: Columbia University Press, 1988.

Sévigné, Mme de. *Selected Letters,* ed. L. Tanock. London and New York: Penguin, 1982.

Shennan, Andrew. *De Gaulle.* London: Longman 1993.

Smith, P. *Feminism and the Third Republic: Women's Political and Civil Rights in France 1918–1945.* Oxford; Clarendon Press, 1996.

Solnon, J.-F. *La Cour de France.* Paris: Fayard, 1987.

Sorel, A. *L'Europe et la révolution française,* 8 vols. Paris: Plon, 1885–1904.

Sorlin, P. *La Société française,* 2 vols. Paris: Arthaud, 1969–71.

Stora, B. *La Gangrène et l'oubli. La Mémoire de la guerre d'Algérie.* Paris: La Découverte, 1992.

Stovall, T. *Paris Noir: African Americans in the City of Light.* New York: University Press of America, 1996.

Taine, H. *Origines de la France contemporaine: la révolution.* Paris: Hachette, 1878–84.

Tallemant des Reaux, G. *Les Histoirettes,* 2 vols., ed. A. Adam. Paris; Gallimard, 1960–61.

Tallet, F., and N. Atkin, eds. *Religion, Society and Politics in France since 1789.* London: Hambleton, 1991.

Tavernier, Y., et al., eds. *L'Univers politique des paysans.* Paris: Colin, 1972.

Thébaud, F. *Écrire l'histoire des femmes.* Fontenay/Saint-Cloud: ENS Editions, 1998.

Thomson, D. *Democracy in France Since 1870.* New York: Oxford University Press, 1969.

Tocqueville, A. de. *Recollections.* Garden City: Doubleday, 1970.

Touchard, J. *Le Gaullisme, 1940–1969.* Paris: Éditions du Seuil, 1978.

Touraine, A. *Anti-Nuclear Protest. The Opposition to Nuclear Energy in France.* Cambridge/Paris: Cambridge University Press/Maison des Sciences de l'Homme, 1983.

Tourzel, L. de. *Mémoires de Madame la duchesse de Tourzel, gouvernante des enfants de France de 1789 à 1795,* J. Chalon ed. Paris: Mercure de France, 1969.

Viansson-Ponté, P. *Histoire de la république Gaullienne,* 2 vols. Paris: Fayard, 1970–71.

Viennot, E. *La Démocratie 'à la française' ou les femmes indésirables.* Paris: Centre d'Études et de Recherches Féministes, Publications de l'Université, Paris-VII Denis Diderot, 1996.

Weber, Eugen. *The Hollow Years: France in the 1930s.* London: Oxford University Press, 1995.

———. *Peasants into Frenchmen: The Modernization of Rural France.* Stanford: Calif. Stanford University Press, 1976.

Weiss, J. *The Popular Culture of Modern Art: Picasso, Duchamp, and Avant-Gardism.* New Haven, Conn.: Yale University Press, 1994.

Wells, P. *Law and Citizenship in Early Modern France.* Baltimore: Johns Hopkins University Press, 1995.

Williams, H. M. *An Eye-Witness Account of the French Revolution by Helen Maria Williams: Letters Containing a Sketch of the Politics of France,* J. Fruchtman Jr., ed. New York: Peter Lang, 1997.

Williams, P. *Crisis and Compromise: Politics in the Fourth Republic.* London: Longmans, 1964.

———. *The French Revolution of 1870–1871.* Paris: Éditions du Seuil, 1971.

Willis, F. Roy. *France, Germany and the New Europe, 1945–1967.* Oxford: Oxford University Press, 1967.

Winock, M. *Nationalisme, antisémitisme et fascisme en France.* Paris: Éditions du Seuil, 1982.

Wolfe, M. *The Conversion of Henri IV.* Cambridge, Mass.: Harvard University Press, 1993.

Wood J. *The King's Army.* Cambridge: Cambridge University Press, 1996.

Woronoff, D. *Histoire de l'industries en France.* Paris: Éditions du Seuil, 1994.

Wright, G. *France in Modern Times.* New York: Norton, 1981.

Wylie, L. *Village in the Vaucluse.* New York: Harper, 1964.

Young, A. *Travel during the Years 1787, 1788 and 1789,* 3 vols. London: W. Richardson, 1794.

Zeldin, T. *France 1848–1945.* Oxford: Oxford University Press, 1977.

# INDEX